GW00363374

GUIDE TO GOLF

OVER 2500 ENTRIES
FOR BRITAIN AND IRELAND
COLOUR PHOTOGRAPHS THROUGHOUT

Produced by AA Publishing

Maps prepared by the Cartographic Department of
The Automobile Association
Maps © The Automobile Association 1999
Directory generated by the AA Establishment Database,
Information Research, Hotel and Touring Services
Editor: David Hancock
Design by The Company of Designers, Basingstoke, Hampshire

The Automobile Association would like to thank the following photographers and libraries for their
assistance in the preparation of this book.

AA Photo Library 1 (Eric Hepworth), 19 (Steve Day), 315 (Jeff Beazley),
391 (C. Molyneau), 419 (J. Blandford),
Phil Sheldon Front & back cover; 3, 4, 8,
La Bretesche Golf Course 6-7

Editorial contributors: John Ingham, Association of Golf Writers and
Charlie Mulqueen of the Cork Examiner

Advertisement Production
Karen Weeks: Tel 01256 491545

Typeset/Repro by Avonset, 11 Kelso Place, Bath BA1 3AU

Printed in Italy by Rotolito Lombarda SpA

Published by AA Publishing, which is a trading name of Automobile Association Developments Limited
whose registered office is Norfolk House, Priestley Road, Basingstoke, Hampshire RG24 9NY,
Registered number 1878835.

ISBN 0 7495 2185 6

CONTENTS

GOLF FOR CHANNEL-HOPPERS

It's just a pitch shot across the water – to France

Call me a dreamer, or an optimist, but I always believe the journey is as interesting as almost any destination. For that reason you hear no complaints from this wandering golf scribe. However, after a million miles worldwide, it does come as a welcome relief if the journey is not too far, and not too complicated, writes John Ingham.

My suggestion is to pack the suitcase, stow some golf balls in the bag, and head for the somewhat under-rated fairways of La Belle France. However, I must trot out the obvious caution. Just because you cross the Channel doesn't mean you are guaranteed perfect weather. The rain can be as wetting as it is in Dover. And another thing! While some courses in France are quite good, they are not in the same class as the best in Britain and Ireland.

Some of the French clubhouses are fantastic gems but certain courses have a rural feel having been literally carved out of unprofitable farmland. Also, you may find yourself playing behind the planets slowest fourball.

But offset this with the fun of a new challenge, new tests and sometimes unusual shots - plus the interesting people

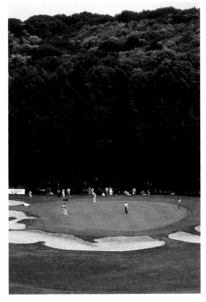

La Boulie Golf Course, Paris.

you'll meet along the route. In other words, it's fun to play away! And, if you're married, well you can take your partner because in France you see more mixed golf than almost anywhere else. You may laugh, but in certain clubs I won't mention, mixed golf is not madly popular and the men-only bar is defended, and could be for the next twenty years, despite words from Brussels.

With all this in mind, I recommend a trip across the Channel where, surprise, surprise, you'll find a welcome from smart clubs who now realise that if they are to survive financially, they are obliged to allow in fee-paying customers, either married, or not.

So, how to get to France with the full kit? Well, thanks to that tunnel they dug under the water, competition has become fierce, with profit margins slashed to the bone, which is good news for travellers like us. I recommend you take the car, go by ferry, and head for Brittany, Normandy, Paris or the Pas de Calais region. Prices allow up to five passengers on Brittany Ferries and the voyage is fun, particularly if you share a bottle of wine, and avoid football hooligans.

But be warned. Don't arrive plastered because piloting a car into France can be awkward, with the first 500 metres being the most dangerous, as I found out when steering a borrowed Renault Twingo up a one-way road - but not in the recommended direction!

Travel, one the great luxuries of life, can prove expensive. So search around for the best offers. The various High Street agents take bookings for all destinations, but take a cut. I often think that if you buy direct, from the offers in magazines or newspapers, you save. But watch out for those prices 'from' a certain figure. If you choose to book direct, with famous outfits like P&O or Page and Moy, opting to sail from Portsmouth, you accept a longer voyage than the more direct route to Calais. But if you intend to play your golf in Normandy or Brittany, arriving in Cherbourg gets you in there, to the heart of the action.

BRITTANY AND NORMANDY

Here, your fourball can take in the sights at Mont St Michel or Bayeux and there are some excellent eating places. From a golf point of view, some tend to favour the old-established courses which are mature, and do not have newly-planted saplings, staked in up and down the edge of the course 'for future generations'. Old clubs don't boast pretentious clubhouses and are often located in historic buildings, once the stately home of some long-dead royalist.

Anyway, if you have chosen to arrive at Cherbourg, or more conveniently St Malo, **Dinard**, built in 1887, is just 15km west of St Malo at St Briac-sur-Mer while there is also **Pen Guen**, established 1926 at St-Cast-le-Guildo. However, there are 20 other courses in Brittany, all built since the 1939-45 war, so visitors can pick-and-mix as they tour.

Senior Americans, involved in the Normandy landings, like to call in at **Omaha Beach Golf Club**, 8km south of Bayeux. Designed by a Frenchman in 1986, it may have been aimed at tourists, and possibly you won't feel like being involved. I know, for instance, that I didn't personally enjoy Rouen, but I didn't sample the nearby course of **Rouen-Mont St Aigan**. Built in 1911, it probably would have been worth a try.

If you intend to land at Cherbourg you are on the Normandy doorstep and will save miles of driving from further down the coast. You can also find two dozen courses in this neck of the woods. **Coutainville**, on the Avenue du Golf, requires visitors to present a handicap certificate, signed by your golf club secretary, which, so they say, proves you are a qualified driver of a golf ball, and won't cause hold-up. This certificate is required by the 'better' clubs who want decent players, who understand etiquette. At the **New Golf Deauville**, built in 1929 by two Englishmen, a welcome awaits visitors, but you must book in advance. It's worth doing, so call (00 33) 2 31 14 24 24 but be prepared to part with 250 francs a head.

If you look through the advertisements, you probably will notice that *Great Escapes* offer a selection of what they call hand-picked hotels and chateaux in northern France. A freephone call to them on 0800 7312929 and you surely will hear about the Hotel de France, 2-stars at Abbeville, some 80km drive from Calais. However, I like the sound of Moulin de Mombreux, 3-stars of 18th-century watermill, converted into a hotel and restaurant with 24 rooms and golf nearby. Prices are very reasonable, for a short break including breakfast, dinner with the only real query being: 'How do they do it?' Well, they are apparently part of the Allez France Holiday Group, and say golfers will enjoy fine cuisine, and they provide directions and all necessary information.

VAL DE LOIRE

For ambitious travellers who enjoy motoring the extra kilometre, head into the Val de Loire, or into Western Loire, and you won't be far from **La Baule**, a fine holiday area I know well, with a golf course designed by Peter Alliss and Dave Thomas, two successful tournament players of a few years back.

Another course I know, although I didn't play it because of unseasonal fog, is **La Bretesche** between Nantes and Vannes, just 8km north west of Pontchateau. When you see the turreted clubhouse, you think of royal homes of days gone by. The outbuildings have been converted into apartments and a phone call (00 33) 2 51 76 86 86 will reveal all.

AROUND PARIS

If you are in the mood to take in Paris and the surrounds, and can bear to tear yourself away from this spectacular city, then there are golf courses worth exploring. The problem is that many are exclusive and closed to visitors at weekends. During the week, they open to recognised players with a handicap, but are inclined to charge quite high fees, as you would expect. **La Boulie**, 15km south west of Paris, charge 430 francs for a midweek round and if there are four of you, we're talking serious money, particularly as you might wish to eat, and enjoy a glass of wine.

While I long to return to the south of France, it is a long hike. So, staying around Paris, try for a game at **St Cloud**, built before the first world war by Harry Colt, an English architect, famous worldwide for wondrous creations. St Cloud is 9km west of the city, at Porte Dauphine and it is a place that oozes pedigree. On Sunday, they require 600 francs a head. So try Monday.

Another expensive, but worthwhile course, is **St Nom-la-Breteche**, 24km west of Paris, on the A-13. Designed by anoth-

La Bretesche Golf Course, Val de Loire

er Englishman, Fred Hawtree, it only allows you in during the week, and at 485 francs a round, I wonder how many visitors they attract. I've enjoyed happy days there during the Lancome tournament, staged each year, and had some terrific meals, paid for by someone else. However, I don't rate the course as the most interesting - let's look for something less costly...

While I personally detest water-covered modern courses, designed by

Americans, you might prefer to pay 150 francs midweek to play the **National Golf Club**, built in 1990 by Van Hagge of the United States. In its favour: location, beyond Versailles on the D36, which is south west of Paris. It boasts two full courses as well as a nine-holer and has every modern facility such as you find in Florida!

To the east of Paris, you might play the **Disneyland Paris Golf Club**, also as the name suggests, built by an American. I notice, on certain days, green fees are 120 francs, which is reasonable. The place is 32km from the centre, via the A4 and you've probably guessed I've never been near it, not even for a tournament.

There are seventeen courses in the region of Paris and I reckon I'd choose **St Germain**, west of Paris by about 24km. Try midweek, but telephone first on (00 33) 1 39 10 30 30. It has 27 holes to choose from, and the hand of architect Colt can be seen in the layout.

JUST ACROSS THE CHANNEL

But now, frankly, I've saved the best until last. We'll suppose you only have the time to pop across to Calais. A treat lies in store, because the area is probably the most famous golfing neck of the woods in France. It deserves its reputation. Succulent food is offered, foie gras patés, local fish, maybe truffles, liqueurs, local fruit and vegetables - and if you can stagger out of the restaurant, the two courses at **Hardelot**, 15km south of Boulogne, are first class, kept in fine condition with the fees reasonable. Don't miss these two, so call on (00 33) 3 21 83 73 10 and say you've heard about its terrific reputation.

While you are in this location which is, let's face it, only just across the Channel, go to **Le Touquet**. There are three courses on offer. I played La Foret, the oldest, with a young professional. At the furthest point from the clubhouse, we were suddenly hit for six by a freak electric storm, with fork lightning terrifying my partner who said he was going to drop his steel-shafted clubs, and leg it to the clubhouse. At the age of 21, this fellow, Andrew Phillips, said he had no intention of ending his life. I told him I, on my part, had no intention of leaving my clubs on the ground, in any part of France - so we both walked in, drenched by the off-seas storm.

Interestingly, some clubs in northern France actively pursue visitors. You can read anything into this - shortage of those keen to walk their fairways for various reasons, or the fact that they are new to the scene. The **Dunkerque Golf Club**, just 20 minutes from Calais (0033) 3 28 61 07 43 charge 190 francs on weekdays and you can make your own reservations. They say take exit 31 from the A-16 motorway, and you can't miss it. The course was built in 1991 and is modern, with fairway-side water that beckons an erratic shot. But the place, they say, is well kept.

Another venue with similar green fees, and nearby, is **Le Golf D'Arras** (00 33) 3 21 50 24 24 reached from Calais on the A-26 road to Reims. The course winds through ponds, rivers, hills, woods - but the architect put in no tank traps. Why do they make golf courses so tough, you ask!

St Germain Golf Course, Paris

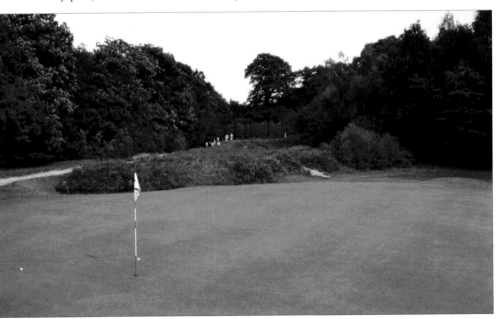

If you are serious about **Le Touquet,** you could try the 3-star Le Manoir Hotel, fashionable with Noel Coward and other English eccentrics in the 1930s, and just a knocked-down 9-iron from the club-house, direct on (00 33) 3 21 06 17 17. Worth a call.

If you've read the advertisements, you'll see that less expensive hotels in Le Touquet, such as the Hotel Red Fox (00 33) 3 21 05 27 58) offer special prices for groups. *Golf France* offer 4 nights for the price of three at the Westminster Hotel, where I've stayed in 4-star comfort. The firm can get 10% off green fees at both Le Touquet and Hardelot and, in addition, two other fine golf courses at **Belles Dunes and Wimereux** all, as they say, within an hour of Calais. Call 0181 644 1225. *French Golf Holidays* (01227 374374) organise golfing holidays in France and say 12 of Europe's top 50 courses are in their programmes. However, they must compete with *Cresta* (0870 2412424) who offer one night free at several selected hotels, and can get you pre-reserved tee-off times at almost 60 courses in France.

It's interesting how the companies encourage us to travel to France, and Le Shuttle and the tunnel has worked wonders. *3D Golf plc* is worth a call on 0800 333333 or 01292 263331 or try Alan and Susan Field of *Fields Fairway* on (00 33) 3 21 33 65 64. Their company is new to me, and they claim you pay no extra for allowing them to find a decent guest house (their own) or a hotel.

Anyway, if you have any queries on a golfing visit to the area, call Le Touquet Tourist Board on (00 33) 3 21 06 72 58 and they can help.

How to Get There

By Air:
From Biggin Hill, off the M25. *Love Air* can arrange flight times to suit, even one-day trips. They arrange everything. Call 01279 681434. From Lydd Airport, near Folkestone *Sky-Trek* (01797 320000) can help.

By Train:
Eurostar (0345 303030).
Le Shuttle (0990 353535).

By Ferry:
Hoverspeed (0990 240241)
Dover – Calais
Folkestone - Boulogne

Condor Ferries (0870 0102178)
Poole or Weymouth – St Malo

Holyman Sally Ferries (0990 595522)
Ramsgate – Dunkirk

Brittany Ferries (0990 360360)
Portsmouth – Caen & St Malo
Poole – Cherbourg
Plymouth – Roscoff
Cork – Roscoff

P&O Ferries (0990 980980)
Dover - Calais
Portsmouth - Le Havre & Cherbourg

Stena Line (0990 707070)
Dover - Calais
Newhaven - Dieppe

SeaFrance (0990 711711)
Dover - Calais

Telephone Numbers
To call France from the UK dial 00 followed by 33 (country code) and the 9-digit number. For calls inside France dial 0 before the 9-digit number eg Paris 01 .. ..

ALL YOU NEED TO KNOW

We have endeavoured to supply all the information you need to know before your visit by telling you what kind of course you can expect, what club facilities are available, including catering, any leisure facilities and the green fees you can expect to pay. We have also included AA-recommended accommodation – whether it be at the course itself or slightly further away.

Arranging a Visit
Some courses want advance notice of any visit, and possibly a letter of introduction from your own club. They may also require a handicap certificate. If this is the case the directory will include this information. However, it is always a good idea to check with any course in advance as details in the directory can change, particularly green fees, during the currency of the guide.

Course Notes
Courses that are considered to be of particular merit or interest have been placed within a shaded box. They may be very historic clubs or they may have been chosen because their courses are particularly testing or enjoyable to play. Some have been included because they are in holiday areas and have proved popular with visiting golfers. Such a selection cannot be either exhaustive or totally objective, and these courses do not represent any formal category on quality or other grounds.

Major Championship courses have special treatment with a full page entry, includ-

ing a selection of places at which to eat as well as to stay.

The Directory
The directory is arranged in countries: England, Northern Ireland and the Republic of Ireland are listed in alphabetical location within each country. Scotland and Wales are listed in alphabetical location within regions – the counties

that comprise each region are listed below the region heading. If you are not sure where your chosen course may be, there is an alphabetical index of courses at the end of the directory. The maps at the end of the book will also help to locate any golf course.

Map References
Should you be travelling in an unfamiliar part of the country and want to know the choice of courses available to you, consult the atlas at the end of the book. In its directory entry, each course has a map number and National Grid reference and there are directions to the course giving the nearest place located on the

map. The grid references for the Irish Republic are unique to the atlas at the back of this book.

Symbols and Abbreviations
In order to maximise the space available, we have used certain symbols and abbreviations within the directory entries and these are explained in the panel below.

04 TQ21	atlas page and National Grid reference		🏪	well-stocked shop
☎	telephone number		⛳	clubs for hire
IR£	Irish Punts (Republic only – the rates of exchange between Punts and pounds sterling are liable to fluctuate)		🛵	motorised cart/trolley for hire
			🛒	buggies for hire
			🛒	trolley for hire
✕	lunch		🏌	driving range
🍽	dinner		★	hotel classification
🍺	bar snacks		✿	Restaurant classification (applicable to championship course entry only)
☕	tea/coffee			
🍸	bar open midday and evenings		Q	Guest house classification
🛏	accommodation at club		B	AA Branded group hotels
🚿	changing rooms		TH	Town House hotels

Entries in Bold Italics
NB Although we make every effort to obtain up-to-date information from golf clubs, in some cases we have been unable to verify details with the club's management. Where this is the case the course name is shown in bold italics and you would be strongly advised to check with the club in advance of your visit.

Telephone Codes
The area codes shown against telephone numbers under Republic of Ireland courses are applicable within the Republic only. Similarly the area codes shown for entries in Great Britain and Northern Ireland cannot be used direct

from the Republic. Check your telephone directory for details. Please note that some area codes and local telephone numbers will change during the currency of the guide (See pages 17 & 18).

Accommodation

For each course listed, we recommend a nearby AA-appointed hotel, giving its classification, full name and address, telephone number and total number of bedrooms, including the number with private bath or shower. In some cases the hotel will be within the grounds of the golf course itself. The hotels recommended in the Golf Guide are mostly in the ★★, ★★★, and ★★★★ star categories. Where there is no AA-appointed hotel nearby, we have recommended AA Guest Accommodation. These are classified by a quality assessment, or Q rating, of 1-5 Q.

Club Accommodation

Some courses offer accommodation at their club. Where this facility exists, the 'bed'

symbol will appear in the entry under club facilities. This has been listed as a further option for those who might wish to stay at the course. However, unless the club accommodation has an AA star-rating, the only accommodation recommended by the AA is the star-rated hotel that appears at the foot of each entry.

HOW THE AA CLASSIFIES HOTELS

Hotel guests can expect to find the following minimum standards at all star levels:

- clean, comfortable, secure bedrooms equipped with modern amenities.
- beds, bedding and other bedroom furniture and appointments in good condition
- proper attention to hygiene in bathrooms and WCs
- all bedrooms with en suite bath/shower rooms at all except the one star level, where some may not be fully en suite
- adequate heating and

independent temperature controls
- a sufficient hot water supply at reasonable times.
- unless there is 24-hour room service, tea and coffee making facilities in the room
- amenities such as an iron and ironing board available on request
- at all but the one star level, TV and/or radio should be standard in every room
- from the three star level upward, direct dial telephones should be standard
- well prepared, wholesome meals presented in an appetising manner

★ What the star classification denotes

Star classification is a quality scheme at five levels. The assessment rises from one star, denoting hotels with the simplest range of facilities, to five stars, denoting large, luxury hotels with a range of services and facilities that meet the best international standards. In addition to the star classification, the AA also makes two further quality assessments to help intending guests in their choice of hotel: Red Star awards and the Quality Percentage Score, explained below.

★ Red Star Awards

AA star classifications are usually depicted in black on signs and in the AA's guides and electronic products. However, at each of the five classification levels, the AA recognises exceptional quality of accommodation and hospitality by awarding Red Stars for excellence.

A hotel with Red Stars, therefore, has been judged to be the best in its star classifi-

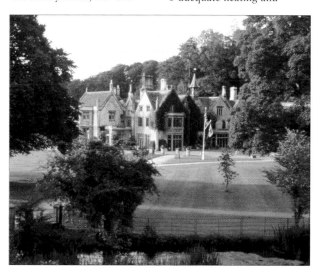

cation and recognises that the hotel offers outstanding levels of comfort, hospitality and customer care.

QUALITY PERCENTAGE SCORE

When they visit an hotel, AA inspectors supplement their general report with a subjective assessment of the quality of everything the hotel offers, including hospitality, based on what they experience as the 'mystery guest'. This enables them to award a percentage score for overall quality.

A one star hotel may receive as high a quality percentage score within its classification as a four or five star hotel, because the percentage score offers a comparison of quality within the star classification.

An intending guest, therefore, can see at a glance that a two star hotel, for example, with a percentage score of 69, offers a higher quality experience within its star classification than a two star hotel with a percentage score of 59.

To gain AA recognition in the first place, a hotel must achieve a minimum quality score of 50 per cent. If it achieves more than 80 per cent, it is almost certain to qualify for Red Stars. The percentage score for hotels with Red Stars is not shown in our guides.

Effectively, therefore, the quality percentage score for the ordinary star classification runs between 50 and 80 per cent, and Red Star hotels, as a general rule, achieve from 81 to 100 per cent.

Minimum Requirements for AA Recognition
★ One Star Hotels
Hotels in this classification are likely to be small and independently owned, with a family atmosphere. Services may be provided by the owner and family on an informal basis. There may be a limited range of facilities and meals may be fairly simple. Lunch, for example, may not be served. Some bedrooms may not have en suite bath/shower rooms. Maintenance, cleanliness and comfort should, however, always be of an acceptable standard.

★★ Two Star Hotels
In this classification hotels will typically be small to medium sized and offer more extensive facilities than at the one star level. Some business hotels come into the two star classification and guests can expect comfortable, well equipped, overnight accommodation, usually with an en suite bath/shower room. Reception and other staff will aim for a more professional presentation that at the one star level, and offer a wider range of straightforward services, including food and drink.

★★★ Three Star Hotels
At this level, hotels are usually of a size to support higher staffing levels, and a significantly greater quality and range of facilities than at the lower star classifications. Reception and the other public rooms will be more spacious and the restaurant will normally also cater for non-residents. All bedrooms will have fully en suite bath and shower rooms and offer a good standard of comfort and equipment, such as a hair dryer, direct dial telephone, toiletries in the bathroom. Some room service can be expected, and some provision for business travellers.

★★★★ Four Star Hotels
Expectations at this level include a degree of luxury as well as quality in the furnishings, decor and equipment, in every area of the hotel. Bedrooms will also usually offer more space than at the lower star levels, and well designed, co-ordinated furnishings and decor. The en suite bathrooms will have both bath and fixed shower. There will be a high enough ratio of staff to guests to provide services like porterage, 24-hour room service, laundry and dry-cleaning. The restaurant will demonstrate a serious approach to its cuisine.

★★★★★ Five Star Hotels
Here you should find spacious and luxurious accommodation throughout the hotel, matching the best international standards. Interior design should impress with its quality and attention to detail, comfort and elegance. Furnishings should be immaculate. Services should be formal, well supervised and flawless in attention to guests' needs, without being intrusive. The restaurant will demonstrate a high level of technical skill, producing dishes to the highest international standards. Staff will be knowledgeable, helpful, well versed in all aspects of customer care, combining efficiency with courtesy.

HOW THE AA ASSESSES RESTAURANTS FOR ROSETTE AWARDS

The AA's rosette award scheme is the only home-grown, nation-wide scheme for assessing the quality of food served by restaurants and hotels. The rosette scheme is an award scheme, not a classification scheme and although there is necessarily an element of subjectivity when it comes to assessing taste, we aim for a consistent approach to our awards throughout the UK. It is important, however, to remember that many places serve enjoyable food but do not qualify for an AA award.

Our awards are made solely on the basis of a meal visit or visits by one or more of our hotel and restaurant inspectors who have an unrivalled breadth and depth of experience in assessing quality. They award rosettes annually on a rising scale of one to five.

Recommendations from users of the guides are always welcome and will be passed on to the inspectors on merit for their consideration, but we do not guarantee a meal visit or an entry in the guide. Rosette awards are made or withdrawn only on the basis of our own inspectors' meal visits.

SO WHAT MAKES A RESTAURANT WORTHY OF A ROSETTE AWARD?

For our inspectors, frequently eating alone, the top and bottom line is the food. They are not swayed by a fashionable or luxurious setting, by the friendliness or immaculate uniforms of the staff, by fussy, over-elaborate presentation, or even by the size of the bill.

The taste of the food is what counts for them, and whether the dish successfully delivers to the diner what the menu promises. A restaurant is only as good as its worst meal.

Although presentation and competent service should be appropriate to the style of the restaurant and the quality of the food, they cannot affect the rosette assessment as such, either up or down.

The following summaries attempt to explain what our inspectors look for, but are intended only as guidelines. The AA is constantly reviewing its award criteria and competition usually results in an all-round improvement in standards, so it becomes increasingly difficult for restaurants to reach award level.

❀ One rosette
At the simplest level, one rosette, the chef should display a mastery of basic techniques and be able to produce dishes of sound quality and clarity of flavours, using good, fresh ingredients:

❀❀ Two rosettes
To gain two rosettes, the chef must show greater technical skill, more consistency and judgement in combining and balancing ingredients and a clear ambition to achieve high standards. Inspectors will look for evidence of innovation to test the dedication of the kitchen brigade, and the use of seasonal ingredients sourced from quality suppliers.

❀❀❀ Three rosettes
This award takes a restaurant into the big league, and, in a typical year, fewer than 10 per

cent of restaurants in our scheme achieve this distinction. Expectations of the kitchen are high, and inspectors find little room for inconsistencies. Exact technique, flair and imagination will come through in every dish, and balance and depth of flavour are all-important.

❀❀❀❀ Four rosettes
This is an exciting award because, at this level, not only should all technical skills be exemplary, but there should also be daring ideas, and they must work. There is no room for disappointment. Flavours should be accurate and vibrant.

❀❀❀❀❀ Five rosettes
This award is the ultimate awarded only when the cooking is at the pinnacle of achievement. Technique should be of such perfection that flavours, combinations and textures show a faultless sense of balance, giving each dish an extra dimension. The sort of cooking that never falters and always strives to give diners a truly memorable taste experience.

NEVADA BOB

THE LARGEST CHAIN OF PROFESSIONAL GOLF SHOPS IN THE WORLD

Already the UK's lowest prices

Major stockist of every top brand at prices that cannot be beaten

In-store driving range and putting green at all stores

Nevada Bob have got the largest range of GOLF CLUBS at the lowest possible prices of any golf chain in the world, with huge ranges from every leading brand. Try your clubs first and fully qualified assistants will be able to give you a personalised assessment to advise on the right clubs for your swing, stature and aspirations. These exceptional services at Nevada Bob mean you cannot buy better.

Why Pay More

NEVADA BOB 10% discount
off your next purchase of clubs*, bags, trolleys & clothing

Exclusively with this voucher

Phone freephone 0800 600 900
for your nearest Nevada Bob golf superstore (over 30 nation-wide)

THE UK's TOP SELLING ACCOMMODATION GUIDES

Illustrated with hundreds of colour photographs to help you choose the hotel or B & B that suits you. AA accommodation guides are fully updated every year and hotels and B & Bs are annually inspected.

The Hotel Guide gives full details of prices and facilities for star-rated hotels and also shows comparative quality in each star band. Accommodation ranges from luxurious five-star hotels, to good value places for overnight stays near motorways, to peaceful country house retreats and family holiday hotels. **Readers prize draw to win a relaxing weekend away.**

Bed & Breakfast Guide entries are graded on the new AA Quality Standards, shown by diamond symbols. Places range from inns and farmhouses to small, personally run hotels, which may be historic manor houses, old mills, converted schoolhouses and a host of other interesting buildings.

Breakfasts are graded for quality on a scale of one to three and good evening meals are highlighted. **Readers prize draw to win a relaxing weekend away.**

AA Lifestyle Guides

TELEPHONE CODE & NUMBER CHANGES

From 22 April 2000 there will be new dialling codes beginning with 02 in London, Cardiff, Coventry, Portsmouth, Southampton and right across Northern Ireland. At the same time, all local numbers in these areas will become eight-digit numbers.

PORTSMOUTH AREA TELEPHONE NUMBER CHANGES

From the 22 April 2000, all dialling codes listed as (01705) will change to **(023)**, followed by an eight-digit local number, starting with **92**.
For example, **(01705)** 123456 will become **(023) 92**12 3456.

SOUTHAMPTON AREA TELEPHONE NUMBER CHANGES

From 22 April 2000, all dialling codes listed as (01703) will change to **(023)**, followed by an eight-digit local number, starting with **80**.
For example, **(01703)** 123456 will become **(023) 80**12 3456.

COVENTRY AREA TELEPHONE NUMBER CHANGES

From the 22 April 2000, all dialling codes listed as (01203) will change to **(024)**, followed by an eight-digit local number. starting with **76**.
For example, **(01203)** 123456 will become **(024) 76**12 3456.

CARDIFF AREA TELEPHONE NUMBER CHANGES

From the 22 April 2000, all dialling codes listed as (01222) will change to **(029)**, followed by an eight-digit local number, starting with **20**.
For example, (01222) 123456 will become **(029) 20**12 3456.

LONDON TELEPHONE NUMBER CHANGES

From the 22 April 2000, the dialling code for the whole of London with be **(020)**, followed by an eight-digit local number.
For example, **(0171)** 123 4567 will become **(020) 7**123 4567,
(0181) 123 4567 will become **(020) 8**123 4567.

IN CASE OF DIFFICULTIES, PLEASE CONSULT DIRECTORY ENQUIRIES

REPUBLIC OF IRELAND – TELEPHONE NUMBER CHANGES

Some telephone codes have changed during the production of this guide. Only the new numbers can be dialled when contacting golf courses located in the areas listed below.

National Dialling Code (NDC)	Numbering Area	Leading Digits of Current Numbers	New Prefix
41	Drogheda	2, 3, 4, 7, 8	98
41	Ardee	5, 6	68
42	Dundalk	2, 3, 5, 7, 8	93
42	Carrickmoss	6, 90, 91, 92, 94, 98	96
42	Castleblayney	4, 95	97
49	Cavan	3, 6, 7	43
49	Cootehill	5	55
49	Oldcastle	4	85
49	Belturbet	2	95
65	Ennis	2, 3, 4, 6	68
65	Ennistymon	7, 8	70
65	Kilrush	5	90
66	Tralee	2, 3, 4, 8	71
66	Dingle	5	91
66	Cahirciveen	7	94
66	Killorglin	6, 9	97

Number Changes in the Cork Area

In the Cork area there will be a two-phase process. Local numbers beginning with 40, 43 or 33 will be prefixed with a 2 or a 7 (see Phase 1 below). In phase two, these new 2 or 7 numbers will be prefixed with a 4 (see Phase 2 below), as will the other first digits.

National Dialling Code (NDC)	Numbering Area	Leading Digit of Current Numbers	New Prefix
PHASE 1			
21	Cork	40	2
21	Coachford	43, 33	7
PHASE 2			
21	Cork	2, 3, 5, 8, 9	4
21	Midleton		4
21	Kinsale	7	4

NORTHERN IRELAND TELEPHONE NUMBER CHANGES

From the 22 April 2000, the dialling code for the whole of Northern Ireland will be **(028)**, followed by an eight-digit local number. For example, **(01232)** 123456 will become **(028) 90**12 3456, **(012477)** 123456 will become **(028) 247** 12345.

IN CASE OF DIFFICULTIES, PLEASE CONSULT DIRECTORY ENQUIRIES

NGLAND

John Ingham writes: Although I detest most of them, motorways have made our world seem a smaller place. And, for golfers, the construction of these speed traps altered attitudes to those who now find an away-day, with eighteen holes included, a realistic possibility. In short, our range is increased, with targets galore!

World travellers, coming here, are astonished at the variety of English courses, particularly in and around the major cities. Near Manchester you have the finest stretches of coastal links anywhere, with places like Formby and Hillside, not to mention Southport and Ainsdale, supporting the more famous championship tests at Birkdale, and Lytham. And thirty miles around London are wondrous courses which, if planted anywhere on this planet, would be worthy of a book in themselves.

Go to Birmingham, or Wolverhampton and not far away are Lindrick, and Woodhall Spa, my two favourites, and such courses as Hollinwell (Notts) and the much under-rated Sherwood Forest. And up in Yorkshire, they are rightly proud of Ganton while I have vivid memories of Moortown having played, and failed to win, the English championship when in my twenties.

People ask which, of all the courses in all of England, is my favourite. It's an absurd question, like asking which is your favourite wine, or ice-cream! But when pushed, I mention that I like a course that doesn't make golfers feel inadequate, that doesn't require them to hit the ball 200 yards over artificial duckponds, and won't tolerate rounds of four hours. On that score I name my home course of Royal Wimbledon - and might mention the world's finest nine-holer at Royal Worlington, although I haven't been there since I played Leonard Crawley, so cannot vouch for the quality of the lunches - most important!

But most writers of things golf will say that Sunningdale Old, or New, tops their list of favourites with, maybe, the Berkshire or Royal St George's (Sandwich) added for good measure. The golfing menu in England is totally remarkable, and nobody will argue with that.

ENGLAND

BEDFORDSHIRE

ASPLEY GUISE   Map 04 SP93

Aspley Guise & Woburn Sands West Hill MK17 8DX
☎ 01908 583596 Fax 01908 582974 (Pro Shop)
A fine undulating course in expansive heathland interspersed with many attractive clumps of gorse, broom and bracken. Some well-established silver birch are a feature. The 7th, 8th and 9th are really tough holes to complete the first half.
18 holes, 6079yds, Par 71, SSS 70, Course record 67.
Club membership 560.
Visitors   with member only at weekends.
Societies Wed & Fri normally booked 6 mths ahead.
Green Fees £29 per day; £23 per round.
Cards   💳 💳 💳 💳 💳
Prof   David Marsden
Designer   Sandy Herd
Facilities ⊗ ⍟ ⏳ 🏌 🍷 ⚑ 🛒 🏪 ➤ ✏
Location   2m W of M1 junc 13

Hotel   ★★★ 68% Moore Place Hotel, The Square, ASPLEY GUISE ☎ 01908 282000 39 ⇄ ♖ Annexe15 ⇄ ♖

BEDFORD   Map 04 TL04

Bedford Great Denham Golf Village MK40 4BF
☎ 01234 320022 Fax 01234 320023
American styled course with 89 bunkers, 8 large water features and large contoured greens. Built on sand and gravel the course is open all year round.
18 holes, 6471yds, Par 72, SSS 72.
Club membership 600.
Visitors   contact in advance, limited weekends.
Societies telephone for details.
Green Fees £20 (£28 weekends and bank holidays).
Cards   💳 💳 💳 💳 💳
Prof   Jermiah Richardson
Designer   David Pottage
Facilities ⊗ ⍟ ⏳ 🏌 🍷 ⚑ ⛳ 🛒 🏪 ➤ ✏ ♙
Location   2.5m W of Bedford off A428

Hotel   ★★★ 74% Woodlands Manor Hotel, Green Ln, Clapham, BEDFORD ☎ 01234 363281   30 ⇄ ♖ Annexe3 ⇄ ♖

Bedford & County Green Ln, Clapham MK41 6ET
☎ 01234 352617 Fax 01234 357195
A mature parkland course established in 1912 with views over Bedford and surrounding countryside. Beware of the brook that discreetly meanders through the 7th, 10th, 11th and 15th holes. The testing par 4 15th is one of the most challenging holes in the area.
18 holes, 6347yds, Par 70, SSS 70.
Club membership 600.
Visitors   handicap certificate required, weekends with member only.
Societies welcome Mon,Tue,Thu & Fri, telephone in advance.

Green Fees not confirmed.
Prof   R Tattersall
Facilities ⌖ ⚑ ♖ ✏
Location   2m N off A6

Hotel   ★★★ 74% Woodlands Manor Hotel, Green Ln, Clapham, BEDFORD ☎ 01234 363281 30 ⇄ ♖ Annexe3 ⇄ ♖

Bedfordshire Bromham Rd, Biddenham MK40 4AF
☎ 01234 261669 Fax 01234 261669
An attractive and easy walking parkland course with plenty of trees providing a problem for 'off-line' golfers.
18 holes, 6305yds, Par 70, SSS 70, Course record 63.
Club membership 700.

Visitors   may not play at weekends except with member.
Societies must telephone in advance/confirm in writing.
Green Fees not confirmed.
Prof   Peter Saunders
Facilities ⌖ ⚑ ⛳ ✏
Location   1m W on A428

Hotel   ★★★ 74% Woodlands Manor Hotel, Green Ln, Clapham, BEDFORD ☎ 01234 363281   30 ⇄ ♖ Annexe3 ⇄ ♖

Mowsbury Cleat Hill, Kimbolton Rd MK41 8DQ
☎ 01234 771041 & 216374 (prof)
Parkland municipal course in rural surroundings. Long and testing 14-bay driving range and squash facilities.
18 holes, 6514yds, Par 72, SSS 71, Course record 66.
Club membership 800.
Visitors   no restrictions.
Societies apply in writing.
Green Fees £7.50 per day/round (£9.90 weekends and bank holidays.
Prof   Malcolm Summers
Designer   Hawtree
Facilities ⊗ ⍟ ⏳ 🏌 🍷 ⚑ 🏪 ⛳ ✏ ♙
& Leisure squash.
Location   2m N of town centre on B660

Hotel   ★★★ 74% Woodlands Manor Hotel, Green Ln, Clapham, BEDFORD ☎ 01234 363281   30 ⇄ ♖ Annexe3 ⇄ ♖

Entries with a shaded background
identify courses that are
considered to be particularly interesting

CHALGRAVE   Map 04 TL02

Chalgrave Manor Dunstable Rd LU5 6JN
☎ 01525 876556 Fax 01525 876556
Undulating course constructed in 1994 offering a good test of
golf for all standards of golfer. Feature holes include the
short 10th (150 yards) that requires an accurate shot across
water to a splendid sloping green, and the Par 4 11th which
incorporates an elevated tee, a ditch, several bunkers, a pond
and perilously close out of bounds.
18 holes, 6382yds, Par 72, SSS 70, Course record 69.
Club membership 450.

Visitors	welcome, dress code smart casual, after 11am at weekends.
Societies	apply in writing or telephone, in advance.
Green Fees	£15 per round (£20 weekends).
Prof	Martin Brewer
Designer	M Palmer
Facilities	⊗ ⏃ 🏌 🍴 ♀ ⚲ 🏠 🕐 🔨 ♂ ⚑ ♣
Location	From M1 junct 12 take A5120 through Toddington, entrance about 1m out, well signposted
Hotel	★★★ 68% Old Palace Lodge Hotel, Church St, DUNSTABLE ☎ 01582 662201 68 ⇆ 🐾

COLMWORTH   Map 04 TL15

Colmworth & North Bedfordshire New Rd MK44 2NU
☎ 01234 378181 Fax 01234 376235
An easy walking course with well-bunkered greens, opened
in 1991. The course is often windy and plays longer than the
yardage suggests. Water comes into play on 3 holes.
18 holes, 6459yds, Par 71, SSS 71, Course record 69.
Club membership 230.

Visitors	advisable to contact in advance, tee reserved for members Sat & Sun until 9.30 am & between 12.30 & 2pm.
Societies	telephone in advance.
Green Fees	£10 per 18 holes; £8 per 12 holes; £6 per 9 holes (£17/£10/£9 weekends and bank holidays).
Prof	Adrian Clifford
Designer	John Glasgow
Facilities & Leisure	⊗ ⏃ by prior arrangement 🏌 🍴 ♀ ⚲ 🏠 🕐 ⚑ fishing.
Location	7m NE of Bedford, off B660
Hotel	★★★ 72% The Barns Hotel, Cardington Rd, BEDFORD ☎ 01234 270044 48 ⇆ 🐾

DUNSTABLE   Map 04 TL02

Dunstable Downs Whipsnade Rd LU6 2NB
☎ 01582 604472 Fax 01582 478700
A fine downland course set on two levels with far-
reaching views and frequent sightings of graceful
gliders. The 9th hole is one of the best short holes in the
country. There is a modernised clubhouse.
18 holes, 6255yds, Par 70, SSS 70, Course record 64.
Club membership 600.

Visitors	welcome Mon,Tue and Fri, weekends with member only. Handicap certificate required.
Societies	apply in advance.
Green Fees	£35 per day; £22.50 per round.
Prof	Michael Weldon
Designer	James Braid
Facilities	⊗ ⏃ 🏌 🍴 ♀ ⚲ 🏠 🔨 ♂
Location	2m S off B4541
Hotel	★★★ 68% Old Palace Lodge Hotel, Church St, DUNSTABLE ☎ 01582 662201 68 ⇆ 🐾

Griffin Chaul End Rd, Caddington LU1 4AX
☎ 01582 415573 Fax 01582 415314
A challenging 18-hole course with ponds, lakes and a SSS of
69.
18 holes, 6161yds, Par 71, SSS 69.
Club membership 480.

Visitors	welcome Mon-Fri & after 2pm weekends no need to book.
Societies	welcome midweek book by telephone.
Green Fees	not confirmed.
Facilities	⊗ 🏌 🍴 ♀ ⚲ 🏠
Location	Off A505 Luton/Dunstable
Hotel	★★★ 68% Old Palace Lodge Hotel, Church St, DUNSTABLE ☎ 01582 662201 68 ⇆ 🐾

LEIGHTON BUZZARD   Map 04 SP92

Leighton Buzzard Plantation Rd LU7 7JF
☎ 01525 373811 Fax 01525 373843
Parkland course with easy walking. The 17th and 18th holes
are challenging tree-lined finishing holes with tight fairways.
11th par 3 is signature hole.
18 holes, 5945yds, Par 71, SSS 70, Course record 66.
Club membership 700.

Visitors	may play yellow tees, may not play Tue (Ladies Day). May only play with member weekends and bank holidays. Handicap certificate required unless playing with member.
Societies	prior booking required.
Green Fees	not confirmed.
Prof	Lee Scarbrow
Facilities	⊗ ⏃ 🏌 🍴 ♀ ⚲ 🏠 🕐 🐾 🔨 ⚑
Location	1.5m N of town centre off A4146
Hotel	★★★ 55% Swan Hotel, High St, LEIGHTON BUZZARD ☎ 01525 372148 38 ⇆ 🐾

LOWER STONDON   Map 04 TL13

Mount Pleasant Station Rd SG16 6JL ☎ 01462 850999
A 9-hole course which, when played over 18 totals some 6003
yards. The course is undulating meadowland with mature
hedges and trees and also 10,000 new trees. Two small ponds
are crossed and there is a significant ditch in play on
2,7,8,9,11,16,17,18th holes. The 9,11 14th holes are all
400yds and play long into the prevailing West wind. Visitors
consider the greens some of the best conditioned in the area
and with good drainage the course rarely has to close.
9 holes, 6003yds, Par 70, SSS 69.
Club membership 300.

Visitors	no restrictions, can book 2 days in advance, booking advisable weekends & evenings May-Sep.
Societies	telephone or apply in writing.
Green Fees	not confirmed.
Cards	🌐 ▭ ▭ ▭ ▭ 🌀
Prof	Mike Roberts

▶

Designer	Derek Young
Facilities	▣ ▦ ♀ ⚲ 🏠 ⛳ ⛴ ✐
Location	0.75m W of A600

Hotel ★★★ 79% Flitwick Manor Hotel, Church Rd, FLITWICK ☎ 01525 712242 15 ⇔ ♠

LUTON   Map 04 TL02

South Beds Warden Hill LU2 7AE
☎ 01582 591500 Fax 01582 495381
18 and 9 hole downland courses, slightly undulating.
Galley Course: 18 holes, 6389yds, Par 71, SSS 71, Course record 64.
Warden Course: 9 holes, 4914yds, Par 64, SSS 64.
Club membership 1000.
Visitors	must contact in advance and have a handicap certificate.
Societies	telephone for details.
Green Fees	Galley Course: £29 per day; £19 per round (£38/£26 weekends & bank holidays). Warden Course: £5.50 (£6.50 weekends & bank holidays).
Prof	Eddie Cogle
Designer	1892
Facilities	⊗ by prior arrangement ▦ by prior arrangement ▣ ▦ ♀ ⚲ 🏠 ✐
Location	2m N of Luton on A6

Hotel ★★★ 66% Thistle Luton, Arndale Centre, LUTON ☎ 01582 734199 150 ⇔ ♠

Stockwood Park London Rd LU1 4LX ☎ 01582 413704
Well laid out municipal parkland course with established trees and several challenging holes.
18 holes, 6049yds, Par 69, SSS 69, Course record 67.
Club membership 800.
Visitors	no restrictions.
Societies	Mon, Tue & Thu only, telephone for application.
Green Fees	not confirmed.
Prof	Glyn McCarthy
Facilities	⊗ ▦ ▣ ▦ ♀ ⚲ 🏠 ⛳ ⛴ ✐ ♪
Location	1m S

Hotel ★★★ 58% The Chiltern, Waller Av, Dunstable Rd, LUTON ☎ 01582 575911 91 ⇔ ♠

MILLBROOK   Map 04 TL03

Lyshott Heath Millbrook Village MK45 2JB
☎ 01525 840252 Fax 01525 406249
Long parkland course, on rolling countryside high above the Bedfordshire plains. Laid out on well-drained sandy soil with many fairways lined with silver birch, pine and larch.
18 holes, 7100yds, Par 74, SSS 73, Course record 69.
Club membership 550.
Visitors	must contact in advance, may not play after 11am on Thu or after 12.30am at weekends.
Societies	telephone for details.
Green Fees	£20 (£30 weekends).
Prof	David Armor
Designer	William Sutherland
Facilities	⊗ ▦ ▣ ▦ ♀ ⚲ 🏠 ✐
Location	E side of village off A507

Hotel ★★★ 79% Flitwick Manor Hotel, Church Rd, FLITWICK ☎ 01525 712242 15 ⇔ ♠

PAVENHAM   Map 04 SP95

Pavenham Park MK43 7PE
☎ 01234 822202 Fax 01234 826602
Mature, undulating parkland course with fast contoured greens.
18 holes, 6400yds, Par 72, SSS 71, Course record 63.
Club membership 790.
Visitors	welcome weekdays, weekends as members guests only.
Societies	telephone in advance.
Green Fees	£30 per day; £20 per round weekdays.
Cards	💳 💳 💳 💳 💳
Prof	Zac Thompson
Designer	Zac Thompson
Facilities	⊗ ▦ ▣ ▦ ♀ ⚲ 🏠 ⛳ ⛴ ✐
Location	1.5m from A6, N of Bedford

Hotel ★★ 65% The Laws Hotel, High St, TURVEY ☎ 01234 881213 & 881655 Fax 01234 888864 23rm(20 ⇔ ♠)

SANDY   Map 04 TL14

John O'Gaunt Sutton Park SG19 2LY
☎ 01767 260360 Fax 01767 262834
Two magnificent parkland courses - John O'Gaunt and Carthagena - covering a gently undulating and tree-lined terrain. The John O'Gaunt course makes the most of numerous natural features, notably a river which crosses the fairways of four holes. The Carthagena course has larger greens, longer tees and from the back tees is a challenging course. Fine clubhouse.
John O'Gaunt Course: 18 holes, 6513yds, Par 71, SSS 71, Course record 64.
Carthagena Course: 18 holes, 5869yds, Par 69, SSS 69.
Club membership 1500.
Visitors	must contact in advance.
Societies	must pre-book.
Green Fees	£45 per day/round (£50 weekends & bank holidays).
Prof	Peter Round
Designer	John O'Gaunt/Others
Facilities	⊗ ▦ ▣ ▦ ♀ ⚲ 🏠 ⛳ ⛴ ✐
Location	3m NE of Biggleswade on B1040

Hotel ★★ 64% Abbotsley Golf Hotel, Potton Rd, Eynesbury Hardwicke, ST NEOTS ☎ 01480 474000 17 ⇔ ♠

SHEFFORD   Map 04 TL13

Beadlow Manor Hotel & Golf & Country Club SG17 5PH
☎ 01525 860800 Fax 01525 861345
A 36-hole golf and leisure complex. The Baroness Manhattan and the Baron Manhattan golf courses are undulating with water hazards on numerous holes. These are good challenging courses for both the beginner and low handicap player.
Baroness Course: 18 holes, 6072yds, Par 71, SSS 69, Course record 67.
Baron Course: 18 holes, 6619yds, Par 73, SSS 72.
Club membership 600.
Visitors	book in advance & must adhere to dress code.
Societies	apply in writing or telephone in advance.
Green Fees	not confirmed.

Prof	Phil Bradley/G Dixon
Facilities	⊗ 🏛 🏐 💺 ♀ 🛎 🍴 🏌 🐎 🚌 ♛ ⚐
& Leisure	sauna, solarium, gymnasium.
Location	2m W on A507

| Hotel | ★★★ 58% Beadlow Manor, Beadlow, SHEFFORD ☎ 01525 860800 33 ⇦ 🐾 |

TILSWORTH   Map 04 SP92

Tilsworth Dunstable Rd LU7 9PU
☎ 01525 210721/2 Fax 01525 210465
An undulating parkland course upgraded from 9 to 18 holes
in 1992. 30-bay floodlit driving range.
18 holes, 5306yds, Par 69, SSS 66, Course record 66.
Club membership 400.

Visitors	may book up to 7 days in advance. May not play before 10am Sundays.
Societies	welcome weekdays, apply in advance.
Green Fees	£10 per 18 holes; £6.50 per 9 holes (£12/£7.50 weekends).
Cards	💳 💳 💳 💳
Prof	Nick Webb
Facilities	⊗ 🏛 🏐 💺 ♀ 🛎 🍴 🐎 🚌 ♛ ⚐
Location	0.5m NE off A5

| Hotel | ★★★ 68% Old Palace Lodge Hotel, Church St, DUNSTABLE ☎ 01582 662201 68 ⇦ 🐾 |

WHIPSNADE   Map 04 TL01

Whipsnade Park Studham Ln, Dagnall HP4 1RH
☎ 01442 842330 Fax 01442 842090
Parkland course situated on downs overlooking the Chilterns
adjoining Whipsnade Zoo. Easy walking, good views.
18 holes, 6800yds, Par 73, SSS 72, Course record 66.
Club membership 600.

Visitors	welcome weekdays, with member only at weekends. Must contact in advance.
Societies	by prior arrangement.
Green Fees	£34 per day; £24 per round.
Cards	💳 💳 💳
Prof	Michael Lewendon
Facilities	⊗ 🏛 🏐 💺 ♀ 🛎 🐎 🚌 ⚐
Location	1m E off B4506

| Hotel | ★★★ 68% Old Palace Lodge Hotel, Church St, DUNSTABLE ☎ 01582 662201 68 ⇦ 🐾 |

WOBURN   Map 04 SP93

For Woburn Golf Course see Bow Brickhill,
Buckinghamshire.

WYBOSTON   Map 04 TL15

Wyboston Lakes MK44 3AL
☎ 01480 223004 Fax 01480 407330
Parkland course, with narrow fairways, small greens, set
around four lakes and a river which provide the biggest
challenge on this very scenic course.
18 holes, 5803yds, Par 70, SSS 69, Course record 65.
Club membership 300.

| Visitors | a booking system is in operation at weekends, book no more than 8 days in advance. |
| Societies | telephone in advance. |

Green Fees	not confirmed.
Prof	Paul Ashwell
Designer	N Oakden
Facilities	⊗ 🏛 🏐 💺 ♀ 🛎 🍴 🐎 🚌 ♛ ⚐
& Leisure	fishing, sauna, solarium, gymnasium.
Location	1m S of St Neots off A1/A428

| Hotel | ★★★ 74% Woodlands Manor Hotel, Green Ln, Clapham, BEDFORD ☎ 01234 363281 30 ⇦ 🐾 Annexe3 ⇦ 🐾 |

BERKSHIRE

ASCOT   Map 04 SU96

Berkshire Swinley Rd SL5 8AY ☎ 01344 621496
Two heathland courses with splendid tree-lined fairways.
Red Course: 18 holes, 6369yds, Par 72, SSS 71.
Blue Course: 18 holes, 6260yds, Par 71, SSS 71.
Club membership 1000.

Visitors	weekdays only on application to secretary.
Societies	applications in writing only.
Green Fees	not confirmed.
Prof	P Anderson
Designer	H Fowler
Facilities	⊗ 🏐 💺 ♀ 🛎 🍴 🐎 🚌 ⚐
Location	2.5m NW of M3 jct 3 on A332

| Hotel | ★★★★ 61% The Berystede, Bagshot Rd, Sunninghill, ASCOT ☎ 01344 623311 91 ⇦ 🐾 |

Lavender Park Swinley Rd SL5 8BD
☎ 01344 890940 & 886096
Public parkland course, ideal for the short game featuring
challenging narrow fairways. Driving range with 9-hole par 3
course, floodlit until 22.30 hrs.
9 holes, 1102yds, Par 27, SSS 28.

Visitors	no restrictions.
Societies	welcome, notice prefered.
Green Fees	not confirmed.
Prof	Wayne Ower/Andy Piper
Facilities	💺 ♀ 🍴 ⚐
Location	3.5m SW of Ascot, on A332

| Hotel | ★★★★ 61% The Berystede, Bagshot Rd, Sunninghill, ASCOT ☎ 01344 623311 91 ⇦ 🐾 |

Mill Ride Mill Ride SL5 8LT
☎ 01344 886777 Fax 01344 886820
Opened for play in 1991, this 18-hole course combines links
and parkland styles. The holes require as much thinking as
playing.
18 holes, 6752yds, Par 72, SSS 72, Course record 64.
Club membership 400.

Visitors	must contact in advance, limited access at weekends.
Societies	apply in advance.
Green Fees	not confirmed.
Cards	🔲 🔲 🔲 🔲
Prof	Mark Palmer
Designer	Donald Steel
Facilities	⊗ �🁢 🖺 🌟 ♀ ⚲ 🏠 ⛳ 🏌 ♂ 🏌
& Leisure	sauna, steamroom.
Location	2m W of Ascot
Hotel	★★★★ 61% The Berystede, Bagshot Rd, Sunninghill, ASCOT ☎ 01344 623311 91 ⇔ 🏨

Royal Ascot Winkfield Rd SL5 7LJ
☎ 01344 625175 Fax 01344 872330
Heathland course inside Ascot racecourse and exposed to
weather.
18 holes, 5716yds, Par 68, SSS 68, Course record 65.
Club membership 620.

Visitors	must be guest of member or contact secretary in advance. Not weekends.
Societies	telephone for provisional booking.
Green Fees	£15 with member only.
Prof	Alistair White
Designer	J H Taylor
Facilities	⊗ �🁢 🖺 🌟 ♀ ⚲ 🏠 🏌
Location	0.5m N on A330
Hotel	★★★★ 61% The Berystede, Bagshot Rd, Sunninghill, ASCOT ☎ 01344 623311 91 ⇔ 🏨

Swinley Forest Coronation Rd SL5 9LE
☎ 01344 874979 (Secretary) Fax 01344 874733
An attractive and immaculate course of heather and pine
situated in the heart of Swinley Forest. The 17th is as
good a short hole as will be found, with a bunkered
plateau green and the 12th hole is one of the most
challenging par 4's.
18 holes, 6100yds, Par 69, SSS 70, Course record 62.
Club membership 325.

Visitors	on introduction of a member or by invitation only.
Societies	must contact in writing.
Green Fees	£65 per day.
Prof	R C Parker
Designer	Harry Colt
Facilities	⊗ �🁢 🖺 🌟 ♀ ⚲ 🏠 ⛳ 🏌 ♂ 🏌
Location	1.5m S, off A330
Hotel	★★★★ 61% The Berystede, Bagshot Rd, Sunninghill, ASCOT ☎ 01344 623311 91 ⇔ 🏨

BINFIELD
Map 04 SU87

Blue Mountain Golf Centre Wood Ln RG42 4EX
☎ 01344 300200 Fax 01344 360960
An 18-hole Pay and Play course with many testing holes with
water hazards. Greens are large, undulating and strategically
placed bunkers provide a fair challenge.
18 holes, 6097yds, Par 70, SSS 70, Course record 61.
Club membership 1250.

Visitors	tee times bookable in person at the Golf Shop up to 9 days in advance.
Societies	must contact in advance.
Green Fees	£16 per 18 holes; £12 per 9 holes (£20/£12 weekends).
Cards	🔲 🔲 🔲 🔲 🔲
Prof	Iain Looms
Facilities	⊗ ⍟ ⍫ �🁢 🖺 🌟 ♀ ⚲ 🏠 ⛳ 🏌 ♂ 🏌
& Leisure	golf academy tuition.
Location	2m from junct 10 of the M4
Hotel	★★★★ 76% Coppid Beech, John Nike Way, BRACKNELL ☎ 01344 303333 205 ⇔ 🏨

CHADDLEWORTH
Map 04 SU47

West Berkshire RG20 7DU
☎ 01488 638574 & 638851 Fax 01488 638781
Challenging and interesting downland course with testing
635 yds 5th hole, one of the longest par 5's in southern
England. Bunkers are well placed from tees and around the
greens to catch any wayward shots.
18 holes, 7059yds, Par 73, SSS 74.
Club membership 650.

Visitors	must contact in advance, may play weekends pm only.
Societies	telephone in advance
Green Fees	£30 per day; £20 per round (£24 weekends pm only).
Cards	🔲 🔲
Prof	Paul Simpson
Designer	Robin Stagg
Facilities	⊗ ⍟ ⍫ 🖺 🌟 ♀ ⚲ 🏠 ⛳ 🏌 ♂ 🏌
Location	1m S of village off A338
Hotel	★★★ 63% The Chequers, Oxford St, NEWBURY ☎ 01635 38000 45 ⇔ 🏨 Annexe11 ⇔ 🏨

> Entries with a shaded background
> identify courses that are
> considered to be particularly interesting

COOKHAM   Map 04 SU88

Winter Hill Grange Ln SL6 9RP
☎ 01628 527613 (Secretary)
Parkland course set in a curve of the Thames with wonderful views across the river to Cliveden.
18 holes, 6408yds, Par 72, SSS 71, Course record 63.
Club membership 850.
Visitors   not permitted weekends.
Societies   welcome Wed & Fri, telephone initially.
Green Fees   not confirmed.
Prof   Mark Booth
Designer   Charles Lawrie
Facilities   ⊗ 占 ☕ ♀ 𝓪 ⍩ ⚐ ⚲ ⚑
Location   1m NW off B4447

Hotel   ★★★★ 72% The Compleat Angler, Marlow Bridge, MARLOW
                  ☎ 01628 484444   65 ⇆ ↑

CROWTHORNE   Map 04 SU86

East Berkshire Ravenswood Ave RG45 6BD
☎ 01344 772041 Fax 01344 777378
An attractive heathland course with an abundance of heather and pine trees. Walking is easy and the greens are exceptionally good. Some fairways become tight where the heather encroaches on the line of play. The course is testing and demands great accuracy.
18 holes, 6344yds, Par 69, SSS 70.
Club membership 766.
Visitors   must contact in advance and have a handicap certificate; must play with member at weekends & bank holidays.
Societies   telephone for availability.
Green Fees   £37 per day.
Prof   Arthur Roe
Designer   P Paxton
Facilities   ⊗ ⍟ by prior arrangement 占 ☕ ♀ 𝓪 ⍩
                  ⚐ ⚲
Location   W side of town centre off B3348

Hotel   ★★★★★ 72% Pennyhill Park Hotel, London Rd, BAGSHOT
                  ☎ 01276 471774
                  28 ⇆ ↑ Annexe86 ⇆ ↑

DATCHET   Map 04 SU97

Datchet Buccleuch Rd SL3 9BP
☎ 01753 543887 & 541872 Fax 01753 541872
Meadowland course, easy walking.
9 holes, 5978yds, Par 70, SSS 69, Course record 63.
Club membership 430.
Visitors   may play weekdays before 3pm.
Societies   Tue only. (Other times by prior arrangement)
Green Fees   £24 per 36 holes; £16 per round.
Facilities   ⊗ ⍟ 占 ☕ ♀ 𝓪 ⚲
Location   NW side of Datchet off B470

Hotel   ★★★ 68% The Castle Hotel, High St, WINDSOR ☎ 01753 851011 111 ⇆ ↑

MAIDENHEAD   Map 04 SU88

Bird Hills Drift Rd, Hawthorn Hill SL6 3ST
☎ 01628 771030 Fax 01628 631023
A gently undulating course with easy walking and many water hazards. Some challenging holes are the Par 5 6th dogleg, Par 3 9th surrounded by water and bunkers, and the 16th which is a long uphill Par 4 and a two-tier green.
18 holes, 6176yds, Par 72, SSS 69, Course record 65.
Club membership 400.
Visitors   to book ring 7 days in advance.
Societies   write or telephone in advance.
Green Fees   not confirmed.
Cards   ⌐ ▬ 🖂
Prof   Nick Slimming
Facilities   ⊗ ⍟ 占 ☕ ♀ 𝓪 ⍩ ⚐ ⚲ ⚑
Location   4m SW of Bray on A330

Hotel   ★★★ 73% Stirrups Country House, Maidens Green, BRACKNELL
                  ☎ 01344 882284   28 ⇆

Castle Royle Golf & Country Club Bath Rd, Knowl Hill RG10 9XA ☎ 01628 829252 Fax 01628 829299
Designed to championship standard, Castle Royle has six lakes and is well drained and irrigated. In attractive countryside with views of Windsor Castle, this gently undulating parkland course is very well bunkered with wide fairways and there are Par 3's with all four aspects to the prevailing wind as each faces a different direction.
18 holes, 6828yds, Par 72, SSS 73.
Club membership 500.
Visitors   must contact in advance.
Societies   must telephone in advance.
Green Fees   not confirmed.
Prof   Mike Herbert
Designer   Neil Coles
Facilities   ⊗ ⍟ 占 𝓪 ⍩ ↖ 🏌 ⚲ ⚑
& Leisure   heated indoor swimming pool, sauna, solarium, gymnasium.
Location   Bath road A4

Hotel   ★★★★ Fredrick's Hotel, Shoppenhangers Rd, MAIDENHEAD ☎ 01628 581000   37 ⇆ ↑

Maidenhead Shoppenhangers Rd SL6 2PZ
☎ 01628 624693 Fax 01628 624693
A pleasant parkland course on level ground with easy walking to good greens. Perhaps a little short but there are many natural features and some first-rate short holes.
18 holes, 6364yds, Par 70, SSS 70.
Club membership 650.
Visitors   may not play after noon on Fri or at weekends. Must contact in advance and have a handicap certificate.
Societies   must contact in writing.
Green Fees   £35 per day; £30 per round.
Prof   Steve Geary
Designer   Alex Simpson
Facilities   ⊗ ⍟ 占 ☕ ♀ 𝓪 ⍩ ⚐ ⚲
Location   S side of town centre off A308

Hotel   ★★★★ Fredrick's Hotel, Shoppenhangers Rd, MAIDENHEAD
                  ☎ 01628 581000   37 ⇆ ↑

Temple Henley Rd, Hurley SL6 5LH
☎ 01628 824795 Fax 01628 828119

An open parkland course offering extensive views over the Thames Valley. Firm, relatively fast greens rely on natural slopes and subtle contours to provide a challenging test to golfers of all abilities. Excellent drainage assures play during inclement weather.
18 holes, 6207yds, Par 70, SSS 70, Course record 63.
Club membership 480.

Visitors	must contact in advance, limited weekend access.
Societies	apply in writing for formal bookings.
Green Fees	£45 per day; £30 per round (£50/£35 weekends & bank holidays).
Cards	🖃 🖩 🏧
Prof	James Whiteley
Designer	Willie Park (Jnr)
Facilities	⊗ 🖳 🍽 ♀ 🏖 🏠 ⛳ ⚲ 🛒 ♂
Location	Exit M4 jct 8/9 take A404M then A4130,or M40 exit jct 4 take A404 then A4130,signposted Henley
Hotel	★★★★ 72% The Compleat Angler, Marlow Bridge, MARLOW ☎ 01628 484444 65 ⇔ ♣

NEWBURY   Map 04 SU46

Donnington Valley Old Oxford Rd, Donnington RG14 3AG
☎ 01635 32488 Fax 0165 569481

Undulating, testing course with mature trees and elevated greens, some protected by water.
18 holes, 6500yds, Par 71, SSS 71.
Club membership 520.

Visitors	booking system up to 7 days in advance, members have priority weekends.
Societies	write or telephone in advance.
Green Fees	not confirmed.
Cards	🖃 🖩 🏧
Prof	Edward Lainchbury
Designer	Cox family
Facilities	⊗ 🞐 🖳 🏖 🏠 ⛳ 🛒 ♂ ♪
& Leisure	hard tennis courts.
Location	2m N of Newbury
Hotel	★★★★ 80% Donnington Valley Hotel & Golf Course, Old Oxford Rd, Donnington, NEWBURY ☎ 01635 551199 58 ⇔ ♣

Newbury & Crookham Bury's Bank Rd, Greenham RG19 8BZ ☎ 01635 40035 Fax 01635 40045

A well-laid out, attractive course running mostly through woodland, and giving more of a challenge than its length suggests.
18 holes, 5940yds, Par 69, SSS 68.
Club membership 800.

Visitors	must play with member on weekends & bank holidays. Handicap certificate required.
Societies	must contact in advance.
Green Fees	£30 per day, £20 per round.
Prof	David Harris
Facilities	⊗ 🞐 🖳 🍽 ♀ 🏠 ⛳ ♂
Location	2m SE off A34
Hotel	★★★ 63% The Chequers, Oxford St, NEWBURY ☎ 01635 38000 45 ⇔ ♣ Annexe11 ⇔ ♣

READING   Map 04 SU77

Calcot Park Bath Rd, Calcot RG31 7RN
☎ 0118 942 7124 Fax 0118 945 3373

A delightfully sporting parkland course just outside the town. Hazards include a lake and many trees. The 6th is the longest, 507 yard par 5, with the tee-shot hit downhill over cross-bunkers to a well-guarded green. The 13th (194 yards) requires a big carry over a gully to a plateau green.
18 holes, 6283yds, Par 70, SSS 70, Course record 63.
Club membership 730.

Visitors	must have handicap certificate or letter of introduction from club. May play weekdays only, excluding bank holidays.
Societies	must apply in writing.
Green Fees	£36 per day/round; £22 after 4pm.
Prof	Ian Campbell
Designer	H S Colt
Facilities	⊗ 🞐 🖳 🍽 ♀ 🏖 🏠 ⛳ ♂
& Leisure	fishing.
Location	1.5m from M4 junct 12 on A4 towards Reading
Hotel	★★★ 77% The Copper Inn Hotel & Restaurant, Church Rd, PANGBOURNE ☎ 0118 984 2244 14 ⇔ ♣ Annexe8 ⇔ ♣

Hennerton Crazies Hill Rd, Wargrave RG10 8LT
☎ 0118 940 1000 Fax 0118 940 1042

Overlooking the Thames Valley, this Par 68 course has many of existing natural features and an good number of hazards such as bunker, mature trees and two small lakes. The most memorable hole is probably the 7th which is a par 3, 183 yards crossing a sharp valley to the green from which there are spectacular views of the whole course.
9 holes, 5460yds, Par 68, SSS 67, Course record 66.
Club membership 450.

Visitors	telephone in advance.
Societies	telephone or write for information.
Green Fees	not confirmed.
Prof	William Farrow
Designer	Col D Beard
Facilities	⊗ 🞐 🖳 🍽 ♀ 🏖 🏠 ⛳ ♂ ♪
Location	Follow signs from A321 Wargrave High Street
Hotel	★★★ 70% Red Lion Hotel, Hart St, HENLEY-ON-THAMES ☎ 01491 572161 27 ⇔ ♣

Mapledurham Chazey Heath, Mapledurham RG4 7UD
☎ 0118 946 3353 Fax 0118 946 3363 ▶

SUNNINGDALE

SUNNINGDALE *Berks* ☎ **01344 621681**
Fax 01344 624154   **Map 04 SU96**

John Ingham writes: Many famous golfers maintain that Sunningdale, on the borders of Berkshire, is the most attractive inland course in Britain. The great Bobby Jones once played the 'perfect' round of 66 made up of threes and fours on the Old Course. Later, Norman von Nida of Australia shot a 63 while the then professional at the club, Arthur Lees, scored a 62 to win a huge wager.

To become a member of this club takes years of waiting. Maybe it is the quality of the courses, maybe the clubhouse atmosphere and perhaps the excellence of the professionals shop has something to do with it; but added up, it has to be the most desirable place to spend a day.

Founded in 1900, the Old Course was designed by Willie Park, while H.S. Colt created the New Course in 1923. Most golfers will agree that there isn't one indifferent hole on either course. While the Old Course, with silver birch, heather and perfect turf, is lovely to behold, the New Course alongside is considered by many to be its equal. But just as golfers want to play the Old Course at St Andrews, and miss the redesigned Jubilee, so visitors to Sunningdale opt for the Old, and fail to realise what they are overlooking by not playing the New.

The classic Old Course is not long, measuring just 6341 yards, and because the greens are normally in excellent condition, anyone with a 'hot' putter can have an exciting day, providing they keep teeshots on the fairway and don't stray into the gorse and the pine trees that lie in wait. On a sunny day, if you had to be anywhere in the world playing well, then we opt for the elevated 10th tee on the Old. What bliss!

Visitors	May not play Fri, Sat, Sun or public holidays. Must contact in advance and have a handicap certificate and letter of introduction
Societies	Tue, Wed, Thu by arrangement.
Green fees	Old Course £105 per day, New Course £75; Combined £130. ▬ ▬ ▬ ▬ ▨
Facilities	⊗ ⊾ ▼ ♀ ⚐ ⚑ 𝆑 Professional Keith Maxwell
Location	Ridgemount Rd Sunningdale, Ascot SL5 9RR (1m S of Sunningdale, off A30)

36 holes. Old Course: 18 holes, 6341yds, Par 70, SSS 70
New Course: 18 holes 6433yds, Par 71, SSS 71

WHERE TO STAY AND EAT NEARBY

HOTELS:
ASCOT
★★★★ ❀ ❀ 70% The Royal Berkshire, London Rd, Sunninghill. ☎ 01344 623322. 63 ⇌ ⁞

★★★★ 61% The Berystede, Bagshot Rd, Sunninghill. ☎ 01344 23311. 91 (90 ⇌ ⁞ 1 ⁞)

★★ 74% Highclere, 19 Kings Rd, Sunninghill. ☎ 01344 625220. 11 ⁞

★★ 66% Brockenhurst, Brockenhurst Rd. ☎ 01344 873252. 11 ⇌ ⁞ Annexe 4 ⇌ ⁞

BAGSHOT
★★★★★ ❀ ❀ 72% Pennyhill Park, London Rd. ☎ 01276 471774 21 ⇌ ⁞ Annexe 84 ⇌ ⁞

RESTAURANTS:
ASCOT
❀ Jade Fountain, 38 High St, Sunningdale. ☎ 01344 27070
BRAY
❀ ❀ ❀ ❀ Waterside Inn, Ferry Road. ☎ 01628 620691.

18-hole course designed by Bob Sandow. Flanked by hedgerows and mature woods, it is testing for players of all levels.
18 holes, 5750yds, Par 69, SSS 68, Course record 66 or 57 holes.
Club membership 340.
Visitors dress code and advanced booking required
Societies must contact in advance.
Green Fees not confirmed.
Cards ▬▬ 🟦🟦🟦 ▤
Prof Symon O'Keefe
Designer Bob Sandow
Facilities ⊗ ⅷ ㄴ ♣ ♀ ♧ 🏠 ⛳ ◊
Location On A4074 to Oxford

Hotel ★★★★ 59% Holiday Inn, Caversham Bridge, Richfield Av, READING
☎ 0118 925 9988 111 ➡ ☏

Reading 17 Kidmore End Rd, Emmer Green RG4 8SG
☎ 0118 947 2909 (Manager)
Pleasant tree-lined parkland course, part hilly and part flat with interesting views and several challenging par 3's.
18 holes, 6212yds, Par 70, SSS 70, Course record 67.
Club membership 700.
Visitors contact the professional. Welcome weekdays, with member only weekends.
Societies apply by telephone.
Green Fees not confirmed.
Prof Andrew Wild
Facilities ⊗ ⅷ ㄴ ♣ ♀ ♧ 🏠 ◊ ℓ
Location 2m N off B481

Hotel ★★★ 63% Ship Hotel, 4-8 Duke St, READING ☎ 0118 958 3455 52 ➡ ☏

SINDLESHAM   Map 04 SU76

Bearwood Mole Rd RG41 5DB ☎ 0118 976 0060
Flat parkland course with one water hazard, the 40 acre lake which features on the challenging 6th and 7th holes. Also driving range.
9 holes, 5610yds, Par 70, SSS 68, Course record 66.
Club membership 500.
Visitors welcome weekdays and weekend afternoons (contact in advance for pm weekend bookings)
Societies apply in writing.
Green Fees £18 per 18 holes; £10 per 9 holes (£22/£15 weekends).
Cards ▬▬ 🟦🟦 🟥🟦 ▤
Prof Bayley Tustin
Designer Barry Tustin
Facilities ⊗ ㄴ ♣ ♀ ♧ 🏠 ◊ ℓ
Location 1m SW on B3030

Hotel ★★★★ 66% Reading Moat House, Mill Ln, Sindlesham, WOKINGHAM
☎ 0118 949 9988 96 ➡ ☏

SONNING   Map 04 SU77

Sonning Duffield Rd RG4 6GJ
☎ 0118 969 3332 Fax 0118 944 8409
A quality parkland course and the scene of many county championships. Wide fairways, not overbunkered, and very good greens. Holes of changing character through wooded belts.

18 holes, 6366yds, Par 70, SSS 70, Course record 65.
Club membership 750.
Visitors weekdays only. Handicap certificate or proof of membership of another club required.
Societies must apply in writing. Wed only.
Green Fees £35 per day; £25 after 10.30am.
Prof R McDougall
Designer Hawtree
Facilities ⊗ ⅷ by prior arrangement ㄴ ♣ ♀ ♧ 🏠 ◊

Location 1m S off A4

Hotel ★★★ 76% The French Horn, SONNING
☎ 0118 969 2204 12 ➡ ☏ Annexe8 ➡ ☏

STREATLEY   Map 04 SU58

Goring & Streatley RG8 9QA
☎ 01491 873229 Fax 01491 875224
A parkland/moorland course that requires 'negotiating'. Four well-known first holes lead up to the heights of the 5th tee, to which there is a 300ft climb. Wide fairways, not overbunkered, with nice rewards on the way home down the last few holes. A delightful course that commands magnificent views of the Ridgeway and the River Thames.
18 holes, 6320yds, Par 71, SSS 70, Course record 65.
Club membership 740.
Visitors must contact in advance, with member only at weekends. Handicap certificate required.
Societies apply in writing.
Green Fees £30 per day; £22 per round.
Prof Roy Mason
Facilities ⊗ ⅷ ㄴ ♣ ♀ ♧ 🏠 ⛳ ◊
Location N of village off A417

Hotel ★★★★ 67% The Swan Diplomat Hotel, High St, STREATLEY
☎ 01491 873737 46 ➡ ☏

SUNNINGDALE   Map 04 SU96

SUNNINGDALE See page 27

Sunningdale Ladies Cross Rd SL5 9RX ☎ 01344 620507
A short 18-hole course with a typical Surrey heathland layout. A very tight course, making for a challenging game.
18 holes, 3616yds, Par 60, SSS 60, Course record 51.
Club membership 350.
Visitors telephone in advance.
Societies Ladies societies only.
Green Fees £18-£27 per day.
Facilities ⊗ ㄴ ♣ ♀ ♧ 🏠 ◊
& Leisure Practice net.
Location 1m S off A30

Hotel ★★★★ 61% The Berystede, Bagshot Rd, Sunninghill, ASCOT
☎ 01344 623311 91 ➡ ☏

WOKINGHAM   Map 04 SU86

Downshire Easthampstead Park RG40 3DH
☎ 01344 302030 Fax 01344 301020
Beautiful municipal parkland course with mature trees.
Water hazards come into play on the 14th and 18th holes,
and especially on the short 7th, a testing downhill 169 yards
over the lake. Pleasant easy walking. Challenging holes: 7th
(par 4), 15th (par 4), 16th (par 3).
18 holes, 6416yds, Par 73, SSS 71.
Club membership 1000.
Visitors	must book six days in advance by telephone or seven days in person, weekend times available.
Societies	must telephone in advance.
Green Fees	not confirmed.
Prof	Wayne Owers
Facilities	⊗ ⅃ 🛒 ♀ 🛆 🏠 ⛳ ↘ ⚒ ♂ ⚑
& Leisure	9 hole pitch & putt.
Location	3m SW of Bracknell

Hotel   ★★★★ 76% Coppid Beech, John Nike Way,
BRACKNELL ☎ 01344 303333 205 ⇌ ♞

Sand Martins Finchampstead Rd RG40 3RQ
☎ 0118 977 0265 Fax 0118 977 0282
Two different 9-hole loops: the front nine is mostly tree-lined
with ponds and the back nine is similar to a links course.
18 holes, 6204yards, Par 70, SSS 70, Course record 65.
Club membership 800.

Visitors	no restrictions, but with member only at weekends.
Societies	prior arrangement by telephone.
Green Fees	on request.
Cards	💳 💳 💳 💳 💳
Prof	Andrew Hall
Designer	Edward Fox
Facilities	⊗ ⅃ by prior arrangement ⅃ 🛒 ♀ 🛆 🏠 ⛳ ↘ ⚒ ♂ ⚑
Location	1m S of Wokingham

Hotel   ★★★★ 66% Reading Moat House, Mill Ln,
Sindlesham, WOKINGHAM
☎ 0118 949 9988 96 ⇌ ♞

BRISTOL

BRISTOL   Map 03 ST57

Bristol and Clifton Beggar Bush Ln, Failand BS8 3TH
☎ 01275 393474 Fax 01275 394611
A downland course with splendid turf and fine tree-lined
fairways. The 222-yard (par 3) 13th with the green well
below, and the par 4 16th, with its second shot across an
old quarry, are outstanding. There are splendid views
over the Bristol Channel towards Wales.
18 holes, 6316yds, Par 70, SSS 70, Course record 65.
Club membership 950.
Visitors	must have a handicap certificate. Weekends restricted.
Societies	telephone to enquire.
Green Fees	£32 per day (£35 weekends).
Prof	Peter Mawson
Designer	Peter McEvoy
Facilities	⊗ by prior arrangement ⅃ 🛒 ♀ 🛆 🏠 ⛳ ↘ ♂
Location	4m W on B3129 off A369

Hotel   ★★★ 67% Redwood Lodge Hotel, Beggar
Bush Ln, Failand, BRISTOL
☎ 01275 393901 112 ⇌ ♞

Filton Golf Course Ln, Filton BS34 7QS
☎ 0117 969 4169 Fax 0117 931 4359
Challenging parkland course situated on high ground in a
pleasant suburb to the north of the city. Extensive views can
be enjoyed from the course, especially from the second tee
and the clubhouse, where on a clear day the Cotswold Hills
and the Brecon Beacons can be seen. Good par 4 testing hole
'dog-leg' 383 yds.
18 holes, 6310yds, Par 70, SSS 70, Course record 68.
Club membership 730.
Visitors	advisable to contact in advance for availability, may not play at weekends unless with member.
Societies	apply in writing/phone for details.
Green Fees	£25 per day; £20 per round.
Prof	J C N Lumb
Facilities	⊗ ⅲ ⅃ 🛒 ♀ 🛆 🏠 ⛳ ↘ ⚒ ♂
Location	5m NW off A38

Hotel   B Posthouse Bristol, Filton Rd, Hambrook,
BRISTOL ☎ 0117 956 4242 198 ⇌ ♞

Henbury Henbury Hill, Westbury-on-Trym BS10 7QB
☎ 0117 950 0044 & 950 2121 (Prof) Fax 0117 959 192
8
A parkland course tree-lined and on two levels. The
River Trym comes into play on the 7th drop-hole with its
green set just over the stream. The last nine holes have
the beautiful Blaise Castle woods for company.
18 holes, 6039yds, Par 70, SSS 70, Course record 65.
Club membership 760.
Visitors	handicap certificate required, with member only at weekends. Advisable to contact in advance for availability.
Societies	apply in writing or telephone well in advance. Tue & Fri only.
Green Fees	not confirmed.
Prof	Nick Riley

▶

Facilities ⊗ ⅲ by prior arrangement 🏌 ⚑ ♀ ⚑ 🏠
⛳ ✎

Location 3m NW of city centre on B4055 off A4018

Hotel ★★★ 63% Henbury Lodge Hotel, Station
Rd, Henbury, BRISTOL
☎ 0117 950 2615 12 ⇆ ⌂ Annexe9 ⇆ ⌂

Knowle West Town Ln, Brislington BS4 5DF
☎ 0117 977 0660 Fax 0117 972 0615
A parkland course with nice turf. The first five holes
climb up and down hill but the remainder are on a more
even plane.
18 holes, 6016yds, Par 69, SSS 69, Course record 61.
Club membership 700.
Visitors must have handicap certificate, must
telephone professional 01179 779193 for
weekends.
Societies Thu only, apply in writing.
Green Fees £27 per 36 holes; £22 per 18 holes (£32/£27
weekends).
Prof Gordon Brand Snr
Designer Hawtree/J H Taylor
Facilities ⊗ 🏌 ⚑ ♀ ⚑ 🏠 ⛳ 🛒 ✎
Location 3m SE of city centre off A37

Hotel ★★★ Hunstrete House Hotel,
HUNSTRETE ☎ 01761 490490 23 ⇆ ⌂

Mangotsfield Carsons Rd, Mangotsfield BS17 3LW
☎ 0117 956 5501
An easy hilly parkland course. Caravan site.
18 holes, 5337yds, Par 68, SSS 66, Course record 61.
Club membership 400.
Visitors no restrictions.
Societies bookings in advance to Craig Trewin.
Green Fees not confirmed.
Prof Craig Trewin
Designer John Day
Facilities ⊗ 🏌 ⚑ ♀ ⚑ 🏠 ⛳ 🛒 ✎
& Leisure sauna.
Location 6m NE of city centre off B4465

Hotel B Posthouse Bristol, Filton Rd, Hambrook,
BRISTOL ☎ 0117 956 4242 198 ⇆ ⌂

Shirehampton Park Park Hill, Shirehampton BS11 0UL
☎ 0117 982 3059 & 9822083 Fax 0117 982 2083
A lovely parkland course with views across the Avon Gorge.
18 holes, 5430yds, Par 67, SSS 66.
Club membership 600.
Visitors with member only at weekends. Must have a
handicap certificate.
Societies weekdays (book through Secretary)
Green Fees £28 per day; £18 per round (weekdays).
Prof Brent Ellis
Facilities ⊗ ⅲ 🏌 ⚑ ♀ ⚑ 🏠 ⛳ ✎
Location 2m E of junct 18 M5 on B4054

Hotel ★★★ 67% Redwood Lodge Hotel, Beggar
Bush Ln, Failand, BRISTOL
☎ 01275 393901 112 ⇆ ⌂

Woodlands Woodlands Ln, Almondsbury BS12 4JZ
☎ 01454 619319 Fax 01454 619397
Situated on the edge of the Severn Valley, bordered by
Hortham Brook and Shepherds Wood this interesting
parkland course, features five testing par 3's set around the
course's five lakes, notably the 206 yd 5th hole which
extends over water.
18 holes, 6068yds, Par 69, SSS 67.
Club membership 101.
Visitors no restrictions.
Societies telephone in advance.
Green Fees not confirmed.
Designer Cliff Chapman
Facilities ⊗ 🏌 ⚑ ♀ ⚑ 🏠 ⛳ 🛒 ✎
& Leisure fishing.
Location N of Bristol off A38

Hotel B Posthouse Bristol, Filton Rd, Hambrook,
BRISTOL ☎ 0117 956 4242 198 ⇆ ⌂

BUCKINGHAMSHIRE

AYLESBURY
Map 04 SP81

Aylesbury Golf Centre Hulcott Ln, Bierton HP22 5GA
☎ 01296 393644
A parkland course with magnificent views to the Chiltern
Hills. A good test of golf with out of bounds coming into
play on 9 of the holes, also a number of water hazards and
bunkers.
18 holes, 5965yds, Par 71, SSS 69.
Club membership 200.
Visitors no restrictions, but booking advisable.
Societies telephone for details.
Green Fees £10 per round (£12 weekends & bank holidays).
Cards 〰 💳 💳
Prof Mitch Kierstenson
Designer T S Benwell
Facilities ⊗ ⅲ 🏌 ⚑ ♀ ⚑ 🏠 ⛳ ✎ ⚑
Location 1m N of Aylesbury on A418

Hotel B Posthouse Aylesbury, Aston Clinton Rd,
AYLESBURY ☎ 01296 393388 94 ⇆ ⌂

Aylesbury Park Oxford Rd HP17 8QQ
☎ 01296 399196 Fax 01296 399196
Parkland course with mature trees, located just south-west of
Aylesbury.
18 holes, 6148yds, Par 70, SSS 69, Course record 69.
Club membership 340.
Visitors may book up to 1 week in advance.
Societies telephone for Society Pack
Green Fees not confirmed.
Cards 〰 💳 💳 💳 🔲
Prof David Boot
Designer H Hawtree
Facilities 🏌 ⚑ ♀ ⚑ 🏠 ⛳ 🛒 ✎ ⚑
Location 0.5m SW of Aylesbury, on the A418

Ellesborough Butlers Cross HP17 0TZ
☎ 01296 622114 Fax 01296 622114
Once part of the property of Chequers, and under the
shadow of the famous monument at the Wendover end of
the Chilterns. A downland course, it is rather hilly with
most holes enhanced by far-ranging views over the
Aylesbury countryside.
18 holes, 6360yds, Par 71, SSS 71, Course record 64.
Club membership 700.

Visitors	welcome on weekdays, handicap certificate required.
Societies	Wed & Thu only, by prior arrangement with General Manager.
Green Fees	not confirmed.
Prof	Mark Squire
Designer	James Braid
Facilities	⊗ ⅃ ⚑ ▼ ♀ ♨ 🖻 ♂
Location	1m E of Ellesborough on B4010
Hotel	★★★ 73% The Bell Inn, ASTON CLINTON ☎ 01296 630252 5 ⇆ ♜ Annexe15 ⇆ ♜

BEACONSFIELD   Map 04 SU99

Beaconsfield Seer Green HP9 2UR
☎ 01494 676545 Fax 01494 681148
An interesting and, at times, testing tree-lined and
parkland course which frequently plays longer than
appears on the card! Each hole differs to a considerable
degree and here lies the charm. Walking is easy, except
perhaps to the 6th and 8th. Well bunkered.
18 holes, 6493yds, Par 72, SSS 71, Course record 63.
Club membership 850.

Visitors	must contact in advance and have a handicap certificate. May not play weekends.
Societies	phone for details
Green Fees	£40 per day; £30 per round.
Prof	Michael Brothers
Designer	H S Colt
Facilities	⊗ ⅃ ⚑ ▼ ♀ ♨ 🖻 ♂ ♂ ⚲
Location	2m E,S of Seer Green
Hotel	★★★★ 67% Bellhouse Hotel, Oxford Rd, BEACONSFIELD ☎ 01753 887211 136 ⇆ ♜

BLETCHLEY   Map 04 SP83

Windmill Hill Tattenhoe Ln MK3 7RB
☎ 01908 631113 Fax 01908 630034
Long, open-parkland course, the first championship course
designed by Henry Cotton, opened in 1972. Proprietary Pay
& Play. No winter greens.
18 holes, 6720yds, Par 73, SSS 72, Course record 68.
Club membership 400.

Visitors	booking system in operation up to 7 days in advance.
Societies	packages available, contact for details.
Green Fees	not confirmed.
Cards	💳
Prof	Colin Clingan
Designer	Henry Cotton

Facilities	⊗ ⅃ ⚑ ▼ ♀ ♨ 🖻 ♂ ♂ ⚲ ⚬
Location	W side of town centre on A421
Hotel	★★ 70% Shenley Church Inn, Burchard Crescent, Shenley Church End, MILTON KEYNES ☎ 01908 505467 50 ⇆ ♜

BOW BRICKHILL   Map 04 SP93

WOBURN See page 33

BUCKINGHAM   Map 04 SP63

Buckingham Tingewick Rd MK18 4AE
☎ 01280 815566 Fax 01280 821812
Undulating parkland course with a stream and river affecting
8 holes.
18 holes, 6082yds, Par 70, SSS 69, Course record 67.
Club membership 690.

Visitors	welcome Mon-Fri, with member only at weekends.
Societies	by prior arrangement.
Green Fees	not confirmed.
Prof	Tom Gates
Facilities	⊗ ⅃ ⚑ ▼ ♀ ♨ 🖻 ♂
Location	1.5m W on A421
Hotel	★★★ 66% Buckingham Four Pillars Hotel, Buckingham Ring Rd South, BUCKINGHAM ☎ 01280 822622 70 ⇆ ♜

BURNHAM   Map 04 SU98

Burnham Beeches Green Ln SL1 8EG
☎ 01628 661448 Fax 01628 668968
In the centre of the lovely Burnham Beeches
countryside. Wide fairways, carefully maintained greens,
some hills, and some devious routes to a few holes. A
good finish.
18 holes, 6449yds, Par 70, SSS 71.
Club membership 670.

Visitors	must contact in advance. May play on weekdays only.
Societies	welcome Apr-Oct, write or telephone for information.
Green Fees	not confirmed.
Prof	Ronnie Bolton
Facilities	⊗ ⅃ ⚑ ▼ ♀ ♨ 🖻 ♂ ♝ ♣ ♂
Location	0.5m NE of Burnham
Hotel	★★★ 70% Burnham Beeches, Grove Rd, BURNHAM ☎ 01628 429955 82 ⇆ ♜

Lambourne Dropmore Rd SL1 8NF
☎ 01628 666755 Fax 01628 663301
A championship standard 18-hole parkland course.
Undulating terrain with many trees and several lakes, notably
on the tricky 7th hole which has a tightly guarded green
reached via a shot over a lake. Seven par 4's over 400yds
with six picturesque lakes, excellent drainage and full
irrigation.
18 holes, 6771yds, Par 72, SSS 73, Course record 67.
Club membership 730.

▶

Visitors must contact in advance & have a handicap certificate. May not play at weekends.
Green Fees £36 (£45 weekends).
Cards ▨ ▨ ▨ ▨ ▨ ▨ ▨
Prof David Hart
Designer Donald Steel
Facilities ⊗ ⫟ ⬛ ♨ ♀ ⚲ ☎ ⚐ ⚒ ⛳ ⚑ ✓ ⟨
& Leisure sauna.
Location Access via M4 junct 7 towards Burnham or M40 junct 2 towards Slough/Burnham

Hotel ★★★ 70% Burnham Beeches, Grove Rd, BURNHAM ☎ 01628 429955 82 ⇄ ⓔ

CHALFONT ST GILES   Map 04 SU99

Harewood Downs Cokes Ln HP8 4TA
☎ 01494 762308 Fax 01494 766869
A testing undulating parkland course with sloping greens and plenty of trees.
18 holes, 5958yds, Par 69, SSS 69, Course record 64.
Visitors must contact in advance.
Societies apply in writing or telephone.
Green Fees £25 per day/round (£30 weekends & bank holidays).
Prof G C Morris
Facilities ⊗ ⫟ ⬛ ♨ ♀ ⚲ ☎ ⚐ ✓
Location 2m E of Amersham on A413

Hotel ★★★★ 67% Bellhouse Hotel, Oxford Rd, BEACONSFIELD ☎ 01753 887211 136 ⇄ ⓔ

CHARTRIDGE   Map 04 SP90

Chartridge Park HP5 2TF ☎ 01494 791772
A family run, easy walking parkland course set high in the beautiful Chiltern Hills, affording breathtaking views.
18 holes, 5516yds, Par 69, SSS 67, Course record 65.
Club membership 700.
Visitors may not play before 10.30am weekends.
Societies must telephone in advance.
Green Fees £20 (£25 weekends).
Cards ▨ ▨ ▨ ▨ ▨
Prof Peter Gibbins
Designer John Jacobs
Facilities ⊗ ⫟ ⬛ ♨ ♀ ⚲ ☎ ⚐ ⚒ ⛳ ✓
Location 3m NW of Chesham

Hotel ★★★ 66% The Crown, High St, AMERSHAM ☎ 01494 721541 19 ⇄ ⓔ Annexe4 ⇄ ⓔ

CHESHAM   Map 04 SP90

Chesham & Ley Hill Ley Hill Common HP5 1UZ
☎ 01494 784541 Fax 01494 785506
Wooded parkland course on hilltop with easy walking.
9 holes, 5296yds, Par 66, SSS 65, Course record 62.
Club membership 400.
Visitors may play Mon & Thu all day, Wed after noon, Fri up to 4pm.
Societies subject to approval, Thu only.
Green Fees £20 per day; £12 per round.
Facilities ⊗ ⫟ ⬛ ♨ ♀ ⚲
Location 2m E of Chesham

Hotel ★★★ 66% The Crown, High St, AMERSHAM ☎ 01494 721541 19 ⇄ ⓔ Annexe4 ⇄ ⓔ

DENHAM   Map 04 TQ08

Buckinghamshire Denham Court Dr UB9 5BG
☎ 01895 835777 Fax 01895 835210
A John Jacobs designed championship-standard course. Visitors only welcome as guests of members to this beautiful course in 269 acres of lovely grounds including mature trees, five lakes and two rivers. The testing 7th hole requires a 185 yd carry over a stream, followed by a second shot over a river to a green guarded by a lake.
18 holes, 6880yds, Par 72, SSS 73, Course record 70.
Club membership 500.
Visitors must contact in advance, with member only or introduced by member. Weekdays only.
Societies must contact in advance.
Green Fees £70 per 18 holes (£80 weekends & bank holidays).
Cards ▨ ▨ ▨ ▨ ▨
Prof John O'Leary
Designer John Jacobs
Facilities ⊗ ⫟ ⬛ ♨ ♀ ⚲ ☎ ⚐ ✓ ⟨
& Leisure sauna.
Location Just beyond junct 1 on M40

Hotel ★★★★ 67% Bellhouse Hotel, Oxford Rd, BEACONSFIELD ☎ 01753 887211 136 ⇄ ⓔ

Denham Tilehouse Ln UB9 5DE
☎ 01895 832022 Fax 01895 835340
A beautifully maintained parkland/heathland course, home of many county champions. Slightly hilly and calling for good judgement of distance in the wooded areas.
18 holes, 6456yds, Par 70, SSS 71, Course record 66.
Club membership 790.
Visitors must contact in advance & have handicap certificate. Must play with member Fri-Sun.
Societies Tue-Thu. Must book in advance.
Green Fees £52 per day; £36 per round.
Prof Stuart Campbell
Designer H S Colt
Facilities ⊗ ⫟ ⬛ ♨ ♀ ⚲ ☎ ⚐ ✓
Location 0.5m N of North Orbital Road, 2m from Uxbridge

Hotel ★★★★ 67% Bellhouse Hotel, Oxford Rd, BEACONSFIELD ☎ 01753 887211 136 ⇄ ⓔ

FLACKWELL HEATH   Map 04 SU89

Flackwell Heath Treadaway Rd, High Wycombe HP10 9PE
☎ 01628 520929 Fax 01628 530040
Open sloping heath and tree-lined course on hills overlooking Loudwater and the M40. Some good challenging par 3's and a several testing small greens.
18 holes, 6211yds, Par 71, SSS 70, Course record 65.
Club membership 800.
Visitors with member only at weekends. Must contact in advance and hold a handicap certificate.
Societies Wed & Thu only, by prior booking.
Green Fees £30 per day; £20 per round.   ▶

WOBURN

BOW BRICKHILL *Bucks* ☎ 01908 370756
Fax 01908 378436   Map O4 SP93

John Ingham writes: Come off the M1 motorway at Junction 13 and you are quickly at Woburn, with its magnificent stately home, wildlife safari park and surrounding echoes of Henry VIII and the Dukes of Bedford. Within the last 25 years two new attractions have been added - two golf courses designed by the famed Charles Lawrie of Cotton Pennink.

To create these beautiful courses, the bulldozers got among pine and chestnut and literally cut fairways through some of the most picturesque country in all England - but it had been country seen by very few. From the very back tees, both courses are somewhat long for the weekend amateur. The Duke's measures 6961 yards and makes for a stiff test for any class of golfer, while the 'easier' Duchess, measuring a very respectable 6651 yards, requires a high degree of skill on its fairways guarded by towering pines.

Today, under the direction of Alex Hay, a Scottish TV golf commentator, the Dukes course has become the home of the increasingly popular Weetabix Women'sBritish Open. It has been held at Woburn since 1990.

The town of Woburn and the Abbey are both within Bedfordshire, while the golf and country club actually lie over the border in Buckinghamshire. Although just 45 miles from London, you will feel very much in the wilds and the local pubs and people, plus some wonderful countryside, make this area an excellent place to stay for a few days.

And, if you can hit the ball straight, you might get near the course record of 63 achieved by Peter Baker and Ian Woosnam!

Visitors	must play with a member at weekends. Midweek by prior arrangement
Societies	must contact in advance.
Green fees	All credit & charge cards.
Facilities	⊗ ☻ ♀ ♨ ⬒ ᵔᶠ ➤ ᴥ ♂ Professional (Luther Blacklock),
Leisure	outdoor swimming pool (heated)
Location	Bow Brickhill, Milton Keynes MK17 9LJ. (SE of Bow Brickhill) 4m W of J13 M1, off A5130

**36 holes. Dukes Course: 18 holes, 6973 yds, Par 72, SSS 74.
Duchess Course: 18 holes, 6651yds, Par 72, SSS 72.**

WHERE TO STAY AND EAT NEARBY

HOTELS:
ASPLEY GUISE
★★★ ⊛ 68% Moore Place, The Square ☎ 01908 282000, 39 ⇄ ℝ Annexe 15 ⇄ ℝ

FLITWICK
★★★ ⊛ ⊛ ⊛ 75% Flitwick Manor, Church Rd. ☎ 01525 712242. 15 ⇄ℝ

WOBURN
★★★ 70% Thistle Bedford Arms, George St. ☎ 01525 290441 53 ⇄ ℝ

RESTAURANTS:
WOBURN
⊛ ⊛ Paris House, Woburn Park ☎ 01525 290692.

Prof	Paul Watson
Facilities	⊗ 🏶 🖺 ♥ ♀ ♨ 📠 ∂
Location	NE side of town centre

Hotel ★★★★ 67% Bellhouse Hotel, Oxford Rd, BEACONSFIELD ☎ 01753 887211 136 ⇋ ♟

GERRARDS CROSS   Map 04 TQ08

Gerrards Cross Chalfont Park SL9 0QA
☎ 01753 883263 Fax 01753 883593
A wooded parkland course which has been modernised in recent years and is now a very pleasant circuit with infinite variety. The best part lies on the plateau above the clubhouse where there are some testing holes.
18 holes, 6295yds, Par 69, SSS 70, Course record 64.
Club membership 773.

Visitors	must contact professional in advance, a handicap certificate is required, may not play Tuesday, weekends or public holidays.
Societies	booking well in advance necessary, handicap certicates required, packages to suit.
Green Fees	£44 per day; £32 per 18 holes.
Prof	Matthew Barr
Designer	Bill Pedlar
Facilities	⊗ 🏶 by prior arrangement 🖺 ♥ ♀ ♨ 📠 ∂
Location	NE side of town centre off A413

Hotel ★★★★ 67% Bellhouse Hotel, Oxford Rd, BEACONSFIELD
☎ 01753 887211 136 ⇋ ♟

HALTON   Map 04 SP81

Chiltern Forest Aston Hill HP22 5NQ
☎ 01296 631267 Fax 01296 631267
Extended to 18 holes in 1992, this very hilly wooded parkland course is on two levels. It is a true test of skill to the low handicap golfer, as well as being a fair challenge to higher handicap golfers. The surrounding woodland makes the course very scenic.
18 holes, 5765yds, Par 70, SSS 70, Course record 69.
Club membership 650.

Visitors	welcome weekdays, must play with member at weekends.
Societies	contact in advance for booking form.
Green Fees	£23 per day; £18 per round.
Cards	▭▭ 🖃 ▭▭ ▭▭ 🖸
Prof	A Lavers
Facilities	⊗ 🖺 ♥ ♀ ♨ 📠 🛒 ∂
Location	1m NE off A4011

Hotel ★★★ 64% Rose & Crown Hotel & Restaurant, High St, TRING ☎ 01442 824071 27 ⇋ ♟

HIGH WYCOMBE   Map 04 SU89

Hazlemere Golf & Country Club Penn Rd, Hazlemere HP15 7LR ☎ 01494 714722 Fax 01494 713914
Undulating parkland course in beautiful countryside with water hazards in play on some holes. Two long par 5s and a fine par 4 closing hole.
18 holes, 5873yds, Par 70, SSS 68, Course record 62.
Club membership 700.

Visitors	weekdays all day. Weekends by prior arrangement through Pro. shop telephone 01494 718298.
Societies	by prior telephone arrangement.
Green Fees	on application.
Cards	▭▭ 🖃 ▭▭ 🖸
Prof	Alistair McKay/Paul Harrison
Designer	Terry Murray
Facilities	⊗ 🖺 ♥ ♀ ♨ 📠 ┅ 🛒 ∂
Location	2m NE, A404 towards Amersham

Hotel ★★★ 66% The Crown, High St, AMERSHAM
☎ 01494 721541 19 ⇋ ♟ Annexe4 ⇋ ♟

IVER   Map 04 TQ08

Iver Hollow Hill Ln, Langley Park Rd SL0 0JJ
☎ 01753 655615 Fax 01753 654225
Fairly flat, pay and play parkland course with challenging par 5s, plenty of hazards - water and ditches - and strong crosswinds to contend with.
9 holes, 6288yds, Par 72, SSS 72, Course record 66.
Club membership 250.

Visitors	competitions at weekends, telephone to pre book tee times.
Societies	telephone in advance.
Green Fees	£11 per 18 holes; £6 per 9 holes (£14.50/£7.50 weekends and bank holidays).
Cards	▭▭ 🖃 ▭ ▭▭ ▭▭ 🖸
Prof	Karl Teschner
Facilities	⊗ 🖺 ♥ ♀ ♨ 📠 ┅ ∂ ♟
Location	1.5m SW off B470

Hotel ★★★★ 66% Slough/Windsor Marriott, Ditton Rd, Langley, SLOUGH
☎ 01753 544244 380 ⇋ ♟

Richings Park Golf & Country Club North Park SL0 9DL
☎ 01753 655370 Fax 01753 655409
Set amongst mature trees and attractive lakes, this testing par 70 parkland course provides a suitable challenge to golfers of all abilities. Well irrigated greens and abundant wildlife. There is an academy course with 5 short holes and teaching facilities on the driving range.
18 holes, 6144yds, Par 70, SSS 69.
Club membership 620.

Visitors	welcome but may not play until after 12 noon at weekends.
Societies	apply in writing or telephone.
Green Fees	£27 per day; £20 per round (£30 at weekends).
Cards	▭▭ 🖃 ▭▭ ▭▭ 🖸
Prof	Seab Kelly
Designer	Alan Higgins
Facilities	⊗ 🏶 🖺 ♥ ♀ ♨ 📠 ┅ 🐾 🛒 ∂ ♟
& Leisure	5 hole academy course.
Location	Junct 5 on M4, A4 towards Heathrow, left at lights, Sutton Lane, right at next lights North Park

Hotel ★★★ 68% Courtyard by Marriott Slough/Windsor, Church St, SLOUGH
☎ 01753 551551 148 ⇋ ♟

LITTLE CHALFONT — Map 04 SU99

Little Chalfont Lodge Ln HP8 4AJ
☎ 01494 764877 Fax 01494 762860
Gently undulating parkland course surrounded by mature trees.
9 holes, 5852yds, Par 68, SSS 68, Course record 66.
Club membership 300.
Visitors no restrictions, please phone to ensure there are no competitions in progress. Must contact for weekend play.
Societies please telephone in advance.
Green Fees £10 per 18 holes (£12 weekends).
Cards
Prof M Dunne
Facilities ⊗ ℳ by prior arrangement 🏌 ♣ ♀ ♨ 🍴 ⚒
& Leisure one motorised cart for hire by arrangement.
Location Between Little Chalfont & Chorleywood

Hotel ★★★ 66% The Crown, High St, AMERSHAM
☎ 01494 721541   19 ⇌ ⚹ Annexe4 ⇌ ⚹

LOUDWATER — Map 04 SU89

Wycombe Heights Golf Centre Rayners Ave HP10 9SW
☎ 01494 816686 Fax 01494 816728
Opened in 1991 and designed by the John Jacobs Partnership. The golf centre includes a 24-bay driving range.
18 holes, 6253yds, Par 70, SSS 72, Course record 69.
Club membership 950.
Visitors booking advisable 6 days in advance.
Societies telephone in advance & confirm in writing.
Green Fees £11.50 (£15.95 weekends & bank holidays).
Cards
Prof Adam Bishop
Designer John Jacobs
Facilities ⊗ ℳ 🏌 ♣ ♀ ♨ 🍴 ⚒ ⚹

Hotel B Posthouse High Wycombe, Handy Cross, HIGH WYCOMBE
☎ 01494 442100 106 ⇌ ⚹

MARLOW — Map 04 SU88

Harleyford Harleyford Estate, Henley Rd SL7 2SP
☎ 01628 402300 Fax 01628 478434
Set in 160 acres, this Donald Steel designed course, founded in 1996, makes the most of the natural rolling contours of the beautiful parkland of the historic Harleyford Estate. A challenging course to golfers of all handicaps. Stunning views across the Thames Valley.
18 holes, 6604yds, Par 72, Course record 72.
Club membership 800.
Visitors soft spikes only. Must contact in advance and have a handicap certificate.
Societies handicap cert required, Tel 01628 402344 Groups co-ordinator.
Green Fees £40 per round (£60 weekends & bank holidays).
Cards
Prof Alasdair Barr
Designer Donald Steel
Facilities ♨ 🍴 ⚒ ⚹
Location S side A4156 Marlow/Henley road, close to A404 Marlow bypass linking junct 4 M40/junct 8/9 M4

Hotel ★★★★ 74% Danesfield House, Henley Rd, MARLOW-ON-THAMES
☎ 01628 891010   87 ⇌ ⚹

MENTMORE — Map 04 SP91

Mentmore Golf & Country Club LU7 0UA
☎ 01296 662020 Fax 01296 662592
Two 18-hole courses - Rosebery and Rothschild - set within the wooded estate grounds of Mentmore Towers. Gently rolling parkland course with mature trees and lakes and two interesting feature holes; the long par 5 (606 yds) 9th on the Rosebery course with fine views of the Chilterns and the par 4 (340yd) 14th on the Rothschild course, in front of the Towers.
Rosebery Course: 18 holes, 6777yds, Par 72, SSS 72, Course record 68.
Rothschild Course: 18 holes, 6763yds, Par 72, SSS 72.
Club membership 1100.
Visitors must contact in advance, may not play weekends before 11am.
Societies by prior arrangement.
Green Fees £40 per day.
Cards
Prof Pip Elson
Designer Bob Sandow
Facilities ⊗ ℳ 🏌 ♣ ♀ ♨ 🍴 ⚒ ⚹
& Leisure hard tennis courts, heated indoor swimming pool, fishing, sauna, gymnasium.
Location 4m S of Leighton Buzzard

Hotel ★★★ 55% Swan Hotel, High St, LEIGHTON BUZZARD ☎ 01525 372148   38 ⇌ ⚹

MILTON KEYNES — Map 04 SP83

Abbey Hill Monks Way, Two Mile Ash MK8 8AA
☎ 01908 562408
Undulating municipal course within the new city. Tight fairways and well-placed bunkers. Stream comes into play on five holes. Also Par 3 course.
18 holes, 6122yds, Par 71, SSS 69, Course record 71.
Club membership 500.
Visitors no restrictions.
Societies must telephone (01908) 562408 in advance.
Green Fees not confirmed.
Cards
Prof Keith Bond
Facilities ⊗ ℳ 🏌 ♣ ♀ ♨ 🍴 ⚒ ⚹
Location 2m W of new town centre off A5

Hotel ★★★ 64% Quality Hotel & Suites Milton Keynes, Monks Way, Two Mile Ash, MILTON KEYNES ☎ 01908 561666   88 ⇌ ⚹

Three Locks Great Brickhill MK17 9BH
☎ 01525 270470 & 270050 Fax 01525 270470
Parkland course offering a challenge to beginners and experienced golfers, with water coming into play on ten holes. Magnificent views.
18 holes, 6036yds, Par 71, SSS 68, Course record 69.
Club membership 350.
Visitors telephone 01525 270050 to book tee times.
Societies write or telephone for details.
Green Fees £21 per day; £13.50 per round (£27/£16 weekends & bank holidays).
Cards ▶

Facilities ⊗ 🏌 💺 ♀ 🛆 🏠 🍴 🏏 🥤 🚜 ♂
& Leisure fishing.
Location A4146 between Leighton Buzzard/Bletchley

Hotel ★★ 70% Shenley Church Inn, Burchard Crescent, Shenley Church End, MILTON KEYNES ☎ 01908 505467 50 ⇔ 🛏

PRINCES RISBOROUGH Map 04 SP80

Whiteleaf Upper Icknield Way, Whiteleaf HP27 0LY
☎ 01844 274058
Short, hilly and tricky 9-hole parkland course, requiring great accuracy, set high in the Chilterns with beautiful views.
9 holes, 5391yds, Par 66, SSS 66, Course record 64.
Club membership 400.
Visitors advisable to contact in advance, with member only at weekends.
Societies on Thu only, must contact the secretary in advance.
Green Fees £25 per day; £18 per round.
Prof Ken Ward
Facilities ⊗ 🏌 🏌 💺 ♀ 🛆 🏠 🍴 ♂
Location 1m NE off A4010

Hotel ★★★ 73% The Bell Inn, ASTON CLINTON ☎ 01296 630252 5 ⇔ 🛏 Annexe15 ⇔ 🛏

STOKE POGES Map 04 SU98

Farnham Park Park Rd SL2 4PJ
☎ 01753 643332 & 647065 Fax 01753 643332 & 647065
Fine, public parkland course in pleasing setting.
18 holes, 6172yds, Par 71, SSS 70, Course record 68.
Club membership 600.
Visitors telephone in advance for tee times.
Societies apply in writing.
Green Fees £9 per round (£12.50 weekends & bank holidays).
Prof Paul Warner
Designer Hawtree
Facilities ⊗ 🏌 💺 ♀ 🛆 🏠 🍴 ♂
Location W side of village off B416

Hotel ★★★★ 66% Slough/Windsor Marriott, Ditton Rd, Langley, SLOUGH ☎ 01753 544244 380 ⇔ 🛏

Stoke Poges Stoke Park, Park Rd SL2 4PG
☎ 01753 717171 Fax 01753 717181
Judgement of the distance from the tee is all important on this first-class parkland course. Fairways are wide and the challenge seemingly innocuous. The 7th hole being the model for the well known 12th hole at Augusta. Voted 'Golf Club of the Year' in 1997', Stoke Poges is a 27 hole course and is considered the best traditional course in the British Isles.
Course 1: 18 holes, 6721yds, Par 71, SSS 72.
Course 2: 18 holes, 6551yds, Par 72, SSS 73.
Course 3: 18 holes, 6318yds, Par 71, SSS 70.
Club membership 750.
Visitors must contact in advance.
Societies telephone in advance.
Green Fees £65 per 18 holes (£150 weekends).
Cards 💳💳💳💳💳
Prof David Woodward

Designer Harry Shapland Colt
Facilities ⊗ 🏌 🏌 💺 ♀ 🛆 🏠 🍴 🏏 🥤 🚜 ♂ ♀
& Leisure hard tennis courts, fishing, croquet and snooker.
Location Turn off A4 at Slough into Stoke Poges Lane B416, club is 1.5m on left

WAVENDON Map 04 SP93

Wavendon Golf Centre Lower End Rd MK17 8DA
☎ 01908 281811 Fax 01908 281257
Pleasant parkland course set within mature oak and lime trees and incorporating several small lakes as water hazards. Easy walking.
18 holes, 5540yds, Par 68, SSS 68.
Club membership 300.
Visitors booking advised.
Societies must contact in advance by telephone.
Green Fees £10 weekdays (£15 weekends).
Cards 💳💳💳💳💳
Prof Greg Iron
Designer J Drake/N Elmer
Facilities ⊗ 🏌 💺 ♀ 🛆 🏠 🍴 🥤 🚜 ♂ ♀
Location Just off A421

Hotel ★★★ 68% Moore Place Hotel, The Square, ASPLEY GUISE ☎ 01908 282000 39 ⇔ 🛏 Annexe15 ⇔ 🛏

WESTON TURVILLE Map 04 SP81

Weston Turville Golf & Squash Club New Rd HP22 5QT
☎ 01296 424084 Fax 01296 395376
Parkland course situated at the foot of the Chiltern Hills and providing an excellent challenge for the accomplished golfer, yet not too daunting for the higher handicap player. Flat easy walking with water hazards and many interesting holes, notably the testing dog-leg 5th (418yds).
18 holes, 6008yds, Par 69, SSS 69, Course record 68.
Club membership 600.
Visitors no restrictions.
Societies must contact in advance.
Green Fees £20 per round (£25 weekends).
Cards 💳💳💳💳
Prof Gary George
Facilities ⊗ 🏌 💺 ♀ 🛆 🏠 🍴 🥤 🚜 ♂
& Leisure squash.
Location 2m SE of Aylesbury, off A41

Hotel ★★★ 73% The Bell Inn, ASTON CLINTON ☎ 01296 630252 5 ⇔ 🛏 Annexe15 ⇔ 🛏

WEXHAM STREET Map 04 SU98

Wexham Park SL3 6ND
☎ 01753 663271 Fax 01753 663318
Gently undulating parkland course. Three courses. One 18 hole, one challenging 9 hole and another 9 hole suitable for beginners.
Blue: 18 holes, 5346yds, Par 68, SSS 66.
Red: 9 holes, 2822yds, Par 34, SSS 68.
Green: 9 holes, 2283yds, Par 32, SSS 32.
Club membership 800.
Visitors no restrictions
Societies must contact in advance.

Green Fees 18 holes: £11 per round (£14.50 weekend). 9 hole: £6 (£7.50 weekends).

Cards	~~ 💳 💳 💳
Prof	David Morgan
Designer	E Lawrence/D Morgan
Facilities	⊗ 🄱 💻 ♀ ⚴ 🖻 🍴 🚞 ♂ ⬥
Location	0.5m S
Hotel	★★★★ 66% Slough/Windsor Marriott, Ditton Rd, Langley, SLOUGH
	☎ 01753 544244 380 ⇥ 🎨

WING   Map 04 SP82

Aylesbury Vale Stewkley Rd LU7 0UJ
☎ 01525 240196 Fax 01525 240848
The course set in quiet countryside is gently undulating, it was opened in the autumn of 1991. There are five ponds to add interest, notably on the par 4 420 yd 13th - unlucky for some - where the second shot is all downhill with an inviting pond spanning the approach to the green. In addition there is a 10-bay driving range and practice putting green.
18 holes, 6612yds, Par 72, SSS 72, Course record 69.
Club membership 545.

Visitors	must adhere to dress regulations. Must contact in advance.
Societies	telephone to book in advance.
Green Fees	£12 weekdays (£21 weekends).
Cards	~~ 💳 💳 💳
Prof	Chris Skeet
Designer	D Wright
Facilities	⊗ 🍴 🄱 💻 ♀ ⚴ 🖻 🍴 🟢 🚞 ♂ ⬥
Location	2m NW on unclassified Stewkley road, between Wing/Stewkley
Hotel	★★★ 55% Swan Hotel, High St, LEIGHTON BUZZARD ☎ 01525 372148 38 ⇥ 🎨

CAMBRIDGESHIRE

BAR HILL   Map 05 TL36

Cambridgeshire Moat House Moat House Hotel, Bar Hill CB3 8EU
☎ 01954 780098 & 249971 Fax 01954 780010
Undulating parkland course with lake and water hazards, easy walking. Many leisure facilities.
18 holes, 6734yds, Par 72, SSS 72, Course record 73.
Club membership 650.

Visitors	must book in advance.
Societies	must telephone in advance.
Green Fees	£18 per round (£23 per round weekends & bank holidays).
Cards	~~ 💳 💳 💳
Prof	Paul Simpson
Facilities	⊗ 🍴 🄱 💻 ♀ ⚴ 🖻 🍴 🚞 ♂ ⬥
& Leisure	hard tennis courts, heated indoor swimming pool, gymnasium, beauty salon.
Location	5m NW of Cambridge on A604
Hotel	★★★ 66% Cambridgeshire Moat House, BAR HILL ☎ 01954 249988 99 ⇥ 🎨

BRAMPTON   Map 04 TL27

Brampton Park Buckden Rd PE18 8NF
☎ 01480 434700 Fax 01480 411145
Set in truly attractive countryside, bounded by the River Great Ouse and bisected by the River Lane. Great variety with mature trees, lakes and water hazards. One of the most difficult holes is the 4th, a Par 3 island green, 175 yards in length.
18 holes, 6300yds, Par 71, SSS 72, Course record 64.
Club membership 650.

Visitors	must contact in advance.
Societies	apply in advance.
Green Fees	£25 per day/round (£35 weekends & bank holidays).
Prof	Alisdair Currie
Designer	Simon Gidman
Facilities	⊗ 🄱 💻 ♀ ⚴ 🖻 🚞 ⬥
Location	Follow signs from A1 or A14 to RAF Brampton
Hotel	★★ 65% The George Coaching Inn, Great North Rd, Buckden, HUNTINGDON
	☎ 01480 810307 16 ⇥ 🎨

CAMBRIDGE   Map 05 TL45

Gog Magog Shelford Bottom CB2 4AB
☎ 01223 247626 Fax 01223 414990
Situated just outside the centre of the university town, Gog Magog, established in 1901, is known as the nursery of Cambridge undergraduate golf. The courses are on high ground, and it is said that if you stand on the highest point and could see far enough to the east the next highest ground would be the Ural Mountains! The courses are open but there are enough trees and other hazards to provide plenty of problems. Views from the high parts are superb. The nature of the ground ensures good winter golf. The area has been designated a Site of Special Scientific Interest (SSSI).
Old Course: 18 holes, 6400yds, Par 70, SSS 70, Course record 60.
Wandlebury: 18 holes, 6735yds, Par 72, SSS 72.
Club membership 1280.

Visitors	Must contact in advance. Mon-Fri only.
Societies	Tue & Thu by reservation.
Green Fees	£42 per day; £35 per round.
Prof	Ian Bamborough
Designer	Hawtree Ltd
Facilities	⊗ 🍴 🄱 💻 ♀ ⚴ 🖻 🍴 🟢 ⬥
Location	3m SE on A1307
Hotel	★★★ 70% Gonville Hotel, Gonville Place, CAMBRIDGE
	☎ 01223 366611 & 221111
	Fax 01223 315470 64 ⇥ 🎨

ELY   Map 05 TL58

Ely City Cambridge Rd CB7 4HX
☎ 01353 662751 (Office) Fax 01353 668636
Parkland course slightly undulating with water hazards formed by lakes and natural dykes. Demanding par 4 5th hole (467yds), often into a headwind, and a testing par 3 2nd hole (160yds) played over 2 ponds Magnificent views of Cathedral. Lee Trevino is the professional record holder.
18 holes, 6627yds, Par 72, SSS 72, Course record 66.
Club membership 850.

                                                 ▶

Visitors	advisable to contact the club in advance.
Societies	Tue to Fri, advisable to contact club well in advance.
Green Fees	£28 per day (£34 weekends & bank holidays).
Prof	Andrew George
Designer	Sir Henry Cotton
Facilities	⊗)Ⅲ ⅙ 🛈 ⌾ ♨ 🛆 🏠 🕈 ✧
& Leisure	snooker room.
Location	S of city on A10

Hotel	★ 65% The Nyton Hotel, 7 Barton Rd, ELY ☎ 01353 662459 10 ⇆ 🅕

GIRTON   Map 05 TL46

Girton Dodford Ln CB3 0QE
☎ 01223 276169 Fax 01223 277150
Flat, open parkland course with many trees and ditches. Easy walking.
18 holes, 6085yds, Par 69, SSS 69, Course record 66.
Club membership 800.

Visitors	with member only at weekends. Contact professional in advance (01223 276991).
Societies	apply writing.
Green Fees	£16 per day.
Prof	Scott Thomson
Designer	Allan Gow
Facilities	⊗)Ⅲ ⅙ 🛈 ⌾ ♨ 🛆 🕈 ✧
Location	NW side of village

Hotel	B Posthouse Cambridge, Lakeview, Bridge Rd, Impington, CAMBRIDGE ☎ 01223 237000 118 ⇆ 🅕

HEMINGFORD ABBOTS   Map 04 TL27

Hemingford Abbots Cambridge Rd PE18 9HQ
☎ 01480 495000 & 493900 Fax 01480 4960000
Interesting 9-hole course featuring a par 5 dog-leg 4th with a testing tapering fairway, two ponds at the entrance to the 8th green and an island green on the 9th.
9 holes, 5468yds, Par 68, SSS 68, Course record 69.
Club membership 170.

Visitors	advisable to phone in advance, particularly for weekends.
Societies	advise in writing or telephone.
Green Fees	not confirmed.
Prof	Craig Watson
Designer	Ray Paton
Facilities	⊗)Ⅲ ⅙ 🛈 ⌾ ♨ 🛆 🏠 🕈 ✧ ⚑
Location	A14 Hemingford Abbots turning

Hotel	★★★ 75% The Old Bridge Hotel, 1 High St, HUNTINGDON ☎ 01480 452681 25 ⇆ 🅕

MARCH   Map 05 TL49

March Frogs Abbey, Grange Rd PE15 0YH
☎ 01354 652364 Fax 01354 652364
Nine-hole parkland course with a particularly challenging par 3 9th hole, with out of bounds on the right and high hedges to the right.
9 holes, 6204yds, Par 70, SSS 70, Course record 65.
Club membership 413.

Visitors	contact in advance, with member only at weekends.
Societies	must contact in advance.

Green Fees	£16.50 per day.
Cards	▬ 💳 💳 📇
Prof	Jason Hadland
Facilities	⊗ by prior arrangement)Ⅲ by prior arrangement ⅙ by prior arrangement 🛈 ⌾ 🛆 🏠 ✧
Location	0.5m off A141, March bypass

Hotel	★★ 64% Olde Griffin Hotel, High St, MARCH ☎ 01354 652517 20rm(19 ⇆ 🅕)

PETERBOROUGH   Map 04 TL19

Elton Furze Bullock Rd, Haddon PE7 3TT
☎ 01832 280189 Fax 01832 280299
A new course opened in 1993. Wooded parkland 18-hole course in lovely surroundings.
18 holes, 6289yds, Par 70, SSS 70, Course record 67.

Visitors	welcome, preferably Tue & Thu, weekends only with prior permission (phone in advance).
Societies	by prior arrangement telephone for details.
Green Fees	£30 per day; £22 per round weekdays (£32 per round weekends).
Prof	Frank Kiddie
Designer	Roger Fitton
Facilities	⊗)Ⅲ ⅙ 🛈 ⌾ ♨ 🛆 🏠 🛆 ✧ ♩
Location	4m SW of Peterborough, off A605

Hotel	★★★★ 64% Swallow Hotel, Peterborough Business Park, Lynchwood, PETERBOROUGH ☎ 01733 371111 163 ⇆ 🅕

Orton Meadows Ham Ln, Orton Waterville PE2 0UU
☎ 01733 237478
Pretty public parkland course set within the Nene Valley Country Park with large lakes and water hazards. Challenging 3rd hole (616yards from white tee) incorporating lots of water and 'out of bounds' areas. Also 12-hole pitch and putt course.
18 holes, 5269yds, Par 67, SSS 68, Course record 69.
Club membership 650.

Visitors	no restrictions.
Societies	apply in advance.
Green Fees	not confirmed.
Cards	▬ 💳 💳 💳
Prof	N Grant/J Mitchell
Designer	D & R Fitton
Facilities	⊗)Ⅲ ⅙ 🛈 ⌾ ♨ 🛆 🕈 ⚑ ✧
& Leisure	12 hole pitch & putt.
Location	3m W of town on A605

Hotel	★★★ 69% Orton Hall Hotel, Orton Longueville, PETERBOROUGH ☎ 01733 391111 66 ⇆ 🅕

Peterborough Milton Milton Ferry PE6 7AG
☎ 01733 380489 Fax 01733 380489
Designed by James Braid, this well-bunkered parkland course is set in the grounds of the Milton Estate, many of the holes being played in full view of Milton Hall. Challenging holes are the difficult dog-leg 10th and 15th. Easy walking.
18 holes, 6205yds, Par 71, SSS 70, Course record 66.
Club membership 800.

Visitors	must contact in advance.
Societies	bookings in writing to secretary.
Green Fees	£25 per day; £20 per round (£25 per round weekends & bank holidays).
Prof	Michael Gallagher

Designer	James Braid
Facilities	⊗ 㸐 ⅃ ㉒ ♀ ⚘ 🏠 ⚷ ↾
Location	2m W of Peterborough on A47

Hotel ★★★ 63% Butterfly Hotel, Thorpe Meadows, Longthorpe Parkway, PETERBOROUGH ☎ 01733 64240 70 ⇄ ↾

Thorpe Wood Thorpe Wood, Nene Parkway PE3 6SE
☎ 01733 267701
Gently undulating, parkland course designed by Peter Alliss and Dave Thomas. Challenging holes include the 5th, the longest hole usually played with prevailing wind and the 14th, entailing a difficult approach shot over water to a two-tier green.
18 holes, 7086yds, Par 73, SSS 74, Course record 68.
Club membership 750.

Visitors	phone for reservations 7 days in advance.
Societies	must telephone in advance, society bookings taken up to year ahead.
Green Fees	£10.20 per round (£13 weekends & bank holidays).
Cards	▭ VISA ▭ ▭ ▭
Prof	Dennis & Roger Fitton
Designer	Peter Allis/Dave Thomas
Facilities	⊗ 㸐 ⅃ ㉒ ♀ ⚘ 🏠 🍴 ⚷
Location	3m W of city centre on A47

Hotel ★★★ 67% Peterborough Moat House, Thorpe Wood, PETERBOROUGH ☎ 01733 289988 125 ⇄ ↾

PIDLEY   Map 05 TL37

Lakeside Lodge Fen Rd PE17 3DD
☎ 01487 740540 Fax 01487 740852
A well designed, spacious course incorporating eight lakes, 12,000 trees and a modern clubhouse. The 9th and 18th holes both finish dramatically alongside a lake in front of the clubhouse. Also 9-hole Par 3 and 25-bay driving range. The Manor provides an interseting contrast with its undulating fairways and angular greens.
Lodge Course: 18 holes, 6821yds, Par 72, SSS 73, Course record 72.
The Manor: 9 holes, 2601yds, Par 68.
Club membership 500.

Visitors	no restrictions.
Societies	must telephone in advance.
Green Fees	£11 per 18 holes (£17 weekends).
Cards	▭ VISA
Prof	Scott Waterman
Designer	A W Headley
Facilities	⊗ 㸐 ⅃ ㉒ ♀ ⚘ 🏠 🍴 ⇄ ⚘ ⚷ ↾
& Leisure	fishing, ten pin bowling.

Hotel ★★★ 67% Slepe Hall Hotel, Ramsey Rd, ST IVES ☎ 01480 463122 16 ⇄ ↾

RAMSEY   Map 04 TL28

Old Nene Golf & Country Club Muchwood Ln, Bodsey PE17 1XQ ☎ 01487 813519 & 815622
A flat well-drained course with water hazards. There are excellent greens and there are many challenging holes across water in either a head wind or cross wind. Eastern Area Environmental Winner 1996.
9 holes, 2788yds, Par 68, SSS 68, Course record 66.
Club membership 200.

Visitors	book in advance especially evenings & weekends. Dress code must be adhered to.
Societies	arrange in advance with Secretary.
Green Fees	£10 per 18 holes; £7 per 9 holes (£15/£9 weekends & bank holidays).
Prof	Stewart Mills
Designer	R Edrich
Facilities	㉒ 🏠 ⚘ ⚘ ⚷ ↾
& Leisure	fishing, practice area.
Location	0.75m N of Ramsey towards Ramsey Mereside

Hotel ★★★ 75% The Old Bridge Hotel, 1 High St, HUNTINGDON ☎ 01480 452681 25 ⇄ ↾

Ramsey 4 Abbey Ter PE17 1DD
☎ 01487 812660 Fax 01487 815746
Flat, parkland course with water hazards and well irrigated greens, mature tees and fairways, assuring a good surface whatever the conditions. It gives the impression of wide open spaces, but the wayward shot is soon punished.
18 holes, 5830yds, Par 71, SSS 68, Course record 65.
Club membership 750.

Visitors	contact professional in advance 01487 813022, may only play with member at weekends & bank holidays.
Societies	apply in writing.
Green Fees	£25 per day.
Prof	Stuart Scott
Designer	J Hamilton Stutt
Facilities	⊗ 㸐 ⅃ ㉒ ♀ ⚘ 🏠 🍴 ⚷
& Leisure	snooker tables,6 rink bowls green.
Location	12m SE of Peterborough on B1040

Hotel ★★★ 75% The Old Bridge Hotel, 1 High St, HUNTINGDON ☎ 01480 452681 25 ⇄ ↾

ST IVES   Map 05 TL37

St Ives (Cambs) Westwood Rd PE17 4RS
☎ 01480 468392 Fax 01480 468392
Picturesque parkland course.
9 holes, 6100yds, Par 70, SSS 69, Course record 68.
Club membership 500.

Visitors	may not play weekends.
Societies	welcome Wednesday & Fridays.
Green Fees	not confirmed.
Prof	Darren Glasby
Facilities	⚘ 🏠 🍴 ⚷
Location	W side of town centre off A1123

Hotel ★★★ 67% Slepe Hall Hotel, Ramsey Rd, ST IVES ☎ 01480 463122 16 ⇄ ↾

ST NEOTS   Map 04 TL16

Abbotsley Golf & Squash Club PE19 4XN
☎ 01480 474000 & 215153 Fax 01480 471018
Two courses - main Abbotsley course featuring mature parkland with tree-lined fairways, plenty of water hazards and a particularly testing par 3 2nd hole - the 'Mousehole'. Cromwell course, opened in 1991, is less demanding with tricky driving holes and sloping greens. Courses surround moated country house and hotel. Residential golf schools 30 weeks of the year plus floodlit, covered driving range, par 3 course and grass practice area..
Abbotsley Course: 18 holes, 6311yds, Par 73, SSS 72, Course record 69.   ▶

Cromwell Course: 18 holes, 6087yds, Par 70, SSS 69.
Club membership 550.

Visitors welcome all times. Necessary to book weekends.
Societies prior booking essential.
Green Fees £36 per day; £25 per round (£30 per round weekends).
Cards ⬛⬛ 🅥🅢🅐 💳
Prof Vivien Saunders
Designer D Young/V Saunders
Facilities ⊗ ⅢⅬ 🄱 ♟ ♨ ⌣ 🏠 🕌 ⮞ 🛺 ♐ ↾
& Leisure squash, gymnasium.
Location 2m SE off B1046

Hotel ★★ 64% Abbotsley Golf Hotel, Potton Rd, Eynesbury Hardwicke, ST NEOTS
☎ 01480 474000 17 ⇆ ♟

St Neots Crosshall Rd PE19 4AE ☎ 01480 472363
Undulating and very picturesque parkland course with lake and water hazards and exceptional greens, close to the Kym and Great Ouse rivers. Easy, level walking.
18 holes, 6074yds, Par 69, SSS 69, Course record 64.
Club membership 630.

Visitors must book in advance. with member only at weekends.
Societies must contact in advance.
Green Fees not confirmed.
Prof Graham Bithrey
Designer H Vardon
Facilities ⌣ 🏠 🕌 ⮞ 🛺 ♐
Location Just off the A1 with the jct B1048 heading into St Neots

Hotel ★★ 64% Abbotsley Golf Hotel, Potton Rd, Eynesbury Hardwicke, ST NEOTS
☎ 01480 474000 17 ⇆ ♟

THORNEY   Map 04 TF20

Thorney English Drove, Thorney PE6 0TJ
☎ 01733 270570 Fax 01733 270842
The 18-hole Fen course is ideal for the beginner, while the Lakes course, opened in June 1995, has a challenging links-style layout with eight holes around water.
Fen Course: 18 holes, 6104yds, Par 70, SSS 69, Course record 66.
Lakes Course: 18 holes, 6401yds, Par 71, SSS 71, Course record 66.
Club membership 400.

Visitors book in advance for Fen course, limited weekend play Lakes course.
Societies contact in advance.
Green Fees Fen: £6.50 (£8.50 weekends & bank holidays). Lakes: £11 (£17.50 weekends & bank holidays).
Prof Mark Templeman
Designer A Dow
Facilities ⊗ ⅢⅬ 🄱 ♟ ♨ ⌣ 🏠 🕌 ⮞ 🛺 ♐ ↾
Location Off A47, 7m NE of Peterborough

Hotel ★★★ 63% Butterfly Hotel, Thorpe Meadows, Longthorpe Parkway, PETERBOROUGH
☎ 01733 64240 70 ⇆ ♟

> Entries with a shaded background
> identify courses that are
> considered to be particularly interesting

TOFT   Map 05 TL35

Cambridge Meridian Comberton Rd CB3 7RY
☎ 01223 264700 Fax 01223 264701
Opened in 1993. Set in 207 acres to a Peter Allis/Clive Clark design with sweeping fairways, lakes and well bunkered greens. The 4th hole has bunker complexes, a sharp dog-leg and a river with the green heavily guarded by bunkers. The 9th and 10th holes challenge the golfer with river crossings.
18 holes, 6651yds, Par 73, SSS 72, Course record 72.
Club membership 600.

Visitors must contact in advance.
Societies telephone for provisional booking
Green Fees £14 per round (£18 weekends) prices for off peak times.
Cards ⬛⬛ 🅥🅢🅐
Prof Michael Clemons
Designer Peter Allis/Clive Clark
Facilities ⊗ Ⅼ 🄱 ♟ ♨ ⌣ 🏠 🕌 ⮞ 🛺 ♐
Location 3m W of Cambridge, on B1046

Hotel ★★ 64% Abbotsley Golf Hotel, Potton Rd, Eynesbury Hardwicke, ST NEOTS
☎ 01480 474000 17 ⇆ ♟

CHESHIRE

ALDERLEY EDGE   Map 07 SJ87

Alderley Edge Brook Ln SK9 7RU ☎ 01625 585583
Well-wooded, undulating pastureland course. A stream crosses 7 of the 9 holes.
9 holes, 5823yds, Par 68, SSS 68, Course record 62.
Club membership 400.

Visitors by arrangement on Thu.
Societies Thu only, apply in writing or telephone.
Green Fees not confirmed.
Prof Peter Bowring
Facilities ⊗ ⅢⅬ 🄱 ♟ ♨ ⌣ 🏠 ♐
Location 1m NW on B5085

Hotel ★★★ 71% Alderley Edge Hotel, Macclesfield Rd, ALDERLEY EDGE
☎ 01625 583033 46 ⇆ ♟

ALSAGER   Map 07 SJ75

Alsager Golf & Country Club Audley Rd ST7 2UR
☎ 01270 875700 Fax 01270 882207
An 18-hole parkland course situated in rolling Cheshire countryside and offering a challenge to all golfers whatever their standard. Clubhouse is well appointed with good facilities and a friendly atmosphere.
18 holes, 6225yds, Par 70, SSS 70.
Club membership 640.

Visitors must contact in advance, can only play with member at weekends.
Societies must contact in advance.
Green Fees not confirmed.
Prof Richard Brown
Facilities ⊗ ⅢⅬ 🄱 ♟ ♨ ⌣ 🏠 🕌 ♐
Location 2m NE of M6 junct 16

Hotel ★★★ 73% Manor House Hotel, Audley Rd,
ALSAGER ☎ 01270 884000 57 ⇄ ♠

CHESTER Map 07 SJ46

Carden Park Hotel Carden Park CH3 9DQ
☎ 01829 731000 Fax 01829 731032
A superb golf resort set in 750 acres of beautiful Cheshire
countryside. Facilities include the mature parkland Cheshire
Course, the new Nicklaus Course, the 9 hole par 3 Azalea
Course, Europe's first Jack Nicklaus Residential Golf School
and a luxurious clubhouse.
Cheshire: 18 holes, 6891yds, Par 72, SSS 71, Course record 69.
Nicklaus: 18 holes, 7045yds, Par 72, SSS 71.
Club membership 250.

Visitors must contact in advance, handicap certificate
required for the Nicklaus Course. To help
maintain the highest quality metal spikes cannot
be worn.
Societies contact for details, tel: 01829 731594.
Green Fees Cheshire £30; Nicklaus £60.
Cards
Prof Simon Edwards
Facilities ⊗ ⅏ ᖤ ☕ ♥ ♀ ⚲ ☖ ♥ ⛳ ♂ ✦
& Leisure hard tennis courts, heated indoor swimming
pool, sauna, solarium, gymnasium, residential
golf school.
Location Off A534

Hotel ★★★★ 72% Carden Park Hotel Golf Resort &
Spa, Carden Park, BROXTON
☎ 01829 731000 115 ⇄ ♠ Annexe77 ⇄ ♠

Chester Curzon Park CH4 8AR
☎ 01244 677760 Fax 01244 676667
Meadowland course on two levels contained within a loop of
the River Dee. The car park overlooks the racecourse across
the river.
18 holes, 6508yds, Par 72, SSS 71, Course record 66.
Club membership 820.
Visitors must contact in advance.
Societies must telephone or write in advance.
Green Fees £23 per day (£28 weekends).
Prof George Parton
Facilities ⊗ ⅏ ᖤ ☕ ♀ ⚲ ☖ ⛳ ✦
Location 1m W of city centre

Hotel ★★★★ 66% Chester Moat House, Trinity St,
CHESTER ☎ 01244 899988 152 ⇄ ♠

Upton-by-Chester Upton Ln, Upton-by-Chester CH2 1EE
☎ 01244 381183 Fax 01244 376955
Pleasant, tree-lined, parkland course. Not easy for low-
handicap players to score well. Testing holes are 2nd (par 4),
14th (par 4) and 15th (par 3).
18 holes, 5808yds, Par 69, SSS 68, Course record 63.
Club membership 800.
Visitors must contact in advance.
Societies apply in writing.
Green Fees £22 per day (£27 per round weekends).
Prof P A Gardner
Facilities ⊗ ⅏ ᖤ ☕ ♀ ⚲ ☖ ⛳ ✦
Location N side off A5116

Hotel ★★★★ 66% Mollington Banastre Hotel,
Parkgate Rd, CHESTER
☎ 01244 851471 63 ⇄

Vicars Cross Tarvin Rd, Great Barrow CH3 7HN
☎ 01244 335174 Fax 01244 335686
Tree-lined parkland course, with undulating terrain.
18 holes, 6365yds, Par 72, SSS 70, Course record 64.
Club membership 750.
Visitors advisable to contact in advance, visitors may not
play competition days or Wed.
Societies Tue & Thu only. Must book in advance.
Green Fees £25 per day.
Prof J A Forsythe
Designer J Richardson
Facilities ⊗ ⅏ ᖤ ☕ ♀ ⚲ ☖ ✦
Location 4m E on A51

Hotel ★★★ 68% Rowton Hall Hotel, Whitchurch Rd,
Rowton, CHESTER
☎ 01244 335262 42 ⇄ ♠

CONGLETON Map 07 SJ86

Astbury Peel Ln, Astbury CW12 4RE
☎ 01260 272772 & 279139
Parkland course in open countryside, bisected by a canal. The
testing 12th hole involves a long carry over a tree-filled
ravine. Large practice area.
18 holes, 6296yds, Par 71, SSS 70, Course record 61.
Club membership 720.
Visitors weekdays ring for availability 01260 298663,
with member only at weekends, contact for
further details.
Societies contact for details.
Green Fees not confirmed.
Prof Ashley Salt
Facilities ⊗ ᖤ ☕ ♀ ⚲ ☖ ✦
Location 1.5m S between A34 and A527

Hotel ★★★ 61% Lion & Swan Hotel, Swan Bank,
CONGLETON ☎ 01260 273115 21 ⇄ ♠

Congleton Biddulph Rd CW12 3LZ ☎ 01260 273540
Superbly-manicured parkland course with views over three
counties from the balcony of the clubhouse.
9 holes, 5103yds, Par 68, SSS 65.
Club membership 400.
Visitors may not play during competitions. Must contact
in advance.
Societies must apply in writing to Secretary.
Green Fees £20 per round (£30 weekends).
Prof John Colclough ▶

Facilities 🏌 ♀ ⚲ 📷
Location   1.5m SE on A527

Hotel   ★★★ 61% Lion & Swan Hotel, Swan Bank,
               CONGLETON ☎ 01260 273115 21 ⇆ ☞

CREWE   Map 07 SJ75

Crewe Fields Rd, Haslington CW1 5TB
☎ 01270 584099 Fax 01270 584099
Undulating parkland course.
18 holes, 6424yds, Par 71, SSS 71, Course record 66.
Club membership 674.
Visitors   contact for details.
Societies   Tue only, prior arrangement with the secretary.
Green Fees not confirmed.
Prof   Mike Booker
Facilities ⊗ 🏌 💻 ♀ ⚲ 📷 ♂
Location   2.25m NE off A534

Hotel   ★★★ 64% Hunters Lodge Hotel, Sydney Rd,
               Sydney, CREWE ☎ 01270 583440 47 ⇆ ☞

Queen's Park Queen's Park Dr CW2 7SB
☎ 01270 666724 Fax 01270 569902
A short but testing municipal course, the 9 holes are
highlighted by the tight dogleg 4th holes and 450yard Par 4
7th hole. There is a testing Par 4 on finishing hole with a
bomb crater on left and outerbounds on the right.
9 holes, 4920yds, Par 68, SSS 64, Course record 67.
Club membership 400.
Visitors   booking for weekends, cannot play Wed or Sun
                before 10.30am.
Societies   must book at least 2 weeks in advance.
Green Fees £5 per 18 holes; £4 per 9 holes (£7/£5 weekends
                & bank holidays).
Cards   ⚊ 💳 💳 💳 💳 💳
Prof   David Evanson
Facilities ⊗ 🏌 💻 ♀ ⚲ 📷 ♂ ♂
& Leisure   hard tennis courts, bowling green.
Location   Located behind Queen's Park. Well signposted

Hotel   ★★★ 64% Hunters Lodge Hotel, Sydney Rd,
               Sydney, CREWE
               ☎ 01270 583440 47 ⇆ ☞

DELAMERE   Map 07 SJ56

Delamere Forest Station Rd CW8 2JE
☎ 01606 883264 (Office) 883307 (Pro)
Fax 01606 883800 (Sec)
Played mostly on undulating open heath there is great

charm in the way this course drops down into the
occasional pine sheltered valley. Six of the first testing
nine hole are between 420 and 455 yards in length.
18 holes, 6328yds, Par 72, SSS 70, Course record 63.
Club membership 500.
Visitors   must contact in advance.
Societies   apply in writing or by telephone.
Green Fees £45 per day; £30 per round (£35 per round
                weekends & bank holidays).
Prof   Ellis B Jones
Designer   H Fowler
Facilities ⊗ 🍴 by prior arrangement 🏌 💻 ♀ ⚲ 📷
                🍴 ⚲ ♂

Location   1.5m NE, off B5152

Hotel   ★★★♨♨ Nunsmere Hall Country House
               Hotel, Tarporley Rd, Oakmere,
               SANDIWAY ☎ 01606 889100 36 ⇆ ☞

DISLEY   Map 07 SJ98

Disley Stanley Hall Ln SK12 2JX
☎ 01663 762071 & 764001 (Sec)
Straddling a hilltop site above Lyme Park, this undulating
parkland/moorland course affords good views and requires
accuracy of approach to almost all the greens which lie on
either a ledge or plateau. Testing holes are the 3rd and 4th.
18 holes, 6015yds, Par 71, SSS 69, Course record 63.
Club membership 658.
Visitors   contact in advance, may not normally play at
                weekends.
Societies   by prior arrangement.
Green Fees £25 per round also all inclusive packages
                available.
Prof   Andrew Esplin
Facilities ⊗ 🍴 🏌 💻 ♀ ⚲ 📷 ♂ ♂
Location   NW side of village off A6

Hotel   ★★★ 66% County Hotel Bramhall, Bramhall
               Ln South, BRAMHALL
               ☎ 0161 455 9988 65 ⇆ ☞

ELLESMERE PORT   Map 07 SJ47

Ellesmere Port Chester Rd, Childer Thornton L66 1QF
☎ 0151 339 7689 Fax 0151 339 7689
Municipal parkland course that is easy walking, with natural
hazards of woods, brook and ponds.
18 holes, 6432yds, Par 71, SSS 70.
Club membership 300.
Visitors   must book with professional & send a deposit.
Societies   by arrangement with professional.
Green Fees not confirmed.
Prof   Tony Roberts
Designer   Cotton, Pennick & Lawrie
Facilities ⊗ 🍴 🏌 💻 ♀ ⚲ 📷 ♂ ♂
& Leisure   squash, golf simulator for hire with professional.
Location   NW side of town centre on A41

Hotel   ★★★ 64% Quality Hotel Chester, Welsh Rd,
               Little Sutton, WIRRAL
               ☎ 0151 339 5121 53 ⇆ ☞

Entries with a shaded background
identify courses that are
considered to be particularly interesting

FRODSHAM   Map 07 SJ57

Frodsham Simons Ln WA6 6HE
☎ 01928 732159 Fax 01928 734070
Undulating parkland course with pleasant views from all
parts. Emphasis on accuracy over the whole course, the long
and difficult par 5 18th necessitating a drive across water to
the green. Crossed by two footpaths so extreme care needed.
18 holes, 6298yds, Par 70, SSS 70.
Club membership 600.
Visitors   must contact in advance. May not play at
                weekends.
Societies   telephone for bookings.
Green Fees £30 per round.
Cards
Prof   Graham Tonge
Designer   John Day
Facilities
Location   1.5m SW

Hotel   ★★★ 67% Forest Hills Hotel & Leisure
                Complex, Bellemonte Rd, Overton Hill,
                FRODSHAM ☎ 01928 735255 57

HELSBY   Map 07 SJ47

Helsby Towers Ln WA6 0JB
☎ 01928 722021 Fax 01928 725384
Parkland course with several tree plantations and natural pits
as water hazards. Total of 46 bunkers.
18 holes, 6229yds, Par 70, SSS 70, Course record 69.
Club membership 590.
Visitors   must contact in advance. Weekends and bank
                holidays with member only.
Societies   Tue & Thu. Booking through Hon Secretary.
Green Fees £22 per round (£30 weekends).
Prof   Matthew Jones
Designer   James Braid (part)
Facilities
Location   1m S off A56

Hotel   ★★★★★ 75% The Chester Grosvenor Hotel,
                Eastgate, CHESTER
                ☎ 01244 324024 85

KNUTSFORD   Map 07 SJ77

Heyrose Budworth Rd, Tabley WA16 0HZ
☎ 01565 733664 Fax 01565 734267
An 18-hole course in wooded and gently undulating terrain.
The par 3 16th (237yrds), bounded by a small river in a
wooded valley, is an interesting and testing hole - one of the
toughest par 3s in Cheshire. Several water hazards. Both the
course and the comfortable clubhouse have attractive views.
18 holes, 6515yds, Par 73, SSS 71, Course record 66.
Club membership 600.
Visitors   not before 3.30pm Sat, ladies priority Wed and
                seniors priority Thu am.
Societies   must contact in advance.
Green Fees £24 per day; £19 per round (£29/£24 weekends
                & bank holidays).
Cards
Prof   Martin Redrup
Designer   C N Bridge
Facilities   by prior arrangement
Location   1.5m from junc 19 on M6

Hotel   ★★★★ 69% Cottons Hotel, Manchester Rd,
                KNUTSFORD ☎ 01565 650333 99

Knutsford Mereheath Ln WA16 6HS ☎ 01565 633355
Parkland course set in a beautiful old deer park. It demands
some precise iron play.
9 holes, 6288yds, Par 70, SSS 70.
Club membership 230.
Visitors   are not permitted weekends and restricted Wed.
                Must contact in advance.
Societies   Thursday only by prior arrangement.
Green Fees £25 per round (£30 weekends & bank holidays).
Prof   A Gillies
Facilities
Location   N side of town centre off A50

Hotel   ★★★★ 69% Cottons Hotel, Manchester Rd,
                KNUTSFORD ☎ 01565 650333 99

Mere Golf & Country Club Chester Rd, Mere
WA16 6LJ ☎ 01565 830155 Fax 01565 830713
A gracious parkland championship course designed by
James Braid in the Cheshire sand belt, with several holes
close to a lake. The round has a tight finish with four
testing holes.
18 holes, 6817yds, Par 71, SSS 73, Course record 64.
Club membership 540.

Visitors   by prior arrangement only, not able to play
                Wed, Fri, Sat & Sun.
Societies   Mon,Tue & Thu only by prior arrangement.
Green Fees not confirmed.
Cards
Prof   Peter Eyre
Designer   James Braid
Facilities
& Leisure   hard tennis courts, heated indoor swimming
                pool, squash, fishing, sauna, solarium,
                gymnasium.
Location   1m E of junc 19 of M6

Hotel   ★★★★ 69% Cottons Hotel, Manchester Rd,
                KNUTSFORD ☎ 01565 650333 99

LYMM   Map 07 SJ68

Lymm Whitbarrow Rd WA13 9AN
☎ 01925 752177 & 755020 Fax 01925 755020
First ten holes are gently undulating with the Manchester
Ship Canal running alongside the 9th hole. The remaining
holes are comparatively flat.   ▶

18 holes, 6304yds, Par 71, SSS 70.
Club membership 650.
Visitors may not play at weekends except with member.
Societies Wed only, must contact in advance.
Green Fees not confirmed.
Prof Steve McCarthy
Facilities ⛏🏠🏌
Location 0.5m N off A6144

Hotel ★★★ 65% Lymm Hotel, Whitbarrow Rd, LYMM ☎ 01925 752233. 20 ⇆ ♟ Annexe43 ⇆ ♟

MACCLESFIELD Map 07 SJ97

Macclesfield The Hollins SK11 7EA
☎ 01625 615845 (Secretary) Fax 01625 260061
Hillside heathland course situated on the edge of the Pennines with excellent views across the Cheshire Plain. A pleasant course providing a good test for players of all abilities.
18 holes, 5769yds, Par 70, SSS 68, Course record 66.
Club membership 620.
Visitors apply in advance and have a handicap certificate.
Societies telephone initially.
Green Fees £20 per day/round (£25 weekends & bank holidays).
Prof Tony Taylor
Designer Hawtree & Son
Facilities ⊗ ⅲ ⅃ 💺 ♟ ⛏ 🏠 ⛳ ♥ 🏌
Location SE side of town centre off A523

Hotel ★★★ 67% Belgrade Hotel & Restaurant, Jackson Ln, Kerridge, Bollington, MACCLESFIELD ☎ 01625 573246 54 ⇆ ♟

Shrigley Hall Hotel Shrigley Park, Pott Shrigley SK10 5SB
☎ 01625 575757 Fax 01625 573323
Parkland course set in 262-acre estate with breathtaking views over the Peak District and Cheshire Plain. Designed by Donald Steel, this championship standard course provides a real sporting challenge while the magnificent hotel provides a wealth of sporting facilities as well as accommodation and food.
18 holes, 6281yds, Par 71, SSS 71, Course record 68.
Club membership 500.

Visitors must contact in advance by telephone.
Societies contact in advance.
Green Fees £35 per day; £30 per round (£45/£35 weekends & bank holidays).
Cards 💳 💳 🗇
Prof Tony Stevens
Designer Donald Steel

Facilities ⊗ ⅲ ⅃ 💺 ♟ ⛏ 🏠 ⛳ 🏌 🚣 🏌
& Leisure hard tennis courts, heated indoor swimming pool, fishing, sauna, solarium, gymnasium.

Hotel ★★★★ 62% Shrigley Hall Hotel Golf & Country Club, Shrigley Park, Pott Shrigley, MACCLESFIELD ☎ 01625 575757 150 ⇆ ♟

Tytherington Dorchester Way, Tytherington SK10 2JP
☎ 01625 434562 Fax 01625 430882
Modern championship course in beautiful, mature parkland setting with numerous water features. Testing holes, notably the signature 12th hole (par 5), played from an elevated tee with adjacent snaking ditch and a lake guarding the green. Headquarters of the Women's European Tour and venue of the WPGET English Open and County matches. Country club facilities.
18 holes, 6750yds, Par 72, SSS 74.
Club membership 3100.
Visitors advisable to contact in advance and be of handicap standard.
Societies weekdays only by prior arrangement.
Green Fees not confirmed.
Cards 💳 💳 💳 💳 💳 💳
Prof Gordon McLeod
Designer Dave Thomas/Patrick Dawson
Facilities ⊗ ⅲ ⅃ 💺 ♟ ⛏ 🏠 ♥ 🚣 🏌 ⛳
Location 1m N of Macclesfield off A523

Hotel ★★★★ 62% Shrigley Hall Hotel Golf & Country Club, Shrigley Park, Pott Shrigley, MACCLESFIELD ☎ 01625 575757 150 ⇆ ♟

NANTWICH Map 07 SJ65

Reaseheath Reaseheath College CW5 6DF ☎ 01270 625131
The course at Reaseheath is attached to Reaseheath College, which is one of the major centres of greenkeeper training in the UK. It is a short 9-hole which can only be played with a member.
9 holes, 1766yds, Par 62, SSS 58.
Club membership 350.
Visitors with member only.
Societies by prior arrangement, apply in writing.
Green Fees not confirmed.
Designer D Mortram
Location 1.5m NE of Nantwich, off A51

OSCROFT Map 07 SJ56

Pryors Hayes Willington Rd CH3 8NL
☎ 01829 741250 Fax 01829 741250
Picturesque 18-hole parkland course set in the heart of Cheshire. Gently undulating fairways demand accurate drives, and numerous trees and water hazards make the course a challenging test of golf.
18 holes, 6074yds, Par 69, SSS 69.
Club membership 625.
Visitors no restrictions.
Societies apply for application form.
Green Fees not confirmed.
Prof Colin Iddon
Designer John Day
Facilities ⊗ ⅲ ⅃ 💺 ♟ ⛏ 🏠 🚣 🏌
Location Between A54 & A51 roads, approx 6m E of Chester, village of Oscroft near Tarvin

Hotel　★★ 62%　Royal Oak Hotel, Warrington Rd,
Mickle Trafford, CHESTER
☎ 01244 301391　36 ⇔ ﾚ

POYNTON　　　　　　　　　　　　Map 07 SJ98

Davenport Worth Hall, Middlewood Rd SK12 1TS
☎ 01625 876951 Fax 01625 877489
Undulating parkland course. Extensive view over Cheshire
Plain from elevated 5th tee. Testing 17th hole, par 4.
18 holes, 6027yds, Par 69, SSS 69, Course record 64.
Club membership 700.
Visitors　contact professional in advance, 01625 858387.
May not play Wed or Sat.
Societies　Tue and Thu only. Must apply in advance.
Green Fees £27 per round (£32 weekends & bank holidays).
Prof　Gary Norcott
Facilities　⊗ by prior arrangement ﾙﾘ by prior arrangement
ﾗ ♥ ♀ ♋ ﾐ ♂
Location　1m E off A523

Hotel　★★★ 66%　County Hotel Bramhall, Bramhall
Ln South, BRAMHALL
☎ 0161 455 9988 65 ⇔ ﾚ

PRESTBURY　　　　　　　　　　　Map 07 SJ97

Prestbury Macclesfield Rd SK10 4BJ
☎ 01625 828241 Fax 01625 828241
Rather strenuous parkland course, undulating hills, with
many plateau greens. The 9th hole has a challenging
uphill 3-tier green and the 17th is over a valley. Host to
county and inter-county championships as well as
England v USA competitions.
18 holes, 6359yds, Par 71, SSS 71, Course record 64.
Club membership 702.

Visitors　must contact in advance and have an
introduction from own club, with member
only at weekends.
Societies　apply in writing, Thu only.
Green Fees £38 per day.
Cards　[cards]
Prof　Nick Summerfield
Designer　Harry S Colt
Facilities　⊗ ﾙﾘ ﾗ ♥ ♀ ♋ ﾐ ♂ ♂ ￤
Location　S side of village off A538

Hotel　★★★★ 68%　Mottram Hall Hotel,
Wilmslow Rd, Mottram St Andrew,
Prestbury ☎ 01625 828135 132 ⇔ ﾚ

RUNCORN　　　　　　　　　　　Map 07 SJ58

Runcorn Clifton Rd WA7 4SU ☎ 01928 574214
Parkland course with tree-lined fairways and easy walking.
Fine views over Mersey and Weaver valleys. Testing holes:
7th par 5; 14th par 5; 17th par 4.
18 holes, 6035yds, Par 69, SSS 69, Course record 58.
Club membership 570.
Visitors　weekends restricted to playing with member
only, Tuesday Ladies Day.
Societies　telephone in advance.
Green Fees £18 per day.
Prof　A Franklin
Facilities　⊗ ﾙﾘ ﾗ ♥ ♀ ♋ ﾐ ♂ ♂
Location　1.25m S of Runcorn Station

Hotel　B Posthouse Warrington/Runcorn, Wood Ln,
Beechwood, RUNCORN
☎ 01928 714000 135 ⇔ ﾚ

SANDBACH　　　　　　　　　　Map 07 SJ76

Malkins Bank Betchton Rd, Malkins Bank CW11 4XN
☎ 01270 765931 Fax 01270 764730
Parkland course. Tight 13th hole with stream running
through.
18 holes, 6071yds, Par 70, SSS 69, Course record 65.
Club membership 500.
Visitors　no restrictions. Advisable to book in advance.
Societies　apply for booking form to course professional
Green Fees £7.75 per round (£8.85 weekends).
Prof　David Wheeler
Designer　Hawtree
Facilities　⊗ ﾙﾘ ﾗ ♥ ♀ ♋ ﾐ ♂ ♂
Location　1.5m SE off A533

Hotel　★★★ 64%　Saxon Cross Hotel, Holmes Chapel
Rd, SANDBACH ☎ 01270 763281　52 ⇔ ﾚ

SANDIWAY　　　　　　　　　　Map 07 SJ67

Sandiway Chester Rd CW8 2DJ
☎ 01606 883247 (Secretary) Fax 01606 888548
Delightful undulating wood and heathland course with
long hills up to the 8th, 16th and 17th holes. Many dog-
legged and tree-lined holes give opportunities for the
deliberate fade or draw.
18 holes, 6404yds, Par 70, SSS 72, Course record 67.
Club membership 700.
Visitors　book through secretary, members have
reserved tees 8.30-9.30 and 12.30-1.30
(11.30-12.30 winter). Handicap certificate
required
Societies　book in advance through
Secretary/Manager.
Green Fees £40 per day; £35 per round (£45/£40
weekends & bank holidays).
Prof　William Laird
Designer　Ted Ray
Facilities　⊗ ﾙﾘ ﾗ ♥ ♀ ♋ ﾐ ♂ ♂
Location　2m W of Northwich on A556

Hotel　★★ 65%　Wincham Hall, Hall Ln,
Wincham, NORTHWICH
☎ 01606 43453 10rm(9 ⇔ ﾚ)

TARPORLEY   Map 07 SJ56

Portal Golf & Country Club Cobbler's Cross Ln CW6 0DJ
☎ 01829 733933 Fax 01829 733928
Opened in 1991, there are two 18-hole courses here -
Championship and Premier - and one 9-hole course -
Arderne. They are set in mature, wooded parkland. There are
fine views over the Cheshire Plain and numerous water
hazards. The Championship 14th is just a short iron through
trees, but its green is virtually an island surrounded by water.
*Championship Course: 18 holes, 7037yds, Par 73, SSS 74,
Course record 64.*
*Premier Course: 18 holes, 6508yds, Par 71, SSS 72, Course
record 64.*
Arderne Course: 9 holes, 1724yds, Par 30.
Club membership 250.

Visitors	must contact in advance.
Societies	must pre-book.
Green Fees	Championship: £45 per round. Premier: £35 per round. Arderne £10 per round.
Cards	🖳 💳 💳 🅾
Prof	Mike Slater/Malcolm Thorniley
Designer	Donald Steel
Facilities	⊗ ⅷ ⛳ 🏌 🍺 ♀ ⚐ 🍴 🏌 🛒 ✍ ⚑
& Leisure	hard tennis courts, golf academy.
Location	Off A49

Hotel	★★★ 64% The Wild Boar, Whitchurch Rd, Beeston, TARPORLEY ☎ 01829 260309 37 ⇄ 🏌

WARRINGTON   Map 07 SJ68

Birchwood Kelvin Close, Science Park North, Birchwood
WA3 7PB
☎ 01925 818819 (Club) & 816574 (Pro) Fax 01925 822403
Very testing parkland course with many natural water
hazards and the prevailing wind creating a problem on each
hole. The 11th hole is particularly challenging.
*Pilgrims: 18 holes, 6727yds, Par 71, SSS 73, Course record
66.*
Progress: 18 holes, 6359yds, Par 71, SSS 72.
*Mayflower (ladies course): 18 holes, 5849yds, Par 74, SSS
74.*
Club membership 720.

Visitors	advisable to check with the professional to determine if course is being used.
Societies	Mon, Wed & Thu. Apply in writing, or telephone.
Green Fees	£26 per day; £18 per round (£34 weekends & bank holidays).

Cards	🖳 💳 💳 🅾
Prof	Paul McEwan
Designer	T J A Macauley
Facilities	⊗ ⅷ ⛳ 🏌 🍺 ♀ ⚐ 🍴 ✍
& Leisure	sauna.
Location	4m NE on A574

Hotel	B Posthouse Haydock, Lodge Ln, HAYDOCK ☎ 01942 717878 138 ⇄ 🏌

Leigh Kenyon Hall, Broseley Ln, Culcheth WA3 4BG
☎ 01925 762943 (Secretary) Fax 01925 765097
A pleasant, well-wooded parkland course. Any
discrepancy in length is compensated by the wide variety
of golf offered here. The course is well maintained and
there is a comfortable clubhouse.
18 holes, 5853yds, Par 69, SSS 68, Course record 64.
Club membership 550.

Visitors	contact professional for details.
Societies	Mon (ex bank holidays) & Tue, apply by telephone.
Green Fees	£26 per day.
Prof	Andrew Baguley
Designer	James Braid
Facilities	⊗ ⅷ ⛳ 🏌 🍺 ♀ ⚐ 🍴 ✍
Location	5m NE off A579

Hotel	★★★ 66% Fir Grove Hotel, Knutsford Old Rd, WARRINGTON ☎ 01925 267471 40 ⇄ 🏌

Poulton Park Dig Ln, Cinnamon Brow, Padgate WA2 0SH
☎ 01925 822802 Fax 01925 822802
Tight, flat parkland course with good greens and many trees.
A straight drive off each tee is important. The 4/13th has a
fairway curving to the left with water and out-of-bounds on
left and trees on right.
9 holes, 4978mtrs, Par 68, SSS 66, Course record 66.
Club membership 350.

Visitors	midweek only. Contact professional for details 01925 825220.
Societies	apply in advance.
Green Fees	£17.
Prof	Darren Newing
Facilities	⊗ ⅷ ⛳ 🏌 🍺 ♀ ⚐ 🍴
Location	3m from Warrington on A574

Hotel	★★★ 66% Fir Grove Hotel, Knutsford Old Rd, WARRINGTON ☎ 01925 267471 40 ⇄ 🏌

Walton Hall Warrington Rd, Higher Walton WA4 5LU
☎ 01925 263061 (bookings)
A quiet, wooded, municipal parkland course on Walton Hall
estate.
18 holes, 6801yds, Par 72, SSS 73, Course record 70.
Club membership 250.

Visitors	must book 6 days in advance.
Societies	must contact in writing.
Green Fees	not confirmed.
Prof	John Jackson
Facilities	⊗ ⅷ ⛳ 🏌 🍺 ♀ ⚐ 🍴 🏌 ✍
Location	2m from junct 11 of M56

Hotel	★★★ 66% Fir Grove Hotel, Knutsford Old Rd, WARRINGTON ☎ 01925 267471 40 ⇄ 🏌

Warrington Hill Warren, London Rd, Appleton WA4 5HR
☎ 01925 261775 (Secretary) Fax 01925 265933
Meadowland, with varied terrain and natural hazards. Major
work has recently been carried out on both the clubhouse and
the course to ensure high standards. The course is a constant
challenge with with ponds, trees and bunkers threatening the
errant shot!
18 holes, 6305yds, Par 72, SSS 70, Course record 61.
Club membership 840.
Visitors   contact in advance.
Societies   by prior arrangement with Secretary.
Green Fees £27 per day (£32 weekends & bank holidays).
Prof   Reay Mackay
Designer   James Braid
Facilities   ⊗ by prior arrangement ▥ by prior arrangement
                         ⓑ ⬛ ♀ ⛌ 🏠 ⚐ ⚑ ✿
Location   1.5m N of junct 10 of M56 on A49

Hotel   ★★ 74% Rockfield Hotel, Alexandra Rd,
                        Grappenhall, WARRINGTON
                        ☎ 01925 262898 6 ⇔ ⚑ Annexe6 ⇔ ⚑

WAVERTON   Map 07 SJ46

Eaton Guy Ln, Waverton CH3 7PH
☎ 01244 335885 & 335826 Fax 01244 335782
Eaton Golf Club has moved to a new course. Designed by
Donald Steel, the course was opened in 1993 and is parkland
with a liberal covering of both mature trees and new planting
enhanced by natural water hazards. The old course at
Eccleston has been returned to nature.
18 holes, 6562yds, Par 72, SSS 71, Course record 69.
Club membership 550.

Eaton Golf Club

Visitors   must contact in advance particularly for
                         weekends.
Societies   must contact in advance. May not play
                         weekends or Wednesdays.
Green Fees £25 per round/day (£30 weekends & bank
                         holidays).
Cards   ▤
Prof   Neil Dunroe
Designer   Donald Steel
Facilities   ⊗ ▥ ⓑ ⬛ ♀ ⛌ 🏠 ⚐ ⚑ ✿ ⚓ ✿
Location   3m SE of Chester off A41

Hotel   ★★★★★ 75% The Chester Grosvenor Hotel,
                        Eastgate, CHESTER
                        ☎ 01244 324024 85 ⇔ ⚑

WIDNES   Map 07 SJ58

St Michael Jubilee Dundalk Rd WA8 8BS
☎ 0151 424 6230 Fax 0151 495 2124
Municipal parkland course dominated by the 'Stewards
Brook'. It is divided into two sections which are split by the
main road and joined by an underpass.
18 holes, 5925yds, Par 69, SSS 67.
Visitors   welcome.
Societies   must contact in writing.
Green Fees not confirmed.
Prof   Darren Chapman
Facilities   ⊗ ⓑ ⬛ ♀ ⛌ 🏠 ⚑

Hotel   ★★★ 64% Everglades Park Hotel, Derby Rd,
                        WIDNES ☎ 0151 495 2040 65 ⇔ ⚑

Widnes Highfield Rd WA8 7DT
☎ 0151 424 2440 Fax 0151 495 2849
Parkland course, easy walking.
18 holes, 5719yds, Par 69, SSS 68.
Visitors   may play after 9am & after 4pm on competition
                         days. Must contact in advance.
Societies   must contact the secretary in writing.
Green Fees not confirmed.
Prof   J O'Brien
Facilities   ⊗ ▥ ⓑ ⬛ ♀ ⛌ 🏠

Hotel   ★★★ 64% Everglades Park Hotel, Derby Rd,
                        WIDNES ☎ 0151 495 2040 65 ⇔ ⚑

WILMSLOW   Map 07 SJ88

Mottram Hall Wilmslow Rd, Mottram St Andrew SK10
4QT ☎ 01625 828135 Fax 01625 828950
Championship standard course with flat meadowland on the
front nine and undulating woodland on the back with well
guarded greens. The course was designed in 1989 and
opened in May 1991. The course is unusual as each half
opens and closes with Par 5's. The hotel offers many leisure
facilities.
18 holes, 7006yds, Par 72, SSS 74, Course record 65.
Club membership 500.
Visitors   must contact in advance. Cannot play before
                         11am Sat/Sun.
Societies   must contact in advance.
Green Fees £39 (£44 weekends).
Cards   ▤ ▤ VISA ▤ ▤ ▤ ▤
Prof   Tim Rastall
Designer   Dave Thomas
Facilities   ⊗ ▥ ⓑ ⬛ ♀ ⛌ 🏠 ⚐ ⚑ ⚓ ✿ ⚓ ✿ ✿
& Leisure   hard tennis courts, heated indoor swimming
                         pool, squash, sauna, solarium, gymnasium.
Location   On A538 between Wilmslow and Preston

Hotel   ★★★★ 68% Mottram Hall Hotel, Wilmslow
                        Rd, Mottram St Andrew, Prestbury
                        ☎ 01625 828135 132 ⇔ ⚑

Styal Station Rd, Styal SK9 4JN
☎ 01625 531359 Fax 01625 530063
Well designed flat parkland course with testing bunkers and
water hazards. Boasts the longest hole in Cheshire!
18 holes, 6301yds, Par 71, SSS 70.
Club membership 700.   ▶

Visitors	contact to reserve tee time.
Societies	telephone in advance.
Green Fees	£14 weekdays (£18 weekends).
Cards	▬▬ VISA CONNECT 🔷
Prof	Simon Forrest
Designer	Tony Holmes
Facilities	⊗ ⑪ 🍴 ᒫ ♥ 𝟈 ⅄ 🆑 🐪 ♞ 🏌 ⚡ ♪
& Leisure	9 hole par3 under construction.
Location	M56 junct5, 5min drive from Wilmslow

Hotel   ★★★★ 63% Belfry House Hotel, Stanley Rd,
HANDFORTH ☎ 0161 437 0511 80 ⇆ ♜

Wilmslow Great Warford, Mobberley WA16 7AY
☎ 01565 872148 Fax 01565 872172
A fine parkland championship course, of middle length,
fair to all classes of player and almost in perfect
condition.
18 holes, 6607yds, Par 72, SSS 72, Course record 62.
Club membership 800.

Visitors	must contact in advance.
Societies	Tue & Thu only application in writing.
Green Fees	£50 per day; £40 per round (£60/£50 weekends).
Prof	John Nowicki
Facilities	⊗ ⑪ 🍴 ᒫ ♥ 𝟈 ⅄ 🆑 🏌 ♪
Location	2m SW off B5058

Hotel   ★★★ 71% Alderley Edge Hotel,
Macclesfield Rd, ALDERLEY EDGE
☎ 01625 583033 46 ⇆ ♜

WINSFORD   Map 07 SJ66

Knights Grange Grange Ln CW7 2PT ☎ 01606 552780
Attractive, well maintained municipal parkland course with
water hazards. Within a large recreation complex including a
public house and childrens' play area.
9 holes, 2719yds, Par 33, SSS 68.

Visitors	24 hr booking system for weekly play, after 10am Wed for weekend bookings.
Societies	apply in writing.
Green Fees	not confirmed.
Prof	Graham Moore
Facilities	ᒫ ⅄ 🆑 🏌 ♪
& Leisure	hard and grass tennis courts.
Location	N side of town off A54

Hotel   ★★ 65% Wincham Hall, Hall Ln, Wincham,
NORTHWICH ☎ 01606 43453 10rm(9 ⇆ ♜)

Entries with a shaded background
identify courses that are
considered to be particularly interesting

Call the AA Hotel Booking Service on
0870 5050505 to book at AA recognised hotels and B & Bs
in the UK and Ireland, or through our Internet site:
http://www.theaa.co.uk/hotels

CORNWALL & ISLES OF SCILLY

BODMIN   Map 02 SX06

Lanhydrock Lostwithiel Rd, Lanhydrock PL30 5AQ
☎ 01208 73600 Fax 01208 77325
An acclaimed parkland/moorland course adjacent to the
National Trust property Lanhydrock house. Nestling in a
picturesque wooded valley of oak and birch, this undulating
course provides an exciting and enjoyable challenge to all
abilities with discreet use of water and bunkers.
18 holes, 6100yds, Par 70, SSS 70, Course record 66.
Club membership 300.

Visitors	no restrictions.
Societies	please telephone in advance.
Green Fees	£34 per day; £26 per 18 holes.
Cards	▬▬ ▬▬ VISA CONNECT 🔷
Prof	Jason Broadway
Designer	Hamilton Stutt
Facilities	⊗ ⑪ 🍴 ᒫ ♥ 𝟈 ⅄ 🆑 🐪 ♞ 🏌 ⚡ ♪
Location	1m S of Bodmin from B3268

Hotel   ★★★ 65% Restormel Lodge Hotel, Hillside
Gardens, LOSTWITHIEL
☎ 01208 872223 21 ⇆ ♜ Annexe12 ⇆

BUDE   Map 02 SS20

Bude & North Cornwall Burn View EX23 8DA
☎ 01288 352006 Fax 01288 356855
Seaside links course with natural sand bunkers, superb greens
and breathtaking views. Club established in 1893.
18 holes, 6205yds, Par 71, SSS 70.
Club membership 1000.

Visitors	book by telephone 6 days in advance for starting time - or before 6 days with a deposit.
Societies	apply in writing or by telephone/fax.
Green Fees	£20 per round; £8 per additional round (£25/£8 weekends & bank holidays).
Prof	John Yeo
Facilities	⊗ ⑪ 🍴 ᒫ ♥ 𝟈 ⅄ 🆑 ♪
Location	N side of town

Hotel   ★★ 61% Camelot Hotel, Downs View, BUDE
☎ 01288 352361 21 ⇆ ♜

BUDOCK VEAN   Map 02 SW73

Budock Vean Golf & Country House Hotel
Mawnan Smith TR11 5LG
☎ 01326 250288 (Hotel) & 252102 (shop)
Fax 01326 250892
Set in 65 acres of mature grounds with a private foreshore to
the Helford River, this 18 tee undulating parkland course has
a tough par 4 5th hole (456yds) which dog-legs at halfway
around an oak tree. The newly extended 16th hole measures
572 yds, par 5.
9 holes, 5227yds, Par 68, SSS 65, Course record 61.
Club membership 140.

Visitors	must contact in advance.
Societies	apply in writing or telephone in advance.
Green Fees	£18 per day (£20 Sun & bank holidays).
Cards	▬▬ ▬▬ VISA CONNECT 🔷
Prof	Tony Ramsden
Designer	James Braid

Facilities ⊗ ⁾⫼ ᴸᴮ ♨ ♥ ♀ ⚐ 🏠 🕈 ⋈ ⤏ 🏌 ♂
& Leisure   hard tennis courts, heated indoor swimming pool.
Location   1.5m SW

Hotel   ★★★★ 73% Budock Vean Golf & Country House Hotel, MAWNAN SMITH
☎ 01326 250288 & 252100
Fax 01326 250892   58 ⇋ 🐾

CAMBORNE   Map 02 SW64

Tehidy Park TR14 0HH
☎ 01209 842208 Fax 01209 843680
A well-maintained parkland course providing good holiday golf.
18 holes, 6241yds, Par 72, SSS 71, Course record 62.
Club membership 850.
Visitors   must contact in advance and have a handicap certificate.
Societies   telephone followed by letter.
Green Fees £22 per day/round (£27 weekends).
Prof   James Dumbreck
Facilities ⊗ ⁾⫼ ᴸᴮ ♨ ♥ ♀ ⚐ 🏠 🕈 ♂
Location   On Portreath/Pool road, 2m S of Camborne

Hotel   ★★★ 66% Penventon Hotel, REDRUTH
☎ 01209 214141   50 ⇋ 🐾

CAMELFORD   Map 02 SX18

Bowood Park Lanteglos PL32 9RF
☎ 01840 213017 Fax 01840 212622
A testing parkland course situated in Bowood Park, formerly the largest deer park in Cornwall. The first nine holes are designed around rolling hills; the back nine holes are played through the River Allen Valley. Plenty of wildlife, water and trees.
18 holes, 6692yds, Par 72, SSS 72.
Club membership 300.

Visitors   booking system in operation
Societies   contact for details.
Green Fees £35 per day; £25 per round.
Cards ▭▭ ▭▭ ▭▭ 🔲 🖃
Prof   Richard Jenkins
Designer   Sandow
Facilities ⊗ ⁾⫼ ᴸᴮ ♨ ♥ ♀ ⚐ 🏠 🕈 ⋈ ⤏ 🏌 ♂ ⟨
Location   Through Camelford, 0.5m turn right Tintagel/Boscastle B3266, 1st left at garage

Hotel   ★★♣♣ 78% Trebrea Lodge, Trenale, TINTAGEL
☎ 01840 770410 6 ⇋ 🐾 Annexe1 ⇋ 🐾

CARLYON BAY   Map 02 SX05

Carlyon Bay Hotel Sea Rd PL25 3RD
☎ 01726 814250
Championship-length, cliff-top course moving into parkland. Magnificent views surpassed only by the quality of the course. The 230-yard (par 3) 18th with railway and road out-of-bounds, holds the player's interest to the end.
18 holes, 6549yds, Par 72, SSS 71, Course record 66.
Club membership 500.
Visitors   must contact in advance.
Societies   must contact in advance.
Green Fees £35 high season; £28 mid season; £24 low season.
Cards ▭▭ ▭▭ ▭▭ 🔲 🖃
Prof   Mark Rowe
Facilities ⊗ ⁾⫼ ᴸᴮ ♨ ♥ ♀ ⚐ 🏠 🕈 ⋈ ⤏ 🏌 ♂
& Leisure   hard tennis courts, outdoor and indoor heated swimming pools, sauna, solarium, 9 hole approach course.

Hotel   ★★★★ 73% Carlyon Bay Hotel, Sea Rd, Carlyon Bay, ST AUSTELL
☎ 01726 812304   73 ⇋ 🐾
See Advertisement on page 54.

CONSTANTINE BAY   Map 02 SW87

Trevose PL28 8JB
☎ 01841 520208 Fax 01841 521057
Well known links course with early holes close to the sea on excellent springy turf. A championship course affording varying degrees of difficulty appealing to both the professional and higher handicap player. It is a good test with well-positioned bunkers, and a meandering stream, and the wind playing a decisive role in preventing low scoring. Self-catering accommodation is available at the club.
Championship Course: 18 holes, 6461yds, Par 71, SSS 71, Course record 66.
Club membership 1500.
Visitors   subject to reservations, handicap certificate required for championship course. Advisable to contact in advance.
Societies   telephone or write to the secretary.
Green Fees £22-£35 per day.
Cards ▭▭ ▭▭ ▭▭ 🔲 🖃
Prof   Gary Alliss
Designer   H S Colt
Facilities ⊗ ⁾⫼ by prior arrangement ᴸᴮ ♥ ♀ ⚐ 🏠 🕈 ⋈ ⤏ 🏌 ♂
& Leisure   hard tennis courts, heated outdoor swimming pool, 2 x 9 hole courses, snooker & games room.
Location   N of Constantine Bay, off B3276

Hotel   ★★★ 77% Treglos Hotel, CONSTANTINE BAY ☎ 01841 520727   44 ⇋ 🐾

FALMOUTH   Map 02 SW83

Falmouth Swanpool Rd TR11 5BQ
☎ 01326 311262 & 01326 314296 Fax 01326 317783
Seaside/parkland course with outstanding coastal views. Sufficiently bunkered to punish any inaccurate shots. Five acres of practice grounds.   ▶

18 holes, 5937yds, Par 71, SSS 70.
Club membership 500.

Visitors	please book for tee time.
Societies	must contact in advance.
Green Fees	£26 per 36 holes; £20 per 18 holes.
Cards	
Prof	Bryan Patterson
Facilities	⊗ ∭ ⓑ 🍷 ♀ ⚒ 🛍 🛈 🐂 🏌 ✧ ⅋
Location	SW side of town centre

Hotel	★★★★ 71% Royal Duchy Hotel, Cliff Rd, FALMOUTH ☎ 01326 313042 43 ⇆ ⋔

Falmouth

HOLYWELL BAY — Map 02 SW75

Holywell Bay TR8 5PW
☎ 01637 830095 Fax 01637 831000
Holywell Golf Club is situated beside a family fun park with many amenities. The course is an 18 hole Par 3 with excellent sea views. Fresh Atlantic winds make the course hard to play and there are several tricky holes, particularly the 18th over the trout pond. The site also has and excellent 18 hole Pitch & Putt course for the whole family.
18 holes, 2784yds, Par 61, Course record 58.
Club membership 100.

Visitors	no restrictions.
Societies	telephone in advance.
Green Fees	£7.50 per round.
Designer	Hartley
Facilities	⊗ ∭ ⓑ 🍷 ♀ 🛈 🏌 ✧
& Leisure	hard tennis courts, heated outdoor swimming pool, fishing.
Location	Off A3075 Newquay/Perranporth road

Hotel	★★ 67% Crantock Bay Hotel, West Pentire, CRANTOCK ☎ 01637 830229 34 ⇆ ⋔

LAUNCESTON — Map 02 SX38

Launceston St Stephens PL15 8HF
☎ 01566 773442 Fax 01566 777506
Undulating parkland course with views over Tamar Valley to Dartmoor and Bodmin Moor. Dominated by the 'The Hill' up which the 8th and 11th fairways rise, and on which the 8th, 9th, 11th and 12th greens sit.
18 holes, 6407yds, Par 70, SSS 71, Course record 65.
Club membership 800.

Visitors	must contact in advance, may not play weekends Apr-Oct.
Societies	telephone in first instance.
Green Fees	not confirmed.
Prof	John Tozer
Facilities	⊗ ∭ ⓑ 🍷 ♀ ⚒ 🛍 🏌 ✧
Location	NW side of town centre on B3254

Hotel	★★ 61% Eagle House, Castle St, LAUNCESTON ☎ 01566 772036 14 ⇆ ⋔

Trethorne Kennards House PL15 8QE
☎ 01566 86324 Fax 01566 86903
Rolling parkland course with well maintained fairways and computer irrigated greens. Plenty of trees and natural water hazards make this well respected course a good challenge.
18 holes, 6432yds, Par 71, SSS 71.
Club membership 630.

Visitors	must contact in advance.
Societies	write or telephone Colin Willis.
Green Fees	£25 per day; £19 per round.
Cards	
Prof	Mark Boundy
Designer	Frank Frayne
Facilities	⊗ ∭ ⓑ 🍷 ♀ ⚒ 🛍 🏌 🛈 🐂 🏌 ✧ ⅋
Location	Just off the A30, 3m W of Launceston, on junct with the A395 (Camelford)

Hotel	★★ 77% Penhallow Manor Country House Hotel, ALTARNUN ☎ 01566 86206 7 ⇆ ⋔

LELANT — Map 02 SW53

West Cornwall TR26 3DZ
☎ 01736 753401 & 753177 Fax 01736 753401
A seaside links with sandhills and lovely turf adjacent to the Hayle estuary and St Ives Bay. A real test of the player's skill, especially 'Calamity Corner' starting at the 5th on the lower land by the River Hayle. A small (3 hole) course is available for practice.
18 holes, 5884yds, Par 69, SSS 69, Course record 63.
Club membership 748.

Visitors	must prove handicap certificate, be a member of a club affiliated to the EGU, advisable to contact in advance.
Societies	must apply in writing.
Green Fees	£30 per day (£35 weekends & bank holidays); 5 Day ticket £85, 7 Day ticket £105.
Prof	Paul Atherton
Designer	Reverend Tyack
Facilities	⊗ ∭ ⓑ 🍷 ♀ ⚒ 🛍 🏌 ✧
Location	N side of village off A3074

Hotel	★★ 68% Pedn-Olva Hotel, The Warren, ST IVES ☎ 01736 796222 28 ⇆ ⋔ Annexe7rm(4 ⇆ ⋔)

LOOE   Map 02 SX25

Looe Widegates PL13 1PX
☎ 01503 240239 Fax 01503 240864
Designed by Harry Vardon in 1935, this downland/parkland course commands panoramic views over south-east Cornwall and the coast. Easy walking.
18 holes, 5940yds, Par 70, SSS 68, Course record 64.
Club membership 600.

Visitors	handicap certificate preferred, booking in advance recommended, no limitations subject to availability.
Societies	telephone in advance, booking to be confirmed in writing.
Green Fees	£30 per 36/27 holes; £22 per 18 holes; £13 per 9 holes (£35/£27/£16 weekends).
Cards	
Prof	Alistair Macdonald
Designer	Harry Vardon
Facilities	
& Leisure	practice nets.
Location	3.5m NE off B3253

Hotel	★★★ 65% Hannafore Point Hotel, Marine Dr, West Looe, LOOE ☎ 01503 263273 37

LOSTWITHIEL   Map 02 SX15

Lostwithiel Hotel, Golf & Country Club Lower Polscoe PL22 0HQ ☎ 01208 873550 Fax 01208 87479
An undulating, parkland course with water hazards. Overlooked by Restormel Castle and the River Fowey flows alongside the course. Driving range.
18 holes, 5984yds, Par 72, SSS 71, Course record 67.
Club membership 500.

Visitors	must contact in advance.
Societies	contact in advance.
Green Fees	£19 (£23 weekends). Thu £10.
Cards	
Prof	Tony Nash
Designer	S Wood
Facilities	
& Leisure	hard tennis courts, heated indoor swimming pool, fishing, gymnasium.
Location	1m outside Lostwithiel off A390

Hotel	★★★ 66% Lostwithiel Hotel Golf & Country Club, Lower Polscoe, LOSTWITHIEL ☎ 01208 873550 18

MAWGAN PORTH   Map 02 SW86

Merlin TR8 4DN ☎ 01841 540222 Fax 01841 541031
A heathland course. The most challenging hole is the Par 5 12th with out of bounds along the lefthand side. ▶

18 holes, 5227yds, Par 67, SSS 67.
Club membership 350.

Visitors   no restrictions, except during club competitions.
Societies   telephone in advance.
Green Fees £12 per day.
Designer   Ross Oliver
Facilities   ⊗ ⅷ ଐ 🍴 ♀ ♨ 🏠 ⛳ 🏌 ♣ ⛴ ✎ ℓ
Location   On the coast rd Newquay/Padstow. After
       Mawgan Porth follow signs for St Eval, golf
       course on right

Hotel   ★★ 67% Tredragon Hotel, MAWGAN
       PORTH ☎ 01637 860213   26 ⇔ 🐾

MAWNAN SMITH   Map 02 SW72

See **Budock Vean**

MULLION   Map 02 SW61

Mullion Cury TR12 7BP ☎ 01326 240685
Founded in 1895, a clifftop and links course with
panoramic views over Mounts Bay. A steep downhill
slope on 6th and the 10th descends to the beach with a
deep ravine alongside the green. Most southerly course
in the British Isles.
18 holes, 6037yds, Par 70, SSS 70.
Club membership 654.

Visitors   preferable to contact in advance, restricted
       during club competitions.
Societies   must contact in advance.
Green Fees £20 per day/round (£25 weekends).
Prof   Phil Blundell
Designer   W Sich
Facilities   ⊗ ⅷ ଐ 🍴 ♀ ♨ 🏠 ⛳ 🏌 ♣ ⛴ ✎
& Leisure   golf academy.
Location   1.5m NW of Mullion, off A3083

Hotel   ★★★ 74% Polurrian Hotel, MULLION
       ☎ 01326 240421   39 ⇔ 🐾

NEWQUAY   Map 02 SW86

Newquay Tower Rd TR7 1LT
☎ 01637 874354 & 872091 Fax 01637 874066
Gently undulating seaside course running parallel to the
beach and open to wind. Breathtaking views.
18 holes, 6140yds, Par 69, SSS 69, Course record 63.
Club membership 700.

Visitors   please telephone in advance.
Societies   apply in writing or telephone.
Green Fees not confirmed.
Cards   ⚊ 💳 💳
Prof   Andrew J Cullen
Designer   H Colt
Facilities   ⊗ ⅷ ଐ 🍴 ♀ ♨ 🏠 ⛳ ✎
& Leisure   hard tennis courts.
Location   W side of town

Hotel   ★★★ 69% Hotel Bristol, Narrowcliff,
       NEWQUAY ☎ 01637 875181   74 ⇔ 🐾

Treloy TR8 4JN ☎ 01637 878554 Fax 01637 871710
An Executive course constructed in 1991 to American
specifications with large contoured and mounded greens.
Offers an interesting round for all categories of player.
9 holes, 2143yds, Par 32, SSS 31, Course record 63.

Visitors   no restrictions.
Societies   telephone in advance.
Green Fees not confirmed.
Cards   ⚊ 💳
Designer   M R M Sandow
Facilities   ଐ 🍴 ♀ ♨ 🏠 ⛳ ♣ ⛴ ✎
Location   On A3059 Newquay to St Columb Major Road

Hotel   ★★ 71% Whipsiderry Hotel, Trevelgue Rd,
       Porth, NEWQUAY
       ☎ 01637 874777 24rm(5 ⇔ 14 🐾)

PADSTOW   Map 02 SW97

See **Constantine Bay**

PERRANPORTH   Map 02 SW75

Perranporth Budnick Hill TR6 0AB
☎ 01872 573701 Fax 01872 573701
There are three testing par 5 holes on the links course (2nd,
5th, 11th) and a fine view over Perranporth Beach from all
holes.
18 holes, 6288yds, Par 72, SSS 72, Course record 62.
Club membership 832.

Visitors   no reserved tee times.
Societies   by prior arrangement.
Green Fees £25 per day (£30 weekends & bank holidays).
Cards   ⚊ 💳
Prof   D Michell
Designer   James Braid
Facilities   ⊗ ⅷ ଐ 🍴 ♀ ♨ 🏠 ⛳ 🏌 ⛴ ✎
& Leisure   snooker & pool.
Location   0.75m NE on B3285

Hotel   ★★ 63% Beach Dunes Hotel, Ramoth Way,
       Reen Sands, PERRANPORTH
       ☎ 01872 572263 6rm(5 ⇔ 🐾) Annexe3 ⇔ 🐾

PRAA SANDS   Map 02 SW52

Praa Sands Germoe Cross Roads TR20 9TQ
☎ 01736 763445 Fax 01736 763399
A beautiful parkland course, overlooking Mount's Bay with
outstanding sea views from every tee and green.

9 holes, 4122yds, Par 62, SSS 60, Course record 59.
Club membership 220.

Visitors	restricted Sun 8-12.30pm, no need to phone.
Societies	telephone in advance for details.
Green Fees	£20 per day; £14.50 per 18 holes; £10 per 9 holes.
Designer	R Hamilton
Facilities	⊗ ⑂ ⟐ 🖥 ♀ ♨ 🏠 ⛿ ♂
& Leisure	pool, darts.
Location	A394 midway between Penzance/Helston
Hotel	★★ 78% Nansloe Manor Hotel, Meneage Rd, HELSTON ☎ 01326 574691 7rm(6 ⇆ ℝ)

ROCK   Map 02 SW97

St Enodoc PL27 6LD
☎ 01208 863216 Fax 01208 862976
Classic links course with huge sand hills and rolling fairways. James Braid laid out the original 18 holes in 1907 and changes were made in 1922 and 1935. English County Final and English Ladies Closed Amateur Championships held recently. On the Church, the 10th is the toughest par 4 on the course and on the 6th is a truly enormous sand hill known as the Himalayas. The Holywell is not as exacting as the Church, it is less demanding on stamina but still a real test of skill for golfers of any handicap.
Church Course: 18 holes, 6243yds, Par 69, SSS 70, Course record 64.
Holywell Course: 18 holes, 4103yds, Par 63, SSS 61.
Club membership 1500.

Visitors	may not play on bank holidays. Must have a handicap certificate of 24 or below for Church Course. Must contact in advance.
Societies	must contact in writing.
Green Fees	Church: £50 per day; £35 per round (£55/£40 weekends). Holywell: £21 per day; £15 per round.
Prof	Nick Williams
Designer	James Braid
Facilities	⊗ ⑂ ⟐ 🖥 ♀ ♨ 🏠 ⛿ ♘ 🛒 ♂ ♙
Location	W side of village
Hotel	★★ 74% Cornish Cottage Hotel & Restaurant, New Polzeath, POLZEATH ☎ 01208 862213 13 ⇆ ℝ

ST AUSTELL   Map 02 SX05

Porthpean Portpean PL26 6AY ☎ 01726 64613
A picturesque 18 hole course, the outward holes are in a pleasant parkland setting whilst the return holes command spectacular views over St Austell Bay.
18 holes, 5209yds, Par 67, SSS 67.
Club membership 300.

Visitors	no restrictions
Societies	telephone in advance.
Green Fees	All week £12 per round/day, £7 per 9 holes.
Facilities	⊗ 🖥 ♀ ♨ 🏠 ⛿ ♂ ♙
Location	1.5m from St Austell by-pass
Hotel	★★ 66% The Pier House, Harbour Front, Charlestown, ST AUSTELL ☎ 01726 67955 26 ⇆ ℝ

St Austell Tregongeeves Ln PL26 7DS
☎ 01726 72649 Fax 01726 74756
Very interesting inland parkland course designed by James Braid and offering glorious views of the surrounding countryside. Undulating, well-covered with tree plantations and well-bunkered. Notable holes are 8th (par 4) and 16th (par 3).
18 holes, 6089yds, Par 69, SSS 69, Course record 67.
Club membership 700.

Visitors	advisable to contact in advance, weekend play is limited. Must be a member of a recognised golf club and hold a handicap certificate.
Societies	must apply in writing.
Green Fees	£20 per round.
Prof	Tony Pitts
Facilities	⊗ 🖥 ♀ ♨ 🏠 ⛿ ♂ ♙
Location	1m W of St Austell on A390
Hotel	★★★ 65% Porth Avallen Hotel, Sea Rd, Carlyon Bay, ST AUSTELL ☎ 01726 812802 24 ⇆ ℝ
Additional hotel	★★★ 63% Cliff Head Hotel, Sea Rd, Carlyon Bay, ST AUSTELL ☎ 01726 812345 Fax 01726 815511 54 ⇆ ℝ

ST IVES   Map 02 SW54

Tregenna Castle Hotel, Golf & Country Club TR26 2DE
☎ 01736 797381 Fax 01736 796066
Parkland course surrounding a castellated hotel and overlooking St Ives Bay and harbour.
18 holes, 3260yds, Par 60, SSS 58.
Club membership 140.

▶

ST MELLION

ST MELLION *Cornwall* ☎ 01579 351351
Fax 01579 350537   **Map 02 SX36**

John Ingham writes: Five miles north west of Saltash, St Mellion is set in Sherlock Holmes country, not far from the famous moor. Opened in 1976, the big course was created by two farming brothers, Martin and Hermon Bond who decided the Tamar Valley, not far from Plymouth, deserved a golf course – and they were prepared to sacrifice their farm to achieve that end.

The first problem was to get hold of an architect who would not be overwhelmed by the problem of converting the rugged countryside into eighteen holes. They had set their hearts on a Jack Nicklaus layout and to ensure he would take on the task, they sent him a letter and a cheque, said to be for £1 million and their determination concentrated the mind of Nicklaus comprehensively!

I have known Tony Moore, the one-time tournament professional (now living locally), for thirty odd years and he suggested I play the course, with his long-hitting son Bobby. But first we were to enjoy a dinner at the heart of this St Mellion International Golf & Country Club, which they thought, would be the ideal preparation for the task of facing a course with four holes in excess of 500 yards!

Tony's son Bobby was one of those strapping lads who lashed the ball miles. But in the first few holes he was missing the fairway, and lost four balls fairly quickly, putting me in what I thought was an unbeatable position. But his erratic play did not last, neither did my lead despite a birdie two at the short 11th, a delightful hole across water from a tee almost overlooked by the ancient church in the background. The two courses (the Old Course was designed by H. J Stutt) are both rugged tests, and St Mellion has staged several top-flight tournaments.

When Jack Nicklaus played here he said: 'I knew it was going to be good, but not this good – it's everything I had hoped for and more ... St Mellion is potentially the finest course in Europe'. This may be true. But it is a tough one, and for some it's too severe a challenge.

Visitors	telephone in advance 01579 352002 or 352007 for golf infoline & course condition report.
Societies	please apply in writing or telephone.
Green fees	Nicklaus Course £42.50 per round. Old Course £30 per round. ⊟ ▆ ▆ ▆ ◑ ▨
Facilities	⊗ ⍜ ▥ ⬚ ▆ ♀ ⊨ ⚲ ⬚ ⋔ ❧ 🥄 🚕 ⚸ ↿
	Professionals Andrew Milton/David Moon
Leisure	hard tennis courts, indoor swimming (heated), squash, health spa
Location	Saltash PL12 6SD (0.5m NW off A388)

36 holes. Nicklaus Course: 18 holes, 6651yds, Par72 SSS 72 Course record 63
The Old Course: 18 holes, 5742yds, Par 68 SSS 68

WHERE TO STAY AND EAT NEARBY

HOTELS:
ST MELLION
★★★ ❀ 72% St Mellion International, ☎ 01579 351351. Annexe 38 ⊟ ☞

LISKEARD
★★ ❀ ❀ ❀ ♨ Well House, St Keyne ☎ 01579 342001. 9 ⊟ ☞

★★ 63% Lord Eliot, Castle St. ☎ 01579 342717. 15 ⊟ ☞

RESTAURANTS:
CALSTOCK
❀ ❀ Danescombe Valley, Lower Kelly ☎ 01822 832414

Visitors   no booking needed. Dress code in operation.
Societies   telephone for details.
Green Fees not confirmed.
Cards   ▭ 🗝 🗝 🗝 🗝
Designer   Abercrombie
Facilities   ⊗ ⊪ ⅃ 🖐 ♥ ⌇ 🖐 ⊶ 🖐 ♂
& Leisure   hard tennis courts, outdoor and indoor heated
swimming pools, squash, sauna, solarium,
gymnasium, snooker, steam room, jaccuzzi,
beauty treatment.
Location   From A30 Penzance road turn off just past
Hayle onto A3074

Hotel   ★★★ 71% Carbis Bay Hotel, Carbis Bay, ST
IVES ☎ 01736 795311   30 🛏 🐾

ST JUST (NEAR LAND'S END)   Map 02 SW33

Cape Cornwall Golf & Country Club Cape Cornwall
TR19 7NL ☎ 01736 788611 Fax 01736 788611
Coastal parkland, walled course. The walls are an integral
part of its design. Country club facilities.
18 holes, 5650yds, Par 70, SSS 68, Course record 69.
Club membership 630.
Visitors   may not play before 11.30am at weekends.
Societies   must contact in advance.
Green Fees £20 (£10 twilight, 6-9pm).
Cards   ▭ 🗝 🗝 🗝
Prof   Paul Atherton
Designer   Bob Hamilton
Facilities   ⊗ ⅃ ♥ ⌇ 🖐 🖐 ⊶ 🖐 ♂
& Leisure   heated indoor swimming pool, sauna, solarium,
gymnasium.
Location   1m W of St Just

Hotel   ★★★▲▲ 65% Higher Faugan Hotel, Newlyn,
PENZANCE ☎ 01736 362076   11 🛏 🐾

ST MELLION   Map 02 SX36

ST MELLION   See page 55

ST MINVER   Map 02 SW97

Roserrow Golf & Country Club Roserrow PL27 6QT
☎ 01208 863000 Fax 01208 863002
Challenging par72 course in an undulating wooded valley.
Stunning views over the Cornish countryside and out to
Hayle Bay. Accommodation and numerous facilities on site.
18 holes, 6551yds, Par 72, SSS 72.
Club membership 400.

Visitors   by arrangement weekdays or weekends, must
pre book tee times.
Societies   apply in writing or telephone in advance.
Green Fees Apr-Oct: £30 per day, £24 per round; Nov-Mar:
£16 per day/round.
Cards   ▭ 🗝 🗝 🗝 🗝
Prof   Andrew Cullen
Facilities   ⊗ ⊪ ⅃ ♥ ⌇ 🖐 🖐 ⊶ 🖐 🖐 ♂ (
& Leisure   hard tennis courts, heated indoor swimming
pool, sauna, gymnasium.
Location   Between Wadebridge and Polzeath off the
B3314

Hotel   ★★ 64% The Molesworth Arms Hotel,
Molesworth St, WADEBRIDGE
☎ 01208 812055 16rm(14 🛏 🐾)

SALTASH   Map 02 SX45

China Fleet Country Club PL12 6LJ
☎ 01752 848668 Fax 01752 848456
A parkland course with river views. The 14th tee shot has to
carry a lake of approximately 150yards.
18 holes, 6551yds, Par 72, SSS 72, Course record 69.
Club membership 550.
Visitors   may play anytime and can book up to 7 days in
advance.
Societies   telephone for provisional booking.
Green Fees not confirmed.
Cards   ▭ 🗝 🗝
Prof   Robert Moore
Designer   Hawtree
Facilities   ⊗ ⊪ ⅃ ♥ ⌇ 🖐 🖐 ⊶ 🖐 🖐 ♂ (
& Leisure   hard tennis courts, heated indoor swimming
pool, squash, sauna, solarium, gymnasium.
Location   1m from the Tamar Bridge

Hotel   B Travelodge, Callington Rd, Carkeel,
SALTASH ☎ Central Res 0800 850950
Fax 01752 849028   32 🛏 🐾

TORPOINT   Map 02 SX45

Whitsand Bay Hotel Golf & Country Club Portwrinkle
PL11 3BU ☎ 01503 230276 Fax 01503 230329
Testing seaside course laid-out on cliffs overlooking
Whitsand Bay. Easy walking after 1st hole. The par 3 (3rd)
hole is acknowledged as one of the most attractive holes in
Cornwall.
18 holes, 5998yds, Par 69, SSS 68, Course record 62.
Club membership 400.

Visitors	visitors welcome.
Societies	must contact in advance.
Green Fees	not confirmed.
Cards	[icons]
Prof	Stephen Poole
Designer	Fernie
Facilities	⊗ ⫽⫽ ㄴ ㅌ ▮ ㅇ △ 🐱 ⫯ 🐟 ⅄ 🚃 ♂
& Leisure	heated indoor swimming pool, sauna, solarium, gymnasium.
Location	5m W off B3247

Hotel	★★ 66% Whitsand Bay Hotel, Golf & Country Club, Portwrinkle, TORPOINT ☎ 01503 230276 51rm(36 ⇔ 🕪)

TRURO — Map 02 SW84

Killiow Park Killiow, Kea TR3 6AG
☎ 01872 270246 Fax 01872 240915
Picturesque parkland course with mature oaks and woodland and five holes played across or around water hazards. Floodlit, all-weather driving range and practice facilities.
18 holes, 3829yds, Par 61.
Club membership 500.

Visitors	may not play until after 9.30am at weekends.
Societies	apply in writing, limited catering facilities at present.
Green Fees	not confirmed.
Designer	Ross Oliver
Facilities	ㄴ ㅇ △ 🐱 ⫯ ♂ (
Location	3m SW of Truro, off A39

Hotel	★★★ 72% Alverton Manor, Tregolls Road, TRURO ☎ 01872 276633 34 ⇔ 🕪

Truro Treliske TR1 3LG
☎ 01872 278684 (manager) & 272640 (club)
Fax 01872 278684
Picturesque and gently undulating parkland course with small greens requiring accurate play. Lovely views over the cathedral city of Truro and the surrounding countryside.
18 holes, 5306yds, Par 66, SSS 66, Course record 60.
Club membership 900.

Visitors	must have handicap certificate, advisable to ring for availability although casual fees welcome.
Societies	telephone for details.
Green Fees	£20 per day (£25 weekends & bank holidays).
Prof	Nigel Bicknell
Designer	Colt, Alison & Morrison
Facilities	⊗ ⫽⫽ ㄴ ㅌ ▮ ㅇ △ 🐱 🐟 🚃 ♂
Location	1.5m W on A390 towards Redruth, adjacent to Treliske Hospital

Hotel	★★★ 72% Alverton Manor, Tregolls Rd, TRURO ☎ 01872 276633 34 ⇔ 🕪

WADEBRIDGE — Map 02 SW97

St Kew St Kew Highway PL30 3EF
☎ 01208 841500 Fax 01208 841500
An interesting, well-laid out 9-hole parkland course with 6 holes with water and 15 bunkers. In a picturesque setting there are 10 par 4s and 8 par 3s. No handicap certificate required but some experience of the game is essential. 9 extra tees have now been provided allowing a different teeing area for the back nine.
18 holes, 4543yds, Par 64, SSS 62, Course record 63.
Club membership 240.

Visitors	no restrictions. Start time system in operation allowing prebooking.
Societies	apply in writing, telephone or fax (same as phone number).
Green Fees	£13 per 18 holes; £8.50 per 9 holes.
Cards	[icons]
Prof	Nick Rogers
Designer	David Derry
Facilities	⊗ ㄴ ▮ ㅇ △ 🐱 ⫯ 🐟 🚃 ♂ (
& Leisure	fishing.
Location	2m N, main A39

Hotel	★★ 64% The Molesworth Arms Hotel, Molesworth St, WADEBRIDGE ☎ 01208 812055 16rm(14 ⇔ 🕪)

CUMBRIA

ALSTON — Map 12 NY74

Alston Moor The Hermitage, Middleton in Teesdale Rd CA9 3DB ☎ 01434 381675
Parkland and Fell, in process of upgrading to full 18 holes, stunning views of the North Pennines.
10 holes, 5518yds, Par 68, SSS 66, Course record 67.
Club membership 170.

Visitors	usually turn up and play but for weekends telephone secretary for information and availability.
Societies	telephone or write in advance.
Green Fees	£9 per day; £5 after 5pm (£11 weekends & bank holidays).
Facilities	ㄴ ▮ ㅇ △
Location	1 S of Alston on B6277

Hotel	★★ 68% Lowbyer Manor Country House Hotel, ALSTON ☎ 01434 381230 8 ⇔ 🕪 Annexe4 ⇔

APPLEBY-IN-WESTMORLAND — Map 12 NY62

Appleby Brackenber Moor CA16 6LP
☎ 017683 51432
This remotely situated heather and moorland course offers interesting golf with the rewarding bonus of several long par-4 holes that will be remembered. There are superb views of the Pennines and the Lakeland hills.
18 holes, 5901yds, Par 68, SSS 68, Course record 63.
Club membership 800.

Visitors	phone for details.
Societies	must contact in advance by letter.
Green Fees	not confirmed.
Prof	Paul Jenkinson
Designer	Willie Fernie
Facilities	⊗ ⫽⫽ ㄴ ㅌ ▮ ㅇ △ 🐱 ⫯ 🐟 ♂
& Leisure	snooker.
Location	2m E of Appleby 0.5m off A66

Hotel	★★★🏖 76% Appleby Manor Country House Hotel, Roman Rd, APPLEBY-IN-WESTMORLAND ☎ 017683 51571 23 ⇔ 🕪 Annexe7 ⇔ 🕪 *See advertisement on page 58*

ASKAM-IN-FURNESS   Map 07 SD27

Dunnerholme Duddon Rd LA16 7AW
☎ 01229 462675 & 465095 Fax 01229 462675
Unique 10-hole (18 tee) links course with view of the Cumbrian mountains and a stream running through.
10 holes, 6154yds, Par 72, SSS 70.
Club membership 400.
Visitors   restricted times on Sun.
Societies   apply in writing to the secretary.
Green Fees £10 per round (£12 weekends & bank holidays).
Facilities   ♨ ♀ ♨
Location   1m N on A595

Hotel   ★★ 64% Lisdoonie Hotel, 307/309 Abbey Rd, BARROW-IN-FURNESS
☎ 01229 827312   12 ⊨ ♠

BARROW-IN-FURNESS   Map 07 SD26

Barrow Rakesmoor Ln, Hawcoat LA14 4QB
☎ 01229 825444 & 832121 (Prof) Fax 01229 832121
Pleasant course laid out two levels on meadowland with extensive views of the nearby Lakeland fells. Upper level is affected by easterly winds.
18 holes, 6184yds, Par 71, SSS 70, Course record 66.
Club membership 700.
Visitors   must be a member of a recognised golf club or hold a handicap certificate, advisable to contact the professional regarding tee time.
Societies   small groups ring professional for details, groups over 12 apply to the secretary in advance.

Green Fees £20 per day.
Prof   Jim McLeod
Facilities   ⊗ ♨ by prior arrangement ♨ ♨ ♀ ♨ ♨ ♠ ♂
Location   2m from Barrow off A590

Hotel   ★★ 64% Lisdoonie Hotel, 307/309 Abbey Rd, BARROW-IN-FURNESS
☎ 01229 827312   12 ⊨ ♠

Furness Central Dr LA14 3LN ☎ 01229 471232
Links golf with a fairly flat first half but a much sterner second nine played across subtle sloping ground. There are good views of the Lakes, North Wales and the Isle of Man.
18 holes, 6363yds, Par 71, SSS 71, Course record 65.
Club membership 630.
Visitors   must contact the secretary in advance.
Societies   apply in writing, must be member of recognised club with handicap certificate.
Green Fees £17 per day.
Facilities   ⊗ ♨ ♨ ♀ ♨ ♨ ♂
& Leisure snooker table.
Location   1.75 W of town centre off A590 to Walney Island

Hotel   ★★ 64% Lisdoonie Hotel, 307/309 Abbey Rd, BARROW-IN-FURNESS
☎ 01229 827312   12 ⊨ ♠

BOWNESS-ON-WINDERMERE   Map 07 SD49

Windermere Clearbarrow LA23 3NB
☎ 015394 43123 Fax 015394 43123
Enjoyable holiday golf on a short, slightly hilly but sporting course in this delightful area of the Lake District National Park, with superb views of the mountains as the backcloth to the lake and the course.
18 holes, 5122yds, Par 67, SSS 65, Course record 58.
Club membership 1043.
Visitors   contact pro shop 7 days before day of play, 10-12 & 2-4.30 or before 9am by arrangement.
Societies   by arrangement contact the secretary.
Green Fees £24 per day (£28 weekends & bank holidays).
Prof   W S M Rooke
Designer   G Lowe
Facilities   ⊗ ♨ ♨ ♀ ♨ ♨ ♨ ♠ ♂
& Leisure snooker.
Location   B5284 1.5m from Bowness

Hotel   ★★★ 68% Wild Boar Hotel, Crook, WINDERMERE
☎ 015394 45225 36 ⊨ ♠
See advertisement on page 62.

BRAMPTON   Map 12 NY56

Brampton Talkin Tarn CA8 1HN
☎ 016977 2255 & 2000 Fax 016877 41487
Challenging golf across glorious rolling fell country demanding solid driving and many long second shots. A number of particularly fine holes, the pick of which may arguably be, the 3rd and 11th. The course offers unrivalled panoramic views from its hilly position.
18 holes, 6407yds, Par 72, SSS 71, Course record 64.
Club membership 800.

Visitors	visitors intending to play at weekends are recommended to telephone in advance.
Societies	apply in writing to M Ogilvie (Hon Commercial Sec), 3 Warwick St, Carlisle, Cumbria CA3 8QW or telephone 01228 401996.
Green Fees	£22 per day/round (£28 weekends & bank holidays).
Prof	Stewart Wilkinson
Designer	James Braid
Facilities & Leisure	⊗ ⦀ ⮂ 🍴 ♟ 🏆 ⌂ ☂ ♂ games room.
Location	1.5m SE of Brampton on B6413
Hotel	★★ 65% The Tarn End House Hotel, Talkin Tarn, BRAMPTON ☎ 016977 2340 7 ⇄ 🐾

CARLISLE   Map 11 NY35

Carlisle Aglionby CA4 8AG
☎ 01228 513029 Fax 01228 513303
Majestic looking parkland course with great appeal. A complete but not too severe test of golf, with fine turf, natural hazards, a stream and many beautiful trees. A qualifying course for the Open Championship.
18 holes, 6278yds, Par 71, SSS 70, Course record 63.
Club membership 800.

Visitors	may not play before 9am and between 12-1.30 and when tee is reserved. Very limited play Sunday and with member only Saturday and Tuesday.
Societies	Mon, Wed & Fri, contact in advance for details.
Green Fees	£40 per day; £25 per round (Sun £60/£40).
Prof	Martin Heggie
Designer	Mackenzie Ross
Facilities	⊗ ⦀ ⮂ 🍴 ♟ 🏆 ⌂ 🛒 ♂
Location	On A69 0.5m E of M6 junc 43

Hotel	★★★ 70% Crown Hotel, Wetheral, CARLISLE ☎ 01228 561888 49 ⇄ 🐾 Annexe2 ⇄ 🐾

Stony Holme Municipal St Aidans Rd CA1 1LS
☎ 01228 625511
Municipal parkland course, bounded on three sides by the River Eden.
18 holes, 5783yds, Par 69, SSS 68, Course record 68.
Club membership 350.

Visitors	advance booking recommended at weekends.
Societies	must telephone pro shop 01228 34856 in advance.
Green Fees	not confirmed.
Prof	S Ling
Facilities	⊗ ⦀ ⮂ 🍴 ♟ 🏆 ⌂ 🛒 ♂
Location	2m W of M6 (junct 43) and A69
Hotel	B Posthouse Carlisle, Parkhouse Rd, CARLISLE ☎ 01228 531201 127 ⇄ 🐾

COCKERMOUTH   Map 11 NY13

Cockermouth ▶

Cockermouth Embleton CA13 9SG
☎ 017687 76223 & 76941 Fax 017687 76941
Fell-land course, fenced, with exceptional views and a hard
climb on the 3rd and 11th holes. Testing holes: 10th and 16th
(rearranged by James Braid).
18 holes, 5496yds, Par 69, SSS 67, Course record 62.
Club membership 600.
Visitors restricted Wed, Sat & Sun.
Societies apply in writing to the secretary.
Green Fees not confirmed.
Designer J Braid
Facilities 🏌 💪 🍴 ⚑ ⛳
Location 3m E off A66

Hotel ★★★ 71% The Trout Hotel, Crown St,
COCKERMOUTH ☎ 01900 823591 30 ➪ 🐾

CROSBY-ON-EDEN   Map 12 NY45

Eden CA6 4RA
☎ 01228 573003 & 573013 Fax 01228 818435
Open, championship-length parkland course following the
River Eden. A large number of water hazards, including the
river on certain holes, demands acuracy, as do the well
designed raised greens. Flood-lit driving range and excellent
clubhouse facilities.
18 holes, 6368yds, Par 72, SSS 72, Course record 64.
Club membership 500.

Visitors must contact in advance.
Societies telephone to check availability.
Green Fees £20 (£25 weekends & bank holidays).
Cards ▬ 💳 💳 💳
Prof Steve Harrison
Facilities ⊗ ⅲ 🏌 💪 🍴 ⛳ ⚑ 🍴 ⚑ ⛳ 🍴
& Leisure hard tennis courts.
Location 5m from M6 junc 44,on A689 towards
Brampton & Newcastle-Upon-Tyne

Hotel ★★★ 🏌 76% Crosby Lodge Country House
Hotel, High Crosby, Crosby-on-Eden,
CARLISLE
☎ 01228 573618 9 ➪ 🐾 Annexe2 ➪ 🐾

GRANGE-OVER-SANDS   Map 07 SD47

Grange Fell Fell Rd LA11 6HB
☎ 015395 32536 Fax 015395 35357
Hillside course with magnificent views over Morecambe
Bay and the surrounding Lakeland mountains.
9 holes, 5278yds, Par 70, SSS 66, Course record 65.
Club membership 400.

Visitors may normally play Mon-Sat.
Green Fees £12 per day (£17 weekends & bank
holidays).
Facilities 💪 🍴 ⛳
Location 1m W on Grange-Over-Sands/Cartmel

Hotel ★★★ 69% Netherwood Hotel, Lindale Rd,
GRANGE-OVER-SANDS
☎ 015395 32552 28 ➪ 🐾

Grange-over-Sands Meathop Rd LA11 6QX
☎ 015395 33180 or 33754 Fax 015395 33754
Interesting parkland course with well sited tree plantations,
ditches and water features. The four par 3s are considered to
be some of the best in the area.
18 holes, 5958yds, Par 70, SSS 69, Course record 68.
Club membership 650.
Visitors must be a member of Golf Club or recognised
Golf Society, advisable to contact in advance for
play at weekends.
Societies apply in writing but very limited availability at
weekends and bank holidays.
Green Fees £24 per day; £18 per round (£28/£24 weekends
& bank holidays).
Prof Steve Sumner-Roberts
Designer Mackenzie (part)
Facilities ⊗ ⅲ 🏌 💪 🍴 ⛳ ⚑ 🍴 ⚑
Location NE of town centre off B5277

Hotel ★★★ 64% Graythwaite Manor Hotel, Fernhill
Rd, GRANGE-OVER-SANDS
☎ 015395 32001 & 33755
Fax 015395 35549 21 ➪ 🐾

KENDAL   Map 07 SD59

Carus Green Burneside Rd LA9 6EB
☎ 01539 721097 Fax 01539 721097
Bounded by the Kent and Sprint rivers (brought into play on
5 holes), this flat course enjoys open views to the Lakeland
Fells.
18 holes, 5691yds, Par 70, SSS 68.
Club membership 400.
Visitors no restrictions except during Club competitions
at weekend, check by phone.
Societies telephone for details.
Green Fees £10 per round (£12 weekends).
Designer W Adamson
Facilities ⊗ by prior arrangement 🏌 💪 🍴 ⛳ ⚑ 🍴 ⚑
Location From rdbt N end of Kendal (A591

Hotel ★★ 63% Garden House Hotel, Fowl-ing Ln,
KENDAL ☎ 01539 731131 11 ➪ 🐾

Kendal The Heights LA9 4PQ ☎ 01539 723499
Elevated parkland/fell course affording breathtaking views of
Lakeland fells and surrounding district.
18 holes, 5765yds, Par 70, SSS 67, Course record 60.
Club membership 737.
Visitors must have a handicap certificate, weekends
subject to availability. Telephone to reserve tee-
off time.
Societies must contact in advance.
Green Fees £20 per day (£25 weekends & bank holidays).
Prof D J Turner

Facilities ⊗ 〗 ⓛ 💻 ♀ ⌂ 🕯 ✓
Location 1m W of town centre

Hotel ★★ 63% Garden House Hotel, Fowl-ing Ln, KENDAL ☎ 01539 731131 11 ⇔ ℕ

KESWICK   Map 11 NY22

Keswick Threlkeld Hall CA12 4SX
☎ 017687 79324 Fax 017687 79861
Varied fell and tree-lined course with commanding views of Lakeland scenery.
18 holes, 6225yds, Par 71, SSS 72, Course record 67.
Club membership 866.
Visitors booking up to 7 days in advance 017687 79010. Restricted on competition days.
Societies apply in writing to secretary.
Green Fees £18 per day (£23 weekends & bank holidays).
Prof Craig Hamilton
Designer Eric Brown
Facilities ⊗ 〗 ⓛ 💻 ♀ ⌂ 🕯 ✓
& Leisure fishing.
Location 4m E of Keswick, off A66

Hotel ★★★★ 64% Keswick Country House Hotel, Station Rd, KESWICK
☎ 017687 72020 74 ⇔ ℕ

KIRKBY LONSDALE   Map 07 SD67

Kirkby Lonsdale Scaleber Ln, Barbon LA6 2LJ
☎ 015242 76365
Parkland course on the east bank of the River Lune and crossed by Barbon Beck. Mainly following the lie of the land, the gently undulating course uses the beck to provide water hazards.
18 holes, 6472yds, Par 72, SSS 71, Course record 68.
Club membership 600.
Visitors restricted on Sunday, must telephone in advance or call in at pro shop.
Societies apply in writing for society package.
Green Fees £20 per day (£25 weekends & bank holidays).
Prof Chris Barrett
Designer Bill Squires
Facilities ⊗ 〗 ⓛ 💻 ♀ ⌂ 🕯 ✓
Location 3m NE of Kirkby Lonsdale on A683

Hotel ★★ 68% Pheasant Inn, CASTERTON
☎ 015242 71230 11 ⇔ ℕ

MARYPORT   Map 11 NY03

Maryport Bankend CA15 6PA ☎ 01900 812605
A tight seaside links course exposed to Solway breezes. Fine views across Solway Firth. Course comprises 9 holes links and 9 holes parkland and small streams can be hazardous on several holes.
18 holes, 6088yds, Par 70, SSS 69, Course record 65.
Club membership 400.
Visitors contact club in advance. Dress code must be observed.
Societies must apply in writing.
Green Fees not confirmed.
Facilities ⊗ 〗 ⓛ 💻 ♀ ⌂ 🕯
Location 1m N on B5300

Hotel ★★★ 63% Broughton Craggs Hotel, Great Broughton, COCKERMOUTH
☎ 01900 824400 14 ⇔ ℕ

PENRITH   Map 12 NY53

Penrith Salkeld Rd CA11 8SG
☎ 01768 891919 Fax 01768 891919
A beautiful and well-balanced course, always changing direction, and demanding good length from the tee. It is set on rolling moorland with occasional pine trees and some fine views.
18 holes, 6047yds, Par 69, SSS 69, Course record 63.
Club membership 850.
Visitors contact in advance. Handicap certificate required.
Societies telephone in advance.
Green Fees not confirmed.
Prof Garry Key
Facilities ⊗ 〗 ⓛ 💻 ♀ ⌂ 🕯 ✓ ℓ
Location 0.75m N off A6

Hotel ★★ 71% George Hotel, Devonshire St, PENRITH ☎ 01768 862696 31 ⇔ ℕ

ST BEES   Map 11 NX91

St Bees CA27 0EJ ☎ 01946 824300
Links course, down hill and dale, with sea views.
9 holes, 5082yds, Par 64, SSS 65.
Club membership 275.
Visitors no restrictions.
Green Fees not confirmed.
Location 0.5m W of village off B5345

Hotel ★★★ 74% Ennerdale Country House Hotel, CLEATOR ☎ 01946 813907 30 ⇔ ℕ

SEASCALE   Map 06 NY00

Seascale The Banks CA20 1QL
☎ 019467 28202 Fax 019467 28202
A tough links requiring length and control. The natural terrain is used to give a variety of holes and considerable character. Undulating greens add to the challenge. Fine views over the Western Fells, the Irish Sea and Isle of Man.
18 holes, 6416yds, Par 71, SSS 71, Course record 65.
Club membership 670.
Visitors no restrictions, but advisable to contact for tee reservation times.
Societies telephone to make provisional booking.
Green Fees £25 per day; £20 per round (£30/£25 weekends & bank holidays).
Prof Craig Hamilton
Designer Willie Campbell
Facilities ⊗ 〗 ⓛ 💻 ♀ ⌂ 🕯 ✓ ℓ
Location NW side of village off B5344

Hotel ★★ 69% Westlakes Hotel, GOSFORTH
☎ 019467 25221 9 ⇔ ℕ

SEDBERGH
Map 07 SD69

Sedbergh Catholes, Abbot Holme LA10 5SS
☎ 015396 21551 (Club) & 20993 (Sec)
A tree-lined grassland course with superb scenery in the Yorkshire Dales National Park. Feature hole is the par 3 2nd (110yds) where the River Dee separates the tee from the green.
9 holes, 5624yds, Par 70, SSS 68, Course record 66. Club membership 250.
Visitors must book to play on weekends & bank holidays.
Societies must contact in advance.
Green Fees not confirmed.
Designer W G Squires
Facilities ⊗ ⅷ ㄴ ♥ ♀ ㅗ ㅎ ☂ ♂
Location 1m S off A683, 5m junct 37 M6

Hotel ★★ 63% Garden House Hotel, Fowl-ing Ln, KENDAL ☎ 01539 731131 11 ⇄ ♠

SILECROFT
Map 06 SD18

Silecroft LA18 4NU ☎ 01229 774250
Seaside links course parallel to the coast of the Irish Sea. Often windy. Easy walking. Spectacular views inland of Lakeland hills.
9 holes, 5877yds, Par 68, SSS 68, Course record 66. Club membership 300.
Visitors may be restricted competition days & bank holidays
Societies must contact in writing.
Green Fees not confirmed.
Facilities ♥ ♀ ㅗ
Location 1m SW

SILLOTH
Map 11 NY15

Silloth on Solway The Clubhouse CA5 4BL
☎ 016973 31304 & 32404 Fax 016973 31782
Billowing dunes, narrow fairways, heather and gorse and the constant subtle problems of tactics and judgement make these superb links on the Solway an exhilarating and searching test. The 13th is a good long hole. Superb views.
18 holes, 6614yds, Par 72, SSS 73, Course record 65. Club membership 700.
Visitors must contact in advance.
Societies telephone for times available.
Green Fees £25 per day (£32 per round weekends).
Cards ▭ ▭
Prof Alan Mackenzie
Designer David Grant/Willie Park Jnr
Facilities ⊗ ⅷ ㄴ ㅗ ㅎ ♂
Location S side of village off B5300

Hotel ★★ 64% Golf Hotel, Criffel St, SILLOTH ☎ 016973 31438 22 ⇄ ♠

ULVERSTON
Map 07 SD27

Ulverston Bardsea Park LA12 9QJ
☎ 01229 582824 Fax 01229 588910
Inland golf with many medium length holes on undulating parkland. The 17th is a testing par 4. Overlooking Morecambe Bay the course offers extensive views to the Lakeland Fells.
18 holes, 6201yds, Par 71, SSS 70, Course record 64. Club membership 750.
Visitors must contact in advance, be a member of an accredited golf club with a handicap certificate. May not play on Sat competition days or on Tue Ladies day.
Societies by arrangement in writing.
Green Fees not confirmed.
Prof M R Smith
Designer A Herd/H S Colt (1923)
Facilities ⊗ ⅷ ㄴ ♥ ♀ ㅗ ㅎ ☂ ♂
Location 2m S off A5087

Hotel ★★★ 65% Whitewater Hotel, The Lakeland Village, NEWBY BRIDGE ☎ 015395 31133 35 ⇄ ♠

WINDERMERE

See **Bowness-on-Windermere**

WORKINGTON   Map 11 NX92

Workington Branthwaite Rd CA14 4SS
☎ 01900 67828 Fax 01900 607123
Meadowland course, undulating, with natural hazards created
by stream and trees. Good views of Solway Firth and
Lakeland Hills. 10th, 13th and 15th holes are particularly
testing.
18 holes, 6217yds, Par 72, SSS 70.
Club membership 735.
Visitors   advisable to contact pro for weekday, weekends
             are generally very busy & Tue is Ladies Day.
Societies   booking required for over 8 people.
Green Fees   £20 per day (£25 weekends & bank holidays).
Prof   Aidrian Drabble
Designer   James Braid
Facilities   ⊗ ⫞ ⓛ ♭ ♥ ♀ ♨ 🖾 🚲 ♂
Location   1.75m E off A596

Hotel   ★★★ 75% Washington Central Hotel,
             Washington St, WORKINGTON
             ☎ 01900 65772 47 ⇆ ♠

DERBYSHIRE

ALFRETON   Map 08 SK45

Alfreton Wingfield Rd, Oakerthorpe DE66 7LH
☎ 01773 832070
A small parkland course with tight fairways and many
natural hazards.
11 holes, 5393yds, Par 67, SSS 66.
Club membership 300.
Visitors   must contact in advance.
Societies   apply in writing or telephone in advance.
Green Fees   not confirmed.
Prof   Julian Mellor
Facilities   ⊗ by prior arrangement ⫞ by prior arrangement
             ⓛ ♥ ♀ ♨ 🖾
Location   1m W on A615

Hotel   ★★★★ 69% Swallow Hotel, Carter Ln East,
             SOUTH NORMANTON
             ☎ 01773 812000 160 ⇆ ♠

ASHBOURNE   Map 07 SK14

Ashbourne Wyaston Rd DE6 2GJ
☎ 01335 342078 Fax 01335 347937
Undulating parkland course.
18 holes, 6402yds, Par 72, SSS 72.
Club membership 650.
Visitors   must contact professional in advance, may not
             play on competition days. With member only at
             weekends.
Societies   telephone in advance.
Green Fees   £28 per day; £20 per round (£30 per round
             weekends).
Prof   Andrew Smith
Designer   D Hemstock
Facilities   ⊗ ⫞ ⓛ ♭ ♥ ♀ ♨ 🖾 ♂
Location   Off Wyaston Road

Hotel   ★★★♨ 75% Callow Hall, Mappleton Rd,
             ASHBOURNE ☎ 01335 343403 & 342412
             Fax 01335 343624   16 ⇆ ♠

BAKEWELL   Map 08 SK26

Bakewell Station Rd DE45 1GB ☎ 01629 812307
Parkland course, hilly, with plenty of natural hazards to test
the golfer. Magnificent views across the Wye Valley.
9 holes, 5240yds, Par 68, SSS 66.
Club membership 325.
Visitors   limited at weekends due to competitions,
             generally available mid week but occasional
             matches/competitions.
Societies   apply in writing.
Green Fees   £15 per day (£20 weekends & bank holidays).
Facilities   ⫞ ⓛ ♥ ♀ ♨
Location   E side of town off A6

Hotel   ★★♨ 74% Croft Country House Hotel, Great
             Longstone, BAKEWELL
             ☎ 01629 640278 9 ⇆ ♠

BAMFORD   Map 08 SK28

Sickleholme Saltergate Ln S33 0BN ☎ 01433 651306
Undulating downland course in the lovely Peak District, with
rivers and ravines and spectacular scenery.
18 holes, 6064yds, Par 69, SSS 69, Course record 62.
Club membership 700.
Visitors   must contact in advance, restricted weekends.
Societies   telephone in advance.
Green Fees   not confirmed.
Prof   P H Taylor
Facilities   ⊗ ⫞ ⓛ ♭ ♥ ♀ ♨ 🖾 ♂
Location   0.75m S on A6013

Hotel   ★★ 66% Yorkshire Bridge Inn, Ashopton Rd,
             Yorkshire Bridge, BAMFORD
             ☎ 01433 651361   10 ⇆ ♠

BREADSALL   Map 08 SK33

Marriot Breadsall Priory Hotel & Country Club Moor
Rd, Morley DE7 6DL ☎ 01332 832235 Fax 01332 833509
Set in 200 acres of mature parkland, the Old Course is built
on the site of a 13th-century priory. Full use had been made
of natural features and fine old trees. In contrast the
Moorland Course, opened in Spring 1992, designed by
Donald Steel and built by Brian Piersen, features Derbyshire
stone walls and open moors heavily affected by winds. Open
when most other clubs are closed in winter.
*Priory Course: 18 holes, 6100yds, Par 72, SSS 69, Course
record 63.*
Moorland Course: 18 holes, 6087yds, Par 70, SSS 69.
Club membership 900.
Visitors   must contact in advance.
Societies   telephone in advance.
Green Fees   Priory: £20-£32 per round. Moorland: £25-£28
             per round.
Cards   💳 💳 💳 💳 💳 💳 💳
Prof   Darren Steels
Designer   D Steel

▶

Facilities ⊗ 〗 ᴸᴮ 🏆 ♀ ⚎ 🏠 ⛳ 🛺 ✄ ⚑
& Leisure hard tennis courts, heated indoor swimming
pool, sauna, solarium, gymnasium.
Location 0.75m W

Hotel ★★★★ 66% Marriott Breadsall Priory Hotel,
Country Club, Moor Rd, MORLEY
☎ 01332 832235   12 ⇥ ⟋ Annexe100 ⇥ ⟋

BUXTON   Map 07 SK07

Buxton & High Peak Townend, Waterswallows Rd
SK17 7EN ☎ 01298 23453
Bracing, well-drained meadowland course; the highest in
Derbyshire. Challenging course where wind direction is a
major factor on some holes; others require blind shots to
sloping greens.
18 holes, 5966yds, Par 69, SSS 69, Course record 65.
Club membership 670.
Visitors contact Mrs S Arnfield.
Societies apply in writing to Mrs S Arnfield.
Green Fees not confirmed.
Prof Gary Brown
Designer J Morris
Facilities ⊗ 〗 ᴸᴮ 🏆 ♀ ⚎ 🏠 ⛳ 🛺 ✄ ⚑
Location 1m NE off A6

Hotel ★★★ 67% Palace Hotel, Palace Rd, BUXTON
☎ 01298 22001 122 ⇥ ⟋

Cavendish Gadley Ln SK17 6XD
☎ 01298 23494 Fax 01298 79708
This parkland/moorland course with its comfortable
clubhouse nestles below the rising hills. Generally open
to the prevailing west wind, it is noted for its excellent
surfaced greens which contain many deceptive subtleties.
Designed by Dr Alastair McKenzie, good holes include
the 8th, 9th and 18th.
18 holes, 5833yds, Par 68, SSS 68, Course record 61.
Club membership 650.
Visitors must contact in advance, weekends are
restricted by competitions. Ladies day
Thursday
Societies telephone professional on 01298 25052.
Green Fees £26 per round (£35 weekends).
Cards 💳 💳 💳 💳
Prof Paul Hunstone
Designer Dr Mackenzie
Facilities ⊗ 〗 ᴸᴮ 🏆 ♀ ⚎ 🏠 ⛳ ✄
Location 0.75m W of town centre off A53

Hotel ★★★ 74% Best Western Lee Wood Hotel,
The Park, BUXTON
☎ 01298 23002 35 ⇥ ⟋ Annexe2 ⇥ ⟋

CHAPEL-EN-LE-FRITH   Map 07 SK08

Chapel-en-le-Frith The Cockyard, Manchester Rd SK23 9UH
☎ 01298 812118 & 813943 (sec) Fax 01298 814990
Scenic parkland course, with testing holes at the 14th (par 4)
and 18th (517 yds), par 5. Good views.
18 holes, 6054yds, Par 70, SSS 69, Course record 67.
Club membership 676.
Visitors must contact professional or secretary in
advance.
Societies apply in advance to Secretary.
Green Fees £22 per day (£30 weekends & bank holidays).
Prof David J Cullen
Facilities ⊗ 〗 ᴸᴮ 🏆 ♀ ⚎ 🏠 ⛳ ✄
Location On B5470

Hotel ★★★ 74% Best Western Lee Wood Hotel, The
Park, BUXTON
☎ 01298 23002 35 ⇥ ⟋ Annexe2 ⇥ ⟋

CHESTERFIELD   Map 08 SK37

Chesterfield Walton S42 7LA
☎ 01246 279256 Fax 01246 276622
A varied and interesting, undulating parkland course with
trees picturesquely adding to the holes and the outlook alike.
Stream hazard on back nine. Views over four counties.
18 holes, 6326yds, Par 71, SSS 70, Course record 65.
Club membership 600.
Visitors must contact in advance and must play with
member at weekends and bank holidays. A
handicap certificate is generally required.
Societies apply in writing.
Green Fees £30 per day; £25 per round.
Prof Mike McLean
Facilities ⊗ 〗 ᴸᴮ 🏆 ♀ ⚎ 🏠 ✄
Location 2m SW off A632

Hotel ★★★ 60% The Chesterfield Hotel, Malkin St,
CHESTERFIELD ☎ 01246 271141   73 ⇥ ⟋

Grassmoor Golf Centre North Wingfield Rd, Grassmoor
S42 5EA ☎ 01246 856044 Fax 01246 853486
An 18-hole heathland course with interesting and challenging
water features. 26-bay floodlit driving range, practice
bunkers and putting area.
18 holes, 5723yds, Par 69, SSS 69, Course record 67.
Club membership 420.
Visitors contact Manager in advance.
Societies telephone Manager in advance.
Green Fees £10 (£12 weekends).
Cards 💳 💳 💳 💳 💳
Prof Gary Hagues
Designer Hawtree
Facilities ⊗ 〗 ᴸᴮ 🏆 ♀ ⚎ 🏠 ⛳ ✄ ⚑
Location Between Chesterfield & Grassmoor, off B6038

Hotel ★★★ 60% The Chesterfield Hotel, Malkin St,
CHESTERFIELD ☎ 01246 271141   73 ⇥ ⟋

Stanedge Walton Hay Farm, Stonedge, Ashover S45 0LW
☎ 01246 566156
Moorland course in hilly situation open to strong winds. Some tricky short holes with narrow fairways, so accuracy is paramount. Magnificent views over four counties. Extended course now open.
9 holes, 5786yds, Par 69, SSS 69, Course record 72.
Club membership 310.
Visitors   with member only Sat & Sun, and may not play after 2pm weekdays.
Societies   apply in writing.
Green Fees   £15 per round (18 holes).
Facilities   by prior arrangement by prior arrangement 🔡 💻♀♨
Location   5m SW off B5057 nr Red Lion public house

Hotel   ★★★ 60% The Chesterfield Hotel, Malkin St, CHESTERFIELD ☎ 01246 271141 73 ⇄ ⁋

Tapton Park Municipal Tapton Park, Tapton S41 0EQ
☎ 01246 239500
Municipal parkland course with some fairly hard walking. The 620 yd (par 5) 5th is a testing hole.
Tapton Main: 18 holes, 6013yds, Par 71, SSS 69.
Dobbin Clough: 9 holes, 2613yds, Par 34.
Club membership 750.
Visitors   must contact in advance. No caddies allowed.
Societies   apply in writing.
Green Fees   not confirmed.
Prof   Fraser Scott
Facilities   ♀♨♡⁋
Location   0.5m E of Chesterfield Station

Hotel   ★★★ 60% The Chesterfield Hotel, Malkin St, CHESTERFIELD ☎ 01246 271141 73 ⇄ ⁋

CODNOR   Map 08 SK44

Ormonde Fields Golf & Country Club Nottingham Rd DE5 9RG ☎ 01773 570043 (Secretary) & 742987 (Pro) Fax 01773 742987
Parkland course with undulating fairways and natural hazards. There is a practice area.
18 holes, 6502yds, Par 71, SSS 72, Course record 68.
Club membership 500.
Visitors   must contact in advance.
Societies   telephone in advance.
Green Fees   £17.50 per day (£22.50 per round weekends).
Cards   ▪
Prof   Peter Buttifant
Designer   W Hawtree
Facilities   ⊗ ♏🔡 💻♀♨♡⁋
Location   1m SE on A610

Hotel   ★★★ 72% Makeney Hall Country House Hotel, Makeney, Milford, BELPER ☎ 01332 842999 27 ⇄ ⁋ Annexe18 ⇄ ⁋

DERBY   Map 08 SK33

Allestree Park Allestree Hall, Duffield Rd, Allestree DE22 2EU ☎ 01332 550616 Fax 01332 541195
Public course, picturesque and undulating set in 300 acre park with views across Derbyshire.
18 holes, 5806yds, Par 68, SSS 68.

Visitors   start times may be booked in advance by telephone, visitors welcome any day.
Societies   apply in writing or by telephone in advance.
Green Fees   £10.60.
Cards   ▪ ▪ VISA ▪ ▪
Prof   John Siddons
Facilities   ⊗ ♏🔡 💻♀♨♡⁋
& Leisure   fishing.
Location   N of Derby, from A38 take A6 towards north, course in 1.5m on left

Hotel   ★★★★ 66% Marriott Breadsall Priory Hotel, Country Club, Moor Rd, MORLEY ☎ 01332 832235 12 ⇄ ⁋ Annexe100 ⇄ ⁋

Mickleover Uttoxeter Rd, Mickleover DE3 5AD
☎ 01332 518662 Fax 01332 512092
Undulating parkland course in pleasant setting, affording splendid country views. Some attractive par 3s and a number of elevated greens.
18 holes, 5708yds, Par 68, SSS 68, Course record 64.
Club membership 800.
Visitors   must contact Professional in advance.
Societies   apply in writing.
Green Fees   £22 per round (£25 weekends).
Cards   ▪
Prof   Tim Coxon
Designer   J Pennink
Facilities   ⊗ ♏🔡 💻♀♨♡⁋
Location   3m W off A516/B5020

Hotel   ★★★★ 75% Mickleover Court Hotel, Etwall Rd, Mickleover, DERBY ☎ 01332 521234 80 ⇄ ⁋

Sinfin Wilmore Rd, Sinfin DE24 9HD
☎ 01332 766462 Fax 01332 769004
Municipal parkland course with tree lined fairways an excellent test of golf. Generally a flat course it is suitable for golfers of all ages.
18 holes, 6163yds, Par 70, SSS 69.
Visitors   starting time must be booked in advance by telephone, visitors welcome any day.
Societies   apply in writing or by telephone in advance.
Green Fees   £10.60 per round.
Cards   ▪ ▪ ▪
Prof   Steven Lamb
Facilities   ⊗ ♏🔡 💻♀♨♡⁋
Location   3.5m S of city centre

Hotel   ★★★ 65% International Hotel, 288 Burton Rd, DERBY ☎ 01332 369321 41 ⇄ ⁋ Annexe21 ⇄ ⁋

DRONFIELD   Map 08 SK37

Hallowes Hallowes Ln S18 1UR
☎ 01246 411196 Fax 01246 411196
Attractive moorland/parkland course set in the Derbyshire hills. Several testing par 4's and splendid views.
18 holes, 6342yds, Par 71, SSS 71, Course record 64.
Club membership 630.
Visitors   may only play with member at weekends. Must contact in advance.
Societies   contact in advance, various packages.
Green Fees   £35 per day; £30 per round.
Prof   Philip Dunn

▶

Facilities ⊗ ⊞ 🏌 🍺 🍽 ♨ 🏠 🪣
& Leisure short game practice area, snooker.
Location S side of town

Hotel ★★ 66% Chantry Hotel, Church St,
DRONFIELD ☎ 01246 413014 7 🛏 🏴

DUFFIELD Map 08 SK34

Chevin Golf Ln DE56 4EE
☎ 01332 841864 Fax 01332 841864
A mixture of parkland and moorland, this course is rather hilly which makes for some hard walking, but with most rewarding views of the surrounding countryside. The 8th hole, aptly named "Tribulation", requires an accurate tee shot, and is one of the most difficult holes in the country.
18 holes, 6057yds, Par 69, SSS 69, Course record 64.
Club membership 750.
Visitors not before 9.30am or off first tee between 12.30 and 2pm. Proof of handicap required.
Societies contact in advance.
Green Fees not confirmed.
Prof Willie Bird
Facilities ⊗ ⊞ 🏌 🍺 🍽 ♨ 🏠 🪣 🏐 🪣
Location N side of town off A6

Hotel ★★★ 72% Makeney Hall Country House Hotel, Makeney, Milford, BELPER
☎ 01332 842999 27 🛏 🏴 Annexe18 🛏 🏴

GLOSSOP Map 07 SK09

Glossop and District Hurst Ln, off Sheffield Rd SK13 7PU
☎ 01457 865247
Moorland course in good position, excellent natural hazards. Difficult closing hole (9th & 18th).
11 holes, 5800yds, Par 68, SSS 68.
Club membership 250.
Visitors may not play on bank holidays or Sat (Apr-Nov).
Societies must apply in writing to professional.
Green Fees not confirmed.
Prof Daniel Marsh
Facilities ⊗ ⊞ 🏌 🍺 🍽 ♨ 🏠 🪣
Location 1m E off A57

Hotel ★★ 70% York House Hotel, York Place, Richmond St, ASHTON-UNDER-LYNE
☎ 0161 330 9000 24 🛏 🏴 Annexe10 🛏 🏴

HORSLEY Map 08 SK34

Horsley Lodge Smalley Mill Rd DE21 5BL
☎ 01332 780838 Fax 01332 781118
This lush meadowland course, opened in 1991 and set in 100 acres of Derbyshire countryside, has some challenging holes. Also Par 3 course and floodlit driving range. Recently installed USGA world class greens designed by former World Champion Peter McEvoy.
18 holes, 6400yds, Par 72, SSS 71, Course record 72.
Club membership 650.
Visitors must contact professional in advance and have handicap. May not play weekends.
Societies must telephone in advance.
Green Fees £25 per round.
Cards 💳 VISA 💳 💳 💳

Prof Paul Kent
Designer Bill White
Facilities ♨ 🏠 🪣 🐟 🪣 🏐 🪣 🪣
& Leisure fishing, sauna, solarium.
Location 4m NE of Derby, off A38 at Belper then follow tourist signs

Hotel ★★★★ 66% Marriott Breadsall Priory Hotel, Country Club, Moor Rd, MORLEY
☎ 01332 832235 12 🛏 🏴 Annexe100 🛏 🏴

KEDLESTON Map 08 SK34

Kedleston Park DE22 5JD
☎ 01332 840035 Fax 01332 842329
The course is laid out in flat mature parkland with fine trees and background views of historic Kedleston Hall (National Trust). Many testing holes are included in each nine and there is an excellent modern clubhouse.
18 holes, 6583yds, Par 71, SSS 72, Course record 63.
Club membership 868.
Visitors must contact in advance. With member only at weekends.
Societies weekdays only, apply in writing.
Green Fees £45 per day; £30 per round.
Prof David J Russell
Designer James Braid
Facilities ⊗ ⊞ 🏌 🍺 🍽 ♨ 🏠 🪣 🐟 🪣 🪣
& Leisure sauna.
Location Signposted Kedleston Hall from A38

Hotel ★★★ 60% Mackworth Hotel, Ashbourne Rd, DERBY
☎ 01332 824324 13 🛏 🏴 Annexe1 🛏 🏴

MATLOCK Map 08 SK36

Matlock Chesterfield Rd, Matlock Moor DE4 5LZ
☎ 01629 582191
Moorland course with fine views of the beautiful Peak District.
18 holes, 5804yds, Par 70, SSS 68, Course record 64.
Club membership 700.
Visitors with member only weekends & bank holidays. Members only weekdays 12.30-1.30pm.
Societies prior arrangement with Secretary.
Green Fees £30 per day; £25 per round.
Prof M A Whithorn
Designer Tom Williamson
Facilities ⊗ by prior arrangement ⊞ by prior arrangement 🏌 🍺 🍽 ♨ 🏠 🪣
Location 1.5m NE of Matlock on A632

Hotel ★★★ 65% New Bath Hotel, New Bath Rd, MATLOCK ☎ 01629 583275 55 🛏 🏴

MICKLEOVER Map 08 SK33

Pastures Cocial Centre, Hospital Ln DE3 5DQ
☎ 01332 521074
Challenging course laid-out on undulating meadowland with good views across the Trent valley.
9 holes, 5095yds, Par 64, SSS 65, Course record 67.
Club membership 320.

Visitors	must be accompanied by a member, may not play on Sun & between noon-4pm Sat.
Societies	Mon & Tue, must contact in advance.
Green Fees	on application.
Designer	J F Pennik
Facilities	⊗ 𝍌 ፱ ⬛ 🍺 ♀ ⛾ 🏠
& Leisure	bowling green.
Location	1m SW off A516

Hotel	★★★ 65% International Hotel, 288 Burton Rd, DERBY ☎ 01332 369321 41 ⇆ 🐾 Annexe21 ⇆ 🐾

MORLEY   Map 08 SK34

Morley Hayes Main Rd DE7 6DG
☎ 01332 780480 Fax 01332 781094
Peaceful pay and play course set in a splendid valley and incorporating charming water features and woodland. Floodlit driving range. Challenging 9 hole short course (Tower Course).
Manor Course: 18 holes, 6744yds, Par 72.

Visitors	welcome. Tower 9 hole course now open.
Societies	booking essential telephone for details.
Green Fees	£15 per 18 holes (£20 weekends & bank holidays).
Cards	⚊ 🔳 🔳 🔳 🔳 🔳
Prof	Mark Whithorn
Facilities	⊗ 𝍌 ፱ ⬛ 🍺 ♀ ⛾ 🏠 ⛳ ⚑ ✎ (
Location	A608

Hotel	★★★★ 66% Marriott Breadsall Priory Hotel, Country Club, Moor Rd, MORLEY ☎ 01332 832235 12 ⇆ 🐾 Annexe100 ⇆ 🐾

NEW MILLS   Map 07 SK08

New Mills Shaw Marsh SK12 4QE ☎ 01663 743485
Moorland course with panoramic views and first-class greens.
9 holes, 5633yds, Par 68, SSS 67.
Club membership 365.

Visitors	telephone in advance, cannot play during competitions.
Societies	must contact secretary or professional in advance.
Green Fees	not confirmed.
Prof	Stephen James
Facilities	⊗ 𝍌 ፱ ⬛ 🍺 ♀ ⛾ 🏠 ⛳ ⚑ 🥄 ✎ (
Location	0.5m N off B6101

Hotel	★★ 67% Red Lion Inn, 112 Buxton Rd, High Ln, STOCKPORT ☎ 01663 765227 6 ⇆ 🐾

RENISHAW   Map 08 SK47

Renishaw Park Club House, Mill Ln S21 3UZ
☎ 01246 432044 & 435484
Part parkland and part meadowland with easy walking.
18 holes, 6262yds, Par 71, SSS 70, Course record 65.
Club membership 750.

Visitors	must contact in advance. Visitors not allowed Thu, weekends or competition days.
Societies	by arrangement.
Green Fees	£32 per day; £23.50 per round (£36.50 per day/round weekends).
Prof	John Oates

Designer	Sir George Sitwell
Facilities	⊗ 🍺 ⬛ ♀ ⛾ 🏠 ✎
Location	1.5m W of junct 30 M1

Hotel	★★★ 60% Sitwell Arms Hotel, Station Rd, RENISHAW ☎ 01246 435226 30 ⇆ 🐾

RISLEY   Map 08 SK43

Maywood Rushy Ln DE72 3ST ☎ 0115 939 2306
Wooded parkland course with numerous water hazards.
18 holes, 6424yds, Par 72, SSS 71, Course record 70.
Club membership 450.

Visitors	advisable to contact in advance during summer, may not play during competitions. Standard dress code applies.
Societies	by prior arrangement.
Green Fees	not confirmed.
Prof	Colin Henderson
Designer	P Moon
Facilities	🍺 ⬛ ♀ ⛾ 🏠 ✎
Location	Near junct 25 on M1

Hotel	★★★ 73% Risley Hall Hotel, Derby Rd, RISLEY ☎ 0115 9399000 16 ⇆ 🐾

SHIRLAND   Map 08 SK45

Shirland Lower Delves DE55 6AU ☎ 01773 834935
Rolling parkland and tree-lined course with extensive views of Derbyshire countryside.
18 holes, 6072yds, Par 71, SSS 70, Course record 70.
Club membership 600.

Visitors	contact professional in advance.
Societies	contact Professional.
Green Fees	not confirmed.
Prof	Neville Hallam
Facilities	⊗ 𝍌 ፱ ⬛ 🍺 ♀ ⛾ 🏠 ⛳ ✎
Location	S side of village off A61

Hotel	★★★★ 69% Swallow Hotel, Carter Ln East, SOUTH NORMANTON ☎ 01773 812000 160 ⇆ 🐾

STANTON-BY-DALE   Map 08 SK43

Erewash Valley DE7 4QR
☎ 0115 932 3258 Fax 0115 932 2984
Parkland/meadowland course overlooking valley and M1. Unique 4th and 5th in Victorian quarry bottom: 5th-testing par 3.
18 holes, 6557yds, Par 72, SSS 71, Course record 67.
Club membership 750.

Visitors	no restrictions except when club events in progress.
Societies	contact in advance.
Green Fees	£27.50 per day; £22.50 per round (£27.50 per round weekends).
Prof	M J Ronan
Designer	Hawtree
Facilities	⊗ 𝍌 by prior arrangement 🍺 ⬛ ♀ ⛾ 🏠 ⛳ ✎ (
& Leisure	snooker tables.
Location	1m W, 2m from junct 25 on M1

Hotel	★★★ 73% Risley Hall Hotel, Derby Rd, RISLEY ☎ 0115 9399000 16 ⇆ 🐾

UNSTONE   Map 08 SK37

Birch Hall Sheffield Rd S18 4DB
☎ 01246 291979 Fax 01246 412912
Very testing woodland/moorland course demanding respect
and a good straight game if one is to walk away with a
respectable card. Sloping fairways gather wayward drives
into thick gorse and deep ditches. Signature holes are the
tough 6th and scenic 13th, the latter begs a big-hitter to go
for a shot to the green.
18 holes, 6379yds, Par 73, SSS 71, Course record 72.
Club membership 320.

Visitors	welcome at all times except before noon at weekends, midweek medals held regularly telephone for details. Advisable to telephone in advance at all times
Societies	apply in writing to secretary or telephone course.
Green Fees	£10 per round.
Prof	Pete Ball
Designer	D Tucker
Facilities	⊗ 川 ﾐ ♥ ♀ ☂
Location	Turn off A61 between Sheffield and Chesterfield, outskirts of Unstone village

Hotel	★★ 66% Chantry Hotel, Church St, DRONFIELD ☎ 01246 413014 7 ➪ ℩

DEVON

AXMOUTH   Map 03 SY29

Axe Cliff EX12 4AB
☎ 01297 21754 & 24371 Fax 01297 24371
Undulating links course with coastal views.
18 holes, 6000yds, Par 70, SSS 70, Course record 70.
Club membership 400.

Visitors	may only play after 11am on Wed & Sun.
Societies	must contact in advance.
Green Fees	not confirmed.
Prof	Mark Dack
Facilities	⊗ 川 ﾐ ♥ ♀ ☂ 🏠
Location	0.75m S on B3172

Hotel	★★ 66% Anchor Inn, Fore St, BEER ☎ 01297 20386 8rm(5 ➪ ℩)

BIGBURY-ON-SEA   Map 03 SX64

Bigbury TQ7 4BB ☎ 01548 810207 Fax 01548 810557
Clifftop, heathland course with easy walking. Exposed to
winds, but with fine views over the sea and River Avon. 7th
hole particularly tricky.
18 holes, 6048yds, Par 70, SSS 69, Course record 65.
Club membership 850.

Visitors	must have handicap certificate.
Societies	must apply in writing.
Green Fees	£24 per day (£26 weekends & bank holidays).
Cards	🏧 📶
Prof	Simon Lloyd
Designer	J H Taylor

Facilities	⊗ 川 by prior arrangement ﾐ ♥ ♀ ☂ 🏠 ⑂ ⚓ 🏇 ✍
Location	1m S on B3392

Hotel	★★★★ 71% Thurlestone Hotel, THURLESTONE ☎ 01548 560382 65 ➪ ℩

BLACKAWTON   Map 03 SX85

Dartmouth Golf & Country Club TQ9 7DE
☎ 01803 712686 & 712650 Fax 01803 712628
The 9-hole Club course and the 18-hole Championship
course are both worth a visit and not just for the beautiful
views. The Championship is one of the most challenging
courses in the West Country with a 4th hole visitors will
always remember.
Championship Course: 18 holes, 6663yds, Par 72, SSS 72.
Club Course: 9 holes, 5166yds, Par 66, SSS 65.
Club membership 800.

Visitors	must contact in advance, visitors welcome subject to availability.
Societies	telephone in advance.
Green Fees	not confirmed.
Cards	🌐 📶 📶 📶
Prof	Steve Dougan
Designer	Jeremy Pern
Facilities	⊗ 川 ﾐ ♥ ♀ ☂ 🏠 ⑂ 🏇 ⚓ ✍ ℩
& Leisure	heated indoor swimming pool, sauna, solarium, gymnasium.
Location	On A3122 Totnes/Dartmouth road

Hotel	★★★ 65% Stoke Lodge Hotel, Stoke Fleming, DARTMOUTH ☎ 01803 770523 25 ➪ ℩

BUDLEIGH SALTERTON   Map 03 SY08

East Devon North View Rd EX9 6DQ
☎ 01395 443370 Fax 01395 445547
An interesting course with downland turf, much heather
and gorse, and superb views over the bay. The early
holes climb to the cliff edge. The downhill 17th has a
heather section in the fairway, leaving a good second to
the green.
18 holes, 6239yds, Par 70, SSS 70, Course record 64.
Club membership 850.

Visitors	advisable to contact in advance, no visitors before 10am. Visitors must be member of a recognised club and must produce proof of handicap.
Societies	must contact in advance.
Green Fees	£35 per day; £27 per round (£42/£35 weekends & bank holidays).
Cards	🌐 📶 📶
Prof	Trevor Underwood
Facilities	⊗ 川 ﾐ ♥ ♀ ☂ 🏠 ⑂ ✍
Location	W side of town centre

Hotel	★★★ 62% The Imperial, The Esplanade, EXMOUTH ☎ 01395 274761 57 ➪ ℩

CHITTLEHAMHOLT Map 03 SS62

Highbullen Hotel EX37 9HD
☎ 01769 540561 Fax 01769 540492
Mature parkland course with water hazards and outstanding
scenic views to Exmoor and Dartmoor. Excellent facilities
offered by the hotel.
18 holes, 5755yds, Par 68, SSS 67.
Club membership 100.

Visitors	to book tee time telephone 01769 540530 daytime, 01769 540561 evenings.
Societies	must contact in advance.
Green Fees	from £14 (from £16 weekends).
Cards	🃏 ▨ 💳 🌐
Prof	Paul Weston
Designer	M Neil/ J Hamilton
Facilities	⊗ 🍴 🛈 🍺 ♀ 🛎 ⛳ 🚜 🏌 🛒 ⚷
& Leisure	hard tennis courts, outdoor and indoor heated swimming pools, squash, fishing, sauna, solarium, gymnasium.
Location	0.5m S of village

Hotel	★★★❄ 68% Highbullen Hotel, CHITTLEHAMHOLT ☎ 01769 540561 12 ⇄ Annexe25 ⇄ 🐾

CHRISTOW Map 03 SX88

Teign Valley EX6 7PA
☎ 01647 253026 Fax 01647 253026
A scenically spectacular 18 hole course set beside the River
Teign in the Dartmoor National Park. Offering a good
challenge to both low and high handicap golfers, it features
two lakeside holes, rolling fairways and fine views.
18 holes, 5913yds, Par 70, SSS 68.
Club membership 300.

Visitors	no restrictions, but need to book by telephone.
Societies	write or telephone for bookings.
Green Fees	not confirmed.
Prof	Richard Stephenson
Designer	P Nicholson
Facilities	⊗ 🍴 🛈 🍺 ♀ 🛎 ⛳ 🏌 🚜 ⚷
Location	Take Teignvalley exit off A38, Exeter/Plymouth Expressway and follow GC signs up valley on B3193

Hotel	★★ 70% The White Hart Hotel, The Square, MORETONHAMPSTEAD ☎ 01647 440406 17 ⇄ 🐾 Annexe3 ⇄ 🐾

CHULMLEIGH Map 03 SS61

Chulmleigh Leigh Rd EX18 7BL
☎ 01769 580519 Fax 01769 580519
Situated in a scenic area with views to distant Dartmoor, this
undulating meadowland course offers a good test for the
most experienced golfer and is enjoyable for newcomers to
the game. Short 18 hole summer course with a tricky 1st
hole; in winter the course is changed to 9 holes and made
longer for players to extend their game.
Summer Short Course: 18 holes, 1450yds, Par 54, SSS 54,
Course record 49.
Winter Course: 9 holes, 2310yds, Par 54, SSS 54.
Club membership 77.

Visitors	welcome anytime.
Societies	telephone in advance.
Green Fees	£9 per 36 holes; £6.50 per 18 holes.
Designer	John Goodban
Facilities	🛈 🍺 ♀ 🛎 ⛳ 🏌 ⚷
Location	SW side of village just off A377

Hotel	★★★ 74% Northcote Manor, BURRINGTON ☎ 01769 560501 11 ⇄ 🐾

CHURSTON FERRERS Map 03 SX95

Churston Dartmouth Rd TQ5 0LA
☎ 01803 842751 & 842218 Fax 01803 845738
A cliff-top downland course with splendid views over
Brixham harbour and Tor Bay. There is some gorse with
a wooded area inland. A variety of shot is called for,
with particularly testing holes at the 3rd, 9th and 15th, all
par 4. Conference facilities and a well equipped shop are
also available.
18 holes, 6219yds, Par 70, SSS 70, Course record 64.
Club membership 700.

Visitors	must telephone in advance and be a member of recognised golf club with a handicap certificate.
Societies	apply in writing or telephone.
Green Fees	£25 per round (£30 weekends).
Cards	💳
Prof	Neil Holman
Facilities	⊗ 🍴 🛈 🍺 ♀ 🛎 ⛳ 🏌 ⚷
Location	NW side of village on A379

Hotel	★★ 65% Dainton Hotel, 95 Dartmouth Rd, Three Beaches, Goodrington, PAIGNTON ☎ 01803 550067 11 ⇄ 🐾

CREDITON Map 03 SS80

Downes Crediton Hookway EX17 3PT
☎ 01363 773025 & 774464 Fax 01363 775060
Recently refurbished and extended clubhouse. Parkland
course with water features. Flat front nine. Hilly and wooded
back nine.
18 holes, 5934yds, Par 70, SSS 68.
Club membership 700.

Visitors	handicap certificate required, must contact in advance, restricted at weekends.
Societies	must contact in advance.
Green Fees	£27.50 per day; £20 per round (£25 per round weekends).
Prof	Howard Finch

▶

Facilities ⊗ ⫪ 👤 ▀ ♀ ⚘ 📷 ⚑ ✐
Location 1.5m SE off A377

Hotel ★★★ 73% Barton Cross Hotel & Restaurant, Huxham, Stoke Canon, EXETER
☎ 01392 841245 9 ⇔ 🐾

CULLOMPTON   Map 03 ST00

Padbrook Park EX15 1RU
☎ 01884 38286 Fax 01884 34359
A 9-hole, 18 tee parkland course with many water and woodland hazards and spectacular views. The dog-leg 2nd and pulpit 7th are of particular challenge to golfers of all standards.
9 holes, 6108yds, Par 70, SSS 70, Course record 67.
Club membership 250.
Visitors welcome at all times, tee must be reserved by telephoning in advance.
Societies apply in writing or telephone.
Green Fees £12 per 18 holes, £8 per 9 holes (£16/£10 weekends).
Cards 💳
Prof Stewart Adwick/Ross Troake
Designer Bob Sandow
Facilities ⊗ ⫪ 👤 ▀ ♀ ⚘ ⚑ ✐
& Leisure fishing, gymnasium.
Location Southern edge of Cullompton on B3181

Hotel ★★★ 67% The Tiverton Hotel, Blundells Rd, TIVERTON ☎ 01884 256120 74 ⇔ 🐾

DAWLISH WARREN   Map 03 SX97

Warren EX7 0NF
☎ 01626 862255 & 864002 Fax 01626 888005
Typical flat, genuine links course lying on spit between sea and Exe estuary. Picturesque scenery, a few trees but much gorse. Testing in windy conditions. The 7th hole provides the opportunity to go for the green across a bay on the estuary.
18 holes, 5965yds, Par 69, SSS 69.
Club membership 600.
Visitors must contact in advance & have handicap certificate.
Societies prior arrangement essential.
Green Fees £21.50 per day (£24.50 weekends & bank holidays).
Prof Andrew Naldrett
Facilities ⊗ ⫪ 👤 ▀ ♀ ⚘ 📷 ✐
Location E side of village

Hotel ★★★ 66% Langstone Cliff Hotel, Dawlish Warren, DAWLISH
☎ 01626 868000 64 ⇔ 🐾 Annexe4 ⇔ 🐾

DOWN ST MARY   Map 03 SS70

Waterbridge EX17 5LG ☎ 01363 85111
A testing course of 9-holes set in a gently sloping valley. The Par of 32 will not be easily gained with 1 par 5, 3 par 4's and 5 par 3's, although the course record holder has Par 29! The 3rd hole which is a raised green is surrounded by water and the 4th (439 yards) is demanding for beginners.
9 holes, 3910yds, Par 64, SSS 64.
Visitors no restrictions.
Societies no restrictions.

Green Fees £10 per 18 holes; £6 per 9 holes (£12/£7 weekends & bank holidays).
Prof David Ridyard
Designer D Taylor
Facilities ▀ ⚑ ✐
Location From Exeter on A377 towards Barnstaple

Hotel ★★★ 74% Northcote Manor, BURRINGTON
☎ 01769 560501 11 ⇔ 🐾

EXETER   Map 03 SX99

Exeter Golf & Country Club Topsham Rd, Countess Wear EX2 7AE ☎ 01392 874139 Fax 01392 874139
A sheltered parkland course with some very old trees and known as the flattest course in Devon. 15th & 17th are testing par 4 holes. Small, well guarded greens.
18 holes, 6000yds, Par 69, SSS 69, Course record 62.
Club membership 800.
Visitors welcome but may not play during match or competitions, very busy pre booking needed up to 1 week in advance. Must have handicap certificate.
Societies welcome Thu only, booking available by telephone to manager tel 01392 874139.
Green Fees £26 per day.
Cards 💳
Prof Mike Rowett
Designer J Braid
Facilities ⊗ ⫪ 👤 ▀ ♀ ⚘ 📷 ✐
& Leisure hard tennis courts, heated indoor plus outdoor swimming pool, squash, sauna, solarium, gymnasium.
Location SE side of city centre off A379

Hotel B Travel Inn, 398 Topsham Rd, EXETER
☎ 01392 875441 44 ⇔ 🐾

Woodbury Park Woodbury Castle, Woodbury EX5 1JJ
☎ 01395 233382 Fax 01395 233384
Two courses set in the lovely wooded parkland of Woodbury Castle.
Oaks: 18 holes, 6870yds, Par 72, SSS 72, Course record 66.
Acorn: 9 holes, 3000yds, Par 35, SSS 70, Course record 64.
Club membership 750.
Visitors welcome, please reserve tee times in advance.
Societies contact in advance.
Green Fees £35 per 18 holes.
Cards 💳
Prof Alan Richards
Designer J Hamilton-Stutt
Facilities ⊗ ⫪ 👤 ▀ ♀ ⚘ 📷 ⚑ 🏌 🛒 ✐ ⚑
& Leisure hard tennis courts, heated indoor swimming pool, squash, fishing, sauna, gymnasium.

Hotel ★★★ 68% Ebford House Hotel, Exmouth Rd, EBFORD ☎ 01392 877658 16 ⇔ 🐾

HIGH BICKINGTON   Map 02 SS52

Libbaton EX37 9BS
☎ 01769 560269 & 560167 Fax 01769 560342
Parkland course on undulating land with no steep slopes. Floodlit driving range.
18 holes, 6494yds, Par 73, SSS 72, Course record 72.
Club membership 500.
Visitors book in advance. No jeans, trainers or collarless shirts.

Societies   telephone to book in advance.
Green Fees   £18 per day; £15 per 18 holes (£20/£18 bank
             holidays & weekends).
Cards   ▭▭ ▬▬
Designer   H Col Badham
Facilities   ⓧ ⑂ 🏌 ♥ ♟ 🏀 ⚐ 🏪 🚬 ⚘ ⚙ ♪
& Leisure   fishing.

Hotel   ★★★🏆 68% Highbullen Hotel,
             CHITTLEHAMHOLT
             ☎ 01769 540561   12 ⇄ Annexe25 ⇄ ♠

HOLSWORTHY   Map 02 SS30

Holsworthy Killatree EX22 6LP
☎ 01409 253177 Fax 01409 253177
Pleasant parkland course with gentle slopes and numerous
trees.
18 holes, 6062yds, Par 70, SSS 69, Course record 64.
Club membership 600.
Visitors   may not play Sun am.
Societies   by arrangement with secretary or professional.
Green Fees   £20 per day/round (£25 weekends & bank
             holidays).
Prof   Simon Chapman
Facilities   ⓧ ⑂ 🏌 ♥ ♟ 🏀 ⚐ 🏪 ♪
Location   1.5m W on A3072

Hotel   ★★★ 70% Falcon Hotel, Breakwater Rd,
             BUDE ☎ 01288 352005   26 ⇄ ♠

HONITON   Map 03 ST10

Honiton Middlehills EX14 8TR ☎ 01404 44422 & 42943
Level parkland course on a plateau 850ft above sea level.
Easy walking and good views. The 4th hole is a testing par 3.
The club was founded in 1896.
18 holes, 5902yds, Par 69, SSS 68.
Club membership 800.
Visitors   must contact in advance.
Societies   society bookings on Thursdays.
Green Fees   not confirmed.
Prof   Adrian Cave
Facilities   ⓧ ⑂ 🏌 ♥ ♟ 🏀 🏪 ♪
Location   1.25m SE of Honiton

Hotel   ★★ 74% Home Farm Hotel & Restaurant,
             Wilmington, HONITON
             ☎ 01404 831278 & 831246
             Fax 01404 831411 6 ⇄ Annexe7 ⇄ ♠

ILFRACOMBE   Map 02 SS54

Ilfracombe Hele Bay EX34 9RT
☎ 01271 862176 Fax 01271 867731
A sporting, clifftop, heathland course with views over the
Bristol Channel and moors from every tee and green.
18 holes, 5893yds, Par 69, SSS 69, Course record 66.
Club membership 642.
Visitors   recommended to make tee reservation prior to
             visit, member only 12-2 daily and before 10 am
             on weekends.
Societies   telephone in advance.
Green Fees   £19 (£22 weekends & bank holidays).
Prof   David Hoare
Designer   T K Weir
Facilities   ⓧ ⑂ 🏌 ♥ ♟ 🏀 ⚐ 🏪 ♪
Location   1.5m E off A399

Hotel   ★★ 71% Elmfield Hotel, Torrs Park,
             ILFRACOMBE
             ☎ 01271 863377   11 ⇄ ♠ Annexe2 ⇄ ♠

IPPLEPEN   Map 03 SX86

Dainton Park Totnes Rd, Ipplepen TQ12 5TN
☎ 01803 813812 Fax 01803 813390
A challenging parkland type course in typical Devon
countryside, with gentle contours, tree-lined fairways and
raised tees. Water hazards make the two opening holes
particularly testing. The 8th, a dramatic 180yard drop hole
totally surrounded by sand, is one of four tough Par 3's on
the course. It is advisable to book start times.
18 holes, 6207yds, Par 71, SSS 70, Course record 70.
Club membership 600.
Visitors   prior booking by phone advisable to guarantee
             start time.
Societies   apply in writing.
Green Fees   £15 per round (£18 weekends).
Cards   ▭▭ ▬▬ ▬▬ ♫
Prof   Martin Tyson
Designer   Adrian Stiff
Facilities   ⓧ ⑂ 🏌 ♥ ♟ 🏀 ⚐ 🏪 ♪
Location   2m S of Newton Abbot on A381

Hotel   ★★ 67% Old Church House Inn, Torbryan,
             IPPLEPEN ☎ 01803 812372   12 ⇄ ♠

Glazebrook House Hotel
★★   South Brent, Devon, England TQ10 9JE.
AA   Telephone: South Brent (01364) 73322.
              Facsimile: (01364) 72350

A unique family run hotel with superb restaurant facilities.
Ideal location in Devon, with easy access to many major golf
courses, including St. Mellion and Nigel Mansell's at
Woodbury. We are also located superbly for touring with
both the South Devon coast and Dartmoor on our doorstep.
The hotel offers an extensive lounge bar and gardens with
plenty of room to relax. Chef Dave Merryman offers a wide
range of Table d'Hôte and A la Carte menu's cooked to the
highest of standards.
Special deals available for groups staying more than 1 night.
10 en-suite, CTV in all rooms, No smoking in bedrooms,
French and English cuisine, V. Meals. Last Orders 8.30pm.
Rooms including breakfast S. £48. D. £68 - £118

## IVYBRIDGE											Map 02 SX65

Dinnaton Sporting & Country Club Blachford Rd PL21
9HU ☎ 01752 892512 & 892452 Fax 01752 698334
Challenging 9-hole moorland course overlooking the South
Hams. With 5 par 4 and 4 par 3 holes, three lakes and tight
fairways; excellent for improving the short game. Floodlit
practice area.
9 holes, 4089yds, Par 64, SSS 60.
Club membership 275.

Visitors	no restrictions.
Societies	telephone in advance.
Green Fees	not confirmed.
Prof	David Ridyard
Designer	Cotton & Pink
Facilities	⊗ ⅏ ⅃⅃⅃
& Leisure	hard tennis courts, heated indoor swimming pool, squash, sauna, solarium, gymnasium.
Location	Leave A38 at Ivybridge junct and continue towards town centre. At first rdbt follow signs for club

Hotel ★★ 74% Glazebrook House Hotel &
Restaurant, SOUTH BRENT
☎ 01364 73322 11 ⇄ 🐾
See advertisement on page 71.

## MORETONHAMPSTEAD									Map 03 SX78

Manor House Hotel TQ13 8RE
☎ 01647 440998 Fax 01647 440961
This enjoyable parkland course has enough hazards to
make any golfer think. Most hazards are natural such as
the Rivers Bowden and Bovey which meander through
the first eight holes.
18 holes, 6016yds, Par 69, SSS 69, Course record 63.
Club membership 120.

Visitors	must contact in advance and pre-arrange starting times.
Societies	must telephone for reservation in advance.
Green Fees	£30 per day; £25 per round (£37/£32 weekends).
Cards	🔲🔲🔲🔲
Prof	Richard Lewis
Designer	J Abercrombie
Facilities	⊗ ⅏ ⅃⅃⅃
& Leisure	hard tennis courts, fishing, Par 3 course.
Location	3m W of Moretonhampstead, off B3212

Hotel ★★★★ 66% Manor House Hotel,
MORETONHAMPSTEAD
☎ 01647 440355 90 ⇄ 🐾

## MORTEHOE											Map 02 SS44

Mortehoe & Woolacombe EX34 7EH
☎ 01271 870225
Attached to a camping and caravan site, this 9-hole course
has 2 par 3s and 7 par 4s. The gently sloping clifftop course
has spectacular views across Morte Bay.
9 holes, 4690yds, Par 66, SSS 63, Course record 66.
Club membership 245.

Visitors	no restrictions.
Societies	must telephone or write in advance.
Green Fees	£12 per 18 holes; £7 per 9 holes.
Designer	D Hoare

Facilities	⊗ ⅏ ⅃⅃⅃
& Leisure	heated indoor swimming pool, indoor bowls, skittles, table tennis, pool table.
Location	0.25m before Mortehoe on station road

Hotel ★★★ 74% Watersmeet Hotel, Mortehoe,
WOOLACOMBE ☎ 01271 870333 23 ⇄ 🐾

## NEWTON ABBOT										Map 03 SX87

Newton Abbot (Stover) Bovey Rd TQ12 6QQ
☎ 01626 352460 (Secretary) Fax 01626 330210
Wooded parkland course with a stream coming into play on
eight holes. Fairly flat.
18 holes, 5862yds, Par 69, SSS 68, Course record 63.
Club membership 800.

Visitors	must have proof of membership of recognised club or current handicap certificate.
Societies	by arrangement on Thu only.
Green Fees	not confirmed.
Prof	Malcolm Craig
Designer	James Braid
Facilities	⊗ ⅏ ⅃⅃⅃
Location	3m N on A382

Hotel ★★ 65% Queens Hotel, Queen St, NEWTON
ABBOT ☎ 01626 363133 & 354106
Fax 01626 364922 22rm(20 ⇄ 🐾)

## OKEHAMPTON										Map 02 SX59

Okehampton Tors Rd EX20 1EF
☎ 01837 52113 Fax 01837 52734
A good combination of moorland, woodland and river make
this one of the prettiest, yet testing courses in Devon.
18 holes, 5243yds, Par 68, SSS 67, Course record 66.
Club membership 600.

Visitors	advance booking recommended, limited times available at weekends. Saturdays by prior arrangement only.
Societies	by prior arrangement.
Green Fees	£20 per day (£25 Sat, £20 Sun).
Prof	Simon Jefferies
Designer	J F Taylor
Facilities	⊗ ⅏ ⅃⅃⅃
Location	1m S off A30

Hotel ★★ 66% Oxenham Arms, SOUTH ZEAL
☎ 01837 840244 & 840577
Fax 01837 840791 8rm(7 ⇄ 🐾)

## PLYMOUTH											Map 02 SX45

Elfordleigh Plympton PL7 5EB
☎ 01752 336428 Fax 01752 344581
Charming, saucer-shaped parkland course with alternate tees
for 18 holes. Tree-lined fairways and three lakes. Fairly hard
walking.
9 holes, 5664yds, Par 68, SSS 67, Course record 66.
Club membership 600.

Visitors	must contact in advance and hold a handicap certificate.
Societies	by arrangement.
Green Fees	£15 per day (£20 weekend & bank holidays).
Cards	🔲🔲🔲🔲

Designer J H Taylor
Facilities ⊗ ⷨ ⮂ 🍴 ⚑ 🛢 🅿 ⛳ 🏌 ✓ ⟨
& Leisure hard tennis courts, heated outdoor swimming pool, squash, gymnasium.
Location 8m NE off B3416

Staddon Heights Plymstock PL9 9SP
☎ 01752 402475 Fax 01752 401998
Seaside course affording spectacular views across Plymouth Sound, Dartmoor and Bodmin Moor. Testing holes include the par 3 17th with its green cut into a hillside and the par 4 14th across a road. Easy walking.
18 holes, 5869yds, Par 68, SSS 70, Course record 66.
Club membership 750.
Visitors must have handicap certificate and contact the pro or secretary in advance.
Societies apply by telephone in advance.
Green Fees not confirmed.
Prof Ian Marshall
Designer Hamilton Stutt
Facilities 🛢 ⚑ 🏌 🅿 ✓
Location 5m SW of city centre

Hotel B Posthouse Plymouth, Cliff Rd, The Hoe, PLYMOUTH ☎ 01752 662828 106 ⇄ 🐾

SAUNTON   Map 02 SS43

Saunton EX33 1LG
☎ 01271 812436 Fax 01271 814241
Two traditional championship links courses. Windy, with natural hazards.
East Course: 18 holes, 6729yds, Par 71, SSS 73, Course record 65.
West Course: 18 holes, 6403yds, Par 71, SSS 72, Course record 67.
Club membership 1100.

Visitors prior booking recommended and must have handicap certificate.

Societies must apply in advance, handicap certificates required.
Green Fees £60 per day, £40 per round (£75/£50 weekends & bank holidays).
Cards 💳 ▬▬ ▬▬ 🏧 🅿
Prof A T MacKenzie
Designer F Pennick
Facilities ⊗ ⷨ ⮂ 🍴 🛢 ⚑ 🅿 ✓
Location S side of village off B3231

Hotel ★★★★ 69% Saunton Sands Hotel, SAUNTON ☎ 01271 890212 92 ⇄ 🐾
Additional hotel ★★ 69% Kittiwell House Hotel & Restaurant, St Mary's Rd, CROYDE ☎ 01271 890247 Fax 01271 890460 12 ⇄ 🐾

SIDMOUTH   Map 03 SY18

Sidmouth Cotmaton Rd, Peak Hill EX10 8SX
☎ 01395 513451 & 516407 Fax 01395 514661
Situated on the side of Peak Hill, offering beautiful coastal views. Club founded in 1889.
18 holes, 5100yds, Par 66, SSS 65, Course record 59.
Club membership 700.
Visitors by prior arrangement.
Societies by prior arrangement with the secretary.
Green Fees not confirmed.
Cards 💳 ▬▬ 🏧 ▬ 🅿
Prof Gaele Tapper
Designer J H Taylor
Facilities ⊗ ⷨ ⮂ 🍴 🛢 ⚑ 🅿 ✓
Location W side of town centre

Hotel ★★★★ 72% Victoria Hotel, Esplanade, SIDMOUTH ☎ 01395 512651 61 ⇄ 🐾

SOUTH BRENT   Map 03 SX66

Wrangaton (S Devon) Golf Links Rd, Wrangaton TQ10 9HJ
☎ 01364 73229 Fax 01364 73229
Unique 18 hole course with 9 holes on moorland and 9 holes on parkland. The course lies within Dartmoor National Park. Spectacular views towards sea and rugged terrain. Natural fairways and hazards include bracken, sheep and ponies.
18 holes, 6083yds, Par 70, SSS 69, Course record 66.
Club membership 700.
Visitors play any time. Must have a handicap certificate and contact in advance.
Societies write or telephone.
Green Fees not confirmed.
Prof Adrian Whitehead
Designer D M A Steel   ▶

Facilities ⊗ 🏻 🖢 ☕ ♀ 🏌 🏠 🥄 🚜 ⚐
Location 2.25 m SW off A38

Hotel ★★ 74% Glazebrook House Hotel & Restaurant, SOUTH BRENT
☎ 01364 73322 11 ⇌ ↾

SPARKWELL   Map 02 SX55

Welbeck Manor & Sparkwell Golf Course Blacklands PL7 5DF ☎ 01752 837219 Fax 01752 837219
A mature parkland course with several challenging holes, it features fairway and greenside bunkers, mature trees and streams. The house on the site, now the hotel, was built by Isambard Kingdom Brunel. Several of the holes have been named to commemorate some of his famous works - the 6th being The Great Western. This is a very challenging Par 5 tee which is out of bounds all the way up the left.
9 holes, 2886yds, Par 68, SSS 68, Course record 68.
Club membership 200.
Visitors   no restrictions
Societies telephone in advance.
Green Fees £10 per 18 holes; £6 per 9 holes (£12/£7 weekends).
Cards 🔲 🔲
Designer John Gabb
Facilities ⊗ 🏻 🖢 ☕ ♀ 🏠 🏌 🥄 ⚐
Location 1m N of A38 Plymouth/Ivybridge road

Hotel ★★★ 68% Boringdon Hall, Colebrook, Plympton, PLYMOUTH
☎ 01752 344455 41 ⇌ ↾

TAVISTOCK   Map 02 SX47

Hurdwick Tavistock Hamlets PL19 8PZ ☎ 01822 612746
This Executive parkland course with many bunkers and fine views opened in 1990. The idea of Executive golf originated in America and the concept is that a round should take no longer than 3 hours whilst offering solid challenge, thus suiting the busy business person.
18 holes, 5200yds, Par 68, SSS 67.
Club membership 180.
Visitors   no restrictions.
Societies must contact in advance.
Green Fees £14 per day.
Designer Hawtree
Facilities 🖢 ☕ ♀ 🏠 🏌 🥄 ⚐
Location 1m N of Tavistock

Hotel ★★★ 65% Bedford Hotel, Plymouth Rd, TAVISTOCK
☎ 01822 613221 31rm(30 ⇌ ↾)

Tavistock Down Rd PL19 9AQ
☎ 01822 612344 Fax 01822 612344
Set on Whitchurch Down in south-west Dartmoor with easy walking and magnificent views over rolling countryside into Cornwall. Downland turf with some heather, and interesting holes on undulating ground.
18 holes, 6250yds, Par 70, SSS 70, Course record 64.
Club membership 700.
Visitors   advisable to contact in advance.
Societies by arrangement with secretary.
Green Fees £22 per day/round (£27 weekends).

Prof   D Rehaag
Designer H Fowler
Facilities ⊗ 🏻 🖢 ☕ ♀ 🏠 🥄 ⚐
Location 1m SE of town centre, on Whitchurch Down

Hotel ★★★ 65% Bedford Hotel, Plymouth Rd, TAVISTOCK ☎ 01822 613221 31rm(30 ⇌ ↾)

TEDBURN ST MARY   Map 03 SX89

Fingle Glen EX6 6AF ☎ 01647 61817
9-hole course containing six par 4's and three par 3's set in 52 acres of rolling countryside. Testing 4th, 5th and 9th holes. 12-bay floodlit driving range.
9 holes, 4818yds, Par 66, SSS 63, Course record 63.
Club membership 400.
Visitors   must contact in advance.
Societies write or telephone in advance.
Green Fees not confirmed.
Prof   Stephen Gould
Designer Bill Pilz
Facilities ⊗ 🏻 🖢 ☕ ♀ 🏠 🏌 🥄 ⚐ ↾
Location 5m W of Exeter, off A30

TEIGNMOUTH   Map 03 SX97

Teignmouth Haldon Moor TQ14 9NY
☎ 01626 777070 Fax 01626 777070
This fairly flat heathland course is high up with a fine panoramic views of sea, moors and river valley. Good springy turf with some heather and an interesting layout makes for very enjoyable holiday golf. Designed by Dr Alister MacKenzie, the world famous architect who also designed Augusta GC USA.
18 holes, 6200yds, Par 71, SSS 70, Course record 65.
Club membership 900.
Visitors   handicap certificate required, groups must contact in advance, restricted tee off times at weekends.
Societies telephone in advance and confirm in writing.
Green Fees not confirmed.
Prof   Peter Ward
Designer Dr Alister Mackenzie
Facilities ⊗ 🏻 🖢 ☕ ♀ 🏠 🥄 ⚐
Location 2m NW off B3192

Hotel ★★ 70% Ness House Hotel, Marine Dr, Shaldon, TEIGNMOUTH
☎ 01626 873480 7 ⇌ ↾ Annexe5 ⇌ ↾

THURLESTONE   Map 03 SX64

Thurlestone TQ7 3NZ
☎ 01548 560405 Fax 01548 560405
Situated on the edge of the cliffs with typical downland turf and good greens. The course, after an interesting opening hole, rises to higher land with fine seaviews, and finishes with an excellent 502-yard downhill hole to the clubhouse.
18 holes, 6340yds, Par 71, SSS 70, Course record 65.
Club membership 770.

Visitors	must contact in advance & have handicap certificate from a recognised club.
Green Fees	£28 per day.
Prof	Peter Laugher
Designer	Harry S Colt
Facilities	⊗ ⅫΠ by prior arrangement ⅃ ⚐ ⚑ ⚐
& Leisure	hard and grass tennis courts.
Location	S side of village
Hotel	★★★★ 71% Thurlestone Hotel, THURLESTONE ☎ 01548 560382 65 ⇄ ⚐

TIVERTON   Map 03 SS91

Tiverton Post Hill EX16 4NE
☎ 01884 252187 Fax 01884 252187
A parkland course where the many different species of
tree are a feature and where the lush pastures ensure
some of the finest fairways in the south-west. There are a
number of interesting holes which visitors will find a real
challenge.
18 holes, 6236yds, Par 71, SSS 71, Course record 65.
Club membership 725.

Visitors	must have a current handicap certificate.
Societies	apply in writing or telephone.
Green Fees	not confirmed.
Prof	David Sheppard
Designer	Braid
Facilities	⊗ ⅫΠ by prior arrangement ⅃ ⚐ ⚑ ⚐
Hotel	★★ 74% Bark House Hotel, Oakford Bridge, BAMPTON ☎ 01398 351236 5rm(2 ⇄2 ⚐)

TORQUAY   Map 03 SX96

Torquay 30 Petitor Rd, St Marychurch TQ1 4QF
☎ 01803 329113 Fax 01803 316116
Unusual combination of cliff and parkland golf, with
wonderful views over the sea and Dartmoor.
18 holes, 6175yds, Par 69, SSS 70, Course record 65.
Club membership 700.

Visitors	must contact in advance.
Societies	must apply in writing.
Green Fees	£24-£28 per day/round.
Prof	Martin Ruth
Facilities	⊗ ⅫΠ ⅃ ⚐ ⚑ ⚐
Location	1.25m N
Hotel	★★ 60% Norcliffe Hotel, 7 Babbacombe Downs Rd, Babbacombe, TORQUAY ☎ 01803 328456 27 ⇄ ⚐

TORRINGTON   Map 02 SS41

Torrington Weare Trees, Great Torrington EX38 7EZ
☎ 01805 622229
Hard walking on hilly commonland 9 hole course.
Challenging par 3 4th hole with a sloping green and difficult
crosswinds. Small greens and outstanding views.
9 holes, 4419yds, Par 64, SSS 62, Course record 58.
Club membership 420.

Visitors	cannot play Sat & Sun before noon.
Societies	by arrangement.
Green Fees	not confirmed.

Facilities	⊗ ⅫΠ by prior arrangement ⅃ ⚐ ⚑ ⚐
Location	1m W of Torringdon
Hotel	★★ 65% Beaconside Hotel, Landcross, BIDEFORD ☎ 01237 477205 8rm(6 ⇄ ⚐)

UPOTTERY   Map 03 ST20

Otter Valley Golf Centre
☎ 01404 861266, Fax 01404 861266 (5m NW of H
oniton off A30, on Upottery Rd)
This Golf School set in beautiful Devon countryside
was established in 1989. There are practice facilities
with driving range, approach green, chipping green w
ith bunkers and 8 practice holes. Weekend and 5 day
courses are available and there is self catering accom
modation, telephone for details. All coaching is given
personally by Andrew Thompson P.G.A.

WESTWARD HO!   Map 02 SS42

Royal North Devon Golf Links Rd EX39 1HD
☎ 01237 473817 Fax 01237 423456
Oldest links course in England with traditional links
features and a museum in the clubhouse.
18 holes, 6644yds, Par 71, SSS 72, Course record 68.
Club membership 1000.

Visitors	advisable to telephone and book tee time, handicap certificate preferred or letter of introduction from club
Societies	apply in writing or telephone.
Green Fees	£34 per day; £28 per round (£40/£34 weekends & bank holidays).
Cards	▭ ▭
Prof	Iain Higgins
Designer	Old Tom Morris
Facilities	⊗ ⅫΠ ⅃ ⚐ ⚑ ⚐
& Leisure	indoor practice room, snooker.
Location	N side of village off B3236
Guest house	▭▭▭ Culloden House Hotel, Fosketh Hill, WESTWARD HO! ☎ 01237 479421 9rm

WOOLFARDISWORTHY   Map 02 SS32

Hartland Forest Woolsery EX39 5RA
☎ 01237 431442 Fax 01237 431734
Exceptionally varied course with many water hazards.
18 holes, 6015yds, Par 71, SSS 69.
Club membership 240.

Visitors	no restrictions.
Societies	telephone in advance or apply in writing.
Green Fees	£25 per day; £20 per round (£5 discount with handicap certificate).
Cards	▭ ▭ ▭ ▭
Facilities	⊗ ⅫΠ ⚐ ⚑ ⚐
& Leisure	hard tennis courts, heated indoor swimming pool, fishing, sauna, solarium, gymnasium.
Location	1.7m E of A39
Hotel	★★★ 73% Penhaven Country House, PARKHAM ☎ 01237 451388 & 451711 Fax 01237 451878 12 ⇄ ⚐

YELVERTON   Map 02 SX56

Yelverton Golf Links Rd PL20 6BN
☎ 01822 852824 Fax 01822 852824
An excellent course on Dartmoor with plenty of gorse
and heather. Tight lies in the fairways, fast greens and
challenging hazards. Boasts 3 of the best holes in Devon
(12th, 13th & 16th). Outstanding views.
18 holes, 6363yds, Par 71, SSS 72, Course record 68.
Club membership 650.

Visitors	must have handicap certificate and subject to availability, advisable to contact in advance.
Societies	must be booked in advance, by telephone initially.
Green Fees	£30 per day (£40 weekends & bank holidays).
Cards	
Prof	Tim McSherry
Designer	Herbert Fowler
Facilities	⊗ ⫫ ⏚ 💺 ⏛ △ 🏠 ⛳ ♂
Location	1m S of Yelverton, off A386

Hotel   ★★★ 73% Moorland Links Hotel,
                   YELVERTON ☎ 01822 852245   45 ⇄ ✆

DORSET

BEAMINSTER   Map 03 ST40

Chedington Court South Perrott DT8 3HU
☎ 01935 891413 Fax 01935 891217
This beautiful 18 hole parkland course is set on the Dorset-
Somerset borders with mature trees and interesting water
hazards.
18 holes, 5924yds, Par 70, SSS 70, Course record 72.
Club membership 400.

Visitors	must book tee time in advance at weekends.
Societies	apply in writing or telephone.
Green Fees	£16 (£20 weekends).
Cards	
Prof	Barry Austin
Designer	David Hemstock
Facilities	⊗ ⫫ ⏚ 💺 ⏛ △ 🏠 ⛳ ♂
Location	5m NE of Beaminster on A356 Dorchester-Crewkerne

Hotel   ★★★ 71% Bridge House Hotel, 3 Prout
                   Bridge, BEAMINSTER
                   ☎ 01308 862200 9 ⇄ ✆ Annexe4 ⇄ ✆

BELCHALWELL   Map 03 ST70

Dorset Heights DT11 0EG
☎ 01258 861386 Fax 01258 860900
Set in an area of outstanding natural beauty, rich in wildlife,
which provides a picturesque backdrop to this stimulating,
undulating course. Modern clubhouse with magnificent views.
18 holes, 6138yds, Par 70, SSS 70, Course record 74.
Club membership 270.

Visitors	must contact in advance, dress restrictions.
Societies	must telephone in advance.
Green Fees	not confirmed.
Cards	
Prof	Andy Stuart
Designer	David Astill
Facilities	⊗ ⏚ 💺 ♀ △ 🏠 ⛳ ♂

Hotel   ★★★ 65% Crown Hotel, West St, BLANDFORD
                   FORUM ☎ 01258 456626   33 ⇄ ✆

BERE REGIS   Map 03 SY89

East Dorset BH20 7NT
☎ 01929 472244 Fax 01929 471294
Lakeland is a long 18-hole parkland course with natural
water features. The Woodland is a second 9-hole, 18-tee
course is set amongst trees and rhododendrons. Floodlit
22-bay driving range, golf shop.
*Lakeland Course: 18 holes, 6580yds, Par 72, SSS 73,
Course record 66.*
Woodland Course: 9 holes, 4887yards, Par 66, SSS 64.
Club membership 550.

Visitors	must book in advance and handicap certificate required for Lakeland course.
Societies	apply in advance.
Green Fees	Lakeland: £34 per day; £29 per round (£39/£34 weekends). Woodland: £22 per day; £20 per round (£24/£22 weekends).
Cards	
Prof	Derwynne Honan
Designer	Martin Hawtree
Facilities	⊗ ⫫ ⏚ 💺 ♀ △ 🏠 ⛳ 🏡 ♂
Location	5m from Bere Regis on Wool Road

Hotel   ★★ 70% Kemps Country House Hotel,
                   East Stoke, WAREHAM
                   ☎ 01929 462563 5rm(4 ⇄ ✆)
                   Annexe10 ⇄ ✆

BLANDFORD FORUM   Map 03 ST80

Ashley Wood Wimborne Rd DT11 9HN
☎ 01258 452253 Fax 01258 450190
Undulating and well drained downland course with superb
views over the Tarrant and Stour Valleys.
18 holes, 6276yds, Par 70, SSS 70, Course record 65.
Club membership 700.

Visitors	phone in advance. Handicap certificate required weekends unless with member.
Societies	apply to Secretary.
Green Fees	£26 per day; £18 after noon (£28 after 1pm weekends).
Prof	Spencer Taylor
Designer	P Tallack
Facilities	⊗ �‖ ⮝ ■ ⛳ ♨ 🏌 ♂
Location	2m E on B3082
Hotel	★★★ 65% Crown Hotel, West St, BLANDFORD FORUM ☎ 01258 456626 33 ⇋ ♠

BOURNEMOUTH   Map 04 SZ09

Bournemouth & Meyrick Central Dr, Meyrick Park BH2
6LH ☎ 01202 292425
Picturesque muncipal parkland course founded in 1890.
18 holes, 5852yds, Par 70, SSS 69, Course record 64.
Club membership 500.

Visitors	advance booking is essential.
Societies	telephone in advance.
Green Fees	not confirmed.
Prof	Lee Thompson
Facilities	⛳ ♨ 🏌 ♂
& Leisure	squash.
Hotel	★★★ 63% Burley Court Hotel, Bath Rd, BOURNEMOUTH ☎ 01202 552824 & 556704 Fax 01202 298514 38 ⇋ ♠

Knighton Heath Francis Av, West Howe BH11 8NX
☎ 01202 572633 Fax 01202 590774
Undulating heathland course on high ground inland from
Poole.
18 holes, 6084yds, Par 70, SSS 69.
Club membership 700.

Visitors	may not play weekend. Phone for availability.
Societies	must book in advance.
Green Fees	£25 per day; £20 per round.
Prof	Jane Miles
Facilities	⊗ �‖ ⮝ ■ ⛳ ♨ ♂
Location	N side of town centre, junct of A348/A3409 signposted at rdbt
Hotel	★★ Beechleas Hotel, 17 Poole Rd, WIMBORNE MINSTER ☎ 01202 841684 5 ⇋ ♠ Annexe4 ⇋ ♠

Queen's Park Queens Park Dr West BH8 9BY
☎ 01202 396198 & 302611 Fax 01202 302611
Undulating parkland course of pine and heather, with narrow,
tree-lined fairways. Public course played over by 'Boscombe
Golf Club' and 'Bournemouth Artisans Golf Club'.
18 holes, 6305yds, Par 72, SSS 70, Course record 69.

Visitors	Thu (ladies day)
Societies	must contact in advance.
Green Fees	not confirmed.

Cards	▭▭ ▭▭
Prof	Richard Hill
Facilities	⊗ ℼ ⮝ ■ ⛳ ♨ 🏌 ♂
Location	2m NE of town centre off A338
Hotel	★★ 67% Hotel Riviera, West Cliff Gardens, BOURNEMOUTH ☎ 01202 552845 34 ⇋ ♠

BRIDPORT   Map 03 SY49

Bridport & West Dorset East Cliff, West Bay DT6 4EP
☎ 01308 421491 & 421095 Fax 01308 421095
Seaside links course on the top of the east cliff, with fine
views over Lyme Bay and surrounding countryside. A
popular feature is the pretty and deceptive 14th hole, its
sunken green lying 90 feet below the tee and guarded by
natural hazards and bunkers.
18 holes, 6488yds, Par 73, SSS 71.
Club membership 700.

Visitors	must contact in advance.
Societies	must contact in writing in advance.
Green Fees	£24 per day (£17 after 12 noon, £10 after 5pm).
Cards	▭▭ ▭▭
Prof	David Parsons
Designer	Hawtree
Facilities	⊗ ⮝ ■ ⛳ ♨ ♂
& Leisure	pitch & putt (holiday season).
Location	2m S of Bridport
Hotel	★★★ 65% Haddon House Hotel, West Bay, BRIDPORT ☎ 01308 423626 & 425323 Fax 01308 427348 12 ⇋ ♠

BROADSTONE   Map 04 SZ09

Broadstone (Dorset) Wentworth Dr BH18 8DQ
☎ 01202 692595 Fax 01202 692595
Undulating and demanding heathland course with the
2nd, 7th, 13th and 16th being particularly challenging
holes.
18 holes, 6315yds, Par 70, SSS 70, Course record 66.
Club membership 700.

Visitors	restricted at weekends & bank holidays. Must contact in advance.
Societies	contact in advance.
Green Fees	£25 per round.
Prof	Nigel Tokely
Designer	Colt/Dunn
Facilities	⊗ by prior arrangement ℼ ⮝ ■ ⛳ ♨ 🏌 ♂
Location	N side of village off B3074
Hotel	★★★ 60% King's Head Hotel, The Square, WIMBORNE ☎ 01202 880101 27 ⇋ ♠

CHRISTCHURCH   Map 04 SZ19

Dudmoor Farm Dudmoor Farm Rd BH23 6AQ
☎ 01202 483980
A testing par 3 & 4 woodland course in an area of
outstanding natural beauty.
9 holes, 1428mtrs, Par 31.

Visitors	no restrictions.
Societies	telephone in advance.
Green Fees	£6 per 18 holes.

▶

Facilities 🍽 ⚒ ⛳ 🏌
& Leisure squash, fishing.

Hotel ★★★ 76% Waterford Lodge Hotel, 87 Bure Ln, Friars Cliff, Mudeford, CHRISTCHURCH ☎ 01425 272948 20 ⇥

Iford Bridge Barrack Rd BH23 2BA ☎ 01202 473817
Parkland course with the River Stour running through. Driving range.
9 holes, 2165yds, Par 34, SSS 32.
Club membership 350.
Visitors must contact in advance.
Societies must contact in advance.
Green Fees not confirmed.
Prof Peter Troth
Facilities ⚒ 🍽 ♀ 🏠 ⛳ 🚜 ✐ ⌇
& Leisure hard and grass tennis courts.
Location W side of town centre on A35

Hotel ★★★ 76% Waterford Lodge Hotel, 87 Bure Ln, Friars Cliff, Mudeford, CHRISTCHURCH ☎ 01425 272948 20 ⇥

DORCHESTER   Map 03 SY69

Came Down Came Down DT2 8NR
☎ 01305 813494 (manager) & 812670 (pro) Fax 01305 813494
Scene of the West of England Championships on several occasions, this fine course lies on a high plateau commanding glorious views over Portland. Three par 5 holes add interest to a round. The turf is of the springy, downland type.
18 holes, 6244yds, Par 70, SSS 71.
Club membership 750.
Visitors advisable to phone in advance, must have handicap certificate. May play after 9am weekdays & after noon Sun.
Societies by arrangement on Wed only.
Green Fees £22 per day (£27.50 weekends).
Cards ▦▦▦ ▦ 🖳
Prof David Holmes
Designer J H Taylor
Facilities ⊗ 🥛 ⚒ 🍽 ♀ ⚒ 🏠 ⛳ 🚜 ✐
Location 2m S off A354

Guest ◯◯◯◯◯ Yalbury Cottage Hotel &
house Restaurant, Lower Bockhampton, DORCHESTER ☎ 01305 262382 8 ⇥ 🐾

FERNDOWN   Map 04 SU00

Dudsbury Christchurch Rd BH22 8ST
☎ 01202 593499 Fax 01202 594555
Set in 150 acres of beautiful Dorset countryside rolling down to the River Stour. Wide variety of interesting and challenging hazards, notably water which comes into play on 14 holes.
Championship Course: 18 holes, 6763yds, Par 71, SSS 73, Course record 64.
Club membership 700.
Visitors welcome by arrangement with secretary or golf professional.
Societies telephone in advance.
Green Fees £30 per round (£35 weekends).
Cards ▦▦ ▦

Prof Roger Tuddenham
Designer Donald Steel
Facilities ⊗ 🥛 ⚒ 🍽 ♀ ⚒ 🏠 ⛳ 🏌 🚜 ✐ ⌇
& Leisure fishing, 6 Hole Par 3 Academy Course.
Location 3m N of Bournemouth on B3073, between Parley and Longham

Hotel ★★★★ 67% The Dormy, New Rd, FERNDOWN ☎ 01202 872121 115 ⇥ 🐾

Ferndown 119 Golf Links Rd BH22 8BU
☎ 01202 874602 Fax 01202 873926
Fairways are gently undulating amongst heather, gorse and pine trees giving the course a most attractive appearance. There are a number of dog-leg holes, and, on a clear day, there are views across to the Isle of Wight.
Championship Course: 18 holes, 6452yds, Par 71, SSS 71, Course record 65.
Presidents Course: 9 holes, 5604yds, Par 70, SSS 68, Course record 65.
Club membership 700.
Visitors must contact in advance & have handicap certificate, no visitors on Thursdays except on Presidents course, numbers restricted at weekends.
Societies welcome Tue & Fri only, telephone in advance.
Green Fees Championship: £42 per round (£55 weekends). Presidents: £15 per round (£20 weekends).
Cards ▦▦ 🖳
Prof Iain Parker
Designer Harold Hilton
Facilities ⊗ 🥛 ⚒ 🍽 ♀ ⚒ 🏠 ⛳ 🚜 ✐
Location S side of town centre off A347

Hotel ★★★★ 67% The Dormy, New Rd, FERNDOWN ☎ 01202 872121 115 ⇥ 🐾

Ferndown Forest Forest Links Rd BH22 9QE
☎ 01202 876096 Fax 01202 894095
Flat parkland course dotted with mature oak trees, several interesting water features, and some tight fairways.
18 holes, 5400yds, Par 67, SSS 65.
Club membership 700.
Visitors advisable to contact in advance,
Societies apply in writing.
Green Fees £10 per day (£12 weekends and bank holidays).
Cards ▦▦ ▦
Prof Kevin Spurgeon
Designer Guy Hunt/Richard Graham
Facilities ⊗ 🥛 ⚒ 🍽 ♀ ⚒ 🏠 ⛳ ✐ ⌇
& Leisure fishing.
Location From London M3 then A31, end of dual carriageway Dolmans Crossing rdbt right exit Forest Links Rd

Hotel ★★★ 65% Bridge House Hotel, 2 Ringwood Rd, Longham, FERNDOWN ☎ 01202 578828 37 ⇥ 🐾

HALSTOCK   Map 03 ST50

Halstock Common Ln BA22 9SF
☎ 01935 891689 Fax 01935 891839
Halstock is a short tight course, but presents an interesting challenge to players of all abilities. The terrain is gently undulating in places and there are plenty of trees and water hazards.
18 holes, 4351yds, Par 65, SSS 61, Course record 61.
Club membership 200.
Visitors must telephone in advance. Restricted Sun am.
Societies telephone in advance.
Green Fees £10 per 18 holes; £5.50 per 9 holes (£12/£7 weekends).
Cards ⬜ 🏧 💳 💳 🅿
Facilities ⬛ 🍴 🏠 🍴 🛒 🏌
Location 6m S of Yeovil

Hotel ★★★⛳ Summer Lodge, EVERSHOT ☎ 01935 83424 11 🛏 🐾 Annexe6 🛏 🐾

HIGHCLIFFE   Map 04 SZ29

Highcliffe Castle 107 Lymington Rd BH23 4LA
☎ 01425 272210 Fax 01425 272210
Picturesque parkland course with easy walking.
18 holes, 4776yds, Par 64, SSS 63, Course record 58.
Club membership 500.
Visitors must have handicap certificate and be a member of recognised club. Telephone in advance.
Societies write or telephone in advance.
Green Fees £25.50 per day (£35.50 weekends & bank holidays 9.30am-noon); £15.50 any day after 4pm.
Facilities ⊗ 🏋 ⬛ 🍴 🍻
Location SW side of town on A337

Hotel ★★★ 76% Waterford Lodge Hotel, 87 Bure Ln, Friars Cliff, Mudeford, CHRISTCHURCH ☎ 01425 272948 20 🛏

HURN   Map 04 SZ19

Parley Parley Green Ln BH23 6BB ☎ 01202 591600
Flat parkland course with few hazards and only one Par 5. Friendly atmosphere.
9 holes, 4584yds, Par 66, SSS 64, Course record 69.
Club membership 238.
Visitors good standard of dress expected.
Societies write or telephone.
Green Fees £7 per 18 holes; £5 per 9 holes (£8/£5.50 weekends).
Prof Ken Gilhespy
Designer P Goodfellow
Facilities ⊗ 🏋 🏋 ⬛ 🍻 🍴 🛒 🏌
Location Opposite Bournemouth airport

Hotel ★★ 67% Fisherman's Haunt Hotel, Sailsbury Rd, Winkton, CHRISTCHURCH ☎ 01202 477283 & 484071 Fax 01202 478883 4 🛏 🐾 Annexe14 🛏 🐾

Entries with a shaded background
identify courses that are
considered to be particularly interesting

LYME REGIS   Map 03 SY39

Lyme Regis Timber Hill DT7 3HQ ☎ 01297 442963
Undulating cliff-top course with magnificent views of Golden Cap and Lyme Bay.
18 holes, 6283yds, Par 71, SSS 70, Course record 67.
Club membership 575.
Visitors must contact in advance & have handicap certificate or be a member of recognised golf club. No play on Thu & Sun mornings.
Societies Tue, Wed & Fri; must contact in writing.
Green Fees £24 per day; £20 per round.
Prof Andrew Black
Designer Donald Steel
Facilities 🏠 🏠 🏌
Location 1.5m N on A3052

Hotel ★★★ 69% Alexandra Hotel, Pound St, LYME REGIS ☎ 01297 442010 27rm(26 🛏 🐾)

LYTCHETT MATRAVERS   Map 03 SY99

Bulbury Woods Bulbury Ln BH16 6HR
☎ 01929 459574 Fax 01929 459000
Parkland course amidst ancient woodland, with a mixture of American and traditional style greens and extensive views over the Purbecks and Poole Harbour.
18 holes, 6065yds, Par 72, SSS 70, Course record 68.
Club membership 700.
Visitors must contact in advance.
Societies must contact in advance.
Green Fees not confirmed.
Cards ⬜ 🏧 💳 💳 🅿
Prof Nigel Gravelle
Facilities ⊗ 🏋 🏋 ⬛ 🍻 🍴 🏠 🏏 🥄 🏌
Location A35 Poole to Dorchester, 3m from Poole centre

Hotel ★★★⛳ Priory Hotel, Church Green, WAREHAM ☎ 01929 551666 15 🛏 🐾 Annexe4 🛏 🐾

POOLE   Map 04 SZ09

Parkstone Links Rd, Parkstone BH14 9QS
☎ 01202 707138 Fax 01202 796027
Very scenic heathland course with views of Poole Bay. Club founded in 1910.
18 holes, 6250yds, Par 72, SSS 70, Course record 63.
Club membership 700.
Visitors must contact in advance and have handicap certificate.
Societies apply in writing.
Green Fees £44 per day; £33 per round (£55/£44 weekends & bank holidays).
Prof Andy Peach
Designer Willie Park Jnr
Facilities ⊗ 🏋 by prior arrangement 🏋 ⬛ 🍻 🍴 🏠 🍴 🏌
Location E side of town centre off A35

Hotel ★★★ 80% Salterns Hotel, 38 Salterns Way, Lilliput, POOLE ☎ 01202 707321 20 🛏 🐾 *See advertisement on page 80*

☆ ☆ ☆
SALTERNS
·HOTEL·

AA 3 star & 80% rating –
2 AA Rosettes

Superb Waterside hotel with outstanding food. 20 beautifully furnished bedrooms overlooking Poole Harbour and Brownsea Island. Many top national awards presented for exceptionally high levels of customer care and outstanding service. Only a pitch and a put away (¼ mile) from Parkstone Golf Club!

38 Salterns Way, Lilliput, Poole, Dorset, BH14 8JR Tel: 01202 707321

Best Western

SHERBORNE   Map 03 ST61

Sherborne Higher Clatcombe DT9 4RN
☎ 01935 814431 Fax 01935 814218
A sporting course of first-class fairways with far-reaching views over the lovely Blackmore Vale and the Vale of Sparkford. Parkland in character, the course has many well-placed bunkers. The dog-leg 2nd calls for an accurately placed tee shot, and another testing hole is the 7th, a 194-yard, par 3. There is a practice area.
18 holes, 5882yds, Par 70, SSS 68, Course record 63.
Club membership 900.
Visitors   must contact in advance & have handicap certificate.
Societies   prior booking only (Tue & Wed only).
Green Fees   £25 per day, £20 per round (£30/£25 weekends & bank holidays).
Prof   Stewart Wright
Designer   James Braid (part)
Facilities   ⊗ ⅢⅡ ⅃ ♨ ♀ ♋ ☎ ⚐
Location   2m N off B3145

Hotel   ★★★ 63% The Sherborne Hotel, Horsecastles Ln, SHERBORNE
                 ☎ 01935 813191   59 ⊨ ⚑

STURMINSTER MARSHALL   Map 03 ST90

Sturminster Marshall Moor Ln BH21 4AH
☎ 01258 858444 Fax 01258 858262
Privately owned club with pay & play facilities set in beautiful Dorset countryside. Played off 18 different tees the course is ideal for golfers of all standards.

---

9 holes, 4882yds, Par 68, SSS 64.
Club membership 350.
Visitors   no restrictions.
Societies   must contact in advance.
Green Fees   £11 per 18 holes; £7 per 9 holes.
Cards   ▭ ▭
Prof   Graham Howell
Designer   John Sharkey/David Holdsworth
Facilities   ⊗ ⅢⅡ ⅃ ♨ ♀ ♋ ☎ ☎ ⚐ ⚐ ⚐
Location   On A350. Signposted from village

Hotel   ★★★ 65% Crown Hotel, West St, BLANDFORD FORUM
                 ☎ 01258 456626   33 ⊨ ⚑

SWANAGE   Map 04 SZ07

Isle of Purbeck BH19 3AB
☎ 01929 450361 & 450354 Fax 01929 450501
A heathland course sited on the Purbeck Hills with grand views across Swanage, the Channel and Poole Harbour. Holes of note include the 5th, 8th, 14th, 15th, and 16th where trees, gorse and heather assert themselves. The very attractive clubhouse is built of the local stone.
Purbeck Course: 18 holes, 6295yds, Par 70, SSS 71, Course record 66.
Dene Course: 9 holes, 4014yds, Par 60.
Club membership 500.

Visitors   advisable to telephone.
Societies   must contact in advance.
Green Fees   £40 per day, £30 per round (£42/£35 weekends & bank holidays).
Cards   ▭ ▭ ▭ ▭
Prof   Ian Brake
Designer   H Colt
Facilities   ⊗ ⅢⅡ by prior arrangement ⅃ ♨ ♀ ♋ ☎ ⚐ ⚐ ⚐
Location   2.5m N on B3351

Hotel   ★★★ 68% The Pines Hotel, Burlington Rd, SWANAGE
                 ☎ 01929 425211   49 ⊨ ⚑

VERWOOD   Map 04 SU00

Crane Valley BH31 7LE
☎ 01202 814088 Fax 01202 813407
Two secluded parkland courses set amid rolling Dorset countryside and mature woodland - a 9-hole Pay and Play and an 18-hole Valley course for golfers holding a handicap certificate. The 6th nestles in the bend of the River Crane and there are 4 long Par 5's ranging from 499 to 545 yards.

Valley: 18 holes, 6445yds, Par 72, SSS 71, Course record 66.
Woodland: 9 holes, Par 66, SSS 60.
Club membership 700.

Visitors	must have handicap certificate for Valley course. Woodland course is pay and play.
Societies	telephone in advance.
Green Fees	Valley: £20 (£30 weekends); Woodland: £5.50 (£6.50 weekends).
Cards	〰️ 💳
Prof	Paul Cannings
Designer	Donald Steel
Facilities	⊗ ⫝̸ ⅃ 🍷 ♀ ⚲ 🍴 🏌 🐟 🛒 ✇ ⌇
Location	6m W of Ringwood on B3081

Hotel	★★★★ 67% The Dormy, New Rd, FERNDOWN ☎ 01202 872121 115 ⇆ 🐾

WAREHAM   Map 03 SY98

Wareham Sandford Rd BH20 4DH
☎ 01929 554147 & 554156 Fax 01929 554147
At the entrance to the Purbecks with splendid views over poole Harbour and Wareham Forest. A mixture of undulating parkland and heathland fairways. A challenge for golfers of all abilities.
18 holes, 5603yds, Par 69, SSS 67, Course record 66.
Club membership 500.

Visitors	must contact the club in advance and hold a handicap certificate. Must be accompanied by a member at weekends & bank holidays.
Societies	weekdays only. Must contact in advance.
Green Fees	£25 per day; £20 per round.
Facilities	⊗ ⅃ 🍷 ♀ ⚲ ✇
Location	Adjacent to A351, nr Wareham railway station

Hotel	★★★ 71% Springfield Country Hotel & Leisure Club, Grange Rd, WAREHAM ☎ 01929 552177 48 ⇆ 🐾

WEYMOUTH   Map 03 SY67

Weymouth Links Rd DT4 0PF
☎ 01305 773981 (Secretary) & 773997 (Prof) Fax 01305 78 8029
Seaside parkland course. The 5th is played off an elevated tee over copse.
18 holes, 5981yds, Par 70, SSS 69, Course record 63.
Club membership 750.

Visitors	advisable to contact in advance.
Societies	apply in writing/telephone
Green Fees	£24 per day/round (£30 weekends & bank holidays).
Cards	〰️ 💳 🏦 📇 💳
Prof	Des Lochrie
Designer	James Braid
Facilities	⊗ ⫝̸ ⅃ 🍷 ♀ ⚲ 📸 🍴 ✇
Location	N side of town centre off B3157

Hotel	★★ 67% Hotel Rex, 29 The Esplanade, WEYMOUTH ☎ 01305 760400 31 ⇆ 🐾

Call the AA Hotel Booking Service on
0870 5050505 to book at AA recognised hotels and B & Bs
in the UK and Ireland, or through our Internet site:
http://www.theaa.co.uk/hotels

BARNARD CASTLE   Map 12 NZ01

Barnard Castle Harmire Rd DL12 8QN
☎ 01833 638355 & 631980 Fax 01833 638355
Perched high on the steep bank of the River Tees, the extensive remains of Barnard Castle with its splendid round tower dates back to the 12th and 13th centuries. The parkland course is flat and lies in open coutryside.
18 holes, 6406yds, Par 73, SSS 71, Course record 66.
Club membership 650.

Visitors	must contact in advance, restricted at weekends. Handicap certificate required.
Societies	apply in writing.
Green Fees	£18 per round (£25 weekends).
Prof	Darren Pearce
Designer	A Watson
Facilities	⊗ ⫝̸ ⅃ 🍷 ♀ ⚲ 📸 🍴 ✇
Location	1m N of town centre on B6278

Hotel	★★ 76% Rose & Crown Hotel, ROMALDKIRK ☎ 01833 650213 7 ⇆ 🐾 Annexe5 ⇆ 🐾

BEAMISH   Map 12 NZ25

Beamish Golf Club DH9 0RH
☎ 0191 370 1382 Fax 0191 370 2937
Parkland course. Designed by Henry Cotton and W Woodend.
18 holes, 6204yds, Par 71, SSS 70, Course record 64.
Club membership 630.

Visitors	must contact in advance and may only play weekdays.
Societies	telephone in advance.
Green Fees	not confirmed.
Prof	Chris Cole
Designer	H Cotton
Facilities	⊗ ⫝̸ ⅃ 🍷 ♀ ⚲ 📸 🍴 ✇
Location	1m NW off A693

Hotel	★★★ 66% Beamish Park Hotel, Beamish Burn Rd, MARLEY HILL ☎ 01207 230666 47 ⇆ 🐾

BILLINGHAM   Map 08 NZ42

Billingham Sandy Ln TS22 5NA
☎ 01642 533816 & 554494 Fax 01642 533816
Parkland course on edge of urban-rural district, with hard walking and water hazards.
18 holes, 6404yds, Par 73, SSS 71, Course record 63.
Club membership 1050.

Visitors	contact professional in advance on 01642 557060 a handicap certificate may be requested.
Societies	apply in writing to Secretary/Manager.
Green Fees	£20 per day (£33 weekends).
Prof	Michael Ure
Designer	F Pennick
Facilities	⊗ ⫝̸ ⅃ 🍷 ♀ ⚲ 📸 🍴 ✇
Location	1m W of town centre E of A19

Hotel   ★★★ 70% Parkmore Hotel, 636 Yarm Rd,
          Eaglescliffe, STOCKTON-ON-TEES
          ☎ 01642 786815 55 ⇌ ⋔

BISHOP AUCKLAND   Map 08 NZ22

Bishop Auckland High Plains, Durham Rd DL14 8DL
☎ 01388 663648 661618 (pro)
A rather hilly parkland course with many well-
established trees offering a challenging round. A small
ravine adds interest to several holes including the short
7th, from a raised tee to a green surrounded by a stream,
gorse and bushes. Pleasant views down the Wear Valley
and over the residence of the Bishop of Durham.
18 holes, 6420yds, Par 72, SSS 71, Course record 64.
Club membership 950.
Visitors   parties must contact in advance. Handicap
              certificate advisable. Dress rules apply.
Societies   weekdays only; must contact in advance.
Green Fees   £24 per day; £20 per round (£26 per round
              weekends).
Cards   ▭▭ ▭▭ ▭ ▭ ▭ ▭
Prof   David Skiffington
Designer   James Kay
Facilities   ⊗ Ⅲᴸ 🍴 🍺 ♀ 🛆 🖚 ♂ ⓣ
& Leisure   snooker tables.
Location   1m NE on A689

Hotel   ★★★ 69% Eden Arms Swallow Hotel,
              RUSHYFORD ☎ 01388 720541 45 ⇌ ⋔

BURNOPFIELD   Map 12 NZ15

Hobson Municipal Hobson NE16 6BZ
☎ 01207 271605 Fax 01207 271069
Meadowland course opened in 1981. Very easy walking.
18 holes, 6403yds, Par 69, SSS 68, Course record 65.
Club membership 700.
Visitors   must book in advance at weekends.
Societies   must contact in advance.
Green Fees   £20 per day; £13 per round; £8.50 after 6pm
              (£16 per round, £11 after 6pm weekends & bank
              holidays).
Prof   Jack Ord
Facilities   ⊗ Ⅲᴸ 🍴 🍺 ♀ 🛆 🖚 ♂
Location   0.75m S on A692

Hotel   ★★★ 68% Swallow Hotel, High West St,
              GATESHEAD ☎ 0191 477 1105 103 ⇌ ⋔

CHESTER-LE-STREET   Map 12 NZ25

Chester-le-Street Lumley Park DH3 4NS
☎ 0191 388 3218 (Secretary) Fax 0191 388 1220
Parkland course in castle grounds, good views, easy walking.
18 holes, 6437yds, Par 71, SSS 71, Course record 71.
Club membership 650.
Visitors   must contact in advance and have an
              introduction from own club or handicap
              certificate.
Societies   must apply in writing.
Green Fees   not confirmed.
Prof   David Fletcher
Designer   J H Taylor
Facilities   ⊗ Ⅲᴸ 🍴 🍺 ♀ 🛆 🖚 ♂
Location   0.5m E off B1284

Hotel   ★★★ 72% Ramside Hall Hotel, Carrville,
          DURHAM ☎ 0191 386 5282 80 ⇌ ⋔

Roseberry Grange Grange Villa DH2 3NF
☎ 0191 370 0670 Fax 0191 370 0660
Testing holes on this parkland course include the uphill par 3
12th (147yds) and the par 4 8th (438yds) with a ditch
crossing the fairway.
18 holes, 5628yds, Par 70, SSS 69.
Club membership 550.
Visitors   after 11.30am Sun & 10.30am Sat in summer,
              pay and play Mon-Fri.
Societies   booking form available on request.
Green Fees   not confirmed.
Cards   ▭▭ ▭ ▭
Prof   Alan Hartley
Facilities   ⊗ Ⅲᴸ 🍴 🍺 ♀ 🛆 🖚 🖚 ♂ ⓣ

Hotel   ★★★ 67% George Washington Golf &
              Country Club, Stone Cellar Rd, District 12,
              High Usworth, WASHINGTON
              ☎ 0191 402 9988 103 ⇌ ⋔

CONSETT   Map 12 NZ15

Consett & District Elmfield Rd DH8 5NN
☎ 01207 502186 Fax 01207 505060
Undulating parkland/moorland course with views across the
Derwent Valley to the Cheviot Hills.
18 holes, 6023yds, Par 71, SSS 69, Course record 63.
Club membership 900.
Visitors   advised to contact Professional in advance on
              01207 580210.
Societies   apply in writing.
Green Fees   not confirmed.
Prof   Craig Dilley
Facilities   🍺 ♀ 🛆 🖚
& Leisure   snooker room.
Location   N side of town on A691

Hotel   ★★ 69% Lord Crewe Arms Hotel,
              BLANCHLAND
              ☎ 01434 675251 9 ⇌ ⋔ Annexe10 ⇌ ⋔

CROOK   Map 12 NZ13

Crook Low Jobs Hill DL15 9AA
☎ 01388 762429 & 767926
Meadowland/parkland course in elevated position with
natural hazards, varied holes and terrain. Panoramic views
over Durham and Cleveland Hills.
18 holes, 6102yds, Par 70, SSS 69, Course record 64.
Club membership 660.
Visitors   must contact Secretary for weekend play,
              limited availability.
Societies   apply in writing to Secretary.
Green Fees   £18 per day (£25 weekends & bank holidays).
Facilities   ⊗ Ⅲᴸ 🍴 🍺 ♀ 🛆
Location   0.5m E off A690

Hotel   ★★ 66% Kensington Hall Hotel, Kensington
              Ter, WILLINGTON
              ☎ 01388 745071 10 ⇌ ⋔

DARLINGTON   Map 08 NZ21

Blackwell Grange Briar Close, Blackwell DL3 8QX
☎ 01325 464458 Fax 01325 464458
Pleasant parkland course with good views, easy walking.
18 holes, 5621yds, Par 68, SSS 67, Course record 63.
Club membership 950.
Visitors restricted Wed & weekends.
Societies welcome weekdays except Wed (Ladies Day).
Green Fees £25 per day; £20 per round (£30 weekends & bank holidays).
Prof Ralph Givens
Designer F Pennink
Facilities ⊗ ⅷ ⅼ ⌷ ♀ ⌂ ⅲ ⌀
Location 1m SW off A66, turn into Blackwell, signposted

Hotel ★★★★ 59% Blackwell Grange, Blackwell Grange, DARLINGTON
☎ 01325 509955 99 ⇆ ⌦

Darlington Haughton Grange DL1 3JD
☎ 01325 355324 Fax 01325 488126
Fairly flat parkland course with tree-lined fairways, and large first-class greens. Championship standard.
18 holes, 6271yds, Par 71, SSS 70, Course record 64.
Club membership 850.
Visitors may not play weekends unless accompanied by member.
Societies by prior arrangement with the Secretary but not at weekends.
Green Fees £25 per holes; £20 per round.
Prof Mark Rogers
Designer McKenzie (part)
Facilities ⊗ ⅷ ⅼ ⌷ ♀ ⌂ ⅲ ⌀
Location N side of town centre off A1150

Hotel ★★★♣♣ 69% Headlam Hall Hotel, Headlam, Gainford, DARLINGTON
☎ 01325 730238 19 ⇆ ⌦ Annexe17 ⇆ ⌦

Hall Garth Golf & Country Club Hotel Coatham Mundeville DL1 3LU ☎ 01325 320246 Fax 01325 310083
A 6900yard course with mature trees and Victorian deer folly. Three greens have been newly laid. The challenging 165 yard Par 3 3rd requires teeing over water, whilst the 500 yard Par 5 6th hole features the picturesque River Swale running alongside the fairway and the green.
9 holes, 6621yds, Par 72, SSS 72.
Visitors advisable to book at least 1 week in advance.
Societies prior booking by telephone.
Green Fees £10 per 18 holes (£12.50 weekends).
Cards ⌹ ⌹ ⌹ ⌹ ⌹
Designer Brian Moore
Facilities ⊗ ⅷ ⅼ ⌷ ♀ ⌂ ⅲ ⌀
& Leisure grass tennis courts, heated indoor swimming pool, sauna, solarium, gymnasium.
Location 0.5m from A1(M) off A167

Hotel ★★★ 70% Hall Garth Golf and Country Club Hotel, Coatham Mundeville, DARLINGTON
☎ 01325 300400 30 ⇆ ⌦ Annexe11 ⇆ ⌦

Stressholme Snipe Ln DL2 2SA ☎ 01325 461002
Picturesque municipal parkland course, long but wide, with 98 bunkers and a par 3 hole played over a river.
18 holes, 6511yds, Par 71, SSS 71.
Club membership 650.

Visitors must contact in advance.
Societies apply to the steward or professional.
Green Fees £9.50 per 18 holes (£11.50 weekends).
Prof Mark Watkins
Facilities ⊗ ⅷ ⅼ ⌷ ♀ ⌂ ⅲ ⌀ ⅼ
Location SW side of town centre on A67

Hotel ★★★★ 59% Blackwell Grange, Blackwell Grange, DARLINGTON
☎ 01325 509955 99 ⇆ ⌦

DURHAM   Map 12 NZ24

Brancepeth Castle Brancepeth Village DH7 8EA
☎ 0191 378 0075 Fax 0191 3783835
Parkland course overlooked at the 9th hole by beautiful Brancepeth Castle.
18 holes, 6234yds, Par 70, SSS 70, Course record 64.
Club membership 780.
Visitors must contact in advance, restricted weekends.
Societies must contact in advance.
Green Fees £29 per day (£35 weekends & bank holidays).
Cards ⌹ ⌹ ⌹
Prof David Howdon
Designer H S Holt
Facilities ⊗ ⅷ ⅼ ⌷ ♀ ⌂ ⅲ ⌀
Location 4m from Durham A690 towards Crook, left at xrds in Brancepath, left turn at Castle Gates,400yds

Hotel ★★★★ 72% Royal County Hotel, Old Elvet, DURHAM ☎ 0191 386 6821 151 ⇆ ⌦

Durham City Littleburn, Langley Moor DH7 8HL
☎ 0191 378 0806 & 378 0029 Fax 0191 378 4265
Undulating parkland course bordered on several holes by the River Browney.
18 holes, 6321yds, Par 71, SSS 70, Course record 67.
Club membership 750.
Visitors restricted on competition days.
Societies apply in writing or telephone the club professional on 0191 378 0029
Green Fees £22 per day/round (£30 weekends & bank holidays).
Prof Steve Corbally
Designer C Stanton
Facilities ⊗ ⅷ ⅼ ⌷ ♀ ⌂ ⅲ ⌀
& Leisure practice bunker & driving nets.
Location 2m W of Durham City, turn left off A690 into Littleburn Ind Est

Hotel ★★★ 70% Three Tuns Swallow Hotel, New Elvet, DURHAM ☎ 0191 386 4326 50 ⇆ ⌦

Mount Oswald South Rd DH1 3TQ
☎ 0191 386 7527 Fax 0191 386 0975
Flat, wooded parkland course with a Georgian clubhouse and good views of Durham cathedral on the back nine.
18 holes, 6101yds, Par 71, SSS 69.
Club membership 120.
Visitors must contact in advance for weekends but may not play before 10am on Sun.
Societies must telephone in advance.
Green Fees £11 Mon-Thu; £12.50 Fri-Sun & bank holidays).
Cards ⌹ ⌹ ⌹ ⌹
Facilities ⊗ ⅷ ⅼ ⌷ ♀ ⌂ ⅲ ⌀
Location On A177, 1m SW og city centre   ▶

Hotel ★★ 67% Bridge Toby Hotel, Croxdale, DURHAM ☎ 0191 378 0524 46 ⇄ ↟

Ramside Hall Carrville DH1 1TD
☎ 0191 386 9514 Fax 0191 386 9519
Three recently constructed 9-hole parkland courses - Princes, Bishops, Cathedral - with 14 lakes and panoramic views surrounding an impressive hotel. Excellent golf academy and driving range.
Princes: 9 holes, 3235yds, Par 36, SSS 36.
Bishops: 9 holes, 3285yds, Par 36.
Cathedral: 9 holes, 2874yds, Par 34.
Club membership 400.
Visitors open at all times subject to tee availability.
Societies telephone in advance.
Green Fees £33 per day; £27 per round; £15 per 9 holes (£40/£33/£17 weekends).
Cards ▰▰ ▰▰ ▰▰ ▰▰ ▰▰
Prof Robert Lister
Designer Johnathan Gaunt
Facilities ⊗ ⏖ ⮂ ♣ ♀ ⚲ 🏠 ⛟ ✎ ↾
Location 500m from A1/A690 interchange

Hotel ★★★ 72% Ramside Hall Hotel, Carrville, DURHAM ☎ 0191 386 5282 80 ⇄ ↟

EAGLESCLIFFE   Map 08 NZ41

Eaglescliffe and District Yarm Rd TS16 0DQ
☎ 01642 780098 Fax 01642 780238
This hilly course offers both pleasant and interesting golf to all classes of player. It lies in a delightful setting on a rolling plateau, shelving to the River Tees. There are fine views to the Cleveland Hills.
18 holes, 6275yds, Par 72, SSS 70, Course record 63.
Club membership 550.
Visitors restricted Tue, Thu, Fri & weekends.
Societies must contact in advance, apply to secretary on 01642 780238
Green Fees £24 per day (£30 weekends & bank holidays).
Prof Paul Bradley
Designer J Braid/H Cotton
Facilities ⊗ ⏖ ⮂ ♣ ♀ ⚲ 🏠 ⛟ ✎
Location E side of village off A135

Hotel ★★★★ 66% Swallow Hotel, John Walker Square, STOCKTON-ON-TEES ☎ 01642 679721 0800 7317549 Fax 01642 601714 125 ⇄ ↟

HARTLEPOOL   Map 08 NZ53

Castle Eden & Peterlee Castle Eden TS27 4SS
☎ 01429 836510
Beautiful parkland course alongside a nature reserve. Hard walking but trees provide wind shelter.
18 holes, 6262yds, Par 70, SSS 70, Course record 65.
Club membership 750.
Visitors with member only during 12-1.30pm & 4-6.30pm. Must contact in advance.
Societies must contact in advance tel: 01429 836510.
Green Fees £22 per day/round (£30 weekends & bank holidays).
Prof Graham J Laidlaw
Designer Henry Cotton

Facilities ⊗ ⏖ ⮂ ♣ ♀ ⚲ 🏠 ⛟ ↾ ✎
Location 2m S of Peterlee on B1281 off A19

Hotel ★★ 69% Hardwicke Hall Manor Hotel, PETERLEE/HARTLEPOOL ☎ 01429 836326 15 ⇄ ↟

Hartlepool Hart Warren TS24 9QF
☎ 01429 274398 Fax 01429 274129
A seaside course, half links, overlooking the North Sea. A good test and equally enjoyable to all handicap players. The 10th, par 4, demands a precise second shot over a ridge and between sand dunes to a green down near the edge of the beach, alongside which several holes are played.
18 holes, 6215yds, Par 70, SSS 70, Course record 63.
Club membership 700.
Visitors with member only on Sun.
Societies must apply in writing in advance.
Green Fees £20 per day (£30 weekends).
Prof Malcolm E Cole
Designer Partly Braid
Facilities ⊗ ⏖ ⮂ ♣ ♀ ⚲ 🏠 ⛟ ✎
Location N of Hartlepool, off A1086

Hotel ★★ 66% Ryedale Moor, 3 Beaconsfield St, Headland, HARTLEPOOL ☎ 01429 231436 16 ⇄ ↟

MIDDLETON ST GEORGE   Map 08 NZ31

Dinsdale Spa Neasham Rd DL2 1DW
☎ 01325 332297 Fax 01325 332297
A mainly flat, parkland course on high land above the River Tees with views of the Cleveland Hills. Water hazards in front 10th tee and green, the prevailing west wind affects the later holes. There is a practice area by the clubhouse.
18 holes, 6090yds, Par 71, SSS 69, Course record 65.
Club membership 870.
Visitors welcome Mon & Wed-Fri, contact for further details.
Societies bookings through office, no weekends or Tue. Apply in writing or telephone.
Green Fees £25 per day.
Prof Neil Metcalfe
Facilities ⊗ ⏖ ⮂ ♣ ♀ ⚲ 🏠 ✎
Location 1.5m SW

Hotel ★★★ 63% The St George, Middleton St George, TEES-SIDE AIRPORT ☎ 01325 332631 59 ⇄ ↟

NEWTON AYCLIFFE   Map 08 NZ22

Oakleaf School Aycliffe Ln DL5 4EF
☎ 01325 310820
A parkland course in a country setting.
18 holes, 5732yds, Par 69, SSS 70.
Club membership 165.
Visitors dress code enforced and must contact in advance for weekends.
Societies apply in writing.
Green Fees not confirmed.

| Facilities & Leisure | squash. |
| Location | 6m N of Darlington, off A6072 |

| Hotel | ★★★★ 71% Redworth Hall Hotel & Country Club, REDWORTH ☎ 01388 772442 100 |

Woodham Golf & Country Club Burnhill Way DL5 4PN
☎ 01325 320574 Fax 01325 315254
Beautiful parkland course offering golfers a full and varied challenge with plenty of trees, numerous lakes and meandering streams.
18 holes, 6771yds, Par 73, SSS 72, Course record 68.
Club membership 694.

Visitors	must book in advance for weekends.
Societies	telephone or write in advance.
Green Fees	£20 per day; £15 per round (£24 per round weekends & bank holidays).
Prof	Ernie Wilson
Designer	James Hamilton Stutt
Facilities	⊗ ⅲ 🏌 🍺 🎾 🏠 🍴 👜 🚜 🛒 ∂
Location	Off A167

| Hotel | ★★★ 69% Eden Arms Swallow Hotel, RUSHYFORD ☎ 01388 720541 45 |

SEAHAM   Map 12 NZ44

Seaham Dawdon SR7 7RD
☎ 0191 581 2354 & 581 1268 (Sec)
Heathland links course with several holes affected by strong prevailing winds.
18 holes, 6017yds, Par 70, SSS 69, Course record 64.
Club membership 600.

Visitors	contact professional at all times, with member only weekends until 3.30pm.
Societies	must apply in advance.
Green Fees	not confirmed.
Prof	Glyn Jones
Facilities	⊗ by prior arrangement ⅲ by prior arrangement 🏌 🍺 🎾 🏠 🍴 ∂
Location	3m E of A19, exit for Seaham

| Hotel | ★★★★ 67% Swallow Hotel, Queen's Pde, Seaburn, SUNDERLAND ☎ 0191 529 2041 98 |

SEATON CAREW   Map 08 NZ52

Seaton Carew Tees Rd TS25 1DE
☎ 01429 261040 & 266249
A championship links course taking full advantage of its dunes, bents, whins and gorse. Renowned for its par 4 (17th); just enough fairway for an accurate drive followed by another precise shot to a pear-shaped, sloping green that is severely trapped.
The Old Course: 18 holes, 6604yds, Par 72, SSS 72.
Brabazon Course: 18 holes, 6849yds, Par 73, SSS 73.
Club membership 650.

Visitors	restricted until after 10am at weekends & bank holidays.
Societies	must apply in writing.
Green Fees	£29 per day (£40 weekends & bank holidays).
Prof	W Hector

Designer	McKenzie
Facilities	⊗ ⅲ 🏌 🍺 🎾 🏠 👜 🚜 ∂
Location	SE side of village off A178

| Hotel | ★★ 66% Ryedale Moor, 3 Beaconsfield St, Headland, HARTLEPOOL ☎ 01429 231436 16 |

SEDGEFIELD   Map 08 NZ32

Knotty Hill Golf Centre TS21 2BB
☎ 01740 620320 Fax 01740 622227
The 18-hole Princes course is set in rolling parkland with many holes routed through shallow valleys. Several holes are set wholly or partially within woodland and water hazards abound. Bishops Course, a new, challenging 18-hole course, is currently under construction; 9 holes were playable at time of going to press, the remaining 9 holes are scheduled to open i Autumn 1999.
Princes Course (A+B): 18 holes, 6577yds, Par 72, SSS 71.
B+C: 18 holes, 6150yds, Par 71, SSS 71.
C+A: 18 holes, 6577yds, Par 73, SSS 71.

Visitors	must telephone in advance for tee reservations.
Societies	package available on request.
Green Fees	Mon-Fri:£24 per 36 holes, £20 per 27 holes, £12 per 18 holes, £8 per 9 holes.
Prof	Nick Walton
Designer	C Stanton
Facilities	⊗ ⅲ 🏌 🍺 🎾 🏠 🍴 👜 🚜 ∂ ⌁
& Leisure	practice bunker, target golf.
Location	1m N of Sedgefield on A177, 2m from junct 60 on A1(M)

| Hotel | ★★★ 64% Hardwick Hall Hotel, SEDGEFIELD ☎ 01740 620253 17 |

STANLEY   Map 12 NZ15

South Moor The Middles, Craghead DH9 6AG
☎ 01207 232848 Fax 01207 284616
Moorland course with natural hazards designed by Dr Alistair McKenzie in 1926 and remains one the most challenging of its type in north east England. Out of bounds features on 11 holes from the tee and the testing par 5 12th hole is uphill and usually against a strong headwind.
18 holes, 6445yds, Par 72, SSS 71, Course record 66.
Club membership 650.

Visitors	must contact in advance but may only play Sun with member. Handicap certificate required.
Societies	apply in writing to Secretary.
Green Fees	£22 per day; £16 per round (£26 per day/round weekends & bank holidays).
Prof	Shaun Cowell
Designer	Dr Alistair Mackenzie
Facilities	⊗ ⅲ 🏌 🍺 🎾 🏠 🍴 🚜 ∂
Location	1.5m SE on B6313

| Hotel | ★★★ 66% Beamish Park Hotel, Beamish Burn Rd, MARLEY HILL ☎ 01207 230666 47 |

Entries with a shaded background
identify courses that are
considered to be particularly interesting

STOCKTON-ON-TEES   Map 08 NZ41

Norton Norton TS20 1SU ☎ 01642 676385
An interesting parkland course with long drives from the 7th
and 17th tees. Several water hazards.
18 holes, 5855yds, Par 70.
Visitors   no visiting party tee times booked on weekends.
Societies   apply in advance.
Green Fees   £9 per 18 holes (£10 weekends).
Cards   🖭 🏧 VISA 🏧 📇
Facilities   ⊗ ⅷ 🍴 🍺 ♀ 🏌
Location   At Norton 2m N off A19

Hotel   ★★★ 70% Parkmore Hotel, 636 Yarm Rd,
                  Eaglescliffe, STOCKTON-ON-TEES
                  ☎ 01642 786815 55 ⇄ 🐾

Teesside Acklam Rd, Thornaby TS17 7JS
☎ 01642 616516 & 673822 (pro) Fax 01642 676252
Flat parkland course, easy walking.
18 holes, 6535yds, Par 72, SSS 71, Course record 64.
Club membership 700.
Visitors   with member only weekdays after 4.30pm,
                  weekends after 11am.
Societies   must contact in writing.
Green Fees   £26 per day.
Prof   Ken Hall
Designer   Makepiece & Dr Somerville
Facilities   ⊗ ⅷ 🍴 🍺 ♀ 🏌 🏠 🏌
Location   1.5m SE on A1130, off A19 at Mandale
                  interchange

Hotel   B Posthouse Teesside, low Ln, Stainton Village,
                  Thornaby, STOCKTON-ON-TEES
                  ☎ 01642 591213 136 ⇄ 🐾

ESSEX

ABRIDGE   Map 05 TQ49

Abridge Golf and Country Club Epping Ln,
Stapleford Tawney RM4 1ST
☎ 01708 688396 Fax 01708 688550
A parkland course with easy walking. The quick drying
course is by no means easy to play. This has been the
venue of several professional tournaments. Abridge is a
Golf and Country Club and has all the attendant
facilities.
18 holes, 6692yds, Par 72, SSS 72, Course record 67.
Club membership 650.
Visitors   must have current handicap certificate,
                  contact in advance. Play with member only
                  at weekends.
Societies   telephone in advance.
Green Fees   not confirmed.
Prof   Stuart Layton
Designer   Henry Cotton
Facilities   ⊗ 🍴 🍺 ♀ 🏌 🏠 🏌 🏌 🏌 🏌 🏌
& Leisure   heated outdoor swimming pool, sauna.
Location   1.75m NE

Hotel   B Posthouse Epping, High Rd, Bell
                  Common, EPPING
                  ☎ 01992 573137 Annexe79 ⇄ 🐾

BASILDON   Map 05 TQ78

Basildon Clay Hill Ln, Kingswood SS16 5JP
☎ 01268 533297 Fax 01268 533849
Undulating municipal parkland course. Testing 13th hole
(par 4).
18 holes, 6236yds, Par 72, SSS 70.
Club membership 350.
Visitors   contact professional in advance 01268 533532.
Societies   may contact for details.
Green Fees   £9 per round (£15 weekends).
Prof   M Oliver
Designer   A Cotton
Facilities   ⊗ ⅷ by prior arrangement 🍺 🍺 ♀ 🏌 🏠 🏌
                  🏌 🏌
Location   1m S off A176

Hotel   B Posthouse Basildon, Cranes Farm Rd,
                  BASILDON ☎ 01268 533955 149 ⇄ 🐾

BENFLEET   Map 05 TQ78

Boyce Hill Vicarage Hill, South Benfleet SS7 1PD
☎ 01268 793625 & 752565
Hilly parkland course with good views.
18 holes, 5983yds, Par 68, SSS 68, Course record 61.
Club membership 700.
Visitors   must have a handicap certificate, must contact
                  24hrs in advance, may not play at weekends.
Societies   Thu only, book well in advance by telephone.
Green Fees   not confirmed.
Prof   Graham Burroughs
Designer   James Braid
Facilities   ⊗ ⅷ 🍴 🍺 ♀ 🏌 🏠 🏌 🏌
Location   0.75m NE of Benfleet Station

Hotel   B Posthouse Basildon, Cranes Farm Rd,
                  BASILDON ☎ 01268 533955 149 ⇄ 🐾

BILLERICAY   Map 05 TQ69

The Burstead Tye Common Rd, Little Burstead CM12 9SS
☎ 01277 631171 Fax 01277 632766
The Burstead is an attractive parkland course set amidst some
of the most attractive countryside in south Essex. It is an
excellent test of golf to players of all standards with the
greens showing maturity beyond their years. Challenging
holes include the Par 4 16th hole which at 348yds requires an
accurate tee shot to leave a second shot played over a lake
protecting an attractive contoured green. The 18th is the
longest hole on the course.
18 holes, 6275yds, Par 71, SSS 70, Course record 67.
Club membership 900.
Visitors   must have handicap certificate and may only
                  play weekdays.
Societies   apply in writing and/or telephone for
                  reservation.
Green Fees   not confirmed.
Cards   🖭 VISA 🏧
Prof   Keith Bridges
Designer   Patrick Tallack
Facilities   ⊗ ⅷ 🍴 🍺 ♀ 🏌 🏠 🏌 🏌 🏌

Hotel ★★★ 67% Chichester Hotel, Old London Rd, Wickford, BASILDON
☎ 01268 560555 2 ⇔ ↑ Annexe32 ⇔ ↑

Stock Brook Golf & Country Club Queens Park Av, Stock CM12 0SP ☎ 01277 653616 & 650400 Fax 01277 633063
Set in 250 acres of picturesque countryside the 27 holes comprise three undulating 9's, offering the challenge of water on a large number of holes. Any combination can be played, but the Stock and Brook courses make the 18-hole, 6750 yard championship course. There are extensive clubhouse facilities.
Stock & Brook Courses: 18 holes, 6728yds, Par 72, SSS 72, Course record 66.
Manor Course: 9 holes, 2997yds, Par 35.
Club membership 750.

Visitors handicap certificate required, must contact 24hrs in advance.
Societies apply in writing or telephone.
Green Fees £25 per day (incl £2.50 towards lunch) (£30 per round weekends).
Cards ⎯ 🟦 🟥 🟩
Prof Kevin Merry
Designer Martin Gillet
Facilities ⊗ ⍢ ﹣ ♨ ♀ 🏊 🏠 🍴 🛄 ⌀ ⎰
& Leisure tennis courts, heated outdoor swimming pool, sauna, gymnasium.

Hotel ★★★ 66% The Heybridge Hotel, Roman Rd, INGATESTONE ☎ 01277 355355 22 ⇔ ↑

BRAINTREE   Map 05 TL72

Braintree Kings Ln, Stisted CM7 8DA
☎ 01376 346079 Fax 01376 334117
Parkland course with many unique mature trees. Good par 3s with the 14th -'Devils Lair'-regarded as one of the best in the county.
18 holes, 6174yds, Par 70, SSS 69, Course record 65.
Club membership 750.
Visitors weekdays only, contact the pro shop in advance 01376 343465.
Societies society days Wed & Thu early booking advised.
Green Fees £30 per day; £20 per round.
Prof Tony Parcell
Designer Hawtree
Facilities ⊗ ⍢ ﹣ ♨ ♀ 🏊 🏠 🛄 ⎰ ⌀
Location 1m E, off A120

Hotel ★★★ 62% White Hart Hotel, Bocking End, BRAINTREE ☎ 01376 321401 31 ⇔ ↑

Towerlands Panfield Rd CM7 5BJ
☎ 01376 326802 Fax 01376 552487
Undulating, grassland course. Driving range and sports hall.
9 holes, 2749yds, Par 34, SSS 66.
Club membership 300.
Visitors must not play before 12.30pm weekends. Correct dress at all times.
Societies must contact in advance by telephone.
Green Fees not confirmed.
Designer G Shiels
Facilities ⊗ ⍢ ﹣ ♨ ♀ 🏊 🏠 🍴 ⌀ ⎰
& Leisure squash.
Location On B1053

Hotel ★★★ 62% White Hart Hotel, Bocking End, BRAINTREE ☎ 01376 321401 31 ⇔ ↑

BRENTWOOD   Map 05 TQ59

Bentley Ongar Rd CM15 9SS
☎ 01277 373179 Fax 01277 375097
Parkland course with water hazards.
18 holes, 6709yds, Par 72, SSS 72.
Club membership 600.
Visitors should contact in advance, may not play at weekends.
Societies must write or telephone in advance.
Green Fees not confirmed.
Prof Nick Garrett
Designer Alec Swann
Facilities ﹣ ♨ ♀ 🏊 🏠 ⌀
Location 3m NW on A128

Hotel B Posthouse Brentwood, Brook St, BRENTWOOD ☎ 01277 260260 145 ⇔ ↑

Hartswood King George's Playing Fields, Ingrave Rd CM14 5AE ☎ 01277 218850 & 214830
Municipal parkland course, easy walking.
18 holes, 5648yds, Par 70, SSS 69, Course record 64.
Club membership 500.
Visitors pre-booking usually essential am.
Societies weekdays only, must contact in advance.
Green Fees £9 (£13 weekends).
Cards ⎯ 🟦 🟥 🟩
Prof Stephan Cole
Facilities ⊗ ﹣ ♨ ♀ 🏊 🏠 🍴 ⌀
Location 0.75m SE on A128

Hotel B Posthouse Brentwood, Brook St, BRENTWOOD ☎ 01277 260260 145 ⇔ ↑

Warley Park Magpie Ln, Little Warley CM13 3DX
☎ 01277 224891 Fax 01277 200679
Parkland course with reasonable walking. Numerous water hazards. There is also a golf-practice ground.
1st & 2nd: 18 holes, 5967yds, Par 69, SSS 68, Course record 67.
1st & 3rd: 18 holes, 6232yds, Par 71, SSS 69, Course record 65.
2nd & 3rd: 18 holes, 6223yds, Par 70, SSS 69, Course record 70.
Club membership 800.
Visitors must have handicap certificate and contact in advance. May not play at weekends.
Societies telephone in advance for provisional booking.
Green Fees £36 per day; £25 per round. ▶

Cards ⎯ 💳 ∅
Prof Jason Groat
Designer Reg Plumbridge
Facilities ⊗ 🏌 🍴 ♀ 🏖 🍺 🐚 🚾 ✐ ♨
Location 0.5m N off junct 29 of M25/A127

Hotel B Posthouse Brentwood, Brook St,
BRENTWOOD ☎ 01277 260260 145 ⇄ ♟

Weald Park Coxtie Green Rd, South Weald CM14 5RJ
☎ 01277 375101 Fax 01277 374888
Tranquil parkland course with many mature oak trees, lakes, ponds and plentiful wildlife. The undulating terrain and the numerous hedges and ponds make this par 71 course a fair test of golf for all abilities.
18 holes, 6612yds, Par 71, SSS 70, Course record 65.
Club membership 570.
Visitors telephone booking preferable, no weekday restrictions
Societies apply in writing or telephone for package.
Green Fees £16 per round (£20 weekends).
Cards ⎯ 💳 📠 🏧 ∅
Prof Ian Parker
Designer Reg Plumbridge
Facilities ⊗ 🏌 🍴 ♀ 🏖 🍺 🚾 ✐
Location 3m from M25

Hotel ★★★★ 71% Marygreen Manor, London Rd,
BRENTWOOD
☎ 01277 225252 3 ⇄ ♟ Annexe40 ⇄ ♟

BULPHAN   Map 05 TQ68

Langdon Hills Golf Centre Lower Dunton Rd RM14 3TY
☎ 01268 548444 Fax 01268 490084
Well situated with the Langdon Hills on one side and dramatic views across London on the other, the Centre offers an interchangeable 27 hole course, a floodlit 22-bay driving range and three academy holes.
Langdon Course: 9 holes, 3132yds, Par 35, SSS 71.
Horndon Course: 9 holes, 3054yds, Par 36, SSS 70.
Bulpman Course: 9 holes, 3054yds, Par 36, SSS 70.
Club membership 600.
Visitors preference given to members on weekend mornings.
Societies apply in writing or telephone.
Green Fees not confirmed.
Facilities ⊗ 🏌 🍴 ♀ 🏖 🍺 ⚑ 🥤 🐚 🚾 ✐ ♨
Location Between A13 & A127 N of A128 S of Basildon

Hotel ★★★★ 71% Marygreen Manor, London Rd,
BRENTWOOD
☎ 01277 225252 3 ⇄ ♟ Annexe40 ⇄ ♟

BURNHAM-ON-CROUCH   Map 05 TQ99

Burnham-on-Crouch Ferry Rd, Creeksea CM0 8PQ
☎ 01621 782282 Fax 01621 784489
Undulating meadowland course, easy walking, windy.
18 holes, 6056yds, Par 70, SSS 69, Course record 66.
Club membership 586.
Visitors welcome weekdays. Must play with member at weekends.
Societies apply in writing or telephone.
Green Fees £22 per day (weekdays only).
Cards ⎯ 💳

Designer Swan
Facilities ⊗ 🏌 🍴 ♀ 🏖 🍺 🐚 🚾 ✐
Location 1.25m W off B1010

CANEWDON   Map 05 TQ99

Ballards Gore Gore Rd SS4 2DA
☎ 01702 258917 Fax 01702 258571
A parkland course with several lakes.
18 holes, 7062yds, Par 73, SSS 74, Course record 69.
Club membership 500.
Visitors may not play at weekends.
Societies weekdays only, apply in advance.
Green Fees £25 per day; £20 per round.
Cards ⎯ 💳
Prof Richard Emery
Facilities ⊗ 🏌 🍴 ♀ 🏖 🍺 🚾 ✐
Location 2m NE of Rochford

Hotel ★★★ 68% Hotel Renouf, Bradley Way,
ROCHFORD ☎ 01702 541334 24 ⇄ ♟

CANVEY ISLAND   Map 05 TQ78

Castle Point Somnes Av SS8 9FG ☎ 01268 510830
A flat seaside links and part parkland course with water hazards on 13 holes and views of the estuary and Hadleigh Castle. Always a test for any golfer when the wind starts to blow.
18 holes, 6176yds, Par 71, SSS 69, Course record 69.
Club membership 275.
Visitors must book for weekends.
Societies phone or write for details.
Green Fees £9.50 per round (£13.50 weekends).
Prof Michael Utteridge
Facilities 🏖 🍺 ⚑ 🚾 ✐ ♨
Location SE of Basildon, A130 to Canvey Island

Hotel ★★★ 67% Chichester Hotel, Old London Rd,
Wickford, BASILDON
☎ 01268 560555 2 ⇄ ♟ Annexe32 ⇄ ♟

CHELMSFORD   Map 05 TL70

Channels Belstead Farm Ln, Little Waltham CM3 3PT
☎ 01245 440005 Fax 01245 442032
The Channels course is built on land from reclaimed gravel pits, 18 very exciting holes with plenty of lakes providing an excellent test of golf. Belsteads a nine hole course is mainly flat but has 3 holes where water has to be negotiated.
Channels Course: 18 holes, 6300yds, Par 71, SSS 71, Course record 67.
Belsteads: 9 holes, 2467yds, Par 34, SSS 32.
Club membership 650.
Visitors Channels Course; must contact in advance and may only play with member at weekends. Belsteads Course; available anytime.
Societies telephone starter on 01245 443311.
Green Fees Channels: £35 per day; £20 per round. Belsteads: £18 per 18 holes; £12 per 9 holes.
Cards ⎯ 💳 🏧 ∅
Prof Ian Sinclair
Designer Cotton & Swan
Facilities ⊗ 🏌 🍴 ♀ 🏖 🍺 🐚 🚾 ✐ ♨
& Leisure fishing.
Location 2m NE on A130

Hotel   ★★★ 67% County Hotel, Rainsford Rd, CHELMSFORD
☎ 01245 491911   28 ⇌ ℉ Annexe8 ⇌ ℉

Chelmsford Widford Rd CM2 9AP
☎ 01245 256483 Fax 01245 256483
An undulating parkland course, hilly in parts, with 3 holes in woods and four difficult par 4's. From the reconstructed clubhouse there are fine views over the course and the wooded hills beyond.
18 holes, 5981yds, Par 68, SSS 69, Course record 66.
Club membership 650.

Visitors   must contact in advance. Society days Wed/Thu, Ladies Day Tue. With member only at weekends.
Societies   must contact in advance.
Green Fees £36 per day; £27 per round.
Cards   ▭ ▬
Prof   Mark Welch
Designer   Tom Dunn
Facilities   ⊗ by prior arrangement ▙ ♥ ♀ ⚲ 🏠 ❧ 🛺 ∅
Location   1.5m S of town centre off A12

Hotel   ★★★★ 67% Pontlands Park Country Hotel, West Hanningfield Rd, Great Baddow, CHELMSFORD
☎ 01245 476444   17 ⇌ ℉

CHIGWELL   Map 05 TQ49

Chigwell High Rd IG7 5BH
☎ 0181 500 2059 Fax 0181 501 3410
A course of high quality, mixing meadowland with parkland. For those who believe 'all Essex is flat' the undulating nature of Chigwell will be a refreshing surprise. The greens are excellent and the fairways tight with mature trees.
18 holes, 6279yds, Par 71, SSS 70, Course record 66.
Club membership 670.

Visitors   must contact in advance & have handicap certificate, but must be accompanied by member at weekends.
Societies   recognised societies welcome by prior arrangement.
Green Fees not confirmed.
Prof   Ray Beard
Designer   Hawtree/Taylor
Facilities   ⊗ ▥ by prior arrangement ▙ ♥ ♀ ⚲ 🏠 ∅
Location   0.5m S on A113

Hotel   ★★ 68% Roebuck Hotel, North End, BUCKHURST HILL
☎ 0181 505 4636 29 ⇌ ℉

CHIGWELL ROW   Map 05 TQ49

Hainault Forest Romford Rd, Chigwell Row IG7 4QW
☎ 0181 500 2131 Fax 0181 501 5196
Club playing over Borough of Redbridge public courses; hilly parkland subject to wind. Two courses, driving range.
No 1 Course: 18 holes, 5687yds, Par 70, SSS 67, Course record 65.
No 2 Course: 18 holes, 6238yds, Par 71, SSS 71.

Club membership 600.
Visitors   no restrictions.
Societies   must contact in writing.
Green Fees not confirmed.
Prof   Chris Hope
Designer   Taylor & Hawtree
Facilities   ⊗ ▙ ♥ ♀ ⚲ 🏠 ❧ 🛺 ∅
Location   0.5m S on A1112

Hotel   ★★★ 66% County Hotel Epping Forest, Oak Hill, WOODFORD GREEN
☎ 0181 787 9988 99 ⇌ ℉

CLACTON-ON-SEA   Map 05 TM11

Clacton West Rd CO15 1AJ
☎ 01255 421919 Fax 01255 424602
Windy, seaside course.
18 holes, 6494yds, Par 71, SSS 69.
Club membership 650.

Visitors   must contact in advance.
Societies   must contact in writing.
Green Fees not confirmed.
Prof   S J Levermore
Facilities   ⚲ 🏠 ❧ 🛺 ∅
Location   1.25m SW of town centre

Hotel   ★★ 71% Maplin Hotel, Esplanade, FRINTON-ON-SEA
☎ 01255 673832 11rm(10 ⇌ ℉)

COLCHESTER   Map 05 TL92

Birch Grove Layer Rd, Kingsford CO2 0HS
☎ 01206 734276
A pretty, undulating course surrounded by woodland - small but challenging with excellent greens. Challenging 6th hole cut through woodland with water hazards and out of bounds.
9 holes, 4038yds, Par 62, SSS 60, Course record 58.
Club membership 250.

Visitors   restricted Sun mornings.
Societies   apply in writing or telephone.
Green Fees £15 per day; £12 per 18 holes; £8 per 9 holes.
Facilities   ⊗ ▥ ▙ ♥ ♀ ⚲ 🏠 ∅
Location   2.5m S on B1026

Hotel   ★★★ 70% George Hotel, 116 High St, COLCHESTER ☎ 01206 578494   48 ⇌ ℉

Colchester Braiswick CO4 5AU
☎ 01206 853396 Fax 01206 852698
A fairly flat, yet scenic, parkland course with tree-lined fairways and small copses. Mainly level walking.
18 holes, 6307yds, Par 70, SSS 70, Course record 64.
Club membership 700.

Visitors   by prior arrangement.
Societies   apply in writing or by telephone, Mon, Thu & Fri only.
Green Fees £20 per round (£30 per weekends).
Prof   Mark Angel
Designer   James Braid
Facilities   ⊗ ▥ by prior arrangement ▙ ♥ ♀ ⚲ 🏠 ∅ ℓ
Location   1.5m NW of town centre on B1508

Hotel   ★★★ 70% George Hotel, 116 High St, COLCHESTER ☎ 01206 578494   48 ⇌ ℉

Colchester & Lexden Golf Centre Bakers Ln CD3 4AU
☎ 01206 843333 Fax 01206 854775
New 18-hole course within easy reach of the town centre.
Also a 9-hole pitch and putt course, and a floodlit driving
range.
18 holes, 5500yds, Par 67.
Club membership 500.

Visitors	welcome.
Societies	telephone for details.
Green Fees	£15 (£17 weekends).
Cards	▭ 🟦 ▭ ▭ 🟢
Prof	Phil Grice
Designer	J Johnson
Facilities	⊗ ⵏ ⅋ 🝚 ♀ ⚖ 🏠 🕈 ♂ ⚑
& Leisure	9 hole par 3.
Location	Adjacent to A12. Take Colchester Central from A12 and then follow tourist signs

Hotel ★★★ 68% Marks Tey Hotel, London Rd,
Marks Tey, COLCHESTER
☎ 01206 210001 110 ⇥ ☏

Stoke-by-Nayland Keepers Ln, Leavenheath CO6 4PZ
☎ 01206 262836 Fax 01206 263356
Two undulating courses (Gainsborough and Constable)
situated in Dedham Vale. Some water hazards and hedges.
On Gainsborough the 10th (par 4) takes 2 shots over a lake;
very testing par 3 at 11th.
Gainsborough Course: 18 holes, 6581yds, Par 72, SSS 71,
Course record 63.
Constable Course: 18 holes, 6544yds, Par 72, SSS 71,
Course record 67.
Club membership 1360.

Visitors	write or telephone for details.
Societies	write or telephone for brochures and booking forms.
Green Fees	not confirmed.
Prof	Kevin Lovelock
Facilities	⊗ ⅋ 🝚 ♀ ⚖ 🏠 ♂ ⚑
& Leisure	fishing.
Location	1.5m NW of Stoke-by-Nayland on B1068

Hotel ★★★🏖 Maison Talbooth, Stratford Rd,
DEDHAM ☎ 01206 322367 10 ⇥ ☏

EARLS COLNE   Map 05 TL82

Colne Valley Station Rd CO6 2LT
☎ 01787 224233 Fax 01787 224126
An 18-hole course along the valley of the River Colne.
Opened in 1991.
18 holes, 6301yds, Par 70, SSS 70, Course record 68.
Club membership 600.

Visitors	only after 10.30am at weekends, must dress correctly, no sharing of clubs. Must contact in advance.
Societies	apply in writing, minimum of 12 persons.
Green Fees	not confirmed.
Prof	Scott Clark
Designer	Howard Swan
Facilities	⊗ ⵏ ⅋ 🝚 ♀ ⚖ 🏠 ♂ ⚑
& Leisure	sauna.
Location	Off A604

Hotel ★★★ 68% Marks Tey Hotel, London Rd,
Marks Tey, COLCHESTER
☎ 01206 210001 110 ⇥ ☏

Essex Golf & Country Club CO6 2NS
☎ 01787 224466 Fax 01787 224410
Created on the site of a World War II airfield, this
challenging course contains 12 lakes. Also 9-hole course as
well as a variety of leisure facilities.
County Course: 18 holes, 6982yds, Par 73, SSS 73, Course
record 67.
Garden Course: 9 holes, 2190yds, Par 34, SSS 34.
Club membership 600.

Visitors	contact golf reception for bookings up to 1 week in advance.
Societies	apply in writing to the Functions Manager.
Green Fees	Country Course £20 per round (£25 weekends); Garden Course £15 per 18 holes; £10 per 9 holes.
Cards	▭ 🟦 ▭ ▭ 🟢
Prof	Mark Spooner
Designer	Reg Plumbridge
Facilities	⊗ ⵏ ⅋ 🝚 ♀ ⚖ 🏠 🕈 ♂ 🏹 ⚑
& Leisure	hard tennis courts, heated indoor swimming pool, fishing, sauna, solarium, gymnasium, indoor practice bunker, video teaching studio, injury clinic.
Location	Off the A120 onto the B1024

Hotel ★★★ 68% Marks Tey Hotel, London Rd,
Marks Tey, COLCHESTER
☎ 01206 210001 110 ⇥ ☏

EPPING   Map 05 TL40

Nazeing Middle St, Nazeing EN9 2LW
☎ 01992 893798 Fax 01992 893882
Parkland course built with American sand based greens and
tees and five strategically placed lakes. One of the most
notable holes is the difficult par 3 13th with out of bounds
and a large lake coming into play.
18 holes, 6598yds, Par 72, SSS 71, Course record 68.
Club membership 400.

Visitors	not compulsory to contact except for weekends when pm only available.
Societies	prior arrangement required in writing.
Green Fees	£20 Tue-Fri; £16 Mon (£28 weekends after 12.30pm).
Cards	▭ 🟦 ▭ ▭ 🟢
Prof	Robert Green
Designer	M Gillete
Facilities	⊗ ⵏ ⅋ 🝚 ♀ ⚖ 🏠 🕈 ♂ ⚑
Location	Just outside Waltham Abbey

Hotel ★★★ 64% Harlow Moat House, Southern
Way, HARLOW ☎ 01279 829988 119 ⇥ ☏

FRINTON-ON-SEA   Map 05 TM22

Frinton 1 The Esplanade CO13 9EP
☎ 01255 674618 Fax 01255 674618
Deceptive, flat seaside links course providing fast, firm and
undulating greens that will test the best putters and tidal
ditches that cross many of the fairways, requiring careful
placement of shots. Its open character means that every shot
has to be evaluated with both wind strength and direction in
mind. Easy walking.
Long Course: 18 holes, 6265yds, Par 71, SSS 70, Course
record 64.
Short Course: 9 holes, 1367yds, Par 58.
Club membership 850.

Visitors	must contact in advance.
Societies	by arrangement, apply in writing to the secretary, Wed, Thu and some Fri.
Green Fees	£25 per round.
Prof	Peter Taggart
Designer	Willy Park Jnr
Facilities	⊗ ⍬ by prior arrangement ⌾ ⬛ ♀ ♨ 🏠 ↑ ⬥ ⚘ ⚲
& Leisure	Snooker.
Location	SW side of town centre

Hotel ★★ 71% Maplin Hotel, Esplanade, FRINTON-ON-SEA ☎ 01255 673832 11rm(10 ⇆ ☏)

GOSFIELD — Map 05 TL72

Gosfield Lake The Manor House, Hall Dr CO9 1SE
☎ 01787 474747 Fax 01787 476044
Parkland course with bunkers, lakes and water hazards. Designed by Sir Henry Cotton/Mr Howard Swan and opened in 1988. Also 9-hole course; ideal for beginners and improvers.
Lakes Course: 18 holes, 6615yds, Par 72, SSS 72.
Meadows Course: 9 holes, 4180yds, Par 66, SSS 63.
Club membership 650.

Visitors	Lakes Course: must contact in advance, handicap certificate required, Sat & Sun from noon only. Meadows Course: restricted during competitions, handicap certificate not required, advisable to contact.
Societies	welcome Mon-Fri by arrangement, telephone or write.
Green Fees	not confirmed.
Prof	Richard Wheeler
Designer	Henry Cotton/Howard Swan
Facilities	⊗ ⍬ ⌾ ⬛ ♀ ♨ 🏠 ⬥ ⚘ ⚲
& Leisure	sauna.
Location	1m W of Gosfield off B1017

Hotel ★★★ 62% White Hart Hotel, Bocking End, BRAINTREE ☎ 01376 321401 31 ⇆ ☏

HARLOW — Map 05 TL40

Canons Brook Elizabeth Way CM19 5BE
☎ 01279 421482 Fax 01279 626393
Challenging parkland course designed by Henry Cotton in 1963. Accuracy is the key requiring straight driving from the tees, especially on the par 5 11th to fly a gap with out of bounds left and right before setting up the shot to the green.
18 holes, 6800yds, Par 73, SSS 72, Course record 65.
Club membership 850.

Visitors	may not play at weekends.
Societies	welcome Mon, Wed and Fri, must book in advance by telephone.
Green Fees	£23 per round.
Prof	Alan McGinn
Designer	Henry Cotton
Facilities	⊗ ⍬ ⌾ ⬛ ♀ ♨ 🏠 ↑ ⚘ ⚲
Location	3m NW of junct 7 on M11

Hotel ★★★ 73% Swallow Churchgate Hotel, Churchgate St Village, Old Harlow, HARLOW ☎ 01279 420246 85 ⇆ ☏

North Weald Rayley Ln, North Weald CM16 6AR
☎ 01992 522118 Fax 01992 522881
Although only opened in November 1995, the blend of lakes and meadowland give this testing course an air of maturity.
18 holes, 6052yds, Par 71, SSS 70, Course record 66.
Club membership 500.

Visitors	must contact in advance, limited at weekends.
Societies	contact in advance.
Green Fees	£20 (£27.50 weekends).
Cards	▦
Prof	Michael Janes
Facilities	⊗ ⌾ ⬛ ♀ ♨ 🏠 ⬥ ⚘ ⚲ ⚲
Location	M11 exit 7,off A414 towards Chipping Ongar

Hotel ★★★ 64% Harlow Moat House, Southern Way, HARLOW ☎ 01279 829988 119 ⇆ ☏

HARWICH — Map 05 TM23

Harwich & Dovercourt Station Rd, Parkeston CO12 4NZ
☎ 01255 503616 Fax 01255 503323
Flat parkland course with easy walking.
9 holes, 5900yds, Par 70, SSS 69, Course record 58.
Club membership 420.

Visitors	visitors with handicap certificate may play by prior arrangement, with member only at weekends.
Societies	prior arrangement essential.
Green Fees	£17 per 18 holes; £8.50 per 9 holes.
Facilities	⊗ ⌾ ⬛ ♀ ♨ 🏠 ⚘ ⚲
Location	Off A120 near Ferry Terminal

Hotel ★★ 72% The Pier at Harwich, The Quay, HARWICH ☎ 01255 241212 6 ⇆

INGRAVE — Map 05 TQ69

Thorndon Park CM13 3RH
☎ 01277 811666 Fax 01277 810645
Among the best of the Essex courses with a fine new purpose-built clubhouse and a lake. The springy turf is easy on the feet. Many newly planted young trees now replace the famous old oaks that were such a feature of this course.
18 holes, 6492yds, Par 71, SSS 71.
Club membership 670.

Visitors	must contact in advance, at weekends with member only.
Societies	welcome Tue and Fri but must apply in writing.
Green Fees	£50 per day; £35 per round.
Prof	Brian White
Designer	Colt/Alison
Facilities	♨ 🏠 ↑ ⚲
Location	W side of village off A128

Hotel B Posthouse Brentwood, Brook St, BRENTWOOD ☎ 01277 260260 145 ⇆ ☏

LOUGHTON — Map 05 TQ49

High Beech Wellington Hill IG10 4AH ☎ 0181 508 7323
Short 9-hole course set in Epping Forest.
9 holes, 1477, Par 27, Course record 25 or 9 holes, 847, Par 27. ▶

Visitors welcome.
Green Fees not confirmed.
Prof Clark Baker
Facilities 🏠 ⛏ ⚲
Location Close to M25 Waltham Abbey junct

Loughton Clays Ln, Debden Green IG10 2RZ
☎ 0181 502 2923
Hilly 9-hole parkland course on the edge of Epping Forest.
9 holes, 4652yds, Par 66, SSS 63, Course record 65.
Club membership 180.
Visitors must contact in advance.
Societies telephone in advance.
Green Fees £8.50 per 18 holes; £6 per 9 holes (£10.50/£7 weekends & bank holidays).
Prof Richard Layton
Facilities 🏌 🍴 ♟ ♨ 🏠 ⛏ ⚲
Location 1.5m SE of Theydon Bois

Hotel B Posthouse Epping, High Rd, Bell Common, EPPING ☎ 01992 573137 Annexe79 ⇌ ♗

MALDON Map 05 TL80

Forrester Park Beckingham Rd, Great Totham CM9 8EA
☎ 01621 891406 Fax 01621 891406
Tight, undulating parkland course with tree-lined fairways and good views over the Blackwater estuary. Easy walking. Attractive 16th-century clubhouse.
18 holes, 6073yds, Par 71, SSS 69, Course record 69.
Club membership 1000.
Visitors must contact in advance but may not play before noon weekends & bank holidays.
Societies must apply in advance.
Green Fees £23 per day; £18 per round (£20 per round weekends).
Cards 💳 💳 💳
Prof Gary Pike
Designer T R Forrester-Muir
Facilities ⊗ 🍴 🏌 ♟ 🍴 ♨ ♨ 🏠 🚗 ⚲
& Leisure hard tennis courts.
Location 3m NE of Maldon off B1022

Hotel ★★★★ 67% Pontlands Park Country Hotel, West Hanningfield Rd, Great Baddow, CHELMSFORD ☎ 01245 476444 17 ⇌ ♗

Maldon Beeleigh, Langford CM9 6LL ☎ 01621 853212
Flat, parkland course in a triangle of land bounded by the River Chelmer, the Blackwater Canal and an old railway embankment. Alternate tees on 2nd nine holes. Testing par 3 14th (166yds) demanding particular accuracy to narrow green guarded by bunkers and large trees.
9 holes, 6253yds, Par 71, SSS 70, Course record 71.
Club membership 380.
Visitors telephone to check availability, may only play with member at weekends. Handicap certificate required.
Societies intially telephone then confirm in writing.
Green Fees £20 per day; £15 per round (Mon-Fri).
Designer Thompson of Felixstowe
Facilities ⊗ 🍴 by prior arrangement 🏌 ♟ ♨ 🏠
Location 1m NW off B1019

Hotel ★★★★ 67% Pontlands Park Country Hotel, West Hanningfield Rd, Great Baddow, CHELMSFORD ☎ 01245 476444 17 ⇌ ♗

ORSETT Map 05 TQ68

Orsett Brentwood Rd RM16 3DS
☎ 01375 891352 Fax 01375 892471
A very good test of golf - this heathland course with its sandy soil is quick drying and provides easy walking. Close to the Thames estuary it is seldom calm and the main hazards are the prevailing wind and thick gorse. Any slight deviation can be exaggerated by the wind and a lost ball in the gorse results. The clubhouse has been modernised.
18 holes, 6614yds, Par 72, SSS 72, Course record 68.
Club membership 750.
Visitors restricted weekends & bank holidays. Must contact in advance and have a handicap certificate.
Societies must contact in advance.
Green Fees not confirmed.
Prof Paul Joiner
Designer James Braid
Facilities ⊗ 🍴 🏌 ♟ ♨ 🏠 🚗 ⚲
Location At junct of A13 off A128

Hotel B Posthouse Basildon, Cranes Farm Rd, BASILDON ☎ 01268 533955 149 ⇌ ♗

PURLEIGH Map 05 TL80

Three Rivers Stow Rd CM3 6RR
☎ 01621 828631 Fax 01621 828060
Set in 265 acres of landscaped wooded parkland, Three Rivers is a fully matured 18-hole course affording good valley views over the Crouch, Blackwater and Roach rivers that give the course its name. With ponds and dog-legs among the challenges it is ideal for beginners and seasoned golfers who have the opportunity to improve their short game.
Kings Course: 18 holes, 6536yds, Par 73, SSS 71.
Jubilee Course: 18 holes, 4800yds, Par 65.
Club membership 800.
Visitors telephone before visit.
Societies apply in writing or telephone.
Green Fees not confirmed.
Cards 💳 💳 💳 💳 💳
Prof Pat O'Connor
Designer Hawtree
Facilities ⊗ 🍴 🏌 ♟ 🍴 ♨ 🏠 ⛏ 🚗 🚗 ⚲ ♘
& Leisure hard tennis courts, squash.
Location 1m from Purleigh on B1012

Hotel ★★★★ 67% Pontlands Park Country Hotel, West Hanningfield Rd, Great Baddow, CHELMSFORD ☎ 01245 476444 17 ⇌ ♗

ROCHFORD Map 05 TQ89

Rochford Hundred Hall Rd SS4 1NW
☎ 01702 544302 Fax 01702 541343
Parkland course with ponds and ditches as natural hazards.
18 holes, 6292yds, Par 72, SSS 70, Course record 64.
Club membership 800.
Visitors must have handicap certificate. Visitors may not play Tue morning (Ladies) or Sun without a member.
Societies must contact in writing.
Green Fees £30 per day.

Prof	Graham Hill
Designer	James Braid
Facilities	⊗ 🏌 ▆ ♀ ♨ 🍴 🛒 ✎
Location	W on B1013

| Hotel | ★★★ 68% Hotel Renouf, Bradley Way, ROCHFORD ☎ 01702 541334 24 ⇔ 🐾 |

SAFFRON WALDEN — Map 05 TL53

Saffron Walden Windmill Hill CB10 1BX
☎ 01799 522786 Fax 01799 522786
Undulating parkland course, beautiful views.
18 holes, 6606yds, Par 72, SSS 72, Course record 63.
Club membership 950.

Visitors	must contact in advance and have a handicap certificate. With member only at weekends.
Societies	must contact in advance.
Green Fees	£30 per day/round.
Prof	Philip Davis
Facilities	⊗ 🏌 ▆ ▆ ♀ ♨ 🍴 🐾 🛒 ✎ ♪
Location	NW side of town centre off B184

| Hotel | ★★ 67% The Crown House, GREAT CHESTERFORD ☎ 01799 530515 8 ⇔ 🐾 Annexe10 ⇔ 🐾 |

SOUTHEND-ON-SEA — Map 05 TQ88

Belfairs Eastwood Rd North, Leigh on Sea SS9 4LR
☎ 01702 525345
Municipal parkland course run by the Borough Council.
Tight second half through thick woods, easy walking.
18 holes, 5840yds, Par 70, SSS 68, Course record 68.
Club membership 350.

Visitors	contact for booking, correct dress code must be adhered to.
Societies	contact 01702 610455.
Green Fees	not confirmed.
Prof	Martin Foreman
Designer	H S Colt
Facilities	⊗ 🏌 ▆ ▆ 🍴 🐾 ✎
& Leisure	hard tennis courts.
Location	3m W, N of A13

| Hotel | ★★★ 64% Balmoral Hotel, 34 Valkyrie Rd, Westcliffe-on-Sea, SOUTHEND-ON-SEA ☎ 01702 342947 29 ⇔ 🐾 |

Thorpe Hall Thorpe Hall Av, Thorpe Bay SS1 3AT
☎ 01702 582205
Parkland course with narrow fairways where placement rather than length is essential.
18 holes, 6286yds, Par 71, SSS 71, Course record 64.
Club membership 995.

Visitors	must contact in advance, with member only weekends & bank holidays.
Societies	apply in writing, only a certain number a year.
Green Fees	£30 per day/round.
Cards	▬ 💳
Prof	Bill McColl
Facilities	⊗ 🏌 ▆ ▆ ♀ ♨ 🍴 🐾 🛒 ✎
& Leisure	squash, sauna, snooker room.
Location	2m E off A13

| Hotel | ★★★ 64% Balmoral Hotel, 34 Valkyrie Rd, Westcliffe-on-Sea, SOUTHEND-ON-SEA ☎ 01702 342947 29 ⇔ 🐾 |

SOUTH OCKENDON — Map 05 TQ58

Belhus Park Belhus Park RM15 4PX
☎ 01708 854260 Fax 01708 851952
A well established 18 hole course set in beautiful parkland.
18 holes, 5255yds, Par 68, SSS 68, Course record 63.
Club membership 200.

Visitors	no restrictions. Must have proper golf shoes and shirts to be worn at all times. Booking advisable at weekends.
Societies	contact in writing or telephone
Green Fees	£9 per round (£13.50 weekends), Day ticket available weekdays.
Prof	Gary Lunn
Designer	Capability Brown
Facilities	⊗ 🏌 ▆ ▆ ♀ ♨ 🍴 🐾 ✎ ♪ ♪
& Leisure	heated indoor swimming pool, solarium, gymnasium.
Location	Off the B1335, 10mins from Lakeside Shopping Centre

| Hotel | ★★★ 69% Lakeside Moat House, High Rd, North Stifford, GRAYS ☎ 01708 719988 97 ⇔ 🐾 |

Top Meadow Fen Ln, North Ockendon RM14 3PR
☎ 01708 852239
Set in the Essex countryside with a panoramic view of the area. Some holes are very difficult with the variable wind directions, especially 1st, 6th, 7th and 13th.
Top Meadow: 18 holes, 6348yds, Par 72, SSS 71, Course record 68.
Club membership 600.

Visitors	welcome Mon-Fri.
Societies	telephone in advance.
Green Fees	not confirmed.
Prof	Paul King/Kevin Smith
Designer	Burns/Stock
Facilities	⊗ 🏌 ▆ ▆ ♀ ♨ 🍴 🐾 🐎 🐾 🛒 ✎ ♪
& Leisure	fishing.

| Hotel | B Travelodge, EAST HORNDON ☎ 01277 810819 22 ⇔ 🐾 |

STANFORD-LE-HOPE — Map 05 TQ68

St Clere's Hall London Rd SS17 0LX
☎ 01375 361565 Fax 01375 361565
All year round golf with views of the Thames, with several challenging par 3's, notably the 223 yard 13th.
18 holes, 6474yds, Par 72, SSS 71, Course record 71.
Club membership 460.

Visitors	welcome after 9.30am Mon-Fri, and 10am Sat &Sun. Telephone for times.
Societies	welcome Mon, Tue and Thu, telephone for details.
Green Fees	£15 per 18 holes; £7.50 per 9 holes (£20/£10 weekends).
Cards	▬ 💳 💳
Prof	David Wood
Designer	A Stiff
Facilities	⊗ 🏌 ▆ ▆ ♀ ♨ 🍴 🐾 🛒 ✎ ♪
Location	5m from M25 E of London on A13, take Stanford turn off in direction Linford, St Clere on the left

| Hotel | ★★★ 69% Lakeside Moat House, High Rd, North Stifford, GRAYS ☎ 01708 719988 97 ⇔ 🐾 |

STAPLEFORD ABBOTTS   Map 05 TQ59

Stapleford Abbotts Horsemanside, Tysea Hill RM4 1JU
☎ 01708 381108 Fax 01708 386345
Abbotts course, provides a challenging test for players of all
abilities as mature trees, large greenside bunkers and many
lakes are all brought into play.
Abbotts Course: 18 holes, 6501yds, Par 72, SSS 71.
Priors Course: 18 holes, 5720yds, Par 69, SSS 69.
Friars Course: 9 holes, 1140yds, Par 27, SSS 27.
Club membership 800.

Visitors	Abbotts Course midweek only. Priors and Friars, 7 days per week. Advisable to telephone starter on 01277 373344 for Priors and 01277 381108 for Abbotts and Friars.
Societies	must be pre booked.
Green Fees	not confirmed.
Cards	⬚ 🆅🅸🆂🅰 💳 ⬚ ⬚ ⬚
Prof	Dominic Eagle
Designer	Henry Cotton/Howard Swan
Facilities	⊗ 🏧 🖥 🛒 ♀ 🛆 🏠 ⛳ 🛒 ♂
& Leisure	sauna.
Location	1m E of Stapleford Abbotts, off B175
Hotel	★★★★ 71% Marygreen Manor, London Rd, BRENTWOOD ☎ 01277 225252 3 ⇥ ☎ Annexe40 ⇥ ☎

THEYDON BOIS   Map 05 TQ49

Theydon Bois Theydon Rd CM16 4EH
☎ 01992 812460 & 813054 Fax 01992 813054
The course was originally nine-holes built into Epping
Forest. It was later extended to 18-holes which were
well-planned and well-bunkered but in keeping with the
'forest tradition. The old nine in the Forest are short and
have two bunkers between them, but even so a wayward
shot can be among the trees. The autumn colours here
are truly magnificent.
18 holes, 5480yds, Par 68, SSS 68, Course record 64.
Club membership 600.

Visitors	may not play Wed, Thu, Sat & Sun mornings, ring 01992 812460 in advance to be sure tee is available.
Societies	book through the secretary.
Green Fees	not confirmed.
Prof	R Hall
Designer	James Braid
Facilities	⊗ 🏧 by prior arrangement 🖥 🛒 ♀ 🛆 🏠 ⛳ ♂
Location	2m from junct 26 on M25
Hotel	B Posthouse Epping, High Rd, Bell Common, EPPING ☎ 01992 573137 Annexe79 ⇥ ☎

TOLLESHUNT KNIGHTS   Map 05 TL91

Five Lakes Hotel Golf & Country Club Colchester Rd
CM9 8HX ☎ 01621 868888
Two 18-hole courses. The Links is a seaside course with a
number of greenside ponds and strategically placed bunkers,
while the Lakes is a championship course with large water
features and mounding between fairways.

*Links Course: 18 holes, 6250yds, Par 71, SSS 70, Course
record 67.*
*Lakes Course: 18 holes, 6767yds, Par 72, SSS 72, Course
record 63.*
Club membership 600.

Visitors	must contact in advance.
Societies	must contact in advance.
Green Fees	not confirmed.
Cards	⬚ 🆅🅸🆂🅰 💳 ⬚ ⬚ ⬚
Prof	Gary Carter
Designer	Lakes Neil Cole
Facilities	⊗ 🏧 🖥 🛒 ♀ 🛆 🏠 ⛳ 🍴 🛢 🛒 ♂ 🏌
& Leisure	hard tennis courts, heated indoor swimming pool, squash, sauna, solarium, gymnasium, putting green.
Location	1.75m NE on B1026
Hotel	★★★★ 72% Five Lakes Hotel, Golf & Country Club, Colchester Rd, TOLLESHUNT KNIGHTS ☎ 01621 868888 114 ⇥ ☎

TOOT HILL   Map 05 TL50

Toot Hill School Rd CM5 9PU
☎ 01277 365523 Fax 01277 364509
Pleasant course with several water hazards and sand greens.
18 holes, 6053yds, Par 70, SSS 69, Course record 65.
Club membership 400.

Visitors	welcome Mon-Fri by prior arrangement, handicap certificate may be required.
Societies	Tue & Thu contact in advance.
Green Fees	£35 per day; £25 per round (£25 per round after 1pm weekends).
Prof	Mark Bishop
Designer	Martin Gillett
Facilities	⊗ 🏧 🖥 🛒 ♀ 🛆 🏠 ⛳ 🛢 🛒 ♂ 🏌
Location	7m SE of Harlow, off A414
Hotel	B Posthouse Epping, High Rd, Bell Common, EPPING ☎ 01992 573137 Annexe79 ⇥ ☎

WITHAM   Map 05 TL81

Benton Hall Wickham Hill CM8 3LH
☎ 01376 502454 Fax 01376 521050
Set in rolling countryside and surrounded by dense
woodland, this challenging course provides a severe test even
to the very best golfers. The River Blackwater dominates the
front nine and natural lakes come into play on five other
holes.
18 holes, 6574yds, Par 72, SSS 72, Course record 64.
Club membership 470.

Visitors	visitors can book 6 days in advance

Societies	telephone in advance.
Green Fees	£25 per round (£30 weekends).
Cards	
Prof	John Hudson/Peter McBride
Designer	Alan Walker/Charles Cox
Facilities	
Location	Witham turn off on A12, signposted
Hotel	★★★ 62% White Hart Hotel, Bocking End, BRAINTREE ☎ 01376 321401 31

Braxted Park Braxted Park Estate CM8 3EN
☎ 01376 572372 Fax 01621 892840
A Pay and Play course in ancient parkland, surrounded by lakes and extremely pretty countryside. Suitable for beginners and experienced players.
9 holes, 2940yds, Par 35, SSS 34.
Club membership 83.

Visitors	welcome weekdays from 7.30am onwards.
Societies	telephone to arrange.
Green Fees	not confirmed.
Prof	Tony Parcell
Designer	Sir Allen Clark
Facilities & Leisure	fishing.
Location	2m from A12 near Kelvedon/Witham, at Gt Braxted
Hotel	★★★ 62% White Hart Hotel, Bocking End, BRAINTREE ☎ 01376 321401 31

WOODHAM WALTER   Map 05 TL80

Bunsay Downs Little Baddow Rd CM9 6RW
☎ 01245 222648 Fax 01245 223989
Attractive 9-hole public course. Also Par 3 course.
9 holes, 2932yds, Par 70, SSS 68.
Badgers: 9 holes, 1319yds, Par 54.
Club membership 400.

Visitors	no restrictions.
Societies	Mon-Fri only. Must contact in advance.
Green Fees	not confirmed.
Prof	Mickey Walker
Facilities	by prior arrangement
Hotel	★★★ 67% County Hotel, Rainsford Rd, CHELMSFORD ☎ 01245 491911 28 Annexe8

Warren CM9 6RW ☎ 01245 223258 Fax 01245 223989
Attractive parkland course with natural hazards and good views.
18 holes, 6229yds, Par 70, SSS 70, Course record 65.
Club membership 765.

Visitors	contact in advance, weekend pm only, Wed pm only.
Societies	arrange by telephone, confirm in writing, weekdays ex Wed.
Green Fees	not confirmed.
Prof	Mickey Walker
Facilities	by prior arrangement
Location	0.5m SW
Hotel	★★★ 67% County Hotel, Rainsford Rd, CHELMSFORD ☎ 01245 491911 28 Annexe8

CHELTENHAM   Map 03 SO92

Cotswold Hills Ullenwood GL53 9QT
☎ 01242 515264 Fax 01242 515263/4
A gently undulating course with open aspects and views of the Cotswolds.
18 holes, 6889yds, Par 71, SSS 74.
Club membership 750.

Visitors	telephone in advance, handicap certificate preferred.
Societies	must apply in writing or telephone.
Green Fees	not confirmed.
Cards	
Prof	Noel Boland
Designer	M D Little
Facilities	
Location	3m SE on A435 and A436
Hotel	B Posthouse Gloucester, Crest Way, Barnwood, GLOUCESTER ☎ 01452 613311 122

Lilley Brook Cirencester Rd, Charlton Kings GL53 8EG
☎ 01242 526785 Fax 01242 256880
Undulating parkland course. Magnificent views over Cheltenham and surrounding coutryside.
18 holes, 6212yds, Par 69, SSS 70, Course record 61.
Club membership 800.

Visitors	advisable to enquire of availability. Handicap certificate required.
Societies	apply in writing.
Green Fees	£30 per day; £25 round (£35/£30 weekends). ▶

Cards	⬛ 🟦 🟥 📇
Prof	Forbes Hadden
Designer	Mackenzie
Facilities	⊗ ⅏ 🝙 ■ ♀ ♨ 🏠 🖈 🐾 🛺 ♂
Location	2m S of Cheltenham on A435

Hotel	★★★★ 67% Cheltenham Park Hotel, Cirencester Rd, Charlton Kings, CHELTENHAM ☎ 01242 222021 144 ⇥ 🖈
	See advertisement on page 95.

Shipton Shipton Oliffe, Andoverford GL54 4HT
☎ 01242 890237 Fax 01242 820336
Deceptive, easy walking course situated in the heart of the Cotswolds and providing a fair challenge and panoramic views.
9 holes, 2516yds, Par 34, Course record 33.

Visitors	pay & play course no bookings taken.
Societies	welcome.
Green Fees	not confirmed.
Facilities	■ ♨ 🏠 🖈 ♂
Location	On A436, south of junct with A40

Hotel	★★★ 62% The Frogmill, Shipton Oliffe, ANDOVERSFORD ☎ 01242 820547 11 ⇥ 🖈 Annexe5 ⇥ 🖈

CHIPPING SODBURY Map 03 ST78

Chipping Sodbury BS37 6PU
☎ 01454 319042 Fax 01454 319042
Parkland courses of Championship proportions. The old course may be seen from the large opening tee by the clubhouse at the top of the hill. Two huge drainage dykes cut through the course and form a distinctive hazard on eleven holes.
New Course: 18 holes, 6912yds, Par 73, SSS 73, Course record 65.
Old Course: 9 holes, 6184yds, Par 70, SSS 69.
Club membership 800.

Visitors	no restriction on Old Course, must have a handicap certificate and may only play until after noon at weekends on New Course.
Societies	must contact in writing.
Green Fees	not confirmed.
Prof	Mike Watts
Designer	Hawtree
Facilities	⊗ ⅏ 🝙 ■ ♀ ♨ 🏠 🖈 🐾 🛺 ♂
Location	0.5m N

Hotel	★★ 58% Cross Hands Hotel, OLD SODBURY ☎ 01454 313000 24rm(3 ⇥ 17 🖈)

CIRENCESTER Map 04 SP00

Cirencester Cheltenham Rd, Bagendon GL7 7BH
☎ 01285 653939 Fax 01285 650665
Undulating open Cotswold course with excellent views.
18 holes, 6055yds, Par 70, SSS 69, Course record 65.
Club membership 800.

Visitors	restricted availability at weekends, contact professional shop in advance on 01285 656124.
Societies	telephone Secretary/Manager.
Green Fees	£25 per day; £20 per round (£30/£25 weekends & bank holidays).

Prof	Peter Garratt
Designer	J Braid
Facilities	⊗ ⅏ 🝙 ■ ♀ ♨ 🏠 🐾 🛺 ♂ ℓ
Location	2 N of Cirencester on A435

Hotel	★★★ 68% Stratton House Hotel, Gloucester Rd, CIRENCESTER ☎ 01285 651761 41 ⇥ 🖈

CLEEVE HILL Map 03 SO92

Cleeve Hill GL52 3PW ☎ 01242 672025
Undulating and open heathland course affected by crosswinds.
18 holes, 6411yds, Par 72, SSS 71, Course record 69.
Club membership 450.

Visitors	bookings taken 7 days in advance. Limited play weekends.
Societies	telephone in advance.
Green Fees	not confirmed.
Prof	Richard Jenkins
Facilities	⊗ ⅏ 🝙 ■ ♀ ♨ 🏠 🖈 ♂
Location	1m NE on B4632

Hotel	★★★ 66% Rising Sun Hotel, CLEEVE HILL ☎ 01242 676281 24 ⇥ 🖈

COLEFORD Map 03 SO51

Forest Hills Mile End Rd GL16 7BY
☎ 01594 810620 Fax 01594 810623
A parkland course on a plateau with panoramic views of Coleford and Forest of Dean. Some testing holes with the par-5 13th hole sitting tight on a water hazard, and the challenging 18th with 2nd shot over large pond to a green protected by another pond and bunker - all in front of the clubhouse.
18 holes, 6740yds, Par 68, SSS 68, Course record 64.
Club membership 350.

Visitors	no restrictions.
Societies	contact in advance.
Green Fees	£15 per round (£20 weekends).
Cards	⬛ 🟥 📇
Prof	Richard Ballard
Designer	A Stiff
Facilities	⊗ ⅏ 🝙 ■ ♀ ♨ 🏠 🖈 🐾 🛺 ♂ ℓ

Hotel	★★★ 69% The Speech House, COLEFORD ☎ 01594 822607 15 ⇥ 🖈

Forest of Dean Golf Club & Bells Hotel Lords Hill GL16 8BD ☎ 01594 832583 Fax 01594 832584
Established in 1973 and now matured into an extremely pleasant parkland course. Well bunkered with light rough, a few blind tee shots and water in play on several holes.
18 holes, 6033yds, Par 70, SSS 69.
Club membership 500.

Visitors	are required to book tee-off times.
Societies	must telephone in advance.
Green Fees	£18 per round.
Cards	⬛ 🟥 📇
Prof	John Hansel
Designer	John Day
Facilities	⊗ ⅏ 🝙 ■ ♀ ♨ 🏠 🖈 🐾 🛺 ♂
& Leisure	hard tennis courts, bowling green.
Location	0.25m from Coleford town centre on B4431 Coleford to Parkend road

Hotel	★★★ 69% The Speech House, COLEFORD ☎ 01594 822607 15 ⊷ ♠

DURSLEY   Map 03 ST79

Stinchcombe Hill Stinchcombe Hill GL11 6AQ
☎ 01453 542015 Fax 01453 549545
High on the hill with splendid views of the Cotswolds, the River Severn and the Welsh hills. A downland course with good turf, some trees and an interesting variety of greens. Protected greens make this a challenging course in windy conditions.
18 holes, 5734yds, Par 68, SSS 68, Course record 63.
Club membership 550.

Visitors	restricted at weekends. Must contact professional in advance 01453 543878.
Societies	must apply in advance.
Green Fees	£20 in summer; £13 in winter (£25/£20 weekends.
Prof	Paul Bushell
Designer	Arthur Hoare
Facilities	⊗ ⫴ ⓛ ⌿ ♀ ⌂ ⌂ ⌀
Location	1m W off A4135
Hotel	★★★ 66% Prince Of Wales Hotel, BERKELEY ☎ 01453 810474 43 ⊷ ♠

GLOUCESTER   Map 03 SO81

Brickhampton Court Cheltenham Rd, Churchdown GL2 9QF ☎ 01452 859444 Fax 01452 859333
27 holes, including the county's first intermediate course (9-hole par 31) for the new and developing golfer, set in undulating parkland. The Spa course offers a good golfing challenge, featuring lakes, streams and well placed bunkers.
Spa: 18 holes, 6449yds, Par 71, SSS 71.
Glevum: 9 holes, 1859yds, Par 31.
Club membership 700.

Visitors	advance booking recommended, recognised golfing attire to be worn and evidence of golfing ability preferred.
Societies	contact for information and booking form,
Green Fees	Spa: £25 per day; £16 per round (£30/£22.50 weekends). Glevum: £10 per 18 holes; £6.50 per 9 holes (£12/£8 weekends).
Cards	⊟ 🟦 VISA 🟥 📇 📇
Prof	David Finch
Designer	Simon Gidman
Facilities	⊗ ⫴ ⓛ ♀ ⌂ 🖜 🛵 ⌀ ⚑
Location	Junct 11 M5, A40 towards Gloucester, at Elmbridge Court rdbt B4063 signed Churchdown, approx 2m
Hotel	★★★ 62% Hatherley Manor Hotel, Down Hatherley Ln, GLOUCESTER ☎ 01452 730217 56 ⊷ ♠

Jarvis Gloucester Hotel & Country Club Matson Ln, Robinswood Hill GL4 6EA ☎ 01452 411331
Undulating, wooded course, built around a hill with superb views over Gloucester and the Cotswolds. The 12th is a drive straight up a hill, nicknamed 'Coronary Hill'.
18 holes, 6170yds, Par 70, SSS 69, Course record 65.
Club membership 600.

Visitors	can book up to 7 days in advance.
Societies	telephone in advance.
Green Fees	not confirmed.
Prof	Peter Darnell
Facilities	⌂ ⌂ ⌿ 🖜 🛵 ⌀
& Leisure	hard tennis courts, heated indoor swimming pool, squash, sauna, solarium, gymnasium.
Location	2.5m SE of Gloucester, off B4073
Hotel	★★★ 76% Hatton Court, Upton Hill, Upton St Leonards, GLOUCESTER ☎ 01452 617412 17 ⊷ ♠ Annexe28 ⊷ ♠

Rodway Hill Newent Rd, Highnam GL2 8DN
☎ 01452 384222
A challenging 18-hole course with superb panoramic views. Testing front 5 holes and the par 3 13th and par 5 16th being affected by strong croswinds off the River Severn.
18 holes, 6070yds, Par 70, SSS 69, Course record 71.
Club membership 400.

Visitors	no restrictions.
Societies	telephone in advance.
Green Fees	£10 per 18 holes; £8 per 9 holes (£14 per 18 holes/£10 per 9 holes weekends).
Cards	⊟ ⊟ 🟥
Prof	Tony Grubb
Designer	John Gabb
Facilities	⊗ ⫴ ⓛ ♀ ⌂ 🖜 ⌿ ⌀
Location	2m outside Gloucester on B4215
Hotel	★★★ 62% Hatherley Manor Hotel, Down Hatherley Ln, GLOUCESTER ☎ 01452 730217 56 ⊷ ♠

LYDNEY   Map 03 SO60

Lydney Lakeside Av GL15 5QA ☎ 01594 842614
Flat parkland/meadowland course with prevailing wind along fairways.
9 holes, 5298yds, Par 66, SSS 66, Course record 63.
Club membership 350.

Visitors	with member only at weekends & bank holidays.
Societies	apply in writing to the Secretary.
Green Fees	not confirmed.
Facilities	⌂
Location	SE side of town centre
Hotel	★★★ 69% The Speech House, COLEFORD ☎ 01594 822607 15 ⊷ ♠

MINCHINHAMPTON   Map 03 SO80

Minchinhampton (New Course) New Course GL6 9BE
☎ 01453 833866 Fax 01453 833860
The Cherington course is set in undulating upland. Large contoured greens, pot bunkers, and, at times, a stiff breeze present a very fair test of skill. The Avening course has a variety of holes including water on the 10th and 13th.
Avening: 18 holes, 6279yds, Par 70, SSS 70, Course record 65.
Cherington: 18 holes, 6320yds, Par 71, SSS 70.
Club membership 1200.

▶

Visitors   must contact in advance.
Societies   must contact by telephone.
Green Fees not confirmed.
Prof   Chris Steele
Designer   Hawtree & Son
Facilities   ⊗ ⫫ 🏌 💪 ♀ 👥 🏠 ⛳ ♂ ℓ
Location   2m SE

Hotel   ★★★ 67% Burleigh Court, Minchinhampton,
          STROUD
          ☎ 01453 883804   11 ⇆ 🐾 Annexe6 ⇆ 🐾

Minchinhampton (Old Course) Old Course GL6 9AQ
☎ 01453 832642 & 836382
An open grassland course 600 feet above sea level. The
numerous humps and hollows around the greens tests the
golfer's ability to play a variety of shots - often in difficult
windy conditions. Panoramic Cotswold views.
18 holes, 6019yds, Par 71, SSS 69.
Club membership 700.
Visitors   must contact in advance.
Societies   must contact in advance.
Green Fees £12 per day (£15 weekends & bank holdays).
Facilities   ⊗ ⫫ 🏌 💪 ♀ 👥 🏠
Location   1m NW

Hotel   ★★★ 67% Burleigh Court, Minchinhampton,
          STROUD
          ☎ 01453 883804   11 ⇆ 🐾 Annexe6 ⇆ 🐾

NAUNTON   Map 04 SP12

Naunton Downs GL54 3AE
☎ 01451 850090 Fax 01451 850091
Naunton Downs course plays over beautiful Cotswold
countryside. A valley running through the course is one of
the main features, creating 1 par 3 hole that crosses over it.
The prevailing wind adds extra challenge to the par 5's
(which play into the wind), combined with small undulating
greens.
18 holes, 6078yds, Par 71, SSS 70, Course record 67.
Club membership 900.
Visitors   must contact in advance.
Societies   telephone for details.
Green Fees £19 per round (£25 weekends).
Prof   Martin Seddon
Designer   J Pott
Facilities   ⊗ ⫫ 🏌 💪 ♀ 👥 🏠 ⛳ 🔧 🛒 ♂
& Leisure   hard tennis courts.
Location   B4068 Stow/Cheltenham

Hotel   ★★★ 81% Lords of the Manor, UPPER
          SLAUGHTER ☎ 01451 820243   27 ⇆ 🐾

PAINSWICK   Map 03 SO80

Painswick GL6 6TL ☎ 01452 812180
Downland course set on Cotswold Hills at Painswick
Beacon, with fine views. Short course more than
compensated by natural hazards and tight fairways.
18 holes, 4895yds, Par 67, SSS 65, Course record 61.
Club membership 480.
Visitors   member only on Sat pm & Sun.
Societies   must apply in advance.
Green Fees £20 per day; £15 per round (£20 per round Sat
          pm).
Cards   [cards]

Facilities   ⊗ ⫫ 🏌 💪 ♀ 👥 🏠 ⛳ ♂
Location   1m N on A46

Hotel   ★★★ 77% Painswick Hotel, Kemps Ln,
          PAINSWICK ☎ 01452 812160   19 ⇆ 🐾

TEWKESBURY   Map 03 SO83

Stakis Puckrup Hall Hotel Puckrup GL20 6EL
☎ 01684 296200 Fax 01684 850788
Set in 140 acres of undulating parkland with lakes, existing
trees and marvellous views of the Malvern hills. There are
water hazards at the 5th and a cluster of bunkers on the long
14th before the challenging tee shot across the water to the
par-3 18th.
18 holes, 6189yds, Par 70, SSS 70.
Club membership 500.

Visitors   must be a regular golfer familiar with rules and
          etiquette, must book a tee time, may book up to
          5 days in advance.
Societies   telephone in advance.
Green Fees £30 per day; £25 per round (£33/£30 weekends).
Cards   [cards]
Prof   Kevin Pickett
Designer   Simon Gidman
Facilities   ⊗ ⫫ 🏌 💪 ♀ 👥 🏠 🏥 🛒 🛺 ♂
& Leisure   heated indoor swimming pool, sauna, solarium,
          gymnasium.
Location   4m N, on main A38

Hotel   ★★★ 66% Old Schoolhouse Hotel &
          Restaurant, SEVERN STOKE
          ☎ 01905 371368 & 371464
          Fax 01905 371591   13 ⇆ 🐾

Tewkesbury Park Hotel Golf & Country Club
Lincoln Green Ln GL20 7DN
☎ 01684 295405 Fax 01684 292386
A parkland course overlooking the Abbey and rivers
Avon and Severn. The par 3, 5th is an exciting hole
calling for accurate distance judgment. The hotel and
country club offer many sports and club facilities
including a well equipped gym with cardio theatre.
18 holes, 6533yds, Par 73, SSS 72, Course record 66.
Club membership 650.
Visitors   must book in advance via pro shop/hotel
          reservations.
Societies   telephone initially.
Green Fees £20 per round (£25 weekend).
Cards   [cards]
Prof   Robert Taylor

Designer	Frank Pennick
Facilities	⊗ ⫴ ⬜ 🍴 ♀ ⛾ 🏠 ⛳ 🏌 ↘ ⛏ 🖊 (
& Leisure	hard tennis courts, heated indoor swimming pool, squash, sauna, solarium, gymnasium, 6 hole par 3 pitch & putt.
Location	1m SW off A38

Hotel	★★★ 68% Tewkesbury Park Hotel, Lincoln Green Ln, TEWKESBURY ☎ 01684 295405 78 ⇋ ☞

THORNBURY   Map 03 ST69

Thornbury Golf Centre Bristol Rd BS35 3XL
☎ 01454 281144 Fax 01454 281177
Two 18 hole pay & play courses designed by Hawtree and set in undulating terrain with estensive views towards the Severn estuary. The Low 18 is a Par 3 with holes ranging from 80 to 207 yards and is ideal for beginners. The High course puts to test the more experienced golfer. Excellent 25 bay floodlit driving range.
High Course: 18 holes, 6154yds, Par 71, SSS 69.
Low Course: 18 holes, 2120yds, Par 54.
Club membership 420.

Visitors	welcome at all times, please contact in advance.
Societies	apply in writing for brochure.
Green Fees	£23 per day; £14.50 per round £9 per 9 holes (£26/£17/£9 weekends & bank holidays).
Cards	💳 💳 💳
Prof	Simon Hubbard
Designer	Hawtree
Facilities	⊗ ⫴ ⬜ 🍴 ♀ ⛾ 🏠 ⛳ 🏌 🖊 (
Location	Off A38

Hotel	★★★🏆 Thornbury Castle, Castle St, THORNBURY ☎ 01454 281182 20 ⇋ ☞

WESTONBIRT   Map 03 ST88

Westonbirt Westonbirt School GL8 8QG ☎ 01666 880242
A parkland course with good views.
9 holes, 4504yds, Par 64, SSS 64.
Club membership 150.

Visitors	no restrictions.
Societies	no reserved tees.
Green Fees	not confirmed.
Facilities	⬧
Location	E side of village off A433

Hotel	★★★ 67% Hare & Hounds Hotel, Westonbirt, TETBURY ☎ 01666 880233 24 ⇋ ☞ Annexe8 ⇋ ☞

WICK   Map 03 ST77

Tracy Park Tracy Park, Bath Rd BS30 5RN
☎ 0117 937 2251 Fax 0117 937 4288
Two 18 hole championship courses on the south-western escarpment of the Cotswolds, affording fine views. Both courses present a challenge to all levels of player, with water playing a part on a number of occasions. The clubhouse dates back to 1600 and is a building of great beauty and elegance, set in the 221 acre estate of this golf and country club.
Crown Course: 18 holes, 6423yds, Par 70, SSS 70.
Cromwell Course: 18 holes, 6003yds, Par 70, SSS 69.
Club membership 900.

Visitors	no restrictions.
Societies	must telephone or write to Graham Packer.
Green Fees	£24 per round (£30 weekends).
Cards	💳 💳 💳 💳 💳
Prof	Richard Berry
Designer	Grant Aitken
Facilities	⊗ ⫴ ⬜ 🍴 ♀ ⛾ 🏠 ⛳ 🏌 ↘ ⛏ 🖊 (
& Leisure	hard tennis courts, squash.
Location	S side of village off A420

Hotel	★★★ The Queensberry Hotel, Russel St, BATH ☎ 01225 447928 29 ⇋ ☞

WOTTON-UNDER-EDGE   Map 03 ST79

Cotswold Edge Upper Rushmire GL12 7PT
☎ 01453 844167 Fax 01453 845120
Meadowland course situated in a quiet Cotswold valley with magnificent views. First half flat and open, second half more varied.
18 holes, 6170yds, Par 71, SSS 71.
Club membership 800.

Visitors	preferable to contact in advance, at weekends may only play with member.
Societies	must in writing or telephone in advance.
Green Fees	£15 per day/round.
Prof	David Gosling
Facilities	⊗ ⬜ 🍴 ♀ ⛾ 🏠 ⛳ 🖊
Location	N of town on B4058 Wotton-Tetbury road

Hotel	★★ 70% Egypt Mill Hotel, NAILSWORTH ☎ 01453 833449 8 ⇋ ☞ Annexe10 ⇋ ☞

GREATER LONDON

London Telephone Number Changes

From the 22 April 2000, the dialling code for the whole of London with be (020), followed by an eight-digit local number. For example, **(0171)** 123 4567 will become **(020) 7**123 4567, **(0181)** 123 4567 will become **(020) 8**123 4567.

Those courses which fall within the confines of the London Postal District area (ie have London postcodes - W1, SW1 etc) are listed under the county heading of London in the gazetteer (see page 178).

GREATER LONDON

ADDINGTON   Map 05 TQ36

The Addington 205 Shirley Church Rd CR0 5AB
☎ 0181 777 1055
A world of heather, bracken, silver birch and pine referred to by Henry Longhurst as his favourite inland course. It is one where thought is required at every hole.
18 holes, 6242yds, Par 71, SSS 71, Course record 66.
Visitors   may not play weekends. Must belong to recognised club.
Societies   weekdays only, telephone for prior arrangement.
Green Fees £35 per day weekdays only.
Designer   Abercromby
Facilities   ⊗ ▆ ♥ ♀ ♨ ♂
& Leisure   practice area.

Hotel   ★★★★ 69% Selsdon Park Hotel, Addington Rd, Sanderstead, CROYDON
☎ 0181 657 8811 204 ⇔ ♠

Addington Court Featherbed Ln CR0 9AA
☎ 0181 657 0281 (booking) 651 5270 (admin)
Fax 0181 651 0282
Challenging, well-drained courses designed by F. Hawtree. Two 18-hole courses, 9-hole course and a pitch-and-putt course designed to suit all standards.
Championship Course: 18 holes, 5577yds, Par 68, SSS 67, Course record 60.
Falconwood: 18 holes, 5472yds, Par 68, SSS 67.
9 Hole: 9 holes, 1733yds, Par 31.
Club membership 350.
Visitors   no restrictions. Advisable to phone in advance to play on Championship Course.
Societies   must telephone in advance.
Green Fees Championship: £14 per round (£17 weekends); Falconwood: £12 per round (£15 weekends); 9 hole £8. 18 hole replay £5, 9 hole replay free.
Cards   ⚊ 💳 💳 💳
Prof   Russ Critcher
Designer   Hawtree Snr
Facilities   ⊗ �𝕄 ▆ ♥ ♀ ♨ 🍴 🚬 ♂ ♘
Location   1m S off A2022

Hotel   ★★★★ 69% Selsdon Park Hotel, Addington Rd, Sanderstead, CROYDON
☎ 0181 657 8811 204 ⇔ ♠

Addington Palace Addington Park, Gravel Hill CR0 5BB
☎ 0181 654 3061 Fax 0181 655 3632
Hard-walking parkland course, with two (par 4) testing holes (2nd and 10th).
18 holes, 6286yds, Par 71, SSS 71, Course record 63.
Club membership 700.
Visitors   telephone in advance, must play with member at weekends & bank holidays.
Societies   Tue, Wed & Fri only, telephone in advance.
Green Fees £30 per day/round.
Prof   Roger Williams
Designer   J H Taylor
Facilities   ⊗ ▆ ♥ ♀ ♨ 🍴 ♂
Location   0.5m SW on A212

Hotel   ★★★★ 69% Selsdon Park Hotel, Addington Rd, Sanderstead, CROYDON
☎ 0181 657 8811 204 ⇔ ♠

BARNEHURST   Map 05 TQ57

Barnehurst Mayplace Rd East DA7 6JU
☎ 01322 523746 Fax 01322 554612
Public parkland course with well matured greens. Easy walking.
9 holes, 5320yds, Par 66, SSS 66.
Club membership 300.
Visitors   restricted Tue, Thu, Sat (pm) & Sun.
Societies   by arrangement.
Green Fees not confirmed.
Facilities   ⊗ ▆ ♥ ♀ ♨ 🍴 ♂
Location   0.75m NW of Crayford off A2000

Hotel   B Posthouse Bexley, Black Prince Interchange, Southwold Rd, BEXLEY
☎ 01322 526900 103 ⇔ ♠

BARNET   Map 04 TQ29

Arkley Rowley Green Rd EN5 3HL
☎ 0181 449 0394 Fax 0181 440 5214
Wooded parkland course situated on highest spot in Hertfordshire with fine views.
9 holes, 6117yds, Par 69, SSS 69.
Club membership 450.
Visitors   may play weekdays only (ex Tue).
Societies   must contact in advance.
Green Fees £20 per day/round.
Prof   Martin Porter
Designer   Braid
Facilities   ⊗ ▆ ♥ ♀ ♨ 🍴 ♂
Location   Off A1 at Arkley sign

Hotel   ★★★ 73% Edgwarebury Hotel, Barnet Ln, ELSTREE ☎ 0181 953 8227 47 ⇔ ♠

Dyrham Park Country Club Galley Ln EN5 4RA
☎ 0181 440 3361 Fax 0181 441 9836
Parkland course.
18 holes, 6369yds, Par 71, SSS 70, Course record 65.
Club membership 1200.
Visitors   must be guest of member.
Societies   Wed only, must book in advance.
Green Fees not confirmed.
Prof   Bill Large
Facilities   ⊗ ⟨all day⟩ ♨ 🍴 🚬 ♂
& Leisure   hard tennis courts, heated outdoor swimming pool, fishing, caddies available.

Location   3m NW off A1081

Hotel   B Posthouse South Mimms, SOUTH MIMMS
☎ 01707 643311 143 ⇆ ☇

Old Fold Manor Old Fold Ln, Hadley Green EN5 4QN
☎ 0181 440 9185 Fax 0181 441 4863
Heathland course, good test of golf.
18 holes, 6481yds, Par 71, SSS 71, Course record 66.
Club membership 520.
Visitors   with member only weekends & bank holidays.
Societies   must apply in writing.
Green Fees   £20 per 18 holes; Public Days Mon/Wed £12
per round.
Prof   Garry Potter
Facilities   ⊗ ⁇ ⅃ ⚑ ♀ ⌂ ☇
& Leisure   snooker.
Location   Off A1000 between Barnet/Potters Bar

Hotel   ★★★★♨ 71% West Lodge Park Hotel,
Cockfosters Rd, HADLEY WOOD
☎ 0181 440 8311 46 ⇆ ☇ Annexe9 ⇆ ☇

Beckenham Place Park The Mansion, Beckenham Place
Park BR3 2BP ☎ 0181 650 2292 Fax 0181 663 1201
Picturesque course in the grounds of a public park. The
course varies from open to tight surroundings with the back
nine providing a challenge for both the novice and low
handicapper. A water-filled ditch comes into play on several
holes.
18 holes, 5722yds, Par 68, SSS 68.
Visitors   booked tee times operate contact for details.
Societies   apply in writing or telephone for Society pack.
Green Fees   not confirmed.
Cards   ▭ ▪ VISA ▪ ▫ ▫
Prof   Huw Davis-Thomas
Facilities   ⊗ ⅃ ⚑ ♀ ⌂ ☇
& Leisure   hard tennis courts.
Location   Main Catford/Beckenham road, just off A21

Hotel   ★★★ 70% Bromley Court Hotel, Bromley
Hill, BROMLEY ☎ 0181 464 5011 115 ⇆ ☇

Langley Park Barnfield Wood Rd BR3 6SZ
☎ 0181 658 6849 Fax 0181 658 6310
This is a pleasant, but difficult, well-wooded, parkland
course with natural hazards including a lake at the 18th
hole.
18 holes, 6488yds, Par 69, SSS 71, Course record 65.
Club membership 700.
Visitors   must contact in advance and may not play
weekends.
Societies   Wed & Thu only, telephone to book.
Green Fees   not confirmed.
Prof   Colin Staff
Designer   J H Taylor
Facilities   ⊗ ⁇ by prior arrangement ⅃ ⚑ ♀ ⌂
⚐ ☇
Location   0.5 N on B2015

Hotel   ★★★ 70% Bromley Court Hotel, Bromley
Hill, BROMLEY
☎ 0181 464 5011 115 ⇆ ☇

Bexleyheath Mount Rd DA6 8JS ☎ 0181 303 6951
Undulating course.
9 holes, 5162yds, Par 66, SSS 66, Course record 65.
Club membership 330.
Visitors   must contact Secretary in advance, may not play
weekends.
Societies   telephone in advance.
Green Fees   not confirmed.
Facilities   ♀ ⌂
Location   1m SW

Hotel   B Posthouse Bexley, Black Prince Interchange,
Southwold Rd, BEXLEY
☎ 01322 526900 103 ⇆ ☇

Cherry Lodge Jail Ln TN16 3AX
☎ 01959 572250 Fax 01959 540672
Undulating parkland course set 600feet above sea level with
panoramic views of the surrounding Kent countryside. An
enjoyable test of golf for all standards. The 14th is 434 yards
across a valley and uphill, requiring two good shots to reach
the green.
18 holes, 6652yds, Par 72, SSS 73, Course record 69.
Club membership 700.
Visitors   must contact in advance but may not play at
weekends.
Societies   must telephone in advance.
Green Fees   £40 per day; £30 per round.
Prof   Nigel Child
Designer   John Day
Facilities   ⊗ ⁇ ⅃ ⚑ ♀ ⌂ ☚ ⚐ ☇ ☇
Location   1m E

Hotel   ★★★ 68% Kings Arms Hotel, Market Square,
WESTERHAM ☎ 01959 562990 17 ⇆ ☇

Bromley Magpie Hall Ln BR2 8JF ☎ 0181 462 7014
Flat course, ideal for beginners.
9 holes, 2745yds, Par 70, SSS 67.
Visitors   no restrictions.
Societies   apply in writing.
Green Fees   not confirmed.
Cards   ▭ ▪ VISA ▪ ▫ ▫
Prof   Danny Williams
Facilities   ⚑ ⌂ ⚐ ☇
Location   2m SE off A21

Hotel   ★★★ 70% Bromley Court Hotel, Bromley
Hill, BROMLEY ☎ 0181 464 5011 115 ⇆ ☇

Shortlands Meadow Rd, Shortlands BR2 0PB
☎ 0181 460 8828
Easy walking parkland course with a brook as a natural
hazard.
9 holes, 5261yds, Par 65, SSS 66, Course record 59.
Club membership 410.
Visitors   must be guest of member.
Green Fees   £10 per round.
Prof   John Murray
Facilities   ⊗ ⅃ ⚑ ♀ ⌂ ☇
Location   0.75m W off A222   ▶

Hotel ★★★ 70% Bromley Court Hotel, Bromley Hill, BROMLEY ☎ 0181 464 5011 115 ⇄ ⋔

Sundridge Park Garden Rd BR1 3NE
☎ 0181 460 0278 Fax 0181 289 3050
The East course is longer than the West but many think the shorter of the two courses is the more difficult. The East is surrounded by trees while the West is more hilly, with good views. Both are certainly a good test of golf.
East Course: 18 holes, 6516yds, Par 71, SSS 71, Course record 63.
West Course: 18 holes, 6019yds, Par 69, SSS 69, Course record 65.
Club membership 1200.
Visitors may only play on weekdays. Must contact in advance and must have a handicap certificate. No advance booking necessary.
Societies must contact well in advance.
Green Fees £40 per day.
Prof Bob Cameron
Designer Willie Park
Facilities ⊗ ⋔ ⅃ ⊑ ♥ ♀ ♨ 🏠 ♂
Location N side of town centre off A2212

Hotel ★★★ 70% Bromley Court Hotel, Bromley Hill, BROMLEY
☎ 0181 464 5011 115 ⇄ ⋔

CARSHALTON Map 04 TQ26

Oaks Sports Centre Woodmansterne Rd SM5 4AN
☎ 0181 643 8363 Fax 0181 770 7303
Public parkland course with floodlit, covered driving range.
18 Holes: 18 holes, 6025yds, Par 70, SSS 69, Course record 65.
The Oaks: 9 holes, 1443yds, Par 28, SSS 28.
Club membership 864.

Visitors no restrictions.
Societies must apply in writing.
Green Fees 18 Hole: £13 per round (£15 weekends). The Oaks: £6 per round (£7 weekends).
Prof Horley/Russell/Pilkington
Facilities ⅃ ♥ ♀ ♨ 🏠 ♂ ♖ ♘ ♂ ⌘
& Leisure squash.
Location 0.5m S on B278

Hotel B Posthouse Croydon, Purley Way, CROYDON ☎ 0181 688 5185 83 ⇄ ⋔

CHESSINGTON Map 04 TQ16

Chessington Garrison Ln KT9 2LW
☎ 0181 391 0948 Fax 0181 397 2068
Tree-lined parkland course designed by Patrick Tallack.
9 holes, 1400yds, Par 27, SSS 28.
Club membership 100.
Visitors must book 7.30am-noon weekends only.
Societies must telephone 1 month in advance.
Green Fees not confirmed.
Designer Patrick Tallack
Facilities ⊗ ⋔ ⅃ ⊑ ♥ ♀ ♨ 🏠 ♂ ♂ ♖
Location Opposite Chessington South Station nr Zoo

Hotel ★★ 64% Haven Hotel, Portsmouth Rd, ESHER
☎ 0181 398 0023 16 ⇄ ⋔ Annexe4 ⇄ ⋔

CHISLEHURST Map 05 TQ47

Chislehurst Camden Park Rd BR7 5HJ
☎ 0181 467 2782 Fax 0181 295 0974
Pleasantly wooded undulating parkland/heathland course. Magnificent clubhouse with historical associations.
18 holes, 5106yds, Par 66, SSS 65, Course record 61.
Club membership 800.
Visitors with member only weekends.
Societies weekdays only.
Green Fees £25 per day.
Prof Mark Lawrence
Designer Park
Facilities ⊗ ⅃ ⊑ ♥ ♀ ♨ 🏠 ♂ ♖ ♂

Hotel ★★★ 70% Bromley Court Hotel, Bromley Hill, BROMLEY ☎ 0181 464 5011 115 ⇄ ⋔

COULSDON Map 04 TQ25

Coulsdon Manor Hotel Coulsdon Court Rd CR5 2LL
☎ 0181 660 6083 Fax 0181 668 3118
Set in its own 140 acres of landscaped parkland.
18 holes, 6037yds, Par 70, SSS 68.

Visitors must telephone up to 5 days in advance.
Societies by arrangement.
Green Fees £14 per round (£17.25 weekends & bank holidays).
Cards 🖰🖰🖰🖰🖰🖰
Prof David Copsey
Designer Harry Colt
Facilities ⊗ ⋔ ⅃ ⊑ ♥ ♀ ♨ 🏠 ♂ ♗ ♖ ♂
& Leisure hard tennis courts, squash, sauna, solarium, gymnasium.

Location 0.75m E off A23 on B2030

Hotel ★★★★ 77% Coulsdon Manor, Coulsdon Court Rd, Coulsdon, CROYDON
☎ 0181 668 0414 35 ⇆ ↑

Woodcote Park Meadow Hill, Bridle Way CR5 2QQ
☎ 0181 668 2788 Fax 0181 668 2788
Slightly undulating parkland course.
18 holes, 6669yds, Par 71, SSS 72, Course record 66.
Club membership 650.
Visitors handicap certificate required, contact professional for details. Visitors may not play weekends.
Societies must contact Secretary in advance.
Green Fees £40 per day; £30 per round.
Prof I Golding
Facilities ⊗ ⅲ ᴸ ♣ ♀ ♨ ♋ ♂
Location 1m N of town centre off A237

Hotel B Posthouse Croydon, Purley Way,
CROYDON ☎ 0181 688 5185 83 ⇆ ↑

CROYDON   Map 04 TQ36

Croham Hurst Croham Rd CR2 7HJ
☎ 0181 657 5581 Fax 0181 657 3229
Parkland course with tree-lined fairways and bounded by wooded hills. Easy walking.
18 holes, 6290yds, Par 70, SSS 70.
Club membership 800.
Visitors must contact in advance & have handicap certificate. With member only weekends & bank holidays.
Societies must book 1 year in advance.
Green Fees £35 per round/day (£42 weekends & bank holidays).
Prof Eric Stillwell
Facilities ⊗ ᴸ ♣ ♀ ♨ ♋ ♂ ♂
Location 1.5m SE, between South Croydon and Selsdon on B269

Hotel ★★★★ 69% Selsdon Park Hotel, Addington Rd, Sanderstead, CROYDON
☎ 0181 657 8811 204 ⇆ ↑

Selsdon Park Addington Rd, Sanderstead CR2 8YA
☎ 0181 657 8811 Fax 0181 651 6171
Parkland course. Full use of hotel's sporting facilities by residents.
18 holes, 6473yds, Par 73, SSS 71.
Visitors welcome, booking advisable, booking 1 week in advance for weekends.
Societies telephone in advance.

Green Fees not confirmed.
Cards ▬ ▩▩ ◫ ▬ ▩ ◱
Prof Malcolm Churchill
Designer J H Taylor
Facilities ⊗ ⅲ ᴸ ♣ ♀ ♨ ♋ ♂ ♂ ⅔ ♂ ♂ ♂
& Leisure hard and grass tennis courts, outdoor and indoor heated swimming pools, squash, sauna, solarium, gymnasium.
Location 3m S on A2022

Hotel ★★★★ 69% Selsdon Park Hotel, Addington Rd, Sanderstead, CROYDON
☎ 0181 657 8811 204 ⇆ ↑

Shirley Park 194 Addiscombe Rd CR0 7LB
☎ 0181 654 1143
This parkland course lies amid fine woodland with good views of Shirley Hills. The more testing holes come in the middle section of the course. The remarkable 7th hole calls for a 187-yard iron or wood shot diagonally across a narrow valley to a shelved green set right-handed into a ridge. The redesigned 13th hole, 160yds, is considered to be one of the finest short holes in the county.
18 holes, 6210yds, Par 71, SSS 70, Course record 66.
Club membership 600.

Visitors should contact in advance. With member only at weekends.
Societies by arrangement.
Green Fees £30 per day/round weekdays.
Prof Paul Webb
Facilities ♨ ♋ ♂ ♂
Location E side of town centre on A232

Hotel ★★★★ 69% Selsdon Park Hotel, Addington Rd, Sanderstead, CROYDON
☎ 0181 657 8811 204 ⇆ ↑

DOWNE   Map 05 TQ46

High Elms High Elms Rd BR6 7JL
☎ 01689 853232 & 858175 bookings
Municipal parkland course. Very tight 13th, 230 yds (par 3).
18 holes, 6210yds, Par 71, SSS 70, Course record 68.
Club membership 450.
Visitors   no restrictions.
Societies   telephone to book. Tel 01689 861813.
Green Fees not confirmed.
Cards   ▭▭ ▭▭ ▭▭ ▭
Prof   Peter Remy
Designer   Hawthorn
Facilities   ⊗ ⨯ ㄴ ▤ ♀ ゐ ☎ ㏓ ⛏ ♣ ⚒ ✓
Location   1.5m NE

Hotel   ★★★ 70% Bromley Court Hotel, Bromley
Hill, BROMLEY ☎ 0181 464 5011 115 ⇔ ▸

West Kent West Hill BR6 7JJ
☎ 01689 851323 Fax 01689 858693
Partly hilly downland course.
18 holes, 6399yds, Par 70, SSS 70.
Club membership 700.
Visitors   with member only at weekends. Must contact in
advance.
Societies   must apply in writing.
Green Fees not confirmed.
Prof   Roger Fidler
Facilities   ⊗ ㄴ ▤ ♀ ゐ ☎ ✓
& Leisure   practice area.
Location   0.75m SW

Hotel   ★★★ 70% Bromley Court Hotel, Bromley
Hill, BROMLEY ☎ 0181 464 5011 115 ⇔ ▸

ENFIELD   Map 04 TQ39

Crews Hill Cattlegate Rd, Crews Hill EN2 8AZ
☎ 0181 363 6674 Fax 0181 364 5641
Parkland course in country surroundings.
18 holes, 6250yds, Par 70, SSS 70, Course record 65.
Club membership 600.
Visitors   all day Mon, 7-9.30am Tue-Fri and after 2pm
Wed & Fri, must play with member at
weekends. Handicap certificate required.
Societies   Wed-Fri; must apply in writing.
Green Fees £12.50 per round.
Cards   ▭▭
Prof   Neil Wichelow
Designer   Harry Colt
Facilities   ゐ ☎ ⛏ ⚒ ✓
Location   3m NW off A1005

Hotel   ★★ 70% Oak Lodge Hotel, 80 Village Rd,
Bush Hill Park, ENFIELD
☎ 0181 360 7082 7 ⇔ ▸

Enfield Old Park Rd South EN2 7DA
☎ 0181 363 3970 Fax 0181 342 0381
Parkland course. Salmons Brook crosses 7 holes.
18 holes, 6154yds, Par 72, SSS 70, Course record 61.
Club membership 700.
Visitors   must contact the Professionalin advance.
Societies   must contact the secretary in advance.
Green Fees on application.
Prof   Lee Fickling

Designer   James Braid
Facilities   ⊗ ⨯ ㄴ ▤ ♀ ゐ ☎ ✓
Location   M25 jnct 24, A1005 to Enfield to rdbt with
church on left, right down Slades Hill, 1st left to
end

Hotel   ★★ 70% Oak Lodge Hotel, 80 Village Rd,
Bush Hill Park, ENFIELD
☎ 0181 360 7082 7 ⇔ ▸

Whitewebbs Park Whitewebbs Ln EN2 9JN
☎ 0181 363 4454 Fax 0181 363 4454
Gently undulating wooded parkland course with an attractive
brook running through four holes.
18 holes, 5863yds, Par 68, SSS 68, Course record 61.
Club membership 190.
Visitors   can play all times, can book in advance
Societies   must apply in writing or by phone to Course
Manager.
Green Fees £12 per round (£15 weekends).
Cards   ▭▭ ▭▭ ▭▭ ▭
Prof   Peter Garlick
Facilities   ⊗ ⨯ ㄴ ▤ ゐ ☎ ✓
Location   N side of town centre

Hotel   ★★ 70% Oak Lodge Hotel, 80 Village Rd,
Bush Hill Park, ENFIELD
☎ 0181 360 7082 7 ⇔ ▸

GREENFORD   Map 04 TQ18

C & L Golf & Country Club Westend Rd, Northolt
UB5 6RD ☎ 0181 845 5662
Parkland course.
18 holes, 4438yds, Par 64, SSS 63.
Club membership 150.
Visitors   welcome, but may not play Sun mornings.
Societies   contact for details.
Green Fees not confirmed.
Prof   Richard Kelly
Designer   Patrick Tallack
Facilities   ⊗ ⨯ ㄴ ▤ ♀ ゐ
& Leisure   hard tennis courts, outdoor swimming pool,
squash, sauna, solarium, gymnasium.
Location   Junct Westend Road/A40

Hotel   ★★★ 69% The Bridge Hotel, Western Av,
GREENFORD ☎ 0181 566 6246 68 ⇔ ▸

Ealing Perivale Ln UB6 8SS
☎ 0181 997 0937 Fax 0181 998 0756
Flat, parkland course relying on natural hazards; trees, tight
fairways, and the River Brent which affects 9 holes.
18 holes, 6216yds, Par 70, SSS 70, Course record 64.
Club membership 600.
Visitors   Mon-Fri only on application to pro shop.
Societies   Mon, Wed & Thu only by arrangement.
Green Fees £30 per day/round.
Prof   Ian Parsons
Designer   H S Colt
Facilities   ⊗ ⨯ by prior arrangement ㄴ ▤ ♀ ゐ ☎ ⚒
✓
Location   Off A40 travelling W from London

Hotel   ★★★ 69% The Bridge Hotel, Western Av,
GREENFORD ☎ 0181 566 6246 68 ⇔ ▸

Horsenden Hill Whitten Av, Woodland Rise UB6 0RD
☎ 0181 902 4555
A well-kept, tree-lined short course.
9 holes, 1632yds, Par 28, SSS 28.
Club membership 135.
Visitors   no restrictions.
Societies   telephone for details.
Green Fees   not confirmed.
Prof   Simon Hoffman
Facilities   ⊗ ⑪ ⓑ 🛐 ♀ ♨ 🏠 ⚑ ♂
Location   3m NE on A4090

Hotel   ★★★ 69% The Bridge Hotel, Western Av,
                  GREENFORD ☎ 0181 566 6246 68 ⇄ 🐾

Lime Trees Park Ruislip Rd, Northolt UB5 6QZ
☎ 0181 842 0442
Parkland course.
9 holes, 5836yds, Par 71, SSS 69.
Club membership 300.
Visitors   no restrictions, but advisable to book for
                  weekends.
Societies   contact for details.
Green Fees   not confirmed.
Prof   Ian Godleman
Facilities   ⊗ ⓑ 🛐 ♀ ♨ 🏠 ⚑ ♂ ⚑
Location   300yds off A40 at Polish War Memorial/A4180
                  towards Hayes

Hotel   ★★★ 69% The Bridge Hotel, Western Av,
                  GREENFORD ☎ 0181 566 6246 68 ⇄ 🐾

Perivale Park Stockdove Way UB6 8TJ
☎ 0181 575 7116
Parkland course.
9 holes, 2667yds, Par 68, SSS 67.
Club membership 250.
Visitors   no restrictions.
Societies   one weeks notice required.
Green Fees   not confirmed.
Prof   Peter Bryant
Facilities   ⊗ ⑪ ⓑ 🛐 ♀ ♨ 🏠 ⚑ ♂
Location   E side of town centre, off A40

Hotel   B Hilton National Wembley, Empire Way,
                  WEMBLEY ☎ 0181 902 8839 306 ⇄ 🐾

HADLEY WOOD   Map 04 TQ29

Hadley Wood Beech Hill EN4 0JJ
☎ 0181 449 4328 & 4486 Fax 0181 364 8633
A parkland course on the northwest edge of London. The
gently undulating fairways have a friendly width inviting
the player to open his shoulders, though the thick rough
can be very punishing to the unwary. The course is
pleasantly wooded and there are some admirable views.
18 holes, 6457yds, Par 72, SSS 71, Course record 66.
Club membership 600.
Visitors   handicap certificate required, may not play
                  Tue mornings & Sat. Must contact in
                  advance.
Societies   must contact in advance.
Green Fees   on application.
Prof   Peter Jones
Designer   Alistair Mackenzie
Facilities   ⓑ ♀ ♨ 🏠 ⚑ ♂ ⚑
Location   E side of village

Hotel   ★★★★♨♨ 71% West Lodge Park Hotel,
                  Cockfosters Rd, HADLEY WOOD
                  ☎ 0181 440 8311 46 ⇄ 🐾 Annexe9 ⇄ 🐾

HAMPTON   Map 04 TQ17

Fulwell Wellington Rd, Hampton Hill TW12 1JY
☎ 0181 977 3844 & 0181-977 2733
Championship-length parkland course with easy walking.
The 575-yd, 17th, is notable.
18 holes, 6544yds, Par 71, SSS 71.
Club membership 750.
Visitors   may not play Tue & weekends. Must contact in
                  advance and have a handicap certificate.
Societies   must apply in writing.
Green Fees   not confirmed.
Prof   Nigel Turner
Facilities   ⊗ ⑪ ⓑ 🛐 ♀ ♨ 🏠 ⚑ ♂ ⚑
Location   1.5m N on A311

Hotel   ★★★ 69% Richmond Hill, Richmond Hill,
                  RICHMOND UPON THAMES
                  ☎ 0181 940 2247 & 940 5466
                  Fax 0181 940 5424 138 ⇄ 🐾

HAMPTON WICK   Map 04 TQ16

Home Park KT1 4AD ☎ 0181 977 2423
Flat, parkland course with easy walking.
18 holes, 6611yds, Par 71, SSS 71.
Club membership 550.
Visitors   welcome all week subject to club competitions.
Societies   apply in writing.
Green Fees   not confirmed.
Prof   Len Roberts
Facilities   ⊗ ⑪ ⓑ 🛐 ♀ ♨ 🏠
Location   Off A308 on W side of Kingston Bridge

Hotel   ★★★ 69% Richmond Hill, Richmond Hill,
                  RICHMOND UPON THAMES
                  ☎ 0181 940 2247 & 940 5466
                  Fax 0181 940 5424 138 ⇄ 🐾

HILLINGDON   Map 04 TQ08

Hillingdon 18 Dorset Way UB10 0JR
☎ 01895 233956 & 239810 Fax 01895 233956
Parkland course west of London.
9 holes, 5490yds, Par 68, SSS 67.
Club membership 400.
Visitors   must contact in advance. May not play Thu,
                  weekends, or bank holidays. Handicap
                  certificate required.
Societies   must apply in writing.
Green Fees   not confirmed.
Prof   Neil Wichelow
Facilities   ⊗ ⓑ ♀ ♨ 🏠 ♂
Location   W side of town off A4020

Hotel   ★★★ 69% Novotel, Junction 4 M4, Cherry Ln,
                  WEST DRAYTON
                  ☎ 01895 431431 178 ⇄ 🐾

HOUNSLOW   Map 04 TQ17

Airlinks Southall Ln TW5 9PE ☎ 0181 561 1418
Meadowland/parkland course designed by P. Allis and D.
Thomas.
18 holes, 6000yds, Par 71, SSS 69.
Club membership 500.
Visitors   welcome all times.
Societies   must apply in writing.
Green Fees   not confirmed.
Cards   ▦ ▩ ▨ ▥
Prof   Tony Martin
Designer   P Alliss/D Thomas
Facilities   ⊗ ⅷ ⅃ 🍴 ♀ ⚘ 🛒 🕏 🛺 ♂ ⟨
& Leisure   Sports centre.
Location   W of Hounslow off M4 junc 3

Hotel   ★★★ 64% Master Robert Hotel, Great West
                    Rd, HOUNSLOW ☎ 0181 570 6261 94 ⇆ ➤

Hounslow Heath Municipal Staines Rd TW4 5DS
☎ 0181 570 5271
Heathland course in a conservation area, planted with an
attractive variety of trees. The 15th hole lies between the fork
of two rivers.
18 holes, 5901yds, Par 69, SSS 68, Course record 62.
Club membership 300.
Visitors   pay & play, bookings taken for weekends &
                    bank holidays seven days in advance.
Societies   must telephone and confirm at least 14 days in
                    advance.
Green Fees   £8 (£11.50 weekends & bank holidays).
Prof   Joe Smith
Designer   Fraser M Middleton
Facilities   ⊗ ⅷ ⅃ 🍴 ⚘ 🕏 ♂
Location   On A315 towards Bedfont

Hotel   ★★★★ 67% Forte Crest Heathrow, Sipson Rd,
                    WEST DRAYTON ☎ 0181 759 2323 610 ⇆ ➤

ILFORD   Map 05 TQ48

Ilford Wanstead Park Rd IG1 3TR
☎ 0181 554 2930 Fax 0181 554 0822
Fairly flat parkland course with the River Roding running
through it. The river borders four holes, and is crossed by
three holes. Whilst not a relatively long course, the small
greens, and many holes requiring brains rather than brawn,
provide a challenging test to all ranges of golfer.
18 holes, 5299yds, Par 67, SSS 66, Course record 61.
Club membership 500.
Visitors   must contact in advance, book with pro on
                    0181 554 0094.
Societies   telephone for provisional date and booking
                    form.
Green Fees   £22 per day; £16 per round (£20 per round
                    weekends).
Cards   ▬ ▦ ▩ ▨ ▥
Prof   S Dowsett
Designer   Whitehead
Facilities   ⊗ ⅷ 🍴 ♀ ⚘ 🕏 ♂
& Leisure   snooker tables.
Location   NW side of town centre off A12

Hotel   ★★★ 66% County Hotel Epping Forest, Oak
                    Hill, WOODFORD GREEN
                    ☎ 0181 787 9988 99 ⇆ ➤

ISLEWORTH   Map 04 TQ17

Wyke Green Syon Ln TW7 5PT
☎ 0181 847 0685 (Prof) Fax 0181 569 8392
Fairly flat parkland course.
18 holes, 6211yds, Par 69, SSS 70, Course record 64.
Club membership 650.
Visitors   may not play before 3pm weekends and bank
                    holidays, must have a handicap certificate or
                    equivalent.
Societies   must apply in writing or telephone in advance.
Green Fees   not confirmed.
Prof   Neil Smith
Facilities   ⊗ ⅷ ⅃ 🍴 ♀ ⚘ 🕏 🛺 ♂
Location   1.5m N on B454 off A4

Hotel   ★★★ 64% Master Robert Hotel, Great West
                    Rd, HOUNSLOW ☎ 0181 570 6261 94 ⇆ ➤

KINGSTON UPON THAMES   Map 04 TQ16

Coombe Hill Golf Club Dr, Coombe Ln West KT2 7DF
☎ 0181 336 7600 Fax 0181 336 7601
A splendid course in wooded terrain. The undulations
and trees make it an especially interesting course of great
charm. And there is a lovely display of rhododendrons in
May and June.
18 holes, 6293yds, Par 71, SSS 71, Course record 67.
Club membership 600.
Visitors   must contact in advance. With member only
                    at weekends.
Societies   must book in advance.
Green Fees   £65 per day.
Cards   ▦ ▩
Prof   Craig Defoy
Designer   J F Abercromby
Facilities   ⊗ ⅃ 🍴 ♀ ⚘ 🕏 🛺 ♂
& Leisure   sauna.
Location   1.75m E on A238

Hotel   ★★★ 69% Kingston Lodge Hotel,
                    Kingston Hill, KINGSTON UPON
                    THAMES ☎ 0181 541 4481 62 ⇆ ➤

Coombe Wood George Rd, Kingston Hill KT2 7NS
☎ 0181 942 0388 Fax 0181 942 0388
Mature parkland course with seven varied and challenging
par 3's.
18 holes, 5299yds, Par 66, SSS 66, Course record 61.
Club membership 640.
Visitors   must play with member at weekends.
Societies   Wed, Thu & Fri; must contact in advance.
Green Fees   £23 per round.
Prof   David Butler
Designer   Tom Williamson
Facilities   ⊗ ⅷ by prior arrangement ⅃ 🍴 ♀ ⚘ 🕏 ♂
Location   1.25m NE on A308

Hotel   ★★★ 69% Kingston Lodge Hotel, Kingston
                    Hill, KINGSTON UPON THAMES
                    ☎ 0181 541 4481 62 ⇆ ➤

> Entries with a shaded background
> identify courses that are
> considered to be particularly interesting

MITCHAM
Map 04 TQ26

Mitcham Carshalton Rd CR4 4HN
☎ 0181 648 4280 Fax 0181 647 4197
A wooded heathland course on a gravel base.
18 holes, 5935yds, Par 69, SSS 68, Course record 65.
Club membership 500.
Visitors	must telephone & book in advance, restricted play at weekends.
Societies	must phone in advance.
Green Fees	not confirmed.
Prof	Jeff Godfrey
Designer	T Scott/T Morris
Facilities	⊗ ⑪ ⌾ ♥ ♀ ♨ 🏌 ✎
Location	1m S

Hotel ★★★ B Posthouse Croydon, Purley Way, CROYDON ☎ 0181 688 5185 83 ⇆ ⚑

NEW MALDEN
Map 04 TQ26

Malden Traps Ln KT3 4RS
☎ 0181 942 0654 Fax 0181 336 2219
Parkland course with the hazard of the Beverley Brook which affects 4 holes (3rd, 7th, 8th and 12th).
18 holes, 6295yds, Par 71, SSS 70.
Club membership 800.
Visitors	restricted weekends and bank holidays. Advisable to telephone.
Societies	must apply in writing.
Green Fees	not confirmed.
Prof	Robert Hunter
Facilities	⊗ ⌾ ♥ ♀ ♨ 🏌 🔔 ⛳ ✎
Location	N side of town centre off B283

Hotel ★★★ 69% Kingston Lodge Hotel, Kingston Hill, KINGSTON UPON THAMES ☎ 0181 541 4481 62 ⇆ ⚑

NORTHWOOD
Map 04 TQ09

Haste Hill The Drive HA6 1HN
☎ 01923 822877 Fax 01923 824683
Parkland course with stream running through. Excellent views.
18 holes, 5787yds, Par 68, SSS 68, Course record 67.
Club membership 250.
Visitors	advised to book in advance 01923 825224
Societies	must apply in advance.
Green Fees	£12.15 per round (£17.60 weekends).
Facilities	⊗ ⑪ by prior arrangement ⌾ ♥ ♀ ♨ 🏌 🔔 ⛳ ✎
Location	0.5m S off A404

Hotel ★★★ 67% Quality Harrow Hotel, Roxborough Bridge, 12-22 Pinner Rd, HARROW ☎ 0181 427 3435 53 ⇆ ⚑ Annexe23 ⇆ ⚑

Northwood Rickmansworth Rd HA6 2QW
☎ 01923 821384 Fax 01923 840150
A very old club to which, it is said, golfers used to drive from London by horse-carriage. They would find their golf interesting as present-day players do. The course is relatively flat although there are some undulations, and trees and whins add not only to the beauty of the course but also to the test of golf.

18 holes, 6553yds, Par 71, SSS 71, Course record 67.
Club membership 650.
Visitors	must contact in advance. May not play weekends.
Societies	must apply in writing.
Green Fees	£35 per day; £27 per round.
Prof	C J Holdsworth
Facilities	⊗ ⑪ ⌾ ♥ ♀ ♨ 🏌 ✎
Location	On main A404

Hotel ★★★ 67% Quality Harrow Hotel, Roxborough Bridge, 12-22 Pinner Rd, HARROW ☎ 0181 427 3435 53 ⇆ ⚑ Annexe23 ⇆ ⚑

Sandy Lodge Sandy Lodge Ln HA6 2JD
☎ 01923 825429 Fax 01923 824319
A links-type, very sandy, heathland course.
18 holes, 6347yds, Par 71, SSS 71, Course record 64.
Club membership 780.
Visitors	must contact in advance, may not play at weekends. Handicap certificate required.
Societies	must telephone in advance.
Green Fees	not confirmed.
Prof	Jeff Pinsent
Designer	H Vardon
Facilities	⊗ ⑪ ⌾ ♥ ♀ ♨ 🏌 ✎ ⚐
Location	N side of town centre off A4125

Hotel ★★★ 64% The White House, Upton Rd, WATFORD ☎ 01923 237316 60 ⇆ ⚑ Annexe26 ⇆ ⚑

ORPINGTON
Map 05 TQ46

Chelsfield Lakes Golf Centre Court Rd BR6 9BX
☎ 01689 896266 Fax 01689 824577
A downland course but some holes are played through the orchards which used to occupy the site. The 9th and 18th holes are separated by a hazardous lake.
18 holes, 6077yds, Par 71, SSS 69, Course record 64.
Warren: 9 holes, 1188yds, Par 27.
Club membership 438.
Visitors	must book in advance.
Societies	telephone in advance.
Green Fees	Chelsfield Lakes: £15 (£18 weekends); Warren: £6 per day, £4 per round (£7.50/£5 weekends).
Cards	MasterCard VISA Barclays CONNECT 💳 📇
Prof	N Lee/B Hodkin
Designer	M Sandow
Facilities	⊗ ⑪ ⌾ ♥ ♀ ♨ 🏌 ✎ ⚐ ⚑
Location	Exit M25 junct 4, on A224 Court Rd

Hotel ★★★ 70% Bromley Court Hotel, Bromley Hill, BROMLEY ☎ 0181 464 5011 115 ⇆ ⚑

Cray Valley Sandy Ln, St Paul's Cray BR5 3HY
☎ 01689 837909 & 871490 Fax 01689 891428
An easy walking open parkland course comprising an 18 hole par70 and a 9 hole par32. Challenging for all standards of golfers.
18 holes, 5669yds, Par 70, SSS 67.
Club membership 640.
Visitors	no restrictions, may book up to 7 days in advance.

▶

Societies   by arrangement.
Green Fees £15 per round (£20 weekends).
Prof   Andy Langdon
Facilities   ⊗ 🏌 🛍 🍺 ♀ ♿ 🏠 ⛳ 🏌 🛒 ⚷ ⛳
Location   1m off A20, Critley's Corner junction

Hotel   ★★★ 70% Bromley Court Hotel, Bromley Hill, BROMLEY ☎ 0181 464 5011 115 ⇥ ⮡

Lullingstone Park Parkgate Rd, Chelsfield BR6 7PX
☎ 01959 533793 & 533794 Fax 01959 533795
Popular 27-hole public course set in 690 acres of undulating parkland. Championship length 18-holes, plus 9-hole course and a further 9-hole pitch and putt.
Main Course: 18 holes, 6778yds, Par 72, SSS 72, Course record 71.
9 hole course: 9 holes, 2432yds, Par 33, SSS 31.
Club membership 400.
Visitors   telephone for details.
Societies   must telephone in advance.
Green Fees Main Course: £10 (£12.50 weekends, £15 7.30-10.30am); 9 hole course: £6 (£8 weekends).
Cards   💳 💳 VISA 💳 💳 💳
Prof   Mark Watt
Facilities   ⊗ 🏌 🛍 🍺 ♀ ♿ 🏠 ⛳ 🛒 ⚷ ⛳
Location   Leave M25 junct 4 and take Well Hill turn

Hotel   ★★★ 70% Bromley Court Hotel, Bromley Hill, BROMLEY ☎ 0181 464 5011 115 ⇥ ⮡

Ruxley Park Golf Centre Sandy Ln, St Paul's Cray BR5 3HY ☎ 01689 871490 Fax 01689 891428
Undulating parkland course with public, floodlit driving range. Difficult 6th hole, par 4. Easy walking and good views.
18 holes, 5703yds, Par 70, SSS 68, Course record 63.
Club membership 450.
Visitors   may book 7 days in advance and regular dress code expected.
Societies   telephone for details 01689 839677.
Green Fees £15 per round (£20 weekends); Par3 £4 at all times.
Cards   💳 💳 VISA 💳 💳 💳 💳
Prof   Andy Langdon
Facilities   ⊗ 🏌 🛍 🍺 ♀ ♿ 🏠 ⛳ 🛒 ⚷ ⛳
Location   2m NE on A223

Hotel   ★★★ 70% Bromley Court Hotel, Bromley Hill, BROMLEY ☎ 0181 464 5011 115 ⇥ ⮡

PINNER   Map 04 TQ18

Grims Dyke Oxhey Ln, Hatch End HA5 4AL
☎ 0181 428 4539 Fax 0181 421 5494
Pleasant, undulating parkland course.
18 holes, 5600yds, Par 69, SSS 67, Course record 61.
Club membership 580.
Visitors   must contact in advance, may not play weekends.
Societies   by arrangement, booked in advance.
Green Fees not confirmed.
Prof   John Rule
Designer   Braid
Facilities   ⊗ 🏌 🛍 🍺 ♀ ♿ 🏠 ⛳ ⚷
Location   3m N of Harrow on A4008

Pinner Hill Southview Rd, Pinner Hill HA5 3YA
☎ 0181 866 0963 Fax 0181 868 4817
A hilly, wooded parkland course.
18 holes, 6086yds, Par 71, SSS 69.
Club membership 770.
Visitors   are required to have handicap certificate on Mon, Tue & Fri. Public days Wed & Thu. Contact in advance.
Societies   Mon, Tue & Fri only, by arrangement.
Green Fees £25 per day (£32 per day weekends).
Prof   Mark Grieve
Designer   J H Taylor
Facilities   ⊗ 🏌 🛍 🍺 ♀ ♿ 🏠 ⛳ 🛒 ⛳
Location   2m NW off A404

Hotel   ★★★ 67% Quality Harrow Hotel, Roxborough Bridge, 12-22 Pinner Rd, HARROW ☎ 0181 427 3435 53 ⇥ ⮡ Annexe23 ⇥ ⮡

PURLEY   Map 05 TQ36

Purley Downs 106 Purley Downs Rd CR2 0RB
☎ 0181 657 8347 Fax 0181 651 5044
Hilly downland course which is a good test for golfers.
18 holes, 6275yds, Par 70, SSS 70, Course record 64.
Club membership 650.
Visitors   must contact in advance & play on weekends only with member.
Societies   must contact in advance.
Green Fees £30 per day; £25 per round.
Prof   Graham Wilson
Designer   J Taylor/H S Colt
Facilities   ♿ 🏠 🛒 ⚷
Location   E side of town centre off A235

Hotel   B Posthouse Croydon, Purley Way, CROYDON ☎ 0181 688 5185 83 ⇥ ⮡

RICHMOND UPON THAMES   Map 04 TQ17

Richmond Sudbrook Park, Petersham TW10 7AS
☎ 0181 940 4351
A beautiful and historic wooded, parkland course on the edge of Richmond Park, with six par-3 holes. The 4th is often described as the best short hole in the south of England. Low scores are uncommon because cunningly sited trees call for great accuracy. The clubhouse is one of the most distinguished small Georgian mansions in England.
18 holes, 6007yds, Par 70, SSS 69.
Club membership 700.
Visitors   may not play weekends.
Societies   must apply in writing.
Green Fees not confirmed.
Prof   Nick Job
Facilities   ⊗ 🛍 🍺 ♀ ♿ 🏠 ⛳ ⚷ ⛳
Location   1.5m S off A307

Hotel   ★★★ 69% Richmond Hill, Richmond Hill, RICHMOND UPON THAMES ☎ 0181 940 2247 & 940 5466 Fax 0181 940 5424 138 ⇥ ⮡

Royal Mid-Surrey Old Deer Park TW9 2SB
☎ 0181 940 1894 Fax 0181 332 2957
A long playing parkland course. The flat fairways are
cleverly bunkered. The 18th provides an exceptionally
good par 4 finish with a huge bunker before the green to
catch the not quite perfect long second.
Outer Course: 18 holes, 6343yds, Par 69, SSS 70,
Course record 62.
Inner Course: 18 holes, 5544yds, Par 68, SSS 67.
Club membership 1250.

Visitors	may not play at weekends. Must contact in advance and bring a handicap certificate.
Societies	must apply in writing.
Green Fees	£42 per day winter; £63 per day summer, late start£26 summer only.
Cards	💳 💳 💳 💳 💳
Prof	David Talbot
Designer	J H Taylor
Facilities	⊗ 🖤 ♀ 👤 🏌 🖤 🎯 🔨 ✓
Location	0.5m N of Richmond upon Thames off A316
Hotel	★★★ 69% Richmond Hill, Richmond Hill, RICHMOND UPON THAMES ☎ 0181 940 2247 & 940 5466 Fax 0181 940 5424 138 ⇋ 🏌

ROMFORD   Map 05 TQ58

Maylands Golf Club & Country Park Colchester Rd,
Harold Park RM3 0AZ
☎ 01708 346466 Fax 01708 373080
Picturesque undulating parkland course.
18 holes, 6361yds, Par 71, SSS 70, Course record 65.
Club membership 700.

Visitors	handicap certificate required.
Societies	Mon, Wed & Fri only, by arrangement.
Green Fees	£30 per 36 holes; £20 per round (£40/£30 weekends & bank holidays).
Cards	💳 💳 💳
Prof	J Hopkin/T Wheals
Designer	H S Colt
Facilities	⊗ 🖤 🖤 ♀ 👤 🏌 🖤 🎯 🔨 ✓
Hotel	B Posthouse Brentwood, Brook St, BRENTWOOD ☎ 01277 260260 145 ⇋ 🏌

Risebridge Golf Centre Risebridge Chase, Lower Bedfords
Rd RM1 4DG ☎ 01708 741429 Fax 01708 741429
A well matured parkland golf course, with many challenging
holes especially the long 12th, the Par 4 13th and Par 5 14th
with water and a two tiered green.
18 holes, 6000yds, Par 71, SSS 70, Course record 66.
Club membership 300.

Visitors	no restrictions.
Societies	must telephone in advance.
Green Fees	not confirmed.
Prof	Paul Jennings
Designer	Hawtree
Facilities	👤 🖤 🎯 ✓ ｌ
& Leisure	pitch & putt.
Location	Between Colier Row and Harold Hill
Hotel	★★★ 61% Palms Hotel, Southend Arterial Rd, HORNCHURCH ☎ 01708 346789 138 ⇋ 🏌

Romford Heath Dr, Gidea Park RM2 5QB
☎ 01708 740986
A many-bunkered parkland course with easy walking. It
is said there are as many bunkers as there are days in the
year. The ground is quick drying making a good course
for winter play when other courses might be too wet.
18 holes, 6389yds, Par 72, SSS 70.
Club membership 693.

Visitors	with member only weekends & bank holidays. Must contact in advance & have handicap certificate. Must contact in advance.
Societies	must telephone in advance.
Green Fees	not confirmed.
Prof	Harry Flatman
Designer	H Colt
Facilities	🖤 ♀ 👤 🏠
Location	1m NE on A118
Hotel	B Posthouse Brentwood, Brook St, BRENTWOOD ☎ 01277 260260 145 ⇋ 🏌

RUISLIP   Map 04 TQ08

Ruislip Ickenham Rd HA4 7DQ
☎ 01895 638081 & 638835 Fax 01895 635780
Municipal parkland course. Many trees.
18 holes, 5700yds, Par 69, SSS 68, Course record 65.
Club membership 500.

Visitors	telephone in advance.
Societies	must contact in advance.
Green Fees	not confirmed.
Prof	Paul Glozier/Stephen Bryan
Designer	Sand Herd
Facilities	⊗ 🖤 🖤 🖤 ♀ 👤 🏠 🏌 🖤 🎯 🔨 ✓ ｌ
Location	0.5m SW on B466
Hotel	★★★ 67% Quality Harrow Hotel, Roxborough Bridge, 12-22 Pinner Rd, HARROW ☎ 0181 427 3435 53 ⇋ 🏌 Annexe23 ⇋ 🏌

SIDCUP   Map 05 TQ47

Sidcup 7 Hurst Rd DA15 9AE ☎ 0181 300 2150
Easy walking parkland course with natural water hazards.
9 holes, 5722yds, Par 68, SSS 68.
Club membership 370.

Visitors	contact in advance and may not play weekends.
Societies	must contact in advance.
Green Fees	not confirmed.
Designer	James Braid
Facilities	⊗ 🖤 🖤 🖤 ♀ 👤 🏠
Location	N side of town centre off A222
Hotel	★★★★ 71% Swallow Hotel, 1 Broadway, BEXLEYHEATH ☎ 0181 298 1000 142 ⇋ 🏌

SOUTHALL   Map 04 TQ17

West Middlesex Greenford Rd UB1 3EE
☎ 0181 574 3450 Fax 0181 574 2383
Gently undulating parkland course.
18 holes, 6242yds, Par 69, SSS 69, Course record 64.
Club membership 700.

▶

Visitors	must contact in advance and may not play at weekends.
Societies	must apply in advance.
Green Fees	not confirmed.
Prof	I P Harris
Facilities	👥 🏠 ⛳
& Leisure	squash.
Location	W side of town centre on A4127 off A4020

Hotel ★★ 63% Beach Dunes Hotel, Ramoth Way, Reen Sands, PERRANPORTH
☎ 01872 572263 6rm(5 ⇔ ↟) Annexe3 ⇔ ↟

STANMORE   Map 04 TQ19

Stanmore 29 Gordon Av HA7 2RL ☎ 0181 954 2599
North London parkland course.
18 holes, 5860yds, Par 68, SSS 68, Course record 61.
Club membership 560.

Visitors	may not play weekends. Contact professional 0181 954 2646.
Societies	phone in advance for booking sheet.
Green Fees	£33 per day, £26 per round.
Prof	V Law
Facilities	⊗ 𝍝 by prior arrangement 👥 🍺 ⛾ 👥 🏠 ⛳
Location	S side of town centre, between Stanmore & Belmont

Hotel ★★★ 67% Quality Harrow Hotel, Roxborough Bridge, 12-22 Pinner Rd, HARROW
☎ 0181 427 3435 53 ⇔ ↟ Annexe23 ⇔ ↟

SURBITON   Map 04 TQ16

Surbiton Woodstock Ln KT9 1UG
☎ 0181 398 3101 (Secretary) & 398 6619 (Pro)
Fax 0181 339 0992
Parkland course with easy walking.
18 holes, 6055yds, Par 70, SSS 69, Course record 63.
Club membership 700.

Visitors	with member only at weekends & bank holidays. No visitors Tue am (Ladies Day).
Societies	Mon & Fri only. Apply year in advance.
Green Fees	£45 per day £30 per round.
Prof	Paul Milton
Designer	Tom Dunn
Facilities	⊗ 👥 🍺 ⛾ 👥 🏠 ⛳
Location	2m S off A3, take A309 from Hook junct of A3,turn left into Woodstock Lane

Hotel ★★ 64% Haven Hotel, Portsmouth Rd, ESHER ☎ 0181 398 0023
16 ⇔ ↟ Annexe4 ⇔ ↟

TWICKENHAM   Map 04 TQ17

Strawberry Hill Wellesley Rd, Strawberry Hill TW2 5SD
☎ 0181 894 0165
Parkland course with easy walking.
9 holes, 4762yds, Par 64, SSS 62, Course record 59.
Club membership 300.

Visitors	must contact in advance, with member only at weekends.
Societies	must apply in writing.
Green Fees	not confirmed.
Prof	Peter Buchan
Designer	J H Taylor

Facilities	👥 🍺 ⛾ 👥 🏠 ⛳
Location	S side of town centre off A311

Hotel ★★★ 69% Richmond Hill, Richmond Hill, RICHMOND UPON THAMES
☎ 0181 940 2247 & 940 5466
Fax 0181 940 5424 138 ⇔ ↟

Twickenham Staines Rd TW2 5JD
☎ 0181 783 1748 & 1698 Fax 0181 941 9134
Interesting tree lined parkland course with water feature.
9 holes, 3180yds, Par 36, SSS 69.

Visitors	must book in advance for weekends & bank holidays.
Societies	apply in advance
Green Fees	not confirmed.
Cards	💳 💳 💳 💳 💳
Prof	Suzy Watt
Facilities	⊗ 👥 🍺 ⛾ 👥 🏠 ⛳ ⛳
& Leisure	putting green.
Location	2m W on A305

Hotel ★★★ 69% Richmond Hill, Richmond Hill, RICHMOND UPON THAMES
☎ 0181 940 2247 & 940 5466
Fax 0181 940 5424 138 ⇔ ↟

UPMINSTER   Map 05 TQ58

Upminster 114 Hall Ln RM14 1AU
☎ 01708 222788 (Secretary) 220000 (Pro)
Fax 01708 222788
The meandering River Ingrebourne features on several holes of this partly undulating parkland course situated on one side of the river valley. It provides a challenge for golfers of all abilities. The clubhouse is a beautiful Grade II listed building.
18 holes, 6076yds, Par 69, SSS 69, Course record 66.
Club membership 1000.

Visitors	contact in advance, may not play at weekends.
Societies	telephone initially.
Green Fees	£30 per day; £25 per round.
Prof	Neil Carr
Designer	W G Key
Facilities	⊗ 𝍝 👥 🍺 ⛾ 👥 🏠 ⛳
Location	2m W from A127 junct with M25

Hotel ★★★ 61% Palms Hotel, Southend Arterial Rd, HORNCHURCH ☎ 01708 346789 138 ⇔ ↟

UXBRIDGE   Map 04 TQ08

Stockley Park Stockley Park UB11 1AQ
☎ 0181 813 5700 561 6339 (tee times) Fax 0181 813 5655
Hilly and challenging parkland championship course designed by Trent Jones in 1993 and situated within two miles of Heathrow Airport.
18 holes, 6548yds, Par 72, SSS 71.

Visitors	6 day in advance reservation facility.
Societies	please telephone for details.
Green Fees	not confirmed.
Cards	💳 💳 💳 💳 💳
Prof	Alex Knox
Designer	Robert Trent Jones Snr
Facilities	⊗ 𝍝 👥 🍺 ⛾ 👥 🏠 ⛳ ⛳
Location	2m N of junct4 M4

Hotel   ★★★★ 76% Crowne Plaza London -
Heathrow, Stockley Rd, WEST DRAYTON
☎ 01895 445555 458 ⇔ ♦

Uxbridge The Drive, Harefield Place UB10 8AQ
☎ 01895 237287 Fax 01895 813539
Municipal parkland course, undulating and tricky.
18 holes, 5750yds, Par 68, SSS 68, Course record 66.
Club membership 400.
Visitors   no restrictions.
Societies   by arrangement.
Green Fees not confirmed.
Cards   ▭▭ ▭▭ ▭▭ ▭
Prof   Phil Howard
Facilities ⊗ ⫫ ⯈ ⯆ ♀ ⏦ ☎ ⫚ ♦ ⯈ ✓
Location   2m N off B467

Hotel   ★★★★ 76% Crowne Plaza London -
Heathrow, Stockley Rd, WEST DRAYTON
☎ 01895 445555 458 ⇔ ♦

WEMBLEY   Map 04 TQ18

Sudbury Bridgewater Rd HA0 1AL
☎ 0181 902 3713 Fax 0181 903 2966
Undulating parkland course very near centre of London.
18 holes, 6282yds, Par 69, SSS 70.
Club membership 650.
Visitors   must have handicap certificate. With member
only at weekends.
Societies   must apply in writing.
Green Fees not confirmed.
Prof   Neil Jordan
Facilities ⊗ ⫫ ⯈ ⯆ ♀ ⏦ ☎ ⯈ ⫚ ✓
Location   SW side of town centre on A4090

Hotel   ★★★ 69% The Bridge Hotel, Western Av,
GREENFORD ☎ 0181 566 6246 68 ⇔ ♦

WEST DRAYTON   Map 04 TQ07

Heathpark Stockley Rd UB7 9NA
☎ 01895 444232 Fax 01895 445122
Fairly large, testing, hilly par 4 course suitable both for
beginners and scratch players.
9 holes, 2032yds, Par 64, Course record 50.
Club membership 80.
Visitors   no restrictions.
Societies   by arrangement.
Green Fees £6 per round (£7 weekends).
Designer   Niel Coles
Facilities ⊗ ⫫ ⯈ ⯆ ♀ ⏦ ☎ ⯈ ⫚ ✓
& Leisure   heated indoor swimming pool, sauna, solarium,
gymnasium.
Location   1m SE off A408 via junct 4 on M4

Hotel   ★★★★ 76% Crowne Plaza London -
Heathrow, Stockley Rd, WEST DRAYTON
☎ 01895 445555 458 ⇔ ♦

WOODFORD GREEN   Map 05 TQ49

Woodford Sunset Av IG8 0ST
☎ 0181 504 3330 & 504 0553 Fax 0181 559 0504
Forest land course on the edge of Epping Forest. Views over
the Lea Valley to the London skyline.

9 holes, 5806yds, Par 70, SSS 68, Course record 66.
Club membership 420.
Visitors   advisable to contact in advance. May not play
Sat or Sun afternoon.
Societies   telephone for details.
Green Fees £15 per day; £12 per round.
Prof   Ashley Johns
Designer   Tom Dunn
Facilities ⊗ ⯆ ♀ Tue-Sat ⏦ ☎
Location   NW side of town centre off A104

Hotel   ★★★ 66% County Hotel Epping Forest, Oak
Hill, WOODFORD GREEN
☎ 0181 787 9988 99 ⇔ ♦

GREATER MANCHESTER

ALTRINCHAM   Map 07 SJ78

Altrincham Stockport Rd WA15 7LP ☎ 0161 928 0761
Municipal parkland course with easy walking, water on many
holes, rolling contours and many trees. Driving range in
grounds.
18 holes, 6162yds, Par 71, SSS 69.
Club membership 350.
Visitors   must book in advance via course office.
Societies   by prior arrangement.
🍂 **Green Fees** £8.50 per round (£9.50 weekends & bank
holidays).
Cards   ▭▭
Prof   Scott Partington
Facilities ⏦ ☎ ⯈ ✓ ⏦
Location   0.75 E of Altrincham on A560

Hotel   ★★★ 65% Cresta Court Hotel, Church St,
ALTRINCHAM ☎ 0161 927 7272 138 ⇔ ♦

Dunham Forest Oldfield Ln WA14 4TY
☎ 0161 928 2605 Fax 0161 929 8975
Attractive parkland course cut through magnificent beech
woods.
18 holes, 6636yds, Par 72, SSS 72.
Club membership 680.
Visitors   by prior arrangement. May not play weekends &
bank holidays.
Societies   apply in writing or telephone in advance.
Green Fees not confirmed.
Prof   Ian Wrigley
Designer   Dave Thomas
Facilities ⊗ ⯈ ⯆ ♀ ⏦ ☎ ⯈ ⫚ ♦ ⯈ ✓
& Leisure   hard tennis courts, squash.
Location   1.5m W off A56

Hotel   ★★★ 67% Quality Hotel Altrincham,
Langham Rd, Bowdon, ALTRINCHAM
☎ 0161 928 7121 89 ⇔ ♦

Ringway Hale Mount, Hale Barns WA15 8SW
☎ 0161 980 8432 (pro) & 0161 904 9609
Parkland course, with interesting natural hazards. Easy
walking, good views.
18 holes, 6494yds, Par 71, SSS 71, Course record 67.
Club membership 700.   ▶

Visitors	must have handicap certificate, may not play before 9.30am or between 1-2pm, play restricted Tue, Fri & Sat.
Societies	Thu only May-Sep.
Green Fees	£31 per round (£37 weekends and bank holidays).
Prof	Nick Ryan
Designer	Colt
Facilities	⊗ ⫿⫿⫿ 🖳 💺 🍵 ⛳ 🏌
Location	M56 junct 6, take A538 signposted Hale & Altrincham

| Hotel | ★★★ 65% Cresta Court Hotel, Church St, ALTRINCHAM ☎ 0161 927 7272 138 ⇔ ♠ |

ASHTON-IN-MAKERFIELD   Map 07 SJ59

Ashton-in-Makerfield Garswood Park, Liverpool Rd
WN4 0YT ☎ 01942 727267 & 719330
Well-wooded parkland course. Easy walking.
18 holes, 6250yds, Par 70, SSS 70.
Club membership 800.

Visitors	with member only weekends & bank holidays. No visitors Wed.
Societies	apply in writing.
Green Fees	£30 per day; £25 per round.
Prof	Peter Allan
Facilities	⊗ ⫿⫿⫿ 🖳 💺 🍵 ⛳ 🏌
Location	0.5m W of M6 (junc 24) on A58

| Hotel | B Posthouse Haydock, Lodge Ln, HAYDOCK ☎ 01942 717878 138 ⇔ ♠ |

ASHTON-UNDER-LYNE   Map 07 SJ99

Ashton-under-Lyne Gorsey Way, Higher Hurst OL6 9HT
☎ 0161 330 1537 Fax 0161 330 1537
A testing, varied moorland course, with large greens. Easy
walking. Three new holes have improved the course.
18 holes, 6209yds, Par 70, SSS 70, Course record 67.
Club membership 550.

Visitors	must contact in advance, with member only weekends & bank holidays.
Societies	apply in advance.
Green Fees	£27 per day/round (weekdays only).
Prof	Colin Boyle
Facilities	⊗ ⫿⫿⫿ 🖳 💺 🍵 🏌
& Leisure	snooker table.
Location	N off B6194

| Hotel | ★★ 70% York House Hotel, York Place, Richmond St, ASHTON-UNDER-LYNE ☎ 0161 330 9000 24 ⇔ ♠ Annexe10 ⇔ ♠ |

Dukinfield Lyne Edge, Yew Tree Ln SK16 5DF
☎ 0161 338 2340
Recently extended, tricky hillside course with several
difficult Par 3s and a very long par 5.
18 holes, 5303yds, Par 67, SSS 66.
Club membership 400.

Visitors	may not play on Wed afternoons & must play with member at weekends, advisable to contact in advance.
Societies	apply in writing or telephone.
Green Fees	not confirmed.
Prof	Jason Peel
Facilities	⊗ ⫿⫿⫿ 🖳 💺 🍵 🏌
Location	S off B6175

| Hotel | ★★ 70% York House Hotel, York Place, Richmond St, ASHTON-UNDER-LYNE ☎ 0161 330 9000 24 ⇔ ♠ Annexe10 ⇔ ♠ |

BOLTON   Map 07 SD70

Bolton Lostock Park, Chorley New Rd BL6 4AJ
☎ 01204 843067 & 843278 Fax 01204 843067
This well maintained heathland course is always a
pleasure to visit. The 12th hole should be treated with
respect and so too should the final four holes which have
ruined many a card.
18 holes, 6237yds, Par 70, SSS 70, Course record 66.
Club membership 612.

Visitors	not able to play Tue before 2.30pm or on competition days, before 10am and between 12-2pm.
Societies	write or telephone in advance, not accepted Tue, Sat or Sun.
Green Fees	£36 per day; £30 per round (£40/£33 weekends & bank holidays).
Prof	R Longworth
Facilities	⊗ ⫿⫿⫿ 🖳 💺 🍵 🏌
Location	3m W of Bolton, on A673

| Hotel | ★★★ 62% The Beaumont Hotel, Beaumont Rd, BOLTON ☎ 01204 651511 101 ⇔ ♠ |

Breightmet Red Bridge, Ainsworth BL2 5PA
☎ 01204 527381
Long parkland course.
9 holes, 6416yds, Par 72, SSS 71, Course record 68.
Club membership 350.

Visitors	may not play Wed or weekends.
Societies	welcome Mon, Tue, Thu & Fri only, apply in advance in writing.
Green Fees	not confirmed.
Facilities	⊗ 🖳 💺 🍵
Location	E side of town centre off A58

| Hotel | ★★★ 66% Egerton House Hotel, Blackburn Rd, Egerton, BOLTON ☎ 01204 307171 32 ⇔ ♠ |

Deane Broadford Rd, Deane BL3 4NS
☎ 01204 61944 (Professional) Fax 01204 651808
Undulating parkland course with small ravines on approaches
to some holes.
18 holes, 5652yds, Par 68, SSS 67, Course record 64.
Club membership 470.

Visitors	must be a member of a golf club or member's guest. Restricted weekends.
Societies	must telephone in advance and confirm in writing.
Green Fees	not confirmed.
Prof	David Martindale
Facilities	⊗ ⓛ 🖤 ⓨ 🛆 🏌
Location	1m from exit 5 on M61 towards Bolton

Hotel	★★★ 62% The Beaumont Hotel, Beaumont Rd, BOLTON ☎ 01204 651511 101 ⇔ 🏌

Dunscar Longworth Ln, Bromley Cross BL7 9QY
☎ 01204 303321
A scenic moorland course with panoramic views. A warm friendly club.
18 holes, 6085yds, Par 71, SSS 69, Course record 65.
Club membership 600.

Visitors	must telephone 01204 592992 in advance and have a handicap certificate.
Societies	must apply in writing.
Green Fees	£20 per round (£30 weekends & bank holidays).
Cards	▬▬ 💳 💳 💳
Prof	Gary Treadgold
Facilities	⊗ 🏛 ⓛ 🖤 ⓨ 🛆 🏠 🏌
Location	2m N off A666

Hotel	★★★ 66% Egerton House Hotel, Blackburn Rd, Egerton, BOLTON ☎ 01204 307171 32 ⇔ 🏌

Great Lever & Farnworth Plodder Ln, Farnworth BL4 0LQ ☎ 01204 656137 Fax 01204 656137
Downland course with easy walking.
18 holes, 6064yds, Par 70, SSS 69, Course record 67.
Club membership 600.

Visitors	must contact in advance, weekend by prior arrangement.
Societies	must contact in advance.
Green Fees	£20 per day (£27 weekends & bank holidays).
Prof	Tony Howarth
Facilities	⊗ 🏛 ⓛ 🖤 ⓨ 🛆 🏠 ⚲ 🏌
Location	1m junct 4 M61

Hotel	★★★ 62% The Beaumont Hotel, Beaumont Rd, BOLTON ☎ 01204 651511 101 ⇔ 🏌

Harwood Springfield, Roading Brook Rd, Harwood BL2 4JD ☎ 01204 522878 & 524233 (Sec)
Mainly flat parkland course.
18 holes, 5778yds, Par 70, SSS 69.
Club membership 574.

Visitors	must be members of a golf club and hold a current handicap certificate. May not play at weekends.
Societies	contact the Secretary by telephone or in writing.
Green Fees	£20 per round.
Prof	M Dance
Facilities	⊗ ⓛ 🖤 ⓨ 🛆 🏠
Location	2.5m NE off B6196

Hotel	★★★ 66% Egerton House Hotel, Blackburn Rd, Egerton, BOLTON ☎ 01204 307171 32 ⇔ 🏌

Old Links Chorley Old Rd, Montserrat BL1 5SU
☎ 01204 842307 Fax 01204 842307 ext 25
Championship moorland course.

18 holes, 6406yds, Par 72, SSS 72.
Club membership 600.

Visitors	must contact in advance and may only play weekends with member.
Societies	apply by letter or telephone.
Green Fees	not confirmed.
Prof	Paul Horridge
Designer	Dr Alistair MacKenzie
Facilities	⊗ 🏛 ⓛ 🖤 ⓨ 🛆 🏠 🏌
Location	NW of town centre on B6226

Hotel	★★★ 62% The Beaumont Hotel, Beaumont Rd, BOLTON ☎ 01204 651511 101 ⇔ 🏌

Regent Park Links Rd, Chorley New Rd BL2 9XX
☎ 01204 844170
Parkland course.
18 holes, 6130yds, Par 70, SSS 69, Course record 67.
Club membership 200.

Visitors	must book 6 days in advance.
Societies	must telephone 01204 495421 in advance.
Green Fees	for green fees telephone 01204 495421.
Cards	💳
Prof	P A Wells
Facilities	⊗ 🏛 ⓛ 🖤 ⓨ 🛆 🏠 ⚲ 🏌
Location	3.5m W off A673

Hotel	★★★ 62% The Beaumont Hotel, Beaumont Rd, BOLTON ☎ 01204 651511 101 ⇔ 🏌

BRAMHALL   Map 07 SJ88

Bramall Park 20 Manor Rd SK7 3LY
☎ 0161 485 3119 & 7101 (secretary) Fax 0161 485 7101
Well-wooded parkland course with splendid views of the Pennines.
18 holes, 6043yds, Par 70, SSS 69.
Club membership 600.

Visitors	must contact in advance.
Societies	apply in writing.
Green Fees	not confirmed.
Prof	M Proffitt
Facilities	🛆 🏠 🏌
Location	NW side of town centre off B5149

Hotel	★★★ 66% County Hotel Bramhall, Bramhall Ln South, BRAMHALL ☎ 0161 455 9988 65 ⇔ 🏌

Bramhall Ladythorn Rd SK7 2EY
☎ 0161 439 6092 Fax 0161 439 0264
Undulating parkland course, easy walking.
18 holes, 6340yds, Par 70, SSS 70.
Club membership 700.

Visitors	must contact in advance.
Societies	apply in writing.
Green Fees	not confirmed.
Prof	Richard Green
Facilities	⊗ 🏛 ⓛ 🖤 ⓨ 🛆 🏠 ⚲
Location	E side of town centre off A5102

Hotel	★★★ 66% County Hotel Bramhall, Bramhall Ln South, BRAMHALL ☎ 0161 455 9988 65 ⇔ 🏌

▶

BROMLEY CROSS — Map 07 SD71

Turton Wood End Farm, Chapeltown Rd BL7 9QH
☎ 01204 852235
Moorland course with panoramic views. A wide variety of holes which challenge any golfer's technique.
18 holes, 6159yds, Par 70, SSS 70, Course record 70.
Club membership 450.

Visitors avoid 11.30-2pm Wed Ladies day. Sat tee available after last competition. Restricted Sun.
Societies must contact in writing.
Green Fees £16 per day (£20 per round weekends & bank holidays).
Designer Alex Herd
Facilities ⊗ ⓑ ♥ ♀ ♨
Location 3m N on A666

Hotel ★★★ 66% Egerton House Hotel, Blackburn Rd, Egerton, BOLTON ☎ 01204 307171 32 ⇄ 🏶

BURY — Map 07 SD81

Bury Unsworth Hall, Blackford Bridge, Manchester Rd BL9 9TJ ☎ 0161 766 4897 Fax 0161 796 3480
Moorland course, difficult in part. Tight and good test of golf.
18 holes, 5961yds, Par 69, SSS 68, Course record 64.
Club membership 650.

Visitors may not normally play at weekends. Must contact in advance.
Societies telephone 0161 766 4897.
Green Fees not confirmed.
Prof S Crake
Designer Mackenzie
Facilities ⊗ ⓜ ⓑ ♥ ♀ ♨ 🏶 ✎
Location 2m S on A56

Hotel ★★★ 65% Bolholt Country Park Hotel, Walshaw Rd, BURY ☎ 0161 762 4000 66 ⇄ 🏶

Lowes Park Hilltop, Lowes Rd BL9 6SU
☎ 0161 764 1231 Fax 0161 763 9503
Moorland course, with easy walking. Exposed outlook with good views.
9 holes, 6009yds, Par 70, SSS 69, Course record 65.
Club membership 400.

Visitors may not play Wed & Sat, by appointment Sun. Must contact in advance.
Societies apply in writing.
Green Fees £17 per day (£23 Sun & bank holidays).
Facilities ⊗ ⓜ ⓑ ♥ ♀ ♨
Location N side of town centre off A56

Hotel ★★★ 65% Bolholt Country Park Hotel, Walshaw Rd, BURY ☎ 0161 762 4000 66 ⇄ 🏶

Walmersley Garretts Close, Walmersley BL9 6TE
☎ 0161 764 1429 & 0161 764 7770 Fax 01706 827618
Moorland hillside course, with wide fairways, large greens and extensive views. Testing holes: 2nd (484 yds) par 5; 5th par 4 with severe dogleg and various hazards.
18 holes, 5341yds, Par 69, SSS 67.
Club membership 475.

Visitors welcome by arrangement with secretary. May only play with member at weekend,
Societies must apply in writing.
Green Fees £20 per day.

Prof S Crake
Designer S Marnoch
Facilities ⊗ ⓜ ⓑ ♥ ♀ ♨ 🏶
Location 2m N off A56

Hotel ★★★ 69% Normandie Hotel, Elbut l n, Birtle, BURY ☎ 0161 764 3869 & 764 1170 Fax 0161 764 4866 20 ⇄ 🏶 Annexe3 ⇄ 🏶

CHEADLE — Map 07 SJ88

Cheadle Cheadle Rd SK8 1HW ☎ 0161 491 4452
Parkland course with hazards on every hole, from sand bunkers and copses to a stream across six of the fairways.
9 holes, 5006yds, Par 64, SSS 65.
Club membership 425.

Visitors may not play Tue & Sat, & restricted Sun. Must contact in advance and have a handicap certificate and be member of a bona-fide golf club.
Societies apply in writing to secretary
Green Fees £20 per day (£25 weekends).
Prof S Booth
Designer T Renouf
Facilities ⊗ ⓜ ⓑ ♥ ♀ ♨ 🏶 ✎
Location S side of village off A5149

Hotel ★★ 67% The Wycliffe Hotel, 74 Edgeley Rd, Edgeley, STOCKPORT ☎ 0161 477 5395 20 ⇄ 🏶

DENTON — Map 07 SJ99

Denton Manchester Rd M34 2NU ☎ 0161 336 3218
Easy, flat parkland course with brook running through. Notable hole is one called 'Death and Glory'.
18 holes, 6541yds, Par 72, SSS 71, Course record 66.
Club membership 585.

Visitors must contact in advance & may not play summer weekends.
Societies apply in advance.
Green Fees not confirmed.
Prof M Hollingworth
Designer R McCauley
Facilities ⊗ ⓜ ⓑ ♥ ♀ ♨ 🏶 ✎
Location 1.5m W on A57

Hotel ★★ 70% York House Hotel, York Place, Richmond St, ASHTON-UNDER-LYNE ☎ 0161 330 9000 24 ⇄ 🏶 Annexe10 ⇄ 🏶

FAILSWORTH — Map 07 SD80

Brookdale Medlock Rd M35 9WQ
☎ 0161 681 4534 Fax 0161 681 4534
Undulating parkland course, with river crossed 5 times in play. Hard walking.
18 holes, 5841yds, Par 68, SSS 68, Course record 64.
Club membership 600.

Visitors advisable to contact in advance. May only play as guest of member at weekends.
Societies must contact in advance.
Green Fees not confirmed.
Prof Tony Cuppello
Facilities ⊗ ⓜ ⓑ ♥ ♀ ♨ 🏶 ✎
Location N side of Manchester

Hotel ★★ 70% York House Hotel, York Place, Richmond St, ASHTON-UNDER-LYNE
☎ 0161 330 9000 24 ⇆ ⋔ Annexe10 ⇆ ⋔

FLIXTON   Map 07 SJ79

William Wroe Municipal Pennybridge Ln, Flixton Rd M41 5DX ☎ 0161 748 8680
Parkland course, with easy walking.
18 holes, 4395yds, Par 68, SSS 65.
Visitors must book in advance.
Societies contact for details.
Green Fees not confirmed.
Prof Scott Partington
Facilities ⛳🏠⋔
Location E side of village off B5158

Hotel ★★★ 60% Trafford Hall Hotel, St Agnes Laned, Hales St, MANCHESTER
☎ 0161 848 7791 31 ⇆ ⋔ Annexe3 ⇆ ⋔

GATLEY   Map 07 SJ88

Gatley Waterfall Farm, Styal Rd, Heald Green SK8 3TW ☎ 0161 437 2091
Parkland course. Moderately testing.
9 holes, 5934yds, Par 68, SSS 68.
Visitors may not play Tue & Sat. With member only weekends. Handicap certificate required.
Societies apply in writing.
Green Fees not confirmed.
Prof Simon Reeves
Facilities ⛳🏠
& Leisure squash.
Location S side of village off B5166

Hotel ★★★★ 63% Belfry House Hotel, Stanley Rd, HANDFORTH ☎ 0161 437 0511 80 ⇆ ⋔

HALE   Map 07 SJ78

Hale Rappax Rd WA15 0NU ☎ 0161 980 4225
Beautiful, undulating parkland course, with the River Bollin winding round fairways.
9 holes, 5780yds, Par 70, SSS 68, Course record 65.
Club membership 300.
Visitors may not play before 4.30pm Thu; with member only weekends.
Societies apply in writing
Green Fees not confirmed.
Prof Mike Grantham
Facilities ⊗ 🎿 by prior arrangement 📖 ☕ ♀ ⛳ 🏠
Location Off Bankhall Lane close to Altrincham Priory Hospital

Hotel ★★★ 67% Quality Hotel Altrincham, Langham Rd, Bowdon, ALTRINCHAM
☎ 0161 928 7121 89 ⇆ ⋔

HAZEL GROVE   Map 07 SJ98

Hazel Grove Buxton Rd SK7 6LU ☎ 0161 483 3978
Testing parkland course with tricky greens and water hazards coming into play on several holes.
18 holes, 6310yds, Par 71, SSS 71.
Club membership 600.

Visitors must contact in advance tel: 0161 483 7272.
Societies must apply in writing, Thu & Fri only.
Green Fees not confirmed.
Prof M E Hill
Facilities ⛳🏠⋔ ♂
Location 1m E off A6

Hotel ★★★ 66% County Hotel Bramhall, Bramhall Ln South, BRAMHALL
☎ 0161 455 9988 65 ⇆ ⋔

HINDLEY   Map 07 SD60

Hindley Hall Hall Ln WN2 2SQ ☎ 01942 255131
Parkland course with mostly easy walking.
18 holes, 5913yds, Par 69, SSS 68, Course record 64.
Club membership 430.
Visitors must contact in advance.
Societies apply in advance to Secretary
Green Fees £20 per round.
Prof Neil Brazell
Facilities ⊗ 🎿 📖 ☕ ♀ ⛳ 🏠 ♂
Location 1m N off A58

Hotel ★★★ 64% Quality Hotel Wigan, Riverway, WIGAN ☎ 01942 826888 88 ⇆ ⋔

LITTLEBOROUGH   Map 07 SD91

Whittaker Whittaker Ln OL15 0LH ☎ 01706 378310
Moorland 9-hole course with outstanding views of Hollingworth Lake Countryside Park and the Pennine Hills.
9 holes, 5632yds, Par 68, SSS 67, Course record 61.
Club membership 210.
Visitors welcome except for Tue pm and Sun.
Societies apply to Secretary.
Green Fees £12 per day (£16 weekends).
Facilities ♀ ⛳
Location 1.5m out of Littleborough off A58

Hotel ★★★ 68% Norton Grange Hotel, Manchester Rd, Castleton, ROCHDALE
☎ 01706 630788 51 ⇆ ⋔

MANCHESTER   Map 07 SJ89

Blackley Victoria Ave East, Blackley M9 7HW
☎ 0161 643 2980 & 654 7770
Parkland course. Course crossed by footpath.
18 holes, 6237yds, Par 70, SSS 70.
Club membership 760.
Visitors with member only Thu, weekends and bank holidays.
Societies apply in advance.
Green Fees £24.
Prof Craig Gould
Facilities ⊗ 🎿 📖 ☕ ♀ ⛳ 🏠 🛒 ♂
Location 4m N of city centre, on Rochdale Rd

Hotel ★★★ 63% Bower Hotel, Hollinwood Av, Chadderton, OLDHAM
☎ 0161 682 7254 63 ⇆ ⋔

▶

Chorlton-cum-Hardy Barlow Hall, Barlow Hall Rd,
Chorlton-cum-Hardy M21 7JJ
☎ 0161 881 5830 Fax 0161 881 5830
Meadowland course with trees, stream and several ditches.
18 holes, 5980yds, Par 70, SSS 69, Course record 64.
Club membership 802.
Visitors   handicap certificate required.
Societies   on Thu only by prior booking.
Green Fees £22 per day (£27 weekends & bank holidays).
Prof   David Screeton
Facilities   ⊗ ⅢⅢ ⅃ ♥ ♀ ♤ ⌂ ☞ ♂
Location   4m S of Manchester A5103/A5145

Hotel   ★★ 63% Willow Bank Hotel, 340-342
            Wilmslow Rd, Fallowfield, MANCHESTER
            ☎ 0161 224 0461 116 ⊟ ☏

Davyhulme Park Gleneagles Rd, Davyhulme M41 8SA
☎ 0161 748 2260 Fax 0161 747 4067
Parkland course.
18 holes, 6237yds, Par 72, SSS 70, Course record 67.
Club membership 680.
Visitors   may play Mon, Tue & Thu.
Societies   telephone in advance.
Green Fees £30 per day; £24 per round.
Prof   Dean Butler
Facilities   ⊗ ⅃ ♥ ♀ ♤ ⌂ ♂
& Leisure   snooker.
Location   8m S adj to Trafford General Hospital

Hotel   ★★★ 60% Trafford Hall Hotel, St Agnes
            Laned, Hales St, MANCHESTER
            ☎ 0161 848 7791 31 ⊟ ☏ Annexe3 ⊟ ☏

Didsbury Ford Ln, Northenden M22 4NQ
☎ 0161 998 9278 Fax 0161 998 9278
Parkland course.
18 holes, 6273yds, Par 70, SSS 70, Course record 63.
Club membership 750.
Visitors   advised to check dates/times with manager or
              professional.
Societies   Thu & Fri, must contact in advance.
Green Fees £26 per day (£30 weekends).
Cards   ▭ ▬
Prof   Peter Barber
Facilities   ⊗ ⅢⅢ ⅃ ♥ ♀ ♤ ⌂ ♘ ♂ ♂
Location   6m S of city centre off A5145

Hotel   B Posthouse Manchester, Palatine Rd,
            Northenden, MANCHESTER
            ☎ 0161 998 7090 190 ⊟ ☏

Fairfield "Boothdale", Booth Rd, Audenshaw M34 5GA
☎ 0161 370 1641 & 370 2292
Parkland course set around a reservoir. Course demands
particularly accurate placing of shots.
18 holes, 4956yds, Par 68, SSS 68, Course record 65.
Club membership 450.
Visitors   may not play mornings at weekends & may be
              restricted on Wed & Thu.
Societies   prior booking through Secretary.
Green Fees not confirmed.
Prof   Stephen Pownell
Facilities   ⊗ by prior arrangement ⅢⅢ by prior arrangement
              ⅃ ♥ ♀ ♤ ⌂ ♂
Location   5m E of Manchester, off A635

Hotel   ★★ 70% York House Hotel, York Place,
            Richmond St, ASHTON-UNDER-LYNE
            ☎ 0161 330 9000 24 ⊟ ☏ Annexe10 ⊟ ☏

Marriott Manchester Hotel & Country Club Worsley Park
M28 2QT ☎ 0161 975 2000
Set in the 200 acres of Worsley Park, the course provides a
challenge to golfers of all abilities.
18 holes, 6611yds, Par 71, SSS 71, Course record 69.
Club membership 340.
Visitors   must contact at least 7 days in advance.
Societies   telephone in advance.
Green Fees £60 per day; £40 per round (£70/£50 weekends).
Cards   ▬ ▭ ▬ 👁 🖊
Prof   David Screeton
Facilities   ⊗ ⅢⅢ ⅃ ♥ ♀ ♤ ⌂ ☞ ♙ ♨ ♂ ♭
Location   junct 13 off M60/M62 signed Worsley.

Hotel   ★★★★ 67% ❀ Marriott Manchester Hotel &
            Country Club, Worsley Park, Worsley,
            MANCHESTER M28 2QT
            ☎ 0161 799 6341   159 ⊟ ☏

Northenden Palatine Rd, Northenden M22 4FR
☎ 0161 998 4738 Fax 0161 998 5592
Parkland course surrounded by the River Mersey.
18 holes, 6503yds, Par 72, SSS 71, Course record 64.
Club membership 800.
Visitors   Must contact in advance.
Societies   Tue & Fri only, apply in advance to Secretary.
Green Fees £27 per day (£30 weekends & bank holidays).
Prof   P A Scott
Designer   Renouf
Facilities   ⊗ ⅢⅢ ⅃ ♥ ♀ ♤ ⌂ ♂
Location   6.5m S of city centre on B1567 off A5103

Hotel   B Posthouse Manchester, Palatine Rd,
            Northenden, MANCHESTER
            ☎ 0161 998 7090 190 ⊟ ☏

Withington 243 Palatine Rd, West Didsbury M20 2UE
☎ 0161 445 9544 Fax 0161 445 5210
Flat parkland course bordering the river Mersey. Easy
walking with an extremely tough finish.
18 holes, 6410yds, Par 71, SSS 71.
Club membership 600.
Visitors   welcome except Thu, must contact in advance,
              restricted at weekends.
Societies   telephone in advance, welcome except Thu, Sat
              & Sun.

Green Fees not confirmed.
Prof R J Ling
Facilities ⊗ ⅷ ⅃ ♨ ♀ ♿ 🏠 ♂
Location 4m SW of city centre off B5167

Hotel B Posthouse Manchester, Palatine Rd,
Northenden, MANCHESTER
☎ 0161 998 7090 190 ⇔ ☎

Worsley Stableford Av, Worsley M30 8AP
☎ 0161 789 4202 Fax 0161 789 3200
Well-wooded parkland course.
18 holes, 6252yds, Par 72, SSS 70, Course record 65.
Club membership 600.
Visitors must contact professional in advance restricted
during club competitions.
Societies apply in advance.
Green Fees not confirmed.
Prof Ceri Cousins
Designer James Braid
Facilities ⊗ ⅷ ⅃ ♨ ♀ ♿ 🏠 ♂ ♂
Location 6.5m NW of city centre off A572

Hotel ★★★ 65% Novotel, Worsley Brow,
WORSLEY ☎ 0161 799 3535 119 ⇔ ☎

MELLOR   Map 07 SJ98

Mellor & Townscliffe Gibb Ln, Tarden SK6 5NA
☎ 0161 427 2208 (secretary) & 427 5759 (pro)
Scenic parkland and moorland course, undulating with some
hard walking. Good views. Testing 200 yd, 9th hole, par 3.
18 holes, 5925yds, Par 70, SSS 69.
Club membership 650.
Visitors with member only weekends & bank holidays.
Societies apply by letter.
Green Fees not confirmed.
Prof Gary R Broadley
Facilities ⊗ ⅃ ♨ ♀ ♿ 🏠 ♂
Location 7m SE of Stockport off A626

Hotel ★★ 70% Springfield Hotel, Station Rd,
MARPLE ☎ 0161 449 0721 7 ⇔ ☎

MIDDLETON   Map 07 SD80

Manchester Hopwood Cottage, Rochdale Rd M24 2QP
☎ 0161 643 3202 Fax 0161 643 9174
Moorland golf of unique character over a spaciously laid
out course with generous fairways sweeping along to
large greens. A wide variety of holes will challenge the
golfer's technique, particularly the testing last three
holes.
18 holes, 6519yds, Par 72, SSS 70, Course record 65.
Club membership 650.
Visitors must contact in advance, limited play
weekends and Wed.
Societies telephone in advance.
Green Fees £40 per day; £30 per round (£50/£45
weekends).
Cards ▭ ▬ ▯
Prof Brian Connor
Designer Shapland Colt
Facilities ⊗ by prior arrangement ⅷ by prior
arrangement ⅃ ♨ ♀ ♿ 🏠 ⚑ ♂ ♭
Location 2.5m N off A664. M62 junct 20

Hotel ★★ 62% Midway Park Hotel, Manchester
Rd, Castleton, ROCHDALE
☎ 01706 32881 24 ⇔ ☎

North Manchester Rhodes House, Manchester Old Rd
M24 4PE ☎ 0161 643 9033
A long, tight heathland course with natural water hazards.
Excellent views of the Yorkshire Wolds.
18 holes, 6527yds, Par 72, SSS 72, Course record 66.
Club membership 750.
Visitors contact Pro Shop on 0161 643 7094 for
availability.
Societies telephone in advance.
Green Fees £25 per round (£30 weekends).
Prof Frank Accleton
Designer J Braid
Facilities ⊗ ⅷ ⅃ ♨ ♀ ♿ 🏠 ♂
Location W side of town centre off A576

Hotel ★★★ 63% Bower Hotel, Hollinwood Av,
Chadderton, OLDHAM
☎ 0161 682 7254 63 ⇔ ☎

MILNROW   Map 07 SD91

Tunshill Kiln Ln OL16 3TS ☎ 01706 342095
Testing moorland course, particularly 6th and 15th (par 5's).
9 holes, 5743yds, Par 70, SSS 70.
Club membership 275.
Visitors must contact in advance, restricted weekends &
evenings.
Societies apply in writing.
Green Fees £15.
Facilities ⊗ ⅷ ⅃ ♨ ♀ ♿
Location 1m NE M62 exit junc 21 off B6225

Hotel ★★★ 68% Norton Grange Hotel, Manchester
Rd, Castleton, ROCHDALE
☎ 01706 630788 51 ⇔ ☎

OLDHAM   Map 07 SD90

Crompton & Royton Highbarn OL2 6RW
☎ 0161 624 0986 Fax 0161 624 0986
Undulating moorland course.
18 holes, 6214yds, Par 70, SSS 70, Course record 65.
Club membership 500.
Visitors must contact in advance and may not play Tue
or Sat, limited play Sun pm and Wed.
Societies apply in advance
Green Fees £20 per day (£30 weekends & bank holidays).
Prof David Melling
Facilities ⊗ ⅷ ⅃ ♨ ♀ ♿ 🏠 ♂
Location 0.5m NE of Royton

Hotel ★★★ 63% Bower Hotel, Hollinwood Av,
Chadderton, OLDHAM
☎ 0161 682 7254 63 ⇔ ☎

Oldham Lees New Rd OL4 5PN ☎ 0161 624 4986
Moorland course, with hard walking.
18 holes, 5122yds, Par 66, SSS 65, Course record 62.
Club membership 370.
Visitors no restrictions.
Societies must contact in advance.   ▶

Green Fees £16 (£22 weekends & bank holidays).
Prof Jason Peel
Facilities ⊗ ⫪ ⬚ ■ ♀ ♋ ⬚ ✐
Location 2.5m E off A669

Hotel ★★ 70% York House Hotel, York Place, Richmond St, ASHTON-UNDER-LYNE
☎ 0161 330 9000 24 ⇄ ♠ Annexe10 ⇄ ♠

Werneth Green Ln, Garden Suburb OL8 3AZ
☎ 0161 624 1190
Semi-moorland course, with a deep gulley and stream crossing eight fairways. Testing hole: 3rd (par 3).
18 holes, 5363yds, Par 68, SSS 66.
Club membership 460.
Visitors may not play on Tue or Thu and weekends. ⸰Must contact in advance.
Societies must contact in advance.
Green Fees not confirmed.
Prof Roy Pennet
Facilities ⊗ ⫪ ⬚ ■ ♀ ♋ ⬚ ✐
Location S side of town centre off A627

Hotel ★★ 70% York House Hotel, York Place, Richmond St, ASHTON-UNDER-LYNE
☎ 0161 330 9000 24 ⇄ ♠ Annexe10 ⇄ ♠

PRESTWICH Map 07 SD80

Heaton Park Municipal Heaton Park, Middleton Rd M25 2SW ☎ 0161 654 9899 Fax 0161 653 2003
A parkland style course in historic Heaton Park with rolling hills and lakes, boasting some spectacular holes. A good test of skill for golfers of all abilities.
18 holes, 5815yds, Par 70, SSS 70.
Club membership 190.
Visitors restricted to club members only between 8-10am Sat & Sun.
Societies apply in writing or by telephone to Matthew Riley
Green Fees not confirmed.
Cards ⬚⬚ ⬚⬚
Prof Dennis Durnian
Designer J H Taylor
Facilities ⊗ ⫪ ⬚ ■ ♀ ♋ ⬚ ⬚ ✐ ✦
Location N of Manchester near junct 18 of M62

Hotel ★★★★ 63% Bolton Moat House, 1 Higher Bridge St, BOLTON
☎ 01204 879988 128 ⇄ ♠

Prestwich Hilton Ln M25 9XB
☎ 0161 773 2544 Fax 0161 773 1404
Parkland course, near to Manchester city centre.
18 holes, 4806yds, Par 64, SSS 63, Course record 60.
Club membership 507.
Visitors handicap certificate, weekdays by arrangement, restricted at weekends.
Societies apply in writing or telephone.
Green Fees not confirmed.
Prof Simon Wakefield
Facilities ♋ ⬚ ⬚ ✐
Location N side of town centre on A6044

Hotel ★★★ 65% Novotel, Worsley Brow, WORSLEY ☎ 0161 799 3535 119 ⇄ ♠

ROCHDALE Map 07 SD81

Castle Hawk Chadwick Ln, Castleton OL11 3BY
☎ 01706 640841 Fax 01706 860587
Two parkland courses, with challenging par 3s, and a driving range.
New Course: 9 holes, 2699yds, Par 34, SSS 34, Course record 30.
Old Course: 18 holes, 3276yds, Par 55, SSS 55.
Club membership 220.
Visitors no restrictions.
Societies must contact in advance.
Green Fees £8 per day (£10 Sundays).
Cards ⬚⬚ ⬚⬚ ⬚⬚ ⬚⬚ ⬚
Prof Mike Vipond
Designer T Wilson
Facilities ⊗ ⫪ ⬚ ■ ♀ ♋ ⬚ ⬚ ✐ ✦
Location S of Rochdale, nr junc 20 (M62)

Hotel ★★★ 68% Norton Grange Hotel, Manchester Rd, Castleton, ROCHDALE
☎ 01706 630788 51 ⇄ ♠

Rochdale Edenfield Rd OL11 5YR
☎ 01706 643818 Fax 01706 643818
Parkland course with enjoyable golf and easy walking.
18 holes, 6050yds, Par 71, SSS 69, Course record 65.
Club membership 750.
Visitors must telephone in advance.
Societies apply in writing or telephone
Green Fees £27 per day/round (£32 weekends & bank holidays).
Prof Andrew Laverty
Designer George Lowe
Facilities ⊗ ⫪ ⬚ ■ ♀ ♋ ⬚ ⬚ ✐
Location 1.75m W on A680

Hotel ★★ 62% Midway Park Hotel, Manchester Rd, Castleton, ROCHDALE
☎ 01706 32881 24 ⇄ ♠

Springfield Park Springfield Park, Bolton Rd OL11 4RE
☎ 01706 56401 (weekend only)
Parkland-moorland course situated in a valley. The River Roch adds an extra hazard to the course.
18 holes, 5237yds, Par 67, SSS 66, Course record 64.
Club membership 300.
Visitors must contact professional in advance.
Societies telephone in advance.
Green Fees not confirmed.
Prof David Wills
Facilities ⬚ ⬚
Location 1.5m SW off A58

Hotel ★★ 62% Midway Park Hotel, Manchester Rd, Castleton, ROCHDALE
☎ 01706 32881 24 ⇄ ♠

ROMILEY Map 07 SJ99

Romiley Goose House Green SK6 4LJ
☎ 0161 430 2392 Fax 0161 430 7258
Semi-parkland course on the edge of the Derbyshire Hills, providing a good test of golf with a number of outstanding holes, notably the 6th, 9th, 14th and 16th. The latter enjoys magnificent views from the tee.
18 holes, 6454yds, Par 70, SSS 71, Course record 66.
Club membership 700.

Visitors	are advised to contact in advance, may not play Thu or Sat before 4pm.
Societies	Tue & Wed, must book in advance.
Green Fees	£40 per day; £30 per round (£50 weekends & bank holidays).
Prof	Gary Butler
Facilities	⊗ by prior arrangement ⚲ by prior arrangement ⌊ ▦ 𝄆 ⌣ ♨ ✎
Location	E side of town centre off B6104

Hotel	★★ 67% Red Lion Inn, 112 Buxton Rd, High Ln, STOCKPORT ☎ 01663 765227 6 ⇥ ↾

SALE   Map 07 SJ79

Ashton on Mersey Church Ln M33 5QQ
☎ 0161 976 4390 & 962 3727 Fax 0161 976 4390
Parkland course with easy walking alongside the River Mersey.
9 holes, 6146yds, Par 71, SSS 69, Course record 66.
Club membership 485.

Visitors	with member only Sun & bank holidays, not Sat or Tue.
Societies	Thu only. Apply in writing.
Green Fees	£18 per day.
Prof	Mike Williams
Facilities	⊗ ▦ ⌊ ▬ 𝄆 ⌣ ♨ ✎
& Leisure	sauna.
Location	1m W of M60 (M63) junc 7, off Glebelands Road

Hotel	★★★ 65% Cresta Court Hotel, Church St, ALTRINCHAM ☎ 0161 927 7272 138 ⇥ ↾

Sale Golf Rd M33 2XU
☎ 0161 973 1638 (Gen Man) Fax 0161 962 4217
Tree-lined parkland course. Feature holes are the 13th - Watery Gap - and the par 3 (117yd) 17th.
18 holes, 6352yds, Par 71, SSS 70.
Club membership 700.

Visitors	contact professional in advance.
Societies	apply by letter.
Green Fees	£28 per round (£33 weekends and bank holidays).
Prof	Mike Stewart
Facilities	⊗ ▦ ⌊ ▬ 𝄆 ⌣ ♨ ✎
Location	0.5m from M60 J6, NW side of town centre off A6144

Hotel	★★★ 65% Cresta Court Hotel, Church St, ALTRINCHAM ☎ 0161 927 7272 138 ⇥ ↾

SHEVINGTON   Map 07 SD50

Gathurst 62 Miles Ln WN6 8EW
☎ 01257 255235 (Secretary) & 254909 (Pro)
Testing parkland course, slightly hilly.
18 holes, 6016yds, Par 70, SSS 69, Course record 64.
Club membership 575.

Visitors	may play anytime except competition days.
Societies	welcome Mon, Tue, Thu & Fri. Apply in writing to Secretary.
Green Fees	£24 per day excluding Wed, weekends & bank holidays.
Prof	Rob Eastwood
Designer	N Pearson
Facilities	⊗ ▦ ⌊ ▬ 𝄆 ⌣ ♨ ✎

Location	W side of village B5375 off junc 27 of M6

Hotel	★★★ 65% Wigan/Standish Moat House, Almond Brook Rd, Standish, WIGAN ☎ 01257 499988 124 ⇥ ↾

STALYBRIDGE   Map 07 SJ99

Stamford Oakfield House, Huddersfield Rd SK15 3PY
☎ 01457 832126 & 834829
Undulating moorland course.
18 holes, 5701yds, Par 70, SSS 68, Course record 62.
Club membership 600.

Visitors	limited play at weekends.
Societies	apply in writing or telephone 0161 633 5211
Green Fees	not confirmed.
Facilities	⊗ ▦ ⌊ ▬ 𝄆 ⌣ ♨ ✎
Location	2m NE off A635

Hotel	★★ 70% York House Hotel, York Place, Richmond St, ASHTON-UNDER-LYNE ☎ 0161 330 9000 24 ⇥ ↾ Annexe10 ⇥ ↾

STANDISH   Map 07 SD51

Standish Court Rectory Ln WN6 0XD
☎ 01257 425777 Fax 01257 425888
Undulating 18 hole parkland course, not overly long but provides a good test for all level of players. Front nine more open with room for errors, back nine very scenic through woodland, a number of tight driving holes. Greens in excellent condition.
18 holes, 5625yds, Par 68, SSS 66.
Club membership 500.

Visitors	can play anytime, phone in advance for tee time, standard golfing dress required.
Societies	telephone in advance.
Green Fees	not confirmed.
Prof	J Kershaw
Designer	P Dawson
Facilities	♨ ⛳ ✎
Location	Off M6 junct 27, just through traffic lights in Standish village

Hotel	★★★★ 67% Kilhey Court Hotel, Chorley Rd, Standish, WIGAN ☎ 01257 472100 62 ⇥ ↾

STOCKPORT   Map 07 SJ89

Heaton Moor Heaton Mersey SK4 3NX
☎ 0161 432 0846
Parkland course, easy walking.
18 holes, 5968, Par 70, SSS 69, Course record 66.
Club membership 400.

Visitors	restricted Tue, bank holidays & Sat (summer).
Societies	apply in writing.
Green Fees	not confirmed.
Prof	Simon Marsh
Facilities	⊗ ▦ ⌊ ▬ 𝄆 ⌣ ♨ ⛳ ✎
Location	N of town centre off B5169

Hotel	★★ 67% Saxon Holme Hotel, 230 Wellington Rd, STOCKPORT ☎ 0161 432 2335 33 ⇥ ↾

Houldsworth Houldsworth Park, Reddish SK5 6BN
☎ 0161 442 9611 & 0161 442 1712 Fax 0161 442 1712
Flat parkland course, tree-lined and with water hazards.
Testing holes 9th (par 5) and 13th (par 5).
18 holes, 6209yds, Par 71, SSS 70.
Club membership 680.
Visitors   may not play weekends & bank holidays unless
              by prior arrangement with professional.
Societies   by prior arrangement.
Green Fees   contact professional on 0161 442 1714.
Prof   David Naylor
Designer   Dave Thomas
Facilities   ⊗ ⪢ ⽕ ♭ ♥ ♀ ♤ 🏠 ✎
Location   4m SE of city centre off A6

Hotel   ★★ 63% Willow Bank Hotel, 340-342
              Wilmslow Rd, Fallowfield, MANCHESTER
              ☎ 0161 224 0461 116 ⇥ ♠

Marple Barnsfold Rd, Hawk Green, Marple SK6 7EL
☎ 0161 427 2311 Fax 0161 427 1125
Parkland course.
18 holes, 5552yds, Par 68, SSS 67, Course record 66.
Club membership 640.
Visitors   restricted Thu afternoon & weekend competition
              days.
Societies   apply in writing to professional.
Green Fees   £20 per day (£30 weekends & bank holidays).
Prof   David Myers
Facilities   ⊗ ⪢ ⽕ ♭ ♥ ♀ ♤ 🏠 ✎
Location   S side of town centre

Hotel   ★★ 67% Red Lion Inn, 112 Buxton Rd, High
              Ln, STOCKPORT ☎ 01663 765227 6 ⇥ ♠

Reddish Vale Southcliffe Rd, Reddish SK5 7EE
☎ 0161 480 2359 Fax 0161 477 8242
Undulating heathland course designed by Dr. A Mackenzie
and situated in the River Tame valley.
18 holes, 6100yds, Par 69, SSS 69, Course record 64.
Club membership 550.
Visitors   must play with member at weekends. No
              societies at weekends.
Societies   must contact in writing.
Green Fees   £22 per round.
Prof   Bob Freeman
Designer   Dr A Mackenzie
Facilities   ⊗ ⪢ ⽕ ♭ ♥ ♀ ♤ 🏠 ⌐ ✎
Location   1.5m N off Sandy Lane

Hotel   ★★ 67% The Wycliffe Hotel, 74 Edgeley Rd,
              Edgeley, STOCKPORT
              ☎ 0161 477 5395 20 ⇥ ♠

Stockport Offerton Rd, Offerton SK2 5HL
☎ 0161 427 8369 (Secretary) & 427 2421 (Pro)
Fax 0161 449 8293
A beautifully situated course in wide open countryside with
views of the Cheshire and Derbyshire hills. It is not too long
but requires that the player plays all the shots, to excellent
greens. Demanding holes include the dog-leg 3rd, 12th, and
18th and the 460 yard opening hole is among the toughest in
Cheshire.
18 holes, 6326yds, Par 71, SSS 71, Course record 66.
Club membership 500.
Visitors   must contact professional in advance, limited
              play weekends.

Societies   Wed & Thu only, apply in writing to Secretary.
Green Fees   £35 per round (£45 weekends & bank holidays).
Prof   Mike Peel
Designer   P Barrie/A Herd
Facilities   ⊗ ⪢ ⽕ ♭ ♥ ♀ ♤ 🏠 ⌐ ✎
Location   4m SE on A627

Hotel   ★★ 67% Red Lion Inn, 112 Buxton Rd, High
              Ln, STOCKPORT ☎ 01663 765227 6 ⇥ ♠

SWINTON   Map 07 SD70

Swinton Park East Lancashire Rd M27 5LX
☎ 0161 794 0861 Fax 0161 281 0698
One of Lancashire's longest inland courses.
18 holes, 6726yds, Par 73, SSS 72, Course record 66.
Club membership 600.
Visitors   may not play weekends or Thu. Must
              contact in advance and have handicap
              certificate.
Societies   apply by letter.
Green Fees   not confirmed.
Prof   James Wilson
Designer   James Braid
Facilities   ⊗ ⪢ ⽕ ♭ ♥ ♀ ♤ 🏠 ✎
Location   1m W off A580

Hotel   ★★★ 65% Novotel, Worsley Brow,
              WORSLEY ☎ 0161 799 3535 119 ⇥ ♠

UPPERMILL   Map 07 SD90

Saddleworth Mountain Ash OL3 6LT
☎ 01457 873653 Fax 01457 820647
Moorland course, with superb views of Pennines.
18 holes, 5976yds, Par 71, SSS 69, Course record 61.
Club membership 800.
Visitors   must contact in advance, restricted at weekends.
Societies   contact in advance.
Green Fees   £23 per day (£30 weekends & bank holidays).
Prof   Robert Johnson
Designer   George Lowe/Dr McKenzie
Facilities   ⊗ ⪢ ⽕ ♭ ♥ ♀ ♤ 🏠 ⊐ 🗲 ⌐ ✎
Location   E side of town centre off A670

Hotel   ★★★ 70% Hotel Smokies Park, Ashton Rd,
              Bardsley, OLDHAM
              ☎ 0161 624 3405 47 ⇥ ♠

URMSTON   Map 07 SJ79

Flixton Church Rd, Flixton M41 6EP
☎ 0161 748 2116
Meadowland course bounded by River Mersey.
9 holes, 6410yds, Par 71, SSS 71.
Club membership 430.
Visitors   contact professional in advance, with member
              only weekends & bank holidays.
Societies   apply in writing.
Green Fees   £16 per day.
Prof   Daniel Procter
Facilities   ⊗ ⪢ by prior arrangement ♭ ♥ ♀ ♤ 🏠 ✎
& Leisure   snooker.
Location   S side of town centre on B5213

Hotel   ★★★★ 65% Copthorne Manchester, Clippers Quay, Salford Quays, MANCHESTER
☎ 0161 873 7321 166 ⇄ ฿

WALKDEN   Map 07 SD70

Brackley Municipal M38 9TR ☎ 0161 790 6076
Mostly flat course.
9 holes, 3003yds, Par 35, SSS 69.
Visitors   no restrictions.
Green Fees not confirmed.
Facilities   🏠
Location   2m NW on A6

Hotel   ★★★ 65% Novotel, Worsley Brow,
WORSLEY ☎ 0161 799 3535 119 ⇄ ฿

WESTHOUGHTON   Map 07 SD60

Westhoughton Long Island, School St BL5 2BR
☎ 01942 811085 & 608958 Fax 01942 608958
Compact downland course.
9 holes, 2886yds, Par 70, SSS 68, Course record 64.
Club membership 280.
Visitors   with member only at weekends.
Societies   telephone in advance or apply in writing.
Green Fees £16 for visitor.
Prof   Jason Seed
Facilities   ⊗ ⅏ ᴸ ☕ ♀ ♨ 🏠
Location   0.5m NW off A58

Hotel   ★★★ 62% The Beaumont Hotel, Beaumont
Rd, BOLTON ☎ 01204 651511 101 ⇄ ฿

WHITEFIELD   Map 07 SD80

Stand The Dales, Ashbourne Grove M45 7NL
☎ 0161 766 3197 Fax 0161 796 3234
A semi-parkland course with five moorland holes. A fine test of golf with a very demanding finish.
18 holes, 6411yds, Par 72, SSS 71, Course record 67.
Club membership 500.
Visitors   must contact professional in advance.
Societies   Wed & Fri, apply by telephone.
Green Fees not confirmed.
Prof   Mark Dance
Designer   G Lowe/A Herd
Facilities   ♨ 🏠 ♖ ✓
Location   1m W off A667

Hotel   ★★★ 65% Bolholt Country Park Hotel,
Walshaw Rd, BURY
☎ 0161 762 4000 66 ⇄ ฿

Whitefield Higher Ln M45 7EZ
☎ 0161 766 2904 & 2728 Fax 0161 7679502
Fine sporting parkland course with well-watered greens.
18 holes, 6045yds, Par 69, SSS 69, Course record 64.
Club membership 540.
Visitors   play restricted Tue & Sun. Booking essential weekends and bank holidays, contact the proffesional shop on 0161 7663096.
Societies   must contact in advance.
Green Fees £25 per day; £18 per round (£35 per round weekends & bank holidays).
Cards   💳 VISA 🔲 🔲 🔲

Prof   Paul Reeves
Facilities   ⊗ ⅏ ᴸ ☕ ♀ ♨ 🏠 ♖ ♘ ⚒ ✓ ₤
& Leisure   hard tennis courts, snooker room.
Location   N side of town centre on A665

Hotel   ★★★★ 60% Thistle Manchester, 3/5 Portland St, Piccadilly Gardens, MANCHESTER
☎ 0161 228 3400 205 ⇄ ฿

WIGAN   Map 07 SD50

Haigh Hall Haigh Country Park, Aspull WN2 1PE
☎ 01942 831107
Municipal parkland course, with hard walking, and a canal forms the west boundary. Adjacent to 'Haigh Country Park' with many facilities.
18 holes, 6423yds, Par 70, SSS 71, Course record 65.
Club membership 250.
Visitors   must contact professional in advance.
Societies   apply in writing to professional.
Green Fees not confirmed.
Prof   Ian Lee
Designer   Frank Pennink
Facilities   ᴸ ☕ 🏠 ♖ ✓
Location   2m NE off B5238

Hotel   ★★ 63% Bel-Air Hotel, 236 Wigan Ln,
WIGAN ☎ 01942 241410 11 ⇄ ฿

Wigan Arley Hall, Haigh WN1 2UH
☎ 01257 421360
Among the best of Lancashire's 9-hole courses. The fine old clubhouse is the original Arley Hall, and is surrounded by a 12th century moat.
9 holes, 6036yds, Par 70, SSS 69.
Club membership 200.
Visitors   must contact in advance. May not play Tue or Sat.
Societies   apply by telephone.
Green Fees £25 per round.
Facilities   ⊗ ⅏ ᴸ ☕ ♀ ♨
Location   3m NE off B5238

Hotel   ★★★ 65% Wigan/Standish Moat House,
Almond Brook Rd, Standish, WIGAN
☎ 01257 499988 124 ⇄ ฿

WOODFORD   Map 07 SJ88

Avro Old Hall Ln SK7 1QR ☎ 0161 439 2709
An attractive, tight and challenging 9-hole course.
9 holes, 5735yds, Par 69, SSS 68.
Club membership 400.
Visitors   restricted weekends and competition days. not able to take societies.
Green Fees not confirmed.
Facilities   ☕ ♨
Location   W side of village on A5102

Hotel   ★★★ 66% County Hotel Bramhall, Bramhall Ln South, BRAMHALL
☎ 0161 455 9988 65 ⇄ ฿

> Entries with a shaded background
> identify courses that are
> considered to be particularly interesting

WORSLEY   Map 07 SD70

Ellesmere Old Clough Ln M28 7HZ
☎ 0161 799 0554 (office) & 790 8591 (pro)
Parkland course with natural hazards. Testing holes: 3rd (par 5), 9th (par 3), 15th (par 5). Hard walking.
18 holes, 6248yds, Par 70, SSS 70, Course record 67.
Club membership 700.

Visitors	welcome except club competition days & bank holidays.
Societies	apply in advance.
Green Fees	£25 per day; £19 per round (£26 per round weekends & bank holidays).
Prof	Terry Morley
Facilities	⊗ 〗 ⅙ ☒ ♀ ⚲ 🏡 ⚘
Location	N side of village off A580
Hotel	★★★ 65% Novotel, Worsley Brow, WORSLEY ☎ 0161 799 3535 119 ⇥ ⋔

HAMPSHIRE

Portsmouth Area Telephone Number Changes

From the 22 April 2000, all dialling codes listed as **(01705)** will change to **(023)**, followed by an eight-digit local number, starting with **92**. For example, **(01705)** 123456 will become **(023) 92**12 3456.

Southampton Area Telephone Number Changes

From 22 April 2000, all dialling codes listed as **(01703)** will change to **(023)**, followed by an eight-digit local number, starting with **80**. For example, **(01703)** 123456 will become **(023) 80**12 3456.

ALDERSHOT   Map 04 SU85

Army Laffans Rd GU11 2HF
☎ 01252 337272 Fax 01252 337562
The second oldest course in Hampshire. Picturesque heathland course with three par 3's, over 200 yds.
18 holes, 6550yds, Par 71, SSS 71, Course record 67.
Club membership 825.

Visitors	may not play weekends.
Societies	apply in writing.
Green Fees	not confirmed.
Cards	▦ ▦ ▦ ▦ ▦
Prof	Graham Cowley
Facilities	⊗ 〗 ⅙ ☒ ♀ ⚲ 🏡 ⚘
Location	1.5m N of town centre off A323/A325
Hotel	★★★ 69% Potters International Hotel, 1 Fleet Rd, ALDERSHOT ☎ 01252 344000 97 ⇥ ⋔

ALRESFORD   Map 04 SU53

Alresford Cheriton Rd, Tichborne Down SO24 0PN
☎ 01962 733746 Fax 01962 736040
A testing downland course on well drained chalk.Now expanded to 18 holes, incorporating the original 12, but changing direction of play to give two starting points and two closing greens near clubhouse.

18 holes, 5905yds, Par 69, SSS 68, Course record 64.
Club membership 750.

Visitors	must contact in advance.
Societies	must telephone in advance.
Green Fees	not confirmed.
Prof	Malcolm Scott
Designer	Scott Webb Young
Facilities	⊗ 〗 ⅙ ☒ ♀ ⚲ 🏡 ⚘ ⋔
Location	1m S on B3046
Hotel	★★ 59% Swan Hotel, 11 West St, ALRESFORD ☎ 01962 732302 & 734427 Fax 01962 735274 11rm(3 ⇥ 7 ⋔) Annexe12 ⇥ ⋔

ALTON   Map 04 SU73

Alton Old Odiham Rd GU34 4BU
☎ 01420 82042 & 86518
Undulating meadowland course.
9 holes, 5744yds, Par 68, SSS 68, Course record 52.
Club membership 350.

Visitors	must contact in advance and must have a handicap certificate to play at weekends.
Societies	must contact in advance.
Green Fees	not confirmed.
Prof	Paul Brown
Designer	James Braid
Facilities	⚲ 🏡 ⚘
Location	2m N of Alton off B3349 at Golden Pot
Hotel	★★★ 67% Alton House Hotel, Normandy St, ALTON ☎ 01420 80033 39 ⇥ ⋔

Worldham Park Cakers Ln, East Worldham GU34 3BF
☎ 01420 543151 Fax 01420 84124
The course is in a picturesque woodland setting with an abundance of challenging holes (doglegs, water and sand). Increased to 18-holes in the summer of 1995.
18 holes, 5800yds, Par 71, SSS 68.
Club membership 500.

Visitors	are advised to book in advance at weekends.
Societies	Mon-Fri only. Must contact in advance.
Green Fees	£11 per round (£13 weekends and bank holidays).
Cards	▦ ▦ ▦ ▦ ▦
Prof	Jon Le Roux
Designer	F J Whidborne
Facilities	⊗ 〗 ⅙ ☒ ♀ ⚲ 🏡 ⚘ ⋔ ⚘
Location	B3004, 2mins from Alton
Hotel	★★★ 68% Alton Grange Hotel, London Rd, ALTON ☎ 01420 86565 26 ⇥ ⋔ Annexe4 ⇥ ⋔

AMPFIELD   Map 04 SU42

Ampfield Par Three Winchester Rd SO51 9BQ
☎ 01794 368480
Pretty parkland course designed by Henry Cotton in 1963. Well-bunkered greens.
18 holes, 2478yds, Par 54, SSS 53, Course record 49.
Club membership 470.

Visitors	must contact in advance & have a handicap certificate to play at weekends & bank holidays, recognised golfshoes must be worn.
Societies	must contact in advance.

Green Fees £15 per day; £9 per round (£15.50 per round weekends & bank holidays).
Prof Richard Benfield
Designer Henry Cotton
Facilities ⊗ ⓑ 🍺 ♀ 🏔 🛍 🏌 ♂
Location 4m NE of Romsey on A31

Hotel ★★★ 68% Potters Heron Hotel, Winchester Rd, Ampfield, ROMSEY
🕾 01703 266611 54 ⇄ ♔

ANDOVER   Map 04 SU34

Andover 51 Winchester Rd SP10 2EF 🕾 01264 358040
Undulating downland course combining a good test of golf for all abilities with breathtaking views across Hampshire countryside. Well guarded greens and a notable par 3, 9th (225yds) with the tee perched on top of a hill, 100ft above the green.
9 holes, 6096yds, Par 70, SSS 69, Course record 66.
Club membership 450.
Visitors must contact professional in advance tel: 01264 324151.
Societies Mon-Wed only. Must contact in advance.
Green Fees £10 per 18 holes; (£22 weekends & bank holidays).
Prof D Lawrence
Designer J H Taylor
Facilities ⊗ by prior arrangement ⫿ by prior arrangement ⓑ 🍺 ♀ 🏔 🛍 ♂
Location 0.5m S on A3057

Hotel ★★★ 62% Ashley Court Hotel, Micheldever Rd, ANDOVER
🕾 01264 357344 9 ⇄ ♔ Annexe26 ⇄ ♔

ASHLEY HEATH   Map 04 SU10

Moors Valley Moors Valley Country Park, Horton Rd BH24 2ET 🕾 01425 479776 Fax 01425 472057
This municipal course is set in the beautiful surroundings of a country park. It offers a test for all standards. It is gently undulating, with water hazards on six holes.
18 holes, 6200yds, Par 72, SSS 70.
Club membership 250.
Visitors must contact in advance.
Societies telephone for availability.
Green Fees £11 per 18 holes (£13 weekends).
Cards --- 🖃 🖃 🖃 ⑤
Prof Michael Torrens
Designer Hawtree & Son
Facilities ⊗ ⫿ ⓑ 🍺 ♀ 🏔 🛍 ♂ ⑂
& Leisure various family activities and 4 hole pitch & putt.
Location Signposted from A31 Ashley Heath roundabout

Hotel ★★★ 64% St Leonards Hotel, Ringwood Rd (A31), ST LEONARDS
🕾 01425 471220 34 ⇄ ♔

BARTON-ON-SEA   Map 04 SZ29

Barton-on-Sea Milford Rd BH25 5PP
🕾 01425 615308 Fax 01425 621457
Though not strictly a links course, it is right on a cliff edge with views over the Isle of Wight and Christchurch Bay. On a still day it is very forgiving - but when it blows the course undergoes a complete change in character. Recently reconstructed to create 27 holes.

Becton-Needles: 18 holes, 6505yds, Par 72, SSS 71.
Needles-Stroller: 18 holes, 6453yds, Par 72, SSS 71.
Stroller-Becton: 18 holes, 6296yds, Par 72, SSS 70.
Club membership 940.
Visitors must contact in advance and have a handicap certificate.
Societies must telephone in advance.
Green Fees £30 per day (£35 weekends & bank holidays).
Prof Pat Coombs
Designer Hamilton Stutt
Facilities ⊗ ⫿ ⓑ 🍺 ♀ 🏔 🛍 🏌 🐾 🛒 ♂
Location B3058 SE side of town

Hotel ★★★★★♣♣ Chewton Glen Hotel, Christchurch Rd, NEW MILTON
🕾 01425 275341 52 ⇄ ♔ Annexe2 ⇄ ♔

BASINGSTOKE   Map 04 SU65

Basingstoke Kempshott Park RG23 7LL
🕾 01256 465990 Fax 01256 331793
A well-maintained parkland course with wide and inviting fairways. You are inclined to expect longer drives than are actually achieved - partly on account of the trees. There are many two-hundred-year-old beech trees, since the course was built on an old deer park.
18 holes, 6350yds, Par 70, SSS 70, Course record 66.
Club membership 700.
Visitors must contact in advance and play Mon-Fri only (ex bank holidays).
Societies must contact in advance.
Green Fees £36 per day; £26 per round.
Cards 🖃 🖃
Prof Guy Shoesmith
Designer James Braid
Facilities ⊗ ⫿ ⓑ 🍺 ♀ 🏔 🛍 🏌 🐾 🛒 ♂
Location 3.5m SW on A30 M3 exit 7

Hotel B Posthouse Basingstoke, Grove Rd, BASINGSTOKE
🕾 01256 468181 84 ⇄ ♔

Dummer Dummer RG25 2AR
🕾 01256 397888 Fax 01256 397889
Opened in July 1993 and designed by Peter Alliss/Clive Clark with several water hazards. Gentle terrain makes the course suitable for players of all ages.
18 holes, 6427yds, Par 72.
Club membership 750.

Visitors	must contact in advance, adhere to dress code, handicap required, limited at weekends.
Societies	contact in advance.
Green Fees	£27 per round (£30 weekends).
Cards	▭ ▭ ▭ ▭
Prof	Gary Stubbington
Designer	Peter Allis
Facilities	⊗ ℿ ㎏ ♥ ⚴ ⌂ ⚑ ⚒ ✐
& Leisure	sauna.
Location	Off junc 7 of M3 towards Dummer village

Hotel	★★★ 69% Centrecourt Hotel, Tennis & Health Club, Centre Dr, Chineham, BASINGSTOKE ☎ 01256 816664 50 ⇔ ♞

Weybrook Park Rooksdown Ln RG24 9NT
☎ 01256 320347 Fax 01256 812973
A course designed to be enjoyable for all standards of player.
Easy walking with fablous views.
18 holes, 6468yds, Par 71, SSS 71.
Club membership 600.

Visitors	telephone for availability.
Societies	telephone in advance for availability and confirm in writing.
Green Fees	£30.50 per day; £17.50 per round (£40.50/£22.50 weekends).
Cards	▭ ▭
Prof	Anthony Dillon
Facilities	⊗ ℿ ㎏ ♥ ♀ ⚴ ⌂ ➤ ⚒ ✐
Location	2m W of town centre, entrance via A339

Hotel	★★★ 61% Ringway Hotel, Popley Way, Aldermaston Roundabout, Ringway North (A339), BASINGSTOKE ☎ 01256 320212 134 ⇔ ♞

BORDON   Map 04 SU73

Blackmoor Firgrove Rd, Whitehill GU35 9EH
☎ 01420 472775 Fax 01420 487666
A first-class moorland course with a great variety of
holes. Fine greens and wide pine tree-lined fairways are
a distinguishing feature. The ground is mainly flat and
walking easy.
18 holes, 6164yds, Par 69, SSS 69, Course record 65.
Club membership 750.

Visitors	must contact in advance and may not play at weekends.
Societies	must telephone in advance.
Green Fees	£45 per 36 holes; £40 per 27 holes; £33 per 18 holes.
Prof	Stephen Clay
Designer	H S Colt
Facilities	⊗ ℿ ㎏ ♥ ♀ ⚴ ⌂ ✐
Location	Travelling S on A325, 6m beyond Farnham, pass through Whitehill and turn right at crossroads

Hotel	★★★ 67% Alton House Hotel, Normandy St, ALTON ☎ 01420 80033 39 ⇔ ♞

BOTLEY   Map 04 SU51

Botley Park Hotel, Golf & Country Club Winchester Rd,
Boorley Green SO32 2UA
☎ 01489 796000 Fax 01489 789242

Pleasantly undulating course with water hazards. Driving
range and country club facilities.
18 holes, 6341yds, Par 70, SSS 70, Course record 67.
Club membership 750.

Visitors	must play with member. Must contact in advance & have handicap certificate.
Societies	contact in advance.
Green Fees	not confirmed.
Cards	▭ ▭ ▭ ▭ ▭ ▭
Prof	Tim Barter
Designer	Ewan Murray
Facilities	⊗ ℿ ㎏ ♥ ♀ ⚴ ⌂ ⚑ ⛳ ➤ ⚒ ✐ ↿
& Leisure	hard tennis courts, heated indoor swimming pool, squash, sauna, solarium, gymnasium, extensive leisure club.
Location	1m NW of Botley on B3354

Hotel	★★★★ 67% Botley Park Hotel Golf & Country Club, Winchester Rd, Boorley Green, BOTLEY ☎ 01489 780888 100 ⇔ ♞

BROCKENHURST   Map 04 SU20

Brokenhurst Manor Sway Rd SO42 7SG
☎ 01590 623332 (Secretary) Fax 01590 624140
An attractive woodland/heathland course set at the edge
of the New Forest, with the unusual feature of three
loops of six holes each to complete the round.
Fascinating holes include the short 5th and 12th, and the
4th and 17th, both dog-legged. A stream also features on
seven of the holes.
18 holes, 6222yds, Par 70, SSS 70, Course record 63.
Club membership 850.

★★
The Watersplash Hotel
Brockenhurst in the New Forest

The Watersplash Hotel is recommended for its excellent food, friendly service and accommodation. Brockenhurst Manor Golf Club, situated just half a mile away, is one of ten courses within easy reach of the hotel. Personally supervised by resident proprietor Robin Foster who specialise in catering for the individual and small golf parties. Well-stocked bar and extensive wine list. All 23 bedrooms have private bathroom, colour TV, tea and coffee making facilities, direct dial telephone and radio. Four-poster Room with double Jacuzzi Bath. Heated outdoor pool in season. For further details ask for our colour brochure.

The Watersplash Hotel, The Rise, Brockenhurst, Hampshire SO42 7ZP. Tel: (01590) 622344 Fax: (01590) 624047

Visitors	must contact in advance, numbers limited. Must have a handicap certificate.
Societies	Thu only, apply in writing.
Green Fees	£42 per day; £32 per round (£58 weekends & bank holidays).
Prof	John Lovell
Designer	H S Colt
Facilities	⊗ 〉Ⅲ ⮮ ▆ ♀ ⚲ 🖃 ✧
Location	1m S on B3055

Hotel	★★★ 67% Balmer Lawn Hotel, Lyndhurst Rd, BROCKENHURST ☎ 01590 623116 55 ⇆ ↾
Additional hotel	★★ 68% Watersplash Hotel, The Rise, BROCKENHURST ☎ 01590 622344 Fax 01590 624047 23 ⇆ ↾

BURLEY

Map 04 SU20

Burley Cott Ln BH24 4BB
☎ 01425 402431 & 403737 Fax 01425 402431
Undulating heather and gorseland. The 7th requires an accurately placed tee shot to obtain par 4. Played off different tees on second nine.
9 holes, 6149yds, Par 71, SSS 69, Course record 68.
Club membership 520.

Visitors	must contact in advance & preferably have a handicap certificate or be a member of a recognised golf club. May not play before 4pm Sat.
Societies	telephone in advance, parties up to 14 only.

Green Fees	£20 per day; £15 per round (£25/£18 weekends & bank holidays).
Facilities	⊗ by prior arrangement ⮮ ▆ ♀ ⚲ ✧
Location	E side of village

Hotel	★★★ 63% Moorhill House, BURLEY ☎ 01425 403285 24 ⇆ ↾

CORHAMPTON

Map 04 SU62

Corhampton Sheep's Pond Ln SO32 3LP
☎ 01489 877279
Free draining downland course situated in the heart of the picturesque Meon Valley.
18 holes, 6444yds, Par 71, SSS 71.
Club membership 800.

Visitors	weekdays only and must contact in advance.
Societies	Mon & Thu only, contact in writing or telephone.
Green Fees	£31 per 36 holes; £21 per 18 holes.
Prof	Ian Roper
Facilities	⊗ ⮮ ▆ ⚲ 🖃 ⚓ ✧
Location	1m W of Corhampton, off B3035

Hotel	★★ 75% Old House Hotel, The Square, WICKHAM ☎ 01329 833049 9 ⇆ ↾

CRONDALL

Map 04 SU74

Oak Park Heath Ln GU10 5PB
☎ 01252 850880 & 850850 Fax 01252 850851
Village: Gently undulating parkland course overlooking pretty village. 16-bay floodlit driving range, practice green and practice bunker. Woodland: Undulating on holes 10 to 13. Panoramic views, mature trees, very challenging.
Woodland: 18 holes, 6240yds, Par 70, SSS 70.
Village: 9 holes, 3279yds, Par 36.
Club membership 600.

Visitors	no restrictions for Village Course. Must book in advance and have a handicap certificate for Woodland Course.
Societies	must telephone in advance.
Green Fees	Woodland: £20 (£30 per round weekends pm only). Village: £10 (£12 per round weekends pm only).
Cards	— ▆▆ ▆▆
Prof	Simon Coaker
Designer	Patrick Dawson
Facilities & Leisure	⊗ 〉Ⅲ ⮮ ▆ ♀ ⚲ 🖃 ⚓ ⚓ ✧ ↾ gymnasium, steam room.
Location	0.5m E of village off A287 Farnham-Odiham

Hotel	★★★★ 60% Farnham House Hotel, Alton Rd, FARNHAM ☎ 01252 716908 25 ⇆ ↾

DIBDEN

Map 04 SU40

Dibden Main Rd SO45 5TB ☎ 01703 207508
Municipal parkland course with views over Southampton Water. A pond guards the green at the par 5, 3rd hole. Twenty-bay driving range.
Course 1: 18 holes, 5900yds, Par 70, SSS 69, Course record 63.
Course 2: 9 holes, 1520yds, Par 29.
Club membership 600.

▶

Visitors	must book in advance.
Societies	must contact in writing.
Green Fees	£10.75 per 18 holes (£12.75 weekends).
Cards	～ ▭ 🔲
Prof	Alan Bridge
Designer	Hamilton Stutt
Facilities	♨🖼🏌♿🍴
Location	2m NW of Dibden Purlieu, off A326 to Hythe
Hotel	★★★ 63% Forest Lodge Hotel, Pikes Hill, Romsey Rd, LYNDHURST ☎ 01703 283677 28 ⇄ ℝ

EASTLEIGH   Map 04 SU41

Fleming Park Magpie Ln SO50 9LS ☎ 01703 612797
Parkland course with stream-'Monks Brook'-running through.
18 holes, 4436yds, Par 65, SSS 62, Course record 62.
Club membership 300.

Visitors	must contact in advance, no restrictions.
Societies	must contact in advance.
Green Fees	£13 per day; £7.10 per 18 holes; £4.60 per 9 holes (£19/£10.50/£7.30 weekends & bank holidays).
Prof	Chris Strickett
Designer	David Miller
Facilities	⊗🖼🏌♿🍴
Location	E side of town centre
Hotel	B Posthouse Eastleigh/Southampton, Leigh Rd, EASTLEIGH ☎ 01703 619700 116 ⇄ ℝ

EAST WELLOW   Map 04 SU32

Wellow Ryedown Ln SO51 6BD
☎ 01794 323833 & 322872 Fax 01794 323832
Three 9-hole courses set in 217 acres of parkland surrounding Embley Park, former home of Florence Nightingale.
Ryedown & Embley: 18 holes, 5966yds, Par 70, SSS 69.
Embley & Blackwater: 18 holes, 6295yds, Par 72, SSS 70.
Blackwater & Ryedown: 18 holes, 5819yds, Par 70, SSS 68.
Club membership 500.

Visitors	advisable to contact in advance weekdays only.
Societies	apply in writing or telephone, Mon-Fri not bank holidays.
Green Fees	£20 per day; £16 per 18 holes.
Prof	Neil Bratley
Designer	W Wiltshire
Facilities	⊗🖼🏌♿🍴
Location	Exit2 of M27, then A36 to Salisbury then 1m right
Hotel	★★★ 61% The White Horse, Market Place, ROMSEY ☎ 01794 512431 33 ⇄ ℝ

FAREHAM   Map 04 SU50

Cams Hall Cams Hill PO16 8UP
☎ 01329 827222 Fax 01329 827111
Two Peter Alliss/Clive Clark designed golf courses opened in 1993. The Creek Course is coastal and has salt and fresh water lakes and the fairways are lined with undulating hills. The Park Course is designed in the grounds of Cams Hall.
Creek Course: 18 holes, 6244yds, Par 71, SSS 70, Course record 69.

Park Course: 9 holes, 3247yds, Par 36, SSS 35.
Club membership 950.

Visitors	must contact in advance, tee times available any time.
Societies	telephone for details and society golf day pack.
Green Fees	£30 per day; £19 per round (£35/£25 weekends).
Cards	▭ 💳 🔲
Prof	Jason Neve
Designer	Peter Alliss
Facilities	⊗🖼🏌♿🍴
& Leisure	sauna.
Location	M27 exit 11 to A27
Hotel	★★★ 62% Lysses House Hotel, 51 High St, FAREHAM ☎ 01329 822622 21 ⇄ ℝ

FARNBOROUGH   Map 04 SU85

Southwood Ively Rd, Cove GU14 0LJ
☎ 01252 548700 Fax 01252 515855
Municipal parkland course with stream running through.
18 holes, 5738yds, Par 69, SSS 68, Course record 61.
Club membership 650.

Visitors	must book in advance.
Societies	must contact in advance.
Green Fees	£13 (£15.50 weekends).
Cards	▭ 💳 🔲
Prof	Bob Hammond
Designer	Hawtree & Son
Facilities	⊗🖼🏌♿🍴
Location	0.5m W
Hotel	B Posthouse Farnborough, Lynchford Rd, FARNBOROUGH ☎ 01252 545051 143 ⇄ ℝ

FLEET   Map 04 SU85

North Hants Minley Rd GU13 8RE
☎ 01252 616443 Fax 01252 811627
Picturesque tree-lined course with much heather and gorse close to the fairways. A comparatively easy par-4 first hole may lull the golfer into a false sense of security, only to be rudely awakened at the testing holes which follow. The ground is rather undulating and, though not tiring, does offer some excellent 'blind' shots, and more than a few surprises in judging distance.
18 holes, 6257yds, Par 69, SSS 70, Course record 65.
Club membership 600.

Visitors	must contact at least 48 hours in advance. Must play with member at weekends.
Societies	Tue & Wed only. Must telephone in advance.

Green Fees	£30 per round; £40 two rounds.
Prof	Steve Porter
Designer	James Braid
Facilities	⊗ ⍾ 🏌 🖚 ☕ ♟ ⚑ 🏪 ✎
Location	0.25m N of Fleet station on B3013
Hotel	★★★ 62% Lismoyne Hotel, Church Rd, FLEET ☎ 01252 628555 44 ⇆ ♠

GOSPORT
Map 04 SZ69

Gosport & Stokes Bay Off Fort Rd, Haslar PO12 2AT
☎ 01705 527941 Fax 01705 527941
A testing links course overlooking the Solent, with plenty of gorse and short rough. Changing winds.
9 holes, 5999yds, Par 70, SSS 69, Course record 65.
Club membership 499.

Visitors	may not play Sun and Thu.
Societies	must contact in writing.
Green Fees	£15 per round.
Facilities	⊗ ⍾ 🏌 🖚 ☕ ♟ ⚑ 🏪 ✎
Location	A32 S from Fareham, E on Fort rd to Haslar
Hotel	★★★ 62% Belle Vue Hotel, 39 Marine Pde East, LEE-ON-THE-SOLENT ☎ 01705 550258 24 ⇆ ♠ Annexe3 ⇆ ♠

HARTLEY WINTNEY
Map 04 SU75

Hartley Wintney London Rd RG27 8PT
☎ 01252 844211 (Sec) 843779 (Prof) Fax 01252 844211
Easy walking, parkland course in pleasant countryside.
Played off different tees on back nine, with testing par 4s at 4th and 13th.
9 holes, 6096yds, Par 70, SSS 69, Course record 63.
Club membership 475.

Visitors	must contact in advance.
Societies	Tue & Thu only by prior arrangement.
Green Fees	£25 per day; £17 per round.
Cards	▭▭ ▭▭ ▭▭ ▭
Prof	Martin Smith
Facilities	⊗ 🏌 🖚 ☕ ♟ ⚑ 🏪 ✎
Location	NE side of village on A30
Hotel	★★★ 62% Lismoyne Hotel, Church Rd, FLEET ☎ 01252 628555 44 ⇆ ♠

HAYLING ISLAND
Map 04 SU70

Hayling Links Ln PO11 0BX
☎ 01705 464446 Fax 01705 464446
A delightful links course among the dunes offering fine sea-scapes and views across to the Isle of Wight. Varying sea breezes and sometimes strong winds ensure that the course seldom plays the same two days running. Testing holes at the 12th and 13th, both par 4. Club selection is important.
18 holes, 5521yds, Par 71, SSS 71, Course record 65.
Club membership 800.

Visitors	must contact in advance and have a handicap certificate, no jeans or denims allowed.
Societies	welcome Tue & Wed, or half days Mon & Thu, apply in writing or telephone.

Green Fees	£35 per day; £28 per round (£45/£35 weekends).
Prof	Raymond Gadd
Designer	Taylor 1905, Simpson 1933
Facilities	⊗ ⍾ by prior arrangement 🖚 ☕ ♟ ⚑ 🏪 ✎
Location	SW side of island at West Town
Hotel	B Posthouse Havant, Northney Rd, HAYLING ISLAND ☎ 01705 465011 92 ⇆ ♠

KINGSCLERE
Map 04 SU55

Sandford Springs Wolverton RG26 5RT
☎ 01635 297883 & 297881 Fax 01635 298065
The course has unique variety in beautiful surroundings and offers three distinctive loops of 9 holes. There are water hazards, woodlands and gradients to negotiate, providing a challenge for all playing categories. From its highest point there are extensive views.
The Park: 9 holes, 2963yds, Par 34.
The Lakes: 9 holes, 2891yds, Par 35.
The Wood: 9 holes, 3072yds, Par 36.
Club membership 650.

Visitors	must contact in advance. Restricted at weekends.
Societies	must contact in advance.
Green Fees	£29 per day; £23 per round.
Cards	▭▭ ▭▭ ▭▭ ▭
Prof	Gary Edmunds/Kim Brake
Designer	Hawtree & Son
Facilities	⊗ ⍾ 🏌 🖚 ☕ ♟ ⚑ 🏪 ✎ 🚜 ⚑
Location	On A339
Hotel	★★★ 50% Millwaters Hotel & Restaurant, London Rd, NEWBURY ☎ 01635 528838 30 ⇆ ♠

KINGSLEY
Map 04 SU73

Dean Farm GU35 9NG ☎ 01420 489478 & 472313
Undulating downland course.
9 holes, 1500yds, Par 29.

Visitors	no restrictions. Course closed Mon until 1pm.
Societies	must contact in writing.
Green Fees	£4 per 9 holes.
Facilities	🏌 🖚 ☕ ♟ 🏪 ✎
& Leisure	hard tennis courts.
Location	W side of village off B3004
Hotel	★★★ 68% Alton Grange Hotel, London Rd, ALTON ☎ 01420 86565 26 ⇆ ♠ Annexe4 ⇆ ♠

LECKFORD
Map 04 SU33

Leckford SO20 6JG ☎ 01264 810320
A testing downland course with good views.
9 holes, 6444yds, Par 70, SSS 71.
Club membership 200.

Green Fees	not confirmed.
Facilities	☕
Location	1m SW off A3057 ▶

Hotel ★★★ 63% Grosvenor Hotel, High St, STOCKBRIDGE ☎ 01264 810606 25 ⇥ ⋔

LEE-ON-THE-SOLENT
Map 04 SU50

Lee-on-Solent Brune Ln PO13 9PB
☎ 01705 551170 Fax 01705 554233
A modest parkland/heathland course, yet a testing one. The five short holes always demand a high standard of play and the 13th is rated one of the best in the country. A new clubhouse completed in 1997.
18 holes, 5755yds, Par 69, SSS 69, Course record 64.
Club membership 750.
Visitors may not play before 9am. Handicap certificate required.
Societies must contact in advance.
Green Fees £30 per day/round (£35 weekends).
Prof John Richardson
Facilities ⊗ ⫪ ⓑ ⚑ ♀ ♨ ⌂ ♂ ↾
Location 1m N off B3385

Hotel ★★★ 62% Belle Vue Hotel, 39 Marine Pde East, LEE-ON-THE-SOLENT
☎ 01705 550258 24 ⇥ ⋔ Annexe3 ⇥ ⋔

LIPHOOK
Map 04 SU83

Liphook Wheatsheaf Enclosure GU30 7EH
☎ 01428 723271 & 723785 Fax 01428 724853
Heathland course with easy walking and fine views.
18 holes, 6167yds, Par 70, SSS 69, Course record 67.
Club membership 800.

Visitors must contact in advance; may not play Tue, competition days etc.
Societies Wed-Fri only. Must contact in advance.
Green Fees £40 per day; £30 per round (£50/£40 weekends).
Prof Ian Large
Designer A C Croome
Facilities ⊗ ⓑ ⚑ ♀ ♨ ⌂ ♂ ↾ ♂
Location 1m S on B2030 (old A3)

Hotel ★★★★ 71% Lythe Hill Hotel, Petworth Rd, HASLEMERE
☎ 01428 651251 41 ⇥ ⋔

Old Thorns Hotel, Golf & Country Club
Griggs Green GU30 7PE ☎ 01428 724555
A challenging 18-hole championship-standard course designed around magnificent oaks, beeches and Scots pine.
18 holes, 6041yds, Par 72, SSS 70.
Visitors no restrictions.
Societies must telephone in advance.
Green Fees £50 per day; £35 per round (£65/£45 weekends).
Cards ⬚ ⬚ ⬚ ⬚ ⬚ ⬚ ⬚
Prof P Loxley
Designer Peter Alliss/Dave Thomas
Facilities ⊗ ⫪ ⓑ ⚑ ♀ ♨ ⌂ ♂ ⛵ ⛱ ♂ ↾
& Leisure hard tennis courts, heated indoor swimming pool, sauna, solarium.
Location Leave A3 at Griggs Green, S of Liphook, signposted 'Old Thorns'

| Hotel | ★★★ 73% Old Thorns Hotel, Golf & Country Club, Longmoor Rd, Griggs Green, LIPHOOK |
| | ☎ 01428 724555 28 ⇄ 🐾 Annexe4 🐾 |

LYNDHURST   Map 04 SU20

Bramshaw Brook SO43 7HE
☎ 01703 813433 Fax 01703 813958
Two 18-hole courses. The Manor Course is landscaped parkland with excellent greens, and features mature trees and streams. The Forest course is set amidst beautiful open forest. Easy walking. The Bell Inn Hotel, attached to the club, provides fine accommodation just a wedge shot from the first tee, and reserved tee times for its guests.
Manor Course: 18 holes, 6517yds, Par 71, SSS 71, Course record 66.
Forest Course: 18 holes, 5774yds, Par 69, SSS 68, Course record 65.
Club membership 950.

Visitors	must be accompanied by member at weekends and bank holidays.
Societies	apply in writing or telephone in advance.
Green Fees	not confirmed.
Prof	Clive Bonner
Facilities	⊗ ⫪ 𝄄 🖥 ♀ ⚐ 🏠 🎯 🏸 🛒 ✎
& Leisure	golfing rates at Bell Inn.
Location	On B3079 1m W of M27 junc 1

| Hotel | ★★★ 68% Bell Inn, BROOK |
| | ☎ 01703 812214 25 ⇄ |

New Forest Southampton Rd SO43 7BU
☎ 01703 282752 Fax 01703 282484
This picturesque heathland course is laid out in a typical stretch of the New Forest on high ground a little above the village of Lyndhurst. Natural hazards include the inevitable forest ponies. The first two holes are somewhat teasing, as is the 485-yard (par 5) 9th. Walking is easy.
18 holes, 5742yds, Par 69, SSS 68.
Club membership 700.

Visitors	must contact in advance.
Societies	must contact in advance.
Green Fees	£16 per day; £12 per round.
Prof	Danny Harris
Facilities	⊗ ⫪ by prior arrangement 𝄄 🖥 ♀ ⚐ 🏠 ✎
Location	0.5m NE off A35

| Hotel | ★★★ 70% Crown Hotel, High St, LYNDHURST |
| | ☎ 01703 282922 39 ⇄ 🐾 |

NEW MILTON   Map 04 SZ29

Chewton Glen Hotel Christchurch Rd BH25 6QS
☎ 01425 275341 Fax 01425 272310
A 9-hole, Par 3 course within the hotel grounds plus a practice area. ONLY open to residents of the hotel or as a guest of a member of the club.
9 holes, 854yds, Par 27.
Club membership 150.

Visitors	non residents must play with member.
Societies	must contact in advance.
Green Fees	not confirmed.
Cards	💳 💳 💳 💳 💳
Facilities	⊗ ⫪ 𝄄 🖥 ♀ ⚐ 🏠 🎯 🛒 ⛳
& Leisure	hard tennis courts, outdoor and indoor heated swimming pools, sauna, gymnasium.

| Hotel | ★★★★★ 🏵 Chewton Glen Hotel, Christchurch Rd, NEW MILTON |
| | ☎ 01425 275341 52 ⇄ 🐾 Annexe2 ⇄ 🐾 |

OVERTON   Map 04 SU54

Test Valley Micheldever Rd RG25 3DS ☎ 01256 771737
A downland course with prominent bunker features and lakes. Teeing variations at most holes enabling the course to be played from 5000 to 7000yds. Free drainage for consistent all-year play. The 2nd, 4th, 12th and 17th holes are particularly challenging but every hole has its own appealing individual character. Has hosted Hampshire Open and many PGA events.
18 holes, 6811yds, Par 72, SSS 73, Course record 66.
Club membership 500.

Visitors	advisable to ring in advance. Must play after 11am weekends & bank holidays.
Societies	apply in writing or telephone in advance.
Green Fees	not confirmed.
Cards	💳 💳 💳 💳
Prof	Alastair Briggs
Designer	Don Wright
Facilities	⊗ ⫪ 𝄄 🖥 ♀ ⚐ 🏠 🎯 ✎
Location	1.5m N of A303

| Hotel | ★★★ 69% Centrecourt Hotel, Tennis & Health Club, Centre Dr, Chineham, BASINGSTOKE |
| | ☎ 01256 816664 50 ⇄ 🐾 |

OWER   Map 04 SU31

Paultons Golf Centre Old Salisbury Rd SO51 6AN
☎ 01703 813992
A Pay and Play 18-hole course built within the original Paultons parkland which was laid out by 'Capability' Brown. There is also a 9-hole academy course, ideal fo beginners or players wishing to improve their short games as well as a 20-bay floodlit driving range.
18 holes, 6238yds, Par 71, SSS 70, Course record 72.
Academy: 9 holes, 1324yds, Par 27, SSS 27, Course record 24.
Club membership 500.

Visitors	pay & play.
Societies	telephone for details.
Green Fees	not confirmed.
Prof	John Cave & Heath Teschner
Designer	J R Smith
Facilities	⊗ ⫪ 𝄄 🖥 ♀ ⚐ 🏠 🎯 🏸 🛒 ⛳

| Hotel | ★★★ 69% Bartley Lodge, Lyndhurst Rd, CADNAM ☎ 01703 812248 31 ⇄ 🐾 |

PETERSFIELD   Map 04 SU72

Petersfield (New Course) Tankerdale Ln, Liss GU33 7QY
☎ 01730 895165 (office) & 895216 (pro)
Fax 01730 894713
A new course designed by Martin Hawtree in an area of outstanding natural beauty with magnificent panoramic views. The Old course 1.5m away also belongs to the Petersfield Golf Club.

▶

18 holes, 6387yds, Par 72, SSS 71, Course record 70.
Club membership 725.

Visitors	start times required.
Societies	booking forms and deposit required.
Green Fees	£25 per round (£30 weekends & bank holidays).
Prof	Greg Hughes
Facilities	⊗ ⫴ ⑄ 🍵 ♥ ♀ ⌂ 🏌 🚃 ✍
Location	Off the A3 (M), between the Liss/Petersfield exits southbound

Hotel	★★★ 77% Spread Eagle Hotel and Health Spa, South St, MIDHURST
	☎ 01730 816911 35 ⊨ 🏌 Annexe4 🏌

Petersfield (Old Course) Sussex Rd GU31 4EJ
☎ 01730 895165 Fax 01730 894713
9 hole parkland course on level ground in an area of
outstanding natural beauty. Numerous trees and water
features. Part of Petersfield Golf Club although 1.5m away
from the 18 hole New Course.
9 holes, 3005yds, Par 72, SSS 69.

Visitors	starting times required, pay & play at all times.
Societies	booking form must be completed & deposit paid.
Green Fees	£10 per 18 holes; £6 per 9 holes (£12/£7 weekends & bank holidays).
Prof	Greg Hughes
Facilities	♥ ⌂ 🏌 ✍
Location	Off Sussex Road , B214

Hotel	★★★ 77% Spread Eagle Hotel and Health Spa, South St, MIDHURST
	☎ 01730 816911 35 ⊨ 🏌 Annexe4 🏌

PORTSMOUTH & SOUTHSEA   Map 04 SU60

Great Salterns Public Course Burrfields Rd,PO3 5HH
☎ 01705 664549 Fax 01705 650525
Easy walking, seaside course with open fairways and testing
shots onto well-guarded, small greens. Testing 13th hole, par
4, requiring 130yd shot across a lake.
18 holes, 5575yds, Par 70, SSS 67, Course record 64.
Club membership 700.

Visitors	no restrictions.
Societies	must contact in advance.
Green Fees	£16.30 per day; £10.30 per round (£12.30 per round weekends).
Cards	💳 💳 💳 💳
Prof	Terry Healy
Facilities	⊗ ⫴ ⑄ 🍵 ♥ ♀ ⌂ 🏌 🚃 ✍ ♪
Location	NE of town centre on A2030

Hotel	★★★ 66% Innlodge Hotel, Burrfields Rd, PORTSMOUTH
	☎ 01705 650510 73 ⊨ 🏌

Southsea The Clubhouse, Burrfields Rd PO3 5JJ
☎ 01705 664549
Municipal, meadowland course.
18 holes, 5800yds, Par 71, SSS 68, Course record 64.
Club membership 479.

Visitors	no restrictions. Booking advisable.
Societies	must contact in advance, tel: 01705 664549.
Green Fees	£10.30 weekdays (£12.30 weekends & bank holidays).
Prof	Terry Healy
Facilities	⊗ ⫴ ⑄ 🍵 ♥ ♀ ⌂ 🏌 🚃 ✍ ♪
Location	0.5m off M27

Hotel	★★★ 66% Innlodge Hotel, Burrfields Rd, PORTSMOUTH
	☎ 01705 650510 73 ⊨ 🏌

ROMSEY   Map 04 SU32

Dunwood Manor Shootash Hill SO51 0GF
☎ 01794 340549 Fax 01794 34215
Undulating parkland course with fine views. Recently
redesigned with fine holes running through mature
woodland.
18 holes, 5771yds, Par 68, SSS 68, Course record 61.
Club membership 720.

Visitors	always welcome advisable to contact in advance; essential for weekends after 11am.
Societies	must contact in advance.
Green Fees	not confirmed.
Prof	Heath Teschner
Facilities	⊗ ⫴ ⑄ 🍵 ♥ ♀ ⌂ 🏌 🚃 🛒 🚃 ✍
Location	4m W off A27

Hotel	★★★ 68% Bell Inn, BROOK
	☎ 01703 812214 25 ⊨

Romsey Romsey Rd, Nursling SO16 0XW
☎ 01703 734637 Fax 01703 741036
Parkland/woodland course with narrow tree-lined fairways.
Six holes are undulating, rest are sloping. There are superb
views over the Test valley.
18 holes, 5851yds, Par 69, SSS 68.
Club membership 900.

Visitors	welcome Mon-Fri, must play with member weekends and bank holidays.
Societies	Mon, Tue & Thu, must contact in advance.
Green Fees	not confirmed.
Prof	Mark Desmond
Facilities	⊗ ⫴ ⑄ 🍵 ♥ ♀ ⌂ 🏌 ✍
Location	3m S on A3057

Hotel	★★★ 61% The White Horse, Market Place, ROMSEY
	☎ 01794 512431 33 ⊨ 🏌

ROTHERWICK   Map 04 SU75

Tylney Park RG27 9AY
☎ 01256 762079 Fax 01256 763079
Parkland course. Practice area.
18 holes, 6109yds, Par 70, SSS 69, Course record 67.
Club membership 730.

Visitors	must be with member at weekends or have a handicap certificate.
Societies	must apply by phone in advance.
Green Fees	not confirmed.
Prof	Chris de Bruin
Designer	W Wiltshire
Facilities	⊗ ⫴ ⑄ 🍵 ♥ ♀ ⌂ 🏌 🦅 🚃 ✍
Location	0.5m SW of Rotherwick, 2m NW of Hook, 2.5m from M3 junct 5 via Newnham

Hotel	★★★★ 🎖 Tylney Hall Hotel, Tylney Hall, ROTHERWICK
	☎ 01256 764881 35 ⊨ 🏌 Annexe75 ⊨ 🏌

ROWLANDS CASTLE — Map 04 SU71

Rowlands Castle 31 Links Ln PO9 6AE
☎ 01705 412784 Fax 01705 413649
Reasonably dry in winter, the flat parkland course is a
testing one with a number of tricky dog-legs and bunkers
much in evidence. The Par 4 13th is a signature hole
necessitating a drive to a narrow fairway and a second shot
to a two-tiered green. The 7th, at 522yds, is the longest
hole on the course and leads to a well-guarded armchair
green.
18 holes, 6612yds, Par 72, SSS 72, Course record 69.
Club membership 800.

Visitors	may not play Sat; must contact in advance and hold a handicap certificate.
Societies	Tue & Thu only; must contact in writing.
Green Fees	£25 per day (£30 weekends).
Prof	Peter Klepacz
Designer	Colt
Facilities	⊗ ⅲ ᴸ ♥ ♀ ᗉ ᗉ ❥ ᴪ ✎
Location	W side of village off B2149

Hotel ★★★ 69% Brookfield Hotel, Havant Rd,
EMSWORTH ☎ 01243 373363 & 376383
Fax 01243 376342 40 ⊨ ℟

SHEDFIELD — Map 04 SU51

Marriott Meon Valley Hotel & Country Club Sandy
Ln SO32 2HQ ☎ 01329 833455 Fax 01329 834411
It has been said that a golf course architect is as good as
the ground on which he has to work. Here Hamilton Stutt
had magnificent terrain at his disposal and a very good
and lovely parkland course is the result. There are three
holes over water. The hotel provides many sports
facilities. The Championship Meon Course plays host to
the Phillips PFA Golf Classic in 1998 and 1999, a true
testament to the challenge it offers.
Meon Course: 18 holes, 6520yds, Par 71, SSS 71,
Course record 66.
Valley Course: 9 holes, 2721yds, Par 35, SSS 33.
Club membership 910.

Visitors	may book up to seven days in advance, not available at weekends and bank holidays.
Societies	telephone in advance, written confirmation.
Green Fees	Meon:£35 per round (£40 weekends); Valley: £16 per round (£20 weekends).
Cards	▭▭ ▭▭ ▭▭ ▭▭ ▭▭
Prof	Jason O'Malley
Designer	Hamilton Stutt

Facilities	⊗ ⅲ ᴸ ♥ ♀ ᗉ ᗉ ᴪ ❤ ➤ ➤ ✎ ∤
& Leisure	hard tennis courts, heated indoor swimming pool, sauna, solarium, gymnasium, health & beauty salon, spa bath, aerobics studio.
Location	Off A334 between Botley and Wickham. Access via junct 7 M27

Hotel ★★★★ 69% Marriott Meon Valley Hotel
& Country Club, Sandy Ln, SHEDFIELD
☎ 01329 833455 113 ⊨ ℟

SOUTHAMPTON — Map 04 SU41

Chilworth Main Rd, Chilworth SO16 7JP ☎ 01703 740544
A course with two loops of nine holes, with a restricted
booking system to allow undisturbed play. The first nine are
fairly long and undulating and include water hazards. The
remaining nine are flatter, but still quite a stiff test.
Manor Golf Course: 18 holes, 5740yds, Par 69, SSS 69,
Course record 68.
Club membership 600.

Visitors	must book in advance.
Societies	telephone in advance and complete booking form, various packages available.
Green Fees	not confirmed.
Prof	M Butcher/Jon Barnes/Andy Vass
Designer	J Garner
Facilities	⊗ ⅲ ᴸ ♥ ♀ ᗉ ✎ ∤
Location	A27 towards Romsey

Hotel ★★★ 60% County Hotel Southampton,
Highfield Ln, Portswood, SOUTHAMPTON
☎ 01703 359955 66 ⊨ ℟

Southampton Golf Course Rd, Bassett SO16 7AY
☎ 01703 760478 & 760546 (booking) Fax 01703 760472
This beautiful municipal parkland course always ensures a
good game, fast in summer, slow in winter. Three par 4's
over 450 yds.
18 holes, 6103yds, Par 69, SSS 70.
9 holes, 2395yds, Par 33.

Visitors	18 hole course: min 2 players (3 weekends and bank holidays) booking advisable but not always necessary. 9 hole course: 1-4 players per tee
Societies	welcome, book up to 1yr in advance.
Green Fees	18 hole course: £8.60 per round (£11.90 weekends & bank holidays); 9 hole course: £3.80 per round (£5.50 weekends & bank holidays).
Prof	John Waring
Designer	Hockley/A P Taylor
Facilities	⊗ ᴸ ♥ ♀ ᗉ ᗉ ᴪ ✎
Location	4m N of city centre off A33

Hotel ★★ 61% The Star Hotel & Restaurant, 26 High
St, SOUTHAMPTON
01703 339939 43rm(37 ⊨ ℟)

Stoneham Monks Wood Close, Bassett SO16 3TT
☎ 01703 769272 Fax 01703 766320
A hilly, heather course with sand or peat sub-soil; the fairways are separated by belts of woodland and heather to present a varied terrain. The interesting 4th is a difficult par 4 and the fine 11th has cross-bunkers about 150 yards from the tee.
18 holes, 6310yds, Par 72, SSS 70, Course record 63.
Club membership 800.

Visitors	advisable to contact in advance, handicap certificate required.
Societies	Mon, Thu & Fri only. Must telephone in advance or apply in writing.
Green Fees	£36 per day, £29 per round (£40 weekends & bank holidays).
Prof	Ian Young
Designer	Willie Park
Facilities	⊗ ⫼ ⅋ ⚑ ♀ ♨ 🖻 ⛳ 🏌 ⚐
Location	4m N of city centre off A27
Hotel	★★★ 60% County Hotel Southampton, Highfield Ln, Portswood, SOUTHAMPTON ☎ 01703 359955 66 ⇆ ☏

SOUTHWICK   Map 04 SU60

Southwick Park Naval Recreation Centre Pinsley Dr
PO17 6EL ☎ 01705 380131 Fax 01705 210289
Set in 100 acres of parkland.
18 holes, 5992yds, Par 69, SSS 69, Course record 64.
Club membership 700.

Visitors	contact in advance, welcome weekends after 2pm
Societies	Tue only, telephone in advance.
Green Fees	£15 per round (£17 weekends).
Prof	John Green
Designer	C Lawrie
Facilities	⊗ ⅋ ⚑ ♀ ♨ 🖻 ⛳ ⚐
Location	0.5m SE off B2177
Hotel	★★ 75% Old House Hotel, The Square, WICKHAM ☎ 01329 833049 9 ⇆ ☏

TADLEY   Map 04 SU66

Bishopswood Bishopswood Ln RG26 4AT
☎ 0118 9812200 Fax 0118 9408606
Wooded course, fairly tight, with stream and natural water hazards.
9 holes, 6474yds, Par 72, SSS 71, Course record 66.
Club membership 485.

Visitors	must contact in advance. No play weekends or bank holidays.
Societies	must contact by telephone.
Green Fees	£10 per 9 holes, £15 per 18 holes.
Cards	⚏ ⚏
Prof	Steve Ward
Designer	M W Phillips/G Blake
Facilities	⊗ ⫼ ⅋ ⚑ ♀ ♨ 🖻 ⚐ ⚒
Location	6m N of Basingstoke off the A340
Hotel	★★★ 76% Romans Country House Hotel, Little London Rd, SILCHESTER ☎ 0118 970 0421 11 ⇆ ☏ Annexe14 ⇆ ☏

WATERLOOVILLE   Map 04 SU60

Portsmouth Crookhorn Ln, Purbrook PO7 5QL
☎ 01705 372210 Fax 01705 200766
Hilly, challenging course with good views of Portsmouth Harbour. Rarely free from the wind and the picturesque 6th, 17th and 18th holes can test the best.
18 holes, 6139yds, Par 69, SSS 70, Course record 64.
Club membership 700.

Visitors	must book in advance.
Societies	must book in advance, in writing or by telephone.
Green Fees	£16.30 per day, day ticket weekdays only; £10.30 per round (£12.30 per round weekends).
Cards	⚏ ⚏ ⚏ ⚏
Prof	Jason Banting
Designer	Hawtree
Facilities	⊗ ⫼ ⅋ ⚑ ♀ ♨ 🖻 ⛳ ⚐
Location	2m S, off A3
Hotel	★★★ 63% The Bear Hotel, East St, HAVANT ☎ 01705 486501 42 ⇆ ☏

Waterlooville Cherry Tree Av, Cowplain,PO8 8AP
☎ 01705 263388 Fax 01705 347513
Parkland course, easy walking. Challenging course with 5 par 5's over 500 yards and featuring 4 ponds and a stream running through.
18 holes, 6602yds, Par 72, SSS 72, Course record 64.
Club membership 800.

Visitors	must contact in advance & may only play on weekdays.
Societies	Thu only; apply by letter or telephone.
Green Fees	not confirmed.
Prof	John Hay
Designer	Henry Cotton
Facilities	⊗ ⅋ ⚑ ♀ ♨ 🖻 ⚐
Location	NE side of town centre off A3
Hotel	B Posthouse Havant, Northney Rd, HAYLING ISLAND ☎ 01705 465011 92 ⇆ ☏

WINCHESTER   Map 04 SU42

Hockley Twyford SO21 1PL
☎ 01962 713165 Fax 01962 713612
High downland course with good views.
18 holes, 6336yds, Par 71, SSS 70, Course record 64.
Club membership 750.

Visitors	are advised to phone in advance. Handicap certificate required.
Societies	must telephone in advance and confirm in writing with deposit.
Green Fees	£28 for 18 holes; £35 for 36 holes.
Prof	Terry Lane
Designer	James Braid
Facilities	⊗ ⫼ ⅋ ⚑ ♀ ♨ 🖻 ⚐
Location	Jct 11 M3, follow sign to Twyford
Hotel	★★★★ 61% The Wessex, Paternoster Row, WINCHESTER ☎ 01962 861611 94 ⇆ ☏

LAINSTON HOUSE HOTEL
★★★★ ◎◎

where English Tradition remains our hallmark

Set in sixty three acres of tranquil Hampshire downland, just 2½ miles from the Historic Cathedral City of Winchester. Lainston House is an elegant William and Mary House with thirty eight individually designed bedrooms and suites. The charm of the reception rooms is enhanced by the peace and serenity of this period house. The highly praised restaurant offers gourmet food freshly prepared with local ingredients and the superb service is complemented by breathtaking views over the tranquil parkland. Lainston House offers weekend tariffs and special events throughout the year.

Golf can be arranged at The Royal Winchester Golf Club which is 2 miles away

Lainston House Hotel & Restaurant, Sparsholt, Winchester, Hampshire SO21 2LT
Telephone: (01962) 863588 Fax: (01962) 776672.
Situated on the B3049 Stockbridge Road out of Winchester

Royal Winchester Sarum Rd SO22 5QE
☎ 01962 852462 Fax 01962 865048
The Royal Winchester course is a sporting downland course centred on a rolling valley, so the course is hilly in places. After a disastrous fire in 1994, a new clubhouse was built (opened August 1995). Royal Winchester must be included in any list of notable clubs, because of its age (it dates from 1888) and also because the club was involved in one of the very first professional matches.
18 holes, 6204yds, Par 71, SSS 70, Course record 65.
Club membership 800.
Visitors must play with member at weekends. Must contact in advance and have a handicap certificate.
Societies must contact in writing or by telephone.
Green Fees £35 per day; £28 per round (Mon-Fri only).
Cards ⬛⬛⬛
Prof Steven Hunter
Facilities ⊗ � 曲 ☕ ♀ ♨ 🏌
Location 1.5m W off A3090

Hotel ★★★★♨ 78% Lainston House Hotel, Sparsholt, WINCHESTER ☎ 01962 863588 38 ⇄ 🐓

South Winchester Romsey Rd SO22 5QW
☎ 01962 877800 Fax 01962 877900
Opened in September 1993, this Peter Alliss/Dave Thomas designed course incorporates downland, meadows and seven lakes. Home of the Hampshire PGA and the venue for European Ladies Tour Pro-Ams.

18 holes, 7086yds, Par 72, SSS 74, Course record 68.
Club membership 750.
Visitors guests only by arrangement.
Societies must contact in advance.
Green Fees not confirmed.
Cards ⬛⬛⬛
Prof Richard Adams
Designer Dave Thomas/Peter Allis
Facilities ⊗ 曲 ☕ ♀ ♨ 🏌
Location On A3090 Romsey road

Hotel ★★★ 68% Royal Hotel, Saint Peter St, WINCHESTER ☎ 01962 840840 75 ⇄ 🐓

HEREFORD Map 03 SO53

Belmont Lodge Belmont HR2 9SA
☎ 01432 352666 Fax 01432 358090
Parkland course designed in two loops of nine. The first nine take the higher ground, offering magnificent views over Herefordshire. The second nine run alongside the river Wye with five holes in play against the river.
18 holes, 6511yds, Par 72, SSS 71, Course record 66.
Club membership 450.
Visitors advised to contact in advance at weekends. Tel: 01432 352666 or 352717.
Societies must telephone in advance. ▶

Green Fees £17 per round (£25 weekends).
Cards   —▪︎▪︎▪︎▪︎
Prof   Mike Welsh
Designer Bob Sandow
Facilities ⊗⫼📒💺♀⚲🏠⛳🏌🛺↙
& Leisure hard tennis courts, fishing, snooker room.
Location 2m S off A465

Hotel   ★★★ 62% Belmont Lodge & Golf Course,
Belmont, HEREFORD
☎ 01432 352666 30 ⇆ ☛

Burghill Valley Tillington Rd, Burghill HR4 7RW
☎ 01432 760456 Fax 01432 761654
The course is situated in typically beautiful Herefordshire
countryside. The walking is easy on gently rolling fairways
with a background of hills and woods and in the distance, the
Welsh mountains. Some holes are played through mature
cider orchards and there are two lakes to negotiate. A fair but
interesting test for players of all abilities.
18 holes, 6239yds, Par 71, SSS 70, Course record 69.
Club membership 700.
Visitors   contact in advance.
Societies apply in writing or telephone in advance.
Green Fees £18 per round (£25 weekends & bank holidays).
Cards   —▪︎▪︎▪︎
Prof   Nigel Clarke
Designer M Barnett
Facilities ⊗⫼📒💺♀⚲🏠🏌🛺↙
Location 4m NW of Hereford

Hotel   ★★★ 61% The Green Dragon, Broad St,
HEREFORD ☎ 01432 272506 83 ⇆ ☛

Hereford Municipal Hereford Leisure Centre, Holmer Rd
HR4 9UD ☎ 01432 344376 Fax 01432 266281
This municipal parkland course is more challenging than first
appearance. The well-drained greens are open all year round
with good drainage for excellent winter golf.
9 holes, 3060yds, Par 35, SSS 69.
Club membership 160.
Visitors   restrictions on race days.
Societies telephone in advance.
Green Fees not confirmed.
Prof   Philip Brookes
Designer J Leek/J McCleoud
Facilities ⊗⫼📒💺♀⚲🏠🏌🛺↙
& Leisure squash, sauna, gymnasium.
Location Adjacent to race course & leisure centre

Hotel   ★★ 63% The Merton Hotel & Governors
Restaurant, 28 Commercial Rd, HEREFORD
☎ 01432 265925 19 ⇆ ☛

KINGTON   Map 03 SO25

Kington Bradnor Hill HR5 3RE
☎ 01544 230340 & 231320
The highest 18-hole course in England, with magnificent
views over seven counties. A natural heathland course
with easy walking on mountain turf cropped by sheep.
There is bracken to catch any really bad shots but no
sand traps.
18 holes, 5980yds, Par 70, SSS 68, Course record 63.
Club membership 640.
Visitors   contact the professional.
Societies must book in advance through the Hon
             Secretary.

Green Fees £20 per day; £15 per round (£25/£20
             weekends).
Prof   Dean Oliver
Designer Major Hutchison
Facilities ⊗⫼📒💺♀⚲🏠🏌↙(
Location 0.5m N of Kington, off B4355

Hotel   ★★ 66% Talbot Hotel, West St,
LEOMINSTER
☎ 01568 616347 20 ⇆ ☛

LEOMINSTER   Map 03 SO45

Leominster Ford Bridge HR6 0LE
☎ 01568 611402 (Prof) & 610055 (Sec/Mngr)
Fax 01568 610055
On undulating parkland with the lower holes running
alongside the River Lugg and others on the higher part of the
course affording fine panoramic views over the surrounding
countryside.
18 holes, 6029yds, Par 70, SSS 69.
Club membership 550.
Visitors   must contact in advance.
Societies must telephone in advance.
Green Fees Tue-Fri: £19 per day; £15.50 per round; Mon:
             £15 per day; £8 per round (£25/£22 weekends &
             bank holidays).
Prof   Andrew Ferriday
Designer Bob Sandow
Facilities ⊗⫼📒💺♀⚲🏠🏌↙
& Leisure fishing.
Location 3m S of Leominster on A49. Clearly signposted
            from Leominster by-pass

Hotel   ★★ 60% Royal Oak Hotel, South St,
LEOMINSTER ☎ 01568 612610   17 ⇥
♟ Annexe1 ⇥ ♟

Additional   ★★ 66% Talbot Hotel, West St,
hotel   LEOMINSTER
☎ 01568 616347 Fax 01568 614880   20 ⇥ ♟

ROSS-ON-WYE   Map 03 SO62

Ross-on-Wye Two Park, Gorsley HR9 7UT
☎ 01989 720267 Fax 01989 720212
The undulating, parkland course has been cut out of a
silver birch forest; the fairways being well-screened
from each other. The fairways are tight, the greens
good and the bunkers have recently been re-
structured.
18 holes, 6451yds, Par 72, SSS 73, Course record 68.
Club membership 760.
Visitors   must contact professional in advance 01989
     720439.
Societies   must telephone in advance.
Green Fees not confirmed.
Prof   Nick Catchpole
Facilities   ⊗ ⅷ ᴮ 🍴 ♀ ♨ 🏠 ♪ ♨
Location   On B4221 N side of M50 junc 3

Hotel   ★★★ 77% Pengethley Manor, Pengethley
Park, ROSS-ON-WYE ☎ 01989 730211
11 ⇥ ♟ Annexe14 ⇥ ♟
See advertisement on page 412.

UPPER SAPEY   Map 03 SO66

Sapey WR6 6XT
☎ 01886 853288 & 853567 Fax 01886 853485
Parkland course with views of the Malvern Hills. Trees, lakes
and water hazards. Not too strenuous a walk.
18 holes, 5935yds, Par 69, SSS 68, Course record 63.
Club membership 520.
Visitors   must contact in advance.
Societies   must contact in advance.
Green Fees £24 per day; £16 per round (£30/£22 weekends
     & bank holidays).
Cards   ⚊ 🟦 ▧ 🔳
Prof   Chris Knowles
Designer   R McMurray
Facilities   ⊗ ⅷ by prior arrangement ᴮ 🍴 ♀ ♨ 🏠 ♪
     ♨ ♨ ♪
& Leisure   bowling green.
Location   B4203 Bromyard/Stourport Rd

Hotel   ★★★ 78% The Elms, ABBERLEY
☎ 01299 896666   16 ⇥ ♟

WORMSLEY   Map 03 SO44

Herefordshire Ravens Causeway HR4 8LY
☎ 01432 830219 & 830465 (pro)
Undulating parkland course with expansive views.
18 holes, 6036yds, Par 70, SSS 69, Course record 61.
Club membership 800.
Visitors   must contact in advance, possibility of weekend
     play if no competitions are taking place.
Societies   must apply in advance.
Green Fees £25 per day; £19 per round (£30/£22 weekends
     & bank holidays).

Cards   ⚊ 🟦 🔳
Prof   David Hemming
Facilities   ⊗ ⅷ ᴮ 🍴 ♀ ♨ 🏠 ♪ 🏇 ♨ ♨
Location   E side of village

Hotel   ★★★ 61% The Green Dragon, Broad St,
HEREFORD
☎ 01432 272506   83 ⇥ ♟

HERTFORDSHIRE

ALDBURY   Map 04 SP91

Stocks Hotel Golf & Country Club Stocks Rd HP23 5RX
☎ 01442 851341 Fax 01442 851253
An 18-hole parkland course is one of the many facilities at
this country club. The course plays off blue, white (6,804
yards), yellow and red tees. There is also a driving range.
18 holes, 6804yds, Par 72, SSS 73, Course record 65.
Visitors   must contact in advance and have a handicap
     certificate. May not play before 2pm at
     weekends.
Societies   must contact well in advance.
Green Fees £30 per round (£40 weekends by arrangement).
Cards   ⚊ 🟦 ▧ 🔳 🔳
Prof   Peter Lane
Designer   Mike Billcliffe
Facilities   ⊗ ⅷ ᴮ 🍴 ♀ ♨ 🏠 ♪ 🏇 ♨ ♨ ♪
& Leisure   hard tennis courts, heated outdoor swimming
     pool, sauna, solarium, gymnasium, snooker,
     table tennis, jacuzzi.
Location   2m from A41 at Tring

Hotel   ★★★★ 60% Pendley Manor, Cow Ln, TRING
☎ 01442 891891   71 ⇥ ♟

ALDENHAM   Map 04 TQ19

Aldenham Golf and Country Club Church Ln WD2 8AL
☎ 01923 853929 Fax 01923 858472
Undulating parkland course.
Old Course: 18 holes, 6480yds, Par 70, SSS 71.
White Course: 9 holes, 4700yds, Par 33, SSS 32.
Club membership 550.
Visitors   Old Course restricted weekends before noon.
     White Course no restrictions.
Societies   must contact in advance.
Green Fees Old Course: £24 per day (£32 weekends & bank
     holidays). White Course:£10 (£12 weekends).
Cards   ⚊ 🟦 ▧ 🔳 🔳
Prof   Tim Dunstan
Facilities   ⊗ ⅷ ᴮ 🍴 ♀ ♨ 🏠 ♪ ♨ ♪
Location   W side of village

Hotel   ★★★ 63% Watford Moat House, 30-40 St
Albans Rd, WATFORD
☎ 01923 429988   90 ⇥ ♟

Entries with a shaded background
identify courses that are
considered to be particularly interesting

BERKHAMSTED
Map 04 SP90

Berkhamsted The Common HP4 2QB
☎ 01442 865832 Fax 01442 863730
There are no sand bunkers on this Championship
heathland course but this does not make it any easier to
play. The natural hazards will test the skill of the most
able players, with a particularly testing hole at the 11th,
568 yards, par 5. Fine Greens, long carries and heather
and gorse. The clubhouse is very comfortable.
18 holes, 6605yds, Par 71, SSS 72, Course record 65.
Club membership 700.

Visitors	must contact in advance.
Societies	must contact in advance.
Green Fees	£35 per day; £25 per round (£35 weekends after 11.30am).
Prof	Basil Proudfoot
Designer	Colt/Braid
Facilities	⊗ ⅢⅬ ⬛ ♀♨ ☎ ♂
Location	1.5m E

Hotel	★★★★ 60% Pendley Manor, Cow Ln, TRING ☎ 01442 891891 71 ⇔ ♠

BISHOP'S STORTFORD
Map 05 TL42

Bishop's Stortford Dunmow Rd CM23 5HP
☎ 01279 654715 Fax 01279 655215
Parkland course, fairly flat.
18 holes, 6404yds, Par 71, SSS 71, Course record 66.
Club membership 900.

Visitors	must have a valid handicap certificate, must play with member at weekends. Must contact in advance in writing.
Societies	must contact in writing.
Green Fees	£35 per day; £25 per 18 holes.
Cards	
Prof	Vince Duncan
Designer	James Braid
Facilities	⊗ ⅢⅬ ⬛ ♀♨ ☎ ♈ ♥ ⚒ ♂
& Leisure	snooker tables.
Location	0.5m W of M11 junc 8 on A1250

Hotel	★★★★ 66% Down Hall Country House Hotel, Hatfield Heath, BISHOP'S STORTFORD ☎ 01279 731441 103 ⇔ ♠

Entries with a shaded background
identify courses that are
considered to be particularly interesting

Great Hadham Golf & Country Club Great Hadham Rd,
Much Hadham SG10 6JE
☎ 01279 843558 Fax 01279 842122
An undulating open meadowland/links course offering excellent
country views and a challenge with its ever present breeze.
18 holes, 6854yds, Par 72, SSS 73, Course record 67.
Club membership 700.

Visitors	welcome all times except am Mon, Wed, Sat & Sun.
Societies	by advance booking in writing.
Green Fees	£30 per day; £18 per round (£25 per round weekends & bank holidays).
Cards	
Prof	Kevin Lunt
Designer	Iain Roberts
Facilities	⊗ ⅢⅬ ⬛ ♀♨ ☎ ♈ ♂ ¿
& Leisure	sauna, solarium, gymnasium, health club.
Location	On the B1004, 3m SW of Bishop's Stortford

Hotel	★★★★ 66% Down Hall Country House Hotel, Hatfield Heath, BISHOP'S STORTFORD ☎ 01279 731441 103 ⇔ ♠

BRICKENDON
Map 05 TL30

Brickendon Grange SG13 8PD
☎ 01992 511258 Fax 01992 511258
Undulating parkland course with some fine par 4's. 17th hole
reputed to be best in the county.
18 holes, 6395yds, Par 71, SSS 70, Course record 66.
Club membership 680.

Visitors	must have handicap certificate. With member only at weekends & bank holidays.
Societies	by arrangement.
Green Fees	£35 per day; £30 per round.
Prof	John Hamilton
Designer	C K Cotton
Facilities	⊗ ⅢⅬ ⬛ ♀♨ ☎ ♥ ⚒ ♂
Location	W side of village

Hotel	★★★ 66% The White Horse, Hertingfordbury, HERTFORD ☎ 01992 586791 42 ⇔ ♠

BROOKMANS PARK
Map 04 TL20

Brookmans Park Golf Club Rd AL9 7AT
☎ 01707 652487 Fax 01707 661851
Brookman's Park is an undulating parkland course, with
several cleverly constructed holes. But it is a fair course,
although it can play long. The 11th, par 3, is a testing
hole which plays across a lake.
18 holes, 6460yds, Par 71, SSS 71, Course record 66.
Club membership 750.

Visitors	must contact professional in advance 01707 652468 and have a handicap certificate; must play with member at weekends & bank holidays.
Societies	must telephone or write in advance.
Green Fees	£40 per day; £30 per round.
Prof	Ian Jelley
Designer	Hawtree/Taylor
Facilities	⊗ ⅢⅬ ⬛ ♀♨ ☎ ♥ ⚒ ♂
Location	N side of village off A1000

Hotel	B Posthouse South Mimms, SOUTH MIMMS ☎ 01707 643311 143 ⇔ ♠

BUNTINGFORD

Map 05 TL32

East Herts Hamels Park SG9 9NA ☎ 01920 821922 (Pro)
An attractive undulating parkland course with magnificent
specimen trees.
18 holes, 6456yds, Par 71, SSS 71.
Club membership 750.
Visitors	must contact in advance & have handicap certificate, but may not play on Wed & weekends.
Societies	apply in writing.
Green Fees	£33 per day; £26 per round.
Prof	S Bryan
Facilities	⊗ 🐄 💺 ♥ 🏌 🍴 🛒 ⚒
Location	1m N of Puckeridge off A10

Hotel	★★★ 62% Vintage Court Hotel, Vintage Corner, PUCKERIDGE ☎ 01920 822722 25 ➡ ⎮⏇

BUSHEY

Map 04 TQ19

Bushey Golf & Country Club High St WD2 1BJ
☎ 0181 950 2283 Fax 0181 386 1181
Undulating parkland with challenging 2nd and 9th holes. The
latter has a sweeping dolgleg left, playing to a green in front
of the club house. For the rather too enthusiatic golfer,
Bushey offers its own physiotherapist!
9 holes, 6120yds, Par 70, SSS 69, Course record 67.
Club membership 411.
Visitors	must contact in advance.
Societies	apply in writing or by telephone.
Green Fees	£15 per 18 holes; £9 per 9 holes (£18/£11 weekends).
Cards	💳 💳
Prof	Michael Lovegrove
Facilities	⊗ 🐄 💺 ♥ 🏌 🍴 🛒 ⚒
& Leisure	sauna, solarium, gymnasium.

Hotel	★★★ 73% Edgwarebury Hotel, Barnet Ln., ELSTREE ☎ 0181 953 8227 47 ➡ ⎮⏇

Bushey Hall Bushey Hall Dr WD2 2EP
☎ 01923 225802 & 222253 Fax 01923 229759
Tree lined parkland course.
18 holes, 6099yds, Par 70, SSS 69.
Club membership 500.

Visitors	may book 7 days in advance.
Societies	must contact in writing.
Green Fees	Mon-Tue £15 per round, Wed-Fri £18.50 per round (£26 per round weekends).
Cards	💳 💳

Prof	Ken Wickham
Designer	Clouston
Facilities	⊗ 🐄 💺 ♥ 🏌 🍴 🛒 ⚒
Location	1.5m NW on A4008

Hotel	★★★ 63% Watford Moat House, 30-40 St Albans Rd, WATFORD ☎ 01923 429988 90 ➡ ⎮⏇

Hartsbourne Golf & Country Club Hartsbourne Ave WD2
1JW ☎ 0181 950 1133
Parkland course with good views.
18 holes, 6305yds, Par 71, SSS 70, Course record 62.
Club membership 750.
Visitors	must be guest of a member.
Societies	phone for details.
Green Fees	not confirmed.
Prof	Geoff Hunt
Facilities	⊗ 🐄 💺 ♥ 🏌 🍴 🛒 ⚒ ⎮
Location	5m SE of Watford

Hotel	★★★ 63% Watford Moat House, 30-40 St Albans Rd, WATFORD ☎ 01923 429988 90 ➡ ⎮⏇

CHESHUNT

Map 05 TL30

Cheshunt Cheshunt Park, Park Ln EN7 6QD
☎ 01992 624009
Municipal parkland course, well-bunkered with ponds, easy
walking.
18 holes, 6613yds, Par 71, SSS 71.
Club membership 350.
Visitors	must book Tee-times through Reception. Must contact in advance.
Societies	must apply in writing.
Green Fees	£10.50-£14.50 per round.
Cards	💳 💳 💳 💳
Prof	Andy Traynor
Designer	P Wawtry
Facilities	⊗ 🐄 💺 ♥ 🏌 🍴 🛒 ⚒
Location	1.5m NW off B156

Hotel	★★★★ 65% Cheshunt Marriott Hotel, Halfhide Ln, Turnford, BROXBOURNE ☎ 01992 451245 143 ➡ ⎮⏇

CHORLEYWOOD

Map 04 TQ09

Chorleywood Common Rd WD3 5LN
☎ 01923 282009 Fax 01923 286739
Very attractive mix of woodland and heathland with natural
hazards and good views.
9 holes, 5676yds, Par 68, SSS 67.
Club membership 300.
Visitors	must contact in advance, restricted weekends.
Societies	initial contact by telephone.
Green Fees	£16 per day; £20 weekends & bank holidays.
Facilities	⊗ 🐄 💺 ♥ 🏌
Location	E side of village off A404

Hotel	★★★ 72% The Bedford Arms Chenies, CHENIES ☎ 01923 283301 10 ➡ ⎮⏇

ELSTREE   Map 04 TQ19

Elstree Watling St WD6 3AA
☎ 0181 953 6115 Fax 0181 207 6390
Parkland course.
18 holes, 6556yds, Par 73, SSS 72.
Club membership 650.

Visitors	advisable to contact in advance, no restrictions weekdays, may not play until after 2pm weekends unless tee time available day prior.
Societies	telephone in advance.
Green Fees	£30 per day; £20 per round (£25 per 18 holes after midday weekends & bank holidays).
Cards	— 🗖 VISA ⬛
Prof	Marc Warwick
Designer	Donald Steel
Facilities	⊗ ∭ by prior arrangement 🏌 ☕ ♀ 🏖 🏠 ⛳ ⚷
Location	A5183 between Radlett and Elstree

Hotel ★★★ 73% Edgwarebury Hotel, Barnet Ln, ELSTREE ☎ 0181 953 8227 47 ⇔ ♜

ESSENDON   Map 04 TL20

Hatfield London Country Club Bedwell Park AL9 6JA
☎ 01707 642624 Fax 01707 646187
Parkland course with many varied hazards, including ponds, a stream and a ditch. 19th-century manor clubhouse. 9-hole pitch and putt.
18 holes, 6880yds, Par 72, SSS 72.
Club membership 250.

Visitors	must contact in advance.
Societies	must contact in advance.
Green Fees	not confirmed.
Prof	Norman Greer
Designer	Fred Hawtry
Facilities	⊗ 🏌 ☕ ♀ 🏖 🏠 ⛳ ⚷
& Leisure	hard tennis courts.
Location	On B158 1m S

Hotel ★★★ 66% Quality Hotel Hatfield, Roehyde Way, HATFIELD ☎ 01707 275701 76 ⇔ ♜

GRAVELEY   Map 04 TL22

Chesfield Downs Jack's Hill SG4 7EQ
☎ 01462 482929 Fax 01462 482930
A revolutionary new golf course with the emphasis on facilities for the entire family. Its undulating, open downland course has an inland links feel. There is a 25-bay floodlit, covered driving range, a 9-hole Par 3 and many other facilities.
18 holes, 6648yds, Par 71, SSS 72.
Club membership 500.

Visitors	no restrictions.
Societies	must telephone in advance.
Green Fees	not confirmed.
Prof	Jane Fernley
Designer	J Gaunt
Facilities	⊗ ∭ by prior arrangement 🏌 ☕ ♀ 🏖 🏠 ⛳ 🛒 ⚷ ♜
& Leisure	par3 9 hole course.
Location	Jct 8 of A1, B197 to Graveley

Hotel ★★★ 60% Hertfordpark Hotel, Danestrete, STEVENAGE ☎ 01438 779955 98 ⇔ ♜

HARPENDEN   Map 04 TL11

Aldwickbury Park Piggottshill Ln AL5 1AB
☎ 01582 760112 Fax 01582 760113
Attractive parkland course with large areas of mature woodland and good views across the Lee Valley.
Park: 18 holes, 6352yds, Par 71, SSS 70, Course record 66.
Club membership 700.

Visitors	telephone in advance.
Societies	telephone for brochure, various packages available.
Green Fees	Park: £20 (£24 weekends).
Cards	— 🗖 VISA ⬛ 🗖
Prof	Dalvyn Germeney
Designer	Ken Brown/Martin Fillett
Facilities	⊗ ∭ 🏌 ☕ ♀ 🏖 🏠 ⛳ 🛒 ⚷
Location	Located just off Wheathampstead Road, between Harpenden/Wheathampstead, 10mins from junct 9 of M1

Hotel ★★★ 67% Harpenden House, 18 Southdown Rd, HARPENDEN ☎ 01582 449955 18 ⇔ ♜ Annexe35 ⇔ ♜

Harpenden Hammonds End, Redbourn Ln AL5 2AX
☎ 01582 712580 Fax 01582 712725
Gently undulating parkland course, easy walking.
18 holes, 6381yds, Par 70, SSS 70, Course record 67.
Club membership 800.

Visitors	must contact in advance. May not play Thu & weekends.
Societies	must apply in writing.
Green Fees	not confirmed.
Prof	Peter Cherry
Designer	Hawtree & Taylor
Facilities	⊗ ∭ 🏌 ☕ ♀ 🏖 🏠 ⛳ ⚷ ♜
Location	1m S on B487

Hotel ★★★ 67% Harpenden House, 18 Southdown Rd, HARPENDEN ☎ 01582 449955 18 ⇔ ♜ Annexe35 ⇔ ♜

Harpenden Common Cravells Rd, East Common AL5 1BL
☎ 01582 715959 Fax 01582 715959
Flat, easy walking, good greens, typical common course.
18 holes, 6214yds, Par 70, SSS 70, Course record 67.
Club membership 710.

Visitors	must contact in advance.
Societies	Thu & Fri only. Must apply in writing.
Green Fees	£30 per day; £25 per round.
Prof	Danny Fitzsimmons
Facilities	⊗ 🏌 ☕ ♀ 🏖 🏠 ⛳ ⚷
Location	1m S on A1081

Hotel ★★★ 73% Glen Eagle Hotel, 1 Luton Rd, HARPENDEN ☎ 01582 760271 60 ⇔ ♜

HEMEL HEMPSTEAD   Map 04 TL00

Boxmoor 18 Box Ln, Boxmoor HP3 0DJ
☎ 01442 242434
Challenging, very hilly, moorland course with sloping fairways divided by trees. Fine views. Testing holes: 3rd (par 3), 4th (par 4).
9 holes, 4812yds, Par 64, SSS 63, Course record 62.
Club membership 280.

Visitors may not play on Sun & bank holidays. Restricted some Sat.
Societies must contact in advance.
Green Fees not confirmed.
Facilities ⊗ ▯ ♀ ⚲
Location 2m SW on B4505

Hotel ★★ 70% The Two Brewers, The Common, CHIPPERFIELD ☎ 01923 265266 20 ⇥ ♠

Little Hay Box Ln, Bovingdon HP3 0DQ ☎ 01442 833798
Semi-parkland, inland links.
18 holes, 6678yds, Par 72, SSS 72.
Visitors advisable to contact in advance.
Societies telephone for details.
Green Fees £11.60 (£15.50 weekends).
Cards ▬ ▭ ▬
Prof D Johnson/M Campbell
Designer Hawtree
Facilities ⊗ ⏁ ⮭ ▯ ♀ ⚲ ⌂ ⚶ ⚲ ⚶ ⚭
Location 1.5m SW on B4505 off A41

Hotel B Posthouse Hemel Hempstead, Breakspear Way, HEMEL HEMPSTEAD ☎ 01442 251122 145 ⇥ ♠

Shendish Manor London Rd, Apsley HP3 0AA
☎ 01442 251806 Fax 01442 230683
A hilly course with plenty of trees and good greens. A tough course for any golfer.
18 holes, 5660yds, Par 70, SSS 67.
Club membership 100.
Visitors no restrictions but advisable to book in advance
Societies must contact in advance.
Green Fees not confirmed.
Cards ▬ ▭
Prof Murray White
Designer D Steel
Facilities ⊗ ⏁ by prior arrangement ⮭ ▯ ♀ ⚲ ⌂ ⚶ ⚭ ⚶
& Leisure sauna, solarium, gymnasium.
Location Just off A4251

Hotel ★★★★ 60% Pendley Manor, Cow Ln, TRING ☎ 01442 891891 71 ⇥ ♠

KNEBWORTH   Map 04 TL22

Knebworth Deards End Ln SG3 6NL
☎ 01438 812752 Fax 01438 815216
Parkland course, easy walking.
18 holes, 6492yds, Par 71, SSS 71, Course record 66.
Club membership 900.
Visitors must have handicap certificate , but must play with member at weekends.
Societies Mon, Tue & Thu. Must contact in advance.
Green Fees £30 per day/round.
Cards ▬ ▭ ▬ ▬ ⚶
Prof Garry Parker
Designer W Park (Jun)
Facilities ⊗ ⏁ by prior arrangement ⮭ ▯ ♀ ⚲ ⌂ ⚭ ⚶
Location N side of village off B197

Hotel B Posthouse Stevenage, Old London Rd, Broadwater, STEVENAGE ☎ 01438 365444 54 ⇥ ♠

LETCHWORTH   Map 04 TL23

Letchworth Letchworth Ln SG6 3NQ
☎ 01462 683203 Fax 01462 484567
Planned more than 50 years ago by Harry Vardon, this adventurous, parkland course is set in a peaceful corner of 'Norman' England. To its variety of natural and artificial hazards is added an unpredictable wind.
18 holes, 6181yds, Par 70, SSS 69, Course record 65.
Club membership 750.
Visitors with member only at weekends. Must contact in advance and have a handicap certificate.
Societies Wed, Thu & Fri only, must telephone in advance.
Green Fees not confirmed.
Prof J Mutimer
Designer Harry Vardon
Facilities ⊗ ⏁ ⮭ ▯ ♀ ⚲ ⌂ ⚭ ⚶
Location S side of town centre off A505

Hotel ★★★ 64% Thistle Stevenage / Hitchin, Blakemore End Rd, Little Wymondley, HITCHIN ☎ 01438 355821 82 ⇥ ♠

LITTLE GADDESDEN   Map 04 SP91

Ashridge HP4 1LY
☎ 01442 842244 Fax 01442 843770
Good parkland course, challenging but fair. Good clubhouse facilities.
18 holes, 6547yds, Par 72, SSS 71, Course record 63.
Club membership 720.
Visitors must contact in advance , be a member of a recognised club & have handicap certificate, may not play weekends & bank holidays.
Societies must apply in writing and complete booking form.
Green Fees not confirmed.
Prof Andrew Ainsworth
Designer Sir G Campbell/C Hutchinson/N Hutchinson
Facilities ⊗ ⏁ ⮭ ▯ ♀ ⚲ ⌂ ⚭ ⚶
Location 5m N of Berkhamsted on the B4506

Hotel ★★★ 73% The Bell Inn, ASTON CLINTON ☎ 01296 630252 5 ⇥ ♠ Annexe15 ⇥ ♠

MUCH HADHAM   Map 05 TL41

Much Hadham Little Hadham Rd SG10 6HD
☎ 01279 843253 Fax 01920 468686
Naturally undulating course with good views extending to Canary Wharf in London on a clear day.
18 holes, 6516yds, Par 71, Course record 71.
Visitors no restrictions.
Societies telephone in advance.
Green Fees not confirmed.
Designer Martin Gillett
Facilities ⮭ ▯ ♀ ⚲ ⌂ ⚭
Location 1.5m S of A120 fom Little Hadham traffic lights

Hotel ★★★ 62% Vintage Court Hotel, Vintage Corner, PUCKERIDGE ☎ 01920 822722 25 ⇥ ♠

POTTERS BAR   Map 04 TL20

Potters Bar Darkes Ln EN6 1DE ☎ 01707 652020
Undulating parkland course with water in play on many
holes.
18 holes, 6279yds, Par 71, SSS 70.
Club membership 650.
Visitors   with member only at weekends, Ladies Day
                 Wed morning.
Societies   Mon-Fri & Wed (pm only) by arrangement with
                 Secretary.
Green Fees   not confirmed.
Cards   ⌐ 🟦
Prof   Gary A'Ris
Designer   James Braid
Facilities   ⊗ ⓑ 🍺 ♀ ☖ 🏠 ⛳ 🏌 🛒 ⌀
Location   1m N of M25 junct 24

Hotel   B Posthouse South Mimms, SOUTH MIMMS
                 ☎ 01707 643311 143 ⇄ ↑

RADLETT   Map 04 TL10

Porters Park Shenley Hill WD7 7AZ ☎ 01923 854127
A splendid, undulating parkland course with fine trees
and lush grass. The holes are all different and interesting
- on many accuracy of shot to the green is of paramount
importance.
18 holes, 6313yds, Par 70, SSS 70, Course record 64.
Club membership 820.
Visitors   must book 24hrs in advance. With member
                 only weekends.
Societies   Wed & Thu only, must apply in writing.
Green Fees   not confirmed.
Prof   David Gleeson
Designer   Braid
Facilities   ⊗ ⓑ 🍺 ♀ ☖ 🏠 ⌀ ↑
Location   NE side of village off A5183

Hotel   ★★★★ 71% Thistle St Albans,
                 Watford Rd, ST ALBANS
                 ☎ 01727 854252 111 ⇄ ↑

REDBOURN   Map 04 TL11

Redbourn Kinsbourne Green Ln AL3 7QA
☎ 01582 793493 Fax 01582 794362
Testing parkland course (Five par 4's over 400 yds). Also 9-
hole par 3 course.
*Ver Course: 18 holes, 6506yds, Par 70, SSS 71, Course
record 67.*
Kingsbourne Course: 9 holes, 1361yds, Par 27.
Club membership 750.
Visitors   must contact up to 3 days in advance for Ver
                 Course. No restrictions for Par 3.
Societies   must telephone in advance.
Green Fees   not confirmed.
Cards   ⌐ 🟦 🟩 🟥 🗎
Prof   Stephen Wunter
Facilities   ⊗ ⑪ ⓑ 🍺 ♀ ☖ 🏠 ⛳ 🏌 🛒 ⌀ ↑
Location   1m N off A5183

Hotel   ★★★ 67% Harpenden House,
                 18 Southdown Rd, HARPENDEN
                 ☎ 01582 449955 18 ⇄ ↑ Annexe35 ⇄ ↑

RICKMANSWORTH   Map 04 TQ09

Moor Park WD3 1QN
☎ 01923 773146 Fax 01923 777109
Two parkland courses.
*High Golf Course: 18 holes, 6713yds, Par 72, SSS 72,
Course record 63.*
West Golf Course: 18 holes, 5815yds, Par 69, SSS 68.
Club membership 1700.
Visitors   must contact in advance but may not play at
                 weekends, bank holidays or before 1pm on
                 Tue & Thu.
Societies   must contact in advance.
Green Fees   High: £50 per round. West: £30 per round
                 (all day £80).
Prof   Lawrence Farmer
Designer   H S Colt
Facilities   ⊗ ⓑ 🍺 ♀ ☖ 🏠 ⛳ 🏌 🛒 ⌀
& Leisure   hard and grass tennis courts.
Location   1.5m SE off A4145

Hotel   ★★★ 63% Watford Moat House,
                 30-40 St Albans Rd, WATFORD
                 ☎ 01923 429988 90 ⇄ ↑

Rickmansworth Public Course Moor Ln WD3 1QL
☎ 01923 775278
Undulating, municipal parkland course.
18 holes, 4469yds, Par 63, SSS 62.
Club membership 240.
Visitors   must contact the club in advance, 7 day booking.
Societies   must contact in advance.
Green Fees   not confirmed.
Cards   ⌐ 🟦 🟩 🟥 🗎
Prof   Alan Dobbins
Designer   Colt
Facilities   ⊗ ⑪ ⓑ 🍺 ♀ ☖ 🏠 ⛳ 🏌 🛒 ⌀
Location   2m S of town off A4145

Hotel   ★★★ 63% Watford Moat House,
                 30-40 St Albans Rd, WATFORD
                 ☎ 01923 429988 90 ⇄ ↑

ROYSTON   Map 05 TL34

Barkway Park Nuthampstead Rd, Barkway SG8 8EN
☎ 01763 849070 & 848215
An undulating course criss-crossed by ditches which come
into play on several holes. The challenging par 3 7th features
a long, narrow green with out of bounds close to the right
edge of the green.
18 holes, 6997yds, Par 74, SSS 74.
Club membership 270.
Visitors   telephone for tee times.
Societies   apply for booking form.
Green Fees   £25 per day; £15 per 18 holes; £10 per 9 holes
                 (£30/£20/£12 weekends & bank holidays).
Cards   ⌐ 🟦 🟩 🟥
Prof   Lee Jones
Designer   Vivien Saunders
Facilities   ⊗ ⑪ ⓑ 🍺 ♀ ☖ 🏠 🛒 ⌀
Location   Off B1368 from A10

Hotel   ★★★ 70% Duxford Lodge Hotel,
                 Ickleton Rd, DUXFORD
                 ☎ 01223 836444 11 ⇄ ↑ Annexe4 ⇄ ↑

Heydon Grange Golf & Country Club Heydon SG8 7NS
☎ 01763 208988 Fax 01763 208926
Three 9-hole parkland courses - the Essex, Cambridgeshire
and Hertfordshire - situated in gently rolling countryside.
Courses are playable all year round.
Essex: 9 holes, 3138yds, Par 36, SSS 35, Course record 67.
Cambridgeshire: 9 holes, 3323yds, Par 36, SSS 36.
Hertfordshire: 9 holes, 3180yds, Par 36, SSS 36.
Club membership 250.

Visitors	must contact to book tee times, welcome all times weekends included.
Societies	telephone in advance for booking form.
Green Fees	£15 (£17 weekends).
Cards	⬛ 🔲 💳
Prof	Stuart Smith
Designer	Cameron Sinclair
Facilities	⊗ ⫝ ⯊ 🍴 ☕ 🏖 ⛳ 🏌 🛒 ⛳ 🏇
Location	A505 between Royston/Duxford, off junct 10 on M11

Hotel ★★★ 70% Duxford Lodge Hotel,
Ickleton Rd, DUXFORD
☎ 01223 836444   11 ⇄ ☗ Annexe4 ⇄ ☗

Kingsway Cambridge Rd, Melbourn SG8 6EY
☎ 01763 262727 Fax 01763 263298
Short and deceptively tricky 9-hole course providing a good
test for both beginners and experienced golfers. Out of
bounds and strategically placed bunkers come into play on
several holes, in particular the tough par 3 7th.
9 holes, 2455yds, Par 33, SSS 32.
Club membership 150.

Visitors	welcome.
Societies	telephone for details.
Green Fees	£5 weekdays (£7 weekends).
Prof	Denise Hastings/Mat Larman
Facilities	⊗ ⯊ ☕ 🏖 ⛳ 🏇
Location	Off the A10

Hotel ★★★ 70% Duxford Lodge Hotel,
Ickleton Rd, DUXFORD
☎ 01223 836444   11 ⇄ ☗ Annexe4 ⇄ ☗

Royston Baldock Rd SG8 5BG
☎ 01763 242696 Fax 01763 242696
Heathland course on undulating terrain and fine fairways.
The 8th, 10th and 15th are the most notable holes on this all
weather course.
18 holes, 6052yds, Par 70, SSS 69, Course record 65.
Club membership 850.

Visitors	Mon-Fri only subject to availability. Must contact in advance.
Societies	by arrangement Mon-Fri.
Green Fees	£20 per round.
Prof	Sean Clark
Facilities	⊗ ⫝ ⯊ 🍴 ☕ 🏖 ⛳ 🏇
Location	0.5m W of town centre

Hotel ★★★ 70% Duxford Lodge Hotel,
Ickleton Rd, DUXFORD
☎ 01223 836444   11 ⇄ ☗ Annexe4 ⇄ ☗

Call the AA Hotel Booking Service on
0870 5050505 to book at AA recognised hotels and B & Bs
in the UK and Ireland, or through our Internet site:
http://www.theaa.co.uk/hotels

ST ALBANS   Map 04 TL10

Abbey View Westminster Lodge Leisure Ctr, Hollywell Hill
AL1 2DL ☎ 01727 868227 Fax 01727 863017
Abbey View is a public golf course designed for beginners,
but is sufficiently challenging for experienced golfers who
only have time for a short game. There is a resident
professional for assistance and lessons.
9 holes, 1383yds, Par 29.

Visitors	welcome but no sharing clubs, suitable footwear & wide wheel trolleys.
Societies	telephone or write in advance.
Green Fees	£5 per 9 holes.
Prof	Ian Goosey
Facilities & Leisure	⊗ ⫝ ⯊ ☕ 🏖 ⛳ 🏇 hard and grass tennis courts, heated indoor swimming pool, sauna, solarium, gymnasium.
Location	Centre of St Albans, off Holywell hill

Hotel ★★ 66% Lake Hotel, 234 London Rd,
ST ALBANS
☎ 01727 840904   43 ⇄ ☗

Batchwood Hall Batchwood Dr AL3 5XA
☎ 01727 844250 Fax 01727 858506
Municipal parkland course designed by J H Taylor and
opened in 1935.
18 holes, 6487yds, Par 71, SSS 71.
Club membership 200.

Visitors	must contact in advance, in person.
Societies	must contact in advance.
Green Fees	not confirmed.
Cards	⬛ 🔲 💳
Prof	Mark Flitton
Facilities & Leisure	⊗ ⫝ ⯊ ☕ 🏖 ⛳ 🏇 hard tennis courts, squash, solarium, gymnasium.
Location	1m NW off A5183

Hotel ★★★ 76% The Manor St Michael's Village,
Fishpool St, ST ALBANS
☎ 01727 864444   23 ⇄ ☗

Verulam London Rd AL1 1JG
☎ 01727 853327 Fax 01727 812201
Easy walking parkland course with fourteen holes having
out-of-bounds. Water affects the 12th, 13th and 14th holes.
Samuel Ryder was Captain here in 1927 when he began the
now celebrated Ryder Cup Competition.
18 holes, 6448yds, Par 72, SSS 71, Course record 67.
Club membership 650.

Visitors	must contact pro shop in advance. With member only at weekends.
Societies	must contact advance.
Green Fees	Mon: £25 per day, £15 per round (Winter: £20 unlimited play); Tue-Fri: £35 per day, £25 per round.
Prof	Nick Burch
Designer	Braid
Facilities	⊗ ⫝ ⯊ ☕ 🏖 ⛳ 🏇
Location	1m from junc 22 of M25 off A1081

Hotel ★★★★ 76% Sopwell House Hotel & Country
Club, Cottonmill Ln, Sopwell, ST ALBANS
☎ 01727 864477   92 ⇄ ☗

SAWBRIDGEWORTH   Map 05 TL41

Manor of Groves Golf & Country Club
High Wych CM21 0LA ☎ 01279 722333
The course is set out over 150 acres of established parkland
and rolling countryside and is a true test of golf for the club
golfer.
18 holes, 6280yds, Par 71, SSS 70, Course record 65.
Club membership 450.
Visitors   telephone bookings preferred, may not play until
            after 12 noon at weekends.
Societies   Mon-Fri by prior arrangement, telephone in
            advance.
Green Fees not confirmed.
Prof   Craig Laurence
Facilities ♿ ⛳ 🍴 ⛏ 🏌 ♿ ♨ ⚲
& Leisure   hard tennis courts, outdoor swimming pool,
            gymnasium.
Location   1.5m on west side of town

Hotel   ★★★ 73% Swallow Churchgate Hotel,
            Churchgate St Village, Old Harlow, HARLOW
            ☎ 01279 420246 85 ⇔ ☞

STANSTEAD ABBOTS   Map 05 TL31

Briggens House Hotel Briggens Park, Stanstead Rd
SG12 8LD ☎ 01279 793742 Fax 01279 793685
An attractive 9-hole course set in the grounds of a 80 acres of
countryside.
9 holes, 2793yds, Par 36, SSS 69, Course record 31.
Club membership 230.
Visitors   may not play Thu 5-6pm and Sun am. No jeans.
            Must have own clubs and golf shoes.
Societies   must contact in advance.
Green Fees not confirmed.
Prof   Alan McGinn
Facilities ♿ ⛳ 🍴 ⛏ 🏌 ♿ ♨ ⚲
& Leisure   hard tennis courts, heated outdoor swimming
            pool, fishing.
Location   Off Stanstead road A414

Hotel   ★★★★ 61% Briggens House, Stanstead Rd,
            STANSTEAD ABBOTS
            ☎ 01279 829955 54 ⇔ ☞

STEVENAGE   Map 04 TL22

Stevenage Golf Centre Aston Ln SG2 7EL
☎ 01438 880424 & 880223 Fax 01438 880040
Municipal course designed by John Jacobs, with natural
water hazards and some wooded areas.
18 holes, 6451yds, Par 72, SSS 71.
Club membership 600.
Visitors   no restrictions.
Societies   must contact 1 week in advance. Deposit
            required.
Green Fees £10.90 (£14.50 weekends & bank holidays).
Cards   ▭▭ ▭▭ ▭▭ ▭▭ ▭▭ ▭
Prof   Steve Barker
Designer   John Jacobs
Facilities ⊗ � 🍴 ⛳ ♿ ⛏ 🏌 ♿ ♨ ⚲ ⚑
& Leisure   par3 course.
Location   4m SE off B5169

Hotel   B Posthouse Stevenage, Old London Rd,
            Broadwater, STEVENAGE
            ☎ 01438 365444 54 ⇔ ☞

WARE   Map 05 TL31

Chadwell Springs Hertford Rd SG12 9LE
☎ 01920 461447
Quick drying moorland course on high plateau subject to
wind. The first two holes are par 5 and notable.
9 holes, 6418yds, Par 72, SSS 71, Course record 68.
Club membership 650.
Visitors   with member only at weekends.
Societies   bookings accepted, Mon, Wed & Fri only.
Green Fees not confirmed.
Prof   Mark Wall
Facilities ⊗ ⍫ ⛏ 🍴 ♿ ♨ ⛳ ♿ ⚲
Location   0.75m W on A119

Hotel   ★★★ 62% County Hotel Ware, Baldock St,
            WARE ☎ 01920 409955 50 ⇔ ☞

Marriott Hanbury Manor Hotel & Country Club SG12
0SD ☎ 01920 487722 Fax 01920 487692
Superb parkland course designed by Jack Nicklaus II. Large
oval tees, watered fairways and undulating greens make up
the first 9 holes. Attractive lakes and deep-faced bunkers are
strategically sited. Second 9 holes offer open panoramas and
challenging holes and are based on the original Harry Vardon
9 hole design.
18 holes, 6622yds, Par 72, SSS 72, Course record 61.
Club membership 800.
Visitors   with handicap certificate, members guest and
            hotel residents welcome. Must contact in
            advance.
Societies   must be booked in advance. Mon, Tue & Wed
            only.
Green Fees £75 per round as hotel guest.
Cards   ▭▭ ▭▭ ▭▭ ▭▭ ▭▭ ▭
Prof   Peter Blaze
Designer   Jack Nicklaus II
Facilities ⊗ ⍫ ⛏ 🍴 ♿ ♨ ⛳ ⛏ 🏌 ♿ ♨ ⚲ ⚑
& Leisure   hard tennis courts, heated indoor swimming
            pool, sauna, solarium, gymnasium.
Location   Adjacent to A10. From the N just past the
            Thunderidge sign

Hotel   ★★★★★ 78% Marriott Hanbury Manor Hotel
            & Country Club, WARE
            ☎ 01920 487722 69 ⇔ ☞ Annexe27 ⇔ ☞

Whitehill Dane End SG12 0JS ☎ 01920 438495
Undulating course providing a good test for both the average
golfer and the low handicapper. Several lakes in challenging
positions.
18 holes, 6681yds, Par 72, SSS 72.
Club membership 600.
Visitors   handicap certificate must be produced or
                competence test taken (free), appropriate
                clothing must be worn.
Societies   telephone or write for booking form.
Green Fees   not confirmed.
Prof   David Ling
Facilities   ⊗ ⽾ ⽫ ⽭ ⽰ ⽲ ⽳ ⽴ ⽵ ⽶ ⽷ ⽸

Hotel   ★★★ 62% County Hotel Ware, Baldock St,
                 WARE ☎ 01920 409955 50 ⇆ ⋔

WATFORD   Map 04 TQ19

West Herts Cassiobury Park WD1 7SL
☎ 01923 236484
Another of the many clubs that were inaugurated in the
1890's when the game of golf was being given a
tremendous boost by the performances of the first
star professionals, Braid, Vardon and Taylor. The West
Herts course is close to Watford but its tree-lined setting
is beautiful and tranquil. Set out on a plateau the course
is exceedingly dry. It also has a very severe finish with
the 17th, a hole of 378 yards, the toughest on the course.
The last hole measures over 480 yards.
18 holes, 6400yds, Par 72, SSS 71, Course record 66.
Club membership 700.
Visitors   must contact in advance.
Societies   must telephone in advance and confirm in
                 writing.
Green Fees   £30 per 36 holes; £20 per 18 holes (£30 18
                 holes weekends).
Cards   ⌹ ⌹ ⌹ ⌹ ⌹ ⌹
Prof   Charles Gough
Designer   Tom Morris
Facilities   ⊗ ⽾ ⽫ ⽭ ⽰ ⽲ ⽳ ⽴ ⽵ ⽶
Location   W side of town centre off A412

Hotel   ★★★ 63% Watford Moat House,
                 30-40 St Albans Rd, WATFORD
                 ☎ 01923 429988 90 ⇆ ⋔

WELWYN GARDEN CITY   Map 04 TL21

Mill Green Gypsy Ln AL6 4TY
☎ 01707 276900 & 270542 (Pro shop) Fax 01707 276898
The course plays over the second 9 holes around the lakes
and sweeps back through the woods. The first 9 holes are
subject to the prevailing winds. The par 3 9-hole gives a
good test for improving the short game.
18 holes, 6615yds, Par 72, SSS 72, Course record 64.
Club membership 700.
Visitors   must contact in advance by telephone. 7 day
                 booking arrangement.
Societies   apply in writing for details.
Green Fees   £19 per round (£25 weekends).
Cards   ⌹ ⌹ ⌹ ⌹ ⌹ ⌹
Prof   Alan Hall
Designer   Alliss & Clark

Facilities   ⊗ ⽾ ⽫ ⽭ ⽰ ⽲ ⽳ ⽴ ⽵ ⽶ ⽷ ⽸
& Leisure   9 hole par 3 course..
Location   Exit 4 of A1(M), A414 to Mill Green

Hotel   ★★★ 64% Quality Hotel Welwyn, The Link,
                 WELWYN ☎ 01438 716911 96 ⇆ ⋔

Panshanger Golf & Squash Complex Old Herns Ln
AL7 2ED ☎ 01707 333350 & 333312 Fax 01707 390010
Picturesque, mature course overlooking Mimram Valley.
18 holes, 6347yds, Par 72, SSS 70, Course record 65.
Club membership 600.
Visitors   no restrictions.
Societies   telephone for details.
Green Fees   not confirmed.
Cards   ⌹ ⌹ ⌹ ⌹
Prof   Bryan Lewis/Mick Corlass
Designer   Peter Kirkham
Facilities   ⊗ ⽾ ⽫ ⽭ ⽰ ⽲ ⽳ ⽴ ⽵ ⽶
& Leisure   squash, Par 3 course.
Location   N side of town centre signposted off B1000

Hotel   ★★★ 64% Quality Hotel Welwyn, The Link,
                 WELWYN ☎ 01438 716911 96 ⇆ ⋔

Welwyn Garden City Mannicotts, High Oaks Rd AL8 7BP
☎ 01707 325243 Fax 01707 393213
Undulating parkland course with a ravine. A former course
record holder is Nick Faldo.
18 holes, 6074yds, Par 70, SSS 69, Course record 64.
Club membership 975.
Visitors   must contact in advance but may not play Sun
                 am.
Societies   must contact in advance.
Green Fees   £20 per day (£35 weekends).
Cards   ⌹ ⌹ ⌹
Prof   Richard May
Facilities   ⊗ ⽫ ⽭ ⽰ ⽲ ⽳ ⽴ ⽵
Location   W side of city, exit 6 off A1

Hotel   ★★★ 64% Quality Hotel Welwyn, The Link,
                 WELWYN ☎ 01438 716911 96 ⇆ ⋔

WHEATHAMPSTEAD   Map 04 TL11

Mid Herts Lamer Ln, Gustard Wood AL4 8RS
☎ 01582 832242 Fax 01582 834834
Commonland, wooded with heather and gorse-lined
fairways.
18 holes, 6060yds, Par 69, SSS 69.
Club membership 760.
Visitors   may not play Tue, Wed afternoons & weekends.
Societies   must contact in writing.
Green Fees   not confirmed.
Prof   Nick Brown
Facilities   ⽰ ⽲ ⽵
Location   1m N on B651

Hotel   ★★★ 67% Harpenden House,
                 18 Southdown Rd, HARPENDEN
                 ☎ 01582 449955 18 ⇆ ⋔ Annexe35 ⇆ ⋔

KENT

ADDINGTON   Map 05 TQ65

West Malling London Rd ME19 5AR
☎ 01732 844785 Fax 01732 844795
Two 18-hole parkland courses.
Spitfire Course: 18 holes, 6142yds, Par 70, SSS 70, Course record 67.
Hurricane Course: 18 holes, 6281yds, Par 70, SSS 70, Course record 69.
Visitors   must contact in advance, may not play weekends until 2pm.
Societies   prior booking required.
Green Fees   £35 per day; £25 per round (£35 per round after noon weekends & bank holidays).
Cards   ⬜ ⬜ ⬜ ⬜ ⬜
Prof   Duncan Lambert
Designer   Max Falkner
Facilities   ⊗ ⫘ ⅃ ⬛ ♀ ⚲ 🏠 🖢 ♣ ♂
& Leisure   steam room jacuzzi.
Location   1m S off A20

Hotel   ★★★ 63% Larkfield Priory Hotel, London Rd, Larkfield, MAIDSTONE
☎ 01732 846858 51 ⇥ ♣

ASH   Map 05 TQ66

The London South Ash Manor Estate TN15 7EN
☎ 01474 879899 Fax 01474 879912
Visitors may only play the courses at LGC as guests of members or prospective members by invitation.The courses, the Heritage and the International were designed by Jack Nicklaus: both include a number of lakes, generous fairways framed with native grasses and many challenging holes. A state-of-the-art drainage system ensures continuous play.
Heritage Course: 18 holes, 6771yds, Par 72, SSS 73, Course record 68.
International Course: 18 holes, 6574yds, Par 72, SSS 72, Course record 66.
Club membership 400.
Visitors   guest of member & prospective members invited by the membership office only.
Green Fees   not confirmed.
Cards   ⬜ ⬜ ⬜ ⬜
Prof   Keith Morgan
Designer   Jack Nicklaus
Facilities   ⚲ 🏠 🖢 ♣ ♣ ♂ ⫯
& Leisure   sauna.
Location   A20, 2m from Brands Hatch

Hotel   ★★★ 63% Larkfield Priory Hotel, London Rd, Larkfield, MAIDSTONE
☎ 01732 846858 51 ⇥ ♣

ASHFORD   Map 05 TR04

Ashford Sandyhurst Ln TN25 4NT
☎ 01233 622655 Fax 01233 622655
Parkland course with good views and easy walking. Narrow fairways and tightly bunkered greens ensure a challenging game.
18 holes, 6263yds, Par 71, SSS 70, Course record 65.
Club membership 650.

Visitors   must contact in advance & have handicap certificate.
Societies   Tue & Thu only, by arrangement.
Green Fees   £32 per day; £22 per round (£30 after 11.30am weekends and bank holidays).
Prof   Hugh Sherman
Designer   Cotton
Facilities   ⊗ ⫘ ⅃ ⬛ ♀ ⚲ 🏠 ♂
Location   1.5m NW off A20

Hotel   ★★★★ 62% Ashford International, Simone Weil Av, ASHFORD
☎ 01233 219988 200 ⇥ ♣

Homelands Bettergolf Centre Ashford Rd, Kingsnorth TN26 1NJ ☎ 01233 661620 Fax 01233 720553
Challenging 9-hole course designed by Donald Steel to provide a stern test for experienced golfers and for others to develop their game. With 4 par 3s and 5 par 4s it demands accuracy rather than length. Floodlit driving range.
9 holes, 2205yds, Par 32, SSS 31.
Club membership 200.
Visitors   no restrictions, but booking essential for weekend and summer evenings.
Societies   prior arrangements are essential.
Green Fees   £10.50 per 18 holes; £7 per 9 holes (£14/£8 weekends & bank holidays).
Cards   ⬜ ⬜ ⬜
Prof   Tony Bowers
Designer   Donald Steel
Facilities   ⅃ ⬛ ♀ ⚲ 🏠 🖢 ♣ ♂ ⫯
Location   Take exit 10 off M20, follow A2070, course signposted from 2nd rdbt to Kingsnorth

Hotel   ★★★ 64% Master Spearpoint Hotel, Canterbury Rd, Kennington, ASHFORD
☎ 01233 636863 34 ⇥ ♣

BARHAM   Map 05 TR25

Broome Park The Broome Park Estate CT4 6QX
☎ 01227 831701 Fax 01227 831973
Championship standard parkland course in a valley, with a 350-year-old mansion clubhouse.
18 holes, 6610yds, Par 72, SSS 72, Course record 66.
Club membership 700.
Visitors   advisable to contact in advance, must have handicap certificate, but may not play Sat/Sun mornings.
Societies   Mon-Fri and Sat-Sun after 12 only, apply in writing or by telephone.
Green Fees   not confirmed.
Cards   ⬜ ⬜
Prof   Tienne Britz
Designer   Donald Steel
Facilities   ⊗ ⫘ ⅃ ⬛ ♀ ⚲ 🏠 🖢 ♣ ♣ ♂ ⫯
& Leisure   hard tennis courts, heated outdoor swimming pool, squash, sauna, solarium.
Location   1.5m SE on A260

Hotel   ★★★ 64% The Chaucer, Ivy Ln, CANTERBURY ☎ 01227 464427 42 ⇥ ♣

Entries with a shaded background
identify courses that are
considered to be particularly interesting

BEARSTED   Map 05 TQ85

Bearsted Ware St ME14 4PQ
☎ 01622 738198 Fax 01622 738198
Parkland course with fine views of the North Downs.
18 holes, 6437yds, Par 72, SSS 71.
Club membership 780.
Visitors   must have handicap certificate and may not play
                  weekends unless with member. Must contact in
                  advance.
Societies   write for reservation forms.
Green Fees   £36 per day; £27 per round.
Prof   Tim Simpson
Facilities   ⊗ ⅢⅡ ⌁ 🍺 🍴 ☕ 🛍 🏌
Location   2.5m E of Maidstone off A20

Hotel   ★★★★ 68% Marriott Tudor Park Hotel &
                  Country Club, Ashford Rd, Bearsted,
                  MAIDSTONE ☎ 01622 734334 118 ⇆ 🐾

BIDDENDEN   Map 05 TQ83

Chart Hills Weeks Ln TN27 8JX
☎ 01580 292222 Fax 01580 292233
Created by Nick Faldo and completed in 1993, this huge
course of grand design measures 7,000 yards from the back
tees. Facilities include a David Leadbetter Golf Academy.
18 holes, 7119yds, Par 72, SSS 74, Course record 66.
Club membership 380.

Visitors   welcome Sun-Fri, contact for details.
Societies   telephone for details.
Green Fees   on application.
Cards   ⊷ 💳 💳 💳 📷 🖭
Prof   Danny French
Designer   Nick Faldo
Facilities   ⊗ ⅢⅡ ⌁ 🍺 🍴 ☕ 🛍 🏌 ⚒ 🏌 🏌
& Leisure   sauna, solarium, gymnasium.
Location   1m N of Biddenden off A274

Hotel   ★★🛏 Kennel Holt Hotel, Goudhurst Rd,
                  CRANBROOK ☎ 01580 712032 10 ⇆ 🐾

BOROUGH GREEN   Map 05 TQ65

Wrotham Heath Seven Mile Ln TN15 8QZ
☎ 01732 884800 Fax 01732 887370
Heathland woodland course with magnificent views of North
Downs.
18 holes, 5954yds, Par 70, SSS 69.
Club membership 550.

Visitors   must contact in advance, weekends with
                  member only.
Societies   Thu & Fri only, by arrangement.
Green Fees   £25 per round.
Prof   Harry Dearden
Designer   Donald Steel (part)
Facilities   ⊗ ⅢⅡ ⌁ 🍺 🍴 ☕ 🛍 🏌
Location   2.25m E on B2016

Hotel   B Posthouse Maidstone/Sevenoaks,
                  London Rd, Wrotham Heath, WROTHAM
                  ☎ 01732 883311 106 ⇆ 🐾

BRENCHLEY   Map 05 TQ64

Moatlands Watermans Ln TN12 6ND
☎ 01892 724400 Fax 01892 723300
A rolling parkland course with dramatic views over the
Weald of Kent. The challenging holes are the Par 4 8th with
its tough dogleg, the 10th where there is a wooded copse
with a Victorian bath-house to be avoided and the 14th where
the approach to the green is guarded by oak trees.
18 holes, 6693yds, Par 72, SSS 72, Course record 63.
Club membership 620.
Visitors   must book in advance.
Societies   apply in writing or telephone.
Green Fees   £45 per day; £29 per round (£55/£39 weekends
                  and bank holidays.
Cards   ⊷ 💳 💳 💳 📷 🖭
Prof   Simon Wood
Designer   H Sugio
Facilities   ⊗ ⅢⅡ ⌁ 🍺 🍴 ☕ 🛍 🏌 🏌 ⚒ 🏌 🏌
& Leisure   hard tennis courts, heated indoor swimming
                  pool, sauna, gymnasium.
Location   3m N of Brenchley off B2160

Hotel   ★★ 65% Russell Hotel, 80 London Rd,
                  TUNBRIDGE WELLS
                  ☎ 01892 544833 19 ⇆ 🐾 Annexe5 ⇆ 🐾

BROADSTAIRS   Map 05 TR36

North Foreland Convent Rd, Kingsgate CT10 3PU
☎ 01843 862140 Fax 01843 862663
A picturesque course situated where the Thames Estuary
widens towards the sea. North Foreland always seems to
have a breath of tradition of golf's earlier days about it.
Perhaps the ghost of one of its earlier professionals, the
famous Abe Mitchell, still haunts the lovely turf of the
fairways. Walking is easy and the wind is deceptive. The
8th and 17th, both par 4, are testing holes. There is also
an 18 hole approach and putting course.
18 holes, 6430yds, Par 71, SSS 71, Course record 65.
Club membership 1100.
Visitors   for Main course are required to book in
                  advance & have handicap certificate. May
                  play afternoons only Mon and Tue,
                  weekends restricted and no visitors Sun
                  morning. Northcliffe course has no restrictio
Societies   Wed & Fri only, by arrangement.
Green Fees   £40 per day; £30 per round.
Cards   ⊷ 💳 💳 🖭
Prof   Neil Hansen
Designer   Fowler & Simpson

▶

Facilities	⊗ ⫿ by prior arrangement 🏌 ♣ ♀ 🏖 🏠
	⛳ 🍴 🏌 ✐
& Leisure	hard tennis courts.
Location	1.5m N off B2052

Hotel	★★★ 61% Royal Albion Hotel,
	Albion St, BROADSTAIRS
	☎ 01843 868071 19 ⇔ 📞

CANTERBURY   Map 05 TR15

Canterbury Scotland Hills, Littlebourne Rd CT1 1TW
☎ 01227 453532 Fax 01227 784277
Undulating parkland course, densely wooded in places, with
elevated trees and difficult drives on several holes.
18 holes, 6249yds, Par 70, SSS 70, Course record 64.
Club membership 650.
Visitors   may only play after 3pm weekends & bank
                  holidays. Must have a handicap certificate.
Societies   by arrangement.
Green Fees   £27 per 18 holes (£36 weekends).
Prof   Paul Everard
Designer   Harry Colt
Facilities   ⊗ by prior arrangement 🏌 ♣ ♀ 🏖 🏠 ✐
Location   1.5m E on A257

| **Hotel** | ★★★ 64% The Chaucer, Ivy Ln, |
| | CANTERBURY ☎ 01227 464427 42 ⇔ 📞 |

CHART SUTTON   Map 05 TQ84

The Ridge Chartway St, East Sutton ME17 3DL
☎ 01622 844382
Opened in 1993, this flat parkland course was designed by
Patrick Dawson around mature orchards to challenge all
levels of player. The par 5, 18th has two lakes to negotiate.
18 holes, 6254yds, Par 71, SSS 70, Course record 68.
Club membership 650.
Visitors   weekdays only, must have handicap certificate.
Societies   Tue & Thu, by arrangement.
Green Fees   not confirmed.
Prof   Matthew Rackham
Designer   Tyton Design
Facilities   ⊗ ⫿ 🏌 ♣ ♀ 🏖 🏠 ⛳ 🍴 🏌 ✐ ⎰
& Leisure   solarium, gymnasium.
Location   5m S of Bearsted, off A274

Hotel	★★★★ 68% Marriott Tudor Park Hotel &
	Country Club, Ashford Rd, Bearsted,
	MAIDSTONE ☎ 01622 734334 118 ⇔ 📞

CRANBROOK   Map 05 TQ73

Executive Golf Club at Cranbrook Golford Rd TN17 4AL
☎ 01580 712833 Fax 01580 714274
Scenic, parkland course with easy terrain, backed by
Hemstead Forest and close to Sissinghurst Castle (1m) and
Bodiam Castle (6m). The course has been transformed over
recent years with the introduction of over 5,000 mature pine
trees. Keeping the ball straight is paramount, a challenging
test of golf for all levels.
18 holes, 6305yds, Par 70, SSS 71.
Visitors   welcome weekdays after 8.30 am. weekends
                  after 11.30 am. Tee reservations may be booked
                  up to 1 calendar month in advance.
Societies   minimum of 12 write or telephone to book.

Green Fees £23 per 18 holes (£30 weekends).
Cards   ▭▬ 💳
Prof   Alan Gillard
Designer   Commander J Harris
Facilities   ⊗ ⫿ by prior arrangement 🏌 ♣ ♀ 🏖 🏠 ✐ ⎰
Location   2m E

Hotel	★★ 69% Hartley Mount Country House,
	Hartley Rd, CRANBROOK
	☎ 01580 712230 6 ⇔ 📞

DARTFORD   Map 05 TQ57

Birchwood Park Birchwood Rd, Wilmington DA2 7HJ
☎ 01322 662038 & 660554 Fax 01322 667283
The main course offers highly challenging play and will test
golfers of all abilities. Beginners and those requiring a quick
game or golfers wishing to improve their short game will
appreciate the 9 hole course where holes range from 96 to
258yards.
18 holes, 6364yds, Par 71, SSS 70, Course record 64.
Club membership 500.

Visitors   must contact in advance.
Societies   telephone for details.
Green Fees   not confirmed.
Cards   ▭▬ 🗔
Prof   Cranfield Golf Academy
Designer   Howard Swann
Facilities   ⊗ ⫿ 🏌 ♣ ♀ 🏖 🏠 ⛳ 🍴 🏌 ✐ ⎰
& Leisure   sauna, solarium, gymnasium, health & fitness
                  centre.
Location   B258 between Dartford & Swanley

| **Hotel** | ★★★★ 71% Swallow Hotel, 1 Broadway, |
| | BEXLEYHEATH ☎ 0181 298 1000 142 ⇔ 📞 |

Dartford Upper Heath Ln, Dartford Heath DA1 2TN
☎ 01322 226455
Heathland course.
18 holes, 5914yds, Par 69, SSS 69, Course record 63.
Club membership 700.
Visitors   may not play at weekends. Must have a
                  handicap certificate.
Societies   Mon & Fri only by prior arrangement with
                  Secretary.
Green Fees   £30 per 2 rounds; £21 per round.
Prof   John Gregory
Designer   James Braid
Facilities   ⊗ ⫿ 🏌 ♣ ♀ 🏖 🏠 ✐

Hotel	B Posthouse Bexley, Black Prince Interchange,
	Southwold Rd, BEXLEY
	☎ 01322 526900 103 ⇔ 📞

DEAL
Map 05 TR35

Royal Cinque Ports Golf Rd CT14 6RF
☎ 01304 374007 Fax 01304 379530
Famous championship seaside links, windy but with easy walking. Outward nine is generally considered the easier, inward nine is longer and includes the renowned 16th, perhaps the most difficult hole. On a fine day there are wonderful views across the Channel.
18 holes, 6785yds, Par 72, SSS 72.
Club membership 850.

Visitors	restricted Wed mornings, weekends & bank holidays. Must contact in advance and have a handicap certificate. Men max 18 handicap; Ladies max 28 handicap.
Societies	must contact in advance.
Green Fees	£60 per day/round; £50 per round after 1pm. (plus £2 charge on credit cards).
Cards	
Prof	Andrew Reynolds
Designer	James Braid
Facilities	⊗ ┣ ♥ ♀ ♨ 🏠 ⛳ 🏌 🛱 ⚐ ₵
Location	Along seafront at N end of Deal
Hotel	★★ 72% Dunkerleys Hotel & Restaurant, 19 Beach St, DEAL ☎ 01304 375016 16rm

EDENBRIDGE
Map 05 TQ44

Edenbridge Golf & Country Club Crouch House Rd TN8 5LQ ☎ 01732 865097 & 867381 Fax 01732 867029
Parkland course with water on many holes, quiet with excellent views of rural Kent.
Old Course: 18 holes, 6646yds, Par 73.
Skeynes Course: 18 holes, 5605yds, Par 67.
Club membership 1100.

Visitors	must contact in advance for Old Course. All tee times bookable 7 days in advance.
Societies	contact in advance.
Green Fees	not confirmed.
Prof	Keith Burkin
Facilities	⊗ ┃ ┣ ♥ ♀ ♨ 🏠 ⛳ 🏌 🛱 ⚐ ₵
& Leisure	hard tennis courts, gymnasium.
Location	0.75m W of town centre, signposted 'Golf Course'
Hotel	★★★♨ Gravetye Manor Hotel, EAST GRINSTEAD ☎ 01342 810567 18 🛱 ⚐

Sweetwoods Park Cowden TN8 7JN ☎ 01342 850729 (Pro shop) & 850942 (Secretary) Fax 01342 850866
An undulating and mature parkland course with fast greens, testing water hazards and fine views across the Weald from four holes. A good challenge off the back tees. Signature holes include the 2nd, 4th and 14th.
18 holes, 6512yds, Par 71, SSS 71, Course record 67.
Club membership 800.

Visitors	no restrictions.
Societies	Mon-Fri after 9am, contact for details.
Green Fees	not confirmed.
Cards	
Prof	Bob Wynn/Ben Clover
Designer	P Strand
Facilities	⊗ ┃ ┣ ♥ ♀ ♨ 🏠 ⚐ ₵
Location	5m E of East Grinstead on the A264

Hotel	★★★ 65% Woodbury House Hotel, Lewes Rd, EAST GRINSTEAD ☎ 01342 313657 14 🛱 ₵

EYNSFORD
Map 05 TQ56

Austin Lodge Upper Austin Lodge Rd DA4 0HU
☎ 01322 863000 Fax 01322 862406
A well drained course designed to lie naturally in three secluded valleys in rolling countryside. Over 7000 yds from the medal tees. Practice ground, nets and a putting green add to the features.
18 holes, 6600yds, Par 73, SSS 71, Course record 68.
Club membership 600.

Visitors	must contact in advance, may not play until after 1pm on weekends and bank holidays.
Societies	telephone for bookings.
Green Fees	£16 per round (£25 weekends & bank holidays).
Cards	
Prof	Paul Edwards
Designer	P Bevan
Facilities	⊗ ┃ ┣ ♥ ♀ ♨ 🏠 ⛳ 🏌 🛱 ⚐ ₵
Location	6m S of Dartford
Hotel	★★★★ 63% Thistle Brands Hatch, BRANDS HATCH ☎ 01474 854900 121 🛱 ₵

FAVERSHAM
Map 05 TR06

Boughton Brickfield Ln ME13 9AJ
☎ 01227 752277 Fax 01227 752361
Rolling parkland/downland course set in 160 acres of Kent countryside, providing a good test of golf, even for the more accomplished players.
18 holes, 6452yds, Par 72, SSS 71, Course record 70.
Club membership 325.

Visitors	booking by telephone advisable.
Societies	telephone for details.
Green Fees	not confirmed.
Cards	
Prof	Trevor Dungate
Designer	P Sparks
Facilities	⊗ ┃ ┣ ♥ ♀ ♨ 🏠 ⛳ 🏌 🛱 ⚐ ₵
Location	Off junct 7 of M2 - Brenley Corner
Hotel	★★★★♨ 78% Eastwell Manor, Eastwell Park, Boughton Lees, ASHFORD ☎ 01233 213000 23 🛱 ₵ Annexe39 🛱 ₵

Faversham Belmont Park ME13 0HB
☎ 01795 890561 Fax 01795 890760
A beautiful inland course laid out over part of a large estate with pheasants walking the fairways quite tamely. Play follows two heavily wooded valleys but the trees affect only the loose shots going out of bounds. Fine views.
18 holes, 6030yds, Par 70, SSS 69, Course record 63.
Club membership 800.

Visitors	must have handicap certificate. With member only at weekends. Contacting the club in advance is advisable.
Societies	must contact in advance.
Green Fees	£35 per day; £35 per round.
Prof	Stuart Rokes

▶

| Facilities | ⊗ 〰 ╚ ♨ ♀ ⚐ ⚑ 🏌 ⛳ |
| Location | 3.5m S |

Hotel	★★★★🏖 78% Eastwell Manor,
	Eastwell Park, Boughton Lees, ASHFORD
	☎ 01233 213000
	23 ⇌ 🏌 Annexe39 ⇌ 🏌

FOLKESTONE   Map 05 TR23

Etchinghill Canterbury Rd, Etchinghill CT18 8FA
☎ 01303 863863 Fax 01303 863210
A varied course incorporating parkland on the outward 9
holes and an interesting downland landscape with many
challenging holes on the back 9.
18 holes, 6121yds, Par 70, SSS 69, Course record 67.
Club membership 600.

Visitors	advisable to reserve tee time in advance.
Societies	telephone or write, packages available.
Green Fees	not confirmed.
Prof	Chris Hodgson
Designer	John Sturdy
Facilities	⊗ 〰 ╚ ♨ ♀ ⚐ ⚑ 🏌 ⛳ 🏌
& Leisure	9 hole par3.
Location	N of M20, access from junct 11 or 12

Hotel	★★★ 62% Wards Restaurant & Hotel,
	39 Earls Ave, FOLKESTONE
	☎ 01303 245166 10 ⇌ 🏌

GILLINGHAM   Map 05 TQ76

Gillingham Woodlands Rd ME7 2AP
☎ 01634 853017 (office) & 855862 (pro)
Fax 01634 574749
Parkland course.
18 holes, 5557yds, Par 69, SSS 67, Course record 64.
Club membership 800.

Visitors	contact in advance, weekends only with
	member, must have handicap certificate.
Societies	must apply in writing.
Green Fees	£25 per day; £18 per round.
Prof	Barry Coomber
Designer	James Braid
Facilities	⊗ 〰 ╚ ♨ ♀ ⚐ ⚑ 🏌 ⛳ 🏌
Location	1.5m SE on A2

Hotel	B Posthouse Rochester, Maidstone Rd,
	ROCHESTER
	☎ 01634 687111 145 ⇌ 🏌

GRAVESEND   Map 05 TQ67

Mid Kent Singlewell Rd DA11 7RB
☎ 01474 568035 Fax 01474 564218
A well-maintained downland course with some easy
walking and some excellent greens. The first hole is
short, but nonetheless a real challenge. The slightest
hook and the ball is out of bounds or lost.
18 holes, 6199yds, Par 69, SSS 69, Course record 60.
Club membership 900.

Visitors	must contact in advance & have handicap
	certificate. May not play weekends.
Societies	Tue only, apply in writing.
Green Fees	£30 per day; £20 per round.
Prof	Mark Foreman
Designer	Frank Pennick
Facilities	⊗ 〰 ╚ ♨ ♀ ⚐ ⚑ 🏌 ⛳
Location	S side of town centre off A227

Hotel	★★★ 60% Overcliffe Hotel,
	15-16 The Overcliffe, GRAVESEND
	☎ 01474 322131 19 🏌 Annexe10 ⇌ 🏌

HALSTEAD   Map 05 TQ46

Broke Hill Sevenoaks Rd TN14 7HR
☎ 01959 533225 Fax 01959 532680
Testing downland course featuring 80 bunkers, strategically
placed water hazards and good views.
18 holes, 6454yds, Par 72, SSS 71, Course record 69.
Club membership 650.

Visitors	weekdays only. Must book in advance.
Societies	telephone for details.
Green Fees	£50 per day; £30 per round.
Cards	🇻 💳 🇻 🇳 💲
Prof	Chris West
Designer	David Williams
Facilities	⊗ 〰 ╚ ♨ ♀ ⚐ ⚑ 🏌 ⛳
& Leisure	sauna.
Location	Off junct 4 of M25, opposite Knockholt railway
	station

| Hotel | ★★★ 68% Kings Arms Hotel, Market Square, |
| | WESTERHAM ☎ 01959 562990   17 ⇌ 🏌 |

HAWKHURST   Map 05 TQ73

Hawkhurst High St TN18 4JS
☎ 01580 754074 & 752396 Fax 01580 754074
Undulating parkland course.
9 holes, 5751yds, Par 70, SSS 68, Course record 69.
Club membership 508.

Visitors	may play weekdays, weekends with member
	only.
Societies	must apply in advance.
Green Fees	£20 per day; £15 per round.
Prof	Tony Collins
Designer	W A Baldock
Facilities	⊗ 〰 ╚ ♨ ♀ ⚐ ⚑ 🏌 ⛳
& Leisure	squash.
Location	W side of village off A268

Hotel	★★★ 70% Tudor Court Hotel,
	Rye Rd, HAWKHURST
	☎ 01580 752312 18 ⇌ 🏌

HEADCORN   Map 05 TQ84

Weald of Kent Maidstone Rd TN27 9PT
☎ 01622 891671 Fax 01622 891793
Enjoying delightful views over the Weald of Kent, this pay
and play course features a range of natural hazards, including
lakes, trees, ditches and undulating fairways. A good test to
golfers of every standard.
18 holes, 6240yds, Par 70, SSS 70, Course record 64.
Club membership 450.

Visitors   can book 3 days in advance, smart casual dress
        no jeans.
Societies   apply in writing or by telephone.
Green Fees not confirmed.
Designer   John Millen
Facilities   ⊗ ⅏ ⅃ ♥ ♀ ♨ 🏠 ⛳ ⛴ 🛒 ⚷
Location   Through Leeds village take A274 towards
        Headcorn, golf course on left

Hotel   ★★★★ 68% Marriott Tudor Park Hotel &
        Country Club, Ashford Rd, Bearsted,
        MAIDSTONE ☎ 01622 734334 118 ⇥ ⋔

HERNE BAY   Map 05 TR16

Herne Bay Eddington CT6 7PG ☎ 01227 374727
Parkland course with bracing air.
18 holes, 5567yds, Par 68, SSS 68.
Club membership 500.

Visitors   may not play mornings at weekends.
Societies   apply in advance.
Green Fees £18 (£25 weekends and bank holidays).
Prof   S Dordoy
Designer   James Braid
Facilities   ⊗ ⅏ by prior arrangement ⅃ ♥ ♀ ♨ 🏠 ⛳ ⚷
Location   On A299 at Herne Bay/Canterbury junct

Hotel   ★★★ 67% Falstaff Hotel,
        St Dunstans St, Westgate, CANTERBURY
        ☎ 01227 462138 24 ⇥ ⋔

HEVER   Map 05 TQ44

Hever Edenbridge TN8 7NG
☎ 01732 700771 Fax 01732 700775
The newly established Hever course has recently been voted
one of the top ten developments in the British Isles. The 27-
hole parkland course is set in 250 acres with water hazards
and outstanding holes like the Par 3 12th which is similar to
the 12th at Augusta.
27 holes, 7002yds, Par 72, SSS 75, Course record 69.
Club membership 620.

Visitors   must book tee times Mon-Fri.
Societies   telephone for details.
Green Fees £42 per day; £45 per 18 holes (£65/£54
        weekends & bank holidays).
Cards   ▭▬ ▨▨▨ ▨▨▨ 🅾
Prof   Richard Tinworth
Designer   Dr Nicholas
Facilities   ⊗ ⅏ ⅃ ♥ ♀ ♨ 🏠 ⛳ ⛴ 🛒 ⚷ ⋔
& Leisure   hard tennis courts, heated indoor swimming
        pool, fishing, sauna, solarium, gymnasium.
Location   10mins from M25

Hotel   ★★★ 76% The Spa Hotel, Mount Ephraim,
        TUNBRIDGE WELLS
        ☎ 01892 520331 74 ⇥

HILDENBOROUGH   Map 05 TQ54

Nizels Nizels Ln TN11 9LU
☎ 01732 838926 (Bookings) Fax 01732 833764
Woodland course with many mature trees, wildlife and lakes
that come into play on several holes. The 2nd hole is a 553yd
Par 5, the green being guarded by bunkers hidden by a range
of hillocks. The Par 4 7th has water on both sides of the
fairway and a pitch over water to the green. The 10th is
539yd Par 5 with a sharp dogleg to the right, followed by a
very narrow entry between trees for the 2nd shot.
18 holes, 6408yds, Par 72, SSS 71, Course record 66.
Club membership 650.

Visitors   telephone professional shop for tee reservation
        01732 838926 at least 4 days in advance.
Societies   weekdays only, telephone initially.
Green Fees not confirmed.
Cards   ▭▬ ▨▨▨ ▨▨▨ ▨▨▨ 🅾
Prof   Sue Hodge
Designer   Donaldson/Edwards Partnership
Facilities   ⊗ ⅏ ⅃ ♥ ♀ ♨ 🏠 ⛳ ⛴ 🛒 ⚷
Location   Off B245

Hotel   ★★★ 62% Rose & Crown Hotel, 125 High St,
        TONBRIDGE ☎ 01732 357966 48 ⇥ ⋔

HOO   Map 05 TQ77

Deangate Ridge Dux Court Rd ME3 8RZ
☎ 01634 251180 Fax 01634 250537
Parkland, municipal course designed by Fred Hawtree. 18-
hole pitch and putt.
18 holes, 6300yds, Par 71, SSS 70, Course record 65.
Club membership 500.
Visitors   no restrictions.
Societies   please telephone 01634 255370.   ▶

Green Fees not confirmed.
Cards ⊟ 🖃 VISA ⬚⬚⬚⬚ 🖃 🖃
Prof Richard Fox
Facilities ⊗ ⏀ ₤ 🖤 ♀ ₤ 🏠 ⛳ 🏌 🖉 ✆
& Leisure hard tennis courts.
Location 4m NE of Rochester off A228

Hotel B Posthouse Rochester, Maidstone Rd,
ROCHESTER ☎ 01634 687111 145 ⇄ 🖡

HYTHE   Map 05 TR13

Hythe Imperial Princes Pde CT21 6AE
☎ 01303 267441 Fax 01303 264610
A 9-hole 18 tee links course bounded by the Royal Military
Canal and the English Channel. Although the course is
relatively flat, its aspect offers an interesting and challenging
round to a wide range of golfers.
9 holes, 5560yds, Par 68, SSS 66, Course record 61.
Club membership 300.
Visitors course closed some Sun until 11am for
competitions.
Societies must apply in writing.
Green Fees £15.
Prof Gordon Ritchie
Facilities ⊗ ⏀ ₤ 🖤 ♀ ₤ 🏠 ⛳ 🏌 ⚓ 🏹 🖉
& Leisure hard and grass tennis courts, heated indoor
swimming pool, squash, sauna, solarium,
gymnasium, croquet, snooker, hair & beauty
salon.
Location SE side of town

Hotel ★★★★ 76% The Hythe Imperial Hotel,
Princes Pde, HYTHE
☎ 01303 267441 100 ⇄ 🖡
Additional ★★★ 74% Stade Court, West Pde, HYTHE
hotel ☎ 01303 268263 Fax 01303 261803 42 ⇄ 🖡

Sene Valley Sene CT18 8BL
☎ 01303 268513 (Manager) & 268514 (Pro)
A two-level downland course which provides interesting golf
over an undulating landscape with sea views.
18 holes, 6196yds, Par 71, SSS 70, Course record 61.
Club membership 600.
Visitors must contact professional in advance.
Societies telephone in advance.
Green Fees £20 (£25 weekends).
Prof Nick Watson
Designer Henry Cotton
Facilities ⊗ ⏀ ₤ 🖤 ♀ ₤ 🏠 🖉 ✆
& Leisure snooker room.
Location 1m NE off B2065

Hotel ★★★★ 76% The Hythe Imperial Hotel,
Princes Pde, HYTHE
☎ 01303 267441 100 ⇄ 🖡

KINGSDOWN   Map 05 TR34

Walmer & Kingsdown The Leas CT14 8EP
☎ 01304 373256 & 363017 Fax 01304 382336
This course near Deal has through the years been
overshadowed by its neighbours at Deal and Sandwich,
yet it is a testing circuit with many undulations. The
course is famous as being the one on which, in 1964,
Assistant Professional, Roger Game became the first
golfer in Britain to hole out in one at two successive

holes; the 7th and 8th. The course is situated on top of
the cliffs, with fine views.
18 holes, 6444yds, Par 72, SSS 71, Course record 66.
Club membership 650.
Visitors must contact in advance. Not before 9.30am
weekdays and noon weekends & bank
holidays.
Societies apply in advance.
Green Fees £30 per day; £25 per round (£30 weekends).
Prof Matthew Paget
Designer James Braid
Facilities ⊗ ⏀ ₤ 🖤 ♀ ₤ 🏠 ⛳ 🖉
Location 1.5m E of Ringwould off A258 Dover-Deal
road

Hotel B Posthouse Dover, Singledge Ln,
Whitfield, DOVER
☎ 01304 821222 67 ⇄ 🖡

LAMBERHURST   Map 05 TQ63

Lamberhurst Church Rd TN3 8DT
☎ 01892 890591 Fax 01892 891140
Parkland course crossing river twice. Fine views.
18 holes, 6345yds, Par 72, SSS 70, Course record 65.
Club membership 700.
Visitors may only play after noon weekends unless with
member, handicap certificate required.
Societies Tue, Wed & Thu only from Apr-Oct, by
arrangement.
Green Fees £33 per day; £22 per round (£36 weekends pm).
Credit cards accepted in pro shop.
Prof Brian Impett
Facilities ⊗ ⏀ by prior arrangement ₤ 🖤 ♀ ₤ 🏠 ⛳ 🏹
⚓ 🖉
Location N side of village on B2162

Hotel ★★★ 76% The Spa Hotel,
Mount Ephraim, TUNBRIDGE WELLS
☎ 01892 520331 74 ⇄

LITTLESTONE   Map 05 TR02

Littlestone St Andrew's Rd TN28 8RB
☎ 01797 363355 Fax 01797 362740
Located in the Romney Marshes, this flattish seaside
links course calls for every variety of shot. The 8th, 15th,
16th and 17th are regarded as classics by international
golfers. Allowance for wind must always be made.
Extensive practice area.
18 holes, 6471yds, Par 71, SSS 72, Course record 67.
Club membership 550.
Visitors must contact in advance, no visitors before
3pm weekends and bank holidays.
Societies must apply in advance.
Green Fees £45 per day; £33 per round (£50/£45
weekends and bank holidays).
Cards ⊟ 🖃 VISA ⬚⬚⬚⬚ 🖃
Prof Stephen Watkins
Designer Laidlaw Purves
Facilities ⊗ ⏀ ₤ 🖤 ♀ ₤ 🏠 ⛳ 🏹 🖉
& Leisure hard tennis courts.
Location 1m from New Romney off Littlestone road
B2070

Hotel ★★★★ 76% The Hythe Imperial Hotel, Princes Pde, HYTHE
☎ 01303 267441 100 ⇆ ✿

Romney Warren St Andrews Rd TN28 8RB
☎ 01797 362231 Fax 01797 362740
A traditional links course, newly developed alongside the 9-hole course at Littlestone. Flat providing easy walking and play challenged by sea breezes.
18 holes, 5126yds, Par 67, SSS 65, Course record 69.
Club membership 300.
Visitors contact professional in advance.
Societies contact in advance.
Green Fees not confirmed.
Cards ⎯ 🖳 🖳 💳
Prof Stephen Watkins
Facilities ⊗ ⎍ ♥ ♀ ⚑ ✿ ✓
Location N side of Littlestone

Hotel ★★★★ 76% The Hythe Imperial Hotel, Princes Pde, HYTHE
☎ 01303 267441 100 ⇆ ✿

LYDD   Map 05 TR02

Lydd Romney Rd TN29 9LS
☎ 01797 320808 Fax 01797 321482
A links-type course offering some interesting challenges, including a number of eye-catching water hazards, wide fairways and plenty of semi-rough. A good test for experienced golfers and appealing to the complete novice.
18 holes, 6517yds, Par 71, Course record 65.
Club membership 415.
Visitors contact in advance on 01797 321201.
Societies telephone in advance.
Green Fees £15 per round (£20 weekends).
Cards ⎯ 🖳
Prof Andrew Jones
Designer Mike Smith
Facilities ⊗ ⎋ ⎍ ♥ ♀ ⚑ ✿ ✓
Location B2075

Hotel ★★★ 61% The George, High St, RYE
☎ 01797 222114 22 ⇆ ✿

MAIDSTONE   Map 05 TQ75

Cobtree Manor Park Chatham Rd, Sandling ME14 3AZ
☎ 01622 753276 Fax 01634 262003
An undulating parkland course with some water hazards.
18 holes, 5611yds, Par 69, SSS 69, Course record 66.
Club membership 500.
Visitors no restrictions but advisable to telephone in advance.
Societies Mon-Fri only, by arrangement tel: 01622 751881.
Green Fees £14 (£18 weekends).
Cards ⎯ 🖳 🖳 💳
Prof Paul Foston
Facilities ⊗ ⎋ ⎍ ♥ ♀ ⚑ ✿ ✓
Location On A229 0.25m N of M20 junc 6

Hotel ★★★ 65% Russell Hotel, 136 Boxley Rd, MAIDSTONE ☎ 01622 692221 42 ⇆ ✿

Leeds Castle Ashford Rd ME17 1PL
☎ 01622 880467 Fax 01622 735616
Situated around Leeds Castle, this is one of the most picturesque courses in Britain. Re-designed in the 1980s by Neil Coles, it is a challenging 9-hole course with the added hazard of the Castle moat. 18-holes may be played on weekdays.
9 holes, 2880yds, Par 33, SSS 33, Course record 30.

Visitors Bookings taken from 6 days in advance.
Societies must telephone in advance.
Green Fees £17 per 18 holes; £11 per 9 holes (£22/£12 weekends).
Cards ⎯ 🖳
Prof Stephen Purves
Designer Neil Coles
Facilities ⊗ ⎋ ⎍ ♥ ♀ ⚑ ✿ ✓
Location On A20 towards Lenham, 4m E of Maidstone via M20 junct 8

Hotel ★★★★ 68% Marriott Tudor Park Hotel & Country Club, Ashford Rd, Bearsted, MAIDSTONE
☎ 01622 734334 118 ⇆ ✿

Marriott Tudor Park Hotel & Country Club Ashford Rd, Bearsted ME14 4NQ
☎ 01622 734334 Fax 01622 735360
The course is set in a 220 acre former deerpark with the pleasant undulating Kent countryside as a backdrop. The natural features of the land have been incorporated into this picturesque course to form a challenge for those of both high and intermediate standard. The Par 5 14th is particularly interesting. It can alter your score dramatically should you gamble with a drive to a narrow fairway. This hole has to be carefully thoughtout from tee to green depending on the wind direction.
18 holes, 6041yds, Par 70, SSS 69, Course record 64.
Club membership 750.
Visitors may not play Sat & Sun before noon. Contact pro shop 01622 739412 for bookings.
Societies please call the Golf Manager.
Green Fees £25 (£35 weekends).
Cards ⎯ 🖳 🖳 💳 🖳 💳
Designer Donald Steel
Facilities ⊗ ⎋ ⎍ ♥ ♀ ⚑ ✿ ✓
& Leisure hard tennis courts, heated indoor swimming pool, sauna, solarium, gymnasium.
Location On A20, 1.25m W of M20 junct 8

Hotel ★★★★ 68% Marriott Tudor Park Hotel & Country Club, Ashford Rd, Bearsted, MAIDSTONE ☎ 01622 734334 118 ⇥ ↑

RAMSGATE Map 05 TR36

St Augustine's Cottington Rd, Cliffsend CT12 5JN
☎ 01843 590333 Fax 01843 590444
A comfortably flat course in this famous bracing Championship area of Kent. Neither as long nor as difficult as its lordly neighbours, St Augustine's will nonetheless extend most golfers. Dykes run across the course.
18 holes, 5197yds, Par 69, SSS 65, Course record 61.
Club membership 670.
Visitors must contact in advance.
Societies must contact in advance.
Green Fees £21.50 per day; £14 after 12 noon (£23.50/£16.50 weekends & bank holidays).
Prof Derek Scott
Designer Tom Vardon
Facilities ⊗ ⫢ ⓛ 🍺 ♀ ⚘ 🏠 🚣 ♐ ✓
Location Off A256 Ramsgate/Sandwich

Hotel ★★★ 66% San Clu Hotel, Victoria Pde, East Cliff, RAMSGATE ☎ 01843 592345 44 ⇥ ↑

ROCHESTER Map 05 TQ76

Rochester & Cobham Park Park Pale ME2 3UL
☎ 01474 823411 Fax 01474 824446
A first-rate course of challenging dimensions in undulating parkland. All holes differ and each requires accurate drive placing to derive the best advantage. The clubhouse and course are situated a quarter of a mile from the western end of the M2. The club was formed in 1891 and the course was redesigned by Donald Steel in 1995.
18 holes, 6596yds, Par 71, SSS 71, Course record 67.
Club membership 720.
Visitors must contact in advance & have handicap certificate. No visitors weekends.
Societies apply in advance.
Green Fees £30 per round; £40 per 2 rounds.
Prof Joe Blair
Designer Donald Steel
Facilities ⊗ ⫢ ⓛ 🍺 ♀ ⚘ 🏠 🚣 ✓ ↾
Location 2.5m W on A2

Hotel ★★★★ 77% Bridgewood Manor Hotel, Bridgewood Roundabout, Walderblade Woods, CHATHAM ☎ 01634 201333 100 ⇥ ↑

SANDWICH Map 05 TR35

Prince's Prince's Dr, Sandwich Bay CT13 9QB
☎ 01304 611118 Fax 01304 612000
With 27 championship holes, Prince's Golf Club enjoys a world wide reputation as a traditional links of the finest quality and is a venue that provides all that is best in modern links golf. The purpose built clubhouse, located at the centre of the three loops of nine, can seat 200 diners and offers panoramic views over Sandwich Bay and the course.
Dunes: 9 holes, 3343yds, Par 36, SSS 36.
Himalayas: 9 holes, 3321yds, Par 35, SSS 35.
Shore: 9 holes, 3455yds, Par 36, SSS 36.
Club membership 200.

Visitors available all week, must contact in advance.
Societies welcome all week, please contact in advance.
Green Fees £50 per day; £42 per round (£55/£47 Sat, £55/£50 Sun).
Cards ▭▭ ▭▭ ▭▭ 📷
Prof Derek Barbour
Designer (1951 Sir Guy Campbell & J S F Morrison)
Facilities ⊗ ⫢ ⓛ 🍺 ♀ ⚘ 🏠 ♐ 🐍 🚣 ✓ ↾
& Leisure golf academy.
Location 2m E via toll road, follow signs from Sandwich

Hotel ★★★ 66% San Clu Hotel, Victoria Pde, East Cliff, RAMSGATE ☎ 01843 592345 44 ⇥ ↑

ROYAL ST GEORGE'S See page 153

SEVENOAKS Map 05 TQ55

Knole Park Seal Hollow Rd TN15 0HJ
☎ 01732 452150 Fax 01732 463159
The course is set in a majestic park with many fine trees and deer running loose. It has a wiry turf seemingly impervious to rain. Certainly a pleasure to play on. Excellent views of Knole House and the North Downs. Outstanding greens.
18 holes, 6266yds, Par 70, SSS 70, Course record 62.
Club membership 800.
Visitors must have a handicap certificate and contact the secretary in advance, may not play at weekends or bank holidays.
Societies telephone initially.
Green Fees £46 per 36 holes; £35 per 18 holes.

ROYAL ST. GEORGE'S

SANDWICH *Kent* ☎ 01304 613090
Fax 01304 611245   **Map 05 TR35**

John Ingham writes: Sandwich is one of the most beautiful and unspoiled towns in southern England. Driving to this part of Kent is much like stepping back into history. The big golf course here, Royal St George's, is where Sandy Lyle won the Open Championship in 1985 by one shot from that colourful American, Payne Stewart.

Like the region, the clubhouse is old-fashioned and the seats near the window in the bar seem to have been there forever. The bar staff may know as much about fishing or lifeboats as they know about beer, and make a visit there a delight, providing you are not looking for modern sophistication.

The course itself is the truest links you will find in all England and the Royal & Ancient, in its wisdom, choose Royal St George's (designed by Dr Laidlaw Purves in 1887) for major championships knowing it will find the pedigree player at the end of a week. Close to the sea, overlooking Pegwell Bay, any kind of wind can make this man-size test even tougher. The sweeping rough at the 1st can be daunting, so can the bunkers and the huge sandhills. But there are classic shots here.

Off-sea breezes can turn to incredible gales, and it is possible to find the course virtually unplayable. A smooth swing can be blown inside out and stories of three good woods to reach certain greens, into wind, are commonplace. Often the problem in high winds is simply to stand up and address the ball. Putting, too, can be almost impossible, with the ball blown off the surface and maybe into the sand.

Visitors	must contact in advance and have a handicap certificate. All golf is two ball golf. May not play at weekends or BHs
Societies	Mon-Wed must apply in writing
Green fees	Midweek only £90 per day, £65 per round.
Facilities	⊗ ⊁Ⅲ (by arrangement) ⓛ ⬛ ♀ ♨ ♠ 🏠 ⛳ ♂ Professional (Andrew Brooks)
Location	Sandwich CT13 9PB (1.5m E of town)

**18 holes, 6565yds, Par 70, SSS 72.
Course record 63**

WHERE TO STAY AND EAT NEARBY

HOTELS:
CANTERBURY
★★★ 67% Falstaff, St Dunstans St.
☎ 01227 462138. 24 (22 ⇆ ♠ 2 ♠)
★★★ 64% The Chaucer, Ivy Lane
☎ 01227 464427. 42 (41 ⇆ ♠ 1 ♠)
★★ ⊛ ⊛ 68% Canterbury, 71 New Dover Rd. ☎ 01227 450551 25 (15 ⇆ 10 ♠)

DOVER
★★★70% The Churchill, Dover Waterfront. ☎ 01304 203633. 68 (52 ⇆ ♠ 15 ♠)
★★★ 61% County, Townwall St.
☎ 01304 509955. 79 ⇆ ♠
★★ ⊛ ⊛ 76% Wallets Court, West Cliffe, St Margarets-at-Cliffe
☎ 01304 852424 3 ⇆ ♠ Annexe 10 ⇆ ♠

RESTAURANTS:
CANTERBURY
⊛ Ristorante Tuo e Mio, 16 The Borough. ☎ 01227 761471

Prof	P E Gill
Designer	J A Abercromby
Facilities	⊗ ⅷ 🍴 🛒 ☕ ♀ ⚒ 🏠 ♂
& Leisure	squash.
Location	SE side of town centre off B2019
Hotel	★★★ 68% Donnington Manor, London Rd, Dunton Green, SEVENOAKS ☎ 01732 462681 62 ⇋ ☎

SHEERNESS   Map 05 TQ97

Sheerness Power Station Rd ME12 3AE
☎ 01795 662585 Fax 01795 666840
Semi-links, marshland course, few bunkers, but many ditches
and water hazards.
18 holes, 6460yds, Par 72, SSS 71, Course record 66.
Club membership 750.

Visitors	with member only at weekends.
Societies	Tue-Thu only, telephone in advance.
Green Fees	£20 per day; £15 per round.
Prof	D Hawkins
Facilities	⊗ ⅷ by prior arrangement 🛒 ☕ ♀ ⚒ 🏠 ♂
Location	1.5m E off A249
Hotel	★★★★77% Bridgewood Manor Hotel, Bridgewood Roundabout, Walderblade Woods, CHATHAM ☎ 01634 201333 100 ⇋ ☎

SHOREHAM   Map 05 TQ56

Darenth Valley Station Rd TN14 7SA
☎ 01959 522944 & 522922 Fax 01959 525089
Easy walking parkland course in beautiful valley. Testing
12th hole, par 4.
18 holes, 6327yds, Par 72, SSS 71, Course record 64.

Visitors	must book in advance.
Societies	contact in advance.
Green Fees	£15 per 18 holes, £7.50 per 9 holes (£20/£10 weekends and bank holidays).
Cards	⊝⊝ 💳 🖃
Prof	Scott Fotheringham
Facilities	⊗ ⅷ by prior arrangement 🛒 ☕ ♀ ⚒ 🏠 ⛳ ♂
& Leisure	fishing.
Location	1m E on A225
Hotel	★★★68% Donnington Manor, London Rd, Dunton Green, SEVENOAKS ☎ 01732 462681 62 ⇋ ☎

SITTINGBOURNE   Map 05 TQ96

The Oast Golf Centre Church Rd, Tonge ME9 9AR
☎ 01795 473527
A Par 3 Approach course of 9 holes with 18 tees augmented
by a 17-bay floodlit driving range and a putting green.
9 holes, 1664yds, Par 54, SSS 54.

Visitors	no restrictions.
Societies	telephone in advance.
Green Fees	£6.50 per 18 holes; £4.50 per 9 holes.
Designer	D Chambers
Facilities	🛒 ☕ ♀ ⛳ ♂ ♭
Location	2m NE, A2 between Bapchild/Teynham
Hotel	★★★★77% Bridgewood Manor Hotel, Bridgewood Roundabout, Walderblade Woods, CHATHAM ☎ 01634 201333 100 ⇋ ☎

Sittingbourne & Milton Regis
Wormdale, Newington ME9 7PX
☎ 01795 842261 Fax 01795 844117
A downland course with pleasant vistas. There are a few
uphill climbs, but the course is far from difficult. The new
back line holes are very testing.
18 holes, 6291yds, Par 71, SSS 70, Course record 63.
Club membership 670.

Visitors	by prior arrangement or letter of introduction. Must contact in advance, may not play at weekends.
Societies	Tue & Thu, apply in advance.
Green Fees	£32 per 36 holes; £20 per 18 holes.
Prof	John Hearn
Designer	Donald Steel
Facilities	⊗ ⅷ 🍴 🛒 ☕ ♀ ⚒ 🏠 ♘ ♞ ♂
Location	Turn off Chestnut Street (old A249) at Danaway
Hotel	★★★★77% Bridgewood Manor Hotel, Bridgewood Roundabout, Walderblade Woods, CHATHAM ☎ 01634 201333 100 ⇋ ☎

Upchurch River Valley Golf Centre
Oak Ln, Upchurch ME9 7AY
☎ 01634 379592 Fax 01634 387784
Undulating parkland course set in picturesque countryside.
Testing water hazards on several holes. Excellent winter
course. The 9-hole course is ideal for beginners and for those
keen to sharpen up their short game.
18 holes, 6237yds, Par 70, SSS 70.
Club membership 421.

Visitors	can play anytime, book for weekend 5 days in advance, weekdays 2 days in advance.
Societies	telephone 01634 360626 for details.
Green Fees	not confirmed.
Cards	⊝⊝ 💳 🖃 🖃
Prof	Roger Cornwell
Designer	David Smart
Facilities	⊗ ⅷ 🍴 🛒 ☕ ♀ ⚒ 🏠 ♘ ♞ ♂ ♭
& Leisure	heated outdoor swimming pool.
Location	A2 between Rainham and Newington
Hotel	★★★65% Russell Hotel, 136 Boxley Rd, MAIDSTONE ☎ 01622 692221 42 ⇋ ☎

SNODLAND   Map 05 TQ76

Oastpark Malling Rd ME6 5LG
☎ 01634 242661 Fax 01634 240744
A challenging parkland course for golfers of all abilities. The
course has water hazards, orchards and views across the
Valley of Dean.
18 holes, 6173yds, Par 69, SSS 69, Course record 71.
Club membership 300.

Visitors	may book 7 days in advance.
Societies	early booking with deposits required.
Green Fees	not confirmed.
Prof	John Gregory
Designer	J D Banks
Facilities	⊗ 🛒 ☕ ♀ ⚒ 🏠 ♂
Location	Access via junct 4 on M20
Hotel	★★★63% Larkfield Priory Hotel, London Rd, Larkfield, MAIDSTONE ☎ 01732 846858 51 ⇋ ☎

TENTERDEN   Map 05 TQ83

Tenterden Woodchurch Rd TN30 7DR
☎ 01580 763987 (sec) & 762409 (shop) Fax 01580 763987
Set in tranquil undulating parkland with beautiful views, the course is challenging with several difficult holes.
18 holes, 6071yds, Par 70, SSS 69, Course record 63.
Club membership 600.

Visitors	contact secretary. May only play with member weekends and bank holidays.
Societies	must apply in writing.
Green Fees	£22 per day.
Facilities	⊗ ⊓ ┗ ♉ ♈ ♌ ⌂ ⌐ ♉ ♉
Location	0.75m E on B2067

Hotel ★★ 69% Hartley Mount Country House, Hartley Rd, CRANBROOK
☎ 01580 712230 6 ⇆ ♄

TONBRIDGE   Map 05 TQ54

Poultwood Higham Ln TN11 9QR
☎ 01732 364039 Fax 01732 353781
There are two public 'pay and play' parkland courses in an idyllic woodland setting. The courses are ecologically designed, over predominantly flat land offering challenging hazzards and interesting playing conditions for all standards of golfer.
18 holes, 5569yds, Par 68, SSS 67 or 9 holes, 1281yds, Par 28.

Visitors	non registered golfers may book up to 2 days in advance for 18 hole course, or take available tee times, pay and play system on 9 hole.
Societies	apply in advance to the clubhouse manager tel 01732 366180.
Green Fees	18 holes; £10.50-£11 (£15.50-£16 weekends). 9 hole course; £4.60-£4.90 (£5.80-£6.20 weekends).
Cards	⚊ 💳 💳 💳 ☑
Prof	Chris Miller
Facilities & Leisure	⊗ ⊓ ┗ ♉ ♈ ♌ ⌂ ⌐ ♉ squash.
Location	Off A227, 3m N of Tonbridge

Hotel ★★★ 62% Rose & Crown Hotel, 125 High St, TONBRIDGE ☎ 01732 357966 48 ⇆ ♄

TUNBRIDGE WELLS (ROYAL)   Map 05 TQ53

Nevill Benhall Mill Rd TN2 5JW
☎ 01892 525818 Fax 01892 517861
Just within Sussex, the county boundary with Kent runs along the northern perimeter of the course. Open undulating ground, well-wooded with some heather and gorse for the first half. The second nine holes slope away from the clubhouse to a valley where a narrow stream hazards two holes.
18 holes, 6349yds, Par 71, SSS 70, Course record 66.
Club membership 900.

Visitors	must contact 48 hours in advance, handicap certificate required, permission from secretary for weekends play.
Societies	must apply in writing one month in advance.
Green Fees	not confirmed.
Prof	Paul Huggett
Designer	Henry Cotton
Facilities	⊗ ⊓ ┗ ♉ ♈ ♌ ⌂ ⌐ ♉ ♉
Location	S of Tunbridge Wells, off forest road

Hotel ★★★ 76% The Spa Hotel, Mount Ephraim, TUNBRIDGE WELLS
☎ 01892 520331 74 ⇆

Tunbridge Wells Langton Rd TN4 8XH
☎ 01892 523324 Fax 01892 536918
Somewhat hilly, well-bunkered parkland course with lake; trees form natural hazards.
9 holes, 4725yds, Par 65, SSS 62, Course record 59.
Club membership 450.

Visitors	must contact in advance, limited availability weekends.
Societies	weekdays, apply in advance.
Green Fees	£25 per day; £15 per 18 holes (£25 per round weekends).
Cards	⚊ 💳 ☑
Prof	Mike Barton
Facilities	⊗ ⊓ by prior arrangement ┗ ♉ ♈ ♌ ⌂ ⌐ ♉
Location	1m W on A264

Hotel ★★★ 76% The Spa Hotel, Mount Ephraim, TUNBRIDGE WELLS
☎ 01892 520331 74 ⇆

WESTERHAM   Map 05 TQ45

Westerham Valence Park, Brasted Rd TN16 1LJ
☎ 01959 563700 Fax 01959 563787
Originally completeley wooded forestry land with thousands of mature pines. The storms of 1987 created natural fairways and the mature landscape makes the course both demanding and spectacular.
18 holes, 6272yds, Par 72, SSS 72.
Club membership 700.

Visitors	welcome but may not play Sat & Sun am.
Societies	telephone General Manager for details.
Green Fees	not confirmed.
Cards	⚊ 💳 💳 💳 ☑ 💳 💳 ☑
Prof	Ewan Campbell
Designer	D Williams
Facilities	⊗ ⊓ ┗ ♉ ♈ ♌ ⌂ ⌐ ♉ ♉ ♉
Location	A25 between Westerham and Brasted

Hotel ★★★ 68% Kings Arms Hotel, Market Square, WESTERHAM ☎ 01959 562990 17 ⇆ ♄

WESTGATE ON SEA   Map 05 TR37

Westgate and Birchington 176 Canterbury Rd CT8 8LT
☎ 01843 831115
Seaside course.
18 holes, 4926yds, Par 64, SSS 64, Course record 60.
Club membership 320.

Visitors	Mon-Sat after 10am, Sun and bank holidays after 11am, must contact in advance & have handicap certificate, restricted at weekends.
Societies	must contact the secretary.
Green Fees	£13 (£15 weekends & bank holidays).
Prof	Roger Game
Facilities	┗ ♉ ♈ ♌ ⌂ ⌐ ♉
Location	E side of town centre off A28

▶

Hotel ★★★ 61% Royal Albion Hotel,
Albion St, BROADSTAIRS
☎ 01843 868071 19 ⊟ ❛

WEST KINGSDOWN   Map 05 TQ56

Woodlands Manor Woodlands TN15 6AB
☎ 01959 523806 & 524161
Interesting, challenging & undulating parkland course with
testing 1st, 9th and 15th holes. Set in a designated area of
outstanding natural beauty.
18 holes, 6100yds, Par 69, SSS 68, Course record 64.
Club membership 650.
Visitors welcome, at weekends by arrangement.
Societies apply in advance.
Green Fees not confirmed.
Cards ▬ ▬ ▧ ▣ ▨ ▧ ▨
Prof Philip Womack
Designer Lyons/Coles
Facilities ⊗ ⊞ ⓺ ♥ ♀ ♧ ⊟ ❜ ❞ ♣ ⚘ ⚲ ❛
& Leisure hard tennis courts.
Location 2m S off A20

Hotel ★★★★ 63% Thistle Brands Hatch,
BRANDS HATCH ☎ 01474 854900 121 ⊟ ❛

WHITSTABLE   Map 05 TR16

Chestfield (Whitstable) 103 Chestfield Rd CT5 3LU
☎ 01227 794411 & 792243 Fax 01227 794454
Gently undulating parkland course with sea views. The Par 3
3rd is generally played into the wind and the Par 4th has a
difficult lefthand dogleg.
18 holes, 5834yds, Par 69, SSS 68, Course record 65.
Club membership 650.
Visitors visitors welcome Mon-Fri except Thur, weekend
with a member only.
Societies must apply in writing.
Green Fees £28 per day; £18 per round.
Prof John Brotherton
Facilities ⊗ by prior arrangement ⓺ ♥ ♀ ♧ ⊟ ♣ ⚘
⚲ ❛
Location 0.5m S by Chesterfield Railway Station

Hotel ★★★ 64% The Chaucer, Ivy Ln,
CANTERBURY
☎ 01227 464427 42 ⊟ ❛

Whitstable & Seasalter Collingwood Rd CT5 1EB
☎ 01227 272020
Links course.
9 holes, 5357yds, Par 66, SSS 63, Course record 62.
Club membership 300.
Visitors must contact in advance. Weekend play by prior
arrangement.
Green Fees £15 per 18 holes; £8 per 9 holes.
Facilities ⊗ ⊞ ⓺ ♥ ♀ ♧
Location W side of town centre off B2205

Hotel ★★★ 64% The Chaucer, Ivy Ln,
CANTERBURY
☎ 01227 464427 42 ⊟ ❛

LANCASHIRE

ACCRINGTON   Map 07 SD72

Accrington & District Devon Av, Oswaldtwistle BB5 4LS
☎ 01254 381614 Fax 01254 381614
Moorland course with pleasant views of the Pennines and
surrounding areas.
18 holes, 6044yds, Par 70, SSS 69, Course record 63.
Club membership 600.
Visitors must contact in advance.
Societies contact in advance.
Green Fees not confirmed.
Prof Bill Harling
Designer J Braid
Facilities ⊗ ⊞ ⓺ ♥ ♀ ♧ ⊟ ❜ ♣ ⚘ ⚲ ❛
Location Mid way between Accrington & Blackburn

Hotel ★★★ 64% Dunkenhalgh Hotel, Blackburn Rd,
Clayton-le-Moors, ACCRINGTON
☎ 01254 398021 37 ⊟ ❛ Annexe42 ⊟ ❛

Baxenden & District Top o' th' Meadow, Baxenden
BB5 2EA ☎ 01254 234555
Moorland course with a long par 3 to start.
9 holes, 5740yds, Par 70, SSS 68, Course record 67.
Club membership 340.
Visitors may not play Sat, Sun and bank holidays except
with member.
Societies must contact in advance.
Green Fees £15 per round weekdays.
Facilities ⊗ ⊞ ⓺ ♥ ♀ ♧
Location 1.5m SE off A680

Hotel ★★★ 64% Dunkenhalgh Hotel, Blackburn Rd,
Clayton-le-Moors, ACCRINGTON
☎ 01254 398021 37 ⊟ ❛ Annexe42 ⊟ ❛

Green Haworth Green Haworth BB5 3SL
☎ 01254 237580 Fax 01254 396176
Moorland course dominated by quarries and difficult in
windy conditions.
9 holes, 5556yds, Par 68, SSS 67, Course record 65.
Club membership 320.
Visitors may not play Sun, Mar-Oct.
Societies apply in writing. Weekdays only before 5pm. Or
contact secretary on above telephone number.
Green Fees £15 per day/round (£20 weekends & bank
holidays).
Facilities ⊗ ⊞ ⓺ ♥ ♀ ♧
Location 2m S off A680

Hotel ★★★ 61% County Hotel Blackburn,
Preston New Rd, BLACKBURN
☎ 01254 899988 101 ⊟ ❛

BACUP   Map 07 SD82

Bacup Maden Rd OL13 8HY
☎ 01706 873170 & 877726 Fax 01706 877726
Moorland course, predominantly flat except climbs to 1st and
10th holes.
9 holes, 6008yds, Par 70, SSS 69.
Club membership 350.

Visitors no restrictions. Club competitions in season on Sat & some Sun, advisable to contact in advance.
Societies must contact in writing.
Green Fees £14 (£17 weekends).
Facilities ⌂
Location W side of town off A671

Hotel ★★ 62% Comfort Inn, Keirby Walk, BURNLEY ☎ 01282 427611 50 ⊖ ♠

BARNOLDSWICK — Map 07 SD84

Ghyll Skipton Rd BB18 6JH ☎ 01282 842466
Excellent, parkland course with outstanding views, especially from the 8th tee where you can see the Three Peaks. Testing 8th hole is an uphill par 4. 11 holes in total 9 in Yorkshire and 2 in Lancashire.
9 holes, 5790yds, Par 68, SSS 66, Course record 62.
Club membership 345.
Visitors may not play Tue, Fri after 4.30pm & Sun.
Societies must contact in writing.
Green Fees £14 per day (£18 weekends).
Facilities ⌂ evenings only ⌂
Location 1m NE on B6252

Hotel ★★★ 67% Stirk House Hotel, GISBURN ☎ 01200 445581 36 ⊖ ♠ Annexe10 ⊖ ♠

BLACKBURN — Map 07 SD62

Blackburn Beardwood Brow BB2 7AX
☎ 01254 51122 Fax 01254 665578
Parkland course on a high plateau with stream and hills. Superb views of Lancashire coast and the Pennines.
18 holes, 6144yds, Par 71, SSS 70.
Club membership 550.
Visitors must contact professional in advance.
Societies must contact in advance.
Green Fees £24 per day (£28 weekends).
Prof Alan Rodwell
Facilities ⊗ ⌂ ⌂ ⌂ ⌂ ⌂ ⌂ ⌂ ♂
Location 1.25m NW of town centre off A677

Hotel ★★★ 61% County Hotel Blackburn, Preston New Rd, BLACKBURN ☎ 01254 899988 101 ⊖ ♠

BLACKPOOL — Map 07 SD33

Blackpool North Shore Devonshire Rd FY2 0RD
☎ 01253 352054 Fax 01253 591240
Undulating parkland course.
18 holes, 6432yds, Par 71, SSS 71, Course record 63.
Club membership 900.
Visitors may not play Thu & Sat. Advisable to contact in advance.
Societies must contact in advance.
Green Fees £27.50 per day; £20 per round.
Prof Brendan Ward
Facilities ⊗ ⌂ ⌂ ⌂ ⌂ ⌂ ⌂ ♂
Location On A587 N of town centre

Hotel ★★ 70% Brabyns Hotel, 1-3 Shaftesbury Av, North Shore, BLACKPOOL ☎ 01253 354263 22 ⊖ ♠ Annexe3 ⊖ ♠

De Vere Blackpool (Herons Reach) East Park Blackpool FY3 8LL ☎ 01253 766156 & 838866 Fax 01253 798800
The course was designed by Peter Alliss and Clive Clarke. There are 10 man-made lakes and several existing ponds. Built to a links design, well mounded but fairly easy walking. Water comes into play on 9 holes, better players can go for the carry or shorter hitters can take the safe route. The course provides an excellent and interesting challenge for golfers of all standards.
18 holes, 6461yds, Par 72, SSS 71, Course record 64.
Club membership 550.

Visitors may book up to 2 weeks in advance tel 01253 766156, (hotel guest/visiting society no limit to how far in advance bookings can be made). Handicap essential, etiquette and dress rules must be adhered to
Societies telephone or write to golf sales office 01253 838866.
Green Fees £30 per round (£35 weekends).
Cards ⌂ ⌂ ⌂ ⌂ ⌂
Prof Dominik Naughton
Designer Peter Alliss/Clive Clark
Facilities ⊗ ⌂ ⌂ ⌂ ⌂ ⌂ ⌂ ⌂ ⌂ ⌂ ♂ ♠
& Leisure hard tennis courts, heated indoor swimming pool, squash, sauna, solarium, gymnasium.
Location Off A587 adjacent to Stanley Park & Zoo

Hotel ★★★★ 67% De Vere Hotel, East Park Dr, BLACKPOOL ☎ 01253 838866 164 ⊖ ♠

Stanley Park Municipal North Park Dr FY3 8LS
☎ 01253 397916 Fax 01253 397916
The golf course, situated in Stanley Park is municipal. The golf club (Blackpool Park) is private but golfers may use the clubhouse facilities if playing the course. An abundance of grassy pits, ponds and open dykes.
18 holes, 6087yds, Par 70, SSS 69, Course record 64.
Club membership 600.
Visitors must apply to Mrs A Hirst, Town Hall, Talbot Square, Blackpool.
Societies must apply in writing to Mrs A Hirst, Blackpool Borough Council, Town Hall, Talbot Square, Blackpool.
Green Fees £10.50 (£12.50 weekends & bank holidays).
Prof Brian Purdie
Designer Mckenzie
Facilities ⊗ ⌂ ⌂ ⌂ ⌂ ⌂ ⌂ ♂
Location 1m E of Blackpool Tower

Hotel ★★★ 57% Clifton Hotel, Talbot Square, The Promenade, BLACKPOOL ☎ 01253 621481 77 ⊖ ♠

BURNLEY   Map 07 SD83

Burnley Glen View BB11 3RW
☎ 01282 421045 & 451281
Moorland course with hilly surrounds.
18 holes, 5911yds, Par 69, SSS 69, Course record 64.
Club membership 750.
Visitors   must contact in advance. May not play on
               Saturdays.
Societies   must apply in writing.
Green Fees £20 per day (£25 weekends & bank holidays).
Prof   William Tye
Facilities   ⊗ ⋈ ⅃ ⬛ ♀ ⚐ 🖐 ♂
Location   1.5m S off A646

Hotel   ★★ 62% Comfort Inn, Keirby Walk,
               BURNLEY ☎ 01282 427611   50 ⇄ ♏

Towneley Towneley Park, Todmorden Rd BB11 3ED
☎ 01282 438473
Parkland course, with other sporting facilities.
18 holes, 5811yds, Par 70, SSS 68, Course record 67.
Club membership 290.
Visitors   must contact in advance.
Societies   must contact in advance in writing.
Green Fees £8 (£9.25 weekends).
Cards   ▭ ▬▬ ▬▬ ⑤
Facilities   ⊗ ⅃ ⬛ ♀ ⚐ 🖐 ♂ ⚐
Location   1m SE of town centre on A671

Hotel   ★★★ 73% Oaks Hotel, Colne Rd, Reedley,
               BURNLEY ☎ 01282 414141   53 ⇄ ♏

CHORLEY   Map 07 SD51

Charnock Richard Preston Rd, Charnock Richard PR7 5LE
☎ 01257 470707 Fax 01257 794343
Flat parkland course, established in 1994, with plenty of
Americanised water hazards. Signature hole the 6th Par 5
with an island green.
18 holes, 6234yds, Par 71, SSS 70, Course record 68.
Club membership 550.
Visitors   strict full dress code, members time 8.30-
               9.30pm and 12.00-1.00pm weekdays, telephone
               for weekend play.
Societies   contact club secretary in writing.
Green Fees £15 per round (£20 weekends).
Cards   ▭ ▬▬ ⑤
Designer   Chris Court
Facilities   ⊗ ⋈ ⅃ ⬛ ♀ ⚐ 🖐 ♂ ⚐
Location   On the main A49, 0.25m from Camelot Theme
               Park

Hotel   ★★★ 66% Park Hall Hotel, Park Hall Rd,
               Charnock Richard, CHORLEY
               ☎ 01257 452090   54 ⇄ ♏ Annexe86 ⇄ ♏

Chorley Hall o' th' Hill, Heath Charnock PR6 9HX
☎ 01257 480263 Fax 01257 480722
A splendid moorland course with plenty of fresh air. The
well-sited clubhouse affords some good views of the
Lancashire coast and of Angelzarke, a local beauty spot.
Beware of the short 3rd hole with its menacing out-of-
bounds.
18 holes, 6307yds, Par 71, SSS 70, Course record 63.
Club membership 550.

Visitors   must contact in advance and may not play
               weekends or bank holidays.
Societies   must contact in advance. Tue-Fri only.
Green Fees not confirmed.
Prof   Gavin Mutch
Designer   J A Steer
Facilities   ⊗ by prior arrangement ⅃ ⬛ ♀ ⚐ 🖐 ♂
               ⚐ ♂
Location   2.5m SE on A673

Hotel   ★★★ 66% Pines Hotel, Clayton le Woods,
               CHORLEY ☎ 01772 338551   37 ⇄ ♏

Duxbury Jubilee Park Duxbury Hall Rd PR7 4AS
☎ 01257 265380 & 241634
Municipal parkland course.
18 holes, 6390yds, Par 71, SSS 70.
Club membership 250.
Visitors   must contact 6 days in advance via Pro shop.
Societies   must contact in advance by letter.
Green Fees not confirmed.
Prof   S Middelman
Designer   Hawtree & Sons
Facilities   ⚐ 🖐 ♂ ⚐
Location   2.5m S off A6

Hotel   B Welcome Lodge, Mill Ln, Charnock Richard,
               CHORLEY ☎ 01257 791746 100 ⇄ ♏

Shaw Hill Hotel Golf & Country Club Preston Rd,
Whittle-Le-Woods PR6 7PP
☎ 01257 269221 Fax 01257 261223
A fine course designed by one of Europe's most
prominent golf architects and offering a considerable
challenge as well as tranquillity and scenic charm. Seven
lakes guard par 5 and long par 4 holes.
18 holes, 6405yds, Par 72, SSS 71, Course record 65.
Club membership 500.
Visitors   must contact in advance, denims and
               trainers not allowed on course or in
               clubhouse. Jacket and tie required in
               restaurant.
Societies   must telephone in advance.
Green Fees £30 per 18 holes (£40 Fri-Sun).
Cards   ▭ ▬▬ ▬▬ ▬▬ 🔲 ⑤
Prof   David Clark
Facilities   ⊗ ⋈ ⅃ ⬛ ♀ ⚐ 🖐 ♂ 🏐 🖐 ⚐ ♂
& Leisure   heated indoor swimming pool, sauna,
               solarium, gymnasium.
Location   On A6 1.5m N

Hotel   ★★★ 68% Shaw Hill Hotel Golf &
               Country Club, Preston Rd,
               Whittle-le-Woods, CHORLEY
               ☎ 01257 269221   26 ⇄ ♏ Annexe4 ⇄ ♏

CLITHEROE   Map 07 SD74

Clitheroe Whalley Rd, Pendleton BB7 1PP
☎ 01200 422292 Fax 01200 422292
One of the best inland courses in the country. Clitheroe
is a parkland-type course with water hazards and good
scenic views, particularly on towards Longridge, and
Pendle Hill. The Club has been the venue for the

Lancashire Amateur Championships, the 1991 County
Championships Tournament and the English Ladies
(Intermediate) Championship.
18 holes, 6326yds, Par 71, SSS 71, Course record 67.
Club membership 750.
Visitors   must contact in advance.
Societies   must contact in advance.
Green Fees £33 per day (£39 weekends & bank
               holidays).
Prof   John Twissell
Designer   James Braid
Facilities   ⊗ 州 🄻 🍴 ♀ 🗼 📷 ⛳ ♂ ⬤
Location   2m S of Clitheroe on Whalley Road

Hotel   ★★ 68% Shireburn Arms Hotel,
               Whalley Rd, HURST GREEN
               ☎ 01254 826518   18 ➦ 🐾

COLNE   Map 07 SD84

Colne Law Farm, Skipton Old Rd BB8 7EB
☎ 01282 863391
Moorland course with scenic surroundings.
9 holes, 5961yds, Par 70, SSS 69, Course record 63.
Club membership 356.
Visitors   restricted Thu. Must contact in advance.
Societies   must contact in advance.
Green Fees not confirmed.
Facilities   🗼
Location   1m E off A56

Hotel   ★★★ 67% Stirk House Hotel, GISBURN
               ☎ 01200 445581   36 ➦ 🐾 Annexe10 ➦ 🐾

DARWEN   Map 07 SD62

Darwen Winter Hill BB3 0LB
☎ 01254 701287 & 776370 (pro)
First 9 holes on parkland, the second 9 on moorland.
18 holes, 5863yds, Par 69, SSS 68, Course record 63.
Club membership 600.
Visitors   may not play on Tue or Sat.
Societies   must contact in advance.
Green Fees £36 per day; £22 per round (£40/£30 weekends).
Prof   Wayne Lennon
Facilities   ⊗ 州 🄻 🍴 ♀ 🗼 📷 ⬤
Location   1m NW

Hotel   ★★★ 66% Whitehall Hotel,
               Springbank, Whitehall, DARWEN
               ☎ 01254 701595   17 ➦ 🐾

FLEETWOOD   Map 07 SD34

Fleetwood Princes Way FY7 8AF
☎ 01253 873661 & 773573 Fax 01253 773573
Championship length, flat seaside links where the player
must always be alert to changes of direction or strength
of the wind.
18 holes, 6723yds, Par 72, SSS 72.
Club membership 600.
Visitors   may not play on competition days or Tue.
Societies   must contact in advance. A deposit of £5
               per player is required.
Green Fees £30 per 27 holes £24 per 18 holes (£40/30
               weekends & bank holidays).
Prof   S McLaughlin
Designer   J A Steer
Facilities   ⊗ 州 🄻 🍴 ♀ 🗼 📷 🏌 ⬤
Location   W side of town centre

Hotel   ★★ 70% Brabyns Hotel, 1-3 Shaftesbury
               Av, North Shore, BLACKPOOL
               ☎ 01253 354263   22 ➦ 🐾 Annexe3 ➦ 🐾

GARSTANG   Map 07 SD44

Garstang Country Hotel & Golf Club Garstang Rd,
Bowgreave PR3 1YE
☎ 01995 600100 Fax 01995 600950
Fairly flat parkland course following the contours of the
Rivers Wyre and Calder and providing a steady test of
ability, especially over the longer back nine. Exceptional
drainage makes the course playable all year round.
18 holes, 6050yds, Par 68, SSS 68.
Visitors   tee times bookable 6 days in advance.
Societies   telephone for availability and confirm in
               writing.
Green Fees £12 per round; £7.50 per 9 holes (£14 weekends
               & bank holidays).
Cards   ▬ 🖃 VISA ◻ ▦ 🔲 ⬤
Prof   Robert Head
Designer   Richard Bradbeer
Facilities   ⊗ 州 🄻 🍴 ♀ 🗼 📷 🏌 🚗 ♂ ⬤
Location   Situated on B6430 1m S of Garstang

GREAT HARWOOD　　　　Map 07 SD73

Great Harwood Harwood Bar, Whalley Rd BB6 7TE
☎ 01254 884391
Flat parkland course with fine views of the Pendle region.
9 holes, 6411yds, Par 73, SSS 71, Course record 68.
Club membership 320.
Visitors　　must contact in advance.
Societies　　welcome mid-week only, apply in writing.
Green Fees £16 per day (£22 weekends & bank holidays).
Facilities　　⊗ ⽊ ⅄ ☕ ♀ ☂
Location　　E side of town centre on A680

Hotel　　★★★ 64% Dunkenhalgh Hotel, Blackburn Rd,
　　　　　　Clayton-le-Moors, ACCRINGTON
　　　　　　☎ 01254 398021　37 ⇄ ☞ Annexe42 ⇄ ☞

HASLINGDEN　　　　Map 07 SD72

Rossendale Ewood Ln Head BB4 6LH
☎ 01706 831339 & 213616 (Pro) Fax 01706 228669
Testing meadowland course, mainly flat, situated on a
plateau with panoramic views.
18 holes, 6293yds, Par 72, Course record 64.
Club membership 700.
Visitors　　must contact in advance. Must play with
　　　　　　member on Sat.
Societies　　must telephone in advance & confirm in writing.
Green Fees £25 per day (£30 weekends & bank holidays).
Prof　　　　Stephen Nicholls
Facilities　　⊗ ⽊ ⅄ ☕ ♀ (ex Mon) ⚘ ☎ ☂
Location　　0.5m S off A56

Hotel　　★★★ 61% County Hotel Blackburn,
　　　　　　Preston New Rd, BLACKBURN
　　　　　　☎ 01254 899988 101 ⇄ ☞

HEYSHAM　　　　Map 07 SD46

Heysham Trumacar Park, Middleton Rd LA3 3JH
☎ 01524 851011 Fax 01524 853030
Seaside parkland course, partly wooded. The 15th is a 459
yard Par 4 hole nearly always played into the prevailing
south west wind.
18 holes, 6258yds, Par 69, SSS 70, Course record 64.
Club membership 1100.
Visitors　　book in advance via the professional, restricted
　　　　　　at weekends.
Societies　　must contact in advance.
Green Fees £24 per day; £19 per round (£29 weekends &
　　　　　　bank holidays).
Prof　　　　Ryan Done
Designer　　Alex Herd
Facilities　　⊗ ⽊ ⅄ ☕ ♀ ⚘ ☎ ☂ ☂
Location　　0.75m S off A589

Hotel　　★★ 62% Clarendon Hotel, Marine Rd West,
　　　　　　West End Promenade, MORECAMBE
　　　　　　☎ 01524 410180 31rm(28 ⇄ ☞)

Call the AA Hotel Booking Service on
0870 5050505 to book at AA recognised hotels and B & Bs
in the UK and Ireland, or through our Internet site:
http://www.theaa.co.uk/hotels

KNOTT END-ON-SEA　　　　Map 07 SD34

Knott End Wyreside FY6 0AA
☎ 01253 810576 Fax 01253 810576
Pleasant, undulating parkland course on banks of River
Wyre. Open to sea breezes.
18 holes, 5789yds, Par 69, SSS 68, Course record 63.
Club membership 500.
Visitors　　book via professional up to 7 days in advance.
Societies　　must contact in advance.
Green Fees not confirmed.
Prof　　　　Paul Walker
Designer　　Braid
Facilities　　⽊ ⅄ ☕ ♀ ⚘ ☎ ☂
Location　　W side of village off B5377

Hotel　　★★ 70% Brabyns Hotel, 1-3 Shaftesbury Av,
　　　　　　North Shore, BLACKPOOL
　　　　　　☎ 01253 354263　22 ⇄ ☞ Annexe3 ⇄ ☞

LANCASTER　　　　Map 07 SD46

Lancaster Golf Club Ashton Hall, Ashton-with-
Stodday LA2 0AJ ☎ 01524 751247 Fax 01524 752742
This course is unusual for parkland golf as it is exposed
to the winds coming off the Irish Sea. It is situated on the
Lune estuary and has some natural hazards and easy
walking. There are however several fine holes among
woods near the old clubhouse.
18 holes, 6282yds, Par 71, SSS 71, Course record 66.
Club membership 925.
Visitors　　residential visitors only at weekends. Must
　　　　　　contact in advance and have a handicap
　　　　　　certificate.
Societies　　Mon-Fri only. Must contact in advance.
　　　　　　Handicap certificate required.
Green Fees not confirmed.
Cards　　　　🖃 ▦ ▤ ⊘
Prof　　　　David Sutcliffe
Designer　　James Braid
Facilities　　⊗ ⽊ ⅄ ☕ ♀ ⚘ ☎ ⛟ ☂
Location　　3m S on A588

Hotel　　★★★★ 69% Lancaster House Hotel,
　　　　　　Green Ln, Ellel, LANCASTER
　　　　　　☎ 01524 844822　80 ⇄ ☞

Lansil Caton Rd LA1 3PE ☎ 01524 61233
Challenging parkland course.
9 holes, 5608yds, Par 70, SSS 67, Course record 68.
Club membership 375.
Visitors　　may not play before 1pm on Sunday.
Societies　　weekdays only; must contact in writing.
Green Fees £12 per day.
Facilities　　⚘
Location　　N side of town centre on A683

Hotel　　B Posthouse Lancaster, Waterside Park, Caton
　　　　　　Rd, LANCASTER ☎ 01524 65999 157 ⇄ ☞

LANGHO　　　　Map 07 SD73

Mytton Fold Hotel & Golf Complex Whalley Rd BB6 8AB
☎ 01254 240662 Fax 01254 248119
The course has panoramic views across the Ribble Valley
and Pendle Hill. Tight fairways and water hazards are
designed to make this a challenging course for any golfer.

18 holes, 6082yds, Par 72, SSS 69, Course record 70.
Club membership 310.

Visitors	must contact in advance.
Societies	telephone in advance.
Green Fees	£14 per day (£16 weekends & bank holidays).
Cards	
Prof	Gary P Coope
Designer	Frank Hargreaves
Facilities	
Location	On A59 between Langho and Whalley
Hotel	★★★ 72% Northcote Manor, Northcote Rd, LANGHO ☎ 01254 240555 14

LEYLAND   Map 07 SD52

Leyland Wigan Rd PR5 2UD
☎ 01772 436457 Fax 01772 436457
Parkland course, fairly flat and usually breezy.
18 holes, 6123yds, Par 69, SSS 70, Course record 64.
Club membership 650.

Visitors	must contact in advance. Welcome weekdays, with member only at weekends.
Societies	must contact in advance.
Green Fees	£25.
Prof	Colin Burgess
Facilities	
Location	E side of town centre on A49
Hotel	★★★ 66% Pines Hotel, Clayton le Woods, CHORLEY ☎ 01772 338551 37

LONGRIDGE   Map 07 SD63

Longridge Fell Barn, Jeffrey Hill PR3 2TU
☎ 01772 783291 Fax 01772 783022
One of the oldest clubs in England. A moorland course with panoramic views of the Ribble Valley, Trough of Bowland, The Fylde and Welsh Mountains.
18 holes, 5975yds, Par 70, SSS 69, Course record 65.
Club membership 700.

Visitors	welcome. Must contact in advance. May not play at weekends Jul-Aug.
Societies	welcome by prior arrangement.
Green Fees	£20 per day, £15 per round (£25 weekends).
Prof	Stephen Taylor
Facilities	
Location	8m NE of Preston off B6243
Hotel	★★ 68% Shireburn Arms Hotel, Whalley Rd, HURST GREEN ☎ 01254 826518 18

LYTHAM ST ANNES   Map 07 SD32

Fairhaven Lytham Hall Park, Ansdell FY8 4JU
☎ 01253 736741 (Secretary) 736976 (Pro)
A flat, but interesting parkland links course of good standard. There are natural hazards as well as numerous bunkers and players need to produce particularly accurate second shots.
18 holes, 6883yds, Par 74, SSS 73, Course record 66.
Club membership 750.

Visitors	telephone professional in advance.
Societies	must contact in advance.
Green Fees	not confirmed.
Prof	Brian Plucknett
Designer	J A Steer

Facilities	
Location	E side of town centre off B5261
Hotel	★★★ 65% Bedford Hotel, 307-311 Clifton Dr South, LYTHAM ST ANNES ☎ 01253 724636 36

Lytham Green Drive Ballam Rd FY8 4LE
☎ 01253 737390 Fax 01253 731350
Pleasant parkland course, ideal for holidaymakers.
18 holes, 6163yds, Par 70, SSS 69, Course record 64.
Club membership 740.

Visitors	must contact in advance. May not play at weekends.
Societies	must apply in writing.
Green Fees	not confirmed.
Prof	Andrew Lancaster
Designer	Steer
Facilities	
Location	E side of town centre off B5259
Hotel	★★★★ 63% Clifton Arms, West Beach, Lytham, LYTHAM ST ANNES ☎ 01253 739898 44

ROYAL LYTHAM ST ANNES   See page 163

St Annes Old Links Highbury Rd FY8 2LD
☎ 01253 723597
Seaside links, qualifying course for Open Championship; compact and of very high standard, particularly greens. Windy, very long 5th, 17th and 18th holes. Famous hole: 9th (171 yds), par 3. Excellent club facilities.
18 holes, 6616yds, Par 72, SSS 72.
Club membership 950.

Visitors	may not play on Sat or before 9.15am & between noon-2pm weekdays. Sundays by prior arrangement only. Handicap certificate requested.
Societies	must contact in advance.
Green Fees	not confirmed.
Prof	G Hardiman
Designer	George Lowe
Facilities	
Location	N side of town centre
Hotel	★★★ 65% Bedford Hotel, 307-311 Clifton Dr South, LYTHAM ST ANNES ☎ 01253 724636 36

MORECAMBE   Map 07 SD46

Morecambe Bare LA4 6AJ
☎ 01524 412841 Fax 01524 412841
Holiday golf at its most enjoyable. The well-maintained, wind-affected seaside parkland course is not long but full of character. Even so the panoramic views across Morecambe Bay and to the Lake District and Pennines make concentration difficult. The 4th is a testing hole.
18 holes, 5770yds, Par 67, SSS 68, Course record 69.
Club membership 850.

Visitors	may play from yellow tees, must contact in advance.
Societies	must contact in advance.
Green Fees	£28 per day; £23 per round (£33/£28 weekends).

Prof	Simon Fletcher
Designer	Dr Alister Mackenzie
Facilities	⊗ ⅷ ▙ ▟ ♀ ♨ 🖭 ✎
& Leisure	snooker tables.
Location	N side of town centre on A5105
Hotel	★★★ 66% Elms Hotel,
	Bare Village, MORECAMBE
	☎ 01524 411501 40 ⇄ ⌕

NELSON   Map 07 SD83

Marsden Park Townhouse Rd BB9 8DG ☎ 01282 661912
A semi-parkland course offering panoramic views of
surrounding countryside, set in the foothills of Pendle
Marsden Park, a testing 18 holes for golfers of all abilities.
18 holes, 5813yds, Par 70, SSS 68, Course record 66.
Club membership 298.

Visitors	welcome at any time, advised to book in advance at weekends.
Societies	Must contact in writing.
Green Fees	£8 per day (£9 weekends & bank holidays).
Cards	💳 🚇 💳
Prof	Martin Ross
Facilities	⊗ ⅷ by prior arrangement ▙ ▟ ♀ ♨ 🖭 ⚲ ✎
Location	E side of town centre off A56
Hotel	★ 61% Smuggler's Haunt Hotel & Restaurant,
	Church Hill East, BRIXHAM
	☎ 01803 853050 & 859416
	Fax 01803 858738 14 ⇄ ⌕

Nelson King's Causeway, Brierfield BB9 0EU
☎ 01282 611834 & 617000 Fax 01282 606226
Moorland course, usually windy, with good views. Testing
8th hole, par 4.
18 holes, 5967yds, Par 70, SSS 69, Course record 63.
Club membership 500.

Visitors	must telephone 01282 617000 in advance, may not play before 9.30am or between 12.30-1.30pm.
Societies	must contact in writing.
Green Fees	£25 per day (£30 weekends & bank holidays).
Prof	Nigel Sumner
Designer	Dr Mackenzie
Facilities	⊗ ⅷ ▙ ▟ ♀ ♨ 🖭 ✎
Location	1.5m SE
Hotel	★★★ 73% Oaks Hotel, Colne Rd, Reedley,
	BURNLEY ☎ 01282 414141 53 ⇄ ⌕

ORMSKIRK   Map 07 SD40

Hurlston Hall Hurlston Ln, Southport Rd, Scarisbrick
L40 8JD ☎ 01704 840400 & 841120 (pro shop)
Fax 01704 841404
Designed by Donald Steel and opened in 1994, this gently
undulating course offers fine views across the Pennines and
Bowland Fells. With generous fairways, large tees and
greens, two streams and seven lakes, it provides a good test
of golf for players of all standards. Luxurious colonial-style
clubhouse.
18 holes, 6746yds, Par 72, SSS 72, Course record 66.

Visitors	welcome, but may be asked for handicap certificate or letter of introduction from own club. Preferable to book in advance.

Societies	registered Golf Societies and others approved by club, write or telephone for details.
Green Fees	Summer: £25 per round (£30 weekends and bank holidays); Winter: £20 per round (£25 weekends and bank holidays).
Cards	💳 🚇 💳 💳
Prof	Jon Escalapez
Designer	Donald Steel
Facilities	⊗ ⅷ ▙ ▟ ♀ ♨ 🖭 ⚲ ⚐ ✎ ⌕
& Leisure	fishing.
Location	Situated 6m from Southpark and 2m from Ormskirk along A570
Hotel	★★★ 62% Beaufort Hotel,
	High Ln, Burscough, ORMSKIRK
	☎ 01704 892655 20 ⇄ ⌕

Ormskirk Rranes Ln, Lathom L40 5UJ
☎ 01695 572227 Fax 01695 572227
A pleasantly secluded, fairly flat, parkland course with
much heath and silver birch. Accuracy from the tees will
provide an interesting variety of second shots.
18 holes, 6358yds, Par 70, SSS 70, Course record 63.
Club membership 300.

Visitors	restricted Sat.
Societies	must telephone or contact in writing.
Green Fees	£40 per day, £30 per round (£45/£35 weekends and Wednesday).
Prof	Jack Hammond
Facilities	♨ 🖭 ✎
Location	1.5m NE
Hotel	★★★ 66% Holland Hall Hotel,
	6 Lafford Ln, UPHOLLAND
	☎ 01695 624426 36 ⇄ ⌕

PLEASINGTON   Map 07 SD62

Pleasington BB2 5JF
☎ 01254 202177 Fax 01254 201028
Plunging and rising across lovely moorland turf this
course tests judgement of distance through the air to
greens of widely differing levels. The 11th and 17th are
testing holes.
18 holes, 6417yds, Par 71, SSS 71.
Club membership 700.

Visitors	may play Mon & Wed-Fri only.
Societies	must contact in advance.
Green Fees	£32 per round (£40 weekends & bank holidays).
Prof	Ged Furey
Facilities	⊗ ⅷ ▙ ▟ ♀ ♨ 🖭 ✎
Location	W side of village
Hotel	★★★ 61% County Hotel Blackburn,
	Preston New Rd, BLACKBURN
	☎ 01254 899988 101 ⇄ ⌕

POULTON-LE-FYLDE   Map 07 SD33

Poulton-le-Fylde Breck Rd FY6 7HJ
☎ 01253 892444 Fax 01253 892444
Municipal parkland course, with easy walking.
9 holes, 3028yds, Par 70, SSS 68.
Club membership 200.

▶

ROYAL LYTHAM AND ST ANNES

LYTHAM ST ANNES *Lancs* ☎ 01253 724206
Fax 01253 780946   **Map 07 SD32**

John Ingham writes: Venue for many Open Championships, the most famous winner here was amateur Bobby Jones who, in 1926, put together a four-round total of 291 using wooden clubs and the old-fashioned ball. In the last round, when level with Al Watrous with two to play, Jones bunkered his teeshot at the 17th while Watrous hit a perfect drive and then a fine second on to the green. Jones climbed into the bunker, decided a 175-yard shot was needed if he had any chance, and hit a club similar to today's 4-iron. The shot was brilliant and finished, not only on the green, but nearer than his rival. Shaken, Watrous 3-putted, Jones got his four and finished with a perfect par while Watrous, rattled, had taken six. The club placed a plaque by the famous bunker and it's there to this day.

Since that time the course, which runs close to the railway but slightly inland from the sea, has staged other historic Opens. Bob Charles of New Zealand became the only left-hander to win the title while Tony Jacklin, in 1969, signalled the re-awakening of British golf by winning.

This huge links, founded in 1886 not far from Blackpool, is not easy. When the wind gets up it can be a nightmare. And not everyone approves a championship course that starts with a par 3 hole and it is, in fact, a rare thing in Britain. Some object to the close proximity of red-bricked houses, and aren't keen on trains that rattle past. Now there is an additional nine-hole course and a driving range.

But it's a test full of history and deserves to be played.

Visitors	Mon & Thu only (unless guest at Dormy House). Must contact in advance, and have a handicap certificate
Societies	must apply to Secretary (large groups Mon & Thur only)
Green fees	£82 per round (includes lunch)
Facilities	⊗ ⫙ ⅃ ▚ ♀ ⋈ ⚲ 📷 ✐ ⚑ Professional (E.Birchenough)
Leisure	snooker
Location	Links Gate, Lytham FY8 3LQ (0.5m E of St Annes town)

18 holes, 6334 yds, Par 71, SSS 71,

WHERE TO STAY AND EAT NEARBY

HOTELS:

LYTHAM ST ANNES
★★★★ 63% Clifton Arms, West Beach, Lytham ☎ 01253 739898 44 ⚑ ⇔

★★★ 66% Chadwick, South Promenade. ☎ 01253 720061. 75 ⇔ ⚑

★★★ 65% Bedford, 307-311 Clifton Drive South. ☎ 01253 724636. 36 (14 ⚑ 22 ⇔ ⚑)

★★ 67% Glendower, North Promenade. ☎ 01253 723241. 60 ⇔ ⚑

★★ 66% St Ives, 7-9 South Promenade. ☎ 01253 720011. 70 (3 ⚑ 60 ⇔)

RESTAURANT:

BLACKPOOL
❀ ❀ September Brasserie, 15-17 Queen St. ☎ 01253 623282

THORNTON
❀ ❀ Didier's Bistro, Trunnah Rd ☎ 01253 860619

Visitors	no restrictions.
Societies	contact in advance by telephone or in writing.
Green Fees	£10-£15 per day.
Cards	— ▨ 🖃
Prof	Lewis Ware
Designer	E Astbury
Facilities	⊗ ೬ ▼ ♀ ♨ 🖆 ⬮ ✆ ⚲
& Leisure	heated indoor swimming pool.
Location	N side of town

Hotel ★★ 70% Brabyns Hotel, 1-3 Shaftesbury Av, North Shore, BLACKPOOL
🕾 01253 354263 22 ⇄ ℕ Annexe3 ⇄ ℕ

PRESTON   Map 07 SD52

Ashton & Lea Tudor Av, Lea PR4 0XA
🕾 01772 726480 & 735282 Fax 01772 735762
Fairly flat parkland course with pond and streams, offering pleasant walks and some testing holes for golfers of all standards.
18 holes, 6370yds, Par 71, SSS 70, Course record 65.
Club membership 650.

Visitors	must contact professional on 01772 720374 or secretary on 01772 735282.
Societies	must contact in writing or by telephone.
Green Fees	£23 (£25 weekends & bank holidays).
Prof	M Greenough
Designer	J Steer
Facilities	⊗ ೬ ▼ ♀ ♨ 🖆 ✆
Location	3m W of Preston on A5085

Hotel B Posthouse Preston, Ringway, PRESTON
🕾 01772 259411 119 ⇄ ℕ

Fishwick Hall Glenluce Dr, Farringdon Park PR1 5TD
🕾 01772 798300 & 795870
Meadowland course overlooking River Ribble. Natural hazards.
18 holes, 6045yds, Par 70, SSS 69, Course record 66.
Club membership 750.

Visitors	advisable to contact in advance.
Societies	must contact in advance.
Green Fees	not confirmed.
Prof	Mike Hadfield
Facilities	⊗ ೬ ▼ ♀ ♨ 🖆 ✆

Hotel B Posthouse Preston, Ringway, PRESTON
🕾 01772 259411 119 ⇄ ℕ

Ingol Tanterton Hall Rd, Ingol PR2 7BY
🕾 01772 734556
Long, high course with natural water hazards.
18 holes, 6296yds, Par 72, SSS 70, Course record 67.
Club membership 600.

Visitors	must contact in advance but may not play on competition days.
Societies	must contact.
Green Fees	not confirmed.
Cards	— ▨ 🖃
Prof	Robert Eastwood
Facilities	⊗ ೬ ▼ ♀ ♨ 🖆 ✆
& Leisure	squash.
Location	2m NW junc 32 of M55 off B5411

Hotel B Posthouse Preston, Ringway, PRESTON
🕾 01772 259411 119 ⇄ ℕ

Penwortham Blundell Ln, Penwortham PR1 0AX
🕾 01772 744630 Fax 01772 744630
A progressive golf club set close to the banks of the River Ribble. The course has tree-lined fairways, excellent greens, and provides easy walking. Testing holes include the 178-yd, par 3 third, the 480-yd, par 5 sixth, and the 398-yd par 4 sixteenth.
18 holes, 6056yds, Par 69, SSS 69.
Club membership 975.

Visitors	must contact in advance; restricted Sun.
Societies	must apply in writing.
Green Fees	£24 per round (£31 weekends).
Prof	Norman Marshall
Facilities	⊗ ⫶ ೬ ▼ ♀ 🖆 ✆
Location	1.5m W of town centre off A59

Hotel ★★★ 66% Tickled Trout, Preston New Rd, Samlesbury, PRESTON
🕾 01772 877671 72 ⇄ ℕ

Preston Fulwood Hall Ln, Fulwood PR2 8DD
🕾 01772 700011 Fax 01772 794234
Pleasant inland golf at this course set in very agreeable parkland. There is a well-balanced selection of holes, undulating amongst groups of trees, and not requiring great length.
18 holes, 6254yds, Par 71, SSS 70.
Club membership 800.

Visitors	may play midweek only. Must contact in advance and have a handicap certificate.
Societies	must contact in writing/telephone.
Green Fees	£31 per day; £26 per round.
Prof	Andrew Greenbank
Designer	James Braid
Facilities	⊗ ⫶ ೬ ▼ ♀ ♨ 🖆 ✆
Location	N side of town centre

Hotel ★★★★ 69% Preston Marriott, Garstang Rd, Broughton, PRESTON
🕾 01772 864087 98 ⇄ ℕ

RISHTON   Map 07 SD73

Rishton Eachill Links, Hawthorn Dr BB1 4HG
🕾 01254 884442 Fax 01254 601205
Undulating moorland course.
9 holes, 6097yds, Par 70, SSS 69, Course record 68.
Club membership 270.

Visitors	must play with member on weekends and bank holidays.
Societies	must contact in writing.
Green Fees	not confirmed.
Facilities	⊗ ⫶ ೬ ▼ ♀ by arrangement ♨
Location	S side of town off A678

Hotel ★★★ 64% Dunkenhalgh Hotel, Blackburn Rd, Clayton-le-Moors, ACCRINGTON
🕾 01254 398021 37 ⇄ ℕ Annexe42 ⇄ ℕ

SILVERDALE   Map 07 SD47

Silverdale Redbridge Ln LA5 0SP
🕾 01524 701300 Fax 01524 702074
Difficult heathland course with rock outcrops. Excellent views.

12 holes, 5463yds, Par 69, SSS 67.
Club membership 500.
Visitors   may only play on Sun in summer if
              accompanied by a member.
Societies   must contact in writing.
Green Fees   £15 per day (£18 weekends & bank holidays).
Facilities   ⊗ ⅷ ⅃ ⬛ ♀ ⚲
Location   Opposite Silverdale Station

Hotel   ★★ 60% Royal Station Hotel, Market St,
              CARNFORTH ☎ 01524 732033 & 733636
              Fax 01524 720267   12 ⊨ ⋔

UPHOLLAND   Map 07 SD50

Beacon Park Beacon Ln WN8 7RU
☎ 01695 622700 Fax 01695 633066
Undulating/hilly parkland course, designed by Donald Steel,
with magnificent view of the Welsh hills. Twenty-four-bay
floodlit driving range open 9am-9pm in summer.
18 holes, 6000yds, Par 72, SSS 69, Course record 68.
Club membership 200.
Visitors   may book 6 days in advance.
Societies   must contact in advance.
Green Fees   £7 (£10 weekends & bank holidays).
Prof   Ray Peters
Designer   Donald Steel
Facilities   ⊗ ⅷ by prior arrangement ⅃ by prior
              arrangement ⬛ ♀ ⚲ ⌂ ⍓ ⚲ ⎀
Location   S of Ashurst Beacon Hill

Hotel   ★★★ 66% Holland Hall Hotel, 6 Lafford Ln,
              UPHOLLAND ☎ 01695 624426   36 ⊨ ⋔

Dean Wood Lafford Ln WN8 0QZ
☎ 01695 622219 Fax 01695 622245
This parkland course has a varied terrain - flat front nine,
undulating back nine. Beware the par 4, 11th and 17th
holes, which has ruined many a card. If there were a
prize for the best maintained course in Lancashire, Dean
Wood would be a strong contender.
18 holes, 6179yds, Par 71, SSS 71, Course record 66.
Club membership 800.
Visitors   must play with member Tue, Wed &
              weekends.
Societies   must contact in advance.
Green Fees   £27 per day (£30 weekends).
Prof   Tony Coop
Designer   James Braid
Facilities   ⊗ ⅷ ⅃ ⬛ ♀ ⚲ ⌂ ⚲
Location   1m from junct 26 of M6

Hotel   ★★★ 66% Holland Hall Hotel,
              6 Lafford Ln, UPHOLLAND
              ☎ 01695 624426   36 ⊨ ⋔

WHALLEY   Map 07 SD73

Whalley Long Leese Barn, Clerk Hill Rd BB7 9DR
☎ 01254 822236
Parkland course near Pendle Hill, overlooking the Ribble
Valley. Superb views. Ninth hole over pond.
9 holes, 6258yds, Par 72, SSS 70, Course record 69.
Club membership 400.
Visitors   must telephone 01254 824766 in advance.
Societies   must apply in writing.

Green Fees £16 per day (£20 weekends & bank holidays).
Prof   H Smith
Facilities   ⊗ ⅷ ⅃ ⬛ ♀ ⚲ ⌂ ⚲
Location   1m SE off A671

Hotel   ★★★★ 64% Clarion Hotel & Suites Foxfields,
              Whalley Rd, Billington, BLACKBURN
              ☎ 01254 822556   70 ⊨ ⋔

WHITWORTH   Map 07 SD81

Lobden Lobden Moor OL12 8XJ
☎ 01706 343228 Fax 01706 343228
Moorland course, with hard walking. Windy.
9 holes, 5697yds, Par 70, SSS 68, Course record 66.
Club membership 250.
Visitors   must contact in advance. May not play Sat.
Societies   must apply in writing to Secretary.
Green Fees   £10 per day (£15 weekends & bank holidays).
Facilities   ⊗ ⅷ ⅃ ⬛ ♀ ⚲
Location   E side of town centre off A671

Hotel   ★★ 62% Midway Park Hotel,
              Manchester Rd, Castleton, ROCHDALE
              ☎ 01706 32881 24 ⊨ ⋔

WILPSHIRE   Map 07 SD63

Wilpshire Whalley Rd BB1 9LF
☎ 01254 248260 Fax 01254 248260
Parkland/moorland course with varied and interesting holes.
Magnificent views of Ribble Valley, the coast and the
Yorkshire Dales.
18 holes, 5921yds, Par 69, SSS 66, Course record 68.
Club membership 500.
Visitors   must contact in advance.
Societies   must contact by telephone and confirm in
              writing.
Green Fees   £25.50 per day (£30.50 weekends & bank
              holidays).
Prof   Walter Slaven
Designer   James Braid
Facilities   ⊗ ⅷ ⅃ ⬛ ♀ ⚲ ⌂ ⍓ ⚲
Location   2m NE of Blackburn, on A666 towards
              Clitheroe

Hotel   ★★★ 61% County Hotel Blackburn, Preston
              New Rd, BLACKBURN
              ☎ 01254 899988 101 ⊨ ⋔

LEICESTERSHIRE

ASHBY-DE-LA-ZOUCH   Map 08 SK31

Willesley Park Measham Rd LE65 2PF
☎ 01530 414596 Fax 01530 414596
Undulating heathland and parkland course with quick
draining sandy sub-soil.
18 holes, 6304yds, Par 70, SSS 70, Course record 64.
Club membership 600.
Visitors   must contact in advance. Restricted weekends.
              Handicap certificate required.   ▶

Societies Wed-Fri only. Must apply in writing.
Green Fees £30 (£35 weekends and bank holidays).
Prof C J Hancock
Designer J Braid
Facilities ⊗ ⍔ ᗷ ☕ ♀ ⚲ 🏠 ⚙ ⚙
Location SW side of town centre on A453

Hotel ★★★ 62% The Fallen Knight,
Kilwardby St, ASHBY-DE-LA ZOUCH
☎ 01530 412230 24 ⇆ ♠

BIRSTALL   Map 04 SK50

Birstall Station Rd LE4 3BB
☎ 0116 267 4322 Fax 0116 267 4322
Parkland course with trees, shrubs, ponds and ditches.
18 holes, 6222yds, Par 70, SSS 70.
Club membership 650.
Visitors with member only weekends; may not play Tue,
Wed & Fri after 9am.
Societies apply in writing.
Green Fees £25 per day; £20 per round.
Prof David Clark
Facilities ⊗ ᗷ ☕ ♀ ⚲ 🏠 ⚙
& Leisure snooker & pool room.
Location 3m N of Leicester on A6

Hotel ★★★ 60% Hotel Saint James, Abbey St,
LEICESTER ☎ 0116 251 0666 73 ⇆ ♠

BOTCHESTON   Map 04 SK40

Forest Hill Markfield Ln LE9 9FJ
☎ 01455 824800 Fax 01455 828522
Parkland course with many trees, four Par 4s, but no steep
gradients.
18 holes, 6039yds, Par 72, SSS 69.
Club membership 450.
Visitors must contact in advance for weekends.
Societies Mon-Fri, must telephone in advance.
Green Fees not confirmed.
Prof Philip Harness
Facilities ⊗ ⍔ ᗷ ☕ ♀ ⚲ 🏠 ⚙ ⚙

Hotel ★★★ 65% Field Head Hotel, Markfield Ln,
MARKFIELD ☎ 01530 245454 28 ⇆ ♠

COSBY   Map 04 SP59

Cosby Chapel Ln, Broughton Rd LE9 1RG
☎ 0116 286 4759 Fax 0116 286 4484
Undulating parkland course with a number of tricky, tight
driving holes.
18 holes, 6410yds, Par 71, SSS 71, Course record 68.
Club membership 750.
Visitors welcome weekdays before 4pm. May not play at
weekends. Recommended to telephone in
advance. Handicap certificate required.
Societies book with secretary.
Green Fees £26 per day; £18 per round.
Prof Martin Wing
Designer Hawtree
Facilities ⊗ by prior arrangement ⍔ by prior arrangement
ᗷ ☕ ♀ ⚲ 🏠 ⚙ ⚙
Location S side of village

Hotel B Posthouse Leicester, Braunstone Ln East,
LEICESTER ☎ 0116 263 0500 172 ⇆ ♠

EAST GOSCOTE   Map 08 SK61

Beedles Lake 170 Broome Ln LE7 3WQ ☎ 0116 260 6759
Fairly flat parkland course, founded in 1992, with an
adjoining lake and well maintained greens.
18 holes, 6625yds, Par 72, SSS 72, Course record 71.
Club membership 400.
Visitors telephone booking required for weekends.
Societies welcome Mon-Fri
Green Fees £9.50 per round (£12.50 weekends) £7.50
twilight round.
Prof Sean Byrne
Designer D Tucker
Facilities ⊗ ⍔ ᗷ ☕ ♀ ⚲ 🏠 ⚙ ⚙ ⚙
& Leisure fishing.
Location Off A46, just N of Leicester through village of
Ratcliffe on the Wreake

Hotel ★★★ 61% Rothley Court,
Westfield Ln, ROTHLEY
☎ 0116 237 4141 13 ⇆ ♠ Annexe21 ⇆ ♠

ENDERBY   Map 04 SP59

Enderby Mill Ln LE9 5HL
☎ 0116 284 9388 Fax 0116 284 9388
A gently undulating 9-hole course at which beginners are
especially welcome. The longest hole is the 2nd at 407 yards
and there are 5 Par 3's.
9 holes, 2133yds, Par 31, SSS 31, Course record 27.
Club membership 150.
Visitors no restrictions.
Societies must telephone in advance.
Green Fees not confirmed.
Prof Chris D'Araujo
Designer David Lowe
Facilities ᗷ ☕ ♀ ⚲ 🏠 ⚙ ⚙
& Leisure heated indoor swimming pool, squash, sauna,
solarium, gymnasium.
Location 2m S, M1 junct21 on Narborough road. Right
turn off roundabout at Foxhunter pub, 0.5m on
left

Hotel ★★ 65% Charnwood Hotel,
48 Leicester Rd, Narborough, LEICESTER
☎ 0116 286 2218 20 ⇆ ♠

HINCKLEY   Map 04 SP49

Hinckley Leicester Rd LE10 3DR
☎ 01455 615124 & 615014 Fax 01455 890841
Rolling parkland with lake features, and lined fairways.
18 holes, 6517yds, Par 71, SSS 71, Course record 65.
Club membership 1000.
Visitors with member only weekends and bank holidays.
Must contact in advance and have a handicap
certificate.
Societies must contact in advance.
Green Fees £30 per day; £25 per round.
Cards 🖃 🖃 🖃 🖃
Prof Richard Jones
Facilities ⊗ ⍔ ᗷ ☕ ♀ ⚲ 🏠 ⚙ ⚙ ⚙ ⚙
Location 1.5m NE on B4668

Hotel ★★ 67% Longshoot Toby Hotel,
Watling St, NUNEATON
☎ 01203 329711 Annexe47 ⇆ ♠

KETTON   Map 04 SK90

Luffenham Heath PE9 3UU
☎ 01780 720205 Fax 01780 722146
This undulating heathland course with low bushes, much gorse and many trees, lies in a conservation area for flora and fauna. From the higher part of the course there is a magnificent view across the Chater Valley.
18 holes, 6273yds, Par 70, SSS 70, Course record 64.
Club membership 550.
Visitors   must contact in advance.
Societies   write or telephone in advance.
Green Fees £35 (£40 weekends).
Cards   ▭
Prof   Ian Burnett
Designer   James Braid
Facilities ⊗ by prior arrangement ⁋⁋⁋ by prior arrangement ⫫ ♛ ♟ ⚑ ⚐ ⛳ ✎
Location   1.5m SW of Ketton by Fosters Railway Bridge on A6121

Hotel   ★★★ 75% The George of Stamford, 71 St Martins, STAMFORD
                ☎ 01780 750750 47 ⇆ ฿

KIBWORTH   Map 04 SP69

Kibworth Weir Rd, Beauchamp LE8 0LP
☎ 0116 279 2301 Fax 0116 279 2301
Parkland course with easy walking. A brook affects a number of fairways
18 holes, 6333yds, Par 71, SSS 70, Course record 65.
Club membership 700.
Visitors   must contact in advance. With member only weekends.
Societies   must contact in advance.
Green Fees £30 per day; £23 per round.
Prof   Bob Larratt
Facilities ⊗ ⁋⁋⁋ ⫫ ♛ ♟ ⚑ ⚐ ⛳ ✎ ฿
Location   S side of village off A6

Hotel   ★★★ 68% Three Swans Hotel, 21 High St, MARKET HARBOROUGH
                ☎ 01858 466644 20 ⇆ ฿ Annexe16 ⇆ ฿

KIRBY MUXLOE   Map 04 SK50

Kirby Muxloe Station Rd LE9 2EP
☎ 0116 239 3457 Fax 0116 239 3457
Pleasant parkland course with a lake in front of the 17th green and a short 18th.
18 holes, 6351yds, Par 70, SSS 70, Course record 65.
Club membership 890.
Visitors   must contact in advance and a handicap certificate is required. No visitors on Tue or at weekends.
Societies   must contact in advance.
Green Fees £30 per day; £25 per round.
Prof   Bruce Whipham
Facilities ⊗ ⁋⁋⁋ ⫫ ♛ ♟ ⚑ ⚐ ⛳ ✎ ฿
Location   S side of village off B5380

Hotel   ★★★★ 59% Holiday Inn, St Nicholas Circle, LEICESTER ☎ 0116 253 1161 188 ⇆ ฿

LEICESTER   Map 04 SK50

Humberstone Heights Gypsy Ln LE5 0TB
☎ 0116 276 3680 & 299 5570 (Pro Shop
Municipal parkland course with 9 hole pitch and putt and 30 bay driving range.
18 holes, 6343yds, Par 70, SSS 70, Course record 66.
Club membership 400.
Visitors   must telephone in advance at weekends.
Societies   must telephone in advance.
Green Fees Summer: £8.75-£10.25; Winter: £7.75-£9.25.
Cards   ▭ ▭▭ ▭▭ ⊘
Prof   John Allcock
Designer   Hawtry & Sons
Facilities ⊗ by prior arrangement ⁋⁋⁋ by prior arrangement ♛ ♟ ⚑ ♟ ⚐ ⛳ ✎ ⚑ ⛳ ✎ ฿
Location   2.5m NE of city centre

Hotel   ★★★ 72% Belmont House Hotel, De Montfort St, LEICESTER
                ☎ 0116 254 4773 75rm(74 ⇆ ฿)

Leicestershire Evington Ln LE5 6DJ
☎ 0116 273 8825 Fax 0116 273 8825
Pleasantly undulating parkland course.
18 holes, 6326yds, Par 68, SSS 70, Course record 63.
Club membership 800.
Visitors   must contact in advance. May not play Sat. Must hold a handicap certificate.
Societies   must contact in advance.
Green Fees £29 per day; £24 per round (£35/£30 weekends & bank holidays).
Prof   John R Turnbull
Designer   Hawtree
Facilities ⊗ ⁋⁋⁋ ⫫ ♛ ♟ ⚑ ⚐ ⛳ ✎
Location   2m E of city off A6030

Hotel   ★★★ 67% Hermitage Hotel, Wigston Rd, Oadby, LEICESTER ☎ 0116 256 9955 57 ⇆ ฿

Western Scudamore Rd, Braunstone Frith LE3 1UQ
☎ 0116 299 5566 Fax 0116 299 5568
Pleasant, undulating parkland course with open aspect fairways in two loops of nine holes.Not too difficult but a good test of golf off the back tees.
18 holes, 6518yds, Par 72, SSS 71.
Club membership 400.
Visitors   must contact in advance.
Societies   must contact the professional in advance.
Green Fees £8.75 (£10.25 weekends).
Cards   ▭ ▭▭ ▭▭ ⊘
Prof   Dave Butler
Facilities ⊗ ⁋⁋⁋ ⫫ ♛ ♟ ⚑ ⚐ ⛳ ✎ ฿
Location   1.5m W of city centre off A47

Hotel   B Posthouse Leicester, Braunstone Ln East, LEICESTER ☎ 0116 263 0500 172 ⇆ ฿

LOUGHBOROUGH   Map 08 SK51

Longcliffe Snell's Nook Ln, Nanpantan LE11 3YA
☎ 01509 239129 Fax 01509 231286
A re-designed course of natural heathland with outcrops of granite forming natural hazards especially on the 1st and 15th. The course is heavily wooded and has much bracken and gorse. There are a number of tight fairways and one blind hole. ▶

18 holes, 6625yds, Par 72, SSS 72.
Club membership 660.
Visitors must contact in advance. With member only at weekends.
Societies telephone for availability, handicap certificate required.
Green Fees £34 per day; £27 per round.
Prof Ian D Bailey
Designer Williamson
Facilities ⊗ ⵿ ⅃ ┗ ■ ♀ ⚑ ╒ ✓
Location 3m SW off B5350

Hotel ★★★ 63% Quality Hotel, New Ashby Rd, LOUGHBOROUGH ☎ 01509 211800 94 ⇔ ⋔

LUTTERWORTH   Map 04 SP58

Kilworth Springs South Kilworth Rd, North Kilworth LE17 6HJ ☎ 01858 575082 & 575974 Fax 01858 575078
An 18-hole course of two loops of 9: the front 9 are links style while the back 9 are in parkland with 4 lakes. On a windy day it is a very challenging course and the 6th hole is well deserving of its nickname 'the Devil's Toenail'.
18 holes, 6543yds, Par 72, SSS 71, Course record 66.
Club membership 800.
Visitors welcome subject to availability. May only play after 12am at weekends.
Societies contact in advance.
Green Fees £17 per round (£21 weekends).
Cards 〰
Prof N Melvin
Facilities ⊗ ⵿ ⅃ ┗ ■ ♀ ⚑ ╒ ⚒ ✓ ╏
Location 4m E of M1 junc 20, A4304 to Mkt Harborough

Hotel ★★★ 55% Denbigh Arms Hotel, High St, LUTTERWORTH ☎ 01455 553537 31 ⇔ ⋔

Lutterworth Rugby Rd LE17 4HN
☎ 01455 552532 Fax 01455 553586
Hilly course with River Swift running through.
18 holes, 6226yds, Par 70, SSS 70.
Club membership 700.
Visitors must play with member at weekends.
Societies must contact in advance.
Green Fees not confirmed.
Prof Roland Tisdall
Facilities ⊗ ⵿ ⅃ ┗ ■ ♀ ⚑ ╒ ⚒ ➔ ✓ ╏
Location 0.5m S on A426

Hotel ★★★ 55% Denbigh Arms Hotel, High St, LUTTERWORTH ☎ 01455 553537 31 ⇔ ⋔

MARKET HARBOROUGH   Map 04 SP78

Market Harborough Oxendon Rd LE16 8NF
☎ 01858 463684
A parkland course situated close to the town. There are wide-ranging views over the surrounding countryside. Lakes a feature on 4 holes; challenging last 3 holes.
18 holes, 6070yds, Par 70, SSS 69, Course record 63.
Club membership 600.
Visitors must play with member at weekends.
Societies must apply in writing.

Green Fees £25 per day; £20 per round.
Prof Frazer Baxter
Designer H Swan
Facilities ⊗ ⵿ ⅃ ┗ ■ ♀ ⚑ ╒ ✓
Location 1m S on A508

Hotel ★★★ 68% Three Swans Hotel, 21 High St, MARKET HARBOROUGH ☎ 01858 466644 20 ⇔ ⋔ Annexe16 ⇔ ⋔

Stoke Albany Ashley Rd, Stoke Albany LE16 8PL
☎ 01858 535208 Fax 01858 535505
Parkland course in the picturesque Welland Valley. Affording good views, the course should appeal to the mid-handicap golfer, and provide an interesting test to the more experienced player.
18 holes, 6132yds, Par 71, SSS 69.
Club membership 400.
Visitors welcome at all times.
Societies please telephone secretary.
Green Fees £13 per 18 holes (£18 weekends).
Prof Adrian Clifford
Designer Hawtree
Facilities ⊗ ⵿ ⅃ ┗ ■ ♀ ⚑ ╒ ✓
Location Located N off A427 Market Harborough/Corby Road, follow Stoke Albany 500m towards Ashley village

Hotel ★★★ 68% Three Swans Hotel, 21 High St, MARKET HARBOROUGH ☎ 01858 466644 20 ⇔ ⋔ Annexe16 ⇔ ⋔

MELTON MOWBRAY   Map 08 SK71

Melton Mowbray Waltham Rd, Thorpe Arnold LE14 4SD
☎ 01664 562118 Fax 01664 562118
Downland but flat course providing easy walking.
18 holes, 6222yds, Par 70, SSS 70.
Club membership 650.
Visitors must contact professional on 01664 569629.
Societies must contact in advance.
Green Fees £20 (£23 weekends).
Prof James Hetherington
Facilities ⊗ ⅃ ┗ ■ ♀ ⚑ ╒ ⚒ ✓
Location 2m NE of Melton Mowbray on A607

Hotel ★★★ 64% Sysonby Knoll Hotel, Asfordby Rd, MELTON MOWBRAY ☎ 01664 563563 23 ⇔ ⋔ Annexe1 ⇔ ⋔

OADBY   Map 04 SK60

Glen Gorse Glen Rd LE2 4RF
☎ 0116 271 4159 Fax 0116 271 4159
Fairly flat 18-hole parkland course with some strategically placed mature trees, new saplings and ponds affecting play on 6 holes. Ridge and furrow is a feature of 5 holes.
18 holes, 6648yds, Par 72, SSS 72, Course record 67.
Club membership 600.
Visitors must contact in advance. Must play with member at weekends.
Societies must telephone secretary in advance.
Green Fees £28.50 per day; £24 per round.
Prof Dominic Fitzpatrick
Facilities ⊗ ⵿ ⅃ ┗ ■ ♀ ⚑ ╒ ✓
& Leisure snooker.
Location On A6 trunk road between Oadby/Great Glen

Hotel ★★★ 67% Hermitage Hotel,
Wigston Rd, Oadby, LEICESTER
☎ 0116 256 9955 57 ⇆ ♠

Oadby Leicester Rd LE2 4AJ ☎ 0116 270 9052
Municipal parkland course.
18 holes, 6376yds, Par 72, SSS 70, Course record 60.
Club membership 500.
Visitors no restrictions.
Societies by arrangement contact pro shop.
Green Fees not confirmed.
Prof Alan Kershaw
Facilities ⊗ ⅲ ⓛ ♥ ♀ ♧ ♠ ♍ ⌀
Location West of Oadby, off A6

Hotel ★★★ 67% Hermitage Hotel,
Wigston Rd, Oadby, LEICESTER
☎ 0116 256 9955 57 ⇆ ♠

ROTHLEY
Map 08 SK51

Rothley Park Westfield Ln LE7 7LH
☎ 0116 230 2809 Fax 0116 230 2809
Parkland course in picturesque situation.
18 holes, 6477yds, Par 71, SSS 71, Course record 67.
Club membership 600.
Visitors must contact professional on 0116 230 3023.
Weekends and bankholidays with member only.
Societies apply in writing to secretary.
Green Fees £30 per day; £25 per round.
Prof Andrew Collins
Facilities ⊗ ⅲ ⓛ ♥ ♀ ♧ ♠ ♍ ⌀
Location Off A6 N of Leicester

Hotel ★★★ 61% Rothley Court,
Westfield Ln, ROTHLEY
☎ 0116 237 4141 13 ⇆ ♠ Annexe21 ⇆ ♠

SCRAPTOFT
Map 04 SK60

Scraptoft Beeby Rd LE7 9SJ ☎ 0116 241 8863
Pleasant, inland country course.
18 holes, 6166yds, Par 70, SSS 70.
Club membership 650.
Visitors with member only weekends. Handicap
certificate required.
Societies apply in writing.
Green Fees not confirmed.
Prof Simon Wood
Facilities ⊗ ⅲ ⓛ ♥ ♀ ♧ ♠ ♍ ⌀
Location 1m NE

Hotel ★★★ 67% Hermitage Hotel,
Wigston Rd, Oadby, LEICESTER
☎ 0116 256 9955 57 ⇆ ♠

SEAGRAVE
Map 08 SK61

Park Hill Park Hill LE12 7NG
☎ 01509 815454 & 815775 (pro) Fax 01509 816062
A new rolling parkland course with tree lined fairways and
views over Charnwood Forest. The opening hole is 420yards
with a forced water carry 100yards short of the green. The
10th is a 610yard Par 5 against the prevailing wind and there
are 2 Par 5's to finish.

18 holes, 7219yds, Par 73, SSS 74, Course record 71.
Club membership 500.
Visitors must contact in advance.
Societies apply in advance.
Green Fees £28 per 36 holes, £24 per 27 holes, £20 per 18
holes (£36/£30/£24 weekends and bank
holidays).
Prof David C Mee
Facilities ⊗ ⅲ ⓛ ♥ ♀ ♧ ♠ ⌀
Location 6m N of Leicester on A46

Hotel ★★★ 63% Quality Hotel,
New Ashby Rd, LOUGHBOROUGH
☎ 01509 211800 94 ⇆ ♠

ULLESTHORPE
Map 04 SP58

Ullesthorpe Frolesworth Rd LE17 5BZ
☎ 01455 209023 Fax 01455 202537
Set in 130 acres of parkland surrounding a 17th-century
manor house, this championship length course can be very
demanding and offers a challenge to both beginners and
professionals. Excellent leisure facilities. Water plays a part
on 3 holes.
18 holes, 6650yds, Par 72, SSS 72, Course record 67.
Club membership 650.
Visitors must contact in advance. With member only Sat,
no play on Sun.
Societies contact well in advance.
Green Fees Mon-Fri: £29 per day, £17 per round.
Cards ▬ ▬ ▣ ▬ ▬ ▣
Prof David Bowring
Facilities ⊗ ⅲ ⓛ ♥ ♀ ♧ ♠ ♍ ⛳ ➤ ⚒ ⌀
& Leisure hard tennis courts, heated indoor swimming
pool, sauna, solarium, gymnasium, snooker
tables, beauty room, steam room.
Location 0.5m N off B577

Hotel ★★★ 70% Ullesthorpe Court Country Hotel &
Golf Club, Frolesworth Rd, ULLESTHORPE
☎ 01455 209023 38 ⇆ ♠

WHETSTONE
Map 04 SP59

Whetstone Cambridge Rd, Cosby LE9 1SJ
☎ 0116 286 1424 Fax 0116 286 1424
Small and very flat parkland course adjacent to motorway.
18 holes, 5795yds, Par 68, SSS 68.
Club membership 500.
Visitors limited times at weekends.
Societies must contact in advance.
Green Fees £20 per 36 holes; £14 per 18 holes (£16 per 18
holes). ▶

Cards

Prof David Raitt

Facilities ⓧ 〠 ⅃ ⅃ ♥ ⅄ ⅄ ♜ ♘ ⌀ ⏋

Location 1m S of village

Hotel ★★★ 66% Time Out Hotel & Leisure, Enderby Rd, Blaby, LEICESTER ☎ 0116 278 7898 28 ⇄ 🐾

WILSON   Map 08 SK42

Breedon Priory Green Ln DE73 1AT ☎ 01332 863081
A relatively short and forgiving course set in undulating countryside with magnificent views from several holes.
18 holes, 5530yds, Par 70, SSS 67, Course record 67.
Club membership 779.

Visitors may play any time if tee available, must book for weekends.

Societies apply in writing or telephone for booking form.

Green Fees not confirmed.

Prof Ben Hill

Designer David Snell

Facilities ⅃ ♥ ⅄ ⅄ ♜ ♘ ⌀ ⏋

Location 4m W of A42/M1 junct 24

Hotel ★★★ 69% The Priest House on the River, Kings Mills, CASTLE DONINGTON ☎ 01332 810649 25 ⇄ 🐾 Annexe20 ⇄ 🐾

WOODHOUSE EAVES   Map 08 SK51

Charnwood Forest Breakback Ln LE12 8TA
☎ 01509 890259 Fax 01509 890925
Hilly heathland course with hard walking, but no bunkers.
9 holes, 5960yds, Par 69, SSS 69, Course record 64.
Club membership 210.

Visitors must contact in advance.

Societies Wed & Thu only. Must contact in advance. Mon & Fri by special arrangement.

Green Fees £10-£25 (£25 per 18 holes weekdays & bank holidays).

Designer James Braid

Facilities ⓧ ⅃ ♥ ⅄ ⅄

Location 3m from junct 22 or 23 of M1

Hotel ★★★★ 71% Quorn Country Hotel, Charnwood House, Leicester Rd, QUORN ☎ 01509 415050 23 ⇄ 🐾

Lingdale Joe Moore's Ln LE12 8TF ☎ 01509 890703
Parkland course located in Charnwood Forest with some hard walking at some holes. The par 3, (3rd) and par 5, (8th) are testing holes. Several holes have water hazards.
18 holes, 6545yds, Par 71, SSS 71, Course record 68.
Club membership 610.

Visitors must telephone professional in advance for weekend play.

Societies must contact in advance.

Green Fees not confirmed.

Prof Peter Sellears

Designer David Tucker

Facilities ⓧ 〠 ⅃ ♥ ⅄ ⅄ ♜ ⌀

Location 1.5m S off B5330

Hotel ★★★★ 71% Quorn Country Hotel, Charnwood House, Leicester Rd, QUORN ☎ 01509 415050 23 ⇄ 🐾

BELTON   Map 08 SK93

Belton Woods Hotel NG32 2LN
☎ 01476 593200 Fax 01476 574547
Two challenging 18-hole courses, a 9-hole Par 3 and a driving range. The Lakes Course has 13 lakes, while The Woodside boasts the third longest hole in Europe at 613 yards. Many leisure facilities.
The Lakes Course: 18 holes, 6808yds, Par 72, SSS 72, Course record 68.
The Woodside Course: 18 holes, 6605yds, Par 73, SSS 72.
Spitfire Course: 9 holes, 1116yds, Par 27, SSS 27.
Club membership 500.

Visitors book tee times in advance with exception of the Spitfire. Dress code ie. no jeans and spike shoes must be worn.

Societies welcome all week, reservations to be made by telephone or letter.

Green Fees Lakes or Woodside: £26 Mon-Thu; £30 Fri-Sun. Spitfire £5.

Cards

Prof Myles Foster

Facilities ⓧ 〠 ⅃ ♥ ⅄ ⅄ ♜ ♘ ⌀ ⏋

& Leisure hard tennis courts, heated indoor swimming pool, squash, sauna, solarium, gymnasium, tuition, beauty salon, fitness assessment.

Location On A607, 2m N of Grantham

Hotel ★★★★ 73% Belton Woods Hotel, BELTON ☎ 01476 593200 136 ⇄ 🐾

BLANKNEY   Map 08 TF06

Blankney LN4 3AZ
☎ 01526 320263 Fax 01526 322521
Open parkland course with mature trees; fairly flat.
18 holes, 6634yds, Par 72, SSS 73, Course record 69.
Club membership 640.

Visitors must contact in advance, may not play Wed mornings, restricted at weekends.

Societies not Wed mornings, booking required.

Green Fees £25 per day; £20 per round (£35/£30 weekends & bank holidays).

Prof Graham Bradley

Designer C Sinclair

Facilities ⓧ 〠 ⅃ ♥ ⅄ ⅄ ♜ ⌀

& Leisure snooker.

Location 10m SW on B1188

Hotel ★★★ 60% Moor Lodge Hotel, Sleaford Rd, BRANSTON ☎ 01522 791366 24 ⇔ ⋔

BOSTON — Map 08 TF34

Boston Cowbridge, Horncastle Rd PE22 7EL
☎ 01205 350589 Fax 01205 350589
Parkland course many water hazards in play on ten holes.
18 holes, 6490yds, Par 72, SSS 71, Course record 69.
Club membership 650.
Visitors evidence of handicap may be requested, contact in advance for tee time.
Societies apply in writing.
Green Fees £24 per day; £18 per round (£30/£24 weekends & bank holidays).
Prof Terry Squires
Facilities ⊗ ⊞ ⓛ ☕ ♀ △ 🏠 ⋔ ∂
Location 2m N of Boston on B1183

Hotel ★★★ 61% New England, 49 Wide Bargate, BOSTON ☎ 01205 365255 25 ⇔ ⋔

Kirton Holme Holme Rd, Kirton Holme PE20 1SY
☎ 01205 290669
A young parkland course designed for mid to high handicappers. It is flat but has 2500 young trees, two natural water course plus water hazards. The 2nd is a challenging, 386yard Par 4 dogleg.
9 holes, 5778yds, Par 70, SSS 68, Course record 71.
Club membership 350.
Visitors no restrictions but booking advisable for weekends & summer evenings.
Societies by prior arrangement.
Green Fees £8 per day; £4.50 per 9 holes (£9/£5.50 weekends & bank holidays).
Designer D W Welberry
Facilities ⊗ ⓛ ☕ ♀ △ ⋔ ∂
Location 4m W of Boston off A52

Hotel ★★ 67% Comfort Inn, Donnington Rd, Bicker Bar, BOSTON ☎ 01205 820118 55 ⇔ ⋔

BOURNE — Map 08 TF02

Toft Hotel Toft PE10 0JT
☎ 01778 590614 Fax 01778 590264
Parkland course on the verge of the Lincoln Edge. Includes lake and uses contours of the hills to full effect.
18 holes, 6486yds, Par 72, SSS 71, Course record 63.
Club membership 450.

Visitors advisable to book for weekends.
Societies apply in advance by telephone.
Green Fees £25 per 36 holes; £16 per 18 holes (£33/£20 weekends).
Cards ▬ 🟦 🟦 🟦 💳
Prof Mark Jackson
Designer Roger Fitton
Facilities ⊗ ⊞ ⓛ ☕ ♀ △ 🏠 ⋔ 🏐 ╲ 🛒 ∂ ✦
Location On A6121 Bourne/Stamford road

Hotel ★★ 57% Angel Hotel, Market Place, BOURNE ☎ 01778 422346 14 ⇔ ⋔

CLEETHORPES — Map 08 TA30

Cleethorpes Kings Rd DN35 0PN ☎ 01472 814060
Flat meadowland seaside course intersected by large dykes.
18 holes, 6349yds, Par 70, SSS 69, Course record 64.
Club membership 720.
Visitors restricted Wed afternoons, handicap certificate preferred.
Societies Tue, Thu or Fri only. Must contact in advance.
Green Fees not confirmed.
Prof Paul Davies
Designer Harry Vardon
Facilities ⊗ ⊞ ⓛ ☕ ♀ △ 🏠 ∂
Location 1.5m S off A1031

Hotel ★★★ 70% Kingsway Hotel, Kingsway, CLEETHORPES ☎ 01472 601122 50 ⇔ ⋔

Tetney Station Rd, Tetney DN36 5HY
☎ 01472 211644 & 811344 Fax 01472 211644
18-hole parkland course set at the foot of the Linclolnshire Wolds. Noted for its challenging water features.
18 holes, 6100yds, Par 71, SSS 69.
Club membership 450.
Visitors contact in advance.
Societies apply in writing.
Green Fees £10 per 18 holes; £7.50 per 11 holes; £5 per 7 holes (£11/£7.50/£5 weekends).
Cards 🟦 🟦 💳
Prof Jason Abrams
Designer J S Grant
Facilities ⊗ ⊞ ⓛ ☕ ♀ △ 🏠 ⋔ 🏐 🛒 ∂
Location 1m off A16 Louth/Grimsby road

Hotel ★★★ 70% Kingsway Hotel, Kingsway, CLEETHORPES ☎ 01472 601122 50 ⇔ ⋔

ELSHAM — Map 08 TA01

Elsham Barton Rd DN20 0LS ☎ 01652 680291
Parkland course in country surroundings. Easy walking.
18 holes, 6429yds, Par 71, SSS 71, Course record 67.
Club membership 650.
Visitors with member only weekends & bank holidays. Must contact in advance.
Societies must apply in writing.
Green Fees £24 per day/round.
Prof Stuart Brewer
Facilities ⊗ ⊞ ⓛ ☕ ♀ △ 🏠 🛒 ∂
Location 2m SW on B1206

Hotel ★★★ 66% Wortley House Hotel, Rowland Rd, SCUNTHORPE ☎ 01724 842223 38 ⇔ ⋔

GAINSBOROUGH   Map 08 SK88

Gainsborough Thonock DN21 1PZ
☎ 01427 613088 Fax 01427 810172
Thonock Park course, founded in 1894 and redesigned in
1987, is an attractive parkland course with many deciduous
trees. Karsten Lakes course is a new championship course
designed by Neil Coles and opened in April 1997. Set in
rolling countryside the lakes and well bunkered greens
provide a true test of golf. Floodlit driving range.
*Thonock Park: 18 holes, 6266yds, Par 72, SSS 70, Course
record 63.*
*Karsten Lakes: 18 holes, 6721yds, Par 72, SSS 72, Course
record 65.*
Club membership 600.
Visitors Thonock Park: welcome weekdays. Ladies Day
Thu morning. Karsten Lakes: welcome 7 days,
advance booking available.
Societies must telephone in advance.
Green Fees Thonock Park £25 per day, £18 per round.
Karsten Lakes £35 per day, £25 per round.
Cards ⊟ 💳 📇 📇 🗘
Prof Stephen Cooper
Designer Neil Coles
Facilities ⊗ �竹 🖢 🖳 ♀ 🛆 🖾 ⛳ 🐾 �', '🏌 ❗
Location 1m N off A159. Signposted off A631

Hotel ★★★ 64% West Retford Hotel, 24 North Rd,
RETFORD ☎ 01777 706333 Annexe60 ⇄ 🏌

GEDNEY HILL   Map 08 TF31

Gedney Hill West Drove PE12 0NT
☎ 01406 330922 Fax 01406 330323
Flat parkland course similar to a links course. Made testing
by Fen winds and small greens. Also a 10-bay driving range.
18 holes, 5493yds, Par 70, SSS 66, Course record 67.
Club membership 300.
Visitors no restrictions.
Societies telephone in advance.
Green Fees £6.25 (£10.50 weekends).
Cards ⊟ 💳
Prof David Hutton
Designer Monkwise Ltd
Facilities ⊗ �竹 🖢 🖳 ♀ 🛆 🖾 ⛳ 🏌 ❗
& Leisure bowling green, snooker room.
Location 5m SE of Spalding

Hotel ★★ 63% Rose & Crown Hotel, Market Place,
WISBECH ☎ 01945 589800 20 ⇄ 🏌

GRANTHAM   Map 08 SK93

Belton Park Belton Ln, Londonthorpe Rd NG31 9SH
☎ 01476 567399 Fax 01476 592078
Three 9-hole courses set in classic mature parkland of Lord
Brownlow's country seat, Belton House. Gently undulating
with streams, ponds, plenty of trees and beautiful scenery,
including a deer park. Famous holes: 5th, 12th, 16th and
18th. Combine any of the three courses for a testing 18-hole
round.
*Brownlow: 18 holes, 6420yds, Par 71, SSS 71, Course record
65.*
Ancaster: 18 holes, 6252yds, Par 70, SSS 70.
Belmont: 18 holes, 6016yds, Par 69, SSS 69.
Club membership 850.

Visitors contact for tee booking.
Societies apply in advance.
Green Fees £30 per day; £24 per round (£36/£30 weekends
& bank holidays).
Cards ⊟ 💳
Prof Brian McKee
Designer Williamson/Allis
Facilities ⊗ �竹 🖢 🖳 ♀ 🛆 🖾 ⛳ 🏌
Location 1.5m NE of Grantham

Hotel ★★★ 68% Kings Hotel, North Pde,
GRANTHAM ☎ 01476 590800 21 ⇄ 🏌

Sudbrook Moor Charity St, Carlton Scroop NG32 3AT
☎ 01400 250796 Fax 01400 250796
A testing 9-hole parkland/meadowland course in a
picturesque valley setting with easy walking.
9 holes, 4811yds, Par 66, SSS 64, Course record 69.
Visitors telephone in advance.
Green Fees Summer: £6 per day (£9 weekends); Winter: £5
per day (£7 weekends).
Cards ⊟ 💳
Prof Tim Hutton
Designer Tim Hutton
Facilities ⊗ 🖳 ♀ 🛆 🖾 ⛳ 🏌
Location 6m NE of Grantham on A607

Hotel ★★★ 68% Kings Hotel, North Pde,
GRANTHAM ☎ 01476 590800 21 ⇄ 🏌

GRIMSBY   Map 08 TA21

Grimsby Littlecoates Rd DN34 4LU
☎ 01472 342630 Fax 01472 342630
Undulating parkland course.
18 holes, 6098yds, Par 70, SSS 69, Course record 66.
Club membership 730.
Visitors contact in advance.
Societies by prior arrangement with secretary.
Green Fees not confirmed.
Prof Richard Smith
Designer Colt
Facilities ⊗ ⲕ 🖢 🖳 ♀ 🛆 🖾 ⛳
Location 1m from A180 & 1m from A46

Hotel B Posthouse Grimsby, Littlecoates Rd,
GRIMSBY ☎ 01472 350295 52 ⇄ 🏌

HORNCASTLE   Map 08 TF26

Horncastle West Ashby LN9 5PP ☎ 01507 526800
Heathland course with many water hazards and bunkers; very
challenging. There is a 25-bay floodlit driving range.
18 holes, 5717yds, Par 70, SSS 70, Course record 71.
Club membership 200.
Visitors dress code must be adhered to, welcome
anytime, may contact in advance.
Societies apply in writing or telephone in advance.
Green Fees £15 per day; £10 per round.
Prof E C Wright
Designer E C Wright
Facilities ⊗ ⲕ 🖢 🖳 ♀ 🛆 ⛳ 🖾 🏌 ❗
& Leisure fishing.
Location Off A158 Lincoln/Skegness road at Edlington,
off A153 at West Ashby

Hotel ★★ 70% Admiral Rodney Hotel, North St,
HORNCASTLE ☎ 01507 523131 31 ⇄ 🏌

The Admiral Rodney Hotel is situated in the Market Town of Horncastle, well known for its many Antique Shops, and has a reputation for friendliness. All bedrooms are en-suite, and the hotel benefits from a full refurbishment. The splendid furnishings and unique decor of the Courtyard Restaurant provides a delightful setting for dinner and the popular Rodney Bar, with it's 'Nautical Theme' serves a selection of Real Ales.

SPECIAL GOLFING BREAKS AVAILABLE WITH LOUTH AND HORNCASTLE GOLF CLUB

AA
★★

North Street, Horncastle, Lincoln LN9 5DX
Telephone: 01507 523131   Fax: 01507 523104
10 minutes drive from Woodhall Spa's Famous Courses

IMMINGHAM   Map 08 TA11

Immingham St Andrews Ln, off Church Ln DN40 2EU
☎ 01469 575298 Fax 01469 577636
An excellent, flat parkland course noted for its numerous dykes which come into play on most holes.
18 holes, 6215yds, Par 71, SSS 70, Course record 69.
Club membership 700.
Visitors   telephone in advance.
Societies   telephone (am) to arrange date.
Green Fees   £15 per round (£22 per round weekends; £23 bank holidays).
Prof   Nick Harding
Designer   Hawtree & Son
Facilities   ⊗ by prior arrangement ⫞ by prior arrangement ♨ ⬛ ♀ ⚲ ☎ ⚑ ⚐ ♂
Location   7m NW off Grimsby

Hotel   ★★ 65% Old Chapel Hotel & Restaurant, 50 Station Rd, Habrough, IMMINGHAM ☎ 01469 572377 14 ⇄ ⟨

LACEBY   Map 08 TA20

Manor Barton St, Laceby Manort DN37 7EA
☎ 01472 873468 Fax 01472 276706
Upgraded to 18 holes in the summer of 1995. The first nine holes as a parkland course, all the fairways lined with young trees. The newly created second nine are mainly open fairways. The 18th hole green is surrounded by water.
18 holes, 6354yds, Par 71, SSS 70.
Club membership 550.
Visitors   welcome but requested to book tee times.
Societies   telephone in advance.
Green Fees   £15 per 18 holes.
Cards   ▭ ▭ ▭ ▭ ⬮
Prof   Paul Rushworth
Facilities   ⊗ ⫞ ♨ ⬛ ♀ ⚲ ☎ ⚑ ♂
& Leisure   fishing.
Location   A18 Barton St - Laceby/Louth

Hotel   ★★★ 57% St James, St James's Square, GRIMSBY ☎ 01472 359771 124 ⇄ ⟨

LINCOLN   Map 08 SK97

Canwick Park Canwick Park, Washingborough Rd
LN4 1EF ☎ 01522 522166 & 542912
Parkland course with views of Lincoln Cathedral. Testing 5th hole (200 yd par 3).
18 holes, 6160yds, Par 70, SSS 69, Course record 65.
Club membership 650.

Visitors   with member only Sat also Sun before 3pm.
Societies   weekdays only by prior arrangement in writing.
Green Fees   not confirmed.
Prof   S Williamson
Designer   Hawtree & Sons
Facilities   ⊗ ♨ ⬛ ♀ ⚲ ☎ ⚑ ♂ ⚐ ♂
Location   1m E of Lincoln

Hotel   B Posthouse Lincoln, Eastgate, LINCOLN ☎ 01522 520341 70 ⇄ ⟨

Carholme Carholme Rd LN1 1SE
☎ 01522 523725 Fax 01522 533733
Parkland course where prevailing west winds can add interest. Good views. 1st hole out of bounds left and right of fairway, pond in front of bunkered green at 5th, lateral water hazards across several fairways.
18 holes, 6243yds, Par 71, SSS 70, Course record 69.
Club membership 625.
Visitors   must contact in advance. Weekends may not play before 2.30pm.
Societies   apply in writing.
Green Fees   £15 per round.
Prof   James Johnson
Facilities   ⊗ ⫞ by prior arrangement ♨ ⬛ ♀ ⚲ ☎ ⚑ ♂
Location   1m W of city centre on A57

Hotel   ★★★★ 59% The White Hart, Bailgate, LINCOLN ☎ 01522 526222 49 ⇄ ⟨

LOUTH   Map 08 TF38

Louth Crowtree Ln LN11 9LJ
☎ 01507 603681 Fax 01507 603681
Undulating parkland course, fine views in an area of outstanding natural beauty.
18 holes, 6424yds, Par 72, SSS 71, Course record 64.
Club membership 700.

▶

Visitors must contact in advance to make sure tee is not reserved for competition.
Societies a booking form will be sent on request.
Green Fees £22 day; £16 per round (£30/£25 weekends & bank holidays).
Prof A Blundell
Facilities ⊗ ⅢⅡ ㄴ ♥ ⬤ ⚲ 🐦 🖐 🏌 ∮
& Leisure squash.
Location W side of Louth between A157/A153

Hotel ★★★ 68% Beaumont Hotel, 66 Victoria Rd, LOUTH ☎ 01507 605005 16 ⇆ 𝄐

MARKET RASEN   Map 08 TF18

Market Rasen & District Legsby Rd LN8 3DZ
☎ 01673 842319
Picturesque, well-wooded heathland course, easy walking, breezy with becks forming natural hazards. Good views of Lincolnshire Wolds.
18 holes, 6045yds, Par 70, SSS 69, Course record 66.
Club membership 600.
Visitors must play with member at weekends and must contact in advance.
Societies Tue & Fri only; must contact in advance.
Green Fees £25 per day; £18 per round.
Prof A M Chester
Facilities ⊗ ⅢⅡ ㄴ ♥ ⬤ ⚲ ∮
Location 1m E, off A46

Hotel ★★★ 68% Beaumont Hotel, 66 Victoria Rd, LOUTH ☎ 01507 605005 16 ⇆ 𝄐

Market Rasen Race Course (Golf Course) Legsby Rd LN8 3EA ☎ 01673 843434 Fax 01673 844532
This is a public course set within the bounds of Market Rasen race course - the entire racing area is out of bounds. The longest hole is the 4th at 454yards with the race course providing a hazard over the whole length of the drive.
9 holes, 2532yds, Par 32.

Visitors closed racedays apart from evening meetings when open until noon.
Societies telephone in advance to arrange.
Green Fees £4 per round (£5 weekends).
Designer Edward Stenton
Facilities 🐦
Location 2m E of Market Rasen

Hotel ★★★ 68% Beaumont Hotel, 66 Victoria Rd, LOUTH ☎ 01507 605005 16 ⇆ 𝄐

NORMANBY   Map 08 SE81

Normanby Hall Normanby Park DN15 9HU
☎ 01724 720226 (Pro shop) 762105 (Secretary)
Well maintained course set in secluded mature parkland. A challenge to golfers of all abilities.
18 holes, 6561yds, Par 71, SSS 71, Course record 66.
Club membership 850.
Visitors book in advance by contacting professional.
Societies must contact in advance: Rachael Lennox, 01724 297860.
Green Fees £19 per day; £11.85 per round (£13.50 per round weekends & bank holidays).
Cards ⚊ 🟦 💳 📇 ▨
Prof Christopher Mann
Designer Hawtree & Son
Facilities ⊗ ⅢⅡ ㄴ ♥ ⬤ ⚲ 🐦 🖐 🏌 ∮
& Leisure free hire of handigolf buggies for disabled.
Location 3m N of Scunthorpe adj to Normanby Hall on B1130

Hotel ★★★ 67% Royal Hotel, Doncaster Rd, SCUNTHORPE ☎ 01724 282233 33 ⇆ 𝄐

SCUNTHORPE   Map 08 SE81

Ashby Decoy Burringham Rd DN17 2AB
☎ 01724 866561 Fax 01724 271708
Pleasant, flat parkland course to satisfy all tastes, yet test the experienced golfer.
18 holes, 6281yds, Par 71, SSS 71, Course record 66.
Club membership 650.
Visitors may not play Sun, Tue or bank holidays. Sat with member only.
Societies apply in advance.
Green Fees not confirmed.
Prof A Miller
Facilities ⊗ ⅢⅡ ㄴ ♥ ⬤ ⚲ ∮
& Leisure billiards room.
Location 2.5m SW on B1450 near Asda Superstore

Hotel ★★★ 67% Royal Hotel, Doncaster Rd, SCUNTHORPE ☎ 01724 282233 33 ⇆ 𝄐

Forest Pines - Briggate Lodge Inn Hotel Ermine St, Broughton DN20 0AQ
☎ 01652 650770 & 650756 Fax 01652 650495
Set in 185 acres of mature parkland and open heathland and constructed in a similar design to that of Wentworth or Sunningdale, Forest Pines offers three challenging 9-hole courses - Forest, Pines and Beeches. Any combination can be played. Facilities include a 17-bay driving range and a spacious clubhouse. Has been voted best new golf club in England by Golf World magazine.
Forest Course: 9 holes, 3291yds, Par 36, SSS 36.
Pines Course: 9 holes, 3591yds, Par 37, SSS 37.
Beeches: 9 holes, 3102yds, Par 35, SSS 35.
Club membership 330.
Visitors must contact in advance.
Societies telephone in advance.
Green Fees £35 per day; £30 per round.
Cards ⚊ 🟦 💳 📇 ▨
Prof David Edwards
Designer John Morgan
Facilities ⊗ ⅢⅡ ㄴ ♥ ⬤ ⚲ 🐦 🛏 🖐 🏌 ∮ ℓ
& Leisure Leisure club due to open June 1999.
Location 200yds from junct 4 M180

Hotel   ★★★ 74% Briggate Lodge Inn,
Ermine St, Broughton, SCUNTHORPE
☎ 01652 650770   86 ⇌ 🌣

Holme Hall Holme Ln, Bottesford DN16 3RF
☎ 01724 862078 Fax 01724 862078
Heathland course with sandy subsoil. Easy walking.
18 holes, 6404yds, Par 71, SSS 71, Course record 65.
Club membership 724.
Visitors   must play with member at weekends & bank
holidays. Must contact in advance.
Societies   must contact in advance.
Green Fees £22 per day; £20 per round.
Prof   Richard McKiernan
Facilities   ⊗ ⅏ ⅃ 💺 ♀ ⚐ 🖈 ✐
Location   3m SE

Hotel   ★★★ 67% Royal Hotel, Doncaster Rd,
SCUNTHORPE ☎ 01724 282233   33 ⇌ 🌣

Kingsway Kingsway DN15 7ER ☎ 01724 840945
Parkland course with many par 3's.
9 holes, 1915yds, Par 29, Course record 28.
Visitors   no restrictions.
Green Fees not confirmed.
Prof   Chris Mann
Facilities   ⚐ ⚐ 🖈 ✐
Location   W side of town centre off A18

Hotel   ★★★ 67% Royal Hotel, Doncaster Rd,
SCUNTHORPE ☎ 01724 282233   33 ⇌ 🌣

SKEGNESS   Map 09 TF56

North Shore Hotel & Golf Club North Shore Rd PE25 1DN
☎ 01754 763298 Fax 01754 761902
A half-links, half-parkland course designed by James Braid
in 1910. Easy walking and good sea views.

18 holes, 6200yds, Par 71, SSS 71, Course record 67.
Club membership 450.
Visitors   tee times must be booked if possible.
Societies   write or telephone in advance.
Green Fees £29 per day; £19 per round (£39/£29 weekdays).
Cards   [card logos]
Prof   J Cornelius
Designer   James Braid
Facilities   ⊗ ⅏ ⅃ 💺 ♀ ⚐ 🖈 ✐
Location   1m N of town centre off A52

Hotel   ★★ 63% North Shore Hotel & Golf Course,
North Shore Rd, SKEGNESS
☎ 01754 763298   30 ⇌ 🌣 Annexe3 ⇌ 🌣

Seacroft Drummond Rd, Seacroft PE25 3AU
☎ 01754 763020 Fax 01754 763020
A typical seaside links with flattish fairways separated
by low ridges and good greens. Easy to walk round. To
the east are sandhills leading to the shore. Southward lies
'Gibraltar Point Nature Reserve'.
18 holes, 6479yds, Par 71, SSS 71, Course record 67.
Club membership 590.
Visitors   must be a member of an affiliated golf club.
Societies   contact in advance.
Green Fees £35 per day; £25 per round (£40/£30
weekends & bank holidays).
Prof   Robin Lawie
Designer   Tom Dunn
Facilities   ⊗ ⅏ ⅃ 💺 ♀ ⚐ 🖈 ✐
Location   S side of town centre

Hotel   ★★★ 62% Crown Hotel,
Drummond Rd, Seacroft, SKEGNESS
☎ 01754 610760   27 ⇌ 🌣

SLEAFORD   Map 08 TF04

Sleaford Willoughby Rd, South Rauceby NG34 8PL
☎ 01529 488273 Fax 01529 488326
Inland links-type course, moderately wooded and fairly flat.
18 holes, 6443yds, Par 72, SSS 71, Course record 64.
Club membership 650.
Visitors   may not play Sun in winter.
Societies   telephone enquiry to fixture secretary or
professional. Written confirmation required.
Green Fees £21 per day; £15 per round (£36 weekends &
bank holidays).
Prof   James Wilson
Designer   T Williamson
Facilities   ⊗ ⅏ ⅃ 💺 ♀ ⚐ 🖈 ✐
Location   2m W of Sleaford, off A153   ▶

Hotel   ★★★ 59%   Angel & Royal Hotel, High St,
GRANTHAM ☎ 01476 565816   29 ⇔ ☞

SOUTH KYME   Map 08 TF14

South Kyme Skinners Ln LN4 4AT
☎ 01526 861113 Fax 01526 861113
A challenging fenland course described as an 'Inland links'.
More water hazards, trees and fairway hazards added during
1995 so the course is improving all the time.
18 holes, 6568yds, Par 72, SSS 71, Course record 67.
Club membership 360.
Visitors   must telephone in advance for tee times.
Societies   telephone for booking form.
Green Fees £14 per round (£16 weekends).
Cards   ⬚
Prof   Peter Chamberlain
Designer   G Bradley
Facilities   ⊗ ⑴ ⑤ ⬛ ☕ ⚐ ⩙ ☜ ⚏ ⚘
Location   Off B1395 in South Kyme village

Hotel   B Travelodge, Holdingham, SLEAFORD
☎ 01529 414752   40 ⇔ ☞

SPALDING   Map 08 TF22

Spalding Surfleet PE11 4EA
☎ 01775 680988 (office) & 680474 (pro)
Fax 01775 680988
A pretty, well laid-out course in a fenland area. The River
Glen runs beside the 1st, 2nd and 4th holes, and ponds and
lakes are very much in play on the 9th, 10th and 11th holes.
Challenging holes include the river dominated 2nd and the
10th which involves a tight drive and dog-leg left to reach a
raised three-tier green.
18 holes, 6478yds, Par 72, SSS 71, Course record 62.
Club membership 750.
Visitors   must contact in advance. Handicap certificate
required.
Societies   write to the secretary, Societies on Thu all day
and Tue pm.
Green Fees £25 per day, £20 per round (£30 weekends &
bank holidays, £20 after 2pm Sun).
Prof   John Spencer
Designer   Price/ Spencer/Ward
Facilities   ⊗ ⑴ ⑤ ⬛ ☕ ⚐ ⩙ ☜ ⚘
Location   4m N of Spalding adjacent to A16

Hotel   ★★ 64%   Cley Hall Hotel,
22 High St, SPALDING
☎ 01775 725157 4 ⇔ ☞ Annexe8 ⇔ ☞

STAMFORD   Map 08 TF00

Burghley Park St Martins PE9 3JX
☎ 01780 762100 & 753789 Fax 01780 753789
Open parkland course with superb greens, many new trees,
ponds and bunkers. Situated in the grounds of Burghley
House.
18 holes, 6236yds, Par 70, SSS 70, Course record 64.
Club membership 775.
Visitors   with member only weekends. Must contact in
advance & have handicap certificate.
Societies   prior arrangement in writing, preferably by 1st
Dec previous year.
Green Fees £21 per day.

Prof   Glenn Davies
Designer   Rev J Day (1938)
Facilities   ⊗ ⑤ ⬛ ☕ ⚐ ⩙ ☜ ⚏ ⚘
Location   1m S of town on B1081

Hotel   ★★★ 75%   The George of Stamford,
71 St Martins, STAMFORD
☎ 01780 750750   47 ⇔ ☞

STOKE ROCHFORD   Map 08 SK92

Stoke Rochford NG33 5EW ☎ 01476 530275
Parkland course designed by C. Turner and extended in 1936
to 18 holes by Major Hotchkin.
18 holes, 6252yds, Par 70, SSS 70, Course record 65.
Club membership 525.
Visitors   must contact in advance, restricted to 9am
weekdays, 10.30am weekends & bank holidays.
Societies   contact one year in advance, in writing.
Green Fees not confirmed.
Prof   Angus Dow
Designer   Major Hotchkin
Facilities   ⚐ ☜ ☜ ⚏ ⚘
Location   Off A1 5m S of Grantham

Hotel   ★★★ 68%   Kings Hotel, North Pde,
GRANTHAM ☎ 01476 590800   21 ⇔ ☞

SUTTON BRIDGE   Map 09 TF42

Sutton Bridge New Rd PE12 9RQ ☎ 01406 350323
Parkland course built around Victorian dock basin, near river
Nene.
9 holes, 5724yds, Par 70, SSS 68.
Club membership 350.
Visitors   may not play competition days, weekends &
bank holidays, must contact in advance. Must
have handicap certificate.
Societies   write or telephone in advance.
Green Fees £19 per day/round.
Prof   D Woolley
Facilities   ⊗ ⑴ ⑤ ⬛ ☕ ⚐ ⩙ ☜ ⚘
Location   E side of village off A17

Hotel   ★★★ 66%   The Duke's Head, Tuesday Market
Place, KING'S LYNN
☎ 01553 774996   71 ⇔ ☞

SUTTON ON SEA   Map 09 TF58

Sandilands Roman Bank LN12 2RJ
☎ 01507 441432 Fax 01507 441617
Flat links course on the sea shore.
18 holes, 5995yds, Par 70, SSS 69.
Club membership 200.
Visitors   no restrictions.
Societies   telephone in advance.
Green Fees £18 per day; £12 per round (£25/£15 weekends
& bank holidays).
Cards   ⬚
Facilities   ⊗ ⑴ ⑤ ⬛ ☕ ⚐ ⩙ ☜ ⚏ ⚘
& Leisure grass tennis courts, gymnasium.
Location   1.5m S off A52

Hotel   ★★★ 63%   Grange & Links Hotel,
Sea Ln, Sandilands, MABLETHORPE
☎ 01507 441334   23 ⇔ ☞

WOODHALL SPA

WOODHALL SPA *Lincs* ☎ 01526 352511
Fax 01526 352778   **Map 08 TF16**

John Ingham writes: Opened in 1905 and regarded as the finest inland course in the British Isles, it has been purchased for £8 million by the English Golf Union to use as a headquarters. Many miles from the nearest towns, the heathland course is covered with silver birch and the fairways are made up of dry, springy turf and several big competitions have been played here.

In the 1960s I played in the Central England Mixed Foursomes and enjoyed the hospitality of the then owner, Neil Hotchkin, who had somehow helped create a wonderful clubhouse atmosphere, with country people behind the bar, giving the place a friendly glow. It remains the same today.

Although 18 miles south-east of Lincoln, I now understand it is wise to telephone to see whether the course can receive visitors for the day. If the answer is 'yes' then be prepared for a treat. Tony Jacklin brought his friend Tom Weiskopf to play and the American was thrilled with the shot-making that is required.

Designed by the Col. S.V. Hotchkin, the course is a pleasant and fairly flat walk but because of the clever shaping of the holes, and the delightful isolation of almost each hole, hidden like a corridor through a stately home, the course becomes a most private place for a friendly four-ball. Measuring 6942 yards, it doesn't appear that long because of the fast-running fairways. The club don't like men visitors to have a handicap above 20 or the women above 30 and since the course is renowned for its huge bunkers, it is to the advantage of players to know how to escape from sand traps. In many ways, Woodhall Spa is like Sunningdale and as those who know that course would readily admit, there is no greater compliment.

Visitors	must be a member of a golf club affilliated to the appropriate Golf Union. Handicap certificate must be produced
Societies	apply by telephone
Green fees	£65 per day, £40 per round. ⊞ ▦ ▤ ▦ ▨
Facilities	⊗ ⋔ ⓛ ☕ ♀ ♨ 🏠 ⚐ ♪ Professional (C C Elliot)
Location	The Broadway LN10 6PU (NE side of village B1191)

18 holes, 6921yards, Par 73 SSS 73
Course record 68

WHERE TO STAY AND EAT NEARBY

HOTELS:
WOODHALL SPA
★★★ 67% Petwood Hotel, Stixwould Rd ☎ 01526 352411. 47 ⇋ 🅜
★★★ 61% Golf Hotel, The Broadway ☎ 01526 353535. 50 (36 ⇋ 🅜 14 🅜)
★★ 59% Eagle Lodge, The Broadway ☎ 01526 353231 23 ⇋ 🅜

RESTAURANT:
HORNCASTLE
🏵 🏵 Magpies, 71-75 East St. ☎ 01507 527004.

TORKSEY   Map 08 SK87

Lincoln LN1 2EG ☎ 01427 718721 Fax 01427 718721
A mature testing inland course on near ideal golfing terrain.
18 holes, 6438yds, Par 71, SSS 71, Course record 67.
Club membership 700.
Visitors welcome on non event days.
Societies apply in writing or telephone.
Green Fees £28 per day; £24 per round.
Prof Ashley Carter
Facilities ⊗ ⫚ ⑃ ♥ ♀ ⚲ 🏠 ♦ ⚷
Location NE side of village, off A156 midway between
Lincoln & Gainsborough

Hotel ★★★★ 59% The White Hart, Bailgate,
LINCOLN ☎ 01522 526222 49 ⇔ ℟

Millfield Sandfield Farm, Laughterton LN1 2LB
☎ 01427 718255 Fax 01427 718255
This golf complex offers a range of facilities to suit every
golfer. The Millfield is designed to suit the more experienced
golfer and follows the natural contours of the landscape. The
Grenville Green is designed for more casual golfers and the
Par 3 is suitable for beginners, family games or for warm-up
and practice play.
18 holes, 5974yds, Par 72, SSS 69, Course record 68.
Green 18: 18 holes, 4485yds, Par 65.
Par 3 course: 9 holes, 1500.
Visitors Millfield: shoes must be worn, no jeans etc.
Green 18 hole no restrictions. Par 3 9 hole no
restrictions.
Societies telephone personal
Green Fees Main: £10 per day, £7 per round; Green 18 hole:
£5 per day; Par 3: £2 per day.
Designer C W Watson
Facilities ⑃ ♥ ♀ 🏠 ⇔ ⚷ ℩
Location On A1133 1m N of A57

Hotel ★★★★ 59% The White Hart, Bailgate,
LINCOLN ☎ 01522 526222 49 ⇔ ℟

WOODHALL SPA   Map 08 TF16

Petwood Hotel

WOODHALL SPA See page 177

WOODTHORPE   Map 09 TF48

Woodthorpe Hall LN13 0DD
☎ 01507 450000 Fax 01507 450000
Parkland course.

18 holes, 5140yds, Par 67, SSS 65, Course record 68.
Club membership 300.
Visitors contact in advance for weekends.
Societies Mon-Fri, apply to the secretary at least one
month prior to visit.
Green Fees £10 per day.
Facilities ⊗ ⫚ ⑃ ♥ ♀ ⚷
& Leisure fishing.
Location 3m NNW of Alford on B1373

Hotel ★★★ 63% Grange & Links Hotel,
Sea Ln, Sandilands, MABLETHORPE
☎ 01507 441334 23 ⇔ ℟

LONDON

London Telephone Number Changes

From the 22 April 2000, the dialling code for the whole of
London with be (020), followed by an eight-digit local
number. For example, **(0171)** 123 4567 will become
(020) 7123 4567, **(0181)** 123 4567 will
become **(020) 8**123 4567.

**Courses within the London Postal District area (ie those
that have London Postcodes - W1, SW1 etc) are listed
here in postal district order commencing East then North,
South and West.** Courses outside the London Postal area,
but within Greater London are to be found listed under the
county of **Greater London** in the gazetteer (see page 100).

LONDON

E4 CHINGFORD

Royal Epping Forest Forest Approach, Chingford E4 7AZ
☎ 0181 529 2195
Woodland course. 'Red' garments must be worn.
18 holes, 6342yds, Par 71, SSS 70.
Club membership 400.
Visitors booking system in operation.
Societies must contact secretary in advance.
Green Fees not confirmed.
Prof J Francis
Facilities 🏠 ⑃ ⚷
Location 300 yds S of Chingford station

Hotel ★★★ 66% County Hotel Epping Forest,
Oak Hill, WOODFORD GREEN
☎ 0181 787 9988 99 ⇔ ℟

West Essex Bury Rd, Sewardstonebury, Chingford E4 7QL
☎ 0181 529 7558 Fax 0181 524 7870
Testing parkland course within Epping Forest. Notable holes
are 8th (par 4), 16th (par 4), 18th (par 5).
18 holes, 6289yds, Par 71, SSS 70.
Club membership 645.
Visitors must have handicap certificate but may not play
on Tue morning, Thu afternoon & weekends.
Societies must contact in advance.

Green Fees £35 per day; £28 per round.
Prof Robert Joyce
Designer James Braid
Facilities ⊗ ⅲ ㄥ ♥ ♀ ⅍ 🏠 �充 ♂ ⎰
Location 1.5m N of Chingford station. Access via M25 junct 26

Hotel ★★ 68% Roebuck Hotel, North End, BUCKHURST HILL
☎ 0181 505 4636 29 ⇄ 🏕

E11 LEYTONSTONE & WANSTEAD

Wanstead Overton Dr, Wanstead E11 2LW
☎ 0181 989 3938 Fax 0181 532 9138
A flat, picturesque parkland course with many trees and shrubs and providing easy walking. The par 3, 16th, involves driving across a lake.
18 holes, 6004yds, Par 69, SSS 69, Course record 62.
Club membership 600.
Visitors must contact in advance and may only play Mon, Tue & Fri.
Societies by prior arrangement.
Green Fees £28 per day.
Prof David Hawkins
Designer James Braid
Facilities ⊗ ⅲ ㄥ ♥ ♀ ⅍ 🏠 ♂ ⎰
& Leisure fishing.
Location From central London A12 NE to Wanstead

Hotel ★★★ 66% County Hotel Epping Forest, Oak Hill, WOODFORD GREEN
☎ 0181 787 9988 99 ⇄ 🏕

N2 EAST FINCHLEY

Hampstead Winnington Rd N2 0TU
☎ 0181 455 0203 Fax 0181 731 6194
Undulating parkland course with many mature trees.
18 holes, 5822yds, Par 68, SSS 68, Course record 64.
Club membership 526.
Visitors restricted Tue and weekends. Contact Professional in advance on 0181 455 7089.
Societies small societies by prior arrangement.
Green Fees £40 per day; £30 per round (£35 per round weekends).
Prof Peter Brown
Designer Tom Dunn
Facilities ㄥ ♥ ♀ ⅍ 🏠 ♂ ⎰
Location Off Hampstead Lane

Hotel B Posthouse Hampstead, 215 Haverstock Hill, LONDON ☎ 0171 794 8121 140 ⇄ 🏕

N6 HIGHGATE

Highgate Denewood Rd N6 4AH
☎ 0181 340 5467 Fax 0181 348 9152
Parkland course.
18 holes, 5985yds, Par 69, SSS 69, Course record 66.
Club membership 800.
Visitors may not play Wed & weekends.
Societies by arrangement.
Green Fees not confirmed.
Prof Robin Turner
Facilities ⊗ ㄥ ♀ ⅍ 🏠 ♂ ⎰

Hotel ★★★★ 68% London Marriott Hotel Regents Park, 128 King Henry's Rd, LONDON
☎ 0171 722 7711 303 ⇄ 🏕

N9 LOWER EDMONTON

Lee Valley Leisure Picketts Lock Sports Centre, Meridian Way, Edmonton N9 0AS
☎ 0181 803 3611
Tricky municipal parkland course with some narrow fairways and the River Lea providing a natural hazard.
18 holes, 4902yds, Par 66, SSS 64, Course record 66.
Club membership 200.
Visitors may telephone for advance bookings.
Societies must telephone in advance.
Green Fees not confirmed.
Prof R Gerken
Facilities ⊗ ⅲ ㄥ ♥ ♀ ⅍ 🏠 ⅋ ♂ ⎰
& Leisure heated indoor swimming pool, squash, sauna, solarium, gymnasium.

Hotel ★★ 70% Oak Lodge Hotel, 80 Village Rd, Bush Hill Park, ENFIELD
☎ 0181 360 7082 7 ⇄ 🏕

N14 SOUTHGATE

Trent Park Bramley Rd, Oakwood N14 4UW
☎ 0181 366 7432
Parkland course set in 150 acres of green belt area. Seven holes played across Merryhills brook. Testing holes are 2nd (423 yds) over brook, 190 yds from the tee, and up to plateau green; 7th (463 yds) dog-leg, over brook, par 4.
18 holes, 6085yds, Par 70, SSS 69, Course record 68.
Club membership 1200.
Visitors must contact 7 days in advance.
Societies must telephone in advance.
Green Fees not confirmed.
Prof Mike Plumbridge
Designer D McGibbon
Facilities ⊗ ⅲ ㄥ ♥ ♀ ⅍ 🏠 ⅋ ♂ ⎰
Location Opposite Oakwood underground station

Hotel ★★★★🛏 71% West Lodge Park Hotel, Cockfosters Rd, HADLEY WOOD
☎ 0181 440 8311 46 ⇄ 🏕 Annexe9 ⇄ 🏕

N20 WHETSTONE

North Middlesex The Manor House, Friern Barnet Ln, Whetstone N20 0NL
☎ 0181 445 1604 & 0181 445 3060 Fax 0181 445 5023
Short parkland course renowned for its tricky greens.
18 holes, 5625yds, Par 69, SSS 67, Course record 64.
Club membership 580.
Visitors advisable to contact in advance, contact professional shop.
Societies bookings in advance, winter offers & summer packages by prior arrangement.
Green Fees Summer: £27 per day; Winter: £22.
Prof Steve Roberts
Designer Willie Park Jnr
Facilities ⊗ ⅲ ㄥ ♥ ♀ ⅍ 🏠 ⅋ ♂ ⎰

Hotel ★★★ 73% Edgwarebury Hotel, Barnet Ln, ELSTREE ☎ 0181 953 8227 47 ⇄ 🏕

South Herts Links Dr, Totteridge N20 8QU
☎ 0181 445 2035 Fax 0181 445 7569
An open undulating parkland course officially in
Hertfordshire, but now in a London postal area. It is,
perhaps, most famous for the fact that two of the greatest
of all British professionals, Harry Vardon and Dai Rees,
CBE were professionals at the club. The course is
testing, over rolling fairways, especially in the prevailing
south-west wind.
18 holes, 6432yds, Par 72, SSS 71, Course record 63.
Club membership 850.

Visitors	must be members of recognised golf club & have handicap certificate of 24 or less. May not play at weekends.
Societies	Wed-Fri only, must apply in writing.
Green Fees	£35 per day; £25 per round.
Prof	Bobby Mitchell
Designer	Harry Vardon
Facilities	🏌️🍴⛳🛒🏌️ ♂
Location	2m E of A1 at Apex Corner
Hotel	B Posthouse South Mimms, SOUTH MIMMS ☎ 01707 643311 143 🖨 ℞

N21 WINCHMORE HILL

Bush Hill Park Bush Hill, Winchmore Hill N21 2BU
☎ 0181 360 5738 Fax 0181 360 5583
Pleasant parkland course surrounded by trees. Contains a
large number of both fairway sandtraps and green side
bunkers. Undulating, but not too harsh.
18 holes, 5809yds, Par 70, SSS 68.
Club membership 700.

Visitors	may not play Wed mornings or weekends & bank holidays.
Societies	by arrangement.
Green Fees	not confirmed.
Prof	Adrian Andrews
Facilities	⊗🍴🏌️♀🏌️🏡♂
Hotel	★★ 70% Oak Lodge Hotel, 80 Village Rd, Bush Hill Park, ENFIELD ☎ 0181 360 7082 7 🖨 ℞

N22 WOOD GREEN

Muswell Hill Rhodes Av, Wood Green N22 4UT
☎ 0181 888 1764 Fax 0181 889 9380
Narrow parkland course featuring numerous water hazards.
18 holes, 6438yds, Par 71, SSS 71, Course record 65.
Club membership 560.

Visitors	must contact in advance, restricted weekends.
Societies	apply in writing or telephone.
Green Fees	not confirmed.
Prof	David Wilton
Facilities	⊗🍴🏌️♀🏌️🏌️🏡♂
Location	Off N Circular Rd at Bounds Green
Hotel	★★★ 68% Raglan Hall Hotel, 8-12 Queens Ave, Muswell Hill, LONDON ☎ 0181 883 9836 46 🖨 ℞

NW4 HENDON   Map 04 TQ28

The Metro Golf Centre Barnet Copthall Sports Centre, Gt
North Way NW4 1PF
☎ 0181 202 1202 Fax 0181 203 1203
Located just seven miles from London's West End, the
Metro Golf Centre represents a new generation of golf
facility dedicated to the development of all standards of
golfer. Facilities include a 48 bay two-tiered driving range, a
testing 9-hole par 3 course with water hazards, pot bunkers
and postage stamp greens, a short game practice area, and a
Golf Academy offering unique teaching methods.
9 holes, 898yds, Par 27, SSS 27, Course record 24.
Club membership 500.

Visitors	welcome any time between 8am-10pm all week for lessons, to play on the course or use driving range.
Societies	telephone in advance.
Green Fees	not confirmed.
Cards	💳 💳 💳 💳
Prof	Barney Puttick
Designer	Cousells
Facilities	⊗🍴🏌️🍴♀🏡🏌️♂ ℞
& Leisure	comprehensive teaching academy.
Location	Just off A41 and A1 at junct 2 of the M1, within the Barnet Copthall Sporting Complex
Hotel	★★★ 70% Holiday Inn Garden Court, Tilling Rd, Brent Cross, LONDON ☎ 0181 455 4777 Res & 0181 201 8686 Fax 0181 455 4660 153 🖨 ℞

NW7 MILL HILL

Finchley Nether Court, Frith Ln, Mill Hill NW7 1PU
☎ 0181 346 2436 & 346 5086 Fax 0181 343 4205
Easy walking on wooded parkland course.
18 holes, 6411yds, Par 72, SSS 71.
Club membership 500.

Visitors	must contact in advance.
Societies	must apply in writing.
Green Fees	on application.
Cards	💳 💳 💳 💳
Prof	David Brown
Designer	James Braid
Facilities	⊗🍴 by prior arrangement 🍴🏌️♀🏡🏌️🛒♂
Location	Near Mill Hill East Tube Station
Hotel	★★★ 73% Edgwarebury Hotel, Barnet Ln, ELSTREE ☎ 0181 953 8227 47 🖨 ℞

Hendon Ashley Walk, Devonshire Rd, Mill Hill NW7 1DG
☎ 0181 346 6023 Fax 0181 343 1974
Easy walking, parkland course with a good variety of trees,
and providing testing golf.
18 holes, 6266yds, Par 70, SSS 70.
Club membership 540.

Visitors	must contact in advance. Restricted weekends & bank holidays.
Societies	Tue-Fri. Must contact in advance.
Green Fees	£35 per day; £28 per round (£35 per round weekends & bank holidays).
Cards	💳 💳 💳 💳
Prof	Stuart Murray
Designer	H S Colt
Facilities	⊗🍴🏌️♀🏡🏌️♂

Location	10 mins from junc 2 of M1 southbound
Hotel	★★★ 73% Edgwarebury Hotel, Barnet Ln, ELSTREE ☎ 0181 953 8227 47 ⇥ ♣

Mill Hill 100 Barnet Way, Mill Hill NW7 3AL
☎ 0181 959 2339 Fax 0181 906 0731
Undulating parkland course with tree and shrub lined fairways, water features strongly on holes 2,10 and 17.
18 holes, 6247yds, Par 70, SSS 70, Course record 65.
Club membership 550.

Visitors	restricted weekends & bank holidays. Must contact in advance.
Societies	must contact in advance.
Green Fees	Summer: £25 (£30 weekends); Winter: £20 (£25 weekends).
Prof	Gary Harvey
Designer	J F Abercrombie/H S Colt
Facilities	⊗ ⅷ by prior arrangement ╠ ♥ ♀ ⌂ ☎ ♔ ♂
Location	On A1 S bound carriageway
Hotel	★★★ 73% Edgwarebury Hotel, Barnet Ln, ELSTREE ☎ 0181 953 8227 47 ⇥ ♣

SE9 ELTHAM

Eltham Warren Bexley Rd, Eltham SE9 2PE
☎ 0181 850 4477 & 850 1166
Parkland course with narrow fairways and small greens. The course is bounded by the A210 on one side and Eltham Park on the other.
9 holes, 5840yds, Par 69, SSS 68, Course record 66.
Club membership 440.

Visitors	may not play at weekends. Must contact in advance and have a handicap certificate.
Societies	Thu only. Must book in advance. Deposit required.
Green Fees	£25 per day.
Prof	Gary Brett
Designer	James Braid
Facilities	⊗ ⅷ by prior arrangement ╠ ♥ ♀ ⌂ ☎ ♂
& Leisure	snooker tables.
Location	0.5m from Eltham station on A210
Hotel	★★★ 70% Bromley Court Hotel, Bromley Hill, BROMLEY ☎ 0181 464 5011 115 ⇥ ♣

Royal Blackheath Court Rd SE9 5AF
☎ 0181 850 1795 Fax 0181 859 0150
A pleasant, parkland course of great character as befits the antiquity of the Club; the clubhouse dates from the 17th century. Many great trees survive and there are two ponds. The 18th requires a pitch to the green over a thick clipped hedge, which also crosses the front of the 1st tee.
18 holes, 6219yds, Par 70, SSS 70.
Club membership 720.

Visitors	must contact in advance but may play mid-week only, handicap certificate is required.
Societies	must apply in writing.
Green Fees	£45 per day; £35 per round.
Cards	▧ ▩ ▨ ▣
Prof	Ian McGregor
Designer	James Braid
Facilities	⊗ ⅷ ╠ ♥ ♀ ⌂ ☎ ♔ ♘ ♂
& Leisure	golf museum.
Location	From M25 junct 3 take A20 towards London. Turn right at 2nd traffic lights to club 500yds on right
Hotel	★★★ 70% Bromley Court Hotel, Bromley Hill, BROMLEY ☎ 0181 464 5011 115 ⇥ ♣

SE18 WOOLWICH　　　　　　　　　　Map 05 TQ47

Shooters Hill Eaglesfield Rd, Shooters Hill SE18 3DA
☎ 0181 854 6368 Fax 0181 854 0469
Hilly and wooded parkland course with good view and natural hazards.
18 holes, 5721 yds, Par 69, SSS 68, Course record 63.
Club membership 900.

Visitors	must have handicap certificate and be a member of a recognised golf club but may not play at weekends, unless with member.
Societies	Tue & Thu only, by arrangement.
Green Fees	£27 per day; £22 per round.
Prof	Michael Ridge
Designer	Willie Park
Facilities	⊗ ⅷ ╠ ♥ ♀ ⌂ ☎ ♘ ♂
Location	Shooters Hill Rd from Blackheath
Hotel	B Posthouse Bexley, Black Prince Interchange, Southwold Rd, BEXLEY ☎ 01322 526900 103 ⇥ ♣

SE21 DULWICH

Dulwich & Sydenham Hill Grange Ln, College Rd
SE21 7LH ☎ 0181 693 3961 & 693 8491
Parkland course overlooking London. Hilly with narrow fairways.
18 holes, 6008yds, Par 69, SSS 69, Course record 63.
Club membership 850.

Visitors	must contact in advance and have a handicap certificate. May not play weekends or bank holidays.
Societies	must telephone in advance & confirm in writing.
Green Fees	not confirmed.
Prof	David Baillie
Facilities	⊗ ⅷ ╠ ♥ ♀ ⌂ ☎ ♔ ♘ ♂
Hotel	★★★ 70% Bromley Court Hotel, Bromley Hill, BROMLEY ☎ 0181 464 5011 115 ⇥ ♣

SE22 EAST DULWICH

Aquarius Marmora Rd, Honor Oak, Off Forest Hill Rd SE22
0RY ☎ 0181 693 1626
Course laid-out on two levels around and over covered
reservoir; hazards include vents and bollards.
9 holes, 5246yds, Par 66, SSS 66, Course record 66.
Club membership 350.
| Visitors | must be accompanied by member and have a handicap certificate. |
Green Fees not confirmed.
Prof Frederick Private
Facilities ⬛♟⛳🏠

Hotel ★★★ 70% Bromley Court Hotel,
Bromley Hill, BROMLEY
☎ 0181 464 5011 115 ⇥ ♠

SE28 WOOLWICH

Riverside Summerton Way, Thamesmead SE28 8PP
☎ 0181 310 7975
A delightful undulating course with a mix of mature trees,
new trees and water hazards. The 4th hole is a challenging
515yards down a narrow fairway.
9 holes, 5462yds, Par 70, SSS 66.
Club membership 150.
Visitors no restrictions.
Societies book by telephone or in writing.
Green Fees not confirmed.
Cards 💳
Prof Mark Nicholls
Designer Heffernan
Facilities ⊗⫼⬛♟⛳🏠♠
Location Off A2 near Woolwich ferry

Hotel ★★★ 64% Bardon Lodge Hotel, 15-17
Stratheden Rd, LONDON
☎ 0181 853 4051 32 ⇥ ♠

SW15 PUTNEY

Richmond Park Roehampton Gate, Priory Ln
SW15 5JR ☎ 0181 876 1795 Fax 0181 878 1354
Two public parkland courses.
Princes Course: 18 holes, 5868yds, Par 69, SSS 68,
Course record 64.
Dukes Course: 18 holes, 6036yds, Par 69, SSS 68.
Visitors must contact in advance or pay and play.
Societies must contact in advance.
Green Fees £13.50 (£16.80 weekends & bank holidays).
Cards 💳
Prof Stuart Hill & David Bown
Designer Fred Hawtree
Facilities ⛳🏠♠
Location Inside Richmond Park Roehampton gate

Hotel ★★★ 69% Richmond Hill, Richmond Hill,
RICHMOND UPON THAMES
☎ 0181 940 2247 & 940 5466
Fax 0181 940 5424 138 ⇥ ♠

Entries with a shaded background
identify courses that are
considered to be particularly interesting

SW18 WANDSORTH

Central London Golf Centre Burntwood Ln, Wandsworth
SW17 0AT ☎ 0181 871 2468 Fax 0181 874 7447
Attractive flat parkland course in the middle of London. The
longest drive is the 430 yard 3rd to one of the course's
superb greens. Well placed bunkers trap the careless shot and
the course rewards the accurate player.
9 holes, 2277yds, Par 62, SSS 62.
Club membership 200.
Visitors must contact in advance.
Societies telephone or write to the secretary.
Green Fees not confirmed.
Cards 💳
Prof Jeremy Robson
Designer Patrick Tallock
Facilities ⊗⫼⬛♟⛳🏠♠
& Leisure putting green, practice area.
Location Between Garatt Lane and Trinity Road

Hotel ★★★★ 77% Cannizaro House,
West Side, Wimbledon Common, LONDON
☎ 0181 879 1464 46 ⇥ ♠

SW19 WIMBLEDON

Royal Wimbledon 29 Camp Rd SW19 4UW
☎ 0181 946 2125 Fax 0181 944 8652
A club steeped in the history of the game, it is also of
great age, dating back to 1865. Of sand and heather like
so many of the Surrey courses its 12th hole (par 4) is
rated as the best on the course.
18 holes, 6300yds, Par 70, SSS 70, Course record 66.
Club membership 1050.
Visitors must be guests of current club member or contact club in advance, weekdays only.
Societies welcome Wed-Thu. Must apply in writing.
Green Fees £55 per round.
Prof Hugh Boyle
Designer H Colt
Facilities ⊗⫼ by prior arrangement ⬛♟⛳🏠♠

Hotel ★★★★ 77% Cannizaro House, West Side,
Wimbledon Common, LONDON
☎ 0181 879 1464 46 ⇥ ♠

Wimbledon Common Camp Rd SW19 4UW
☎ 0181 946 0294 Fax 0181 946 7571
Quick-drying course on Wimbledon Common. Well wooded,
with tight fairways, challenging short holes but no
bunkers.The course is also played over by London Scottish
Golf Club (0181 788 0135). All players must wear plain red
upper garments.
18 holes, 5438yds, Par 68, SSS 66.
Club membership 250.
Visitors with member only at weekends.
Societies must telephone in advance.
Green Fees not confirmed.
Prof J S Jukes
Facilities ⊗⫼⬛♟⛳🏠

Hotel ★★★★ 77% Cannizaro House, West Side,
Wimbledon Common, LONDON
☎ 0181 879 1464 46 ⇥ ♠

Wimbledon Park Home Park Rd, Wimbledon SW19 7HR
☎ 0181 946 1250 Fax 0181 944 8688
Easy walking on parkland course. Sheltered lake provides hazard on 3 holes.
18 holes, 5465yds, Par 66, SSS 66.
Club membership 700.
Visitors restricted weekends & bank holidays. Must contact in advance and have handicap certificate or letter of introduction.
Societies must apply in writing.
Green Fees £40 per day/round.
Prof Dean Wingrove
Designer Willie Park Jnr
Facilities ⊗ ⑪ ⓛ ♥ ♀ ⌂ ⌐ ✧
Location 400 yds from Wimbledon Park Station

Hotel ★★★ 69% Richmond Hill, Richmond Hill, RICHMOND UPON THAMES
☎ 0181 940 2247 & 940 5466
Fax 0181 940 5424 138 ⇆ ℟

W7 HANWELL

Brent Valley 138 Church Rd, Hanwell W7 3BE
☎ 0181 567 1287
Municipal parkland course with easy walking. The River Brent winds through the course.
18 holes, 5426yds, Par 67, SSS 66.
Club membership 350.
Visitors no restrictions.
Societies one month's notice required.
Green Fees not confirmed.
Cards — ▭ ▭ ▭ ▭
Prof Peter Bryant
Facilities ⊗ ⓛ ♥ ♀ ⌂ ⌐ ✧

Hotel ★★★ 64% Master Robert Hotel, Great West Rd, HOUNSLOW
☎ 0181 570 6261 94 ⇆ ℟

MERSEYSIDE

BEBINGTON   Map 07 SJ38

Brackenwood Brackenwood Golf Course, Bracken Ln L63 2LY ☎ 0151 608 3093
Municipal parkland course with easy walking, a very testing but fair course in a fine rural setting, usually in very good condition.
18 holes, 6208yds, Par 70, SSS 70, Course record 66.
Club membership 320.
Visitors must book for weekends one week in advance.
Societies must apply in advance.
Green Fees £7 per round.
Prof Ken Lamb
Facilities ⌂ ⌐ ✧
Location 0.75m N of M53 junc 4 on B5151

Hotel ★★★ 68% Thornton Hall Hotel, Neston Rd, THORNTON HOUGH
☎ 0151 336 3938 5 ⇆ ℟ Annexe58 ⇆ ℟

BIRKENHEAD   Map 07 SJ38

Arrowe Park Woodchurch L49 5LW
☎ 0151 677 1527
Pleasant municipal parkland course.
18 holes, 6435yds, Par 72, SSS 71, Course record 66.
Club membership 220.
Visitors no restrictions, Booking at weekends 1wk in advance.
Societies must telephone in advance.
Green Fees £7 per round.
Prof Colin Disbury
Facilities ⊗ ⑪ ⓛ ♥ ♀ ⌂ ⌐ ⚒ ✧
& Leisure tennis courts, pitch & putt.
Location 1m from M53 junc 3 on A551

Hotel ★★★ 69% Bowler Hat Hotel, 2 Talbot Rd, Oxton, BIRKENHEAD
☎ 0151 652 4931 32 ⇆ ℟

Prenton Golf Links Rd, Prenton L42 8LW
☎ 0151 608 1053 Fax 0151 609 1580
Parkland course with easy walking and views of the Welsh Hills.
18 holes, 6429yds, Par 71, SSS 71.
Club membership 610.
Visitors no restrictions.
Societies must telephone in advance and confirm in writing.
Green Fees £30 per day (£35 weekends & bank holidays).
Prof Robin Thompson
Designer James Braid
Facilities ⊗ ⑪ ⓛ ♥ ♀ ⌂ ⌐ ℟ ✧
Location M53 junct 3 off A552 towards Birkenhead

Hotel ★★ 66% Riverhill Hotel, Talbot Rd, Oxton, BIRKENHEAD
☎ 0151 653 3773 16 ⇆ ℟

Wirral Ladies 93 Bidston Rd, Oxton L43 6TS
☎ 0151 652 1255 Fax 0151 653 4323
Heathland course with heather and birch.
18 holes, 4948yds, Par 69, SSS 69.
Club membership 430.
Visitors may not play before 11am weekends or over Christmas and Easter holidays.
Societies must telephone in advance. Weekdays only.
Green Fees £30 per day; £25.50 per round.
Prof Angus Law
Facilities ⊗ ⑪ ⓛ ♥ ♀ ⌂ ⌐ ✧
Location W side of town centre on B5151

Hotel ★★★ 69% Bowler Hat Hotel, 2 Talbot Rd, Oxton, BIRKENHEAD
☎ 0151 652 4931 32 ⇆ ℟

BLUNDELLSANDS   Map 07 SJ39

West Lancashire Hall Rd West L23 8SZ
☎ 0151 924 1076 Fax 0151 931 4448
Challenging, traditional links with sandy subsoil overlooking the Mersey Estuary. The course provides excellent golf throughout the year. The four short holes are very fine.
18 holes, 6763yds, Par 72, SSS 73, Course record 66.
Club membership 650.
▶

Visitors	must have a handicap certificate. May not play before 9.30am Mon-Fri and on competition days and weekends only after 3.30pm.
Societies	must contact in advance.
Green Fees	£50 per day; £35 per round (£60 per 18 holes weekends & bank holidays).
Prof	Tim Hastings
Designer	C K Cotton
Facilities	⊗ ⫙ ⪮ 🍺 ♀ ⛘ 📷 ⌀
Location	N side of village
Hotel	★★★ 65% Carlton Blundellsands, The Serpentine, BLUNDELLSANDS ☎ 0151 924 6515 30 ⇌ 📻

BOOTLE   Map 07 SJ39

Bootle 2 Dunnings Bridge Rd L30 2PP ☎ 0151 928 6196
Municipal seaside course, with prevailing north-westerly wind. Testing holes: 5th (200 yds) par 3; 7th (415 yds) par 4.
18 holes, 6362yds, Par 70, SSS 70, Course record 64.
Club membership 380.

Visitors	must contact Golf Shop on 0151 928 1371 not between 9-9.45am Sat and 7.45-12 Sun.
Societies	must apply in writing.
Green Fees	£7.50.
Prof	Alan Bradshaw
Facilities	⊗ ⫙ ⪮ 🍺 ♀ 📷 ⛘ ⌀
Location	2m NE on A5036
Hotel	★★★ 65% Carlton Blundellsands, The Serpentine, BLUNDELLSANDS ☎ 0151 924 6515 30 ⇌ 📻

BROMBOROUGH   Map 07 SJ38

Bromborough Raby Hall Rd L63 0NW
☎ 0151 334 2155 Fax 0151 334 0303
Parkland course.
18 holes, 6650yds, Par 72, SSS 73, Course record 67.
Club membership 800.

Visitors	are advised to contact professional on 0151 334 4499 in advance.
Societies	normal society day Wed ; must apply in advance.
Green Fees	£28 per day.
Prof	Geoff Berry
Designer	J Hassall
Facilities	⊗ ⫙ ⪮ 🍺 ♀ ⛘ 📷 ⚑ ⌀
Location	0.5m W of Station
Hotel	B Travel Inn, High St, Bromborough Cross, BROMBOROUGH ☎ 0151 334 2917 31 ⇌ 📻

CALDY   Map 07 SJ28

Caldy Links Hey Rd L48 1NB
☎ 0151 625 5660 Fax 0151 6257394
A parkland course situated on the estuary of the River Dee with many of the fairways running parallel to the river. Of Championship length, the course offers excellent golf all year, but is subject to variable winds that noticeably alter the day to day playing of each hole. There are excellent views of North Wales and Snowdonia.

18 holes, 6668yds, Par 72, SSS 73, Course record 68.
Club membership 800.

Visitors	may play on weekdays only.
Societies	must telephone in advance.
Green Fees	not confirmed.
Prof	K Jones
Facilities	⊗ by prior arrangement ⫙ by prior arrangement ⪮ 🍺 ♀ ⛘ 📷 ⚒ ⌀
Location	SE side of village, from Caldy rdbt on A540 follow signs to Caldy and golf club
Hotel	★★★ 68% Thornton Hall Hotel, Neston Rd, THORNTON HOUGH ☎ 0151 336 3938 5 ⇌ 📻 Annexe58 ⇌ 📻

EASTHAM   Map 07 SJ38

Eastham Lodge 117 Ferry Rd L62 0AP
☎ 0151 327 3003 Fax 0151 327 3003
A parkland course with many mature trees, recently upgraded to 18 holes.
18 holes, 5706yds, Par 68, SSS 68.
Club membership 800.

Visitors	advisable to telephone in advance to check availability, tel 0151 327 3008 professionals shop, start times available up to 2 weeks in advance, with member only at weekends.
Societies	welcome Tue. Must apply in writing.
Green Fees	£22 per day/round.
Prof	R Boobyer
Designer	Hawtree/D Hemstock
Facilities	⊗ ⫙ ⪮ 🍺 ♀ ⛘ 📷 ⌀
Location	1.5m N
Hotel	B Travel Inn, High St, Bromborough Cross, BROMBOROUGH ☎ 0151 334 2917 31 ⇌ 📻

FORMBY   Map 07 SD30

Formby Golf Rd L37 1LQ
☎ 01704 872164 Fax 01704 833028
Championship seaside links through sandhills and partly through pine trees. Partly sheltered from the wind by high dunes it features firm, springy turf, fast seaside greens and natural sandy bunkers. Well drained it plays well throughout the year.
18 holes, 6701yds, Par 72, SSS 72, Course record 65.
Club membership 680.

Visitors	must contact in advance, very limited on Sat & Wed.
Societies	must contact well in advance.
Green Fees	£60 per day/round.
Cards	💳 💳 💳 💳
Prof	Gary Butler
Designer	Park/Colt
Facilities	⊗ ⫙ ⪮ 🍺 ♀ ⛘ 📷 ⚑ ⌀
Location	N side of town
Hotel	★★★ 65% Carlton Blundellsands, The Serpentine, BLUNDELLSANDS ☎ 0151 924 6515 30 ⇌ 📻

184

Formby Ladies Golf Rd L37 1YH
☎ 01704 873493 Fax 01704 873493
Seaside links - one of the few independent ladies clubs in the country. The course has contrasting hard-hitting holes in flat country and tricky holes in sandhills and woods.
18 holes, 5374yds, Par 71, SSS 71.
Club membership 570.
Visitors   must contact in advance and may not play Thu or before 11am Sat & Sun.
Societies   must apply in advance.
Green Fees £30 per day (£35 weekends & bank holidays).
Prof   Gary Butler
Facilities   ⊗ ᛉ by prior arrangement ᛒ 🍵 ♀ ⚲ 🖅 🗸
Location   N side of town

Hotel   ★★★ 65% Carlton Blundellsands,
The Serpentine, BLUNDELLSANDS
☎ 0151 924 6515 30 ⇨ 🏴

HESWALL   Map 07 SJ28

Heswall Cottage Ln L60 8PB
☎ 0151 342 1237 Fax 0151 342 1237
A pleasant parkland course in soft undulating country over-looking the estuary of the River Dee. There are excellent views of the Welsh hills and coastline, and a good test of golf. The clubhouse is modern and well-appointed with good facilities.
18 holes, 6492yds, Par 72, SSS 72, Course record 62.
Club membership 940.
Visitors   must contact in advance.
Societies   must apply in advance.
Green Fees not confirmed.
Prof   Alan Thompson
Facilities   ⊗ ᛉ ᛒ 🍵 ♀ ⚲ 🖅 🗸
Location   1m S off A540

Hotel   ★★★ 68% Thornton Hall Hotel,
Neston Rd, THORNTON HOUGH
☎ 0151 336 3938 5 ⇨ 🏴 Annexe58 ⇨ 🏴

HOYLAKE   Map 07 SJ28

Hoylake Carr Ln, Municipal Links L47 4BG
☎ 0151 632 2956
Flat, generally windy semi-links course. Tricky fairways.
18 holes, 6313yds, Par 70, SSS 70, Course record 67.
Club membership 303.
Societies   must telephone 0151 632 4883 club steward or 0151 632 2956 club professional.
Green Fees not confirmed.
Prof   Simon Hooton
Facilities   ⊗ ᛉ ᛒ ♀ (ex Fri) ⚲ 🖅 ⚑ 🗸
Location   SW side of town off A540

Hotel   ★★★ 66% Leasowe Castle Hotel, Leasowe Rd,
MORETON ☎ 0151 606 9191 47 ⇨ 🏴

Royal Liverpool Meols Dr L47 4AL
☎ 0151 632 3101 & 632 3102 Fax 0151 632 6737
A world famous, windswept seaside links course, venue for ten Open Championships and 17 Amateur Championships.
18 holes, 6199yds, Par 72, SSS 71.
Club membership 650.

Visitors   must contact in advance & have a handicap certificate. Restricted before 9.30am & between 1-2pm. No play Thu am (ladies day). Limited play weekends (pm only).
Societies   must contact in advance.
Green Fees £85 per day; £60 per round (£100 per round weekends & bank holidays).
Cards   🌐 🔲 🟥 VISA 🟨 🔵 🔲
Prof   John Heggarty
Designer   R Chambers/G Morris
Facilities   ⊗ ᛉ by prior arrangement ᛒ 🍵 ♀ ⚲ 🖅
⚑ 🗸 ᛣ
Location   SW side of town on A540

Hotel   ★★★ 66% Leasowe Castle Hotel,
Leasowe Rd, MORETON
☎ 0151 606 9191 47 ⇨ 🏴

HUYTON   Map 07 SJ49

Bowring Bowring Park, Roby Rd L36 4HD
☎ 0151 489 1901
Flat parkland course.
18 holes, 5651yds, Par 70.
Club membership 200.
Visitors   no restrictions.
Green Fees not confirmed.
Facilities   ᛒ 🍵 🖅
Location   On A5080 adjacent M62 junc 5

Hotel   ★ 61% Rockland Hotel, View Rd, RAINHILL
☎ 0151 426 4603 11rm(9 ⇨1 🏴)

Huyton & Prescot Hurst Park, Huyton Ln L36 1UA
☎ 0151 489 3948 Fax 0151 489 0797
An easy walking, parkland course providing excellent golf.
18 holes, 5779yds, Par 68, SSS 68, Course record 65.
Club membership 700.
Visitors   must contact in advance.
Societies   must apply in writing.
Green Fees £22.50 per day.
Prof   Gerry Bond
Facilities   ⊗ ᛉ by prior arrangement ᛒ 🍵 ♀ ⚲ 🖅 🗸
& Leisure practice bays.
Location   1.5m NE off B5199

Hotel   ★ 61% Rockland Hotel, View Rd, RAINHILL
☎ 0151 426 4603 11rm(9 ⇨1 🏴)

LIVERPOOL   Map 07 SJ39

Allerton Park Allerton Manor Golf Estate,
Allerton Rd L18 3JT ☎ 0151 428 1046
Parkland course.
18 holes, 5459yds, Par 67, SSS 67.
Visitors   must book with professional in advance.
Societies   by prior arrangement with professional.
Green Fees not confirmed.
Prof   Barry Large
Facilities   🖅 ⚑ 🗸
Location   5.5m SE of city centre off A562 and B5180

Hotel   ★★★★ 59% Thistle Liverpool, Chapel St,
LIVERPOOL ☎ 0151 227 4444 226 ⇨ 🏴

The Childwall Naylors Rd, Gateacre L27 2YB
☎ 0151 487 0654 Fax 0151 487 0882
Parkland golf is played here over a testing course, where accuracy from the tee is well-rewarded. The course is very popular with visiting societies for the clubhouse has many amenities. Course designed by James Braid.
18 holes, 6425yds, Par 72, SSS 71, Course record 66.
Club membership 650.

Visitors	must contact in advance.
Societies	must apply in writing.
Green Fees	£26 (£35 weekends).
Prof	Nigel M Parr
Designer	James Braid
Facilities	ⓧ ⫼ ⑤ ☕ ♀ ♂ 🏠 🕾 ⚤ ⟨
Location	7m E of city centre off B5178

Hotel	★ 61% Rockland Hotel, View Rd, RAINHILL ☎ 0151 426 4603 11rm(9 ⇔1 🏠)

Kirkby-Liverpool Municipal Ingoe Ln, Kirkby L32 4SS
☎ 0151 546 5435
Flat, easy course.
18 holes, 6704yds, Par 72, SSS 72, Course record 68.
Club membership 150.

Societies	must contact 1 week in advance.
Green Fees	not confirmed.
Prof	Dave Weston
Facilities	ⓧ ⫼ ⑤ ☕ ♀ ♂ 🏠 🕾 ⚤
Location	7.5m NE of city centre on A506

Hotel	★★★★ 58% Liverpool Moat House Hotel, Paradise St, LIVERPOOL ☎ 0151 471 9988 251 ⇔ 🏠

Lee Park Childwall Valley Rd L27 3YA
☎ 0151 487 3882 Fax 0151 487 3882
Flat parkland course with ponds in places and plenty of trees.
18 holes, 6095yds, Par 72, SSS 69.
Club membership 600.

Visitors	must dress acceptably. Must contact in advance.
Societies	must contact in advance.
Green Fees	£23 per day (£28 weekends & bank holidays).
Designer	G Cotton
Facilities	ⓧ ⫼ ⑤ ☕ ♀ ⚤
Location	7m E of city centre off B5178

Hotel	★★★★ 58% Liverpool Moat House Hotel, Paradise St, LIVERPOOL ☎ 0151 471 9988 251 ⇔ 🏠

West Derby Yew Tree Ln, West Derby L12 9HQ
☎ 0151 254 1034 Fax 0151 259 0505
A parkland course always in first-class condition, and so giving easy walking. The fairways are well-wooded. Care must be taken on the first nine holes to avoid the brook which guards many of the greens. A modern well-designed clubhouse with many amenities, overlooks the course.
18 holes, 6277yds, Par 72, SSS 70, Course record 65.
Club membership 550.

Visitors	may not play before 9.30am. May not play weekends and bank holidays.
Societies	may not play on Sat, Sun & bank holidays; must contact in advance.

Green Fees	£27 per 28 holes; £25 per round.
Prof	Andrew Witherup
Facilities	⚤ 🏠 ⚤
Location	4.5m E of city centre off A57

Hotel	★★★★ 59% Thistle Liverpool, Chapel St, LIVERPOOL ☎ 0151 227 4444 226 ⇔ 🏠

Woolton Speke Rd, Woolton L25 7TZ
☎ 0151 486 2298 Fax 0151 486 1664
Parkland course providing a good round of golf for all standards.
18 holes, 5717yds, Par 69, SSS 68.
Club membership 700.

Visitors	must contact in advance. Restricted at weekends.
Societies	must contact in advance.
Green Fees	not confirmed.
Prof	Alan Gibson
Facilities	ⓧ ⫼ ⑤ ☕ ♀ 🏠 ⚤ ⚤
Location	7m SE of city centre off A562

Hotel	★★★★ 59% Thistle Liverpool, Chapel St, LIVERPOOL ☎ 0151 227 4444 226 ⇔ 🏠

NEWTON-LE-WILLOWS   Map 07 SJ59

Haydock Park Newton Ln WA12 0HX
☎ 01925 228525 Fax 01925 228525
A well-wooded parkland course, close to the well-known racecourse, and always in excellent condition. The pleasant undulating fairways offer some very interesting golf and the 6th, 9th, 11th and 13th holes are particularly testing. The clubhouse is very comfortable.
18 holes, 6043yds, Par 70, SSS 69, Course record 65.
Club membership 560.

Visitors	welcome weekdays except Tue, with member only weekends & bank holidays. Must contact in advance.
Societies	must contact in advance.
Green Fees	£26 per day.
Prof	Peter Kenwright
Designer	James Braid
Facilities	ⓧ ⫼ ⑤ ☕ ♀ 🏠 ⚤
Location	0.75m NE off A49

Hotel	B Posthouse Haydock, Lodge Ln, HAYDOCK ☎ 01942 717878 138 ⇔ 🏠

RAINHILL   Map 07 SJ49

Blundells Hill Blundells Ln L35 6NA
☎ 01744 24892 Fax 01744 28861
Blundells Hill Club: 18 holes, 6256yds, Par 71, SSS 70.
Club membership 600.

Visitors	may not play off white tees.
Societies	telephone for prices and availability.
Green Fees	not confirmed.
Cards	🔲 🟥 🟦 🟩
Prof	Richard Leach
Designer	Steve Marnoch
Facilities	ⓧ ⫼ ⑤ ☕ ♀ 🏠 ⚤ ⟨
Location	3 mins from junct 7 (eastbound M62)

▶

186

THE ROYAL BIRKDALE

SOUTHPORT *Merseyside* ☎ 01704 567920
Fax 01704 562327   **Map 07 SD31**

John Ingham writes: There are few seaside links in the world that can be described as 'great', but Royal Birkdale, with its expanse of towering sandhills and willow scrub, is one of them. There have been some changes since the club (designed by George Lowe) was founded in 1889 and they have hosted everything that matters here, including the Open and the Ryder Cup. Some changes have been made even since Arnold Palmer hit that wondrous recovery shot that helped him win an Open in the early sixties, and led to a plaque being erected at the spot from which the divot was taken.

Well bunkered, the sandhills run along the edges of the fairways and make ideal platforms from which to view the Open Championship - played frequently here because the examination is supreme in the United Kingdom.

The links, in a wind, may be too difficult for the weekender. Certainly it found out Dai Rees in 1961 when he was chasing Palmer for the title. In the last round the course struck at the very first hole. Rees had hit his teeshot a mite to the left, and then had to wait for the players to hole out on the green ahead, before attempting a powerful shot with a lofted wood from the fairway. The ball smacked into the back of a bunker, and fell back into sand. Rees took an awful seven and Palmer beat him for the trophy - by one shot. The Welshman had stormed back in 31 but his chance to win an Open had gone forever. But Rees still touched his hat to the links, and held it in great respect as, indeed, does Arnold Palmer.

But for the amateur, another problem is simply hitting the ball far enough. If you play this terrific course from the Open Championship back tees, it measures 6726 yards and par 72 takes some getting, even with your handicap allowance!

Visitors must contact in advance, and have a handicap certificate. Normally not Fri & Sat, and restricted on Sun
Societies must apply in advance.
Green fees not confirmed ▬ ▬ ▬
Facilities ⊗ ⅷ ঌ ⬛ ♀ ⚐ 🖴
         ⛵ ✐ Professional
         (Richard Bradbeer)
Location Waterloo Road, Birkdale, Southport PR8 2LX (2m S of town on A565)

18 holes, 6726yds, Par 72, SSS 73, Course record 65

WHERE TO STAY AND EAT NEARBY

HOTELS:
SOUTHPORT
★★★❀ 69% Royal Clifton, Promenade. ☎ 01704 533771. 106 (100 ⇆ ♜ 6 ♜)
★★★ 68% Stutelea Hotel & Leisure Club, Alexandra Rd. ☎ 01704 544220. 20 ⇆ ♜

★★★ 67% Scarisbrick, Lord St. ☎ 01704 543000. 77 (76 ⇆ ♜ 1 ♜)

★★ 68% Balmoral Lodge, 41 Queens Rd. ☎ 01704 544298. 15 ⇆ ♜

RESTAURANT:
WRIGHTINGTON
❀ High Moor Inn, Highmoor Ln (jct 27 off M6, take B5239). ☎ 01257 252364

Hotel   ★ 61% Rockland Hotel, View Rd, RAINHILL
☎ 0151 426 4603 11rm(9 ⇆1 ⋒)

ST HELENS   Map 07 SJ59

Grange Park Prescot Rd WA10 3AD
☎ 01744 26318 Fax 01744 26318
A course of Championship length set in plesant country
surroundings - playing the course it is hard to believe
that industrial St Helens lies so close at hand. The course
is a fine test of golf and there are many attractive holes
liable to challenge all grades. The course has recently
undergone a programme of modernisation.
18 holes, 6422yds, Par 72, SSS 71, Course record 65.
Club membership 730.
Visitors	play allowed any day except public holidays. Advisable to contact professional in advance (01744 28785)
Societies	apply in writing
Green Fees	£25 upto 27 holes (£37.50 per 18 holes weekends).
Prof	Paul Roberts
Designer	James Braid
Facilities	⊗ ⨇ ┗ ☕ ♀ 🏖 🏠 ✐
Location	1.5m SW on A58

Hotel   ★★ 62% Kirkfield Hotel,
2/4 Church St, NEWTON LE WILLOWS
☎ 01925 228196 15rm(14 ⇆ ⋒)

Houghwood Golf Billinge Hill, Crank Rd, Crank
WA11 8RL ☎ 01744 894444 Fax 01744 894754
In a perfect setting Houghwood has magnificent panoramic
views over Lancashire plain and Welsh Hills. With large
USGA greens this undulating course is a superb test of golf
for all abilities.
18 holes, 6202yds, Par 70, SSS 69, Course record 68.
Club membership 700.
Visitors	no restrictions but dress code must be adhered to.
Societies	telephone enquiries welcome, deposit secures booking.
Green Fees	£14.50 per round (£17.50 weekends and bank holidays).
Cards	💳 💳 💳 💳
Prof	Paul Dickenson
Designer	Neville Pearsons
Facilities	⊗ ⨇ ┗ ☕ ♀ 🏖 🏠 ✐ 🛒 ♿ ✐
Location	From M6 junct 23 follow A580 to A571 to Billinge

Hotel   ★★★★ 68% Thistle Haydock, Penny Ln,
HAYDOCK ☎ 01942 272000 139 ⇆ ⋒

Sherdley Park Sherdley Rd WA9 5DE ☎ 01744 813149
Fairly hilly course with ponds in places.
18 holes, 5941yds, Par 70, SSS 69.
Club membership 160.
Visitors	no restrictions.
Green Fees	not confirmed.
Facilities	🏖 🏠 ✐
Location	2m S off A570

Hotel   ★★ 62% Kirkfield Hotel,
2/4 Church St, NEWTON LE WILLOWS
☎ 01925 228196 15rm(14 ⇆ ⋒)

SOUTHPORT   Map 07 SD31

The Hesketh Cockle Dick's Ln, off Cambridge Rd
PR9 9QQ ☎ 01704 536897 Fax 01704 539250
The Hesketh is the oldest of the six clubs in Southport,
founded in 1885. The 'Links' are of Championship
standard having hosted the Lancashire County
Championship in 1995, the British Senior Amateur and
British Girls Amateur. Used as a final qualifying course
for the Open Championship.
18 holes, 6572yds, Par 72, SSS 72, Course record 67.
Club membership 600.
Visitors	welcome, with handicap certificate, at all time other than Tues am (Ladies) and 12.30-2pm daily. Must contact in advance.
Societies	please contact Martyn G Senior in advance.
Green Fees	£45 per day; £35 per round (£50 weekends).
Prof	John Donoghue
Designer	J F Morris
Facilities	⊗ ⨇ ┗ ☕ ♀ 🏖 🏠 ✐ ✐
Location	1m NE of town centre off A565

Hotel   ★★★ 68% Stutelea Hotel & Leisure Club,
Alexandra Rd, SOUTHPORT
☎ 01704 544220 20 ⇆ ⋒

Hillside Hastings Rd, Hillside PR8 2LU
☎ 01704 567169 Fax 01704 563192
Championship links course with natural hazards open to
strong wind.
18 holes, 6850yds, Par 72, SSS 74, Course record 66.
Club membership 700.
Visitors	must contact in advance through secretary.
Societies	must apply to secretary in advance.
Green Fees	not confirmed.
Prof	Brian Seddon
Designer	Hawtree
Facilities	⊗ ⨇ ┗ ☕ ♀ 🏖 🏠 ✐ 🛒 ♿ ✐ ⸙
Location	3m S of town centre on A565

Hotel   ★★★ 69% Royal Clifton Hotel,
Promenade, SOUTHPORT
☎ 01704 533771 106 ⇆ ⋒

ROYAL BIRKDALE See page 187

Southport & Ainsdale Bradshaws Ln, Ainsdale
PR8 3LG ☎ 01704 578000 Fax 01704 570896
'S and A', as it is known in the North is another of the
fine Championship courses for which this part of the
country is famed. This Club has staged many important
events and offers golf of the highest order.
18 holes, 6603yds, Par 72, SSS 73, Course record 62.
Club membership 815.
Visitors	welcome except Thu am & bank holidays. Must contact club in advance & have handicap certificate.
Societies	must apply in advance.
Green Fees	£45 per day; £35 per round (£45 per round weekends).
Cards	💳 💳 💳 💳 💳
Prof	M Houghton
Designer	James Braid

Facilities	⊗ ⑊ 🍴 🍺 ♀ 🏌 🏠 ⛳ ♂
Location	3m S off A565
Hotel	★★★ 69% Royal Clifton Hotel, Promenade, SOUTHPORT ☎ 01704 533771 106 ⇔ 🐾

Southport Municipal Park Rd West PR9 0JR
☎ 01704 535286
Municipal seaside links course. Played over by Southport
Municipal, Alt and Park golf clubs.
18 holes, 6400yds, Par 70, SSS 69, Course record 67.
Club membership 750.

Visitors	no restrictions.
Societies	must telephone 6 days in advance.
Green Fees	not confirmed.
Cards	🌐 💳 🌐
Prof	Bill Fletcher
Facilities	⊗ 🍴 🍺 ♀ 🏌 🏠 ⛳ 🏌 ♂
Location	N side of town centre off A565
Hotel	★★★ 69% Royal Clifton Hotel, Promenade, SOUTHPORT ☎ 01704 533771 106 ⇔ 🐾

Southport Old Links Moss Ln, Churchtown PR9 7QS
☎ 01704 228207 Fax 01704 505353
Seaside course with tree-lined fairways and easy walking.
One of the oldest courses in Southport, Henry Vardon won
the 'Leeds Cup' here in 1922.
9 holes, 6244yds, Par 72, SSS 71, Course record 68.
Club membership 450.

Visitors	advisable to contact in advance.
Societies	apply in writing.
Green Fees	£25.50 per day; £18.50 per round (£25.50 per round weekends).
Facilities	⊗ ⑊ 🍴 🍺 ♀ 🏌
Location	NW side of town centre off A5267
Hotel	★★ 65% Bold Hotel, 585 Lord St, SOUTHPORT ☎ 01704 532578 23rm(9 ⇔11 🐾)

WALLASEY
Map 07 SJ29

Bidston Bidston Link Rd L44 2HR ☎ 0151 638 3412
Parkland course, with westerly winds.
18 holes, 6140yds, Par 70, SSS 71, Course record 66.
Club membership 650.

Visitors	must contact in advance, restricted weekends.
Societies	must apply in writing.
Green Fees	not confirmed.
Prof	J Law
Facilities	⊗ 🍴 🍺 ♀ 🏌 🏠
Location	0.5m W of M53 junc 1 entrance off A551
Hotel	★★★ 66% Leasowe Castle Hotel, Leasowe Rd, MORETON ☎ 0151 606 9191 47 ⇔ 🐾

Leasowe Moreton L46 3RD
☎ 0151 677 5852 Fax 0151 677 5852
Rather flat, semi-links, seaside course.
18 holes, 6227yds, Par 71, SSS 71.
Club membership 637.

Visitors	telephone professional (0151 678 5460). Handicap certificate required. Not Sat play and not before noon on Sun.

Societies	contact in advance.
Green Fees	not confirmed.
Cards	🌐 🌐
Prof	Andrew Ayres
Designer	John Ball Jnr
Facilities	⊗ ⑊ 🍴 🍺 ♀ 🏌 🏠 ⛳ ♂
Location	2m W on A551
Hotel	★★★ 66% Leasowe Castle Hotel, Leasowe Rd, MORETON ☎ 0151 606 9191 47 ⇔ 🐾

Wallasey Bayswater Rd L45 8LA
☎ 0151 691 1024 Fax 0151 638 8988
A well-established sporting links, adjacent to the Irish
Sea, with huge sandhills and many classic holes where
the player's skills are often combined with good fortune.
Large, firm greens and fine views but not for the fainthearted.
18 holes, 6607yds, Par 72.
Club membership 605.

Visitors	must contact one month in advance.
Societies	must apply in writing or telephone.
Green Fees	not confirmed.
Prof	Mike Adams
Designer	Tom Morris
Facilities	🍴 🍺 ♀ 🏠 ⛳ ♂
Location	N side of town centre off A554
Hotel	★★★ 66% Leasowe Castle Hotel, Leasowe Rd, MORETON ☎ 0151 606 9191 47 ⇔ 🐾

Warren Grove Rd L45 0JA ☎ 0151 639 8323
Short, undulating links course with first-class greens and
prevailing winds off the sea.
9 holes, 5854yds, Par 72, SSS 68.
Club membership 150.

Visitors	welcome except Sun 7-11am.
Green Fees	not confirmed.
Prof	Steve Konrad
Facilities	🍺 🏠 ⛳ ♂
Location	N side of town centre off A554
Hotel	★★★ 66% Leasowe Castle Hotel, Leasowe Rd, MORETON ☎ 0151 606 9191 47 ⇔ 🐾

NORFOLK

BARNHAM BROOM
Map 05 TG00

Barnham Broom Hotel,Golf,Conference,Leisure
Honingham Rd NR9 4DD
☎ 01603 759393 759552 golf shop Fax 01603 758224
Valley course meanders through the River Yare Valley,
parkland and mature trees. Hill course has wide
fairways, heavily guarded greens and spectacular views.
Valley Course: 18 holes, 6603yds, Par 72, SSS 72.
Hill Course: 18 holes, 6495yds, Par 71, SSS 71.
Club membership 500.

Visitors	must contact in advance.
Societies	must contact in advance.

▶

Green Fees	contact golf shop for details.
Cards	▨ ▨ ▨ ▨ ▨ ▨ ▨
Prof	P Ballingall/A Sheard
Designer	Frank Pennink
Facilities	⊗ ∭ ⬚ ♨ ♀ ⚘ ➔ ⛳ ⚑ ➘ 🏌 ⚐
& Leisure	hard tennis courts, heated indoor swimming pool, squash, sauna, solarium, gymnasium, golf & leisure packages.
Location	1m N, S of A47
Hotel	★★★ 72% Barnham Broom Hotel, BARNHAM BROOM ☎ 01603 759393 53 ⇄ ℜ *See advertisement on page 193.*

BAWBURGH   Map 05 TG10

Bawburgh Glen Lodge, Marlingford Rd NR9 3LU
☎ 01603 740404 Fax 01603 740403
Undulating course, mixture of parkland & heathland. Excellent 18th hole to finish.
18 holes, 5959yds, Par 70, SSS 69.
Club membership 700.

Visitors	must contact in advance, limited play at weekends.
Societies	must contact in advance.
Green Fees	£18 per weekday (£20 weekends and bank holidays).
Cards	▨ ▨ ▨
Prof	Chris Potter
Designer	Shaun Mansell
Facilities	⊗ ⬚ ♨ ♀ ⚘ ➘ 🏌 ⚐ ⚐
Location	S of Royal Norfolk Showground, on A47
Hotel	★★★ 70% Park Farm Hotel, HETHERSETT ☎ 01603 810264 6 ⇄ ℜ Annexe30 ⇄ ℜ

BRANCASTER   Map 09 TF74

Royal West Norfolk PE31 8AX
☎ 01485 210223 Fax 01485 210087
If you want to see what golf courses were like years ago, then go to the Royal West Norfolk where tradition exudes from both clubhouse and course. Close by the sea, the links are laid out in the grand manner and are characterised by sleepered greens, superb cross-bunkering and salt marshes.
18 holes, 6428yds, Par 71, SSS 71, Course record 66.
Club membership 740.

Visitors	must contact well in advance. Restrictions at weekends and in Aug.
Societies	must contact Secretary in advance.

Green Fees	£50 (£60 weekends).
Cards	▨ ▨ ▨ ▨ ▨
Prof	S Rayner
Designer	Holcombe-Ingleby
Facilities	⊗ ∭ ⬚ ♨ ♀ ⚘ ➔ 🏌 ⚐
Location	7m E of Hunstanton. In Brancaster village turn N at the beach/Broad Lane junct with A149 for 1m
Hotel	★★ 72% Titchwell Manor Hotel, TITCHWELL ☎ 01485 210221 11rm(7 ⇄ ℜ) Annexe4 ⇄ ℜ

CROMER   Map 09 TG24

Royal Cromer 145 Overstrand Rd NR27 0JH
☎ 01263 512884 Fax 01263 512884
Seaside course set out on cliff edge, hilly and subject to wind.
18 holes, 6508yds, Par 72, SSS 72, Course record 67.
Club membership 650.

Visitors	must contact in advance & have handicap certificate. Restricted at weekends.
Societies	must contact in advance.
Green Fees	£33 per day (£40 weekends & bank holidays). Reduced fees after 4pm also in winter.
Prof	Robin Page
Designer	J H Taylor
Facilities	⊗ ∭ ⬚ ♨ ♀ ⚘ ➔ 🏌
Location	1m E on B1159
Hotel	★★ 66% Red Lion, Brook St, CROMER ☎ 01263 514964 12 ⇄ ℜ

DENVER   Map 05 TF60

Ryston Park PE38 0HH
☎ 01366 382133 Fax 01366 383834
Parkland course.
9 holes, 6310yds, Par 70, SSS 70, Course record 66.
Club membership 330.

Visitors	must contact in advance. May not play weekends or bank holidays.
Societies	must apply in writing.
Green Fees	£20 per round (£15 per round Oct-Apr).
Designer	James Braid
Facilities	⊗ ∭ ⬚ ♨ ♀ ⚘ ➔ 🏌 ⚐
Location	0.5m S on A10
Hotel	★★ 69% Castle Hotel, High St, DOWNHAM MARKET ☎ 01366 384311 10 ⇄ ℜ

DEREHAM   Map 09 TF91

Dereham Quebec Rd NR19 2DS
☎ 01362 695900 & 695904 Fax 01362 695904
Parkland course.
9 holes, 6225yds, Par 71, SSS 70, Course record 64.
Club membership 400.
Visitors must contact in advance and have a handicap certificate; must play with member at weekends.
Societies must apply in writing.
Green Fees not confirmed.
Prof Robert Curtis
Facilities ⊗ �𝕄 ⌸ ♌ ⅄ ♨ ⌂ ⋞
Location N side of town centre off B1110

Hotel ★★★ 72% Barnham Broom Hotel, BARNHAM BROOM ☎ 01603 759393 53 ⇌ ♜

The Norfolk Golf & Country Club Hingham Rd, Reymerston NR9 4QQ
☎ 01362 850297 Fax 01362 850614
The course meanders through more than 200 acres of rolling Norfolk countryside, including ancient ditches, hedging and woodland. Large greens are built to USGA secification.
18 holes, 6609yds, Par 72, SSS 72.
Club membership 400.
Visitors contact Golf reception, bookings up to 1 week in advance.
Societies apply in writing to the General Manager.
Green Fees £18 per round (£22 weekends).
Cards 💳 VISA
Prof Tony Varney
Facilities ⊗ 𝕄 ⌸ ♌ ⅄ ♨ ⌂ ⋞ ⛟ ⛳ ⋞
& Leisure sauna, solarium, gymnasium, pitch & putt.
Location 12m W of Norwich, off B1135

Hotel ★★★ 72% Barnham Broom Hotel, BARNHAM BROOM ☎ 01603 759393 53 ⇌ ♜

DISS   Map 05 TM18

Diss Stuston IP22 3JB
☎ 01379 641025 Fax 01379 641025
Commonland course with natural hazards.
18 holes, 6238yds, Par 73, SSS 70.
Club membership 750.
Visitors must contact in advance but may not play weekends & bank holidays.
Societies by arrangement.
Green Fees £20 per day.
Prof N J Taylor
Facilities ⊗ 𝕄 ⌸ ♌ ⅄ ♨ ⌂ ⛟ ⛳ ⋞
Location 1.5m SE on B1118

Hotel ★★★ 70% Cornwallis Arms, BROME ☎ 01379 870326 10 ⇌ ♜ Annexe6 ⇌ ♜

FAKENHAM   Map 09 TF92

Fakenham Gallow Sports Centre, The Race Course N21 7NY ☎ 01328 863534
A well-wooded 9-hole course.
9 holes, 6174yds, Par 71, SSS 70, Course record 65.
Club membership 460.

Visitors any time with member, restricted until after noon weekends and bank holidays.
Societies apply in writing or telephone.
Green Fees not confirmed.
Prof Colin Williams
Facilities ⊗ ⌸ ♌ ⅄ ♨ ⌂ ⋞
& Leisure hard tennis courts, squash.

Hotel ★★ 66% Crown Hotel, Market Place, FAKENHAM ☎ 01328 851418 12 ⇌ ♜

GORLESTON-ON-SEA   Map 05 TG50

Gorleston Warren Rd NR31 6JT
☎ 01493 661911 & 662103 Fax 01493 661911
Cliff top course, the most easterly in the British Isles.
18 holes, 6391yds, Par 71, SSS 71, Course record 68.
Club membership 860.
Visitors advisable to contact in advance, must have handicap.
Societies must apply in writing.
Green Fees £21 per day/round (£25 weekends & bank holidays).
Prof Nick Brown
Designer J H Taylor
Facilities ⊗ 𝕄 ⌸ ♌ ⅄ ♨ ⌂ ⛳ ⋞
Location S side of town centre

Hotel ★★★ 74% Cliff Hotel, Gorleston, GREAT YARMOUTH ☎ 01493 662179 39 ⇌ ♜

GREAT YARMOUTH   Map 05 TG50

Caldecott Hall Golf & Leisure Caldecott Hall, Beccles Rd, Fritton NR31 9EY ☎ 01493 488488 Fax 01493 488561
Facilities at Caldecott Hall include an 18-hole course with testing dog-leg fairways, a short par 3 9-hole course, a floodlit driving range, and good practising areas.
Club membership 500.

Societies arrangements in advance.
Prof Mark Snazell
Facilities ⊗ 𝕄 ⌸ ♌ ⅄ ♨ ⌂ ⛳ ⛟ ⋞ ♟
& Leisure equestrian centre with tuition and 400 acres of woodland hacking.
Location On the A143 Beccles/Gt Yarmouth road at Fritton

Hotel ★★★ 74% Cliff Hotel, Gorleston, GREAT YARMOUTH ☎ 01493 662179 39 ⇌ ♜

Great Yarmouth & Caister Beach House,
Caister-on-Sea NR30 5TD ☎ 01493 728699
This great old club, which celebrated its centenary in
1982, has played its part in the development of the game.
It is a fine old-fashioned links where not many golfers
have bettered the SSS in competitions. The 468-yard 8th
(par 4), is a testing hole and the 7th is an extremely fine
short hole. A feature of the course is a number of
sleepered bunkers, a line of 4 bisecting the 4th.
18 holes, 6330yds, Par 70, SSS 70, Course record 66.
Club membership 720.

Visitors	must contact in advance. Restricted weekends.
Societies	must apply in writing or telephone.
Green Fees	£27 per day (£30 weekends & bank holidays).
Prof	James Hill
Designer	H Colt
Facilities	⊗ ⑂ ⓛ ♥ ♀ ♨ ⬧ ✎
& Leisure	snooker.
Location	0.5m N off A149
Hotel	★★★ 66% Imperial Hotel, North Dr, GREAT YARMOUTH ☎ 01493 851113 39 ⇋ ♠

HUNSTANTON   Map 09 TF64

Hunstanton Golf Course Rd PE36 6JQ
☎ 01485 532811 Fax 01485 532319
A championship links course set among some of the
most natural golfing country in East Anglia. Keep out of
the numerous bunkers and master the fast greens to play
to your handicap - then you only have the wind to
contend with! Good playing conditions all year round.
18 holes, 6735yds, Par 72, SSS 72, Course record 65.
Club membership 675.

Visitors	must contact in advance and be a club member with current handicap certificate. Restricted at weekends & may not play bank holiday weekends. Play in two ball format ie singles or foursomes.
Societies	apply in advance.
Green Fees	£50 per day (£60 weekends). £30 after 4pm weekdays.
Prof	John Carter
Designer	James Braid
Facilities	⊗ ⑂ by prior arrangement ⓛ ♥ ♀ ♨ ✎ ⬧ ♠ ♣ ✎
Location	Off A149 in Old Hunstanton Village signposted
Hotel	★★ 72% Caley Hall Motel, Old Hunstanton Rd, HUNSTANTON ☎ 01485 533486 Annexe33 ⇋

KING'S LYNN   Map 09 TF62

Eagles 39 School Rd, Tilney All Saints PE34 4RS
☎ 01553 827147 Fax 01553 829777
Parkland course with plenty of water hazards and bunkers.
Also Par-3 course and floodlit, covered driving range.
9 holes, 4284yds, Par 64, SSS 61, Course record 64.
Club membership 200.

Visitors	no restrictions.
Societies	must contact in advance.

Green Fees £13 per 18 holes, £6.50 per 9 holes (£15/£7.50 weekends & bank holidays).

Cards	▨ ▨ ▨ ▨ ▨ ▨
Prof	Nigel Pickerell
Designer	D W Horn
Facilities	⊗ ⓛ ♥ ♀ ♨ ✎ ♣ ⬧ ♠
& Leisure	hard tennis courts.
Location	Off A47 at roundabout to Tilney All Saints
Hotel	★★★ 66% The Duke's Head, Tuesday Market Place, KING'S LYNN ☎ 01553 774996 71 ⇋ ♠

King's Lynn Castle Rising PE31 6BD
☎ 01553 631654
Challenging, wooded parkland course.
18 holes, 6609yds, Par 72, SSS 72.
Club membership 1000.

Visitors	must contact in advance.
Societies	must contact in advance.
Green Fees	not confirmed.
Prof	Chris Hanlon
Designer	Thomas & Allis
Facilities	⊗ ⑂ ⓛ ♥ ♀ ♨ ✎ ♣ ✎
Location	4m NE off A149
Hotel	★★★ 66% The Duke's Head, Tuesday Market Place, KING'S LYNN ☎ 01553 774996 71 ⇋ ♠

MATTISHALL   Map 09 TG01

Mattishall South Green NR20 3JZ
☎ 01362 850111
Mattishall has the distinction of having the longest hole in
Norfolk at a very demanding 615yds.
9 holes, 3109yds, Par 35, SSS 69.
Club membership 120.

Visitors	no restrictions.
Societies	welcome.
Green Fees	not confirmed.
Designer	B Todd
Facilities	♥ ♀ ♨ ✎ ♣ ✎
Hotel	★★★ 72% Barnham Broom Hotel, BARNHAM BROOM ☎ 01603 759393 53 ⇋ ♠

MIDDLETON   Map 09 TF61

Middleton Hall Hall Orchards PE32 1RH
☎ 01553 841800
The setting is one of natural undulations, and mature
specimen trees, offering a most attractive environment for the
game of golf. The architecturally designed course provides a
challenge for the competent golfer, there is also a covered
floodlit driving range and practice putting green.
18 holes, 6007yds, Par 71, SSS 69.
Club membership 600.

Visitors	no restrictions.
Societies	must contact in advance.
Green Fees	£25 per day; £20 per round (£30/£25 weekends).
Prof	Peter Bowler
Designer	D Scott
Facilities	⊗ ⑂ ⓛ ♥ ♀ ♨ ✎ ✎ ♠
Location	4m from King's Lynn off A47
Hotel	★★★ 65% Butterfly Hotel, Beveridge Way, Hardwick Narrows, KING'S LYNN ☎ 01553 771707 50 ⇋ ♠

AA ★★★
BARNHAM BROOM HOTEL
GOLF • CONFERENCE • LEISURE

Set in 250 acres of countryside this modern hotel, golf and leisure complex has 53 en-suite bedrooms, a spacious lounge, sports bar café, restaurant and a host of leisure facilities including Hair and Beauty Salons. Two 18 hole courses in Yare river valley and undulating hillside setting. Practice ground and 3-hole academy area. Residential and non-residential golf schools and personal tuition provided by Peter Ballingall Golf School. The complex also contains excellent conference and banqueting facilities.

Golf and Leisure Packages available
Host: Richard Bond
For further information and brochure please telephone 01603 759393

Access: From London and the South via A11; from Midlands and the North via A47. 8 miles south west of Norwich.

Barnham Broom, Norwich NR9 4DD
Tel: (01603) 759393
Fax: (01603) 758224

MUNDESLEY
Map 09 TG33

Mundesley Links Rd NR11 8ES
☎ 01263 720279 & 720095 Fax 01263 720279
Parkland course, undulating with panoramic views, short but competitive. One mile from the sea.
9 holes, 5377yds, Par 68, SSS 66, Course record 63.
Club membership 450.
Visitors restricted Wed & weekends, also Tue 4-6pm, dress regulations, no sharing clubs, golf shoes must be worn.
Societies must contact one month in advance.
Green Fees £20 per day; £18 per round; £12 per 9 holes.
Prof T G Symmons
Facilities ⊗ 🐾 🍺 ♀ ⚲ 🏠 🌶 ⌀ ⌁
Location W side of village off B1159

Hotel ★★ 66% Red Lion, Brook St, CROMER
☎ 01263 514964 12 ⇄ 🐾

NORWICH
Map 05 TG20

Costessey Park Old Costessey NR8 5AL
☎ 01603 746333 & 747085 Fax 01603 746185
The course lies in the gently contoured Two River valley, providing players with a number of holes that bring the river and man-made lakes into play.
18 holes, 5820yds, Par 71, SSS 68, Course record 68.
Club membership 600.
Visitors may not play competition days, prior booking required for weekends.
Societies welcome by prior arrangement.
Green Fees not confirmed.

Cards ⌸ 🃏 🃏 🃏
Prof Simon Cook
Facilities ⊗ 🎱 🐾 🍺 ♀ ⚲ 🏠 🌶 🐦 🚜 ⌀

Hotel ★★★ 66% Quality Hotel, 2 Barnard Rd, Bowthorpe, NORWICH
☎ 01603 741161 80 ⇄ 🐾

Eaton Newmarket Rd NR4 6SF
☎ 01603 451686 & 452881 Fax 01603 451686
An undulating, tree-lined parkland course with excellent trees. Easy opening par 5 followed by an intimidating par 3 that is well bunkered with deep rough on both sides. The challenging 17th hole is uphill to a small hidden green and always needs more club than expected.
18 holes, 6114yds, Par 70, SSS 69, Course record 64.
Club membership 800.
Visitors restricted before 11.30am weekends. Advised to contact in advance.
Societies must contact in advance.
Green Fees not confirmed.
Prof Mark Allen
Facilities ⊗ 🐾 🍺 ♀ ⚲ 🏠 ⌀
Location 1.5m SW of city centre off A11

Hotel ★★★ 70% Park Farm Hotel, HETHERSETT
☎ 01603 810264 6 ⇄ 🐾 Annexe30 ⇄ 🐾

Royal Norwich Drayton High Rd, Hellesdon NR6 5AH
☎ 01603 429928 Fax 01603 417945
Undulating mature parkland course complimented with gorse. Largely unchanged since the alterations carried out by James Braid in 1924. A challenging test of golf.
18 holes, 6506yds, Par 72, SSS 72, Course record 65.
Club membership 700.
Visitors must contact in advance. Restricted weekends & bank holidays.
Societies must contact in advance.
Green Fees £30 per day (£36 weekends & bank holidays).
Prof Dean Futter
Designer James Braid
Facilities ⊗ 🎱 by prior arrangement 🐾 🍺 ♀ ⚲ 🏠 ⌀ 🐦 ⌀
Location 2.5m NW of city centre on A1067

Hotel ★★★ 66% Quality Hotel, 2 Barnard Rd, Bowthorpe, NORWICH
☎ 01603 741161 80 ⇄ 🐾

Sprowston Park Wroxham Rd NR7 8RP
☎ 01603 410657 Fax 01603 788884
A Pay & Play course set in 100 acres of parkland. A very tight course, so accuracy is required for good golf. The facilities include a 27-bay driving range, a practice area and tuition from a team of professionals.
18 holes, 5843yds, Par 70, SSS 68, Course record 63.
Club membership 640.
Visitors no restrictions.
Societies must contact in advance.
Green Fees £17 (£21 weekends & bank holidays).
Cards ⌸ 🃏 🃏 🃏
Prof Guy D Ireson
Facilities ⊗ 🎱 🐾 🍺 ♀ ⚲ 🏠 🌶 🐦 🚜 ⌀ ⌁
Location 4m NE from city centre on A1151

Hotel ★★★★ 74% Swallow Sprowston Manor, Sprowston Park, Wroxham Rd, Sprowston, NORWICH ☎ 01603 410871 94 ⇄ 🐾
See advertisement on page 194.

Wensum Valley Hotel, Golf & Country Club Beech Av, Taverham NR8 6HP ☎ 01603 261012 Fax 01603 261664
An undulating, picturesque golf course situated on the side of a valley. The greens in particular are very undulating and always give the average golfer a testing time. The 12th hole from a raised tee provides a blind and windy tee shot and a very slopey green.
Valley Course: 18 holes, 6172yds, Par 71, SSS 69, Course record 67.
Wensum Course: 9 holes, 5812yds, Par 70, SSS 68.
Club membership 900.
Visitors	no restrictions but advisable to book tee times at weekends.
Societies	apply in writing or by telephone.
Green Fees	£18.
Cards	▦▦▦▦▦
Prof	Peter Whittle
Designer	B Todd
Facilities	ⓧ ⽇ ⼁ ▦ ⼁ ⼁ ▦ ⼁ ⼁ ⼁
& Leisure	fishing, bowls green.
Location	5m N of Norwich

Hotel	★★★ 69% Swallow Nelson Hotel, Prince of Wales Rd, NORWICH ☎ 01603 760260 132 ⇔ ☞

SHERINGHAM · Map 09 TG14

Sheringham Weybourne Rd NR26 8HG
☎ 01263 823488 & 822038 Fax 01263 825189
Splendid cliff-top links with gorse, good 'seaside turf' and plenty of space. Straight driving is essential for a low score. The course is close to the shore and can be very windswept, but offers magnificent views.
18 holes, 6464yds, Par 70, SSS 71, Course record 65.
Club membership 680.
Visitors	must contact in advance & have handicap certificate. Restricted weekends.
Societies	must apply in writing.
Green Fees	£37 per day/round (£42 weekends & bank holidays).
Prof	M W Jubb
Designer	Tom Dunn
Facilities	ⓧ ⽇ ⼁ ▦ ⼁ ⼁ ⼁
Location	W side of town centre on A149

Hotel	★★ 70% Beaumaris Hotel, South St, SHERINGHAM ☎ 01263 822370 21 ⇔ ☞

SWAFFHAM · Map 05 TF80

Swaffham Cley Rd PE37 8AE ☎ 01760 721611
Heathland course and designated wildlife site.
9 holes, 6252yds, Par 72, SSS 70.
Club membership 385.
Visitors	must contact in advance. With member only at weekends.
Societies	must contact in advance.
Green Fees	£20 per day/round.
Prof	Peter Field
Facilities	ⓧ ⽇ ⼁ ▦ ⼁ ⼁ ⼁
Location	1.5m SW

Hotel	★★★ 64% George Hotel, Station Rd, SWAFFHAM ☎ 01760 721238 27 ⇔ ☞

S PROWSTON PARK Golf Course, located 4 miles North East of Norwich, A1151 to Wroxham and the Norfolk Broads. This four star country house hotel lies at the end of an oak lined driveway in ten acres of parkland, surrounded by the hotel's 18-hole golf course. Inclusive packages available – society meetings welcome.

Sprowston Park, Wroxham Road, Norwich NR7 8RP
Telephone Reservations: (01603) 410871

THETFORD · Map 05 TL88

Feltwell Thor Ave, Feltwell IP26 4AY ☎ 01842 827644
In spite of being an inland links, this 9-hole course is still open and windy.
9 holes, 6256yds, Par 70, SSS 70, Course record 68.
Club membership 400.
Visitors	dress restriction, no jeans, tracksuits or collarless shirts, golf shoes to be worn.
Societies	apply in writing or telephone in advance.
Green Fees	£15 per day (£22 weekends & bank holidays).
Prof	Peter Field
Facilities	ⓧ ⽇ ⼁ ▦ ⼁ (closed Mon) ⼁ ⼁ ⼁
Location	On B1112

Hotel	★★★ 62% The Bell, King St, THETFORD ☎ 01842 754455 47 ⇔ ☞

Thetford Brandon Rd IP24 3NE
☎ 01842 752169 Fax 01842 766212
This is a course with a good pedigree. It was laid-out by a fine golfer, C.H. Mayo, later altered by James Braid and then again altered by another famous course designer, Mackenzie Ross. It is a testing heathland course with a particularly stiff finish.
18 holes, 6879yds, Par 72, SSS 73, Course record 66.
Club membership 850.
Visitors	pre booking advisable, may not play weekends or bank holidays except with member. Handicap certificate required.
Societies	must contact in advance, Wed-Fri only.
Green Fees	£32 per day/round.
Cards	▦▦▦▦▦

Prof	Gary Kitley
Facilities	⊗ ♨ ᛤ 🏌 ♀ ⚑ 🏠 🏴 ⚙
Location	2m W of Thetford on B1107
Hotel	★★★ 62% The Bell, King St, THETFORD ☎ 01842 754455 47 ⇄ ♠

WATTON   Map 05 TF90

Richmond Park Saham Rd IP25 6EA
☎ 01953 881803 Fax 01953 881817
Compact parkland course with mature and young trees.
These together with the Little Wissey river and other water
hazards create an interesting but not daunting challenge.
18 holes, 6289yds, Par 71, SSS 70, Course record 69.
Club membership 600.

Visitors   not before 10.30am weekends & bank holidays
Societies   must contact in advance.
Green Fees £24 per day; £18 per round (£24 per day/round
             weekends).
Cards   ▭ ▭ VISA
Prof   Alan Hemsley
Designer   D Jessup/D Scott
Facilities   ⊗ ♨ ᛤ 🏌 ♀ ⚑ 🏠 🏴 🛒 🗼 ⚙ ⛳
& Leisure   gymnasium.
Location   500yds NW of town centre

Hotel   ★★★ 64% George Hotel, Station Rd,
            SWAFFHAM ☎ 01760 721238   27 ⇄ ♠

WESTON LONGVILLE   Map 09 TG11

Weston Park NR9 5JW
☎ 01603 872363 Fax 01603 873040
Testing course set in 200 acres of mature parkland with
specimen trees.
18 holes, 6603yds, Par 72, SSS 72, Course record 69.
Club membership 400.

Visitors   must telephone for tee times on 01603 872998
Societies   must telephone for prices and tee times.
Green Fees £35 per day; £26 per 18 holes (£40/£31
             weekends).
Prof   Michael Few
Facilities   ⊗ ᛤ 🏌 ♀ 🏠 🛒 🗼 ⚙
& Leisure   hard tennis courts, chipping green.
Location   Off the A1067 Norwich/Fakenham road, 9m
            NW of Norwich

Hotel   ★★★ 66% Quality Hotel, 2 Barnard Rd,
            Bowthorpe, NORWICH
            ☎ 01603 741161   80 ⇄ ♠

WEST RUNTON   Map 09 TG14

Links Country Park Hotel & Golf Club NR27 9QH
   ☎ 01263 838215 Fax 01263 838264
Parkland course 500 yds from the sea, with superb views
overlooking West Runton. The hotel offers extensive leisure
facilities.
9 holes, 4842yds, Par 66, SSS 64.
Club membership 250.

Visitors   restrictions weekends.
Societies   must telephone in advance.
Green Fees £20 per day (£25 weekends & bank holidays).
Cards   ▭ VISA ▭ ▭ ⚙
Prof   Lee Patterson
Designer   J.H Taylor
Facilities   ⊗ ♨ ᛤ 🏌 ♀ 🏠 🏴 🛒 🥄 🗼 ⚙
& Leisure   hard tennis courts, heated indoor swimming
            pool, sauna, solarium.
Location   S side of village off A149

Hotel   ★★ 70% Beaumaris Hotel,
            South St, SHERINGHAM
            ☎ 01263 822370   21 ⇄ ♠

NORTHAMPTONSHIRE

CHACOMBE   Map 04 SP44

Cherwell Edge OX17 2EN
   ☎ 01295 711591 Fax 01295 712404
Parkland course open since 1980. The front nine is short and
tight with mature trees. The back nine is longer and more
open.
18 holes, 5947yds, Par 70, SSS 68, Course record 64.
Club membership 650.

Visitors   no restrictions but golf shoes to be worn (can be
            hired) and tidy appearance expected.
Societies   must apply in advance.
Green Fees £12 (£16 weekends).
Cards   ▭ VISA ▭ ▭ ⚙
Prof   Joe Kingston
Designer   R Davies
Facilities   ⊗ ᛤ 🏌 ♀ 🏠 🏴 🥄 🗼 ⚙ ⛳
Location   Exit M40 junct 11, 0.5m S off B4525

Hotel   ★★★ 68% Whately Hall, Banbury Cross,
            BANBURY ☎ 01295 263451   72 ⇄ ♠

COLD ASHBY
Map 04 SP67

Cold Ashby Stanford Rd NN6 6EP
☎ 01604 740548 Fax 01604 740548
Undulating parkland course, nicely matured, with superb views. The 27 holes consist of three loops of nine which can be interlinked with each other. All three loops have their own challenge and any combination of two loops will give an excellent course. The start of the Elkington loop offers 5 holes of scenic beauty and testing golf and the 3rd on the Winwick loop is a 200-yard par 3 from a magnificent plateau tee.
Ashby-Elkington: 18 holes, 6308yds, Par 72, SSS 70, Course record 69.
Winwick-Ashby: 18 holes, 6004yds, Par 70, SSS 69, Course record 68.
Elkington-Winwick: 18 holes, 6250yds, Par 70, SSS 70, Course record 70.
Club membership 700.
Visitors start time must be reserved at weekends.
Societies must contact in advance.
Green Fees £25 per day; £16 per 18 holes; £9 per 9 holes (£197 per 18 holes; £10 per 9 holes weekends).
Cards ⌐ 💳 🔜 🔄
Prof Shane Rose
Designer David Croxton
Facilities ⊗ ⵊ ⅃ ⅃ ⵊ ☕ ♊ 🏌 ⚐
Location Close to junct 1 A14 & junct 18 M1 midway between Rugby, Leicester & Northampton

Hotel B Posthouse Northampton/Rugby, CRICK
☎ 01788 822101 88 ⇆ 🏃

COLLINGTREE
Map 04 SP75

Collingtree Park Windingbrook Ln NN4 0XN
☎ 01604 700000 Fax 01604 702600
Superb 18-hole resort course designed by former U.S. and British Open champion Johnny Miller. Stunning island green at the 18th hole. The Golf Academy includes a driving range, practice holes, indoor video teaching room.
18 holes, 6695yds, Par 72, SSS 72, Course record 66.
Visitors must contact in advance & have handicap certificate.
Societies contact in advance.
Green Fees not confirmed.
Prof Geoff Pook
Designer Johnny Miller
Facilities ⊗ ⵊ ⅃ ⅃ ⵊ ☕ ♊ 🏌 ⚐ ⚐
& Leisure fishing.
Location M1-junc 15 on A508 to Northampton

Hotel ★★★★ 68% Swallow Hotel, Eagle Dr, NORTHAMPTON
☎ 01604 768700 120 ⇆ 🏃

CORBY
Map 04 SP88

Corby Public Stamford Rd, Weldon NN17 3JH
☎ 01536 260756
Municipal course laid out on made-up quarry ground and open to prevailing wind. Wet in winter. Played over by Priors Hall Club.
18 holes, 6677yds, Par 72, SSS 72.
Club membership 600.

Visitors are advised to book in advance.
Societies must contact in advance.
Green Fees £8.50 per 18 holes; £4.75 per 9 holes (£11/£6.30 weekends).
Designer F Hawtree
Facilities ⊗ ⵊ ⅃ ⅃ ⵊ ☕ ♊ 🏌 ⚐ ⚐
Location 4m NE on A43

Hotel ★★★ 67% The Talbot, New St, OUNDLE
☎ 01832 273621 39 ⇆ 🏃

DAVENTRY
Map 04 SP56

Daventry & District Norton Rd NN11 5LS
☎ 01327 702829
A hilly course with hard walking.
9 holes, 5812yds, Par 69, SSS 68, Course record 68.
Club membership 360.
Visitors restricted Sun mornings & weekends (Oct-Mar).
Societies contact the club secretary.
Green Fees £10 (£15 weekends & bank holidays).
Facilities ⵊ ⅃ ⅃ ⵊ ☕
Location 1m NE

Hotel ★★★★ 62% Hanover International Hotel & Club Daventry, Sedgemoor Way, off Ashby Rd, DAVENTRY ☎ 01327 301777 138 ⇆ 🏃

FARTHINGSTONE
Map 04 SP65

Farthingstone Hotel & Golf Course NN12 8AH
☎ 01327 361533 & 361291 Fax 01327 361645
A mature and challenging course set in picturesque countryside.
18 holes, 6299yds, Par 70, SSS 70, Course record 68.
Club membership 500.
Visitors must contact in advance.
Societies must contact in advance.
Green Fees £12.50-£16.50 (£18-£27 weekends).
Cards ⌐ 💳 🔜 🔄
Prof Austin Curtis
Designer Don Donaldson
Facilities ⊗ ⵊ ⅃ ⅃ ⵊ ☕ ♊ 🏌 ⚐ ⚐
& Leisure squash, Snooker, Pool table, Indoor practice bay.
Location 1m W

Hotel ★★ 65% Globe Hotel, High St, WEEDON
☎ 01327 340336 15 ⇆ 🏃 Annexe3 ⇆ 🏃

HELLIDON
Map 04 SP55

Hellidon Lakes Hotel & Country Club NN11 6LN
☎ 01327 262550 Fax 01327 262559
Spectacular parkland course designed by David Snell.
18 holes, 6691yds, Par 72, SSS 72 or 9 holes, 2791yds, Par 70, SSS 67.
Club membership 500.
Visitors 18 hole course; must contact in advance & have handicap certificate at weekends. 9 hole; open to beginners.
Societies must telephone in advance.
Green Fees not confirmed.
Prof Gary Wills
Designer D Snell

Facilities ⊗ 🎱 ⛳ 🏌 ♀ ⚓ 📷 ⛳ 🦢 ✉ ⚷ ℓ
& Leisure hard tennis courts, heated indoor swimming pool, fishing, sauna, solarium, gymnasium.

Hotel ★★★★ 70% Hellidon Lakes Hotel & Country Club, HELLIDON ☎ 01327 262550 45 ⇆ 🏌

KETTERING   Map 04 SP87

Kettering Headlands NN15 6XA ☎ 01536 511104
A very pleasant, mainly flat meadowland course with easy walking.
18 holes, 6081yds, Par 69, SSS 69, Course record 64.
Club membership 700.
Visitors welcome but with member only weekends & bank holidays.
Societies Wed & Fri only, apply in writing.
Green Fees £24 per day.
Prof Kevin Theobald
Designer Tom Morris
Facilities ⊗ 🎱 ⛳ 🏌 ♀ ⚓ 📷 ⛳ ⚷
Location S side of town centre

Hotel ★★★★ 70% Kettering Park Hotel, Kettering Parkway, KETTERING ☎ 01536 416666 119 ⇆ 🏌

NORTHAMPTON   Map 04 SP76

Brampton Heath Sandy Ln, Church Brampton NN6 8AX
☎ 01604 843939 Fax 01604 843885
Appealing to both the novice and experienced golfer, this beautiful, well drained heathland course affords panoramic views over Northampton.
18 holes, 6366yds, Par 71, SSS 70, Course record 69.
Club membership 500.
Visitors advisable to book especially for weekends, may book up to 8 days in advance.
Societies write or telephone for details.
Green Fees £12 per 18 holes; £7.20 per 9 holes (£16/£9.60 weekends).
Cards ⚊ 💳 💳 💳 📇
Prof Richard Hudson
Designer D Snell
Facilities ⊗ 🎱 ⛳ 🏌 ♀ ⚓ 📷 ⛳ 🦢 ⚓ ⚷ ℓ
& Leisure short course par 3.
Location Signposted off old A50 Kingsthorpe to Welford road, 2m N of Kingsthorpe

Hotel ★★★ 71% Lime Trees Hotel, 8 Langham Place, Barrack Rd, NORTHAMPTON ☎ 01604 632188 27 ⇆ 🏌

Delapre Golf Complex Eagle Dr, Nene Valley Way NN4 7DU ☎ 01604 764036 Fax 01604 706378
Rolling parkland course, part of municipal golf complex, which includes two 9-hole, par 3 courses, pitch-and-putt and 40 bay floodlit driving-range.
Main Course: 18 holes, 6269yds, Par 70, SSS 70, Course record 66.
Hardingstone Course: 9 holes, 2109yds, Par 32, SSS 32.
Club membership 900.
Visitors no restrictions but advance booking advised for weekends.
Societies must book and pay full green fees 2 weeks in advance.
Green Fees not confirmed.
Prof John Corby

Designer John Jacobs/John Corby
Facilities ⊗ 🎱 ⛳ 🏌 ♀ ⚓ 📷 ⛳ ⚷ ℓ
Location 2m SE

Hotel ★★★ 65% Quality Hotel Northampton, Ashley Way, Weston Favell, NORTHAMPTON ☎ 01604 739955 31 ⇆ 🏌 Annexe35 ⇆ 🏌
See advertisement on page 262.

Kingsthorpe Kingsley Rd NN2 7BU
☎ 01604 710610 Fax 01604 710610
A compact, undulating parkland course set within the town boundary. Not a long course but testing enough to attract a competitive membership that boasts several County players.
18 holes, 5918yds, Par 69, SSS 69, Course record 63.
Club membership 630.
Visitors must contact in advance and have handicap certificate. With member only weekends.
Societies must contact in advance.
Green Fees £25 per day.
Prof Paul Armstrong
Designer Mr Alison
Facilities ⊗ 🎱 ⛳ 🏌 ♀ ⚓ 📷 ⚷
Location N side of town centre on A5095 between the Racecourse and Kingsthorpe

Hotel ★★★ 65% Quality Hotel Northampton, Ashley Way, Weston Favell, NORTHAMPTON ☎ 01604 739955 31 ⇆ 🏌 Annexe35 ⇆ 🏌

Northampton Harlestone NN7 4EF
☎ 01604 845155 Fax 01604 820262
Parkland course with water in play on three holes.
18 holes, 6615yds, Par 72, SSS 72, Course record 67.
Club membership 750.
Visitors must contact in advance and have handicap certificate. With member only at weekends, no visitors on Wed.
Societies must contact in advance.
Green Fees Weekdays: £30 per day/round.
Cards ⚊ 💳 💳 💳 💳 📇
Prof Kevin Dickens
Designer Sinclair Steel
Facilities ⊗ 🎱 ⛳ 🏌 ♀ ⚓ 📷 ⚷
Location NW of town centre on A428

Hotel ★★★ 67% Northampton Moat House, Silver St, NORTHAMPTON ☎ 01604 739988 141 ⇆ 🏌

Northamptonshire County Golf Ln, Church Brampton NN6 8AZ
☎ 01604 843025 Fax 01604 843025
A fine, traditional course situated on undulating heathland with areas of gorse, heather and extensive coniferous and deciduous woodland. A river and a railway line pass through the course.
18 holes, 6503yds, Par 70, SSS 71, Course record 65.
Club membership 750.
Visitors restricted weekends. May not play on bank holidays. Must contact in advance and have a handicap certificate.
Societies Wed/Thu only, must contact in advance.
Green Fees £40 per day/round.
Prof Tim Rouse
Designer H S Colt
Facilities ⊗ 🎱 ⛳ 🏌 ♀ ⚓ 📷 ⛳ ⚷ ℓ
Location 5m NW of Northampton, off A50   ▶

Hotel   ★★★ 65% Quality Hotel Northampton, Ashley Way, Weston Favell, NORTHAMPTON ☎ 01604 739955   31 ⇆ ໃ Annexe35 ⇆ ໃ

Overstone Park Billing Ln NN6 0AP
☎ 01604 647666 Fax 01604 642635
A testing parkland course, gently undulating within panoramic views of local stately home. Excellent drainage and fine greens make the course great all year round. Water comes into play on three holes.
18 holes, 6602yds, Par 72, SSS 72, Course record 68.
Club membership 500.
Visitors   contact in advance, only after 2pm at weekends. Must contact in advance.
Societies   write or telephone.
Green Fees   Weekdays £35 per day; £25 per round (£27.50/£20 winter).
Cards   ▬ ▬▬ ▬▬ ▣ ▬ ◪ ▨
Prof   Brain Mudge
Designer   Donald Steel
Facilities   ⊗ ⫛ ⅃ ➘ ♥ ⅒ △ ₢ ╬ ⅂ ⚲ ⤙ ✎
& Leisure   hard tennis courts, heated indoor swimming pool, fishing, sauna, solarium, gymnasium, horse riding locally.
Location   Exit M1 junct15, follow A45 to Billing Aquadrone turn off, course is 2m on Gt Billing Way

Hotel   ★★ 67% Thorplands Toby Hotel, Talavera Way, Round Spinney, NORTHAMPTON ☎ 01604 494241   31 ⇆ ໃ

OUNDLE   Map 04 TL08

Oundle Benefield Rd PE8 4EZ
☎ 01832 273267 (Gen Manager) Fax 01832 273267
Undulating parkland course, shortish but difficult. A small brook affects some of the approaches to the greens.
18 holes, 6235yds, Par 71, SSS 70, Course record 72.
Club membership 600.
Visitors   may not play Tue (Ladies Day) or before 10.30am weekends unless with member.
Societies   must apply in advance.
Green Fees   £25.50 per day (£35.50 weekends).
Prof   Richard Keys
Facilities   ⊗ ⫛ ⅃ ➘ ♥ ⅂ ⚲ △ ₢ ⅒ ✎
Location   1m W on A427

Hotel   ★★★ 67% The Talbot, New St, OUNDLE ☎ 01832 273621   39 ⇆ ໃ

STAVERTON   Map 04 SP56

Staverton Park NN11 6JT ☎ 01327 302000
Open course, fairly testing with good views.
18 holes, 6661yds, Par 71, SSS 72, Course record 65.
Club membership 300.
Visitors   restricted weekends. Must contact in advance. Handicap certificates preferred.
Societies   must contact in advance.
Green Fees   not confirmed.
Prof   Richard Mudge
Designer   Cmdr John Harris
Facilities   ⊗ ⫛ ⅃ ➘ ♥ ⅂ ⚲ △ ₢ ⅒ ✎ ⚲ ♭
& Leisure   sauna, gymnasium.
Location   0.75m NE of Staverton on A425

Hotel   ★★★★ 62% Hanover International Hotel & Club Daventry, Sedgemoor Way, off Ashby Rd, DAVENTRY ☎ 01327 301777 138 ⇆ ໃ

WELLINGBOROUGH   Map 04 SP86

Rushden Kimbolton Rd, Chelveston NN9 6AN
☎ 01933 418511
Parkland course with brook running through the middle.
10 holes, 6335yds, Par 71, SSS 70, Course record 68.
Club membership 400.
Visitors   may not play Wed afternoon. With member only weekends.
Societies   must apply in writing.
Green Fees   £18 per day/round.
Facilities   ⊗ ⫛ ⅃ ➘ ♥ ⅂ ⚲ △
Location   2m E of Higham Ferrers on Kimbolton Rd

Hotel   ★★★ 65% Hind Hotel, Sheep St, WELLINGBOROUGH ☎ 01933 222827   34 ⇆ ໃ

Wellingborough Great Harrowden Hall NN9 5AD
☎ 01933 677234 Fax 01933 679379
An undulating parkland course with many trees. The 514-yd, 14th is a testing hole. The clubhouse is a stately home.
18 holes, 6617yds, Par 72, SSS 72, Course record 68.
Club membership 820.
Visitors   may not play at weekends & bank holidays or Tue between 10am and 2.30pm.
Societies   must apply in writing.
Green Fees   £35 per day; £25 per round.
Prof   David Clifford
Designer   Hawtree
Facilities   ⊗ ⫛ ⅃ ➘ ♥ ⅂ ⚲ △ ₢ ⅒ ✎
& Leisure   outdoor swimming pool, snooker.
Location   2m N on A509

Hotel   ★★★ 65% Hind Hotel, Sheep St, WELLINGBOROUGH ☎ 01933 222827   34 ⇆ ໃ

WHITTLEBURY   Map 04 SP64

Whittlebury Park Golf & Country Club NN12 8XW
☎ 01327 858092 Fax 01327 858009
The 36 holes incorporate three courses of tournament-standard nines plus a short course. The 1905 Course is a reconstruction of the original parkland course built at the turn of the century, the Royal Whittlewood is a lakeland course playing around copses and the Grand Prix, next to Silverstone Motor Racing circuit has a strong links feel playing over gently undulating grassland with challenging lake features.
Grand Prix: 9 holes, 3339yds, Par 36, SSS 36.
Royal Whittlewood: 9 holes, 3323yds, Par 36, SSS 36.
1905: 9 holes, 3256yds, Par 36, SSS 36.
Club membership 450.
Visitors   must contact in advance.
Societies   telephone 01327 858092 in advance.
Green Fees   £10-£20 weekdays (£30 weekends).
Cards   ▬ ▬▬▬ ▨
Prof   Martin Leung
Designer   Cameron Sinclair
Facilities   ⊗ ⫛ ➘ ♥ ⅂ ⚲ △ ₢ ⅒ ⤙ ✎ ♭
Location   A413 Buckingham Road

Hotel   ★★★ 66% Buckingham Four Pillars Hotel,
               Buckingham Ring Rd South, BUCKINGHAM
               ☎ 01280 822622 70 ⇥ ☏

NORTHUMBERLAND

ALLENDALE   Map 12 NY85

Allendale High Studdon, Allenheads Rd NE47 9DH
☎ 01434 683926 & 683623 Fax 01434 683668
Challenging and hilly parkland course set 1000 feet above
sea level with superb views of Allendale. New club house.
18 holes, 4541yds, Par 66, SSS 62, Course record 69.
Club membership 270.
Visitors   may not play Aug bank holiday until after 3pm.
Societies   must apply in writing to Secretary.
Green Fees   £20 per day; £12 per 18 holes.
Facilities   ☏ ♀ ⚒
Location   1.5m S on B6295

Hotel   ★★★ 68% Beaumont Hotel, Beaumont St,
               HEXHAM ☎ 01434 602331 25 ⇥ ☏

ALNMOUTH   Map 12 NU21

Alnmouth Foxton Hall NE66 3BE
☎ 01665 830231 Fax 01665 830922
Coastal course with pleasant views.
18 holes, 6429yds, Par 69, SSS 69, Course record 64.
Club membership 850.
Visitors   may not play Wed, Fri, weekends & bank
               holidays.
Societies   Mon, Tue or Thu only.
Green Fees   £29 per day; £22 per round after 2pm Mon, Tue
               & Thu only.
Designer   H S Colt
Facilities   ☒ ⏶ ⛟ ☏ ♀ ⚒ 🍴 ⌑ 🛏 ⚐ ⚒ ♂
& Leisure   snooker.
Location   1m NE

Hotel   ★★★ 63% White Swan Hotel,
               Bondgate Within, ALNWICK
               ☎ 01665 602109 58 ⇥ ☏

Alnmouth Village Marine Rd NE66 2RZ
☎ 01665 830370
Seaside course with part coastal view.
9 holes, 6078yds, Par 70, SSS 70, Course record 63.
Club membership 480.
Visitors   may not play before 11am on competition days.
Societies   must contact in advance.
Green Fees   not confirmed.
Facilities   ☒ ⏶ ⛟ ☏ ♀ ⚒
Location   E side of village

Hotel   ★★★ 63% White Swan Hotel,
               Bondgate Within, ALNWICK
               ☎ 01665 602109 58 ⇥ ☏

ALNWICK   Map 12 NU11

Alnwick Swansfield Park NE66 2AT ☎ 01665 602632
Parkland course offering a fair test of golfing skills.
18 holes, 6284yds, Par 70, SSS 70, Course record 66.
Club membership 550.
Visitors   no restrictions.
Societies   must contact secretary in advance.
Green Fees   £17 per day; £13 per round (£22/£17 weekends
               & bank holidays).
Designer   Rochester
Facilities   ☒ ⏶ ⛟ ☏ ♀ ⚒
Location   S side of town

Hotel   ★★★ 63% White Swan Hotel,
               Bondgate Within, ALNWICK
               ☎ 01665 602109 58 ⇥ ☏

BAMBURGH   Map 12 NU13

Bamburgh Castle NE69 7DE
☎ 01668 214378 (club) & 214321 (sec)
Superb coastal course with excellent greens that are both
fast and true, natural hazards of heather and whin bushes
abound. Magnificent views of Farne Islands, Holy
Island, Lindisfarne Castle, Bamburgh Castle and Cheviot
Hils.
18 holes, 5621yds, Par 68, SSS 67, Course record 64.
Club membership 700.
Visitors   must contact in advance. Restricted
               weekends, bank holidays and competition
               days.
Societies   apply in writing. Weekdays only.
Green Fees   £30 per day/round (£35 per day;£30 per
               round weekends & bank holidays).
Designer   George Rochester
Facilities   ☒ ⏶ ⛟ ☏ ♀ ⚒ 🛏 ♂
Location   6m E of A1 via B1341 or B1342

Hotel   ★★ 67% Lord Crewe Arms,
               Front St, BAMBURGH
               ☎ 01668 214243 24rm(21 ⇥ ☏)

BEDLINGTON   Map 12 NZ28

Bedlingtonshire Acorn Bank NE22 6AA
☎ 01670 822087
Meadowland/parkland course with easy walking. Under
certain conditions the wind can be a distinct hazard.
18 holes, 6813mtrs, Par 73, SSS 73, Course record 68.
Club membership 960.
Visitors   must contact in advance.
Societies   must apply in writing.
Green Fees   not confirmed.
Prof   Marcus Webb
Designer   Frank Pennink
Facilities   ☒ ⏶ ⛟ ☏ ♀ ⚒ 🍴 ♂
Location   1m SW on A1068

Hotel   ★★★★ 63% Holiday Inn,
               Great North Rd, SEATON BURN
               ☎ 0191 201 9988 150 ⇥ ☏

BELFORD   Map 12 NU13

Belford South Rd NE70 7DP
☎ 01668 213433 Fax 01668 213919
An east coast parkland course. Crosswinds affect the 4th but
the compensation is spectacular views over Holy Island.
9 holes, 3152yds, Par 72, SSS 70, Course record 72.
Club membership 200.
Visitors   no restrictions.
Societies   must contact in advance.
Green Fees £14 per 18 holes; £10 per 9 holes (£17/£11
            weekends and bank holidays).
Designer   Nigel Williams
Facilities 🄫 💌 ♀ ♤ ⌂ ⛳ ⚐ ♐ ⚒
Location   Off A1, midway between Alnwick & Berwick
            on Tweed

Hotel   ★★★ 68% Blue Bell Hotel, Market Place,
         BELFORD ☎ 01668 213543 17 ⇔ ⋔

BELLINGHAM   Map 12 NY88

Bellingham Boggle Hole NE48 2DT
☎ 01434 220530 (Secretary) Fax 01434 220160
This highly regarded 18-hole golf course is situated between
Hadrian's Wall and the Scottish Border. A rolling parkland
course with many natural hazards. There is a mixture of
testing par threes, long par fives and tricky par fours.
18 holes, 6077yds, Par 70, SSS 70, Course record 68.
Club membership 650.
Visitors   welcome all week, advisable to contact in
            advance as starting sheet in operation.
Societies   must contact in advance.
Green Fees £20 per day/round (£25 weekends & bank
            holidays).
Designer   E Johnson/I Wilson
Facilities 🄫 ⧫ 🄫 💌 ♀ ♤ ⛳ ⚒ ⚐
Location   N side of village on B6320

Hotel   ★★ 69% Riverdale Hall Hotel,
         BELLINGHAM ☎ 01434 220254 20 ⇔ ⋔

BERWICK-UPON-TWEED   Map 12 NT95

Berwick-upon-Tweed (Goswick) Goswick TD15 2RW
☎ 01289 387256
Natural seaside links course, with undulating fairways,
elevated tees and good greens.
18 holes, 6465yds, Par 72, SSS 71, Course record 69.
Club membership 600.

Visitors   must contact in advance for weekends,
            advisable at other times.
Societies   must telephone in advance (apply in writing
            Apr-Sep).
Green Fees not confirmed.
Prof   Paul Terras
Designer   James Braid
Facilities 🄫 ⧫ 🄫 💌 ♀ ♤ ⛳ ⚐ ♐ ⚒
Location   6m S off A1

Hotel   ★★★ 68% Blue Bell Hotel, Market Place,
         BELFORD ☎ 01668 213543 17 ⇔ ⋔

Magdalene Fields Magdalene Fields TD15 1NE
☎ 01289 306384 & 306130 Fax 01289 306384
Seaside course with natural hazards formed by sea bays. All
holes open to winds. Testing 8th hole over bay (par 3).
18 holes, 6407yds, Par 72, SSS 71, Course record 65.
Club membership 400.
Visitors   must contact in advance for weekend play.
Societies   must contact in advance.
Green Fees £16 per round (£18 weekends).
Designer   Willie Park
Facilities 🄫 ⧫ 🄫 💌 ♀ ♤ ⛳ ⚒ ⚐
Location   0.5m on E side of town centre

Hotel   ★★★🌢 72% Tillmouth Park Hotel,
         CORNHILL-ON-TWEED
         ☎ 01890 882255 12 ⇔ ⋔ Annexe2 ⇔ ⋔

BLYTH   Map 12 NZ38

Blyth New Delaval, Newsham NE24 4DB
☎ 01670 540110 (sec) & 356514 (pro) Fax 01670 540134
Course built over old colliery. Parkland with water hazards.
18 holes, 6456yds, Par 72, SSS 71, Course record 65.
Club membership 820.
Visitors   with member only after 3pm & at weekends.
            Must contact in advance.
Societies   apply in writing.
Green Fees £20 per day; £18 per round (£22 per round after
            3pm weekends).
Prof   Andrew Brown
Designer   Hamilton Stutt
Facilities 🄫 🄫 💌 ♀ ♤ ⛳ ⚒
Location   6m N of Whitley Bay

Hotel   ★★★ 64% Windsor Hotel,
         South Pde, WHITLEY BAY
         ☎ 0191 251 8888 63 ⇔ ⋔

CRAMLINGTON — Map 12 NZ27

Arcot Hall NE23 7QP
☎ 0191 236 2794 Fax 0191 217 0370
A wooded parkland course, reasonably flat.
18 holes, 6380yds, Par 70, SSS 70, Course record 65.
Club membership 660.

Visitors	must contact in advance. May not play weekends.
Societies	must contact in advance.
Green Fees	£26 per day (weekdays only).
Prof	Graham Cant
Designer	James Braid
Facilities	⊗ Ⅻↈ ⌶ ♀ ♨ 🛆 📷 ⌁ ⌀
Location	2m SW off A1

Hotel ★★★★ 63% Holiday Inn, Great North Rd, SEATON BURN ☎ 0191 201 9988 150 ⇆ ♞

EMBLETON — Map 12 NU22

Dunstanburgh Castle NE66 3XQ
☎ 01665 576562 Fax 01665 576562
Rolling links designed by James Braid, adjacent to the beautiful Embleton Bay. Historic Dunstanburgh Castle is at one end of the course and a National Trust lake and bird sanctuary at the other. Superb views.
18 holes, 6298yds, Par 70, SSS 69, Course record 69.
Club membership 394.

Visitors	advisable to contact in advance at weekends and holiday periods.
Societies	must contact in advance.
Green Fees	£15 per day (£25 per day; £20 per round weekends & bank holidays).
Designer	James Braid
Facilities	⊗ Ⅻↈ ⌶ ♀ ♨ 🛆 📷 ⌁ ⌀
Location	7m NE of Alnwick off A1

Hotel ★★ 68% Beach House Hotel, Sea Front, SEAHOUSES ☎ 01665 720337 14 ⇆ ♞

GREENHEAD — Map 12 NY66

Haltwhistle Banktop CA6 7HL
☎ 016977 47367 & 01434 344000 (sec) Fax 01434 344311
Interesting course with panoramic views of Northumberland National Park. The 515yard Par 5 14th hole is a real test of golf skill, played from the highest point of the course through an undulating fairway to a viciously sloping green. The 188yard Par 3 now the 1st hole, played uphill, is particularly difficult playing into the prevailing west wind.
18 holes, 5522yds, Par 69, SSS 67, Course record 70.
Club membership 391.

Visitors	no visitors Sun mornings.
Societies	apply in writing to: Hon Secretary, John Gilbertson, Parkhead Farmhouse, Bardon Mill, Northumberland NE47 7JS.
Green Fees	£12 per day (£15 weekends).
Facilities	⊗ Ⅻↈ ⌶ ♀ ♨
Location	N on A69 past Haltwhistle on Gilsland Road

Hotel ★★★♨♨ Farlam Hall Hotel, Hallbankgate, BRAMPTON ☎ 016977 46234 11 ⇆ ♞ Annexe1 ⇆ ♞

HEXHAM — Map 12 NY96

De Vere Slaley Hall, Golf Resort & Spa Slaley NE47 0BY
☎ 01434 673350 (hotel) & 673154 (pro) Fax 01434 673152
Measuring 7073yds from the championship tees, this Dave Thomas designed course incorporates forest, parkland and moorland with an abundance of lakes and streams. The challenging par 4 9th (452yds) is played over water through a narrow avenue of towering trees and dense rhododendrons. An official PGA European Tour venue and hosts the COMPAQ European Grand Prix. The Priestman course designed by PGA Chairman, Neil Coles will be of equal length and standard as the Hunting course. Opening in spring 1999 the Priestman is situated in 280 acres on the western side of the estate, giving panoramic views over the Tyndale Valley.
Hunting Course: 18 holes, 7073yds, Par 72, SSS 73, Course record 65.
Priestman Course: 18 holes, 7010yds, Par 72, SSS 71.
Club membership 350.

Visitors	must contact in advance, times subject to availability. May not play weekends or public holidays.
Societies	apply in writing to bookings co-ordinator, small groups 8 or less may book through pro shop.
Green Fees	not confirmed.
Cards	🗀 🗀 🗀 🗀 🗀 🗀
Prof	Mark Stancer
Designer	Dave Thomas/Neil Coles
Facilities	⊗ Ⅻↈ ⌶ ♀ ♨ 🛆 📷 ⌁ 🛏 ☞ ⚓ ⌀ ⟊
& Leisure	heated indoor swimming pool, fishing, sauna, solarium, gymnasium.
Location	8m S of Hexham off A68

Hotel ★★★★ 70% De Vere Slaley Hall, Slaley, HEXHAM ☎ 01434 673350 139 ⇆ ♞

Hexham Spital Park NE46 3RZ
☎ 01434 603072 Fax 01434 601865
A very pretty well drained parkland course with interesting natural contours. Exquisite views from parts of the course, of the Tyne valley below. As good a parkland course as any in the North of England.
18 holes, 6000yds, Par 70, SSS 68, Course record 64.
Club membership 700.

Visitors	advance booking advisable.
Societies	welcome weekdays, contact in advance.
Green Fees	£35 per day; £25 per round (£35 per round weekends & bank holidays).
Cards	🗀 🗀 🗀 🗀 🗀 🗀
Prof	Martin Forster
Facilities	⊗ Ⅻↈ ⌶ ♀ ♨ 🛆 📷 ⌁ ⌀
& Leisure	squash.
Location	1m NW on B6531

Hotel ★★★ 68% Beaumont Hotel, Beaumont St, HEXHAM ☎ 01434 602331 25 ⇆ ♞
See advertisement on page 202.

LONGHORSLEY — Map 12 NZ19

Linden Hall NE65 8XF
☎ 01670 788050 Fax 01670 788544
Set within the picturesque Linden Hall Estate, with views of the Cheviot Hills and the Northumberland coast, this newly

►

THE BEAUMONT HOTEL,
Hexham, Northumberland
NE46 3LT
Tel: (01434) 602331
Email: Beaumont.hotel@btinternet.com

The perfect base for 3 of the North East's finest
Golf Courses: Slaley, Hexham
& Matfen Hall.
25 Bedrooms, with full facilities, excellent food
and choice of bars make a wonderful 'Golfing
Hotel'. Special Golf Rates on Request

AA ★★★

---

established course features mature woodland and several
burns and lakes.
18 holes, 6809yds, Par 72, SSS 73.
Club membership 240.

Visitors   must book in advance.
Societies   must be of reasonable standard of play, observe
                   dress code & etiquette, preferably have handicap
                   certificate.
Green Fees   £25 per round (£27.50 weekends).
Cards   ▭▭ ▭▭ ▭▭ ▭
Prof   David Curry
Designer   Jonathan Gaunt
Facilities   ⊗ ⊪ ⅙ ▼ ♀ ♨ 🏠 🛉 🏄 ➘ ♨ ♂ ♩
& Leisure   hard tennis courts, heated indoor swimming
                   pool, sauna, solarium, gymnasium, ballooning,
                   croquet, clay pigeon shooting, quad bikes.
Location   From A1 N/S take A697 to Coldstream, approx
                   4m to Longhorsley, Linden Hall 0.5m past
                   village

Hotel   ★★★★♨♨ 70% Linden Hall Hotel,
                   Health Spa & Golf Course, LONGHORSLEY
                   ☎ 01670 516611 50 ⇄ 🏺

MATFEN   Map 12 NZ07

Matfen Hall NE20 0RQ
☎ 01661 886500 Fax 01661 886055
An 18-hole parkland course set in beautiful countryside with
many natural and man-made hazards. Also a challenging 9-
hole par 3 course and a driving range.
18 holes, 6609yds, Par 73, SSS 72, Course record 67.
Club membership 450.

Visitors   contact in advance, restricted on weekends
                   between 8-10am.
Societies   telephone for details.
Green Fees   £35 per day; £22 per round (£40/£26 weekends).
Cards   ▭▭ ▭▭ ▭▭ ▭ ▭
Prof   John Harrison
Facilities   ⊗ ⊪ ⅙ ▼ ♀ ♨ 🏠 🛉 🏄 ➘ ♨ ♩
& Leisure   9 hole par3.
Location   Just off B6318 Military road 15m W of
                   Newcastle

Hotel   ★★ 69% Angel Inn, Main St, CORBRIDGE
                   ☎ 01434 632119 5 ⇄ 🏺

MORPETH   Map 12 NZ28

Morpeth The Common NE61 2BT ☎ 01670 504942
Parkland course with views of the Cheviots.
18 holes, 6206yds, Par 71, SSS 69, Course record 65.
Club membership 700.

Visitors   restricted weekends & bank holidays. Must
                   contact in advance and have a handicap
                   certificate.
Societies   apply in writing.
Green Fees   £25 per day; £20 per round (£33/£25 weekends
                   & bank holidays).
Prof   Martin Jackson
Designer   Harry Vardon
Facilities   ⊗ ⊪ ⅙ ▼ ♀ ♨ 🏠 ➘ ♂
Location   S side of town centre on A197

Hotel   ★★★★♨♨ 70% Linden Hall Hotel,
                   Health Spa & Golf Course, LONGHORSLEY
                   ☎ 01670 516611 50 ⇄ 🏺

NEWBIGGIN-BY-THE-SEA   Map 12 NZ38

Newbiggin-by-the-Sea Prospect Place NE64 6DW
☎ 01670 817344 Fax 01670 520236
Seaside-links course.
18 holes, 6452yds, Par 72, SSS 71, Course record 65.
Club membership 570.

Visitors   must contact professional on arrival and may not
                   play before 10am.
Societies   must apply in writing.
Green Fees   £16 per day (£22 weekends).
Prof   Marcus Webb
Facilities   ⊗ ⊪ ⅙ ▼ ♀ ♨ 🏠 🛉 ♂
& Leisure   snooker.
Location   N side of town

Hotel   ★★★★♨♨ 70% Linden Hall Hotel,
                   Health Spa & Golf Course, LONGHORSLEY
                   ☎ 01670 516611 50 ⇄ 🏺

PONTELAND   Map 12 NZ17

Ponteland 53 Bell Villas NE20 9BD ☎ 01661 822689
Open parkland course offering testing golf and good views.
18 holes, 6524yds, Par 72, SSS 71, Course record 66.
Club membership 720.

Visitors   with member only Fri, weekends & bank
                   holidays.
Societies   welcome Tue & Thu only. Must contact in
                   advance.
Green Fees   not confirmed.
Prof   Alan Crosby

Facilities ⊗ �)Ⅲ ᴸᴮ ♥ ♀ ♨ 🏠 ⚐
Location 0.5m E on A696

Hotel ★★★ 64% Newcastle Airport Moat House, Woolsington, NEWCASTLE UPON TYNE AIRPORT
☎ 0191 401 9988 100 ⇄ ╠

PRUDHOE Map 12 NZ06

Prudhoe Eastwood Park NE42 5DX
☎ 01661 832466 Fax 01661 830710
Parkland course with natural hazards and easy walking along undulating fairways.
18 holes, 5812yds, Par 69, SSS 68, Course record 60.
Club membership 700.
Visitors must contact in advance. Weekends after 4.30pm
Societies must contact in writing.
Green Fees £20 per day/round (£25 weekends).
Prof John Crawford
Facilities ⊗)Ⅲ ᴸᴮ ♥ ♀ ♨ 🏠
Location E side of town centre off A695

Hotel ★★★ 70% Gibside Arms Hotel, Front St, WHICKHAM
☎ 0191 488 9292 45 ⇄ ╠

ROTHBURY Map 12 NU00

Rothbury Old Race Course NE65 7TR
☎ 01669 620718 & 621271
Very flat parkland course alongside the River Coquet.
9 holes, 5681yds, Par 68, SSS 67, Course record 65.
Club membership 350.
Visitors may play at weekends by arrangement only.
Societies Must contact secretary in advance.
Green Fees £11 per day (£16 weekends).
Designer J Radcliffe
Facilities ᴸᴮ ♥ ♀ ♨
Location SW side of town off B6342

Hotel ★★★ 63% White Swan Hotel, Bondgate Within, ALNWICK
☎ 01665 602109 58 ⇄ ╠

SEAHOUSES Map 12 NU23

Seahouses Beadnell Rd NE68 7XT
☎ 01665 720794 Fax 01665 721994
Typical links course with many hazards, including the famous 10th, 'Logans Loch', water hole.
18 holes, 5516yds, Par 67, SSS 67, Course record 63.
Club membership 750.
Visitors must contact in advance.
Societies must contact in advance. May not play Sun.
Green Fees £18 per day (£25 weekends).
Facilities ⊗)Ⅲ ᴸᴮ ♥ ♀ ♨ ⚐
Location S side of village on B1340

Hotel ★★ 68% Bamburgh Castle Hotel, SEAHOUSES
☎ 01665 720283 20 ⇄ ╠

STOCKSFIELD Map 12 NZ06

Stocksfield New Ridley Rd NE43 7RE
☎ 01661 843041 Fax 01661 843046
Challenging course: parkland (9 holes), woodland (9 holes). Some elevated greens and water hazards.
18 holes, 5978yds, Par 70, SSS 70, Course record 63.
Club membership 550.
Visitors welcome except Wed am & weekends until 4pm.
Societies must contact in advance.
Green Fees £25 per day; £20 per round (£25 per round weekends & bank holidays).
Prof David Mather
Designer Pennick
Facilities ⊗)Ⅲ by prior arrangement ᴸᴮ ♥ ♀ ♨ 🏠 ⚐ ⚐
Location 2.5m SE off A695

Hotel ★★★ 68% Beaumont Hotel, Beaumont St, HEXHAM
☎ 01434 602331 25 ⇄ ╠

SWARLAND Map 12 NU10

Swarland Hall Coast View NE65 9JG
☎ 01670 787010
Parkland course set in mature woodland. There are seven Par 4 holes in excess of 400 yards.
18 holes, 6628yds, Par 72, SSS 72.
Club membership 400.
Visitors restricted on competition days. Advisable to contact in advance.
Societies apply in advance.
Green Fees £18 per day; £14 per round (£25/£18 weekends & bank holidays).
Prof David Fletcher/Linzi Hardy
Facilities ⊗)Ⅲ ᴸᴮ ♥ ♀ ♨ 🏠 ⚐ 🏌 ♨ ⚐
Location Approx 1m W of A1

Hotel ★★★★♨♨ 70% Linden Hall Hotel, Health Spa & Golf Course, LONGHORSLEY
☎ 01670 516611 50 ⇄ ╠

WARKWORTH Map 12 NU20

Warkworth The Links NE65 0SW
☎ 01665 711596
Seaside links course, with good views and alternative tees for the back nine.
9 holes, 5870yds, Par 70, SSS 68, Course record 66.
Club membership 470.
Visitors welcome except Tue & Sat.
Societies must contact in advance.
Green Fees not confirmed.
Designer T Morris
Facilities ⊗ ᴸᴮ ♥ ♀ ♨
Location 0.5m E of village off A1068

Hotel ★★★ 63% White Swan Hotel, Bondgate Within, ALNWICK
☎ 01665 602109 58 ⇄ ╠

> Entries with a shaded background identify courses that are considered to be particularly interesting

WOOLER   Map 12 NT92

Wooler Dod Law, Doddington NE71 6EA
☎ 01668 282135
Hilltop, moorland course with spectacular views over the
Glendale valley. Nine greens played from 18 tees. A very
challenging course when windy with one Par 5 of 580 yards.
The course is much under used during the week so is always
available.
9 holes, 6358yds, Par 72, SSS 70, Course record 72.
Club membership 300.
Visitors   normally no restrictions.
Societies   by prior arrangement with secretary.
Green Fees £10 (£15 weekends & bank holidays).
Facilities   ⊗ ⓑ ♥ ⚐ ♨ ♣
Location   At Doddington on B6525 Wooler/Berwick Rd

Hotel   ★★ 64% Tankerville Arms Hotel, Cottage Rd,
                    WOOLER ☎ 01668 281581 16 ⇆ ⏚

NOTTINGHAMSHIRE

CALVERTON   Map 08 SK64

Ramsdale Park Golf Centre Oxton Rd NG14 6NU
☎ 0115 965 5600 Fax 0115 965 4105
The High course is a challenging and comprehensive test for
any standard of golfer. A relatively flat front nine is followed
by an undulating back nine that is renowned as one of the
best 9 holes of golf in the county. The Low course is an 18
hole Par 3 course gaining a reputation as one of the best in
the country. Hole lengths vary from 100 to 207yds.
*High Course: 18 holes, 6546yds, Par 71, SSS 71, Course
record 70.*
Low Course: 18 holes, 2844yds, Par 54.
Club membership 400.
Visitors   may book up to 7 days in advance.
Societies   welcome midweek, apply in writing or
                    telephone.
Green Fees Low Course: £7.80 (weekends £8.20); High
                    Course: £14 (weekends £16.50).
Cards   ⚊ ⚏ ⚟ ⚞
Prof   Robert Macey
Designer   Hawtree
Facilities   ⊗ ⟊ ⓑ ♥ ⚐ ♨ 🖰 ♣ ♨ ⚑ ♣
Location   8m NE of Nottingham, off B6386

Hotel   ★★★ 58% Saracen's Head, Market Place,
                    SOUTHWELL ☎ 01636 812701 27 ⇆ ⏚

Springwater Moor Ln NG14 6FZ ☎ 0115 965 2129
1998 will see this attractive golf course, set in rolling
countryside close to Nottingham, extended to 18 holes. It
offers an interesting and challenging game of golf to players
of all handicaps, as well as fine views over the Trent Valley.
18 holes, 6224yds, Par 71, SSS 70.
Visitors   5 day advance booking by telephone, booking
                    available all week subject to competitions and
                    Society/Corporate reservations.
Societies   apply in writing or telephone for Society Pack.
Green Fees not confirmed.
Prof   Paul Wharmsby

Designer   Neil Footitty/Paul Wharmsby
Facilities   ⊗ ⟊ ⓑ ♥ ⚐ ♨ 🖰 ♣ ♨ ⚑ ♣
& Leisure   short game academy.
Location   300yds on the left from the turning to Calverton
                    off A6097

Hotel   ★★★ 58% Saracen's Head, Market Place,
                    SOUTHWELL ☎ 01636 812701 27 ⇆ ⏚

EAST LEAKE   Map 08 SK52

Rushcliffe Stocking Ln LE12 5RL
☎ 01509 852959 Fax 01509 852688
Hilly, tree-lined and picturesque parkland course.
18 holes, 6013yds, Par 70, SSS 69, Course record 63.
Club membership 700.
Visitors   welcome but may not play Tue and restricted
                    weekends & bank holidays 9.30-11am & 3-
                    4.30pm.
Societies   must apply in advance.
Green Fees £24 per day (£28 weekends).
Prof   Chris Hall
Facilities   ⊗ ⟊ ⓑ ♥ ⚐ 🖰 ♣
Location   1m N

Hotel   ★★★ 66% Yew Lodge Hotel & Conference
                    Centre, Packington Hill, KEGWORTH
                    ☎ 01509 672518 64 ⇆ ⏚

HUCKNALL   Map 08 SK54

Leen Valley Golf Centre Wigwam Ln NG15 7TA
☎ 0115 964 2037 Fax 0115 964 2724
An interesting and challenging parkland course, featuring
several lakes, the River Leen and the Baker Brook. Suitable
for all standards of golfers.
18 holes, 6233yds, Par 72, SSS 70.
Club membership 750.
Visitors   tee times can be booked in advance and are
                    advisable for Fri, Sat & Sun.
Societies   by arrangement.
Green Fees £9 (£12.50 weekends). Reduced rates in winter.
Cards   ⚊ ⚏ ⚟ ⚞ ⚞
Prof   John Lines
Designer   Tom Hodgetts
Facilities   ⊗ ⟊ ⓑ ♥ ⚐ ♨ 🖰 ♣ ♨ ⚑ ♣
Location   0.5m from Hucknall Town Centre, follow signs
                    for railway station and turn right into Wigwam
                    Lane

Hotel   ★★★ 63% Bestwood Lodge, Bestwood
                    Country park, Arnold, NOTTINGHAM
                    ☎ 0115 920 3011 40 ⇆ ⏚

KEYWORTH   Map 08 SK63

Stanton on the Wolds Golf Rd, Stanton-on-the-Wolds
NG12 5BH ☎ 0115 937 4885 & 937 2044
Fax 0115 937 4885
Parkland course, fairly flat with stream running through four
holes.
18 holes, 6437yds, Par 73, SSS 71, Course record 67.
Club membership 705.
Visitors   must contact in advance. Must play with
                    member at weekends and may not play Tue.
Societies   must apply in writing.
Green Fees £ 20 per day/round.
Prof   Nick Hernon

Designer   Tom Williamson
Facilities   ⊗ ⊞ by prior arrangement ⓑ 🍺 ♀ 🕹 🏠 ⚲ ♂
Location   E side of village

Hotel   ★★ 65% Rufford Hotel, 53 Melton Rd,
West Bridgford, NOTTINGHAM
☎ 0115 981 4202 34 ⇆ 🍴

KIRKBY IN ASHFIELD   Map 08 SK55

Notts Derby Rd NG17 7QR
☎ 01623 753225 Fax 01623 753655
Undulating heathland Championship course.
18 holes, 7030yds, Par 72, SSS 74, Course record 64.
Club membership 500.
Visitors   must contact in advance & have handicap
certificate. With member only weekends &
bank holidays.
Societies   must apply in advance.
Green Fees £65 per day; £45 per round.
Prof   Alasdair Thomas
Designer   Willie Park
Facilities   ⊗ ⊞ ⓑ 🍺 ♀ 🕹 🏠 ⚲ ♂ ⚲ 🍴
Location   1.5m SE off A611

Hotel   ★★★★ 69% Swallow Hotel,
Carter Ln East, SOUTH NORMANTON
☎ 01773 812000 160 ⇆ 🍴

LONG EATON   Map 08 SK43

Trent Lock Golf Centre Lock Ln, Sawley NG10 2FY
☎ 0115 9464398 Fax 01159 461183
Main course has two par 5, five par 3 and eleven par 4 holes,
plus water features and three holes adjacent to the river. A
challenging test of golf.
*Main Course: 18 holes, 5717yds, Par 69, SSS 68, Course
record 73.*
9 hole: 9 holes, 2929YDS, Par 36.
Club membership 500.
Visitors   no restriction Mon-Fri am but booking system
12pm Fri-closing Sun.
Societies   apply in writing or telephone in advance.
Green Fees 18 hole course £12 (£15 weekends). 9 hole £5.
Cards   [card symbols]
Prof   M Taylor
Designer   E McCausland
Facilities   ⊗ ⊞ ⓑ 🍺 ♀ 🕹 🏠 ⚲ 🍴

Hotel   ★★★ 67% Novotel, Bostock Ln,
LONG EATON ☎ 0115 946 5111 108 ⇆ 🍴

MANSFIELD   Map 08 SK56

Sherwood Forest Eakring Rd NG18 3EW
☎ 01623 626689 Fax 01623 420412
As the name suggests, the Forest is the main feature of
this natural heathland course with its heather, silver birch
and pine trees. The homeward nine holes are particularly
testing. The 11th to the 14th are notable par 4 holes on
this well-bunkered course designed by the great James
Braid.
18 holes, 6698yds, Par 71, SSS 73, Course record 64.
Club membership 750.
Visitors   weekdays only by prior arrangement with
the Secretary.

Societies   by arrangement with the Secretary.
Green Fees on application.
Prof   Ken Hall
Designer   W S Colt/James Braid
Facilities   ⊗ ⊞ ⓑ 🍺 ♀ 🕹 🏠 ⚲ ♂
& Leisure snooker.
Location   E of Mansfield

Hotel   ★★ 67% Pine Lodge Hotel,
281-283 Nottingham Rd, MANSFIELD
☎ 01623 622308 20 ⇆ 🍴

MANSFIELD WOODHOUSE   Map 08 SK56

Mansfield Woodhouse Leeming Ln North NG19 9EU
☎ 01623 623521
Easy walking on heathland.
9 holes, 2446yds, Par 68, SSS 64.
Club membership 130.
Visitors   no restrictions.
Societies   must contact by telephone.
Green Fees £3.30 (9 holes); £5 (18 holes).
Prof   Leslie Highfield
Designer   A Highfield & F Horfman
Facilities   ⊗ ⊞ ⓑ 🍺 ♀ 🏠 ⚲
Location   N side of town centre off A60

Hotel   ★★ 67% Pine Lodge Hotel, 281-283
Nottingham Rd, MANSFIELD
☎ 01623 622308 20 ⇆ 🍴

NEWARK-ON-TRENT   Map 08 SK75

Newark Coddington NG24 2QX
☎ 01636 626282 Fax 22245 626497
Wooded, parkland course in secluded situation with easy
walking.
18 holes, 6421yds, Par 71, SSS 71, Course record 66.
Club membership 600.
Visitors   must contact in advance and have handicap
certificate. May not play Tue (Ladies Day) or
weekends.
Societies   must contact in advance.
Green Fees £27 per day; £22 per round.
Prof   P A Lockley
Facilities   ⊗ ⊞ ⓑ 🍺 ♀ 🕹 🏠 ⚲
Location   4m E on A17

Hotel   ★★ 71% Grange Hotel,
73 London Rd, NEWARK
☎ 01636 703399 10 ⇆ 🍴 Annexe5 ⇆ 🍴

NOTTINGHAM   Map 08 SK53

Beeston Fields Old Dr, Wollaton Rd, Beeston NG9 3DD
☎ 0115 925 7062 Fax 0115 925 4280
Parkland course with sandy subsoil and wide, tree-lined
fairways. The par 3, 14th has elevated tee and small bunker-
guarded green.
18 holes, 6402yds, Par 71, SSS 71, Course record 64.
Club membership 800.
Visitors   must contact professional on 0115 922 0872 for
availability.
Societies   must apply in advance.

▶

Green Fees £35 per 36 holes; £25 per round (£35 per round weekends).
Prof Alun Wardle
Designer Tom Williamson
Facilities ⊗ ⅷ by prior arrangement 🍴 ☕ ♀ ♟ 🏠 ⛳ ✐
Location 400mtrs SW off A52 Nottingham/Derby road

Hotel B Posthouse Nottingham/Derby, Bostocks Ln, SANDIACRE ☎ 0115 9397800 93 ⇌ 🐾

Bramcote Hills Thoresby Rd, off Derby Rd, Bramcote NG9 3EP ☎ 0115 928 1880
A Pay and Play, 18-hole Par 3 course with challenging greens.
18 holes, 1500yds, Par 54.
Visitors no restrictions.
Societies telephone in advance.
Green Fees not confirmed.
Facilities ⛳
Location Off A52 Derby rd

Hotel ★★ 63% Priory Hotel, Derby Rd, Wollaton Vale, NOTTINGHAM ☎ 0115 922 1691 31 ⇌ 🐾

Bulwell Forest Hucknall Rd, Bulwell NG6 9LQ ☎ 0115 977 0576
Municipal heathland course with many natural hazards. Very tight fairways and subject to wind.
18 holes, 5606yds, Par 68, SSS 67, Course record 62.
Club membership 350.
Visitors restricted weekends. Must contact in advance.
Societies must apply in advance.
Green Fees £16 per day; £11 per round.
Cards 🖻 🖻 🖻 🖻 🖻
Prof Lee Rawlings
Facilities ⊗ ⅷ by prior arrangement 🍴 ☕ ♀ ♟ 🏠 ⛳ ✐
& Leisure hard tennis courts.
Location 3m from junct 26 on M1. 4m NW of city centre on A611

Hotel ★★★ 64% Nottingham Moat House, Mansfield Rd, NOTTINGHAM ☎ 0115 935 9988 172 ⇌ 🐾

Chilwell Manor Meadow Ln, Chilwell NG9 5AE ☎ 0115 925 8958 Fax 0115 922 0575
Flat parkland course.
18 holes, 6379yds, Par 70, SSS 70, Course record 66.
Club membership 750.
Visitors with member only weekends. Must contact in advance and have a handicap certificate.
Societies welcome Mon, must apply in advance.
Green Fees £18 per day/round (£20 per round weekends).
Prof Paul Wilson
Designer Tom Williamson
Facilities ⊗ ⅷ 🍴 ☕ ♀ ♟ 🏠 ✐
Location 4m SW on A6005

Hotel ★★ 63% Europa Hotel, 20-22 Derby Rd, LONG EATON ☎ 0115 972 8481 15 ⇌ 🐾

Edwalton Municipal Wellin Ln, Edwalton NG12 4AS ☎ 0115 923 4775
Gently sloping, 9-hole parkland course. Also 9-hole Par 3 and large practice ground.
9 holes, 3336yds, Par 72, SSS 72, Course record 71.
Club membership 900.

Visitors booking system in operation.
Societies prior booking necessary.
Green Fees not confirmed.
Prof John Staples
Facilities ⊗ 🍴 ☕ ♀ ♟ 🏠 ⛳ ✐
Location S of Nottingham, off A606

Hotel ★★ 65% Rufford Hotel, 53 Melton Rd, West Bridgford, NOTTINGHAM ☎ 0115 981 4202 34 ⇌ 🐾

Mapperley Central Av, Plains Rd, Mapperley NG3 5RH ☎ 0115 955 6672
Hilly meadowland course but with easy walking.
18 holes, 6283yds, Par 71, SSS 70, Course record 68.
Club membership 650.
Visitors must contact in advance. May not play Tue or Sat.
Societies must telephone in advance.
Green Fees not confirmed.
Prof Malcolm Allen
Designer John Mason
Facilities ⊗ ⅷ 🍴 ☕ ♀ ♟ 🏠 ⛳ ✐
& Leisure pool table.
Location 3m NE of city centre off B684

Hotel B Posthouse Nottingham City, St James's St, NOTTINGHAM ☎ 0115 947 0131 130 ⇌ 🐾

Nottingham City Lawton Dr, Bulwell NG6 8BL ☎ 0115 927 6916 & 927 2767 Fax 0115 927 6916
A pleasant municipal parkland course on the city outskirts.
18 holes, 6218yds, Par 69, SSS 70, Course record 65.
Club membership 425.
Visitors restricted Sat 7am-3pm.
Societies welcome, contact professional.
Green Fees not confirmed.
Prof Cyril Jepson
Designer H Braid
Facilities ♟ 🏠 ⛳ ✐
Location 4m NW of city centre off A6002

Hotel ★★★ 64% Nottingham Moat House, Mansfield Rd, NOTTINGHAM ☎ 0115 935 9988 172 ⇌ 🐾

Wollaton Park Limetree Av, Wollaton Park NG8 1BT ☎ 0115 978 7574 Fax 0115 978 7574
A pleasant, fairly level course set in a park close to the centre of Nottingham, with red and fallow deer herds. The fairways are tree-lined. The 502-yd dog-leg 15th is a notable hole. The stately home - Wollaton Hall - is situated in the park.
18 holes, 6445yds, Par 71, SSS 71, Course record 64.
Club membership 650.
Visitors may not play Wed or competition days.
Societies must apply in advance.
Green Fees £36 per day; £26 per round (£41/£31 weekends).
Prof John Lower
Designer W Williamson
Facilities ⊗ ⅷ 🍴 ☕ ♀ ♟ 🏠 ⛳ ✐
Location 2.5m W of city centre off A52

Hotel ★★★ 58% Swans Hotel & Restaurant, 84-90 Radcliffe Rd, West Bridgford, NOTTINGHAM ☎ 0115 981 4042 30 ⇌ 🐾

OLLERTON   Map 08 SK66

Rufford Park Golf Centre Rufford Ln, Rufford NG22 9DG
☎ 01623 825253 Fax 01623 825254
Rufford Park is noted for its pictuesque 18 holes with its
especially challenging Par 3's. From the unique 173yard Par
3 17th over water to the riverside 596yard 13th, the course
offers everything the golfer needs from beginner to
professional.
18 holes, 6155yds, Par 70, SSS 69.
Club membership 550.
Visitors	are advised to book in advance. Unable to play weekend mornings.
Societies	society packages on request, need to be booked in advance.
Green Fees	£14 per round (£18 weekends).
Cards	⬛⬛⬛⬛⬛⬛
Prof	John Vaughan/James Thompson
Designer	David Hemstock
Facilities	⊗ �)Ⅲ ⅙ �🖴 ⅌ ⚲ 🏠 ⏰ 🛆 🚲 ♂ ⚲
Location	S Of Ollerton off A614. Take the 'Rufford Mill' turn

Hotel	★★★ 69% Clumber Park Hotel, Clumber Park, WORKSOP ☎ 01623 835333 48 ⇋ 🐾

OXTON   Map 08 SK65

Oakmere Park Oaks Ln NG25 0RH
☎ 0115 965 3545 Fax 0115 965 5628
Set in rolling parkland in the heart of picturesque Robin
Hood country. The par 4 (16th) and par 5 (1st) are notable.
Twenty-bay floodlit driving range.
Admirals: 18 holes, 6617yds, Par 72, SSS 72.
Commanders: 9 holes, 6407yds, Par 72, SSS 72.
Club membership 450.
Visitors	correct golf attire required, please book for weekends.
Societies	please apply in writing or telephone.
Green Fees	Admirals: £18 per round (£25 weekends). Commanders: £12 per 18 holes (£16 weekends).
Cards	⬛
Prof	Daryl St-John Jones
Designer	Frank Pennick
Facilities	⊗ ⊗ ⅙ ⅙ 🖴 ⅌ ⚲ 🏠 ⏰ 🛆 ♂ ⚲
Location	1m NW off A6097

Hotel	★★★ 58% Saracen's Head, Market Place, SOUTHWELL ☎ 01636 812701 27 ⇋ 🐾

RADCLIFFE-ON-TRENT   Map 08 SK63

Cotgrave Place Golf & Country Club Main Rd,
Stragglethorpe NG12 3HB
☎ 0115 933 3344 Fax 0115 933 4567
The course now offers 36 holes of championship golf. The
front nine of the Open Course are placed around a beautiful
lake, man made ponds and the Grantham Canal. The back
nine is set in magnificent parkland with mature trees and
wide fairways. Masters has an opening nine set amongst
hedgerows and coppices. The huge greens with their
interesting shapes are a particularly challenging test of nerve.
The Peter Aliss designed second nine opened in 1998 and is
proving to be a challenge to even the best golfers. the par 5,
17th hole is one of the toughest in the country.

Open course: 18 holes, 6303yds, Par 71, SSS 70.
Masters course: 18 holes, 5887yds, Par 69, SSS 68.
Club membership 800.
Visitors	must contact in advance.
Societies	telephone in advance.
Green Fees	not confirmed.
Cards	⬛⬛⬛⬛⬛⬛
Prof	Robert Smith
Facilities	⊗ ⊗ ⅙ ⅙ 🖴 ⅌ ⚲ 🏠 🛆 🚲 ♂ ⚲
Location	Off A52, 6miles from Nottingham

Hotel	★★🏵 69% Langar Hall, LANGAR ☎ 01949 860559 10 ⇋ 🐾

Radcliffe-on-Trent Dewberry Ln, Cropwell Rd NG12 2JH
☎ 0115 933 3000 Fax 0115 9116991
Fairly flat, parkland course with three good finishing holes:
16th (427 yds) par 4; 17th (180 yds) through spinney, par 3;
18th (331 yds) dog-leg par 4. Excellent views.
18 holes, 6381yds, Par 70, SSS 71, Course record 64.
Club membership 670.
Visitors	must contact in advance.
Societies	welcome Wed. Must contact in advance.
Green Fees	£23 per day (£28 weekends).
Prof	Robert Ellis
Designer	Tom Williamson
Facilities	⊗ ⊗ ⅙ ⅙ 🖴 ⅌ ⚲ 🏠 ⏰ 🚲 ♂
Location	Take the A52 to Nottingham, turn L at 2nd set of traffic lights, 400yds on left

Hotel	★★★ 58% Swans Hotel & Restaurant, 84-90 Radcliffe Rd, West Bridgford, NOTTINGHAM ☎ 0115 981 4042 30 ⇋ 🐾

RETFORD   Map 08 SK78

Retford Brecks Rd, Ordsall DN22 7UA
☎ 01777 860682 (Secretary) & 703733 (Pro)
Fax 01777 710412
A wooded, parkland course.
18 holes, 6409yds, Par 72, SSS 72, Course record 67.
Club membership 700.
Visitors	advisable to contact in advance, with member only at weekends and holidays.
Societies	apply in writing or telephone. Not welcome Tue morning or bank holidays, limited availability weekends.
Green Fees	£20 per day; £15 per round.
Prof	Craig Morris
Designer	Tom Williamson
Facilities	⊗ ⊗ ⅙ ⅙ 🖴 ⅌ ⚲ 🏠 ⏰ 🚲 🛆 ♂
Location	1.5m S A620, between Worksop & Gainsborough

Hotel	★★★ 64% West Retford Hotel, 24 North Rd, RETFORD ☎ 01777 706333 Annexe60 ⇋ 🐾

RUDDINGTON   Map 08 SK53

Ruddington Grange Wilford Rd NG11 6NB
☎ 0115 984 6141
Undulating parkland course with water hazards on 12 holes.
18 holes, 6543yds, Par 72, SSS 72, Course record 69.
Club membership 650.
Visitors	a handicap certificate is required, contact in advance if possible. Play may be restricted Sat & Wed mornings. ▶

Societies must contact in advance.
Green Fees not confirmed.
Cards ⬛ 🔲
Prof Robert Simpson
Facilities ⊗ ⏍ ⮴ 🍺 🏆 ♨ 🛍 🏌
Location 5m S of Nottingham, A60 to Ruddington

Hotel ★★★ 58% Swans Hotel & Restaurant, 84-90 Radcliffe Rd, West Bridgford, NOTTINGHAM ☎ 0115 981 4042 30 ⇥ 🏌

SERLBY   Map 08 SK68

Serlby Park DN10 6BA
☎ 01777 818268 Fax 01302 536336
Parkland course.
11 holes, 5325yds, Par 66, SSS 66, Course record 63.
Club membership 250.
Visitors must be introduced by and play with member.
Societies apply in writing before 31 Dec for following year.
Green Fees not confirmed.
Designer Galway
Facilities ⊗ ⏍ ⮴ 🍺 🏆 ♨
Location E side of village off A638

Hotel ★★★ 69% Charnwood Hotel, Sheffield Rd, BLYTH ☎ 01909 591610 34 ⇥ 🏌

SUTTON IN ASHFIELD   Map 08 SK45

Coxmoor Coxmoor Rd NG17 5LF
☎ 01623 557359 Fax 01623 557359
Undulating moorland/heathland course with easy walking and excellent views. The clubhouse is modern with a well-equipped games room. The course lies adjacent to Forestry Commission land over which there are several footpaths and extensive views.
18 holes, 6571yds, Par 73, SSS 72, Course record 65.
Club membership 700.
Visitors must play with member weekends & bank holidays. Must contact in advance.
Societies must apply in advance.
Green Fees £30 per 18 holes; £38 per 27 holes; £42 per 36 holes.
Prof David Ridley
Facilities ⊗ ⏍ ⮴ 🍺 🏆 ♨ 🛍
Location 2m SE off A611. 4m from junct 27 on M1

Hotel ★★★★ 69% Swallow Hotel, Carter Ln East, SOUTH NORMANTON ☎ 01773 812000 160 ⇥ 🏌

WORKSOP   Map 08 SK57

Bondhay Golf & Country Club Bondhay Ln, Whitwell S80 3EH ☎ 01909 724709 & 723608 Fax 01909 720226
The wind usually plays quite an active role in making this pleasantly undulating course testing. Signatures holes are the 1st which requires a 2nd shot over water into a basin of trees; the 2nd comes back over the same expanse of water and requires a mid to short iron to a long, narrow green; the 18th is a Par 5 with a lake right in lay up distance - the dilemma is whether to lay up short or go for the carry.
Devonshire Course: 18 holes, 6720yds, Par 72, SSS 71, Course record 67.

Family Course: 9 holes, 1118yds, Par 27, Course record 24.
Club membership 400.
Visitors must contact in advance.
Societies must telephone in advance.
Green Fees not confirmed.
Cards ⬛ 🔲 🔲 🔲
Prof Martin Bell
Designer Donald Steel
Facilities ⊗ ⏍ ⮴ 🍺 🏆 ♨ 🛍 🏌 🛒 ♨ 🏌 🏌
& Leisure fishing.
Location 5m W of Worksop, off A619

Hotel ★★★ 60% Sitwell Arms Hotel, Station Rd, RENISHAW ☎ 01246 435226 30 ⇥ 🏌

Kilton Forest Blyth Rd S81 0TL ☎ 01909 486563
Slightly undulating, parkland course on the north edge of Sherwood Forest. Includes three ponds. Excellent conditions all the year round.
18 holes, 6424yds, Par 72, SSS 71, Course record 69.
Club membership 350.
Visitors must contact in advance.
Societies must contact in advance.
Green Fees £8.40 per round (£10.90 weekends).
Prof Stuart Betteridge
Facilities ⊗ ⏍ ⮴ 🍺 🏆 ♨ 🛍 🏌 🏌
Location 1m NE of town centre on B6045

Hotel ★★ 71% Lion Hotel, 112 Bridge St, WORKSOP ☎ 01909 477925 32 ⇥ 🏌

Lindrick Lindrick Common S81 8BH
☎ 01909 475282 Fax 01909 488685
Heathland course with some trees and masses of gorse.
18 holes, 6486yds, Par 71, SSS 72, Course record 65.
Club membership 490.
Visitors must contact in advance. Restricted Tue & weekends. Handicap certificate required.
Societies welcome except Tue (am) & weekends by prior arrangement with the Secretary.
Green Fees £45 per day weekdays (£45 per round weekends).
Prof John R King
Facilities ⊗ ⏍ ⮴ 🍺 🏆 ♨ 🛍
& Leisure buggies for disabled only.
Location 4m NW on A57

Hotel ★★ 71% Lion Hotel, 112 Bridge St, WORKSOP ☎ 01909 477925 32 ⇥ 🏌

Worksop Windmill Ln S80 2SQ
☎ 01909 472696 & 477731 Fax 01909 477731
Adjacent to Clumber Park this course has a heathland-type terrain, with gorse, broom, oak and birch trees. Fast, true greens, dry all year round.
18 holes, 6660yds, Par 72, SSS 73.
Club membership 600.
Visitors by arrangement with professional tel: 01909 477732.
Societies must apply in advance.
Green Fees £35 per day; £25 per round (£35 per round weekends & bank holidays).
Prof C Weatherhead
Facilities ⊗ ⏍ ⮴ 🍺 🏆 ♨ 🛍
Location Off A57 Ringroad, B6034 to Edwinstowe

Hotel   ★★★ 69% Clumber Park Hotel, Clumber Park, WORKSOP ☎ 01623 835333 48 ⇆ ↑

OXFORDSHIRE

ABINGDON   Map 04 SU49

Drayton Park Steventon Rd, Drayton Village OX14 2RR
☎ 01235 550607 Fax 01235 525731
Set in the heart of the Oxfordshire countryside, an 18-hole parkland course designed by Hawtree. Five lakes and sand based greens.
18 holes, 5500yds, Par 67, SSS 67.
Club membership 500.
Visitors   may phone to book, must have golf shoes, no jeans or tracksuits.
Societies   contact in advance.
Green Fees not confirmed.
Prof   Dinah Masey
Designer   Hawtree
Facilities ⊗ ⅏ by prior arrangement ♁ ♥ ♀ ♐ ☎ ♨ ♣ ♂ ↾
& Leisure   9 hole par 3 course.
Location   Between Oxford & Newbury,off A34 at Didcot

Hotel   ★★★ 67% The Upper Reaches, Thames St, ABINGDON ☎ 01235 522311 31 ⇆ ↑

BANBURY   Map 04 SP44

Rye Hill Milcombe OX15 4RU
☎ 01295 721818 Fax 01295 720089
Well drained course features wide fairways, large undulating greens, water hazards on the 10th, and fine views of the surrounding countryside.
18 holes, 6692yds, Par 71, SSS 72.
Club membership 400.
Visitors   advisable to book in advance, especially at weekends. May not play Sat before 11am.
Societies   telephone for details of Packages available.
Green Fees £14 per round (£17 weekends and bank holidays).
Cards   ⚊ ▦ ▨ ⬛ ▨
Prof   Tony Pennock
Facilities ⊗ ♁ ♥ ♀ ♐ ☎ ♨ ♣ ♂ ↾
& Leisure   fishing.
Location   Junct 11 M40. A361 towards Chipping Norton, signed 1m out of Bloxham

Hotel   ★★★ 69% Banbury House, Oxford Rd, BANBURY ☎ 01295 259361 63 ⇆ ↑

BURFORD   Map 04 SP21

Burford Swindon Rd OX18 4JG ☎ 01993 822583
Created out of open-farmland, this parkland course has high quality fairways and greens.
18 holes, 6414yds, Par 71, SSS 71, Course record 64.
Club membership 830.
Visitors   must contact in advance. May not play weekends.

Societies   apply in writing.
Green Fees £29 per day weekdays.
Prof   Norman Allen
Designer   John H Turner
Facilities ⊗ ⅏ ♁ ♥ ♀ ♐ ☎ ↾
Location   0.5m S off A361

Hotel   ★★ 65% Golden Pheasant Hotel, 91 High St, BURFORD ☎ 01993 823223 12rm(11 ⇆ ↑)

CHESTERTON   Map 04 SP52

Chesterton Golf & Country Club OX6 8TE
☎ 01869 242023
Laid out over one-time farmland. Well-bunkered, and water hazards increase the difficulty of the course.
18 holes, 6229yds, Par 71, SSS 70, Course record 68.
Club membership 400.
Visitors   may pre-book upto 4 days ahead.
Societies   must contact in advance.
Green Fees £15 (£18 weekends & bank holidays).
Prof   J Wilkshire
Designer   R Stagg
Facilities ♁ ♥ ♀ ♐ ☎ ♂
& Leisure   Snooker.
Location   0.5m W off A4095, 1m E of B430 at Weston-on-the-Green

Hotel   ★★ 67% Jersey Arms Hotel, MIDDLETON STONEY ☎ 01869 343234 & 343505 Fax 01869 343565 6 ⇆ Annexe10 ⇆

CHIPPING NORTON   Map 04 SP32

Chipping Norton Southcombe OX7 5QH
☎ 01608 642383 Fax 01608 645422
Pleasant downland course open to winds.
18 holes, 6241yds, Par 71, SSS 70, Course record 62.
Club membership 900.
Visitors   with member only at weekends & bank holidays.
Societies   telephone in advance.
Green Fees £22 per day.
Prof   Derek Craik
Facilities ⊗ ⅏ ♁ ♥ ♀ ♐ ☎ ↾ ♣ ♂ ♂
Location   1.5m E on A44

Hotel   ★★ 62% The White Hart Hotel, 16 High St, CHIPPING NORTON ☎ 01608 642572 14 ⇆ ↑ Annexe5 ⇆

Lyneham Lyneham OX7 6QQ
☎ 01993 831841 Fax 01993 831775
Lyneham was designed to use the natural features. It is set in 170 acres on the fringe of the Costwolds and blends superbly with its surroundings. Lakes and streams enhance the challenge of the course with water coming into play on 8 of the 18 holes. All greens are sand based, built to USGA specification.
18 holes, 6669yds, Par 72, SSS 72, Course record 67.
Club membership 725.
Visitors   must contact in advance.
Societies   apply in advance.
Green Fees £23 per day; £16 per round (£28/£20 weekends).
Prof   Richard Jefferies   ▶

Designer	D G Carpenter
Facilities	⊗ �𝄃⃫ ⃛ ➊ ▦ ♟ ♣ 🛋 ♥ 🖊 ⚷
Location	Off A361, between Burford/Chipping Norton
Hotel	★★ 66% Shaven Crown Hotel, SHIPTON-UNDER-WYCHWOOD ☎ 01993 830330 9rm(8 ⇆ ✆)

DIDCOT   Map 04 SU59

Hadden Hill Wallingford Rd OX11 9BJ
☎ 01235 510410 Fax 01235 510410
A challenging course on undulating terrain with excellent drainage so visitors can be sure of playing no matter what the weather conditions have been. Two loops of nine holes.
18 holes, 6563yds, Par 71, SSS 71, Course record 65.
Club membership 400.

Visitors	telephone to book tee times.
Societies	telephone to arrange times & dates & receive booking form.
Green Fees	£13 per 18 holes; £7.50 per 9 holes (£18/£9.50 weekends).
Cards	▭ ▬ 🟦 🟢 🟥 💠
Prof	Adrian Waters
Designer	Michael V Morley
Facilities	⊗ 𝄃⃫ ⃛ ➊ ▦ ♟ ♣ 🛋 ♥ 🖊 ⚷
Location	On A4130 1m E of Didcot
Hotel	★★★ 68% Abingdon Four Pillars Hotel, Marcham Rd, ABINGDON ☎ 01235 553456 63 ⇆ ✆

FARINGDON   Map 04 SU29

Carswell Carswell Home Farm, Carswell SN7 8PU
☎ 01367 870422 Fax 01367 870592
An attractive course set in undulating wooded countryside close to Faringdon. Mature trees, five lakes and well placed bunkers add interest to the course. Floodlit driving range.
18 holes, 6133yds, Par 72, SSS 70.

Visitors	book in advance to avoid dissapointment.
Societies	on weekdays only telephone to check availability, deposit required,
Green Fees	£15 per round (£22 weekends & bank holidays).
Prof	Geoff Robbins
Facilities	⊗ 𝄃⃫ ⃛ ➊ ▦ ♟ 🛋 ♥ 🖊 ⚷
& Leisure	sauna, gymnasium.
Location	Just off the A420 between Oxford and Swindon
Hotel	★★★ 72% Sudbury House Hotel & Conference Centre, London St, FARINGDON ☎ 01367 241272 49 ⇆ ✆

FRILFORD   Map 04 SU49

Frilford Heath OX13 5NW
☎ 01865 390864 Fax 01865 390823
54 holes in three distinctive layouts of significantly differing character. The Green course is a fully mature heathland course of some 6000 yards. The Red course is of championship length at 6800 yards with a parkland flavour and a marked degree of challenge. The Blue course is of modern design, opened in 1994 at 6728 yards, it incorporates water hazards and large shallow sand traps.
Red Course: 18 holes, 6884yds, Par 73, SSS 73, Course record 68.

Green Course: 18 holes, 6006yds, Par 69, SSS 69, Course record 63.
Blue Course: 18 holes, 6728yds, Par 72, SSS 72, Course record 66.
Club membership 1300.

Visitors	contact in advance. Handicap certificates required.
Societies	apply in advance.
Green Fees	Summer: £45 per day (£60 weekends). Winter: £35 per day (£45 weekends).
Cards	▭ ▬ 🟦 💠
Prof	Derek Craik
Designer	J Taylor/D Cotton/S Gidman
Facilities	♟ ♣ 🛋 ♥ 🖊 ⚷
Location	3m W of Abingdon off A338 Oxford-Wantage road
Hotel	★★★ 68% Abingdon Four Pillars Hotel, Marcham Rd, ABINGDON ☎ 01235 553456 63 ⇆ ✆

HENLEY-ON-THAMES   Map 04 SU78

Aspect Park Remenham Hill RG9 3EH
☎ 01491 577562 & 578306
Parkland course.
18 holes, 6643yds, Par 72, SSS 72.
Club membership 500.

Visitors	must contact in advance, suitable golf attire required on course, no jeans in the clubhouse.
Societies	must contact in advance.
Green Fees	not confirmed.
Prof	Terry Notley
Designer	Tim Winsland
Facilities	⊗ 𝄃⃫ ⃛ ➊ ▦ ♟ ♣ 🛋 ♥ 🖊 ⚷
Hotel	★★★ 70% Red Lion Hotel, Hart St, HENLEY-ON-THAMES ☎ 01491 572161 27 ⇆ ✆

Badgemore Park RG9 4NR
☎ 01491 573667 Fax 01491 576899
Mature parkland course with easy walking. The 13th is a very difficult par 3 hole played over a valley to a narrow green and accuracy off the tee is essential.
18 holes, 6112yds, Par 69, SSS 69, Course record 65.
Club membership 600.

Visitors	contact professional shop on 01491 574175. Tuesday morning Ladies only, bookings to be made for all other times.
Societies	contact General Manager to book.
Green Fees	£26 per day, £18 per round (£28 per round weekends).
Cards	▭ ▬ 🟦 💠
Prof	Jonathon Dunn
Designer	Robert Sandow
Facilities	⊗ 𝄃⃫ ⃛ ➊ ▦ ♟ ♣ 🛋 ♥ 🖊 ⚷
Location	From Henley take B290 to Rotherfield Greys Club, 1.5m on R
Hotel	★★★ 70% Red Lion Hotel, Hart St, HENLEY-ON-THAMES ☎ 01491 572161 27 ⇆ ✆

Henley Harpsden RG9 4HG
☎ 01491 575742 Fax 01491 412179
Undulating parkland course. 6th hole, blind (par 4), with
steep hill.
18 holes, 6329yds, Par 70, SSS 70, Course record 63.
Club membership 800.
Visitors   must contact in advance. Weekend only with a
                member.
Societies   Wed & Thu, apply in writing.
Green Fees   £30 per day.
Prof   Mark Howell
Designer   James Braid
Facilities   ⓑ 💺 ♀ ⚒ 🏚 ♂
Location   1.25m S off A4155

Hotel   ★★★ 70% Red Lion Hotel, Hart St,
                HENLEY-ON-THAMES
                ☎ 01491 572161   27 ➡ 🐾

HORTON-CUM-STUDLEY   Map 04 SP51

Studley Wood The Straight Mile OX33 1BF
☎ 01865 351122 & 351144 Fax 01865 351166
Woodland course set in a former deer park with twelve lakes
and specimen oak trees providing challenging natural hazards
on almost all the holes.
18 holes, 6811yds, Par 73, SSS 73, Course record 65.
Club membership 700.
Visitors   must play to handicap standard, tee times
                booked up to 4 days in advance.
Societies   contact secretary for details.
Green Fees   not confirmed.
Cards   ⸺ 💳 🏦 🔲 🖵
Prof   Tony Williams
Designer   Simon Gidman
Facilities   ⊗ ⯍ ⓑ 💺 ♀ ⚒ 🏚 🖘 🏌 ♂ ₹
Location   4m from Oxford follow signs for Horton-cum-
                Studley from Headington rdbt on Oxford
                ringroad

Hotel   ★★★↟ 78% Studley Priory Hotel,
                HORTON-CUM-STUDLEY
                ☎ 01865 351203 & 351254
                Fax 01865 351613 18 ➡ 🐾

KIRTLINGTON   Map 04 SP41

Kirtlington Lince Ln OX5 3JY
☎ 01869 351133 Fax 01869 351143
A three year old inland links type course with challenging
greens.
18 holes, 6084yds, Par 70, SSS 69.
Club membership 300.
Visitors   must book for weekends and advisable to book
                for weekdays. Must contact in advance.
Societies   contact for Society packages.
Green Fees   £15 per 18 holes, £9 per 9 holes (£20/£12
                weekends & bank holidays).
Cards   ⸺ 💳 🔲 🖵
Prof   Peter Hughes
Designer   Graham Webster
Facilities   ⊗ ⯍ ⓑ 💺 ♀ ⚒ 🏚 🖘 🏌 🚣 ♂ ₹
Location   On A4095 just outside village of Kirtlington

Hotel   ★★★ 66% Weston Manor Hotel, WESTON-
                ON-THE-GREEN
                ☎ 01869 350621 16 ➡ 🐾 Annexe20 ➡ 🐾

MILTON COMMON   Map 04 SP60

The Oxfordshire Rycote Ln OX9 2PU
☎ 01844 278300 Fax 01844 278003
Designed by Rees Jones, The Oxfordshire is considered
to be one of the most exciting courses in the country.
With four man-made lakes and 135 bunkers, it is a
magnificent test of shot-making where almost every hole
deserves special mention. Unfortunately it is only open
to members and their guests.
18 holes, 6856yds, Par 72, SSS 75, Course record 65.
Club membership 750.
Visitors   members guests only.
Green Fees   on application.
Cards   💳 💳 🏦 🔲 🖵
Prof   Neil Pike
Designer   Rees Jones
Facilities   ⚒ 🏚 🖘 🖘 🚣 ♂ ₹
Location   1.5m from junct 7, M40 on A329

Hotel   ★★★ 75% Spread Eagle Hotel,
                Cornmarket, THAME
                ☎ 01844 213661 33 ➡ 🐾

NUFFIELD   Map 04 SU68

Huntercombe RG9 5SL
☎ 01491 641207 Fax 01491 642060
This heathland/woodland course overlooks the
Oxfordshire plain and has many attractive and interesting
fairways and greens. Walking is easy after the 3rd which
is a notable hole. The course is subject to wind and grass
pot bunkers are interesting hazards.
18 holes, 6301yds, Par 70, SSS 70, Course record 63.
Club membership 800.
Visitors   must contact in advance and have a
                handicap certificate.
Societies   must contact in advance.
Green Fees   not confirmed.
Prof   John B Draycott
Designer   Willy Park
Facilities   ⚒ 🏚 ♂
Location   N off A423

Hotel   ★★★ 64% Shillingford Bridge Hotel,
                Shillingford, WALLINGFORD
                ☎ 01865 858567 34 ➡ 🐾 Annexe8 ➡ 🐾

OXFORD   Map 04 SP50

North Oxford Banbury Rd OX2 8EZ
☎ 01865 554924 Fax 01865 515921
Gently undulating parkland course.
18 holes, 5736yds, Par 67, SSS 67, Course record 62.
Club membership 700.
Visitors   at weekends & bank holidays may only play
                after 4pm.
Societies   must contact in advance.
Green Fees   £25 per day £13 twilight (after 5pm).
Cards   ⸺ 💳 🅓 🏦 🔲 🖵
Prof   Robert Harris
Facilities   ⊗ ⯍ ⓑ 💺 ♀ ⚒ 🏚 🖘 ♂
Location   3m N of city centre on A423

                                                    ▶

Hotel ★★★ 66% Oxford Moat House, Godstow Rd, Wolvercote Roundabout, OXFORD
☎ 01865 489988 155 ⇄ ₣

Southfield Hill Top Rd OX4 1PF
☎ 01865 242158 Fax 01865 242158
Home of the City, University and Ladies Clubs, and well-known to graduates throughout the world. A challenging course, in varied parkland setting, providing a real test for players.
18 holes, 6328yds, Par 70, SSS 70, Course record 61.
Club membership 850.
Visitors	with member only at weekends.
Societies	must apply in writing.
Green Fees	not confirmed.
Cards	⬛ ⬛ ⬛ ⬛ ⬛ ⬛
Prof	Tony Rees
Designer	H S Colt
Facilities	⊗ ⵊ ᴸ ♥ ⵙ ⚐ ⚑ ⛳ 🏌 ✓
Location	1.5m SE of city centre off B480

Hotel ★★★ 65% Eastgate Hotel, The High, Merton St, OXFORD
☎ 01865 248244 64 ⇄ ₣

SHRIVENHAM   Map 04 SU28

Shrivenham Park Penny Hooks SN6 8EX
☎ 01793 783853 Fax 01793 782999
Parkland course with easy walking. The par 5, 17th is a difficult dog-leg.
18 holes, 5713yds, Par 69, SSS 69, Course record 64.
Club membership 450.
Visitors	phone in advance.
Societies	phone for details.
Green Fees	phone for prices.
Cards	⬛ ⬛ ⬛ ⬛ ⬛ ⬛
Prof	Barry Randall
Designer	Gordon Cox
Facilities	⊗ ⵊ ᴸ ♥ ⵙ ⚐ ⚑ 🏌 ✓
Location	0.5m NE of town centre

Hotel ★★★ 72% Sudbury House Hotel & Conference Centre, London St, FARINGDON
☎ 01367 241272 49 ⇄ ₣

TADMARTON   Map 04 SP33

Tadmarton Heath OX15 5HL
☎ 01608 737278 Fax 01608 730548
A mixture of heath and sandy land, the course, which is open to strong winds, incorporates the site of an old Roman encampment. The clubhouse is an old farm building with a 'holy well' from which the greens are watered. The 7th is a testing hole over water.
18 holes, 5917yds, Par 69, SSS 69, Course record 63.
Club membership 600.
Visitors	weekday by appointment, with member only at weekends.
Societies	by arrangement with club office.
Green Fees	not confirmed.
Prof	Tom Jones
Designer	Col Hutchinson

Facilities	⊗ ⵊ ᴸ ♥ ⵙ ⚐ ⚑ ⛳ 🏌 ✓
& Leisure	fishing.
Location	1m SW of Lower Tadmarton off B4035, 4m from Banbury

Hotel ★★★ 69% Banbury House, Oxford Rd, BANBURY ☎ 01295 259361 63 ⇄ ₣

WATERSTOCK   Map 04 SP60

Waterstock Thame Rd OX33 1HT
☎ 01844 338093 Fax 01844 338036
A 6,500yard course designed by Donald Steel with USGA greens and tees fully computer irrigated. Four Par 3's facing North, South, East and West. A brook and hidden lake affect six holes, with doglegs being 4th and 10th holes. Five Par 5's on the course, making it a challenge for players of all standards.
18 holes, 6535yds, Par 73, SSS 71, Course record 68.
Club membership 500.
Visitors	no restrictions.
Societies	apply in writing or telephone.
Green Fees	not confirmed.
Cards	⬛ ⬛ ⬛ ⬛
Prof	Julian Goodman
Designer	Donald Steel
Facilities	⊗ ⵊ ᴸ ♥ ⵙ ⚐ ⚑ ⛳ 🏌 ✓
& Leisure	fishing.
Location	On junc 8 of M40

Hotel ★★★ 75% Spread Eagle Hotel, Cornmarket, THAME ☎ 01844 213661 33 ⇄ ₣

WITNEY   Map 04 SP31

Witney Lakes Downs Rd OX8 5SY
☎ 01993 779000 Fax 01993 778866
A lakeland style course with 5 large lakes coming into play on 8 holes. An excellent test of golf that will use every club in your bag.
18 holes, 6700yds, Par 71.
Club membership 400.
Visitors	may pre-book 5 days in advance.
Societies	telephone or write in advance.
Green Fees	£13 per round (£18 weekends).
Cards	⬛ ⬛ ⬛ ⬛ ⬛ ⬛
Designer	Simon Gidman
Facilities	⊗ ⵊ ᴸ ♥ ⵙ ⚐ ⚑ ⛳ 🏌 ✓
& Leisure	heated indoor swimming pool, sauna, solarium, gymnasium, health & fitness club.
Location	2m W of Witney town centre, off B4047 Witney/Burford road

Hotel ★★★ 70% Witney Four Pillars Hotel, Ducklington Ln, WITNEY
☎ 01993 779777 74 ⇄ ₣

Entries with a shaded background
identify courses that are
considered to be particularly interesting

RUTLAND

SHROPSHIRE

GREAT CASTERTON
Map 08 TF00

Rutland County PE9 4AQ
☎ 01780 460330 Fax 01780 460437
Inland links-style course with gently rolling fairways, large tees and greens. Playable all year round due to good drainage.
18 holes, 6401yds, Par 71, SSS 71.
Club membership 530.
Visitors   must book in advance at the shop, tel 01780 460239.
Societies   contact office by phone, must be booked in advance.
Green Fees   £30 per 36 holes; £20 per 18 holes (£35/£25 weekends).
Cards   ▨▨ ▨▨ ▨▨ 🄳 ▨▨ ▨▨ 🄲
Prof   James Darroch
Designer   Cameron Sinclair
Facilities   ⊗ 🏲 🝙 🝙 🝙 ♣ 🛢 ↑ ⛟ 🏌 ♂ ↑
Location   2m N of Stamford on A1

Hotel   ★★ 67% The White Horse Inn, Main St, EMPINGHAM
☎ 01780 460221 & 460521
Fax 01780 460521 4 ⇄ 🐾 Annexe9 ⇄ 🐾

GREETHAM
Map 08 SK91

Greetham Valley Wood Ln LE15 7NP
☎ 01780 460004 Fax 01780 460623
Set in 260 acres, including mature woodland, undulating natural valley, water hazards, Greetham Valley was opened in Spring 1992. The complex comprises 2x18 hole courses The Lakes and The Valley. A luxurious clubhouse, 9 hole par3, floodlit driving range and teaching academy.
Lakes: 18 holes, 6779yds, Par 72, SSS 72, Course record 64.
Valley: 18 holes, 5595yds, Par 68, SSS 67.
Club membership 850.
Visitors   must contact in advance.
Societies   must contact in advance.
Green Fees   £32 per day; £24 per round; £12 per 9 holes (£35/£28/£16 weekends).
Cards   ▨▨ ▨▨ ▨▨ 🄲
Prof   John Pengelly
Designer   F E Hinch
Facilities   ⊗ 🏲 🝙 🝙 🝙 ♣ 🛢 ↑ ⛟ 🏌 ♂ ↑
& Leisure   bowls green.
Location   Take the B668 Oakham road off the A1 and follow signs to the course which are clearly marked

Hotel   ★★★ 72% Barnsdale Lodge, The Avenue, Rutland Water, North Shore, OAKHAM
☎ 01572 724678   45 ⇄ 🐾

BRIDGNORTH
Map 07 SO79

Bridgnorth Stanley Ln WV16 4SF
☎ 01746 763315 Fax 01746 761381
A pleasant course laid-out on parkland on the bank of the River Severn.
18 holes, 6673yds, Par 73, SSS 73, Course record 65.
Club membership 725.
Visitors   must contact in advance but may not play on Wed. Restricted weekends.
Societies   must contact in writing.
Green Fees   £18-£22 (£24-£30 weekends).
Prof   Paul Hinton
Facilities   ⊗ 🏲 🝙 🝙 🝙 ♣ 🛢 🏌 ♂
& Leisure   fishing.
Location   1m N off B4373, 0.5m from town centre

Hotel   ★★ 66% Croft Hotel, Saint Mary's St, BRIDGNORTH
☎ 01746 762416 12rm(4 ⇄ 6 🐾)

CHURCH STRETTON
Map 07 SO49

Church Stretton Trevor Hill SY6 6JH
☎ 01694 722281
Hillside course designed by James Braid on the lower slopes of the Long Mynd.
18 holes, 5020yds, Par 66, SSS 65, Course record 63.
Club membership 450.
Visitors   Tee reserved for members Sat 9-10.30 & 1-2.30, Sun prior to 10.30 & 1-2.30 (summer).
Societies   must contact in advance.
Green Fees   £14 (£20 weekends & bank holidays).
Prof   J Townsend
Designer   James Braid
Facilities   ⊗ 🏲 🝙 🝙 🝙 ♣ 🛢 🏌
Location   W of the town. From Cardington Valley drive up Trevor Hill, a steep, winding road

Hotel   ★★ 69% Mynd House Hotel, Ludlow Rd, Little Stretton, CHURCH STRETTON
☎ 01694 722212 7 ⇄ 🐾

CLEOBURY MORTIMER

Cleobury Mortimer Wyre Common DY14 8HQ
☎ 01299 271112 Fax 01299 271628
Well designed 27-hole parkland course set in undulating countryside with fine views from all holes, and offering an interesting challenge to golfers of all abilities.
Foxes Run: 9 holes, 2980yds, Par 34, SSS 34.
Badgers Sett: 9 holes, 3271yds, Par 36, SSS 36.
Deer Park: 9 holes, 3167yds, Par 35, SSS 35.
Club membership 650.
Visitors   advisable to book in advance, handicap certificate may be required at weekends.
Societies   write or telephone in advance.
Green Fees   £25 per day; £17.50 per 18 holes, £11.50 per 9 holes (£30/£19.95/£13.50 weekends & bank holidays).
Cards   ▨▨ ▨▨ ▨▨ 🄲
Prof   Graham Farr   ▶

Facilities ⊗ ⵌ Ꮮ 👜 ♀ ⵜ 📷 ➤ 🚿 ⌀ (
& Leisure fishing, chipping and bunker play practise area.
Location 10m W of Kidderminster on A4117 1m N of
Cleobury Mortimer, off B4201

Hotel ★★ 73% Redfern Hotel,
CLEOBURY MORTIMER
☎ 01299 270395 5 ⇆ 📳 Annexe6 ⇆ 📳

HIGHLEY — Map 07 SO78

Severn Meadows WV16 6HZ ☎ 01746 862212
Picturesque course set alongside the River Severn and
providing a tight test of golf with much of the course
bordered by mature trees.
9 holes, 5258yds, Par 68, SSS 67.
Club membership 170.
Visitors booking advisable for weekends.
Societies advance booking necessary.
Green Fees not confirmed.
Facilities ⊗ Ꮮ ♀ ⵜ 📷

Hotel ★★★★ 66% Mill Hotel & Restaurant,
ALVELEY ☎ 01746 780437 21 ⇆ 📳

LILLESHALL — Map 07 SJ71

Lilleshall Hall TF10 9AS ☎ 01952 603840
Heavily-wooded parkland course. Easy walking.
18 holes, 5906yds, Par 68, SSS 68.
Club membership 650.
Visitors must contact in advance and play with member
at weekends.
Societies must apply in writing by Dec for the following
year.
Green Fees £20 per day.
Prof Nigel Bramall
Designer H S Colt
Facilities ⵜ 📷 ⌀
Location 3m SE

Hotel ★★ 68% White House Hotel,
Wellington Rd, Muxton, TELFORD
☎ 01952 604276 & 603603
Fax 01952 670336 32 ⇆ 📳

LUDLOW — Map 07 SO57

Ludlow Bromfield SY8 2BT ☎ 01584 856285
A long-established heathland course in the middle of the
racecourse. Very flat, quick drying, with broom and gorse-
lined fairways.
18 holes, 6277yds, Par 70, SSS 70, Course record 65.
Club membership 700.
Visitors advisable to contact in advance.
Societies apply in advance.
Green Fees £18 per day (£24 weekends & bank holidays).
Prof Russell Price
Facilities ⊗ ⵌ Ꮮ 👜 ♀ ⵜ 📷 ⵏ ⌀
Location 1m N of Ludlow, off A49

Hotel ★★★ 64% The Feathers at Ludlow,
Bull Ring, LUDLOW
☎ 01584 875261 40 ⇆ 📳

MARKET DRAYTON — Map 07 SJ63

Market Drayton Sutton TF9 2HX
☎ 01630 652266 Fax 01630 652266
Parkland course in quiet, picturesque surroundings providing
a good test of golf. Bungalow on course is made available for
golfing holidays.
18 holes, 6290yds, Par 71, SSS 71, Course record 69.
Club membership 550.
Visitors may not play on Sun; must play with member on
Sat. Must contact in advance.
Societies welcome Mon,Wed,Thu & Fri, must contact in
advance.
Green Fees not confirmed.
Prof Russell Clewes
Facilities ⊗ ⵌ Ꮮ 👜 ♀ ⵜ 📷 ⌀
Location 1m SW

Hotel ★★★⚑⚑ 70% Goldstone Hall,
Goldstone, MARKET DRAYTON
☎ 01630 661202 & 661487
Fax 01630 661585 8 ⇆ 📳

MEOLE BRACE — Map 07 SJ41

Meole Brace SY2 6QQ ☎ 01743 364050
Pleasant municipal course.
9 holes, 5830yds, Par 68, SSS 68, Course record 66.
Club membership 300.
Visitors may not play Wed and must book in advance for
weekends & bank holidays.
Societies must contact Mr R Wootton, Shrewsbury &
Atcham Borough Council on 01743 231456.
Green Fees not confirmed.
Prof Ian Doran
Facilities 📷 ⵏ ⌀
Location NE side of village off A49

Hotel ★★★ 63% The Lion, Wyle Cop,
SHREWSBURY ☎ 01743 353107 59 ⇆ 📳

OSWESTRY — Map 07 SJ22

Mile End Mile End, Old Shrewsbury Rd SY11 4JE
☎ 01691 671246 Fax 01691 670580
A gently undulating parkland-type course boasting
challenging holes for all standards of golfing ability. Longest
hole is par 5 14th at 540yds. A number of water features need
to be negotiated including two large ponds on the 3rd and
17th. The course is set in 140 acres, ensuring all holes are
sufficiently isolated.
18 holes, 6194yds, Par 71, SSS 69, Course record 69.
Club membership 550.
Visitors welcome at all times please telephone in
advance to check availability.
Societies must contact in advance, information available.
Green Fees £21 per day; £14 per round (£27/£18 weekends
& bank holidays).
Prof Scott Carpenter
Designer Price/Gough
Facilities ⊗ ⵌ by prior arrangement Ꮮ 👜 ♀ ⵜ 📷 🦃 ⌀
(
Location 1m SE of Oswestry, just off A5

Hotel ★★★ 68% Wynnstay Hotel, Church St,
OSWESTRY ☎ 01691 655261 27 ⇆ 📳

Oswestry Aston Park SY11 4JJ
☎ 01691 610535 Fax 01691 610535
Parkland course laid-out on undulating ground.
18 holes, 6024yds, Par 70, SSS 69, Course record 62.
Club membership 960.

Visitors	must contact in advance. Must have a handicap certificate or play with member.
Societies	must contact in advance.
Green Fees	£25 per day, £20 per round (£33/£28 weekends & bank holidays).
Prof	David Skelton
Designer	James Braid
Facilities	⊗ ⫴ ⅃ ⬛ ♀ ⚲ 🛆 ⚲
Location	2m SE on A5

Hotel ★★★ 68% Wynnstay Hotel, Church St, OSWESTRY ☎ 01691 655261 27 ⇔ ⟨

PANT   Map 07 SJ22

Llanymynech SY10 8LB ☎ 01691 830983
Upland course on the site of an early Iron Age/Roman hillfort with far-reaching views. 15 holes in Wales 3 holes in England, drive off in Wales putt out in England on 4th hole.
18 holes, 6114yds, Par 70, SSS 69, Course record 65.
Club membership 700.

Visitors	prior contact advisable, some weekends restricted.
Societies	must contact Secretary.
Green Fees	£25 per day; £16 per round (£25/£20 weekends).
Prof	Andrew P Griffiths
Facilities	⊗ ⫴ ⅃ ⬛ ♀ 🛆 ⚲ ⚲
Location	6m S of Oswestry on A483. In village of Pant turn at Cross Guns Inn

Hotel ★★★ 68% Wynnstay Hotel, Church St, OSWESTRY ☎ 01691 655261 27 ⇔ ⟨

SHIFNAL   Map 07 SJ70

Shifnal Decker Hill TF11 8QL
☎ 01952 460330 Fax 01952 460330
Well-wooded parkland course. Walking is easy and an attractive country mansion serves as the clubhouse.
18 holes, 6468yds, Par 71, SSS 71, Course record 65.
Club membership 600.

Visitors	must contact in advance, may not play at weekends.
Societies	must contact in advance.
Green Fees	£30 per day; £25 per round.
Prof	Justin Flanagan
Designer	Pennick
Facilities	⊗ ⫴ ⅃ ⬛ ♀ 🛆 ⚲ ⚲
& Leisure	snooker table.
Location	1m N of Shifnal, off B4379

Hotel ★★★★ 63% Park House Hotel, Park St, SHIFNAL ☎ 01952 460128 38 ⇔ ⟨ Annexe16 ⇔ ⟨

SHREWSBURY   Map 07 SJ41

Arscott Arscott, Pontesbury SY5 0XP
☎ 01743 860114 Fax 01743 860114
At 365feet above sea level, the views from Arscott Golf Club of the hills of south Shropshire and Wales are superb. Arscott is a new course, set in mature parkland with water features and holes demanding all sorts of club choice. A challenge to all golfers both high and low handicap.

18 holes, 6178yds, Par 70, SSS 69, Course record 68.
Club membership 550.

Visitors	most times available by prior arrangement.
Societies	apply in writing or telephone for tee reservation.
Green Fees	£22 per day, £16 per round (£25/£20 weekends).
Cards	🟦 🟦
Prof	Ian Doran
Designer	M Hamer
Facilities	⊗ ⫴ ⅃ ⬛ ♀ 🛆 ⚲ ⚲
& Leisure	fishing.
Location	Off A488, S of Shrewsbury 3m from A5

Hotel ★★★ 63% The Lion, Wyle Cop, SHREWSBURY ☎ 01743 353107 59 ⇔ ⟨

Shrewsbury Condover SY5 7BL
☎ 01743 872976, 872977 (sec) & 873751 (pro)
Fax 01743 874647
Parkland course. First nine flat, second undulating with good views of the Long Mynd Range. Several holes with water features. Fast putting surfaces.
18 holes, 6300yds, Par 70, SSS 70.
Club membership 872.

Visitors	must contact in advance and have a handicap certificate.
Societies	must contact in writing.
Green Fees	not confimed.
Prof	Peter Seal
Facilities	⊗ ⫴ ⅃ ⬛ ♀ 🛆 ⚲ 🛆 ⚲ ⚲
Location	4m S off A49

Hotel ★★★ 63% Prince Rupert Hotel, Butcher Row, SHREWSBURY ☎ 01743 499955 69 ⇔ ⟨

TELFORD   Map 07 SJ60

The Shropshire Granville Park, Muxton TF2 8PQ
☎ 01952 677800 Fax 01952 677622
Designed by Martin Hawtree this 27 hole course comprises 3 loops of 9. Each course has an abundance of lakes and water hazards making club selection a vital part of the round. Championship tees are available by pre-arrangement for the low handicap player.
Blue: 9 holes, 3286yds, Par 35, SSS 35.
Silver: 9 holes, 3303yds, Par 36, SSS 36.
Gold: 9 holes, 3334yds, Par 36, SSS 36.
Club membership 400.

Visitors	recommended to book in advance.
Societies	must book in advance.
Green Fees	not confirmed.
Cards	━━ 🟦 🟦 🔲 🟦 🟦 🟦
Prof	Steve Marr
Designer	Martin Hawtree
Facilities	⊗ ⫴ ⅃ ⬛ ♀ 🛆 ⚲ 🛆 ⚲ ⚲
Location	From M54/A5 take B5060 towards Donnington. Take 3rd exit at Granville rdbt and continue

Hotel ★★★ 67% Holiday Inn, St Quentin Gate, TELFORD ☎ 01952 292500 100 ⇔ ⟨

Telford Golf & Country Club Great Hay Dr, Sutton Hill TF7 4DT ☎ 01952 429977 Fax 01952 586602
Rolling parkland course with easy walking. Five lakes and large sand traps are hazards to the fine greens.
18 holes, 6761yds, Par 72, SSS 72, Course record 66.
Club membership 450. ▶

Visitors must contact in advance, be a competent golfer and abide by dress regulations.
Societies must book in advance 01952 429977
Green Fees not confirmed.
Cards ▨▨▨ ▨ ▨ ▨
Prof Ian Doran
Designer Allis/Dromas
Facilities ⊗ ⏶ ⮂ ⯊ ♀ ⮹ ⮩ ⯄ ⭲ ⭷ ⮜ ⭣ ⭰ ⭽
& Leisure heated indoor swimming pool, squash, sauna, solarium, gymnasium, 6 hole par 3 course.
Location 4m S of town centre off A442

Hotel ★★★ 67% Telford Golf & Country Club, Great Hay Dr, Sutton Hill, TELFORD
☎ 01952 429977 86 ⭤ ⭡

WELLINGTON   Map 07 SJ61

Wrekin Ercall Woods, Golf Links Ln TF6 5BX
☎ 01952 244032 Fax 01952 252906
Downland course with some hard walking but rewarding views.
18 holes, 5699yds, Par 67, SSS 66, Course record 64.
Club membership 681.

Visitors must contact in advance. Limited weekends & bank holidays.
Societies must apply in writing/telephone.
Green Fees £25 per day; £20 per round (£28 weekends & bank holidays).
Prof K Housden
Facilities ⊗ ⏶ ⮂ ⯊ ♀ ⮹ ⯄ ⭷
Location 1.25m S off B5061

Hotel ★★★ 69% Buckatree Hall Hotel, The Wrekin, Wellington, TELFORD
☎ 01952 641821 60 ⭤ ⭡

WESTON-UNDER-REDCASTLE   Map 07 SJ52

Hawkstone Park Hotel SY4 5UY
☎ 01939 200611 Fax 01939 200335
The Hawkstone Course plays through the English Heritage designated Grade I landscape of the historic park and follies providing a beautiful, tranquil yet dramatic back drop to a round of golf. The Windmill Course, re-designed and opened in 1995, utilises many American style features and extensive water hazards and is a challenging alternative.
Hawkstone Course: 18 holes, 6491yds, Par 72, SSS 72.
Windmill Course: 18 holes, 6476yds, Par 72, SSS 72.
Academy Course: 6 holes, 741yds, Par 18.
Club membership 750.

Visitors must book and pay in advance.
Societies must contact in advance by telephone.
Green Fees not confirmed.
Cards ▨▨▨ ▨ ▨ ▨
Prof Paul Brown & Paul Wesseling
Designer B Huggett
Facilities ⊗ ⏶ ⮂ ⯊ ♀ ⮹ ⮩ ⯄ ⭲ ⭷ ⭣ ⭰ ⭽
Location N side of village 0.75m E of A49

WHITCHURCH   Map 07 SJ54

Hill Valley Terrick Rd SY13 4JZ
☎ 01948 663584 & 667788 Fax 01948 665927
Two testing parkland courses ideally suited to the club and scratch golfer alike. The Emerald, cleverly designed by Peter Alliss and Dave Thomas, has fairways that thread their way through 160 acres of trees, lakes and streams to American-style greens trapped by sand and water. Shorter Sapphire with smaller greens requiring accurate approach shots.
Emerald: 18 holes, 6628yds, Par 73, SSS 72, Course record 64.
Sapphire: 18 holes, 4801yds, Par 66, SSS 64.
Club membership 600.

Visitors must contact in advance, deposit required
Societies must contact in advance; a deposit will be required.
Green Fees Emerald £25; Sapphire £15.
Cards ▨▨▨ ▨ ▨
Prof A R Minshall & Clive Burgess
Designer Peter Alliss/Dave Thomas
Facilities ⊗ ⏶ ⮂ ⯊ ♀ ⮹ ⮩ ⯄ ⭲ ⭷ ⭣ ⭰ ⭽
& Leisure sauna, solarium, gymnasium, billiards, snooker, function suite.
Location 1m N. Follow signs from Bypass

Hotel ★★ 69% Crown Hotel & Restaurant, High St, NANTWICH
☎ 01270 625283 18 ⭤ ⭡

WORFIELD   Map 07 SO79

Worfield Roughton WV15 5HE
☎ 01746 716372 Fax 01746 716302
Opened in 1991, this undulating course with good-sized greens, well placed bunkers and 3 lakes, rated highly in a golf magazine survey. All year round golf based on sandy soil.
18 holes, 6801yds, Par 73, SSS 73, Course record 68.
Club membership 500.

Visitors must contact in advance, weekends only after 2pm.
Societies contact in advance.
Green Fees £25 per 27/36 holes; £18 per round weekdays.
Cards ▨▨▨ ▨ ▨ ▨
Prof Steve Russell
Designer T Williams
Facilities ⊗ ⏶ ⮂ ⯊ ♀ ⮹ ⯄ ⭲ ⭣ ⭰ ⭷
Location 3m W of Bridgnorth, off A454

Hotel ★★★⛴ 79% Old Vicarage Hotel, WORFIELD
☎ 01746 716497 10 ⭤ ⭡ Annexe4 ⭤ ⭡

SOMERSET

BACKWELL　Map 03 ST46

Tall Pines Cooks Bridle Path, Downside BS48 3DJ
☎ 01275 472076 Fax 01275 474869
Parkland course with views over the Bristol Channel.
18 holes, 6049yds, Par 70, SSS 69.
Club membership 500.
Visitors　must book in advance at weekends.
Societies　prior arrangement by telephone for details.
Green Fees　£14 per round (£16 weekends).
Prof　Alex Murray
Designer　T Murray
Facilities　⊗ ⅏ 🛇 💺 ♀ ♨ 🏠 🎄 🏌 ✎
Location　Adjacent to Bristol Airport, 1m off A38

Hotel　★★ 66% Beachlands Hotel, 17 Uphill Rd North, WESTON-SUPER-MARE
☎ 01934 621401 23 ⇄ ☏

BATH　Map 03 ST76

Bath Sham Castle, North Rd BA2 6JG
☎ 01225 463834 Fax 01225 331027
Considered to be one of the finest courses in the west, this is the site of Bath's oldest golf club. An interesting course situated on high ground overlooking the city and with splendid views over the surrounding countryside. The rocky ground supports good quality turf and there are many good holes. The 17th is a dog-leg right past, or over the corner of an out-of-bounds wall, and thence on to an undulating green.
18 holes, 6438yds, Par 71, SSS 71, Course record 66.
Club membership 750.
Visitors　advisable to contact in advance. Handicap certificates required.
Societies　Wed & Fri by prior arrangement.
Green Fees　£30 per day; £25 per round (£35/£30 weekends & bank holidays).

Hotel　★★★ 69% The Francis, Queen Square, BATH ☎ 01225 424257 94 ⇄ ☏

Entry Hill BA2 5NA ☎ 01225 834248
9 holes, 2065yds, Par 33, SSS 30.
Club membership 650.
Visitors　advisable to book in advance, must wear golf shoes or training shoes.
Societies　bookings required in advance.
Green Fees　£8-£9.50 per 18 holes; £5-£6 per 9 hole.
Prof　Tim Tapley
Facilities　💺 ♨ 🏠 🏌 ✎
Location　Off A367

Lansdown Lansdown BA1 9BT
☎ 01225 422138 Fax 01225 339252
A flat parkland course situated 800 feet above sea level, providing a challenge to both low and high handicap golfers.
18 holes, 6316yds, Par 71, SSS 70, Course record 65.
Club membership 500.
Visitors　must contact in advance to ascertain availability and have a handicap certificate.
Societies　apply in writing or telephone in advance.
Green Fees　£20 per day/round; £10 per 9 holes.

Cards　⬚ 🟦 🟦 🟦 🟢
Prof　Terry Mercer
Designer　C A Whitcombe
Facilities　⊗ ⅏ 🛇 💺 ♀ ♨ 🏠 ✎ ☽
Location　6m SW of exit 18 of M4

Hotel　★★★ 61% Pratt's Hotel, South Pde, BATH
☎ 01225 460441 46 ⇄ ☏

BRIDGWATER　Map 03 ST23

Cannington Cannington College, Cannington TA5 2LS
☎ 01278 655050 Fax 01278 655055
Nine hole golf course of 'links-like' appearance, designed by Martin Hawtree of Oxford. The 4th hole is a challenging 464yard Par 4, slightly up hill and into the prevailing wind.
9 holes, 2929yds, Par 34, SSS 34.
Club membership 200.
Visitors　pay & play anytime ex Wed evening.
Societies　apply in writing.
Green Fees　not confirmed.
Prof　Ron Macrow
Designer　Martin Hawtree
Facilities　♨ 🏠 🏌 ✎
& Leisure　Cannington visitor centre.
Location　4m NW of Bridgwater of A39

Hotel　★★ 66% Friarn Court Hotel, 37 St Mary St, BRIDGWATER ☎ 01278 452859 16 ⇄ ☏

BURNHAM-ON-SEA　Map 03 ST34

Brean Coast Rd, Brean Sands TA8 2QY
☎ 01278 752111 Fax 01278 752111
Level and open moorland course with water hazards. Facilities of 'Brean Leisure Park' adjoining.
18 holes, 5715yds, Par 69, SSS 68, Course record 66.
Club membership 350.
Visitors　may not play on Sat & Sun before 11.30am. Book in advance through professional.
Societies　contact office or professional in advance.
Green Fees　£20 per day; £12 per round (£20 per round weekends).
Cards　⬚ 🟦
Prof　David Haines
Facilities　⊗ by prior arrangement ⅏ by prior arrangement 🛇 💺 ♀ ♨ 🏠 🎄 🏌 ✎
& Leisure　heated indoor plus outdoor swimming pool, fishing, sauna.
Location　4m from junct 22 M5 on coast road

Hotel　★★♨ 65% Batch Country Hotel, Batch Ln, LYMPSHAM ☎ 01934 750371 8 ⇄ ☏
See advertisement on page 218.

Burnham & Berrow St Christopher's Way TA8 2PE
☎ 01278 785760 Fax 01278 795440
Natural championship links course with panoramic views of the Somerset hills sweeping across the famed reed beds and the Bristol channel with the islands of Steepholm and Flatholm against the background of the Welsh coast line.
Championship Course: 18 holes, 6606yds, Par 71, SSS 73, Course record 66.
9 Hole Course: 9 holes, 6308yds, Par 72, SSS 70.
Club membership 900.　▶

BATCH COUNTRY HOTEL AA ★★

Lympsham, Nr. Weston-super-Mare, Somerset BS24 0EX.
Telephone: (01934) 750371 Fax: (01934) 750501
Family run hotel with long reputation for friendly atmosphere and excellent traditional English food, a la carte menu also available. Fully licensed lounge bar.
Situated in own grounds with unlimited parking. Just a short drive from Burnham-on-Sea, Weston-super-Mare and golf courses.
All bedrooms include en suite, colour TV and tea/coffee facilities.
Egon Ronay and Ashley Courtenay recommended.

---

must contact in advance & have handicap certificate (22 or under gentlemen, 30 or under ladies) to play on the Championship course.

Societies	telephone in advance.
Green Fees	£38 per day/round (£50 weekends & bank holidays); 9 hole £12.
Prof	Mark Crowther-Smith
Facilities	⊗ ∭ ⅃ ⚑ 〒 ⅄ ⚘ 🏠 ↑ ⛳ ↘ ⚐
Location	1m N of town on B3140

Hotel	★★ 68% Woodlands Hotel, Hill Ln, BRENT KNOLL ☎ 01278 760232 8 ⇄ 🄵
Additional hotel	★★♨ 65% Batch Country Hotel, Batch Ln, LYMPSHAM ☎ 01934 750371 Fax 01934 750501 8 ⇄ 🄵

CHARD   Map 03 ST30

Windwhistle Golf, Squash & Country Club Cricket St Thomas TA20 4DG ☎ 01460 30231 Fax 01460 30055
Parkland course at 735 ft above sea level with outstanding views over the Somerset Levels to the Bristol Channel and South Wales.
East/West Course: 18 holes, 5812yds, Par 71, SSS 68, Course record 69.
Club membership 600.

Visitors	must contact in advance.
Societies	by prior arrangement.
Green Fees	£18 per day; £15 per round (£20/£18 weekends & bank holidays).
Cards	💳 🟥 🟦
Prof	Duncan Driver
Designer	Braid & Taylor
Facilities	⅃ ⚑ 〒 ⅄ ⚘ 🏠 ↑ ⚐
& Leisure	squash, driving range to open 1999.
Location	3m E of Chard on A30

Hotel	★★★ 63% Shrubbery Hotel, ILMINSTER ☎ 01460 52108 14 ⇄ 🄵

CLEVEDON   Map 03 ST47

Clevedon Castle Rd, Walton St Mary BS21 7AA
☎ 01275 874057 Fax 01275 341228
Situated on the cliff-top overlooking the Severn estuary and with distant views of the Welsh coast. Excellent parkland course in first-class condition overlooking the Severn estuary. Magnificent scenery and some tremendous 'drop' holes. Strong winds.
18 holes, 6117yds, Par 70, SSS 69, Course record 65.
Club membership 750.

Visitors	must contact in advance. No play Wed morning.
Societies	not bank holidays, telephone or apply in writing.
Green Fees	£28 (£40 per weekends & bank holidays).
Cards	💳 🟥 🟦
Prof	Robert Scanlan
Designer	S Herd
Facilities	⊗ ∭ ⅃ ⚑ 〒 ⅄ ⚘ 🏠 ↑ ⚐
Location	1m NE of town centre

Hotel	★★★ 65% Walton Park Hotel, Wellington Ter, CLEVEDON ☎ 01275 874253 40 ⇄ 🄵

CONGRESBURY   Map 03 ST46

Mendip Spring Honeyhall Ln BS49 5JT
☎ 01934 852322 Fax 01934 853021
Set in peaceful countryside with the Mendip Hills as a backdrop, this 18-hole course includes lakes and numerous water hazards covering some 12 acres of the course. The 12th is an island green surrounded by water and there are long drives on the 7th and 13th. The 9-hole Lakeside course is an easy walking course, mainly par 4. Floodlit driving range.
Brinsea Course: 18 holes, 6334yds, Par 71, SSS 70, Course record 64.
Lakeside: 9 holes, 4520yds, Par 68, SSS 68.
Club membership 445.

Visitors	must contact in advance for Brinsea course and handicap certificate required for weekends. Lakeside is play & pay anytime.
Societies	booking in advance by arrangement.
Green Fees	Brinsea: £22 per round (£25 weekends & bank holidays). Lakeside: £7.50 per 9 holes (£8 weekends & bank holidays). Day ticket £29 (£32 weekends).
Cards	💳 🟥 🟦
Prof	John Blackburn
Facilities	⊗ ∭ ⅃ ⚑ 〒 ⅄ ⚘ 🏠 ↑ ↘ ⚐ ⚑
Location	8m E of Weston-Super-Mare between A370 and A38

Hotel	★★★♨ 71% Daneswood House Hotel, Cuck Hill, SHIPHAM ☎ 01934 843145 & 843945 Fax 01934 843824 9 ⇄ 🄵 Annexe3 ⇄ 🄵

Entries with a shaded background identify courses that are considered to be particularly interesting

ENMORE   Map 03 ST23

Enmore Park TA5 2AN
☎ 01278 671481 Fax 01278 671481
Hilly, parkland course with water features on foothills of
Quantocks. Wooded countryside and views of Quantocks and
Mendips. 1st and 10th are testing holes.
18 holes, 6406yds, Par 71, SSS 71, Course record 66.
Club membership 750.

Visitors	phone professional for details, must have handicap certificate for weekends.
Societies	must apply in writing.
Green Fees	£25 per day; £18 per round (£25 per round weekends).
Cards	
Prof	Nigel Wixon
Designer	Hawtree
Facilities	⊗ ⋔ ⓑ � icons
Location	A39 to Minehead, at first set of lights turn left to Spaxton, then 1.5m to reservoir and turn left
Hotel	★★★ 73% Walnut Tree Hotel, North Petherton, BRIDGWATER ☎ 01278 662255 32 🛏

FARRINGTON GURNEY   Map 03 ST65

Farrington Marsh Ln BS39 6TS
☎ 01761 241274 (office) & 214274 (pro)
Fax 01761 241274
USGA spec greens on both challenging 9 and 18 hole
courses. Newly completed 18 hole course with computerised
irrigation, six lakes, four tees per hole and excellent views.
Testing holes include the 12th (282yds) with the green set
behind a lake at the base of a 100ft drop, and the 17th which
is played between two lakes.
Executive Course: 9 holes, 3022yds, Par 54, SSS 53, Course record 56.
Main Course: 18 holes, 6316yds, Par 72, SSS 72, Course record 68.
Club membership 750.

Visitors	must book starting times at weekends.
Societies	welcome except for weekends & bank holidays, telephone or write in advance.
Green Fees	Main course; £27.50 all day; £20 per round (£36/£30 weekends & bank holidays). Executive course; £12 per day; £7 per 9 holes (£14/£9 weekends & bank holidays).
Cards	
Prof	Peter Thompson
Designer	Peter Thompson
Facilities	⊗ ⋔ ⓑ service icons
& Leisure	sauna, video teaching studio.
Hotel	★★ 71% Country Ways Hotel, Marsh Ln, FARRINGTON GURNEY ☎ 01761 452449 6 🛏

FROME   Map 03 ST74

Frome Golf Centre Critchill Manor BA11 4LJ
☎ 01373 453410 Fax 01373 453410
Attractive parkland course, founded in 1993, situated in a
picturesque valley just outside the town, complete with
practice areas and a driving range.
18 holes, 4890yds, Par 66, SSS 64, Course record 62.
Club membership 330.

Visitors	no restrictions.
Societies	telephone in advance.
Green Fees	not confirmed.
Prof	Adrian Wright
Designer	R Flower
Facilities	⊗ ⓑ service icons
Location	A361 Frome/Shepton Mallet, at Nunney Catch rdbt through Nunney, course on left before Frome
Hotel	★★ 68% The George at Nunney, 11 Church St, NUNNEY ☎ 01373 836458 9rm(8 🛏 🐾)

Orchardleigh BA11 2PH
☎ 01373 454200 Fax 01373 454202
Originally designed by Ryder Cup golfer, Brian Huggett, as
two returning nines through mature parkland. Five lakes
bring water into play on seven holes.
18 holes, 6831yds, Par 72, SSS 73.
Club membership 500.

Visitors	no visitors before 11am at weekends.
Societies	apply in writing or telephone in advance.
Green Fees	£30 per round, £35 per 27/36 holes (£40 weekends).
Cards	
Prof	Peter Green/Steve Slinger
Designer	Brian Huggett
Facilities	⊗ ⋔ ⓑ service icons
& Leisure	fishing.
Location	1m W of Frome on the A362
Hotel	★★ 68% The George at Nunney, 11 Church St, NUNNEY ☎ 01373 836458 9rm(8 🛏 🐾)

GURNEY SLADE   Map 03 ST64

Mendip BA3 4UT ☎ 01749 840570 Fax 01749 841439
Undulating downland course offering an interesting test of
golf·on superb fairways and extensive views over the
surrounding countryside.
18 holes, 6383yds, Par 71, SSS 71, Course record 65.
Club membership 900.

Visitors	must contact in advance. Handicap certificates required for play at weekends and bank holidays.
Societies	by arrangement with secretary.
Green Fees	£26 per day; £21 per round (£31 weekends & bank holidays).
Prof	Ron Lee
Facilities	⊗ ⋔ ⓑ service icons
Location	1.5m S off A37
Hotel	★★★ 70% Centurion Hotel, Charlton Ln, MIDSOMER NORTON ☎ 01761 417711 44 🛏 🐾

KEYNSHAM   Map 03 ST66

Stockwood Vale Stockwood Ln BS31 2ER
☎ 0117 986 6505 Fax 0117 986 0509
Undulating and challenging public course in a beautiful
setting with interesting well bunkered holes, in particular the
beautiful and challenging 5th and 13th holes.
18 holes, 6031yds, Par 71, SSS 69.
Club membership 600.

Visitors	no restrictions, but must reserve a start time.
Societies	telephone in advance. ▶

Green Fees £14 per 18 holes (£16 weekends).
Cards 🇻🇸🇦 🇩🇪 🇳🇿 🇬🇧
Prof John Richards
Facilities ⊗ ⫴ ⮧ ♛ ♀ △ 🏠 ♂ ⟨
Location Just off Hicks Gate on A4

Hotel ★★ 66% Chelwood House Hotel,
CHELWOOD ☎ 01761 490730 12 ⇆ ♟

LANGPORT   Map 03 ST42

Long Sutton Long Sutton TA10 9JU
☎ 01458 241017 Fax 01458 241022
Gentle, undulating, Pay and Play course.
18 holes, 6367yds, Par 71, SSS 70, Course record 71.
Club membership 600.
Visitors advisable to phone in advance.
Societies telephone in advance.
Green Fees £24 per day; £16 per round (£30/£20 weekends).
Cards 🇻🇸 🇩🇪 🇳🇿 🇬🇧
Prof Michael Blackwell
Designer Patrick Dawson
Facilities ⊗ ⫴ ⮧ ♛ ♀ △ 🏠 ♞ ♂ 🏌 ⟨
Location 10m NW of Yeovil off A372

Hotel ★★★ 70% The Hollies, Bower Hinton,
MARTOCK ☎ 01935 822232 Annexe32 ⇆ ♟

LONG ASHTON   Map 03 ST57

Long Ashton The Clubhouse, Clarken Coombe BS41 9DW
☎ 01275 392316 Fax 01275 394395
Wooded parkland course with nice turf, wonderful views of
Bristol and surrounding areas and a spacious practice area.
Good testing holes, especially the back nine, in prevailing
south-west winds. The short second hole (126yds) cut from
an old quarry and played over a road can ruin many a card!
Good drainage ensures pleasant winter golf.
18 holes, 6077yds, Par 70, SSS 70, Course record 66.
Club membership 700.
Visitors recommended to telephone the professional.
Societies must contact the secretary in advance.
Green Fees not confirmed.
Prof Denis Scanlan
Designer J H Taylor
Facilities ⊗ ⮧ ♛ ♀ △ 🏠 ⟨
Location 0.5m N on B3128

Hotel ★★★ 67% Redwood Lodge Hotel,
Beggar Bush Ln, Failand, BRISTOL
☎ 01275 393901 112 ⇆ ♟

Woodspring Golf & Country Club Yanley Ln BS18 9LR
☎ 01275 394378 Fax 01275 394473
Set in 180 acres of undulating heathland featuring superb
natural water hazards, protected greens and a rising
landscape. Designed by Peter Alliss and Clive Clark and laid
out by Donald Steel, the course has three individual 9-hole
courses, the Avon, Severn & Brunel. The 9th hole on the
Brunel course is a feature hole here, with an elevated tee shot
over a natural gorge. In undulating hills south of Bristol, long
carries to tight fairways, elevated island tees and difficult
approaches to greens make the most of the 27 holes.
Avon Course: 9 holes, 2960yds, Par 35, SSS 34.
Brunel Course: 9 holes, 3320yds, Par 37, SSS 35.
Severn Course: 9 holes, 3267yds, Par 36, SSS 35.
Club membership 960.

Visitors must contact in advance, weekends may be
limited to play after midday. Dress codes must
be adhered to.
Societies must contact Kevin Pitts in advance.
Green Fees not confirmed.
Cards 🇪🇺 🇩🇪 🇻🇸 🇦🇺 🇳🇿 🇬🇧
Prof Nigel Beer
Designer Clarke/Alliss/Steel
Facilities ⊗ ⫴ ⮧ ♛ ♀ △ 🏠 ♞ ♂ 🏌 ⟨
& Leisure sauna.
Location Off A38 Bridgewater Road

Hotel ★★★ 67% Redwood Lodge Hotel,
Beggar Bush Ln, Failand, BRISTOL
☎ 01275 393901 112 ⇆ ♟

MIDSOMER NORTON   Map 03 ST65

Fosseway Country Club Charlton Ln BA3 4BD
☎ 01761 412214 Fax 01761 418357
Very attractive tree-lined parkland course, not demanding but
with lovely views towards the Mendip Hills.
9 holes, 4565yds, Par 67, SSS 61.
Club membership 250.
Visitors may not play on Wed evenings, Sun mornings &
competitions days.
Societies apply in writing or telephone.
Green Fees £10 per day (£12 weekends & bank holidays).
Cards 🇻🇸 🇩🇪 🇳🇿 🇬🇧
Designer C K Cotton/F Pennink
Facilities ⊗ ⫴ ⮧ ♛ ♀ △ 🏠 ♞ ⟨
& Leisure heated indoor swimming pool, squash.
Location SE of town centre off A367

Hotel ★★★ 70% Centurion Hotel, Charlton Ln,
MIDSOMER NORTON
☎ 01761 417711 44 ⇆ ♟

MINEHEAD   Map 03 SS94

Minehead & West Somerset The Warren TA24 5SJ
☎ 01643 702057 Fax 01643 705095
Flat seaside links, very exposed to wind, with good turf
set on a shingle bank. The last five holes adjacent to the
beach are testing. The 215-yard 18th is wedged between
the beach and the club buildings and provides a good
finish.
18 holes, 6228yds, Par 71, SSS 71, Course record 65.
Club membership 620.
Visitors must contact secretary in advance.
Societies telephone in advance.
Green Fees £22 per day (£25 weekends & bank
holidays).
Prof Ian Read
Facilities ⊗ ⫴ ⮧ ♛ ♀ △ 🏠 ♞ ♂ ⟨
Location E end of esplanade

Hotel ★★ 74% Channel House Hotel, Church
Path, MINEHEAD
☎ 01643 703229 8 ⇆ ♟

SALTFORD   Map 03 ST66

Saltford Golf Club Ln BS31 3AA ☎ 01225 872043
Parkland course with easy walking and panoramic views
over the Avon Valley. The par 4, 2nd and 13th are notable.

18 holes, 6081yds, Par 69, SSS 69.
Club membership 800.

Visitors   must contact in advance & have handicap certificate.
Societies   must telephone in advance.
Green Fees not confirmed.
Prof   Dudley Millinstead
Designer   Harry Vardon
Facilities   ⊗ ⫟ ᝰ ♥ ♀ ⚎ 🏠 ⚐ 🏌 🛆 ✆
Location   S side of village

Hotel   ★★★ Hunstrete House Hotel, HUNSTRETE
     ☎ 01761 490490   23 ⇆ 🐾

SOMERTON   Map 03 ST42

Wheathill Wheathill TA11 7HG
☎ 01963 240667 Fax 01963 240230
A Par 68 parkland course with nice views in quiet countryside. It is flat lying with the 13th hole along the river. There is an Academy 4-hole course and a massive practice area.
18 holes, 5362yds, Par 68, SSS 66.
Club membership 350.

Visitors   no restrictions.
Societies   telephone to arrange.
Green Fees not confirmed.
Prof   A England
Designer   J Pain
Facilities   ⊗ ⫟ ᝰ ♥ ♀ ⚎ 🏠 ⚐ 🏌 🛆 ✆
Location   5m E of Somerton off B3153

Hotel   ★★★ 58% Wessex Hotel, High St, STREET
     ☎ 01458 443383   50 ⇆ 🐾

TAUNTON   Map 03 ST22

Oake Manor Oake TA4 1BA
☎ 01823 461993 Fax 01823 461995
A parkland/lakeland course situated in breathtaking Somerset countryside with views of the Quantock, Blackdown and Brendon Hills. Ten holes feature water hazards such as lakes, cascades and a trout stream. The 15th hole (Par 5, 476yds) is bounded by water all down the left with a carry over another lake on to an island green. The course is challenging yet great fun for all standards of golfer.
18 holes, 6109yds, Par 70, SSS 69.
Club membership 600.

Visitors   no restrictions but visitors must book in advance.
Societies   contact Russell Gardner by telephone.
Green Fees £16.50 (£20 weekends).
Prof   Russell Gardner
Designer   Adrian Stiff
Facilities   🛆 🏠 ⚐ ✆ ⚍
Location   Exit M5 junct 26, take A38 towards Taunton and follow signs to Oake

Hotel   ★★★ 71% Rumwell Manor Hotel, Rumwell, TAUNTON
     ☎ 01823 461902   10 ⇆ 🐾 Annexe10 ⇆ 🐾

Taunton & Pickeridge Corfe TA3 7BY   ☎ 01823 421537
Downland course with extensive views.
18 holes, 5927yds, Par 69, SSS 68, Course record 61.
Club membership 600.

Visitors   must have a handicap certificate

Societies   must telephone in advance.
Green Fees not confirmed.
Prof   Gary Milne
Facilities   ⊗ ⫟ ᝰ ♥ ♀ 🛆 🏠 ✆
Location   4m S off B3170

Hotel   ★★★ 75% The Mount Somerset Hotel, Henlade, TAUNTON
     ☎ 01823 442500   11 ⇆ 🐾

Taunton Vale Creech Heathfield TA3 5EY
☎ 01823 412220 Fax 01823 413583
An 18 hole and a 9 hole golf course in a parkland complex occupying 156 acres in the Vale of Taunton. Complex includes a floodlit driving range.
Charlton Course: 18 holes, 6167yds, Par 70, SSS 69, Course record 65.
Durston Course: 9 holes, 2004yds, Par 64, SSS 60.
Club membership 670.

Visitors   telephone booking essential. Must contact Professional on 01823 412880
Societies   must book in advance.
Green Fees 18 holes: £26 per day, £16 per round (£32/£20 weekends); 9 holes: £12 per day, £8 per round (£15/£10 weekends & bank holidays).
Prof   Martin Keitch
Designer   John Payne
Facilities   ⊗ ⫟ ᝰ ♥ ♀ 🛆 🏠 ⚐ 🏌 🛆 ✆ ⚍
Location   Off A361 between juncts 24 & 25 on M5

Hotel   ★★★ 75% The Mount Somerset Hotel, Henlade, TAUNTON
     ☎ 01823 442500   11 ⇆ 🐾

Vivary Park Municipal Fons George TA1 3JU
☎ 01823 333875
A parkland course, tight and narrow with ponds.
18 holes, 4620yds, Par 63, SSS 63, Course record 59.
Club membership 700.

Visitors   may play anytime except weekends before 9am, bookings can be made 8 days in advance.
Societies   apply in writing.
Green Fees £8.10 per round.
Prof   Mike Steadman
Designer   W H Fowler
Facilities   ⊗ ⫟ ᝰ ♥ ♀ 🛆 🏠 ⚐ ✆
& Leisure   hard tennis courts.
Location   S side of town centre off A38

Hotel   ★★ 61% Falcon Hotel, Henlade, TAUNTON
     ☎ 01823 442502   11 ⇆ 🐾

WEDMORE   Map 03 ST44

Isle of Wedmore Lineage BS28 4QT
☎ 01934 713649 (Office) 712452 (Pro) Fax 01934 713696
Gentle undulating course designed to maintain natural environment. Existing woodland and hedgerow enhanced by new planting. Magnificent panoramic views of Cheddar Valley and Glastonbury Tor.
18 holes, 6006yds, Par 70, SSS 69, Course record 70.
Club membership 620.

Visitors   telephone professional in advance. Not before 9.30am weekends.
Societies   weekdays only, telephone in advance.
Green Fees £22 per day; £18 per round (£25/£22 weekends).
Cards   🖃 VISA 💳 📇 📘   ▶
Prof   Graham Coombe

Designer	Terry Murray
Facilities	⊗ ∭ ⅃ ⊵ ♥ ♀ ♨ 🛍 ↑ ♂
Location	Off B3139 between Wells & Burnham-on-Sea

| Hotel | ★★★ 67% Swan Hotel, Sadler St, WELLS ☎ 01749 678877 38 ⇄ ⋔ |

WELLS   Map 03 ST54

Wells (Somerset) East Horrington Rd BA5 3DS
☎ 01749 675005 Fax 01749 675005
Beautiful wooded course with wonderful views. The
prevailing SW wind complicates the 448-yd, 3rd.
18 holes, 6015yds, Par 70, SSS 69, Course record 66.
Club membership 712.

Visitors	must contact in advance & have handicap certificate weekends. Tee times restricted at weekends to after 9.30pm
Societies	must apply in advance.
Green Fees	£20-£25 per day.
Cards	VISA
Prof	Adrian Bishop
Facilities	⊗ ∭ ⅃ ⊵ ♥ ♀ ♨ 🛍 ↑ ♘ ♣ ♂ ℓ
Location	1.5m E off B3139

| Hotel | ★★★ 67% Swan Hotel, Sadler St, WELLS ☎ 01749 678877 38 ⇄ ⋔ |

WESTON-SUPER-MARE   Map 03 ST36

Weston-super-Mare Uphill Rd North BS23 4NQ
☎ 01934 626968 & 633360 Fax 01934 626968
A compact and interesting layout with the opening hole
adjacent to the beach. The sandy, links-type course is
slightly undulating and has beautifully maintained turf
and greens. The 15th is a testing 455-yard, par 4.
18 holes, 6300yds, Par 70, SSS 70, Course record 65.
Club membership 778.

Visitors	must have handicap certificate to play at weekends.
Societies	apply in writing or telephone.
Green Fees	not confirmed.
Prof	Mike Laband
Designer	T Dunne/Dr Mackenzie
Facilities	⊗ ∭ ⅃ ⊵ ♥ ♀ ♨ 🛍
Location	S side of town centre off A370

| Hotel | ★★ 66% Beachlands Hotel, 17 Uphill Rd North, WESTON-SUPER-MARE ☎ 01934 621401 23 ⇄ ⋔ |

Worlebury Monks Hill BS22 9SX
☎ 01934 625789 Fax 01934 625789
Situated on the ridge of Worlebury Hill, this seaside course
offers fairly easy walking and extensive views of the Severn
estuary and Wales.
18 holes, 5963yds, Par 70, SSS 69, Course record 66.
Club membership 590.

Visitors	must be recognised golfers, handicap certificate or proof of club membership may be required
Societies	apply in writing or telephone in advance.
Green Fees	£20 per day (£30 weekends).
Prof	Gary Marks
Designer	A Hawtree
Facilities	⊗ ∭ by prior arrangement ⅃ ⊵ ♥ ♀ ♨ 🛍 ♂
& Leisure	snooker table.
Location	5m NE off A370

| Hotel | ★★★ 68% Commodore Hotel, Beach Rd, Sand Bay, Kewstoke, WESTON-SUPER-MARE ☎ 01934 415778 12 ⇄ ⋔ Annexe6 ⇄ ⋔ |

YEOVIL   Map 03 ST51

Yeovil Sherborne Rd BA21 5BW
☎ 01935 422965 Fax 01935 411283
On the Old Course the opener lies by the River Yeo
before the gentle climb to high downs with good views.
The outstanding 14th and 15th holes present a challenge,
being below the player with a deep railway cutting on
the left of the green. The 1st on the Newton Course is
played over the river which then leads to a challenging
but scenic golf course.
Old Course: 18 holes, 6144yds, Par 72, SSS 70, Course record 64.
Newton Course: 9 holes, 4891yds, Par 68, SSS 65.
Club membership 1000.

Visitors	must contact in advance. Members only before 9.30am and 12.30-2.
Societies	telephone in advance.
Green Fees	not confirmed.
Prof	Geoff Kite
Designer	Fowler & Allison
Facilities	⊗ ∭ ⅃ ⊵ ♥ ♀ ♨ 🛍 ↑ ♂
Location	1m E on A30

| Hotel | ★★★ 72% Yeovil Court Hotel, West Coker Rd, YEOVIL ☎ 01935 863746 15 ⇄ ⋔ Annexe11 ⇄ ⋔ |

STAFFORDSHIRE

BROCTON   Map 07 SJ91

Brocton Hall ST17 0TH
☎ 01785 661901 Fax 01785 661591
Parkland course with gentle slopes in places, easy walking.
18 holes, 6095yds, Par 69, SSS 69, Course record 66.
Club membership 665.

Visitors	not competition days. Must contact in advance.
Societies	must apply in advance.
Green Fees	£30 per day.
Prof	R G Johnson
Designer	Harry Vardon
Facilities	⊗ ∭ ⅃ ⊵ ♥ ♀ ♨ 🛍 ↑ ♂
Location	NW side of village off A34

| Hotel | ★★★ 65% Garth Hotel, Wolverhampton Rd, Moss Pit, STAFFORD ☎ 01785 256124 60 ⇄ ⋔ |

BURTON-UPON-TRENT   Map 07 SK22

Branston Burton Rd, Branston DE14 3DP
☎ 01283 512211 Fax 01283 566984
Flat semi-parkland course, adjacent to River Trent, on
undulating ground with natural water hazards on 13 holes.
18 holes, 6647yds, Par 72, SSS 72, Course record 65.
Club membership 800.

Visitors may not play before noon or at weekends. Must contact in advance.
Societies must telephone in advance.
Green Fees £38 per day; £28 per round (£40 per round weekends & bank holidays).
Cards ⬚ 🔲 🔲 🔲 🔲 🔲
Prof Sean Stiff
Designer G Ramshall
Facilities ⊗ ⫟ 🝖 🛆 🖤 ♀ 🛆 📷 🏌 ⛳ ♂ ⛳ ⟨
& Leisure heated indoor swimming pool, sauna, solarium, gymnasium.
Location 1.5m SW on A5121

Hotel ★★★ 69% Riverside Hotel, Riverside Dr, Branston, BURTON UPON TRENT
☎ 01283 511234 22 ⇄ 🐾

Burton-upon-Trent 43 Ashby Rd East DE15 0PS
☎ 01283 544551 Fax 01283 544551
Undulating parkland course with trees a major feature. There are testing par 3s at 10th and 12th. The 18th has a lake on the approach to the green.
18 holes, 6579yds, Par 71, SSS 71, Course record 63.
Club membership 600.
Visitors must contact in advance and have a handicap certificate.
Societies must contact in advance.
Green Fees not confirmed.
Prof Gary Stafford
Designer H S Colt
Facilities ⊗ ⫟ 🝖 🛆 🖤 ♀ 🛆 📷 🏌 ⛳
Location 3m E on A511

Hotel ★★★ 69% Riverside Hotel, Riverside Dr, Branston, BURTON UPON TRENT
☎ 01283 511234 22 ⇄ 🐾

Craythorne Craythorne Rd, Stretton DE13 0AZ
☎ 01283 564329 Fax 01283 511908
A relatively short and challenging parkland course with tight fairways and views of the Trent Valley. Excellent greens. Suits all standards but particularly good for society players.
18 holes, 5450yds, Par 68, SSS 67, Course record 66.
Club membership 500.
Visitors must contact in advance.
Societies apply in writing or telephone for details.
Green Fees £30 per day; £20 per round (£25 per round weekends).
Cards ⬚ 🔲
Prof Steve Hadfield
Facilities ⊗ ⫟ 🝖 🛆 🖤 ♀ 🛆 📷 🏌 ⛳ ⟨
Location Off A38 through Stretton village

Hotel ★★★ 69% Riverside Hotel, Riverside Dr, Branston, BURTON UPON TRENT
☎ 01283 511234 22 ⇄ 🐾

Hoar Cross Hall Health Spa Golf Academy Hoar Cross DE13 8QS ☎ 01283 575671
Newly constructed golf academy located in the grounds of a stately home, now a well appointed health spa resort and hotel. Driving range, bunker and practice areas.
Club membership 300.
Visitors day guests & residents.
Societies golfing societies that are resident only.
Green Fees not confirmed.
Prof Gary Prince

Designer Geoffrey Collins
Facilities 🛆 📷 🏌 🚻 ⛳
& Leisure hard tennis courts, heated indoor swimming pool, sauna, solarium, gymnasium.

CANNOCK   Map 07 SJ91

Beau Desert Rugeley Rd, Hazelslade WS12 5PJ
☎ 01543 422626 Fax 01543 451137
Heathland course surrounded by a forest.
18 holes, 6310yds, Par 70, SSS 71, Course record 64.
Club membership 500.
Visitors are advised to contact professional in advance.
Societies must contact in advance.
Green Fees £38 per day (£48 weekends & bank holidays).
Prof Barrie Stevens
Designer Herbert Fowler
Facilities ⊗ ⫟ 🝖 🛆 🖤 ♀ 🛆 📷 🏌 ⛳ ⟨
Location 0.5m NE of village

Hotel ★★★ 65% Roman Way Hotel, Watling St, Hatherton, CANNOCK
☎ 01543 572121 56 ⇄ 🐾

Cannock Park Stafford Rd WS11 2AL
☎ 01543 578850 Fax 01543 578850
Part of a large leisure centre, this parkland-type course plays alongside Cannock Chase. Good drainage, open most of year.
18 holes, 5149yds, Par 67, SSS 65.
Club membership 250.
Visitors must book in advance.
Societies must contact in advance.
Green Fees £8 per round (£10 weekends).
Prof David Dunk
Designer John Mainland
Facilities 🝖 🖤 ♀ 🛆 📷 🏌 ⛳
& Leisure hard tennis courts, heated indoor swimming pool, sauna, solarium, gymnasium.
Location 0.5m N of town centre on A34

Hotel ★★★ 65% Roman Way Hotel, Watling St, Hatherton, CANNOCK
☎ 01543 572121 56 ⇄ 🐾

ENVILLE   Map 07 SO88

Enville Highgate Common DY7 5BN
☎ 01384 872074 (Office) Fax 01384 873396
Easy walking on two fairly flat parkland/moorland courses - the 'Highgate' and the 'Lodge'.
Highgate Course: 18 holes, 6556yds, Par 72, SSS 72, Course record 65.
Lodge Course: 18 holes, 6291yds, Par 70, SSS 70.
Club membership 900.
Visitors must play with member at weekends.
Societies phone initially for details.
Green Fees £40 per 36 holes; £30 per 18 holes.
Prof Sean Power
Facilities 🛆 📷 🏌 🚻 ⛳ ⛳
Location Take A458 towards Bridgnorth, after 4.5m turn right. Golf club signposted

Hotel ★★★ 63% Talbot Hotel, High St, STOURBRIDGE
☎ 01384 394350 30 ⇄ 🐾

GOLDENHILL   Map 07 SJ85

Goldenhill Mobberley Rd ST6 5SS
☎ 01782 234200 Fax 01782 234303
Rolling parkland course with water features on six of the
back nine holes.
18 holes, 5957yds, Par 71, SSS 69.
Club membership 400.
Visitors   contact in advance for weekend play.
Societies   must apply in writing or telephone.
Green Fees not confirmed.
Facilities   ⊗ ⅷ ┗ ♥ ♀ ⌂ ☂ ⚷
Location   On A50, 4m N of Stoke

Hotel   ★★★ 73% Manor House Hotel, Audley Rd,
ALSAGER ☎ 01270 884000   57 ⇥ ♟

HIMLEY   Map 07 SO89

Himley Hall Golf Centre Log Cabin, Himley Hall Park
DY3 4DF ☎ 01902 895207
Parkland course set in grounds of Himley Hall Park, with
lovely views. Large practice area including a pitch-and-putt.
9 holes, 6215yds, Par 72, SSS 70, Course record 65.
Club membership 200.
Visitors   restricted weekends.
Green Fees £5.50 per 9 holes; £8 per 18 holes.
Prof   Jeremy Nichols
Designer   A Baker
Facilities   ⊗ ┗ ♥ ⌂ ⚷
& Leisure   9 hole pitch & putt.
Location   0.5m E on B4176

Hotel   ★★★ 62% Himley Country Hotel, School Rd,
HIMLEY ☎ 01902 896716   73 ⇥ ♟

LEEK   Map 07 SJ95

Leek Birchall, Cheddleton Rd ST13 5RE
☎ 01538 384779 Fax 01538 384535
Undulating, challenging mainly parkland course, reputedly
one of the best in the area.
18 holes, 6218yds, Par 70, SSS 70, Course record 63.
Club membership 750.
Visitors   must contact Professional in advance.
Societies   must apply in advance.
Green Fees £24 (£30 weekends & bank holidays).
Prof   Peter A Stubbs
Facilities   ⊗ ⅷ ┗ ♥ ♀ ⌂ ⚷
Location   0.75m S on A520

Hotel   ★★★ 69% George Hotel, Swan Square,
Burslem, STOKE-ON-TRENT
☎ 01782 577544   39 ⇥ ♟

Westwood (Leek) Newcastle Rd ST13 7AA
☎ 01538 398385 & 398897 (Prof) Fax 01538 382485
A challenging moorland/parkland course set in beautiful
open countryside with an undulating front nine. The back
nine is more open and longer with the River Churnet coming
into play on several holes.
18 holes, 6207yds, Par 70, SSS 69, Course record 66.
Club membership 700.
Visitors   must book in advance.
Societies   apply by phone or in writing.
Green Fees £25 per day; £18 per round (£20 weekends).

Prof   Neale Hyde
Facilities   ⊗ ⅷ ┗ ♥ ♀ ⌂ ☂ ⚷
Location   On A53, S of Leek

Hotel   ★★★ 69% George Hotel, Swan Square,
Burslem, STOKE-ON-TRENT
☎ 01782 577544   39 ⇥ ♟

LICHFIELD   Map 07 SK10

Seedy Mill Elmhurst WS13 8HE
☎ 01543 417333 Fax 01543 418098
A 27 hole course in picturesque parkland scenery. Numerous
holes crossed by meandering mill streams. Undulating greens
defended by hazards lie in wait for the practised approach.
Well appointed clubhouse.
18 holes, 6308yds, Par 72, SSS 70, Course record 68.
Club membership 1200.
Visitors   must contact at least 3 days in advance.
Societies   apply in writing or telephone.
Green Fees £30 per day; £20 per 18 holes (£25 per 18 holes
           weekends).
Cards   ▭ ▩ ▩ ▦ ▩ ⚷
Prof   Simon Jackson
Designer   Hawtree & Son
Facilities   ⊗ ⅷ ┗ ♥ ♀ ⌂ ⌂ ☂ ⚷ ⚷ ⚷
Location   At Elmhurst, 2m N of Lichfield, off A515

Hotel   ★★★ 67% Little Barrow Hotel, Beacon St,
LICHFIELD ☎ 01543 414500   24 ⇥ ♟

Whittington Heath Tamworth Rd WS14 9PW
☎ 01543 432317 Fax 01543 432317
18 magnificent holes winding their way through
heathland and trees, presenting a good test for the serious
golfer. Leaving the fairway can be severely punished.
The dog-legs are most tempting, inviting the golfer to
chance his arm. Local knowledge is a definite advantage.
Clear views of the famous three spires of Lichfield
Cathedral.
18 holes, 6490yds, Par 70, SSS 71, Course record 65.
Club membership 660.
Visitors   must contact in advance. May not play at
           weekends. Handicap certificate required.
Societies   welcome Wed & Thu, must apply in
           writing.
Green Fees £27 per 18 holes.
Cards   ▭ ▩ ▩ ▦ ▩ ⚷
Prof   Adrian Sadler
Designer   Colt
Facilities   ⊗ ⅷ ┗ ♥ ♀ ⌂ ⌂
Location   2.5m SE on A51 Lichfield-Tamworth road

Hotel   ★★★ 67% Little Barrow Hotel, Beacon St,
LICHFIELD ☎ 01543 414500   24 ⇥ ♟

NEWCASTLE-UNDER-LYME   Map 07 SJ84

Newcastle Municipal Newcastle Rd, Keele ST5 5AB
☎ 01782 627596
Open course on the side of a hill without mature trees.
18 holes, 6396yds, Par 71, SSS 70, Course record 64.
Club membership 210.
Visitors   must contact in advance.

Societies   by prior arrangement to Newcastle-Under-Lyme
Borough Council, Civic Offices, Merrial St,
Newcastle-Under-Lyme, Staffs.
Green Fees   £7.30 per round (£8.20 weekends).
Prof   Colin Smith
Facilities   ⊗ ⫽ ⬙ ⬛ ♀ 🏠 ⌖ ♂ ⟨
Location   2m W on A525

Hotel   B Posthouse Stoke on Trent, Clayton Rd,
NEWCASTLE-UNDER-LYME
☎ 01782 717171 119 ⇋ ⋒

Newcastle-Under-Lyme Whitmore Rd ST5 2QB
☎ 01782 617006
Parkland course.
18 holes, 6404yds, Par 72, SSS 71.
Club membership 600.
Visitors   must contact in advance. With member only
weekends.
Societies   must contact in advance.
Green Fees   not confirmed.
Prof   Paul Symonds
Facilities   ⊗ ⫽ ⬙ ⬛ ♀ ⬠ 🏠 ⌖ ♂
Location   1m SW on A53

Hotel   ★★ 63% Comfort Inn, Liverpool Rd,
NEWCASTLE-UNDER-LYME
☎ 01782 717000   45 ⇋ ⋒ Annexe23 ⇋ ⋒

Wolstanton Dimsdale Old Hall, Hassam Pde, Wolstanton
ST5 9DR ☎ 01782 622413 (Sec) & 616995
A challenging undulating suburban course incorporating 6
difficult Par 3 holes. The 6th hole (Par 3) is 233yds from the
Medal Tee.
18 holes, 5807yds, Par 68, SSS 68, Course record 63.
Club membership 700.
Visitors   must contact in advance. May not play Tue
(Ladies Day). With member only at weekends &
bank holidays.
Societies   must contact in advance.
Green Fees   £20 per day/round.
Prof   Simon Arnold
Facilities   ⊗ ⫽ ⬙ ⬛ ♀ ⬠ 🏠 ♂
Location   1.5m from town centre. Turn off A34 at The
Sportsman Inn

Hotel   B Posthouse Stoke on Trent, Clayton Rd,
NEWCASTLE-UNDER-LYME
☎ 01782 717171 119 ⇋ ⋒

ONNELEY
Map 07 SJ74

Onneley CW3 5QF ☎ 01782 750577
A tight, picturesque, hillside parkland course. An ideal test
for the short game
9 holes, 5584yds, Par 70, SSS 67, Course record 67.
Club membership 410.
Visitors   welcome except during competitions, but may
not play on Sun and with member only Sat and
bank holidays.
Societies   packages available apply in writing to secretary.
Green Fees   £15 per 18 holes.
Facilities   ⊗ by prior arrangement ⫽ by prior arrangement
⬙ ⬛ ♀ ⬠
Location   2m from Woore on A525

Hotel   ★★ 69% Wheatsheaf Inn at Onneley,
Barhill Rd, ONNELEY ☎ 01782 751581 6 ⋒

PATTINGHAM
Map 07 SO89

Patshull Park Hotel Golf & Country Club WV6 7HR
☎ 01902 700100 Fax 01902 700874
Picturesque course set in 280 acres of glorious Capability
Brown landscaped parkland. Designed by John Jacobs, the
course meanders alongside trout fishing lakes. Many leisure
facilities.
18 holes, 6400yds, Par 72, SSS 71, Course record 63.
Club membership 330.

Visitors   must contact in advance.
Societies   must contact in advance.
Green Fees   £25 per round (£30 weekends).
Cards   [card logos]
Prof   Richard Bissell
Designer   John Jacobs
Facilities   ⊗ ⫽ ⬙ ⬛ ♀ ⬠ 🏠 ⌖ ♂ ⇘ ⛟ ♂
& Leisure   heated indoor swimming pool, fishing, sauna,
solarium, gymnasium, gymnasium, cardio gym,
steam room, pool/billiards.
Location   Off A464

Hotel   ★★★ 66% Patshull Park Hotel Golf & Country
Club, Patshull Park, PATTINGHAM
☎ 01902 700100   49 ⇋ ⋒

PERTON
Map 07 SO89

Perton Park Wrottesley Park Rd WV6 7HL
☎ 01902 380103 & 380073 Fax 01902 380073
Challenging inland links style course set in the picturesque
Staffordshire countryside.
18 holes, 6620yds, Par 72, SSS 72, Course record 61.
Club membership 500.
Visitors   must book in advance.
Societies   must telephone in advance.
Green Fees   £18 per day; £12 per round (£24/£18 weekends
& bank holidays).
Cards   [card logos]
Prof   Jeremy Harrold
Facilities   ⊗ ⫽ ⬙ ⬛ ♀ ⬠ 🏠 ⌖ ⛟ ♂ ⟨
& Leisure   hard tennis courts, snooker, pool table, bowls,
darts.
Location   6m W of Wolverhampton, off A454

Hotel   ★★ 68% Ely House Hotel, 53 Tettenhall Rd,
WOLVERHAMPTON
☎ 01902 311311   18 ⇋ ⋒

STAFFORD   Map 07 SJ92

Stafford Castle Newport Rd ST16 1BP
☎ 01785 223821
Parkland type course built around Stafford Castle.
9 holes, 6382yds, Par 71, SSS 70, Course record 68.
Club membership 400.
Visitors   must contact in advance. May not play Sun morning.
Societies   must apply in writing or by telephone.
Green Fees   £16 per day (£20 weekends & bank holidays).
Facilities   ⊗ ﹚﬐ ﬐ ﬔ ♥ ﬙ ﬚
Location   SW side of town centre off A518

Hotel   ★★★ 65% Garth Hotel, Wolverhampton Rd, Moss Pit, STAFFORD
☎ 01785 256124   60 ⇄ ♥

STOKE-ON-TRENT   Map 07 SJ84

Burslem Wood Farm, High Ln, Tunstall ST6 7JT
☎ 01782 837006
On the outskirts of Tunstall, a moorland course with hard walking.
9 holes, 5354yds, Par 66, SSS 66, Course record 66.
Club membership 250.
Visitors   except Sun & with member only Sat & bank holidays.
Societies   must telephone in advance.
Green Fees   not confirmed.
Facilities   ⊗ ﹚﬐ ﬐ ﬔ ♥ ﬙
Location   4m N of city centre on B5049

Hotel   ★★★ 69% George Hotel, Swan Square, Burslem, STOKE-ON-TRENT
☎ 01782 577544   39 ⇄ ♥

Greenway Hall Stanley Rd, Stockton Brook ST9 9LJ
☎ 01782 503158
Moorland course with fine views of the Pennines.
18 holes, 5678yds, Par 68, SSS 67.
Club membership 560.
Visitors   may play weekdays only.
Societies   must apply in writing.
Green Fees   not confirmed.
Facilities   ⊗ ﹚﬐ by prior arrangement ﬔ ♥ ﬙ ﬚ ﬙
Location   5m NE off A53

Hotel   ★★★ 69% George Hotel, Swan Square, Burslem, STOKE-ON-TRENT
☎ 01782 577544   39 ⇄ ♥

Trentham 14 Barlaston Old Rd, Trentham ST4 8HB
☎ 01782 658109 Fax 01782 644024
Parkland course. The par 3, 4th is a testing hole reached through a copse of trees.
18 holes, 6644yds, Par 72, SSS 72, Course record 67.
Club membership 600.
Visitors   must contact in advance.
Societies   must contact in advance.
Green Fees   £35 per 18 holes (£40 weekends pm only).
Prof   Sandy Wilson
Designer   Colt & Alison
Facilities   ﬔ ﬙ ﬐ ﬒ ﬙ ﬚ ﬙
& Leisure   squash.
Location   3m S off A5035

Hotel   ★★★ 65% Haydon House Hotel, Haydon St, Basford, STOKE-ON-TRENT
☎ 01782 711311   17 ⇄ ♥ Annexe6 ⇄ ♥

Trentham Park Trentham Park ST4 8AE
☎ 01782 658800 Fax 01782 658800
Fine woodland course.
18 holes, 6425yds, Par 71, SSS 71, Course record 67.
Club membership 850.
Visitors   must contact in advance.
Societies   Wed & Fri, must apply in advance.
Green Fees   £25 per round.
Prof   Brian Rimmer
Facilities   ⊗ ﹚﬐ ﬐ ﬔ ♥ ﬙ ﬚ ﬙
Location   Adjacent to Trentham Gardens, off A34 3m S of Newcastle-under-Lyme

Hotel   B Posthouse Stoke on Trent, Clayton Rd, NEWCASTLE-UNDER-LYME
☎ 01782 717171 119 ⇄ ♥

STONE   Map 07 SJ93

Barlaston Meaford Rd ST15 8UX
☎ 01782 372795 & 372867 Fax 01782 372867
Picturesque meadowland course designed by Peter Alliss.
18 holes, 5800yds, Par 69, SSS 68.
Club membership 650.
Visitors   may not play before 10am or after 4pm Fridays, weekends and bank holidays.
Societies   telephone or apply in writing.
Green Fees   not confirmed.
Prof   Ian Rogers
Designer   Peter Alliss
Facilities   ⊗ ﬐ ﬔ ♥ ﬙ ﬚ ﬙ ﬙

Hotel   ★★★ 64% Stone House Hotel, Stafford Rd, STONE ☎ 01785 815531   50 ⇄ ♥

Izaak Walton Eccleshall Rd, Cold Norton ST15 0NS
☎ 01785 760900
Opened in 1992, a gently undulating meadowland course with streams and ponds as features.
18 holes, 6281yds, Par 72, SSS 72, Course record 72.
Club membership 400.
Visitors   must contact in advance for weekends play.
Societies   must telephone in advance.
Green Fees   not confirmed.
Prof   Julie Brown
Facilities   ⊗ ﹚﬐ ﬐ ﬔ ♥ ﬙ ﬚ ﬙ ﬙ ﬙
Location   On B5026 between Stone & Eccleshall

Hotel   ★★★ 64% Stone House Hotel, Stafford Rd, STONE ☎ 01785 815531   50 ⇄ ♥

Stone Filleybrooks ST15 0NB ☎ 01785 813103
9-hole parkland course with easy walking and 18 different tees.
9 holes, 6299yds, Par 71, SSS 70, Course record 68.
Club membership 310.
Visitors   with member only weekends & bank holidays.
Societies   must apply in writing.
Green Fees   £15 per day/round.
Facilities   ⊗ ﹚﬐ ﬐ ﬔ ♥ ﬙ ﬚ ﬙
Location   0.5m W on A34

Hotel ★★★ 64% Stone House Hotel, Stafford Rd, STONE ☎ 01785 815531 50 ⇄ ℟

TAMWORTH   Map 07 SK20

Drayton Park Drayton Park, Fazeley B78 3TN
☎ 01827 251139 Fax 01827 284035
Parkland course designed by James Braid. Club established since 1897.
18 holes, 6214yds, Par 71, SSS 71, Course record 62.
Club membership 450.
Visitors	with member only weekends. Must book in advance (call either professional or secretary).
Societies	must apply in writing.
Green Fees	£32 per day/round.
Prof	M W Passmore
Designer	James Braid
Facilities	⊗ ∭ ㄴ ☕ ♀ ♙ 🎁 ∅
Location	2m S on A4091, next to Drayton Manor Leisure Park

Hotel ★★★★ 74% The Belfry, WISHAW ☎ 01675 470301 324 ⇄ ℟

Tamworth Municipal Eagle Dr, Amington B77 4EG
☎ 01827 709303 Fax 01827 709304
First-class municipal, parkland course and a good test of golf.
18 holes, 6605yds, Par 73, SSS 72, Course record 63.
Club membership 600.
Visitors	must book in advance at weekends.
Societies	must contact in advance.
Green Fees	£8.65 per 18 holes; £5.65 for 9 holes.
Cards	〰 💳 💳 💳 🔲
Prof	Daryl Scott
Designer	Hawtree & Son
Facilities	⊗ ∭ ㄴ ☕ ♀ ♙ 🎁 ⚑ ⚙ ∅ ℓ
Location	2.5m E off B5000

Hotel ★★ 61% Angel Croft Hotel, Beacon St, LICHFIELD ☎ 01543 258737 10rm(3 ⇄5 ℟) Annexe8 ⇄ ℟

UTTOXETER   Map 07 SK03

Uttoxeter Wood Ln ST14 8JR
☎ 01889 565108 & 566552 (Office) Fax 01889 567501
Undulating course with spectacular views adjacent to the racecourse.
18 holes, 5798yds, Par 70, SSS 69, Course record 66.
Club membership 750.
Visitors	restricted weekends and competition days.
Societies	must apply in writing.
Green Fees	not confirmed.
Prof	Adam McCandless
Facilities	⊗ ∭ ㄴ ☕ ♀ ♙ ∅
Location	1m SE off B5017, follow Racecourse signs town centre

Hotel ★★ 66% Bank House Hotel, Church St, UTTOXETER ☎ 01889 566922 14 ⇄ ℟

WESTON   Map 07 SJ92

Ingestre Park ST18 0RE
☎ 01889 270845 Fax 01889 270845
Parkland course set in the grounds of Ingestre Hall, former home of the Earl of Shrewsbury, with mature trees and pleasant views.
18 holes, 6251yds, Par 70, SSS 70, Course record 67.
Club membership 850.
Visitors	with member only weekends & bank holidays. Must play before 3.30pm weekdays. Advance booking preferred. Handicap certificate required.
Societies	must apply in advance.
Green Fees	£28 per day; £23 per round.
Prof	Danny Scullion
Designer	Hawtree
Facilities	⊗ ∭ ㄴ ☕ ♀ ♙ 🎁 ⚑ ⚙ ∅
Location	2m SE off A51

Hotel ★★★ 65% Tillington Hall Hotel, Eccleshall Rd, STAFFORD ☎ 01785 253531 90 ⇄ ℟

WHISTON   Map 07 SK04

Whiston Hall Whiston Hall ST10 2HZ ☎ 01538 266260
A challenging 18-hole course in scenic countryside, incorporating many natural obstacles and providing a test for all golfing abilities.
18 holes, 5742yds, Par 71, SSS 69, Course record 70.
Club membership 400.
Visitors	reasonable dress on the course. Must telephone in advance at weekends.
Societies	phone for details.
Green Fees	£10 weekdays & weekends if contacted in advance.
Designer	T Cooper
Facilities	⊗ ∭ ㄴ ☕ ♀ ♙ ∅
& Leisure	fishing, snooker room.
Location	Off A52, between Stoke-on-Trent and Ashbourne

Hotel ★★★ 69% George Hotel, Swan Square, Burslem, STOKE-ON-TRENT ☎ 01782 577544 39 ⇄ ℟

SUFFOLK

ALDEBURGH   Map 05 TM45

Aldeburgh Saxmundham Rd IP15 5PE
☎ 01728 452890 Fax 01728 452937
Fine heathland golf course providing a varied and interesting challenge for the handicap golfer. Additional 9 hole course suitable for golfing holiday makers.
18 holes, 6330yds, Par 68, SSS 71, Course record 65.
River Course: 9 holes, 4228yds, Par 64, SSS 61.
Club membership 850.
Visitors	must contact in advance and have a handicap certificate. 2 ball/foursomes only.
Societies	must contact in advance.

▶

Green Fees £40 per day/round, £30 after noon (£50/£35 weekends).
Prof Keith Preston
Facilities ⊗ 🅱 💪 🍷 🛆 🏠 🍴 ✧
Location 1m W on A1094

Hotel ★★★ 73% Wentworth Hotel, Wentworth Rd, ALDEBURGH ☎ 01728 452312 31rm(24 ⇆4 🅵) Annexe7 ⇆ 🅵

BECCLES   Map 05 TM49

Beccles The Common NR34 9YN ☎ 01502 712244
Common course with gorse bushes, no water hazards or bunkers.
9 holes, 2779yds, Par 68, SSS 67.
Club membership 175.
Visitors must play with member on Sun.
Societies must telephone in advance.
Green Fees £8 (£10 weekends & bank holidays).
Facilities 🅱 💪 🍷 🛆 🏠 🍴 ✧
Location NE side of town

Hotel ★★★ 65% Hotel Hatfield, The Esplanade, LOWESTOFT ☎ 01502 565337 33 ⇆ 🅵

BUNGAY   Map 05 TM38

Bungay & Waveney Valley Outney Common NR35 1DS ☎ 01986 892337 Fax 01986 892222
Heathland course partly comprising Neolithic stone workings, easy walking.

WENTWORTH
HOTEL ★★★
Aldeburgh, Suffolk
Tel: (01728) 452312 Fax: (01728) 454343
E-mail: wentworth.hotel@anglianet.co.uk
Website: www.wentworthhotel.com

The Hotel has the comfort and style of a Country House. Two comfortable lounges, with open fires and antique furniture, provide ample space to relax. Each individually decorated bedroom, many with sea views, is equipped with a colour television, radio, hairdryer and tea making facilities. The Restaurant serves a variety of fresh produce whilst a light lunch can be chosen from the Bar menu, eaten outside in the sunken terrace garden. Aldeburgh is timeless and unhurried. There are quality shops, two excellent golf courses within a short distance from the hotel, long walks and some of the best birdwatching at Minsmere Bird reserve. Music and the Arts can be heard at the Internationally famous Snape Malting Concert hall. Lastly, there are miles of beach to sit upon and watch the sea!

---

18 holes, 6044yds, Par 69, SSS 69, Course record 64.
Club membership 730.
Visitors should contact in advance. With member only weekends & bank holidays.
Societies must contact in advance.
Green Fees £26 per day; £20 per round.
Prof Nigel Whyte
Designer James Braid
Facilities ⊗ 🏗 🅱 💪 🍷 🛆 🏠 🍴 🚜 ✧
Location 0.5m NW on A143

Hotel ★★★ 65% Hotel Hatfield, The Esplanade, LOWESTOFT ☎ 01502 565337 33 ⇆ 🅵

BURY ST EDMUNDS   Map 05 TL86

Bury St Edmunds Tut Hill IP28 6LG ☎ 01284 755979
Undulating parkland course with easy walking and attractive short holes.
18 holes, 6678yds, Par 72, SSS 72, Course record 69 or 9 holes, 2217yds, Par 62, SSS 62.
Club membership 850.
Visitors with member only at weekends for 18 hole course.
Societies must apply in writing.
Green Fees not confirmed.
Prof Mark Jillings
Designer Ted Ray
Facilities ⊗ 🏗 by prior arrangement 🅱 💪 🍷 🛆 🏠 ✧
Location 2m NW on B1106 off A45

Hotel ★★★ 71% Angel Hotel, Angel Hill, BURY ST EDMUNDS ☎ 01284 753926 42 ⇆ 🅵

The Suffolk Golf & Country Club Fornham St Genevieve IP28 6JQ ☎ 01284 706777 Fax 01284 706721
A classic parkland course with the river Lark running through it, which comes into play regularly.
The Genevieve Course: 18 holes, 6321yds, Par 72, SSS 71.
Club membership 600.
Visitors contact Golf reception, bookings up to 1week in advance.
Societies apply inwriting to the General Manager.
Green Fees £20 per round (£25 weekends & bank holidays).
Cards 💳 💳 💳 📳
Prof Steve Hall
Facilities ⊗ 🏗 🅱 💪 🍷 🛆 🏠 🍴 🐾 🚜 ✧
& Leisure heated indoor swimming pool, sauna, solarium, gymnasium.
Location Off the A14 onto the B1106 to Fornham

Hotel ★★★♨ 70% Ravenwood Hall Hotel, Rougham, BURY ST EDMUNDS ☎ 01359 270345 7 ⇆ Annexe7 ⇆

CRETINGHAM   Map 05 TM26

Cretingham IP13 7BA ☎ 01728 685275 Fax 01728 685037
Parkland course.
9 holes, 4552yds, Par 66, SSS 64, Course record 61.
Club membership 350.
Visitors booking required for weekends.
Societies must contact in advance.
Green Fees not confirmed.
Cards 💳 💳 📳
Prof Colin Jenkins

Designer	J Austin
Facilities & Leisure	⊗ 🏷 🍺 ♟ 🛍 🏠 ⛳ 🚜 ♂ ♪ hard tennis courts, outdoor swimming pool, pitch & putt.
Location	2m from A1120 at Earl Soham

Hotel ★★ 64% Cedars Hotel, Needham Rd, STOWMARKET ☎ 01449 612668 25 ⇔ ♠

FELIXSTOWE   Map 05 TM33

Felixstowe Ferry Ferry Rd IP11 9RY
☎ 01394 286834 Fax 01394 273679
Seaside links course, pleasant views, easy walking. Testing 491-yd, 7th hole. New 9 hole course now open.
Martello Course: 18 holes, 6272yds, Par 72, SSS 70.
Club membership 900.

Visitors	may not play weekends on Martello Course.
Societies	Tue, Wed & Fri.
Green Fees	not confirmed.
Prof	Ian MacPherson
Designer	Henry Cotton
Facilities	🛍 🏠 🚜 ♪
Location	NE side of town centre. Signposted from A14

Hotel ★★ 70% Waverley Hotel, 2 Wolsey Gardens, FELIXSTOWE ☎ 01394 282811 19 ⇔ ♠

FLEMPTON   Map 05 TL86

Flempton IP28 6EQ ☎ 01284 728291
Breckland course.
9 holes, 6240yds, Par 70, SSS 70.
Club membership 300.

Visitors	must produce handicap certificate. With member only weekends & bank holidays.
Societies	Limited to small societies - must apply in writing.
Green Fees	not confirmed.
Prof	Mark Jillings
Facilities	⊗ 🏷 🍺 ♟ 🛍 🏠 ♪
Location	0.5m W on A1101

Hotel ★★★ 68% The Priory Hotel, Tollgate, BURY ST EDMUNDS
☎ 01284 766181 9 ⇔ ♠ Annexe18 ⇔ ♠

HALESWORTH   Map 05 TM37

Halesworth Bramfield Rd IP19 9XA
☎ 01986 875567 Fax 01986 874565
A 27-hole professionally designed parkland complex of one 18 hole membership course and a 9 hole pay and play.
18 holes, 6580yds, Par 72, SSS 72, Course record 71.
9 holes, 3059yds, Par 33.
Club membership 700.

Visitors	visitors welcome at all times except for Sunday before noon on the 18 hole course. Handicap certificate required for the 18 hole course.
Societies	telephone for booking form.
Green Fees	£15 per round (£20 per round weekends). £7.50 per 9 holes.
Prof	Steven MacPherson
Designer	J W Johnson
Facilities	⊗ 𝄞 🏷 🍺 ♟ 🛍 🏠 ⛳ 🌿 🚜 ♪ ♪
Location	0.75m S of town, signposted on left of A144 road to Bramfield

Hotel ★★★ 70% Swan Hotel, Market Place, SOUTHWOLD ☎ 01502 722186
26rm(25 ⇔ ♠) Annexe17 ⇔ ♠

HAVERHILL   Map 05 TL64

Haverhill Coupals Rd CB9 7UW
☎ 01440 761951 Fax 01440 761951
An 18 hole course lying across two valleys in pleasant parkland. The front nine with undulating fairways is complimented by a saucer shaped back nine, bisected by the River Stour, presenting a challenge to golfers of all standards.
18 holes, 5898yds, Par 70, SSS 68, Course record 65.
Club membership 600.

Visitors	telephone to check for club competitions.
Societies	must contact in advance. Tue & Thu only.
Green Fees	£21 per day; £18 per 18 holes (£26/£22 weekends & bank holidays).
Prof	Simon Mayfield
Facilities	⊗ 𝄞 🏷 🍺 ♟ 🛍 🏠 ⛳ ♪
Location	1m SE off A604

Hotel ★★ 70% Four Seasons Hotel, Walden Rd, THAXTED ☎ 01371 830129 9rm(8 ⇔ ♠)

HINTLESHAM   Map 05 TM04

Hintlesham Hall IP8 3NS
☎ 01473 652761 Fax 01473 652750
Magnificent championship length course blending harmoniously with the ancient parkland surrounding this exclusive hotel. The 6630yd parkland course was designed by Hawtree and Son, one of the oldest established firms of golf course architects in the world. The course is fair but challenging for low and high handicappers alike. Hotel offers beautiful accommodation, excellent cuisine and many facilities.
18 holes, 6638yds, Par 72, SSS 72, Course record 67.
Club membership 350.

Visitors	must contact 48 hours in advance.
Societies	must telephone in advance.
Green Fees	£49 per day; £28 per round.
Cards	💳 💳 💳 💳 💳 💳
Prof	Alastair Spink
Designer	Hawtree & Sons
Facilities	⊗ 𝄞 🏷 🍺 ♟ 🛍 🏠 ⛳ 🚜 🌿 🚜 ♪
& Leisure	hard tennis courts, heated outdoor swimming pool, sauna, solarium, gymnasium.
Location	In village on A1071 ▶

Hotel	★★★★🏊 Hintlesham Hall Hotel, HINTLESHAM ☎ 01473 652334 & 652268 Fax 01473 652463 33 ⇆ 🐾

IPSWICH
Map 05 TM14

Alnesbourne Priory Priory Park IP10 0JT
☎ 01473 727393 Fax 01473 278372
A fabulous outlook facing due south across the River Orwell
is one of the many good features of this course set in
woodland. All holes run among trees with some fairways
requiring straight shots. The 8th green is on saltings by the
river.
9 holes, 1700yds, Par 29.
Club membership 30.
Visitors closed on Tuesday. Closed 6 Jan-28 Feb.
Societies Tue only, telephone in advance.
Green Fees £10 (£11 Sat; £12 Sun & bank holidays).
Facilities ⊗ ⅲ ㏐ ➡ ♀ ♋ 🏌
& Leisure hard tennis courts, heated outdoor swimming
pool.
Location 3m SE, off A14

Hotel	★★★ 68% Courtyard by Marriott Ipswich, The Havens, Ransomes Europark, IPSWICH ☎ 01473 272244 60 ⇆ 🐾

Fynn Valley IP6 9JA ☎ 01473 785267 Fax 01473 785632
Undulating parkland course plus Par-3 nine-hole and driving
range. Many new developments are in hand on this complex.
18 holes, 5873yds, Par 68, SSS 68, Course record 67.
Club membership 700.
Visitors members only Sun until noon.
Societies must apply in advance.
Green Fees £18 per 18 holes (£24 weekends & bank
holidays).
Cards 🖻 🖻 🖻 🖻
Prof Glenn Crane
Designer Tony Tyrrell
Facilities ⊗ ⅲ ㏐ ➡ ♀ ♋ 🏌 🛒 ❖ ⚷ ⓘ
Location 2m N of Ipswich on B1077

Hotel	★★★ 64% Novotel, Greyfriars Rd, IPSWICH ☎ 01473 232400 100 ⇆ 🐾

Ipswich Purdis Heath IP3 8UQ ☎ 01473 728941 Fax 01473 715236 Many golfers are suprised when they hear that Ipswich has, at Purdis Heath, a first-class golf course. In some ways it resembles some of Surrey's better courses; a beautiful heathland/parkland course with two lakes and easy walking. *18 holes, 6405yds, Par 71, SSS 71, Course record 63 or 9 holes, 1930yds, Par 31, SSS 59.* *Club membership 750.*
Visitors must contact in advance & have a handicap certificate for 18 hole courses.
Societies must contact in advance.
Green Fees £35 per day; £25 per round (£38/£28 weekends & bank Holidays).
Prof Stephen Whymark
Designer James Braid
Facilities ⊗ ⅲ ㏐ ➡ ♀ ♋ 🏌 ⚷
Location E side of town centre off A1156

Hotel	★★★ 73% Marlborough Hotel, Henley Rd, IPSWICH ☎ 01473 257677 22 ⇆ 🐾

Rushmere Rushmere Heath IP4 5QQ ☎ 01473 725648
Heathland course with gorse and prevailing winds. Testing
5th hole - dog leg, 419 yards (par 4).
18 holes, 6262yds, Par 70, SSS 70, Course record 66.
Club membership 770.
Visitors not before 2.30pm weekends & bank holidays.
Must have a handicap certificate.
Societies weekdays (ex Wed) by arrangement.
Green Fees £20 per day/round.
Prof N T J McNeill
Facilities ⊗ ㏐ ➡ ♀ ♋ 🏌 ⚷
Location Off A12 N of Ipswich. Signposted

Hotel	★★★ 73% Marlborough Hotel, Henley Rd, IPSWICH ☎ 01473 257677 22 ⇆ 🐾

LOWESTOFT
Map 05 TM59

Rookery Park Carlton Colville NR33 8HJ
☎ 01502 560380 Fax 01502 560380
Parkland course with a 9-hole, Par 3 adjacent.
18 holes, 6714yds, Par 72, SSS 72.
Club membership 1000.
Visitors must have handicap certificate.
Societies by arrangement.
Green Fees £25 per day (£30 weekends & bank holidays).
Prof Martin Elsworthy
Designer C D Lawrie
Facilities ⊗ ⅲ ㏐ ➡ ♀ ♋ 🏌 ⚷
Location 3.5m SW on A146

Hotel	★★★ 65% Hotel Hatfield, The Esplanade, LOWESTOFT ☎ 01502 565337 33 ⇆ 🐾

NEWMARKET
Map 05 TL66

Links Cambridge Rd CB8 0TG
☎ 01638 663000 Fax 01638 661476
Gently undulating parkland.
18 holes, 6574yds, Par 72, SSS 71, Course record 66.
Club membership 780.
Visitors must have handicap certificate, may not play
Sun before 11.30am.
Societies telephone secretary in advance.
Green Fees £28 (£32 weekends & bank holidays).
Prof John Sharkey
Designer Col. Hotchkin
Facilities ⊗ ⅲ ㏐ ➡ ♀ ♋ 🏌 ⚷
Location 1m SW on A1034

Hotel	★★★ 69% Heath Court Hotel, Moulton Rd, NEWMARKET ☎ 01638 667171 41 ⇆ 🐾

NEWTON
Map 05 TL94

Newton Green Newton Green CO10 0QN
☎ 01787 377217 & 377501
Flat, 18-hole commonland course.
18 holes, 5960yds, Par 69, SSS 68.
Club membership 640.
Visitors must contact in advance but may not play on
Tue or Sat & Sun before 12.30.

Societies	apply in advance.
Green Fees	not confirmed.
Prof	Tim Cooper
Facilities	⌂☕🍴🛒
Location	W side of village on A134

Hotel ★★★ 67% The Bull, Hall St, LONG MELFORD ☎ 01787 378494 25 ⇄ ☏

RAYDON   Map 05 TM03

Brett Vale Noakes Rd IP7 5LR
☎ 01473 310718 Fax 01473 312270
Brett Vale course takes you through a nature reserve and on lakeside walks, affording views over Dedham Vale. The excellent fairways demand an accurate tee and good approach shots. 1, 2, 3, 8, 10 and 15 are all affected by crosswinds, but once in the valley it is much more sheltered. Although only 6,000 yards the course is testing and interesting at all levels of golf.
18 holes, 6000yds, Par 70, SSS 69, Course record 65.
Club membership 500.

Visitors	must book tee times and wear appropriate clothing.
Societies	apply in writing or telephone.
Green Fees	£25 per day; £15 per round (£30/£20 weekends).
Cards	💳
Prof	Robert Taylor
Designer	Howard Smith
Facilities	⊗)🍴🛒 💼♀⌂☕🍴🛒
Location	B1070 at Raydon, 2m from A12

Hotel ★★★▲▲ Maison Talbooth, Stratford Rd, DEDHAM ☎ 01206 322367 10 ⇄ ☏

SOUTHWOLD   Map 05 TM57

Southwold The Common IP18 6TB
☎ 01502 723234 & 723248
Commonland course with 4-acre practice ground and panoramic views of the sea.
9 holes, 6052yds, Par 70, SSS 69, Course record 67.
Club membership 450.

Visitors	restricted on competition days (Ladies-Wed, Gents-Sun).
Societies	must contact in advance.
Green Fees	Summer: £18 per round (£22 weekends); Winter: £15 (£18 weekends).
Prof	Brian Allen
Facilities	⌂☕🍴
Location	From A12 - B1140 to Southwold

Hotel ★★★ 70% Swan Hotel, Market Place, SOUTHWOLD ☎ 01502 722186 26rm(25 ⇄ ☏) Annexe17 ⇄ ☏

STOWMARKET   Map 05 TM05

Stowmarket Lower Rd, Onehouse IP14 3DA
☎ 01449 736473 Fax 01449 736826
Parkland course.
18 holes, 6107yds, Par 69, SSS 69, Course record 66.
Club membership 630.

Visitors	must contact in advance.
Societies	Thu or Fri, by arrangement.

Green Fees	£30 per day, £24 per round (£40/£30 weekends and bank holidays).
Prof	Duncan Burl
Facilities	⊗)🍴 by prior arrangement 🛒💼♀⌂☕🍴🛒
Location	2.5m SW off B115

Hotel ★★ 64% Cedars Hotel, Needham Rd, STOWMARKET ☎ 01449 612668 25 ⇄ ☏

THORPENESS   Map 05 TM45

Thorpeness Golf Club & Hotel IP16 4NH
☎ 01728 452176 Fax 01728 453868
The holes of this moorland course are pleasantly varied with several quite difficult par 4's. Natural hazards abound. The 15th, with its sharp left dog-leg, is one of the best holes. Designed by James Braid.
18 holes, 6271yds, Par 69, SSS 71, Course record 66.
Club membership 270.

Visitors	contact in advance.
Societies	telephone in advance, deposit required.
Green Fees	£30 per day (£35 weekends).
Cards	💳
Prof	Frank Hill
Designer	James Braid
Facilities	⊗)🍴🛒💼♀⌂☕🍴🛒
& Leisure	hard tennis courts, snooker room.
Location	W side of village off B1353

Hotel ★★★ 73% White Lion Hotel Ltd, Market Cross Place, ALDEBURGH ☎ 01728 452720 38 ⇄ ☏

WALDRINGFIELD   Map 05 TM24

Waldringfield Heath Newbourne Rd IP12 4PT
☎ 01473 736768 Fax 01473 736436
Easy walking heathland course with long drives on 1st and 13th (590yds) and some ponds.
18 holes, 6141yds, Par 71, SSS 69, Course record 67.
Club membership 630.

Visitors	welcome Mon-Fri, weekends & bank holidays after noon.
Societies	weekdays by arrangement.
Green Fees	£22.50 per day, £15 per round (£18 weekends and bank holidays).
Prof	Robin Mann
Designer	Phillip Pilgrem
Facilities	⊗)🍴🛒💼♀⌂☕🍴
Location	3m NE of Ipswich off old A12

Hotel ★★★▲▲ 74% Seckford Hall Hotel, WOODBRIDGE ☎ 01394 385678 22 ⇄ ☏ Annexe10 ⇄ ☏

WOODBRIDGE   Map 05 TM24

Seckford Seckford Hall Rd, Great Bealings IP13 6NT
☎ 01394 388000 Fax 01394 382818
A challenging course interspersed with young tree plantations, numerous bunkers, water hazards and undulating fairways, providing a tough test for all levels of golfer. The testing 18th is almost completely surrounded by water.
18 holes, 5303yds, Par 68, SSS 66, Course record 62.
Club membership 400.

▶

Visitors	telephone in advance for tee times.
Societies	telephone in advance. Computerised booking system.
Green Fees	£15 per 18 holes (£17.50 weekends).
Cards	
Prof	John Skinner
Designer	J Johnson
Facilities	
& Leisure	heated indoor swimming pool, fishing, sauna, solarium, gymnasium.
Location	(3m W of Woodbridge, 0ff A12)
Hotel	★★★⚓ 74% Seckford Hall Hotel, WOODBRIDGE ☎ 01394 385678 22 🛏 ⬤ Annexe10 🛏 ⬤

Ufford Park Hotel Golf & Leisure Yarmouth Rd, Ufford
IP12 1QW ☎ 01394 383555 Fax 01394 383582
A challenging new course opened in autumn 1992. The 18-hole Par 71 course is set in ancient parkland has many natural features including 11 water hazards retaind from the original parkland. There is also an extensive hotel and leisure complex beside the course.
18 holes, 6325yds, Par 71, SSS 71, Course record 67.
Club membership 320.

Visitors	must book tee time from golf shop 01394 382836
Societies	telephone or fax in advance to book tee time.
Green Fees	from £18 weekdays per day/round.
Cards	
Prof	Stuart Robertson
Designer	Phil Pilgrim
Facilities	
& Leisure	heated indoor swimming pool, sauna, solarium, gymnasium.
Location	Just off A12, on the B1438
Hotel	★★★ 70% Ufford Park Hotel Golf & Leisure, Yarmouth Rd, Ufford, WOODBRIDGE ☎ 01394 383555 42 🛏 ⬤ Annexe2 🛏 ⬤

Woodbridge Bromeswell Heath IP12 2PF
☎ 01394 382038 Fax 01394 382392
A beautiful course, one of the best in East Anglia. It is situated on high ground and in different seasons present golfers with a great variety of colour. Some say that of the many good holes the 14th is the best.
18 holes, 6299yds, Par 70, SSS 70, Course record 64.
Forest Course: 9 holes, 6382yds, Par 70, SSS 70.
Club membership 900.

Visitors	Main Course: must contact in advance, handicap certificate required, with member only weekends. Forest Course: open all days and no handicap certificate required.

Societies	by prior telephone call or in writing.
Green Fees	not confirmed.
Prof	Adrian Hubert
Designer	Davie Grant
Facilities	
Location	2.5m NE off A1152
Hotel	★★★⚓ 74% Seckford Hall Hotel, WOODBRIDGE ☎ 01394 385678 22 🛏 ⬤ Annexe10 🛏 ⬤

WORLINGTON   Map 05 TL67

Royal Worlington & Newmarket IP28 8SD
☎ 01638 712216 Fax 01638 717787
Inland 'links' course. Favourite 9-hole course of many golf writers.
9 holes, 3105yds, Par 35, SSS 70, Course record 67.
Club membership 325.

Visitors	with member only at weekends. Must contact in advance and have a handicap certificate.
Societies	must apply in writing.
Green Fees	£40 per day; £30 after 2pm.
Prof	Malcolm Hawkins
Designer	Tom Dunn
Facilities	
Location	0.5m SE
Hotel	★★★ 67% Riverside Hotel, Mill St, MILDENHALL ☎ 01638 717274 20 🛏 ⬤

SURREY

ADDLESTONE   Map 04 TQ06

New Zealand Woodham Ln KT15 3QD
☎ 01932 345049 Fax 01932 342891
Heathland course set in trees and heather.
18 holes, 6012yds, Par 68, SSS 69, Course record 66.
Club membership 320.

Visitors	must contact in advance.
Societies	telephone initially.
Green Fees	not confirmed.
Prof	Vic Elvidge
Designer	Muir Fergusson/Simpson
Facilities	
Location	1.5m E of Woking
Hotel	★★★ 65% The Ship, Monument Green, WEYBRIDGE ☎ 01932 848364 39 🛏 ⬤

ASHFORD   Map 04 TQ07

Ashford Manor Fordbridge Rd TW15 3RT
☎ 01784 257687 Fax 01784 420355
Tree lined parkland course, looks easy but is difficult.
18 holes, 6352yds, Par 70, SSS 70, Course record 64.
Club membership 700.

Visitors advisable to telephone in advance, handicap certificate required, with member only at weekends but may not play competition days.
Societies welcome weekdays, except Thu am, must contact in advance.
Green Fees £25 per day/round, £10 per round after 5pm.
Prof Mike Finney
Facilities ⊗ ⓑ ♥ ♀ ♨ 🏠 𝄀
Location 2m E of Staines via A308 Staines by-pass

Hotel ★★★ 70% The Thames Lodge, Thames St, STAINES ☎ 01784 464433 44 ⇄ ↾

BAGSHOT   Map 04 SU96

Pennyhill Park Hotel & Country Club London Rd GU19 5ET ☎ 01276 471774 Fax 01276 473217
A nine-hole course set in 11.4 acres of beautiful parkland. It is challenging to even the most experienced golfer.
9 holes, 2095yds, Par 32, SSS 32.
Club membership 100.

Visitors prior booking must be made. telephone in advance.
Green Fees not confirmed.
Facilities ♨ ↾ ⋈
& Leisure hard tennis courts, heated outdoor swimming pool, fishing, sauna.

Hotel ★★★★★ 72% Pennyhill Park Hotel, London Rd, BAGSHOT ☎ 01276 471774 28 ⇄ ↾ Annexe86 ⇄ ↾

Windlesham Grove End GU19 5HY ☎ 01276 452220 Fax 01276 452290
A parkland course with many demanding Par 4 holes over 400 yards. Thoughtfully designed by Tommy Horton.
18 holes, 6600yds, Par 71, SSS 71, Course record 69.
Club membership 800.
Visitors handicap certificate required, contact in advance.
Societies apply in advance.
Green Fees not confirmed.
Prof Alan Barber
Designer Tommy Horton
Facilities ⊗ ⅏ ⓑ ♥ ♀ ♨ 🏠 ↾ ⚒ 𝄀 ⚲
Location Junct of A30/A322

Hotel ★★★★★ 72% Pennyhill Park Hotel, London Rd, BAGSHOT ☎ 01276 471774 28 ⇄ ↾ Annexe86 ⇄ ↾

BANSTEAD   Map 04 TQ25

Banstead Downs Burdon Ln, Belmont, Sutton SM2 7DD
☎ 0181 642 2284 Fax 0181 642 5252
A natural downland course set on a site of botanic interest. A challenging 18 holes with narrow fairways and tight lies.
18 holes, 6194yds, Par 69, SSS 69, Course record 64.
Club membership 835.
Visitors must book in advance and have handicap certificate or letter of introduction. With member only weekends.
Societies Thu, by prior arrangement
Green Fees £30 per day; £20 after noon.
Prof Robert Dickman
Designer J H Taylor/James Braid
Facilities ⊗ ⓑ ♥ ♀ ♨ 🏠 𝄀
Location 1.5m N on A217

Hotel ★★ 64% Driftbridge Hotel, Reigate Rd, EPSOM ☎ 01737 352163 34 ⇄ ↾

Cuddington Banstead Rd SM7 1RD
☎ 0181 393 0952 Fax 0181 786 7025
Parkland course with easy walking and good views.
18 holes, 6436yds, Par 70, SSS 71, Course record 61.
Club membership 694.
Visitors must contact in advance and have a handicap certificate or letter of introduction.
Societies welcome Thu, must apply in advance.
Green Fees not confirmed.
Prof Mark Warner
Designer H S Colt
Facilities ♨ 🏠 ↾ 𝄀
Location N of Banstead station on A2022

Hotel ★★ 64% Driftbridge Hotel, Reigate Rd, EPSOM ☎ 01737 352163 34 ⇄ ↾

BRAMLEY   Map 04 TQ04

Bramley GU5 0AL ☎ 01483 892696 Fax 01483 894673
Parkland course, from the high ground picturesque views of the Wey Valley on one side and the Hog's Back. Full on course irrigation system with three reservoirs on the course.
18 holes, 5990yds, Par 69, SSS 69, Course record 63.
Club membership 850.
Visitors may not play Tue am (Ladies Morning) and must play with member at weekends & bank holidays. Must contact secretary on 01483 892696.
Societies must telephone the secretary in advance.
Green Fees £33 per day; £27 per round.
Prof Gary Peddie
Designer James Braid
Facilities ⊗ ⅏ ⓑ ♥ ♀ ♨ 🏠 ↾ ⚒ ⚲ 𝄀 ⚑
Location 3m S of Guildford on A281

Hotel B Posthouse Guildford, Egerton Rd, GUILDFORD ☎ 01483 574444 162 ⇄ ↾

BROOKWOOD   Map 04 SU95

West Hill Bagshot Rd GU24 0BH
☎ 01483 474365 Fax 01483 474252
Set in the Surrey landscape of heath, heather and tree lined fairways. An interesting and challenging course ▶

with subtle greens and a stream which affects play on seven holes. A premium on the well positioned drive.
18 holes, 6368yds, Par 69, SSS 70, Course record 62.
Club membership 500.

Visitors must contact in advance & have handicap certificate, may not play weekends & bank holidays.
Societies weekdays only (ex Wed). Telephone in advance.
Green Fees £60 per day; £42.50 per round.
Prof John A Clements
Designer C Butchart/W Parke
Facilities ⊗)▥ ⓛ ▛ ♀ ☖ 🖚 🍴 ✑
Location E side of village on A322

Hotel ★★★★★ 72% Pennyhill Park Hotel, London Rd, BAGSHOT ☎ 01276 471774 28 ⇄ 🦌 Annexe86 ⇄ 🦌

CAMBERLEY Map 04 SU86

Camberley Heath Golf Dr GU15 1JG
☎ 01276 23258 Fax 01276 692505
One of the great 'heath and heather' courses so frequently associated with Surrey. Several very good short holes - especially the 8th. The 10th is a difficult and interesting par 4, as also is the 17th, where the drive must be held well to the left as perdition lurks on the right. A fairway irrigation system has been installed.
18 holes, 6147yds, Par 72, SSS 70, Course record 65.
Club membership 600.

Visitors may not play at weekends. Must contact in advance.
Societies must apply in advance.
Green Fees £36 per round.
Cards 🌐 📶 🈺 🄳 🈴 🈯 🄵
Prof Glen Ralph
Designer Harry S Colt
Facilities ⊗ ⓛ ▛ ♀ ☖ 🖚 🍴 ✑ 🦌 ✑ 🍴
Location 1.25m SE of town centre off A325

Hotel ★★★★★ 72% Pennyhill Park Hotel, London Rd, BAGSHOT ☎ 01276 471774 28 ⇄ 🦌 Annexe86 ⇄ 🦌

Pine Ridge Old Bisley Rd, Frimley GU16 5NX
☎ 01276 675444 & 20770 Fax 01276 678837
Pay and play heathland course with challenging par 3s, deceptively demanding par 4s and several birdiable par 5s. Good corporate or society packages.
Pine Ridge Golf Centre: 18 holes, 6458yds, Par 72, SSS 71, Course record 67.

Visitors must pre book, no jeans or trainers.
Societies bookable in advance, packages available to suit.
Green Fees not confirmed.
Cards 🌐 📶 🄳 🈴 🈯 🄵
Prof Andrew Fannon
Designer Clive D Smith
Facilities ⊗ by prior arrangement)▥ by prior arrangement ⓛ ▛ ♀ ☖ 🖚 🍴 🦌 ✑ 🍴
& Leisure ten pin bowling centre for corporate or private functions.
Location Just off B3015, near A30

Hotel ★★★ 69% Frimley Hall, Portsmouth Rd, CAMBERLEY ☎ 01276 28321 86 ⇄ 🦌

CATERHAM Map 05 TQ35

Happy Valley Rook Ln, Chaldon CR3 5AA
☎ 01883 344555 Fax 01883 344422
Opened in May 1999, this technically challenging course is set in beautiful countryside and features fully irrigated greens and fairways. It also has large practice areas.
18 holes, 6900yds, Par 72, SSS 73.
Club membership 750.

Visitors may play weekdays only, and can book in advance.
Societies apply in writing.
Green Fees £45 per day; £27 per round.
Cards 🌐 📶 🈯 🄵
Designer David Williams
Facilities ⊗)▥ ⓛ ▛ ♀ ☖ 🖚 🦌 🍴 ✑ 🍴
Location M25 junct 6 A22

Hotel ★★★★ 77% Coulsdon Manor, Coulsdon Court Rd, Coulsdon, CROYDON ☎ 0181 668 0414 35 ⇄ 🦌

CHERTSEY Map 04 TQ06

Barrow Hills Longcross KT16 0DS ☎ 01344 635770
This parkland course with natural hazards is only open to guests of members.
18 holes, 3090yds, Par 56, SSS 53, Course record 58.
Club membership 355.
Visitors must play with member at all times.
Green Fees not confirmed.
Location 3m W on B386

Hotel ★★★ 70% The Thames Lodge, Thames St, STAINES ☎ 01784 464433 44 ⇄ 🦌

Laleham Laleham Reach KT16 8RP
☎ 01932 564211 Fax 01932 564448
Well-bunkered parkland/meadowland course.
18 holes, 6211yds, Par 70, SSS 70.
Club membership 600.
Visitors members guests only at weekends.
Societies must contact in writing.
Green Fees not confirmed.

Prof Hogan Stott
Facilities ⊗ ⓑ ⚑ ♀ ♨ 🏌 ✐
Location 1.5m N

Hotel ★★★ 70% The Thames Lodge, Thames St, STAINES ☎ 01784 464433 44 ⇔ ⋒

CHIDDINGFOLD Map 04 SU93

Chiddingfold Petworth Rd GU8 4SL
☎ 01428 685888 Fax 01428 685939
With panoramic views across the Surrey Downs, this challenging course offers a unique combination of lakes, mature woodland and wildlife.
18 holes, 5501yds, Par 70, SSS 67.
Club membership 325.
Visitors telephone bookings up to one week in advance.
Societies prior telephone booking required.
Green Fees Mon £10; Tue-Fri £15 (£22 weekends).
Cards 🔳 🔳 🔳 🔳 🔳
Prof Paul Creamer
Designer Johnathan Gaunt
Facilities ⊗ ⓜ ⓑ 🖥 ⚑ ♀ ♨ 🏌 ✎ ⛳ ⚒ ✐ ↀ
& Leisure gymnasium, Small fitness studio.
Location A283

Hotel ★★★★ 71% Lythe Hill Hotel, Petworth Rd, HASLEMERE ☎ 01428 651251 41 ⇔ ⋒

CHIPSTEAD Map 04 TQ25

Chipstead How Ln CR5 3LN
☎ 01737 555781 Fax 01737 555404
Hilly parkland course, hard walking, good views. Testing 18th hole.
18 holes, 5491yds, Par 68, SSS 67, Course record 63.
Club membership 650.
Visitors must contact in advance. May not play weekends or Tue mornings.
Societies must apply in writing.
Green Fees not confirmed.
Prof Gary Torbett
Facilities ⊗ ⓜ ⓑ 🖥 ⚑ ♀ ♨ 🏌 ✎ ⛳ ⚒ ✐ ↀ
Location 0.5m N of village

Hotel ★★★★ 69% Selsdon Park Hotel, Addington Rd, Sanderstead, CROYDON ☎ 0181 657 8811 204 ⇔ ⋒

CHOBHAM Map 04 SU96

Chobham Chobham Rd, Knaphill GU21 2TZ
☎ 01276 855584 Fax 01276 855663
Designed by Peter Allis and Clive Clark, Chobham course sits among mature oaks and tree nurseries offering tree-lined fairways, together with six man-made lakes.
18 holes, 5821yds, Par 69, SSS 67, Course record 67.
Club membership 750.
Visitors booking in advance essential.
Societies by prior arrangement.
Green Fees not confirmed.
Prof Richard Thomas
Designer Peter Alliss/Clive Clark
Facilities ⊗ ⓜ by prior arrangement ⓑ ⚑ ♀ ♨ 🏌 ✐

Hotel ★★★ 60% Falcon Hotel, 68 Farnborough Rd, FARNBOROUGH ☎ 01252 545378 30 ⇔ ⋒

COBHAM Map 04 TQ16

Silvermere Redhill Rd KT11 1EF ☎ 01932 866007
Parkland course with many very tight holes through woodland, 17th has 170-yd carry over the lake. Driving range.
18 holes, 6700yds, Par 73.
Club membership 740.
Visitors may not play at weekends until 1pm. Must contact in advance.
Societies must contact by telephone.
Green Fees not confirmed.
Prof Doug McClelland
Facilities ⊗ ⓜ ⓑ 🖥 ⚑ ♀ ♨ 🏌 ⛳ ✐ ↀ
& Leisure fishing.
Location 2.25m NW off A245

Hotel ★★★★ 67% Woodlands Park Hotel, Woodlands Ln, STOKE D'ABERNON ☎ 01372 843933 59 ⇔ ⋒

CRANLEIGH Map 04 TQ03

Fernfell Golf & Country Club Barhatch Ln GU6 7NG
☎ 01483 268855 Fax 01483 267251
Scenic woodland/parkland course at the base of the Surrey hills, easy walking. Clubhouse in 400-year-old barn.
18 holes, 5257yds, Par 68, SSS 67, Course record 64.
Club membership 1000.
Visitors welcome weekdays except Thu am, for weekends contact professional shop in advance on 01483 277188
Societies telephone in advance.
Green Fees £30 per day, £23 per round (£25 per round weekends & bank holidays.
Cards 🔳 🔳 🔳 🔳
Prof Trevor Longmuir
Facilities ⊗ ⓑ 🖥 ⚑ ♀ ♨ 🏌 ⛳ ✐ ↀ
& Leisure hard tennis courts, heated indoor swimming pool, sauna, gymnasium.
Location Off A281 Guildford to Horsham road, signposted Cranleigh

Hotel ★★★ 62% Gatton Manor Hotel Golf & Country Club, Standon Ln, OCKLEY ☎ 01306 627555 16 ⇔ ⋒

Wildwood Country Club Horsham Rd, Alfold, Cranleigh GU6 8JE ☎ 01403 753255
Parkland with stands of old oaks dominating several holes, a stream fed by a natural spring winds through a series of lakes and ponds. The greens are smooth, undulating and large. The 5th and 16th are the most challenging holes.
18 holes, 6655yds, Par 72, SSS 73, Course record 65.
Club membership 400.
Visitors welcome subject to availability & booking.
Societies apply in writing or telephone for enquiries.
Green Fees not confirmed.
Cards 🔳 🔳 🔳 🔳
Prof Nicholas Parfrement
Designer Hawtree & Sons
Facilities ⊗ ⓑ ⚑ ♀ ♨ 🏌 ⛳ ✐
& Leisure fishing.
Location Off A281, approx 9m S of Guildford

Hotel ★★★ 62% Gatton Manor Hotel Golf & Country Club, Standon Ln, OCKLEY ☎ 01306 627555 16 ⇔ ⋒

DORKING   Map 04 TQ14

Betchworth Park Reigate Rd RH4 1NZ ☎ 01306 882052
Parkland course, with hard walking on southern ridge of
Boxhill.
18 holes, 6266yds, Par 69, SSS 70, Course record 64.
Club membership 725.
Visitors   weekend play Sun pm only. Must contact in
                 advance.
Societies   apply in writing.
Green Fees   not confirmed.
Prof   Tocher
Designer   H Colt
Facilities   ⊗ ⓑ ♨ ♀ ♨ 🏠 ⛳ ♪
Location   1m E on A25

Hotel   ★★★ 67% The White Horse,
                 High St, DORKING
                 ☎ 01306 881138   36 ⇆ 🐾 Annexe32 ⇆ 🐾

Dorking Chart Park, Deepdene Av RH5 4BX
☎ 01306 886917
Undulating parkland course, easy slopes, wind-sheltered.
Testing holes: 5th 'Tom's Puddle' (par 4); 7th 'Rest and Be
Thankful' (par 4); 9th 'Double Decker' (par 4).
9 holes, 5120yds, Par 66, SSS 65, Course record 62.
Club membership 408.
Visitors   may not play Wed am and with member only
                 weekends & bank holidays. Contact in advance.
Societies   Tue & Thu, telephone in advance.
Green Fees   £16 per day; £12 per 18 holes. Twilight £8.
Prof   Paul Napier
Designer   J Braid/Others
Facilities   ⊗ ⫻ by prior arrangement ⓑ ♨ ♀ ♨ 🏠 ⛳ ♪
                 ⚒ ♪
Location   1m S on A24

Hotel   ★★★★ 67% The Burford Bridge,
                 Burford Bridge, Box Hill, DORKING
                 ☎ 01306 884561   57 ⇆ 🐾

EAST HORSLEY   Map 04 TQ05

Drift KT24 5HD ☎ 01483 284641 Fax 01483 284642
Woodland course with secluded fairways and picturesque
setting. A challenging course that punishes the wayward
shot.
18 holes, 6424yds, Par 73, SSS 72, Course record 70.
Club membership 760.
Visitors   book in advance to the pro shop, Mon-Fri only.
Societies   Mon-Fri, telephone in advance.
Green Fees   not confirmed.
Cards   💳
Prof   Peter Fuller
Designer   Sandown
Facilities   ⊗ ⫻ ⓑ ♨ ♀ ♨ 🏠 ⛳ ♪ ⚒ ♪ ♪
Location   1.5m N off B2039

Hotel   ★★ 60% Bookham Grange Hotel,
                 Little Bookham Common, Bookham,
                 LEATHERHEAD
                 ☎ 01372 452742   21 ⇆ 🐾

┌─────────────────────────────────────┐
│   Entries with a shaded background   │
│   identify courses that are   │
│   considered to be particularly interesting │
└─────────────────────────────────────┘

EFFINGHAM   Map 04 TQ15

Effingham Guildford Rd KT24 5PZ
☎ 01372 452203 Fax 01372 459959
Easy-walking downland course laid out on 270-acres
with tree-lined fairways. It is one of the longest of the
Surrey courses with wide subtle greens that provide a
provocative but by no means exhausting challenge. Fine
views.
18 holes, 6524yds, Par 71, SSS 71, Course record 64.
Club membership 800.
Visitors   contact in advance. With member only
                 weekends & bank holidays.
Societies   Wed, Thu & Fri only and must book in
                 advance.
Green Fees   £35 per day; £27.50 per round.
Prof   Steve Hoatson
Designer   H S Colt
Facilities   ⊗ ⫻ ⓑ ♨ ♀ ♨ 🏠 ⛳ ♪ ⚒ ♪ ♪
& Leisure   hard tennis courts.
Location   W side of village on A246

Hotel   ★★ 60% Bookham Grange Hotel,
                 Little Bookham Common, Bookham,
                 LEATHERHEAD
                 ☎ 01372 452742   21 ⇆ 🐾

ENTON GREEN   Map 04 SU94

West Surrey GU8 5AF
☎ 01483 421275 Fax 01483 41519
A good parkland-type course in rolling, well-wooded
setting. Some fairways are tight with straight driving at a
premium. The 17th is a testing hole with a long hill walk.
18 holes, 6259yds, Par 71, SSS 70, Course record 65.
Club membership 600.
Visitors   must contact in advance and have a
                 handicap certificate.
Societies   must apply in writing. All players to have a
                 handicap.
Green Fees   not confirmed.
Prof   Alister Tawse
Designer   Herbert Fowler
Facilities   ⊗ ⫻ ⓑ ♨ ♀ ♨ 🏠 ♪ ♪ ♪
Location   S side of village

Hotel   ★★★ 64% The Bush Hotel, The Borough,
                 FARNHAM ☎ 01252 715237   65 ⇆ 🐾

EPSOM   Map 04 TQ26

Epsom

Epsom Longdown Ln South KT17 4JR
☎ 01372 721666 Fax 01372 817183
Traditional downland course with many mature trees and
well watered greens.
18 holes, 5701yds, Par 69, SSS 68, Course record 62.
Club membership 800.
Visitors   available any day except Tue, Sat & Sun till
12.00 hrs.
Societies   telephone professional on 01372 741867.
Green Fees £33 all day; £22 per round.
Prof   Ron Goudie
Designer   Willie Dunne
Facilities   ⊗ ⛾ ㄴ 🍺 ♀ 🛆 🏠 ♂
Location   SE side of town centre on B288

Hotel   ★★ 64% Driftbridge Hotel, Reigate Rd,
EPSOM ☎ 01737 352163 34 ⇆ ♠

Horton Park Country Club Hook Rd KT19 8QG
☎ 0181 393 8400 & 394 2626 Fax 0181 394 1369
Parkland course in picturesque surroundings within a country
park with a natural lake. Recently re-shaped, the course
offers a challenge to all golfers with dog-legs, water hazards
and the 10th at 160yds with an island green. There is also a
separate full length Par 3 9 hole course.
18 holes, 6257yds, Par 71.
Club membership 450.

Visitors   must book for weekends, recommended booking
for midweek. Dress code in force.
Societies   must telephone in advance to play at weekends
& bank holidays.
Green Fees on request.
Cards   ▭▭ ▭▭ ▭▭ 🔲 🔲
Prof   Jody September/Helen Omidiran
Designer   Dr Peter Nicholson
Facilities   ⊗ ⛾ ㄴ 🍺 ♀ 🛆 🏠 ♂ 🛒 ⛳

Hotel   ★★ 64% Driftbridge Hotel, Reigate Rd,
EPSOM ☎ 01737 352163 34 ⇆ ♠

ESHER   Map 04 TQ16

Moore Place Portsmouth Rd KT10 9LN
☎ 01372 463533 Fax 01372 460274
Public course on attractive, undulating parkland laid out
some 60 years ago by Harry Vardon. Examples of most of
the trees that will survive in the UK are to be found on the
course. Testing short holes at 2nd, 3rd and 9th.
9 holes, 2148yds, Par 32, SSS 30, Course record 25.
Club membership 300.
Visitors   no restrictions.
Societies   must contact in advance.

Green Fees £5.80 per 9 holes (£7.70 weekends & bank
holidays).
Cards   ▭▭ ▭▭ 🔲 🔲
Prof   David Allen
Designer   Harry Vardon/David Allen
Facilities   ⊗ ⛾ ㄴ 🍺 ♀ 🛆 🏠 ♂ 🛒
Location   0.5m from town centre on A307

Hotel   ★★★ 65% The Ship, Monument Green,
WEYBRIDGE ☎ 01932 848364 39 ⇆ ♠

Thames Ditton & Esher Portsmouth Rd KT10 9AL
☎ 0181 398 1551
Commonland course with public right of way across the
course. Although the course is not long, accuracy is essential
and wayward shots are normally punished.
18 holes, 5149yds, Par 66, SSS 65, Course record 63.
Club membership 250.
Visitors   may not play on Sun mornings. Advisable to
telephone for availability.
Societies   must contact in advance.
Green Fees £12 per 18 holes; £7 per 9 holes (£14/£8
weekends).
Prof   Mark Rodbard
Facilities   ⊗ ⛾ by prior arrangement ㄴ 🍺 ♀ 🛆 🏠 ♂
Location   1m NE on A307

Hotel   ★★ 64% Haven Hotel,
Portsmouth Rd, ESHER
☎ 0181 398 0023 16 ⇆ ♠ Annexe4 ⇆ ♠

FARLEIGH   Map 05 TQ36

Farleigh Court Old Farleigh Rd CR6 9PX
☎ 0188362 7711 & 7733 Fax 0188362 7722
Members: 18 holes, 6414yds, Par 72, SSS 71.
Pay & Play: 9 holes, 6562yds, Par 72, SSS 71.
Club membership 450.
Visitors   welcome on the Members Course and the Pay &
Play Course.
Societies   welcome, please and ask for Society Co
ordinator.
Green Fees not confirmed.
Cards   ▭▭ ▭▭ ▭▭ 🔲
Prof   Tom O'Keefe
Designer   John Jacobs
Facilities   ⊗ ⛾ ㄴ 🍺 ♀ 🛆 🏠 ♂ 🌂 ♂ ⛳
& Leisure   sauna.
Location   1.5m from Selsdon

Hotel   ★★★★ 69% Selsdon Park Hotel,
Addington Rd, Sanderstead, CROYDON
☎ 0181 657 8811 204 ⇆ ♠

FARNHAM   Map 04 SU84

Blacknest Binsted GU34 4QL
☎ 01420 22888 Fax 01420 22001
Privately owned pay and play golf centre catering for all ages
and levels of abilities. Facilities include a 15-bay driving
range, gymnasium and a challenging, newly-constructed 18-
hole course featuring water on 14 holes.
18 holes, 6019yds, Par 69, SSS 69, Course record 65.
Club membership 450.
Visitors   welcome at all times but should telephone for
tee times especially weekends. No denims or
collarless shirts.
▶

Societies	prior arrangements necessary telephone or write.
Green Fees	£14.50 per round (£16.50 weekends).
Cards	▨ ▨ ▨ ▨ ▨
Prof	Ian Benson
Designer	Mr Nicholson
Facilities	⊗ ⅲ ▙ ▆ ⊉ △ 🖾 ⋔ ♂ 𝄢
& Leisure	sauna, solarium, gymnasium.
Location	0.5m S of A31 at Bentley

Hotel	★★★▟▟ 60% Farnham House Hotel, Alton Rd, FARNHAM ☎ 01252 716908 25 ⇆ 🖟

Farnham The Sands GU10 1PX
☎ 01252 782109 Fax 01252 781185
A mixture of meadowland and heath with quick drying
sandy subsoil. Several of the earlier holes have
interesting features, the finishing holes rather less.
18 holes, 6325yds, Par 72, SSS 70, Course record 66.
Club membership 700.

Visitors	must contact in advance. Must be member of recognised club & have handicap certificate. With member only weekends.
Societies	must apply in writing.
Green Fees	£37.50 per day; £30 per round.
Prof	Grahame Cowlishaw
Facilities	⊗ ⅲ by prior arrangement ▙ ▆ ⊉ △ 🖾 ♂
Location	3m E off A31

Hotel	★★★ 64% The Bush Hotel, The Borough, FARNHAM ☎ 01252 715237 65 ⇆ 🖟

Farnham Park Folly Hill, Farnham Park GU9 0AU
☎ 01252 715216
Municipal parkland course in Farnham Park.
9 holes, 1163yds, Par 27, SSS 50, Course record 51.
Club membership 80.

Visitors	pay and play everyday.
Societies	telephone in advance.
Green Fees	£4 per 9 holes (£4.50 weekends).
Prof	Peter Chapman
Designer	Henry Cotton
Facilities	⊗ ⅲ ▙ ▆ ⊉🖾 ⋔
Location	N side of town centre on A287, adjacent to Farnham Castle

Hotel	★★★ 64% The Bush Hotel, The Borough, FARNHAM ☎ 01252 715237 65 ⇆ 🖟

GODALMING   Map 04 SU94

Broadwater Park Guildford Rd, Farncombe GU7 3BU
☎ 01483 429955
A Par-3 public course with floodlit driving range.
9 holes, 1287yds, Par 54, SSS 50.
Club membership 160.

Visitors	must book for weekends & bank holidays.
Societies	telephone in advance.
Green Fees	not confirmed.
Cards	▨ ▨ ▨ ▨ ▨
Prof	Kevin D Milton
Designer	Kevin Milton
Facilities	▙ ▆ ⊉🖾 ⋔ ♂ 𝄢
Location	4m SW of Guildford

Hotel	★★★ 78% The Angel Posting House and Livery, 91 High St, GUILDFORD ☎ 01483 564555 11 ⇆ 🖟

Hurtmore Hurtmore Rd, Hurtmore GU7 2RN
☎ 01483 426492 Fax 01483 426121
A Peter Alliss/Clive Clark Pay and Play course with seven
lakes and 100 bunkers. The 15th hole is the longest at
540yards. Played mainly into the wind there are 10 bunkers
to negotiate. The 3rd hole at 440yds stroke Index 1 is a real
test. A dogleg right around a lake and 9 bunkers makes this
hole worthy of its stroke index.
18 holes, 5514yds, Par 70, SSS 67, Course record 69.
Club membership 200.

Visitors	book by telephone up to 6 days in advance.
Societies	telephone in advance.
Green Fees	not confirmed.
Cards	▨ ▨ ▨ ▨ ▨
Prof	Maxine Burton
Designer	Peter Alliss/Clive Clark
Facilities	⊗ ⅲ ▙ ▆ ⊉ △ 🖾 ⋔ ♂
Location	2m NW of Godalming between A3/A3100, access via unclass road

Hotel	★★★ 78% The Angel Posting House and Livery, 91 High St, GUILDFORD ☎ 01483 564555 11 ⇆ 🖟

Shillinglee Park Chiddingfold GU8 4TA
☎ 01428 653237 & 708158 Fax 01428 644391
Manicured parkland course with many natural features
including seven ponds. The 4th and 7th are the signature
holes requiring tee shots and second shots over ponds, to
well-guarded greens.
9 holes, 5032yds, Par 64, SSS 64, Course record 65.
Club membership 400.

Visitors	restricted Sat, Tue and Thu morning, advisable to book any other time.
Societies	apply for details.
Green Fees	£13 per 18 holes; £8.50 per 9 holes (£15/£9.50 weekends).
Cards	▨ ▨ ▨ ▨ ▨
Prof	David Parkinson
Designer	Roger Mace
Facilities	⊗ ⅲ by prior arrangement ▙ ▆ ⊉ △ 🖾 ⋔ ➷ ♣ ♂
Location	5m S of Godalming, off A283

Hotel	★★★★ 71% Lythe Hill Hotel, Petworth Rd, HASLEMERE ☎ 01428 651251 41 ⇆ 🖟

GUILDFORD   Map 04 SU94

Guildford High Path Rd, Merrow GU1 2HL
☎ 01483 563941 Fax 01483 453228
The course is on typical Surrey downland bordered by
attractive woodlands. Situated on chalk, it is
acknowledged to be one of the best all-weather courses
in the area, and the oldest course in Surrey. The holes
provide an interesting variety of play, an invigorating
experience.
18 holes, 6090yds, Par 69, SSS 70, Course record 65.
Club membership 700.

Visitors	must contact in advance. With member only weekends & bank holidays.
Societies	welcome Mon-Fri. Must apply in advance.

Green Fees £38 per day; £28 per round.
Prof P G Hollington
Designer J H Taylor/Hawtree
Facilities ⊗ ᴸ ᴸ ☕ ♀ ♨ 🏠 ⛳ ◥ ✐
& Leisure practice nets.
Location E side of town centre off A246

Hotel ★★★ 70% The Manor,
Newlands Corner, GUILDFORD
☎ 01483 222624 45 ⇌ ↟

Merrist Wood Coombe Ln, Worplesdon GU3 3PE
☎ 01483 884045 Fax 01483 884047
More parkland than heathland, Merrist Wood has a bit of
everything. Water comes into play on five holes, the
bunkering is fierce, the greens slope and the back nine has
plenty of trees. Two holes stand out especially: the
picturesque par 3 11th with a tee shot through the trees and
the dastardly par 4 17th, including a 210yd carry over a lake
and ditches either side of the green.
18 holes, 6600yda, Par 72, SSS 71.
Club membership 650.
Visitors must contact in advance, at weekends only after
11am.
Societies apply in writing.
Green Fees £35 per round (£50 weekends).
Prof Andrew Kirk
Designer David Williams
Facilities ⊗ 〗 by prior arrangement ᴸ ☕ ♀ ♨ 🏠 ✐ ◥
Location 3m out of Guildford on A323 to Aldershot

Hotel ★★★ 78% The Angel Posting House and
Livery, 91 High St, GUILDFORD
☎ 01483 564555 11 ⇌ ↟

Milford Station Ln, Milford GU8 5HS
☎ 01483 419200 Fax 01483 41999
A Peter Alliss/Clive Clark designed course opened summer
1993. The design has cleverly incorporated a demanding
course within an existing woodland and meadow area.
18 holes, 5945yds, Par 69, SSS 68, Course record 67.
Club membership 750.
Visitors must contact in advance, tee booking system,
telephone 01483 416291 up to 1 week in
advance.
Societies telephone in advance.
Green Fees £25 per day (£35 weekends).
Cards ▭ ▭ ▭ ▭ ▭ ▭
Prof Nick English
Designer Peter Allis
Facilities ⊗ 〗 ᴸ ☕ ♀ ♨ 🏠 ⛳ ◥ ☗ ✐
Location 6m SW, leave A3 Milford then A3100 to Enton

Hotel ★★★ 78% The Angel Posting House and
Livery, 91 High St, GUILDFORD
☎ 01483 564555 11 ⇌ ↟

Roker Park Rokers Farm, Aldershot Rd GU3 3PB
☎ 01483 236677 Fax 01483 232324
A Pay and Play 9-hole parkland course. A challenging course
with two Par 5 holes.
9 holes, 3037yds, Par 36, SSS 72.
Club membership 200.
Visitors no restrictions, pay & play, phone for
reservations.

Societies prior arrangement with deposit at least 14 days
before, minimum 12 persons.
Green Fees £13 per 18 holes; £7.50 per 9 holes (£16/£8.80
weekends & bank holidays).
Prof Kevin Warn
Designer W V Roker
Facilities ⊗ 〗 ᴸ ☕ ♀ ♨ 🏠 ⛳ ◥ ☗ ✐ ⸙
Location A323, 3m from Guildford

Hotel ★★★ 78% The Angel Posting House and
Livery, 91 High St, GUILDFORD
☎ 01483 564555 11 ⇌ ↟

HINDHEAD   Map 04 SU83

Hindhead Churt Rd GU26 6HX
☎ 01428 604614 Fax 01428 608508
A good example of a Surrey heath-and-heather course,
and most picturesque. Players must be prepared for some
hard walking. The first nine fairways follow narrow
valleys requiring straight hitting; the second nine are
much less restricted.
18 holes, 6356yds, Par 70, SSS 70, Course record 63.
Club membership 770.
Visitors must contact in advance and have a
handicap certificate.
Societies Wed & Thu only, contact in advance
Green Fees £43 per day; £32 per round (£53/£42
weekends & bank holidays).
Prof Neil Ogilvy
Designer J H Taylor
Facilities ⊗ 〗 by prior arrangement ᴸ ☕ ♀ ♨ 🏠
⛳ ✐
Location 1.5m NW of Hindhead on A287

Hotel ★★★★ 71% Lythe Hill Hotel,
Petworth Rd, HASLEMERE
☎ 01428 651251 41 ⇌ ↟

KINGSWOOD   Map 04 TQ25

Kingswood Sandy Ln KT20 6NE ☎ 01737 832188
Flat parkland course, easy walking.
18 holes, 6880yds, Par 72, SSS 73.
Club membership 700.
Visitors must contact professional at least 24 hrs in
advance. May not play weekend mornings.
Societies must apply in advance.
Green Fees £36 (£50 weekends).
Cards ▭ ▭ ▭ ▭ ▭ ▭
Prof James Dodds
Designer James Braid
Facilities ♨ 🏠 ⛳ ◥ ☗ ✐ ⸙
& Leisure squash.
Location 0.5m S of village off A217

Hotel ★★★ 65% Reigate Manor Hotel, Reigate Hill,
REIGATE ☎ 01737 240125 50 ⇌ ↟

LEATHERHEAD   Map 04 TQ15

Leatherhead Kingston Rd KT22 0EE
☎ 01372 843966 & 843956 Fax 01372 842241
Parkland course with numerous ditches and only two hills, so
walking is easy.
18 holes, 6203yds, Par 71, SSS 69, Course record 67. ▶

Visitors telephone pro shop 01372 843956 up to 10 days in advance.
Societies telephone for booking form.
Green Fees not confirmed.
Prof Simon Norman
Facilities ⊗ 🏌 🍴 🍽 ♀ ⛳ 🏧 🚜 ✏
Location 0.25m from junct 9 of M25, on A243

Hotel ★★★★ 67% Woodlands Park Hotel, Woodlands Ln, STOKE D'ABERNON ☎ 01372 843933 59 ⇔ ↾

Pachesham Park Golf Complex Oaklawn Rd KT22 0BP
☎ 01372 843453 Fax 01372 844076
A 9-hole undulating parkland course playing out over 18 holes at 5,618yds, starting with 5 shorter but tight holes followed by 4 longer more open but testing to finish.
9 holes, 2805yds, Par 70, SSS 67, Course record 67.
Club membership 450.
Visitors book 2 days in advance by phone. May play weekends after 12.30pm.
Societies apply in advance.
Green Fees £15 per 18 holes; £9 per 9 holes (£18/£10 weekends & bank holidays).
Cards 💳 💳 💳 💳 💳
Prof Philip Taylor
Designer Phil Taylor
Facilities ⊗ 🍽 by prior arrangement 🏌 🍴 ♀ ⛳ 🏧 🚜 ✏ ♩
Location On A244, 0.5m from M25 junct 9

Hotel ★★★★ 67% Woodlands Park Hotel, Woodlands Ln, STOKE D'ABERNON ☎ 01372 843933 59 ⇔ ↾

Tyrrells Wood The Drive KT22 8QP
☎ 01372 376025 Fax 01372 360836
Parkland course with easy walking. Snooker.
18 holes, 6282yds, Par 71, SSS 70, Course record 65.
Club membership 700.
Visitors must contact in advance. Restricted weekends.
Societies must apply in advance.
Green Fees not confirmed.
Prof Max Taylor
Designer James Braid
Facilities ♀ ⛳ 🏧 🚜 ✏
& Leisure putting green & limited practice area.
Location 2m SE of town, off A24

Hotel ★★★★ 67% The Burford Bridge, Burford Bridge, Box Hill, DORKING ☎ 01306 884561 57 ⇔ ↾

LIMPSFIELD Map 05 TQ45

Limpsfield Chart Westerham Rd RH8 0SL
☎ 01883 723405
Tight heathland course set in National Trust land, well wooded.
9 holes, 5718yds, Par 70, SSS 68, Course record 64.
Club membership 300.
Visitors with member only or by appointment weekends & not before 3.30pm Thu (Ladies Day).
Societies must apply in advance.
Green Fees £18 per day/round.
Facilities ⊗ by prior arrangement 🍽 by prior arrangement 🏌 ♀
& Leisure putting green, practice area.

Location 1m E on A25 from M25 junct 6

Hotel ★★★ 68% Kings Arms Hotel, Market Square, WESTERHAM ☎ 01959 562990 17 ⇔ ↾

LINGFIELD Map 05 TQ34

Lingfield Park Lingfield Rd, Racecourse Rd RH7 6PQ
☎ 01342 834602 Fax 01342 834602
Difficult and challenging, tree-lined parkland course set in 210 acres of beautiful Surrey countryside. Driving range.
18 holes, 6473yds, Par 71, SSS 72, Course record 69.
Club membership 700.
Visitors must be accompanied by member on Sat & Sun. Advisable to telephone first.
Societies must telephone in advance.
Green Fees £28 per 18 holes.
Cards 💳 💳 💳 💳
Prof Christopher Morley
Facilities ⊗ 🍽 🍴 🍽 ♀ ⛳ 🏧 🚜 ✏ ♩
Location Entrance next to Lingfield race course

Hotel ★★★ 65% Woodbury House Hotel, Lewes Rd, EAST GRINSTEAD ☎ 01342 313657 14 ⇔ ↾

NEWDIGATE Map 04 TQ14

Rusper Rusper Rd RH5 5BX
☎ 01293 871871 (shop) & 871456 (office)
Fax 01293 871456
New course set in mature woodland. The opening two holes give the golfer an encouraging start with the following holes demanding accurate play through the trees. The 5th hole is a challenging Par 5 from the back tee with a gentle dogleg tempting the golfer to take a shortcut. Play is from two sets of tees to 2 pin positions, giving the golfer alternative holes on the second nine.
9 holes, 6218yds, Par 71, SSS 69, Course record 67.
Club membership 270.
Visitors welcome but telephone to reserve time, some restrictions if competitions being played.
Societies telephone in advance for details.
Green Fees £11.50 per 18 holes; £7 per 9 holes (£15.50/£8.50 weekends).
Cards 💳 💳 💳 ✏
Prof Janice Arnold
Designer A Blunden
Facilities ⊗ 🍽 by prior arrangement 🏌 🍴 ♀ ⛳ 🏧 ✏ ♩
Location Between Newdigate/Rusper, off A24

Hotel ★★★★ 67% The Burford Bridge, Burford Bridge, Box Hill, DORKING ☎ 01306 884561 57 ⇔ ↾

OCKLEY Map 04 TQ14

Gatton Manor Hotel Golf & Country Club Standon Ln RH5 5PQ ☎ 01306 627555 Fax 01306 627713
Undulating parkland course through woods and over many challenging water holes.
18 holes, 6629yds, Par 72, SSS 72, Course record 68.
Club membership 300.
Visitors may book up to 10 days in advance. Restricted Sun (am). Tee times to be booked through professional 01306 627557

Societies must apply in advance.
Green Fees Apr-Oct: £21 (£28 weekends); Nov-Mar: £16 (£21 weekends).
Cards
Prof Rae Sargent
Designer Henry Cotton
Facilities
& Leisure grass tennis courts, fishing, sauna, solarium, gymnasium.
Location 1.5m SW off A29

Hotel ★★★ 62% Gatton Manor Hotel Golf & Country Club, Standon Ln, OCKLEY ☎ 01306 627555 16 ⇄ ╠

OTTERSHAW   Map 04 TQ06

Foxhills Stonehill Rd KT16 0EL
☎ 01932 872050 Fax 01932 874762
A pair of parkland courses designed in the grand manner and with American course-design in mind. One course is tree-lined, the other, as well as trees, has massive bunkers and artificial lakes which contribute to the interest. Both courses offer testing golf and they finish on the same long 'double green'. Par 3 'Manor' course also available.
The Bernard Hunt Course: 18 holes, 6734yds, Par 73, SSS 72.
Longcross Course: 18 holes, 6429yds, Par 72, SSS 71.
Manor Course: 9 holes, 1143yds, Par 27, SSS 27.
Visitors contact sales office to reserve times. Restricted before noon weekends.
Societies welcome Mon-Fri, must apply in advance.
Green Fees £50 (£65 weekends after 12pm).
Cards
Prof B Hunt/A Good/R Summerscales
Designer F W Hawtree
Facilities
& Leisure hard tennis courts, outdoor and indoor heated swimming pools, squash, sauna, solarium, gymnasium.
Location 1m NW

Hotel ★★★ 67% The Crown Hotel, 7 London St, CHERTSEY ☎ 01932 564657 Annexe30 ⇄ ╠

PIRBRIGHT   Map 04 SU95

Goal Farm Gole Rd GU24 0PZ
☎ 01483 473183 & 473205
Beautiful lanscaped parkland 'Pay and Play' course with excellent greens.

9 holes, 1273yds, Par 54, SSS 48.
Club membership 300.
Visitors may not play on Sat before 4pm or Thu before 2pm.
Societies telephone in advance.
Green Fees £4 per 9 holes (£4.25 weekends and bank holidays).
Designer Bill Cox
Facilities
Location 1.5m NW on B3012

Hotel B Posthouse Farnborough, Lynchford Rd, FARNBOROUGH ☎ 01252 545051 143 ⇄ ╠

PUTTENHAM   Map 04 SU94

Puttenham Heath Rd GU3 1AL
☎ 01483 810498 Fax 01483 810988
Picturesque tree-lined heathland course offering testing golf, easy walking.
18 holes, 6211yds, Par 71, SSS 70.
Club membership 650.
Visitors weekdays by prior arrangment tel: 01483 810498, with member only weekends & public holidays.
Societies apply in advance to secretary.
Green Fees £30 per day; £23 per round.
Prof Gary Simmons
Facilities
& Leisure lessons available.
Location 1m SE on B3000

Hotel ★★★ 64% The Bush Hotel, The Borough, FARNHAM ☎ 01252 715237 65 ⇄ ╠

REDHILL   Map 04 TQ25

Redhill & Reigate Clarence Rd, Pendelton Rd RH1 6LB
☎ 01737 240777 Fax 01737 242117
Flat well wooded parkland course.
18 holes, 5238yds, Par 67, SSS 66.
Club membership 600.
Visitors may not play before 11am weekends or after 2pm Sun (Jun-Sep). Must contact in advance.
Societies must apply in writing.
Green Fees £12 per round (£18 weekends & bank holidays).
Prof Warren Pike
Facilities
Location 1m S on A23

Hotel ★★★ 65% Reigate Manor Hotel, Reigate Hill, REIGATE ☎ 01737 240125 50 ⇄ ╠

REIGATE   Map 04 TQ25

Reigate Heath Flanchford Rd RH2 8QR
☎ 01737 242610 & 226793 Fax 01737 226793
Gorse, heather, pine and birch trees abound on this popular 9-hole heathland course. Sandy soil gives all year round play even in the wettest winters. Clubhouse enjoys panoramic views of the North Downs and Leith Hill.
9 holes, 5658yds, Par 67, SSS 67, Course record 65.
Club membership 550.
Visitors with member only weekends & bank holidays. Must contact in advance.
Societies must apply in writing.
Green Fees £25 per day; £18 morning; £12 afternoon. ▶

Prof Barry Davies
Facilities ⊗ ⓑ 🍵 ♟ ⚂ 🏠 ⚐
Location 1.5m W off A25

Hotel ★★★ 65% Reigate Manor Hotel,
Reigate Hill, REIGATE
☎ 01737 240125 50 ⇄ 🐾

Reigate Hill Gatton Bottom RH2 0TU
☎ 01737 645577 Fax 01737 642650
Championship standard course opened in 1995 with fully
irrigated tees and greens. Feature holes include the 5th which
is divided by four bunkers and the par 5 14th involving a
tricky second shot across a lake. Very good short holes at 8th
and 12th with panoramic views from the tees.
18 holes, 6175yds, Par 72, SSS 70, Course record 75.
Club membership 650.
Visitors must contact in advance to book tee time, may
not play weekends until 12 noon.
Societies welcome Mon-Fri but must book in advance.
Green Fees £25 per round. (£35 per round weekends after
noon).
Cards 💳 💳 💳 💳
Prof Martin Platts
Designer David Williams
Facilities ⊗ ⓑ 🍵 ♟ ⚂ 🏠 ⚐ ⚐ ♨
Location 1m from junct 8 of M25

Hotel ★★★ 63% Bridge House Hotel, Reigate Hill,
REIGATE ☎ 01737 246801 & 244821
Fax 01737 223756 39 ⇄ 🐾

SHEPPERTON Map 04 TQ06

American Golf at Sunbury Charlton Ln TW17 8QA
☎ 01932 771414 Fax 01932 789300
The new 18 hole course is now open and provides a
challenge for golfers of all levels. The final 27 hole layout is
anticipated for completion in the summer of 1999.
Sunbury Golf Course: 18 holes, 4830yds, Par 66, SSS 64,
Course record 60.
Club membership 300.
Visitors no restrictions.
Societies advance booking necessary.
Green Fees £12 per round (£17 weekends).
Cards 💳 💳 💳 💳 💳 💳
Prof Alistair Hardaway
Facilities ⊗ ⓙ ⓑ 🍵 ♟ ⚂ 🏠 ⚐ ⚐ ⚐ ♨
Location Off junct 1 of the M3

Hotel ★★★ 63% Shepperton Moat House Hotel,
Felix Ln, SHEPPERTON
☎ 01932 241404 156 ⇄ 🐾

TANDRIDGE Map 05 TQ35

Tandridge RH8 9NQ
☎ 01883 712274 Fax 01883 730537
A parkland course with two loops of 9 holes from the
clubhouse. The first 9 is relatively flat. The second 9
undulates and reveals several outstanding views of the
North Downs and the South.
18 holes, 6250yds, Par 70, SSS 70.
Club membership 750.
Visitors must contact in advance. May play Mon,
Wed, Thu
Societies Mon, Wed & Thu, apply in advance.

Green Fees £49 am round/all day; £38 pm round..
Cards 💳 💳 💳 💳 💳 💳
Prof Chris Evans
Designer H S Colt
Facilities ⊗ ⓑ 🍵 ♟ ⚂ 🏠 ⚐ ⚐
Location 2m SE junc 6 M25, 1.5m E of Godstone on
A25

Hotel ★★★★ 71% Nutfield Priory, Nutfield,
REDHILL ☎ 01737 822066 60 ⇄ 🐾

TILFORD Map 04 SU84

Hankley Common GU10 2DD
☎ 01252 792493 Fax 01252 795699
A natural heathland course subject to wind. Greens are
first rate. The 18th, a long par 4, is most challenging, the
green being beyond a deep chasm which traps any but
the perfect second shot. The 7th is a spectacular one-
shotter.
18 holes, 6418yds, Par 71, SSS 71.
Club membership 700.
Visitors handicap certificate required, restricted to
afternoons at weekends.
Societies apply in writing.
Green Fees £55 per day; £42 per round (£55 per round
weekends & bank holidays).
Prof Peter Stow
Facilities ⊗ ⓙ ⓑ 🍵 ♟ ⚂ 🏠 ⚐
Location 0.75m SE

Hotel ★★★ 64% The Bush Hotel,
The Borough, FARNHAM
☎ 01252 715237 65 ⇄ 🐾

VIRGINIA WATER Map 04 TQ06

WENTWORTH See page 243.

WALTON-ON-THAMES Map 04 TQ16

Burhill Burwood Rd KT12 4BL
☎ 01932 227345 Fax 01932 267159
A relatively short and easy parkland course with some
truly magnificent trees. The 18th is a splendid par 4
requiring a well-placed drive and a long firm second.
This course is always in immaculate condition.
18 holes, 6479yds, Par 70, SSS 71, Course record 65.
Club membership 1000.
Visitors may not play Fri-Sun unless introduced by
member. Must contact in advance.
Societies apply in writing.
Green Fees £55 per day, £35 per round.
Prof Lee Johnson
Designer Willie Park
Facilities ⊗ ⓑ 🍵 ♟ ⚂ 🏠 ⚐ ♨
& Leisure squash.
Location 2m S

Hotel ★★★ 65% The Ship, Monument Green,
WEYBRIDGE
☎ 01932 848364 39 ⇄ 🐾

WENTWORTH CLUB

VIRGINIA WATER *Surrey* ☎ **01344 842201**
Fax 01344 842804   **Map O4 TQO6**

John Ingham writes: Among the really famous inland courses in England you have to name Wentworth. The challenge, in terms of sheer yards, is enormous. But the qualities go beyond this, and include the atmosphere, the heathland, the silver birch and fairway-side homes.

The West Course is the one every visitor wishes to play. You can't possibly name the best hole. Bernard Gallacher, the former professional, has his view, but you may select the 7th where the drive rolls downhill and the second shot has to be played high up to a stepped green. The closing holes really sort out the best of them too.

The clubhouse offers facilities not typical of many British golf clubs. The pro shop resembles a plush city store; evening hospitality events are frequent and society meetings here are catered for as at few other centres for sport, and it's all done in five-star style. Probably it is during the World Match-Play championship when Wentworth can be seen at its best. The tents are up, the superstars pile in and out of huge cars and the air is one of luxury and opulence.

One of the attractions of Wentworth is that the great players, including Ben Hogan and Sam Snead, have played here. Gary Player has won marvellously at Wentworth, beating Tony Lema after being seven down in the 36-hole match! Great competitors from the past have stamped their mark here. Arnold Palmer, back in the 1960s, beat Neil Coles in the Match-Play final but then, a generation later, faced young Seve Ballesteros. The Spaniard saved his bacon by pitching in for an eagle three at the last against Palmer, to take the clash into extra holes, where he won.

Visitors	weekdays only. Must contact in advance with letter from own club or a current handicap certificate
Societies	apply in advance
Green fees	(per round) West Course £75-£145; East Course £55-£90 & Edinburgh Course £60-£100. ▬ ▬ ▬ ▬ ⬙ 🗋
Facilities	⊗ ⫫ ⅃ 🍴 ⅃ ⛳ 🏠 ⛿ 🍴 ⚷ ⚭ Professional (David Rennie)
Leisure	tennis (hard court & grass), outdoor heated swimming pool, sauna, solarium, health club, gym.
Location	Wentworth Drive, GU25 4LS (just off A30 at junction with A329 to Ascot)

54 holes. West Course: 18 holes, 6957yds, Par 73, SSS 74, Course record 63
East Course: 18 holes, 6198yds, Par 68, SSS 70, Course record 62
Edinburgh: 18 holes, 6979yds, Par 72, SSS 73, Course record 67

WHERE TO STAY AND EAT NEARBY

HOTELS:
ASCOT
★★★★🏵 🏵 70% The Royal Berkshire, London Rd, Sunninghill ☎ 01344 623322. 63 ⇌ 🐾
🏵★★★ 61% The Berystede, Bagshot Rd, Sunninghill. ☎ 01344 623311 91 (90 ⇌ 🐾 1 🐾)
★★74% Highclere, 19 Kings Road, Sunninghill. ☎ 01344 625220. 11 🐾

BAGSHOT
★★★★★🏵 🏵 🏵 72% Pennyhill Park, London Rd. ☎ 01276 471774 21 ⇌ 🐾 Annexe 84 ⇌ 🐾.

EGHAM
★★★★🏵 🏵 72% Runnymede Hotel & Spa, Windsor Rd. ☎ 01784 436171. 180 ⇌ 🐾.

RESTAURANTS:
BRAY
🏵 🏵 🏵 🏵 Waterside Inn, Ferry Rd. ☎ 01628 620691.

WALTON-ON-THE-HILL   Map 04 TQ25

WALTON HEATH See page 245

WEST BYFLEET   Map 04 TQ06

West Byfleet Sheerwater Rd KT14 6AA
☎ 01932 343433 Fax 01932 340667
An attractive course set against a background of
woodland and gorse. The 13th is the famous 'pond' shot
with a water hazard and two bunkers fronting the green.
No less than six holes of 420 yards or more.
18 holes, 6211yds, Par 70, SSS 70.
Club membership 600.
Visitors	must contact professional in advance, only with member at weekends. Restricted Thu (Ladies Day).
Societies	must apply in writing.
Green Fees	£38 per day; £30 per round.
Cards	▭ ▭ ▭
Prof	David Regan
Designer	C S Butchart
Facilities	⊗ �III 🛝 ♥ ♀ 🛆 🏠 🥄 🚜 ♂
Location	W side of village on A245

Hotel	B Hilton National Cobham, Seven Hills Rd South, COBHAM ☎ 01932 864471 149 ⊋ 🐾

WEST CLANDON   Map 04 TQ05

Clandon Regis Epsom Rd GU4 7TT
☎ 01483 224888 Fax 01483 211781
High quality parkland course with challenging lake holes on
the back nine. European Tour specification tees and greens.
18 holes, 6412yds, Par 72, SSS 71.
Visitors	contact in advance.
Societies	telephone in advance.
Green Fees	not confirmed.
Cards	▭ ▭ ▭ ▭
Prof	Steve Lloyd
Designer	David Williams
Facilities	⊗ III 🛝 ♥ ♀ 🛆 🏠 ♂ ⚑
& Leisure	sauna.
Location	From A246 Guildford/Leatherhead direction

Hotel	★★★ 70% The Manor, Newlands Corner, GUILDFORD ☎ 01483 222624 45 ⊋ 🐾

WEST END   Map 04 SU96

Windlemere Windlesham Rd GU24 5LS ☎ 01276 858727
A parkland course, undulating in parts with natural water
hazards. There is also a floodlit driving range.
9 holes, 2673yds, Par 34, SSS 33, Course record 30.
Visitors	no restrictions.
Societies	advisable to contact in advance.
Green Fees	not confirmed.
Prof	David Thomas
Designer	Clive Smith
Facilities	⊗ 🛝 ♥ ♀ 🛆 🏠 ⚑ ♂ ⚑
Location	N side of village at junct of A319/A322

Hotel	★★★★★ 72% Pennyhill Park Hotel, London Rd, BAGSHOT ☎ 01276 471774 28 ⊋ 🐾 Annexe86 ⊋ 🐾

WEYBRIDGE   Map 04 TQ06

St George's Hill Golf Club Rd, St George's Hill
KT13 0NL ☎ 01932 847758 Fax 01932 821564
Comparable and similar to Wentworth, a feature of this
course is the number of long and difficult par 4s. To
score well it is necessary to place the drive - and long
driving pays handsomely. Walking is hard on this
undulating, heavily wooded course with plentiful heather
and rhododendrons.
*Red & Blue: 18 holes, 6569yds, Par 70, SSS 71, Course
record 64.*
Green: 9 holes, 2869yds, Par 35.
Club membership 600.
Visitors	must contact in advance and have a handicap certificate. Visitors may only play Wed-Fri.
Societies	apply in writing
Green Fees	Wed-Fri only £70 per day; £55 per round.
Prof	A C Rattue
Designer	H S Colt
Facilities	⊗ 🛝 ♥ ♀ 🛆 🏠 ⚑ ♂
Location	2m S off B374

Hotel	★★★★ 73% Oatlands Park, 146 Oatlands Drive, WEYBRIDGE ☎ 01932 847242 134 (120⊋🐾 14🐾)

WOKING   Map 04 TQ05

Hoebridge Golf Centre Old Woking Rd GU22 8JH
☎ 01483 722611 Fax 01483 740369
Three public courses set in parkland on Surrey sand belt. 24-
bay floodlit driving range.
*Main Course: 18 holes, 6536yds, Par 72, SSS 71, Course
record 68.*
Shey Course: 9 holes, 2294yds, Par 33.
Maybury Course: 18 holes, 2230yds, Par 54.
Club membership 600.
Visitors	welcome every day, course and reservation desk open dawn to dusk. Credit card reservations 6 days in advance.
Societies	Mon-Fri only, telephone in advance
Green Fees	not confirmed.
Cards	▭ ▭ ▭ ▭
Prof	Tim Powell
Designer	John Jacobs

▶

WALTON HEATH

WALTON ON THE HILL *Surrey* ☎ **01737 812380**
Fax 01737 814225   **Map O4 TQ25**

John Ingham writes: Several historic names are etched on the Honours Board at Walton Heath, almost 700 feet above sea level. The rare atmosphere here is justified because these Surrey courses can claim to be the toughest inland examination in Britain. Walton Heath is famous for staging the Ryder Cup and the European Open Championship but older players will remember it best for the Match-Play Championship battles that involved Sir Henry Cotton and Dai Rees as well as huge money matches that brought names such as Bobby Locke and Fred Daly to public prominence.

Once owned by the News of the World newspaper, MP's, Lords and significant members of the press would be invited down to Walton Heath by Sir Emsley Carr, who was one of the first to employ a lady as Secretary and manager of a well-known championship venue.

The courses were designed in 1903 by Herbert Fowler, who used natural hollows and channels for drainage, so the fairways equal the best on any seaside links and quickly dry out, even after a severe storm.

Erratic shots, wide of the prepared surface, are wickedly punished and weekend players are tormented in awful fashion. Nobody escapes undamaged from the gorse and bracken but it is the heather, with those tough stems, that really snarl up any attempt at an over-ambitious recovery shot. So be advised - if you're caught off the fairway, don't attempt anything fancy. Play back on the shortest route to comparative security.

While the Old Course is most frequently played by visitors, the New Course is very challenging and requires all the subtle shots required if you are to get the ball near the hole. And, in the clubhouse, they serve a spectacular lunch.

Visitors	limited play weekends. Must contact in advance and have a handicap certificate or letter of introduction
Societies	telephone in advance or apply in writing
Green fees	£72 per day; £60 after 11.30am.
Facilities	⊗ 🛍 🍺 ♀ 🏖 🏠 ⛳ ⚒ Professional (Ken Macpherson)
Location	Deans Lane, Tadworth KT20 7TP (SE side of village, off B2032)

36 holes. **Old Course: 18 holes, 6801yds, Par 72, SSS 73, Course record 65**
New Course: 18 holes, 6659 yds, Par 72, SSS 72

WHERE TO STAY AND EAT NEARBY

HOTELS:

DORKING
★★★★ 67% The Burford Bridge, Burford Bridge, Box Hill (2m NE A24) ☎ 01306 884561. 57 🛏 🐾

REIGATE
★★★ 65% Reigate Manor, Reigate Hill. ☎ 01737 240125. 50 (46 🛏 🐾 4 🐾)
★★★🏵 63% Bridge House, Reigate Hill. ☎ 01737 246801. 39 🛏 🐾

STOKE D'ABERNON
★★★★🏵🏵 67% Woodlands Park, Woodlands Ln. ☎ 01372 843933. 59 🛏 🐾 .

RESTAURANTS:
DORKING
🏵🏵 Partners & Sons, 2-4 West St. ☎ 01306 882826.

Facilities ⊗ 🄱 🖥 ♀ 🛆 🏠 🛅 🛥 ♐ (
Location On B382 Old Woking to West Byfleet road

Hotel ★★★★★ 72% Pennyhill Park Hotel,
London Rd, BAGSHOT
☎ 01276 471774   28 ⇆ 🛏 Annexe86 ⇆ 🛏

Pyrford Warren Ln, Pyrford GU22 8XR
☎ 01483 723555 Fax 01483 729777
Opened in September 1993 this inland links style course was designed by Peter Alliss and Clive Clark. Set between Surrey woodlands, the fairways weave between 23 acres of water courses while the greens and tees are connected by rustic bridges. The signature hole is the Par 5 9th at 595 yards, with a dogleg and final approach over water and a sand shelf.
18 holes, 6230yds, Par 72, SSS 70, Course record 69.
Club membership 600.
Visitors must book in advance.
Societies must contact in advance.
Green Fees not confirmed.
Cards 💳 💳 💳 💳 💳
Prof Richard Pilbury
Designer Peter Allis & Clive Clark
Facilities ⊗ 🅇 🄱 🖥 ♀ 🛆 🏠 🛅 🛥 ♐
Location Off A3 Ripley to Pyrford

Hotel ★★★★★ 72% Pennyhill Park Hotel,
London Rd, BAGSHOT
☎ 01276 471774   28 ⇆ 🛏 Annexe86 ⇆ 🛏

Woking Pond Rd, Hook Heath GU22 0JZ
☎ 01483 760053 Fax 01483 772441
An 18-hole course on Surrey heathland with few changes from the original course designed in 1892 by Tom Dunn. Bernard Darwin a past Captain and President has written ' the beauty of Woking is that there is something distinctive about every hole...'.
18 holes, 6340yds, Par 70, SSS 70, Course record 65.
Club membership 550.
Visitors must contact secretary at least 7 days prior to playing. No visitors weekends & bank holidays.
Societies telephone intially then confrim in writing, normally 12 months notice.
Green Fees not confirmed.
Prof John Thorne
Designer Tom Dunn
Facilities ⊗ 🅇 🄱 🖥 ♀ 🛆 🏠 🛥 ♐ (
Location W of town centre

Hotel ★★★★★ 72% Pennyhill Park Hotel,
London Rd, BAGSHOT
☎ 01276 471774
28 ⇆ 🛏 Annexe86 ⇆ 🛏

Worplesdon Heath House Rd GU22 0RA
☎ 01483 472277
The scene of the celebrated mixed-foursomes competition. Accurate driving is essential on this heathland course. The short 10th across a lake from tee to green is a notable hole, and the 18th provides a wonderfully challenging par-4 finish.
18 holes, 6440yds, Par 71, SSS 71, Course record 64.
Club membership 590.

Visitors must play with member at weekends & bank holidays. Must contact in advance and have a handicap certificate.
Societies must contact in writing.
Green Fees not confirmed.
Prof J Christine
Facilities ⊗ 🄱 🖥 ♀ 🛆 🏠 🛅 ♐
Location 6m N of Guildford, off A322

Hotel ★★★★★ 72% Pennyhill Park Hotel,
London Rd, BAGSHOT
☎ 01276 471774
28 ⇆ 🛏 Annexe86 ⇆ 🛏

WOLDINGHAM   Map 05 TQ35

Duke's Dene Slines New Rd CR3 7HA
☎ 01883 653501 Fax 01883 653502
Located in Halliloo Valley and designed by the American architect Bradford Benz, this pleasant course utilises all the contours and features of the valley.
18 holes, 6393yds, Par 71, SSS 70.
Club membership 744.
Visitors tee times should be booked in advance with pro shop. Weekends available after noon for visitors.
Societies telephone to book.
Green Fees not confirmed.
Cards 💳 💳 💳 💳 💳
Prof Paul Thornley
Designer Bradford Benz
Facilities ⊗ by prior arrangement 🅇 by prior arrangement
🄱 🖥 ♀ 🛆 🏠 🛅 🛥 ♐

Hotel ★★★ 68% Kings Arms Hotel,
Market Square, WESTERHAM
☎ 01959 562990   17 ⇆ 🛏

North Downs Northdown Rd CR3 7AA
☎ 01883 652057 Fax 01883 652832
Downland course, 850 ft above sea-level, with several testing holes and magnificent views.
18 holes, 5843yds, Par 69, SSS 68, Course record 66.
Club membership 700.
Visitors must play with member at weekends and bank holidays. Must contact in advance.
Societies must contact in writing.
Green Fees not confirmed.
Prof M Homewood
Designer Pennink
Facilities ⊗ 🅇 🄱 🖥 ♀ 🛆 🏠 ♐
Location 0.75m S

Hotel ★★★ 68% Kings Arms Hotel,
Market Square, WESTERHAM
☎ 01959 562990   17 ⇆ 🛏

SUSSEX, EAST

BEXHILL   Map 05 TQ70

Cooden Beach Cooden Sea Rd TN39 4TR
☎ 01424 842040 Fax 01424 842040
The course is close by the sea, but is not real links in
character. Despite that, it is dry and plays well
throughout the year. There are some excellent holes such
as the 4th, played to a built-up green, the short 12th, and
three good holes to finish. There are added ponds which
make the player think more about tee shots and shots to
the green.
18 holes, 6470yds, Par 72, SSS 71, Course record 67.
Club membership 730.
Visitors   must have a handicap certificate. Restricted
                  at weekends. Book in advance with
                  professional 01424 843938
Societies   must contact in advance by telephoning
                  secretary.
Green Fees   £29 per day/round (£35 weekends & bank
                  holidays).
Prof   Jeffrey Sim
Designer   W Herbert Fowler
Facilities   ⊗ 🏠 💺 ▼ ♀ 🛆 🏠 🕈 🐾 🚃 ⊘
& Leisure   snooker tables.
Location   2m W on A259

Hotel   ★★★ 76% Lansdowne Hotel, King
                  Edward's Pde, EASTBOURNE
                  ☎ 01323 725174 121 ⇄ 🐾

Highwoods Ellerslie Ln TN39 4LJ
☎ 01424 212625 Fax 01424 216866
Undulating course.
18 holes, 6218yds, Par 70, SSS 70.
Club membership 820.
Visitors   must play with member on Sun. Must contact in
                  advance and have an introduction from own
                  club. Handicap required.
Societies   advance notice advised.
Green Fees   not confirmed.
Prof   M Andrews
Designer   J H Taylor
Facilities   ⊗ 🏠 💺 ▼ ♀ 🛆 🏠 ⊘
Location   1.5m NW

Hotel   ★★★ 64% White Friars Hotel,
                  Boreham St, HERSTMONCEUX
                  ☎ 01323 832355 12 ⇄ 🐾 Annexe8 ⇄ 🐾

BRIGHTON & HOVE   Map 04 TQ30

Brighton & Hove Devils Dyke Rd BN1 8YJ
☎ 01273 556482 Fax 01273 556482
Downland course with sea views. Famous drop hole par 3.
9 holes, 5704yds, Par 68, SSS 68, Course record 65.
Club membership 300.
Visitors   must contact in advance, restricted play Wed,
                  Fri & weekends.
Societies   must contact secretary in advance.
Green Fees   £15 per 18 hole; £10 per 9 holes (£25/£15
                  weekends).
Cards   💳 VISA 📷

Prof   Phil Bonsall
Designer   James Braid
Facilities   ⊗ 🏠 💺 ▼ ♀ 🛆 🏠 🕈 🐾 ⊘
Location   4m NW

Hotel   ★★ 61% St Catherines Lodge Hotel, Seafront,
                  Kingsway, HOVE
                  ☎ 01273 778181 50rm(40 ⇄ 🐾)

Dyke Devils Dyke, Dyke Rd BN1 8YJ
☎ 01273 857296 Fax 01273 857078
This downland course has some glorious views both
towards the sea and inland. The best hole on the course
is probably the 17th; it is one of those teasing short holes
of just over 200 yards, and is played across a gully to a
high green.
18 holes, 6611yds, Par 72, SSS 72, Course record 66.
Club membership 750.
Visitors   advisable to contact in advance. May not
                  play before noon on Sun.
Societies   apply by telephone or in writing.
Green Fees   not confirmed.
Prof   Richard Arnold
Designer   Fred Hawtree
Facilities   ⊗ 🏠 💺 ▼ ♀ 🛆 🏠 🕈 🐾 🚃 ⊘
Location   4m N of Brighton, between A23 & A27

Hotel   ★★ 61% St Catherines Lodge Hotel,
                  Seafront, Kingsway, HOVE
                  ☎ 01273 778181 50rm(40 ⇄ 🐾)

East Brighton Roedean Rd BN2 5RA
☎ 01273 604838 Fax 01273 680277
Undulating downland course, overlooking the sea. Windy.
18 holes, 6346yds, Par 72, SSS 70, Course record 62.
Club membership 650.
Visitors   contact in advance & may only play weekends
                  after 11am.
Societies   must contact in advance, handicap certificate
                  required.
Green Fees   £29 per day; £22 per round (£34/£26 weekends
                  and bank holidays).
Cards   💳 VISA 📷 💷
Prof   Mark Stuart-William
Designer   James Braid
Facilities   ⊗ 🏠 💺 ▼ ♀ 🛆 🏠 🕈 🐾 ⊘
Location   2m E of Palace Pier, overlooking marina

Hotel   ★★★ 65% Quality Hotel Brighton, West St,
                  BRIGHTON ☎ 01273 220033 138 ⇄ 🐾

Hollingbury Park Ditchling Rd BN1 7HS
☎ 01273 552010 (sec) & 500086 (res)
Municipal course in hilly situation on the Downs,
overlooking the sea.
18 holes, 6500yds, Par 72, SSS 71, Course record 65.
Club membership 300.
Visitors   must contact in advance.
Societies   telephone the secretary for details.
Green Fees   not confirmed.
Prof   Graeme Crompton
Facilities   🛆 🏠 🕈 🐾 🚃 ⊘
Location   2m N of town centre

Hotel   ★★★ 72% Old Ship Hotel, King's Rd,
                  BRIGHTON ☎ 01273 329001 152 ⇄ 🐾

Waterhall Saddlescombe Rd BN1 8YN ☎ 01273 508658
Hilly downland course with hard walking and open to the
wind. Private club playing over municipal course.
18 holes, 5773yds, Par 69, SSS 68, Course record 66.
Club membership 300.
Visitors   must contact in advance, may not play at start of
day. Restricted tee times Sat and Sun am.
Societies   must contact the secretary in writing or
telephone.
Green Fees £11.50 per round (£15.50 weekends).
Prof   Paul Charman
Facilities   ⊗ ⅲ ⅃ 및 ♀ ♈ 🗑 ⚑ ∮
Location   2m NE from A27

Hotel   ★★ 61% St Catherines Lodge Hotel,
Seafront, Kingsway, HOVE
☎ 01273 778181 50rm(40 ⇆ ⚲)

West Hove Church Farm, Hangleton BN3 8AN
☎ 01273 419738 & 413494 (pro) Fax 01273 439988
A downland course designed by Hawtree & Sons.
18 holes, 6237yds, Par 70, SSS 70, Course record 69.
Club membership 625.
Visitors   tee times by arrangement.
Societies   by arrangement, telephone or write.
Green Fees £32 per day; £22 per round (£37/£27 weekends).
Prof   Darren Cook
Designer   Hawtree & Sons
Facilities   ⊗ ⅃ 및 ♀ ♈ 🗑 ♓ ♒ ∮ ∤
Location   Easy access from A27, N of Brighton

Hotel   ★★ 61% St Catherines Lodge Hotel,
Seafront, Kingsway, HOVE
☎ 01273 778181 50rm(40 ⇆ ⚲)

CROWBOROUGH — Map 05 TQ53

Crowborough Beacon Beacon Rd TN6 1UJ
☎ 01892 661511

Standing some 800 feet above sea level, this is a testing
heathland course, with panoramic views of the South
Downs, Eastbourne and even the sea on a clear day.
18 holes, 6279yds, Par 71, SSS 70, Course record 66.
Club membership 700.
Visitors   must contact in advance & have handicap
certificate but may only play at weekends &
bank holidays after 2.30pm.
Societies   telephone or apply in writing to secretary.
Green Fees £40 per day; £25 per round (£30 per round
weekends & bank holidays).
Prof   D C Newnham
Facilities   ⊗ ⅃ 및 ♀ ♈ 🗑 ⚑ ∮
Location   1m SW on A26

Hotel   ★★★ 76% The Spa Hotel, Mount
Ephraim, TUNBRIDGE WELLS
☎ 01892 520331 74 ⇆

Dewlands Manor Cottage Hill, Rotherfield TN6 3JN
☎ 01892 852266 Fax 01892 853015
A beautifully kept meadowland course with water featrures.
9 holes, 3186yds, Par 36, SSS 70.
Visitors   must telephone in advance.
Societies   telephone for availability.
Green Fees not confirmed.
Cards
Prof   Nick Godin
Designer   R M & N M Godin
Facilities   ⊗ ⅃ 및 ♀ ♈ 🗑 ⚑ ♓ ♒ ∮
& Leisure   indoor teaching facilities.
Location   0.5m S of Rotherfield

Inn   🅾🅾🅾 Plough & Horses Inn, Walshes Rd,
CROWBOROUGH
☎ 01892 652614 8 ⇆ ⚲

DITCHLING — Map 05 TQ31

Mid Sussex Spatham Ln BN6 8XJ
☎ 01273 846567 Fax 01273 845767
Mature parkland course with many trees, water hazards,
strategically placed bunkers and superbly contoured greens.
The 14th hole, a spectacular par 5, demands accurate
shotmaking to avoid the various hazards along its length.
18 holes, 6431yds, Par 71, SSS 71, Course record 65.
Club membership 600.
Visitors   telephone in advance to book tee times. After
2pm at weekends in summer and after 12.30pm
in winter.
Societies   advance booking required.

Green Fees £22 per round 9-3.30pm; £15 per round before 9am & after 3.30pm (£25 weekends after 2pm).
Cards ⊟ 💳 💳 💳 🔄 ⬜
Prof Chris Connell
Designer David Williams
Facilities ⊗ �III 🖫 🍴 🍷 🏊 🏠 ⚑ 🛒 🏌 ⚒ ⚏
Location 1m E of Ditchling village

Hotel ★★★ 77% The Shelleys, High St, LEWES
☎ 01273 472361 19 ⇆ 📢

EASTBOURNE Map 05 TV69

Eastbourne Downs East Dean Rd BN20 8ES
☎ 01323 720827 Fax 01323 412506
This downland course has spectacular views over the South Downs and Channel. Situated in an area of outstanding natural beauty approximately 1 mile behind Beachy Head.
18 holes, 6601yds, Par 72, SSS 72, Course record 70.
Club membership 650.
Visitors a handicap certificate is required for weekends. Visitors may not play before 9.15am weekdays and before 11am weekends except by arrangement.
Societies contact secretary in advance for details.
Green Fees £21 per day, £17 per round (£24/£21 weekends).
Prof T Marshall
Designer J H Taylor
Facilities ⊗ �III 🖫 🍴 🍷 🏊 🏠 ⚑ ⚒
Location 0.5m W of town centre on A259

Hotel ★★★ 76% Lansdowne Hotel, King Edward's Pde, EASTBOURNE
☎ 01323 725174 121 ⇆ 📢

Royal Eastbourne Paradise Dr BN20 8BP
☎ 01323 729738 Fax 01323 729738
A famous club which celebrated its centenary in 1987. The course plays longer than it measures. Testing holes are the 8th, a par 3 played to a high green and the 16th, a par 5 righthand dogleg.
Devonshire Course: 18 holes, 6109yds, Par 71, SSS 69, Course record 62.
Hartington Course: 9 holes, 2147yds, Par 64, SSS 61.
Club membership 800.
Visitors must contact in advance, may not play weekends except by arrangement. Handicap certificate required for Devonshire course.
Societies must apply in advance.
Green Fees not confirmed.
Cards ⊟ 💳 💳 💳 🔄 ⬜
Prof Richard Wooller
Designer Arthur Mayhewe
Facilities ⊗ �III by prior arrangement 🖫 🍴 🍷 🏊 🏠 ⚑ 🛒 🏌 ⚒
Location 0.5m W of town centre

Hotel ★★★ 76% Lansdowne Hotel, King Edward's Pde, EASTBOURNE
☎ 01323 725174 121 ⇆ 📢

Willingdon Southdown Rd, Willingdon BN20 9AA
☎ 01323 410981 Fax 01323 411510
Unique, hilly downland course set in oyster-shaped amphitheatre.

18 holes, 6118yds, Par 69, SSS 69.
Club membership 570.
Visitors must have handicap, by application, may not play at weekends.
Societies apply in advance.
Green Fees seasonal variations £14-£25 per day/round (£16-£28 weekends, £12 after 4pm).
Prof James Debenham
Designer J Taylor/Dr Mackenzie
Facilities ⊗ 🖫 🍴 🍷 🏊 🏠 ⚑ 🛒 🏌 ⚒
Location 0.5m N of town centre off A22

Hotel ★★★ 61% Wish Tower Hotel, King Edward's Pde, EASTBOURNE
☎ 01323 722676 56 ⇆ 📢

FOREST ROW Map 05 TQ43

Ashdown Forest Golf Hotel Chapel Ln RH18 5BB
☎ 01342 824866 Fax 01342 824869
A natural undulating heathland and woodland course cut out of the Ashdown Forest. No sand bunkers, just equally testing heather dunes with the 14th hole regarded as the best. The hotel specialises in catering for golf breaks and societies.
West Course: 18 holes, 5606yds, Par 68, SSS 67.
Club membership 180.
Visitors must contact in advance, bookings up to 6 days in advance. Prepayment required.
Societies must telephone in advance.
Green Fees £21 per day; £16 per round (£26/£21 weekends).
Cards ⊟ 💳 💳 💳 🔄 ⬜
Prof Martyn Landsborough
Facilities ⊗ �III 🖫 🍴 🍷 🏊 🏠 ⚑ 🛒 🏌 ⚒
& Leisure hard tennis courts, fishing.
Location 4m S of East Grinstead off A22 & B2110

Royal Ashdown Forest Chapel Ln RH18 5LR
☎ 01342 822018 Fax 01342 825211
Old Course on undulating heathland. No bunkers. Long
carries off the tees and magnificent views over the
Forest. Not a course for the high handicapper. West
Course on natural heathland. No bunkers.
*Old Course: 18 holes, 6477yds, Par 72, SSS 71, Course
record 67.*
West Course: 18 holes, 5606yds, Par 68, SSS 67.
Club membership 450.

Visitors	restricted weekends & Tue. Must have a handicap certificate on Old Course. No restrictions on West Course.
Societies	must contact in advance.
Green Fees	Old Course: £40 per day/round (£50 weekends). West Course: £21 per day; £16 per round (£26/£21 weekends).
Cards	
Prof	Martyn Landsborough
Facilities	
Location	SE side of Forest Row village, off B2110
Hotel	★★★ 65% Woodbury House Hotel, Lewes Rd, EAST GRINSTEAD ☎ 01342 313657 14

HAILSHAM   Map 05 TQ50

Wellshurst Golf & Country Club North St,
Hellingly BN27 4EE ☎ 01435 813456 Fax 01435 812444
There are outstanding views of the South Downs and the
Weald Valley from this 18-hole, well-manicured, undulating
course. There are varied features and some water hazards. A
practice sand bunker, putting green and driving range are
available to improve your golf. the clubhouse and leisure
facilities are open to visitors.
18 holes, 5771yds, Par 70, SSS 68, Course record 64.
Club membership 320.

Visitors	no restrictions but advisable to book.
Societies	telephone in advance to book tee times.
Green Fees	£22 per day; £16 per 18 holes (£28/£20 weekends & bank holidays).
Cards	
Prof	Mark Jarvis
Designer	The Golf Corporation
Facilities	
& Leisure	sauna, solarium, gymnasium.
Location	2.5m N of Hailsham, on A267
Hotel	★★ 68% The Olde Forge Hotel & Restaurant, Magham Down, HAILSHAM ☎ 01323 842893 8

HASTINGS & ST LEONARDS   Map 05 TQ80

Hastings Beauport Park Estate, St Leonards TN38 0TA
☎ 01424 852981
Played over Hastings Public Course. Undulating parkland
with stream and fine views.
18 holes, 6248yds, Par 71, SSS 70, Course record 70.
Club membership 400.

Visitors	no restrictions.
Societies	arrangement by telephone.
Green Fees	not confirmed.
Prof	Charles Giddins

Facilities	
& Leisure	hard tennis courts, outdoor swimming pool.
Location	3m N of Hastings on A2100
Hotel	★★★♨ 70% Beauport Park Hotel, Battle Rd, HASTINGS ☎ 01424 851222 23

HEATHFIELD   Map 05 TQ52

Horam Park Chiddingly Rd, Horam TN21 0JJ
☎ 01435 813477 Fax 01435 813677
A pretty woodland course with lakes.
9 holes, 6237yds, Par 70, SSS 68, Course record 64.
Club membership 450.

Visitors	contact for tee times.
Societies	prior booking required.
Green Fees	not confirmed.
Cards	
Prof	Liam Greasley
Designer	Glen Johnson
Facilities	
Location	Off A267
Hotel	★★★ 69% Boship Farm Hotel, Lower Dicker, HAILSHAM ☎ 01323 844826 Annexe47

HOLTYE   Map 05 TQ43

Holtye TN8 7ED
☎ 01342 850635 & 850576 Fax 01342 850576
Undulating forest/heathland course with tree-lined fairways
providing testing golf. Different tees on back nine.

9 holes, 5325yds, Par 66, SSS 66, Course record 62.
Club membership 430.

Visitors	may not play mornings Wed-Thu & weekends.
Societies	Tue & Fri by arrangement.
Green Fees	£16 per day/round (£18 weekends & bank holidays). £10 per 9 holes (£13 weekends).
Prof	Kevin Hinton
Facilities	⊗ ⓚ ♦ ♥ ♀ ♐ ✓
Location	4m E of East Grinstead and 6m W of Tunbridge Wells on A264

Hotel	★★★ 65% Woodbury House Hotel, Lewes Rd, EAST GRINSTEAD ☎ 01342 313657 14 ⇌ ℞

LEWES   Map 05 TQ41

Lewes Chapel Hill BN7 2BB ☎ 01273 483474 & 473245
Downland course. Fine views.
18 holes, 6213yds, Par 71, SSS 70, Course record 65.
Club membership 660.

Visitors	may not play at weekends before 2pm. Bookings taken up to 7 days in advance.
Societies	must contact in advance.
Green Fees	not confirmed.
Prof	Paul Dobson
Designer	Jack Rowe
Facilities	⊗ ⓚ ♦ ♥ ♀ ♐ ♠ ✓
Location	E side of town centre

Hotel	★★★ 67% White Hart Hotel, 55 High St, LEWES ☎ 01273 476694 23rm(19 ⇌ ℞) Annexe29 ⇌ ℞

NEWHAVEN   Map 05 TQ40

Peacehaven Brighton Rd BN9 9UH ☎ 01273 512571
Downland course, sometimes windy. Testing holes: 1st (par 3), 4th (par 4), 9th (par 3), 10th (par 3), 18th (par 3).
9 holes, 5305yds, Par 69, SSS 66.
Club membership 270.

Visitors	may not play before 11am weekends.
Societies	telephone in advance.
Green Fees	not confirmed.
Prof	Gerry Williams
Designer	James Braid
Facilities	⊗ ⓚ ♦ ♥ ♀ ♐ ♠ ✓
Location	0.75m W on A259

Hotel	★★★ 67% The Star Inn, ALFRISTON ☎ 01323 870495 37 ⇌ ℞

RYE   Map 05 TQ92

Rye New Lydd Rd, Camber TN31 7QS
☎ 01797 225241 Fax 01797 225460
Typical links course with superb greens and views.
Old Course: 18 holes, 6317yds, Par 68, SSS 71, Course record 64.
Jubilee Course: 9 holes, 6141yds, Par 71, SSS 70.
Club membership 1100.

Visitors	must be invited/introduced by a member.
Green Fees	on application.
Prof	Michael Lee
Designer	H S Colt
Facilities	⊗ ♥ ♀ ♐ ♠ ✓

Location	2.75m SE off A259
Hotel	★★★ 61% The George, High St, RYE ☎ 01797 222114 22 ⇌ ℞

SEAFORD   Map 05 TV49

Seaford Firle Rd, East Blatchington BN25 2JD
☎ 01323 892442 Fax 01323 89113
The great H. Taylor did not perhaps design as many courses as his friend and rival, James Braid, but Seaford's original design was Taylor's. It is a splendid downland course with magnificent views and some fine holes.
18 holes, 6551yds, Par 69, SSS 71.
Club membership 600.

Visitors	must contact in advance.
Societies	must contact in advance.
Green Fees	£35 per 36 holes; £25 per round.
Cards	💳
Prof	David Mills
Designer	J H Taylor
Facilities	⊗ ⓜ ⓚ ♦ ♥ ♀ ♐ ♠ ⛳ ✓ ♣
Location	Turn inland at war memorial off A259

Hotel	★★★ 67% The Star Inn, ALFRISTON ☎ 01323 870495 37 ⇌ ℞

Seaford Head Southdown Rd BN25 4JS
☎ 01323 890139 & 894843
A links type course situated on the cliff edge giving exception views over the Seven Sisters and coastline. The upper level is reached via a short hole with elevated green - known as the 'Hell Hole' and the 18th Par 5 tee is on the 'Head' being 300 feet above sea level.
18 holes, 5848yds, Par 71, SSS 68, Course record 63.
Club membership 450.

Visitors	No restrictions.
Societies	write or telephone the Pro's shop.
Green Fees	not confirmed.
Prof	Tony Lowles
Facilities	⊗ ⓜ ⓚ ♦ ♥ ♀ ♐ ♠ ⛳ ✓

Hotel	★★★ 64% Deans Place, Seaford Rd, ALFRISTON ☎ 01323 870248 36 ⇌ ℞

SEDLESCOMBE   Map 05 TQ71

Sedlescombe Kent St TN33 0SD
☎ 01424 870898 Fax 01424 870855
Situated in the beautiful Sussex countryside. The natural water and tree line adds to the beauty as well as making it an enjoyable round of golf.
18 holes, 6359yds, Par 71, SSS 70, Course record 68.
Club membership 300.

Visitors	please telephone and reserve tee times.
Societies	please telephone to reserve tee times.
Green Fees	£20 per day; £15 per 18 holes; £10 per 9 holes (£24/£18/£12 weekends).
Cards	💳
Prof	James Andrews
Facilities	⊗ ⓚ ♦ ♥ ♀ ♐ ♠ ⛳ ✓ ♣
Location	A21, 4m N of Hastings

Hotel	★★★ 67% Brickwall Hotel, The Green, SEDLESCOMBE ☎ 01424 870253 23 ⇌ ℞

TICEHURST   Map 05 TQ63

Dale Hill Hotel & Golf Club TN5 7DQ
☎ 01580 200112 Fax 01580 201249
Picturesque course with woodland, water and gently
undulating fairways. Hotel and leisure centre within
grounds.
Dale Hill: 18 holes, 6106yds, Par 70, SSS 69.
Ian Woosnam: 18 holes, 6512yds, Par 71, SSS 71.
Club membership 950.

Visitors	booking only 7 days in advance.
Societies	must contact in advance.
Green Fees	not confirmed.
Cards	▨ ▨ ▨ ▨ ▨
Prof	Andrew Good
Designer	Ian Woosnam
Facilities	⊗ 米 ▮ 📷 🍴 🏌 ⛳ ⚐ ♪
& Leisure	heated indoor swimming pool, sauna, solarium, gymnasium.
Location	N side of village off B2087

Hotel	★★★★ 67% Dale Hill Hotel & Golf Club, TICEHURST ☎ 01580 200112 26 ⇌ ♠

UCKFIELD   Map 05 TQ42

EAST SUSSEX NATIONAL   See page 253

Piltdown Piltdown TN22 3XB
☎ 01825 722033 Fax 01825 724192
Natural heathland course with much heather and gorse. No
bunkers, easy walking, fine views.
18 holes, 6070yds, Par 68, SSS 69, Course record 67.
Club membership 400.

Visitors	must telephone pro shop in advance 01825 722389 and have a handicap certificate. Play on Tue, Thu and weekends is restricted.
Societies	must contact in writing.
Green Fees	£32 per day; £27.50 per round.
Prof	John Amos
Facilities	⊗ ▮ 📷 🍴 🏌 ⛳ ⚐ ♪
Location	3m NW off A272

Hotel	★★★ 63% Halland Forge Hotel & Restaurant, HALLAND ☎ 01825 840456 Annexe20 ⇌ ♠

SUSSEX, WEST

ANGMERING   Map 04 TQ00

Ham Manor BN16 4JE
☎ 01903 783288 Fax 01903 850886
Two miles from the sea, this parkland course has fine
springy turf and provides an interesting test in two loops
of nine holes each.
18 holes, 6267yds, Par 70, SSS 70, Course record 64.
Club membership 780.

Visitors	must have a handicap certificate. Telephone pro shop in advance 01903 783732.
Societies	telephone for details

Green Fees	£26 (£40 weekends).
Prof	Simon Buckley
Designer	Harry Colt
Facilities	⛳ 📷 ♪
Location	Off A259

Hotel	★★★ 62% Chatsworth Hotel, Steyne, WORTHING ☎ 01903 236103 107 ⇌ ♠

ARUNDEL   Map 04 TQ00

Avisford Park Yapton Ln, Walberton BN18 0LS
☎ 01243 554611 Fax 01243 555580
Newly extended course - now 18-holes - enjoying a country
hotel complex setting. The course opens with a real challenge
as there is out of bounds water and tree hazards the whole
length of this 414yard drive.
18 holes, 5703yds, Par 68, SSS 66.
Club membership 100.

Visitors	must contact in advance for weekend play.
Societies	apply in writing or telephone.
Green Fees	not confirmed.
Cards	▨ ▨
Prof	Richard Beach
Facilities	⊗ ▮ 📷 🍴 🏌 ⛳ ⚐ ♪
Location	Off A27, towards Yapton

Hotel	★★★ 68% Norfolk Arms Hotel, High St, ARUNDEL ☎ 01903 882101 21 ⇌ Annexe13 ⇌

BOGNOR REGIS   Map 04 SZ99

Bognor Regis Downview Rd, Felpham PO22 8JD
☎ 01243 821929 (Secretary) Fax 01243 860719
This flattish, well tree lined, parkland course has more
variety than is to be found on some other South Coast
courses. The club is also known far and wide for its
enterprise in creating a social atmosphere. The course is
open to the prevailing wind and the river Rife and many
water ditches need negotiation.
18 holes, 6238yds, Par 70, SSS 70, Course record 64.
Club membership 700.

Visitors	handicap certificate required, must play with member at weekends. Must contact in advance (pro shop 01243 865209).
Societies	phone initially.
Green Fees	£25 per day/round (£30 weekends & bank holidays).
Prof	Stephen Bassil
Designer	James Braid
Facilities	⊗ ▮ 📷 🍴 🏌 ⛳ ♪
Location	0.5m N at Felpham traffic lights on A259

Hotel	★★ 67% Aldwick Hotel, Aldwick Rd, Aldwick, BOGNOR REGIS ☎ 01243 821945 19 ⇌ ♠

BURGESS HILL   Map 04 TQ31

Burgess Hill Cuckfield Rd RH15 8RE
☎ 01444 258585 Fax 247318
Opened May 1998, an academy course bordered by a tributary
of the River Adur. Facilities available for public use include a
floodlit driving range and a large sweeping putting green. ▶

EAST SUSSEX NATIONAL

Uckfield *East Sussex* ☎ **01825 880088**
Fax 01825 880066   **Map 05 TQ42**

John Ingham writes: Designed by Bob Cupp on a grand championship scale and opened in 1989, East Sussex National presents two massive courses, one more than 7000 yards long. Both are ideal for big-hitting professionals and already they have staged the European Open here. Boasting a driving range and a Golf Academy, Bob Cupp, once a designer for Jack Nicklaus, decided to use what they call 'bent' grass from tee to green - and the result is an American-type course to test everyone, depending upon which tee you drive from.

Could either course, brand spanking new, compare with the other Sussex classics of Pulborough (West Sussex) and Royal Ashdown Forest, a gem of a place near Forest Row and a course without a single bunker? When first I drove into the vastness of the car park and eyed the huge redbrick clubhouse, I admit it all looked daunting. The experience is not unlike entering a hotel-country club complex in the United States, signing in as one does at the reception area before walking across a suspended corridor towards the huge and well-stocked professional's shop.

The East Sussex National offers the most modern day's golf in the United Kingdom. The greens on both the East and West courses are immaculate and groomed to perfection. Strike the putt solidly and on-line, and it must go in! While it's true that 50,000 spectators can watch you hole out on the last green, it's just as true that on a quiet day out, you can enjoy letting out plenty of shaft without fear of hitting valuable balls into thick woods.

The West course is reserved for members and their guests, but visitors are welcomed on the other course.

Visitors	Contact Advance Reservations for details.
Societies	must contact Advance Reservations (01825 880231)
Green fees	Telephone 01825 880232 for current details. ⊟ ▦ ▦ ▦ ▣ ▨
Facilities	⊗ ▥ ⊞ ⌷ ♥ ♀ 🛏 ⌂ ♠ ⚲ ⚘ 🏐 ♂ ⚲ Professional (Iain Naylor), David Leadbetter Golf Academy.
Leisure	hard court tennis, indoor swimming, sauna, solarium.
Location	Little Horsted TN22 5ES (2m S on A22)

36 holes. East Course 18 holes, 6760yds, Par72 SSS 72
Course record 63
West Course 18 holes, 6638yds, Par 72, SSS72. Course record 64

WHERE TO STAY AND EAT NEARBY

HOTELS:

UCKFIELD
★★★★🏵 🏵 **71%** Buxted Park Country House Hotel, Buxted ☎ 01825 732711 44 ⇄ ⋔

★★★ 🏵 🏵 🏵 ♨♨ **77%** Horsted Place Sporting Estate & Hotel, Little Horsted ☎ 01825 750581. 17 ⇄ ⋔

HALLAND
★★★ **63%** Halland Forge
☎ 01825 840456. Annexe 20 (3 ⋔ 17 ⇄ ⋔)

NEWICK
★★★🏵 🏵 **75%** Newick Park Country Estate ☎ 01825 723633 13 (9 ⇄⋔ 4 ⋔)

9 holes, 1250yds, Par 27.
Societies   contact in advance.
Green Fees not confirmed.
Cards
Prof   Giles Downer
Designer   Donald Steel
Facilities
Location   N of town on B2036

Hotel   ★★★🛏 77% Ockenden Manor, Ockenden Ln,
                CUCKFIELD ☎ 01444 416111 22 ⇥ 🅁

CHICHESTER   Map 04 SU80

Chichester Hunston Village PO20 6AX
☎ 01243 533833 Fax 01243 539922
Set amongst lush farmland, the Tower course has four lakes
which bring water into play on seven holes. The Florida-style
Cathedral course was opened in spring 1994. There is also a
9-hole par 3 and a floodlit driving range.
*Tower Course: 18 holes, 6175yds, Par 72, SSS 69, Course
record 67.*
*Cathedral Course: 18 holes, 6461yds, Par 72, SSS 69,
Course record 70.*
Club membership 600.
Visitors   a strict dress code is in operation. Must contact
                in advance. Tee reservations up to 7 days in
                advance on 01243 533833.
Societies   must contact in advance.
Green Fees £15 per round (£20 weekends).
Cards
Prof   John Slinger
Designer   Philip Saunders
Facilities
Location   3m S of Chichester, on B2145 at Hunston

Hotel   ★★★ 67% The Ship Hotel, North St,
                CHICHESTER ☎ 01243 778000 34 ⇥ 🅁

COPTHORNE   Map 05 TQ33

Copthorne Borers Arms Rd RH10 3LL
☎ 01342 712033 & 712058 Fax 01342 717682
Despite it having been in existence since 1892, this club
remains one of the lesser known Sussex courses. It is
hard to know why because it is most attractive with
plenty of trees and much variety
18 holes, 6505yds, Par 71, SSS 71, Course record 67.
Club membership 550.
Visitors   advised to contact in advance, may not play
                weekends before 1pm.
Societies   must contact in advance.
Green Fees £38 per day; £30 per round (£32 per round
                after 1pm at weekends).
Prof   Joe Burrell
Designer   James Braid
Facilities
Location   E side of village junc 10 of M23 off A264

Hotel   ★★★★ 70% Copthorne London Gatwick,
                Copthorne Way, COPTHORNE
                ☎ 01342 714971 227 ⇥ 🅁

Effingham Park The Copthorne Effingham Park, Hotel,
West Park Rd RH10 3EU ☎ 01342 716528 Fax 716039
Parkland course.

9 holes, 1769yds, Par 30, SSS 57, Course record 28.
Club membership 390.
Visitors   restricted at weekends before 11am and not after
                4pm Tue, Apr-Oct.
Societies   Mon-Fri, and Sat/Sun after 1pm, must
                write/telephone in advance.
Green Fees not confirmed.
Cards
Prof   Mark Root
Designer   Francisco Escario
Facilities
& Leisure   hard tennis courts, heated indoor swimming
                pool, sauna, solarium, gymnasium.
Location   2m E on B2028

Hotel   ★★★★ 63% Copthorne Effingham Park,
                West Park Rd, COPTHORNE
                ☎ 01342 714994 122 ⇥ 🅁

CRAWLEY   Map 04 TQ23

Cottesmore Buchan Hill, Pease Pottage RH11 9AT
☎ 01293 528256 Fax 01293 522819
The course was originally founded in 1974. The Griffin
course is undulating with four holes are over water. The
newer Phoenix course is shorter and less testing. But both are
lined by silver birch, pine and oak, with rhododendrons
ablaze in June.
Griffin Course: 18 holes, 6248yds, Par 71, SSS 70.
Phoenix Course: 18 holes, 5514yds, Par 69, SSS 67.
Club membership 1500.
Visitors   dress code applies
Societies   must telephone in advance.
Green Fees Griffin: £30 per day; £18 per round (£40/£24
                weekends). Phoenix: £22 per day; £15 per round
                (£28/£20 weekends).
Cards
Prof   Calum J Callan
Designer   Michael J Rogerson
Facilities
& Leisure   hard tennis courts, heated indoor swimming
                pool, squash, sauna, solarium, gymnasium.
Location   3m SW 1m W of M23 junc 11

Hotel   ★★★★ 66% Holiday Inn London-Gatwick,
                Langley Dr, CRAWLEY
                ☎ 01293 529991 223 ⇥ 🅁

Ifield Golf & Country Club Rusper Rd, Ifield RH11 0LN
☎ 01293 520222 Fax 01293 612973
Parkland course.
18 holes, 6330yds, Par 70, SSS 70, Course record 65.
Club membership 750.

Visitors	must contact professional in advance. Must be guest of member at weekends.
Societies	apply in advance.
Green Fees	£32 per day; £22 per round weekdays.
Cards	— 🔤 📇 💳
Prof	Jonathan Earl
Designer	Bernard Darwin
Facilities	⊗ 🛒 🍴 🍽 ♀ ⚞ 🏠 ⛳ 🛶 🏌 ⌀
& Leisure	squash.
Location	1m W side of town centre off A23

Hotel	★★★★ 66% Holiday Inn London-Gatwick, Langley Dr, CRAWLEY ☎ 01293 529991 223 ⇆ 🐾

Tilgate Forest Golf Centre Titmus Dr RH10 5EU
☎ 01293 530103
Designed by former Ryder Cup players Neil Coles and Brian Huggett, the course has been carefully cut through a silver birch and pine forest. It is possibly one of th most beautiful public courses in the country. The 17th is a treacherous Par 5 demanding an uphill third shot to a green surrounded by rhododendrons.
18 holes, 6359yds, Par 72, SSS 69 or 9 holes, 1136yds, Par 27.

Visitors	may book up to 7 days in advance.
Societies	telephone in advance for details.
Green Fees	not confirmed.
Prof	Sean Trussell
Designer	Neil Coles/Brian Huggett
Facilities	⊗ 🛒 🍴 🍽 ♀ ⚞ 🏠 ⛳ ⌀ 🍴
Hotel	★★★★ 66% Holiday Inn London-Gatwick, Langley Dr, CRAWLEY ☎ 01293 529991 223 ⇆ 🐾

GOODWOOD   Map 04 SU80

Goodwood Kennel Hill PO18 0PN
☎ 01243 774968 Fax 01243 781741
Downland course designed by the master architect, James Braid. Many notable holes, particularly the finishing ones: 17 down an avenue of beech trees and 18 along in front of the terrace. Superb views of the downs and the coast.
18 holes, 6434yds, Par 72, SSS 71.
Club membership 930.

Visitors	must have handicap certificate
Societies	Wed & Thu, telephone secretary in advance.
Green Fees	£32 per day (£42 weekends).
Prof	Keith MacDonald
Designer	J Braid
Facilities	⊗ 🛒 by prior arrangement 🛒 🍴 ♀ ⚞ 🏠 🍴 🛶 🏌 ⌀
Location	3m NE of Chichester off A27

Hotel	★★★★ 70% Marriott Goodwood Park Hotel & Country Club, GOODWOOD ☎ 01243 775537 94 ⇆ 🐾

Marriott Goodwood Park Hotel & Country Club
PO18 0QB ☎ 01243 775537 Fax 01243 520120
A parkland course set within the 12,000 acre Goodwood estate.
18 holes, 6579yds, Par 72, SSS 71, Course record 66.
Club membership 700.

Visitors	must hold a current handicap certificate.
Societies	telephone or write.

Green Fees	£28 per round (£35 weekends).
Cards	— 🔤 💳 📇 💳
Prof	Adrian Wratting
Designer	Donald Steele
Facilities	⊗ 🛒 🍴 🍽 ♀ ⚞ 🏠 ⛳ 🛶 🏌 ⌀
& Leisure	hard tennis courts, heated indoor swimming pool, sauna, solarium, gymnasium.
Location	3m N of Chichester, in the grounds of Goodwood House

---

Hotel	★★★★ 70% Marriott Goodwood Park Hotel & Country Club, GOODWOOD ☎ 01243 775537 94 ⇆ 🐾

HASSOCKS   Map 04 TQ31

Hassocks London Rd BN6 9NA
☎ 01273 846630 Fax 01273 846070
Set against the backdrop of the South Downs, Hassocks is an 18 hole par 70 course designed and contoured to blend naturally with the surrounding countryside. A friendly and relaxed course, appealing to golfers of all ages and abilities.
18 holes, 5754yds, Par 70, SSS 68, Course record 73.
Club membership 350.

Visitors	phone Pro. shop in advance.
Societies	apply in writing or telephone in advance.
Green Fees	£14.25 (£17.50 weekends).
Cards	— 🔤 💳 📇 🔤 💳
Prof	Charles Ledger
Designer	Paul Wright
Facilities	⊗ 🛒 🍴 🍽 ♀ ⚞ 🏠 ⛳ 🛶 🏌 ⌀
Location	On the A273 between Burgess Hill and Hassocks

Hotel	★★★ 63% The Hickstead Hotel, Jobs Ln, Bolney, HICKSTEAD ☎ 01444 248023 50 ⇆ 🐾

HAYWARDS HEATH   Map 05 TQ32

Haywards Heath High Beech Ln RH16 1SL
☎ 01444 414457 Fax 01444 458319
Pleasant parkland course with several challenging par 4s and 3s.
18 holes, 6204yds, Par 71, SSS 70, Course record 66.
Club membership 770.

Visitors	must have a handicap certificate. Must contact in advance.
Societies	Wed & Thu only by prior arrangement with the secretary.
Green Fees	not confirmed.
Prof	Michael Henning	▶

Facilities ⚐ 🏠 ⚙ ♂ ⚶
Location 1.25m N off B2028

Hotel ★★★🏖️ 77% Ockenden Manor, Ockenden Ln,
CUCKFIELD ☎ 01444 416111 22 ⇔ ☞

Paxhill Park East Mascalls Ln, Lindfield RH16 2QN
☎ 01444 484467 Fax 01444 482709
A relatively flat parkland course designed by Patrick Tallack.
Water hazard on 5th, 13th and 14th holes.
18 holes, 6117yds, Par 70, SSS 69, Course record 67.
Club membership 430.
Visitors welcome but may not play weekend mornings.
Societies must contact in advance.
Green Fees £25 per day; £15 per round (£20 weekend &
bank holidays).
Cards ⬚ ■ ⬛ ⬛ ⬛ ⬛ ⬛
Prof Paul Lyons
Designer P Tallack
Facilities ⊗ ⌇ by prior arrangement 🍴 ☕ ♀ ⚐ 🏠 ⚙ ♂ ⚶

Hotel ★★★🏖️ 77% Ockenden Manor, Ockenden Ln,
CUCKFIELD ☎ 01444 416111 22 ⇔ ☞

HORSHAM   Map 04 TQ13

See also **Slinfold**

Horsham Worthing Rd RH13 7AX
☎ 01403 271525 Fax 01403 274528
A short but challenging course with six Par 4s and three Par
3s''s, two of which are played across water. Designed for
beginners and intermediates but also challenges better
players with a standard scratch of six below par.
9 holes, 4122yds, Par 33, SSS 30, Course record 55.
Club membership 250.
Visitors no restrictions other than not until after 11am on
Sat.
Societies apply in advance.
Green Fees not confirmed.
Cards ⬚ ■ ⬛ ⬛ ⬛ ⬛ ⬛
Prof Neil Burke
Facilities ⊗ 🍴 ☕ ♀ ⚐ 🏠 ⚙ ♂ ⚶
& Leisure gymnasium.
Location Off A24 rdbt, between Horsham/Southwater, by
garage on B2237

Hotel ★★ 67% Ye Olde King's Head Hotel,
Carfax, HORSHAM
☎ 01403 253126 42rm(41 ⇔ ☞)

HURSTPIERPOINT   Map 04 TQ21

Singing Hills Albourne BN6 9EB
☎ 01273 835353 Fax 01273 835444
Three distinct nines (Lake, River & Valley) can be combined
to make a truly varied game. Gently undulating fairways and
spectacular waterholes make Singing Hills a test of accurate
shotmaking. The opening 2 holes of the Rive Nine have long
drives, while the second hole on the Lake course is an Island
green where the tee is also protected by two bunkers. The
Valley Course demand long, accurate tee shots.
Lake: 9 holes, 3253yds, Par 35, SSS 35.
River: 9 holes, 2826yds, Par 34, SSS 34.
Valley: 9 holes, 3348yds, Par 36, SSS 36.
Club membership 390.

Visitors no restrictions, but strict dress code observed
Societies apply in advance.
Green Fees £28 per day; £18 per 18 holes (£36/£26
weekends & bank holidays).
Cards ⬚ ■ ⬛ ⬛ ⬛ ⬛ ⬛
Prof Wallace Street
Designer M R M Sandow
Facilities ⊗ ⌇ by prior arrangement 🍴 ☕ ♀ ⚐ 🏠 ⚙ ♂
⚶
Location Off A23, on B2117

Hotel ★★★ 63% The Hickstead Hotel, Jobs Ln,
Bolney, HICKSTEAD
☎ 01444 248023 50 ⇔ ☞

LITTLEHAMPTON   Map 04 TQ00

Littlehampton Rope Walk, West Beach BN17 5DL
☎ 01903 717170 Fax 726629
A delightful seaside links in an equally delightful setting
- and the only links course in the area.
18 holes, 6244yds, Par 70, SSS 70, Course record 62.
Club membership 650.
Visitors contact in advance & must have handicap
certificate.
Societies welcome weekdays.
Green Fees not confirmed.
Prof Guy McQuitty
Facilities ⊗ 🍴 ☕ ♀ ⚐ 🏠 ♣ ⚶
Location 1m W off A259

Hotel ★★★ 78% Bailiffscourt Hotel,
CLIMPING ☎ 01903 723511
10 ⇔ ☞ Annexe22 ⇔ ☞

LOWER BEEDING   Map 04 TQ22

Brookfield RH13 6LY ☎ 01403 891191
An 8 hole practice course and a driving range, designed as an
executive course for beginners and those who find if difficult
to play a full 18 holes. It is very popular.
8 holes.
Visitors   no restrictions.
Societies   & groups apply in writing or telephone.
Green Fees   not confirmed.
Facilities   ⊗ ⅲ ⓑ ⓛ ⓟ ♀ ⊨
& Leisure   fishing.

Hotel   ★★ 64% Brookfield Farm Hotel,
                  Winterpit Ln, Lower Beeding, HORSHAM
                  ☎ 01403 891191 17rm
Additional   ★★★★⚘South Lodge Hotel, Brighton Rd,
hotel   LOWER BEEDING
                  ☎ 01403 891711 Fax 01403 891253 39 ⇦

MANNINGS HEATH   Map 04 TQ22

Mannings Heath Fullers, Hammerpond Rd RH13 6PG
☎ 01403 210228 Fax 01403 270974
The course meanders up hill and down dale over
heathland with streams affecting 11 of the holes.
Wooded valleys protect the course from strong winds.
Famous holes at 12th (the 'Waterfall', par 3), 13th (the
'Valley', par 4).
*Waterfall: 18 holes, 6378yds, Par 71, SSS 70, Course
record 66.*
Kingfisher: 18 holes, 6217yds, Par 70, SSS 70.
Club membership 700.
Visitors   may book up to 7 days in advance.
Societies   must contact in advance.
Green Fees   not confirmed.
Cards   ⊟ ⊟ ⟐ ⊟ ⊟
Prof   Clive Tucker
Designer   David Williams
Facilities   ⊗ ⅲ ⓑ ⓛ ⓟ ♀ ⚘ ⓖ ⛳ ♣ ♨ ⚑ ⓕ
& Leisure   hard tennis courts, fishing, sauna, chipping
                  practice area.
Location   M23 junct 11, take A281 from Horsham or
                  Brighton. Club on N side of village

Hotel   ★★★★⚘ South Lodge Hotel, Brighton
                  Rd, LOWER BEEDING
                  ☎ 01403 891711 39 ⇦

MIDHURST   Map 04 SU82

Cowdray Park Petworth Rd GU29 0BB
☎ 01730 813599 Fax 01730 815900
Undulating parkland course with scenic views of surrounding
countryside, including Elizabethan ruins. The course is
situated in a National Park oruginally designed by Capability
Brown in the 18th century.
18 holes, 6212yds, Par 70, SSS 70, Course record 66.
Club membership 720.
Visitors   advised to contact in advance.
Societies   apply in writing/telephone/e-mail/fax.
Green Fees   £26 (£36 weeeknds after 11.30am).
Prof   Richard Gough
Designer   Jack White
Facilities   ⊗ ⅲ ⓑ ⓛ ⓟ ♀ ⚘ ⓖ ♣ ⚑ ⓕ
Location   1m E of Midhurst on A272

Hotel   ★★★ 77% Spread Eagle Hotel and Health Spa,
                  South St, MIDHURST
                  ☎ 01730 816911 35 ⇦ ⓕ Annexe4 ⓕ

PULBOROUGH   Map 04 TQ01

West Sussex Golf Club Ln, Wiggonholt RH20 2EN
☎ 01798 872563 Fax 01798 872033
Heathland course.
18 holes, 6221yds, Par 68, SSS 70, Course record 61.
Club membership 850.
Visitors   must contact in advance, may not play
                  weekends.
Societies   Wed & Thu only, apply in writing.
Green Fees   £55 per 2 rounds; £42.50 per round;
                  (£60/£50 per round weekends.)
Prof   Tim Packham
Designer   Campbell/Hutcheson
Facilities   ⊗ ⓑ ⓛ ⓟ ♀ ⚘ ⓖ ⚑ ⓕ ⓖ ⓕ
Location   1.5m E off A283

Hotel   ★★★ 67% Roundabout Hotel,
                  Monkmead Ln, WEST CHILTINGTON
                  ☎ 01798 813838 23 ⇦ ⓕ

PYECOMBE   Map 04 TQ21

Pyecombe Clayton Hill BN45 7FF
☎ 01273 845372 Fax 01273 843338
Typical downland course on the inland side of the South
Downs. Picturesque with magnificent views.
18 holes, 6278yds, Par 71, SSS 70, Course record 67.
Club membership 700.
Visitors   must contact in advance and may only play after
                  9.15am weekdays and after 2.15pm weekends
Societies   telephone secretary in advance.
Green Fees   £18 per round (£25 weekends).
Prof   C R White
Facilities   ⊗ ⓑ ⓛ ⓟ ♀ ⚘ ⓖ ⚑ ⓕ ⓖ
Location   E side of village on A273

Hotel   ★★★ 64% Courtlands Hotel,
                  21-27 The Drive, HOVE
                  ☎ 01273 731055 56 ⇦ ⓕ Annexe12 ⇦ ⓕ

SELSEY   Map 04 SZ89

Selsey Golf Links Ln PO20 9DR
☎ 01243 602203
Fairly difficult seaside course, exposed to wind and has
natural ditches.
9 holes, 5834yds, Par 68, SSS 68, Course record 64.
Club membership 360.
Visitors   must contact in advance.
Societies   must contact in advance in writing
Green Fees   not confirmed.
Prof   Peter Grindley
Designer   J H Taylor
Facilities   ⊗ ⅲ ⓑ ⓛ ⓟ ♀ ⚘ ⓖ ⓕ
& Leisure   hard tennis courts, bowling, tennis.
Location   1m N off B2145

Hotel   ★★★ 67% The Ship Hotel,
                  North St, CHICHESTER
                  ☎ 01243 778000 34 ⇦ ⓕ

SLINFOLD   Map 04 TQ13

Slinfold Park Golf & Country Club
Stane St RH13 7RE
☎ 01403 791555 Fax 01403 791465
Opened for play in spring 1993, Slinfold course enjoys splendid views among mature trees. The 10th tee is spectacularly located on the centre of one of the two large landscaped lakes. The 166-yard 16th has water running in front of of the tee and everything sloping towards it!
Championship Course: 18 holes, 6407yds, Par 72, SSS 71, Course record 64.
Academy Course: 9 holes, 1315yds, Par 28.
Club membership 611.
Visitors   subject to booking.
Societies   advance booking required, weekends and bank holidays not available.
Green Fees £25 per round.
Cards
Prof   T Clingan
Designer   John Fortune
Facilities
Location   4m W on the A29

Hotel   ★★★ 72% Random Hall Hotel, Stane St, Slinford, HORSHAM
☎ 01403 790558   15

WEST CHILTINGTON   Map 04 TQ01

West Chiltington Broadford Bridge Rd RH20 2YA
☎ 01798 813574 Fax 01798 812631
The Main Course is situated on gently undulating, well-drained greens and offers panoramic views of the Sussex Downs. Three large double greens provide an interesting feature to this new course. Also 9-hole short course and 13-bay driving range.
Windmill: 18 holes, 5888yds, Par 70, SSS 69, Course record 66 or 9 holes, 1360yds, Par 28.
Visitors   book tee times in advance.
Societies   by prior arrangement.
Green Fees not confirmed.
Prof   Barrie Aram
Designer   Brian Barnes
Facilities
Location   On N side of village

Hotel   ★★★ 67% Roundabout Hotel, Monkmead Ln, WEST CHILTINGTON
☎ 01798 813838   23

WORTHING   Map 04 TQ10

Hill Barn Municipal Hill Barn Ln BN14 9QE
☎ 01903 237301
Downland course with views of both Isle of Wight and Brighton.
18 holes, 6224yds, Par 70, SSS 70.
Club membership 1000.
Visitors   no restrictions, but advisable to book tee times.
Societies   must telephone in advance.
Green Fees not confirmed.
Cards
Prof   S Blanchard
Facilities
Location   N side of town at junction of A24/A27

Hotel   ★★★ 62% Chatsworth Hotel, Steyne, WORTHING
☎ 01903 236103 107

Worthing Links Rd BN14 9QZ
☎ 01903 260801 Fax 694664
The Upper Course, short and tricky with entrancing views, will provide good entertainment. 'Lower Course' is considered to be one of the best downland courses in the country.
Lower Course: 18 holes, 6530yds, Par 71, SSS 72, Course record 62.
Upper Course: 18 holes, 5243yds, Par 66, SSS 66.
Club membership 1200.
Visitors   advisable to contact in advance, not weekends during GMT.
Societies   contact in advance.
Green Fees £35 per day; £25 per round Lower Course, £20 per round Upper Course (£40 per day, £30 per round either course weekends & bank holidays).
Prof   Stephen Rolley
Designer   H S Colt
Facilities
Location   N side of town centre off A27

Hotel   ★★★ 71% Ardington Hotel, Steyne Gardens, WORTHING
☎ 01903 230451   45

TYNE & WEAR

BACKWORTH   Map 12 NZ37

Backworth The Hall NE27 0AH ☎ 0191 268 1048
Parkland course with easy walking, natural hazards and good
scenery.
9 holes, 5930yds, Par 71, SSS 69, Course record 64.
Club membership 480.
Visitors   visitors may not play Tue (Ladies Day) &
weekend mornings. Play limited Sat/Sun during Apr-Sep.
Societies   apply in writing to secretary.
Green Fees £12 per round (£14 weekends & bank holidays).
Facilities   ⊗ ⊁ by prior arrangement ⅏ ♨ ♀
& Leisure   bowling green.
Location   W side of town on B1322

Hotel   ★★★★ 63% Holiday Inn, Great North Rd,
                 SEATON BURN ☎ 0191 201 9988 150 ⊨ ♞

BIRTLEY   Map 12 NZ25

Birtley Birtley Ln DH3 2LR ☎ 0191 410 2207
Parkland course.
9 holes, 5660yds, Par 67, SSS 67, Course record 63.
Club membership 270.
Visitors   must play with member at weekends & bank
                 holidays.
Societies   apply in writing, must contact 1 month in
                 advance in summer.
Green Fees £12 per round.
Facilities   ⅏ ♨ ♀ ⚘

Hotel   B Posthouse Washington, Emerson District 5,
                 WASHINGTON ☎ 0191 416 2264 138 ⊨ ♞

BOLDON   Map 12 NZ36

Boldon Dipe Ln, East Boldon NE36 0PQ
☎ 0191 536 5360 & 0191 536 4182 Fax 0191 537 2270
Parkland links course, easy walking, distant sea views,
windy.
18 holes, 6362yds, Par 72, SSS 70, Course record 67.
Club membership 700.
Visitors   may not play after 3.30pm at weekends & bank
                 holidays.
Societies   must contact in advance.
Green Fees not confirmed.
Designer   Harry Varden
Facilities   ⊗ ⊁ ⅏ ♨ ♀ ⚘ 🏠 ⛾ ⚘ ⚘ ⚘
& Leisure   snooker.
Location   S side of village off A184

Hotel   ★★★ 68% Quality Hotel, Witney Way,
                 Boldon, SUNDERLAND
                 ☎ 0191 519 1999 82 ⊨ ♞

CHOPWELL   Map 12 NZ15

Garesfield NE17 7AP
☎ 01207 561309 Fax 01207 561309
Undulating parkland course with good views and picturesque
woodland surroundings.
18 holes, 6458yds, Par 72, SSS 71, Course record 68.
Club membership 746.

Visitors   weekends after 4.30pm only, unless with
                 member. Must contact in advance. No visiting
                 parties Mondays or Saturdays.
Societies   must contact secretary in advance.
Green Fees not confirmed.
Prof   David Race
Designer   Harry Fernie
Facilities   ⊗ ⊁ ⅏ ♨ ♀ ♨ 🏠 ⛾ ⚘   ⚘
Location   From A1 take A694 to Rowlands Gill. Turn
                 right (signed Ryton) to High Spen. Turn left for
                 Chopwell

Hotel   ★★★ 65% Quality Hotel Newcastle,
                 Newgate St, NEWCASTLE UPON TYNE
                 ☎ 0191 232 5025 93 ⊨ ♞

FELLING   Map 12 NZ26

Heworth Gingling Gate, Heworth NE10 8XY
☎ 0191 469 9832
Fairly flat, parkland course.
18 holes, 6437yds, Par 71, SSS 71.
Club membership 800.
Visitors   may not play Sat & before 10am Sun, Apr-Sep.
Societies   must apply in writing.
Green Fees not confirmed.
Facilities   ⊗ ⊁ ⅏ ♨ ♀ ♨
Location   On A195, 0.5m NW of junc with A1(M)

Hotel   B Posthouse Washington, Emerson District 5,
                 WASHINGTON
                 ☎ 0191 416 2264 138 ⊨ ♞

GATESHEAD   Map 12 NZ26

Ravensworth Moss Heaps, Wrekenton NE9 7UU
☎ 0191 487 2843
Moorland/parkland course 600 ft above sea-level with fine
views. Testing 13th hole (par 3).
18 holes, 5966yds, Par 69, SSS 69.
Club membership 600.
Visitors   apply in advance.
Societies   apply in writing to secretary.
Green Fees not confirmed.
Prof   Shaun Cowell
Designer   J W Fraser
Facilities   ⊗ by prior arrangement ⊁ by prior arrangement
                 ⅏ ♨ ♀ ♨ 🏠 ⚘
Location   3m SE off A6127

Hotel   ★★★ 68% Swallow Hotel, High West St,
                 GATESHEAD
                 ☎ 0191 477 1105 103 ⊨ ♞

GOSFORTH   Map 12 NZ26

Gosforth Broadway East NE3 5ER ☎ 0191 285 3495
Parkland course with natural water hazards, easy walking.
18 holes, 6024yds, Par 69, SSS 68, Course record 65.
Club membership 500.
Visitors   must contact in advance. Restricted play on
                 competition days.
Societies   telephone in advance.
Green Fees £20 per day.
Prof   G Garland
Facilities   ⊗ ⊁ ⅏ ♨ ♀ ♨ 🏠 ⚘
Location   N side of town centre off A6125   ▶

Hotel   ★★★★ 75% Swallow Gosforth Park Hotel, High Gosforth Park, Gosforth, NEWCASTLE UPON TYNE ☎ 0191 236 4111 178 ⇔ 🏠

Parklands Gosforth Park Golfing Complex, High Gosforth Park NE3 5HQ ☎ 0191 236 4867 & 236 4480
Parklands course is set in pleasant parkland with challenging shots around and sometimes over attractive water hazards. The first 9 holes are easier but the second 9 test even the most experienced golfer.
18 holes, 6060yds, Par 71, SSS 69, Course record 66.
Club membership 750.

Visitors	a daily start sheet operates with bookings taken from 4.30pm the previous day during weekdays, and from 8am Fri & Sat for weekends.
Societies	by prior arrangement with club secretary.
Green Fees	£15 per 18 holes (£18 weekends & bank holidays).
Prof	Brian Rumney
Facilities	⊗ �📶 ⫶ 🍴 ☕ ♀ ♨ 🏠 ⚡ ⛳
Location	3m N, at the end A1 Western by Pass

Hotel   ★★★★ 75% Swallow Gosforth Park Hotel, High Gosforth Park, Gosforth, NEWCASTLE UPON TYNE ☎ 0191 236 4111 178 ⇔ 🏠

HOUGHTON-LE-SPRING   Map 12 NZ35

Elemore Elemore Ln, Hetton-le-Hole DH5 0QB ☎ 0191 517 3061 Fax 0191 5173054
Elmore course tests a players ability in all aspects of the game, with drives over water as well as wedges. The greens are firm all year round and there are well positioned bunkers.
18 holes, 5947yds, Par 69, Course record 68.
Club membership 100.

Visitors	no restrictions. Phone to avoid society days.
Societies	apply in writing, telephone enquiries welcome.
Green Fees	£8.10 per round (£10 weekends & bank holidays).
Prof	Stephen Bryan
Designer	J Gaunt
Facilities	⊗ �📶 ⫶ 🍴 ☕ ♀ ♨ 🏠 ⚡ 🦢 ⛳
Location	4m S of Houghton-Le-Spring on the A182

Hotel   ★★ 59% Chilton Lodge Country Pub & Motel, Black Boy Rd, Chilton Moor, Fencehouses, HOUGHTON-LE-SPRING ☎ 0191 385 2694 25 ⇔ 🏠

Houghton-le-Spring Copt Hill DH5 8LU ☎ 0191 584 1198 & 584 0048
Hilly, downland course with natural slope hazards.
18 holes, 6443yds, Par 72, SSS 71, Course record 64.
Club membership 600.

Visitors	may not play on Sun until 4pm.
Societies	must contact secretary in advance.
Green Fees	not confirmed.
Prof	Kevin Gow
Facilities	⊗ �📶 ⫶ 🍴 ☕ ♀ ♨ 🏠
Location	0.5m E on B1404

Hotel   ★★ 59% Chilton Lodge Country Pub & Motel, Black Boy Rd, Chilton Moor, Fencehouses, HOUGHTON-LE-SPRING ☎ 0191 385 2694 25 ⇔ 🏠

NEWCASTLE UPON TYNE   Map 12 NZ26

City of Newcastle Three Mile Bridge NE3 2DR ☎ 0191 285 1775 Fax 0191 2840700
A well-manicured parkland course in the Newcastle suburbs, subject to wind.
18 holes, 6528yds, Par 72, SSS 71, Course record 64.
Club membership 460.

Visitors	no restrictions but advisable to telephone first.
Societies	telephone in advance
Green Fees	£24 per day (£28 weekends & bank holidays).
Prof	Steve McKenna
Designer	Harry Varden
Facilities	⊗ �📶 ⫶ 🍴 ☕ ♀ ♨ 🏠 ⚡ ⛳
Location	3m N on B1318

Hotel   ★★★ 64% Newcastle Airport Moat House, Woolsington, NEWCASTLE UPON TYNE AIRPORT ☎ 0191 401 9988 100 ⇔ 🏠

Newcastle United Ponteland Rd, Cowgate NE5 3JW ☎ 0191 286 9998 Fax 0191 286 4323
Moorland course with natural hazards.
18 holes, 6617yds, Par 72, SSS 72, Course record 68.
Club membership 600.

Visitors	must play with member at weekends.
Societies	must contact in writing.
Green Fees	£18 per day.
Facilities	⊗ ⫶ 🍴 ☕ ♀ ♨ 🏠 ⚡ ⛳
Location	1.25m NW of city centre off A6127

Hotel   ★★★ 69% Imperial Swallow Hotel, Jesmond Rd, NEWCASTLE UPON TYNE ☎ 0191 281 5511 122 ⇔ 🏠

Northumberland High Gosforth Park NE3 5HT ☎ 0191 236 2498 Fax 0191 236 2498
Many golf courses have been sited inside racecourses, although not so many survive today. One which does is the Northumberland Club's course at High Gosforth Park. Naturally the course is flat but there are plenty of mounds and other hazards to make it a fine test of golf. It should be said that not all the holes are within the confines of the racecourse, but both inside and out there are some good holes. This is a Championship course.
18 holes, 6629yds, Par 72, SSS 72, Course record 65.
Club membership 580.

Visitors	may not play at weekends or competition days. Must contact in advance.
Societies	must apply in writing.
Green Fees	£45 per day; £35 per round.
Designer	Colt/Braid
Facilities	⊗ �📶 ⫶ 🍴 ☕ ♀ ♨ ⛳
Location	4m N of city centre off A1

Hotel   ★★★★ 75% Swallow Gosforth Park Hotel, High Gosforth Park, Gosforth, NEWCASTLE UPON TYNE ☎ 0191 236 4111 178 ⇔ 🏠

Westerhope Whorlton Grange, Westerhope NE5 1PP ☎ 0191 286 7636
Attractive parkland course with tree-lined fairways, and easy walking. Good open views towards the airport.
18 holes, 6444yds, Par 72, SSS 71, Course record 64.
Club membership 778.

Visitors	with member only at weekends. Must contact in advance.
Societies	must contact Secretary in advance.
Green Fees	not confirmed.
Prof	Nigel Brown
Facilities	⊗ ⅲ ⅙ ⬆ ☕ ♀ ⚲ 🏠 ❦ 🛒 ✧
Location	4.5m NW of city centre off B6324
Hotel	★★★★ 75% Swallow Gosforth Park Hotel, High Gosforth Park, Gosforth, NEWCASTLE UPON TYNE ☎ 0191 236 4111 178 ➪ ⑃

RYTON　　　　　　　　　　　　　　　　Map 12 NZ16

Ryton Clara Vale NE40 3TD
☎ 0191 413 3737 Fax 0191 413 1642
Parkland course.
18 holes, 5950yds, Par 70, SSS 69, Course record 68.
Club membership 600.

Visitors	with member only at weekends.
Societies	apply in advance.
Green Fees	not confirmed.
Facilities	⊗ ⅲ ⅙ ⬆ ☕ ♀ ⚲
Location	NW side of town off A695
Hotel	★★★ 70% Gibside Arms Hotel, Front St, WHICKHAM ☎ 0191 488 9292 45 ➪ ⑃

Tyneside Westfield Ln NE40 3QE
☎ 0191 413 2742 Fax 0191 413 2742
Open parkland course, water hazard, hilly, practice area.
18 holes, 6042yds, Par 70, SSS 69, Course record 65.
Club membership 900.

Visitors	must contact in advance to play at weekends (after 3pm)
Societies	must apply in advance.
Green Fees	£25 per day; £20 per round (weekends after 3pm £15 per round).
Cards	⋯ 💳 💳 📇
Prof	Malcolm Gunn
Designer	H S Colt
Facilities	⊗ ⅲ ⅙ ⬆ ☕ ♀ ⚲ 🏠 ✧
Location	NW side of town off A695
Hotel	★★★ 70% Gibside Arms Hotel, Front St, WHICKHAM ☎ 0191 488 9292 45 ➪ ⑃

SOUTH SHIELDS　　　　　　　　　　　Map 12 NZ36

South Shields Cleadon Hills NE34 8EG ☎ 0191 456 8942
A slightly undulating downland course on a limestone base ensuring good conditions underfoot. Open to strong winds, the course is testing but fair. There are fine views of the coastline.
18 holes, 6264yds, Par 71, SSS 70, Course record 64.
Club membership 800.

Visitors	must contact in advance.
Societies	by arrangement.
Green Fees	£20 per day (£25 weekends & bank holidays).
Prof	Gary Parsons
Designer	McKenzie-Braid
Facilities	⊗ ⅲ ⅙ ⬆ ☕ ♀ ⚲ 🏠 ♟ ✧
Location	SE side of town centre off A1300
Hotel	★★★ 64% Sea Hotel, Sea Rd, SOUTH SHIELDS ☎ 0191 427 0999 33 ➪ ⑃

Whitburn Lizard Ln NE34 7AF
☎ 0191 529 4944 Fax 0191 529 4944
Parkland course.
18 holes, 5900yds, Par 69, SSS 68, Course record 64.
Club membership 650.

Visitors	restricted weekends & Tue. Contact professional in advance.
Societies	must apply in writing to secretary
Green Fees	£20 per day (£26 weekends & bank holidays).
Prof	David Stephenson
Designer	Colt, Alison & Morrison
Facilities	⊗ ⅲ ⅙ ⬆ ☕ ♀ ⚲ 🏠 ✧
Location	2.5m SE off A183
Hotel	★★★★ 67% Swallow Hotel, Queen's Pde, Seaburn, SUNDERLAND ☎ 0191 529 2041 98 ➪ ⑃

SUNDERLAND　　　　　　　　　　　　Map 12 NZ35

Ryhope Leechmore Way, Ryhope SR2 0DH
☎ 0191 523 7333
A municipal course recently extended to 18 holes.
18 holes, 4601yds, Par 65, SSS 63.
Club membership 350.

Visitors	no restrictions.
Societies	apply in writing, telephone enquiries welcome.
Green Fees	not confirmed.
Facilities	♀ ⚲ 🏠 ♟
Location	3.5m S of city centre
Hotel	★★★★ 67% Swallow Hotel, Queen's Pde, Seaburn, SUNDERLAND ☎ 0191 529 2041 98 ➪ ⑃

Wearside Coxgreen SR4 9JT
☎ 0191 534 2518 Fax 0191 5342518
Open, undulating parkland course rolling down to the River Wear and beneath the shadow of the famous Penshaw Monument. Built on the lines of an Athenian temple it is a well-known landmark. Two ravines cross the course presenting a variety of challenging holes.
18 holes, 6373yds, Par 71, SSS 74, Course record 63.
Club membership 648.

Visitors	may not play before 9.30am, between 12.30-1.30 or after 4pm.
Societies	must apply in writing.
Green Fees	£26 per day (£33 weekends & bank holidays).
Prof	Doug Brolls
Facilities & Leisure	⊗ ⅲ ⅙ ⬆ ☕ ♀ ⚲ 🏠 ✧ 4 hole pqr 3 practice course.
Location	3.5m W off A183
Hotel	★★★★ 67% Swallow Hotel, Queen's Pde, Seaburn, SUNDERLAND ☎ 0191 529 2041 98 ➪ ⑃

TYNEMOUTH　　　　　　　　　　　　Map 12 NZ36

Tynemouth Spital Dene NE30 2ER
☎ 0191 257 4578 Fax 0191 259 5193
Well-drained parkland course, easy walking.
18 holes, 6401yds, Par 70, SSS 71, Course record 64.
Club membership 824.

▶

Visitors must play with member weekends & bank holidays.
Societies must contact in writing.
Green Fees not confirmed.
Prof J P McKenna
Designer Willie Park
Facilities 🅰️🏠🍴🛒⛳
Location 0.5m W

Hotel ★★★ 66% Grand Hotel, Grand Pde,
TYNEMOUTH ☎ 0191 293 6666 40 ⇄ ♞

WALLSEND   Map 12 NZ26

Wallsend Rheydt Av, Bigges Main NE28 8SU
☎ 0191 262 1973
Parkland course.
18 holes, 6608yds, Par 72, SSS 72, Course record 66.
Club membership 750.
Visitors may not play before 12.30pm weekends. Must book in advance
Societies must apply in writing.
Green Fees £13 per round (£15 weekends).
Prof Ken Phillips
Facilities 🅱️🍴🏠🛒⛳
Location NW side of town centre off A193

Hotel ★★★ 69% Imperial Swallow Hotel,
Jesmond Rd, NEWCASTLE UPON TYNE
☎ 0191 281 5511 122 ⇄ ♞

WASHINGTON   Map 12 NZ25

George Washington Hotel Golf & Country Club Stone Cellar Rd, High Usworth NE37 1PH
☎ 0191 402 9988 Fax 0191 4151166
Championship-standard course. Also a 9-hole (par 3) course, putting green and 21-bay floodlit driving range.
18 holes, 6267yds, Par 73, SSS 71.
Club membership 600.

Visitors must contact in advance. May not play before 10am or between noon & 2pm at weekends.
Societies book in advance.
Green Fees not confirmed.
Cards 💳💳💳💳💳
Prof Warren Marshall
Facilities ⊗🍴🅱️♨️🍴🏠🛒🚗⛳
& Leisure heated indoor swimming pool, squash, sauna, solarium, gymnasium.

Hotel ★★★ 67% George Washington Golf & Country Club, Stone Cellar Rd, District 12, High Usworth, WASHINGTON
☎ 0191 402 9988 103 ⇄ ♞

WHICKHAM   Map 12 NZ26

Whickham Hollinside Park, Fellside Rd NE16 5BA
☎ 0191 488 1576 Fax 0191 488 1576
Undulating parkland course with attractive panoramic views.
18 holes, 5878yds, Par 68, SSS 68, Course record 61.
Club membership 660.
Visitors must contact Professional in advance.
Societies by arrangement.
Green Fees £20 per day/round (£25 Sun).
Prof Graeme Lisle
Facilities ⊗🍴 by prior arrangement 🅱️🍴🏠🛒⛳
& Leisure snooker.
Location 1.5m S

Hotel ★★★ 68% Swallow Hotel, High West St,
GATESHEAD ☎ 0191 477 1105 103 ⇄ ♞

WHITLEY BAY   Map 12 NZ37

Whitley Bay Claremont Rd NE26 3UF
☎ 0191 252 0180 Fax 0191 297 0030
Downland course close to the sea. A stream runs through the undulating terrain.
18 holes, 6600yds, Par 71, SSS 71, Course record 66.
Club membership 800.

Visitors	may not play at weekends.
Societies	telephone initially.
Green Fees	£30 per day; £22 per round.
Prof	Gary Shipley
Facilities	⊗ ⊞ 🏌 💻 ♀ ♨ 🏠 ✐
Location	NW side of town centre off A1148

| Hotel | ★★★ 64% Windsor Hotel, South Pde, WHITLEY BAY ☎ 0191 251 8888 63 ⇄ 🏴 |

WARWICKSHIRE

Coventry Area Telephone Number Changes

From the 22 April 2000, all dialling codes listed as **(01203)** will change to **(024)**, followed by an eight-digit local number. starting with **76**. For example, **(01203)** 123456 will become **(024) 76**12 3456.

ATHERSTONE   Map 04 SP39

Atherstone The Outwoods, Coleshill Rd CV9 2RL
☎ 01827 713110
Scenic parkland course, established in 1894 and laid out on hilly ground.
18 holes, 6006yds, Par 72, SSS 70, Course record 69.
Club membership 520.

Visitors	handicap certificate required. With member only weekends and bank holidays but not Sun. Also with holder of handicap certificate by permission of Club Secretary.
Societies	contact in advance.
Green Fees	£20 per day/round.
Designer	Hawtree & Gaunt Mornoch
Facilities	⊗ ⊞ 🏌 💻 ♀ ♨ 🏴
Location	0.5m S on B4116

| Hotel | ★★ 75% Chapel House Hotel, Friar's Gate, ATHERSTONE ☎ 01827 718949 14 ⇄ 🏴 |

BIDFORD-ON-AVON   Map 04 SP15

Bidford Grange Stratford Rd B50 4LY
☎ 01789 490319 Fax 01789 778184
Designed by Howard Swan & Paul Tillman, this very long, championship standard course is built to represent a links course and is fully irrigated. There are water hazards on the first 7 holes, and particularly challenging holes on the 16th (223yds,par 3), 8th (600yds, par 5) and an uphill par 4 at the 13th.
18 holes, 7233yds, Par 72, SSS 74, Course record 66.
Club membership 200.

Visitors	no restrictions.
Societies	apply in writing or phone, minimum 12, maximum 36.
Green Fees	£12 per 18 holes (£15 weekends).
Cards	▬ ▬ ▬ 🔲 💳
Facilities	🏌 💻 ♀ ♨ 🖚 🏳 🏴 ✐
& Leisure	fishing.
Location	4m W of Stratford upon Avon, B439

| Hotel | ★★★ 75% Salford Hall Hotel, ABBOT'S SALFORD ☎ 01386 871300 14 ⇄ 🏴 Annexe19 ⇄ 🏴 |

BRANDON   Map 04 SP47

City of Coventry-Brandon Wood Brandon Ln, Wolston CV8 3GQ ☎ 01203 543141
Municipal parkland course surrounded by fields and bounded by River Avon on east side. Floodlit driving range.
18 holes, 6610yds, Par 72, SSS 72, Course record 68.
Club membership 500.

Visitors	telephone for details.
Societies	telephone secretary for details
Green Fees	not confirmed.
Prof	Chris Gledhill
Facilities	⊗ ⊞ 🏌 💻 ♀ ♨ 🏠 🏳 🖚 ✐
Location	Off A45 southbound

| Hotel | ★★★ 65% The Brandon Hall, Main St, BRANDON ☎ 01203 542571 60 ⇄ 🏴 |

COLESHILL   Map 04 SP28

Maxstoke Park Castle Ln B46 2RD
☎ 01675 466743 Fax 01675 466743
Parkland course with easy walking. Numerous trees and a lake form natural hazards.
18 holes, 6442yds, Par 71, SSS 71, Course record 64.
Club membership 720.

Visitors	with member only at weekends & bank holidays.
Societies	contact in advance.
Green Fees	£38 per day; £33 per 27 holes; £25 per 18 holes.
Prof	Neil McEwan
Facilities	⊗ ⊞ 🏌 💻 ♀ ♨ 🏠 🏳 ✐
Location	3m NE of Coleshill on B4114 turn right for Maxstoke then 1m on right

| Hotel | ★★★ 64% Coleshill Hotel, 152 High St, COLESHILL ☎ 01675 465527 15 ⇄ 🏴 Annexe8 ⇄ 🏴 |

HENLEY-IN-ARDEN   Map 04 SP16

Henley Golf & Country Club Birmingham Rd B95 5QA
☎ 01564 793715 Fax 01564 795754
Founded in 1994, this improving course is maturing well and provides a good golfing challenge for all handicaps.
18 holes, 6933yds, Par 73, SSS 73.
Club membership 675.

Visitors	may book up to 7 days in advance.
Societies	apply in writing or telephone in advance.
Green Fees	£20 (£25 weekends).
Cards	▬ ▬ ▬ 🔲 💳
Prof	Simon Edwin
Designer	N Selwyn Smith
Facilities	⊗ ⊞ 🏌 💻 ♀ ♨ 🏠 🏳 🏴 ✐
& Leisure	hard tennis courts, 9 hole par 3.
Location	On the left hand side of the Birmingham road, just N of Henley-in Arden

| Hotel | ★★★ 63% Quality Hotel, Pool Bank, Southcrest, REDDITCH ☎ 01527 541511 58 ⇄ 🏴 |

Entries with a shaded background identify courses that are considered to be particularly interesting

KENILWORTH　　　　　　　　　　　Map 04 SP27

Kenilworth Crewe Ln CV8 2EA
☎ 01926 858517 Fax 01926 864453
Parkland course in open hilly situation. Club founded in
1889.
18 holes, 6413yds, Par 73, SSS 71, Course record 62.
Club membership 725.
Visitors　　must contact in advance.
Societies　　apply in writing.
Green Fees　£28 per day/round (£37 weekends).
Cards　　　🖴 🖴 💳 🖴 🖴 🖴
Prof　　　　Steve Yates
Designer　　Hawtree
Facilities　　⊗ ⅷ ⓛ 🍺 ⅴ ⅍ ⅏ ⅆ ➘ ⅾ
& Leisure　　Par 3 chipping green.
Location　　0.5m NE

Hotel　　★★ 63% Clarendon House Hotel,
　　　　　　Old High St, KENILWORTH
　　　　　　☎ 01926 857668 Cen. Res. 0800 616883
　　　　　　Fax 01926 850669　30 ⇄ 🐾

LEA MARSTON　　　　　　　　　　Map 04 SP29

Lea Marston Hotel & Leisure Complex Haunch Ln
B76 0BY ☎ 01675 470468 Fax 01675 470871
Par 3, 'pay-and-play' course, with water hazards, out of
bounds, and large bunkers. The venue for the past two years
of the Midlands Professional Par 3 Competition. Golf driving
range.
9 holes, 783yds, Par 27, SSS 27, Course record 46.
Club membership 150.
Visitors　　no restrictions.
Societies　　must telephone in advance.
Green Fees　not confirmed.
Prof　　　　Andrew Stokes
Designer　　J R Blake
Facilities　　⊗ ⅷ ⓛ 🍺 ⅴ 🖴 ⅏ 🖴 ⅼ
& Leisure　　hard tennis courts, heated indoor swimming
　　　　　　pool, sauna, solarium, gymnasium.

Hotel　　★★★ 72% Lea Marston Hotel & Leisure
　　　　　　Complex, Haunch Ln, LEA MARSTON
　　　　　　☎ 01675 470468　83 ⇄ 🐾

LEAMINGTON SPA　　　　　　　　Map 04 SP36

Leamington & County Golf Ln, Whitnash CV31 2QA
☎ 01926 425961 Fax 01926 425961
Undulating parkland course with extensive views.
18 holes, 6488yds, Par 71, SSS 71, Course record 65.
Club membership 802.
Visitors　　must contact in advance.
Societies　　telephone in advance.
Green Fees　£30 per day; £25 per round (£40 per round
　　　　　　weekends).
Prof　　　　Iain Grant
Designer　　H S Colt
Facilities　　⊗ ⅷ ⓛ 🍺 ⅴ ⅍ 🖴 ➘ 🖴 ⅆ
& Leisure　　snooker room.
Location　　S side of town centre

Hotel　　★★★ 60% Manor House Hotel,
　　　　　　Avenue Rd, LEAMINGTON SPA
　　　　　　☎ 01926 423251　53 ⇄ 🐾

Newbold Comyn Newbold Ter East CV32 4EW
☎ 01926 421157
Municipal parkland course with hilly front nine. The par 4,
9th is a 467-yd testing hole.
18 holes, 6315yds, Par 70, SSS 70, Course record 70.
Club membership 320.
Visitors　　no restrictions.
Societies　　apply to professional.
Green Fees　not confirmed.
Prof　　　　Don Knight
Facilities　　⊗ ⅷ ⓛ 🍺 ⅴ ⅍ 🖴 ⅏ ⅆ
& Leisure　　heated indoor swimming pool, gymnasium.
Location　　0.75m E of town centre off B4099

Hotel　　★★★ 60% Manor House Hotel,
　　　　　　Avenue Rd, LEAMINGTON SPA
　　　　　　☎ 01926 423251　53 ⇄ 🐾

LEEK WOOTTON　　　　　　　　　Map 04 SP26

The Warwickshire CV35 7QT
☎ 01926 409409 Fax 01926 408409
Opened in 1993, this is an unusual championship standard
course. Designed by Karl Litten, the 36 holes are laid out as
four interchangeable loops of 9 holes to create six contrasting
yet superb courses in a parkland and woodland setting.
South East Course: 18 holes, 7000yds, Par 72, SSS 72,
Course record 68.
North West Course: 18 holes, 7400yds, Par 72, SSS 74,
Course record 68.
Club membership 880.
Visitors　　can book up to 7 days in advance.
Societies　　apply to sales office for details.
Green Fees　not confirmed.
Cards　　　🖴 🖴 💳 🖴 🖴 🖴
Prof　　　　J Cook/B Fotheringham
Designer　　Karl Litten
Facilities　　⊗ ⅷ ⓛ 🍺 ⅴ ⅍ 🖴 ⅏ ➘ 🚜 ⅆ ⅼ
Location　　On B4115

Hotel　　★★★ 68% Chesford Grange Hotel,
　　　　　　Chesford Bridge, KENILWORTH
　　　　　　☎ 01926 859331 145 ⇄ 🐾 Annexe9 ⇄ 🐾

NUNEATON　　　　　　　　　　　Map 04 SP39

Nuneaton Golf Dr, Whitestone CV11 6QF
☎ 01203 347810 Fax 01203 327563
Undulating moorland and woodland course.
18 holes, 6429yds, Par 71, SSS 71.
Club membership 675.
Visitors　　must produce evidence of membership of a
　　　　　　recognised golf club or society, with member
　　　　　　only at weekends.
Societies　　apply in writing.
Green Fees　not confirmed.
Prof　　　　Steven Bainbridge
Facilities　　⊗ ⅷ ⓛ 🍺 ⅴ ⅍ 🖴 ⅆ
Location　　2m SE off B4114

Hotel　　★★ 67% Longshoot Toby Hotel,
　　　　　　Watling St, NUNEATON
　　　　　　☎ 01203 329711 Annexe47 ⇄ 🐾

Oakridge Arley Ln, Ansley Village CV10 9PH
☎ 01676 541389 & 540542 Fax 01676 542709
There are a number of water hazards on the back nine which add to the natural beauty of the countryside. The undulating course is affected by winter cross winds on several holes. Overall it will certainly test golfing skills.
18 holes, 6242yds, Par 71, SSS 70.
Club membership 500.
Visitors   contact in advance, with members only at weekends.
Societies   apply in writing or telephone in advance.
Green Fees not confirmed.
Cards   ⬜ 💳 🅳
Prof   Ian Sadler
Designer   Algy Jayes
Facilities   ⊗ ⫘ ⅃ ♥ ♀ ⚲ 🏠 ⚑ ⛏ ➘ 🛒 ⌁
Location   4m W

Hotel   ★★★ 62% Weston Hall, Weston Ln, Weston in Arden, Bulkington, NUNEATON
                  ☎ 01203 312989   40 ⊖ 🛏

Purley Chase Pipers Ln, Ridge Ln CV10 0RB
☎ 01203 393118 Fax 01203 398015
Meadowland course with tricky water hazards on eight holes and undulating greens. 13-bay driving range.
18 holes, 6772yds, Par 72, SSS 72, Course record 67.
Club membership 750.
Visitors   welcome except at weekends.
Societies   telephone for provisional booking (Mon-Fri only).
Green Fees £15 per round.
Cards   ⬜ 💳
Prof   Gary Carver
Facilities   ⊗ ⫘ ⅃ ♥ ♀ ⚲ 🏠 ➘ 🛒 ⌁ ⚲
Location   2m NW off B4114

Hotel   ★★ 67% Longshoot Toby Hotel, Watling St, NUNEATON
                  ☎ 01203 329711 Annexe47 ⊖ 🛏

RUGBY   Map 04 SP57

Rugby Clifton Rd CV21 3RD
☎ 01788 542306 01788 575134 (Pro) Fax 01788 542306
Parkland course with brook running through the middle and crossed by a viaduct.
18 holes, 5457yds, Par 68, SSS 67, Course record 62.
Club membership 700.
Visitors   weekends & bank holidays with member only.
Societies   apply in writing.
Green Fees £20 per day/round.
Prof   Nat Summers
Facilities   ⊗ ⫘ ⅃ ♥ ♀ ⚲ 🏠 ⚑ ⌁
& Leisure   snooker.
Location   1m NE on B5414

Hotel   ★★★ 59% The Rugby Grosvenor Hotel, Clifton Rd, RUGBY
                  ☎ 01788 535686   26 ⊖ 🛏

Whitefields Hotel Golf & Country Club Coventry Rd, Thurlaston CV23 9JR ☎ 01788 815555 Fax 01788 521695
Whitefields has superb natural drainage. There are many water features and the 13th has a stunnning dogleg 442yard Par 4 with a superb view across Draycote Water. The 16th is completely surrounded by water and is particularly difficult.

18 holes, 6223yds, Par 71, SSS 70, Course record 66.
Club membership 400.
Visitors   advisable to book unless hotel guest, available 7 days, contact secretary on 01788 815555.
Societies   contact secretary in advance.
Green Fees £18 weekdays (£25 weekends).
Cards   ⬜ 💳 🅳 🅶
Designer   Reg Mason
Facilities   ⊗ ⫘ ⅃ ♥ ♀ ⚲ 🏠 ⚑ 🏁 ➘ 🛒 ⌁ ⚲
Location   A45 Coventry road, near Dunchurch

Hotel   ★★★ 59% Whitefields Hotel Golf & Country Club, Coventry Rd, Thurlaston, RUGBY
                  ☎ 01788 521800 & 522393
                  Fax 01788 521695   33 ⊖ 🛏

STONELEIGH   Map 04 SP37

Stoneleigh Deer Park The Clubhouse, The Old Deer Park, Coventry Rd CV8 3DR
☎ 01203 639991 Fax 01203 511533
Parkland course in old deer park with many mature trees. The River Avon meanders through the course and comes into play on 4 holes. Also 9-hole course.
Tantara Course: 18 holes, 6023yds, Par 71, SSS 69.
Avon Course: 9 holes, 1251yds, Par 27.
Club membership 800.
Visitors   must contact in advance, no visitors at weekends except by prior arrangement.
Societies   by prior arrangement.
Green Fees Tantara: £20 per day; £14.50 per round (£30/£22.50 weekends); Avon: £5 per round.
Prof   Matt McGuire
Designer   Ken Harrison
Facilities   ⊗ ⫘ ⅃ ♥ ♀ ⚲ 🏠 ⚑ ➘ 🛒 ⌁
Location   3m NE of Kenilworth

Hotel   ★★★ 70% De Montfort Hotel, The Square, KENILWORTH ☎ 01926 855944 104 ⊖ 🛏

STRATFORD-UPON-AVON   Map 04 SP25

Stratford Oaks Bearley Rd, Snitterfield CV37 0EZ
☎ 01789 731980 Fax 01789 731981
American styled, parkland course designed by Howard Swan.
18 holes, 6100yds, Par 71, SSS 69, Course record 66.
Club membership 750.
Visitors   contact in advance.
Societies   telephone in advance.
Green Fees telephone for green fees.
Cards   ⬜ 💳 🅶
Prof   Andrew Dunbar   ▶

Designer	H Swann
Facilities	⊗ ⫝̸ 🛈 💺 ♀ ♨ ☎ ⛳ ♂ ℓ
Location	4m N of Stratford-upon-Avon

Hotel	★★★★ 69% Stratford Manor, Warwick Rd, STRATFORD-UPON-AVON ☎ 01789 731173 103 ⇌ 🐾

Stratford-upon-Avon Tiddington Rd CV37 7BA
☎ 01789 205749
Beautiful parkland course. The par 3, 16th is tricky and the par 5, 17th and 18th, provide a tough end.
18 holes, 6311yds, Par 72, SSS 70, Course record 64.
Club membership 750.

Visitors	restricted on Wed.
Societies	must telephone in advance.
Green Fees	not confirmed.
Prof	D Sutherland
Facilities	⊗ ⫝̸ 🛈 💺 ♀ ♨ ☎ ⛳ 🚜 ♂
Location	0.75m E on B4086

Hotel	★★★★ 67% The Alveston Manor, Clopton Bridge, STRATFORD-UPON-AVON ☎ 01789 204581 114 ⇌ 🐾

Welcombe Hotel Warwick Rd CV37 0NR
☎ 01789 295252 Fax 01789 414666
Wooded parkland course of great character and boasting superb views of the River Avon, Stratford and the Cotswolds. Set within the hotel's 157-acre estate, it has two lakes and water features.
18 holes, 6274yds, Par 70, SSS 70, Course record 64.

Visitors	must contact in advance.
Societies	booking via Hotel.
Green Fees	not confirmed.
Cards	💳 💳 💳 💳 💳 💳
Prof	Carl Masons
Designer	Thomas Macauley
Facilities	⊗ ⫝̸ 🛈 💺 ♀ ♨ ☎ ⛳ 🏨 🕊 🚜 ♂ ℓ
& Leisure	hard tennis courts, fishing, solarium, gymnasium, hairdresser, health & beauty salon, snooker.
Location	1.5m NE off A46

Hotel	★★★★ 73% Welcombe Hotel and Golf Course, Warwick Rd, STRATFORD-UPON-AVON ☎ 01789 295252 67 ⇌ 🐾

TANWORTH-IN-ARDEN   Map 04 SP17

Ladbrook Park Poolhead Ln B94 5ED
☎ 01564 742264 Fax 01564 742909
Parkland course lined with trees.
18 holes, 6427yds, Par 71, SSS 71, Course record 65.
Club membership 700.

Visitors	welcome weekdays, with member at weekends. Must contact in advance & have handicap certificate.
Societies	apply in advance.
Green Fees	£40 per 36 holes, £32 per 28 holes, £25 per 18 holes.
Cards	💳 💳 💳 💳 💳
Prof	Richard Mountford
Designer	H S Colt
Facilities	⊗ ⫝̸ 🛈 💺 ♀ ♨ ☎ ⛳ ♂
Location	2.5m SE of M42 junct 3

Hotel	★★★▲▲ Nuthurst Grange Country House Hotel, Nuthurst Grange Ln, HOCKLEY HEATH ☎ 01564 783972 15 ⇌ 🐾

UPPER BRAILES   Map 04 SP32

Brailes Sutton Ln, Lower Brailes OX15 5BB
☎ 01608 685336
Undulating meadowland on 130 acres of Cotswold countryside. Sutton brook passes through the course and is crossed 5 times. The Par 5 17th offers the most spectacular view of three counties from the tee. There is a prevailing cross wind.
18 holes, 6270yds, Par 71, SSS 70, Course record 67.
Club membership 430.

Visitors	advance telephone advisable to 01608 685633.
Societies	telephone or write for information to the secretary.
Green Fees	£27 per 27/36 holes; £18 per 18 holes (£36/£26 weekends & bank holidays).
Prof	Mike Bendall
Designer	B A Hull
Facilities	⊗ ⫝̸ 🛈 💺 ♀ ♨ ☎ ⛳ 🚜 ♂
Location	4m E of Shipston-on-Stour, on B4035

Hotel	★★ 60% The Red Lion Hotel, Main St, Long Compton, SHIPSTON ON STOUR ☎ 01608 684221 5 ⇌ 🐾

WARWICK   Map 04 SP26

Warwick The Racecourse CV34 6HW ☎ 01926 494316
Parkland course with easy walking. Driving range with floodlit bays.
9 holes, 2682yds, Par 34, SSS 66, Course record 67.
Club membership 150.

Visitors	must contact in advance. May not play Sun before 12.30pm
Societies	contact in advance.
Green Fees	£4.50 per 9 holes (£5 weekends).
Prof	Phil Sharp
Designer	D G Dunkley
Facilities	💺 ♀ ♨ ☎ ⛳ ♂ ℓ
Location	W side of town centre

Hotel	★★ 62% Warwick Arms Hotel, 17 High St, WARWICK ☎ 01926 492759 35 ⇌ 🐾

WEST MIDLANDS

Coventry Area Telephone Number Changes

From the 22 April 2000, all dialling codes listed as **(01203)** will change to **(024)**, followed by an eight-digit local number. starting with **76**. For example, **(01203)** 123456 will become **(024) 76**12 3456.

ALDRIDGE   Map 07 SK00

Druids Heath Stonnall Rd WS9 8JZ
☎ 01922 455595 (Office) & 459523 (Prof)
Testing, undulating heathland course.
18 holes, 6659yds, Par 72, SSS 73.
Club membership 590.

Visitors	contact in advance recommended. Weekend play permitted after 2pm.
Societies	phone initially.
Green Fees	£25 per day (£33 weekends after 2pm).
Prof	Glenn Williams
Facilities	⊗ 〿 ㄴ 🍺 ♀ ⚠ 🖃 ✐
& Leisure	snooker.
Location	NE side of town centre off A454

Hotel	★★★ 75% The Fairlawns at Aldridge, 178 Little Aston Rd, Aldridge, WALSALL ☎ 01922 455122 46 ⇆ ℟

BIRMINGHAM   Map 07 SP08

Brandhall Heron Rd, Oldbury, Warley B68 8AQ
☎ 0121 552 2195
Municipal parkland course, easy walking, good hazards. Testing holes: 1st-502 yds (par 5); 10th-455 yds dog-leg (par 5).
18 holes, 5734yds, Par 70, SSS 68, Course record 66.

Visitors	restricted weekends. Telephone for tee times (access to clubhouse on payment of small entrance fee and subject to prior arrangement).
Societies	by arrangement, apply in writing
Green Fees	£8.50 per round.
Cards	▬▬ 🟦
Prof	Carl Yates
Facilities	⊗ 🍺 🖃 ⚐ ✐
Location	5.5m W of Birmingham city centre off A4123

Hotel	B Posthouse Birmingham Great Barr, Chapel Ln, Great Barr, BIRMINGHAM ☎ 0121 357 7444 192 ⇆ ℟

Cocks Moors Woods Municipal Alcester Rd South, Kings Heath B14 4ER ☎ 0121 444 3584 Fax 0121 441 1305
Although quite short this tree-lined, parkland course has well maintained greens and offers a good test of golf.
18 holes, 5769yds, Par 69, SSS 68.
Club membership 400.

Visitors	no restrictions.
Societies	must contact in advance.
Green Fees	not confirmed.
Prof	Steve Ellis
Facilities	⊗ ㄴ 🍺 ♀ ⚠ 🖃 ⚐ ✐
& Leisure	heated indoor swimming pool, solarium, gymnasium.
Location	5m S of city centre on A435

Hotel	B Posthouse Birmingham City, Smallbrook Queensway, BIRMINGHAM ☎ 0121 643 8171 251 ⇆ ℟

Edgbaston Church Rd, Edgbaston B15 3TB
☎ 0121 454 1736 Fax 0121 454 2395
Set in 144 acres of woodland, lake and parkland, two miles from the centre of Birmingham, this delightful course utilises the wealth of natural features to provide a series of testing and adventurous holes set in the traditional double loop that starts directly in front of the Clubhouse, an imposing Georgian mansion.
18 holes, 6106yds, Par 69, SSS 69, Course record 63.
Club membership 880.

Visitors	recommended to contact in advance through golf reservations, must have handicap certificate. Most weekends pm.

Societies	must apply in writing.
Green Fees	£35 per round (£50 weekends).
Prof	Jamie Cundy
Designer	H S Colt
Facilities	⊗ 〿 ㄴ 🍺 ♀ ⚠ 🖃 ⚐ 🥄 🛒 ✐
Location	1m S of city centre on B4217 off A38

Hotel	★★★ 66% Plough & Harrow, 135 Hagley Rd, EDGBASTON ☎ 0121 454 4111 44 ⇆ ℟

Great Barr Chapel Ln, Great Barr B43 7BA
☎ 0121 357 5270
Parkland course with easy walking. Pleasant views of Barr Beacon National Park.
18 holes, 6523yds, Par 72, SSS 71, Course record 67.
Club membership 600.

Visitors	restricted at weekends.
Societies	must contact in writing.
Green Fees	not confirmed.
Prof	Richard Spragg
Facilities	⊗ 〿 ㄴ 🍺 ♀ ⚠ 🖃 🥄 ✐
Location	6m N of city centre off A 34

Hotel	B Posthouse Birmingham Great Barr, Chapel Ln, Great Barr, BIRMINGHAM ☎ 0121 357 7444 192 ⇆ ℟

Handsworth 11 Sunningdale Close, Handsworth Wood B20 1NP ☎ 0121 554 0599 & 554 3387 Fax 0121 554 3387
Undulating parkland course with some tight fairways but subject to wind.
18 holes, 6267yds, Par 70, SSS 70, Course record 65.
Club membership 800.

Visitors	restricted weekends, bank holidays & Xmas. Must contact in advance and have a handicap certificate.
Societies	must contact in advance.
Green Fees	not confirmed.
Prof	Lee Bashford
Facilities	⚠ 🖃 ✐
& Leisure	squash.
Location	3.5m NW of city centre off A4040

Hotel	★★★ 68% Birmingham/West Bromwich Moat House, Birmingham Rd, WEST BROMWICH ☎ 0121 609 9988 168 ⇆ ℟

Harborne 40 Tennal Rd, Harborne B32 2JE
☎ 0121 427 3058
Parkland course in hilly situation, with brook running through.
18 holes, 6230yds, Par 70, SSS 70, Course record 65.
Club membership 655.

Visitors	must have handicap certificate, contact in advance, may not play weekends except with member, Ladies have priority Tue.
Societies	Mon, Wed-Fri apply to secretary, by phone or letter.
Green Fees	£35 per day; £30 per round.
Prof	Alan Quarterman
Designer	Harry Colt
Facilities	⊗ 〿 ㄴ 🍺 ♀ ⚠ 🖃 ⚐ ✐
Location	3.5 m SW of city centre off A4040

▶

Hotel ★★★ 66% Plough & Harrow, 135 Hagley Rd,
EDGBASTON ☎ 0121 454 4111 44 ⇄ ℜ

Harborne Church Farm Vicarage Rd, Harborne B17 0SN
☎ 0121 427 1204 Fax 0121 428 3126
Parkland course with water hazards and easy walking. Some
holes might prove difficult.
9 holes, 4882yds, Par 66, SSS 64, Course record 62.
Club membership 200.
Visitors   must contact in advance.
Societies   must telephone in advance.
Green Fees contact for details.
Cards   ⚊ ▦ ▦ ▣ ▦ ▧ ▨
Prof   Paul Johnson
Facilities   ⊗ ⅷ ⅃ ➥ ☖ 🏠 ⛳ ∂
Location   3.5m SW of city centre off A4040

Hotel ★★★ 66% Plough & Harrow, 135 Hagley Rd,
EDGBASTON ☎ 0121 454 4111 44 ⇄ ℜ

Hatchford Brook Coventry Rd, Sheldon B26 3PY
☎ 0121 743 9821 Fax 0121 743 3420
Fairly flat, municipal parkland course.
18 holes, 6155yds, Par 69, SSS 69.
Club membership 450.
Visitors   are restricted early Sat & Sun.
Societies   must contact in advance.
Green Fees not confirmed.
Cards   ▦ ▣ ▧
Prof   Mark Hampton
Facilities   ⊗ ➥ ☖ 🏠 ⛳ ∂
Location   6m E of city centre on A45

Hotel B Posthouse Birmingham Airport, Coventry Rd,
BIRMINGHAM ☎ 0121 782 8141 141 ⇄ ℜ

Hilltop Park Ln, Handsworth B21 8LJ ☎ 0121 554 4463
A good test of golf with interesting layout, undulating
fairways and large greens, located in the Sandwell Valley
conservation area.
18 holes, 6208yds, Par 70, SSS 70.
Club membership 400.
Visitors   no restrictions but booking necessary.
Societies   Mon-Fri, telephone Professional in advance.
Green Fees £9 per 18 holes; £5.50 per 9 holes (£10/£6.50
weekends).
Prof   Kevin Highfield
Designer   Hawtree
Facilities   ⊗ ⅷ ➥ ☖ 🏠 ⛳ ∂
Location   On A41, 1m from junct 1 M5

Hotel ★★★ 68% Birmingham/West Bromwich Moat
House, Birmingham Rd, WEST BROMWICH
☎ 0121 609 9988 168 ⇄ ℜ

Lickey Hills Rosehill, Rednal B45 8RR
☎ 0121 453 3159 Fax 0121 457 8779
Hilly municipal course overlooking the city.
18 holes, 5835yds, Par 68, SSS 68.
Club membership 300.
Visitors   may not play between 9 & 10.30am weekends.
Societies   must contact in advance.
Green Fees not confirmed.
Prof   Joe Kelly
Facilities   ☖ 🏠 ⛳
& Leisure   tennis courts.
Location   10m SW of city centre on B4096

Hotel ★★ 70% Norwood Hotel, 87-89 Bunbury Rd,
Northfield, BIRMINGHAM
☎ 0121 411 2202 18 ⇄ ℜ

Moseley Springfield Rd, Kings Heath B14 7DX
☎ 0121 444 2115 Fax 0121 441 4662
Parkland course with a lake, pond and stream to provide
natural hazards. The par-3, 4th goes through a cutting in
woodland to a tree and garden-lined amphitheatre, and the
par-4, 5th entails a drive over a lake to a dog-leg fairway.
18 holes, 6300yds, Par 70, SSS 70, Course record 64.
Club membership 600.
Visitors   may only play by prior arrangement, weekdays
excluding bank holidays.
Societies   by prior arrangement.
Green Fees £37 per day.
Prof   Gary Edge
Facilities   ⊗ ⅷ by prior arrangement ⅃ ➥ ♀ ☖ 🏠 ∂
Location   4m S of city centre on B4146 off A435

Hotel ★★ 70% Norwood Hotel, 87-89 Bunbury Rd,
Northfield, BIRMINGHAM
☎ 0121 411 2202 18 ⇄ ℜ

North Worcestershire Frankley Beeches Rd, Northfield
B31 5LP ☎ 0121 475 1047 Fax 0121 476 8681
Designed by James Braid and established in 1907, this is a
mature parkland course. Tree plantations rather than heavy
rough are the main hazards.
18 holes, 5959yds, Par 69, SSS 68, Course record 64.
Club membership 600.
Visitors   by prior arrangement with professional. Must
play with member at weekends. All visitors
must have an official CONGU handicap.
Societies   apply in advance in writing or by telephone to
the professional tel: 0121 475 5721.
Green Fees £18.50 per round weekdays only.
Prof   Finley Clarke
Designer   James Braid
Facilities   ☖ 🏠 ⛳ ∂
Location   7m SW of Birmingham city centre, off A38

Hotel ★★ 70% Norwood Hotel, 87-89 Bunbury Rd,
Northfield, BIRMINGHAM
☎ 0121 411 2202 18 ⇄ ℜ

Warley Lightswood Hill, Warley B67 5ED
☎ 0121 429 2440 Fax 0121 434 4430
Municipal parkland course in Warley Woods. New out of
bounds areas and bunkers have tightened the course
considerably with further improvement following current tree
planting.
9 holes, 5346yds, Par 68, SSS 66, Course record 64.
Club membership 200.
Visitors   no restrictions. Linc card system for easier
booking.
Societies   booking advised, times very limited for large
parties.
Green Fees not confirmed.
Cards   ▦
Prof   David Owen
Facilities   ⊗ ⅷ ➥ ☖ 🏠 ⛳ ∂
Location   4m W of city centre off A456

Hotel ★★★ 66% Plough & Harrow, 135 Hagley Rd,
EDGBASTON ☎ 0121 454 4111 44 ⇄ ℜ

COVENTRY

Map 04 SP37

Ansty Golf Centre Brinklow Rd, Ansty CV7 9JH
☎ 01203 621341 Fax 01203 602671
18-hole Pay and Play course of two 9-hole loops.
Membership competitions for handicaps. Driving range and
putting green.
18 holes, 6079yds, Par 71, SSS 68, Course record 66.
Club membership 400.
Visitors no restrictions.
Societies welcome, telephone in advance.
Green Fees weekdays: £9 per 18 holes; £5 per 9 holes.
Cards ▭▭ ▭▭ ▣
Prof Craig Philips
Designer David Morgan
Facilities ⊗ ⓑ �␣ ♥ ♀ ♨ ♟ ♦ ♣
Location 3m from city centre via A4600

Hotel ★★★ 64% Novotel, Wilsons Ln,
COVENTRY ☎ 01203 365000 98 ⇔ ⚑

Coventry St Martins Rd, Finham Park CV3 6RJ
☎ 01203 414152 Fax 01203 690131
The scene of several major professional events, this
undulating parkland course has a great deal of quality. More
than that, it usually plays its length, and thus scoring is never
easy, as many professionals have found to their cost.
18 holes, 6601yds, Par 73, SSS 73, Course record 67.
Club membership 500.
Visitors must contact in advance. May not play at
weekends and bank holidays.
Societies must apply in writing.
Green Fees £35 per day.
Cards ▭▭ ▭▭ ▣
Prof Philip Weaver
Designer Vardon Bros/Hawtree
Facilities ⊗ ⓑ ⓛ ⓑ ♥ ♀ ♨ ♣
Location 3m S of city centre on B4133, 2m from jct
of A45/A46

Hotel ★★★ 69% Hylands Hotel, Warwick Rd,
COVENTRY ☎ 01203 501600 54 ⇔ ⚑

Coventry Hearsall Beechwood Av CV5 6DF
☎ 01203 713470
Parkland course with fairly easy walking. A brook provides
an interesting hazard.
18 holes, 6005yds, Par 70, SSS 69.
Club membership 650.
Visitors with member only at weekends.
Societies apply in writing to secretary.
Green Fees £24 per day.
Prof Mike Tarn
Facilities ⊗ ⓛ ⓑ ⓛ ⓑ ♥ ♀ ♨ ♣
Location 1.5m SW of city centre off A429

Hotel ★★★ 69% Hylands Hotel, Warwick Rd,
COVENTRY ☎ 01203 501600 54 ⇔ ⚑

Windmill Village Hotel Golf & Leisure Club
Birmingham Rd, Allesley CV5 9AL
☎ 01203 404040 Fax 01203 404042
An attractive 18-hole course over rolling parkland with
plenty of trees and two lakes that demand shots over open
water. Four challenging Par 5 holes. Good leisure facilities.

18 holes, 5213yds, Par 70, SSS 67, Course record 66.
Club membership 600.
Visitors must contact in advance. Pre-payment required
at peak times.
Societies telephone for booking form.
Green Fees £9.95-£13.95 per 18 holes.
Cards ▭▭ ▭▭ ▣ ▭▭ ▣
Prof Robert Hunter
Designer Robert Hunter
Facilities ⊗ ⓛ ⓑ ⓛ ♥ ♀ ♨ ♟ ♦ ♣ ♧ ♣
& Leisure hard tennis courts, heated indoor swimming
pool, fishing, sauna, solarium, gymnasium,
beauty suite.
Location On A45 W of Coventry

Hotel ★★★ 74% Brooklands Grange Hotel &
Restaurant, Holyhead Rd, COVENTRY
☎ 01203 601601 30 ⇔ ⚑

DUDLEY

Map 07 SO99

Dudley Turner's Hill, Rowley Regis, Warley B65 9DP
☎ 01384 233877
Fairly hilly parkland course.
18 holes, 5714yds, Par 69, SSS 68.
Club membership 550.
Visitors may not play at weekends.
Societies must contact in advance.
Green Fees £25 per round/day.
Prof Paul Taylor
Facilities ⊗ ⓛ ⓑ ⓛ ♥ ♀ ♨ ♣
Location 2m S of town centre off B4171

Hotel ★★★ 62% Himley Country Hotel, School Rd,
HIMLEY ☎ 01902 896716 73 ⇔ ⚑

Swindon Bridgnorth Rd, Swindon DY3 4PU
☎ 01902 897031 & 895226 Fax 01902 326219
Attractive undulating woodland/parkland course, with
spectacular views.
Old Course: 18 holes, 6091yds, Par 71, SSS 69.
New Course: 9 holes, 1135yds, Par 27.
Club membership 700.
Visitors must contact in advance.
Societies must apply in writing.
Green Fees £18 per round.
Cards ▭▭ ▭▭
Prof Phil Lester
Facilities ⊗ ⓑ ⓛ ♥ ♀ ♨ ♣ ♧ ♣
& Leisure fishing.
Location On B4176, 3m from A449 at Himley

Hotel ★★★ 62% Himley Country Hotel, School Rd,
HIMLEY ☎ 01902 896716 73 ⇔ ⚑

HALESOWEN

Map 07 SO98

Corngreaves Hall Corngreaves Rd B64 7NL
☎ 01384 567880
Mature course offering a good challenge to the best golfers
with American specification greens and most holes holding a
testing start. Magnificent views of the Clent Hills.
9 holes, 2800.
Visitors at anytime by prior arrangement.
Societies apply in writing in advance.
Green Fees not confirmed.

▶

Prof S Joyce/C Yates
Facilities ⊗ 🍺 ⛳ ♂

Hotel ★★★ 63% Talbot Hotel, High St,
STOURBRIDGE
☎ 01384 394350 30 ⇶ ♞

Halesowen The Leasowes, Leasowes Ln B62 8QF
☎ 0121 501 3606 Fax 0121 501 3606
Parkland course in convenient position within the only Grade
1 listed park in the Midlands.
18 holes, 5754yds, Par 69, SSS 69, Course record 65.
Club membership 625.
Visitors welcome weekdays, may only play weekends or
bank holidays with member unless previously
agreed.
Societies must apply in writing.
Green Fees £28 per day; £20 per round.
Prof Jon Nicholas
Facilities ⊗ ⊪ ☪ 🍺 ♟ 🏠 ⛳ ♂
Location 1m E junct 3 M5, Leasowes Lane off Manor
Lane

Hotel ★★★ 63% Talbot Hotel, High St,
STOURBRIDGE ☎ 01384 394350 30 ⇶ ♞

KNOWLE   Map 07 SP17

Copt Heath 1220 Warwick Rd B93 9LN
☎ 01564 772650 Fax 01564 771022
Parkland course designed by H. Vardon.
18 holes, 6517yds, Par 71, SSS 71.
Club membership 700.
Visitors must contact in advance and possess official
handicap. May not play weekends & bank
holidays.
Societies must contact in advance.
Green Fees not confirmed.
Prof Brian J Barton
Designer H Vardon
Facilities ⊗ ⊪ ☪ 🍺 ♟ 🏠 🛒 ♂ 🏌
Location On A4141, 0.50m S of junct 5 of M42

Hotel ★★★★ 64% St John's Swallow Hotel,
651 Warwick Rd, SOLIHULL
☎ 0121 711 3000 177 ⇶ ♞

MERIDEN   Map 04 SP28

Marriott Forest of Arden Golf & Country Club Maxstoke
Ln CV7 7HR ☎ 01676 522335 Fax 01676 523711
Two parkland courses, set within the grounds of Packington
Estate, with water hazards and offering a fine test of golf.
On-site hotel with many leisure facilities.
*Arden Course: 18 holes, 6718yds, Par 72, SSS 73, Course
record 62.*
Aylesford Course: 18 holes, 6525yds, Par 71, SSS 72.
Club membership 800.
Visitors book 10 days in advance, 48 hours in advance
for weekends.
Societies by arrangement.

Call the AA Hotel Booking Service on
0870 5050505 to book at AA recognised hotels and B & Bs
in the UK and Ireland, or through our Internet site:
http://www.theaa.co.uk/hotels

Green Fees Arden Course: £50 per round (£60 weekends).
Aylesford: £35 per round (£40 weekends).
Cards 🗎 ▦ 🌐 🅿 ▧ ▧
Prof Kim Thomas
Designer Donald Steele
Facilities ⊗ ⊪ ☪ 🍺 ♟ 🏠 ⛳ 🛒 ♂ 🏌
& Leisure hard tennis courts, heated indoor swimming
pool, fishing, sauna, solarium, gymnasium,
croquet lawn, health and beauty salon, steam
room, jacuzzi, aerobics studio.
Location 1m SW on B4102

Hotel ★★★★ 70% Marriott Forest of Arden Hotel &
Country Club, Maxstoke Ln, MERIDEN
☎ 01676 522335 215 ⇶ ♞

North Warwickshire Hampton Ln CV7 7LL
☎ 01676 522259 Fax 01676 522915
Parkland course with easy walking.
9 holes, 6390yds, Par 72, SSS 70, Course record 65.
Club membership 425.
Visitors must contact in advance.
Societies must apply in writing to secretary.
Green Fees £18 per round.
Prof Andrew Bownes
Facilities ☪ ♟ 🏠 ♂
Location 1m SW on B4102

Hotel ★★★ 72% Manor Hotel, Main Rd, MERIDEN
☎ 01676 522735 114 ⇶ ♞

Stonebridge Golf Centre Somers Rd CV7 7PL
☎ 01676 522442 Fax 01676 522447
The course is set in the beautiful landscape of the Packington
estate, with mature shrubs and trees. Water features are
incorporated to provide an excellent variety for a wide range
of golfing abilities.
18 holes, 6240yds, Par 70, SSS 70, Course record 70.
Club membership 360.
Visitors advisable to book in advance, booking up to 7
days in advance.
Societies apply in writing or telephone in advance.
Green Fees £14 per round (£15 Fri; £16 weekends and bank
holidays).
Cards 🗎 ▦ 🌐 🅿 ▧ ▧ ▧
Prof Steve Harrison
Designer Mark Jones
Facilities ⊗ ⊪ ☪ 🍺 ♟ 🏠 ⛳ 🛒 ♂ 🏌
& Leisure fishing.

Hotel ★★★ 72% Manor Hotel, Main Rd, MERIDEN
☎ 01676 522735 114 ⇶ ♞

SEDGLEY   Map 07 SO99

Sedgley Golf Centre Sandyfields Rd DY3 3DL
☎ 01902 880503
Public Pay and Play course. Undulating contours and mature
trees with extensive views over surrounding countryside.
9 holes, 3147yds, Par 72, SSS 70.
Club membership 150.
Visitors booking advisable for weekends.
Societies must contact in advance.
Green Fees £8 per 18 holes; £6 per 9 holes (£8.50/£6.50
weekends & bank holidays).
Prof Garry Mercer
Designer W G Cox
Facilities ♨ ⚐ ♣ ♨ ♨ ♂ ♪
Location 0.5m from town centre off A463

Hotel ★★★ 62% Himley Country Hotel,
School Rd, HIMLEY
☎ 01902 896716 73 ⇌ ♠

SOLIHULL   Map 07 SP17

Olton Mirfield Rd B91 1JH
☎ 0121 704 1936 & 0121 705 1083 Fax 0121 711 2010
Parkland course with prevailing southwest wind.
18 holes, 6265yds, Par 69, SSS 71, Course record 63.
Club membership 600.
Visitors must contact in advance. No visitors at
weekend.
Societies apply in writing.
Green Fees not confirmed.
Prof Mark Daubney
Designer J H Taylor
Facilities ♨ ⚐ ♣ ♨ ♨ ⚑ ♨ ♂ ♪ ♪
Location Exit M42 junct 5 and take A41 for 1.5m

Hotel ★★★★ 64% St John's Swallow Hotel,
651 Warwick Rd, SOLIHULL
☎ 0121 711 3000 177 ⇌ ♠

Robin Hood St Bernards Rd B92 7DJ
☎ 0121 706 0061 Fax 0121 706 0061
Pleasant parkland course with easy walking and open to good
views.Tree lined fairways and varied holes, culminating in
two excellent finishing holes. Modern clubhouse.
18 holes, 6635yds, Par 72, SSS 72, Course record 68.
Club membership 650.
Visitors must contact in advance. With member only at
weekends.
Societies must contact in advance.
Green Fees £35 per day; £29 per round.
Prof Alan Harvey
Designer H S Colt
Facilities ♨ ⚐ ♣ ♨ ♨ ⚑ ♨ ♂ ♪
Location 2m W off B4025

Hotel ★★★★ 64% St John's Swallow Hotel,
651 Warwick Rd, SOLIHULL
☎ 0121 711 3000 177 ⇌ ♠

Shirley Stratford Rd, Monkpath, Shirley B90 4EW
☎ 0121 744 6001
Fairly flat parkland course.
18 holes, 6510yds, Par 72, SSS 71.
Club membership 600.

Visitors may not play bank holidays & with member
only at weekends. Handicap certificate is
required.
Societies must contact in advance.
Green Fees £25 per round.
Prof S Bottrill
Facilities ♨ ⚐ ♣ ♨ ♨ ♨ ♂ ♪
Location 3m SW off A34

Hotel ★★★★ 62% Regency Hotel,
Stratford Rd, Shirley, SOLIHULL
☎ 0121 745 6119 112 ⇌ ♠

STOURBRIDGE   Map 07 SO98

Hagley Golf & Country Club Wassell Grove, Hagley
DY9 9JW ☎ 01562 883701 Fax 01562 887518
Undulating parkland course set beneath the Clent Hills; there
are superb views. Testing 15th, par 5, 557 yards.
18 holes, 6353yds, Par 72, SSS 72, Course record 66.
Club membership 700.
Visitors welcome weekdays but restricted Wed (Ladies
Day) & with member only at weekends.
Societies Mon-Fri only, must apply in writing.
Green Fees not confirmed.
Prof Iain Clark
Designer Garratt & Co
Facilities ♨ ⚐ ♣ ♨ ♨ ♨ ♂ ♪
& Leisure squash.
Location 1m E of Hagley off A456. 2m from junct 3 0n
M5

Hotel ★★★ 63% Talbot Hotel, High St,
STOURBRIDGE ☎ 01384 394350 30 ⇌ ♠

Stourbridge Worcester Ln, Pedmore DY8 2RB
☎ 01384 395566 Fax 01384 444660
Parkland course.
18 holes, 6231yds, Par 70, SSS 69, Course record 67.
Club membership 857.
Visitors contact secretary, no casual visitors weekends.
Ladies day Wednesday.
Societies must apply in writing.
Green Fees not confirmed.
Prof M Male
Facilities ♨ ♂ ♪
Location 2m from town centre

Hotel ★★★ 63% Talbot Hotel, High St,
STOURBRIDGE ☎ 01384 394350 30 ⇌ ♠

SUTTON COLDFIELD   Map 07 SP19

THE BELFRY See page 273

Boldmere Monmouth Dr B73 6JL
☎ 0121 354 3379 Fax 0121 355 4534
Established municipal course with 10 par 3s and a lake
coming into play on the 16th and 18th holes.
18 holes, 4493yds, Par 63, SSS 62, Course record 57.
Club membership 300.
Visitors must contact in advance.
Societies midweek only, apply in writing.
Green Fees not confirmed.
Prof Trevor Short
Facilities ♨ ♣ ♨ ♨ ⚑ ♨ ♪   ▶

THE BELFRY

WISHAW *North Warwickshire* ☎ 01675 470301
Fax 01675 470178   **Map 07 SP19**

John Ingham writes: When professional people are commissioned to turn a piece of farmland into a golf course and hotel complex, they are flattered - and delighted. This happened to Peter Alliss and Dave Thomas, two celebrated tournament competitors. The challenge they were offered: turn an unsympathetic piece of land into a good golf course.The resulting Belfry Golf Club was opened in 1977.

Since that date the two architects have every reason to be proud. The course, set in 500 acres of Warwickshire countryside, has staged three of the popular Ryder Cup matches, and the two courses - the completely refurbished Brabazon and the Derby - named after two Lords, have received thousands of visitors. These visitors have been entertained with a kindly reception, enhanced by a really excellent hotel. A third course - the PGA National Course opened in Spring 1997. The Belfry is also home to the PGA Training Academy.

Since its establishment, the saplings and newly-created greens have settled down very well and presented a worthwhile face to the world. One of the big challenges of The Belfry are the lakes and many water hazards that gobble up wild shots. Many a famous player, such as Seve Ballesteros, has had balls sinking without trace at the Brabazon's famously testing 18th hole. This monster requires the player to clear the lake twice in its 455-yard drive to reach an uphill, three-tiered, 60-yard long green.

As a public course, The Belfry is open to all-comers every day. This obviously means a great deal of traffic, although there are many other worthwhile courses in the West Midlands such as Hansworth and Little Aston. However, The Belfry is excellently managed and kept in top condition by a team now fully experienced in catering for every golfer. Recently, bunkering and new tees have improved several of the holes and spectator mounding has improved viewing of the golf tournaments.

In its fine parkland setting the club has become well known for its accommodation and fine business facilities and, being so well placed for the NEC, Birmingham and the international airport, it attracts a variety of golfers.

Visitors	must contact in advance. Handicap certificate is required for the Brabazon & PGA courses; 24 or better gentleman, 32 or better Ladies & juniors.
Societies	must telephone in advance
Green fees	not confirmed. ━ ■ ☲ ▨
Facilities	⊗ ⊮ ⅃ � ☕ ♀ 🍴 ♨ 🏌 ⚐ ➹ 🏌 🏇 ✦ ↾ Professional (P McGovern)
Leisure	hard tennis courts, heated indoor swimming pool, squash, sauna, solarium, gym, residential Golf School.
Location	Sutton Coldfield B76 9PR (exit junc 9 M42 4m E)

Brabazon: 18 holes, 6724yds, Par 72, SSS 73.
Derby: 18 holes, 6009yds Par 69, SSS 69
PGA; 18holes, 6639yds Par 72 SSS72

WHERE TO STAY AND EAT NEARBY

HOTELS:
WISHAW
★★★★⊛ ⊛ 74%The Belfry, Lichfield Rd. ☎ 01675 470301. 324 4🛏 320🍽

★★★58% Moxhull Hall, Holly Lane. ☎ 0121-329 2056. 11(3 🛏8 🍽 🛏) Annexe 9🍽 🛏

LEA MARSTON
★★★72% Lea Marston Hotel and Leisure Complex, Haunch Lane. ☎ 01675 470468 83 (81 🍽 🛏 2 🛏)

SUTTON COLDFIELD
★★★★⊛ ⊛ ♣♠ The Thistle New Hall, Walmley Rd. ☎ 0121-378 2442. 60 🍽 🛏
★★★ 62% Sutton Court, 60-66 Lichfield Rd. ☎ 0870 6011160. 56 (9 🛏 47 🍽 🛏) Annexe 8 🍽 🛏

Location	Adjacent to Sutton Park

Hotel ★★★ 72% Moor Hall Hotel, Moor Hall Dr,
Four Oaks, SUTTON COLDFIELD
☎ 0121 308 3751 75 ⇌ 🐾

Little Aston Streetly B74 3AN
☎ 0121 353 2942 Fax 0121 353 2942
Parkland course.
18 holes, 6670yds, Par 72, SSS 73, Course record 64.
Club membership 350.

Visitors	must contact in advance & may not play at weekends.
Societies	must apply in writing.
Green Fees	£50 per day.
Prof	John Anderson
Designer	H Vardon
Facilities	⊗ ⽋ 🍴 ♀ ⚞ 🏠 𝄐
Location	3.5m NW of Sutton Coldfield off A454

Hotel ★★★ 72% Moor Hall Hotel, Moor Hall Dr,
Four Oaks, SUTTON COLDFIELD
☎ 0121 308 3751 75 ⇌ 🐾

Moor Hall Moor Hall Dr B75 6LN
☎ 0121 308 6130 Fax 0121 308 6130
Parkland course. The 14th is a notable hole.
18 holes, 6249yds, Par 70, SSS 70.
Club membership 600.

Visitors	must contact in advance. With member only weekends & bank holidays.
Societies	must apply in writing.
Green Fees	not confirmed.
Prof	Alan Partridge
Facilities	⚞ 🏠 𝄐
Location	2.5m N of town centre off A453

Hotel ★★★ 72% Moor Hall Hotel, Moor Hall Dr,
Four Oaks, SUTTON COLDFIELD
☎ 0121 308 3751 75 ⇌ 🐾

Pype Hayes Eachel Hurst Rd, Walmley B76 1EP
☎ 0121 351 1014 Fax 0121 313 0206
Attractive, fairly flat course with excellent greens.
18 holes, 5927yds, Par 71, SSS 69.
Club membership 400.

Visitors	phone professional in advance.
Societies	contact professional in advance.
Green Fees	not confirmed.
Prof	James Bayliss
Designer	Bobby Jones
Facilities	⊗ ⽋ 🍴 ♀ 🏠 𝄐
Location	2.5m S off B4148

Hotel ★★★ 65% Marston Farm Hotel,
Bodymoor Heath, SUTTON COLDFIELD
☎ 01827 872133 37 ⇌ 🐾

Sutton Coldfield 110 Thornhill Rd, Streetly B74 3ER
☎ 0121 353 9633 Fax 0121 353 5503
A fine natural, all-weather, heathland course, with tight
fairways, gorse, heather and trees. A good challenge for all
standards of golfer.
18 holes, 6541yds, Par 72, SSS 71, Course record 65.
Club membership 600.

Visitors	must contact in advance. Restricted at weekends and bank holidays.
Societies	must apply in writing.

Green Fees	£35 per day.
Prof	Jerry Hayes
Designer	D McKenzie
Facilities	⊗ ⽋ 🍴 ♀ ⚞ 🏠
Location	3m NW on B4138

Hotel ★★★ 72% Moor Hall Hotel, Moor Hall Dr,
Four Oaks, SUTTON COLDFIELD
☎ 0121 308 3751 75 ⇌ 🐾

Walmley Brooks Rd, Wylde Green B72 1HR
☎ 0121 373 0029 & 377 7272 Fax 0121 377 7272
Pleasant parkland course with many trees. The hazards are
not difficult.
18 holes, 6585yds, Par 72, SSS 72, Course record 67.
Club membership 650.

Visitors	must contact in advance. Weekends may only play as guest of member.
Societies	must contact in advance.
Green Fees	£35 per day; £30 per round.
Prof	C J Wicketts
Facilities	⊗ 🍴 ♀ ⚞ 🏠 𝄐
Location	2m S off A5127

Hotel ★★★ 65% Marston Farm Hotel,
Bodymoor Heath, SUTTON COLDFIELD
☎ 01827 872133 37 ⇌ 🐾

WALSALL   Map 07 SP09

Bloxwich Stafford Rd, Bloxwich WS3 3PQ
☎ 01922 405724 (club) & 476593 (sec/man)
Fax 01922 476593
Undulating parkland course with natural hazards and subject
to strong north wind.
18 holes, 6273yds, Par 71, SSS 71, Course record 68.
Club membership 595.

Visitors	may not play at weekends.
Societies	must contact in advance.
Green Fees	not confirmed.
Prof	Richard J Dance
Facilities	⊗ ⽋ 🍴 ♀ ⚞ 🏠 𝄐
Location	3m N of town centre on A34

Hotel ★★★ 75% The Fairlawns at Aldridge,
178 Little Aston Rd, Aldridge, WALSALL
☎ 01922 455122 46 ⇌ 🐾

Calderfields Aldridge Rd WS4 2JS
☎ 01922 640540 Fax 01922 638787
Parkland course with lake.
18 holes, 6590yds, Par 73, SSS 71.
Club membership 550.

Visitors	no restrictions.
Societies	telephone 01922 632243 in advance.
Green Fees	£18 per round.
Cards	💳 📇 🔲 🔳
Prof	Darren Lewis
Designer	Roy Winter
Facilities	⚞ 🏠 𝄐 🛒 ♀ 𝄐
& Leisure	fishing.
Location	On A454

Hotel ★★★ 75% The Fairlawns at Aldridge,
178 Little Aston Rd, Aldridge, WALSALL
☎ 01922 455122 46 ⇌ 🐾

Walsall The Broadway WS1 3EY
☎ 01922 613512 Fax 01922 616460
Well-wooded parkland course with easy walking.
18 holes, 6300yds, Par 70, SSS 70, Course record 65.
Club membership 600.

Visitors	must contact in advance. May not play weekends & bank holidays.
Societies	must apply in writing.
Green Fees	not confirmed.
Prof	Richard Lambert
Designer	McKenzie
Facilities	⛳🍴🏌
Location	1m S of town centre off A34

Hotel	★★★ 62% The Boundary Hotel, Birmingham Rd, WALSALL ☎ 01922 633555 94 ⇆ ♞

WEST BROMWICH   Map 07 SP09

Dartmouth Vale St B71 4DW ☎ 0121 588 2131
Meadowland course with undulating but easy walking. The
617 yd (par 5) first hole is something of a challenge.
9 holes, 6060yds, Par 71, SSS 71, Course record 66.
Club membership 350.

Visitors	with member only at weekends. May not play bank holidays or medal weekends.
Societies	must apply in writing.
Green Fees	not confirmed.
Prof	Guy Dean
Facilities	⛳🍴🏌🏌
Location	E side of town centre off A4041

Hotel	★★★ 68% Birmingham/West Bromwich Moat House, Birmingham Rd, WEST BROMWICH ☎ 0121 609 9988 168 ⇆ ♞

Sandwell Park Birmingham Rd B71 4JJ
☎ 0121 553 4637 Fax 0121 525 1651
Undulating wooded heathland course situated in the
Sandwell Valley.
18 holes, 6468yds, Par 71, SSS 73, Course record 65.
Club membership 550.

Visitors	must contact in advance. May not play at weekends.
Societies	must contact in advance.
Green Fees	£35 per 36 holes; £30 per 18 holes.
Prof	Nigel Wylie
Designer	H S Colt
Facilities	⊗🍴🏌🍺🏌⛳🍴🏌
& Leisure	practice chipping area/green.
Location	On A41, 200yds from juct 1 of the M5

Hotel	★★★ 68% Birmingham/West Bromwich Moat House, Birmingham Rd, WEST BROMWICH ☎ 0121 609 9988 168 ⇆ ♞

WOLVERHAMPTON   Map 07 SO99

Oxley Park Stafford Rd, Bushbury WV10 6DE
☎ 01902 425892 Fax 01902 712241
Rolling parkland course with trees, bunkers and water
hazards.
18 holes, 6222yds, Par 71, SSS 70, Course record 68.
Club membership 550.

Visitors	must contact in advance.
Societies	must contact in advance.
Green Fees	£29 per day; £25 per round.
Prof	Les Burlison
Designer	H S Colt
Facilities	⊗🍴🏌🍺🏌⛳🍴🏌🏌
& Leisure	snooker.
Location	N of town centre off A449

Hotel	★★ 68% Ely House Hotel, 53 Tettenhall Rd, WOLVERHAMPTON ☎ 01902 311311 18 ⇆ ♞

Penn Penn Common, Penn WV4 5JN ☎ 01902 341142
Heathland course just outside the town.
18 holes, 6462yds, Par 70, SSS 71, Course record 68.
Club membership 650.

Visitors	must play with member at weekends.
Societies	must contact in advance.
Green Fees	£25 per day; £20 per round.
Prof	A Briscoe
Facilities	⊗🍴🏌🍺🏌⛳🍴🏌🏌
Location	SW side of town centre off A449

Hotel	★★★ 63% Quality Hotel Wolverhampton, Penn Rd, WOLVERHAMPTON ☎ 01902 429216 66 ⇆ ♞ Annexe27 ⇆ ♞

South Staffordshire Danescourt Rd, Tettenhall WV6 9BQ
☎ 01902 751065 Fax 01902 741753
A parkland course.
18 holes, 6513yds, Par 71, SSS 71.
Club membership 500.

Visitors	must contact in advance but may not play weekends & before 2pm Tue.
Societies	must apply in writing.
Green Fees	not confirmed.
Prof	Jim Rhodes
Designer	Harry Vardon
Facilities	⊗🍴🏌🍺🏌⛳🍴🏌🏌
Location	3m NW off A41

Hotel	★★ 68% Ely House Hotel, 53 Tettenhall Rd, WOLVERHAMPTON ☎ 01902 311311 18 ⇆ ♞

Three Hammers Short Course Old Stafford Rd, Coven
WV10 7PP ☎ 01902 790940
Well maintained short course designed by Henry Cotton and
providing a unique challenge to golfers of all standards.
18 holes, 1438yds, Par 54, SSS 54, Course record 43.

Visitors	no restrictions.
Societies	contact for details.
Green Fees	not confirmed.

▶

Designer Henry Cotton
Facilities ⊗ ⫼ 🏌 ⬛ ♀ ⚲ 🏠 ⛳ ⌕
Location On A449 N of junct 2 M54

Hotel ★★★ 65% Roman Way Hotel, Watling St,
Hatherton, CANNOCK
☎ 01543 572121   56 ⇆ 📻

Wergs Keepers Ln, Tettenhall WV6 8UA
☎ 01902 742225 Fax 01902 744748
Open parkland course.
18 holes, 6949yds, Par 72, SSS 73.
Club membership 250.
Visitors are advised to contact in advance.
Societies must contact in advance.
Green Fees £14.50 per day (£18 weekends & bank
holidays).
Cards 💳 💳 💳
Designer C W Moseley
Facilities ⊗ 🏌 ⬛ ♀ ⚲ 🏠 🗼 ⛳ ✎
Location From Wolverhampton take A41 towards
Newport for 2.5m then R for 0.5m then R again

Hotel ★★ 68% Ely House Hotel, 53 Tettenhall Rd,
WOLVERHAMPTON
☎ 01902 311311   18 ⇆ 📻

WIGHT, ISLE OF

COWES   Map 04 SZ49

Cowes Crossfield Av PO31 8HN ☎ 01983 292303
Fairly level, tight parkland course with difficult par 3s and
Solent views.
9 holes, 5934yds, Par 70, SSS 68, Course record 66.
Club membership 300.
Visitors restricted Thu & Sun mornings.
Societies Mon-Wed, must contact in advance.
Green Fees not confirmed.
Designer Hamilton-Stutt
Facilities ⚲ ⛳ ✎
Location NW side of town

Hotel ★★ 60% The Fountain Hotel, High St,
COWES ☎ 01983 292397   20 ⇆ 📻

EAST COWES   Map 04 SZ59

Osborne Osborne House Estate PO32 6JX
☎ 01983 295421
Undulating parkland course in the grounds of Osborne
House. Quiet and peaceful situation.
9 holes, 6418yds, Par 70, SSS 70, Course record 71.
Club membership 400.
Visitors may not play Tue before 1pm, weekends before
noon & bank holidays before 11am.
Societies telephone initially.
Green Fees £16 per day (£19 weekends & bank holidays).
Facilities ⊗ ⫼ 🏌 ⬛ ♀ ⚲ 🏠 ✎
Location E side of town centre off A3021

Hotel ★★ 60% The Fountain Hotel, High St,
COWES ☎ 01983 292397   20 ⇆ 📻

FRESHWATER   Map 04 SZ38

Freshwater Bay Afton Down PO40 9TZ
☎ 01983 752955 Fax 01983 756704
A downland/seaside links with wide fairways and spectacular
coastal views of the Solent and Channel.
18 holes, 5725yds, Par 69, SSS 68.
Club membership 450.
Visitors may play daily after 9.30 ex Thu & Sun (10.30).
Societies apply to secretary.
Green Fees £20 per day (£24 weekends & bank holidays).
Cards 💳 💳
Designer J H Taylor
Facilities ⊗ 🏌 by prior arrangement 🏌 ⬛ ♀ ⚲ ⛳ ✎
Location 0.5m E of village off A3055

Hotel ★★ 69% Sentry Mead Hotel, Madeira Rd,
TOTLAND BAY ☎ 01983 753212   14 ⇆ 📻

NEWPORT   Map 04 SZ58

Newport St George's Down, Shide PO30 2JB
☎ 01983 525076
Downland course, fine views.
9 holes, 5710yds, Par 68, SSS 68.
Club membership 350.
Visitors may not play Wed noon-3.30pm or before 3pm
Sat & noon Sun.
Societies contact Secretary in advance.
Green Fees not confirmed.
Facilities ⊗ 🏌 by prior arrangement 🏌 ⬛ ♀ ⚲ 🏠 ⛳ ✎
Location 1.5m S off A3020

Hotel ★★ 60% The Fountain Hotel, High St,
COWES ☎ 01983 292397   20 ⇆ 📻

RYDE   Map 04 SZ59

Ryde Binstead Rd PO33 3NF
☎ 01983 614809 Fax 01983 567418
Downland course with wide views over the Solent.
9 holes, 5287yds, Par 66, SSS 66, Course record 65.
Club membership 500.
Visitors may not play Wed afternoons, Sun mornings or
before 10.30am Sat.
Societies must contact in writing.
Green Fees £15 per day/round (£20 weekends & bank
holidays).
Cards 💳
Designer Hamilton-Stutt
Facilities ⊗ 🏌 ⬛ ♀ ⚲ 🏠 ⛳ ✎
Location 1m W on A3054

Hotel ★★ 70% Biskra Beach Hotel & Restaurant,
17 Saint Thomas's St, RYDE
☎ 01983 567913   14 ⇆ 📻

SANDOWN   Map 04 SZ58

Shanklin & Sandown The Fairway, Lake PO36 9PR
☎ 01983 403217 (office) & 404424 (pro)
Fax 01983 403217 (office)/404424 (pro)
Heathland course with some hilly holes. Mostly sandy base
but some clay makes it generally playable all year.
18 holes, 5804yds, Par 70, SSS 68, Course record 64.
Club membership 600.

Visitors	must contact in advance & have handicap certificate. May not play before noon Sat or 9.30am Sun.
Societies	apply in writing.
Green Fees	£25 per day (£30 weekends & bank holidays).
Prof	Peter Hammond
Designer	Braid
Facilities	⊗ ⅏ by prior arrangement 🏌 🍺 🍴 ⚖ 🏠 🥾 ✐
Location	From Sandown drive towards Shanklin past Heights Leisure Centre after 200yds R into Fairway for 1m

Hotel ★★★ 64% Brunswick Hotel, Queens Rd, SHANKLIN ☎ 01983 863245 32rm(27 ⇔ ☏)

VENTNOR   Map 04 SZ57

Ventnor Steephill Down Rd PO38 1BP ☎ 01983 853326
Downland course subject to wind. Fine seascapes.
12 holes, 5767yds, Par 70, SSS 68.
Club membership 297.

Visitors	may not play Fri noon-3pm or Sun mornings.
Societies	telephone initially.
Green Fees	not confirmed.
Facilities	🏌 🍺 🍴 ⚖ 🥾 ✐
Location	1m NW off B3327

Hotel ★★★ 64% Ventnor Towers Hotel, Madeira Rd, VENTNOR ☎ 01983 852277 27 ⇔ ☏

WILTSHIRE

BISHOPS CANNINGS   Map 04 SU06

North Wilts SN10 2LP
☎ 01380 860627 Fax 01380 860877
High, downland course with fine views.
18 holes, 6322yds, Par 71, SSS 70, Course record 65.
Club membership 800.

Visitors	welcome, a handicap certificate is required at weekends.
Societies	must book in advance.
Green Fees	£25 per day; £19 per round (£40/£25 weekends).
Cards	🖃 💳 💳 💳 🔗 🌐
Prof	Graham Laing
Facilities	⊗ ⅏ 🏌 🍺 🍴 ⚖ 🏠 🥾 ✐
Location	2m NW

Hotel ★★★ 66% Bear Hotel, Market Place, DEVIZES ☎ 01380 722444 24 ⇔ ☏

CALNE   Map 03 ST97

Bowood Golf & Country Club Derry Hill SN11 9PQ
☎ 01249 822228 Fax 01249 822218
Designed by Dave Thomas and set in a magnificent Grade I
listed 'Capability Brown' park, this course provides a fine
test for golfers and hosts the European Challenge Tour
Championship. There are fine practice and teaching facilities
and accommodation is available, along with conference
facilities in the historic clubhouse.
18 holes, 6890yds, Par 72, SSS 73, Course record 67.
Club membership 500.

Visitors	welcome except before noon on Sat and Sun. Advisable to book.
Societies	booking by telephone.
Green Fees	£45 per 36 holes; £40 per 27 holes; £34 per 18 holes. Academy Course £6 per hour.
Cards	🖃 💳 💳 💳 💳 🔗 🌐
Prof	N Blenkarne
Designer	Dave Thomas
Facilities	⊗ ⅏ 🏌 🍺 🍴 ⚖ 🏠 🥾 🚗 🏏 ✐ ⚑
& Leisure	Bowood House and Gardens.
Location	M4 junct 17 off A4 between Chippenham & Calne

Hotel ★★ 68% Lansdowne Strand Hotel, The Strand, CALNE ☎ 01249 812488 21 ⇔ ☏ Annexe5 ⇔ ☏

CASTLE COMBE   Map 03 ST87

Manor House SN14 7JW
☎ 01249 782982 Fax 01249 782992
Opened in 1992 and set in one of the finest locations in
England, this 18-hole Peter Alliss/Clive Clark course was
designed to marry neatly with the surrounding conservation
area. Many mature trees have been used to great effect giving
individuality and challenge to every shot. There are
spectacular holes at the 17th & 18th with lakes and waterfalls
making them memorable.
18 holes, 6340yds, Par 73, SSS 71.
Club membership 450.

Visitors	must have a handicap certificate and must contact in advance.
Societies	contact in advance.
Green Fees	£60 per day; £37.50 per round (£80/£50 weekends & bank holidays).
Cards	🖃 💳 💳 💳 🔗 🌐
Prof	Chris Smith
Designer	Peter Alliss/Clive Clark ▶

Facilities ⊗ 〗ⓛ 🏌 💺 ⊊ 🏊 🍴 🅿 🏐 🚣 ⚷ ⍾
& Leisure hard tennis courts, heated outdoor swimming pool, fishing, sauna, Snooker.
Location On B4039, 5m NW of Chippenham

Hotel ★★★★♨ Manor House Hotel, CASTLE COMBE ☎ 01249 782206 21 ⇌ 🛏 Annexe24 ⇌ 🛏

CHAPMANSLADE   Map 03 ST84

Thoulstone Park BA13 4AQ
☎ 01373 832825 Fax 01373 832821
A rolling parkland course with natural lakes and mature trees. Hole 7, stroke index 1 has a second shot over a large lake to the green so a straight drive is essential.
18 holes, 6161yds, Par 71, SSS 69.
Club membership 500.
Visitors restricted Sat & Sun mornings. Dress code applies.
Societies telephone in advance.
Green Fees not confirmed.
Prof Tony Isaac
Facilities ⓛ 🏌 💺 ⊊ 🏊 🍴 🅿 ⚷ ⍾
Location On A36 between Bath/Warminster

Hotel ★★ 73% Woolpack Inn, BECKINGTON ☎ 01373 831244 12 ⇌ 🛏

CHIPPENHAM   Map 03 ST97

Chippenham Malmesbury Rd SN15 5LT
☎ 01249 652040 Fax 01249 446681
Easy walking on downland course. Testing holes at 1st and 15th.
18 holes, 5559yds, Par 69, SSS 67, Course record 64.
Club membership 650.
Visitors must contact in advance.
Societies must contact in writing.
Green Fees £20 per day/round (£25 weekends & bank holidays).
Prof Bill Creamer
Facilities ⊗ 〗ⓛ 🏌 💺 ⊊ 🏊 🍴 🅿 ⚷
Location M4 junct 17, 1m N of Chippenham beside A350

Hotel ★★★★♨ Manor House Hotel, CASTLE COMBE ☎ 01249 782206 21 ⇌ 🛏 Annexe24 ⇌ 🛏

CRICKLADE   Map 04 SU09

Cricklade Hotel & Country Club Common Hill SN6 6HA
☎ 01793 750751 Fax 01793 751767
A challenging 9-hole course with undulating greens and beautiful views. Par 3 6th (128yds) signature hole from an elevated tee to a green protected by a deep pot bunker.
9 holes, 1830yds, Par 62, SSS 57.
Club membership 170.
Visitors may not play weekends or bank holidays unless accompanied by a member.
Societies apply in writing.
Green Fees £25 per day, £16 per 18 holes, weekdays only.
Cards 🔲 💳 💳 💳 💳
Prof Ian Bolt
Designer Ian Bolt/Colin Smith

Facilities ⊗ 〗ⓛ 🏌 💺 ⊊ 🏊 🍴 🅿 🏐 ⚷
& Leisure hard tennis courts, heated indoor swimming pool, solarium, gymnasium, steam room, snooker table, pool table.
Location On the B4040 out of Cricklade, towards Malmesbury

Hotel ★★★ 66% Stanton House Hotel, The Avenue, Stanton Fitzwarren, SWINDON ☎ 01793 861777 86 ⇌ 🛏

ERLESTOKE   Map 03 ST95

Erlestoke Sands SN10 5UA
☎ 01380 831069 Fax 01380 831069
The course is set on the lower slopes of Salisbury Plain with distant views to the Cotswolds and Marlborough Downs. The 7th plunges from an elevated three-tiered tee, high in the woods, to a large green with a spectacular backdrop of a meandering river and hills. The course was built to suit every standard of golfer from the novice to the very low handicapper and its two tiers offer lakes and rolling downland.
18 holes, 6406yds, Par 73, SSS 71, Course record 69.
Club membership 706.
Visitors phone for tee booking in advance 01380 830300. Dress rules apply.
Societies must book in advance.
Green Fees not confirmed.
Prof Adrian Marsh
Designer Adrian Stiff
Facilities ⊗ 〗ⓛ 🏌 💺 ⊊ 🏊 🍴 🅿 🏐 🚣 ⚷ ⍾
Location On B3098 Devizes/Westbury road

Hotel ★★★ 66% Bear Hotel, Market Place, DEVIZES ☎ 01380 722444 24 ⇌ 🛏

GREAT DURNFORD   Map 04 SU13

High Post SP4 6AT
☎ 01722 782356 Fax 01722 782356
An interesting downland course on Wiltshire chalk with good turf and splendid views over the southern area of Salisbury Plain. The par 3, 17th and the two-shot 18th require good judgement.
18 holes, 6305yds, Par 70, SSS 70, Course record 64.
Club membership 580.
Visitors a handicap certificate is required at weekends & bank holidays. Telephone professional in advance 01722 782219.
Societies apply by telephone to manager.
Green Fees £33 per day; £25 per round (£38/£30 weekends & bank holidays).
Prof Ian Welding
Facilities ⊗ 〗ⓛ 🏌 💺 ⊊ 🏊 🍴 ⚷ ⍾
Location 1.75m SE on A345

Hotel ★★★ 68% Rose & Crown Hotel, Harnham Rd, Harnham, SALISBURY ☎ 01722 399955 28 ⇌ 🛏

Entries with a shaded background
identify courses that are
considered to be particularly interesting

HIGHWORTH   Map 04 SU29

Highworth Community Golf Centre Swindon Rd SN6 7SJ
☎ 01793 766014 Fax 01793 766014
Public downland course, situated in a high position affording
good views of the Wiltshire Downs.
9 holes, 3120yds, Par 35, SSS 35, Course record 29.
Club membership 150.
Visitors   no restrictions.
Societies   advisable to contact in advance.
Green Fees £6.50.
Prof   Mark Toombs
Designer   T Watt/ B Sandry/D Lang
Facilities   ⬛🏠🔧♟
Location   Off A361 Swindon to Letchlade road

Hotel   ★★★ 72% Sudbury House Hotel &
                 Conference Centre, London St, FARINGDON
                 ☎ 01367 241272 49 ⇌ ⋔

Wrag Barn Golf & Country Club Shrivenham Rd
SN6 7QQ ☎ 01793 861327 Fax 01793 861325
This course, designed by Hawtree, is some 6,500yards long.
The Par of 72 can be demanding as it maximises the natural
features of gentle contours, trees and water. The Par 3 5th is
particularly tricky. A long approach shot has to carry over a
stream 5 yards in front of the tree-protected green. The large
greenside bunker to the right attracts an alarming number of
balls!
18 holes, 6500yds, Par 72.
Club membership 600.
Visitors   no restrictions but may not play before noon at
                 weekends.
Societies   contact in advance.
Green Fees £30 per day; £22 per round (£30 per round Fri &
                 weekends).
Prof   Barry Loughrey
Designer   Hawtree
Facilities   🏠⬛♟🔧🛒♟
Location   On B4000 Shrivenham Road

Hotel   ★★★ 66% Stanton House Hotel, The Avenue,
                 Stanton Fitzwarren, SWINDON
                 ☎ 01793 861777 86 ⇌ ⋔

KINGSDOWN   Map 03 ST86

Kingsdown SN13 8BS
☎ 01225 742530 Fax 01225 743472
Fairly flat, open downland course with very sparse tree cover
but surrounding wood.
18 holes, 6445yds, Par 72, SSS 71, Course record 64.
Club membership 650.
Visitors   welcome except at weekends. Must contact in
                 advance & have a handicap certificate.
Societies   apply by letter.
Green Fees £23.
Prof   Andrew Butler
Facilities   ⊗🍴🏠⬛♟🔧♟
Location   W side of village

Hotel   ★★★★ Lucknam Park, COLERNE
                 ☎ 01225 742777 23 ⇌ ⋔ Annexe18 ⇌ ⋔

LANDFORD   Map 04 SU21

Hamptworth Golf & Country Club Hamptworth Rd,
Hamptworth SP5 2DU
☎ 01794 390155 Fax 01794 390022
Hamptworth enjoys ancient woodland and an abundance of
wildlife in a beautiful setting on the edge of the New Forest.
The 14th is one of its most challenging holes having a narrow
fairway guarded by established forest oaks. The 2nd is a
dogleg of 543yds and plays differently all year.
18 holes, 6516yds, Par 72, SSS 71, Course record 68.
Club membership 450.
Visitors   telephone to check availability.
Societies   write or telephone in advance.
Green Fees not confirmed.
Cards   ⬛
Prof   Phil Stevens
Designer   Philip Sanders/Brian Pierson
Facilities   ⊗🍴🏠⬛♟🏠🔧🛒♟
& Leisure   gymnasium.
Location   1m NW, A36/B3079

Hotel   ★★★ 69% Bartley Lodge, Lyndhurst Rd,
                 CADNAM ☎ 01703 812248 31 ⇌ ⋔

MARLBOROUGH   Map 04 SU16

Marlborough The Common SN8 1DU
☎ 01672 512147 Fax 01672 513164
Downland course with extensive views over the Og valley
and Marlborough Downs.
18 holes, 6491yds, Par 72, SSS 71.
Club membership 900.
Visitors   restricted at certain times; must have a handicap
                 certificate at weekends. Must contact in
                 advance.
Societies   must contact in advance.
Green Fees £29 per day; £22 per round (£40/£30 weekends).
Cards   ⬛
Prof   S Amor
Facilities   ⊗🍴🏠⬛♟🏠🛒♟
Location   N side of town centre on A346

Hotel   ★★★ 61% The Castle & Ball, High St,
                 MARLBOROUGH
                 ☎ 01672 515201 34 ⇌ ⋔

OAKSEY   Map 03 ST99

Oaksey Park Golf & Leisure SN16 9SB
☎ 01666 577995 Fax 01666 577174
A testing nine-hole parkland course set on the west side of
the Cotswold Water Parks.
9 holes, 3100yds, Par 70, SSS 69, Course record 66.
Club membership 200.
Visitors   no restrictions.
Societies   telephone for details.
Green Fees not confirmed.
Cards   ⬛
Designer   Chapman & Warren
Facilities   ⊗♟⬛♟🏠
& Leisure   fishing, shooting, water sports, horse riding
                 available.
Location   On B road connecting A419 & A429, on
                 outskirts of village of Oaksey. S of Cirencester
                 ▶

Hotel   ★★★ 68% Stratton House Hotel, Gloucester Rd, CIRENCESTER ☎ 01285 651761   41 ⇔ ⟡

OGBOURNE ST GEORGE   Map 04 SU27

Ogbourne Downs SN8 1TB
☎ 01672 841327 Fax 01672 841327
Downland turf and magnificent greens. Wind and slopes make this one of the most challenging courses in Wiltshire. Extensive views.
18 holes, 6353yds, Par 71, SSS 70, Course record 65.
Club membership 890.
Visitors   phone in advance. Handicap certificate required.
Societies   must apply for booking form in advance.
Green Fees £25 per day/round (£35 weekends).
Cards   〓 〓 〓 🖂
Prof   Colin Harraway
Designer   J H Taylor
Facilities   ⊗ ⽕ ⛳ 🍺 ♀ △ 🏠 🛈 ⛋ ⤸ ⚷ ⼃
Location   N side of village on A346

Hotel   ★★★ 74% Ivy House Hotel, High St, MARLBOROUGH ☎ 01672 515333   28 ⇔ ⟡

SALISBURY   Map 04 SU12

Salisbury & South Wilts Netherhampton SP2 8PR
☎ 01722 742645 Fax 01722 742645
Gently undulating and well drained parkland courses in country setting with panoramic views of the cathedral and surrounding country. A 27 hole course played in various configurations.
Main Course: 18 holes, 6528yds, Par 71, SSS 71, Course record 61.
Bibury Course: 9 holes, 2885yds, Par 33.
Club membership 1000.
Visitors   must telephone in advance.
Societies   telephone initially.
Green Fees not confirmed.
Prof   John Cave/Geraldine Teschner
Designer   J H Taylor/S Gidman
Facilities   ⊗ ⽕ ⛳ 🍺 ♀ △ 🏠 🛈 ⚷
Location   2m W on A3094

Hotel   ★★★ 68% Rose & Crown Hotel, Harnham Rd, Harnham, SALISBURY ☎ 01722 399955   28 ⇔ ⟡

SWINDON   Map 04 SU18

Broome Manor Golf Complex Pipers Way SN3 1RG
☎ 01793 532403 Fax 01793 433255
Two courses and a 34-bay floodlit driving range. Parkland with water hazards, open fairways and short cut rough. Walking is easy on gentle slopes.
18 holes, 6283yds, Par 71, SSS 70, Course record 62.
Club membership 800.
Visitors   pre-booking advised for 18 hole course.
Societies   must be prebooked.
Green Fees not confirmed.
Cards   〓 〓 〓 🖂
Prof   Barry Sandry
Designer   Hawtree
Facilities   ⊗ ⽕ ⛳ 🍺 ♀ △ 🏠 🛈 ⚷ ⼃

Location   1.75m SE of town centre off B4006

Hotel   ★★★★ 66% Swindon Marriott, Pipers Way, SWINDON ☎ 01793 512121 153 ⇔ ⟡

TIDWORTH   Map 04 SU24

Tidworth Garrison Bulford Rd SP9 7AF
☎ 01980 842301 Fax 01980 842301
A breezy, dry downland course with lovely turf, fine trees and views over Salisbury Plain and the surrounding area. The 4th and 12th holes are notable. The 564-yard 14th, going down towards the clubhouse, gives the big hitter a chance to let fly.
18 holes, 6320yds, Par 70, SSS 70, Course record 62.
Club membership 700.
Visitors   must contact in advance, weekend & bank holiday bookings may not be made until Thursday prior.
Societies   Tue & Thu, bookings required 12-18 months in advance.
Green Fees £24 per day/round.
Prof   Terry Gosden
Designer   Donald Steel
Facilities   ⊗ ⽕ ⛳ 🍺 ♀ △ 🏠 🛈 ⛋ ⚷
Location   W side of village off A338

Hotel   ★★★ 62% Ashley Court Hotel, Micheldever Rd, ANDOVER ☎ 01264 357344 9 ⇔ ⟡ Annexe26 ⇔ ⟡

TOLLARD ROYAL   Map 03 ST91

Rushmore Park Golf Club SP5 5QB
☎ 01725 516326 Fax 01725 516466
Peaceful and testing parkland course, founded in 1994, situated on Cranborne Chase with far-reaching views. An undulating course with avenues of trees and well drained greens.
18 holes, 5580yds, Par 71, SSS 67.
Club membership 350.
Visitors   booking advisable over weekends.
Societies   welcome by appointment.
Green Fees £13 per 18 holes (£17 weekends).
Cards   〓 〓 Barclays 〓 🖂
Prof   Sean McDonagh
Designer   Tony Crouch
Facilities   ⊗ ⽕ ⛳ 🍺 ♀ △ 🏠 🛈 ⚷ ⼃
Location   16m SW of Salisbury, entrance off the B3081 between Sixpenny Handley and Tollard Royal

Hotel   ★★★ 72% Royal Chase Hotel, Royal Chase Roundabout, SHAFTESBURY ☎ 01747 853355   35 ⇔ ⟡

UPAVON   Map 04 SU15

Upavon Douglas Av SN9 6BQ
☎ 01980 630787 Fax 01980 630787
Downland course set on sides of infamous valley, with some wind affecting play. Includes a par 5 of 602 yards and finishing hole of 170 yards across a ravine.
18 holes, 6407yds, Par 71, SSS 71, Course record 70.
Club membership 600.
Visitors   must contact in advance and may not play before noon at weekends.

Societies telephone in advance.
Green Fees £24 per day; £16 per round.
Cards ⬛⬛⬛⬛⬛
Prof Richard Blake
Designer Richard Blake
Facilities ⊗℡⛳♨♀⚐⛴⚑♪⚙
& Leisure hard tennis courts.
Location 2m E on A342

Hotel ★★★ 66% Bear Hotel, Market Place,
DEVIZES ☎ 01380 722444 24 ⇄ ໕

WARMINSTER   Map 03 ST84

West Wilts Elm Hill BA12 0AU
☎ 01985 212702 Fax 01985 219809
A hilltop course among the Wiltshire downs on
downland turf. Free draining, short, but a very good test
of accurate iron play. Excellent greens and clubhouse
facilities.
18 holes, 5709yds, Par 70, SSS 68, Course record 62.
Club membership 650.
Visitors must contact in advance. Handicap
certificate required.
Societies apply by letter.
Green Fees £28 per day; £20 per round (£36 per
day/round weekends & bank holidays).
Prof Andrew Lamb
Designer J H Taylor
Facilities ⊗℡⛳♨♀⚐⛴⚑♪⚙
Location N side of town centre off A350

Hotel ★★★★ 73% Bishopstrow House,
WARMINSTER
☎ 01985 212312 31 ⇄ ໕

WOOTTON BASSETT   Map 04 SU08

Brinkworth Longmans Farm, Brinkworth SN15 5DG
☎ 01666 510277
Fairly long and open course with ditches and water hazards
on the 2nd and 18th holes. Several testing par 3s with
crosswinds and three long and tricky par 5s, notably the 4th,
8th and 14th holes.
18 holes, 5884yds, Par 70, SSS 70.
Club membership 100.
Visitors welcome any time no contact needed.
Societies telephone in advance or apply in writing.
Green Fees £8 per 18 holes (£10 weekends & bank
holidays).
Designer Jullian Sheppard
Facilities ⛳♨♀⚐⛴♪⚙
Location Just off B4042 between Malmesbury/Wootton
Bassett

Hotel ★★★ 70% Marsh Farm Hotel, Coped Hall,
WOOTTON BASSETT
☎ 01793 848044 4 ⇄ ໕ Annexe29 ⇄ ໕

Wiltshire Vastern SN4 7PB
☎ 01793 849999 Fax 01793 849988
A Peter Alliss/Clive Clark design set in rolling Wiltshire
downland countryside. A number of lakes add a challenge for
both low and high handicappers.
18 holes, 6522yds, Par 72, SSS 71.
Club membership 800.

Visitors must contact in advance.
Societies contact in advance.
Green Fees £30 per day.
Cards ⬛⬛⬛⬛
Prof Andy Gray
Designer Peter Allis & Clive Clark
Facilities ⊗℡⛳♨♀⚐⛴⚑♪⚙⚐⚙
Location Leave M4 at junc 16, on A3102

Hotel ★★★ 70% Marsh Farm Hotel, Coped Hall,
WOOTTON BASSETT
☎ 01793 848044 4 ⇄ ໕ Annexe29 ⇄ ໕

WORCESTERSHIRE

ALVECHURCH   Map 07 SP07

Kings Norton Brockhill Ln, Weatheroak B48 7ED
☎ 01564 826706 & 826789 Fax 01564 826955
A 27 hole Championship venue, 18 hole course 7000yds
par 72 plus 12 hole par 3 course. Parkland with water
hazards.
Weatheroak: 18 holes, 6748yds, Par 72, SSS 72.
Brockhill: 18 holes, 6648yds, Par 72, SSS 72.
Wythall: 18 holes, 6612yds, Par 72, SSS 72.
Club membership 1000.
Visitors must contact in advance. No visitors at
weekends
Societies must telephone in advance.
Green Fees £35 per 27 holes; £30 per 18 holes.
Prof Kevin Hayward
Designer F Hawtree
Facilities ⊗℡⛳♨♀⚐⛴⚑♪⚙⚐⚙
Location M42 junct3, off A435

Hotel ★★★ 72% Pine Lodge Hotel,
Kidderminster Rd, BROMSGROVE
☎ 01527 576600 114 ⇄ ໕

BEWDLEY   Map 07 SO77

Little Lakes Golf and Country Club Lye Head DY12 2UZ
☎ 01299 266385 Fax 01299 266178
A pleasant undulating parkland course extended to 18 holes
in April 1995. The course offers some pleasing views and
several demanding holes.
18 holes, 5644yds, Par 69, SSS 68, Course record 63.
Club membership 400.
Visitors advisable to telephone in advance.
Societies must telephone in advance.
Green Fees £13 per day (£17 per round weekends and bank
holidays).
Cards ⬛⬛⬛⬛
Prof Mark A Laing
Designer M Laing
Facilities ⊗℡⛳♨♀⚐⛴♪⚙⚐⚙
& Leisure hard tennis courts, heated outdoor swimming
pool, fishing.
Location 2.25m W off A456

Hotel ★★ 64% The George Hotel, Load St,
BEWDLEY ☎ 01299 402117 11 ⇄ ໕

Wharton Park Longbank DY12 2QW
☎ 01299 405222 & 405163 Fax 01299 405121
18-hole championship-standard course in 140 acres of
countryside. Some long Par 5s eg the 9th (594yds) as well as
superb par 3 holes at 3rd, 10th, 15th make this a very
challenging course.
18 holes, 6603yds, Par 73, SSS 72, Course record 66.
Club membership 500.
Visitors must contact in advance.
Societies prior booking required.
Green Fees not confirmed.
Cards ▭ ▦ ▦ ▦ 🗐
Prof Angus Hoare
Facilities ⊗ ⅧⅬ🍴♀🏖🏠⚲⛳♐⚑
& Leisure fishing.
Location Off A456 Bewdley bypass

Hotel ★★ 64% The George Hotel, Load St,
BEWDLEY ☎ 01299 402117 11 ⇔ ♠

BISHAMPTON Map 03 SO95

Vale Golf Club Hill Furze Rd WR10 2LZ
☎ 01386 462781 Fax 01386 462597
Opened in 1991 this course offers an American-style layout,
with large greens, trees and bunkers and several water
hazards. Its rolling fairways provide a testing round, as well
as superb views of the Malvern Hills. Picturesque and
peaceful. Also 9-hole course and 20-bay driving range.
International Course: 18 holes, 7114yds, Par 74, SSS 74,
Course record 72.
Lenches Course: 9 holes, 2759yds, Par 35, SSS 34.
Club membership 650.
Visitors booking up to one week in advance.
Societies must apply in advance. May only play weekdays
on 18 hole course.
Green Fees International: £20 (£25 weekends). Lenches:
£10 weekdays & weekends.
Cards ▭ ▦ ▦ 🗐
Prof Caroline Griffiths
Designer Bob Sandon
Facilities ⊗ ⅧⅬ🍴♀🏖🏠⚲♐⚑
& Leisure fishing.
Location Signposted off A4538

Hotel ★★ 68% The Chequers Inn, Chequers Ln,
FLADBURY ☎ 01386 860276 & 860527
Fax 01386 861286 8 ⇔ ♠

BLAKEDOWN Map 07 SO87

Churchill and Blakedown Churchill Ln DY10 3NB
☎ 01562 700018
Pleasant course on hilltop with extensive views.
9 holes, 6472yds, Par 72, SSS 71, Course record 63.
Club membership 380.
Visitors with member only weekends & bank holidays.
Handicap certificate required.
Societies by arrangement through secretary.
Green Fees not confirmed.
Prof K Wheeler
Facilities ⊗ ⅧⅬ🍴♀🏖🏠⚲
Location W side of village off A456

Hotel ★★★★ 64% Stone Manor Hotel, Stone,
KIDDERMINSTER
☎ 01562 777555 52 ⇔ ♠

BRANSFORD Map 03 SO75

Bank House Hotel Golf & Country Club WR6 5JD
☎ 01886 833551 Fax 01886 832461
The Pine Lakes course is designed as a 'Florida' style course
with fairways weaving between water courses, 13 lakes and
sculptured mounds with colouful plant displays. The 6,204yd
course has doglegs, island greens and tight fairways to
challenge all standards of player. The 10th, 16th and 18th
(The Devil's Elbow) are particularly tricky.
18 holes, 6204yds, Par 72, SSS 71, Course record 65.
Club membership 380.

Visitors all tee times must be booked, no play before
9.30am.
Societies contact the golf secretary, all tee times must be
booked in advance.
Green Fees not confirmed.
Prof Craig George
Designer Bob Sandow
Facilities ⊗ ⅧⅬ🍴♀🏖🏠⛳🏇⚲⛳♐⚑
& Leisure outdoor swimming pool, sauna, solarium,
gymnasium.
Location 3m S of Worcester, A4103

Hotel ★★★ 65% Bank House Hotel Golf & Country
Club, Hereford Rd, BRANSFORD
☎ 01886 833551 68 ⇔ ♠

BROADWAY Map 04 SP03

Broadway Willersey Hill WR12 7LG
☎ 01386 853683 Fax 01386 858643
At the edge of the Cotswolds this downland course lies at an
altitude of 900 ft above sea level, with extensive views.
Natural contours and man made hazards mean that drives
have to be placed, approaches carefully judged and the
greens expertly read.
18 holes, 6216yds, Par 72, SSS 70, Course record 65.
Club membership 850.
Visitors may not play Sat between Apr-Sep before 3pm.
Restricted play Sun. Must contact in advance.
Societies Wed-Fri, must contact in advance.
Green Fees £33 per day; £28 per round (£35 weekends &
bank holidays).
Prof Martyn Freeman
Designer James Braid
Facilities ⊗ ⅧⅬ🍴♀🏖🏠⛳⚲
Location 1.5m E on A44

Hotel ★★★ 74% Dormy House Hotel,
Willersey Hill, BROADWAY
☎ 01386 852711 26 ⇔ ♠ Annexe23 ⇔

BROMSGROVE
Map 07 SO97

Blackwell Agmore Rd, Blackwell B60 1PY
☎ 0121 445 1994 Fax 0121 445 4911
Pleasantly undulating parkland with a variety of trees. Laid out in two 9-hole loops.
18 holes, 6230yds, Par 70, SSS 71, Course record 63.
Club membership 385.

Visitors	must contact in advance, must have handicap certificate, may not play at weekends,
Societies	must contact in advance.
Green Fees	£50 per day.
Prof	Nigel Blake
Facilities	⊗ by prior arrangement ⽊ by prior arrangement ⽥ ▐ ⽑ ⽄ ⽢ ⽃ ⽝
Location	2m W of Alvechurch

Hotel	★★★ 72% Pine Lodge Hotel, Kidderminster Rd, BROMSGROVE ☎ 01527 576600 114 ⇄ ℝ

Bromsgrove Golf Centre Stratford Rd B60 1LD
☎ 01527 575886 Fax 01527 570964
Gently undulating parkland course with large contoured greens, generous tee surfaces and superb views over Worcestershire. Tricky par 3 16th across a lake. Also 41 bay floodlit driving range, floodlit practice bunker and new clubhouse with conference facilities.
18 holes, 5880yds, Par 68, SSS 68.
Club membership 900.

Visitors	dress restriction, no T-shirts, jeans, tracksuits etc. 7 day booking facilities available.
Societies	packages available, apply in writing or telephone.
Green Fees	£13.50 per 18 holes; £8 per 9 holes (£17/£10.50 weekends & bank holidays).
Cards	⟶ ▭ ▩ ▣
Prof	Graeme Long/Mark Davies
Designer	Hawtree & Son
Facilities	⊗ ⽊ ⽥ ▐ ⽑ ⽄ ⽢ ⽣ ⽃ ⽝ ⽞
& Leisure	practice bunker.
Location	E side of Bromsgrove, 6m W of Alvechurch

Hotel	★★★ 72% Pine Lodge Hotel, Kidderminster Rd, BROMSGROVE ☎ 01527 576600 114 ⇄ ℝ

DROITWICH
Map 03 SO86

Droitwich Ford Ln WR9 0BQ
☎ 01905 774344 Fax 01905 797 290
Undulating parkland course.

18 holes, 6058yds, Par 70, SSS 69, Course record 62.
Club membership 732.

Visitors	with member only weekends & bank holidays.
Societies	must apply by telephone and letter.
Green Fees	not confirmed.
Prof	C Thompson
Designer	J Braid/G Franks
Facilities	⊗ ⽊ ⽥ ▐ ⽑ ⽄ ⽢ ⽃
& Leisure	snooker.
Location	Off A38 Droitwich to Bromsgrove road, midway between Droitwich and M5 junct 5

Hotel	★★★★ 67% Chateau Impney Hotel, DROITWICH SPA ☎ 01905 774411 67 ⇄ ℝ

Gaudet Luce Middle Ln, Hadzor WR9 7DP
☎ 01905 796375 Fax 01905 796375
A challenging 18-hole course with two contrasting 9-hole loops. The front nine are long and fairly open, the back nine are tight and compact requiring good positional and approach play. Water features on several holes.
18 holes, 5887yds, Par 70, SSS 68.
Club membership 225.

Visitors	welcome, advisable to telephone in advance, proper golfing attire required at all times.
Societies	telephone for details.
Green Fees	not confirmed.
Prof	Mark Laing
Facilities	⽥ ▐ ⽑ ⽄ ⽢
Location	M5 junct 5, left at Tagwell road into Middle Lane, 1st driveway on left to clubhouse

Hotel	★★★★ 67% Chateau Impney Hotel, DROITWICH SPA ☎ 01905 774411 67 ⇄ ℝ

Ombersley Bishops Wood Rd, Lineholt, Ombersley WR9 0LE ☎ 01905 620747 Fax 01905 620047
Undulating course in beautiful countryside high above the edge of the Severn Valley. Covered driving range and putting green.
18 holes, 6139yds, Par 72, SSS 69, Course record 67.
Club membership 750.

Visitors	suitable dress expected, no jeans, T-shirts etc.
Societies	telephone in advance.
Green Fees	not confirmed.
Prof	Graham Glenister
Designer	David Morgan
Facilities	⊗ ⽊ ⽥ ▐ ⽑ ⽄ ⽢ ⽣ ⽃ ⽝ ⽞ ⽟
Location	3m W of Droitwich, off A449. At Mitre Oak pub, take A4025 to Stourport, signposted 400yds on left

Hotel	★★★★ 65% Raven Hotel, Victoria Square, DROITWICH SPA ☎ 01905 772224 72 ⇄ ℝ

FLADBURY
Map 03 SO94

Evesham Craycombe Links, Old Worcester Rd WR10 2QS ☎ 01386 860395
Parkland, heavily wooded, with the River Avon running alongside 5th and 14th holes. Good views. Nine greens played from eighteen different tees.
9 holes, 6415yds, Par 72, SSS 71, Course record 68.
Club membership 383.

▶

Visitors	must contact in advance. With members only at weekends.
Societies	must apply by letter.
Green Fees	not confirmed.
Prof	Charles Haynes
Facilities	⊗ �🍽 🖫 🖳 ♀ 🍴 🏠 ⛳ 🏌 ♂ 𝄪
Location	0.75m N on A4538

Hotel	★★★ 71% The Evesham Hotel, Coopers Ln, Off Waterside, EVESHAM ☎ 01386 765566 & 0800 716969 (Res) Fax 01386 765443 39 ➡ 🐾

HOLLYWOOD   Map 07 SP07

Gay Hill Hollywood Ln B47 5PP
☎ 0121 430 8544 & 474 6001 (pro)
Fax 0121 436 7796
A meadowland course, some 7m from Birmingham.
18 holes, 6532yds, Par 72, SSS 71, Course record 64.
Club membership 740.

Visitors	must contact in advance. May only play at weekends with member.
Societies	telephone in advance.
Green Fees	not confirmed.
Prof	Andrew Potter
Facilities	⊗ 🖫 🖳 ♀ 🏠 🍴 ♂
Location	N side of village

Hotel	★★★★ 62% Regency Hotel, Stratford Rd, Shirley, SOLIHULL ☎ 0121 745 6119 112 ➡ 🐾

KIDDERMINSTER   Map 07 SO87

Habberley Low Trimpley DY11 5RG
☎ 01562 745756 Fax 01562 745756
Very hilly, wooded parkland course.
9 holes, 5481yds, Par 69, Course record 62.
Club membership 300.

Visitors	may only play weekends with a member,
Societies	telephone initially.
Green Fees	not confirmed.
Facilities	⊗ �🍽 🖫 🖳 ♀ 🏠
Location	2m NW of Kidderminster

Hotel	★★★★ 64% Stone Manor Hotel, Stone, KIDDERMINSTER ☎ 01562 777555 52 ➡ 🐾

Kidderminster Russell Rd DY10 3HT
☎ 01562 822303 Fax 01562 862041
Parkland course with natural hazards and some easy walking.
18 holes, 6405yds, Par 72, SSS 71, Course record 66.
Club membership 860.

Visitors	with member only weekends & bank holidays. Must have a handicap certificate.
Societies	Thu only, apply in advance.
Green Fees	not confirmed.
Prof	Nick Underwood
Facilities	🏠 🍴 ♂
Location	0.5m SE of town centre, signposted off A449

Hotel	★★★★ 64% Stone Manor Hotel, Stone, KIDDERMINSTER ☎ 01562 777555 52 ➡ 🐾

Wyre Forest Zortech Av DY10 4JP
☎ 01299 822682 Fax 01299 879433
Making full use of the existing contours, this interesting and challenging course is bounded by woodland and gives extensive views over the surrounding area. Well drained fairways and greens.
18 holes, 5790yds, Par 70, SSS 68, Course record 68.
Club membership 397.

Visitors	preferable to telephone first.
Societies	brochure on request, deposit secures date, write or telephone.
Green Fees	not confirmed.
Cards	🔳 🔳 🔳 🔳 🔳
Prof	Simon Price
Facilities	⊗ �🍽 🖫 🖳 ♀ 🏠 🍴 🏌 ♂
Location	Approx half way between Kidderminster/Stourport, on the A451

Hotel	★★★★ 69% Stourport Manor, Hartlebury Rd, STOURPORT-ON-SEVERN ☎ 01299 289955 68 ➡ 🐾

MALVERN WELLS   Map 03 SO74

Worcestershire Wood Farm, Hanley Rd WR14 4PP
☎ 01684 575992 & 573905 Fax 01684 575992
Fairly easy walking on windy downland course with trees, ditches and other natural hazards. Outstanding views of Malvern Hills and Severn Valley. 17th hole (par 5) is approached over small lake.
18 holes, 6470yds, Par 71, SSS 71, Course record 65.
Club membership 770.

Visitors	only after 10am at weekends or with a member. Must contact in advance. Handicap certificate required.
Societies	Thu & Fri only, apply in writing.
Green Fees	not confirmed.
Cards	🔳
Prof	Richard Lewis
Designer	Colt/Braid
Facilities	⊗ �🍽 🖫 🖳 ♀ 🏠 🏌 ♂
Location	2m S of Gt Malvern on B4209

Hotel	★★★♨ 73% The Cottage in the Wood Hotel, Holywell Rd, Malvern Wells, MALVERN ☎ 01684 575859 8 ➡ 🐾 Annexe12 ➡ 🐾

REDDITCH   Map 07 SP06

Abbey Hotel Golf & Country Club
Dagnell End Rd   B98 7BD
☎ 01527 68006 (golf shop) & 63913 (reception)
Fax 01527 584112
Young parkland course opened in 1985, with rolling
fairways. A 'Site of Special Scientific Interest', the course
includes two fishing lakes and is pleasant to play.
18 holes, 6499yds, Par 72, SSS 72.
Club membership 700.

Visitors	must contact in advance.
Societies	must apply in writing.
Green Fees	£12 per round (£16 weekends).
Prof	S Edwards
Facilities	⊗ ℍ 🛒 🖥 ♀ ♣ 🏠 ⛳ 🏎 ✂ ♞
& Leisure	heated indoor swimming pool, fishing, sauna, solarium, gymnasium, massage & beauty facilities.
Location	1.25m N off A441 on B4101

Hotel	★★★ 68% The Abbey Park Hotel, Hither Green Ln, Dagnel End Rd, Bordesley, REDDITCH ☎ 01527 584140

Pitcheroak Plymouth Rd B97 4PB   ☎ 01527 541054
Woodland course, hilly in places.There is also a putting
green and a practice ground.
9 holes, 4561yds, Par 65, SSS 62.
Club membership 200.

Visitors	no restrictions.
Societies	telephone to book.
Green Fees	£7.50 per 18 holes; £5.75 per 9 holes (£8.65/£6.35 weekends).
Cards	🔲 🔲
Prof	David Stewart
Facilities	⊗ 🛒 🖥 ♀ ♣ 🏠 ⛳ ✂
Location	SW side of town centre off A448

Hotel	★★★ 63% Quality Hotel, Pool Bank, Southcrest, REDDITCH ☎ 01527 541511 58 ⇆ ♟

Redditch Lower Grinsty, Green Ln, Callow Hill B97 5PJ
☎ 01527 543079 Fax 01527 543079
Parkland course, the hazards including woods, ditches and
large ponds. The par 4, 14th is a testing hole. All greens were
rebuilt in 1996/1997.
18 holes, 6671yds, Par 72, SSS 72, Course record 68.
Club membership 650.

Visitors	with member only weekends & bank holidays, no visitors on competition days, advisable to telephone in advance.

Societies	telephone Secretary.
Green Fees	£27.50 per day.
Prof	Frank Powell
Designer	F Pennick
Facilities	⊗ ℍ 🛒 🖥 ♀ ♣ 🏠 ⛳ ♞ 🏎 ✂
Location	2m SW

Hotel	★★★ 63% Quality Hotel, Pool Bank, Southcrest, REDDITCH ☎ 01527 541511 58 ⇆ ♟

TENBURY WELLS   Map 07 SO56

Cadmore Lodge Hotel & Country Club St Michaels,
Berrington Green WR15 8TQ
☎ 01584 810044 Fax 01584 810044
A picturesque 9-hole course in a brook valley. Challenging
holes include the 1st and 6th over the lake, 8th over the
valley and 9th over hedges.
9 holes, 5132yds, Par 68, SSS 65.
Club membership 200.

Visitors	no restrictions but check availability.
Societies	telephone in advance.
Green Fees	£10 (£14 weekends).
Cards	🔲 🔲 🔲 🔲 🔲 🔲
Facilities	⊗ ℍ 🛒 🖥 ♀ ♣ 🏎 ✂
& Leisure	hard tennis courts, heated indoor swimming pool, fishing, sauna, gymnasium, pool table.
Location	From Tenbury take A4112 to Leominster, after approx 2m turn right for Berrington. 0.75 on left

Hotel	★★ 66% Cadmore Lodge Hotel & Country Club, Berrington Green, St Michaels, TENBURY WELLS ☎ 01584 810044 14 ⇆ ♟

WORCESTER   Map 03 SO85

Worcester Golf & Country Club Boughton Park WR2 4EZ
☎ 01905 422555 Fax 01905 749090
Fine parkland course with many trees, a lake, and views of
the Malvern Hills.
18 holes, 6251yds, Par 70, SSS 70, Course record 67.
Club membership 1000.

Visitors	must contact professional in advance. May not play at weekends.
Societies	telephone in advance.
Green Fees	£25 per round.
Prof	Colin Colenso
Designer	Dr A Mackenzie
Facilities	⊗ by prior arrangement ℍ by prior arrangement 🛒 🖥 ♀ ♣ 🏠 ✂
& Leisure	hard and grass tennis courts, squash. ▶

Location   1.5m from city centre on A4103

Hotel   ★★★ 63% The Gifford Hotel, High St,
WORCESTER ☎ 01905 726262 103 ⇄ ♠

WYTHALL   Map 07 SP07

Fulford Heath Tanners Green Ln B47 6BH
☎ 01564 824758 Fax 01564 822629
A mature parkland course encompassing two classic par
threes. The 11th, a mere 149 yards, shoots from an elevated
tee through a channel of trees to a well protected green. The
16th, a 166 yard par 3, elevated green, demands a 140 yard
carry over an imposing lake.
18 holes, 6179yds, Par 70, SSS 70, Course record 66.
Club membership 700.
Visitors   with member only weekend & bank holidays.
Societies   must apply in advance.
Green Fees £34 per day.
Prof   David Down
Designer   Hawtree
Facilities   ⊗ ⊪ ⬥ ♥ ♀ ⚲ 🕾 ♂
Location   1m SE off A435

Hotel   ★★★★ 64% St John's Swallow Hotel,
651 Warwick Rd, SOLIHULL
☎ 0121 711 3000 177 ⇄ ♠

YORKSHIRE, EAST RIDING OF

BEVERLEY   Map 08 TA03

Beverley & East Riding The Westwood HU17 8RG
☎ 01482 868757 Fax 01482 868757
Picturesque parkland course with some hard walking and
natural hazards - trees and gorse bushes. Also cattle (spring
to autumn); horse-riders are an occasional hazard in the early
morning.
Westwood: 18 holes, 6127yds, Par 69, SSS 69,
Course record 65.
Club membership 530.
Visitors   advised to contact pro shop 01482 869519.
Societies   telephone 01482 868757, then written
confirmation.
Green Fees £17 per day; £13 per round (£22/£17 weekends
& bank holidays).
Prof   Ian Mackie
Facilities   ⊗ ⊪ by prior arrangement ⬥ ♥ ♀ ⚲ 🕾 ♂
Location   1m SW on B1230

Hotel   ★★★ 67% Beverley Arms Hotel,
North Bar Within, BEVERLEY
☎ 01482 869241 56 ⇄ ♠

BRANDESBURTON   Map 08 TA14

Hainsworth Park Burton Holme YO25 8RT
☎ 01964 542362
A parkland course with easy walking.
18 holes, 6048yds, Par 71, SSS 69, Course record 62.
Club membership 500.

Visitors   contact in advance.
Societies   telephone initially.
Green Fees not confirmed.
Cards   ⬛⬛
Prof   Paul Binnington
Facilities   ⊗ ⊪ ⬥ ♥ ♀ ⚲ 🕾 ♂ ♥ ♂
& Leisure   grass tennis courts, fishing.
Location   SW side of village on A165

Hotel   ★★ 68% Burton Lodge Hotel,
BRANDESBURTON
☎ 01964 542847 7 ⇄ ♠ Annexe2 ⇄ ♠

BRIDLINGTON   Map 08 TA16

Bridlington Belvedere Rd YO15 3NA
☎ 01262 606367 Fax 01262 606367
Clifftop, seaside course, windy at times, with hazards of
bunkers, ponds, ditches and trees.
18 holes, 6638yds, Par 72, SSS 72, Course record 66.
Club membership 600.
Visitors   must contact in advance, professional 01262
674721 limited at weekends.
Societies   telephone bookings in advance.
Green Fees £22 per day; £15 per round (£25 per day/round
weekends & bank holidays).
Prof   Anthony Howarth
Designer   James Braid
Facilities   ⊗ ⊪ ⬥ ♥ ♀ ⚲ 🕾 ♂ ♂
Location   1m S off A165

Hotel   ★★★ 67% Revelstoke Hotel,
1-3 Flamborough Rd, BRIDLINGTON
☎ 01262 672362 25 ⇄ ♠

Bridlington Links Flamborough Rd, Marton YO15 1DW
☎ 01262 401584 Fax 01262 401702
Coastal links type course with large greens, numerous water
hazards and splendid views towards Flamborough Head.
When the wind blows off the sea, the course becomes a
challenging test of golf for even the experienced golfer.
Main: 18 holes, 6719yds, Par 72, SSS 72, Course record 70.
Club membership 350.
Visitors   telephone to book tee times.
Societies   telephone for booking.
Green Fees not confirmed.
Cards   ⬛⬛⬛
Prof   Steve Raybould
Designer   Swan
Facilities   ⊗ ⊪ ⬥ ♥ ♀ ⚲ 🕾 ♂ ♥ ⚒ ♂ ⚶
Location   On the B1255 between Bridlington and
Flamborough

Hotel   ★★★ 66% Expanse Hotel, North Marine Dr,
BRIDLINGTON
☎ 01262 675347 48 ⇄ ♠

BROUGH   Map 08 SE92

Brough Cave Rd HU15 1HB
☎ 01482 667291 Fax 01482 667291
Parkland course.
18 holes, 6159yds, Par 68, SSS 69, Course record 64.
Club membership 800.
Visitors   must have handicap certificate and contact in
advance.
Societies   apply by letter.

Green Fees not confirmed.
Cards ▭ ▬ ▨ ▧
Prof Gordon Townhill
Facilities ⊗ ⅲ ▤ � ♀ ⚲ 📁 ⛳ ♂
Location 0.5m N

Hotel B Posthouse Hull, Ferriby High Rd, NORTH
FERRIBY ☎ 01482 645212 96 ⇔ ♠

COTTINGHAM Map 08 TA03

Cottingham Woodhill Way HU16 5RZ
☎ 01482 846030 Fax 01482 845932
Gently undulating parkland course incorporating many
natural features, including lateral water hazards, several
ponds on the approach to greens, and rolling fairways.
18 holes, 6459yds, Par 72, SSS 71, Course record 69.
Club membership 650.
Visitors may book by telephone in advance, times
available all day weekdays, after 11am
weekends.
Societies deposit required and confirmation in writing.
Green Fees £14 per round (£20 per round weekends).
Prof Chris Gray
Designer Terry Litten
Facilities ⊗ ⅲ ▤ ▬ ♀ ⚲ 📁 ⛳ ♂ ♭
& Leisure equestrian centre.
Location 4m from A63/M62 on A164. Turn off to
Cottingham on B1233, in 100yds turn left into
Woodhill Way

Hotel ★★★♨♨ 61% Rowley Manor Hotel,
Rowley Rd, LITTLE WEIGHTON
☎ 01482 848248 16 ⇔ ♠

DRIFFIELD (GREAT) Map 08 TA05

Driffield Sunderlandwick YO25 9AD
☎ 01377 253116 Fax 01377 240599
An easy walking, mature parkland course set within the
beautiful Sunderlandwick Estate.
18 holes, 6215yds, Par 70, SSS 69, Course record 67.
Club membership 693.
Visitors must book in advance and adhere to club dress
rule.
Societies apply in writing or telephone.
Green Fees not confirmed.
Prof Dennis Taylor
Facilities ⊗ ⅲ ▤ ▬ ♀ ⚲ 📁 ♂
& Leisure fishing.
Location 2m S off A164

Hotel ★★★ 70% Bell Hotel,
46 Market Place, DRIFFIELD
☎ 01377 256661 14 ⇔ ♠

FLAMBOROUGH Map 08 TA27

Flamborough Head Lighthouse Rd YO15 1AR
☎ 01262 850333 & 850417 Fax 01262 850279
Undulating seaside course.
18 holes, 5976yds, Par 70, SSS 69, Course record 70.
Club membership 500.
Visitors welcome but may not play; before 1pm Sun,
Wed between 10.30 & 1.30, Sat between 11.30
& 12.30.
Societies must contact in advance.

Green Fees £17 per day; £14 per round (£20 weekends &
bank holidays).
Facilities ⊗ ⅲ ▤ ▬ ♀ ⚲ 📁 ♠ ♂
Location 2m E off B1259

Hotel ★ 67% Flaneburg Hotel & Restaurant,
North Marine Rd, FLAMBOROUGH
☎ 01262 850284 14rm(12 ♠)

HESSLE Map 08 TA02

Hessle Westfield Rd, Raywell HU16 5YL
☎ 01482 650171 & 650190 (Prof)
Well-wooded downland course, easy walking, windy.
18 holes, 6604yds, Par 72, SSS 72, Course record 68.
Visitors not Tue between 9-1 and may not play before
11am on Sat & Sun.
Societies by prior arrangement.
Green Fees not confirmed.
Prof Grahame Fieldsend
Designer D Thomas/P Allis
Facilities ⊗ ⅲ ▤ ▬ ♀ ⚲ 📁 ♂
Location 3m SW of Cottingham

Hotel B Posthouse Hull, Ferriby High Rd, NORTH
FERRIBY ☎ 01482 645212 96 ⇔ ♠

HORNSEA Map 08 TA14

Hornsea Rolston Rd HU18 1XG
☎ 01964 532020 Fax 01964 532020
Flat, parkland course with good greens.
18 holes, 6685yds, Par 72, SSS 72, Course record 66.
Club membership 600.
Visitors with member only at weekends & after 3pm.
Must contact in advance.
Societies contact Secretary in advance.
Green Fees £30 per day; £22 per round (£30 per round
weekends).
Prof Brian Thompson
Facilities ⊗ ⅲ ▤ ▬ ♀ ⚲ 📁 ⛳ ♣ ♂
& Leisure snooker table.
Location 1m S on B1242, follow signs for Hornsea
Freeport

Hotel ★★★ 67% Beverley Arms Hotel, North Bar
Within, BEVERLEY
☎ 01482 869241 56 ⇔ ♠

HULL Map 08 TA02

Ganstead Park Longdales Ln, Coniston HU11 4LB
☎ 01482 817754 Fax 01482 817754
Parkland course, easy walking, with water features.
18 holes, 6801yds, Par 72, SSS 73, Course record 67.
Club membership 500.
Visitors contact in advance.
Societies telephone in advance.
Green Fees £24 per day; £18 per round (£26 per round
weekends).
Prof Michael J Smee
Designer P Green
Facilities ⊗ ⅲ ▤ ▬ ♀ ⚲ 📁 ♠ ♂
Location 6m NE on A165

Hotel ★★★ 66% Quality Hotel Hull, 170 Ferensway,
HULL ☎ 01482 325087 155 ⇔ ♠

Hull The Hall, 27 Packman Ln HU10 7TJ
☎ 01482 658919 Fax 01482 658919
Parkland course.
18 holes, 6242yds, Par 70, SSS 70.
Club membership 840.

Visitors	only weekdays. Contact professional 01482 653074.
Societies	only on Tue and Thu by prior arrangement.
Green Fees	£32 per day; £26.50 per round.
Prof	David Jagger
Designer	James Braid
Facilities	⊗ �171 🏌 ➡ ♀ 🛆 🖂 🛒
Location	5m W of city centre off A164

Hotel ★★★ 71% Willerby Manor Hotel, Well Ln,
WILLERBY ☎ 01482 652616 51 ⇔ 🐾

Springhead Park Willerby Rd HU5 5JE ☎ 01482 656309
Municipal parkland course with tight, tree-lined, undulating
fairways.
18 holes, 6402yds, Par 71, SSS 71.
Club membership 667.

Visitors	welcome ex Sun (tee reserved).
Green Fees	not confirmed.
Prof	Barry Herrington
Facilities	🖂 🛒
Location	5m W off A164

Hotel ★★★ 71% Willerby Manor Hotel, Well Ln,
WILLERBY ☎ 01482 652616 51 ⇔ 🐾

Sutton Park Salthouse Rd HU8 9HF
☎ 01482 374242 Fax 01482 701428
Municipal parkland course.
18 holes, 6251yds, Par 70, SSS 69, Course record 67.
Club membership 300.

Visitors	no restrictions.
Societies	prior arrangement via club, telephone and confirm in writing.
Green Fees	£7 per round (£9 weekends & bank holidays).
Prof	Paul Rushworth
Facilities	🛆 🖂 🛒 🛒
Location	3m NE on B1237 off A165

Hotel ★★★ 66% Quality Hotel Hull, 170 Ferensway,
HULL ☎ 01482 325087 155 ⇔ 🐾

South Cave   Map 08 SE93

Cave Castle Hotel & Country Club Church Hill, South
Cave HU15 2EU ☎ 01430 421286 Fax 01430 421118
A young but challenging course at the foot of the Wolds with
superb views. Tuition, golf clinics and golf breaks are
available.
18 holes, 6500yds, Par 73, SSS 71, Course record 71.
Club membership 450.

Visitors	must contact in advance, may not play before 11am weekends/bank holidays.
Societies	by arrangement with Manager.
Green Fees	£12.50 (£18 weekends & bank holidays).
Prof	Stephen MacKinder
Designer	Mrs N Freling
Facilities	⊗ ⚏ 🏌 ➡ ♀ 🛆 🖂 🛒 🎿 🛒
& Leisure	heated indoor swimming pool, fishing, sauna, solarium, gymnasium.
Location	1m from A63

Hotel ★★ 63% Fox & Coney Inn, Market Place,
SOUTH CAVE ☎ 01430 422275 8 ⇔ 🐾

Withernsea   Map 08 TA32

Withernsea Chesnut Av HU19 2PG ☎ 01964 612078
Exposed seaside links with narrow, undulating fairways,
bunkers and small greens.
9 holes, 5907yds, Par 72, SSS 69.
Club membership 300.

Visitors	with member only at weekends before 3pm.
Societies	apply in writing.
Green Fees	not confirmed.
Prof	Graham Harrison
Facilities	⊗ by prior arrangement ⚏ by prior arrangement 🏌 by prior arrangement ➡ ♀ weekends 🛆 🖂
Location	S side of town centre off A1033

Hotel ★★★ 66% Quality Hotel Hull, 170 Ferensway,
HULL ☎ 01482 325087 155 ⇔ 🐾

YORKSHIRE, NORTH

Aldwark   Map 08 SE46

Aldwark Manor YO61 1UF
☎ 01347 838353 Fax 01347 830007
An easy walking, scenic 18-hole parkland course with holes
both sides of the River Ure. The course surrounds the
Victorian Aldwark Manor Golf Hotel. A warm welcome to
society and corporate days.
18 holes, 6171yds, Par 71, SSS 70, Course record 69.
Club membership 400.

Visitors	must contact in advance, restricted weekends.
Societies	must telephone in advance.
Green Fees	£25 per day; £20 per round (£30/£25 weekends & bank holidays).
Cards	💳 💳 💳 💳 💳 💳
Prof	Phil Harrison
Facilities	⊗ ⚏ 🏌 ➡ ♀ 🛆 🖂 🛒 🚗 🛒
& Leisure	fishing.
Location	5m SE of Boroughbridge off A1, 12m NW of York off A19

Hotel ★★★ 70% Aldwark Manor Hotel,
Golf & Country Club, ALDWARK
☎ 01347 838146 & 838251 Fax 01347 838867
25 ⇔ 🐾 Annexe3rm(2 ⇔ 🐾)

Bedale   Map 08 SE28

Bedale Leyburn Rd DL8 1EZ
☎ 01677 422451 Fax 01677 422451
Secluded parkland course with many trees and water
features. A quiet, testing course ideal for beginners and the
more adept golfer.
18 holes, 6610yds, Par 72, SSS 72, Course record 68.
Club membership 600.

Visitors	welcome when course is free, contact Professional or Secretary to book.
Societies	must apply in advance.

Green Fees	£20 per day/round (£30 weekends).
Prof	Tony Johnson
Facilities	⊗ ⅏ ⅄ 💺 ♀ ⅄ 🏠 ⌀
Location	0.25 N of town on A684
Hotel	★ 68% Buck Inn, THORNTON WATLASS
	☎ 01677 422461 7rm(5 ⇥ ♠)

BENTHAM   Map 07 SD66

Bentham Robin Ln LA2 7AG ☎ 01524 262455
Moorland course with glorious views.
9 holes, 5760yds, Par 70, SSS 69, Course record 69.
Club membership 480.

Visitors	no restrictions.
Societies	must apply in advance.
Green Fees	£16 per day (£20 weekends & bank holidays).
Facilities	⊗ ⅏ ⅄ 💺 ♀ ⅄
Location	N side of High Bentham
Hotel	★★ 66% The Traddock, AUSTWICK
	☎ 015242 51224 11 ⇥ ♠

CATTERICK GARRISON   Map 08 SE29

Catterick Leyburn Rd DL9 3QE
☎ 01748 833268 Fax 01748 833268
Scenic parkland/moorland course of Championship standard,
with good views of the Pennines and Cleveland hills. Testing
1st and 6th holes.
18 holes, 6329yds, Par 71, SSS 70, Course record 68.
Club membership 700.

Visitors	tee reservation system in operation telephone professional shop 01748 833671, Tuesday is Ladies day, Thursday Senior priority until 10am.
Societies	by arrangement.
Green Fees	£25 per day/round (£30 weekends).
Prof	Andy Marshall
Designer	Arthur Day
Facilities	⊗ ⅏ ⅄ 💺 ♀ ⅄ 🏠 ⌀ 🏌 ♠ 🛒 ⌀
Location	0.5m W of Catterick Garrison Centre
Hotel	★★ 69% King's Head Hotel, Market Place, RICHMOND
	☎ 01748 850220 26 ⇥ ♠ Annexe4 ⇥ ♠

COPMANTHORPE   Map 08 SE54

Pike Hills Tadcaster Rd YO23 3UW
☎ 01904 700797 Fax 01904 700797
Parkland course surrounding nature reserve. Level terrain.
18 holes, 6146yds, Par 71, SSS 70, Course record 67.
Club membership 750.

Visitors	welcome weekdays, with member only weekends & bank holidays.
Societies	must apply in advance.
Green Fees	£26 per day; £20 per round.
Prof	Ian Gradwell
Facilities	⊗ ⅏ ⅄ 💺 ♀ ⅄ 🏠 🏌 🐾 🛒 ⌀
Location	3m SW of York on A64
Hotel	★★★★ 64% Swallow Hotel, Tadcaster Rd, YORK ☎ 01904 701000 113 ⇥ ♠

EASINGWOLD   Map 08 SE56

Easingwold Stillington Rd YO61 3ET
☎ 01347 821964 (Prof) & 822474 (Sec) Fax 01347 822474
Parkland course with easy walking. Trees are a major feature
and on six holes water hazards come into play.
18 holes, 6060mtrs, Par 72, SSS 72, Course record 65.
Club membership 700.

Visitors	prior enquiry essential.
Societies	prior application in writing essential.
Green Fees	£30 per day; £25 per round (£30 weekends).
Prof	John Hughes
Designer	Hawtree
Facilities	⊗ ⅏ ⅄ 💺 ♀ ⅄ 🏠 🛒 ⌀
Location	1m S of Easingwold, 12m N of York
Hotel	★★ 66% George Hotel, Market Place, EASINGWOLD
	☎ 01347 821698 14 ⇥ ♠

FILEY   Map 08 TA18

Filey West Av YO14 9BQ
☎ 01723 513293 Fax 01723 514952
Parkland course with good views. Stream runs through
course. Testing 9th and 13th holes.
18 holes, 6112yds, Par 70, SSS 69, Course record 64.
Club membership 900.

Visitors	must telephone to reserve tee time.
Societies	contact by telephone.
Green Fees	£21-£27 per day; £16-£21 per round (£30/£28 weekends).
Prof	Gary Hutchinson
Designer	Braid
Facilities	⊗ ⅏ ⅄ 💺 ♀ ⅄ 🏠 🏌 🐾 ⌀
& Leisure	9 hole starter course.
Location	0.5m S of Filey
Hotel	★★ 68% Wrangham House Hotel, 10 Stonegate, HUNMANBY
	☎ 01723 891333 8 ⇥ ♠ Annexe4 ⇥ ♠

GANTON — Map 08 SE97

Ganton YO12 4PA
☎ 01944 710329 Fax 01944 710922
Championship course, heathland, gorse-lined fairways and heavily bunkered; variable winds.
18 holes, 6734yds, Par 73, SSS 74, Course record 65.
Club membership 500.

Visitors	by prior arrangement.
Societies	prior arrangement in writing.
Green Fees	£50 per day/round (£56 weekends & bank holidays).
Cards	〇〇〇〇〇〇
Prof	Gary Brown
Designer	Dunn/Vardon/Braid/Colt
Facilities	⊗ ⅷ 馬 ➌ ♀ ♨ 曲 ィ ↘ ▵ ♂
Location	11m SW of Scarborough on A64
Hotel	★★★ 62% East Ayton Lodge Country House, Moor Ln, Forge Valley, EAST AYTON ☎ 01723 864227 11 ➪ ℝ Annexe20 ➪ ℝ

HARROGATE — Map 08 SE35

Harrogate Forest Ln Head, Starbeck HG2 7TF
☎ 01423 862999 Fax 01423 860073
One of Yorkshire's oldest and best courses was designed in 1897 by 'Sandy' Herd. A perfect example of golf architecture, its greens and fairways offer an interesting but fair challenge. The undulating parkland course once formed part of the ancient Forest of Knaresborough. Excellent clubhouse.
18 holes, 6241yds, Par 69, SSS 70, Course record 64.
Club membership 650.

Visitors	advisable to contact professional in advance, weekend play limited.
Societies	must contact in writing or intially by telephone.
Green Fees	£35 per day; £30 per round (£40 day/round weekends & bank holidays).
Cards	〇〇
Prof	Paul Johnson
Designer	Sandy Herd
Facilities	⊗ ⅷ 馬 ➌ ♀ ▵ 曲 ♂
& Leisure	Snooker.
Location	2.25m N on A59
Hotel	★★★ 66% The White House, 10 Park Pde, HARROGATE ☎ 01423 501388 10 ➪ ℝ

Oakdale Oakdale Glen HG1 2LN
☎ 01423 567162 & 567188 Fax 01423 536030
A pleasant, undulating parkland course which provides a good test of golf for the low handicap player without intimidating the less proficient. A special feature is an attractive stream which comes in to play on four holes. Excellent views from the clubhouse which has good facilities.
18 holes, 6456yds, Par 71, SSS 71, Course record 61.
Club membership 1034.

Visitors	no party bookings weekends.
Societies	telephone followed by letter.
Green Fees	£27 per round (£32 per round weekends & bank holidays).

Prof	Clive Dell
Designer	Dr McKenzie
Facilities	⊗ ⅷ 馬 ➌ ♀ ▵ 曲 ィ ↘ ♂
Location	N side of town centre off A61
Hotel	★★★ 72% Grants Hotel, 3-13 Swan Rd, HARROGATE ☎ 01423 560666 42 ➪ ℝ

Rudding Park House & Hotel HG3 1DJ
☎ 01423 872100 Fax 01423 873011
Opened in Spring 1995, Rudding Park has been designed by Hawtree of Oxford as a parkland course with 5 water features to be operated on a Pay and Play basis.
18 holes, 6871yds, Par 72, SSS 73, Course record 72.

Visitors	handicap certificate required, tee reservation available 7 days in advance.
Societies	apply by telephone in advance.
Green Fees	£19 per round (£21 weekends & bank holidays).
Cards	〇〇〇〇
Prof	Simon Hotham
Designer	Hawtree
Facilities	⊗ ⅷ 馬 ➌ ♀ ▵ 曲 ィ ↩ ↘ ▵ ♂ ₹
& Leisure	heated outdoor swimming pool.
Location	2m SE of Harrogate town centre, off A658 follow brown tourist signs
Hotel	★★★★ 71% Rudding Park House & Hotel, Rudding Park, Follifoot, HARROGATE ☎ 01423 871350 50 ➪ ℝ

HOWDEN — Map 08 SE72

Boothferry Park Spaldington Ln DN14 7NG
☎ 01430 430364
Pleasant meadowland course in the Vale of York with interesting natural dykes creating extra challenge on some holes. The par3 5th over water will test your nerve.
18 holes, 6651yds, Par 73, SSS 72, Course record 64.
Club membership 500.

Visitors	must contact in advance, tee times bookable.
Societies	must contact for booking form.
Green Fees	£10 per round (£15 weekends).
Prof	Nigel Bundy
Designer	Donald Steel
Facilities	⊗ ⅷ 馬 ➌ ♀ ▵ 曲 ィ ▵ ♂ ₹
Location	2.5m N of Howden off B1228
Hotel	★★ 71% Clifton Hotel, 15 Boothferry Rd, GOOLE ☎ 01405 761336 9rm(8 ➪ ℝ)

KIRKBYMOORSIDE — Map 08 SE68

Kirkbymoorside Manor Vale YO62 6EG
☎ 01751 431525 Fax 01751 433190
Hilly parkland course with narrow fairways, gorse and hawthorn bushes. Beautiful views.
18 holes, 6101yds, Par 69, SSS 69, Course record 65.
Club membership 650.

Visitors	are advised to contact in advance, may not play before 9.30 or between 12.30-1.30.
Societies	must apply in advance.
Green Fees	£20 per day (£27 weekends & bank holidays).
Facilities	⊗ ⅷ 馬 ➌ ♀ ▵ ィ ♂
& Leisure	snooker room.
Location	N side of village

Hotel ★★ 70% George & Dragon Hotel, 17 Market Place, KIRKBYMOORSIDE ☎ 01751 433334 12 ⇆ ♠ Annexe7 ⇆ ♠

KNARESBOROUGH　　　　　　　　Map 08 SE35

Knaresborough Boroughbridge Rd HG5 0QQ
☎ 01423 862690 Fax 01423 869345
Undulating parkland course with mature trees and two water features in attractive rural setting.
18 holes, 6433yds, Par 70, SSS 71, Course record 67.
Club membership 802.
Visitors restricted start times summer weekends.
Societies apply by telephone or letter, no bookings for Sat, Sun or Tue.
Green Fees £32 per day; £25 per round (£35/£30 weekends, no visitors bank holidays).
Prof Gary J Vickers
Designer Hawtree
Facilities ⊗ ℐ�┃ ▙ ▆ ♀ ❧ 🏠 ⏀ ⚐
Location 1.25 N on A6055

Hotel ★★★ 70% Dower House Hotel, Bond End, KNARESBOROUGH
☎ 01423 863302
28 ⇆ ♠ Annexe4rm(3 ⇆ ♠)

MALTON　　　　　　　　　　　　Map 08 SE77

Malton & Norton Welham Park, Norton YO17 9QE
☎ 01653 693882 Fax 01653 697912
Parkland course, consisting of 3 nine hole loops, with panoramic views of the moors. Very testing 1st hole (564 yds dog-leg, left).
Welham Course: 18 holes, 6456yds, Par 72, SSS 71.
Park Course: 18 holes, 6242yds, Par 72, SSS 70.
Derwent Course: 18 holes, 6286yds, Par 72, SSS 70.
Club membership 825.
Visitors anytime except during competitions.
Societies telephone and confirm in writing.
Green Fees £22 per day/round (£28 weekends & bank holidays).
Cards ▬ 🟦🟦 🟦
Prof S Robinson
Facilities ⊗ ℐ�┃ ▙ ▆ ♀ ❧ 🏠 ⏀ ⚐
Location 1m S

Hotel ★★★♨♨ 71% Burythorpe House Hotel, Burythorpe, MALTON
☎ 01653 658200 11 ⇆ ♠

MASHAM　　　　　　　　　　　Map 08 SE28

Masham Burnholme, Swinton Rd HG4 4HT
☎ 01765 688054 Fax 01765 688054
Flat parkland course crossed by River Burn, which comes into play on several holes.
9 holes, 6068yds, Par 70, SSS 69.
Club membership 327.
Visitors must play with member at weekends & bank holidays.
Societies write or telephone well in advance.
Green Fees £20 per day; £15 per round.
Facilities ▆ ♀ ❧
Location 8m from junction of B6267 off A1 signposted Thirsk/Masham. Then 1m SW off A6108

Hotel ★ 68% Buck Inn, THORNTON WATLASS ☎ 01677 422461 7rm(5 ⇆ ♠)

MIDDLESBROUGH　　　　　　　Map 08 NZ41

Middlesbrough Brass Castle Ln, Marton TS8 9EE
☎ 01642 311515
Undulating parkland course, prevailing winds. Testing 6th, 12th and 15th holes.
18 holes, 6215yds, Par 70, SSS 70, Course record 64.
Club membership 960.
Visitors restricted Tue & Sat.
Societies Wed, Thu & Fri only. Must contact the club in advance.
Green Fees not confirmed.
Prof Don Jones
Facilities ⊗ ℐ�┃ ▙ ▆ ♀ ❧ 🏠 ↖ 🛒 ⚐
Location 4m S off A172

Hotel ★★★ 70% Parkmore Hotel, 636 Yarm Rd, Eaglescliffe, STOCKTON-ON-TEES
☎ 01642 786815 55 ⇆ ♠

Middlesbrough Municipal Ladgate Ln TS5 7YZ
☎ 01642 315533 Fax 01642 300726
Parkland course with good views. The front nine holes have wide fairways and large, often well-guarded greens while the back nine demand shots over tree-lined water hazards and narrow entrances to subtly contoured greens. Driving range.
18 holes, 6333yds, Par 71, SSS 70, Course record 67.
Club membership 630.
Visitors book on the day weekdays, 7days in advance for weekends & bank holidays.
Societies apply in writing giving at least 2 weeks in advance.
Green Fees £9.50 (£12 weekends & bank holidays).
Prof Alan Hope
Designer Shuttleworth
Facilities ⊗ ▙ ▆ ♀ ❧ 🏠 ↖ 🛒 ⚐ ⚑
Location 2m S of Middlesbrough on the A174

Hotel ★★★ 70% Parkmore Hotel, 636 Yarm Rd, Eaglescliffe, STOCKTON-ON-TEES
☎ 01642 786815 55 ⇆ ♠

NORTHALLERTON　　　　　　　Map 08 SE39

Romanby Yafforth Rd DL7 0PE
☎ 01609 779988 Fax 01609 779084
Set in natural undulating terrain with the River Wiske meandering through the course, this fairly new golf venue offers a testing round of golf for all abilities. In addition to the river, two lakes come into play on the 2nd, 5th and 11th holes. 12-bay floodlit driving range.
18 holes, 6663yds, Par 72, SSS 72, Course record 72.
Club membership 525.
Visitors welcome everyday please book tee time in advance.
Societies contact Grant McDonnell for details, tel 01609 778855.
Green Fees £22.50 per day; £15 per round (£30/£20 weekends and bank holidays).
Cards ▬ 🟦🟦 🟦 🟦 🟦
Prof Tim Jenkins
Designer Will Adamson
Facilities ⊗ ℐ�┃ ▙ ▆ ♀ ❧ 🏠 ↖ 🛒 ⚐ ⚑

▶

Location On the main Northallerton/Richmond road
B6271, 1m W of Northallerton

Hotel ★★ 65% The Golden Lion, High St,
NORTHALLERTON
☎ 01609 777411 26rm(21 ⇥ ⌐)

PANNAL   Map 08 SE35

Pannal Follifoot Rd HG3 1ES
☎ 01423 872628 Fax 01423 870043
Fine championship course. Moorland turf but well-
wooded with trees closely involved with play.
18 holes, 6622yds, Par 72, SSS 72, Course record 62.
Club membership 780.
Visitors preferable to contact in advance, weekends
limited.
Societies apply in advance.
Green Fees £40 per round (18 holes) (£50 per round
weekends & bank holidays).
Prof Murray Burgess
Designer Sandy Herd
Facilities ⊗ ╫ ┗ ♥ ♀ ♣ ♠ ☂ ✐
Location E side of village off A61

Hotel ★★★ 68% The Imperial, Prospect Place,
HARROGATE
☎ 01423 565071 85 ⇥ ⌐

RAVENSCAR   Map 08 NZ90

Raven Hall Hotel Golf Course YO13 0ET
☎ 01723 870353 Fax 01723 870072
Opened by the Earl of Cranbrook in 1898, this 9-hole clifftop
course is sloping and with good quality small greens.
Because of its clifftop position it is subject to strong winds
which make it great fun to play, especially the 6th hole.
9 holes, 1894yds, Par 32, SSS 32.
Club membership 120.
Visitors must contact in advance, busy at weekends,
spikes essential, no jeans/T shirts.
Societies telephone in advance.
Green Fees not confirmed.
Cards ⟼ ▬▬ ▬▬ 🏧
Facilities ⊗ ╫ ┗ ♥ ♀ ☂ 🞖
& Leisure hard tennis courts, heated indoor plus outdoor
swimming pool, sauna.
Location Situated on cliff top

Hotel ★★★ 64% Raven Hall Hotel, RAVENSCAR
☎ 01723 870353 53 ⇥ ⌐

REDCAR   Map 08 NZ62

Cleveland Queen St TS10 1BT
☎ 01642 471798 Fax 01642 471798
The oldest golf club in Yorkshire playing over the only links
championship course in Yorkshire. A true test of traditional
golf, especially when windy. Flat seaside links with easy
walking.
18 holes, 6700yds, Par 72, SSS 72, Course record 67.
Club membership 820.
Visitors advisable to book in advanc.
Societies initially telephone for details.
Green Fees £22 per day; £20 per round (£26/£22 weekends).
Prof Stephen Wynn

Facilities ⊗ ╫ ┗ ♥ ♀ ♣ 🏠
Location 8m E of Middlesborough

Hotel ★★★▲♣ 70% Grinkle Park Hotel,
EASINGTON
☎ 01287 640515 20 ⇥ ⌐

Wilton Wilton TS10 4QY
☎ 01642 465265 (Secretary) & 452730 (Prof)
Fax 01642 465463
Parkland course with some fine views.
18 holes, 6126yds, Par 70, SSS 69, Course record 64.
Club membership 750.
Visitors telephone professional 01642 452730 to check
availability, no visitors Saturday, Ladies
competition have priority Tuesday.
Societies must telephone in advance.
Green Fees £20 per day (£26 Sunday).
Prof P D Smillie
Facilities ⊗ ╫ by prior arrangement ┗ ♥ ♀ ♣ 🏠 ✐
Location 3m W of Redcar, on A174

Hotel ★★★▲♣ 70% Grinkle Park Hotel,
EASINGTON
☎ 01287 640515 20 ⇥ ⌐

RICHMOND   Map 07 NZ10

Richmond Bend Hagg DL10 5EX
☎ 01748 823231(Secretary)
Undulating parkland course. Ideal to play 27 holes, not too
testing but very interesting.
18 holes, 5769yds, Par 70, SSS 68, Course record 63.
Club membership 600.
Visitors may not play before 3.30am on Sun.
Societies must contact in writing or telephone 01748
822457.
Green Fees £20 per day (£30 per day; £25 per round
weekends & bank holidays).
Prof Paul Jackson
Designer P Pennink
Facilities ⊗ ╫ ┗ ♥ ♀ ♣ 🏠 ☂ ✐
Location 0.75m N

Hotel ★★ 69% King's Head Hotel, Market Place,
RICHMOND
☎ 01748 850220 26 ⇥ ⌐ Annexe4 ⇥ ⌐

RIPON   Map 08 SE37

Ripon City Palace Rd HG4 3HH ☎ 01765 603640
Hard-walking on undulating parkland course; two testing par
3's at 5th and 16th.
18 holes, 6084yds, Par 70, SSS 69, Course record 68.
Club membership 675.
Visitors book with professional. Limited play Sat
especially Apr-Aug.
Societies contact in writing or telephone.
Green Fees £27 per 27 holes; £20 per 18 holes (£30 per
round weekends & bank holidays).
Prof S T Davis
Designer H Varden
Facilities ⊗ ┗ ♥ ♀ ♣ 🏠 ☂ 🞖 ✐
Location 1m NW on A6108

Hotel ★★★ 68% Ripon Spa Hotel, Park St, RIPON
☎ 01765 602172 40 ⇥ ⌐

SALTBURN-BY-THE-SEA — Map 08 NZ62

Hunley Hall Golf Club & Hotel Ings Ln, Brotton
TS12 2QQ ☎ 01287 676216 Fax 01287 678250
A picturesque 27 hole coastal course a good test of golf for
all abilities.
*Morgans: 18 holes, 6918yds, Par 73, SSS 73, Course record
68.*
Millennium: 18 holes, 5948yds, Par 68, SSS 69.
Imperial: 18 holes, 6586yds, Par 72, SSS 71.
Club membership 400.
Visitors	tee off times must be reserved in advance, times available between 9.30-11.30 and after 1pm.
Societies	telephone for information and availability.
Green Fees	£20 per day (£30 weekends).
Cards	
Prof	Andrew Brook
Designer	John Morgan
Facilities	
Location	From A174 take St Margarets Way 0.5m to club

Hotel	★★★👥 70% Grinkle Park Hotel, EASINGTON ☎ 01287 640515 20 ⇄ 🐾

Saltburn by the Sea Hob Hill, Guisborough Rd TS12 1NJ
☎ 01287 622812
Undulating meadowland course surrounded by woodland.
Particularly attractive in autumn. There are fine views of the
Cleveland Hills and of Tees Bay.
18 holes, 5846yds, Par 70, SSS 68, Course record 62.
Club membership 900.
Visitors	telephone in advance, no visitors on Saturday.
Societies	apply in writing.
Green Fees	not confirmed.
Prof	Mike Nutter
Designer	J Braid
Facilities	
Location	0.5m out of Saltburn on Guisborough road

Hotel	★★★👥 70% Grinkle Park Hotel, EASINGTON ☎ 01287 640515 20 ⇄ 🐾

SCARBOROUGH — Map 08 TA08

Scarborough North Cliff North Cliff Av YO12 6PP
☎ 01723 360786 Fax 01723 362134
Seaside parkland course begining on cliff top overlooking
bay and castle. Good views.
18 holes, 6425yds, Par 71, SSS 71, Course record 66.
Club membership 895.
Visitors	must be member of a club with handicap certificate. May not play before 10.30am Sun.
Societies	prior booking with secretary for parties of 8-40.
Green Fees	£27 per day; £20 per round (£30/ £24 weekends & bank holidays).
Prof	Simon N Deller
Designer	James Braid
Facilities	
Location	2m N of town centre off A165

Hotel	★★★ 64% Esplanade Hotel, Belmont Rd, SCARBOROUGH ☎ 01723 360382 73 ⇄ 🐾

Scarborough South Cliff Deepdale Av YO11 2UE
☎ 01723 374737
Parkland/seaside course designed by Dr Mackenzie.
18 holes, 6039yds, Par 70, SSS 69, Course record 66.
Club membership 700.

Visitors	contact in advance may not play before 9.30am Mon-Fri, 10am Sat and 10.30am Sun.
Societies	must contact Secretary in advance.
Green Fees	not confirmed.
Prof	A R Skingle
Designer	McKenzie
Facilities	
Location	1m S on A165

Hotel	★★ 63% Bradley Court Hotel, Filey Rd, South Cliff, SCARBOROUGH ☎ 01723 360476 40 ⇄ 🐾

SELBY — Map 08 SE63

Selby Brayton Barff YO8 9LD ☎ 01757 228622
Mainly flat, links-type course; prevailing SW wind. Testing
holes including the 3rd, 7th and 16th.
18 holes, 6246yds, Par 70, SSS 70, Course record 63.
Club membership 840.
Visitors	contact professional on 01757 228785, members and guests only at weekends.
Societies	welcome Mon-Fri, must apply in advance.
Green Fees	£30 per day, £25 per round.
Prof	Andrew Smith
Designer	J Taylor & Hawtree
Facilities	
Location	Off A19 at Brayton

Hotel	★★★👥 68% Monk Fryston Hall, MONK FRYSTON ☎ 01977 682369 30 ⇄ 🐾

SETTLE — Map 07 SD86

Settle Buckhaw Brow, Giggleswick BD24 0DH
☎ 01729 825288 Fax 01729 825288
Picturesque parkland course with stream affecting play on
four holes.
9 holes, 5530yds, Par 68, SSS 66, Course record 59.
Club membership 380.
Visitors	may not play before 4pm on Sun.
Societies	apply in writing or telephone 4 weeks in advance.
Green Fees	£10 per day (£10 per round weekends).
Designer	Tom Vardon
Facilities	
Location	1m N on A65

Hotel	★★★ 67% Falcon Manor Hotel, Skipton Rd, SETTLE ☎ 01729 823814 15 ⇄ 🐾 Annexe5 ⇄ 🐾

SKIPTON — Map 07 SD95

Skipton Off North West By-Pass BD23 1LL
☎ 01756 795657 Fax 01756 796665
Undulating parkland course with some water hazards and
panoramic views.
18 holes, 6049yds, Par 70, SSS 69, Course record 67.
Club membership 800.
Visitors	welcome by prior arrangement.
Societies	must apply in writing.
Green Fees	£23 per day (£25 weekends).
Prof	Peter Robinson
Facilities	
& Leisure	snooker room.
Location	1m N of Skipton on A59

▶

Hotel   ★★★ The Devonshire Arms Country House Hotel, BOLTON ABBEY ☎ 01756 710441   41 ⇔ 𝍠

TADCASTER   Map 08 SE44

Cocksford Cocksford, Stutton LS24 9NG
☎ 01937 834253
Three 9-hole courses; the old 18-hole combination set on undulating meadowland with the famous Cock Beck featuring on 8 of the original 18 holes. Whatever combination you choose the course is relatively short featuring a number of drivable par 4s, but beware danger surrounds many of the greens!
Old Course: 18 holes, 5570yds, Par 71, SSS 69, Course record 65.
Plews Course: 18 holes, 5559yds, Par 70, SSS 68.
Quarry Hills Course: 18 holes, 4951yds, Par 67, SSS 65.
Club membership 450.
Visitors   welcome, contact pro shop.
Societies   telephone the secretary.
Green Fees not confirmed.
Prof   Graham Thompson
Designer   Bill Brodigan
Facilities   ⊗ ℿ ⓛ 🖢 ♥ ♀ � 🖰 ⛟ ⋈ ◥ ⌀
Location   Between York & Leeds, A162 from Tadcaster

Hotel   ★★★⚑⚑ 75% Wood Hall Hotel, Trip Ln, Linton, WETHERBY ☎ 01937 587271   37 ⇔ 𝍠 Annexe6 ⇔ 𝍠

Scathingwell Scarthingwell LS24 9PF
☎ 01937 557864 (pro) 557878 (club) Fax 01937 557909
Testing water hazards and well placed bunkers and trees provide a challenging test of golf for all handicaps at this scenic parkland course, located 4 miles south of Tadcaster.
18 holes, 6771yds, Par 72, SSS 72.
Club membership 500.
Visitors   dress code must be adhered to.
Societies   golf packages available, book one month in advance.
Green Fees £16 per 18 holes (£18 weekends).
Prof   Steve Footman
Facilities   ⊗ ℿ ⓛ 🖢 ♥ ♀ ⚐ 🖰 ⌀
Location   4m S of Tadcaster on the A162 Tadcaster/Perrybridge Road, approx 2m from the A1

Hotel   B Posthouse Leeds/Selby, SOUTH MILFORD ☎ 01977 682711   95 ⇔ 𝍠

THIRSK   Map 08 SE48

Thirsk & Northallerton Thornton-le-Street YO7 4AB
☎ 01845 522170 & 525115
The course has good views of the nearby Hambleton Hills. Testing course, mainly flat land.
18 holes, 6514yds, Par 72, SSS 71.
Club membership 450.
Visitors   must telephone in advance, and have handicap certificate. No play Sun unless with member.
Societies   must apply in writing.
Green Fees £25 per day; £20 per round.
Prof   Robert Garner
Facilities   ⊗ ℿ ⓛ 🖢 ♥ ♀ ⚐ 🖰 ⛟ ⋈ ⌀
Location   2m N on A168

Hotel   ★★ 62% Three Tuns Hotel, Market Place, THIRSK ☎ 01845 523124   11 ⇔ 𝍠

WHITBY   Map 08 NZ81

Whitby Low Straggleton, Sandsend Rd YO21 3SR
☎ 01947 600660 Fax 01947 600660
Seaside course with 4 holes along cliff tops and over ravines. Good views and fresh sea breeze.
18 holes, 6134yds, Par 71, Course record 66.
Club membership 800.
Visitors   may not play on competition days, parties must contact in advance.
Societies   must contact in writing.
Green Fees £20 per day (£25 weekends and bank holidays).
Prof   Richard Wood
Facilities   ⊗ ℿ ⓛ 🖢 ♥ ♀ ⚐ 🖰 ⛟ ⌀
Location   1.5m NW on A174

Hotel   ★★ 67% White House Hotel, Upgang Ln, West Cliff, WHITBY ☎ 01947 600469   11rm(5 ⇔4 𝍠)

YORK   Map 08 SE65

Forest of Galtres Skelton Ln, Wigginton YO32 3RF
☎ 01904 766198 Fax 01904 766198
Level parkland course in the heart of the ancient Forest of Galtres with mature oak trees and interesting water features coming into play on the 5th,6th,14th and 17th holes. Views towards York Minster.
18 holes, 6312yds, Par 72, SSS 70, Course record 67.
Club membership 450.
Visitors   telephone to book, may play any time.
Societies   booking system, telephone for forms.
Green Fees £21 per day; £16 per round (£25/£21 weekends & bank holidays).
Prof   Neil Suckling
Designer   Simon Gidman
Facilities   ⊗ ℿ ⓛ 🖢 ♥ ♀ ⚐ 🖰 ⛟ ⌀
Location   0.5m from the York ring road B1237, just off A19 Thirsk road through the village of Skelton

Hotel   ★★ 69% Beechwood Close Hotel, 19 Shipton Rd, Clifton, YORK ☎ 01904 658378   14 ⇔ 𝍠

Forest Park Stockton-on-the-Forest YO32 9UW
☎ 01904 400425
A parkland/meadowland course, opened in 1991, with natural features including a stream and mature and new trees.
Old Foss Course: 18 holes, 6600yds, Par 71, SSS 72, Course record 73.
The West Course: 9 holes, 3186yds, Par 70, SSS 70.
Club membership 600.
Visitors   welcome, subject to tee availability. Advisable to contact club in advance.
Societies   by prior arrangement.
Green Fees £23 per day; £17 per 18 holes; £8 per 9 holes (£30/£22/£10 weekends & bank holidays)..
Cards   🖃🖃 🖃🖃 🖃 ⌀
Facilities   ⊗ ℿ ⓛ 🖢 ♥ ♀ ⚐ 🖰 ⛟ ⌀ ⅃
Location   4m NE of York, 1.5m from end of A64, York bypass

Hotel　★★★ 72%　York Pavilion Hotel, 45 Main St,
Fulford, YORK ☎ 01904 622099　44 ⇄ ♥

Fulford Heslington Ln YO10 5DY
☎ 01904 413579 Fax 01904 416918
A flat, parkland/moorland course well-known for the
superb quality of its turf, particularly the greens, and
now famous as the venue for some of the best golf
tournaments in the British Isles, in past years.
18 holes, 6775yds, Par 72, SSS 72, Course record 62.
Club membership 700.
Visitors　must contact in advance.
Societies　not Tue am, book with the manager.
Green Fees　£45 per day; £35 per round (£45 per round
weekends & bank holidays).
Prof　Bryan Hessay
Designer　Dr Mckenzie
Facilities　⊗ ⅢⅡ ╚ ♥ ♀ ♨ 🏠 ✎ ❦ ♂
Location　2m S of York off A19

Hotel　★★★★ 64%　Swallow Hotel, Tadcaster
Rd, YORK ☎ 01904 701000 113 ⇄ ♥

Heworth Muncaster House, Muncastergate YO31 9JY
☎ 01904 422389 Fax 01904 426156
11-hole parkland course, easy walking. Holes 3 to 9 played
twice from different tees.
11 holes, 6141yds, Par 70, SSS 69, Course record 69.
Club membership 550.
Visitors　advisable to telephone the professional in
advance, no catering Mondays
Societies　apply in writing.
Green Fees　£18 per day; £14 per round (£20/£18 weekends
& bank holidays).
Prof　Stephen Burdett
Designer　B Cheal
Facilities　⊗ ⅢⅡ ╚ ♥ ♀ ♨ 🏠 ✎ ♂
Location　1.5m NE of city centre on A1036

Hotel　★★★ 65%　Monkbar Hotel, St Maurices Rd,
YORK ☎ 01904 638086　99 ⇄ ♥

Swallow Hall Crockey Hill YO1 4SG
☎ 01904 448889 Fax 01904 448219
A small 18-hole, Par 3 course with 2 par 4s. Attached to a
caravan park.
18 holes, 3100yds, Par 56, SSS 56, Course record 58.
Club membership 100.
Visitors　no restrictions.
Societies　must telephone in advance.
Green Fees　not confirmed.
Designer　Brian Henry
Facilities　♥ ♨ ✎ ➣ ♂ ⎰
& Leisure　hard tennis courts.
Location　Off A19, signposted to Wheldrake

Hotel　★★★ 72%　York Pavilion Hotel, 45 Main St,
Fulford, YORK ☎ 01904 622099　44 ⇄ ♥

York Lords Moor Ln, Strensall YO32 5XF
☎ 01904 491840 Fax 01904 491852
A pleasant, well-designed, heathland course with easy
walking. The course is of good length but being flat the
going does not tire. The course is well bunkered with
excellent greens and there are two testing pond holes.

18 holes, 6301yds, Par 70, SSS 70, Course record 66.
Club membership 700.
Visitors　with member only weekends, must contact in
advance.
Societies　more than 16 contact secretary, under 16 contact
professional.
Green Fees　£36 per 36 holes/£26 per 18 holes Mon-Fri.
Prof　A B Mason
Designer　J H Taylor
Facilities　⊗ ⅢⅡ ╚ ♥ ♀ ♨ 🏠 ✎ ♂
Location　6m NE, E of Strensall village

Hotel　★★★ 74%　Dean Court Hotel,
Duncombe Place, YORK
☎ 01904 625082　39 ⇄ ♥

BARNSLEY　　　　　　　　　　　Map 08 SE30

Barnsley Wakefield Rd, Staincross S75 6JZ
☎ 01226 382856
Undulating municipal parkland course with easy walking
apart from last 4 holes. Testing 8th and 18th holes.
18 holes, 5951yds, Par 69, SSS 69, Course record 64.
Club membership 450.
Visitors　no restrictions.
Societies　by arrangement.
Green Fees　not confirmed.
Prof　Mike Melling
Facilities　⊗ ⅢⅡ ╚ ♥ ♀ ♨ 🏠 ✎ ♂
Location　3m N on A61

Hotel　★★★ 69%　Ardsley House Hotel & Health
Club, Doncaster Rd, Ardsley, BARNSLEY
☎ 01226 309955　73 ⇄ ♥

Sandhill Middlecliffe Ln, Little Houghton S72 0HW
☎ 01226 753444
Opened in 1993, the course is reasonably flat with
generously wide fairways laid out between and amongst 25
acres of newly planted woodlands. Holes of note are the 4th
which is a 311 yard Par 4 to a horseshoe green around a 9-
foot deep bunker; the 7th Par 3 to blind reverse Mackenzie
Green and the 11th 416 yard Par 4 dogleg where the brave
can take on the out of bounds.
18 holes, 6250yds, Par 71, SSS 70, Course record 69.
Club membership 275.
Visitors　welcome by prior booking.
Societies　telephone for availability, write to confirm.
Green Fees　£14 per day; £8.50 per round (£18/£11
weekends).
Cards　🗅 🗅
Designer　John Royston
Facilities　⊗ ⅢⅡ ╚ ♥ ♀ ♨ 🏠 ⎰
Location　5m E of Barnsley, off A635

Hotel　★★★ 69%　Ardsley House Hotel & Health
Club, Doncaster Rd, Ardsley, BARNSLEY
☎ 01226 309955　73 ⇄ ♥

BAWTRY
Map 08 SK69

Austerfield Park Cross Ln, Austerfield DN10 6RF
☎ 01302 710841 Fax 01302 710850
Long moorland course with postage stamp 8th and testing
618-yd 7th. Driving range and Par 3 attached.
18 holes, 6900yds, Par 73, SSS 73, Course record 69.
Club membership 500.
Visitors welcome weekdays, after 10am weekends.
Societies must contact in advance.
Green Fees not confirmed.
Cards 🔲 VISA
Prof Darran Roberts
Facilities ⊗ ⅷ ⅊ ♥ ♀ ⚐ 🏠 ⚑ ✆ ♦
Location 2m from Bawtry on A614

Hotel ★★★ 60% The Crown Hotel, High St,
BAWTRY ☎ 01302 710341 57 ⇔ ♠

CONISBROUGH
Map 08 SK59

Crookhill Park Municipal Carr Ln DN12 2BE
☎ 01709 862979
A naturally sloping parkland course with many holes
featuring tight dog-legs and small, undulating greens. The
signature hole (11th) involves a fearsome tee shot over a
ditch onto a sloping fairway and final shot to an elevated
green surrounded by tall trees and deep bunkers.
18 holes, 5849yds, Par 70, SSS 68, Course record 64.
Club membership 350.
Visitors booking system for general play.
Societies bookings taken in advance, deposits taken
through booking system.
Green Fees not confirmed.
Prof Richard Swaine
Facilities ⅊ ♥ ♀ ⚐ 🏠 ⚑
Location 1.5m SE on B6094

Hotel ★★★ 64% Quality Hotel Doncaster, High St,
DONCASTER ☎ 01302 342261 66 ⇔ ♠

DONCASTER
Map 08 SE50

Doncaster 278 Bawtry Rd, Bessacarr DN4 7PD
☎ 01302 868316 & 865994
Pleasant undulating heathland course with wooded
surroundings. Quick drying, ideal all year round course.
18 holes, 6220yds, Par 69, SSS 70, Course record 66.
Club membership 600.
Visitors must contact in advance. Times restricted on
Wed & weekends.
Societies must contact in advance.
Green Fees £27.50 per day; £22.50 per round
(£32.50/£27.50 weekends & bank holidays).
Prof Graham Bailey
Designer Mackenzie/Hawtree
Facilities ⊗ ⅷ ⅊ ♥ ♀ ⚐ 🏠 ♦
Location 4m SE on A638

Hotel ★★★ 71% Mount Pleasant Hotel,
Great North Rd, ROSSINGTON
☎ 01302 868696 & 868219
Fax 01302 865130 42 ⇔ ♠

Doncaster Town Moor Bawtry Rd, Belle Vue DN4 5HU
☎ 01302 535286 & 533167
Easy walking, but testing, heathland course with good true
greens. Friendly club. Notable hole is 11th (par 4), 464 yds.
Situated in centre of racecourse.
18 holes, 6072yds, Par 69, SSS 69, Course record 66.
Club membership 520.
Societies must contact in advance.
Green Fees not confirmed.
Prof Steven C Poole
Facilities ⊗ ⅷ ⅊ ♥ ♀ ⚐ 🏠
Location 1.5m E, at racecourse, on A638

Hotel ★★★ 64% Quality Hotel Doncaster, High St,
DONCASTER ☎ 01302 342261 66 ⇔ ♠

Owston Park Owston Ln, Owston DN6 8EF
☎ 01302 330821
A flat easy walking course surrounded by woodland. A lot of
mature trees and a few ditches in play. A practice putting
green and chipping area.
9 holes, 2866yds, Par 35, SSS 70.
Visitors no restrictions.
Societies telephone in advance.
Green Fees £4.25 per 9 holes (£4.50 weekends).
Cards 🔲 🔲 VISA 🔲 🔲
Prof Mike Parker
Designer M Parker
Facilities ♥ ♀ ⚐ 🏠 ⚑ ♦
Location 5m N of Doncaster off A19

Hotel ★★★ 64% Quality Hotel Doncaster, High St,
DONCASTER ☎ 01302 342261 66 ⇔ ♠

Thornhurst Park Holme Ln, Owston DN5 0LR
☎ 01302 337799 Fax 01302 721495
Surrounded by Owston Wood, this scenic parkland course
has numerous strategically placed bunkers, and a lake comes
into play at the 7th and 8th holes.
18 holes, 6490yds, Par 72, SSS 72, Course record 72.
Club membership 160.
Visitors must wear trousers, shirt with collar and golf
shoes, can contact 2 days in advance.
Societies telephone or write in advance.
Green Fees £8 per 18 holes; £5 per 9 holes (£10/£6
weekends & bank holidays).
Prof Kevin Pearce
Facilities ⊗ ⅷ ⅊ ♥ ♀ ⚐ 🏠 ♦
Location On the A19 between Bentley/Askern, easy
access from M62 and A1 (M)

Hotel ★★★ 64% Quality Hotel Doncaster, High St,
DONCASTER ☎ 01302 342261 66 ⇔ ♠

Wheatley Armthorpe Rd DN2 5QB
☎ 01302 831655 & 834085
Fairly flat well-bunkered, lake-holed, parkland course.
18 holes, 6405yds, Par 71, SSS 71, Course record 64.
Club membership 600.
Visitors telephone in advance handicap cert required.
Must contact in advance.
Societies must contact professional in advance.
Green Fees not confirmed.
Cards 🔲 🔲 🔲 🔲
Prof S Fox
Designer George Duncan
Facilities ⊗ ⅷ ⅊ ♥ ♀ ⚐ 🏠 ♦

Location	NE side of town centre off A18

Hotel	★★ 70% Regent Hotel, Regent Square, DONCASTER ☎ 01302 364180 50 ⇔ 🐾

HATFIELD   Map 08 SE60

Kings Wood Thorne Rd DN7 6EP ☎ 01405 741343
A flat course with ditches that come into play on several holes, especially on the testing back nine. Notable holes are the 12th par 4, 16th and par 5 18th.
18 holes, 6002yds, Par 70, SSS 69, Course record 69.
Club membership 100.

Visitors	visitors are welcome any time of week, advisable to contact in advance by telephone, especially for weekend play.
Societies	apply in writing to the professional, or telephone in advance.
Green Fees	telephone for prices.
Cards	💳 🖅 🖃 🔳
Prof	Jonathan Drury
Facilities	🍽 🏠 🪝 ♂
Location	2m SW of junct 1 of M180, take A614 to Thorne, then Thorne road to Hatfield

Hotel	★★ 69% Belmont Hotel, Horsefair Green, THORNE ☎ 01405 812320 23 ⇔ 🐾

HICKLETON   Map 08 SE40

Hickleton Lidgett Ln DN5 7BE
☎ 01709 896081 Fax 01709 896081
Undulating, picturesque parkland course designed by Neil Coles and Brian Huggett offering a good test of golf.
18 holes, 6434yds, Par 71, SSS 71, Course record 68.
Club membership 625.

Visitors	restricted weekdays after 9am & weekends after 2.30pm. Must contact in advance.
Societies	must contact in advance.
Green Fees	£21 per day, £17 per round (£26 per day/round weekends).
Prof	Paul Shepherd
Designer	Huggett/Coles
Facilities	⊗ 🍸 🍪 🍽 ♀ 🏠 🪝 ♂
Location	0.5m W on B6411

Hotel	★★★ 64% Quality Hotel Doncaster, High St, DONCASTER ☎ 01302 342261 66 ⇔ 🐾

HIGH GREEN   Map 08 SK39

Tankersley Park S35 4LG ☎ 0114 246 8247
Akin to an inland links, this parkland course is hilly, windy and has good views.
18 holes, 6212yds, Par 69, SSS 70, Course record 64.
Club membership 634.

Visitors	must contact in advance.
Societies	must apply in writing.
Green Fees	£28 per day; £23 per round (£28 per round weekends).
Prof	Ian Kirk
Designer	Hawtree
Facilities	⊗ 🍸 🍪 🍽 ♀ 🏠 🪝 ♂
Location	Off A61/M1 onto A616, Stocksbridge bypass

Hotel	★★★ 70% Tankersley Manor, Church Ln, TANKERSLEY ☎ 01226 744700 70 ⇔ 🐾

RAWMARSH   Map 08 SK49

Wath Abdy Ln S62 7SJ
☎ 01709 872149 & 878609 (office) Fax 01709 878609
Parkland course, not easy in spite of its length; 17th hole (par 3) is a difficult 244yds with narrow driving area.
18 holes, 5857yds, Par 68, SSS 68.
Club membership 550.

Visitors	must play with member at weekends. Must contact in advance and have a handicap certificate.
Societies	must contact in writing, may not play at weekends.
Green Fees	not confirmed.
Prof	Chris Bassett
Facilities	🏠 🪝 ♂
Location	2.5m N off A633

Hotel	★★★ 65% Carlton Park Hotel, 102/104 Moorgate Rd, ROTHERHAM ☎ 01709 849955 75 ⇔ 🐾

ROTHERHAM   Map 08 SK49

Grange Park Upper Wortley Rd S61 2SJ
☎ 01709 559497
Parkland/meadowland course, with panoramic views especially from the back nine. The golf is testing, particularly at the 1st, 4th and 18th holes (par 4), and 8th, 12th and 15th (par 5).
18 holes, 6421yds, Par 71, SSS 71, Course record 65.
Club membership 214.

Visitors	no restrictions.
Societies	apply in writing to professional.
Green Fees	£9.50 per round (£10.50 weekends & bank holidays).
Prof	Eric Clark
Designer	Fred Hawtree
Facilities	⊗ 🍸 🍪 🍽 ♀ 🏠 🪝 ♂ ⓘ
Location	3m NW off A629

Hotel	★★★ 70% Tankersley Manor, Church Ln, TANKERSLEY ☎ 01226 744700 70 ⇔ 🐾

Phoenix Pavilion Ln, Brinsworth S60 5PA
☎ 01709 363864 & 382624 Fax 01709 363788
Undulating meadowland course with variable wind.
18 holes, 6182yds, Par 71, SSS 69, Course record 65.
Club membership 1100.

Visitors	must contact in advance.
Societies	must apply in writing.
Green Fees	not confirmed.
Prof	M Roberts
Designer	C K Cotton
Facilities	⊗ 🍸 🍪 🍽 ♀ 🏠 🪝 ♂ ⓘ
& Leisure	hard tennis courts, squash, fishing, gymnasium.
Location	SW side of town centre off A630

Hotel	★★★ 65% Carlton Park Hotel, 102/104 Moorgate Rd, ROTHERHAM ☎ 01709 849955 75 ⇔ 🐾

Rotherham Golf Club Ltd Thrybergh Park, Doncaster Rd,
Thrybergh S65 4NU
☎ 01709 850812 (Secretary) Fax 01709 855288
Parkland course with easy walking along tree-lined fairways.
18 holes, 6324yds, Par 70, SSS 70, Course record 65.
Club membership 500.
Visitors   must contact in advance.
Societies   must contact secretary in advance.
Green Fees   £30 per day; £26 per round (£35 weekends &
                      bank holidays).
Prof   Simon Thornhill
Facilities   ⛳🏠🏌🚗♂
Location   3.5m E on A630

Hotel   ★★★ 67% Elton Hotel, Main St,
                      Bramley, ROTHERHAM
                      ☎ 01709 545681   13 ⇆ 🛏 Annexe16 ⇆ 🛏

Sitwell Park Shrogswood Rd S60 4BY
☎ 01709 541046 Fax 01709 703637
Parkland course with easy walking.
18 holes, 6209yds, Par 71, SSS 70, Course record 61.
Club membership 450.
Visitors   must contact in advance.
Societies   must contact in advance.
Green Fees   £28 per day; £24 per round (£32/£28 weekends
                      & bank holidays).
Prof   Nic Taylor
Designer   A MacKenzie
Facilities   ⊗🍴🍺🏌♀⛳🏠🚗♂♂

Hotel   ★★★★ 66% Hellaby Hall Hotel,
                      Old Hellaby Ln, Hellaby, ROTHERHAM
                      ☎ 01709 702701   52 ⇆ 🛏

SHEFFIELD   Map 08 SK38

Abbeydale Twentywell Ln, Dore S17 4QA
☎ 0114 236 0763
Parkland course, well-kept and wooded. Testing hole: 12th,
par 3.
18 holes, 6419yds, Par 72, SSS 72.
Club membership 750.
Visitors   by arrangement.
Societies   must apply in writing.
Green Fees   not confirmed.
Prof   Nigel Perry
Designer   Herbert Fowler
Facilities   ⊗🍴🍺🏌♀⛳🏠🏌♂
Location   4m SW of city centre off A621

Hotel   ★★★★ 62% Sheffield Moat House,
                      Chesterfield Rd South, SHEFFIELD
                      ☎ 0114 282 9988 95 ⇆ 🛏

Beauchief Municipal Abbey Ln S8 0DB ☎ 0114 236 7274
Municipal course with natural water hazards. The rolling
land looks west to the Pennines and a 12th-century abbey
adorns the course.
18 holes, 5452yds, Par 67, SSS 66, Course record 65.
Club membership 450.
Visitors   are advised to book in advance in summer.
Societies   weekdays only, must apply in writing to:
                      Recreation Department, Tower Lodge, Firth
                      Park Road, Sheffield S5 6WS.
Green Fees   £9 per round.
Cards   ⚊ 💳 📇
Prof   A Highfield

Facilities   ⊗🍴🍺🍺♀⛳🏠🏌♂
Location   4m SW of city centre off A621

Hotel   ★★★ 69% Beauchief Hotel, 161 Abbeydale Rd
                      South, SHEFFIELD
                      ☎ 0114 262 0500 41 ⇆ 🛏

Birley Wood Birley Ln S12 3BP ☎ 0114 264 7262
Undulating meadowland course with well-varied features,
easy walking and good views. Practice range and green.
18 holes, 5100yds, Par 66, SSS 65, Course record 64.
Club membership 300.
Visitors   no restrictions.
Societies   apply in advance.
Green Fees   not confirmed.
Prof   Peter Ball
Facilities   ⛳🏌
Location   4.5m SE of city centre off A616

Hotel   ★★★ 67% Mosborough Hall Hotel, High St,
                      Mosborough, SHEFFIELD
                      ☎ 0114 248 4353 23 ⇆ 🛏

Concord Park Shiregreen Ln S5 6AE
☎ 0114 234 9802 & 257 7378
Hilly municipal parkland course with some fairways wood-
flanked, good views, often windy. Seven par 3 holes. Course
under development.
18 holes, 4872yds, Par 67, SSS 64, Course record 57.
Club membership 150.
Visitors   no restrictions.
Green Fees   not confirmed.
Prof   W Allcroft
Facilities   🍺🍺♀⛳🏠🏌ℓ
& Leisure   hard tennis courts, heated indoor swimming
                      pool, squash, solarium, gymnasium.
Location   3.5m N of city centre on B6086 off A6135

Hotel   B Posthouse Sheffield, Mancheater Rd,
                      Broomhill, SHEFFIELD
                      ☎ 0114 267 0067 136 ⇆ 🛏

Dore & Totley Bradway Rd, Bradway S17 4QR
☎ 0114 236 0492
Flat parkland course.
18 holes, 6265yds, Par 70, SSS 70, Course record 65.
Club membership 580.
Visitors   must contact in advance a handicap certificate
                      may be requested, may not play weekends.
Societies   must apply in writing.
Green Fees   not confirmed.
Facilities   ⊗🍴🍺🍺♀⛳🏠♂
Location   7m S of city centre on B6054 off A61

Hotel   B Posthouse Sheffield, Mancheater Rd,
                      Broomhill, SHEFFIELD
                      ☎ 0114 267 0067 136 ⇆ 🛏

Hallamshire Golf Club Ltd Sandygate S10 4LA
☎ 0114 230 2153 Fax 0114 230 2153
Situated on a shelf of land at a height of 850 ft.
Magnificent views to the west. Moorland turf, long
carries over ravine. Good natural drainage.
18 holes, 6359yds, Par 71, SSS 71, Course record 63.
Club membership 600.
Visitors   contact professional in advance. Tees
                      reserved for members 8-9.30 and noon-1.30.

Societies	parties of 12+ should book in advance with secretary.
Green Fees	£36 per day (£41 weekends & bank holidays).
Cards	▭▭ ▭
Prof	G R Tickell
Designer	Various
Facilities	⊗ ⫟ ⬚ 🍴 ♀ ⚘ 🛋 ⛳ ✧
Location	Off A57 at Crosspool onto Sandygate Rd, clubhouse 0.75m on right
Hotel	B Posthouse Sheffield, Mancheater Rd, Broomhill, SHEFFIELD ☎ 0114 267 0067 136 ⇆ ⫪

Hillsborough Worrall Rd S6 4BE
☎ 0114 234 9151 (Secretary) & 233 2666 (Pro)
Beautiful moorland/woodland course 500 ft above sea-level, reasonable walking. Challenging first four holes into a prevailing wind and a tight, testing 14th hole.
18 holes, 6216yards, Par 71, SSS 70, Course record 64.
Club membership 650.

Visitors	contact professional in advance. May not play Tue (Ladies Day), Thu and weekends before 2pm
Societies	must apply in writing to secretary.
Green Fees	not confirmed.
Prof	Graham Walker
Facilities	⊗ ⫟ ⬚ 🍴 ♀ ⚘ 🛋 ⛳ ✧ ✦
Location	3m NW of city centre off A616
Hotel	★★★ 63% Rutland Hotel, 452 Glossop Rd, Broomhill, SHEFFIELD ☎ 0114 266 4411 70 ⇆ ⫪ Annexe17 ⇆ ⫪

Lees Hall Hemsworth Rd, Norton S8 8LL
☎ 0114 255 4402
Parkland/meadowland course with panoramic view of city.
18 holes, 6171yds, Par 71, SSS 70, Course record 63.
Club membership 695.

Visitors	welcome.
Societies	must apply in writing.
Green Fees	not confirmed.
Prof	S Berry
Facilities	⫟ by prior arrangement ⬚ 🍴 ♀ ⚘ 🛋 ✧
Location	3.5m S of city centre off A6102
Hotel	B Posthouse Sheffield, Mancheater Rd, Broomhill, SHEFFIELD ☎ 0114 267 0067 136 ⇆ ⫪

Rother Valley Golf Centre Mansfield Rd, Wales Bar
S26 5PQ ☎ 0114 247 3000 Fax 0114 247 6000
The challenging Blue Monster parkland course features a variety of water hazards. Notable holes include the 7th, with its island green fronted by water and dominated by bunkers to the rear. Lookout for the water on the par 5 18th.
18 holes, 6602yds, Par 72, SSS 72, Course record 70.
Club membership 500.

Visitors	2 days in advance booking format.
Societies	apply in writing or telephone in advance.
Green Fees	£7.50 per round Mon; £11 per round Tue-Fri (£16 weekends).
Cards	▭▭ ▭▭ ▭ 🄳 ▭ ▭ 🄶
Prof	Jason Ripley
Designer	Michael Shattock & Mark Roe

Facilities	⊗ ⫟ ⬚ 🍴 ♀ ⚘ 🛋 ⛳ ✧ 🛵 ✦ ✧
Location	Off junct 31 of the M1, follow signs to Rother Valley Country Park
Hotel	★★★ 67% Mosborough Hall Hotel, High St, Mosborough, SHEFFIELD ☎ 0114 248 4353 23 ⇆ ⫪

Tinsley Park Municipal Golf High Hazels Park, Darnall
S9 4PE ☎ 0114 2037435
Undulating meadowland course with plenty of trees and rough. A test for all categories of golfer.
18 holes, 6064yds, Par 71, SSS 69.
Club membership 580.

Visitors	prior booking essential.
Societies	apply in writing to Sheffield City Council, Recreation Dept., Meersbrook Park, Sheffield.
Green Fees	£7.50 per round (£8.50 weekends).
Prof	A P Highfield
Facilities & Leisure	⊗ ⫟ by prior arrangement ⬚ 🍴 ♀ ⚘ 🛋 ⛳ ✧ hard tennis courts.
Location	4m E of city centre off A630
Hotel	★★★ 67% Mosborough Hall Hotel, High St, Mosborough, SHEFFIELD ☎ 0114 248 4353 23 ⇆ ⫪

SILKSTONE   Map 08 SE20

Silkstone Field Head, Elmhurst Ln S75 4LD
☎ 01226 790328
Parkland/downland course, fine views over the Pennines.
Testing golf.
18 holes, 6069yds, Par 70, SSS 70, Course record 64.
Club membership 508.

Visitors	with member only at weekends.
Societies	contact in advance.
Green Fees	£26 per round.
Prof	Kevin Guy
Facilities	⊗ ⫟ ⬚ 🍴 ♀ ⚘ 🛋 🛵 🛢 ✧
Location	1m E off A628
Hotel	★★★ 69% Ardsley House Hotel & Health Club, Doncaster Rd, Ardsley, BARNSLEY ☎ 01226 309955 73 ⇆ ⫪

STOCKSBRIDGE   Map 08 SK29

Stocksbridge & District 30 Royd Ln, Townend, Deepcar
S36 2RZ ☎ 0114 288 2003 (office) & 288 2779 (pro)
Hilly moorland course.
18 holes, 5200yds, Par 65, SSS 65, Course record 60.
Club membership 470.

Visitors	contact the professional.
Societies	apply to secretary.
Green Fees	£20 per day; £16 per round (£30 per day weekends).
Prof	Timothy Brookes
Designer	Dave Thomas
Facilities	⊗ ⫟ ⬚ 🍴 ♀ ⚘ 🛋
Location	S side of town centre
Hotel	B Posthouse Sheffield, Mancheater Rd, Broomhill, SHEFFIELD ☎ 0114 267 0067 136 ⇆ ⫪

THORNE   Map 08 SE61

Thorne Kirton Ln DN8 5RJ
☎ 01405 812084 Fax 01405 741899
Picturesque parkland course with 6000 newly planted trees.
Water hazards on 11th, 14th & 18th holes.
18 holes, 5366yds, Par 68, SSS 66, Course record 62.
Club membership 300.
Visitors   no restrictions.
Societies   telephone in advance.
Green Fees £9 per round (£10 weekends).
Prof   Edward Highfield
Designer   R D Highfield
Facilities   ⊗ ⅏ ᴸᴮ ⬛ ♀ ⚤ 🏠 ⛳ ✓
Location   14m SE of Pontefract off of M18

Hotel   ★★ 69% Belmont Hotel, Horsefair Green,
THORNE ☎ 01405 812320   23 ⇌ 🐾

WORTLEY   Map 08 SK39

Wortley Hermit Hill Ln S35 7DF
☎ 0114 288 8469 Fax 0114 288 8469
Well-wooded, undulating parkland course sheltered from
prevailing wind.
18 holes, 6028yds, Par 69, SSS 68, Course record 62.
Club membership 510.
Visitors   may not play between 11.30am and 1pm. Must
contact professional in advance and hold a
handicap certificate.
Societies   telephone in advance and confirm in writing
with deposit.
Green Fees not confirmed.
Prof   Ian Kirk
Facilities   ⊗ ⅏ by prior arrangement ᴸᴮ ⬛ ♀ ⚤ 🏠 ⛳ ✓
Location   0.5m NE of village off A629

Hotel   B Posthouse Sheffield, Mancheater Rd,
Broomhill, SHEFFIELD
☎ 0114 267 0067 136 ⇌ 🐾

YORKSHIRE, WEST

ALWOODLEY   Map 08 SE24

Alwoodley Wigton Ln LS17 8SA
☎ 0113 268 1680 Fax 0113 293 9458
A fine heathland course with length, trees and abundant
heather. Many attractive situations - together a severe
test of golf.
18 holes, 6686yds, Par 72, SSS 73, Course record 67.
Club membership 462.
Visitors   must contact in advance,
Societies   must apply in advance.
Green Fees £50 per day/round (£60 weekends & bank
holidays).
Prof   John R Green
Designer   Dr Alistair Mackenzie
Facilities   ⊗ ⅏ ᴸᴮ ⬛ ♀ ⚤ 🏠 ⛳ ✓
Location   5m N off A61

Hotel   ★★★ 66% Harewood Arms Hotel,
Harrogate Rd, HAREWOOD
☎ 0113 288 6566 13 ⇌ 🐾 Annexe11 ⇌ 🐾

BAILDON   Map 07 SE13

Baildon Moorgate BD17 5PP ☎ 01274 595162
Moorland course set out in links style with outward front
nine looping back to clubhouse. Panoramic views with
testing short holes in prevailing winds.
18 holes, 6225yds, Par 70, SSS 70, Course record 63.
Club membership 500.
Visitors   contact in advance, restricted Tue & weekends.
Societies   large numbers apply in writing, small numbers
check with the professional.
Green Fees not confirmed.
Prof   Richard Masters
Designer   Tom Morris
Facilities   ⊗ ⅏ ᴸᴮ ⬛ ♀ ⚤ 🏠 ⛳ ✓
Location   3m N of Bradford, off A6038

Hotel   ★★★★ 70% Marriott Hollins Hall Hotel and
Country Club, Hollins Hill, Baildon, SHIPLEY
☎ 01274 530053 122 ⇌ 🐾

BINGLEY   Map 07 SE13

Bingley St Ives Golf Club House, St Ives Estate, Harden
BD16 1AT ☎ 01274 562436 Fax 01274 511788
Parkland/moorland course.
18 holes, 6485yds, Par 71, SSS 71, Course record 69.
Club membership 450.

Visitors   contact professional on 01274 562506, no green
fees Sat.
Societies   telephone in advance, the professional 01274
562506.
Green Fees £29 per day; £24 per round (£28 per round
weekends).
Prof   Ray Firth
Designer   Alastair Mackenzie
Facilities   ⊗ ⅏ ᴸᴮ ⬛ ♀ ⚤ 🏠 🛺 ✓
Location   0.75m W off B6429

Hotel   ★★ 66% Oakwood Hall Hotel, Lady Ln,
BINGLEY ☎ 01274 564123 & 563569
Fax 01274 561477 20 ⇌ 🐾

Shipley Beckfoot Ln BD16 1LX
☎ 01274 563212 (Club) & 563674 (Pro)
Fax 01274 568652
Well established parkland course, founded in 1922, featuring
6 good par 3's
18 holes, 6215yds, Par 71, SSS 70, Course record 65.
Club membership 600.
Visitors   may play Mon, Wed-Fri & Sun, but Tue only
after 2.30pm & Sat after 4pm.
Societies   initial enquiry by phone to secretary 01274
568652 and or by letter.
Green Fees £27 (£32 weekend & bank holidays).
Prof   J R Parry
Designer   Colt, Allison, Mackenzie, Braid
Facilities   ⊗ ⦀ ⬧ 🛈 ⬛ ♀ ⚎ 🏠 ⛳ ♟ ⚬
Location   6m N of Bradford on A650

Hotel   ★★ 66% Oakwood Hall Hotel, Lady Ln,
BINGLEY ☎ 01274 564123 & 563569
Fax 01274 561477   20 ⇄ ⋔

BRADFORD   Map 07 SE13

Bradford Moor Scarr Hall, Pollard Ln BD2 4RW
☎ 01274 771716 & 771718
Moorland course with tricky undulating greens.
9 holes, 5900yds, Par 70, SSS 68, Course record 65.
Club membership 330.
Visitors   no visitors at weekends except with member.
Societies   can book starting times by application in
writing.
Green Fees £8 before 2pm; £12 after 2pm.
Prof   Ron Hughes
Facilities   ⊗ ⦀ ⬧ 🛈 ⬛ ♀ ⚎ 🏠 ⛳ ⚬
Location   2m NE of city centre off A658

Hotel   ★★ 68% Park Drive Hotel, 12 Park Dr,
BRADFORD ☎ 01274 480194   11 ⇄ ⋔

Clayton Thornton View Rd, Clayton BD14 6JX
☎ 01274 880047
Moorland course, difficult in windy conditions.
9 holes, 5407yds, Par 68, SSS 67.
Club membership 300.
Visitors   may not play before 4pm on Sun.
Societies   apply in writing to the Secretary or Captain.
Green Fees £10 per round (£12 weekends & bank holidays).
Facilities   ⊗ ⦀ ⬧ 🛈 ⬛ ♀ ⚎
Location   2.5m SW of city centre on A647

Hotel   ★★★ 62% Novotel,
Merrydale Rd, BRADFORD
☎ 01274 683683 127 ⇄ ⋔

East Bierley South View Rd, East Bierley BD4 6PP
☎ 01274 681023
Hilly moorland course with narrow fairways. Two par 3
holes over 200 yds.
9 holes, 4700yds, Par 64, SSS 63.
Club membership 300.
Visitors   restricted Sat (am), Sun & Mon evening. Must
contact in advance.
Societies   must apply in writing.
Green Fees not confirmed.
Facilities   ⊗ ⦀ ⬧ 🛈 ⬛ ♀ ⚎
Location   4m SE of city centre off A650

Hotel   ★★★ 62% Novotel, Merrydale Rd,
BRADFORD ☎ 01274 683683 127 ⇄ ⋔

Headley Headley Ln, Thornton BD13 3LX
☎ 01274 833481 Fax 01274 833481
Hilly moorland course, short but very testing, windy, fine
views.
9 holes, 5140yds, Par 66, SSS 64, Course record 61.
Club membership 300.
Visitors   must contact in advance, may not play weekends
& bank holidays.
Societies   must contact in advance.
Green Fees not confirmed.
Facilities   ⊗ ⦀ ⬧ 🛈 ⬛ ♀ ⚎
Location   4m W of city centre off B6145 at Thornton

Hotel   ★★ 68% Park Drive Hotel, 12 Park Dr,
BRADFORD ☎ 01274 480194   11 ⇄ ⋔

Queensbury Brighouse Rd, Queensbury BD13 1QF
☎ 01274 882155 & 816864
Undulating woodland/parkland course. Course currently
being reconfigured.
9 holes, 5024yds, Par 66, SSS 65, Course record 63.
Club membership 380.
Visitors   preferable to telephone in advance, restricted at
weekends.
Societies   apply in writing.
Green Fees £15 per 18 holes (£30 weekends & bank
holidays).
Prof   John Ambler
Designer   Jonathan Gaunt
Facilities   ⊗ ⬧ 🛈 ⬛ ♀ ⚎
Location   4m from Bradford on A647

Hotel   ★★ 68% Park Drive Hotel, 12 Park Dr,
BRADFORD ☎ 01274 480194   11 ⇄ ⋔

South Bradford Pearson Rd, Odsal BD6 1BH
☎ 01274 679195
Hilly course with good greens, trees and ditches. Interesting
short 2nd hole (par 3) 200 yds, well-bunkered and played
from an elevated tee.
9 holes, 6068yds, Par 70, SSS 68, Course record 65.
Club membership 300.
Visitors   must contact professional in advance. Weekends
contact for availability. Tuesday Ladies Day.
Societies   must apply in writing to the secretary.
Green Fees £16 per day (£22 weekends) handicap certificate
required.
Prof   Paul Cooke
Facilities   ⊗ ⦀ ⬧ 🛈 ⬛ ♀ ⚎ 🏠 ⚬
Location   2m S of city centre off A638

Hotel   ★★★ 62% Novotel, Merrydale Rd,
BRADFORD ☎ 01274 683683 127 ⇄ ⋔

West Bowling Newall Hall, Rooley Ln BD5 8LB
☎ 01274 393207 (office) & 728036 (pro) Fax 01274 393207
Undulating, tree-lined parkland course. Testing hole: 'the
Coffin' short par 3, very narrow.
18 holes, 5763yds, Par 68, SSS 67.
Club membership 500.
Visitors   must apply in writing, very limited at weekends.
Societies   must apply in writing.
Green Fees £20 per round (£30 weekends & bank holidays).
Prof   Ian A Marshall   ▶

Facilities ⊗ ⫴ ⮾ 🏌 ♀ ⚲ 🏠 ✐
Location   Corner of M606 & A638 (east)

Hotel   ★★★★ 64% Cedar Court Hotel Bradford, Mayo Av, Off Pooley Ln, BRADFORD
☎ 01274 406606 & 406601
Fax 01274 406600 131 ⇄ 🐾

West Bradford Chellow Grange Rd BD9 6NP
☎ 01274 542767
Parkland course, windy, especially 3rd, 4th, 5th and 6th holes. Hilly but not hard.
18 holes, 5741yds, Par 69, SSS 68.
Club membership 440.
Visitors   restricted Sat. Tuesday is Ladies day, can play if available, advisable to telephone 01274 542102 to reserve a time.
Societies   must apply in writing.
Green Fees £19.50 per day/round.
Prof   Nigel M Barber
Facilities ⚲ 🏠 ✐
Location   W side of city centre off B6144

Hotel   ★★★★ 70% Marriott Hollins Hall Hotel and Country Club, Hollins Hill, Baildon, SHIPLEY
☎ 01274 530053 122 ⇄ 🐾

BRIGHOUSE   Map 07 SE12

Willow Valley Golf & Country Club Highmoor Ln, Clifton HD6 4JB ☎ 01274 878624 Fax 01274 852805
A championship length 18-hole course offering a unique golfing experience, featuring island greens, shaped fairways and bunkers, and multiple teeing areas. The 9-hole course offers an exciting challenge to less experienced golfers.
South: 18 holes, 6496yds, Par 72, SSS 72, Course record 75.
North: 9 holes, 2039yds, Par 30, SSS 60.
Club membership 260.
Visitors   tee times may be booked by phone on payment of green fee by credit/debit card.
Societies   telephone in advance for availability and booking form.
Green Fees South: £22 per round (£27 Fri-Sun). North: £6 per nine holes; £10 per 18 (£7/£12.50 Fri-Sun).
Cards 〓 〓 💳 🖃
Prof   Julian Haworth
Designer   Jonathan Gaunt
Facilities ⊗ ⫴ ⮾ 🏌 ♀ ⚲ 🏠 ⛳ ⛏ ✐ ⛴
Location   Junct 25 of M62 follow A644 towards Brighouse, at small rdbt turn right, A643, course is 2m on righ

Hotel   ★★ 70% Healds Hall Hotel, Leeds Rd, Liversedge, DEWSBURY
☎ 01924 409112 25 ⇄ 🐾

CLECKHEATON   Map 08 SE12

Cleckheaton & District Bradford Rd BD19 6BU
☎ 01274 851266 Fax 01274 871382
Parkland course with gentle hills.
18 holes, 5769yds, Par 71, SSS 68.
Club membership 550.
Visitors   parties must arrange in advance, not weekends.
Societies   weekdays only; must contact in advance.
Green Fees £30 per day; £25 per round.
Prof   Mike Ingham

Facilities ⊗ ⫴ ⮾ 🏌 ♀ ⚲ 🏠 ⛴
Location   1.5m NW on A638 junc 26 M62

Hotel   ★★★ 67% Gomersal Park Hotel, Moor Ln, GOMERSAL
☎ 01274 869386 52 ⇄ 🐾

DEWSBURY   Map 08 SE22

Hanging Heaton White Cross Rd WF12 7DT
☎ 01924 461606 Fax 01924 430100
Arable land course, easy walking, fine views. Testing 4th hole (par 3).
9 holes, 5400mtrs, Par 69, SSS 67.
Club membership 550.
Visitors   must play with member at weekends & bank holidays. Must contact in advance.
Societies   must telephone in advance.
Green Fees not confirmed.
Prof   S Hartley
Facilities ⚲ 🏠
Location   0.75m NE off A653

Hotel   ★★ 70% Healds Hall Hotel, Leeds Rd, Liversedge, DEWSBURY
☎ 01924 409112 25 ⇄ 🐾

ELLAND   Map 07 SE12

Elland Hammerstones, Leach Ln HX5 0TA
☎ 01422 372505 & 374886 (pro)
Parkland course.
9 holes, 2815yds, Par 66, SSS 66, Course record 64.
Club membership 450.
Visitors   welcome.
Societies   must contact in writing.
Green Fees £14 per day/round (£25 weekends & bank holidays).
Prof   N Krzywicki
Facilities ⊗ ⫴ ⮾ 🏌 ♀ ⚲ 🏠 ✐
Location   1m SW

Hotel   ★★ 70% Rock Inn Hotel & Churchills, Holywell Green, HALIFAX
☎ 01422 379721 30 ⇄ 🐾

FENAY BRIDGE   Map 08 SE11

Woodsome Hall HD8 0LQ
☎ 01484 602739 Fax 01484 608260
A parkland course with good views and an historic clubhouse.
18 holes, 5807yds, Par 70, SSS 68.
Club membership 800.
Visitors   must contact in advance. Jacket and tie required in most rooms.
Societies   must apply in writing.
Green Fees £35 per day; £27.50 per round (£40/£35 weekends & bank holidays).
Prof   M Higginbotton
Facilities ⊗ ⫴ ⮾ 🏌 ♀ ⚲ 🏠 ✐
Location   1.5m SW off A629

Hotel   ★★★ 69% Bagden Hall, Wakefield Rd, Scissett, HUDDERSFIELD
☎ 01484 865330 17 ⇄ 🐾

GARFORTH   Map 08 SE43

Garforth LS25 2DS ☎ 0113 286 2021
Parkland course with fine views, easy walking.
18 holes, 6005yds, Par 69, SSS 69.
Club membership 500.
Visitors   must contact in advance and have handicap
              certificate. With member only weekends & bank
              holidays.
Societies   must apply in advance.
Green Fees not confirmed.
Prof   Ken Findlater
Facilities   ⊗ ⌂ ℡ ♥ ♀ ♨ 🏠 ⚐ ♂
Location   1m N

Hotel   ★★★ 74% Holdsworth House Hotel,
              Holdsworth, HALIFAX
              ☎ 01422 240024 40 ⇌ ♠

GUISELEY   Map 08 SE14

Bradford (Hawksworth) Hawksworth Ln LS20 8NP
☎ 01943 875570 873719 (Pro) Fax 01943 875570
Moorland course with eight par 4 holes of 360 yds or more.
The course is a venue for county championship events.
18 holes, 6259yds, Par 71, SSS 71, Course record 66.
Club membership 650.
Visitors   must have a handicap certificate and contact in
              advance. May not play Sat.
Societies   make prior arrangements with manager.
Green Fees £30 per day; £25 per round.
Prof   Sydney Weldon
Designer   W H Fowler
Facilities   ⊗ ⌂ ℡ ♥ ♀ ♨ 🏠 ♂
Location   SW side of town centre off A6038

Hotel   ★★★★ 70% Marriott Hollins Hall Hotel and
              Country Club, Hollins Hill, Baildon, SHIPLEY
              ☎ 01274 530053 122 ⇌ ♠

HALIFAX   Map 07 SE02

Halifax Union Ln, Ogden HX2 8XR
☎ 01422 244171 Fax 01422 241459
Hilly moorland course crossed by streams, natural hazards,
and offering fine views. Testing 172-yd 17th (par3).
18 holes, 6037yds, Par 70, SSS 70, Course record 63.
Club membership 700.
Visitors   contact professional for tee times, 01422
              240047. Limited play weekend.
Societies   contact manager for dates.
Green Fees £20 per day; £15 per round (£30/£20 weekends).
Prof   Michael Allison
Designer   A Herd/J Braid
Facilities   ⊗ ℡ ♥ ♀ ♨ 🏠 ⚐ ♂
Location   A629 Halifax/Keighley, 4 miles from Halifax

Hotel   ★★★ 74% Holdsworth House Hotel,
              Holdsworth, HALIFAX
              ☎ 01422 240024 40 ⇌ ♠

Lightcliffe Knowle Top Rd, Lightcliffe HX3 8SW
☎ 01422 202459
Heathland course.
9 holes, 5388yds, Par 68, SSS 68.
Club membership 545.

Visitors   must be a member of a recognised golf club.
              May not play Sun morning/competition days.
Societies   must contact 21 days in advance.
Green Fees not confirmed.
Prof   Robert Kershaw
Facilities   ⌂ 🏠
Location   3.5m E on A58

Hotel   ★★★ 74% Holdsworth House Hotel,
              Holdsworth, HALIFAX
              ☎ 01422 240024 40 ⇌ ♠

West End Paddock Ln, Highroad Well HX2 0NT
☎ 01422 341878 Fax 01422 341878
Semi-moorland course. Tree lined. Two ponds.
18 holes, 5951yds, Par 69, SSS 69, Course record 62.
Visitors   contact in advance.
Societies   must apply in writing to Secretary.
Green Fees £26 per day; £21 per round (£31/£26 weekends
              & bank holidays).
Prof   David Rishworth
Facilities   ⊗ ⌂ ℡ ♥ ♀ ♨ 🏠 ♂
& Leisure   snooker.
Location   W side of town centre off A646

Hotel   ★★★ 74% Holdsworth House Hotel,
              Holdsworth, HALIFAX
              ☎ 01422 240024 40 ⇌ ♠

HEBDEN BRIDGE   Map 07 SD92

Hebden Bridge Mount Skip, Wadsworth HX7 8PH
☎ 01422 842896 & 842732
Moorland course with splendid views.
9 holes, 5242yds, Par 68, SSS 67, Course record 63.
Club membership 300.
Visitors   weekends after 4pm only.
Societies   apply in writing.
Green Fees £12 per day.
Facilities   ⊗ by prior arrangement ⌂ by prior arrangement
              ♀ ♨
Location   1.5m E off A6033

Hotel   ★★★ 66% Carlton Hotel, Albert St, HEBDEN
              BRIDGE ☎ 01422 844400 16 ⇌ ♠

HOLYWELL GREEN   Map 07 SE01

Halifax Bradley Hall HX4 9AN ☎ 01422 374108
Moorland/parkland course, tightened by recent tree planting,
easy walking.
18 holes, 6138yds, Par 70, SSS 70, Course record 65.
Club membership 500.
Visitors   contact in advance.
Societies   must apply in advance.
Green Fees £23 per day; £28 per round (£35/£28 weekends
              & bank holidays).
Prof   Peter Wood
Facilities   ⊗ ⌂ ℡ ♥ ♀ ♨ 🏠 ♂
Location   S on A6112

Hotel   ★★ 70% Rock Inn Hotel & Churchills,
              Holywell Green, HALIFAX
              ☎ 01422 379721 30 ⇌ ♠

HUDDERSFIELD   Map 07 SE11

Bagden Hall Hotel & Golf Course Wakefield Rd, Scissett HD8 9LE ☎ 01484 864839 Fax 01484 861001
Well maintained tree-lined course set in idyllic surroundings and offering a challenging test of golf for all levels of handicap. Lake guarded greens require pin-point accuracy.
9 holes, 3002yds, Par 56, SSS 55, Course record 60.
Club membership 200.

Visitors	anytime.
Societies	company day packages available, telephone Director of golf.
Green Fees	£10 per 18 holes (£13 weekends).
Prof	Ian Darren
Designer	F O'Donnell/R Brathwaite
Facilities	⊗ ╫ ┖ ▐ ♀ ♨ ☎ ╤ ♠ ♂
Location	A636 Wakefield-Denby Dale

Hotel   ★★★ 69% Bagden Hall, Wakefield Rd, Scissett, HUDDERSFIELD ☎ 01484 865330   17 ⇆ ↾

Bradley Park Off Bradley Rd HD2 1PZ
☎ 01484 223772 Fax 01484 451613
Parkland course, challenging with good mix of long and short holes. Also 14-bay floodlit driving range and 9-hole par 3 course, ideal for beginners. Superb views.
18 holes, 6284yds, Par 70, SSS 70, Course record 65.
Club membership 300.

Visitors	may book by phone for weekends and bank holidays from the preceeding Thu. No restrictions on other days.
Societies	welcome midweek, apply in writing to professional.
Green Fees	£12 per round (£14 weekends & bank holidays).
Cards	⬜ ⬜ ⬜ ⬜ ⬜
Prof	Parnell E Reilly
Designer	Cotton/Pennick/Lowire & Ptnrs
Facilities	⊗ ╫ ┖ ▐ ♀ ♨ ☎ ╤ ♠ ♥ ♂ ◖
& Leisure	9 hole par 3 course.
Location	2.5m from junct 25 of M62

Hotel   ★★★ 66% The George Hotel, St George's Square, HUDDERSFIELD ☎ 01484 515444   60 ⇆ ↾

Crosland Heath Felk Stile Rd, Crosland Heath HD4 7AF
☎ 01484 653216
Moorland course with fine views over valley.
18 holes, 5972yds, Par 70, SSS 70.
Club membership 350.

Visitors	welcome, but advisable to check with professional.
Societies	must telephone in advance.
Green Fees	not confirmed.
Prof	Chris Gaunt
Facilities	♨ ☎
Location	SW off A62

Hotel   ★★★ 66% The George Hotel, St George's Square, HUDDERSFIELD ☎ 01484 515444   60 ⇆ ↾

Huddersfield Fixby Hall, Lightridge Rd, Fixby HD2 2EP
☎ 01484 426203 Fax 01484 424623
A testing heathland course of championship standard laid out in 1891.

18 holes, 6432yds, Par 71, SSS 71, Course record 64.
Club membership 759.

Visitors	must book tee times with professional.
Societies	welcome Mon & Wed-Fri, prior arrangement required.
Green Fees	£45 per day; £33 per round (£60/£45 weekends & bank holidays).
Prof	Paul Carman
Facilities	⊗ ╫ ┖ ▐ ♀ ♨ ☎ ♂
Location	2m N off A641

Hotel   ★★★ 66% The George Hotel, St George's Square, HUDDERSFIELD ☎ 01484 515444   60 ⇆ ↾

Longley Park Maple St, Off Somerset Rd HD5 9AX
☎ 01484 422304
Lowland course, surrounded by mature woodland.
9 holes, 5212yds, Par 66, SSS 66, Course record 61.
Club membership 440.

Visitors	by arrangement with professional, must have handicap certificate, restricted Thu & weekends. No catering Mon.
Societies	must apply in writing to secretary.
Green Fees	£13 per 18 holes (£16 weekends).
Prof	Nick Jones
Facilities	⊗ ╫ ┖ ▐ ♀ ♨ ☎ ╤ ♂
Location	0.5m SE of town centre off A629

Hotel   ★★★ 66% The George Hotel, St George's Square, HUDDERSFIELD ☎ 01484 515444   60 ⇆ ↾

ILKLEY   Map 07 SE14

Ben Rhydding High Wood, Ben Rhydding LS29 8SB
☎ 01943 608759
Moorland/parkland course with splendid views over the Wharfe valley.
9 holes, 4711yds, Par 65, SSS 64, Course record 64.
Club membership 260.

Visitors	contact in advance. May only play at weekend as guest of member.
Societies	advance notice in writing. In view of limited resources requests considered by monthly committee meeting.
Green Fees	not confirmed.
Facilities	♀ ♨
Location	SE side of town

Hotel   ★★★ 70% Rombalds Hotel & Restaurant, 11 West View, Wells Rd, ILKLEY ☎ 01943 603201   15 ⇆ ↾

Ilkley Nesfield Rd, Myddleton LS29 0BE
☎ 01943 600214
This beautiful parkland course is situated in Wharfedale and the Wharfe is a hazard on each of the first seven holes. In fact, the 3rd is laid out entirely on an island in the middle of the river.
18 holes, 5953yds, Par 69, SSS 70, Course record 66.
Club membership 450.

Visitors	advisable to contact in advance.
Societies	apply in writing.
Green Fees	£37 (£42 weekends & bank holidays).
Prof	John L Hammond

Facilities	⊗ 🗽 ⑂ ➤ ♀ ⚲ 📷 ⛳ ✐
& Leisure	fishing.
Location	W side of town centre off A65

Hotel	★★★ 70% Rombalds Hotel & Restaurant, 11 West View, Wells Rd, ILKLEY ☎ 01943 603201 15 ⇄ 📞

KEIGHLEY

Map 07 SE04

Branshaw Branshaw Moor, Oakworth BD22 7ES
☎ 01535 643235 (sec) & 647441 (pro) Fax 01535 647441
Picturesque moorland course with fairly narrow fairways and good greens. Extensive views.
18 holes, 6000yds, Par 69, SSS 69, Course record 64.
Club membership 500.

Visitors	welcome most times, restrictions at weekends advisable to ring.
Societies	apply in writing to Professional.
Green Fees	£20 per day; £15 per round (£25/£20 weekends & bank holidays).
Prof	Mark Tyler
Designer	James Braid
Facilities	⊗ 🗽 ⑂ ➤ ♀ ⚲ 📷 ✐
Location	2m SW on B6149

Hotel	★★ 66% Dalesgate Hotel, 406 Skipton Rd, Utley, KEIGHLEY ☎ 01535 664930 20 ⇄ 📞

Keighley Howden Park, Utley BD20 6DH
☎ 01535 604778 Fax 01535 604778
Parkland course with good views down the Aire Valley.
18 holes, 6149yds, Par 69, SSS 70, Course record 64.
Club membership 600.

Visitors	restricted Sat & Sun. Must contact in advance. No catering/bar Mondays, Ladies day on Tuesday.
Societies	must apply in advance.
Green Fees	£28 per day; £24 per round (£34/£28 weekends).
Cards	🟦🟦
Prof	Mike Bradley
Facilities	⊗ 🗽 ⑂ ➤ ♀ ⚲ 📷 ✐
Location	1m NW of town centre off B6143

Hotel	★★ 66% Dalesgate Hotel, 406 Skipton Rd, Utley, KEIGHLEY ☎ 01535 664930 20 ⇄ 📞

LEEDS

Map 08 SE33

Brandon Holywell Ln, Shadwell LS17 8EZ
☎ 0113 273 7471
An 18-hole links type course enjoying varying degrees of rough, water and sand hazards.
18 holes, 4000yds, Par 68.

Visitors	pay & play course booking not usually necessary.
Societies	telephone or write in advance.
Green Fees	not confirmed.
Facilities	➤ ♀ 📷 ⛳ ✐
Location	From Leeds-Wetherby Rd turn left to Shadwell left again up Main St, right at Red Lion Pub

Hotel	★★★ 80% Haley's Hotel & Restaurant, Shire Oak Rd, Headingley, LEEDS ☎ 0113 278 4446 22 ⇄ 📞 Annexe7 ⇄ 📞

Cookridge Hall Golf & Country Club Cookridge Ln
LS16 7NL ☎ 0113 2300641 Fax 0113 2857115
American-style course designed by Karl Litten. Expect plenty of water hazards, tees for all standards. Large bunkers and fairways between mounds and young trees.
18 holes, 6779yds, Par 72, SSS 72.
Club membership 600.

Visitors	must contact in advance. Strict dress code applies.
Societies	telephone in advance.
Green Fees	£25 per day; £18 per round (£30/£20 per round weekends).
Cards	🟦🟦🟦🟦🟦
Prof	Mark Pearson
Designer	Karl Liiten
Facilities	⊗ 🗽 ⑂ ➤ ♀ ⚲ 📷 ⛳ ✐ ♟
& Leisure	heated indoor swimming pool, sauna, solarium, gymnasium, health & fitness club.
Location	On Otley Old Road, off A660, 3m N of Leeds

Hotel	★★★ 80% Haley's Hotel & Restaurant, Shire Oak Rd, Headingley, LEEDS ☎ 0113 278 4446 22 ⇄ 📞 Annexe7 ⇄ 📞

Gotts Park Armley Ridge Rd LS12 2QX
☎ 0113 231 1896
Municipal parkland course; hilly and windy with narrow fairways. Some very steep hills to some greens. A challenging course requiring accuracy rather than length from the tees.
18 holes, 4960yds, Par 65, SSS 64, Course record 63.
Club membership 200.

Visitors	no restrictions.
Green Fees	not confirmed.
Prof	John F Simpson
Facilities	♀ (evenings) 📷 ⛳
Location	3m W of city centre off A647

Hotel	★★★★ 69% Queen's Hotel, City Square, LEEDS ☎ 0113 243 1323 199 ⇄ 📞

Headingley Back Church Ln, Adel LS16 8DW
☎ 0113 267 9573 Fax 0113 281 7334
An undulating course with a wealth of natural features offering fine views from higher ground. Its most striking hazard is the famous ravine at the 18th. Leeds's oldest course, founded in 1892.
18 holes, 6298yds, Par 69, SSS 70, Course record 64.
Club membership 700.

Visitors	must contact in advance, restricted at weekends.
Societies	must telephone in advance and confirm in writing.
Green Fees	£35 per day; £30 per round (£40 per day/round weekends & bank holidays).
Prof	Steven Foster
Designer	Dr Mackenzie
Facilities	⊗ 🗽 ⑂ ➤ ♀ ⚲ 📷 ⛳ ✐
Location	5.5m N of city centre off A660

Hotel	B Posthouse Bramhope, Leeds Rd, BRAMHOPE ☎ 0113 284 2911 124 ⇄ 📞

Horsforth Layton Rise, Layton Rd, Horsforth LS18 5EX
☎ 0113 258 6819 Fax 0113 258 6819
Moorland/parkland course overlooking airport.
18 holes, 6243yds, Par 71, SSS 70, Course record 65.
Club membership 750.

Visitors	restricted Sat & with member only Sun.
Societies	must apply in writing.
Green Fees	£30 per day; £24 per round (£35 weekends).
Prof	Neil Bell
Facilities	⊗ ⽊ ⅃ ⪧ ♥ ⊈ ♨ 🏠 ♂
Location	6.5m NW of city centre off A65

Hotel	B Posthouse Bramhope, Leeds Rd, BRAMHOPE ☎ 0113 284 2911 124 ⇆ 🏲

Leeds Elmete Ln LS8 2LJ ☎ 0113 265 8775
Parkland course with pleasant views.
18 holes, 6097yds, Par 69, SSS 69, Course record 63.
Club membership 600.

Visitors	with member only weekends, yellow tees only. Must contact in advance.
Societies	must apply in writing.
Green Fees	not confirmed.
Prof	Simon Longster
Facilities	⊈ 🏠 ⊤ ♂
Location	5m NE of city centre on A6120 off A58

Hotel	★★★ 80% Haley's Hotel & Restaurant, Shire Oak Rd, Headingley, LEEDS ☎ 0113 278 4446 22 ⇆ 🏲 Annexe7 ⇆ 🏲

Leeds Golf Centre Wike Ridge Ln, Shadwell LS17 9JW
☎ 0113 288 6000 Fax 0113 288 6185
Two courses - the 18-hole Wike Ridge, a traditional
heathland course designed by Donald Steel. The sand-based
greens are constructed to USGA specification and there are
an excellent variety of holes with some very challenging Par
5's. The 12-hole Oaks is complemented by a floodlit driving
range and other practice facilities. The course is the home of
the Leeds Golf Academy.
Wike Ridge Course: 18 holes, 6482yds, Par 72, SSS 71.
Oaks: 12 holes, 1610yds, Par 36.
Club membership 500.

Visitors	no restrictions, telephone booking advisable.
Societies	tee reservation available in advance.
Green Fees	£22 per day; £13.50 per 18 holes (£25 per day; £15 per 18 holes weekends).
Cards	🖅 🖅 🖅 🖅 🖅
Prof	Neil Harvey
Designer	Donald Steel
Facilities	⊗ ⽊ ⅃ ⪧ ♥ ⊈ ♨ 🏠 ⊤ ♭ ♠ ♂ ℓ
Location	5m N, take A58 course on N side of Shadwell

Hotel	★★★ 80% Haley's Hotel & Restaurant, Shire Oak Rd, Headingley, LEEDS ☎ 0113 278 4446 22 ⇆ 🏲 Annexe7 ⇆ 🏲

Middleton Park Municipal Middleton Park, Middleton
LS10 3TN ☎ 0113 270 0449 & 270 9506
Parkland course.
18 holes, 5263yds, Par 68, SSS 66, Course record 63.
Club membership 320.

Visitors	may only use the club 6 times in one year.
Green Fees	not confirmed.
Prof	Jim Pape
Facilities	⊈ 🏠 ⊤
Location	3m S off A653

Hotel	★★★★ 69% Queen's Hotel, City Square, LEEDS ☎ 0113 243 1323 199 ⇆ 🏲

Moor Allerton Coal Rd, Wike LS17 7EA
☎ 0113 266 1154 Fax 0113 237 1124
The Moor Allerton Club, established in 1921, has 27
holes set in 220 acres of undulating parkland, with
testing water hazards and magnificent views extending
across the Vale of York. The Championship Course was
designed by Robert Trent Jones, the famous American
course architect, and provides a challenge to both high
and low handicapped golfers.
Lakes Course: 18 holes, 6470yds, Par 71, SSS 72.
Blackmoor Course: 18 holes, 6673yds, Par 71, SSS 73.
High Course: 18 holes, 6841yds, Par 72, SSS 74.
Club membership 1200.

Visitors	contact professional (0113 266 5209).
Societies	must apply in advance.
Green Fees	not confirmed.
Prof	Richard Lane
Designer	Robert Trent Jones
Facilities	⊗ ⽊ ⅃ ⪧ ♥ ⊈ ♨ 🏠 ⊤ ♭ ♠ ♂ ℓ
& Leisure	hard tennis courts, sauna, crown green bowls, snooker table.
Location	5.5m N of city centre on A61

Hotel	★★★ 66% Harewood Arms Hotel, Harrogate Rd, HAREWOOD ☎ 0113 288 6566 13 ⇆ 🏲 Annexe11 ⇆ 🏲

Moortown Harrogate Rd, Alwoodley LS17 7DB
☎ 0113 268 6521 Fax 0113 268 0986
Championship course, tough but fair. Springy moorland
turf, natural hazards of heather, gorse and streams,
cunningly placed bunkers and immaculate greens.
Original home of Ryder Cup in 1929.
18 holes, 6782yds, Par 72, SSS 73, Course record 66.
Club membership 566.

Visitors	must contact in advance.
Societies	apply in writing in advance.
Green Fees	not confirmed.
Prof	Bryon Hutchinson
Designer	A McKenzie
Facilities	⊈ 🏠 ⊤ ♠ ♂ ℓ
& Leisure	practice area.
Location	6m N of city centre on A61

Hotel	★★★ 66% Harewood Arms Hotel, Harrogate Rd, HAREWOOD ☎ 0113 288 6566 13 ⇆ 🏲 Annexe11 ⇆ 🏲

Oulton Park Rothwell LS26 8EX
☎ 0113 282 3152
27-hole championship-length municipal course. Although municipal, a dress rule is applied. 16-bay driving range.
Main Course: 18 holes, 6450yds, Par 71, SSS 71, Course record 65.
Short Course: 9 holes, 3250yds, Par 35, SSS 35.
Club membership 450.
Visitors must apply 24hrs in advance.
Societies Mon-Fri. Must contact in advance.
Green Fees not confirmed.
Prof Stephen Gromett
Designer Dave Thomas
Facilities ⊗ ⅢⅬ ▆ ♀ ♨ ☐ ☂ ⋔ ⌖ ♕ ⊕ ⚬ ⌁
& Leisure heated indoor swimming pool, squash, sauna, solarium, gymnasium.
Location Junc 30 on M62

Hotel ★★★★★ 70% Oulton Hall Hotel,
Rothwell Ln, Oulton, LEEDS
☎ 0113 282 1000 152 ⇄ ┌

Roundhay Park Ln LS8 2EJ ☎ 0113 266 2695
Attractive municipal parkland course, natural hazards, easy walking.
9 holes, 5223yds, Par 70, SSS 65, Course record 61.
Club membership 300.
Visitors must contact professional at all times.
Societies telephone or write to the professional.
Green Fees not confirmed.
Prof James Pape
Facilities Ⅲ Ⅼ ▆ ♀ ♨ ☐ ⌖ ⚬
Location 4m NE of city centre off A58

Hotel ★★★ 80% Haley's Hotel & Restaurant,
Shire Oak Rd, Headingley, LEEDS
☎ 0113 278 4446 22 ⇄ ┌ Annexe7 ⇄ ┌

Sand Moor Alwoodley Ln LS17 7DJ
☎ 0113 268 5180 Fax 0113 268 5180
A beautiful, undulating course overlooking Lord Harewood's estate and the Eccup Reservoir. The course is wooded with some holes adjacent to water. The 12th is perhaps the most difficult where the fairway falls away towards the reservoir.
18 holes, 6429yds, Par 71, SSS 71, Course record 63.
Club membership 553.
Visitors restricted weekends & bank holidays.
Societies must apply in advance.
Green Fees £40 per day; £32 per round (£44 per round Sun & bank holidays).
Prof Peter Tupling
Designer Dr A Mackenzie
Facilities ⊗ Ⅲ by prior arrangement Ⅼ ▆ ♀ ♨ ☐ ⌖ ⚬
Location 5m N of city centre off A61

Hotel B Posthouse Bramhope, Leeds Rd,
BRAMHOPE ☎ 0113 284 2911 124 ⇄ ┌

South Leeds Gipsy Ln, Beeston LS11 5TU
☎ 0113 277 1676 & 270 2598 (pro)
Parkland course, windy, hard walking, good views.
18 holes, 5769yds, Par 69, SSS 68, Course record 64.
Club membership 500.

Visitors welcome weekdays except competition time, may not play weekends.
Societies must apply in advance.
Green Fees £18 (£26 bank holidays).
Prof Mike Lewis
Facilities ⊗ Ⅲ Ⅼ ▆ ♀ ♨ ☐ ⚬
Location 3m S of city centre off A653

Hotel ★★★★ 69% Queen's Hotel, City Square,
LEEDS ☎ 0113 243 1323 199 ⇄ ┌

Temple Newsam Temple-Newsam Rd LS15 0LN
☎ 0113 264 5624
Two parkland courses. Testing long 13th (563 yds) on second course.
Lord Irwin: 18 holes, 6460yds, Par 69, SSS 71.
Lady Dorothy: 18 holes, 6299yds, Par 70, SSS 70.
Club membership 520.
Visitors no restrictions.
Societies must apply in advance in writing.
Green Fees not confirmed.
Prof Alan Swaine
Facilities ⊗ Ⅼ ▆ ♀ ♨ ☐ ⌖ ⚬
Location 3.5m E of city centre off A63

Hotel ★★★ 80% Haley's Hotel & Restaurant,
Shire Oak Rd, Headingley, LEEDS
☎ 0113 278 4446 22 ⇄ ┌ Annexe7 ⇄ ┌

MARSDEN

Map 07 SE01

Marsden Mount Rd, Hemplow HD7 6NN ☎ 01484 844253
Moorland course with good views, natural hazards, windy.
9 holes, 5702yds, Par 68, SSS 68, Course record 63.
Club membership 200. ▶

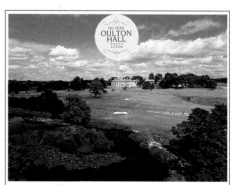

Oulton Hall Hotel is a magnificent hotel surrounded by 19th century formal gardens. The hotel has a special agreement with the Oulton Park Golf Course, venue for the De Vere PGA City of Leeds Championship in July, to guarantee guests preferential tee times. The course is as varied and dramatic as the Yorkshire countryside that influences its challenging character.
Rothwell Lane, Oulton, Leeds, LS26 8HN
Tel: 0113 2821000   Fax: 0113 2828066

Visitors   must play with member at weekends.
Societies   Mon-Fri; must contact in advance.
Green Fees not confirmed.
Prof   Nick Krzywicki
Designer   Dr McKenzie
Facilities   ⊗ ⅲ ᗩ ➘ ♀ ♙ ☖
& Leisure   hard tennis courts.
Location   S side off A62

Hotel   ★★★ 60% Briar Court Hotel, Halifax Rd,
Birchencliffe, HUDDERSFIELD
☎ 01484 519902   48 ⇨ ✿

MELTHAM   Map 07 SE01

Meltham Thick Hollins Hall HD7 3DQ
☎ 01484 850227 Fax 01484 850227
Parkland course with good views. Testing 548 yd, 13th hole
(par 5).
18 holes, 6379yds, Par 71, SSS 70, Course record 67.
Club membership 550.
Visitors   may not play Sat & Wed (Ladies Day), desirable
to contact professional in advance.
Societies   must apply in writing.
Green Fees £25 per day; £20 per round (£30/£25 weekends
& bank holidays).
Prof   Paul Davies
Designer   Alex Herd
Facilities   ⊗ ⅲ ᗩ ➘ ♀ ♙ ☖ ♠ ✓
Location   SE side of village off B6107

Hotel   ★★★ 66% The George Hotel,
St George's Square, HUDDERSFIELD
☎ 01484 515444   60 ⇨ ✿

MIRFIELD   Map 08 SE21

Dewsbury District Sands Ln WF14 8HJ
☎ 01924 492399 & 496030 Fax 01924 492399
Heathland/parkland course with panoramic views and hard
walking. Ponds in middle of 3rd fairway, left of 5th green
and 17th green.
18 holes, 6360yds, Par 71, SSS 71.
Club membership 650.
Visitors   Sun after 1pm, on non competition days.
Telephone in advance.
Societies   telephone bookings.
Green Fees £22.50 per day (£22.50 per round weekends).
Prof   Nigel P Hirst
Designer   Old Tom Morris/ Peter Alliss
Facilities   ⊗ ⅲ ᗩ ➘ ♀ ♙ ☖ ♠ ✓
& Leisure   snooker tables.
Location   Off A644, 6m from junct 25 on M62

Hotel   ★★★ 66% The George Hotel,
St George's Square, HUDDERSFIELD
☎ 01484 515444   60 ⇨ ✿

MORLEY   Map 08 SE22

Howley Hall Scotchman Ln LS27 0NX
☎ 01924 478417 & 473852 Fax 01924 478417
Parkland course with easy walking and good views.
18 holes, 6058yds, Par 71, SSS 69.
Club membership 700.
Visitors   standard course only, may not play Sat.
Handicap certificate required.

Societies   contact for details.
Green Fees not confirmed.
Prof   Gary Watkinson
Facilities   ⊗ ⅲ ᗩ ➘ ♀ ♙ ☖ ♟ ➘ ✓
Location   1.5m S on B6123

Hotel   ★★ 68% Alder House Hotel,
Towngate Rd, Healey Ln, BATLEY
☎ 01924 444777   20 ⇨ ✿

NORMANTON   Map 08 SE32

Normanton Snydale Rd WF6 1PN
☎ 01924 892943 Fax 01924 220134
A pleasant, flat course with tight fairways in places and an
internal out-of-bounds requiring accuracy.
9 holes, 5288yds, Par 66, SSS 66.
Club membership 400.
Visitors   may not play on Sun.
Societies   mid-week only, apply in writing or telephone.
Green Fees not confirmed.
Prof   Ian Hunt
Facilities   ⊗ ⅲ ᗩ ➘ ♀ ♙ ☖ ♟
Location   0.5m SE on B6133

Hotel   ★★★ 66% Quality Hotel Wakefield, Queen St,
WAKEFIELD ☎ 01924 372111   64 ⇨ ✿

OSSETT   Map 08 SE22

Low Laithes Parkmill Ln, Flushdyke WF5 9AP
☎ 01924 274667 & 266067 Fax 01924 266067
Testing parkland course.
18 holes, 6463yds, Par 72, SSS 71, Course record 65.
Club membership 600.
Visitors   may not play before 9.30am and 12.30-1.30
weekdays and before 10am and 12-2
weekends/bank holidays.
Societies   by prior arrangement.
Green Fees £23 per day; £19 per round.
Prof   Paul Browning
Designer   Dr Mackenzie
Facilities   ⊗ ⅲ ᗩ ➘ ♀ ♙ ☖ ♠ ✓
Location   Leave M1 at jct 40 then signposted on
Dewsbury road 0.5m from M1

Hotel   B Posthouse Northampton/Rugby, CRICK
☎ 01788 822101   88 ⇨ ✿

OTLEY   Map 08 SE24

Otley Off West Busk Ln LS21 3NG
☎ 01943 465329 Fax 01943 850387
An expansive course with magnificent views across
Wharfedale. It is well-wooded with streams crossing the
fairway. The 4th is a fine hole which generally needs two
woods to reach the plateau green. The 17th is a good
short hole.
18 holes, 6225yds, Par 70, SSS 70, Course record 66.
Club membership 700.
Visitors   telephone to check tee time. May not play
Tue morning or Sat.
Societies   telephone enquiries welcome, bookings in
writing.
Green Fees £33 per 36 holes, £26 upto 27 holes
(£39/£33 weekends and bank holidays).
Prof   Steven Tomkinson

| Facilities | ⊗ ⊪ ㄴ ♥ ♀ ♨ ㊟ ☂ ⸰ |
| Location | 1.5m SW off A6038 |

| Hotel | B Posthouse Bramhope, Leeds Rd, |
| | BRAMHOPE ☎ 0113 284 2911 124 ⇆ ♘ |

OUTLANE   Map 07 SE01

Outlane Slack Ln, off New Hey Rd HD3 3YL
☎ 01422 311789 & 374762 Fax 01422 311789
Moorland course.
18 holes, 6015yds, Par 71, SSS 70, Course record 66.
Club membership 600.

Visitors	telephone in advance, must be correctly equipped and attired. No play Sat, limited Sun morning.
Societies	apply in writing.
Green Fees	£18 per day/round (£28 weekends & bank holidays).
Prof	David Chapman
Facilities	⊗ ⊪ ㄴ ♥ ♀ ♨ ㊟ ☂ ⸰
Location	S side of village off A640

| Hotel | ★★★ 69% Old Golf House Hotel, New Hey Rd, Outlane, HUDDERSFIELD ☎ 01422 379311 50 ⇆ ♘ |

PONTEFRACT   Map 08 SE42

Mid Yorkshire Havercroft Ln, Darrington WF8 3BP
☎ 01977 704522 Fax 01977 600823
An 18-hole championship-standard course opened in 1993, and widely considered to be one of the finest new courses in Yorkshire.
18 holes, 6500yds, Par 72, SSS 71, Course record 68.
Club membership 500.

Visitors	tee times bookable by telephone, visitors after 12 noon at weekends.
Societies	apply in writing to the secretary.
Green Fees	not confirmed.
Cards	▬
Prof	Alistair Cobbett
Designer	Steve Marnoch
Facilities	⊗ ⊪ ㄴ ♥ ♀ ♨ ㊟ ☂ ⤙ ⸰ ⌕
Location	On the A1, 0.5m south intersection of A1/M62

| Hotel | ★★★ 71% Wentbridge House Hotel, WENTBRIDGE ☎ 01977 620444 16 ⇆ ♘ Annexe4 ⇆ ♘ |

Pontefract & District Park Ln WF8 4QS
☎ 01977 792241 Fax 01977 792241
Undulating parkland course, some elevated tees.
18 holes, 6227yds, Par 72, SSS 70.
Club membership 800.

Visitors	welcome except Wed & weekends, advisable to contact in advance.
Societies	welcome except Wed & weekends.
Green Fees	not confirmed.
Prof	Nick Newman
Facilities	♨ ㊟ ⸰
Location	1.5m W on B6134

| Hotel | ★★★ 71% Wentbridge House Hotel, WENTBRIDGE ☎ 01977 620444 16 ⇆ ♘ Annexe4 ⇆ ♘ |

PUDSEY   Map 08 SE23

Calverley Woodhall Ln LS28 5QY
☎ 0113 256 9244 Fax 0113 256 9244
Parkland course on gently undulating terrain where accurate approach shots are rewarded to small greens.
18 holes, 5590yds, Par 68, SSS 67, Course record 64 or 9 holes, 2137yds, Par 33.
Club membership 510.

Visitors	Advisable to book 18 hole course in advance and may not play Sun morning. 9 hole course. pay and play at all times.
Societies	contact in writing or telephone.
Green Fees	£12 (£17 weekends). 9 holes £5.
Cards	▬ ▬ ▬
Prof	Derek Johnson
Designer	S. Lyle
Facilities	⊗ ⊪ ㄴ ♥ ♀ ♨ ㊟ ☂ ⸰
Location	Signposted Calverley from A647 Leeds/Bradford road

| Hotel | ★★ 68% Park Drive Hotel, 12 Park Dr, BRADFORD ☎ 01274 480194 11 ⇆ ♘ |

Fulneck LS28 8NT ☎ 0113 256 5191
Picturesque parkland course.
9 holes, 5456yds, Par 66, SSS 67, Course record 65.
Club membership 250.

Visitors	with member only weekends & bank holidays.
Societies	must apply in writing.
Green Fees	£14 per day.
Facilities	⊗ by prior arrangement ⊪ by prior arrangement ㄴ ♥ ♀ ♨
Location	Pudsey, between Leeds/Bradford

| Hotel | ★★★ 62% Novotel, Merrydale Rd, BRADFORD ☎ 01274 683683 127 ⇆ ♘ |

Woodhall Hills Calverley LS28 5UN ☎ 0113 255 4594
Meadowland course, prevailing SW winds, fairly hard walking. Testing holes: 8th, 377 yd (par 4); 14th, 206 yd (par 3).
18 holes, 6001yds, Par 70, SSS 69, Course record 63.
Club membership 570.

Visitors	any day advise secretary/professional in advance.
Societies	telephone/write in advance.
Green Fees	not confirmed.
Prof	Warren Lockett
Facilities	⊗ ⊪ ㄴ ♥ ♀ ♨ ㊟ ⸰
Location	1m NW off A647

| Hotel | ★★ 68% Park Drive Hotel, 12 Park Dr, BRADFORD ☎ 01274 480194 11 ⇆ ♘ |

RAWDON   Map 08 SE23

Rawdon Golf & Lawn Tennis Club Buckstone Dr
LS19 6BD ☎ 0113 250 6040
Undulating parkland course.
9 holes, 5980yds, Par 72, SSS 69.
Club membership 700.

Visitors	must contact in advance & have handicap certificate. With member only at weekends.
Societies	must contact in advance.
Green Fees	not confirmed.
Prof	Simon Toot

▶

Facilities ⊗ ≀ ᴸ 🍴 ♀ ♨ 🏠 ⛳ ♂
& Leisure hard and grass tennis courts.
Location S side of town off A65

Hotel ★★★ 65% Apperley Manor, Apperley Ln,
Apperley Bridge, BRADFORD
☎ 0113 250 5626 13 ⇆ 🐾

RIDDLESDEN   Map 07 SE04

Riddlesden Howden Rough BD20 5QN
☎ 01535 602148
Undulating moorland course with prevailing west winds,
some hard walking and beautiful views. Ten par 3 holes and
spectacular 6th and 15th holes played over old quarry sites.
18 holes, 4295yds, Par 63, SSS 61.
Club membership 350.
Visitors restricted before 2pm weekends.
Societies apply by telephone or in writing.
Green Fees £15 (£20 weekends).
Facilities ⊗ ᴸ 🍴 ♀ ♨
Location 1m NW

Hotel ★★ 66% Dalesgate Hotel, 406 Skipton Rd,
Utley, KEIGHLEY
☎ 01535 664930 20 ⇆ 🐾

SCARCROFT   Map 08 SE34

Scarcroft Skye Ln LS14 3BQ ☎ 0113 289 2311
Undulating parkland course with prevailing west wind and
easy walking.
18 holes, 6426yds, Par 71, SSS 69.
Club membership 667.
Visitors must contact in advance.
Societies must contact in advance.
Green Fees £35 per day; £28 per round (£40 per round
weekends & bank holidays, £26 after 4pm).
Prof Darren Tear
Designer Charles Mackenzie
Facilities ⊗ ≀ ᴸ 🍴 ♀ ♨ 🏠 ⛳ ♂
Location 0.5m N of village off A58

Hotel ★★★ 66% Harewood Arms Hotel,
Harrogate Rd, HAREWOOD
☎ 0113 288 6566 13 ⇆ 🐾 Annexe11 ⇆ 🐾

SHIPLEY   Map 07 SE13

Marriott Hollins Hall Hotel & Country Club
Hollins Hill, Baildon BD17 8QW
☎ 01274 534212 & 534211 Fax 01274 534220
Set in natural heathland amongst the beautiful Yorkshire
moors and dales. The course is majestic, challenging and
classically designed in the spirit of the game.
18 holes, 6671yds, Par 71, SSS 71.
Visitors must contact in advance - 10 days max.
Societies telephone in advance 01274 530053.
Green Fees £50 per day; £30 per round.
Cards 💳 💳 💳 💳 💳
Prof to be confirmed
Designer Ross McMurray
Facilities ⊗ ≀ ᴸ 🍴 ♀ ♨ 🏠 ⛳ 🏌 🏊 ♂
& Leisure heated indoor swimming pool, sauna, solarium,
gymnasium, health & beauty salon.
Location 3m N on the A6038 Otley road

Hotel ★★★★ 70% Marriott Hollins Hall Hotel and
Country Club, Hollins Hill, Baildon, SHIPLEY
☎ 01274 530053 122 ⇆ 🐾

Northcliffe High Bank Ln BD18 4LJ
☎ 01274 596731 Fax 01274 596731
Parkland course with magnificent views of moors. Testing
1st hole (18th green 100 feet below tee).
18 holes, 6104yds, Par 71, SSS 69, Course record 64.
Club membership 700.
Visitors no restrictions.
Societies book via secretary in advance, weekdays only.
Green Fees £20 per day/round (£25 weekend and bank
holidays).
Prof M Hillas
Designer James Braid
Facilities ⊗ ≀ ᴸ 🍴 ♀ ♨ 🏠 ⛳ 🏌 ♂
Location 1.25m SW of Shipley, off A650

Hotel ★★★★ 70% Marriott Hollins Hall Hotel and
Country Club, Hollins Hill, Baildon, SHIPLEY
☎ 01274 530053 122 ⇆ 🐾

SILSDEN   Map 07 SE04

Silsden High Brunthwaite BD20 0NH ☎ 01535 652998
Tight downland course which can be windy. Good views of
the Aire Valley.
14 holes, 4870yds, Par 65, SSS 64, Course record 61.
Club membership 300.
Visitors may not play before 11am on Sun.
Societies must apply in advance.
Green Fees not confirmed.
Facilities ⊗ by prior arrangement ♀ ♨
Location 1m E

Hotel ★★ 66% Dalesgate Hotel,
406 Skipton Rd, Utley, KEIGHLEY
☎ 01535 664930 20 ⇆ 🐾

SOWERBY   Map 07 SE02

Ryburn The Shaw, Norland HX6 3QP ☎ 01422 831355
Moorland course, easy walking.
9 holes, 4984yds, Par 66, SSS 64, Course record 64.
Club membership 200.
Visitors must contact in advance.
Societies apply in writing.
Green Fees not confirmed.
Facilities ⊗ ≀ ᴸ 🍴 ♀ ♨
Location 1m S of Sowerby Bridge off A58

Hotel ★★ 69% The Hobbit Hotel, Hob Ln,
Norland, Sowerby Bridge, HALIFAX
☎ 01422 832202 17 ⇆ ☞ Annexe5 ⇆ ☞

TODMORDEN
Map 07 SD92

Todmorden Rive Rocks, Cross Stone Rd OL14 8RD
☎ 01706 812986
Pleasant moorland course.
9 holes, 5382yds, Par 68, SSS 68, Course record 67.
Club membership 240.
Visitors restricted Thu & weekends. Advisable to contact
in advance.
Societies must apply in writing.
Green Fees £15 (£20 weekends and bank holidays).
Facilities ⓑ ♥ ♀ ⚲
Location NE off A646

Hotel ★★★ 66% Scaitcliffe Hall, Burnley Rd,
TODMORDEN ☎ 01706 818888 28 ⇆ ☞

WAKEFIELD
Map 08 SE32

City of Wakefield Lupset Park, Horbury Rd WF2 8QS
☎ 01924 360282
Parkland course.
18 holes, 6319yds, Par 72, SSS 70, Course record 67.
Club membership 600.
Visitors restricted weekends.
Societies must apply in advance to stewardess 01924
367242.
Green Fees not confirmed.
Prof Roger Holland
Designer J S F Morrison
Facilities ⊗ ⅏ ⓑ ♥ ♀ ⚲ ⌂ ⛳ ⚬
Location 1.5m W of city centre on A642

Hotel B Posthouse Wakefield, Queen's Dr, Ossett,
WAKEFIELD ☎ 01924 276388 99 ⇆ ☞

Painthorpe House Painthorpe Ln, Painthorpe, Crigglestone
WF4 3HE ☎ 01924 274527 & 255083 Fax 01924 252022
Undulating meadowland course, easy walking.
9 holes, 4544yds, Par 62, SSS 62, Course record 63.
Club membership 150.
Visitors pay and play Mon-Sat, after 2.30pm on Sun.
Societies must telephone in advance.
Green Fees £5 per 18 holes (£6 weekends).
Cards [VISA]
Facilities ⊗ ⅏ ⓑ ♥ ♀ ⚲
Location 2m S off A636, 0.5m from jct 39 M1

Hotel B Posthouse Wakefield, Queen's Dr, Ossett,
WAKEFIELD ☎ 01924 276388 99 ⇆ ☞

Wakefield Woodthorpe Ln, Sandal WF2 6JH
☎ 01924 258778 (sec) & 255380 (pro) Fax 01924 242752
A well-sheltered meadowland/heath course with easy
walking and good views.
18 holes, 6650yds, Par 72, SSS 72, Course record 66.
Club membership 540.
Visitors contact must be made in advance. Visitors Wed,
Thu and Fri only.
Societies must apply in writing.
Green Fees £27.50 per day; £22 per round (£30 weekends &
bank holidays).

Prof Ian M Wright
Designer McKenzie
Facilities ⊗ ⅏ ⓑ ♥ ♀ ⚲ ⌂ ⚬
Location 3m S of Wakefield, off A61

Hotel B Posthouse Wakefield, Queen's Dr, Ossett,
WAKEFIELD ☎ 01924 276388 99 ⇆ ☞ •

WETHERBY
Map 08 SE44

Wetherby Linton Ln LS22 4JF
☎ 01937 580089 Fax 01937 581915
Parkland course with fine views.
18 holes, 6235yds, Par 71, SSS 70, Course record 63.
Club membership 650.
Visitors may not play Mon & Tues morning.
Societies apply in writing or telephone in advance.
Green Fees £30 per day; £25 per round (£36 per round/day
weekends and bank holidays).
Prof D Padgett
Facilities ⊗ ⅏ ⓑ ♥ ♀ ⚲ ⌂ ⛳ ⚲ ⚬ ⚬
& Leisure putting green, practice area.
Location 1m W off A661

Hotel ★★★★♨ 75% Wood Hall Hotel,
Trip Ln, Linton, WETHERBY
☎ 01937 587271 37 ⇆ ☞ Annexe6 ⇆ ☞

CHANNEL ISLANDS

ALDERNEY

ALDERNEY
Map 16

Alderney Route des Carrieres GY9 3YD ☎ 01481 822835
Undulating seaside course with sea on all sides and offering
magnificent views from its high tees and greens. Course
designed by Frank Pennink.
9 holes, 5006yds, Par 64, SSS 65, Course record 65.
Club membership 400.
Visitors may not play before 10am at weekends.
Advisable to contact in advance.
Societies must contact in advance.
Green Fees not confirmed.
Facilities ⓑ ♥ ♀ ⚲ ⛳ ⚬
Location 1m E of St Annes

Hotel ★★ 72% Inchalla Hotel, St Anne,
ALDERNEY ☎ 01481 823220 9 ⇆ ☞

GUERNSEY

L'ANCRESSE VALE
Map 16.

Royal Guernsey GY3 5BY
☎ 01481 46523 Fax 01481 43960
Not quite as old as its neighbour Royal Jersey, Royal
Guernsey is a sporting course which was re-designed
after World War II by Mackenzie Ross, who has many
fine courses to his credit. It is a pleasant links, well- ▶

maintained, and administered by the States of Guernsey in the form of the States Tourist Committee. The 8th hole, a good par 4, requires an accurate second shot to the green set amongst the gorse and thick rough. The 18th, with lively views, needs a strong shot to reach the green well down below. The course is windy, with hard walking. There is a junior section.
18 holes, 6206yds, Par 70, SSS 70, Course record 64.
Club membership 934.

Visitors	must have a handicap certificate; may not play on Thu, Sat afternoons & Sun.
Green Fees	£35 per day.
Cards	🖸
Prof	Norman Wood
Designer	Mackenzie Ross
Facilities	⊗ � 🍴 ⌷ ⌷ 🏌 🛄 🏌 ↑ 🖊 🏌 (
Location	3m N of St Peter Port
Hotel	★★★★ 70% St Pierre Park Hotel, Rohais, ST PETER PORT ☎ 01481 728282 132 ⇥ 🏌

St Peter Port   Map 16

St Pierre Park Golf Club Rohais GY1 1FD
☎ 01481 728282 Fax 01481 712041
Par 3 parkland course with delightful setting, with lakes, streams and many tricky holes.
9 holes, 2610yds, Par 54, SSS 50, Course record 52.
Club membership 200.

Visitors	contact in advance.
Societies	must contact in advance.
Green Fees	not confirmed.
Cards	🖸 💳 🖸
Prof	Roy Corbet
Designer	Jacklin
Facilities	⊗ ⎗ 🍴 ⌷ ⌷ 🏌 🛄 🏌 ↑ 🖊 🏌 (
& Leisure	hard tennis courts, heated indoor swimming pool, sauna, solarium, gymnasium, health suite with beauty treatment.
Location	1m W off Rohais Rd
Hotel	★★★★ 70% St Pierre Park Hotel, Rohais, ST PETER PORT ☎ 01481 728282 132 ⇥ 🏌

JERSEY

Grouville   Map 16

Royal Jersey JE3 9BD ☎ 01534 854416
A seaside links, historic because of its age: its centenary was celebrated in 1978. It is also famous for the fact that Britain's greatest golfer, Harry Vardon, was born in a little cottage on the edge of the course and learned his golf here.
18 holes, 6059yds, Par 70, SSS 70, Course record 64.
Club membership 1364.

Visitors	restricted to 10am-noon & 2pm-4pm.
Societies	welcome Mon-Fri. Must apply in writing.
Green Fees	£40 per round.
Prof	Tommy Horton

Designer	Harry Vardon
Facilities	⊗ ⎗ 🍴 ⌷ ⌷ 🏌 🛄 ↑ 🖊 🏌
Location	4m E of St Helier off coast rd
Hotel	★★★ 67% Old Court House Hotel, GOREY ☎ 01534 854444 58 ⇥ 🏌

La Moye   Map 16

La Moye La Route Orange JE3 8GQ
☎ 01534 743401 Fax 01534 747289
Seaside championship links course (venue for the Jersey Seniors Open) situated in an exposed position on the south western corner of the island overlooking St Ouens Bay. Offers spectacular views, two start points, full course all year - no temporary greens.
18 holes, 6664yds, Par 72, SSS 72, Course record 68.
Club membership 1300.

Visitors	must contact course ranger in advance 01534 747166. Visitors may play after 2.30pm weekends and bank holidays.
Societies	apply in writing.
Green Fees	£40 per round (£45 weekends).
Cards	💳 🖸 🖸
Prof	Mike Deeley
Designer	James Braid
Facilities	⊗ ⎗ 🍴 ⌷ ⌷ 🏌 🛄 🏌 ↑ 🖊 🏌 (
Location	W side of village off A13
Hotel	★★★★ 75% The Atlantic Hotel, Mont de la Pulente, ST BRELADE ☎ 01534 744101 50 ⇥ 🏌

St Clement   Map 16

St Clement Jersey Recreation Grounds JE2 6PN
☎ 01534 21938
Very tight moorland course. Holes cross over fairways, impossible to play to scratch. Suitable for middle to high handicaps.
9 holes, 2244yds, Par 30.
Club membership 500.

Green Fees	not confirmed.
Facilities	🛄
& Leisure	hard tennis courts.
Location	E side of St Helier on A5
Hotel	★★★★🏌 Longueville Manor Hotel, ST SAVIOUR ☎ 01534 725501 32 ⇥ 🏌

St Ouen   Map 16

Les Mielles Golf & Country Club JE3 7PQ
☎ 01534 482787 Fax 01534 485414
Challenging American-style parkland course with bent grass greens, dwarf rye fairways and picturesque ponds situated in the Island's largest conservation area within St Ouen's Bay.
18 holes, 5633yds, Par 70, SSS 68, Course record 62.
Club membership 1500.

Visitors	welcome all times, prior booking recommended.
Societies	write in advance to avoid disappointment.
Green Fees	not confirmed.
Cards	💳 🖸 🖸 🖸
Prof	Lee Elstone
Designer	J Le Brun/R Whitehead

Facilities   ⊗ ⫫ ⓑ ♥ ♀ ⚐ 🏠 🏌 🛴 🚃 🏌 ⚔

Location   Centre of St Ouen's Bay

Hotel   ★★★ 67% Mermaid Hotel, ST PETER
            ☎ 01534 741255   68 ⇆ ☞

ISLE OF MAN

CASTLETOWN   Map 06 SC26

Castletown Golf Links Fort Island, Derbyhaven IM9 1UA
☎ 01624 822201 & 822211 (pro shop) Fax 01624 824633
Set on the Langness Peninsula, this superb Championship
course is surrounded on three sides by the sea, and holds
many surprises from its Championship tees. The hotel offers
many leisure facilities.
18 holes, 6750yds, Par 72, SSS 72, Course record 64.
Club membership 600.

Visitors   contact in advance. Sat reserved for hotel
              residents and club members. Ladies only Wed
              morning
Societies   must telephone in advance.
Green Fees £28 per day (£33 Fri-Sun & bank holidays).
Cards   ▭▭ ▭ 🂠 ▭
Prof   Murray Crowe
Designer   McKenzie Ross
Facilities   ⊗ ⫫ ⓑ ♥ ♀ ⚐ 🏠 🏌 🛴 🚃 ⚔
& Leisure   heated indoor swimming pool, sauna, solarium.

Hotel   ★★★ 66% Castletown Golf Links Hotel,
            Fort Island, CASTLETOWN
            ☎ 01624 822201   58 ⇆ ☞

DOUGLAS   Map 06 SC37

Douglas Pulrose Park IM2 1AE   ☎ 01624 661558
Hilly, parkland and moorland course under the control of
Douglas Corporation.
18 holes, 5922yds, Par 69, SSS 68, Course record 62.
Club membership 330.
Visitors   no restrictions.
Societies   telephone to book tee time.
Green Fees £8.50 per day (£10.50 weekends).
Prof   Kerry Parry
Facilities   ⊗ ⓑ ♥ ♀ ⚐ 🏠 🏌 ⚔
Location   1m W off A1

Hotel   ★★★ 68% The Empress Hotel,
            Central Promenade, DOUGLAS
            ☎ 01624 661155 102 ⇆ ☞

Mount Murray Hotel & Country Club Mount Murray,
Santon IM4 2HT   ☎ 01624 661111 Fax 01624 611116
A challenging course with many natural features, lakes,
streams etc. Five Par 5's, five Par 3's and the rest Par 4.
18 holes, 6664yds, Par 72, SSS 72.
Club membership 378.

Visitors   must contact in advance. Visitors may not play
              before 9.30am weekends
Societies   telephone in advance.
Green Fees not confirmed.
Cards   ▭▭ ▭ 🂠 ▭ ▭
Prof   Andrew Dyson
Facilities   ⊗ ⫫ ⓑ ♥ ♀ ⚐ 🏠 🏌 🏌 🛴 🚃 ⚔ ⚔
& Leisure   hard tennis courts, heated indoor swimming
              pool, squash, sauna, solarium, gymnasium.
Location   Located on main road 5m from Douglas towards
              airport

Hotel   ★★★★ 67% Mount Murray Hotel & Country
            Club, Santon, DOUGLAS
            ☎ 01624 661111   90 ⇆ ☞

ONCHAN   Map 06 SC47

King Edward Bay Golf & Country Club Howstrake, Groudle
Rd IM3 2JR   ☎ 01624 672709
Club plays over King Edward Bay course. Hilly seaside links
course with natural hazards and good views.
18 holes, 5485yds, Par 67, SSS 65, Course record 63.
Club membership 370.
Visitors   must have a handicap certificate.
Societies   must contact in advance.
Green Fees not confirmed.
Prof   Donald Jones
Designer   Tom Morris
Facilities   ⊗ ⫫ ⓑ ♥ ♀ ⚐ 🏠 🏌 🚃 ⚔
Location   E side of town off A11

Hotel   ★★★ 71% Sefton Hotel, Harris Promenade,
            DOUGLAS ☎ 01624 645500 107 ⇆ ☞

PEEL   Map 06 SC28

Peel Rheast Ln IM5 1BG
☎ 01624 842227 & 843456 Fax 01624 843456
Moorland course, with natural hazards and easy walking.
Good views. 11th hole is a par 4, dog-leg.
18 holes, 5850yds, Par 69, SSS 68, Course record 69.
Club membership 856.
Visitors   limited availability weekends.
Societies   apply in writing.

▶

Green Fees £17 per day (£24 weekends & bank holidays).
Prof Murray Crowe
Designer Robert Braide
Facilities ⊗ ⅃ ♟ ♀ ⚎ 📷 ⛾ ♂
& Leisure snooker.
Location SE side of town centre on A1

Hotel ★★★ 68% The Empress Hotel,
Central Promenade, DOUGLAS
☎ 01624 661155 102 ⇥ ☞

PORT ERIN   Map 06 SC16

Rowany Rowany Dr IM9 6LN
☎ 01624 834108 or 834072 Fax 01624 834108
Undulating seaside course with testing later holes.
18 holes, 5840yds, Par 70, SSS 69, Course record 66.
Club membership 550.
Visitors must contact in advance.
Societies telephone in advance.
Green Fees not confirmed.
Designer G Lowe
Facilities ⊗ ⅃ ♟ ♀ ⚎ 📷 ⛾ ⚒ ♂
Location N side of village off A32

Hotel ★★★ 67% Cherry Orchard Hotel, Bridson St,
PORT ERIN ☎ 01624 833811 31 ⇥ ☞

PORT ST MARY   Map 06 SC26

Port St Mary Kallow Point Rd ☎ 01624 834932
Slightly hilly course with beautiful scenic views over Port St
Mary and the Irish Sea.
9 holes, 5418yds, Par 68, SSS 66, Course record 62.
Club membership 432.

Visitors anytime except between 8-10.30 weekends.
Societies contact for details.
Green Fees £11 (£13 weekends).
Cards ⚊ 🏧 VISA ⚎ 🏦 CONNECT ⚎ ⚎
Designer George Duncan
Facilities ⊗ ⅊ ⅃ ♟ ♀ ⚎ 📷 ⚒ ♂
& Leisure hard tennis courts.
Location Signposted on entering Port St Mary

Hotel ★★★ 67% Cherry Orchard Hotel, Bridson St,
PORT ERIN ☎ 01624 833811 31 ⇥ ☞

RAMSEY   Map 06 SC49

Ramsey Brookfield IM8 2AH
☎ 01624 812244 Fax 01624 812244
Parkland course, with easy walking. Windy. Good views.
Testing holes: 1st, par 5; 18th, par 3.
18 holes, 5960yds, Par 70, SSS 69, Course record 64.
Club membership 1000.
Visitors contact in advance, visitors may not play before
10am weekdays.
Societies must apply in advance.
Green Fees Winter: £10 (£14 weekends & bank holidays).
Summer: £18 (£22 weekends & bank holidays).
Cards ⚊ VISA ⚎ ⚎ ⚎
Prof Calum Wilson
Designer James Braid
Facilities ⊗ ⅊ ⅃ ♟ ♀ ⚎ 📷 ⛾ ♂
Location SW side of town

Hotel ★★★ 68% The Empress Hotel,
Central Promenade, DOUGLAS
☎ 01624 661155 102 ⇥ ☞

SCOTLAND

John Ingham writes: According to most historians, Scotland is the birthplace of golf, even though the Chinese, believe it or not, claim hit-and-walk originated in their country, back in the mists of time.

But it is now a sad truth that certain traditional, if old-fashioned courses in Scotland, are taking their position in world golf a little for granted - and they do so at their peril. In simple terms there are links which need, as a matter of some urgency, to be given a rest, notably St Andrews, the monument to the game, now unfairly exposed to a constant stream of golfing tourists, even allowing trollies over the famous 'umps and 'ollows once trod by Jones, Vardon, Tolley, Wethered - you name them.

But contrast St Andrews with the newly-built Loch Lomond which I've played, and like other visitors, was delighted at the privilege of being there. The whole place is immaculate, as indeed is my personal favourite, Gleneagles (King's and Queen's).

Scotland is dotted with superb golfing tests, some which do not require a bank loan prior to the green fee. I'm told to play Royal Dornoch, Machrihanish, Lundin Links, while I know Muirfield inside out as a golf reporter, I've never been put to the test of what Jack Nicklaus thinks is one of the finest, and one that is not hacked to death by nomads.

You can have terrific fun at Turnberry, although it has a couple of mundane opening holes. Royal Troon is a grand spot for an Open Championship, but I wonder how much joy it is in a gale. I know for a fact that Carnoustie can be a nightmare, but Ben Hogan loved it, even though there wasn't a decent hotel in sight, so he stayed private.

Golf Monthly, a magazine old established, ranks four Scottish courses in the top six in the UK. While I don't agree with them, and point out the editor is a Scot (!) it does indicate the colossal strength of Scotland as a place to go. But it has rivals aplenty....in other parts of this golfer's paradise.

SCOTLAND

The directory which follows has been divided into three geographical regions. Counties have not been shown against individual locations as recent legislation has created a number of smaller counties which will be unfamiliar to the visitor. The postal authorities have confirmed that it is no longer necessary to include a county name in addresses, provided a post code is shown. All locations appear in the atlas section at the end of this guide in their appropriate counties.

HIGHLANDS & ISLANDS

This region includes the counties of Aberdeen City, Aberdeenshire, Highland, Moray, Orkney, Shetland and Western Isles which reflect the recent national changes.

ABERDEEN   Map 15 NJ90

Auchmill Bonnyview Rd, West Heatheryfold AB16 7FQ
☎ 01224 715214
This course is definitely not for beginners - the fairways are tree-lined and very tight on most holes. Three holes are quite hilly and although the remainder is flat there are nice views over Aberdeen. The course is not recommended for anyone over 22 handicap unless they have plenty of golf balls!
18 holes, 5123metres, Par 68, SSS 67, Course record 67. Club membership 300.

Visitors	members have priority Sat & Wed for club competitions.
Societies	apply in writing to Leisure and Recreation Dept, Aberdeen District Council.
Green Fees	not confirmed.
Designer	Neil Coles/Brian Hugget
Facilities	⊗ by prior arrangement ⏏ by prior arrangement 🍴 ⬛ ♀ ⚐
Location	Outskirts Aberdeen, A96 Aberdeen/Inverness
Hotel	★★★ 66% The Craighaar, Waterton Rd, Bankhead, ABERDEEN ☎ 01224 712275 55 ⇆ 🐾

Balnagask St Fitticks Rd AB11 3QT ☎ 01224 876407
Links course. Used by the Nigg Bay Club.
18 holes, 5986yds, Par 70, SSS 69.

Visitors	no restrictions.
Societies	apply to council tel 01224 276276.
Green Fees	not confirmed.
Facilities	⊗ ⏏ 🍴 ⬛ ♀ ⚐
Location	2m E of city centre
Hotel	★★★ 69% Thistle Aberdeen Caledonian, 10 Union Ter, ABERDEEN ☎ 01224 640233 80 ⇆ 🐾

Deeside Golf Rd, Bieldside AB15 9DL
☎ 01224 869457 Fax 01224 869457
An interesting riverside course with several tree-lined fairways. A stream comes into play at 9 of the 18 holes on the main course.
18 holes, 5971yds, Par 71, SSS 69, Course record 63. Club membership 800.

Visitors	must contact in advance, may not play competition days.
Societies	apply in writing.
Green Fees	£25 per day (£30 weekends & bank holidays).
Prof	Frank J Coutts
Facilities	⊗ ⏏ 🍴 🏋 ⬛ ♀ ⚑ ⚐
Location	3m W of city centre off A93
Hotel	★★★★ 70% Ardoe House, South Deeside Rd, Blairs, ABERDEEN ☎ 01224 867355 71 ⇆ 🐾

Hazelhead Public Hazelhead AB1 8BD
☎ No telephone
A tree-lined course.
18 holes, 6595yds, Par 70, SSS 70.

Visitors	no restrictions.
Societies	must contact in advance.
Green Fees	not confirmed.
Facilities	⏏ 🍴 ⚐
Location	4m W of city centre off A944
Hotel	★★★★ 70% Ardoe House, South Deeside Rd, Blairs, ABERDEEN ☎ 01224 867355 71 ⇆ 🐾

Kings Links AB24 1RZ ☎ 01224 632269
A typical links course with no tree lines and plenty of bunkers.The 14th hole is tricky - a long par 4 with a raised green and not much fairway round the green. The course is playable all year. Nearby there is a 6-hole course. The Bon Accord Club, Caledonian Club and Northern Club play over this course.
18 holes, 6384yds, Par 72, SSS 71.

Visitors	contact starters box on 01224 632269 regarding booking of tee times.
Societies	write to the Arts & Recreation Dept, St Nicholas House, Broad Street, Aberdeen.
Green Fees	not confirmed.
Facilities	⏏
Location	0.75m NE of city centre
Hotel	★★★ 69% Thistle Aberdeen Caledonian, 10 Union Ter, ABERDEEN ☎ 01224 640233 80 ⇆ 🐾

Murcar Bridge of Don AB23 8BD
☎ 01224 704354 Fax 01224 704354
Seaside links course, prevailing SW wind, hard-walking. Testing 4th and 14th holes.
Murcar: 18 holes, 6287yds, Par 71, SSS 71, Course record 65.
Strabathie: 9 holes, 2680yds, Par 35, SSS 35.
Club membership 850.

Visitors	must contact in advance.
Societies	advance booking required.
Green Fees	not confirmed.
Cards	▬▬ ▬▬
Prof	Gary Forbes
Designer	Archie Simpson
Facilities	⊗ ⏏ 🍴 🏋 ⬛ ♀ ⚑ ⚐
Location	5m NE of city centre off A92
Hotel	★★★ 66% The Craighaar, Waterton Rd, Bankhead, ABERDEEN ☎ 01224 712275 55 ⇆ 🐾

Royal Aberdeen Links Rd, Balgownie, Bridge of Don
AB23 8AT ☎ 01224 702571 Fax 01224 826591
Championship links course with undulating dunes. Windy,
easy walking.
Balgownie Course: 18 holes, 6372yds, Par 71, SSS 71,
Course record 63.
Silverburn Course: 18 holes, 4066yds, Par 64, SSS 61.
Club membership 500.
Visitors times for visitors 10-11.30 and 2-3.30pm
weekdays, after 3.30pm weekends. Must contact
in advance.
Societies apply in writing.
Green Fees Balgownie: £75 per day,£55 per round (£65 per
round weekends). Silverburn: £27.50 weekdays.
Cards ⊙ ▩ ⊙
Prof Ronnie MacAskill
Designer Baird & Simpson
Facilities ⊗ ⌑ ■ ♀ ⚘ 🏠 ⛳ ⬿
Location 2.5m N of city centre off A92

Hotel ★★★ 69% Thistle Aberdeen Caledonian,
10 Union Ter, ABERDEEN
☎ 01224 640233 80 ⇋ 🐾

Westhill Westhill Heights, Westhill AB32 6RY
☎ 01224 742567 Fax 01224 749124
A highland course.
18 holes, 5921yds, Par 69, SSS 69, Course record 65.
Club membership 930.
Visitors must contact in advance, not Saturdays.
Societies telephone in advance.
Green Fees £18 per day; £12 per round.
Prof George Bruce
Designer Charles Lawrie
Facilities ⊗ ⌑ ■ ♀ ⚘ 🏠 ⛳ ⬿
Location 6m NW of city centre off A944

Hotel ★★★ 66% Westhill Hotel, Westhill,
ABERDEEN
☎ 01224 740388 37 ⇋ 🐾 Annexe13 ⇋ 🐾

ABOYNE Map 15 NO59

Aboyne Formaston Park AB34 5HP
☎ 013398 86328 Fax 013398 87078
Beautiful parkland with outstanding views. Two lochs on
course.
18 holes, 5975yds, Par 68, SSS 69, Course record 62.
Club membership 930.
Visitors no restrictions. Advisable to contact in advance.
Societies prior booking essential.
Green Fees not confirmed.
Prof Innes Wright
Facilities ⊗ ⌑ ⌑ ■ ♀ ⚘ 🏠 ⛳ ⬿
Location E side of village, N of A93

Hotel ★★ 62% Birse Lodge Hotel, 20 Charleston Rd,
ABOYNE ☎ 013398 86253 12 ⇋ 🐾

ALFORD Map 15 NJ51

Alford Montgarrie Rd AB33 8AE
☎ 019755 62178 Fax 019755 62178
A flat parkland course in scenic countryside. Divided into
sections by a road, a narrow-guage railway and a burn.
18 holes, 5483yds, Par 69, SSS 65, Course record 64.
Club membership 600.

Visitors advisable to contact in advance.
Societies telephone in advance.
Green Fees £19 per day; £13 per round (£27/£21 weekends)
£45 5 day ticket.
Facilities ⊗ ⌑ ⌑ ■ ♀ ⚘ 🏠 ⛳ ⬿
Location In the centre of the village on A944

Hotel ★★★🏖 Kildrummy Castle Hotel,
KILDRUMMY ☎ 019755 71288 16 ⇋ 🐾

ALNESS Map 14 NH66

Alness Ardross Rd IV17 0QA ☎ 01349 883877
A testing, parkland course with beautiful views over the
Cromarty Firth and the Black Isle. An additional 9 holes
were developed in 1997, four holes run alongside the Averon
river making the course more scenic and interesting.
18 holes, 4886yds, Par 67, SSS 64, Course record 62.
Club membership 270.
Visitors telephone in advance for weekend play, parties
must telephone for booking
Societies must contact in advance.
Green Fees £10 per day (£12 weekends).
Facilities ⊗ ⌑ by prior arrangement ⌑ ■ ♀ ⚘ ⛳ ⬿
& Leisure fishing.
Location 0.5m N off A9

Hotel ★★★ 70% Morangie House Hotel, Morangie
Rd, TAIN ☎ 01862 892281 26 ⇋ 🐾

ARISAIG Map 13 NM68

Traigh PH39 4NT ☎ 01687 450337
According to at least one newspaper Traigh is 'probably the
most beautifully sited nine-hole golf course in the world'.
Whether that is true or not, Traigh lies by the sea alongside
sandy beaches with views to Skye and the Inner Hebrides.
The feature of the course is a line of grassy hills, originally
sand dunes, that rise to some 60 feet. The course was
completely redesigned in 1995.
9 holes, 2456yds, Par 68, SSS 65, Course record 67.
Club membership 150.
Visitors no restrictions.
Societies contact in advance.
Green Fees £12 per day, £40 per week.
Designer John Salvesen 1994
Facilities ■ 🏠 ⛳ ⬿
Location 2m N of Arisaig on A830

Hotel ★★ 66% Arisaig Hotel, ARISAIG
☎ 01687 450210 13 ⇋ 🐾

AUCHENBLAE Map 15 NO77

Auchenblae AB30 1BU ☎ 01561 320002
Picturesque, small, undulating parkland course offering good
views.
9 holes, 2174yds, Par 33, SSS 32, Course record 62.
Club membership 450.
Visitors restricted Wed & Fri evenings.
Societies must telephone in advance.
Green Fees £9 per day (£12 weekends).
Facilities ■ ⬿
Location 0.5m NE

Hotel ★★ 65% County Hotel & Leisure Club,
Arduthie Rd, STONEHAVEN
☎ 01569 764386 14 ⇋ 🐾

BALLATER   Map 15 NO39

Ballater Victoria Rd AB35 5QX
☎ 013397 55567 Fax 013397 55057
Moorland course with testing long holes and beautiful scenery.
18 holes, 5638yds, Par 67, SSS 67, Course record 62.
Club membership 750.
Visitors must contact in advance.
Societies prior booking recommended.
Green Fees not confirmed.
Cards ⬚ ⬚ 🔄
Prof Bill Yule
Facilities ⊗ ⏏ ⓛ 🍺 ♀ ♨ 🏠 ⚑ ↑ ♂
& Leisure hard tennis courts, fishing, snooker.
Location W side of town

Hotel ★★★ 72% Darroch Learg Hotel, Braemar Rd, BALLATER
☎ 013397 55443 13 🛏 🏨 Annexe5 🛏 🏨

BANCHORY   Map 15 NO69

Banchory Kinneskie Rd AB31 5TA
☎ 01330 822365 Fax 01330 822491
Sheltered parkland course situated beside the River Dee, with easy walking and woodland scenery. 12th and 13th holes are testing. Course was reconstructed during 1996 and several new holes introduced.
18 holes, 5775yds, Par 69, SSS 68, Course record 65.
Club membership 975.
Visitors must contact in advance, telephone for details on 01330 822447
Societies must book in advance, no parties Tue & weekends.
Green Fees £25 per day, £18 per round (£26/£21 weekends).
Cards ⬚ ⬚ 🔄
Prof David Naylor
Facilities ⊗ ⏏ ⓛ 🍺 ♀ ♨ 🏠 ↑ ♂
Location A93, 300 yds from W end of High St

Hotel ★★★🦌 74% Banchory Lodge Hotel, BANCHORY ☎ 01330 822625 22 🛏 🏨

BANFF   Map 15 NJ66

Duff House Royal The Barnyards AB45 3SX
☎ 01261 812062 Fax 01261 812224
Well-manicured flat parkland, bounded by woodlands and River Deveron. Well bunkered and renowned for its large, two-tier greens.
18 holes, 6161yds, Par 68, SSS 69, Course record 63.
Club membership 1000.

Visitors a handicap certificate is preferred. Some time restrictions.
Societies must apply in writing.
Green Fees £24 per day; £18 per round (£30/£25 weekends).
Cards ⬚ ⬚ ⬚ 🔄
Prof Bob Strachan
Designer Dr McKenzie
Facilities ⊗ ⏏ ⓛ 🍺 ♀ ♨ 🏠 ⚑ ♂
Location 0.5m S on A98

Hotel ★★★ 66% Banff Springs Hotel, Golden Knowes Rd, BANFF
☎ 01261 812881 31 🛏 🏨

BOAT OF GARTEN   Map 14 NH91

Boat of Garten PH24 3BQ
☎ 01479 831282 Fax 01479 831523
This heathland course was cut out from a silver birch forest though the fairways are adequately wide. There are natural hazards of broom and heather, good views and walking is easy. A round provides great variety.
18 holes, 5866yds, Par 69, SSS 69, Course record 67.
Club membership 600.
Visitors must contact in advance. Handicap certificate required. Play restricted to 10am-4pm weekends & 9.20am-7pm weekdays
Societies must telephone in advance.
Green Fees £28 per day; £23 per round (£33/£28 weekends).
Cards ⬚ ⬚ ⬚ 🔄
Designer James Braid
Facilities ⊗ ⏏ ⓛ 🍺 ♀ ♨ 🏠 ⚑ ↑ ♂
& Leisure hard tennis courts.
Location E side of village

Hotel ★★★ 65% Boat Hotel, BOAT OF GARTEN ☎ 01479 831258 32 🛏 🏨

BONAR BRIDGE   Map 14 NH69

Bonar Bridge-Ardgay Migdale Rd IV24 3EJ
☎ 01863 766375 Fax 01863 766738
Wooded moorland course with picturesque views of hills and loch.
9 holes, 5284yds, Par 68, SSS 67.
Club membership 250.
Visitors no restrictions.
Societies apply in writing.
Green Fees £12 per day.
Facilities ⊗ 🍺 ♨
Location 0.5m E

★★★ AA

Overlooking the beautiful but challenging
Boat of Garten Golf Course – the
'Gleneagles' of the Highlands –
the Boat Hotel offers you superb value Tee
Break holidays with golf on any of 9 local
courses. Special Rates for Golf Societies
and all golf reserved in advance.
Dine in our two rosetted restaurant.
All 32 rooms en-suite

For Golf Brochure Contact:
Suzanne MacLean, Golf Desk,
The Boat Hotel, Boat of Garten,
Inverness-shire. PH24 3BH
Tel: 01479 831258 Fax: 01479 831414

Hotel   ★★ 69% Dornoch Castle Hotel,
Castle St, DORNOCH
☎ 01862 810216 4 ⇄ ☞ Annexe13 ⇄ ☞

BRAEMAR   Map 15 NO19

Braemar Cluniebank Rd AB35 5XX ☎ 013397 41618
Flat course, set amid beautiful countryside on Royal Deeside,
with River Clunie running through several holes. The 2nd
hole is one of the most testing in the area.
18 holes, 5000yds, Par 65, SSS 64, Course record 59.
Club membership 450.

Visitors	are advised to book 24 hours in advance to play at weekends. Tee reserved until 12.30 on Sat for members only.
Societies	must contact secretary in advance 01224 704471.
Green Fees	£16 per day; £11 per round (£21/£16 weekends).
Designer	Joe Anderson
Facilities	⊗ ⅏ ㄥ ♥ ♀ ♨ ⛤ ✆ ♂
Location	0.5m S

Hotel   ★★★ 68% The Invercauld Arms, BRAEMAR
☎ 013397 41605 68 ⇄ ☞

BRORA   Map 14 NC90

Brora Golf Rd KW9 6QS
☎ 01408 621417 Fax 01408 622157
Typical seaside links with little rough and fine views. Some
testing holes.
18 holes, 6110yds, Par 69, SSS 69, Course record 61.
Club membership 704.

Visitors	advisable to book in advance May-Oct.
Societies	advisable to book in advance.
Green Fees	£20 per round, £10 per 2nd round (£25 weekends).
Designer	James Braid
Facilities	⊗ ⅏ ㄥ ♥ ♀ ♨ ⛤ ✆ ♂
& Leisure	snooker.
Location	E side of village. Follow signs to Beach Car Park

Hotel   ★★★ 66% The Links Hotel, Golf Rd, BRORA
☎ 01408 621225 23 ⇄ ☞

BUCKIE   Map 15 NJ46

Buckpool Barhill Rd, Buckpool AB56 1DU
☎ 01542 832236 Fax 01542 832236
Links course with superlative view over Moray Firth, easy
walking.
18 holes, 6257yds, Par 70, SSS 70, Course record 64.
Club membership 430.

Visitors	parties please apply in advance.
Societies	apply in advance.
Green Fees	£15 per day; £12 per round (£20/15 weekends).
Facilities	⊗ ⅏ ㄥ ♥ ♀ ♨ ♂
& Leisure	squash.
Location	Off A98

Hotel   ★★ 67% Mill House Hotel, Tynet, BUCKIE
☎ 01542 850233 15 ⇄ ☞

Strathlene Portessie AB56 2DJ ☎ 01542 831798
Raised seaside links course with magnificent view. A special
feature of the course is approach shots to raised greens (holes
4,5,6 & 13).
18 holes, 5980yds, Par 69, SSS 69, Course record 65.
Club membership 370.

Visitors	booking essential at weekends.
Societies	telephone for Mon-Fri & apply in writing for weekends.
Green Fees	£18 per day; £12 per round (£20/£16 weekends) discounts for parties at all times.
Facilities	⊗ ㄥ ♥ ♀ ♨ ♂
Location	3m E on A942

Hotel   ★★ 67% Mill House Hotel, Tynet, BUCKIE
☎ 01542 850233 15 ⇄ ☞

CARRBRIDGE   Map 14 NH92

Carrbridge Inverness Rd PH23 3AU ☎ 01479 841623
Short but challenging part-parkland, part-moorland course
with magnificent views of the Cairngorms.
9 holes, 5402yds, Par 71, SSS 68, Course record 64.
Club membership 650.

Visitors	during May-Sep, course not open to visitors after 5pm Wed & before 4pm most Sun.
Societies	small parties welcome, apply in writing.
Green Fees	£11-£12 per day (£13 weekends). Evening (after 6.30pm) £6-£8.
Facilities	♥ ♨ ⛤ ♂
Location	N side of village

Hotel   ★★★⚑ 68% Dalrachney Lodge Hotel,
CARRBRIDGE
☎ 01479 841252 11 ⇄ ☞

RED HOUSE HOTEL
★★

**AULTON ROAD, CRUDEN BAY,
PETERHEAD AB42 0NJ
Tel: 01779 812215 Fax: 01779 812320**

The Red House Hotel must be the ideal choice, for those who wish to play on one of Britain's top links courses, which is always beautifully maintained. The hotel is situated just 30 minutes north of Aberdeen's Airport in the tranquil coastal village of Cruden Bay. The Red House Hotel is also an ideal base for both river and sea anglers, bird watching or walks along its rugged but beautiful coastline. A warm Scottish welcome along with excellent Scots cuisine served in its Slains restaurant which overlooks the course awaits any visitor to the Red House Hotel.

CRUDEN BAY   Map 15 NK03

Cruden Bay Aulton Rd AB42 0NN
☎ 01779 812285 Fax 01779 812945
A typical links course which epitomizes the old fashioned style of rugged links golf. The drives require accuracy with bunkers and protecting greens, blind holes and undulating greens. The 10th provides a panoramic view of the back nine down at beach level, and to the east can be seen the outline of the spectacular ruin of Slains Castle featured in Bram Stoker's Dracula. The figure eight design of the course is quite unusual.
Main Course: 18 holes, 6395yds, Par 70, SSS 72, Course record 65.
St Olaf Course: 9 holes, 2553yds, Par 64, SSS 65.
Club membership 1100.

Visitors	welcome on weekdays, at weekends only when there are no competitions, advisable to contact for details.
Societies	weekdays only telephone in advance.
Green Fees	not confirmed.
Prof	Robbie Stewart
Designer	Thomas Simpson
Facilities	⊗ ⊪ ⒧ 🖥 ♀ ⚘ 🖻 ⛳ ♂ ℓ
Location	SW side of village on A975

Hotel	★★ 66% Red House Hotel, Aulton Rd, CRUDEN BAY ☎ 01779 812215 6rm(5 ⇆ ╏)

CULLEN   Map 15 NJ56

Cullen The Links AB56 4UU ☎ 01542 840685
Interesting links on two levels with rocks and ravines offering some challenging holes. Spectacular scenery.
18 holes, 4610yds, Par 63, SSS 62, Course record 58.
Club membership 600.

Visitors	no restrictions but during summer club medal matches given preference on Mon/Wed/Sat.
Societies	advance applications advisable.
Green Fees	£15 per day; £10 per round (£18/£13 weekends).
Designer	Tom Morris/Charlie Neaves
Facilities	⊗ ⊪ by prior arrangement ⒧ 🖥 ♀ ⚘ ℓ
Location	0.5m W off A98

Hotel	★★ 67% Mill House Hotel, Tynet, BUCKIE ☎ 01542 850233 15 ⇆ ╏

DORNOCH   Map 14 NH78

The Carnegie Club Skibo Castle IV25 3RQ
☎ 01862 894600 Fax 01862 894601
Set within the grounds of an enchanting castle, with the sea on three sides and the hills of Sutherland and Ross-shire all around, this splendid course enjoys a magnificent position. Although not long by modern standards, strong and fickle winds will test even the most experienced golfer. Excellent leisure facilities.
18 holes, 6403yds, Par 71, SSS 71.
Club membership 550.

Visitors	weekdays only by written application to the secretary.
Societies	by prior arrangement
Green Fees	£130 per round.
Cards	▭ ▦ ▦ 💳 ▦ 🖉
Prof	George Finlayson
Designer	J Sutherland/Donald Steel
Facilities	⊗ 🖥 ♀ ⚘ 🖻 ⛳ ⛴ ♂ ℓ
& Leisure	hard tennis courts, heated indoor swimming pool, fishing, sauna, solarium, gymnasium, clay pidgeon/pistol shooting, cycling, archery, horse riding, snooker & kids play area.
Location	Off A9 3m before Dornoch

Hotel	★★ 69% Dornoch Castle Hotel, Castle St, DORNOCH ☎ 01862 810216 4 ⇆ ╏ Annexe13 ⇆ ╏

Royal Dornoch Golf Rd IV25 3LW
☎ 01862 810219 Fax 01862 810792
Very challenging seaside championship links, designed by Tom Morris and John Sutherland.
Championship: 18 holes, 6514yds, Par 70, SSS 73, Course record 65.
Struie Course: 18 holes, 5438yds, Par 69, SSS 66.
Club membership 1650.

Visitors	must have a handicap of 24 for gentlemen (ladies 35) on Championship Course. Must contact in advance.
Societies	must apply in advance.
Green Fees	Championship course: £40-£55 per round (£45-£65 weekends). Struie course: £11-22 per day; £8-16 per round.
Cards	▭ ▦ ▦ 🖉

Prof	A Skinner
Designer	Tom Morris
Facilities	⊗)Ⅲ by prior arrangement ⓛ 🍺 ♀ 🛆 🏠 �🏓 🥢 ⚓ ✐
& Leisure	hard tennis courts, fishing.
Location	E side of town

Hotel	★★ 69% Dornoch Castle Hotel, Castle St, DORNOCH ☎ 01862 810216 4 ⇄ ⚑ Annexe13 ⇄ ⚑

DUFFTOWN   Map 15 NJ33

Dufftown Methercluny, Tomintoul Rd AB55 4BS
☎ 01340 820325 Fax 01340 820325
A short and undulating inland course with spectacular views. Highest hole over 1200 ft above sea level.
18 holes, 5308yds, Par 67, SSS 67, Course record 67.
Club membership 250.

Visitors	tee reserved Tue & Wed 4.30-6.30 & Sun 7.30-9 & 12.30-2.
Societies	apply in writing or by telephone
Green Fees	£15 per day; £10 per round.
Designer	Members
Facilities	⊗ by prior arrangement)Ⅲ by prior arrangement ⓛ by prior arrangement 🍺 ♀ 🛆 �🏓 ✐
Location	0.75m SW off B9009

Hotel	★★★ 75% Craigellachie Hotel, CRAIGELLACHIE ☎ 01340 881204 26 ⇄ ⚑

DURNESS   Map 14 NC46

Durness Balnakeil IV27 4PG
☎ 01971 511364 Fax 01971 511205
A 9-hole course set in tremendous scenery overlooking Balnakeil Bay. Part links and part inland with water hazards.

Off alternative tees for second 9 holes giving surprising variety. Tremendous last hole played across the sea to the green over 100 yards away.
9 holes, 5555yds, Par 70, SSS 69, Course record 71.
Club membership 150.

Visitors	restricted 10am-12.30 on Sun during Jun-Sep.
Societies	must telephone in advance 01971 511364 (ex Sun).
Green Fees	£12 per day; £50 per week.
Designer	F Keith
Facilities	⊗ 🍺 🛆 �🏓 ✐
& Leisure	fishing.
Location	1m W of village overlooking Balnakeil Bay

Guest house	**QQQ** Port-Na-Con House, Loch Eribol, by Sutherland, LAIRG ☎ 01971 511367 3 ⇄ ⚑

ELGIN   Map 15 NJ26

Elgin Hardhillock, Birnie Rd, New Elgin IV30 3SX
☎ 01343 542338 Fax 01343 542341
Possibly the finest inland course in the north of Scotland, with undulating greens and compact holes that demand the highest accuracy. There are thirteen par 4's and one par 5 hole on its parkland layout.
18 holes, 6163yds, Par 68, SSS 69, Course record 64.
Club membership 1000.

Visitors	must contact in advance, weekend play only by prior arrangement
Societies	telephone secretary for details.
Green Fees	£29 per day; £22 per round (£35/£28 weekends).
Prof	Ian P Rodger
Designer	John Macpherson
Facilities	⊗)Ⅲ ⓛ 🍺 ♀ 🛆 🏠 �🏓 🥢 ⚓ ✐ ₹
Location	1m S on A941

Hotel	★★★ 76% Mansion House Hotel, The Haugh, ELGIN ☎ 01343 548811 23 ⇄ ⚑

ELLON   Map 15 NJ93

McDonald Hospital Rd AB41 9AW
☎ 01358 720576 Fax 01358 720001
Tight, parkland course with streams and a pond.
18 holes, 5986yds, Par 70, SSS 69.
Club membership 710.

Visitors	advisable to book in advance
Societies	telephone in advance.
Green Fees	£20 per day; £14 per round(£24-£30/£20-£24 weekends).
Prof	Ronnie Urquhart	▶

Facilities ⊗ ⟩⊪ ⌷ ⯑ ♀ ⚐ ⚐⚑ ♂
Location 0.25m N on A948

Hotel ★★ 70% Udny Arms Hotel, Main St, NEWBURGH ☎ 01358 789444 26 ⇆ ♠

FORRES   Map 14 NJ05

Forres Muiryshade IV36 0RD
☎ 01309 672250 Fax 01309 672250
An all-year parkland course laid on light, well-drained soil in wooded countryside. Walking is easy despite some hilly holes. A test for the best golfers.
18 holes, 6240yds, Par 70, SSS 70, Course record 64.
Club membership 1000.
Visitors welcome although club competitions take priority. Weekends may be restricted in summer.
Societies advised to telephone 2-3 weeks in advance.
Green Fees £22 per day; £18 per day (£30/£25 weekends).
Cards ▭ ▭ ▯
Prof Sandy Aird
Designer James Braid/Willie Park
Facilities ⊗ ⟩⊪ ⌷ ⯑ ♀ ⚐ ⚐⚑ ♠ ♞ ♂
Location SE side of town centre off B9010

Hotel ★★★ 66% Ramnee Hotel, Victoria Rd, FORRES ☎ 01309 672410 20 ⇆ ♠

FORT AUGUSTUS   Map 14 NH30

Fort Augustus Markethill PH32 4AU ☎ 01320 366660
Moorland course, with narrow fairways and good views. Bordered by the tree-lined Caledonian Canal to the north and heather clad hills to the south.
9 holes, 5454yds, Par 67, SSS 67, Course record 67.
Club membership 170.
Visitors may not play Sat 1.30-4 & occasional Sun.
Societies telephone in advance.
Green Fees not confirmed.
Facilities ♀ ⚐ ⚐⚑ ♂
Location 1m SW on A82

Hotel ★★ 67% Lovat Arms Hotel, FORT AUGUSTUS ☎ 01320 366206 & 366204 Fax 01320 366677 23 ⇆ ♠

FORTROSE   Map 14 NH75

Fortrose & Rosemarkie Ness Rd East IV10 8SE
☎ 01381 620529
Seaside links course, set on a peninsula with sea on three sides. Easy walking, good views. Designed by James Braid; the club was formed in 1888.
18 holes, 5858yds, Par 71, SSS 69, Course record 64.
Club membership 770.
Visitors restricted 8.45-10.15am & 1-2.15 then 4.45-6.30pm.
Societies must telephone in advance.
Green Fees £28 per day; £18 per round (£35/£25 weekends & bank holidays).
Cards ▭ ▭
Designer James Braid
Facilities ⊗ ⊪ ⌷ ⯑ ♀ ⚐ ⚐⚑ ♂
Location E side of town centre

FORT WILLIAM   Map 14 NN17

Fort William Torlundy PH33 7SN
☎ 01397 704464
Spectacular moorland location looking onto the cliffs of Ben Nevis. Tees and greens are in excellent condition and major drainage improvements to the fairways were implemented in 1995.
18 holes, 6500yds, Par 72, SSS 71, Course record 67.
Club membership 420.
Visitors no restrictions.
Societies must contact in writing.
Green Fees £18 per day £15 per round.
Designer Hamilton Stutt
Facilities ⊪ ⌷ ⯑ ♀ ⚐ ⚐⚑ ♂
Location 3m NE on A82

Hotel ★★★ 70% Moorings Hotel, Banavie, FORT WILLIAM ☎ 01397 772797 21 ⇆ ♠

FRASERBURGH   Map 15 NJ96

Fraserburgh AB43 8TL ☎ 01346 516616
Testing seaside course, natural links.
Corbie: 18 holes, 6278yds, Par 70, SSS 70, Course record 65.
Rosehill: 9 holes, 3400yds, Par 70, SSS 71.
Club membership 600.
Visitors no restrictions but advised to check availability.
Societies must contact in advance.
Green Fees Corbie: £20 per day, £15 per round (£25/£20 weekends). Rosehill: £10 (£12 weekends).
Designer James Braid
Facilities ⊗ ⟩⊪ ⌷ ⯑ ♀ ⚐ ⚐⚑ ♂
Location 1m SE on B9033

Hotel ★★★ 73% Waterside Inn, Fraserburgh Rd, PETERHEAD ☎ 01779 471121 69 ⇆ ♠ Annexe40 ⇆ ♠

GAIRLOCH   Map 14 NG87

Gairloch IV21 2BE
☎ 01445 712407 Fax 01445 712407
Fine seaside links course running along Gairloch Sands with good views over the sea to Skye. In windy conditions each hole is affected. The par 5 eighth hole is described by one of Scotlands teaching professionals as one of the best natural par 5's in the country.
9 holes, 4514yds, Par 63, SSS 64, Course record 61.
Club membership 250.
Visitors must be competent golfer and member of a recognised club.
Societies apply in writing to secretary.
Green Fees £13.50 per day; £49 per week.
Designer Capt Burgess
Facilities ⊪ ⌷ ⯑ ♀ ⚐ ⚐⚑ ♂
Location 1m S on A832

Hotel ★★ 66% The Old Inn, Flowerdale, GAIRLOCH ☎ 01445 712006 14 ⇆ ♠

> Entries with a shaded background identify courses that are considered to be particularly interesting

GARMOUTH   Map 15 NJ36

Garmouth & Kingston Spey St IV32 7NJ
☎ 01343 870388 Fax 01343 870388
Seaside course with several parkland holes and tidal waters.
Naturally flat and suitable for the elderly.
18 holes, 5874yds, Par 68, SSS 68, Course record 67.
Club membership 500.
Visitors   must contact in advance.
Societies   advisable to phone in advance.
Green Fees   £20 per day; £14 per round (£20/£16 weekends).
Designer   George Smith
Facilities   ⊗ ⓚ ⚏ ♈ ⚒ ♥ ♂
& Leisure   fishing.
Location   In village on B9015

Hotel   ★★★ 76% Mansion House Hotel, The Haugh,
                   ELGIN ☎ 01343 548811 23 ⇌ ꜩ

GOLSPIE   Map 14 NH89

Golspie Ferry Rd KW10 6ST
☎ 01408 633266 Fax 01408 633393
Founded in 1889, Golspie's seaside course offers easy
walking and natural hazards including beach heather and
whins. Spectacular scenery.
18 holes, 5890yds, Par 68, SSS 68, Course record 64.
Club membership 300.
Visitors   contact in advance.
Societies   contact in advance.
Green Fees   £20 per day; £18 per round (£25/20 weekends &
                   bank holidays).
Cards   ⚏ ▭ ▭ ⚏
Designer   James Braid
Facilities   ⊗ ⓚ by prior arrangement ⓚ ⚏ ♈ ⚒ ♥ ♂ ♂
Location   0.5m S off A9

Hotel   ★★★ 66% The Links Hotel, Golf Rd, BRORA
                   ☎ 01408 621225 23 ⇌ ꜩ

GRANTOWN-ON-SPEY   Map 14 NJ02

Grantown-on-Spey Golf Course Rd PH26 3HY
☎ 01479 872079 (Apr-Oct) Fax 01479 873725
Parkland and woodland course. Part easy walking, remainder
hilly. The 7th to 13th really sorts out the golfers.
18 holes, 5710yds, Par 70, SSS 68, Course record 60.
Club membership 720.
Visitors   advisable to contact in advance. No visitors
                   before 10am weekends.
Societies   clubhouse open Apr-Oct, apply in advance to
                   secretary.
Green Fees   £18 per day (£23 weekends) £10 evening round.

Cards   ⚏ ▭ ▭ ⚏ ⚏ ⚏
Designer   A Brown/W Park/J Braid
Facilities   ⊗ ⓚ by prior arrangement ⓚ ⚏ ♈ ⚒ ♥ ♂
                   ♌ ♂
Location   NE side of town centre

Hotel   ★★ 77% Culdearn House, Woodlands Ter,
                   GRANTOWN ON SPEY
                   ☎ 01479 872106 9 ⇌ ꜩ

HELMSDALE   Map 14 ND01

Helmsdale Golf Rd KW8 6JA ☎ 01431 821650
Sheltered, undulating course following the line of the
Helmsdale River.
9 holes, 1860yds, Par 62, SSS 61.
Club membership 90.
Visitors   no restrictions.
Societies   apply in writing.
Green Fees   £15 per day; £8 per round; £40 per week.
Facilities   ⚏
Location   NW side of town on A896

Hotel   ★★★ 66% The Links Hotel, Golf Rd, BRORA
                   ☎ 01408 621225 23 ⇌ ꜩ

HOPEMAN   Map 15 NJ16

Hopeman Clubhouse IV30 5YA
☎ 01343 830578 Fax 01343 830152
Links-type course with beautiful views over the Moray Firth.
The 12th hole, called the Priescach, is a short hole with a
drop of 100 feet from tee to green. It can require anything
from a wedge to a wood depending on the wind.
18 holes, 5590yds, Par 67, SSS 67.
Club membership 750.
Visitors   must contact in advance, restricted tee times at
                   weekend and between 12:45-1:45 weekdays
Societies   contact in advance.
Green Fees   £20 per day; £15 per round (£25/£20 weekends).
Facilities   ⊗ ⓚ ⓚ ⚏ ♈ ⚒ ♥ ♂
Location   E side of village off B9040

Hotel   ★★ 66% Stotfield Hotel, Stotfield Rd,
                   LOSSIEMOUTH ☎ 01343 812011 46 ⇌ ꜩ

HUNTLY   Map 15 NJ53

Huntly Cooper Park AB54 4SH ☎ 01466 792643
A parkland course lying between the Rivers Deveron and
Bogie.
18 holes, 5399yds, Par 67, SSS 66.
Club membership 850.   ▶

Visitors may not play before 8am.
Societies must contact the secretary.
Green Fees not confirmed.
Facilities ⊗ ⅷ ᵬ ▆ ♥ ⅄ ♙ ⅋ ₹
Location N side of Huntly, turn off A96 at bypass roundabout

Hotel ★★★⁴⁴ 64% Castle Hotel, HUNTLY
☎ 01466 792696   19 ⇄ ₹
See advertisement on page 323.

INSCH   Map 15 NJ62

Insch Golf Ter AB52 6JY
☎ 01464 820363 Fax 01464 820363
A challenging 18 hole course, a mixture of flat undulating parkland, with trees, stream and pond.
18 holes, 5500yds, Par 70, SSS 67.
Club membership 400.
Visitors restricted during club competitions and Tee times, ie Mon - Ladies night, Tue - Mens night, Wed - juniors, telephone clubhouse 01464 820363 for information. Pre-booking is advised
Societies apply in writing or telephone, bookings accepted.
Green Fees £15 per round (£20 weekends).
Designer Greens of Scotland
Facilities ᵬ ▆ ♥ ⅄
Location A96

Hotel ★★ 65% Lodge Hotel, OLD RAYNE
☎ 01464 851205 3 ₹ Annexe4 ⇄ ₹

INVERALLOCHY   Map 15 NK06

Inverallochy Whitelink AB43 8XY ☎ 01346 582000
Seaside links course with natural hazards, tricky par 3s and easy walking.
18 holes, 5237yds, Par 65, SSS 65, Course record 57.
Club membership 350.
Visitors restricted at weekends and competition days, contact for availability.
Societies apply in writing.
Green Fees £10 per day (£15 weekends, £10 after 2pm Sun).
Facilities ⊗ ᵬ ▆ ♥ ⅄
Location E side of village off B9107

Hotel ★★★ 73% Waterside Inn,
Fraserburgh Rd, PETERHEAD
☎ 01779 471121   69 ⇄ ₹ Annexe40 ⇄ ₹

INVERGORDON   Map 14 NH76

Invergordon King George St IV18 0BD ☎ 01349 852715
Fairly easy but windy 18-hole parkland course, with woodland, wide fairways and good views over Cromarty Firth. Very good greens and a fair challenge, especially if the wind is from the west.
18 holes, 6030yds, Par 69, SSS 69, Course record 66.
Club membership 240.
Visitors visitors advised to avoid Tue & Thu 4.30-6, Mon & Wed 5-6 and Sat 8.30-10 & 1-2pm.
Societies must contact in advance, call 01349 852608.
Green Fees £20 per day; £15 per round.
Designer A Rae
Facilities ⊗ by prior arrangement ⅷ by prior arrangement ᵬ by prior arrangement ▆ ⅄ ⅋ ₹
Location W side of town centre on B817

Hotel ★★★ 70% Morangie House Hotel, Morangie
Rd, TAIN ☎ 01862 892281   26 ⇄ ₹

INVERNESS   Map 14 NH64

Inverness Culcabock IV2 3XQ
☎ 01463 239882 Fax 01463 239882
Fairly flat parkland course with burn running through it. Windy in winter. The 14th is one of the most difficult Par 4's in the north of Scotland.
18 holes, 6226yds, Par 69, SSS 70.
Club membership 1100.
Visitors restricted at weekends.
Societies must telephone in advance.
Green Fees £32 per day, £23 per round (£35/£27 weekends and bank holidays).
Cards ⎯ ▇ ▧ ⊘
Prof Alistair P Thomson
Facilities ⊗ ⅷ ᵬ ▆ ♥ ⅄ ♙ ⅋ ⅋

Hotel ★★★★ 69% Kingsmills Hotel,
Culcabock Rd, INVERNESS
☎ 01463 237166   76 ⇄ ₹ Annexe6 ⇄ ₹

Loch Ness Fairways, Castle Heather IV21 6AA
☎ 01463 713335 Fax 01463 712695
Challenging parkland course with superb views over Inverness, the Beauly Firth and the Black Isle.
18 holes, 6772yds, Par 73, SSS 72, Course record 69.
Club membership 580.
Visitors please contact in advance, may play at weekends usually after noon.
Societies telephone for details.
Green Fees £20 per day (£25 weekends).
Cards ⎯ ▇ ▧ ⊘
Prof Martin Piggot
Facilities ⊗ ⅷ ᵬ ▆ ♥ ⅄ ♙ ⅋ ⅂ ♟ ⅋ ₹
Location SW outskirts of Inverness, along new bypass

Hotel ★★⁴⁴ Dunain Park Hotel, INVERNESS
☎ 01463 230512 12rm(10 ⇄ ₹)

Torvean Glenurquhart Rd IV3 6JN
☎ 01463 711434 (Starter) & 225651 (Secretary)
Fax 01463 225651
Municipal parkland course, easy walking, good views.
18 holes, 5784yds, Par 69, SSS 68, Course record 64.
Club membership 400.
Visitors must contact in advance.
Societies advance bookings through The Highland Council, Town House, Inverness.
Green Fees not confirmed.
Designer Hamilton
Facilities ▆ ♥ ⅄ ⅋ ⅋
Location 1.5m SW on A82

Hotel ★★⁴⁴ Dunain Park Hotel, INVERNESS
☎ 01463 230512 12rm(10 ⇄ ₹)

INVERURIE   Map 15 NJ72

Inverurie Blackhall Rd AB51 5JB
☎ 01467 624080 Fax 01467 621051
Parkland course, part of which is through wooded area.
18 holes, 5711yds, Par 69, SSS 68, Course record 64.
Club membership 700.

Visitors   book tee time through shop up to 24 hrs in
                 advance 01467 620193.
Societies   telephone administrator.
Green Fees   £18 per day; £14 per round (£24/£18 weekends).
Prof   Mark Lees
Facilities   ⊗ ⫞ ﬁ ⌐ ⚐ ⟁ 🏠 ⛳ ♂
Location   E side of town off A96

Hotel   ★★★ 69% Strathburn Hotel, Burghmuir Dr,
                 INVERURIE ☎ 01467 624422 25 ⇨ ♞

KEITH   Map 15 NJ45

Keith Fife Park AB55 5DF
☎ 01542 882469 Fax 01542 888176
Parkland course, with natural hazards over first 9 holes.
Testing 7th hole, 232 yds, par 3.
18 holes, 5767yds, Par 69, SSS 68.
Club membership 500.
Visitors   no restrictions except competitions.
Societies   by arrangement with outings secretary (01542
                 886114)
Green Fees   £14 per day; £12 per round (£17/£14 weekends).
Facilities   ⌐ ⚐ ⟁ ♂
Location   NW side of town centre off A96, onto B9014
                 and first right

Hotel   ★★★ 75% Craigellachie Hotel,
                 CRAIGELLACHIE
                 ☎ 01340 881204 26 ⇨ ♞

KEMNAY   Map 15 NJ71

Kemnay Monymusk Rd AB51 5RA
☎ 01467 642225 shop & 643746 office Fax 01467 643746
Undulating parkland course with superb views. A stream
crosses four holes.
18 holes, 5903yds, Par 70, SSS 69, Course record 69.
Club membership 800.
Visitors   telephone shop for booking.
Societies   must telephone in advance.
Green Fees   not confirmed.
Prof   Ronnie McDonald
Designer   Greens of Scotland
Facilities   ⊗ ⫞ ﬁ ⌐ ⚐ ⟁ 🏠 ⛳ ♂
Location   W side of village on B993

Hotel   ★★★ 66% Westhill Hotel, Westhill,
                 ABERDEEN ☎ 01224 740388
                 37 ⇨ ♞ Annexe13 ⇨ ♞

KINGUSSIE   Map 14 NH70

Kingussie Gynack Rd PH21 1LR
☎ 01540 661600 Fax 01540 662066
Hilly upland course with natural hazards and magnificent
views. Stands about 1000ft above sea level at its highest
point, and the River Gynack comes into play on five holes.
18 holes, 5500yds, Par 66, SSS 68, Course record 63.
Club membership 800.
Visitors   advisable to book in advance.
Societies   must contact in advance.
Green Fees   £20 per day; £16 per round (£25/£18 weekends).
Designer   Vardon
Facilities   ⊗ ﬁ ⌐ ⚐ ⟁ 🏠 ⛳ ⛏ ♂
Location   0.25m N off A86

Hotel   ★★ 75% The Scot House Hotel, Newtonmore
                 Rd, KINGUSSIE ☎ 01540 661351 9 ⇨ ♞

KINTORE   Map 15 NJ71

Kintore Balbithan AB51 0UR
☎ 01467 632631 Fax 01467 741588
The course covers a large area of ground from the Don
Basin, near the clubhouse, to mature woodland at the far
perimeter. One of the main attractions is the excellent
drainage which results in very few days of lost play.
18 holes, 5997yds, Par 70, SSS 69, Course record 62.
Club membership 700.
Visitors   during season booking system is in operation &
                 slots for visitors are available. Other times can
                 be booked 24 hours in advance.
Societies   apply in writing or telephone.
Green Fees   £18 per day; £13 per round (£24/£19 weekends).
Facilities   ⊗ ⫞ ﬁ ⌐ ⚐ ⟁ ♂
Location   1m from village centre on B977

Hotel   ★★ 65% Torryburn Hotel, School Rd,
                 KINTORE ☎ 01467 632269 9rm(8 ♞)

LEWIS, ISLE OF   Map 13 NB43

STORNOWAY   Map 13 NB43

Stornoway Lady Lever Park HS2 0XP ☎ 01851 702240
Undulating parkland course set in grounds of Lews Castle
with fine views over the Minch to the mainland. A number of
very testing par 3's and the 11th hole the 'Dardanelles' one
of the most testing par 5's in Europe.
18 holes, 5252yds, Par 68, SSS 67, Course record 62.
Club membership 440.
Visitors   no golf on Sun.
Societies   apply in writing.
Green Fees   £15 per day.
Facilities   ﬁ ⌐ ⚐ ⟁ 🏠 ⛳ ♂
Location   0.5m from town centre off A857

Hotel   ★★★ 66% Cabarfeidh Hotel, STORNOWAY
                 ☎ 01851 702604 46 ⇨ ♞

LOCHCARRON   Map 14 NG83

Lochcarron East End IV54 8YU
Seaside links course with some parkland with an interesting
2nd hole. A short course but great accuracy is required.
9 holes, 1789yds, Par 62, SSS 60.
Club membership 150.
Visitors   restricted Mon evening & Sat 2-5pm.
Societies   welcome but restricted Mon evening & Sat 2-
                 5pm.
Green Fees   £40 per week; £10 per day.
Facilities   ⛳
Location   1m E

Hotel   ★★ 66% Lochcarron Hotel,
                 Main St, LOCHCARRON
                 ☎ 01520 722226 10rm(9 ⇨ ♞)

▶

LOSSIEMOUTH
Map 15 NJ27

Moray IV31 6QS
☎ 01343 812018 Fax 01343 815102
Two fine Scottish Championship links courses, known as
Old and New (Moray), and situated on the Moray Firth
where the weather is unusually mild.
*Old Course: 18 holes, 6643yds, Par 71, SSS 73, Course
record 65.*
*New Course: 18 holes, 6004yds, Par 69, SSS 69, Course
record 62.*
Club membership 1550.
Visitors　must contact in advance 01343 812018
　　　　　　Secretary.
Societies　must contact in advance.
Green Fees not confirmed.
Prof　　　Alistair Thomson
Designer　Tom Morris
Facilities　⊗ ⅲ 🏠 🍺 ♀ 🏌 🏠 ⑁ ⌀
Location　N side of town

Hotel　　★★ 66% Stotfield Hotel,
　　　　　　Stotfield Rd, LOSSIEMOUTH
　　　　　　☎ 01343 812011　46 ⇌ ৫

LYBSTER
Map 15 ND23

Lybster Main St KW3 6AE
Picturesque, short heathland course, easy walking.
9 holes, 1896yds, Par 62, SSS 61, Course record 59.
Club membership 140.
Visitors　no restrictions.
Societies　must contact in advance.
Green Fees not confirmed.
Facilities　🏠 🏌
Location　E side of village

Hotel　　★★ 69% Portland Arms, LYBSTER
♪ „⌐　　☎ 01593 721208　19 ⇌ ৫

MACDUFF
Map 15 NJ76

Royal Tarlair Buchan St AB44 1TA ☎ 01261 832897
Seaside clifftop course, can be windy. Testing 13th, 'Clivet'
(par 3).
18 holes, 5866yds, Par 71, SSS 68, Course record 62.
Club membership 520.
Visitors　no restrictions.
Societies　apply in writing.
Green Fees £15 per day; £10 per round (£20/£13 weekends).
Facilities　⊗ ⅲ 🏠 🍺 ♀ 🏠 🏌 ⌀
Location　0.75m E off A98

Hotel　　★★★ 66% Banff Springs Hotel,
　　　　　　Golden Knowes Rd, BANFF
　　　　　　☎ 01261 812881　31 ⇌ ৫

MUIR OF ORD
Map 14 NH55

Muir of Ord Great North Rd IV6 7SX
☎ 01463 870825 Fax 01463 870825
Old established (1875), heathland course with tight fairways
and easy walking. Testing 13th, 'Castle Hill' (par 3).
18 holes, 5557yds, Par 68, SSS 68, Course record 63.
Club membership 650.

Visitors　may not play before 11am weekends without
　　　　　　prior agreement and during club competitions.
Societies　telephone followed by letter of confirmation.
Green Fees not confirmed.
Prof　　　G Leggat
Designer　James Braid
Facilities　⊗ 🏠 🍺 ♀ 🏠 🏌 ⑁ ⌀
& Leisure　snooker & pool tables.
Location　S side of village on A862

Hotel　　★★★ 70% Priory Hotel, The Square,
　　　　　　BEAULY ☎ 01463 782309　36 ⇌ ৫

NAIRN
Map 14 NH85

Nairn Seabank Rd IV12 4HB
☎ 01667 453208 Fax 01667 456328
Championship, seaside links founded in 1887 and
created from a wilderness of heather and whin. Designed
by Archie Simpson, old Tom Morris and James Braid.
Opening holes stretch out along the shoreline with the
turn for home at the 10th. Regularly chosen for national
championships.
18 holes, 6452yds, Par 71, SSS 73, Course record 65.
Club membership 1150.
Visitors　book in advance through secretary, may not
　　　　　　play between 8-11.00 am & 12-2.30 pm (Fri
　　　　　　& Sat).
Societies　subject to availability bookings through
　　　　　　secretary's office.
Green Fees £55 per round (£60 weekends).
Cards　　▭ ▭ ⊡
Prof　　　Robin P Fyfe
Designer　A Simpson/Old Tom Morris/James Braid
Facilities　⊗ ⅲ 🏠 🍺 ♀ 🏠 🏌 ⌀
& Leisure　snooker table, 9 hole course.
Location　16m E of Inverness on A96

Hotel　　★★★★ 67% Golf View Hotel &
　　　　　　Leisure Club, Seabank Rd, NAIRN
　　　　　　☎ 01667 452301　48 ⇌ ৫

Nairn Dunbar Lochloy Rd IV12 5AE
☎ 01667 452741 Fax 01667 456897
Links course with sea views and testing gorse-and whin-lined
fairways. Testing hole: 'Long Peter' (527 yds).
18 holes, 6720yds, Par 72, SSS 73.
Club membership 700.

Visitors　April-Oct only. Weekends restricted, contact in
　　　　　　advance.
Societies　must contact in advance.
Green Fees £35 per day; £28 per round (£45/£33 weekends).

Cards
Prof   David Torrance
Facilities ⊗ 〗 ⅃ ☕ ♀ ⌘ ⌂ ☂ ⚑ ⚷
Location   E side of town off A96

Hotel   ★★ 64% Alton Burn Hotel, Alton Burn Rd,
                NAIRN ☎ 01667 452051
                19rm(14 ⇆3 🐾) Annexe7 ⇆ 🐾

NETHY BRIDGE   Map 14 NJ02

Abernethy PH25 3EB ☎ 01479 821305
Picturesque moorland course.
9 holes, 2551yds, Par 33, SSS 33.
Club membership 350.
Visitors   contact in advance.
Societies   must contact in advance.
Green Fees not confirmed.
Facilities ⌂ ⚑ ⚷
Location   N side of village on B970

Hotel   ★★★ 71% Muckrach Lodge Hotel,
                DULNAIN BRIDGE
                ☎ 01479 851257   10 ⇆ 🐾 Annexe4 ⇆ 🐾

NEWBURGH ON YTHAN   Map 15 NJ92

Newburgh on Ythan Newburgh Links AB41 0AW
☎ 01358 789058 Fax 01358 789956
This seaside course was founded in 1888 and is adjacent to a
bird sanctuary. Testing 550-yd dog leg (par 5). Extended to
18-hole in 1995.
18 holes, 6162yds, Par 72, SSS 69, Course record 70.
Club membership 400.
Visitors   must contact in advance.
Societies   apply in advance.
Green Fees £16 per day (£21 weekends).
Facilities ⊗ ⅃ ☕ ♀ ⌂ ⚷
Location   E side of village on A975

Hotel   ★★ 70% Udny Arms Hotel, Main St,
                NEWBURGH ☎ 01358 789444   26 ⇆ 🐾

NEWMACHAR   Map 15 NJ81

Newmachar Swailend AB21 7UU
☎ 01651 863002 Fax 01651 863055
Hawkshill is a championship-standard parkland course
designed by Dave Thomas and opened in 1991. Several lakes
affect five of the holes and there are well developed birch
and Scots pine trees. Swailend is a parkland course designed
by Dave Thomas and opened in 1997. It povides a test all of
its own with some well positioned bunkering and testing
greens.
Hawkshill Course: 18 holes, 6623yds, Par 72, SSS 74,
Course record 67.
Swailend Course: 18 holes, 6388yds, Par 72, SSS 71.
Club membership 900.
Visitors   must contact in advance & have handicap
                certificate for Hawkshill course.
Societies   apply in writing.
Green Fees Hawkshill: £45 per day; £30 per round (£40 per
                round weekends). Swailend: £25 per day; £15
                per round (£30/£20 weekends).
Cards   — 〓 💳 📧
Prof   Peter Smith

Designer   Dave Thomas/Peter Allis
Facilities ⊗ 〗 ⅃ ☕ ♀ ⌘ ⌂ ☂ ⚑ ⚷ ⚷
Location   2m N of Dyce, off A947

Hotel   ★★★ 69% Strathburn Hotel, Burghmuir Dr,
                INVERURIE ☎ 01467 624422   25 ⇆ 🐾

NEWTONMORE   Map 14 NN79

Newtonmore Golf Course Rd PH20 1AT
☎ 01540 673328 & 673878 Fax 01540 673878
Inland course beside the River Spey. Beautiful views and
easy walking. Testing 17th hole (par 3).
18 holes, 6029yds, Par 70, SSS 69, Course record 68.
Club membership 420.
Visitors   contact in advance.
Societies   apply in writing to secretary.
Green Fees £16 per day; £13 per round (£21/£15 weekends).
Prof   Robert Henderson
Facilities ⊗ 〗 ⅃ ☕ ♀ ⌘ ⌂ ☂ ⚑ ⚷ ⚷
Location   E side of town off A9

Hotel   ★★ 75% The Scot House Hotel, Newtonmore
                Rd, KINGUSSIE ☎ 01540 661351 9 ⇆ 🐾

OLDMELDRUM   Map 15 NJ82

Old Meldrum Kirk Brae AB51 0DJ
☎ 01651 872648 Fax 01651 873555
Parkland course with tree-lined fairways and superb views.
Challenging 196 yard, Par 3, 11th over two ponds to a green
surrounded by bunkers.
18 holes, 5988yds, Par 70, SSS 69, Course record 66.
Club membership 700.
Visitors   may not play during Club competitions.
Societies   apply in writing to secretary
Green Fees £14 (£20 weekends).
Prof   to be appointed
Facilities ⊗ 〗 ⅃ ☕ ♀ ⌘ ⌂ ⚷
Location   E side of village off A947

Hotel   ★★★ 69% Strathburn Hotel, Burghmuir Dr,
                INVERURIE ☎ 01467 624422   25 ⇆ 🐾

ORKNEY   Map 16

KIRKWALL   Map 16 HY41

Orkney Grainbank KW15 1RB ☎ 01856 872457
Open parkland course with few hazards and superb views
over Kirkwall and Islands.
18 holes, 5411yds, Par 70, SSS 67, Course record 65.
Club membership 402.
Visitors   may not play on competition days.
Societies   write or telephone if possible.
Green Fees not confirmed.
Facilities ⅃ ☕ ♀ ⌂ ⚑ ⚷
Location   0.5m W off A965

Hotel   ★★★ 64% Ayre Hotel, Ayre Rd, KIRKWALL
                ☎ 01856 873001   33 ⇆ 🐾

Entries with a shaded background
identify courses that are
considered to be particularly interesting

STROMNESS   Map 16 HY20

Stromness KW16 3DW ☎ 01856 850772
Testing parkland/seaside course with easy walking. Beautiful holiday course with magnificent views of Scapa Flow. New clubhouse opened 1999.
18 holes, 4762yds, Par 65, SSS 63, Course record 61.
Club membership 275.

Visitors	no restrictions except during major competitions.
Societies	no restrictions.
Green Fees	£12 per day/round.
Facilities	⊗ by prior arrangement ⏟ by prior arrangement ᛒ by prior arrangement ♥ ♀ ᐃ
& Leisure	hard tennis courts.
Location	S side of town centre off A965
Hotel	★★★ 64% Ayre Hotel, Ayre Rd, KIRKWALL ☎ 01856 873001 33 ⇄ ℝ

WESTRAY   Map 16 HY44

Westray Rosevale KW17 2DH ☎ 01857 677373
Interesting, picturesque seaside course, easy walking.
9 holes, 2405yds, Par 33.
Club membership 60.

Visitors	no restrictions.
Green Fees	not confirmed.
Facilities	ᛖ
Location	1m NW of Pierowall off B9066
Hotel	★★★ 64% Ayre Hotel, Ayre Rd, KIRKWALL ☎ 01856 873001 33 ⇄ ℝ

PETERCULTER   Map 15 NJ80

Peterculter Oldtown, Burnside Rd AB14 0LN
☎ 01224 734994 Fax 01224 735580
The course is a tight Par 68 (from Yellow tees) with a beautiful Par 2 2nd and two Par 5 holes in excess of 500 yards. Surrounded by wonderful scenery and bordered by the River Dee, there is a variety of birds, deer and foxes on the course, which also has superb views up the Dee Valley.
18 holes, 5947yds, Par 68, SSS 68, Course record 68.
Club membership 1035.

Visitors	contact 3 days in advance, welcome after 2.30pm weekdays & 4pm weekends.
Societies	contact up to 7 days in advance.
Green Fees	not confirmed.
Prof	Dean Vannet
Designer	Greens of Scotland
Facilities	⊗ ⏟ ᛒ ♥ ♀ ᐃ 🏠 ᛖ 🛞 🏌 ⚷
Location	On A93
Hotel	★★★ 66% Westhill Hotel, Westhill, ABERDEEN ☎ 01224 740388 37 ⇄ ℝ Annexe13 ⇄ ℝ

PETERHEAD   Map 15 NK14

Peterhead Craigewan Links, Riverside Dr AB42 1LT
☎ 01779 472149 & 480725 Fax 01779 480725
The Old Course is a natural links course bounded by the sea and the River Ugie. Varying conditions of play depending on wind and weather. The New Course is more of a parkland course.

Old Course: 18 holes, 6173yds, Par 70, SSS 71, Course record 64.
New Course: 9 holes, 4456yds, Par 62, SSS 62.
Club membership 650.

Visitors	welcome any day apart from Saturdays, restricted times on the Old Course. Telephone for details.
Societies	apply in writing, restricted availablility on Saturdays
Green Fees	Old Course: £22 per day; £16 per round (£27/£20 weekends). New Course: £9 per day/round.
Designer	W Park/ L Auchterconie/J Braid
Facilities	⊗ ⏟ ᛒ ♥ ♀ ᐃ ᛖ ⚷
Location	N side of town centre off A952
Hotel	★★★ 73% Waterside Inn, Fraserburgh Rd, PETERHEAD ☎ 01779 471121 69 ⇄ ℝ Annexe40 ⇄ ℝ

PORTLETHEN   Map 15 NO99

Portlethen Badentoy Rd AB12 4YA
☎ 01224 782575 & 781090 Fax 01224 781090
Set in pleasant parkland, this new course features mature trees and a stream which affects a number of holes.
18 holes, 6707yds, Par 72, SSS 72, Course record 63.
Club membership 1000.

Visitors	may not play Sat. Contact in advance.
Societies	apply in advance.
Green Fees	£22 per day; £15 per round (£30/£22 weekends).
Cards	▬ ▬ ▬ 🔲
Prof	Muriel Thomson
Designer	Cameron Sinclair
Facilities	⊗ ⏟ ᛒ ♥ ♀ ᐃ 🏠 ᛖ 🛞 ⚷
Location	Off A90 S of Aberdeen
Hotel	★★ 65% County Hotel & Leisure Club, Arduthie Rd, STONEHAVEN ☎ 01569 764386 14 ⇄ ℝ

REAY   Map 14 NC96

Reay KW14 7RE ☎ 01847 811288
Picturesque seaside links with natural hazards, following the contours of Sandside Bay. Tight and testing.
18 holes, 5884yds, Par 69, SSS 68, Course record 64.
Club membership 325.

Visitors	restricted competition days
Societies	apply in writing.
Green Fees	not confirmed.
Facilities	ᛒ ♥ ♀ ᐃ
Location	0.5m E off A836
Guest house	▬ Tigh-na-Clash Guest House, Tigh-na-Clash, MELVICH ☎ 01641 531262 8 ℝ

ROTHES   Map 15 NJ24

Rothes Blackhall AB38 7AN ☎ 01340 831443 (evenings)
A hilly course opened in 1990 on an elevated site overlooking the remains of Rothes castle and the Spey valley. The 2nd fairway and most of the 3rd are sheltered by woodland. The ground alongside the 5th & 6th falls away steeply.
9 holes, 4972yds, Par 68, SSS 65.
Club membership 280.

Visitors course reserved Mon 5-6.30 & Tue 5-7.30.
Societies apply in writing to secretary.
Green Fees £10 per day (£12 weekends).
Designer John Souter
Facilities ⌂
& Leisure practice net.
Location 9m S of Elgin on A941

SHETLAND   Map 16

LERWICK   Map 16 HU44

Shetland PO Box 18 ZE1 0YW ☎ 01595 840369
Challenging moorland course, hard walking. A burn runs the
full length of the course and provides a natural hazard.
Testing holes include the 3rd (par 4), 5th (par 4).
*Dale Course: 18 holes, 5800yds, Par 68, SSS 68, Course
record 68.*
Club membership 450.
Visitors advisable to contact in advance.
Societies telephone in advance.
Green Fees not confirmed.
Facilities ⊾ ⛻ ⚑ ⌂ ⛳
Location 4m N on A970

Hotel ★★★ 67% Lerwick Hotel, 15 South Rd,
LERWICK ☎ 01595 692166 35 ⇔ ℟

WHALSAY, ISLAND OF   Map 16 HU56

Whalsay Skaw Taing ZE2 9AA
☎ 01806 566450 & 566481 & 566705
The most northerly golf course in Britain, with a large part of
it running round the coastline, offering spectacular holes in
an exposed but highly scenic setting. There are no cut
fairways as yet, these are defined by marker posts, with
preferred lies in operation all year round.
18 holes, 6009yds, Par 70, SSS 68, Course record 65.
Club membership 149.
Visitors no restrictions
Societies telephone in advance.
Green Fees £10 per day; £30 per week.
Facilities ⊾ ⚑ ⌂
Location N end of Island

Hotel ★★★⚘ 64% Busta House Hotel, BRAE
☎ 01806 522506 20 ⇔ ℟

SKYE, ISLE OF   Map 13 NG53

SCONSER   Map 13 NG53

Isle of Skye IV48 8TD
☎ 01478 650351 Fax 01478 650351
Seaside course with spectacular views. 9 holes with 18 tees.
Suitable for golfers of all abilities.
18 holes, 4677yds, Par 66, SSS 64, Course record 62.
Club membership 235.
Visitors no restrictions
Societies apply in advance.
Green Fees £14 per day/round.
Facilities ⛻ ⌂ ⓔ ⛳ ∅
Location A87 between Broadford and Portree

Hotel ★★ 73% Rosedale Hotel, PORTREE
☎ 01478 613131 20 ⇔ ℟ Annexe3 ⇔ ℟

SKEABOST BRIDGE   Map 13 NG44

Skeabost Skeabost House Hotel IV51 9NR
☎ 01470 532202
Short woodland and seaside course featuring some very tight
fairways and greens.
9 holes, 3056yds, Par 62, SSS 60, Course record 58.
Club membership 80.
Visitors must contact in advance.
Societies contact in advance.
Green Fees not confirmed.
Designer John Stuart
Facilities ⊗ ⊪ ⊾ ⚑ ⌂ ⓔ ⛳ ⌾
& Leisure fishing.

Hotel ★★★ 72% Cuillin Hills Hotel, PORTREE
☎ 01478 612003 16 ⇔ ℟ Annexe9 ⇔ ℟

SOUTH UIST, ISLE OF   Map 13 NF72

ASKERNISH   Map 13 NF72

Askernish Lochboisdale PA81 5SY ☎ No telephone
Golfers play on machair (hard-wearing short grass), close to
the Atlantic shore.
9 holes, 5042yds, Par 68, SSS 67, Course record 64.
Club membership 15.
Visitors no restrictions.
Societies welcome.
Green Fees not confirmed.
Designer Tom Morris
Facilities ⊗ ⊪ ⊾ ⚑ ⛳
Location 5m NW of Lochboisdale off A865 via ferry

SPEY BAY   Map 15 NJ36

Spey Bay IV32 7PJ ☎ 01343 820424
Seaside links course over gently undulating banks and well-
drained ground. Good views along Moray coast. Driving
range.
18 holes, 6092yds, Par 70, SSS 69, Course record 66.
Club membership 350.
Visitors telephone for details (especially for Sun)
Societies book by telephone.
Green Fees £15 per day; £10 per round (£18/£13 weekends).
Cards ▭ ▭ ▱
Prof Hamish MacDonald
Designer Ben Sayers
Facilities ⊗ ⊪ ⊾ ⛻ ⚑ ⌂ ⛳ ⌾ ∅ ⚹
& Leisure hard tennis courts.
Location 4.5m N of Fochabers on B9104

Hotel ★★ 67% Mill House Hotel, Tynet, BUCKIE
☎ 01542 850233 15 ⇔ ℟

STONEHAVEN   Map 15 NO88

Stonehaven Cowie AB39 3RH
☎ 01569 762124 Fax 01569 765973
Challenging meadowland course overlooking sea with three
gullies and splendid views.
18 holes, 5103yds, Par 66, SSS 65, Course record 61.
Club membership 850.   ▶

Visitors prefer prior booking, may not play before 4pm Sat.
Societies telephone or fax in advance to W A Donald.
Green Fees £15 per day (£20 weekends).
Cards ▆▆▆▆▆ 🟦
Designer C Simpson
Facilities ⊗ ⅓ ᴸ ♥ ♀ ♨ 🏠 ♂
& Leisure snooker.
Location 1m N off A92

Hotel ★★ 65% County Hotel & Leisure Club, Arduthie Rd, STONEHAVEN ☎ 01569 764386 14 ⇆ ☞

STRATHPEFFER   Map 14 NH45

Strathpeffer Spa IV14 9AS
☎ 01997 421219 & 421011 Fax 01997 421011
Upland course with many natural hazards (few sand bunkers), hard walking and fine views. Testing 3rd hole (par 3) across loch.
18 holes, 4792yds, Par 65, SSS 64, Course record 60.
Club membership 500.
Visitors advisable to contact in advance.
Societies apply in writing.
Green Fees £20 per day; £14 per round; £60 per week (Mon-Fri).
Cards ▆▆▆ ▆▆
Designer Willie Park/Tom Morris
Facilities ⊗ ⅓ ᴸ ♥ ♀ ♨ 🏠 ♂
Location 0.25m N of village off A834

Hotel ★★ 70% Brunstane Lodge Hotel, Golf Rd, STRATHPEFFER ☎ 01997 421261 7rm(6 ⇆ ☞)

TAIN   Map 14 NH78

Tain Chapel Rd IV19 1Pa
☎ 01862 892314 Fax 01862 892099
Heathland/links course with river affecting 3 holes; easy walking, fine views.
18 holes, 6311yds, Par 71, SSS 70, Course record 62.
Club membership 500.
Visitors no restrictions.
Societies must book in advance.
Green Fees £30 per day; £24 per round (£36/£30 weekends).
Cards ▆▆▆ ▆▆
Designer Tom Morris
Facilities ⊗ ⅓ by prior arrangement ᴸ ♥ ♀ ♨ 🏠 ♂ ♨ ♂
Location E side of town centre off B9174

Hotel ★★★ 70% Morangie House Hotel, Morangie Rd, TAIN ☎ 01862 892281 26 ⇆ ☞

TARLAND   Map 15 NJ40

Tarland Aberdeen Rd AB34 4TB
☎ 013398 81000 Fax 013398 81000
Difficult upland course, but easy walking. Some spectacular holes, mainly 4th (par 4) and 5th (par 3) and fine scenery.
9 holes, 5888yds, Par 67, SSS 68, Course record 65.
Club membership 350.
Visitors must contact in advance.
Societies must telephone in advance.
Green Fees £14 per day (£18 weekends).

Designer Tom Morris
Facilities ⊗ ⅓ ᴸ ♥ ♀ ♨ ♂
Location E side of village off B9119

Hotel ★★ 62% Birse Lodge Hotel, 20 Charleston Rd, ABOYNE ☎ 013398 86253 12 ⇆ ☞

THURSO   Map 15 ND16

Thurso Newlands of Geise KW14 7XF
☎ 01847 893807
Parkland course, windy, but with fine views of Dunnet Head and the Orkney Islands.
18 holes, 5828yds, Par 69, SSS 69, Course record 63.
Club membership 301.
Visitors no restrictions.
Societies contact in advance.
Green Fees not confirmed.
Facilities ᴸ ♥ ♀ ♨ ♂ ♂
Location 2m SW on B874

Hotel ★★ 67% Park Hotel, THURSO ☎ 01847 893251 11 ⇆ ☞

TORPHINS   Map 15 NJ60

Torphins Bog Rd AB31 4JU
☎ 013398 82115 Fax 013398 82402
Heathland/parkland course built on a hill with views of the Cairngorms.
9 holes, 4800yds, Par 64, SSS 64, Course record 63.
Club membership 380.
Visitors must contact in advance. Restricted on competition days (alternate Sat and Sun).
Societies apply in advance.
Green Fees £11 per day (£13 weekends).
Facilities ᴸ ♥ ♀ ♨ ♂
Location 0.25m W of village off A980

Hotel ★★★ 74% Tor-na-Coille Hotel, BANCHORY ☎ 01330 822242 23 ⇆ ☞

TURRIFF   Map 15 NJ74

Turriff Rosehall AB53 7HD
☎ 01888 562982 Fax 01888 568050
A well-maintained parkland course alongside the River Deveron in picturesque surroundings. 6th and 12th particularly challenging in a testing course.
18 holes, 6107yds, Par 70, SSS 69, Course record 64.
Club membership 894.
Visitors may not play before 10am weekends. Must contact in advance.
Societies apply in writing to the secretary.
Green Fees £20 per day; £16 per round (£27/£21 weekends).
Prof Robin Smith
Facilities ⊗ ⅓ ᴸ ♥ ♀ ♨ 🏠 ♂
Location 1m W off B9024

Hotel ★★★ 66% Banff Springs Hotel, Golden Knowes Rd, BANFF ☎ 01261 812881 31 ⇆ ☞

Entries with a shaded background
identify courses that are
considered to be particularly interesting

WICK   Map 15 ND35

Wick Reiss KW1 4RW ☎ 01955 602726
Typical seaside links course, fairly flat, easy walking. 9 holes straight out and straight back. Normally breezy.
18 holes, 5976yds, Par 69, SSS 70, Course record 63.
Club membership 352.
Visitors   no restrictions.
Societies   apply in writing or telephone in advance.
Green Fees £15 per day, £10 after 5pm.
Designer   James Braid
Facilities   ⬛ ♀ ⚲ ⛳ ✧
Location   3.5m N off A9

Hotel   ★★ 67% Mackay's Hotel, Union St, WICK
☎ 01955 602323 27rm(19 ⇆ ⁅)

CENTRAL SCOTLAND

This region includes the counties of Angus, Argyll & Bute, Clackmannanshire, City of Edinburgh, Dundee City, East Lothian, Falkirk, Fife, Inverclyde, Midlothian, Perthshire & Kinross, Stirling and West Lothian which reflect the recent national changes.

ABERDOUR   Map 11 NT18

Aberdour Seaside Place KY3 0TX
☎ 01383 860080 Fax 01383 860050
Parkland course with lovely views over Firth of Forth.
18 holes, 5460yds, Par 67, SSS 66, Course record 63.
Club membership 800.
Visitors   must contact in advance, may not play Saturdays.
Societies   telephone or write to secretary in advance
Green Fees £28 per day; £17 per round.
Prof   Gordon McCallum
Facilities   ⊗ ⫵ ⛳ ⬛ ♀ ⚲ ⛫ ⛳ ✧
Location   S side of village

Hotel   ★★ 68% Woodside Hotel, High St,
ABERDOUR ☎ 01383 860328 20 ⇆ ⁅

ABERFELDY   Map 14 NN84

Aberfeldy Taybridge Rd PH15 2BH ☎ 01887 820535
Founded in 1895, this flat, parkland course is situated by River Tay near the famous Wade Bridge and Black Watch Monument and enjoys some splendid scenery. The new layout will test the keen golfer.
18 holes, 5283yds, Par 68, SSS 66, Course record 67.
Club membership 333.
Visitors   are advised to book in advance especially at weekends.
Societies   must contact in advance.
Green Fees £22 per day; £12 per round (£25/£16 weekends).
Designer   Soutars
Facilities   ⊗ ⫵ ⛳ ⬛ ♀ ⚲ ⛫ ⛳ ✧
& Leisure   fishing.
Location   N side of town centre

Hotel   ★★ 69% The Weem, Weem, ABERFELDY
☎ 01887 820381 12 ⇆ ⁅

ABERFOYLE   Map 11 NN50

Aberfoyle Braeval FK8 3UY ☎ 01877 382493
Scenic heathland course with mountain views.
18 holes, 5210yds, Par 66, SSS 66.
Club membership 665.
Visitors   may not tee off before 10.30am Sat & Sun.
Societies   must contact in advance.
Green Fees £16 per day; £12 per round (£24 per day; £16 per round weekends).
Facilities   ⊗ ⫵ ⬛ ♀ ⚲ ✧
Location   1m E on A81

Hotel   ★★★ 69% Forest Hills Hotel, Kinlochard,
ABERFOYLE ☎ 01877 387277 56 ⇆ ⁅

ABERLADY   Map 12 NT47

Kilspindie EH32 0QD
☎ 01875 870358 Fax 01875 870358
Seaside course, short but tight and well-bunkered. Situated on the shores of the river Forth. Testing holes: 2nd, 3rd, 4th and 7th. A new 6200 yard par 71 links course is planned to open in mid 2000.
18 holes, 5480yds, Par 69, SSS 66, Course record 62.
Club membership 1000.
Visitors   must contact in advance, prefered days for visitors Mon-Fri
Societies   contact secretary in advance.
Green Fees £30 per day, £20 per round (£35/£25 weekends).
Prof   Graham J Sked
Facilities   ⊗ ⫵ ⛳ ⬛ ♀ ⚲ ⛫ ⛳ ✧
Location   W side of village off A198

Hotel   ★★ 68% Kilspindie House Hotel, Main St,
ABERLADY ☎ 01875 870682 26 ⇆ ⁅

Luffness New EH32 0QA
☎ 01620 843114 & 843336 Fax 01620 842933
Links course, National Final Qualifying Course for Open Championship.
18 holes, 6122yds, Par 69, SSS 70, Course record 62.
Club membership 700.
Visitors   must contact in advance but may not play at weekends & bank holidays.
Societies   telephone for application form.
Green Fees £50 per day; £35 per round.
Designer   Tom Morris
Facilities   ⊗ ⫵ ⬛ ♀ ⚲ ⛫ ✧
Location   1m E on A198

Hotel   ★★★⚑ Greywalls Hotel,
Muirfield, GULLANE
☎ 01620 842144 17 ⇆ ⁅ Annexe5 ⇆ ⁅

ALLOA   Map 11 NS89

Alloa Schawpark, Sauchie FK10 3AX
☎ 01259 722745 & 724476 Fax 01259 724476
Undulating, wooded parkland course, situated under the Ochil hills, scenery and playing conditions are exceptional.
18 holes, 6229yds, Par 69, SSS 71, Course record 63.
Club membership 910.
Visitors   7 day booking system through professional. Advised to book especially at weekends.
Societies   apply in writing.

▶

Green Fees £30 per day; £20 per round (£35/£25 weekends).
Cards ⊡ ⊟ ▨
Prof Bill Bennett
Designer James Braid
Facilities ⊗ ⫙ ▙ ▚ ♥ ♀ ⚐ 🏠 ⛳ ⤢ ⛟ ✎
Location 1.5m NE on A908

Hotel ★★★ 75% Gean House, Gean Park, Tullibody
Rd, ALLOA ☎ 01259 219275 7 ⇆ ☞

Braehead Cambus FK10 2NT ☎ 01259 725766
Attactive parkland course at the foot of the Ochil Hills, and
offering spectacular views.
18 holes, 6086yds, Par 70, SSS 69, Course record 64.
Club membership 800.
Visitors advisable to telephone in advance.
Societies must contact the clubhouse manager in advance
tel 01259 725766.
Green Fees not confirmed.
Prof Paul Brookes
Designer Robert Tait
Facilities ⊗ ⫙ ▙ ▚ ♥ ♀ ⚐ 🏠 ⛳ ⤢ ⛟ ✎
Location 1m W on A907

Hotel ★★★ 75% Gean House, Gean Park, Tullibody
Rd, ALLOA ☎ 01259 219275 7 ⇆ ☞

ALVA   Map 11 NS89

Alva Beauclerc St FK12 5LD ☎ 01259 760431
A 9-hole course at the foot of the Ochil Hills which gives it
its characteristic sloping fairways and fast greens.
9 holes, 2423yds, Par 66, SSS 64, Course record 63.
Club membership 318.
Visitors may not play during medal competitions or Thu
evening (Ladies night).
Societies apply in writing or telephone in advance.
Green Fees £12 per day (£15 weekends).
Facilities ▙ ▚ ♥ ♀ ⤢
Location 7m from Stirling,A91 Stirling/St Andrews rd

ALYTH   Map 15 NO24

Alyth Pitcrocknie PH11 8HF
☎ 01828 632268 Fax 01828 633491
Windy, heathland course with easy walking.
18 holes, 6205yds, Par 71, SSS 71, Course record 65.
Club membership 1000.
Visitors advance booking advisable, handicap certificate
required and dress etiquette must be observed.
Societies must telephone in advance.
Green Fees not confirmed.
Prof Tom Melville
Designer James Braid
Facilities ⤢ 🏠 ⛳ ⛟ ⤢ ✎ ⚭
Location 1m E on B954

Hotel ★★ 64% Angus Hotel, 46 Wellmeadow,
BLAIRGOWRIE ☎ 01250 872455 81 ⇆ ☞

Strathmore Golf Centre Leroch PH11 8NZ
☎ 01828 633322 Fax 01828 633533
The Rannaleroch course is set on rolling parkland and heath
with splendid views over Strathmore. The course is laid out
in two loops of nine which both start and finish at the
clubhouse. Among the challenging holes is the 480yard 5th
with a 180yard carry over water from a high tee position (a
cop out route available!).

*Rannaleroch Course: 18 holes, 6454yds, Par 72, SSS 72,
Course record 68.*
Leitfie Links: 9 holes, 1666yds, Par 29, SSS 29.
Club membership 300.
Visitors no restrictions, advised to book in advance
Societies phone enquiry recommended.
Green Fees Rannaleroch: £18 per round (£23 weekends).
Leitfie Links: £10 per day (£12 weekends).
Cards ⊡ ⊟ ▨
Prof Colin Smith
Designer John Salvesen
Facilities ⊗ ⫙ ▙ ▚ ♥ ♀ ⚐ 🏠 ⛳ ⤢ ⛟ ✎ ⚭
Location 5m SE of Alyth,off B954 at Meigle onto A926

Hotel ★★★⚑⚑ 75% Old Mansion House Hotel,
AUCHTERHOUSE ☎ 01382 320366 6 ⇆ ☞

ANSTRUTHER   Map 12 NO50

Anstruther Marsfield, Shore Rd KY10 3DZ
☎ 01333 310956
Seaside links course with some excellent par 3 holes; always
in good condition.
9 holes, 4144mtrs, Par 62, SSS 63, Course record 61.
Club membership 700.
Visitors advised to phone in advance.
Societies welcome except Jun-Aug. Must apply in writing.
Green Fees £12 per 18 holes; £8 per 9 holes (£16/£10
weekends).
Designer Tom Morris
Facilities ⊗ ⫙ ▙ ♥ ♀ ⤢ ⛟ ✎
Location SW off A917

Hotel ★★ 63% Smugglers Inn, High St,
ANSTRUTHER ☎ 01333 310506 9 ⇆ ☞

ARBROATH   Map 12 NO64

Arbroath Elliot DD11 2PE
☎ 01241 872069 Fax 01241 875837
Municipal seaside links course, with bunkers guarding
greens. Played upon by Arbroath Artisan Club.
18 holes, 6185yds, Par 70, SSS 69, Course record 64.
Club membership 550.
Visitors contact professional 01241 875837.
Societies contact professional 01241 875837.
Green Fees £23 per 36 holes; £16 per 18 holes (£35/£23
weekends).
Prof Lindsay Ewart
Designer Braid
Facilities ⊗ ⫙ ▙ ▚ ♥ ♀ ⤢ 🏠 ⛳ ✎ ⚭
Location 2m SW on A92

Hotel ★★ 60% Hotel Seaforth, Dundee Rd,
ARBROATH ☎ 01241 872232 21rm(19 ⇆ ☞)

Letham Grange Colliston DD11 4RL
☎ 01241 890373 Fax 01241 890725
Often referred to as the 'Augusta of Scotland', the Old
Course provides championship standards in spectacular
surroundings with attractive lochs and burns. The New
Course is less arduous and shorter using many natural
features of the estate.
*Old Course: 18 holes, 6632yds, Par 73, SSS 73, Course
record 64.*
*New Course: 18 holes, 5528yds, Par 68, SSS 68, Course
record 64.*
Club membership 750.

Visitors no visitors weekends before 9.30am, Old Course before 10am Tue & New Course before 10am Fri.
Societies telephone in advance.
Green Fees not confirmed.
Cards [symbols]
Prof Steven Moie
Designer G K Smith/Donald Steel
Facilities [symbols]
Location 4m N on A933

Hotel ★★★ 69% The Letham Grange Mansion House Hotel, Colliston, ARBROATH ☎ 01241 890373 19 ⇆ ⁿ Annexe22 ⇆ ⁿ
See advertisment on page 337.

AUCHTERARDER   Map 11 NN91

Auchterarder Orchil Rd PH3 1LS
☎ 01764 662804 (Secretary) Fax 01764 662804
Parkland course with easy walking.
18 holes, 5775yds, Par 69, SSS 68, Course record 62.
Club membership 765.
Visitors must contact professional in advance.
Societies must contact in advance.
Green Fees £28 per day; £20 per round (£36/£25 weekends).
Prof Gavin Baxter
Facilities [symbols]
Location 0.75m SW on A824

Hotel ★★★★★ The Gleneagles Hotel, AUCHTERARDER ☎ 01764 662231 229 ⇆ ⁿ

GLENEAGLES   See page 335

BARRY   Map 12 NO53

Panmure Burnside Rd DD7 7RT
☎ 01241 855120 Fax 01241 859737
A nerve-testing, adventurous course set amongst sandhills - its hazards belie the quiet nature of the opening holes. This tight links has been used as a qualifying course for the Open Championship, and features Ben Hogan's favourite hole, the dog-leg 6th, which heralds the toughest stretch, around the turn.
18 holes, 6317yds, Par 70, SSS 71, Course record 62.
Club membership 700.
Visitors may not play Sat. Parties of 5 or more must contact in advance.
Societies must contact secretary in advance.
Green Fees not confirmed.

Cards [symbols]
Prof Neil Mackintosh
Facilities [symbols]
Location S side of village off A930

Hotel ★★ 65% Hogan House Hotel, Links Pde, CARNOUSTIE ☎ 01241 853273 7 ⇆ ⁿ

BATHGATE   Map 11 NS96

Bathgate Edinburgh Rd EH48 1BA
☎ 01506 630553 & 652232 Fax 01506 636775
Moorland course. Easy walking. Testing 11th hole, par 3.
18 holes, 6250yds, Par 71, SSS 70, Course record 58.
Club membership 900.
Visitors casual visitors welcome other than on competition days. Handicap certificate advisable.
Societies apply in writing.
Green Fees £21 per day; £16 per round (£32 per day weekends).
Prof Sandy Strachan
Designer W Park
Facilities [symbols]
Location E side of town off A89

Hotel ★★★ 67% The Hilcroft Hotel, East Main St, WHITBURN ☎ 01501 740818 31 ⇆ ⁿ

BLAIR ATHOLL   Map 14 NN86

Blair Atholl Invertilt Rd PH18 5TG ☎ 01796 481407
Parkland course, river runs alongside 3 holes, easy walking.
9 holes, 5816yds, Par 70, SSS 68, Course record 65.
Club membership 460.
Visitors apply in advance to avoid competition times.
Societies apply in writing.
Green Fees £13 per day (£16 weekends).
Designer Morriss
Facilities [symbols]
Location 0.5m S off B8079

Hotel ★★ 68% Atholl Arms Hotel, BLAIR ATHOLL ☎ 01796 481205 30 ⇆ ⁿ

BLAIRGOWRIE   Map 15 NO14

Blairgowrie Rosemount PH10 6LG
☎ 01250 872622 Fax 01250 875451
Two 18-hole heathland courses, also a 9-hole course.
Rosemount Course: 18 holes, 6590yds, Par 72, SSS 73.
Lansdowne Course: 18 holes, 6802yds, Par 72, SSS 74, Course record 67.
Wee Course: 9 holes, 4654yds, Par 64, SSS 63.
Club membership 1550.
Visitors must contact in advance & have handicap certificate, restricted Wed, Fri & weekends.
Societies must contact in advance.
Green Fees £60 per day for all courses. Rosemount £50 per round; Lansdowne £40 per round; (£75 per day weekends; £40-£55 per round).
Cards [symbols]
Prof Charles Dernie
Designer J Braid/P Allis/D Thomas/Old Tom Morris
Facilities [symbols]
Location (off A93 Rosemount) ▶

Hotel	★★★▲▲ Kinloch House Hotel,
	BLAIRGOWRIE
	☎ 01250 884237 21 ⇄ ↑

BONNYRIGG   Map 11 NT36

Broomieknowe 36 Golf Course Rd EH19 2HZ
☎ 0131 663 9317 Fax 0131 663 2152
Easy walking mature parkland course laid out by Ben Sayers
and extended by James Braid. Elevated site with excellent
views.
18 holes, 6150yds, Par 70, SSS 70, Course record 65.
Visitors   must contact in advance.
Societies   contact for details.
Green Fees £25 day ticket; £17 per round (£20 per round
        weekends).
Prof   Mark Patchett
Designer   Ben Sayers/Hawtree
Facilities ⊗ ⅷ ⅃ ⬛ ♀ △ 🖻 ☞ ✿
Location   0.5m NE off B704

Hotel	★★ 61% Eskbank Hotel, 29 Dalhousie Rd,
	DALKEITH ☎ 0131 663 3234 16 ⇄ ↑

BRECHIN   Map 15 NO56

Brechin Trinity DD9 7PD ☎ 01356 622383
Rolling parkland course, with easy walking and good views
of Strathmore Valley and Grampian Mountains.
18 holes, 6092yds, Par 72, SSS 70, Course record 66.
Club membership 620.
Visitors   contact Professional on 01356 625270 in
        advance. Restricted weekends.
Societies   must contact club steward in advance.
Green Fees £20 per day; £15 per round (£28/£20 weekends).
Prof   Stephen Rennie
Designer   James Braid (partly)
Facilities ⊗ ⅷ ⅃ ⬛ ♀ △ 🖻 ☞ ✿ ⚓ ✿
& Leisure   squash.
Location   1m N on B966

Hotel	★★ 62% Northern Hotel, 2/4 Clerk St,
	BRECHIN ☎ 01356 625505 20rm(5 ⇄ 12 ↑)

BRIDGE OF ALLAN   Map 11 NS79

Bridge of Allan Sunnylaw FK9 4LY ☎ 01786 832332
Parkland course, very hilly with good views of Stirling
Castle and beyond to the Trossachs. Testing 1st hole, 221 yds
(par 3) uphill 6 ft wall 25 yds before green.
9 holes, 4932yds, Par 66, SSS 65, Course record 62.
Club membership 400.

Visitors   restricted Sat.
Societies   must contact in advance.
Green Fees £10 weekday (£15 weekend).
Designer   Tom Morris
Facilities ⅃ ⬛ ♀ △ ✿
Location   0.5m N off A9

Hotel	★★★ 64% Royal Hotel, Henderson St,
	BRIDGE OF ALLAN
	☎ 01786 832284 32 ⇄ ↑

BROXBURN   Map 11 NT07

Niddry Castle Castle Rd, Winchburgh EH52 6RQ
☎ 01506 891097
A 9-hole parkland course. While not very long, it requires
accurate golf to score well.
9 holes, 5514yds, Par 70, SSS 67, Course record 65.
Club membership 510.
Visitors   advisable to contact at weekends, restricted
        during competition time.
Societies   must contact in advance.
Green Fees £13 per round (£19 weekends).
Facilities ⊗ ⅷ ⅃ ⬛ ♀ △
Location   9m W of Edinburgh on B9080

Hotel	★★★ 62% Forth Bridges Hotel,
	1 Ferrymuir Gait, SOUTH QUEENSFERRY
	☎ 0131 469 9955 108 ⇄ ↑

BURNTISLAND   Map 11 NT28

Burntisland Golf House Club Dodhead, Kirkcaldy Rd
KY3 9LQ ☎ 01592 874093 (Manager) & 872116 (Pro)
Fax 01592 874093

This hill course has fine sea views.
18 holes, 5965yds, Par 70, SSS 69, Course record 62.
Club membership 800.   ▶

KINLOCH HOUSE HOTEL
AA ★★★ ◎◎◎

By Blairgowrie, Perthshire, PH10 6SG
Telephone: Blairgowrie (01250) 884 237 Fax: (01250) 884 333
Kinloch House is an award winning, family run, Country house hotel in the heart of
Sporting Perthshire. Located approximately 1½ hours from Glasgow, Edinburgh,
Inverness and Aberdeen, the hotel has 30 golf courses within an hour's drive,
including many Championship ones. Full drying facilities for clothes and equipment
are available, we would be delighted to help plan your golf and book your tee times.
Please write or telephone for a brochure *David and Sarah Shentall*

THE GLENEAGLES HOTEL

AUCHTERARDER *Perthshire & Kinross*
☎ 01764 662231 Fax 01764 694383   Map 11 NN91

John Ingham writes: Between Perth and Stirling you'll find those delightful courses, the King's and Queen's designed by James Braid and opened in 1919 to universal acclaim. There is nothing better – anywhere! They represent the best in beautiful, undulating moorland golf set alongside the massive and famous hotel – once the Caledonian Railway Hotel. The splendid Gleneagles Hotel courses are loved by its residents and for very good reasons – they are the stuff of dreams, of springy fairways, heather, bracken and pheasants that dart away when a shot misses the short grass and plunges into the wild life.

The motto there 'High Above the High' is apt as the 395 yard twelfth on the King's, named Tappit Hen (maybe it should be 'tap it in') is more than 600 feet above sea level with magnificent panoramas providing, of course, that mellow Scottish mists allow.

Only visitors to the hotel can play the courses. Years ago I stayed at the Glen with the late Henry Longhurst. 'We'll just have a quick 18 before dinner' he had said and delighted in showing me round the superb course. Since those days Jack Nicklaus has built his type of course there, the Monarch, in an American style. So now all tastes are catered for at this 5-star escape,

Without doubt the Gleneagles experience will impress any golfer and if the weather is fine, there is no better place to be. I used to go there every autumn for the Gleneagles Foursomes and at that time of the year, with the leaves golden, you feel that anything is possible.

Visitors	A handicap certificate is not required but booking is essential 8 weeks in advance.
Societies	contact for details.
Green fees	Nov-Mar £75; Apr £85; May-Oct £100; Twilight £55. ▪ ▨ ▤ ▥ ▦ ▨
Facilities	⊗ ℿ ┗ ▆ ♀ ⇔ ∆ 🏠 ⚐ ⚑ ⚒ ✀ ℓ
	Professional (Greg Schofield). Golf academy
Leisure	tennis, squash, swimming, gymnasuim, riding, fishing, shooting
Location	Perthshire PH3 1NF (2 miles SW of A823)

**63 holes. Kings: 18 holes, 6471yds, Par 68, SSS 71
Queens: 18 holes, 5965 yds, Par 68, SSS 70
Monarch: 18 holes, 6551yds, Par 72,SSS 73
Wee: 9 holes, 1481yds, Par 27**

WHERE TO STAY AND EAT NEARBY

HOTELS:

AUCHTERARDER

★ ★ ★ ★ ★ ⊛ ⊛ ⊛ The Gleneagles Hotel ☎ 01764 662231. 229 ⇆ ⋔
★★★⊛ ⊛ ▲▲77% Auchterarder House ☎ 01764 663646. 15 ⇆ ⋔
★★⊛ 74% Cairn Lodge, Orchil Road. ☎ 01764 662634. 7 ⇆ ⋔

Visitors weekend play restricted. Book by telephoning professional.
Societies apply in writing to manager.
Green Fees £25 per day; £17 per round (£37/£25 weekends).
Prof Jacky Montgomery
Designer Willie Park Jnr
Facilities ⊗ ⅲ ⅓ ⬛ ♀ ⅃ ⌂ ♉ ⚐ ↺
Location 1m E on B923

Hotel ★★ 64% Inchview Hotel, 69 Kinghorn Rd, BURNTISLAND ☎ 01592 872239 12 ⇌ ↾

BUTE, ISLE OF   Map 10 NS05

KINGARTH   Map 10 NS05

Bute Kingarth, Rothesay PA20 9HN ☎ 01700 504369
Flat seaside course with good fenced greens.
9 holes, 2497yds, Par 68, SSS 64, Course record 65.
Club membership 210.
Visitors restricted Sat until after 12.30pm.
Societies apply in advance.
Green Fees £8 per day.
Facilities ⌖
Location 1m W off A844

Hotel ★★♨ 77% Ardmory House Hotel & Restaurant, Ardmory Rd, ARDBEG ☎ 01700 502346 5 ⇌ ↾

PORT BANNATYNE   Map 10 NS06

Port Bannatyne Bannatyne Mains Rd PA20 0PH ☎ 01700 502009
Seaside hill course with panoramic views. Difficult hole: 4th (par 3).
13 holes, 5085yds, Par 68, SSS 65, Course record 63.
Club membership 200.
Visitors no restrictions.
Societies must telephone in advance.
Green Fees £12 per day; £8 per round (£17/£13 weekends).
Designer Peter Morrison
Facilities ⅓ ⬛ ⌖
Location W side of village off A844

Hotel ★★♨ 77% Ardmory House Hotel & Restaurant, Ardmory Rd, ARDBEG ☎ 01700 502346 5 ⇌ ↾

ROTHESAY   Map 10 NS06

Rothesay Canada Hill PA20 9HN ☎ 01700 503554 Fax 01700 503554
A scenic island course designed by James Braid and Ben Sayers. The course is fairly hilly, with views of the Firth of Clyde, Rothesay Bay or the Kyles of Bute from every hole. Winds are a regular feature which makes the two par 5 holes extremely challenging.
18 holes, 5395yds, Par 69, SSS 66, Course record 62.
Club membership 400.
Visitors pre-booking essential for weekends, telephone professional 01700 503554.
Societies contact in advance, booking essential at weekends.
Green Fees not confirmed.
Cards ▭▭ ▭▭ ▭▭ ▭▭ ▭▭ ▭▭

Prof James M Dougal
Designer James Braid & Ben Sayers
Facilities ⊗ ⅲ ⅓ ⬛ ♀ ⌖ ⌂ ♉ ⚐ ⚐

Hotel ★★♨ 77% Ardmory House Hotel & Restaurant, Ardmory Rd, ARDBEG ☎ 01700 502346 5 ⇌ ↾

CALLANDER   Map 11 NN60

Callander Aveland Rd FK17 8EN
☎ 01877 330090 & 330975 Fax 01877 330062
Challenging parkland course with tight fairways and a number of interesting holes. Designed by Tom Morris Snr and overlooked by the Trossachs.
18 holes, 5151yds, Par 66, SSS 66, Course record 61.
Club membership 750.
Visitors prior booking 24-48 hrs is advised in the playing season. Handicap certificate Wed/Sun.
Societies write or telephone for booking form.
Green Fees not confirmed.
Prof William Kelly
Designer Morris/Fernie
Facilities ⊗ ⅲ ⅓ ♀ ⌖ ⌂ ♉ ⚐
Location E side of town off A84

Hotel ★★★♨ 72% Roman Camp Country House Hotel, CALLANDER ☎ 01877 330003 14 ⇌ ↾

CARDENDEN   Map 11 NT29

Auchterderran Woodend Rd KY5 0NH
☎ 01592 721579
This is a relatively flat course requiring a lot of thought. There are two or three holes to test the best.
9 holes, 5250yds, Par 66, SSS 66, Course record 63.
Club membership 120.
Visitors no visitors between 7-11am & 1-3pm Sat, also some Sun in season.
Societies apply in writing.
Green Fees not confirmed.
Facilities ♀ ⌖
Location N end Cardenden, Kirkcaldy/Glenrothes road

Hotel ★★★ 65% Dean Park Hotel, Chapel Level, KIRKCALDY ☎ 01592 261635 29 ⇌ ↾ Annexe12 ⇌ ↾

CARDROSS   Map 10 NS37

Cardross Main Rd G82 5LB
☎ 01389 841754 Fax 01389 841754
Undulating parkland course, testing with good views.
18 holes, 6469yds, Par 71, SSS 72, Course record 65.
Club membership 800.
Visitors may not play at weekends unless introduced by member. Contact professional in advance 01359 841350
Societies must contact in writing.
Green Fees £35 per day; £25 per round.
Cards ▭▭ ▭▭
Prof Robert Farrell
Designer James Braid
Facilities ⊗ ⅲ ⅓ ⬛ ♀ ⌖ ⌂ ♉ ⚐
Location In centre of village on A814

Hotel   ★★ 61% Commodore Toby Hotel,
112 West Clyde St, HELENSBURGH
☎ 01436 676924   45 ⇆ ♪

CARNOUSTIE   Map 12 NO53

CARNOUSTIE   See page 339

CARNOUSTIE See page 339

CARRADALE   Map 10 NR83

Carradale PA28 6SG ☎ 01583 431335
Pleasant seaside course built on a promontory overlooking
the Isle of Arran. Natural terrain and small greens are the
most difficult natural hazards. Described as the most sporting
9-hole course in Scotland. Testing 7th hole (240 yds), par 3.
Beware of wild goats in summer.
9 holes, 2392yds, Par 66, SSS 64, Course record 64.
Club membership 320.
Visitors   no restrictions
Societies   contact in advance.
Green Fees £8 per day.
Facilities   ⏁ ♂
Location   S side of village, on B842

Hotel   ★★ 67% Seafield Hotel,
Kilkerran Rd, CAMPBELTOWN
☎ 01586 554385 3 ⇆ ♪ Annexe6 ♪

COLONSAY, ISLE OF   Map 10 NR39

LETHAM GRANGE RESORT HOTEL

AA

★★★★

Colliston by Arbroath
Angus DD11 4RL
Tel: 01241 890373 Fax: 01241 890725
E-mail: lethamgrange@sol.co.uk

Situated in the heart of Angus countryside with
many sporting and leisure pursuits on the estate,
Letham Grange offers a tranquil oasis in which
to recharge.

The main house is a beautifully restored
Victorian mansion and the Golf Estate rooms
set in the grounds offer a good quality. Friendly,
efficient staff serving a mix of Scottish and
French cuisine.

Taste of Scotland Recommended

SCALASAIG   Map 10 NR39

Colonsay Machrins Farm PA61 7YP
☎ 01951 200364 Fax 01951 200312
Traditional links course on natural machair (hard wearing
short grass), challenging, primitive. Colonsay Hotel, 2 miles
away, is the headquarters of the club, offering
accommodation and facilities.
18 holes, 4775yds, Par 72, SSS 72.
Club membership 200.
Visitors   no restrictions.
Societies   apply in writing.
Green Fees not confirmed.
Facilities   ⊗ ⫫ ♭ ➚ ♀ ⫔
Location   2m W on A870

Hotel   ★★ 70% Colonsay Hotel, SCALASAIG
☎ 01951 200316 11rm(9 ⇆ ♪)

COMRIE   Map 11 NN72

Laggan Braes PH6 2LR ☎ 01764 760055
Scenic highland course with two tricky par 3 holes.
9 holes, 6040yds, Par 70, SSS 70, Course record 62.
Club membership 315.
Visitors   apply in advance (for party bookings)
Societies   must contact in advance.
Green Fees £12 per day (£16 per day, £12 per round
weekends and bank holidays).
Designer   Col. Williamson
Facilities   ⊗ ♭ ⏁ ⫔ ➘ ♂
& Leisure   fishing.
Location   E side of village off A85

Guest   QQQ Mossgiel Guest House, Burrell St,
house   COMRIE ☎ 01764 670567 3 ♪

COWDENBEATH   Map 11 NT19

Cowdenbeath Seco Place KY4 8PD ☎ 01383 511918
A parkland-based 9-hole golf course, due to be extended to
18 holes in June 1998.
*Dora Course: 9 holes, 6552yds, Par 72, SSS 71, Course
record 68.*
Club membership 400.
Visitors   no restrictions.
Societies   must contact at least 2 weeks in advance.
Green Fees not confirmed.
Facilities   ♭ ♀ ♀ ♂
Location   6m E of Dunfermline

Hotel   ★★ 68% Woodside Hotel, High St,
ABERDOUR ☎ 01383 860328   20 ⇆ ♪

CRAIL   Map 12 NO60

Crail Golfing Society Balcomie Clubhouse, Fifeness
KY10 3XN ☎ 01333 450686 Fax 01333 450416
Perched on the edge of the North Sea on the very point
of the golfing county of Fife, the Crail Golfing Society's
course at Balcomie is picturesque and sporting. And here
again golf history has been made for Crail Golfing
Society began its life in 1786. The course is highly
thought of by students of the game both for its testing
holes and the standard of its greens. Craighead Links has
▶

panoramic seascape and country views. With wide sweeping fairways and large greens it is a testing but fair challenge, be warned there are hungry bunkers a plenty! This second links at Fifeness is set to join Balcomie as one of Scotlands's 'must play' courses.
Balcomie Links: 18 holes, 5922yds, Par 69, SSS 69.
Craighead Links: 18 holes, 6728yds, Par 71, SSS 72.
Club membership 1400.

Visitors	must contact in advance, restricted 10am-noon & 2-4.30pm.
Societies	must contact in advance, as much notice as possible for weekend play.
Green Fees	£35 per day; £22 per round (£45/£27 weekends).
Cards	
Prof	Graeme Lennie
Designer	Tom Morris
Facilities	
Location	2m NE off A917

Hotel	★★ 68% Balcomie Links Hotel, Balcomie Rd, CRAIL ☎ 01333 450237 11 ⇄ ি
Additional Guesthouse	QQQQ The Spindrift, Pittenweem Rd, ANSTRUTHER ☎ 01333 310573 Fax 01333 310573 8 ⇄ ি

CRIEFF   Map 11 NN82

Crieff Ferntower, Perth Rd PH7 3LR
☎ 01764 652909 Fax 01764 655096
This course is what you might call 'up and down' but the turf is beautiful and the highland air fresh and invigorating. There are views from the course over Strathearn. Of the two courses the Ferntower is the more challenging. Both parkland, the Dornock has one water hazard.

Ferntower Course: 18 holes, 6402yds, Par 71, SSS 71, Course record 65.
Dornock Course: 9 holes, 2387yds, Par 32, SSS 63.
Club membership 720.

Visitors	must contact professional in advance.
Societies	must contact professional in advance.
Green Fees	not confirmed.
Prof	David Murchie
Designer	James Braid
Facilities	
Location	0.5m NE on A85

Hotel	★★ 71% Murraypark Hotel, Connaught Ter, CRIEFF ☎ 01764 653731 20 ⇄ ি

CUPAR   Map 11 NO31

Cupar Hilltarvit KY15 5NZ
☎ 01334 653549 Fax 01334 653549
Hilly parkland course with fine views over north east Fife.5th/14th hole is most difficult - uphill and into the prevailing wind.
9 holes, 5500yds, Par 68, SSS 65, Course record 62.
Club membership 450.

Visitors	welcome except Sat.
Societies	must contact in advance.
Green Fees	£12 per round/day (£15 weekends). £50 per week. £25 Family ticket.
Designer	Allan Robertson
Facilities	
Location	0.75m S off A92

Hotel	★★ 69% Eden House Hotel, 2 Pitscottie Rd, CUPAR ☎ 01334 652510 9 ⇄ ি Annexe2 ⇄ ি

DALKEITH   Map 11 NT36

Newbattle Abbey Rd EH22 3AD
☎ 0131 663 2123 & 0131 663 1819 Fax 0131 654 1810
Undulating parkland course on three levels, surrounded by woods.
18 holes, 6005yds, Par 69, SSS 70, Course record 61.
Club membership 700.

Visitors	Mon-Fri ex public holidays, before 4pm.
Societies	welcome weekdays ex public holidays, before 4pm.
Green Fees	£26 per day; £17 per round.
Prof	David Torrance
Designer	S Colt
Facilities	
Location	SW side of town off A68

Hotel	★★ 61% Eskbank Hotel, 29 Dalhousie Rd, DALKEITH ☎ 0131 663 3234 16 ⇄ ি

DALMALLY   Map 10 NN12

Dalmally Old Saw Mill PA33 1AE ☎ 01838 200370
A 9-hole flat parkland course bounded by the River Orchy and surrounded by mountains. Many water hazards and bunkers.
9 holes, 2257yds, Par 64, SSS 63, Course record 64.
Club membership 100.

Visitors	no visitors on Sun between 9-10 & 1-2.

▶

CARNOUSTIE GOLF LINKS

CARNOUSTIE *Angus* ☎ **01241 853789**

Fax 01241 852720   **Map 12 NO53**

John Ingham writes: You love it, or hate it - but you respect it. Carnoustie, designed by James Braid, can be a graveyard. Simply standing up to the buffeting is bad enough, but those closing holes, across the Barry Burn (or into it) are a prospect which can gnaw at the mind. The burn twists through the links like an angry serpent and has to be crossed no fewer than seven times.

Back in 1953 they came to see Ben Hogan play in the Open Championship. This little man from Texas had a magic about him, and the huge terrifying links, the dread of any short hitter, certainly promised to be a platform on which to examine the finest golfer of his day, and maybe of any day.

Not since 1860 had any golfer won the Open on his first attempt. Certainly Hogan hadn't come to this awesome place for the money which, in those days, was a pittance. He had come to prove he was the best player in the world. That was pressure!

When Mr Hogan saw the 'Stone Age' course, dating back to the birth of the game, he was shocked because it lacked trees and colour, and looked drab. But he beat the 7200-yard monster course for the 1953 Championship, which was, as they say, something else.

'Winning the British Open at Carnoustie gave me my greatest pleasure' he told the *Fort Worth Star-Telegram.* 'Certainly the other victories were pleasurable, but none gave me the feeling, the desire to perform, that gripped me in Scotland'.

Sadly, Hogan never returned and then the great links was taken from the Open Championship rota. Now, thankfully, they have built a new clubhouse, and an International hotel is being completed. So the R&A has re-instated it for future major events, including the Open

Visitors	must contact golf links in advance. Must have a handicap certificate for Championship course
Societies	prior arrangement required either in writing or by telephone
Green fees	Championship: £60 per round. Burnside: £30 per day; £20 per round; Buddon Links: £24 per day; £16 per round. Combination day tickets: Championship & Burnside £70; Championship & Buddon Links £68; Burnside & Buddon Links £28
Facilities	⚒ ♟ Professional Lee Vannet
Location	Carnoustie DD7 7JE Links Parade (SW side of town, off A930)

54 holes. Championship Course: 18 holes, 6936 yds, Par 72, SSS 74, Course record 68)
Burnside Course: 18 holes, 6020 yds, Par 68, SSS 69
Buddon Links: 18 holes, 5420 yds, Par 66, SSS 66

WHERE TO STAY AND EAT NEARBY

HOTELS:
ARBROATH
★★ 60% Hotel Seaforth, Dundee Rd, ☎ 01241 872232. 21 (6 🛏 ⊨14 🛏)

CARNOUSTIE
★★ 69% Carlogie House, Carlogie Rd ☎ 01241 853185. 12 (2 🛏 ⊨ 10 ⊨) Annexe 4 ⊨

★★65% Hogan House, Links Pde. ☎ 01241 853273. 7(3 🛏 ⊨ 4 ⊨)

RESTAURANT:
CARNOUSTIE
🍽 11 Park Avenue. ☎ 01241 853336.

INVERKEILOR
🍽 🍽 Gordon's, Homewood House, Main St. ☎ 01241 830364.

Societies   telephone in advance.
Green Fees £10 per day.
Designer   MacFarlane Barrow Co
Facilities   🏐 by prior arrangement ☕ by prior arrangement ⛴ by arrangement ⛳ 🚹
& Leisure   fishing.
Location   On A85, 1.5m W of Dalmally

Hotel   ★★ 60% Polfearn Hotel, TAYNUILT ☎ 01866 822251 16rm(3 ⇌11 🐾)

DOLLAR   Map 11 NS99

Dollar Brewlands House FK14 7EA ☎ 01259 742400
Compact hillside course with magnificent views along the Ochil Hills.
18 holes, 5242yds, Par 69, SSS 66, Course record 62.
Club membership 470.
Visitors   weekdays course available but restricted Wed ladies day, weekends must contact in advance.
Societies   write or telephone in advance.
Green Fees £16 per day; £12 per round (£20 day/round weekends).
Designer   Ben Sayers
Facilities   ⊗ 🎿 🏐 ☕ 🍴 ⛴ 🚹 ⛳ 🐾
Location   0.5m N off A91

Hotel   ★★★ 64% Royal Hotel, Henderson St, BRIDGE OF ALLAN ☎ 01786 832284 32 ⇌ 🐾

DRYMEN   Map 11 NS48

Buchanan Castle G63 0HY
☎ 01360 660307 Fax 01360 870382
Parkland course, with easy walking and good views.
18 holes, 6086yds, Par 70, SSS 69.
Club membership 830.
Visitors   must contact in advance.
Societies   must contact in advance.
Green Fees £40 per day; £30 per round.
Cards   🔲
Prof   Keith Baxter
Designer   James Braid
Facilities   ⊗ 🎿 🏐 ☕ 🍴 ⛴ 🚹 ⛳ 🐾
Location   1m W

Hotel   ★★★ 67% Buchanan Arms Hotel, DRYMEN ☎ 01360 660588 52 ⇌ 🐾

DUNBAR   Map 12 NT67

Dunbar East Links EH42 1LT
☎ 01368 862317 Fax 01368 865202
Another of Scotland's old links. It is said that it was some Dunbar members who first took the game of golf to the North of England. A natural links course on a narrow strip of land, following the contours of the sea shore, there is a wall bordering one side and the shore on the other side making this quite a challenging course for all levels of player. The wind, if blowing from the sea, is a problem.
18 holes, 6406yds, Par 71, SSS 71, Course record 64.
Club membership 1000.
Visitors   may not play Thurs between 12.30-2 weekdays12-2 weekends or before 9.30am any day.
Societies   telephone in advance.
Green Fees not confirmed.

Prof   Derek Small
Designer   Tom Morris
Facilities   ⊗ 🎿 🏐 ☕ 🍴 ⛴ 🚹 ⛳ 🐾
Location   0.5m E off A1087

Hotel   ★★ 65% Bayswell Hotel, Bayswell Park, DUNBAR ☎ 01368 862225 13 ⇌ 🐾

Winterfield North Rd EH42 1AY ☎ 01368 863562
Seaside course with superb views.
18 holes, 5155yds, Par 65, SSS 64.
Club membership 300.

Winterfield Golf Club

Societies   must arrange in advance through professional
Green Fees £19 per day; £14.50 per round (£25/£16.50 weekends).
Prof   Kevin Phillips
Facilities   ⊗ 🎿 🏐 ☕ 🍴 ⛴ 🚹 ⛳ 🐾
Location   W side of town off A1087

Hotel   ★★ 65% Bayswell Hotel, Bayswell Park, DUNBAR ☎ 01368 862225 13 ⇌ 🐾

DUNBLANE   Map 11 NN70

Dunblane New Golf Club Perth Rd FK15 0LJ
☎ 01786 821521 Fax 01786 821522
Well maintained parkland course, with reasonably hard walking. Testing 6th and 9th holes.
18 holes, 5536yds, Par 69, SSS 67.
Club membership 1000.
Visitors   may play 9.30am-noon & 2.30-4pm Mon-Fri. Must contact in advance.
Societies   welcome Mon, Wed-Fri, contact in advance.
Green Fees £32 per day; £20 per round.
Prof   Bob Jamieson
Facilities   ⊗ 🎿 🏐 ☕ 🍴 ⛴ 🚹 ⛳ 🐾
Location   E side of town on A9

Hotel   ★★★ 🔱 Cromlix House Hotel, Kinbuck, DUNBLANE ☎ 01786 822125 14 ⇌ 🐾

DUNDEE   Map 11 NO43

Caird Park Mains Loan DD4 9BX ☎ 01382 453606
Municipal parkland course.
18 holes, 5494yds, Par 69, SSS 68, Course record 67.
Club membership 400.
Visitors   no restrictions.
Societies   must contact in advance 01382 438871.
Green Fees not confirmed.

Prof J Black
Facilities ⊗ 🏌 💪 🍴 ♟ 🏠 🎯 ♂
Location 1.5m N of city centre off A972

Hotel ★★★ 70% Swallow Hotel, Kingsway West, Invergowrie, DUNDEE
☎ 01382 641122 107 ⇔ 🐾

Camperdown Camperdown House, Camperdown Park DD2 4TF ☎ 01382 623398
Parkland course. Testing 2nd hole.
18 holes, 6548yds, Par 71, SSS 72.
Club membership 600.
Visitors must contact in advance.
Societies must contact in advance.
Green Fees not confirmed.
Facilities 🏠
& Leisure hard tennis courts.
Location 3m NW of city centre off A923

Hotel ★★★🏊 75% Old Mansion House Hotel, AUCHTERHOUSE
☎ 01382 320366 6 ⇔ 🐾

Downfield Turnberry Av DD2 3QP
☎ 01382 825595 Fax 01382 813111
A fine inland course of recent Championship rating set in undulating woodland to the north of Dundee. The Gelly burn provides a hazard for several holes.
18 holes, 6803yds, Par 73, SSS 73, Course record 65.
Club membership 750.
Visitors must contact in advance, no visitors at weekends.
Societies must contact in advance.
Green Fees £48 per day; £33 per round.
Cards 💳 💳 💳
Prof Kenny Hutton
Designer C K Cotton
Facilities ⊗ 🏌 💪 🍴 ♟ 🏠 🎯 🛒 🏌 ♂
Location N of city centre off A923

Hotel ★★★🏊 75% Old Mansion House Hotel, AUCHTERHOUSE
☎ 01382 320366 6 ⇔ 🐾

DUNFERMLINE Map 11 NT08

Canmore Venturefair Av KY12 0PE ☎ 01383 724969
Parkland course with excellent turf, ideal for 36 hole play, suitable all ages a good test of golf.
18 holes, 5376yds, Par 67, SSS 66, Course record 61.
Club membership 710.
Visitors Sat not usually available. Limited Sun. Must contact Professional in advance.
Societies apply in writing to secretary.
Green Fees £20 per day; £15 per round (£30/£20 weekends).
Prof Jim McKinnon
Designer Ben Sayers & others
Facilities ⊗ 🏌 💪 🍴 ♟ 🏠 ♂
Location 1m N on A823

Hotel ★★★ 62% King Malcolm, Queensferry Rd, DUNFERMLINE
☎ 01383 722611 48 ⇔ 🐾

Dunfermline Pitfirrane, Crossford KY12 8QW
☎ 01383 723534 & 729061
Gently undulating parkland course with interesting contours. Five Par 5's, Five Par 3's. No water hazards.
18 holes, 6237yds, Par 72, SSS 70, Course record 65.
Club membership 690.
Visitors may not play Sat. Contact to check times.
Societies must contact in advance.
Green Fees not confirmed.
Prof Steve Craig
Designer J R Stutt
Facilities ⊗ 🏌 💪 🍴 ♟ 🏠 ♂
Location 2m W on A994

Hotel ★★★ 62% King Malcolm, Queensferry Rd, DUNFERMLINE ☎ 01383 722611 48 ⇔ 🐾

Pitreavie Queensferry Rd KY11 8PR
☎ 01383 722591 Fax 01383 722591
Picturesque woodland course with panoramic view of the River Forth Valley. Testing golf.
18 holes, 6086yds, Par 70, SSS 69, Course record 65.
Club membership 700.
Visitors welcome except for competition days.
Societies must write or telephone in advance.
Green Fees £26 per day; £19 per round (£38/£24 weekends).
Prof Colin Mitchell
Designer Dr Alaistair McKenzie
Facilities ⊗ 🏌 💪 🍴 ♟ 🏠 🎯 ♂
Location SE side of town on A823

Hotel ★★★ 62% King Malcolm, Queensferry Rd, DUNFERMLINE
☎ 01383 722611 48 ⇔ 🐾

DUNKELD Map 11 NO04

Dunkeld & Birnam Fungarth PH8 0HU
☎ 01350 727524 Fax 01350 728660
Interesting heathland course with spectacular views of surrounding countryside.
9 holes, 5322yds, Par 68, SSS 66, Course record 64.
Club membership 450.
Visitors must contact in advance.
Societies apply in writing.
Green Fees not confirmed, given on application.
Facilities ⊗ 🏌 💪 🍴 ♟ 🏠 🎯 ♂ 🏌
Location 1m N of village on A923

Hotel ★★★🏊 Kinnaird, Kinnaird Estate, DUNKELD ☎ 01796 482440 9 ⇔ 🐾

DUNNING Map 11 NO01

Dunning Rollo Park PH2 0RH ☎ 01764 684747
Parkland course with a series of stone built bridges crossing a burn meandering over a large part of the course.
9 holes, 4836yds, Par 66, SSS 63, Course record 63.
Club membership 580.
Visitors Gents competitions Saturday, Ladies Tue, other than that no restrictions.
Societies must contact in advance in writing.
Green Fees £12 per round (£14 weekends).
Facilities 🍴 🏠 ♂
& Leisure hard tennis courts.
Location 1.5m off A9, 4m N of Auchterarder ▶

Hotel   ★★★ 66% Lovat Hotel, 90 Glasgow Rd,
PERTH ☎ 01738 636555   31 ⇌ ♠

Whitemoss Whitemoss Rd PH2 0QX
☎ 01738 730300 Fax 01738 730300
Undulating parkland course situated in the scenic Strathearn
Valley, ten miles from Perth (off the A9).
18 holes, 5595yds, Par 68, SSS 68, Course record 63.
Club membership 600.

Visitors   advisable to telephone in advance, visitors
welcome all week, may play 9 holes half price.
Societies   please telephone for details.
Green Fees   not confirmed.
Designer   Whitemoss Leisure
Facilities   ⊗ ⅷ ♥ ♨ 🏠 ⚐ ∂
& Leisure   practice range, chipping bunkers, practice net.
Location   Turn off A9 at Whitemoss Road junct, 3m N of
Gleneagles

Hotel   ★★ 74% Cairn Lodge, Orchil Rd,
AUCHTERARDER
☎ 01764 662634 & 662431
Fax 01764 664866 7 ⇌ ♠

DUNOON   Map 10 NS17

Cowal Ardenslate Rd PA23 8LT
☎ 01369 705673 Fax 01369 705673
Moorland course. Panoramic views of Clyde Estuary and
surrounding hills.
18 holes, 6063yds, Par 70, SSS 70, Course record 63.
Club membership 900.
Visitors   advisable to book in advance.
Societies   must telephone in advance.
Green Fees   £22 per round (£32 weekends).
Prof   Russell Weir
Designer   James Braid
Facilities   ⊗ ⅷ ⅊ ♥ ♨ 🏠 ⚐ ∂
Location   1m N

Hotel   ★★ 76% Enmore Hotel, Marine Pde, Kirn,
DUNOON ☎ 01369 702230   10 ⇌ ♠

EDINBURGH   Map 11 NT27

Baberton 50 Baberton Av, Juniper Green EH14 5DU
☎ 0131 453 4911 Fax 0131 453 4911
Parkland course.
18 holes, 6129yds, Par 69, SSS 70, Course record 64.
Club membership 900.
Visitors   may not play at weekends or after 3.30pm
weekdays. Contact in advance.

Societies   must contact in advance.
Green Fees   not confirmed.
Prof   Ken Kelly
Designer   Willie Park Jnr
Facilities   ⊗ ⅷ ♨ ♥ ⅊ ♨ 🏠 ∂
Location   5m W of city centre off A70

Hotel   ★★★★ 62% Swallow Royal Scot Hotel,
111 Glasgow Rd, EDINBURGH
☎ 0131 334 9191 259 ⇌ ♠

Braid Hills Braid Hills Approach EH10 6JZ
☎ 0131 447 6666 Fax 0131 557 5170
Municipal heathland course with superb views of Edinburgh
and the Firth of Forth, quite challenging.
Course No 1: 18 holes, 5692yds, Par 70, SSS 68.
Course No 2: 18 holes, 4602yds, Par 65.

Visitors   two courses Braids 1 & Braids 2 operate from
Apr-Sep, one course only during winter.
Societies   telephone 0131 557 5457 or apply in writing to
Edinburgh Leisure, 23 Waterloo Place,
Edinburgh EH1 3BH
Green Fees   18 holes; £9.65 peak times, £8.80 off peak.
Facilities   ♨ ⚐ ∂
& Leisure   A driving range and pro shop operate as separate
business adjacent to E end of course.
Location   2.5m S of city centre off A702

Hotel   ★★★ 70% Braid Hills Hotel, 134 Braid Rd,
Braid Hills, EDINBURGH
☎ 0131 447 8888 68 ⇌ ♠

Bruntsfield Links Golfing Society 32 Barnton Av EH4 6JH
☎ 0131 336 1479 Fax 0131 336 5538
Mature parkland course with magnificent views over the
Firth of Forth and to the west. Greens and fairways are
generally immaculate. Challenging for all categories of
handicap. The course has hosted British Senior and Boys
Championships and Scottish Youths in 1998.
18 holes, 6407yds, Par 71, SSS 71, Course record 67.
Club membership 1100.
Visitors   must telephone in advance. 0131 336 4050 or
0131 336 1479
Societies   apply in writing.
Green Fees   £50 per day; £36 per round (£55/£42 weekends).
Prof   Brian Mackenzie
Designer   Willie Park Jr
Facilities   ⊗ ⅷ ♥ ⅊ ♨ 🏠 ⚐ ♦ ⚓ ∂ ⅃
Location   4m NW of city centre off A90

Hotel   ★★★ 62% The Barnton, Queensferry Rd,
Barnton, EDINBURGH
☎ 0131 339 1144 50 ⇌ ♠

Carrick Knowe Carrick Knowe Municipal, Glendevon Park EH12 5UZ ☎ 0131 337 1096 557 5457 adv booking
Fax 0131 557 5170
Flat parkland course. Played over by two clubs, Carrick Knowe and Carrick Vale.
18 holes, 6132yds, Par 70, SSS 69.
Visitors   may be restricted at weekends.
Societies   telephone 0131 557 5457 or write to Edinburgh Leisure, 23 Waterloo Place EH1 3BH.
Green Fees £8.80 per round.
Facilities   ⛺ 🏌 ✓
Location   3m W of city centre, S of A8

Hotel   B Posthouse Edinburgh, Corstorphine Rd, EDINBURGH ☎ 0131 334 0390 303 ⇄ 🐾

Craigentinny Fillyside Rd, Lochend EH7 6RG
☎ 0131 554 7501 557 5457 adv booking
Fax 0131 557 5170
To the north east of Edinburgh, Craigentinny course is between Leith and Portobello. It is generally flat although there are some hillocks with gentle slopes. The famous Arthur's Seat dominates the southern skyline.
18 holes, 5418yds, Par 67, SSS 65.
Visitors   must contact in advance.
Societies   telephone 0131 557 5457 or apply in writing to: Edinburgh Leisure, 23 Waterloo Place EH1 3BH.
Green Fees 18 holes £9.65 peak times, £8.80 off peak.
Facilities   ⛺ 🏌 ✓
Location   NE side of city, between Leith & Portobello

Hotel   ★★★ 71% Thistle Edinburgh, 107 Leith St, EDINBURGH ☎ 0131 556 0111 143 ⇄ 🐾

Craigmillar Park 1 Observatory Rd EH9 3HG
☎ 0131 667 0047
Parkland course, with good views.
18 holes, 5851yds, Par 70, SSS 69, Course record 63.
Club membership 750.
Visitors   must contact in advance, welcome Monday-Friday and Sunday afternoons
Societies   must contact in writing.
Green Fees £25.50 per day; £17.50 per round.
Prof   B McGhee
Designer   James Braid
Facilities   ⊗ �🍽 💺 ▤ 🏆 ⛺ 🏠 🏌 🚜 ✓
Location   2m S of city centre off A7

Hotel   ★★ 68% Allison House Hotel, 15/17 Mayfield Gardens, EDINBURGH ☎ 0131 667 8049 23rm(21 🐾)

Duddingston Duddingston Rd West EH15 3QD
☎ 0131 661 7688 Fax 0131 661 4301
Parkland course with burn as a natural hazard. Testing 11th hole. Easy walking and windy.
18 holes, 6647yds, Par 71, SSS 71.
Club membership 700.
Visitors   may not play at weekends.
Societies   Tue & Thu only. Must contact in advance.
Green Fees £40 per day; £28 per round.
Cards   — 🔳 🔳 🔳 🔳 🔳
Prof   Alastair McLean
Facilities   ⊗ ⍟ 💺 ▤ 🏆 ⛺ 🏠 🏌 ✓
Location   2.5m SE of city centre off A1

Hotel   ★★★ 74% Prestonfield House Hotel, Priestfield Rd, EDINBURGH ☎ 0131 668 3346 31rm(30 ⇄ 🐾)

Kingsknowe 326 Lanark Rd EH14 2JD
☎ 0131 441 1145 Fax 0131 441 2079
Hilly parkland course with prevailing SW winds.
18 holes, 5979yds, Par 69, SSS 69, Course record 63.
Club membership 800.
Visitors   contact in advance and subject to availability of tee times.
Societies   apply in writing or telephone secretary.
Green Fees £27 per day; £21 per round (£30 per round weekends).
Prof   Andrew Marshall
Designer   A Herd/James Braid
Facilities   ⊗ ⍟ 💺 ▤ 🏆 ⛺ 🏠 🏌 🚜 ✓
Location   4m SW of city centre on A70

Hotel   ★★★ 73% Bruntsfield Hotel, 69/74 Bruntsfield Place, EDINBURGH ☎ 0131 229 1393 50 ⇄ 🐾

Liberton 297 Gilmerton Rd EH16 5UJ
☎ 0131 664 3009 (sec) & 664 1056 (pro)
Fax 0131 666 0853
Undulating, wooded parkland course.
18 holes, 5306yds, Par 67, SSS 67, Course record 61.
Club membership 675.
Visitors   must contact in advance.
Societies   must contact in writing.
Green Fees £30 per day; £17 per round (£30 per round weekends).
Cards   — 🔳 🔳
Prof   Iain Seath
Facilities   ⊗ ⍟ 💺 ▤ 🏆 ⛺ 🏠 ✓
Location   3m SE of city centre on A7

Hotel   ★★ 61% Eskbank Hotel, 29 Dalhousie Rd, DALKEITH ☎ 0131 663 3234 16 ⇄ 🐾

Lothianburn 106A Biggar Rd, Fairmilehead EH10 7DU
☎ 0131 445 2206 & 0131 445 5067
Hillside course with a 'T' shaped wooded-area, situated in the Pentland foothills. Testing in windy conditions. Fine views of Edinburgh and the Lothians.
18 holes, 5568yds, Par 71, SSS 68, Course record 66.
Club membership 850.
Visitors   weekends after 3.30pm contact professional, weekdays up to 4pm.
Societies   apply to the secretary or telephone in the first instance.
Green Fees £22 per day; £16 per round (£27/£22 weekends).
Prof   Kurt Mungall
Designer   J Braid (re-designed 1928)
Facilities   ⊗ ⍟ 💺 ▤ 🏆 ⛺ 🏠 🏌 ✓
Location   4.5m S of city centre on A702

Hotel   ★★★ 70% Braid Hills Hotel, 134 Braid Rd, Braid Hills, EDINBURGH ☎ 0131 447 8888 68 ⇄ 🐾

> Entries with a shaded background identify courses that are considered to be particularly interesting

Marriott Dalmahoy Hotel Golf & Country Club
Kirknewton EH27 8EB
☎ 0131 333 1845 Fax 0131 333 1433
Two outstanding upland courses, meandering around the
lake and across picturesque streams. The West Course is
the easier of the two whilst the trickier East Course is a
greater challenge, the par 3 15th known as the 'Wee
Wrecker' with good reason.
*East Course: 18 holes, 6638yds, Par 72, SSS 72, Course
record 63.*
*West Course: 18 holes, 5168yds, Par 68, SSS 67, Course
record 60.*
Club membership 700.
Visitors	welcome Mon-Fri, weekend by application, call in advance to book tee times, subject to availability
Societies	telephone or write for information.
Green Fees	not confirmed.
Cards	▬ ▬ ▬ ▬ ⑤
Prof	Brian Anderson/Stuart Callan
Designer	James Braid
Facilities	⊗ ⑪ ⓛ ♥ ♀ ⚘ 🏠 ⚓ ⛳ ➤ ⚑ ⚗
& Leisure	hard tennis courts, heated indoor swimming pool, squash, sauna, solarium, gymnasium.
Location	7m W of city centre on A71

Hotel	★★★★ 72% Marriott Dalmahoy Hotel & Country Club, Kirknewton, EDINBURGH ☎ 0131 333 1845 43 ⇔ ⌂ Annexe108 ⇔ ⌂

Merchants of Edinburgh 10 Craighill Gardens EH10 5PY
☎ 0131 447 1219
Testing hill course.
18 holes, 4889ydss, Par 65, SSS 64, Course record 59.
Club membership 900.
Visitors	must play with member at weekends.
Societies	must contact in secretary in writing.
Green Fees	not confirmed.
Prof	Neil Colquhoun
Designer	R G Ross
Facilities	⊗ ⑪ ⓛ ♥ ♀ ⚘ 🏠 ⛳ ⚗
Location	2m SW of city centre off A702

Hotel	★★★ 70% Braid Hills Hotel, 134 Braid Rd, Braid Hills, EDINBURGH ☎ 0131 447 8888 68 ⇔ ⌂

Mortonhall 231 Braid Rd EH10 6PB
☎ 0131 447 6974 Fax 0131 447 8712
Moorland/parkland course with views over Edinburgh.
18 holes, 6557yds, Par 72, SSS 72, Course record 66.
Club membership 525.
Visitors	advisable to contact by phone.
Societies	may not play at weekends. Must contact in writing.
Green Fees	£40 per day; £30 per round.
Prof	Douglas Horn
Designer	James Braid/F Hawtree
Facilities	ⓛ ♥ ♀ ⚘ 🏠 ⛳ ⚗
Location	3m S of city centre off A702

Hotel	★★★ 70% Braid Hills Hotel, 134 Braid Rd, Braid Hills, EDINBURGH ☎ 0131 447 8888 68 ⇔ ⌂

Murrayfield 43 Murrayfield Rd EH12 6EU
☎ 0131 337 3478 Fax 0131 313 0721
Parkland course on the side of Corstorphine Hill, with fine
views.
18 holes, 5725yds, Par 70, SSS 69.
Club membership 750.
Visitors	contact in advance, may not play at weekends.
Green Fees	not confirmed.
Prof	J J Fisher
Facilities	⊗ ⓛ ♥ ♀ ⚘ 🏠 ⛳ ⚗
Location	2m W of city centre off A8

Hotel	B Posthouse Edinburgh, Corstorphine Rd, EDINBURGH ☎ 0131 334 0390 303 ⇔ ⌂

Portobello Stanley St EH15 1JJ
☎ 0131 669 4361 557 5457 adv booking
Fax 0131 557 5170
Public parkland course, easy walking.
9 holes, 2400yds, Par 32, SSS 32.
Club membership 70.
Visitors	may not play Sat 8.30-10am & 12.30-2pm and on competition days.
Societies	contact in advance, telephone 0131 557 5457 or write to Edinburgh Leisure, 23 Waterloo Place EH1 3BH.
Green Fees	9 holes £4.83 peak times, £4.40 off peak.
Facilities	⚘ ⛳
Location	3m E of city centre off A1

Hotel	★★★ 63% Kings Manor, 100 Milton Rd East, EDINBURGH ☎ 0131 669 0444 69 ⇔ ⌂

Prestonfield Priestfield Rd North EH16 5HS
☎ 0131 667 9665
Parkland course with beautiful views.
18 holes, 6212yds, Par 70, SSS 70, Course record 62.
Club membership 850.
Visitors	contact secretary in advance.
Societies	must contact secretary.
Green Fees	not confirmed.
Cards	▬ ▬ ▬ ⑤
Prof	Graham MacDonald
Designer	James Braid
Facilities	⊗ ⑪ ⓛ ♥ ♀ ⚘ 🏠 ⛳ ⚗
Location	1.5m S of city centre off A68

Hotel	★★★ 74% Prestonfield House Hotel, Priestfield Rd, EDINBURGH ☎ 0131 668 3346 31rm(30 ⇔ ⌂)

Ravelston 24 Ravelston Dykes Rd EH4 5NZ
☎ 0131 315 2486
Parkland course.
9 holes, 5230yds, Par 66, SSS 65, Course record 64.
Club membership 610.
Visitors must contact in advance but may not play at weekends & bank holidays.
Green Fees £15 per day/round Mon-Fri.
Designer James Braid
Facilities 🅱 🍵 ⛳
Location 3m W of city centre off A90

Hotel B Posthouse Edinburgh, Corstorphine Rd, EDINBURGH ☎ 0131 334 0390 303 ⇄ 🐾

> **Royal Burgess** 181 Whitehouse Rd, Barnton EH4 6BY
> ☎ 0131 339 2075 Fax 0131 339 3712
> No mention of golf clubs would be complete without mention of the Royal Burgess, which was instituted in 1735, thus being the oldest golfing society in the world. Its course is a pleasant parkland, and one with very much variety. A club which all those interested in the history of the game should visit.
> *18 holes, 6111yds, Par 71, SSS 69.*
> *Club membership 620.*
> **Visitors** must contact in advance. Gentlemen only.
> **Societies** must contact in advance.
> **Green Fees** £50 per day; £40 per round.
> **Prof** George Yuille
> **Designer** Tom Morris
> **Facilities** ⊗ 🅱 🍵 🍸 ⛳ 🏠 🎿 ♂
> **Location** 5m W of city centre off A90
>
> **Hotel** ★★★ 62% The Barnton, Queensferry Rd, Barnton, EDINBURGH ☎ 0131 339 1144 50 ⇄ 🐾

Silverknowes Silverknowes, Parkway EH4 5ET
☎ 0131 336 3843 557 5457 adv booking
Fax 0131 557 5170
Public links course on coast overlooking the Firth of Forth.
18 holes, 6202yds, Par 71, SSS 70.
Visitors welcome.
Societies telephone 0131 557 5457 or apply in writing to: Edinburgh Leisure, 23 Waterloo Place, Edinburgh EH1 3BH.
Green Fees 18 holes; £9.65 peak times, £8.80 off peak.
Facilities ⛳ 🎿 ♂
Location 4m NW of city centre, easy access from city by-pass

Hotel ★★★ 62% The Barnton, Queensferry Rd, Barnton, EDINBURGH ☎ 0131 339 1144 50 ⇄ 🐾

Swanston 111 Swanston Rd, Fairmilehead EH10 7DS
☎ 0131 445 2239
Hillside course with steep climb at 12th & 13th holes.
18 holes, 5024yds, Par 66, SSS 65, Course record 63.
Club membership 600.
Visitors contact in advance.
Societies must contact in advance.
Green Fees not confirmed.
Prof Ian Taylor
Designer Herbert More
Facilities ⊗ 🍴 🅱 🍵 🍸 ⛳ 🏠 🎿 ♂
Location 4m S of city centre off B701

Hotel ★★★ 70% Braid Hills Hotel, 134 Braid Rd, Braid Hills, EDINBURGH ☎ 0131 447 8888 68 ⇄ 🐾

Torphin Hill Torphin Rd, Colinton EH13 0PG
☎ 0131 441 1100
Beautiful hillside, heathland course, with fine views of Edinburgh and the Forth Estuary.
18 holes, 4580mtrs, Par 67, SSS 66, Course record 63.
Club membership 550.
Visitors must contact in advance, limited access Sat & Sun (only after 2pm)
Societies must contact in advance.
Green Fees £18 per day; £12 per round (£20 per round weekends).
Cards 💳
Prof Jamie Browne
Facilities ⊗ 🍴 🅱 🍵 🍸 ⛳ 🏠
Location 5m SW of city centre S of A720

Hotel ★★★ 70% Braid Hills Hotel, 134 Braid Rd, Braid Hills, EDINBURGH ☎ 0131 447 8888 68 ⇄ 🐾

Turnhouse 154 Turnhouse Rd EH12 0AD ☎ 0131 339 1014
Hilly, parkland/heathland course, good views.
18 holes, 6171yds, Par 69, SSS 70, Course record 62.
Club membership 800.
Visitors with member only at weekends, and no visitors Wed or Medal days. Must contact professional in advance.
Societies must contact in writing.
Green Fees £25 per day, £16 per round.
Prof John Murray
Designer J Braid
Facilities ⊗ 🍴 🅱 🍵 🍸 ⛳ 🏠 🎿 ♂
Location 6m W of city centre N of A8 ▶

Hotel ★★★ 62% The Barnton,
Queensferry Rd, Barnton, EDINBURGH
☎ 0131 339 1144 50 ⇌ ♥

EDZELL   Map 15 NO66

Edzell High St DD9 7TF
☎ 01356 647283 (Secretary) Fax 01356 648094
This delightful course is situated in the foothills of the
Scottish Highlands and provides good golf as well as
conveying to everyone who plays there a feeling of
peace and quiet. The village of Edzell is one of the most
picturesque in Scotland.
18 holes, 6348yds, Par 71, SSS 71, Course record 62.
Club membership 750.

Visitors	may not play 4.45-6.15 weekdays & 7.30-10, 12-2 weekends. Not before 2pm on 1st Sat each month.
Societies	must contact secretary at least 14 days in advance.
Green Fees	£31 per day; £21 per round (£41/£27 weekends).
Prof	A J Webster
Designer	Bob Simpson
Facilities	⊗ ⅲ ⅼ 🛢 ⅋ 🛆 🏠 ⅋ ⅄ 🏌 ∅ ⅼ
Location	S side of village on B966

Hotel ★★★ 62% Glenesk Hotel, High St,
EDZELL ☎ 01356 648319 24 ⇌ ♥

ELIE   Map 12 NO40

Golf House Club KY9 1AS
☎ 01333 330301 Fax 01333 330895
One of Scotland's most delightful holiday courses with
panoramic views over the Firth of Forth. Some of the
holes out towards the rocky coastline are splendid. This
is the course which has produced many good
professionals, including the immortal James Braid.
18 holes, 6273yds, Par 70, SSS 70, Course record 62.
Club membership 600.

Visitors	advisable to contact in advance, limited availability Sat May-Sep and no visitors Sun May-Sep, ballot in operation for tee times during July and August
Societies	must contact in advance.
Green Fees	£45 per day; £32 per round (£55/£40 weekends).
Prof	Robin Wilson
Designer	James Braid
Facilities	⊗ ⅲ ⅼ 🛢 ⅋ 🛆 🏠 ⅋ ∅ ⅼ
& Leisure	hard tennis courts.
Location	W side of village off A917

Golf Hotel

Hotel ★★★ 65% The Golf Hotel, Bank St, ELIE
☎ 01333 330209 22 ⇌ ♥

ERISKA   Map 10 NM94

Isle of Eriska PA37 1SD
☎ 01631 720371 Fax 01631 720531
This remote and most beautiful 6-hole course, set around the
owners hotel, is gradually being upgraded to a testing 9-hole
challenge, complete with stunning views.
6 holes, 1588yds, Par 22.
Club membership 40.

Visitors	contact in advance.
Green Fees	£7.50.
Cards	🖂 🖂 🖂 🖂 🖂
Designer	H Swan
Facilities	ⅼ 🛢 ⅋ 🛆 🏌 🏠 ∅ ⅼ
& Leisure	hard tennis courts, heated indoor swimming pool, sauna, gymnasium.
Location	A828 Connel/Fort William, signposted 4m from North of Benderloch village

Hotel ★★★♨♨ Isle of Eriska, Eriska, BY OBAN
☎ 01631 720371 17 ⇌ ♥

FALKIRK   Map 11 NS88

Falkirk Carmuirs, 136 Stirling Rd, Camellon FK2 7YP
☎ 01324 611061 Fax 01324 639573
Parkland course with trees, gorse and streams.
18 holes, 6230yds, Par 71, SSS 70, Course record 66.
Club membership 800.

Visitors	telephone starter 01324 612219, visiting parties only on Sun. May not play Sat.
Societies	telephone 01324 612219 in advance.
Green Fees	£20 per day; £15 per round (£30 per day Sun).
Designer	James Braid
Facilities	⊗ ⅲ ⅼ 🛢 ⅋ 🛆 🏠 ∅
Location	1.5m W on A9

Hotel ★★★★ 68% Inchyra Grange Hotel,
Grange Rd, POLMONT
☎ 01324 711911 109 ⇌ ♥

FALKLAND   Map 11 NO20

Falkland The Myre KY15 7AA
☎ 01337 857404
A flat, well kept course with excellent greens and views of
East Lomond Hill and Falkland Palace.
9 holes, 5216yds, Par 68, SSS 65, Course record 62.
Club membership 300.

Visitors	parties must make prior arrangements, please check availability at weekends.
Societies	must contact in advance.
Green Fees	£7.50 per day, £5 per round (£10/£8 weekends).
Facilities	⊗ ⅲ ⅼ 🛢 ⅋ 🛆
Location	N side of town on A912

Hotel ★★ 67% Lomond Hills Hotel,
Parliament Square, FREUCHIE
☎ 01337 857329 & 857498
Fax 01337 858180 25 ⇌ ♥

FAULDHOUSE   Map 11 NS96

Greenburn 6 Greenburn Rd EH47 9HG ☎ 01501 770292
Exposed rolling course with sparse tree cover. Water hazards
from a pond and a burn.
18 holes, 6045yds, Par 71, SSS 70, Course record 65.
Club membership 900.
Visitors   contact in advance for details.
Societies   by prior arrangement.
Green Fees   not confirmed.
Prof   Malcolm Leighton
Facilities   ⊗ ⊪ 🝙 🍺 🍴 ⚲ ♂
Location   3m SW of Whitburn

Hotel   ★★★ 67% The Hilcroft Hotel, East Main St,
                  WHITBURN ☎ 01501 740818 31 ⇋ ℞

FORFAR   Map 15 NO45

Forfar Cunninghill, Arbroath Rd DD8 2RL
☎ 01307 463773 Fax 01307 468495
Moorland course with wooded, undulating fairways and fine
views.
18 holes, 6053yds, Par 69, SSS 70, Course record 61.
Club membership 820.
Visitors   may not play before 2.30pm Sat.
Societies   must contact in advance.
Green Fees   £25 per day; £17 per round (£30/£22 weekends
                  & bank holidays).
Prof   Peter McNiven
Designer   James Braid
Facilities   ⊗ ⊪ 🝙 🍺 🍴 ⚲ ♂
Location   1.5m E of Forfar on A932

Hotel   ★★★👪 66% Idvies House Hotel, Letham,
                  FORFAR ☎ 01307 818787 11 ⇋ ℞

GIFFORD   Map 12 NT56

Gifford Edinburgh Rd EH41 4JE ☎ 01620 810267
Parkland course, with easy walking.
9 holes, 6243yds, Par 71, SSS 70, Course record 64.
Club membership 400.
Visitors   restricted weekends, not after 4pm Sat & noon
                  Sun.
Societies   telephone in advance.
Green Fees   £15 per day; £12 per round.
Facilities   🍺 ⚲ ♂
Location   1m SW off B6355

Hotel   ★★ 72% Tweeddale Arms Hotel, GIFFORD
                  ☎ 01620 810240 16 ⇋ ℞

GIGHA ISLAND   Map 10 NR64

Gigha PA41 7AA
☎ 01583 505287 01583 505254 Fax 01583 505244
A 9-hole course with scenic views of the Sound of Gigha to the
east and to the north the Kilberry Hills. The 9th hole is a good
par 3, especially with a strong blow of wind from the west.
9 holes, 5042 yds, Par 66, SSS 65.
Club membership 40.
Visitors   no restrictions.
Societies   telephone for details.
Green Fees   £10 per day/round.
Facilities   ⊯
Location   0.5m N of Druimeonbeg farm shop

GLENROTHES   Map 11 NO20

Glenrothes Golf Course Rd KY6 2LA ☎ 01592 754561
Mature parkland, challenging back nine with burn crossing 4
fairways. Wide fairways offer opportunities for long hitters
and birdy chances for those with good short game.
18 holes, 6444yds, Par 71, SSS 71, Course record 67.
Club membership 750.
Visitors   no restrictions except for some times at
                  weekends . Bookings for parties can be made in
                  advance.
Societies   write to secretary.
Green Fees   not confirmed.
Designer   J R Stutt
Facilities   ⊗ ⊪ 🝙 🍺 🍴 ⚲
Location   W side of town off B921

Hotel   ★★★★👪 Balbirnie House, Balbirnie Park,
                  MARKINCH ☎ 01592 610066 30 ⇋ ℞

GLENSHEE (SPITTAL OF)   Map 15 NO16

Dalmunzie Dalmunzie Estate PH10 7QG
☎ 01250 885226 Fax 01250 885225
Well maintained Highland course with difficult walking.
Testing short course with small but good greens.   ▶

9 holes, 2035yds, Par 30, SSS 30.
Club membership 70.
Visitors restricted Sun 10.30-11.30am.
Societies advance contact preferred.
Green Fees £10 per day; £7 per 9 holes; £40 per week.
Facilities ⊗ ⊪ ⓑ ♥ ♀ 🏠 🍴 🏌
& Leisure hard tennis courts, fishing, mountain bike hire,
pony trekking.
Location 2m NW of Spittal of Glenshee

Hotel ★★♨ 68% Dalmunzie House Hotel,
SPITTAL OF GLENSHEE
☎ 01250 885224 18rm(16 ⇄ ♠)
See advertisement on page 347.

GOREBRIDGE   Map 11 NT36

Vogrie Vogrie Estate Country Park EH23 4NU
☎ 01875 821716
A 9-hole municipal course located within a country park.
The wide fairways are particularly suited to beginners.
9 holes, 2530yds, Par 33.
Visitors book by telephone 24 hrs in advance.
Green Fees not confirmed.
Facilities ⚐
Location Off B6372

Hotel ★★★ 64% The Johnstounburn House,
HUMBIE ☎ 01875 833696
11rm(10 ⇄ ♠) Annexe9 ⇄ ♠

GOUROCK   Map 10 NS27

Gourock Cowal View PA19 1HD
☎ 01475 631001 Fax 01475 631001
Moorland course with hills and dells. Testing 8th hole, par 5.
Magnificent views over Firth of Clyde.
18 holes, 6512yds, Par 73, SSS 73, Course record 64.
Club membership 720.
Visitors must have handicap certificate or letter of
introduction. May not play Sat.
Societies welcome weekdays, must contact in advance.
Green Fees not confirmed.
Prof Gavin Coyle
Designer J Braid/H Cotton
Facilities ⓑ ♥ ♀ ⚐ 🏠 🍴 ✓
Location SW side of town off A770

Hotel ★★★ 63% Manor Park Hotel, LARGS
☎ 01475 520832
10 ⇄ ♠ Annexe13 ⇄ ♠

GREENOCK   Map 10 NS27

Greenock Forsyth St PA16 8RE ☎ 01475 720793
Testing moorland course with panoramic views of Clyde
Estuary.
18 holes, 5838yds, Par 69, SSS 69.
Club membership 730.
Visitors may not play Sat. Must contact in advance and
have a handicap certificate.
Societies must telephone in advance.
Green Fees not confirmed.
Prof Graham Ross
Designer James Braid
Facilities ⊗ ⊪ ⓑ ♥ ♀ ⚐ 🏠 ✓
Location SW side of town off A770

Hotel ★★★ 63% Manor Park Hotel, LARGS
☎ 01475 520832 10 ⇄ ♠ Annexe13 ⇄ ♠

Greenock Whinhill Beith Rd PA16 9LN
☎ 01475 724694 evenings & weekends only
Picturesque heathland public course.
18 holes, 5504yds, Par 68, SSS 68, Course record 64.
Club membership 200.
Visitors may only use club facilities with member.
Green Fees not confirmed.
Facilities ♀ ⚐
Location 1.5m SW off B7054

Hotel ★★★ 63% Manor Park Hotel, LARGS
☎ 01475 520832 10 ⇄ ♠ Annexe13 ⇄ ♠

GULLANE   Map 12 NT48

Gullane West Links Rd EH31 2BB
☎ 01620 842255 Fax 01620 842327
Gullane is a delightful village and one of Scotland's
great golf centres. Gullane club was formed in 1882.
There are three Gullane courses and the No 1 is of
championship standard. It differs from most Scottish
courses in as much as it is of the upland links type and
really quite hilly. The first tee is literally in the village.
The views from the top of the course are magnificent and
stretch far and wide in every direction - in fact, it is said
that 14 counties can be seen from the highest spot.
*Course No 1: 18 holes, 6466yds, Par 71, SSS 72, Course
record 66.*
*Course No 2: 18 holes, 6244yds, Par 71, SSS 70, Course
record 63.*
Course No 3: 18 holes, 5252yds, Par 68, SSS 66.
Club membership 1200.
Visitors advance booking recommended.
Societies advance booking advised.
Green Fees £56 weekdays; £70 weekends.
Cards 💳 🎫 💳 📇 🎫 💳
Prof Jimmy Hume
Designer Willie Park
Facilities ⊗ ⊪ ⓑ ♥ ♀ ⚐ 🏠 🍴 🎿 ♞ ✓ ⓣ
Location At west end of village on A198

Hotel ★★★♨ Greywalls Hotel,
Muirfield, GULLANE
☎ 01620 842144 17 ⇄ ♠ Annexe5 ⇄ ♠

MUIRFIELD (HONOURABLE COMPANY OF EDINBURGH GOLFERS See page 349

HADDINGTON   Map 12 NT57

Haddington Amisfield Park EH41 4PT
☎ 01620 823627 Fax 01620 826058
Inland course, tree-lined and bunkered, but not hilly.
18 holes, 6317yds, Par 71, SSS 70, Course record 68.
Club membership 650.
Visitors may not play between 7am-10am & noon-2pm
at weekends. Must contact in advance.
Societies must contact in advance; deposits required.
Green Fees not confirmed.
Prof John Sandilands
Facilities ⊗ ⊪ ⓑ ♥ ♀ ⚐ 🏠 ♞ 🎿 ✓
Location E side off A613   ▶

MUIRFIELD
(Honourable Company of Edinburgh Golfers)

GULLANE *East Lothian* ☏ 01620 842123
Fax 01620 842977   Map 12 NT 48

*J*ohn Ingham writes: Ask an American superstar to name the best golf course in Great Britain, or maybe even in the entire world, and the likely answer will be Muirfield. It certainly features in the top ten of any meaningful selection.

Purely on shape and balance, the course has everything. Ask competitors in the Open Championship what they think of the last nine holes, and they will tell you it can wreck the stoutest heart. But ask Isoa Aoki of Japan what he thinks, and he will smile and maybe tell of his course record 63 here.

The course was designed by Old Tom Morris in 1891. However, the club was founded in 1744, making it just ten years older than the Royal & Ancient itself but not as old as Royal Blackheath. However, these dates show that Muirfield certainly has seniority and tradition. Quite simply, it is exclusive and entirely excellent. Muirfield has staged some outstanding Open Championships with one, I suspect, standing out in people's minds more than any other.

Back in 1972, Tony Jacklin was Europe's best player and looked set to prove it again at Muirfield when he had appeared to wear down Lee Trevino, the defending champion. At the 71st hole, Trevino seemed to be frittering away strokes as he mis-hit a shot downwind through the dry, fast, green. The next few minutes were truly hair-raising 'I was mad' recalled Trevino. 'My next shot from the bank was strictly a give-up one. And the ball went straight in the hole.' Jacklin had chipped up, well short. Then he missed his putt, turned for the return putt, and missed again. We all did mental arithmetic. Jacklin had blown it and when he bogeyed the last, furious at himself, he suddenly wasn't the winner - Trevino was.

Those of us who were there recall Trevino had holed one bunker shot, and chipped in three times. Muirfield looked on his brilliance with favour and sad Jacklin never won an Open again.

Visitors	contact in advance Tue & Thur only, handicap no greater than 18 for men; 24 for ladies.
Societies	telephone in advance. Tue and Thur only. No more than 12 in a group.
Green fees	£95 per day; £70 per round
Facilities	⊗ ☕ ♀ ♨ ⛳ ♂
Location	Muirfield, Gullane EH31 2EG (off A198 on NE side of village)

18 holes, 6601 yards, Par 70, SSS 73, Course record 63

WHERE TO STAY AND EAT NEARBY

HOTELS:

ABERLADY
★★ 68% Kilspindie House, Main St. ☏ 01875 870682. 26 (8 ♠ 18 ⇆ ♠)

DIRLETON
★★★ ⊛ ⊛ 67% The Open Arms. ☏ 01620 850241. 10 ⇆ ♠

GULLANE
★★★ ⊛ ⊛ ♨ Greywalls, Muirfield. ☏ 01620 842144. 17 (1 ♠ ⇆ 16 ⇆) Annexe 5 ⇆ ♠

NORTH BERWICK
★★★ 64% The Marine, Cromwell Rd. ☏ 01620 892406. 83 ⇆ ♠

★60% Nether Abbey, 20 Dirleton Ave. ☏ 01620 892802. 16 (4 ⇆ 6 ♠)

RESTAURANT:

GULLANE
⊛ ⊛ ⊛ La Potinière, Main St. ☏ 01620 843214.

Hotel ★★ 72% Tweeddale Arms Hotel, GIFFORD
☎ 01620 810240 16 ⇌ ♞

HELENSBURGH · Map 10 NS28

Helensburgh 25 East Abercromby St G84 9HZ
☎ 01436 674173 Fax 01436 671170
Sporting moorland course with superb views of Loch
Lomond and River Clyde.
18 holes, 6104yds, Par 69, SSS 70, Course record 64.
Club membership 880.
Visitors may not play at weekends.
Societies weekdays only, must contact in writing.
Green Fees £30 per day; £20 per round.
Cards ▭ ▬ ▭ ▨
Prof David Fotheringham
Designer Old Tom Morris
Facilities ⊗ ⫴ ⫼ 🏋 🍺 ♀ ⌂ 🏌 ∅
Location NE side of town off B832

Hotel ★★ 61% Commodore Toby Hotel,
112 West Clyde St, HELENSBURGH
☎ 01436 676924 45 ⇌ ♞

INNELLAN · Map 10 NS17

Innellan Knockamillie Rd PA23 7SG
☎ 01369 830242 & 702573
Situated above the village of Innellan, this undulating hilltop
course has extensive views of the Firth of Clyde.
9 holes, 4683yds, Par 64, SSS 64, Course record 63.
Club membership 199.
Visitors welcome but may not play after 5pm on
Mondays.
Societies telephone initially.
Green Fees £12 per day.
Facilities 🏋 🍺 ♀ 🏌
Location 4m S of Dunoon

Hotel ★★ 68% Royal Marine Hotel,
Hunters Quay, DUNOON ☎ 01369 705810
28 ⇌ ♞ Annexe10 ⇌ ♞

INVERARAY · Map 10 NN00

Inveraray North Cromalt PA32 8XT ☎ 01499 302140
Testing parkland course with beautiful views overlooking
Loch Fyne.
9 holes, 5790yds, Par 70, SSS 68, Course record 69.
Club membership 178.
Visitors none
Societies write or telephone to the secretary.
Green Fees £10 per day.
Facilities ⌂
Location 1m S of Inveraray

ISLAY, ISLE OF · Map 10 NR34

PORT ELLEN · Map 10 NR34

Machrie Hotel Machrie PA42 7AN
☎ 01496 302310 Fax 01496 302404
Championship links course opened in 1891, where golf's
first £100 Open Championship was played in 1901. Fine
turf and many blind holes. Par 4.

18 holes, 6226yds, Par 71, SSS 71, Course record 65.
Club membership 340.
Visitors no restrictions.
Societies apply in writing or telephone.
Green Fees £32.50 per day; £25 per round.
Cards ▭ ▬ ▭ ▨
Designer W Campbell
Facilities ⊗ ⫴ 🏋 🍺 ♀ ⌂ 🏌 🛏 ∅ ♟
& Leisure fishing, snooker, pool tables, carpet bowls.
Location 4m N off A846

Hotel ★★ 59% Lochside Hotel, 19 Shore St,
BOWMORE ☎ 01496 810244 8 ⇌ ♞

KENMORE · Map 14 NN74

Kenmore PH15 2HN ☎ 01887 830226 Fax 01887 830211
Testing course in mildly undulating natural terrain. Beautiful
views in tranquil setting by Loch Tay.
9 holes, 6052yds, Par 70, SSS 69, Course record 69.
Club membership 200.
Visitors advance booking advisable.
Societies telephone in advance.
Green Fees £17 per day; £12 per 18 holes; £8.50 per 9 holes
(£18/£13/£10 weekends).
Cards ▭ ▨
Designer Robin Menzies
Facilities ⊗ ⫴ 🏋 🍺 ♀ ⌂ 🏌 🛏 ♙ 🛒 ∅
& Leisure fishing.
Location On A827, beside Kenmore Bridge

Hotel ★★ 63% Fortingall Hotel, FORTINGALL
☎ 01887 830367 & 830368
Fax 01887 830367 10 ⇌ ♞

Taymouth Castle Taymouth Castle Estate PH15 2NT
☎ 01887 830228 Fax 01887 830830
Parkland course set amidst beautiful mountain and loch
scenery. Easy walking. Fishing.
18 holes, 6066yds, Par 69, SSS 69, Course record 62.
Club membership 250.
Visitors parties must book in advance to avoid busy
times.
Societies should contact in advance.
Green Fees £28 per day; £18 round (£38/£22 weekends).
Prof Alex Marshall
Designer James Braid
Facilities ⊗ ⫴ 🏋 🍺 ♀ ⌂ 🏌 🛏 ♙ 🛒 ∅
& Leisure hard tennis courts, fishing.
Location 1m E on A827, 5m W of Aberfeldy

Hotel ★★ 63% Fortingall Hotel, FORTINGALL
☎ 01887 830367 & 830368
Fax 01887 830367 10 ⇌ ♞

KILLIN · Map 11 NN53

Killin FK21 8TX ☎ 01567 820312
Parkland course with good views. Glorious setting.
9 holes, 2600yds, Par 66, SSS 65, Course record 61.
Club membership 250.
Visitors may not play competition days, parties must
book in advance.
Societies previous record of courses visited required.
Apply in writing or telephone in advance.
Green Fees not confirmed.

Designer	John Duncan
Facilities	⊗ 〗🍴 🍺 ⬛ ♀ 🛆 🏠 ⛴ ❦ 🛒 ♂
Location	1m N on A827

Hotel   ★★★ 64% Dall Lodge Country House Hotel, Main St, KILLIN ☎ 01567 820217 10 ⇨ ☞

KILMACOLM   Map 10 NS36

Kilmacolm Porterfield Rd PA13 4PD
☎ 01505 872139 Fax 01505 874007
Moorland course, easy walking, fine views. Testing 7th, 13th and 14th holes.
18 holes, 5961yds, Par 69, SSS 69, Course record 64.
Club membership 850.

Visitors	must contact in advance, visitors welcome Tuesday, Wednesday & Thursday.
Societies	apply in writing.
Green Fees	not confirmed.
Prof	David Stewart
Designer	Willie Campbell
Facilities	⊗ 〗🍴 ⬛ ♀ 🛆 🏠 ♂
Location	SE side of town off A761

Hotel   ★★★★🏅 69% Gleddoch House Hotel, LANGBANK ☎ 01475 540711 39 ⇨ ☞

KINCARDINE   Map 11 NS98

Tulliallan Alloa Rd FK10 4BB
☎ 01259 730798 Fax 01259 730798
Pleasant parkland course with easily negotiable slopes, a meandering burn and scenic views.
18 holes, 5965yds, Par 69, SSS 69.
Club membership 600.

Visitors	restricted at weekends, must contact professional shop
Societies	may not play on Sat; must contact in advance.
Green Fees	£27.50 per day, £15 per round (£35/£20 weekends).
Prof	Steven Kelly
Facilities	⊗ 〗🍴 ⬛ ♀ 🛆 🏠 ⛴ ♂
Location	1m NW on A977

Hotel   ★★★ 64% Dall Lodge Country House Hotel, Main St, KILLIN ☎ 01567 820217 10 ⇨ ☞

KINGHORN   Map 11 NT28

Kinghorn Macduff Cres KY3 9RE ☎ 01592 890345
Municipal course, 300 ft above sea level with views over Firth of Forth and North Sea. Undulating and quite testing. Facilities shared by Kinghorn Ladies.
18 holes, 5269yds, Par 65, SSS 67.
Club membership 190.

Visitors	no restrictions.
Societies	must contact in writing.
Green Fees	not confirmed.
Facilities	⊗ by prior arrangement 〗 by prior arrangement 🍺 by prior arrangement ⬛ by prior arrangement ♀ 🛆
Location	S side of town on A921

Hotel   ★★★ 65% Dean Park Hotel, Chapel Level, KIRKCALDY ☎ 01592 261635 29 ⇨ ☞ Annexe12 ⇨ ☞

KINROSS   Map 11 N010

Green Hotel 2 The Muirs KY13 8AS
☎ 01577 863407 Fax 01577 863180
Two interesting and picturesque parkland courses, with easy walking.
Red Course: 18 holes, 6256yds, Par 73, SSS 71.
Blue Course: 18 holes, 6438yds, Par 71, SSS 72.
Club membership 600.

Visitors	must contact in advance.
Societies	must contact in advance.
Green Fees	£25 per day, £15 per round (£35/25 weekends).
Prof	Stuart Geraghty
Designer	Sir David Montgomery
Facilities	⊗ 〗🍴 🍺 ⬛ ♀ 🛆 🏠 ⛴ ❦ 🛒 ♂
& Leisure	hard tennis courts, heated indoor swimming pool, squash, fishing, sauna, solarium, small fitness area in hotel.
Location	NE side of town on B996

Hotel   ★★★ 73% Green Hotel, 2 The Muirs, KINROSS ☎ 01577 863467 47 ⇨ ☞

KIRKCALDY   Map 11 NT29

Dunnikier Park Dunnikier Way KY1 3LP
☎ 01592 261599
Parkland, rolling fairways, not heavily bunkered, views of Firth of Forth.
18 holes, 6036metres, Par 72, SSS 72, Course record 65.
Club membership 720.

Visitors	visitors must contact course starter in person.
Societies	apply in writing. ▶

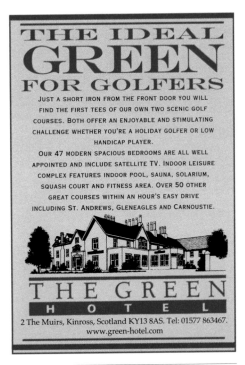

Green Fees £18 per day; £12 per round (£22/£16 weekends).
Prof   Gregor Whyte
Designer   R Stutt
Facilities   ⊗ ⊪ ⅃ ☕ ⌺ ⚑ 🛏 🛒 ♿
Location   2m N on B981

Hotel   ★★★ 65% Dean Park Hotel, Chapel Level,
KIRKCALDY ☎ 01592 261635
29 ⇋ ₨ Annexe12 ⇋ ₨

Kirkcaldy Balwearie Rd KY2 5LT
☎ 01592 205240 & 203258 (Pro Shop)
Challenging parkland course in rural setting, with beautiful
views. On-course watering ensures good conditions all
season.
18 holes, 6004yds, Par 71, SSS 69, Course record 65.
Club membership 822.
Visitors   limited play Sat. Advised to contact pro-shop
01592 203258.
Societies   telephone bookings.
Green Fees £22 per day; £16 per round (£32/£22 weekends).
Prof   Anthony Caira
Facilities   ⊗ ⊪ ⅃ ☕ ⌺ ⚑ 🛒 ♿
Location   SW side of town off A910

Hotel   ★★★ 65% Dean Park Hotel, Chapel Level,
KIRKCALDY ☎ 01592 261635
29 ⇋ ₨ Annexe12 ⇋ ₨

KIRRIEMUIR   Map 15 NO35

Kirriemuir Shielhill Rd, Northmuir DD8 4LN
☎ 01575 573317 Fax 01575 573317
Parkland and heathland course set at the foot of the Angus
glens, with good view.
18 holes, 5553yds, Par 68, SSS 67, Course record 62.
Club membership 750.
Visitors   must play with member at weekends.
Societies ·· must apply in advance, may not play weekends.
Green Fees £24 per day; £18 per round.
Prof   Karyn Dallas
Designer   James Braid
Facilities   ⊗ ⊪ ⅃ ☕ ⌺ ⚑ ♿
Location   1m N off B955

Hotel   ★★★♨ 66% Idvies House Hotel, Letham,
FORFAR ☎ 01307 818787   11 ⇋ ₨

LADYBANK   Map 11 NO30

Ladybank Annsmuir KY15 7RA
☎ 01337 830814 Fax 01337 831505
Picturesque parkland/heathland course, popular with visitors.
Qualifying course for the British Open.
18 holes, 6641yds, Par 71, SSS 72, Course record 63.
Club membership 900.
Visitors   advance booking essential.
Societies   must telephone or write in advance.
Green Fees £40 per day; £28 per round (£35 per round
weekends, no advance booking, very limited).
Cards   ⚊ ▭ ▯
Prof   Martin Gray
Facilities   ⊗ ⊪ ⅃ ☕ ⌺ ⚑ 🛒 ♿
Location   N side of village off B9129

Hotel   ★★★ 63% Fernie Castle, Letham,
LADYBANK ☎ 01337 810381   15 ⇋ ₨

LARBERT   Map 11 NS88

Falkirk Tryst 86 Burnhead Rd FK5 4BD
☎ 01324 562054 & 562415
Links-type course, fairly level with trees and broom, well-
bunkered. Winds can affect play.
18 holes, 6053yds, Par 70, SSS 69, Course record 62.
Club membership 850.
Visitors   must contact in advance no play at weekends.
Societies   visitors welcome Mon-Fri must book or
telephone.
Green Fees £25 per day; £17 per round.
Prof   Steven Dunsmore
Facilities   ⊗ ⊪ ⅃ ☕ ⌺ ⚑ ♿
Location   On A88 between A9 and A905

Hotel   ★★★★ 68% Inchyra Grange Hotel, Grange
Rd, POLMONT ☎ 01324 711911 109 ⇋ ₨

Glenbervie Clubhouse Stirling Rd FK5 4SJ
☎ 01324 562605 Fax 01324 551054
Parkland course with good views.
18 holes, 6423yds, Par 71, SSS 70, Course record 64.
Club membership 600.
Visitors   Mon to Fri till 4pm, parties Tues & Thurs only
Societies   Tue & Thu only. Apply in writing.
Green Fees £47 per day; £32 per round.
Cards   ▭ ▯
Prof   John Chillas
Designer   James Braid
Facilities   ⊗ ⅃ ☕ ⌺ ⚑ ♿
Location   2m NW on A9

Hotel   ★★★★ 68% Inchyra Grange Hotel, Grange
Rd, POLMONT ☎ 01324 711911 109 ⇋ ₨

LESLIE   Map 11 NO20

Leslie Balsillie Laws KY6 3EZ ☎ 01592 620040
Challenging parkland course.
9 holes, 4686yds, Par 63, SSS 64, Course record 63.
Club membership 230.
Visitors   contact secretary in writing.
Societies   letter to the Secretary.
Green Fees £8.50 per day (£10.50 weekends).
Designer   Tom Morris
Facilities   ☕ ⌺ ⚑
Location   N side of town off A911

LEUCHARS   Map 12 NO42

Drumoig Hotel & Golf Course Drumoig KY16 0BE
☎ 01382 541800 Fax 01382 542211
A developing but challenging young championship course.
Set in a parkland environment, the course is links like in
places. Features include Whinstone Quarries and views over
to St Andrews and Carnoustie. Water features are
demanding, especially on the 9th where the fairway runs
between Drumoigs two mini lochs.
18 holes, 7006yds, Par 72, SSS 73.
Club membership 200.
Visitors   advisable to telephone in advance.
Societies   telephone in advance.
Green Fees £22 per round (£28 weekends).
Cards   ⚊ ▭ ▭ ▯ ▮
Facilities   ⊗ ⊪ ⅃ ☕ ⌺ ⚑ 🛏 🛒 ♿

& Leisure Scottish National Golf Centre in grounds.
Location On the A914 between St Andrews and Dundee

Hotel ★★★ 70% Drumoig Golf Hotel, Drumoig, LEUCHARS
☎ 01382 541800 Annexe24 ⇌ ↑

St Michaels KY16 0DX
☎ 01334 839365 & 838666 Fax 01334 838666
Parkland course with open views over Fife and Tayside. The undulating course weaves its way through tree plantations. The short Par 4 17th, parallel to the railway and over a pond to a stepped green, poses an interesting challenge.
18 holes, 5802yds, Par 70, SSS 68, Course record 68.
Club membership 550.
Visitors may not play on Sun before noon.
Societies must apply in writing, limited weekends
Green Fees £25 per day; £18 per round (£27.50/£20 weekends).
Facilities ⊗ ⫿ by prior arrangement ᕪ 🍺 ♀ 占 ✓
Location NW side of village on A919

Hotel ★★ 69% Eden House Hotel, 2 Pitscottie Rd, CUPAR
☎ 01334 652510 9 ⇌ ↑ Annexe2 ⇌ ↑

LEVEN   Map 11 NO30

Leven Links The Promenade KY8 4HS
☎ 01333 428859 & 421390 Fax 01333 428859
Leven has the classic ingredients which make up a golf links in Scotland; undulating fairways with hills and hallows, out of bounds and a 'burn' or stream. A top class championship links course used for British Open final qualifying stages, it has fine views over Largo Bay.
18 holes, 6436yds, Par 71, SSS 70, Course record 62.
Club membership 1000.
Visitors contact in advance. Limited availability Fri pm & Sat, contact for these times no more than 5 days in advance.
Societies apply in advance.
Green Fees £35 per day; £25 per round (£40/£30 weekends).
Designer Tom Morris
Facilities ⊗ ⫿ ᕪ 🍺 ♀ 占 🏠 ✓
Hotel ★★★ 58% Caledonian Hotel, 81 High St, LEVEN ☎ 01333 424101 24 ⇌ ↑

Scoonie North Links KY8 4SP ☎ 01333 423437
A pleasant inland links course suitable for all ages.
18 holes, 4979mtrs, SSS 65.
Club membership 150.
Visitors no restrictions.
Societies apply in writing.
Green Fees not confirmed.
Facilities ♀ 占 🏗

Hotel ★★★ 58% Caledonian Hotel, 81 High St, LEVEN ☎ 01333 424101 24 ⇌ ↑

LINLITHGOW   Map 11 NS97

Linlithgow Braehead EH49 6QF
☎ 01506 842585 (Secretary) & 844356 (Pro)
Fax 01506 842764
Slightly hilly parkland course in beautiful setting.

18 holes, 5800yds, Par 70, SSS 68, Course record 65.
Club membership 450.
Visitors may not play Sat. Must book in advance Sun.
Societies must contact in writing.
Green Fees £25 per day; £17 per round (£30/£25 Sunday).
Prof Steven Rosie
Designer R Simpson of Carnoustie
Facilities ⊗ ⫿ ᕪ 🍺 ♀ 占 🏠 ✓
Location 1m S off Bathgate Road off A803

Hotel ★★★★ 68% Inchyra Grange Hotel, Grange Rd, POLMONT ☎ 01324 711911 109 ⇌ ↑

West Lothian Airngath Hill EH49 7RH
☎ 01506 826030 Fax 01506 826030
Hilly parkland course with superb views of River Forth.
18 holes, 6228yds, Par 71, SSS 71.
Club membership 800.
Visitors weekends by arrangement. Advisable to contact in high season.
Societies apply in writing.
Green Fees £22 day ; £17 per round (£30/£22 weekends).
Cards 🌑 💳 ⬜
Prof Colin Gillies
Designer Fraser Middleton
Facilities ⊗ ᕪ 🍺 ♀ 占 🏠 🏗 ✓
Location 1m S off A706

Hotel ★★★★ 68% Inchyra Grange Hotel, Grange Rd, POLMONT ☎ 01324 711911 109 ⇌ ↑

LIVINGSTON   Map 11 NT06

Deer Park Golf & Country Club Golfcourse Rd EH54 9EG
☎ 01506 431037 Fax 01506 435608
Long testing course, fairly flat, championship standard.
18 holes, 6688yds, Par 72, SSS 72, Course record 65.
Club membership 650.
Visitors proper golfing attire to be worn, must book in advance, Sun after 10am.
Societies telephone or write
Green Fees £30 per day; £20 per round (£40/£30 weekends).
Cards 🌑 💳 ⬛ ⬜
Prof Brian Dunbar
Designer Alliss/Thomas
Facilities ⊗ ⫿ ᕪ 🍺 ♀ 占 🏠 🏗 🦯 🛺 ✓
& Leisure heated indoor swimming pool, squash, sauna, solarium, gymnasium, ten pin bowling, snooker.
Location N side of town off A809

Hotel B Hilton National Livingston, Almondview, LIVINGSTON ☎ 01506 431222 120 ⇌ ↑

Pumpherston Drumshoreland Rd, Pumpherston EH53 0LH
☎ 01506 432869
Undulating parkland course with testing 6th hole (par 4), and view of Pentland Hills.
9 holes, 5382yds, Par 66, SSS 66, Course record 64.
Club membership 440.
Visitors must be accompanied by a member.
Societies apply in writing to the secretary.
Green Fees not confirmed.
Facilities ⊗ ᕪ 🍺 ♀ 占
Location 1m E of Livingston between A71 & A89

Hotel B Hilton National Livingston, Almondview, LIVINGSTON ☎ 01506 431222 120 ⇌ ↑

LOCHGELLY
Map 11 NT19

Lochgelly Cartmore Rd KY5 9PB ☎ 01592 780174
Parkland course with easy walking and often windy.
18 holes, 5491yds, Par 68, SSS 67, Course record 63.
Club membership 650.
Visitors no restrictions, parties must book in advance.
Societies must apply in writing.
Green Fees £20 per day; £12 per round (£27/£18 weekends).
Prof Martin Goldie
Designer Ian Marchbanks
Facilities ⊗ ⊪ 🏠 ♀ 🕊 🏠
Location W side of town off A910

Hotel ★★★ 65% Dean Park Hotel,
Chapel Level, KIRKCALDY
☎ 01592 261635 29 ⇄ ⌂ Annexe12 ⇄ ⌂

Lochore Meadows Lochore Meadows Country Park,
Crosshill, Lochore KY5 8BA
☎ 01592 414300 Fax 01592 414345
Lochside course with natural stream running through, and
woodland nearby. Country park offers many leisure facilities.
9 holes, 5554yds, Par 72, SSS 71.
Club membership 160.
Visitors no restrictions.
Societies must contact in advance.
Green Fees £7.50 per 18 holes; £4.50 per 9 holes (£10/£6.50
weekends & bank holidays).
Facilities 🗯 ᐱ
& Leisure outdoor swimming pool, fishing, horse riding,
water sports centre.
Location 2m N off B920

Hotel ★★★ 73% Green Hotel, 2 The Muirs,
KINROSS ☎ 01577 863467 47 ⇄ ⌂

LOCHGILPHEAD
Map 10 NR88

Lochgilphead Blarbuie Rd PA31 8LE ☎ 01546 602340
A varied course with short but interesting holes. Some
elevated greens and tees and some tight fairways.
9 holes, 2242yds, Par 64, SSS 63, Course record 54.
Club membership 250.
Visitors restricted during weekend club competitions.
Societies apply in advance, restricted wekends.
Green Fees not confirmed.
Designer Dr I McCamond
Facilities 🏠 🗯 ♀ ᐱ 🏠 ✂
Location Adjacent to the hospital. Signposted from the
village.

Hotel ★★ 65% The Stag Hotel, Argyll St,
LOCHGILPHEAD ☎ 01546 602496 17 ⇄ ⌂

LONGNIDDRY
Map 12 NT47

Longniddry Links Rd EH32 0NL
☎ 01875 852141 & 01875 852228 Fax 01875 853371
Undulating seaside links and partial parkland course.
One of the numerous courses which stretch east from
Edinburgh right to Dunbar. The inward half is more open
than the wooded outward half, but can be difficult in
prevailing west wind. No par 5s.
18 holes, 6219yds, Par 68, SSS 70, Course record 63.
Club membership 1140.

Visitors may book tee times up to 7 days in advance,
welcome most times except during
competitions
Societies Mon-Thu, apply in writing, handicap
certificate required.
Green Fees £47 per day; £30 per round (£40 per round
weekends).
Cards 💳 ▆▆ ▄▄
Prof John Gray
Designer H S Colt
Facilities ⊗ ⊪ 🏠 🗯 ♀ ᐱ 🏠 🕊 ✂
Location N side of village off A198

Hotel ★★ 68% Kilspindie House Hotel, Main St,
ABERLADY ☎ 01875 870682 26 ⇄ ⌂

LUNDIN LINKS
Map 12 NO40

Lundin Golf Rd KY8 6BA
☎ 01333 320202 Fax 01333 329743
The Leven Links and the course of the Lundin Club
adjoin each other. The course is part seaside and part
inland. The holes are excellent but those which can be
described as seaside holes have a very different nature
from the inland style ones. The par 3 14th looks
seawards across the Firth of Forth towards Edinburgh
and the old railway line defines out of bounds at several
holes. A number of burns snake across the fairways.
18 holes, 6394yds, Par 71, SSS 71, Course record 63.
Club membership 820.
Visitors visitors welcome weekdays 9-3.30 (3pm
Fridays) and Sat after 2.30pm, no vistors
Sun. Book well in advance.
Societies book well in advance by telephoning
Secretary (mornings).
Green Fees £37 per day; £29 per round. Sat pm £37 per
round.
Cards 💳 ▆▆
Prof David Webster
Designer James Braid
Facilities ⊗ ⊪ 🏠 🗯 ♀ ᐱ 🏠 ✂
Location W side of village off A915

Hotel ★★★ 74% Old Manor Hotel,
Leven Rd, LUNDIN LINKS
☎ 01333 320368 24 ⇄ ⌂

Lundin Ladies Woodielea Rd KY6 6AR ☎ 01333 320832
Short, lowland course with Roman stones on the second
fairway, and coastal views.
9 holes, 2365yds, Par 68, SSS 67, Course record 67.
Club membership 350.
Visitors contact in advance. Competition days Wed and
some weekends.
Societies telephone secretary.
Green Fees £10 per day (£12 weekend).
Designer James Braid
Facilities 🗯 ᐱ ✂
Location W side of village off A915

Hotel ★★★ 74% Old Manor Hotel, Leven Rd,
LUNDIN LINKS ☎ 01333 320368 24 ⇄ ⌂

LUSS
Map 10 NS39

LOCH LOMOND

Luss, Central Scotland   Tel: 01436 655555
Fax: 01436 655500

John Ingham writes - Vikings invaded in the ninth century AD. Later came the dreaded English to plunder. If you know the score, follow the Rob Roy Macgregor trail, but don't brand him a cattle thief. The man is legend from the mists of time. Today, instead of swords and crossbows, visitors are greeted not with a hail of arrows, but with views of glens, castles and, if you have the right connections, the chance to visit and play what I regard as the nation's most important new course, Loch Lomond on the bonnie banks.

I arrived in a new Aston Martin, all the way from London and was invited into what used to be the home of the chiefs of Clan Colquhoun. It is now the splendid clubhouse, boasting the Chinese Drawing Room, portraits in oil, beautiful ceilings and it resembles some wondrous film set. Former Scots Guard Captain Neil Hobday, then club manager, ordered coffee.

And the course? I played on the magnificent stretch, more than 7000 yards and found, from the back tee, the 625-yard 6th, on the very edge of the water, to be a real little Loch Lomond monster. But everywhere you look is a scenic wonder, and the course is so well kept, so interesting and inspiring that Nick Faldo went overboard and claimed it to be the finest new course in Europe. Nobody has denied this.

Designed by two Americans, Jay Morrish and the mighty Tom Weiskopf, it altered my view that few Americans are able to build anything other than artificial-lake covered stretches, similar to the ones you find in Arizona. The main problem is that Loch Lomond is very, very exclusive and getting on the course is about as difficult as getting a pass to play Augusta, or Muirfield.

But this international club is there for ever and Scotland, and all golf, is the beneficiary.

Visitor	are only permitted to play as a guest of members.
Facilities	🛏 ⛏ 🏠 🍴 ⚌ 🏌
	Professional (Colin Campbell)
Location	Rossdhu House, Luss G83 8NT (off A82 north west of Glasgow)

18 holes, 7060yds, Par 71, Course record 62.

WHERE TO STAY AND EAT NEARBY

HOTELS:

BALLOCH
★ ★ ★ ★ 🌸 🌸 🌸 80% Cameron House Hotel. ☎ 01389 755565. 96 🛏 🍴

LUSS
★ ★ ★ 🌸 70% The Lodge on Loch Lomond. ☎ 01436 860201 29 🛏 🍴

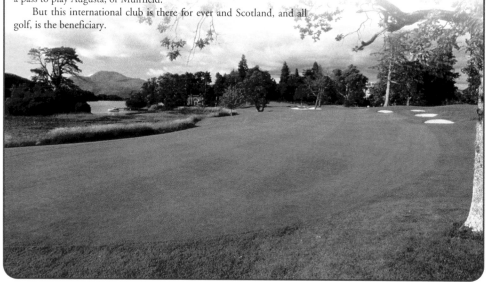

LOCH LOMOND See page 355

MACHRIHANISH   Map 10 NR62

Machrihanish PA28 6PT ☎ 01586 810213
Magnificent seaside links of championship status. The
1st hole is the famous drive across the Atlantic. Sandy
soil allows for play all year round. Large greens, easy
walking, windy. Fishing.
18 holes, 6228yds, Par 70, SSS 71.
Club membership 1035.
Visitors   no restrictions.
Societies   apply in writing.
Green Fees £40 per day; £25 per round (£50/£30 Sat).
Cards   ⚊ 🖃 💳 🖃 📷
Prof   Ken Campbell
Designer   Tom Morris
Facilities   ⊗ ⫚ ⱡ ⌷ 💺 ♀ ⚐ ⌂ ✐
Location   5m W of Campbeltown on B843

Hotel   ★★ 67% Seafield Hotel, Kilkerran Rd,
                 CAMPBELTOWN
                 ☎ 01586 554385 3 ⇋ ⋔ Annexe6 ⋔

MARKINCH˙   Map 11 NO20

Balbirnie Park Balbirnie Park KY7 6NR
☎ 01592 612095 & 752006 (tee times) Fax 01592 612383
A fine example of the best in traditional parkland design,
with natural contours the inspiration behind the layout.
18 holes, 6214yds, Par 71, SSS 70, Course record 65.
Club membership 900.
Visitors   must contact in advance. Numbers restricted
                 weekends and visitors must play from yellow
                 tees, smart but casual dress code.
Societies   booking forms sent out on request by asst
                 secretary.
Green Fees £33 per day; £25 per round (£40/£30 weekends).
Cards   ⚊ 🖃 💳 🖃 📷 📷
Prof   D F G Scott
Facilities   ⊗ ⫚ ⱡ 💺 ♀ ⌂ ⚐ ⌂ ♞ ⫚ ♣ ✐
Location   2m E of Glenrothes

Hotel   ★★★★🏌 Balbirnie House, Balbirnie Park,
                 MARKINCH ☎ 01592 610066 30 ⇋ ⋔

> Entries with a shaded background
> identify courses that are
> considered to be particularly interesting

MILNATHORT   Map 11 NO10

Milnathort South St KY13 9XA ☎ 01577 864069
Undulating inland course with lush fairways and excellent
greens for most of the year. Strategically placed copses of
trees require accurate tee shots. Different tees and greens for
each hole will make for more interesting play.
9 holes, 5969yds, Par 71, SSS 69, Course record 65.
Club membership 600.
Visitors   must contact in advance.
Societies   advisable to book in advance.
Green Fees special visitor packages available.
Facilities   ⊗ ⫚ ⱡ 💺 ♀ ⌂
& Leisure   9 hole putting green.
Location   S side of town on A922

Hotel   ★★ 64% The Glenfarg Hotel & Restaurant,
                 Main St, GLENFARG
                 ☎ 01577 830241 15rm(14 ⇋ ⋔)

MONIFIETH   Map 12 NO43

Monifieth Princes St DD5 4AW
☎ 01382 532767 (Medal) & 532967 (Ashludie)
Fax 01382 535553
The chief of the two courses at Monifieth is the Medal
Course. It has been one of the qualifying venues for the
Open Championship on more than one occasion. A
seaside links, but divided from the sand dunes by a
railway which provides the principal hazard for the first
few holes. The 10th hole is outstanding, the 17th is
excellent and there is a delightful finishing hole. The
Links is to be used as a qualifying course for the 1999
Open which is being held at Carnoustie. The other
course here is the Ashludie, and both are played over by
a number of clubs who share the links.
Medal Course: 18 holes, 6655yds, Par 71, SSS 72,
Course record 63.
Ashludie Course: 18 holes, 5123yds, Par 68, SSS 66.
Club membership 1750.
Visitors   must contact in advance. Restricted to after
                 2pm Sat, 10am Sun & after 9.30pm Mon-
                 Fri.
Societies   must contact in advance by telephone or
                 writing to Medal Starter's Box, Princes St,
                 Monifieth.
Green Fees not confirmed.
Prof   Ian McLeod
Facilities   ⊗ ⫚ ⱡ 💺 ♀ ⌂ ⚐ ⌂ ✐
Location   NE side of town on A930

Hotel   ★★ 69% Carlogie House Hotel,
                 Carlogie Rd, CARNOUSTIE
                 ☎ 01241 853185 12 ⇋ ⋔ Annexe4 ⋔

MONTROSE   Map 15 NO75

Montrose Links Trust Traill Dr DD10 8SW
☎ 01674 672932 Fax 01674 671800
The links at Montrose like many others in Scotland are
on commonland and are shared by three clubs. The
Medal course at Montrose - the fifth oldest in the world -
is typical of Scottish seaside links, with narrow,
undulating fairways and problems from the first hole to
the last. The Broomfield course is flatter and easier.

Medal Course: 18 holes, 6495yds, Par 71, SSS 72, Course record 64.
Broomfield Course: 18 holes, 4800yds, Par 66, SSS 63.
Club membership 1300.

Visitors	may not play on the Medal Course on Sat before 2.30pm & before 10am on Sun. Must have a handicap certificate for Medal Course. Contact in advance. No restrictions on Broomfield Course.
Societies	must contact secretary in advance.
Green Fees	Medal: £35 per day; £25 per round (£45/£30 weekends). Broomfield: £10 per round (£14 weekends).
Cards	⌦ 🌌 📇 🗒
Prof	Kevin Stables
Designer	W Park/Tom Morris
Facilities	⊗ ⨛ 🛋 ☕ ♀ ⚲ 🍴 ⛳ ♂
Location	NE side of town off A92

Hotel	★★★ 65% Park Hotel, 61 John St, MONTROSE ☎ 01674 673415 59rm(53 ⇆ ↿)
Additional hotel	★★★ 67% Links Hotel, Mid Links, MONTROSE ☎ 01674 671000 Fax 01674 672698 22 ⇆ ↿

MUCKHART   Map 11 NO00

Muckhart FK14 7JH ☎ 01259 781423
Scenic heathland/downland course.
Muckhart Course: 18 holes, 6034yds, Par 71, SSS 70, Course record 65.

(MONTROSE LINKS TRUST)
MONTROSE GOLF COURSES

Two links courses: MEDAL COURSE (Par 71, SSS72)
BROOMFIELD COURSE (Par 66, SSS 63)

AN INVITATION TO COME AND PLAY OUR HISTORIC
LINKS WHICH WAS A FINAL QUALIFYING COURSE FOR
THE OPEN IN 1999.

RANKED FIFTH OLDEST IN THE WORLD

VISITORS VERY WELCOME

Individual Round and Day Tickets Available on Both Courses
All Visitors and Parties Very Welcome.

*Special packages available including catering and
in conjunction with local hotels*

Enquiries to:	Mrs M Stewart, Secretary, Montrose Links Trust, Traill Drive, Montrose, Angus DD10 8SW. Tel: 01674 672932 Fax: 01674 671800

Naemoor Course: 9 holes, 3234yds, Par 35.
Club membership 750.

Visitors	telephone to book - steward 01259 781423 or professional 01259 781493.
Societies	booking by prior arrangement.
Green Fees	not confirmed.
Prof	Keith Salmoni
Facilities	⊗ ⨛ 🛋 ☕ ♀ ⚲ 🍴 ⛳ ♂
Location	SW of village off A91

Hotel	★★★ 66% Gartwhinzean Hotel, POWMILL ☎ 01577 840595 23 ⇆ ↿

MULL, ISLE OF   Map 10 NM73

CRAIGNURE   Map 10 NM73

Craignure Scallastle PA65 6PB
☎ 01680 812487 & 812416 Fax 01680 300402
A natural links course designed round the estuary of the
Scallastle Burn that flows into the Sound of Mull.
Completely re designed in 1978/9. Continual improvements
such as 5 new tees in 1998 will provide 18 teeing areas for
the 9 hole layout in 1999.
9 holes, 5233yds, Par 69, SSS 66, Course record 72.
Club membership 100.

Visitors	may not play on competition days, contact for fixture list.
Societies	write to the secretary 10 days in advance.
Green Fees	£11 per day.
Facilities	⚲ 🍴 ⛳ ♂
Location	1.5m N of Craignure A849

Hotel	★★★ 73% Western Isles Hotel, TOBERMORY ☎ 01688 302012 26 ⇆ ↿

TOBERMORY   Map 13 NM55

Tobermory PA75 6PG
☎ 01688 302338 Fax 01688 302140
A beautifully maintained hilltop course with superb views
over the Sound of Mull. Testing 7th hole (par 3). Often
described as the best 9 hole course in Scotland.
9 holes, 4890yds, Par 64, SSS 64, Course record 65.
Club membership 150.

Visitors	no restrictions except competition days.
Societies	preferable to contact in advance.
Green Fees	£13 per day; £50 per week.
Designer	David Adams
Facilities	♀ ⚲ 🍴
Location	0.5m N off A848

Hotel	★★★ 73% Western Isles Hotel, TOBERMORY ☎ 01688 302012 26 ⇆ ↿

MUSSELBURGH   Map 11 NT37

Musselburgh Monktonhall EH21 6SA ☎ 0131 665 2005
Testing parkland course with natural hazards including trees
and a burn, easy walking.
18 holes, 6614yds, Par 71, SSS 73, Course record 65.
Club membership 1000.

Visitors	must contact in advance.
Societies	must contact in advance.
Green Fees	£25 per day; £18 per round (£30/£22 weekends).
Prof	Fraser Mann ▶

Designer   James Braid
Facilities ⊗ ⫿ 🛅 💺 🍴 ⛳ 🏌 ♨ 🚜 ✐
Location   1m S on B6415

Hotel   ★★ 62% Iona Hotel, Strathearn Place,
            EDINBURGH
            ☎ 0131 447 6264 & 0131 447 5050
            Fax 0131 452 8574 17rm(4 ⇌8 ⏑)

Musselburgh Links, The Old Course 10 Balcarres Rd,
Millhill EH21 7SD
☎ 0131 665 5438 (Starter) Fax 0131 665 5438
A links type course.
9 holes, 2808yds, Par 34, SSS 34.
Visitors   must book in advance
Societies   must contact in advance.
Green Fees £4-£7.50 per 9 holes.
Facilities ⊗ by prior arrangement 🛅 by prior arrangement
            💺 by arrangement 🍴 🏌 ✐
Location   1m E of town off A1

Hotel   ★★ 62% Iona Hotel,
            Strathearn Place, EDINBURGH
            ☎ 0131 447 6264 &
            0131 447 5050 Fax 0131 452 8574
            17rm(4 ⇌8 ⏑)

MUTHILL   Map 11 NN81

Muthill Peat Rd PH5 2DA
☎ 01764 681523 Fax 01764 681557
Parkland course with fine views. Not too hilly, tight with
narrow fairways.
9 holes, 4700yds, Par 66, SSS 63, Course record 61.
Club membership 500.
Visitors   no restrictions.
Societies   book in advance.
Green Fees £15 per day; £13 per 18 holes (£20/£16
            weekends).
Facilities ⊗ ⫿ 🛅 💺 from April 🍴 ⛳ 🏌 ✐
Location   W side of village off A822

Hotel   ★★ 71% Murraypark Hotel, Connaught Ter,
            CRIEFF ☎ 01764 653731 20 ⇌ ⏑

NORTH BERWICK   Map 12 NT58

Glen East Links, Tantallon Ter EH39 4LE
☎ 01620 895288 & 892726 Fax 01620 895447
An interesting course with a good variety of holes. The views
of the town, the Firth of Forth and the Bass Rock are
breathtaking.

BRITAIN'S BEST PUBS
*Choose from over 1600 pubs,
inns & village restaurants
in*
AA BEST PUBS & INNS
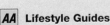 **AA** Lifestyle Guides

18 holes, 6089yds, Par 69, SSS 69, Course record 64.
Club membership 650.
Visitors   booking advisable.
Societies   advance booking recommended.
Green Fees £27 per day; £18 per round (£33/£23 weekends).
Cards   ▬ 💳 £ 🅂
Designer   McKenzie Ross
Facilities ⊗ ⫿ 🛅 💺 🍴 ⛳ 🏌 ✐
Location   1m E of B198

Hotel   ★ 60% Nether Abbey Hotel,
            20 Dirleton Av, NORTH BERWICK
            ☎ 01620 892802 16rm(4 ⇌6 ⏑)

North Berwick Beach Rd EH39 4BB
☎ 01620 892135 Fax 01620 893274
Another of East Lothian's famous courses, the links at
North Berwick is still popular. A classic championship
links, it has many hazards including the beach, streams,
bunkers, light rough and low walls. The great hole on the
course is the 15th, the famous 'Redan', selected for
television's best 18 in the UK. Used by both the
Tantallon and Bass Rock Golf Clubs.
18 holes, 6420yds, Par 71, SSS 71, Course record 64.
Club membership 730.
Visitors   must contact in advance.
Societies   must contact in advance.
Green Fees not confirmed.
Prof   D Huish
Facilities 🍴 ⛳ 🏌 ✐
Location   W side of town on A198

Hotel   ★★★ 65% The Marine,
            Cromwell Rd, NORTH BERWICK
            ☎ 01620 892406 83 ⇌ ⏑

Whitekirk Whitekirk EH39 5PR
☎ 01620 870300 Fax 01620 870330
Scenic coastal course with lush green fairways, gorse
covered rocky banks and stunning views. Natural water
hazards and strong sea breezes make this well designed
course a good test of golf.
18 holes, 6526yds, Par 72, SSS 72, Course record 64.
Club membership 200.
Visitors   no restrictions.
Societies   apply in writing or telephone.
Green Fees £30 per day, £18 per round (£35/£25 weekends).
Cards   ▬ 💳 ▬ 🅂
Prof   Paul Wardell
Designer   Cameron Sinclair
Facilities 🍴 🏌 🛏 ♨ 🚜 ✐ ⏑
Location   3m off the main A1 Edinburgh/Berwick-upon-
            Tweed road A198 North Berwick

Hotel   ★ 60% Nether Abbey Hotel,
            20 Dirleton Av, NORTH BERWICK
            ☎ 01620 892802 16rm(4 ⇌6 ⏑)

OBAN   Map 10 NM83

Glencruitten Glencruitten Rd PA34 4PU
☎ 01631 564604
There is plenty of space and considerable variety of hole
on this downland course - popular with holidaymakers.
In a beautiful, isolated situation, the course is hilly and
testing, particularly the 1st and 12th, par 4's, and 10th
and 15th, par 3's.

18 holes, 4452yds, Par 61, SSS 63, Course record 55.
Club membership 600.
Visitors restricted Thu & weekends
Societies must contact in writing.
Green Fees £15 per round/day.
Cards 💳
Prof Graham Clark
Designer James Braid
Facilities ⊗ ⫿ ⓑ 🍺 ♀ ⚲ 🏠 ⛳ ♂
& Leisure pool table.
Location NE side of town centre off A816

Hotel ★★ 59% Caledonian Hotel,
Station Square, OBAN
☎ 01631 563133 70 ⇥ ⋒

PENICUIK   Map 11 NT25

Glencorse Milton Bridge EH26 0RD
☎ 01968 677189 Fax 01968 674399
Picturesque parkland course with burn affecting ten holes.
Testing 5th hole (237 yds) par 3.
18 holes, 5217yds, Par 64, SSS 66, Course record 60.
Club membership 700.

Visitors contact secretary, unable to play during club competitions
Societies contact secretary for details.
Green Fees £24.50 per day; £18.50 per 18 holes.
Prof Cliffe Jones
Designer J R Strutt
Facilities ⊗ ⫿ ⓑ 🍺 ♀ ⚲ 🏠 ♂ ⓲
Location 1.5m N of Penicuik on A701

Hotel ★★ 63% Roslin Glen Hotel, 2 Penicuik Rd,
ROSLIN ☎ 0131 440 2029 7 ⇥ ⋒

PERTH   Map 11 NO12

Craigie Hill Cherrybank PH2 0NE
☎ 01738 620829 & 622644
Slightly hilly, parkland course. Good views over Perth.
18 holes, 5386yds, Par 66, SSS 67, Course record 60.
Club membership 560.
Visitors restricted access Sat. Telephone up to 3 days in advance.
Societies must contact in writing.
Green Fees not confirmed.
Prof Steven Harrier
Designer Fernie/Anderson
Facilities ⊗ ⫿ ⓑ 🍺 ♀ ⚲ 🏠 ⛳ ♂
Location 1m SW of city centre off A952

Hotel ★★★ 58% The Royal George, Tay St, PERTH
☎ 01738 624455 39rm(37 ⇥ ⋒)

King James VI Moncreiffe Island PH2 8NR
☎ 01738 445132 (Secretary) Fax 01738 445132
Parkland course, situated on island in the middle of River Tay. Easy walking.
18 holes, 6038yds, Par 70, SSS 69, Course record 62.
Club membership 650.
Visitors visitors restricted on competition days. Contact professional for bookings.
Societies book by telephone.
Green Fees not confirmed.
Prof Tony Coles
Designer Tom Morris
Facilities ⓑ 🍺 ♀ ⚲ 🏠 ⛳ 🚵 ♂
Location SE side of city centre

Hotel ★★★ 66% Queens Hotel, Leonard St, PERTH
☎ 01738 442222 51 ⇥ ⋒

Murrayshall Country House Hotel Murrayshall, Scone
PH2 7PH ☎ 01738 552784 & 551171 Fax 01738 552595
This course is laid out in 130 acres of parkland with tree-lined fairways, magnificent views of the Grampian Highlands. Hotel and driving range.
18 holes, 6441yds, Par 73, SSS 72.
Club membership 350.
Visitors no restrictions.
Societies telephone in advance.
Green Fees not confirmed.
Cards 💳
Prof Alan Reid
Designer Hamilton Stutt

MURRAYSHALL HOUSE AND GOLF COURSE
SCONE, BY PERTH SCOTLAND

Set within 300 acres of parkland golf course, this 3 star, STB highly commended country house hotel has 26 bedrooms and a self-contained lodge house. Leisure facilities include sauna, gymnasium, jacuzzi, tennis courts, driving range and indoor golf school.
Special golf packages available
Society welcome groups
Our clubhouse facilities are available to non members
Pro Shop 01738 552784

Facilities ⊗ 〗⑂ ㄴ ■ ♀ ⚲ ⌂ ⌐ ◢ ♣ ⚘ ⟋ ⟨
& Leisure hard tennis courts, sauna, gymnasium.
Location E side of village off A94

Hotel ★★★⚘ 76% Murrayshall Country House
Hotel & Golf Course, New Scone, PERTH
☎ 01738 551171 27 ⇆ ⑂

North Inch North Inch, off Hay St PH1 5PH
☎ 01738 636481
An enjoyable short and often testing course incorporating
mature trees, open parkland with fine views and attractive
riverside.
18 holes, 5178yds, Par 65, Course record 60.
Club membership 476.
Visitors advisable to telephone in advance. Due to a
flood prevention wall to be built late 97/98 there
may be some disruption.
Green Fees not confirmed.
Designer Tom Morris
Facilities ⊗ ■ ♀ ⟋
& Leisure squash, gymnasium.

Hotel ★★★ 58% The Royal George, Tay St, PERTH
☎ 01738 624455 39rm(37 ⇆ ⑂)

PITLOCHRY   Map 14 NN95

Pitlochry Pitlochry Estate Office PH16 5QY
☎ 01796 472792
A varied and interesting heathland course with fine
views and posing many problems. Its SSS permits few
errors in its achievement.
18 holes, 5811yds, Par 69, SSS 69, Course record 63.
Club membership 400.
Visitors Sat & Sun may not play before 9.30am.
Societies must contact in advance.
Green Fees not confirmed.
Prof George Hampton
Designer Willy Fernie
Facilities ⊗ 〗⑂ ㄴ ■ ♀ ⚲ ⌂ ⌐ ◣ ⟋
Location N side of town off A924

Hotel ★★★ 69% Pine Trees Hotel, Strathview
Ter, PITLOCHRY
☎ 01796 472121 19 ⇆ ⑂

POLMONT   Map 11 NS97

Grangemouth Polmont Hill FK2 0YE
☎ 01324 503840 Fax 01324 715818
Windy parkland course. Testing holes: 3rd, 4th (par 4's); 5th
(par 5); 7th (par 3) 216 yds over reservoir (elevated green);
8th, 9th, 18th (par 4's).
18 holes, 6314yds, Par 71, SSS 71, Course record 70.
Club membership 700.
Visitors must contact in advance.
Societies must contact in writing.
Green Fees not confirmed.
Prof Stuart Campbell
Facilities ⊗ 〗⑂ ㄴ ■ ♀ ⚲ ⌂ ⟋
Location On unclass rd 0.5m N of M9 junc 4

Hotel ★★★★ 68% Inchyra Grange Hotel,
Grange Rd, POLMONT
☎ 01324 711911 109 ⇆ ⑂

Polmont Manuelrigg, Maddiston FK2 0LS
☎ 01324 711277 Fax 01324 712504
Parkland course, hilly with few bunkers. Views of the River
Forth and Ochil Hills.
9 holes, 3073yds, Par 72, SSS 69, Course record 66.
Club membership 300.
Visitors no visitors on Sat from Apr-Sep, Mon-Fri must
tee of before 5pm.
Societies apply in writing to club secretary.
Green Fees £8 per 18 holes (£14 Sun).
Facilities ⊗ 〗⑂ ㄴ ■ ♀ ⚲ ⌂
Location A805 from Falkirk, 1st right after fire brigade
headquarters

Hotel ★★★★ 68% Inchyra Grange Hotel, Grange
Rd, POLMONT ☎ 01324 711911 109 ⇆ ⑂

PORT GLASGOW   Map 10 NS37

Port Glasgow Devol Rd PA14 5XE
☎ 01475 704181 & 705671 (shop)
A moorland course set on a hilltop overlooking the Clyde,
with magnificent views to the Cowal hills.
18 holes, 5712yds, Par 68, SSS 68.
Club membership 390.
Visitors may not play on Sat. By prior arrangement or
with member Sun.
Societies apply in writing.
Green Fees £20 per day; £15 per round.
Facilities ⊗ 〗⑂ ㄴ ■ ♀ ⚲ ⌂
Location 1m S

Hotel ★★★★⚘ 69% Gleddoch House Hotel,
LANGBANK ☎ 01475 540711 39 ⇆ ⑂

PRESTONPANS   Map 11 NT37

Royal Musselburgh Prestongrange House EH32 9RP
☎ 01875 810276 Fax 01875 810276
Tree-lined parkland course overlooking Firth of Forth.
18 holes, 6237yds, Par 70, SSS 70, Course record 64.
Club membership 970.
Visitors must contact professional in advance, restricted
Fri afternoons & weekends.
Societies must contact in advance.
Green Fees £35 per day, £25 per round (£35 per round
weekends).
Prof John Henderson
Designer James Braid
Facilities ⊗ 〗⑂ ㄴ ■ ♀ ⚲ ⌂ ⌐ ◣ ⟋
Location W side of town centre off A59, Prestonpans to
North Berwick rd

Hotel ★★ 68% Kilspindie House Hotel, Main St,
ABERLADY ☎ 01875 870682 26 ⇆ ⑂

RATHO   Map 11 NT17

Ratho Park EH28 8NX
☎ 0131 333 2566 & 333 1752 Fax 0131 333 1752
Flat parkland course.
18 holes, 5900yds, Par 69, SSS 68, Course record 62.
Club membership 850.
Visitors must contact in advance.
Societies must contact in writing. Only able to play Tue-
Thu

Green Fees £35 per day £25 per round (£35 per round weekends).
Prof   Alan Pate
Designer James Braid
Facilities ⊗ 🍽 🛍 �🍷 ☕ 👤 🏠 ⛳
Location 0.75m E, N of A71

Hotel   B Posthouse Edinburgh, Corstorphine Rd, EDINBURGH ☎ 0131 334 0390 303 🛏 🐾

ST ANDREWS
Map 12 NO51

British Golf Museum
☎ 01334 478880 (situated opposite Royal & Ancient Golf Club) The museum which tells the history of golf from its origins to the present day, is of interest to golfers and non-golfers alike. Themed galleries and interactive displays explore the history of the major championships and the lives of the famous players, and trace the development of golfing equipment. An audio-visual theatre shows historic golfing moments.
Open: Etr-mid Oct, daily 9.30am-5.30pm (mid Oct-Etr Thu-Mon 11am-3pm, closed Tue & Wed.
Admission: There is a charge. Telephone for details.

Dukes Course Craigtoun KY16 8NS
☎ 01334 474371 Fax 01334 479456
Blending the characteristics of a links course with an inland course, Dukes offers rolling fairways, undulating greens and a testing woodland section, and magnificent views over St Andrews Bay towards Carnoustie.
18 holes, 6749yds, Par 72, SSS 73.
Club membership 325. ▶

Visitors booking should be in advance to avoid disappointment.
Societies apply in writing or fax in advance.
Green Fees £50 (£55 weekends).
Cards [symbols]
Prof John Kelly
Designer Peter Thomson
Facilities ⊗ ⊞ 🛍 💆 ♀ ♨ ☕ ☞ 🚶 🏌 ⚷ 🏑 🏌 ⚷ ⛵
& Leisure heated indoor swimming pool, sauna, solarium, gymnasium, tuition available.
Location Follow M90 from Edinburgh onto A91 to Cupar then to St Andrew turning off for Strathkiness

Hotel ★★★★★ 68% The Old Course Hotel, ST ANDREWS ☎ 01334 474371 125 ⇔ 🐾
Additional QQQ Riverview Guest House, Edenside,
Guesthouse ST ANDREWS ☎ 01334 838009 Fax 01334 839944 7 🐾
See advertisement on page 361.

ST ANDREWS LINKS   See page 363

ST FILLANS   Map 11 NN62

St Fillans South Loch Earn Rd PH6 2NJ ☎ 01764 685312
Fairly flat, beautiful parkland course. Beside the river Earn and set amongst the Perthshire hills. Wonderfully rich in flora, animal and bird life.
9 holes, 5896yds, Par 68, SSS 67, Course record 73.
Club membership 400.
Visitors advisable to contact in advance.
Societies Apr-Oct, apply to starter.
Green Fees not confirmed.
Designer W Auchterlonie
Facilities ⊗ ⊞ 🛍 💆 ♀ ☕ ⚷
Location E side of village off A85

Hotel ★★★ 69% The Four Seasons Hotel, Loch Earn, ST FILLANS ☎ 01764 685333   12 ⇔ 🐾 Annexe6 ⇔ 🐾

SALINE   Map 11 NT09

Saline Kinneddar Hill KY12 9LT ☎ 01383 852591
Hillside parkland course with excellent turf and panoramic view of the Forth Valley.
9 holes, 5302yds, Par 68, SSS 66, Course record 63.
Club membership 400.
Visitors advisable to contact in advance and may not play Sat, some restrictions Sun.
Societies contact in advance.
Green Fees £9 per day (£12 Sun).
Facilities 🛍 💆 ♀ ♨ ⚷
Location 0.5m E at junc B913/914

Hotel ★★★ 62% King Malcolm, Queensferry Rd, DUNFERMLINE ☎ 01383 722611   48 ⇔ 🐾

SOUTHEND   Map 10 NR60

Dunaverty PA28 6RW ☎ 01586 830677
Undulating, seaside course.
18 holes, 4799yds, Par 66, SSS 63, Course record 59.
Club membership 400.
Visitors limited Sat, contact in advance.

Societies apply in advance.
Green Fees not confirmed.
Facilities ⊗ ⊞ by prior arrangement 🛍 💆 ♨ 🏠 ⚷
& Leisure fishing.
Location 10m S of Campbeltown on B842

Hotel ★★ 67% Seafield Hotel, Kilkerran Rd, CAMPBELTOWN
☎ 01586 554385 3 ⇔ 🐾 Annexe6 🐾

SOUTH QUEENSFERRY   Map 11 NT17

Dundas Parks Dundas Estate EH30 9PQ
☎ 0131 331 1588
Parkland course situated on the estate of Dundas Castle, with excellent views. For 18 holes, the 9 are played twice.
9 holes, Par 70, SSS 69, Course record 66.
Club membership 500.
Visitors must contact in advance, only with a member
Societies must contact in writing.
Green Fees £10 per round.
Facilities ♨
Location 0.5m S on A8000

Hotel ★★★ 62% Forth Bridges Hotel, 1 Ferrymuir Gait, SOUTH QUEENSFERRY
☎ 0131 469 9955 108 ⇔ 🐾

STIRLING   Map 11 NS79

Stirling Queens Rd FK8 3AA
☎ 01786 464098 Fax 01786 450748
Undulating parkland course with magnificent views of Stirling Castle and the Grampian Mountains. Testing 15th, 'Cotton's Fancy', 384 yds (par 4).
18 holes, 6438yds, Par 72, SSS 71, Course record 64.
Club membership 1100.
Visitors may reserve tee off times mid week 9-4.30pm. At weekends tee off times may be reserved on day of play subject to availability.
Societies must apply in writing or telephone.
Green Fees £30 per day; £20 per round.
Cards [symbols]
Prof Ian Collins
Designer James Braid/Henry Cotton
Facilities ⊗ ⊞ 🛍 💆 ♀ ♨ ☕ ⚷ 🏌 ⚷ ⛵
Location W side of town on B8051

Hotel ★★ 68% Terraces Hotel, 4 Melville Ter, STIRLING ☎ 01786 472268   18 ⇔ 🐾

STRATHTAY   Map 14 NN95

Strathtay ☎ 01350 727797
A wooded mainly hilly course with pleasing panoramic views. 5th hole 'Spion Kop' is especially difficult. It is steep, with heavy rough on both sides of the hilly fairway and an unsighted green of the back of the hill which is affected by winds.
9 holes, 4082yds, Par 63, SSS 63, Course record 61.
Club membership 158.
Visitors restricted May-Sep; Sun 12.30-5pm & Mon 6-8pm. Also some Wed & Thu evenings.
Societies by letter or telephone to Secretary T D Lind, Lorne Cottage, Dalguise, Dunkeld, Perthshire PH8 0JX.
Green Fees not confirmed.
Facilities ♨   ▶

ST ANDREWS LINKS

ST ANDREWS *Fife* ☎ 01334 466666
Fax 01334 477036
Map 12 N051

John Ingham writes: If golf has a mother, then without doubt it is St Andrews, the most famous links in all the world. Sir Winston Churchill is said to have claimed golf was invented by the Devil, and if this is so then the famous Old Course must be the Devil's playground. How can one reconcile these two thoughts; the birthplace and mother of the game - and yet the very Devil of a test?

The great Bobby Jones started by hating St Andrews and shredded his card into a hundred pieces, letting it blow in the wind. But eventually he came to love the place, and earn the affection of all golf. However you view St Andrews, you cannot ignore it. That master shot-maker from America, Sam Snead, took one look and claimed they should plant cattle fodder on the bumpy acres. Gary Player once said it should be towed out to sea, and sunk. But Jack Nicklaus loved it so much that when he won an Open title here, he threw his putter into the air. And he went away, and copied several of the St Andrews features in other courses that now decorate this earth.

St Andrews is much more than an 18-hole test. It is a whole experience and a walk in history. Name the famous players of yesteryear, and they played here, taking divots from the very spot that you can also take divots - merely by paying for a ticket. You too can wander out with your clubs to conquer some holes, maybe, and to be brought to a humbling halt by others.

Jack Nicklaus won his most remarkable victory on this course, thanks to an historic missed putt of just 3 feet 6 inches by Doug Sanders, who had needed a final hole par 4 to win the 1970 Open Championship. The all-time course record is 62, shot by Curtis Strange in the 1987 Dunhill Cup. Surely nobody, not even Tiger Woods, can ever beat that as they've now added many extra yards to several holes.

Visitors	must telephone in advance
Societies	must book at least a month in advance.
Green fees	Old course: £75; New Course £35; Jubilee £35, Eden £23; Strathtyrum £17, Balgove £7 (18 holes).
Facilities	⊗ ⫴ 🍴 🍷 🛒 ⛱ 🏠 ⛳ 🐟 🛥 ✎
Location	Pilmour Cottage, St. Andrews KY16 9SF (NW of town off the A91)

Old Course: 18 holes, 6566yds, Par 72, SSS 72
New (West Sands Rd): 18 holes, 6604yds, Par 71, SSS 72
Jubilee (West Sands Rd): 18 holes, 6805yds, Par 72, SSS 73
Eden (Dundee Rd): 18 holes, 6112yds, Par 70, SSS 70
Strathtyrum): 18 holes, 5094yds, Par 69, SSS64
Balgove 9 holes 3060 yds, Par 60

WHERE TO STAY AND EAT NEARBY

HOTELS:
ST ANDREWS
★★★★★ ✿ ✿ 68% Old Course St Andrews, Old Station Rd. ☎ 01334 474371 125 ⇄ 🐾

★★★ ✿ ✿ 78% St Andrews Golf, 40 The Scores. ☎ 01334 472611. 22 (20 ⇄ 🐾 2 🐾)

★★★66% Scores, 76 The Scores ☎ 01334 472451 30 (2 🐾 28 ⇄ 🐾)

RESTAURANTS:
CUPAR
✿ ✿ ✿ Ostlers Close, Bonnygate ☎ 01334 655574

Location	Eastern end of minor rd to Weem, off A827

Hotel ★★ 69% The Weem, Weem, ABERFELDY
☎ 01887 820381 12 ⇌ ♙

TARBERT Map 10 NR86

Tarbert PA29 6XX ☎ 01880 820536
Beautiful moorland course. Four fairways crossed by streams.
9 holes, 4460yds, Par 66, SSS 63, Course record 62.
Visitors may not play Sat pm.
Societies apply in writing.
Green Fees £10 per 18 holes; £6 per 9 holes.
Location N1m W on B8024

Hotel ★★★♨ 67% Stonefield Castle Hotel,
TARBERT
☎ 01880 820836 33 ⇌ ♙

TAYPORT Map 12 NO42

Scotscraig Golf Rd DD6 9DZ
☎ 01382 552515 Fax 01382 553130
A rather tight course on downland-type turf with an abundance of gorse. The sheltered position of this Open qualifying course ensures good weather throughout the year.
18 holes, 6550yds, Par 71, SSS 72, Course record 69.
Club membership 850.
Visitors restricted at weekends. Must contact in advance.
Societies advance booking.
Green Fees on application.
Cards 〓 〓 〓 ▨
Prof S J Campbell
Designer Tom Morris
Facilities ⊗ ⊪ ⅃ ♙ ☂ ♟ ☆ 🏠 ⚑ ♂ ♠
Location S side of village off B945

Hotel ★★★♨ 64% Sandford Hotel,
Newport Hill, Wormit, DUNDEE
☎ 01382 541802 16 ⇌ ♙

THORNTON Map 11 NT29

Thornton Station Rd KY1 4DW
☎ 01592 771111 Fax 01592 774955
A relatively flat, lightly tree-lined, parkland course bounded on three sides by a river which come into play at holes 14-16.
18 holes, 6155yds, Par 70, SSS 69, Course record 64.
Club membership 700.
Visitors restricted at weekends before 10am & between 12.30-2pm, also Tue 1-1.30 & Thu 9-10. Booking in advance recommended.
Societies apply in advance.
Green Fees £25 per day; £15 per round (£32/£22 weekends).
Facilities ⊗ ⊪ ⅃ ♙ ☂ ♟ ♠
Location 1m E of town off A92

Hotel ★★★★♨ Balbirnie House,
Balbirnie Park, MARKINCH
☎ 01592 610066 30 ⇌ ♙

TIGHNABRUAICH Map 10 NR97

Kyles of Bute PA21 2EE ☎ 01700 811603
Moorland course which is hilly and exposed to wind. Good views of the Kyles of Bute.
9 holes, 4778yds, Par 66, SSS 64, Course record 62.
Club membership 150.
Visitors may not play Wed pm or Sun am.
Societies telephone in advance.
Green Fees £8 per day/round (£10 weekends).
Facilities ☂ ⚑ ♠
Location 1.25m S off B8000

Hotel ★★ 78% Kilfinan Hotel, KILFINAN
☎ 01700 821201 11 ⇌ ♙

TILLICOULTRY Map 11 NS99

Tillicoultry Alva Rd FK13 6BL ☎ 01259 750124
Parkland course at foot of the Ochil Hills entailing some hard walking.
9 holes, 4904metres, Par 68, SSS 66, Course record 61.
Club membership 400.
Visitors must contact in advance.
Societies apply to the secretary.
Green Fees not confirmed.
Facilities ⊗ ⊪ ⅃ ♙ ☂ ♟ ☂
Location A91, 9m E of Stirling

UPHALL Map 11 NT07

Uphall EH52 6JT ☎ 01506 856404 Fax 01506 855358
Windy parkland course, easy walking.
18 holes, 5588yds, Par 69, SSS 67, Course record 62.
Club membership 500.
Visitors restricted weekends.
Societies must contact in advance.
Green Fees not confirmed.
Prof Gordon Law
Facilities ⊗ ⊪ ⅃ ♙ ☂ ♟ ☆ 🏠 ⚑ ♂
Location W side of village on A899

Hotel ★★★★ 69% Houstoun House Hotel and
Country Club, UPHALL
☎ 01506 853831 25 ⇌ ♙ Annexe47 ⇌ ♙

WEST CALDER Map 11 NT06

Harburn EH55 8RS ☎ 01506 871131 & 871256
Moorland, reasonably flat.
18 holes, 5921yds, Par 69, SSS 69, Course record 62.
Club membership 870.

Visitors	contact secretary, limited weekends.
Societies	must contact in writing.
Green Fees	£24 per day; £18 per round (£28/£21 Fri, £34/£23 weekends & bank holidays).
Prof	Stephen Mills
Facilities	⊗ ⫼ ⯩ ⛾ ⌇ ⚲ ⌂ ⏚ 🛺 ⚘
Location	2m S on B7008

Hotel	★★★ 67% The Hilcroft Hotel, East Main St, WHITBURN ☎ 01501 740818 31 ⇔ ⌁

WHITBURN   Map 11 NS96

Polkemmet Country Park EH47 0AD ☎ 01501 743905
Public parkland course surrounded by mature woodland and rhododendron bushes. 15-bay floodlit driving range.
9 holes, 2969mtrs, Par 37.

Visitors	no restrictions.
Green Fees	£4.50 per round (£5.25 weekends).
Facilities	⊗ ⯩ ⛾ ⌇ ⚘ ⚲
& Leisure	barbecue and childrens play area.
Location	2m W on B7066

Hotel	★★★ 67% The Hilcroft Hotel, East Main St, WHITBURN ☎ 01501 740818 31 ⇔ ⌁

SOUTHERN LOWLANDS & BORDERS

This region includes the counties of City of Glasgow, Dumbarton & Clydebank, Dumfries & Galloway, East Ayrshire, East Dunbartonshire, East Renfrewshire, North Ayrshire, North Lanarkshire, Renfrewshire, Scottish Borders, South Ayrshire and South Lanarkshire which reflect the recent national changes.

AIRDRIE   Map 11 NS76

Airdrie Rochsoles ML6 0PQ ☎ 01236 762195
Picturesque parkland course with good views.
18 holes, 6004yds, Par 69, SSS 69, Course record 64.
Club membership 450.

Visitors	must contact in advance. With member only weekends & bank holidays.
Societies	apply in writing.
Green Fees	not confirmed.
Prof	A McCloskey
Facilities	⛾ ⌇ ⌂
Location	1m N on B802

Hotel	★★★★ 64% Westerwood Hotel Golf & Country Club, 1 St Andrews Dr, Westerwood, CUMBERNAULD ☎ 01236 457171 49 ⇔ ⌁

Easter Moffat Mansion House, Plains ML6 8NP
☎ 01236 842878
Moorland/parkland course.
18 holes, 6221yds, Par 72, SSS 70, Course record 66.
Club membership 450.

Visitors	may only play on weekdays.
Societies	must contact in advance.
Green Fees	£20 per day; £15 per round.
Prof	Graham King

Facilities	⊗ ⫼ ⯩ ⛾ ⌇ ⌂ ⚘
Location	2m E on old Edinburgh-Glasgow road

Hotel	★★★★ 64% Westerwood Hotel Golf & Country Club, 1 St Andrews Dr, Westerwood, CUMBERNAULD ☎ 01236 457171 49 ⇔ ⌁

ARRAN, ISLE OF   Map 10 NR94

BLACKWATERFOOT   Map 10 NR82

Shiskine Shore Rd KA27 8HA
☎ 01770 860226 Fax 01770 860205
Unique 12-hole links course with gorgeous outlook to the Mull of Kintyre.
12 holes, 2990yds, Par 42, SSS 42.
Club membership 670.

Visitors	must contact in advance.
Societies	must contact in writing in advance. Jul and Aug no parties.
Green Fees	£18 per day; £12 per round(£20 per day weekends & bank holidays).
Designer	Fernie of Troon
Facilities	⊗ ⌇ ⌂ ⛾ 🛺 ⚘
& Leisure	hard tennis courts.
Location	W side of village off A841

Hotel	★★🏖 Kilmichael Country House Hotel, Glen Cloy, BRODICK ☎ 01770 302219 6 ⇔ ⌁ Annexe3 ⇔ ⌁

BRODICK   Map 10 NS03

Brodick KA27 8DL
☎ 01770 302349 & 302513 Fax 01770 302349
Short seaside course, very flat.
18 holes, 4736yds, Par 65, SSS 64, Course record 60.
Club membership 631.

Visitors	must contact in advance but may not play at competition times.
Societies	must contact secretary in writing.
Green Fees	£18 per day; £13 per round (£25/£16 weekends). £65 per week, £90 per fortnight.
Prof	Peter McCalla
Facilities	⊗ ⫼ ⯩ ⛾ ⌇ ⌂ ⚘
Location	N side of village

Hotel	★★★ 76% Auchrannie Country House Hotel, BRODICK ☎ 01770 302234 28 ⇔ ⌁

CORRIE   Map 10 NS04

Corrie Sannox KA27 8JD
☎ 01770 810223 Fax 01770 810268
A heathland course on the coast with beautiful mountain scenery. An upward climb to 6th hole, then a descent from the 7th. All these holes are subject to strong winds in bad weather.
9 holes, 1948yds, Par 62, SSS 61, Course record 56.
Club membership 240.

Visitors	welcome except Sat pm and first Thu afternoon of the month.
Societies	maximum size of party 16, apply in advance.
Green Fees	£8 per day. ▶

Facilities ⊗ 🝰 💺 🗃
Location 6m N of A841

Hotel ★★★ 76% Auchrannie Country House Hotel, BRODICK ☎ 01770 302234 28 ⇆ 📷

LAMLASH   Map 10 NS03

Lamlash KA27 8JU
☎ 01770 600296 & 600196 (Starter) Fax 01770 600296
Undulating heathland course with magnificent views of the mountains and sea.
18 holes, 4640yds, Par 64, SSS 64, Course record 60.
Club membership 480.
Visitors book in advance by letter
Societies must contact in writing.
Green Fees £16 per day; £12 per round after 4pm (£20 weekends).
Designer Auchterlonie
Facilities ⊗ 🝰 🝰 💺 💺 ♀ 🝰 🗃 🝰 🝰 ⚘
Location 0.75m N of Lamlash on A841. 3m S of Brodick Ferry Terminal

Hotel ★★★ 76% Auchrannie Country House Hotel, BRODICK ☎ 01770 302234 28 ⇆ 📷

LOCHRANZA   Map 10 NR95

Lochranza KA27 8HL
☎ 01770 830273 Fax 01770 830600
This course opened in 1991 is mainly on the level, set amid spectacular scenery where the fairways are grazed by wild red deer, while overhead buzzards and golden eagles may be seen. There are water hazards including the river which is lined by mature trees. The final three holes, nicknamed the Bermuda Triangle, provide an absorbing finish right to the 18th hole - a 530 yard dogleg through trees and over the river. The large greens are played off 18 tees.
9 holes, 5033mtrs, Par 70, SSS 70, Course record 74.
Visitors no restrictions; course closed Nov-mid Apr.
Societies advance booking preferred.
Green Fees £18 per day; £12 per 18 holes.
Designer re laid 1991 I Robertson
Facilities 🝰 💺 💺 🗃 🝰 ⚘
Location Main road, Lochranza village.

Hotel ★★🝰🝰 Kilmichael Country House Hotel, Glen Cloy, BRODICK ☎ 01770 302219 6 ⇆ 📷 Annexe3 ⇆ 📷

MACHRIE   Map 10 NR83

Machrie Bay KA27 8DZ ☎ 01770 850232
Fairly flat seaside course. Designed at turn of century by William Fernie.
9 holes, 4400yds, Par 66, SSS 62, Course record 70.
Club membership 315.
Visitors no restrictions.
Societies write in advance.
Green Fees £8 per day.
Designer W Fernie
Facilities ⊗ 🝰 💺 🝰 🝰 ⚘
& Leisure hard tennis courts, fishing.
Location 9m W of Brodick via String Rd

Hotel ★★🝰🝰 Kilmichael Country House Hotel, Glen Cloy, BRODICK ☎ 01770 302219 6 ⇆ 📷 Annexe3 ⇆ 📷

WHITING BAY   Map 10 NS02

Whiting Bay KA27 8QT ☎ 01770 700487
Heathland course.
18 holes, 4405yds, Par 63, SSS 63, Course record 59.
Club membership 350.
Visitors tee reserved 8.45-9.30am, also Sun 11.45-1pm.
Societies apply by telephone and confirm in writing with deposit.
Green Fees £17.50 per day; £13.50 per round (£33 weekends).
Facilities ⊗ 🝰 💺 💺 ♀ 🝰 🗃 🝰 🝰 🝰 ⚘
Location NW side of village off A841

Hotel ★★🝰🝰 Kilmichael Country House Hotel, Glen Cloy, BRODICK ☎ 01770 302219 6 ⇆ 📷 Annexe3 ⇆ 📷

AYR   Map 10 NS32

Belleisle Belleisle Park KA7 4DU
☎ 01292 441258 Fax 01292 442632
Parkland course with beautiful sea views. First-class conditions.
Belleisle Course: 18 holes, 6431yds, Par 71, SSS 72, Course record 63.
Seafield Course: 18 holes, 5498yds, Par 68, SSS 66.
Club membership 300.
Visitors advised to contact in advance, telephone to book.
Societies advised to contact in advance, telephone 01292 616255.
Green Fees £19 per round (£21 per round weekends). Day inc. Belleisle & Seafield £27.
Prof David Gemmell
Designer James Braid
Facilities ⊗ 🝰 💺 💺 ♀ 🝰 🗃 🝰 🝰 ⚘
Location 2m S on A719

Hotel ★★★ 58% Quality Hotel Ayr, Burns Statue Square, AYR ☎ 01292 263268 70 ⇆ 📷

Dalmilling Westwood Av KA8 0QY
☎ 01292 263893
Meadowland course, with easy walking.
18 holes, 5724yds, Par 69, SSS 68, Course record 61.
Club membership 140.
Visitors must contact in advance.
Societies must contact in advance.
Green Fees £20 per day; £13 per round (£25/£13.50 weekends).
Cards 🖸 🖸 🖸 🖸
Prof Philip Cheyney
Facilities ⊗ 🝰 💺 💺 ♀ 🝰 🗃 🝰 ⚘
Location 1.5m E of town centre off A719

Hotel ★★ 66% Carlton Toby Hotel, 187 Ayr Rd, PRESTWICK ☎ 01292 476811 34 ⇆ 📷

BALMORE   Map 11 NS57

Balmore Golf Course Rd G64 4AW
☎ 01360 620240 Fax 01360 620284
Parkland course with fine views.
18 holes, 5530yds, Par 66, SSS 67, Course record 63.
Club membership 700.
Visitors   must contact in advance and be accompanied by member, may not play at weekends
Societies   apply in writing.
Green Fees £35 per day; £25 per round.
Designer   James Braid
Facilities   ⊗ ⅶ 🍺 ♀ ⚒
Location   N off A807

Hotel   ★★★ 62% The Black Bull, Main St,
MILNGAVIE ☎ 0141 956 2291 27 ⇄ ⋔

BARASSIE   Map 10 NS33

Kilmarnock (Barassie) 29 Hillhouse Rd KA10 6SY
☎ 01292 313920 Fax 01292 313920
The club now has a 27 hole layout. Magnificent seaside links, relatively flat with much heather and small, undulating greens.
18 holes, 6817yds, Par 72, SSS 74, Course record 72.
New 9 hole course: 9 holes, 2888yds, Par 34, SSS 34.
Club membership 600.
Visitors   with member only Wed & weekends. May not play Fri am. Contact secretary in advance.
Societies   must telephone in advance and confirm in writing.
Green Fees £58 per 36 holes; £48 per 27 holes; £38 per 18 holes;.
Prof   Gregor Howie
Designer   Theodore Moone
Facilities   ⚒ 🏠 🍴 ⚷
Location   E side of village on B746

Hotel   ★★★★ 68% Marine Highland Hotel, Crosbie Rd, TROON
☎ 01292 314444 74 ⇄ ⋔

BARRHEAD   Map 11 NS45

Fereneze Fereneze Av G78 1HJ
☎ 0141 881 1519 Fax 0141 221 0135
Hilly moorland course, with a good view at the end of a hard climb to the 3rd, then levels out.
18 holes, 5821yds, Par 70, SSS 68.
Club membership 700.
Visitors   must contact in advance but may not play at weekends.
Societies   apply in writing.
Green Fees not confirmed.
Facilities   ⊗ ⅶ 🎱 🍺 ♀ ⚒ 🏠 🍴
Location   NW side of town off B774

Hotel   ★★★ 69% Dalmeny Park Country House, Lochlibo Rd, BARRHEAD
☎ 0141 881 9211 20 ⇄ ⋔

BEARSDEN   Map 11 NS57

Bearsden Thorn Rd G61 4BP ☎ 0141 942 2351
Parkland course, with 16 greens and 11 teeing grounds. Easy walking and views over city.
9 holes, 6014yds, Par 68, SSS 69, Course record 67.
Club membership 450.
Visitors   must be accompanied by and play with member.
Societies   apply by writing.
Green Fees not confirmed.
Facilities   ⚒
Location   1m W off A809

Hotel   ★★★ 62% The Black Bull, Main St,
MILNGAVIE ☎ 0141 956 2291 27 ⇄ ⋔

Douglas Park Hillfoot G61 2TJ
☎ 0141 942 2220 Fax 0141 942 0985
Parkland course with wide variety of holes.
18 holes, 5957yds, Par 69, SSS 69.
Club membership 900.
Visitors   must be accompanied by member and must contact in advance, Wednesdays and Thursdays for visiting parties only
Societies   Wed & Thu. Must telephone in advance.
Green Fees £30 per day; £22 per round.
Prof   David Scott
Facilities   ⊗ ⅶ by prior arrangement 🎱 🍺 ♀ ⚒ 🏠 ⚙
Location   E side of town on A81

Hotel   ★★★ 62% The Black Bull, Main St,
MILNGAVIE ☎ 0141 956 2291 27 ⇄ ⋔

Windyhill Baljaffray Rd G61 4QQ
☎ 0141 942 2349 Fax 0141 942 5874
Interesting parkland/moorland course with panoramic views of Glasgow and beyond; testing 12th hole.
18 holes, 6254yds, Par 71, SSS 70, Course record 64.
Club membership 800.
Visitors   may not play at weekends. Must contact professional in advance.
Societies   must apply in writing.
Green Fees £20 per day.
Prof   G Collinson
Designer   James Braid
Facilities   ⊗ ⅶ 🎱 🍺 ♀ ⚒ 🏠 🍴 ⚷
Location   2m NW off B8050

Hotel   ★★★ 62% The Black Bull, Main St,
MILNGAVIE ☎ 0141 956 2291 27 ⇄ ⋔

BEITH   Map 10 NS35

Beith Threepwood Rd KA15 2JR
☎ 01505 503166 Fax 01505 506814
Hilly course, with panoramic views over 7 counties.
18 holes, 5616yds, Par 68, SSS 68.
Club membership 420.
Visitors   contact for details.
Societies   apply in writing to secretary at least 1 month in advance.
Green Fees on application.
Facilities   ⊗ ⅶ 🎱 🍺 ♀ ⚒
Location   1.5m NE off A737

Hotel   ★★★ 66% Bowfield Hotel & Country Club, HOWWOOD ☎ 01505 705225 23 ⇄ ⋔

Bellshill   Map 11 NS76

Bellshill Community Rd, Orbiston ML4 2RZ
☎ 01698 745124
Parkland course.
18 holes, 5900yds, Par 69, SSS 69.
Club membership 500.
Visitors   apply in writing in advance, may not play on
            competition Sat & Sun.
Societies apply in writing in advance.
Green Fees £29 per day (2 rounds of golf plus meals).
Facilities ⊗ ⅢⅢ ⅃ ♥ ♀ ♧ ♧
Location   1m SE off A721

Hotel   ★★ 70% Redstones Hotel,
            8-10 Glasgow Rd, UDDINGSTON
            ☎ 01698 813774 & 814843
            Fax 01698 815319 18rm(16 ⇔ ♠)

Biggar   Map 11 NT03

Biggar The Park, Broughton Rd ML12 6AH
☎ 01899 220319
Flat parkland course, easy walking and fine views.
18 holes, 5600yds, Par 67, SSS 66, Course record 61.
Club membership 340.
Visitors   Must contact in advance. Smart casual wear
            required.
Societies must book in advance, observe dress code.
Green Fees £10 per round (£15 weekends & bank holidays).
Designer   W Park Jnr
Facilities ⊗ ⅢⅢ ⅃ ♥ ♀ ♧ ♧ ♧ ♧
& Leisure hard tennis courts.
Location   S side of town

Hotel   ★★★♨ 70% Shieldhill Hotel, Quothquan,
            BIGGAR ☎ 01899 220035   16 ⇔ ♠

Bishopbriggs   Map 11 NS67

Bishopbriggs Brackenbrae Rd G64 2DX ☎ 0141 772 1810
Parkland course with views to Campsie Hills.
18 holes, 6041yds, Par 69, SSS 69, Course record 63.
Club membership 600.
Visitors   must be accompanied by a member and have
            introduction from own club.
Societies apply in writing to the Committee one month in
            advance.
Green Fees not confirmed.
Facilities ♀ ♧ ♧
Location   0.5m NW off A803

Hotel   ★★★ 62% The Black Bull, Main St,
            MILNGAVIE ☎ 0141 956 2291 27 ⇔ ♠

Cawder Cadder Rd G64 3QD
☎ 0141 772 7101 Fax 0141 772 4463
Two parkland courses; Cawder Course is hilly, with 5th, 9th,
10th, 11th-testing holes. Keir Course is flat.
Cawder Course: 18 holes, 6295yds, Par 70, SSS 71.
Keir Course: 18 holes, 5877yds, Par 68, SSS 68.
Club membership 1150.
Visitors   must contact in advance & may play on
            weekdays only.
Societies must contact in writing, not on Bank Holidays
Green Fees £33 per day; £26 per round.

Cards   ⊷ ⬛⬛ ⬛ ⬛
Prof   Ken Stavely
Designer   James Braid
Facilities ⊗ ⅢⅢ ⅃ ♥ ♀ ♧ ♧ ♧
Location   1m NE off A803

Hotel   ★★★ 62% The Black Bull, Main St,
            MILNGAVIE ☎ 0141 956 2291 27 ⇔ ♠

Littlehill Auchinairn Rd G64 1UT ☎ 0141 772 1916
Municipal parkland course.
18 holes, 6240yds, Par 70, SSS 70.
Visitors   must contact in advance.
Societies advance bookings required in writing
Green Fees not confirmed.
Facilities ♧
Location   3m NE of Glasgow city centre on A803

Bishopton   Map 10 NS47

Erskine PA7 5PH ☎ 01505 862302
Parkland course.
18 holes, 6287yds, Par 71, SSS 70.
Club membership 700.
Visitors   introduced by member or by prior arrangement.
Societies apply in writing.
Green Fees £37 per day; £25 per round.
Prof   Peter Thomson
Facilities ♧ ♧ ♧ ♧
Location   0.75 NE off B815

Hotel   B Posthouse Glasgow/Erskine, North Barr,
            ERSKINE ☎ 0141 812 0123 166 ⇔ ♠

Bonhill   Map 10 NS37

Vale of Leven North Field Rd G83 9ET ☎ 01389 752351
Hilly moorland course, tricky with many natural hazards -
gorse, burns, trees. Overlooks Loch Lomond.
18 holes, 5162yds, Par 67, SSS 66, Course record 61.
Club membership 640.
Visitors   may not play Sat.
Societies apply to the secretary.
Green Fees £24 per day; £16 per round (£30/£20 weekends).
Facilities ⊗ ⅢⅢ ⅃ ♥ ♀ ♧ ♧ ♧
Location   E side of town off A813

Hotel   ★★ 65% Dumbuck Hotel, Glasgow Rd,
            DUMBARTON ☎ 01389 734336   22 ⇔ ♠

Bothwell   Map 11 NS75

Bothwell Castle Blantyre Rd G71 8PJ
☎ 01698 853177 Fax 01698 854052
Flattish tree lined parkland course in residential area.
18 holes, 6200yds, Par 71, SSS 70, Course record 63.
Club membership 1000.
Visitors   may only play Mon-Fri 9.30-10.30am & 2-3pm.
Green Fees not confirmed.
Prof   Gordon Niven
Facilities ⊗ ⅢⅢ ⅃ ♥ ♀ ♧ ♧ ♧ ♧
Location   NW of village off B7071

Hotel   ★★★ 66% Bothwell Bridge Hotel, 89 Main St,
            BOTHWELL ☎ 01698 852246   90 ⇔ ♠

BRIDGE OF WEIR   Map 10 NS36

Ranfurly Castle The Clubhouse, Golf Rd PA11 3HN
☎ 01505 612609 Fax 01505 612609
A highly challenging, 240 acre, picturesque moorland course.
18 holes, 6284yds, Par 70, SSS 71, Course record 65.
Club membership 825.
Visitors   golf club members on weekdays only, contact in advance.
Societies   Tue only, apply in writing.
Green Fees   £40 per day; £30 per round.
Prof   Tom Eckford
Designer   A Kirkcaldy/W Auchterlomie
Facilities   ⊗ ⁇ by prior arrangement ᒪ 🍺 ♀ 🏊 🏠 ⛳
                  🛒 ⚲
Location   5m NW of Johnstone

Hotel   ★★★ 66% Bowfield Hotel & Country Club,
                  HOWWOOD ☎ 01505 705225   23 ⇄ ℝ

BURNSIDE   Map 11 NS66

Blairbeth Fernbrae Av, Fernhill G73 4SF
☎ 0141 634 3355
Parkland course.
18 holes, 5518yds, Par 70, SSS 68, Course record 64.
Club membership 600.
Visitors   must contact in advance & may not play weekends.
Societies   apply in advance.
Green Fees   on application.
Facilities   ⊗ ⁇ ᒪ 🍺 ♀ 🏊
Location   2m S of Rutherglen off Burnside road

Hotel   ★★★ 66% The Macdonald, Eastwood Toll,
                  GIFFNOCK ☎ 0141 638 2225 56 ⇄ ℝ

Cathkin Braes Cathkin Rd G73 4SE
☎ 0141 634 6605 Fax 0141 634 6605
Moorland course, prevailing westerly wind, small loch hazard at 5th hole.
18 holes, 6208yds, Par 71, SSS 71.
Club membership 890.
Visitors   must contact in advance & have handicap certificate but may not play at weekends.
Societies   apply in writing.
Green Fees   not confirmed.
Prof   Stephen Bree
Designer   James Braid
Facilities   ⊗ ⁇ ᒪ 🍺 ♀ 🏊 🏠 🛒 🛒 ⚲
Location   1m S on B759

Hotel   ★★★ 66% The Macdonald, Eastwood Toll,
                  GIFFNOCK ☎ 0141 638 2225 56 ⇄ ℝ

CARLUKE   Map 11 NS85

Carluke Mauldslie Rd, Hallcraig ML8 5HG
☎ 01555 771070 & 770574
Parkland course with views over the Clyde Valley. Testing 11th hole, par 3.
18 holes, 5853yds, Par 70, SSS 68, Course record 63.
Club membership 750.
Visitors   must contact in advance & may not play weekends and bank holidays.
Societies   prior arrangement required.

Green Fees not confirmed.
Prof   Richard Forrest
Facilities   ⊗ ⁇ ᒪ 🍺 ♀ 🏊 🏠 ⚲
Location   1m W off A73

Hotel   ★★★ 68% Popinjay Hotel, Lanark Rd,
                  ROSEBANK ☎ 01555 860441
                  40 ⇄ ℝ Annexe5 ⇄ ℝ

CARNWATH   Map 11 NS94

Carnwath 1 Main St ML11 8JX ☎ 01555 840251
Picturesque parkland course slightly hilly, with small greens calling for accuracy. Panoramic views.
18 holes, 5953yds, Par 70, SSS 69, Course record 63.
Club membership 470.
Visitors   restricted after 5pm, no visitors Sat.
Societies   apply in writing or telephone.
Green Fees   not confirmed.
Facilities   ⊗ ⁇ ᒪ 🍺 ♀ 🏊 🏠 ⚲
Location   W side of village on A70

Hotel   ★★★ 64% Cartland Bridge Hotel, Glasgow
                  Rd, LANARK ☎ 01555 664426   18 ⇄ ℝ

CASTLE DOUGLAS   Map 11 NX76

Castle Douglas Abercromby Rd DG7 1BB
☎ 01556 502801 or 502099
Parkland course, one severe hill.
9 holes, 2704yds, Par 68, SSS 66.
Club membership 500.
Societies   apply by writing to secretary.
Green Fees   not confirmed.
Facilities   ⊗ ᒪ 🍺 ♀ 🏊 🏠 🛒 ⚲
Location   W side of town

Hotel   ★★ 65% Imperial Hotel, 35 King St, CASTLE
                  DOUGLAS ☎ 01556 502086   12 ⇄ ℝ

CLARKSTON   Map 11 NS55

Cathcart Castle Mearns Rd G76 7YL
☎ 0141 638 9449 Fax 0141 638 1201
Tree-lined parkland course, with undulating terrain.
18 holes, 5832yds, Par 68, SSS 68.
Club membership 995.
Visitors   by prior arrangement with professional, must have a handicap certificate from own club.
Societies   Tue & Thu only; must apply in writing.
Green Fees   £40 per day; £28 per round.
Prof   Stephen Duncan
Facilities   ⊗ ⁇ ᒪ 🍺 ♀ 🏊 🏠 🛒 ⚲
Location   0.75m SW off A726

Hotel   ★★★ 66% The Macdonald, Eastwood Toll,
                  GIFFNOCK ☎ 0141 638 2225 56 ⇄ ℝ

CLYDEBANK   Map 11 NS56

Clydebank & District Glasgow Rd, Hardgate G81 5QY
☎ 01389 383831 & 383833 Fax 01389 383831
An undulating parkland course established in 1905 overlooking Clydebank.
18 holes, 5823yds, Par 68, SSS 68, Course record 64.
Club membership 889.

▶

Visitors round only, weekdays only and no bank holidays. Must tee off before 4.30pm. Apply to professional 01389 878686.
Societies must apply in writing.
Green Fees £15.
Designer Members
Facilities ⊗ ℐℙ ⬆ ♥ ♀ ♣ ♠
Location 2m E of Erskine Bridge

Hotel ★★★ 65% Patio Hotel, 1 South Av, Clydebank Business Park, CLYDEBANK ☎ 0141 951 1133 80 ⇥ ↸

Dalmuir Municipal Overtoun Rd, Dalmuir G81 3RE
☎ 0141 952 6372
Hilly, compact parkland course with tough finishing holes.
18 holes, 5349yds, Par 67, SSS 66.
Visitors no restrictions.
Societies contact in advance.
Green Fees not confirmed.
Prof Stewart Savage
Facilities ⊗ ℐℙ ⬆ ♀ ♣ ♠ ♨ ✎
& Leisure bowling, hard tennis court Apr-Sep.
Location 2m NW of town centre

Hotel ★★★ 65% Patio Hotel, 1 South Av, Clydebank Business Park, CLYDEBANK ☎ 0141 951 1133 80 ⇥ ↸

COATBRIDGE

Map 11 NS76

Drumpellier Drumpellier Av ML5 1RX
☎ 01236 424139 Fax 01236 428723
Parkland course.
18 holes, 6227yds, Par 71, SSS 70, Course record 60.
Club membership 827.
Visitors must contact in advance, may not play weekends.
Societies apply in advance.
Green Fees £30 per day; £22 per round.
Prof David Ross
Designer W Fernie
Facilities ⊗ ℐℙ ⬆ ♥ ♀ ♣ ♠ ♨ ✎
Location 0.75m W off A89

Hotel ★★★ 66% Bothwell Bridge Hotel, 89 Main St, BOTHWELL ☎ 01698 852246 90 ⇥ ↸

COLDSTREAM

Map 12 NT83

Hirsel Kelso Rd TD12 4NJ
☎ 01890 882678 & 882233 Fax 01890 882233
A beautifully situated parkland course set in the Hirsel Estate, with panoramic views of the Cheviot Hills. Each hole offers a different challenge especially the 7th, a 170yd par 3 demanding accuracy of flight and length from the tee to ensure achieving a par.
18 holes, 6092yds, Par 70, SSS 70, Course record 65.
Club membership 680.
Visitors contact for details, no restrictions.
Societies write or telephone the secretary in advance.
Green Fees not confirmed.
Facilities ⊗ ℐℙ ⬆ ♥ ♀ ♣ ♠ ♨ ✎
Location At W end of Coldstream on A697

Hotel ★★★⚘ 72% Tillmouth Park Hotel, CORNHILL-ON-TWEED ☎ 01890 882255 12 ⇥ ↸ Annexe2 ⇥ ↸

COLVEND

Map 11 NX85

Colvend Sandyhills DG5 4PY
☎ 01556 630398 & 610878 (Sec)
Picturesque and challenging course on Solway coast. Superb views.
18 holes, 5220yds, Par 68, SSS 67.
Club membership 490.
Visitors restricted Apr-Sep on Tue, 1st tee reserved for weekly Medal 1-1.30 & 4-6pm and some weekends for open competitions.
Societies must telephone in advance.
Green Fees £18 per day; £70 per week.
Designer Allis & Thomas
Facilities ⊗ ℐℙ ⬆ ♥ ♀ ♣ ♠ ♨ ✎
Location 6m from Dalbeattie on A710 Solway Coast Rd

Hotel ★★ 64% Clonyard House Hotel, COLVEND ☎ 01556 630372 15 ⇥ ↸

CUMBERNAULD

Map 11 NS77

Dullatur 1A Glen Douglas Dr G68 0DW
☎ 01236 723230 Fax 01236 727271
Dullatur Carrickstone is a parkland course, with natural hazards and wind. Dullatur Antonine, designed by Dave Thomas, is a modern course opened in 1996.
Carrickstone: 18 holes, 6204yds, Par 70, SSS 70, Course record 68.
Antonine: 18 holes, 5940yds, Par 70, SSS 70.
Club membership 700.
Visitors telephone for availability.
Societies must apply in writing to secretary.
Green Fees £30 per day; £20 per round (£35/£25 weekends).
Cards 💳 ▬▬▬
Prof Duncan Sinclair
Designer James Braid
Facilities ⊗ ℐℙ ⬆ ♥ ♀ ♣ ♠ ♨ 🏐 ⚓ ✎
& Leisure hard tennis courts, sauna, solarium, gymnasium, Bowling.
Location 1.5m N

Hotel ★★★★ 64% Westerwood Hotel Golf & Country Club, 1 St Andrews Dr, Westerwood, CUMBERNAULD ☎ 01236 457171 49 ⇥ ↸

Palacerigg Palacerigg Country Park G67 3HU
☎ 01236 734969 Fax 01236 721461
Well wooded parkland course.
18 holes, 6444yds, Par 72, SSS 71, Course record 65.
Club membership 350.
Visitors anytime except club competitions, advance booking advisable.
Societies apply in writing to the Secretary.
Green Fees not confirmed.
Designer Henry Cotton
Facilities ⊗ ℐℙ ⬆ ♥ ♀ ♣ ♠
Location 2m S of Cumbernauld on Palacerigg road off Lenziemill road B8054

Hotel ★★★★ 64% Westerwood Hotel Golf & Country Club, 1 St Andrews Dr, Westerwood, CUMBERNAULD ☎ 01236 457171 49 ⇥ ↸

Westerwood Hotel Golf & Country Club
1 St Andrews Dr, Westerwood G68 0EW
☎ 01236 457171 Fax 01236 738478
Undulating parkland/woodland course designed by Dave
Thomas and Seve Ballesteros. Holes meander through silver
birch, firs, heaths and heathers, and the spectacular 15th,
'The Waterfall', has its green set against a 40ft rockface.
Buggie track. Hotel facilities.
18 holes, 6616yds, Par 72, SSS 72, Course record 65.
Club membership 1000.

Visitors	advised to book in advance.
Societies	all bookings through golf coordinator on 01236 457171 ext 215.
Green Fees	£35 per day; £22.50 per round (£45/£27.50 weekends).
Cards	⬜⬜⬜⬜⬜
Prof	Steven Killin
Designer	Seve Ballesteros/Dave Thomas
Facilities	⊗ 🏌 🍴 🏪 ♀ ⛳ 🏠 🏌 🎾 🚣 🏊 🏇
& Leisure	hard tennis courts, heated indoor swimming pool, solarium, gymnasium, steam room, beauty salon, aerobics, snooker table, table tennis.
Location	Adjacent to A80, 14m from Glasgow City Centre

Hotel	★★★★ 64% Westerwood Hotel Golf & Country Club, 1 St Andrews Dr, Westerwood, CUMBERNAULD ☎ 01236 457171 49 ⇄ ⭢

CUMMERTREES   Map 11 NY16

Powfoot DG12 5QE
☎ 01461 700276 Fax 01461 700276
This British Championship Course is on the Solway
Firth, playing at this delightfully compact semi-links
seaside course is a scenic treat. Lovely holes include the
2nd, the 8th and the 11th, also 9th with World War II
bomb crater.
18 holes, 6283yds, Par 71, SSS 70, Course record 63.
Club membership 920.

Visitors	contact in advance. May not play before 9am between 11am-1pm and after 3.30pm wekdays, no visitors Sat or before 2pm Sun.
Societies	must book in advance.
Green Fees	£30 per day; £23 per round, also 3/5 day ticket available.
Prof	Gareth Dick
Designer	J Braid
Facilities	⊗ 🏌 🍴 ♀ 🏪 ⛳
Location	0.5m off B724

Hotel	★★ 66% Golf Hotel, Links Av, POWFOOT ☎ 01461 700254 19rm(16 ⇄ ⭢)

DUMBARTON   Map 10 NS37

Dumbarton Broadmeadow G82 2BQ
☎ 01389 732830 Fax 01389 765995
Flat parkland course.
18 holes, 5992yds, Par 71, SSS 69, Course record 64.
Club membership 700.

Visitors	may play Mon, Thu & Fri only.
Societies	must apply in writing to Secretary.
Green Fees	not confirmed.
Facilities	⊗ 🏌 🍴 🏪 ♀ ⛳
Location	0.25m N off A814

Hotel	★★ 65% Dumbuck Hotel, Glasgow Rd, DUMBARTON ☎ 01389 734336 22 ⇄ ⭢

DUMFRIES   Map 11 NX97

Dumfries & County Nunfield, Edinburgh Rd DG1 1JX
☎ 01387 253585
Parkland course alongside River Nith, with views over the
Queensberry Hills.
Nunfield: 18 holes, 5928yds, Par 69, SSS 68,
Course record 63.
Club membership 800.

Visitors	must contact in advance but may not play Saturdays and during competitions on Sundays
Societies	apply in writing.
Green Fees	£25 per day.

▶

Prof Stuart Syme
Designer James Braid
Facilities ⊗ ⑂ ⓛ ╚ ♥ ♀ ♨ ☎ ⑁ ⌀
Location 1m NE of Dumfries on A701

Hotel ★★★ Station Hotel, 49 Lovers Walk, DUMFRIES ☎ 01387 254316 32 ⇔ ⌀
Additional hotel ★★★ 68% Cairndale Hotel & Leisure Club, English St, DUMFRIES
☎ 01387 254111 Fax 01387 250555
76 ⇔ ⌀
See advertisement on page 371.

Dumfries & Galloway 2 Laurieston Av DG2 7NY
☎ 01387 263848
Parkland course.
18 holes, 5803yds, Par 68, SSS 68.
Club membership 800.
Visitors may not play on competition days.
Societies apply in writing.
Green Fees not confirmed.
Prof Joe Fergusson
Facilities ♀ ♨ ☎ ⑁
Location W side of town centre on A75

Hotel ★★★ 68% Cairndale Hotel & Leisure Club, English St, DUMFRIES
☎ 01387 254111 76 ⇔ ⌀

DUNS   Map 12 NT75

Duns Longformacus Rd TD11 3NR
☎ 01361 882717 (Sec) & 882194 (Clubhouse)
Interesting upland course, with natural hazards of water and hilly slopes. Views south to the Cheviot Hills. A burn comes into play at 7 of the holes.
18 holes, 6209yds, Par 70, SSS 70.
Club membership 520.
Visitors welcome except competition days and Mon, Tue and Wed after 4pm. Advisable to contact in advance Apr-Oct.
Societies write or telephone the secretary in advance for booking details.
Green Fees £17 per day; £14 per round (£22/£17 weekends).
Designer A H Scott
Facilities ⊗ by prior arrangement ╚ ♥ ♀ ♨ ⌀
Location 1m W off A6105

Hotel ★★★ 71% Marshall Meadows Country House Hotel, BERWICK-UPON-TWEED
☎ 01289 331133 19 ⇔ ⌀

EAGLESHAM   Map 11 NS55

Bonnyton Kirktonmoor Rd G76 0QA
☎ 01355 302781 Fax 01355 303151
Dramatic moorland course offering spectacular views beautiful countryside as far as snow-capped Ben Lomond. Tree-lined fairways, plateau greens, natural burns and well situated bunkers and a unique variety of holes offer golfers both challenge and reward.
18 holes, 6255yds, Par 72, SSS 71.
Club membership 960.
Visitors welcome weekdays only (ex Tue), must contact in advance.
Societies must telephone in advance.
Green Fees not confirmed.

Prof Kendal McWade
Facilities ⊗ ⑂ ⓛ ╚ ♥ ♀ ♨ ☎ ⑁ ♞ ⌀
Location 0.25m SW off B764

Hotel ★★★ 62% Bruce Hotel, Cornwall St, EAST KILBRIDE ☎ 01355 229771 78 ⇔ ⌀

EAST KILBRIDE   Map 11 NS65

East Kilbride Chapelside Rd, Nerston G74 4PF
☎ 01355 247728
Parkland and hill course. Very windy. Testing 7th, 9th and 14th holes.
18 holes, 6419yds, Par 71, SSS 71.
Club membership 850.
Visitors by appointment.
Societies must telephone in advance & submit formal application.
Green Fees not confirmed.
Prof Willy Walker
Facilities ⊗ by prior arrangement ⑂ ╚ ♥ ♀ ♨ ☎ ⑁ ⌀
Location 0.5m N off A749

Hotel ★★★ 62% Bruce Hotel, Cornwall St, EAST KILBRIDE ☎ 01355 229771 78 ⇔ ⌀

Torrance House Calderglen Country Park, Strathaven Rd G75 0QZ ☎ 01355 248638 Fax 01355 233451
A mature parkland course.
18 holes, 6476yds, Par 72, SSS 69, Course record 71.
Club membership 1000.
Visitors welcome, may book up to six days in advance.
Societies Mon-Fri. Apply in writing to John Dunlop, South Lanarkshire Council, Civic Centre, East Kilbride.
Green Fees £8.10-£9.50 per round.
Prof John Dunlop
Facilities ⊗ ⑂ ⓛ ╚ ♥ ♀ ♨ ☎ ⑁ ⌀
Location 1.5m SE of Kilbride on A726

Hotel ★★★ 62% Bruce Hotel, Cornwall St, EAST KILBRIDE
☎ 01355 229771 78 ⇔ ⌀

EYEMOUTH   Map 12 NT96

Eyemouth Gunsgreen Hill TD14 5SF
☎ 01890 750551 & 750004 (Starter)
A superb course set on the East Berwickshire coast, containing interesting and challenging holes. The clubhouse overlooks the picturesque fishing village of Eyemouth and provides panoramic views over the course and North Sea.
18 holes, 6472yds, Par 72, SSS 71, Course record 67.
Club membership 400.
Visitors may not play before 9am Sat or before 10am Sun.
Societies apply in writing or telephone.
Green Fees £22 per day; £15 per day (£30/£20 weekends).
Prof Paul Terras, Tony McLeman
Designer J R Bain
Facilities ⊗ ⑂ ⓛ ╚ ♥ ♀ ♨ ☎ ⑁ ♝ ⌀
Location E side of town, 8m N of Berwick and 2m off A1

Hotel ★★★ 71% Marshall Meadows Country House Hotel, BERWICK-UPON-TWEED
☎ 01289 331133 19 ⇔ ⌀

GALASHIELS Map 12 NT43

Galashiels Ladhope Recreation Ground TD1 2NJ
☎ 01896 753724
Hillside course, superb views from the top; 10th hole very
steep.
18 holes, 5185yds, Par 67, SSS 66, Course record 61.
Club membership 343.
Visitors	must contact the secretary in advance especially for weekends.
Societies	arrangements with secretary especially for weekends.
Green Fees	not confirmed.
Designer	James Braid
Facilities	⊗ by prior arrangement ⮐ by prior arrangement ▼ by prior arrangement ♀ ⟁ ♂
Location	N side of town centre off A7

Hotel   ★★★ 65% Kingsknowes Hotel, Selkirk Rd,
GALASHIELS ☎ 01896 758375 11 ⇆ ⋒

Torwoodlee TD1 2NE ☎ 01896 752260
Parkland course with natural hazards designed by Willie Park
with a new extension by John Garner, provides a good test
for all abilities of play.
18 holes, 6200yds, Par 70, SSS 69, Course record 68.
Club membership 550.
Visitors	restricted Thu - ladies day and Sat - mens competitions.
Societies	letter to secretary.
Green Fees	£25 per day; £18 per round (£30/£25 weekends), packages available £24-£40.
Cards	💳 💳
Prof	R Elliot
Designer	Willie Park
Facilities	⊗ ⨉ ⮐ ▼ ♀ ⟁ 🏠 🎯 ⬥ ♨ ♂
Location	1.75m NW off A7

Hotel   ★★★ 65% Kingsknowes Hotel, Selkirk Rd,
GALASHIELS ☎ 01896 758375 11 ⇆ ⋒

GALSTON Map 11 NS53

Loudoun Edinburgh Rd KA4 8PA
☎ 01563 821993 & 820551 Fax 01563 822229
Pleasant, fairly flat parkland course with many mature trees.
18 holes, 5773yds, Par 68, SSS 68, Course record 61.
Club membership 750.
Visitors	must contact in advance. Weekdays only, must play with member at weekends/public holidays
Societies	telephone in advance.
Green Fees	£30 per day; £18 per round.
Facilities	⊗ ⨉ ⮐ ▼ ♀ ⟁ 🏠 ♂
Location	NE side of town on A71

Hotel   ★★★ 68% Strathaven Hotel, Hamilton Rd,
STRATHAVEN ☎ 01357 521778 22 ⇆ ⋒

GARTCOSH Map 11 NS66

Mount Ellen Johnston Rd G69 8EY
☎ 01236 872277 Fax 01236 872249
Downland course with 73 bunkers. Testing hole: 10th
('Bedlay'), 156 yds, par 3.
18 holes, 5525yds, Par 68, SSS 67, Course record 67.
Club membership 500.

Visitors	may play Mon-Fri 9am-4pm. Must contact in advance.
Societies	must contact in advance.
Green Fees	£30 per day, £16 per round.
Prof	Iain Bilsborough
Facilities	⊗ ⨉ ⮐ ▼ ♀ ⟁ 🏠 🎯 ⬥ ♨ ♂
Location	0.75m N off A752

Hotel   ★★★★ 64% Copthorne Glasgow,
George Square, GLASGOW
☎ 0141 332 6711 141 ⇆ ⋒

GATEHOUSE-OF-FLEET Map 11 NX55

Gatehouse Laurieston Rd DG7 2BE ☎ 01644 450260
Set against a background of rolling hills with scenic views of
Fleet Bay and the Solway Firth.
9 holes, 2521yds, Par 66, SSS 66, Course record 60.
Club membership 370.
Visitors	restricted Sun before 11.30am.
Societies	telephone in advance.
Green Fees	£10 per day/round.
Designer	Tom Fernie
Facilities	⟁
Location	0.25m N of town

Hotel   ★★★ 64% Murray Arms Hotel,
GATEHOUSE OF FLEET
☎ 01557 814207 12 ⇆ ⋒ Annexe1 ⇆ ⋒
Additional   ★★★★♨ 68% Cally Palace Hotel,
hotel   GATEHOUSE OF FLEET
☎ 01557 814341 Fax 01557 814522 56 ⇆

GIRVAN   Map 10 NX19

Brunston Castle Golf Course Rd, Dailly KA26 9GD
☎ 01465 811471 Fax 01465 811545
Sheltered inland parkland course. A championship design by
Donald Steel, the course is bisected by the River Girvan and
shaped to incorporate all the natural surroundings. It finishes
with the 17th 185 yards over a man made lake. Driving
range.
Burns: 18 holes, 6792yds, Par 72, SSS 73, Course record 71.
Club membership 400.
Visitors   reserved for members at weekends 8-10 &
            12.30-1.30. Must contact in advance.
Societies   telephone 01465 811471 to book.
Green Fees £40 per day; £26 per round (£45/£30 weekends).
Prof   Stephen Forbes
Designer   Donald Steel
Facilities ⊗ ⽸ ⅃ ⌷ ♥ ♀ ⚐ ☎ ⍲ ⚲ ⚑ ⚶ ⚯ ⚘ ⚵
Location   6m SE of Turnberry, 5m E of Girvan

Hotel   ★★★ 77% Malin Court, TURNBERRY
            ☎ 01655 331457 18 ⊋ ⚲

Girvan Golf Course Rd KA26 9HW ☎ 01465 714272
Municipal seaside and parkland course. Testing 17th hole
(223-yds) uphill, par 3. Good views.
18 holes, 5098yds, Par 64, SSS 65, Course record 61.
Club membership 175.
Visitors   telephone to book.
Societies   welcome.
Green Fees £20 per day, £13 per round (£25/£13.50
            weekends).
Cards   ⎓ ▦ ▨ ⯑
Designer   D Kinnell/J Braid
Facilities ⊗ ⽸ ⅃ ⌷ ♥ ♀ ⚐ ⚯
Location   N side of town off A77

Hotel   ★★★ 77% Malin Court, TURNBERRY
            ☎ 01655 331457 18 ⊋ ⚲

GLASGOW   Map 11 NS56

Alexandra Alexandra Park, Alexandra Pde G31 8SE
☎ 0141 556 1294
Parkland course, hilly with some woodland. Many bunkers
and a barrier of trees between 1st and 9th fairway. Work
currently in progress to alter greens and improve course,
9 holes, 2800yds, Par 31, Course record 25.
Club membership 85.

Visitors   no restrictions.
Societies   telephone 24 hrs in advance or by writing one
            week in advance.
Green Fees not confirmed.
Designer   G McArthur
Facilities ⚐
Location   2m E of city centre off M8/A8

Cowglen Barrhead Rd G43 1AU
☎ 0141 632 0556 Fax 01505 503000
Undulating and challenging parkland course with good views
over the Clyde valley to the Campsie Hills. Club and line
selection is most important on many holes due to the
strategic placing of copses on the course.
18 holes, 6079yds, Par 69, SSS 69, Course record 63.
Club membership 805.
Visitors   play on shorter course. Must contact in advance
            and have a handicap certificate. No visitors Tue,
            Fri and weekends.
Societies   must be booked in writing through the secretary.
Green Fees £35 per day; £25 per round.
Prof   John McTear
Designer   David Adams/James Braid
Facilities ⊗ ⽸ ⅃ ⌷ ♥ ♀ ⚐ ☎ ⚯
Location   4.5m SW of city centre on B762

Hotel   ★★★ 66% The Macdonald, Eastwood Toll,
            GIFFNOCK ☎ 0141 638 2225 56 ⊋ ⚲

Haggs Castle 70 Dumbreck Rd, Dumbreck G41 4SN
☎ 0141 427 1157 Fax 0141 427 1157
Wooded, parkland course where Scottish National
Championships and the Glasgow and Scottish Open have
been held. Quite difficult.
18 holes, 6464yds, Par 73, SSS 72.
Club membership 900.
Visitors   may not play at weekends. Must contact in
            advance.
Societies   apply in writing.
Green Fees not confirmed.
Prof   Jim McAlister
Designer   James Baird
Facilities ⚐ ☎ ⚶ ⚘ ⚵ ⚯
Location   2.5m SW of city centre on B768

Hotel   ★★★ 67% Swallow Hotel,
            517 Paisley Rd West, GLASGOW
            ☎ 0141 427 3146 117 ⊋ ⚲

Kirkhill Greenless Rd, Cambuslang G72 8YN
☎ 0141 641 8499 Fax 0141 641 8499
Meadowland course designed by James Braid.
18 holes, 6030yds, Par 70, SSS 70, Course record 63.
Club membership 650.
Visitors　　　must play with member at weekends.
Societies　　must contact in advance.
Green Fees　not confirmed.
Prof　　　　　Duncan Williamson
Designer　　 J Braid
Facilities　　⊗ ⅲ ⅳ ⅴ ⅵ ⅶ ⅷ
Location　　 5m SE of city centre off A749

Hotel　　　　★★★ 61% Stuart Hotel, 2 Cornwall Way,
　　　　　　　Town Centre, EAST KILBRIDE
　　　　　　　☎ 013552 21161 39 ⇔ ℟

Knightswood Lincoln Av G13 5QZ
☎ 0141 959 6358
Flat parkland course within easy reach of city. Two dog-legs.
9 holes, 5584yds, Par 68, SSS 67.
Club membership 40.
Visitors　　　reserved tee Wed and Fri am bookings 1 day in
　　　　　　　advance, no other restrictions.
Societies　　welcome, must book 1 day in advance.
Green Fees　£3 per 9 holes.
Facilities　　Ⅵ
Location　　 4m W of city centre off A82

Hotel　　　　★★★ 66% Jurys Glasgow Hotel,
　　　　　　　Great Western Rd, GLASGOW
　　　　　　　☎ 0141 334 8161 136 ⇔ ℟

Lethamhill 1240 Cumbernauld Rd, Millerston G33 1AH
☎ 0141 770 6220 Fax 1041 770 0520
Municipal parkland course.
18 holes, 5859yds, Par 70, SSS 69.
Visitors　　　must contact in advance.
Societies　　must contact in advance.
Green Fees　not confirmed.
Facilities　　Ⅵ
Location　　 3m NE of city centre on A80

Hotel　　　　★★★★ 64% Copthorne Glasgow,
　　　　　　　George Square, GLASGOW
　　　　　　　☎ 0141 332 6711 141 ⇔ ℟

Linn Park Simshill Rd G44 5EP ☎ 0141 633 0377
Municipal parkland course with six par 3's in outward half.
18 holes, 4952yds, Par 65, SSS 65, Course record 61.
Visitors　　　must contact in advance.
Societies　　advance booking in writing
Green Fees　not confirmed.
Facilities　　Ⅵ
Location　　 4m S of city centre off B766

Hotel　　　　★★★ 62% Bruce Hotel, Cornwall St,
　　　　　　　EAST KILBRIDE ☎ 01355 229771　78 ⇔ ℟

Pollok 90 Barrhead Rd G43 1BG
☎ 0141 632 4351 & 632 1080 Fax 0141 649 1398
Parkland course with woods and river.
18 holes, 6254yds, Par 71, SSS 70, Course record 62.
Club membership 620.
Visitors　　　Members only until 2pm weekends. Must
　　　　　　　contact in advance. Ladies only as part of
　　　　　　　visiting parties

Societies　　must contact in writing.
Green Fees　£40 per day; £30 per round.
Designer　　 James Braid
Facilities　　⊗ ⅲ ⅳ ⅴ ⅵ ⅶ ⅷ ⅸ
Location　　 4m SW of city centre on A762

Hotel　　　　★★★ 64% The Tinto Firs, 470 Kilmarnock Rd,
　　　　　　　GLASGOW ☎ 0141 637 2353 27 ⇔ ℟

Williamwood Clarkston Rd G44 3YR
☎ 0141 637 1783 Fax 0141 571 0166
Undulating parkland course with mature woodlands.
18 holes, 5878yds, Par 67, SSS 69, Course record 61.
Club membership 800.
Visitors　　　apply in writing to secretary, no weekend play.
Societies　　midweek bookings only, apply in writing to
　　　　　　　secretary.
Green Fees　£35 per day; £25 per round.
Prof　　　　　Stewart Marshall
Designer　　 James Braid
Facilities　　⊗ ⅲ ⅳ ⅴ ⅵ ⅶ ⅷ ⅸ
Location　　 5m S of city centre on B767

Hotel　　　　★★★ 66% The Macdonald, Eastwood Toll,
　　　　　　　GIFFNOCK ☎ 0141 638 2225 56 ⇔ ℟

GLENLUCE　　　　　　　　　　　　　Map 10 NX15

Wigtownshire County Mains of Park DG8 0NN
☎ 01581 300420
Seaside links course on the shores of Luce Bay, easy walking
but affected by winds. The 12th hole, a dogleg with out of
bounds to the right,is named after the course's designer,
Gordon Cunnigham.
18 holes, 5847yds, Par 70, SSS 68, Course record 67.
Club membership 450.
Visitors　　　may play any day by prior arrangement ex
　　　　　　　competition days.
Societies　　must contact in advance.
Green Fees　£23 per day ; £18 per round (£25/£20
　　　　　　　weekends).
Designer　　 W Gordon Cunningham
Facilities　　⊗ ⅲ ⅳ ⅴ ⅵ ⅶ ⅷ ⅸ ℡ ⅹ
Location　　 1.5m W off A75

Hotel　　　　★★★★ 69% North West Castle Hotel,
　　　　　　　STRANRAER
　　　　　　　☎ 01776 704413　70 ⇔ ℟ Annexe3 ⇔ ℟

GREAT CUMBRAE ISLAND (MILLPORT)
　　　　　　　　　　　　　　　　　　　　Map 10 NS15

Millport Golf Rd KA28 0HB
☎ 01475 530305 (Prof) & 530311 Fax 01475 530306
Pleasantly situated on the west side of Cumbrae looking over
Bute to Arran and the Mull of Kintyre. Exposure means
conditions may vary according to wind strength and
direction. A typical seaside resort course welcoming visitors.
18 holes, 5828yds, Par 68, SSS 69, Course record 64.
Club membership 525.
Visitors　　　advisable to phone and book tee times especially
　　　　　　　in summer months.
Societies　　telephone or write in advance.
Green Fees　£20 per day; £18 per round.
Designer　　 James Braid
Facilities　　⊗ ⅲ ⅳ ⅴ ⅵ ⅶ ⅷ ⅸ
Location　　 Approx 4m from ferry slip　　　　　　 ▶

Hotel   ★★★ 72% Brisbane House, 14 Greenock Rd, Esplanade, LARGS
☎ 01475 687200   23 ⇥ ↿

GRETNA   Map 11 NY36

Gretna Kirtle View DG16 5HD   ☎ 01461 338464
A nice parkland course on gentle hills. Opened in 1991, it offers a good test of skill.
9 holes, 3214yds, Par 72, SSS 71, Course record 71.
Club membership 250.
Visitors   no restrictions.
Societies   telephone in advance.
Green Fees not confirmed.
Designer   N Williams
Facilities   ⚐ ⌀ ↿
Location   0.5m W of Gretna on B721,signposted

Hotel   ★★ 68% Solway Lodge Hotel, Annan Rd, GRETNA
☎ 01461 338266 3 ⇥ ↿ Annexe7 ⇥ ↿

HAMILTON   Map 11 NS75

Hamilton Carlisle Rd, Ferniegair ML3 7TU
☎ 01698 282872
Beautiful parkland course.
18 holes, 6243yds, Par 70, SSS 71, Course record 62.
Visitors   must contact in advance, may not play weekends.
Societies   apply in writing.
Green Fees not confirmed.
Prof   Maurice Moir
Designer   James Braid
Facilities   ⊗ ⑂ ⚐ ▆ ♀ ⚐ 🖿 ⌀
Location   1.5m SE on A72

Hotel   B Holiday Inn Express, Strathclyde Country Park, HAMILTON ☎ 01698 858585 120 ↿

Strathclyde Park Mote Hill ML3 6BY
☎ 01698 429350
Municipal wooded parkland course with views into the Strathclyde Park sailing loch.
9 holes, 3128yds, Par 36, SSS 70, Course record 64.
Club membership 240.
Visitors   telephone, same day booking system in operation. May book up to 1 week in advance. Weekdays or weekends
Societies   must contact in advance on above telephone number.
Green Fees £3 per 9 holes (£3.50 weekends & bank holidays).
Prof   William Walker
Facilities   ⚐ ▆ ♀ ⚐ 🖿 ↿
Location   N side of town off B7071

Hotel   B Holiday Inn Express, Strathclyde Country Park, HAMILTON ☎ 01698 858585 120 ↿

HAWICK   Map 12 NT51

Hawick Vertish Hill TD9 0NY   ☎ 01450 372293
Hill course with good views.
18 holes, 5929yds, Par 68, SSS 69, Course record 63.
Club membership 600.

Visitors   must contact in advance. Course busy Sat until 3pm. 1st tee off time for visitors on Sun 10.30pm.
Societies   write or telephone for booking arrangement.
Green Fees £24 per day; £18 per round.
Facilities   ⊗ ⑂ ⚐ ▆ ♀ ⚐ 🖿 ⌀
Location   SW side of town

Hotel   ★★ 71% Kirklands Hotel, West Stewart Place, HAWICK
☎ 01450 372263 5 ⇥ ↿ Annexe4 ⇥ ↿

INNERLEITHEN   Map 11 NT33

Innerleithen Leithen Water, Leithen Rd EH44 6NL
☎ 01896 830951
Moorland course, with easy walking. Burns and rivers are natural hazards. Testing 5th hole (100 yds) par 3.
9 holes, 6066yds, Par 70, SSS 69, Course record 65.
Club membership 240.
Visitors   advisable to check for availability for weekends.
Societies   by prior booking.
Green Fees not confirmed.
Designer   Willie Park
Facilities   ⚐ ▆ ♀ ⚐
Location   1.5m N on B709

Hotel   ★★★ 72% Peebles Hydro Hotel, PEEBLES
☎ 01721 720602 137 ⇥ ↿

IRVINE   Map 10 NS33

Glasgow Gailes KA11 5AE
☎ 0141 942 2011 Fax 0141 942 0770
A lovely seaside links. The turf of the fairways and all the greens is truly glorious and provides tireless play. Established in 1882, and is a qualifying course for the Open Championship.
18 holes, 6515yds, Par 71, SSS 72, Course record 64.
Club membership 1200.
Visitors   prior booking through secretary reccomended, no visitors before 2.30pm Sat & Sun.
Societies   initial contact by telephone.
Green Fees £60 per day; £50 per round (£55 per round weekends).
Cards   ▭ ▬ 🖿
Prof   J Steven
Designer   W Park Jnr
Facilities   ⊗ ⑂ by prior arrangement ⚐ ▆ ♀ ⚐ 🖿 ⛳ ⌀
Location   2m S off A737

Hotel   ★★★★ 57% Hospitality Inn Irvine, 46 Annick Rd, IRVINE
☎ 01294 274272 127 ⇥ ↿

Irvine Bogside KA12 8SN ☎ 01294 275979
Testing links course; only two short holes.
18 holes, 6400yds, Par 71, SSS 73, Course record 65.
Club membership 450.
Societies   are welcome weekdays and pm weekends, telephone in advance.
Green Fees not confirmed.
Prof   Keith Erskine
Designer   James Braid

Facilities	⊗ ⑂Ⅲ 🛢 🍺 ⛾ 🍴 🏠 ☂ ✎
Location	N side of town off A737

Hotel   ★★★★ 57% Hospitality Inn Irvine, 46 Annick Rd, IRVINE ☎ 01294 274272 127 ⇄ ⚑

Irvine Ravenspark 13 Kidsneuk Ln KA12 8SR
☎ 01294 271293
Parkland course.
18 holes, 6702yds, Par 71, SSS 71, Course record 65.
Club membership 600.

Visitors	may not play Sat before 2pm.
Societies	not allowed Sat, contact club steward in advance.
Green Fees	not confirmed.
Prof	Peter Bond
Facilities	⊗ ⑂Ⅲ 🛢 ⛾ 🍺 🏠
Location	N side of town on A737

Hotel   ★★★ 73% Montgreenan Mansion House Hotel, Montgreenan Estate, KILWINNING ☎ 01294 557733 21 ⇄ ⚑

Western Gailes Gailes by Irvine KA11 5AE
☎ 01294 311649 Fax 01294 312312
A magnificent seaside links with glorious turf and wonderful greens. The view is open across the Firth of Clyde to the neighbouring islands. It is a well-balanced course crossed by 3 burns. There are 2 par 5's, the 6th and 14th, and the 11th is a testing 445-yd, par 4, dog-leg.
18 holes, 6639yds, Par 71, SSS 73, Course record 65.

Visitors	welcome Mon, Tue (no ladies) Wed, Fri. Must contact in advance and have a handicap certificate.
Societies	must contact in advance.
Green Fees	not confirmed.
Facilities	⊗ ⑂Ⅲ 🛢 🍺 ⛾ ☂ ✎
Location	2m S off A737

Hotel   ★★★ 73% Montgreenan Mansion House Hotel, Montgreenan Estate, KILWINNING ☎ 01294 557733 21 ⇄ ⚑

JEDBURGH   Map 12 NT62

Jedburgh Dunion Rd TD8 6DQ
☎ 01835 863587
Undulating parkland course, windy, with young trees.
9 holes, 5760yds, Par 68, SSS 67, Course record 62.
Club membership 265.

Visitors	welcome before 6pm weekdays, and after 6pm at weekends
Societies	must contact at least one month in advance.
Green Fees	£15 per day/round.
Designer	William Park
Facilities	⊗ by prior arrangement ⑂Ⅲ by prior arrangement 🛢 by prior arrangement 🍺 ⛾ ☂
Location	1m W on B6358

Hotel   ★★ 71% Kirklands Hotel, West Stewart Place, HAWICK ☎ 01450 372263 5 ⇄ ⚑ Annexe4 ⇄ ⚑

JOHNSTONE   Map 10 NS46

Cochrane Castle Scott Av, Craigston PA5 0HF
☎ 01505 320146 Fax 01505 325338
Fairly hilly parkland course, wooded with two small streams running through it.
18 holes, 6223yds, Par 71, SSS 71, Course record 65.
Club membership 660.

Visitors	contact in advance, may not play at weekends.
Societies	apply in writing.
Green Fees	£28 per day; £17 per round.
Prof	Jason Boyd
Designer	J Hunter
Facilities	⊗ ⑂Ⅲ 🛢 🍺 ⛾ ☂ 🏠 ✎
Location	1m from Johnstone town centre, off Beith Rd

Hotel   ★★★ 68% Lynnhurst Hotel, Park Rd, JOHNSTONE ☎ 01505 324331 21 ⇄ ⚑

Elderslie 63 Main Rd, Elderslie PA5 9AZ
☎ 01505 323956 Fax 01505 340346
Parkland course, undulating, with good views.
18 holes, 6175yds, Par 70, SSS 70, Course record 61.
Club membership 940.

Visitors	may not play at weekends & bank holidays. Must contact club in advance and preferably have a handicap certificate.
Societies	must telephone in advance.
Green Fees	not confirmed.
Prof	Richard Bowman
Designer	J Braid
Facilities	⊗ ⑂Ⅲ 🛢 ⛾ ☂ 🦢 ✎
Location	E side of town on A737

Hotel   ★★★ 68% Lynnhurst Hotel, Park Rd, JOHNSTONE ☎ 01505 324331 21 ⇄ ⚑

KELSO   Map 12 NT73

Kelso Racecourse Rd TD5 7SL ☎ 01573 223009
Parkland course. Easy walking.
18 holes, 6046yds, Par 70, SSS 69, Course record 64.
Club membership 500.

Visitors	advisable to telephone in advance.
Societies	apply in writing.
Green Fees	not confirmed.
Designer	James Braid
Facilities	⊗ ⑂Ⅲ 🛢 🍺 ⛾ ☂ 🏠 🍴 ✎
Location	N side of town centre off B6461

Hotel   ★★★ 62% Cross Keys Hotel, 36-37 The Square, KELSO ☎ 01573 223303 28 ⇄ ⚑

Roxburghe TD5 8JZ ☎ 01573 450331 Fax 01573 450611
Opened in 1996 and designed by Dave Thomas, this undulating course is set in 200 acres of mature parkland. Deep challenging bunkers, rolling greens and dramatic water hazards, including the River Teviot, provide a good test for all golfing abilities.
18 holes, 6873yds, Par 72, SSS 73, Course record 67.
Club membership 310.

Visitors	dress code (smart casual, no jeans, no training shoes).
Societies	please telephone in advance, a number of packages available.
Green Fees	£50 per day, £35 per round (£60/£40 weekends).

▶

THE ROXBURGHE
HOTEL & GOLF COURSE

The Roxburghe Golf Course is set in over 200 acres, with a mix of parkland and woodland. Dave Thomas, internationally renowned golf course architect was appointed in March 1995 and his brief was to create a golf course of the highest quality using the existing natural features of the site to maximum effect. The course bears all the unique hallmarks of Dave Thomas, numerous deep challenging bunkers, mature woodland to define fairways, dramatic water hazards and generous rolling greens.

Kelso, Roxburghshire TD5 8JZ
Tel: 01573 450331 Fax: 01573 450611

Cards	⚊ 💳 💳 💳
Prof	Gordon Niven
Designer	Dave Thomas
Facilities	⊗ ℳ ⬛ ⬛ ♀ ⚲ 🏠 🍴 ⛴ 🏌 🏌 ⚲ ↑
& Leisure	hard tennis courts, fishing, shooting school, croquet, health & beauty clinic.
Location	5m E of Jedburgh on A698, 2m W of Kelso on A698

Hotel	★★★🏌 74% The Roxburghe Hotel & Golf Course, Heiton, KELSO ☎ 01573 450331 16 ⇔ ↑ Annexe6 ⇔ ↑

KILBIRNIE   Map 10 NS35

Kilbirnie Place Largs Rd KA25 7AT ☎ 01505 683398
Easy walking parkland course.
18 holes, 5400yds, Par 69, SSS 67.
Club membership 450.
Visitors	no restrictions weekdays, no parties on Sun.
Societies	must apply in writing in advance.
Green Fees	not confirmed.
Facilities	♀ ⚲
Location	1m W on A760

Hotel	★★★ 72% Priory House Hotel, Broomfields, LARGS ☎ 01475 686460 21 ⇔ ↑

KILMARNOCK   Map 10 NS43

Annanhill Irvine Rd KA1 2RT ☎ 01563 521644
Municipal, tree-lined parkland course played over by private clubs.

18 holes, 6269yds, Par 71, SSS 70, Course record 66.
Club membership 394.
Visitors	must book at starters office.
Societies	apply in writing.
Green Fees	on application.
Designer	Jack McLean
Facilities	⚲
Location	1m N on A71

Hotel	★★★ 75% Chapeltoun House Hotel, STEWARTON ☎ 01560 482696 8 ⇔ ↑
Additional hotel	★★★ 73% Montgreenan Mansion House Hotel, Montgreenan Estate, KILWINNING ☎ 01294 557733 Fax 01294 850397 21 ⇔ ↑

Caprington Ayr Rd KA1 4UW
☎ 01563 523702 & 521915 (Gen Enq)
Municipal parkland course.
18 holes, 5740yds, Par 68, SSS 68.
Club membership 400.
Visitors	may not play on Sat.
Societies	must contact in advance.
Green Fees	not confirmed.
Facilities	⊗ by prior arrangement ℳ by prior arrangement ⬛ ♀ ⚲ 🏠 ♂
Location	1.5m S on B7038

Hotel	★★★ 75% Chapeltoun House Hotel, STEWARTON ☎ 01560 482696 8 ⇔ ↑

KILSYTH   Map 11 NS77

Kilsyth Lennox Tak Ma Doon Rd G65 0RS
☎ 01236 824115 Fax 01236 823089
Hilly moorland course, hard walking. Course and facilities revamped with 18-holes after a serious fire early in 1993.
18 holes, 5912yds, Par 70, SSS 70, Course record 66.
Club membership 500.
Visitors	advisable to contact in advance. No restrictions weekdays up to 5pm, may play Sun on application but not Sat.
Societies	must contact in advance.
Green Fees	not confirmed.
Prof	R Abercrombie
Facilities	⊗ ℳ ⬛ ⬛ ♀ ⚲ 🏠 🚜
Location	N side of town off A803

Hotel	★★★ Kirkhouse Inn, STRATHBLANE ☎ 01360 770621 15 ⇔ ↑

KIRKCUDBRIGHT   Map 11 NX65

Brighouse Bay Borgue DG6 4TS
☎ 01557 870409 Fax 01557 870319
A beautifully situated scenic maritime course on free draining coastal grassland and playable all year. Making use of many natural features - water, gullies and rocks - it provides a testing challenge to golfers of all handicaps.
18 holes, 6603yds, Par 72, SSS 72.
Club membership 170.
Visitors	pay as you play - payment at adjacent Leisure Club. Phoning in advance recommended.
Societies	prior arrangement necessary.
Green Fees	£22 per day; £16 per round.
Cards	⚊ 💳 💳 💳
Designer	D Gray

Facilities
& Leisure heated indoor swimming pool, fishing, gymnasium, mini golf, steam room, adjacent to AA Campsite of the Year 1998, quad bikes, ten pin bowling.
Location 3m S of Borgue off B727

Hotel ★★★ 67% Selkirk Arms Hotel, Old High St, KIRKCUDBRIGHT
☎ 01557 330402 14 ⇔ ® Annexe3 ⇔ ®

Kirkcudbright Stirling Crescent DG6 4EZ
☎ 01557 330314
Parkland course. Hilly, with hard walking. Good views over the Harbour town of Kirkcudbright and the Dee Estuary.
18 holes, 5739yds, Par 69, SSS 69, Course record 63.
Club membership 500.
Visitors advisable to contact in advance.
Societies contact in advance.
Green Fees £23 per day; £18 per round.
Facilities ⟁ ⤬ ⛳ ✐
Location NE side of town off A711

Hotel ★★★ 67% Selkirk Arms Hotel, Old High St, KIRKCUDBRIGHT
☎ 01557 330402 14 ⇔ ® Annexe3 ⇔ ®

KIRKINTILLOCH   Map 11 NS67

Hayston Campsie Rd G66 1RN
☎ 0141 776 1244 & 775 0723 (Sec)
An undulating, tree-lined course with a sandy subsoil.
18 holes, 6042yds, Par 70, SSS 70, Course record 62.
Club membership 800.
Visitors must apply in advance, may not play weekends.
Societies Tue & Thu, apply in writing
Green Fees £30 per day; £20 per round.
Prof Steven Barnett
Designer James Braid
Facilities ⊗ ⅲ ⭒ ⚐ ♀ ⟁ ⛫ ✐
Location 1m NW off A803

Hotel ★★★ Kirkhouse Inn, STRATHBLANE
☎ 01360 770621 15 ⇔ ®

Kirkintilloch Campsie Rd G66 1RN ☎ 0141 776 1256
Parkland course in rural setting.
18 holes, 5269yds, Par 70, SSS 66, Course record 61.
Club membership 650.
Visitors must be introduced by member.
Societies apply in writing.
Green Fees on application.
Designer James Braid
Facilities ⊗ ⅲ ⭒ ⚐ ♀ ⟁ ⛫
Location 1m NW off A803

Hotel ★★★ Kirkhouse Inn, STRATHBLANE
☎ 01360 770621 15 ⇔ ®

LANARK   Map 11 NS84

Lanark The Moor, Whitelees Rd ML11 7RX
☎ 01555 663219 & 661456
Chosen as one of the pre-qualifying tests for the Open Championship held at Lanark from 1977 to 1983. The address of the club, 'The Moor', gives some indication as to the kind of golf to be found there. Golf has been played at Lanark for well over a century and the Club dates from 1851.
Old Course: 18 holes, 6423yds, Par 70, SSS 71, Course record 62.
Wee Course: 9 holes, 1489yds, Par 28.
Club membership 880.
Visitors booking advisable, no visitors weekends.
Societies apply in advance.
Green Fees £38 per day; £25 per round April to October.
Prof Alan White
Designer Tom Morris
Facilities ⊗ ⅲ ⭒ ⚐ ♀ ⟁ ⛫ ✎ ⚒ ✐
Location E side of town centre off A73

Hotel ★★★ 64% Cartland Bridge Hotel, Glasgow Rd, LANARK
☎ 01555 664426 18 ⇔ ®

LANGBANK   Map 10 NS37

Gleddoch Golf and Country Club PA14 6YE
☎ 01475 540304 Fax 01475 540201
Parkland and heathland course with other sporting facilities available to temporary members. Good views over Firth of Clyde.
18 holes, 6330yds, Par 71, SSS 71, Course record 64.
Club membership 500.
Visitors must contact in advance.
Societies must contact in advance.
Green Fees £40 per day; £30 per round (£50/£40 weekends).
Cards ⊟ 🔲 🔳 ⚏
Prof Keith Campbell
Designer Hamilton Strutt
Facilities ⊗ ⅲ ⭒ ⚐ ♀ ⟁ ⛫ ⛫ ✎ ⚒ ✐ ℓ
& Leisure squash, horse riding.
Location B789-Old Greenock Road

Hotel ★★★★≜≜ 69% Gleddoch House Hotel, LANGBANK ☎ 01475 540711 39 ⇔ ®

LANGHOLM   Map 11 NY38

Langholm Whitaside DG13 0JR ☎ 013873 80673/81247
Hillside course with fine views, easy to medium walking.
9 holes, 5744yds, Par 70, SSS 68, Course record 63.
Club membership 200.
Visitors restricted Sat & Sun.
Societies apply in writing to secretary.
Green Fees not confirmed.
Facilities ⊗ by prior arrangement ⅲ by prior arrangement ⭒ by prior arrangement ⚐ by prior arrangement ♀
Location E side of village off A7

Hotel ★★ 61% Eskdale Hotel, Market Place, LANGHOLM ☎ 013873 80357 & 81178 Fax 013873 80357 15rm(11 ⇔ ®)

LARGS   Map 10 NS25

Largs Irvine Rd KA30 8EU
☎ 01475 673594 Fax 01475 673594
A parkland, tree-lined course with views to the Clyde coast and Arran Isles. ▶

18 holes, 6115yds, Par 70, SSS 71, Course record 63.
Club membership 850.
Visitors   may not play competition days. Other times by
             arrangement.
Societies   apply in writing.
Green Fees £35 per day; £25 per round (£35 per round
             weekends before 4pm).
Prof   Kenneth Docherty
Facilities ⊗ ⅏ ⅃⅃ ♥ ♀ ♒ ♙ ✈ ⚥
Location 1m S of town centre on A78

Hotel   ★★★ 72% Priory House Hotel, Broomfields,
           LARGS ☎ 01475 686460 21 ⇆ ✆

Routenburn Routenburn Rd KA30 8QA ☎ 01475 673230
Heathland course with fine views over Firth of Clyde.
18 holes, 5675yds, Par 68, SSS 68.
Club membership 500.
Visitors   no restrictions.
Societies   apply in writing.
Green Fees not confirmed.
Cards   ▭
Prof   J Grieg McQueen
Designer   J Braid
Facilities ⊗ ⅏ ⅃⅃ ♥ ♀ ♒ ♙ ⚥
Location 1m N off A78

Hotel   ★★★ 63% Manor Park Hotel, LARGS
           ☎ 01475 520832 10 ⇆ ✆ Annexe13 ⇆ ✆

LARKHALL   Map 11 NS75

Larkhall Burnhead Rd ML9 3AA ☎ 01698 889597
Small, inland parkland course.
9 holes, 6234yds, Par 70, SSS 70, Course record 69.
Club membership 250.
Visitors   restricted Tue & Sat.
Green Fees £3.50-£6.50 weekdays (£4-£8 weekends).
Facilities ♥ ♀
Location E side of town on B7019

Hotel   ★★★ 68% Popinjay Hotel,
           Lanark Rd, ROSEBANK
           ☎ 01555 860441 40 ⇆ ✆ Annexe5 ⇆ ✆

LAUDER   Map 12 NT54

Lauder Galashiels Rd TD2 6RS ☎ 01578 722526
Inland course and practice area on gently sloping hill.
9 holes, 3001yds, Par 72, SSS 70, Course record 66.
Club membership 200.
Visitors   restricted Wed 4.30-5.30pm and Sun before
             noon.
Societies   telephone in advance.
Green Fees £10 per day.
Designer   Willie Park Jnr
Facilities ♒
Location On Galashiels Rd, off A68, 0.5m from Lauder

Hotel   ★★ 66% Lauderdale Hotel, 1 Edinburgh Rd,
           LAUDER ☎ 01578 722231 9 ⇆ ✆

LEADHILLS   Map 11 NS81

Leadhills ML12 6XR ☎ no telephone Fax 01659 74324
A testing, hilly course with high winds. At 1500ft above sea
level it is the highest golf course in Scotland.

9 holes, 4354yds, Par 66, SSS 64.
Club membership 80.
Visitors   no restrictions.
Societies   must contact in advance.
Green Fees not confirmed.
Location E side of village off B797

Hotel   ★★ 65% Blackaddie House Hotel,
           Blackaddie Rd, SANQUHAR
           ☎ 01659 50270 9 ⇆ ✆

LENNOXTOWN   Map 11 NS67

Campsie Crow Rd G65 7HX ☎ 01360 310244
Scenic hillside course.
18 holes, 5507yds, Par 70, SSS 68, Course record 69.
Club membership 640.
Visitors   contact professional 01360 310920.
Societies   wrtten application.
Green Fees not confirmed.
Prof   Mark Brennan
Designer   W Auchterlonie
Facilities ⊗ ⅏ ⅃⅃ ♥ ♀ ♒ 🏠
Location 0.5m N on B822

Hotel   ★★★ Kirkhouse Inn, STRATHBLANE
           ☎ 01360 770621 15 ⇆ ✆

LENZIE   Map 11 NS67

Lenzie 19 Crosshill Rd G66 5DA
☎ 0141 776 1535 & 0141 776 6020 Fax 0141 777 7748
Pleasant parkland course.
18 holes, 5984yds, Par 69, SSS 69, Course record 64.
Club membership 890.
Visitors   must contact in advance (some Sunday dates
             available)
Societies   apply in writing.
Green Fees £28 per day; £18 per round.
Prof   Jim McCallum
Facilities ⊗ ⅏ ⅃⅃ ♥ ♀ ♒ 🏠 ⚲ ⚥
Location N of Glasgow, approx 15 mins from Glasgow
             city centre, Kirkintilloch turn off M80

Hotel   ★★★ Kirkhouse Inn, STRATHBLANE
           ☎ 01360 770621 15 ⇆ ✆

LESMAHAGOW   Map 11 NS83

Holland Bush Acretophead ML11 0JS
☎ 01555 893484 & 893646
Fairly difficult, tree-lined municipal parkland and moorland
course. 1st half is relatively flat, while 2nd half is hilly.
18 holes, 6246yds, Par 71, SSS 69, Course record 63.
Club membership 500.
Visitors   no restrictions.
Societies   contact the professional in advance.
Green Fees £8.20 per round (£9.50 weekends & bank
             holidays).
Prof   Ian Rae
Designer   J Lawson/K Pate
Facilities ⊗ ⅏ ⅃⅃ ♥ ♀ ♒ 🏠 ✈ ⚥

Hotel   ★★★ 68% Strathaven Hotel,
           Hamilton Rd, STRATHAVEN
           ☎ 01357 521778 22 ⇆ ✆

LOCHMABEN
Map 11 NY08

Lochmaben Castlehillgate DG11 1NT ☎ 01387 810552
Attractive parkland course surrounding the Kirk Loch, excellent views on this well maintained course.
18 holes, 5357yds, Par 67, SSS 66, Course record 61.
Club membership 850.
Visitors   advised to contact in advance.
Societies   must contact in advance.
Green Fees £20 per day; £16 per round (£25/£20 weekends).
Designer   James Braid
Facilities   ⊗ ⅲ ⅃ ⬥ ⚑ ⚓ ⚘
& Leisure   fishing, snooker table.
Location   S side of village off A709

Hotel   ★★★ 69% Dryfesdale Hotel, LOCKERBIE
☎ 01576 202427 15rm(9 ⇆ ⬥)

LOCHWINNOCH
Map 10 NS35

Lochwinnoch Burnfoot Rd PA12 4AN
☎ 01505 842153 & 01505 843029 Fax 01505 843668
Well maintained parkland course incorporating natural burns. Throughout the course the majority of fairways are wide with tricky greens, but always in good condition. Very scenic with lots of bunkers.
18 holes, 6243yds, Par 71, SSS 71, Course record 63.
Club membership 650.
Visitors   may not play at weekends and bank holidays unless accompanied by member(check with Pro Shop). Restricted during competition days.
Societies   apply in writing to club administrator.
Green Fees not confirmed.
Cards   ⬝⬝ ⬛⬛
Prof   Gerry Reilly
Facilities   ⊗ ⅲ ⅃ ⬥ ⚑ ⚓ ⚘ ⚒ ⚘ ⚘ ⚘
Location   W side of town off A760, between Johnstone & Beith, off A737 on Largs road A760

Hotel   ★★★ 66% Bowfield Hotel & Country Club, HOWWOOD ☎ 01505 705225   23 ⇆ ⬥

LOCKERBIE
Map 11 NY18

Lockerbie Corrie Rd DG11 2ND
☎ 01576 203363 Fax 01576 203363
Parkland course with fine views and featuring the only pond hole in Dumfriesshire. Pond comes into play at 3 holes.
18 holes, 5614yds, Par 68, SSS 67, Course record 64.
Club membership 620.
Visitors   restricted Sun. Advisable to book in advance.
Societies   must contact secretary in advance.
Green Fees £18 per day; £15 per round (£18 per round weekends).
Designer   James Braid
Facilities   ⊗ ⅲ ⅃ ⬥ ⚑ ⚓ ⚘ ⚘
Location   E side of town centre off B7068

Hotel   ★★★ 69% Dryfesdale Hotel, LOCKERBIE
☎ 01576 202427 15rm(9 ⇆ ⬥)

MAUCHLINE
Map 11 NS42

Ballochmyle Catrine Rd KA5 6LE
☎ 01290 550469 Fax 01290 550469
Wooded parkland course.

18 holes, 5972yds, Par 70, SSS 69, Course record 64.
Club membership 730.
Visitors   welcome.
Societies   apply in writing.
Green Fees not confirmed.
Cards   ⬝⬝ ⬛⬛ ⬛⬛ ⬝
Facilities   ⊗ ⅲ by prior arrangement ⅃ ⬥ ⚑ ⚓ ⚓ ⚘
& Leisure   two full size snooker tables.
Location   1m SE on B705

Hotel   ★ 64% Royal Hotel, 1 Glaisnock St, CUMNOCK ☎ 01290 420822 12rm(6 ⇆ ⬥)

MAYBOLE
Map 10 NS20

Maybole Municipal Memorial Park KA19 7DX
☎ 01655 889770
Hilly parkland course.
9 holes, 2635yds, Par 33, SSS 65, Course record 64.
Club membership 100.
Visitors   no restrictions, telephone to book.
Societies   must contact in advance.
Green Fees £13 per day; £8.80 per round (£15.50/£9.20 weekends).

Hotel   ★★ Ladyburn, MAYBOLE
☎ 01655 740585 8rm(4 ⇆ 3 ⬥)

MELROSE
Map 12 NT53

Melrose Dingleton TD6 9HS
☎ 01896 822855 & 01835 822758
Undulating tree-lined fairways with spendid views. Many bunkers.
9 holes, 5579yds, Par 70, SSS 68, Course record 61.
Club membership 380.
Visitors   competitions all Sats and many Suns Apr-Oct, ladies priority Tue, junior priority Wed am in holidays. No visitors to tee off after 4pm Apr-Oct.
Societies   apply in writing.
Green Fees not confirmed.
Facilities   ⬥ ⚓
Location   Off A68,S side of town centre on B6359

Hotel   ★★★ 66% Burt's Hotel, The Square, MELROSE ☎ 01896 822285   20 ⇆ ⬥

MILNGAVIE
Map 11 NS57

Clober Craigton Rd G62 7HP ☎ 0141 956 1685
Parkland course. Testing 5th hole, par 3.
18 holes, 5042yds, Par 65, SSS 65, Course record 61.
Club membership 600.
Visitors   may not play after 4pm Mon-Fri. Must play with member weekends and bank holidays.
Societies   must contact in advance.
Green Fees not confirmed.
Prof   A Tak
Facilities   ⊗ ⅲ ⅃ ⬥ ⚑ ⚓ ⚓ ⚘
Location   NW side of town

Hotel   ★★★ 62% The Black Bull, Main St, MILNGAVIE ☎ 0141 956 2291 27 ⇆ ⬥

Dougalston Strathblane Rd G62 8HJ
☎ 0141 956 5750 Fax 0141 956 6480
A golf course of tremendous character set in 400 acres dotted with drumlins, lakes and criss-crossed by streams and ▶

ditches. One of the toughest tests of golf in the west of Scotland.
18 holes, 6683yds, Par 72, SSS 71.
Club membership 500.

Visitors	visitors may only play Mon-Fri, tee times may be booked 3 days in advance.
Societies	weekdays only.
Green Fees	not confirmed.
Cards	💳
Designer	Commander Harris
Facilities	⊗ ℍ ⓑ ♥ ♀ ⚲ 🏠 ⛳ ♂
Location	NE side of town on A81

Hotel ★★★ 62% The Black Bull, Main St, MILNGAVIE ☎ 0141 956 2291 27 ⇆ 🐾

Hilton Park Auldmarroch Estate, Stockiemuir Rd G62 7HB ☎ 0141 956 4657 Fax 0141 956 4657
Moorland courses set amidst magnificent scenery.
Hilton Course: 18 holes, 6054yds, Par 70, SSS 70, Course record 65.
Allander Course: 18 holes, 5487yards, Par 69, SSS 67, Course record 65.
Club membership 1200.

Visitors	must contact in advance but may not play at weekends.
Societies	apply in advance to secretary.
Green Fees	£30 per day; £24 per round.
Prof	W McCondichie
Designer	James Braid
Facilities	⊗ ℍ ⓑ ♥ ♀ ⚲ 🏠 ⛳ ♂ 🐾
Location	3m NW of Milngavie, on A809

Hotel ★★★ 62% The Black Bull, Main St, MILNGAVIE ☎ 0141 956 2291 27 ⇆ 🐾

Milngavie Laighpark G62 8EP ☎ 0141 956 1619 Fax 0141 956 4252
Very scenic moorland course, which plays its full length, challenging SSS, testing 1st hole followed by many others.
18 holes, 5818yds, Par 68, SSS 68, Course record 59.
Club membership 700.

Visitors	must contact in advance, may not play weekends.
Societies	apply in writing.
Green Fees	£22 Mon-Fri.
Designer	The Auchterlonie Brothers
Facilities	⊗ ℍ by prior arrangement ⓑ ♥ ♀ ⚲
Location	1.25m N

Hotel ★★★ 62% The Black Bull, Main St, MILNGAVIE ☎ 0141 956 2291 27 ⇆ 🐾

MINTO Map 12 NT52

Minto Denholm TD9 8SH ☎ 01450 870220
Pleasant, undulating parkland course featuring mature trees and panoramic views of Scottish Border country. Short but quite testing.
18 holes, 5460yds, Par 68, SSS 67, Course record 63.
Club membership 670.

Visitors	advisable to telephone in advance, and essential for weekends.
Societies	telephone or write.
Green Fees	not confirmed.
Facilities	⊗ ℍ ⓑ ♥ ♀ ⚲ 🐾 ⛏ ♂
Location	5m from Hawick, 1.25m off A698 at Denholm

Hotel ★★ 71% Kirklands Hotel, West Stewart Place, HAWICK ☎ 01450 372263 5 ⇆ 🐾 Annexe4 ⇆ 🐾

MOFFAT Map 11 NT00

Moffat Coatshill DG10 9SB ☎ 01683 220020
Scenic moorland course overlooking the town, with panoramic views of southern uplands.
18 holes, 5218yds, Par 69, SSS 67, Course record 60.
Club membership 350.

Visitors	advised to contact in advance, no visitors after 12 noon on Wed.
Societies	apply in writing to the clubmistress.
Green Fees	£20 per day; £18.50 per round (£31/£28.50 weekend).
Designer	Ben Sayers
Facilities	⊗ ℍ ⓑ ♥ ♀ ⚲ 🏠 ⛳ ♂
& Leisure	2 snooker tables, pool, darts, table tennis, T.V.
Location	From A74 1m on A701 to Moffat, course signposted

Hotel ★★★ 70% Moffat House Hotel, High St, MOFFAT ☎ 01683 220039 20 ⇆ 🐾

MONREITH Map 10 NX34

St Medan DG8 8NJ ☎ 01988 700358
Links course with panoramic views of the Solway and Isle of Man.
9 holes, 4608yds, Par 64, SSS 63, Course record 60.
Club membership 300.

Visitors	no restrictions.
Societies	apply in advance by telephone or writing
Green Fees	not confirmed.
Designer	James Braid
Facilities	⊗ ℍ ⓑ ♥ ♀ ⚲ ⛳
Location	1m SE off A747

Hotel ★★★♨ 67% Corsemalzie House Hotel, PORT WILLIAM ☎ 01988 860254 14 ⇆ 🐾

MOTHERWELL Map 11 NS75

Colville Park New Jerviston House, Jerviston Estate, Merry St ML1 4UG ☎ 01698 265779 (pro) Fax 01698 230418
Parkland course. First nine, tree-lined, second nine, more exposed. Testing 10th hole par 3, 16th hole par 4.
18 holes, 6250yds, Par 71, SSS 70, Course record 63.
Club membership 800.

Visitors	must contact in advance in writing.
Societies	apply in writing.
Green Fees	£20 per round/day.
Cards	💳 💳 💳
Prof	Alan Forrest
Designer	James Braid
Facilities	⊗ ℍ ⓑ ♥ ♀ ⚲ 🏠
Location	1.25m NE on A723 from Motherwell town centre

Hotel ★★★ 66% Bothwell Bridge Hotel, 89 Main St, BOTHWELL ☎ 01698 852246 90 ⇆ 🐾

MUIRHEAD — Map 11 NS66

Crow Wood Garnkirk House, Cumbernauld Rd G69 9JF
☎ 0141 779 4954 Fax 0141 779 9148
Parkland course.
18 holes, 6261yds, Par 71, SSS 71, Course record 62.
Club membership 800.

Visitors	must contact in advance but may not play weekends, bank holidays or competition days
Societies	apply in advance.
Green Fees	£21 per round.
Cards	—
Prof	Brian Moffat
Designer	James Braid
Facilities	⊗ ⫙ ⬧ ☕ ♀ ☒ 𝄢 ✧
Location	0.5m W on A80

Hotel ★★★ 72% Malmaison Hotel, 278 West George St, GLASGOW ☎ 0141 572 1000 72 ⇄ ♠

NEWCASTLETON — Map 12 NY48

Newcastleton Holm Hill TD9 0QD ☎ 01387 375257
Hilly course with scenic views over the Liddesdale Valley and Newcastleton.
9 holes, 5748yds, Par 70, SSS 68.
Club membership 100.

Visitors	contact the Secretary in advance.
Societies	contact by telephone or in writing in advance.
Green Fees	not confirmed.
Designer	J Shade
Facilities	☒ ⫟
& Leisure	fishing.
Location	W side of village

Hotel ★★ 61% Eskdale Hotel, Market Place, LANGHOLM ☎ 013873 80357 & 81178 Fax 013873 80357 15rm(11 ⇄ ♠)

NEW CUMNOCK — Map 11 NS61

New Cumnock Lochhill, Cumnock Rd KA18 4PN
☎ 01290 338848
Parkland course.
9 holes, 5176yds, Par 68, SSS 68, Course record 63.
Club membership 280.

Visitors	restricted on Sun competition days. After 4 pm only
Societies	apply in writing.
Green Fees	£7 per day/round. Pay at Lochside House Hotel.
Designer	Willie Fernie
Facilities	⊗ ⫙ ⬧ ☕ ♀ ☒ 𝄢
& Leisure	fishing.
Location	0.75m N on A76

Hotel ★ 64% Royal Hotel, 1 Glaisnock St, CUMNOCK ☎ 01290 420822 12rm(6 ⇄ ♠)

NEW GALLOWAY — Map 11 NX67

New Galloway High St DG7 3RN
☎ 01644 420737 & 450685 Fax 01644 450685
Set on the edge of the Galloway Hills and overlooking Loch Ken, the course has excellent tees and first class greens. The course rises through the first two fairways to a plateau with all round viws that many think unsurpassed.

9 holes, 5006yds, Par 68, SSS 67, Course record 63.
Club membership 350.

Visitors	restricted on Sun (competition days). All visitors play off yellow markers.
Societies	contact secretary in advance.
Green Fees	£12.50 per day.
Designer	James Braid
Facilities	⊗ by prior arrangement ⬧ ☕ ♀ ☒
Location	S side of town on A762

Hotel ★★ 70% Douglas Arms, King St, CASTLE DOUGLAS ☎ 01556 502231 24 ⇄ ♠

NEWTON MEARNS — Map 11 NS55

East Renfrewshire Pilmuir G77 6RT
☎ 01355 500258
Undulating moorland with loch; prevailing SW wind.
18 holes, 6097yds, Par 70, SSS 70, Course record 63.
Club membership 900.

Visitors	telephone for details.
Societies	must contact in advance.
Green Fees	£40 per day; £30 per round.
Cards	—
Prof	Gordon Clarke
Designer	James Braid
Facilities	⊗ ⫙ ⬧ ☕ ♀ ☒ 𝄢 ✧
Location	3m SW on A77

Hotel ★★★ 66% The Macdonald, Eastwood Toll, GIFFNOCK ☎ 0141 638 2225 56 ⇄ ♠

Eastwood Muirshield, Loganswell G77 6RX
☎ 01355 500280
An undulating moorland course situated in a scenic setting.
18 holes, 5864yds, Par 68, SSS 69, Course record 62.
Club membership 900.

Visitors	contact in advance, may only play with member at weekends.
Societies	must contact in advance.
Green Fees	£30 per day; £24 per round.
Prof	Allan McGinness
Designer	Theodore Moone
Facilities	⊗ ⫙ ⬧ ☕ ♀ ☒ 𝄢 ✧
Location	2.5m S of Newton Mearns, on A77

Hotel ★★★ 66% The Macdonald, Eastwood Toll, GIFFNOCK ☎ 0141 638 2225 56 ⇄ ♠

Whitecraigs 72 Ayr Rd G46 6SW
☎ 0141 639 4530 & 0141 639 2140 pro
Beautiful parkland course.
18 holes, 6230yds, Par 70, SSS 70, Course record 65.
Club membership 1078.

Visitors	must contact professional in advance and have a handicap certificate. With member only weekends and bank holidays.
Green Fees	not confirmed.
Prof	Alistair Forrow
Facilities	⊗ ⫙ ⬧ ☕ ♀ ☒ 𝄢 ⫟ ✧
Location	1.5m NE on A77

Hotel ★★★ 66% The Macdonald, Eastwood Toll, GIFFNOCK ☎ 0141 638 2225 56 ⇄ ♠ ▶

383

NEWTON STEWART
Map 10 NX46

Newton Stewart Kirroughtree Av, Minnigaff DG8 6PF
☎ 01671 402172
Parkland course in picturesque setting. A good test for all
standards of golfers with a variety of shots required.
18 holes, 5903yds, Par 69, SSS 70, Course record 66.
Club membership 380.
Visitors   must contact in advance.
Societies   must contact in advance.
Green Fees £22 per day; £19 per round (£26/£22 weekends
     & bank holidays).
Facilities ⊗ ⅏ ⅊ ⬛ ♀ ⅃ 🏠 ⟙ ♨ ✓
Location   0.5m N of town centre

Hotel   ★★ 72% Creebridge House Hotel, NEWTON
STEWART ☎ 01671 402121 19 ⇄ ♠

PAISLEY
Map 11 NS46

Barshaw Barshaw Park PA1 3TJ ☎ 0141 889 2908
Municipal parkland course.
18 holes, 5703yds, Par 68, SSS 67, Course record 63.
Club membership 100.
Visitors   no restrictions.
Societies   by prior arrangement with Parks Manager, Dept
of Sports & Leisure, Renfrewshire Council,
Mirren House, 6 Maxwell St, Paisley PA3 2AB.
Green Fees not confirmed.
Prof   John Scott
Facilities ⬛ ⅃ ⟙ ✓
Location   1m E off A737

Hotel   ★★★ 69% Glynhill Hotel & Leisure Club,
Paisley Rd, RENFREW
☎ 0141 886 5555 & 885 1111
Fax 0141 885 2838 125 ⇄ ♠

Paisley Braehead PA2 8TZ
☎ 0141 884 3903 Fax 0141 884 3903
Moorland course, windy but with good views. The course has
been designed in two loops of nine holes.
18 holes, 6215yds, Par 70, SSS 71.
Club membership 800.
Visitors   must contact in advance. Visitors may not play
weekends or public holidays.
Societies   weekdays only, excluding bank holidays.
Contact in advance.
Green Fees not confirmed.
Prof   Gordon Stewart
Facilities ⊗ ⅏ ⅊ ⬛ ♀ ⅃ 🏠 ♨ ✓
Location   S side of town off B774

Hotel   ★★★ 69% Glynhill Hotel & Leisure Club,
Paisley Rd, RENFREW
☎ 0141 886 5555 & 885 1111
Fax 0141 885 2838 125 ⇄ ♠

Ralston Strathmore Av, Ralston PA1 3DT
☎ 0141 882 1349 Fax 0141 883 9837
Parkland course.
18 holes, 6071yds, Par 71, SSS 69, Course record 62.
Club membership 750.
Visitors   Mon -Fri only and must be accompanied by
member.
Societies   written notice required
Green Fees not confirmed.

Prof   John Scott
Designer   J Braid
Facilities ⊗ ⅏ ⅊ ⬛ ♀ ⅃ 🏠 ✓
Location   2m E off A737

Hotel   ★★★ 67% Swallow Hotel,
517 Paisley Rd West, GLASGOW
☎ 0141 427 3146 117 ⇄ ♠

PATNA
Map 10 NS41

Doon Valley Hillside Park KA6 7JT ☎ 01292 531607
Established parkland course located on an undulating
hillside.
9 holes, 5654yds, Par 70, SSS 68.
Club membership 100.
Visitors   no restrictions mid week, advisable to contact in
advance for weekends.
Societies   telephone to arrange.
Green Fees £11 per round.
Facilities ♀ ⅃
& Leisure fishing.
Location   10m S of Ayr on the A713

Hotel   ★★ Ladyburn, MAYBOLE
☎ 01655 740585 8rm(4 ⇄ 3 ♠)

PEEBLES
Map 11 NT24

Peebles Kirkland St EH45 8EU
☎ 01721 720197
Parkland course with fine views.
18 holes, 6160yds, Par 70, SSS 70, Course record 63.
Club membership 750.
Visitors   advisable to ring for information on availability,
no visitors on Sat.
Societies   apply by telephone or in writing in advance.
Green Fees £25 per day; £18 per round (£34/£25 weekends).
Cards   ▭ ▬ 🖃
Prof   Craig Imlah
Designer   H S Colt
Facilities ⊗ ⅏ ⅊ ⬛ ♀ ⅃ 🏠 ⟙ 🦢 ♨ ✓
Location   W side of town centre off A72

Hotel   ★★★ 72% Peebles Hydro Hotel, PEEBLES
☎ 01721 720602 137 ⇄ ♠

PORTPATRICK
Map 10 NX05

Portpatrick Golf Course Rd DG9 8TB
☎ 01776 810273 Fax 01776 810811
Seaside links-type course, set on cliffs overlooking the Irish
Sea, with magnificent views.
*Dunskey Course: 18 holes, 5908yds, Par 70, SSS 68, Course
record 63.*
*Dinvin Course: 9 holes, 1504yds, Par 27, SSS 27, Course
record 23.*
Club membership 750.
Visitors   must contact in advance. £5 deposit required
Societies   must contact in advance.
Green Fees Dunskey: £28 per day; £19 per round (£33/£22
weekends) Dinvin: £12 per day; £8 per 18 holes.
Cards   ▭ ▬ 🖃 🖃
Designer   Charles Hunter
Facilities ⊗ ⅏ ⅊ ⬛ ♀ ⅃ 🏠 ⟙ ✓
Location   On entering village, 300 yds right from war
memorial

Hotel   ★★★ 69% Fernhill Hotel, PORTPATRICK
                 ☎ 01776 810220   14 ⇆ ♞ Annexe6 ⇆ ♞

PRESTWICK   Map 10 NS32

Prestwick 2 Links Rd KA9 1QG
☎ 01292 477404 Fax 01292 477255
Seaside links with natural hazards, tight fairways and
difficult fast undulating greens.
18 holes, 6544yds, Par 71, SSS 73.
Club membership 575.

Visitors	restricted Thu; may not play at weekends. Must contact in advance and have a handicap certificate.
Societies	must contact in writing.
Green Fees	£90 per day; £65 per round.
Cards	⚌ 💳 💳 🖱
Prof	F C Rennie
Designer	Tom Morris
Facilities	⊗ ⓔ 🍴 ♟ ⚑ 🏠 🐾 ⚷
Location	In town centre off A79

Hotel   ★★ 66% Parkstone Hotel, Esplanade,
                 PRESTWICK
                 ☎ 01292 477286   22 ⇆ ♞
Additional   ★★ 66% Carlton Toby Hotel, 187 Ayr Rd,
hotel   PRESTWICK ☎ 01292 476811
                 Fax 01292 474845   34 ⇆ ♞

Prestwick St Cuthbert East Rd KA9 2SX
☎ 01292 477101 Fax 01292 671730
Parkland course with easy walking, natural hazards and
sometimes windy.
18 holes, 6470yds, Par 71, SSS 71, Course record 64.
Club membership 880.

Visitors	must contact in advance but may not play at weekends & bank holidays.
Societies	Mon-Fri, apply in writing.
Green Fees	£30 per day; £22 per round.
Facilities	⊗ ⓔ 🍴 ♟ ⚑ ⚷
Location	0.5m E of town centre off A77

Hotel   ★★ 66% Parkstone Hotel,
                 Esplanade, PRESTWICK
                 ☎ 01292 477286   22 ⇆ ♞

Prestwick St Nicholas Grangemuir Rd KA9 1SN
☎ 01292 477608 Fax 01292 473900
Seaside links course with whins, heather and tight fairways.
It provides easy walking and has an unrestricted view of the
Firth of Clyde.
18 holes, 5952yds, Par 69, SSS 69, Course record 63.
Club membership 750.

Visitors	except Sat, Sun am. Must contact in advance.
Societies	must contact in advance.
Green Fees	£50 per day; £30 per round (£35 per round Sun).
Cards	⚌ 💳 💳 🖱
Designer	Charles Hunter
Facilities	⊗ ⓔ 🍴 ♟ ⚑ 🏠 🐾 ⚷
Location	S side of town off A79

Hotel   ★★ 66% Parkstone Hotel,
                 Esplanade, PRESTWICK
                 ☎ 01292 477286   22 ⇆ ♞

RENFREW   Map 11 NS46

Renfrew Blythswood Estate, Inchinnan Rd PA4 9EG
☎ 0141 886 6692 Fax 0141 886 1808
Tree-lined parkland course.
18 holes, 6818yds, Par 72, SSS 73, Course record 65.
Club membership 800.

Visitors	restricted to Mon, Tue & Thu, apply in advance.
Societies	apply in writing in advance.
Green Fees	£35 per day; £25 per round.
Prof	Stephen Dundas
Designer	Commander Harris
Facilities	⊗ ⓔ 🍴 ♟ ⚑ 🏠 🐾 ⚷
Location	0.75m W off A8

Hotel   ★★★ 69% Glynhill Hotel & Leisure Club,
                 Paisley Rd, RENFREW
                 ☎ 0141 886 5555 & 885 1111
                 Fax 0141 885 2838 125 ⇆ ♞

RIGSIDE   Map 11 NS83

Douglas Water Old School, Ayr Rd ML11 9NP
☎ 01555 880361
A 9-hole course with good variety and some hills and
spectacular views. An interesting course with a challenging
longest hole of 564 yards but, overall, not too testing for
average golfers.
9 holes, 5890yds, Par 72, SSS 69, Course record 65.
Club membership 250.

Visitors	no restrictions weekdays or Sun, competitions on Sat normal restrictions.
Societies	apply in writing/telephone in advance.
Green Fees	£8 weekdays (£10 Sunday & Bank Holidays).
Facilities	⚑ ♟ (prior arrangement) ⚐
Location	Ayr road A70

Hotel   ★★★ 64% Tinto Hotel, Symington, BIGGAR
                 ☎ 01899 308454   29 ⇆ ♞

ST BOSWELLS   Map 12 NT53

St Boswells Braeheads TD6 0DE ☎ 01835 823527
Attractive parkland course by the banks of the River Tweed;
easy walking.
9 holes, 5250yds, Par 66.
Club membership 320.

Visitors	contact in advance.
Societies	booking by writing to secretary.
Green Fees	£12 per round (£15 weekends).
Designer	W Park
Facilities	⊗ by prior arrangement 🍴 ⓔ by prior arrangement ⚑ ⚐
& Leisure	fishing.
Location	500yds off A68 east end of village

Hotel   ★★★⚘⚘ 77% Dryburgh Abbey Hotel,
                 ST BOSWELLS
                 ☎ 01835 822261   37 ⇆ ♞ Annexe1 ⇆ ♞

SANQUHAR   Map 11 NS70

Sanquhar Euchen Golf Course, Blackaddie Rd DG4 6JZ
☎ 01659 50577 & 66095
Parkland course, fine views, easy walking. A good test for all
standards of golfer.   ▶

9 holes, 5594yds, Par 70, SSS 68, Course record 66.
Club membership 200.

Visitors	no restrictions.
Societies	must pre-book.
Green Fees	£10 per day (£12 weekends).
Designer	Willie Fernie
Facilities	⌂
Location	0.5m SW off A76

Hotel	★★ 65% Blackaddie House Hotel, Blackaddie Rd, SANQUHAR ☎ 01659 50270 9 ⇄ ♠

SELKIRK   Map 12 NT42

Selkirk Selkirk Hill TD7 4NW ☎ 01750 20621
Pleasant moorland course set around Selkirk Hill. Unrivalled views.
9 holes, 5620yds, Par 68, SSS 67, Course record 61.
Club membership 364.

Visitors	contact in advance, may not play Mon evening, competition/match days.
Societies	must telephone in advance.
Green Fees	not confirmed.
Facilities	⊗ by prior arrangement ♭ by prior arrangement ♥ by prior arrangement ♀ ⌂ ♔ ♂
Location	1m S on A7

Hotel	★★★ 66% Burt's Hotel, The Square, MELROSE ☎ 01896 822285 20 ⇄ ♠

SHOTTS   Map 11 NS86

Shotts Blairhead ML7 5BJ ☎ 01501 820431
Moorland course.
18 holes, 6205yds, Par 70, SSS 70, Course record 63.
Club membership 800.

Visitors	visitors by arrangement on Sun.
Societies	apply in writing.
Green Fees	not confirmed.
Prof	Sandy Strachan
Designer	James Braid
Facilities	⊗ ♏ ♭ ♥ ♀ ⌂ ♔ ♣ ♂
Location	2m from M8 off Benhar Road

Hotel	★★★ 67% The Hilcroft Hotel, East Main St, WHITBURN ☎ 01501 740818 31 ⇄ ♠

SKELMORLIE   Map 10 NS16

Skelmorlie Beithglass PA17 5ES ☎ 01475 520152
Parkland/moorland course with magnificent views over Firth of Clyde. Designed by James Braid, the club celebrated its centenary in 1991. The first five holes are played twice.
13 holes, 5056yds, Par 64, SSS 65.
Club membership 385.

Visitors	no visitors before 4pm Sat.
Societies	apply by telephone.
Green Fees	not confirmed.
Designer	James Braid
Facilities	♥ ♀ ⌂ ♔
& Leisure	fishing.
Location	E side of village off A78

Hotel	★★★ 63% Manor Park Hotel, LARGS ☎ 01475 520832 10 ⇄ ♠ Annexe13 ⇄ ♠

SOUTHERNESS   Map 11 NX95

Southerness DG2 8AZ
☎ 01387 880677 Fax 01387 880644
Natural links, Championship course with panoramic views. Heather and bracken abound.
18 holes, 6566yds, Par 69, SSS 73, Course record 65.
Club membership 830.

Visitors	must have handicap certificate and contact in advance.
Societies	must contact in advance.
Green Fees	£30 per day (£40 per day weekends & bank holidays).
Cards	▨ ▨ ▨
Designer	McKenzie Ross
Facilities	⊗ ♏ ♭ ♥ ♀ ⌂ ♂
Location	3.5m S of Kirkbean off A710

Hotel	★★ 64% Clonyard House Hotel, COLVEND ☎ 01556 630372 15 ⇄ ♠

STEVENSTON   Map 10 NS24

Ardeer Greenhead KA20 4JX
☎ 01294 464542 Fax 01294 465316
Parkland course with natural hazards.
18 holes, 6500yds, Par 72, SSS 72, Course record 66.
Club membership 650.

Visitors	may not play Sat.
Societies	must contact in advance.
Green Fees	not confirmed.
Prof	Garrie Thompson
Designer	Stutt
Facilities	⊗ ♏ ♭ ♥ ♀ ⌂ ♣
Location	0.5m N off A78

Hotel	★★★★ 57% Hospitality Inn Irvine, 46 Annick Rd, IRVINE ☎ 01294 274272 127 ⇄ ♠

Auchenharvie Moor Park Rd West KA20 3HU
☎ 01294 603103
Long and flat municipal course with narrow greens and a pond affecting the 3rd and 12th holes. Easy walking.
9 holes, 5203yds, Par 65, SSS 64, Course record 67.
Club membership 150.

Visitors	municipal course 6 day advance booking system.
Societies	apply to professional.
Green Fees	£4.60 per 9 holes (£6.70 weekends).
Cards	▨
Prof	Bob Rodgers
Facilities	⊗ ♭ ♥ ♀ ⌂ ♔ ♂ ♣
Location	Off A738

Hotel	★★★ 73% Montgreenan Mansion House Hotel, Montgreenan Estate, KILWINNING ☎ 01294 557733 21 ⇄ ♠

STRANRAER   Map 10 NX06

Stranraer Creachmore by Stranraer DG9 0LF
☎ 01776 870245 Fax 01776 870445
Parkland course with beautiful view of Loch Ryan.
18 holes, 6308yds, Par 70, SSS 72, Course record 66.
Club membership 700.

▶

ROYAL TROON

TROON *South Ayrshire* ☎ 01292 311555
Fax 01292 318204   **Map 10 NS33**

John Ingham writes: When Jack Nicklaus first played Royal Troon in the 1962 Open, he was 22 and hit the ball a long way. At that time Nicklaus told me 'There are only two holes that I might not reach with my second shot. My favourite shot is the drive, which I hit up to 350 yards. Just before I swing,' he said, 'all my concentration is directed on one thing and that is to give the ball as big a hit - and as square a hit - as I physically can.'

While sheer length from the back tees at Royal Troon is a great advantage, bearing in mind the full course measures 7097 yards, where you hit the ball is more important than how far. The reason is that this championship links-type course is peppered with bunkers not visible from the tee.

That particular Open was won by Arnold Palmer, in those days a longish hitter as well. However, Palmer also had a delightful putting touch, essential for Royal Troon greens, which can prove hard to read.

Royal Troon is one of the finest links in the world and in an American list appears at number 36. Created in 1878, it was then mercifully free of jumbo jets from nearby Prestwick and has provided entertaining and testing golf for players from all over the world. Greg Norman holds the record with a 10-under-par round of 64. A round which put him in a tie for the 1989 Open which he lost to Mark Calcavecchia.

In the 1960s I played a round at this grand links with the late Henry Longhurst, a good club single figure man who had once won the German Amateur championship. To my best drives, lashed in the breeze, he would just hiss 'Wrong line' and, sure enough, when we got up the fairway, the ball would be submerged in soft sand. In fact I'm told there are 365 bunkers, one for every day of the year!

The Marine Highland hotel is on the edge of the course and, as there are 22 other courses in the area, this makes a great place for a holiday.

So great is Royal Troon, in fact, that the Royal and Ancient staged the 1997 Open again - for the seventh time since 1923!

Visitors	may play Mon, Tue and Thu only. Must write in advance and have a letter of introduction from own club and a handicap certificate of under 20. Ladies and under 18s may only play on the Portland
Green fees	£115 per day (incl coffee & lunch)
Facilities	⊗ ⫟ (by arrangement) 🍴 ♥ ♀ ♣ 🛍 ☂ 🏌 ♂ (Professional (R. B. Anderson)
Location	Craigend Rd, Troon KA10 6EP (S side of town on B749)

36 holes. Old Course: 18 holes, 6641yds, Par 71, SSS 73. Course record 64
Portland: 18 holes, 6289yds, Par 71, SSS 71

WHERE TO STAY AND EAT NEARBY

HOTELS:
TROON
★★★★⊛ 68% Marine Highland, Crosbie Rd. ☎ 01292 314444, 74 ⇄ ♠

★★★⊛ ⊛ ⊛ ♨ Lochgreen House, Monktenhill Rd, Southwood ☎ 01292 313343. 7 ⇄ ♠

★★★⊛ 75% Highgrove House, Old Loans Rd ☎ 01292 312511. 9 (7 ⇄ ♠ 2 ♠)

★★★⊛ 73% Piersland House, Craigend Rd. ☎ 01292 314747. 15 (9 ⇄ 6 ♠) Annexe 13 ⇄ ♠

Visitors   must contact in advance. Members times reserved throughout year.
Societies   must telephone in advance.
Green Fees £27 per day, £20 per round (£32/£25 weekends).
Designer   James Braid
Facilities ⊗ ⫫ ⓑ ♥ ♀ ⚐ ⌂ ✑
Location   2.5m NW on A718

Hotel   ★★★★ 69% North West Castle Hotel,
                STRANRAER
                ☎ 01776 704413   70 ⇆ ⫫ Annexe3 ⇆ ⫫

STRATHAVEN   Map 11 NS64

Strathaven Glasgow Rd ML10 6NL
☎ 01357 520421 Fax 01357 520421
Gently undulating, tree-lined, Championship parkland course with panoramic views over town and Avon valley.
18 holes, 6224yds, Par 71, SSS 71, Course record 63.
Club membership 950.
Visitors   welcome weekdays up to 4pm only. Must contact in advance.
Societies   apply in writing to general manager.
Green Fees not confirmed.
Prof   Matt McCrorie
Designer   Willie Fernie/J Stutt
Facilities ⚐ ⌂ ♥ ✑
Location   NE side of town on A726

Hotel   ★★★ 68% Strathaven Hotel, Hamilton Rd,
                STRATHAVEN ☎ 01357 521778   22 ⇆ ⫫

THORNHILL   Map 11 NX89

Thornhill Blacknest DG3 5DW ☎ 01848 330546
Moorland/parkland course with fine views over the southern uplands.
18 holes, 6011yds, Par 71, SSS 70, Course record 67.
Club membership 700.
Visitors   apply in advance, restricted competition days.
Societies   apply in writing.
Green Fees £22 per day (£28 weekends & bank holidays).
Prof   James Davidson
Facilities ⊗ ⫫ ⓑ ♥ ♀ ⚐ ⌂ ✑
Location   1m E of town off A76

Hotel   ★★ 73% Trigony House Hotel, Closeburn,
                THORNHILL ☎ 01848 331211 8 ⇆ ⫫

TROON   Map 10 NS33

ROYAL TROON See page 387

Troon Municipal Harling Dr KA10 6NE
☎ 01292 312464 Fax 01292 312578
Three links courses, two Championship.
Lochgreen Course: 18 holes, 6820yds, Par 74, SSS 73.
Darley Course: 18 holes, 6360yds, Par 71, SSS 63.
Fullarton Course: 18 holes, 4870yds, Par 72, SSS 72.
Club membership 3000.
Visitors   no restrictions.
Societies   apply in writing.
Green Fees not confirmed.
Prof   Gordon McKinlay

Facilities ♀ ⚐ ⌂ ⫫
Location   100yds from railway station

Hotel   ★★ 61% Craiglea Hotel, South Beach,
                TROON ☎ 01292 311366 20rm(10 ⇆ ⫫)

TURNBERRY   Map 10 NS20

TURNBERRY GOLF COURSE   See page 389

UDDINGSTON   Map 11 NS66

Calderbraes 57 Roundknowe Rd G71 7TS
☎ 01698 813425
Parkland course with good view of Clyde Valley. Testing 4th hole (par 4), hard uphill.
9 holes, 5046yds, Par 66, SSS 67, Course record 65.
Club membership 230.
Visitors   weekdays before 5pm.
Societies   welcome
Green Fees not conirmed.
Facilities ⊗ ⫫ ⓑ ♥ ♀ ⚐
Location   1.5m NW off A74

Hotel   ★★ 70% Redstones Hotel,
                8-10 Glasgow Rd, UDDINGSTON
                ☎ 01698 813774 & 814843
                Fax 01698 815319 18rm(16 ⇆ ⫫)

UPLAWMOOR   Map 10 NS45

Caldwell G78 4AU
☎ 01505 850366 (Secretary) & 850616 (Pro)
Fax 01505 850604
Parkland course.
18 holes, 6294yds, Par 71, SSS 70, Course record 63.
Club membership 600.
Visitors   must be with member at weekends & bank holidays. Must contact professional in advance.
Societies   writing to Secretary.
Green Fees £33 per day; £23 per round.
Prof   Stephen Forbes
Facilities ⊗ ⫫ ⓑ ♥ ♀ ⚐ ⌂ ✑
Location   0.5m SW A736

Hotel   ★★★ 69% Dalmeny Park Country House,
                Lochlibo Rd, BARRHEAD
                ☎ 0141 881 9211 20 ⇆ ⫫

WEST KILBRIDE   Map 10 NS24

West Kilbride 33-35 Fullerton Dr, Seamill KA23 9HT
☎ 01294 823911 Fax 01294 823911
Seaside links course on Firth of Clyde, with fine views of Isle of Arran from every hole.
18 holes, 5974yds, Par 70, SSS 70, Course record 63.
Club membership 840.
Visitors   may not play at weekends, must contact in advance.
Societies   Tue & Thu only; must contact in advance.
Green Fees on application.
Prof   Graham Ross
Designer   James Braid
Facilities ⚐ ⌂ ⫫ ✑

▶

TURNBERRY HOTEL GOLF COURSES

TURNBERRY *South Ayrshire*

☎ **01655 331000 Fax 01655 331706**   **Map 10 NS20**

John Ingham writes: The hotel is sumptuous, the Ailsa and Arran courses beneath it are total magic. The air reaches down into your inner lung and of all places in Scotland, Turnberry has to be among the finest.

Tunberry is delightfully off the beaten track and, although the courses are principally for residents of the hotel, if you wish to fly in, then Prestwick Airport is only seventeen miles from the first tee. What makes the place so desirable is the warmness of the welcome and, course professional Brian Gunson will tell you, this is literally so on occasions, as the links is on the friendliest of gulf streams.

The Ailsa course has been the venue for the Open in 1977 and 1986 and hosted it again in 1994. It was here in the 1977 Open, that Jack Nicklaus put up such a brave fight against Tom Watson. Then, in 1986, we had a wondrous victory from Greg Norman. He has fond memories of Turnberry, where a few hours after the prize-giving he was able to sit with his wife on the edge of the great links, drinking champagne, and watching the moon roll round the pure white lighthouse out by the 9th green.

Without any doubt, Turnberry is the stuff of dreams and you must go there if you possibly can.

Visitors   The golf courses are principally for residents of the hotel, so must contact in advance

Societies contact in advance as courses are for residents of the hotel only

Green fees on application.

Facilities ⊗ ⪢ 占 ♥ ☲ 🛏 ♨
        🏠 ⛳ ♂ ⚘ Professional (Brian Gunson)

Leisure   tennis (hardcourt), indoor swimming pool, squash, sauna, solarium, gym.

Location Turnberry KA26 9LT. On A719 N side of village

36 holes. Ailsa Course: 18 holes, 6440 yds, Par 69, SSS 72, Course record 63 Arran Course: 18 holes, 6014yds, Par 68, SSS 69. Course record 65

WHERE TO STAY AND EAT NEARBY

HOTELS:

MAYBOLE

★★⚙ Ladyburn

☎ 01655 740585. 8(7 ☲ 🐾)

TURNBERRY

★★★★★ ⚙⚙ Turnberry Hotel, Golf Courses & Spa.

☎ 01655 331000. 132 ☲ 🐾

★★★ ⚙ 76%Malin Court.

☎01655 331457. 17 ☲ 🐾

Location   W side of town off A78

Hotel   ★★★ 72% Priory House Hotel, Broomfields,
LARGS ☎ 01475 686460 21 ⇋ ☏

WEST LINTON   Map 11 NT15

Rutherford Castle Golf Club EH46 7AS
☎ 01968 661 233 Fax 01968 661 233
Undulating parkland set beneath the Pentland hills. With
many challenging holes. A good test for the better player
whilst offering great enjoyment to the average player.
18 holes, 6525yds, Par 72, SSS 71.
Club membership 360.
Visitors   telephone booking anytime.
Societies   application form forwarded on request.
Green Fees £15 per round (£25 weekends).
Designer   Bryan Moore
Facilities   ⓑ ☕ ♀ ⚒ ⚓
& Leisure   fishing.
Location   S of Edinburgh city bypass (A720) on A702
towards Carlisle

Hotel   ★★★ 72% Peebles Hydro Hotel, PEEBLES
☎ 01721 720602 137 ⇋ ☏

West Linton EH46 7HN ☎ 01968 660256
Moorland course with beautiful views of Pentland Hills.
18 holes, 6132yds, Par 69, SSS 70, Course record 63.
Club membership 800.
Visitors   weekdays anytime, weekends not before 1pm.
Societies   contact the secretary in writing.
Green Fees £30 per day; £20 per round (£30 per round
weekends).
Prof   Ian Wright
Designer   Millar/Braid/Fraser
Facilities   ⊗ ⅷ ⓑ ☕ ♀ ⚒ 🏠 ⚐ ⚑ ⚓ ♪
Location   NW side of village off A702

Hotel   ★★★ 72% Peebles Hydro Hotel, PEEBLES
☎ 01721 720602 137 ⇋ ☏

WIGTOWN   Map 10 NX45

Wigtown & Bladnoch Lightlands Ter DG8 9EF
☎ 01988 403354
Slightly hilly parkland course with fine views over Wigtown
Bay to Galloway Hills.
9 holes, 5462yds, Par 68, SSS 67, Course record 62.
Club membership 150.
Visitors   advisable to contact in advance for weekend
play. Course closed to visitors during open
competitions.
Societies   contact secretary in advance.
Green Fees not confirmed.
Designer   W Muir
Facilities   ⊗ by prior arrangement ⅷ by prior arrangement
ⓑ ☕ ♀ ⚒
Location   SW on A714

Hotel   ★★ 72% Creebridge House Hotel, NEWTON
STEWART ☎ 01671 402121 19 ⇋ ☏

WISHAW   Map 11 NS75

Wishaw 55 Cleland Rd ML2 7PH ☎ 01698 372869
Parkland course with many tree-lined areas. Bunkers protect
17 of the 18 greens.
18 holes, 6073yds, Par 69, SSS 69, Course record 64.
Club membership 984.
Visitors   must contact secretary in advance. May not play
Sat but may play alternate Sun.
Societies   apply in writing.
Green Fees £25 per day; £15 per round (£30/£20 Sun).
Prof   Stuart Adair
Designer   James Braid
Facilities   ⊗ ⅷ ⓑ ☕ ♀ ⚒ 🏠 ⚐ ⚓ ♪
Location   NW side of town off A721

Hotel   ★★★ 68% Popinjay Hotel,
Lanark Rd, ROSEBANK
☎ 01555 860441 40 ⇋ ☏ Annexe5 ⇋ ☏

WALES

John Ingham writes: Those not averse to wearing a daffodil in their lapel each St David's Day will tell you Wales not only boasts some great sporting characters, but also some excellent golf courses which don't cost fortunes to play.

Back in 1960, I drove my black Wolseley across the mountain road to Harlech to report a women's championship for the London Evening Standard. The event was staged across Royal St David's, on the coast just eleven miles from Barmouth and built, in 1893, on low-lying ground beneath the famous castle. It is the grandest seaside links, with dunes, rushes, dog roses.

The Principality has other great courses further south. There's Aberdovey, originally played into sunken flower pots in 1892. Today there's a frightening tee shot along a gorge, between hills. From one tee is an amazing pulpit-like view of the estuary, and Cardigan Bay.

Perhaps the most famous course in Wales is Royal Porthcawl which has opened its doors to championships, and Internationals. Begun in 1891 with nine holes and no clubhouse, it became 'Royal' in 1909 and it takes skill to play, particularly if the off-sea winds are zipping in from the Bristol Channel. Curiously, it often misses the rains, on its peninsula as it tends to fall a few miles inland.

By contrast, play at St Pierre, not far from the Severn Bridge near Chepstow, Monmouthshire. The location, parkland with a delightful manor, was found by dear old Bill Graham who bought it, after the war, and with the help of Bill Cox, built it into a splendid and somewhat sumptuous halt for golfers who appreciate more inland, parkland fairways.

Today, everyone tells me if I haven't played the Rolls of Monmouth, west of the town on the B4233, a rare treat lies in store. Created in 1982, it is considered very upmarket. Play it, they say, before you die.

WALES

The directory which follows has been divided into three geographical regions. Counties have not been shown against individual locations as recent legislation has created a number of smaller counties which will be unfamiliar to the visitor. The postal authorities have confirmed that it is no longer necessary to include a county name in addresses, provided a post code is shown. All locations appear in the atlas at the end of this guide in their appropriate counties.

NORTH WALES

This region includes the counties of Conwy, Denbighshire, Flintshire, Gwynedd, Isle of Anglesey and Wrexham which reflect the recent national changes.

ABERDYFI   Map 06 SN69

Aberdovey LL35 0RT
☎ 01654 767493 Fax 01654 767027
A beautiful championship course at the mouth of the Dovey estuary, Aberdovey has all the true characteristics of a seaside links. It has some fine holes among them the 3rd, the 12th, an especially good short hole, and the 11th. There are some striking views to be had from the course.
18 holes, 6445yds, Par 71, SSS 71, Course record 66.
Club membership 1000.
Visitors   handicap certificate required, must contact in advance, restrictions at weekends.
Societies   prior arrangement essential.
Green Fees £42 per day, £29 per round (£50/£35 weekends).
Cards   ⬜ ⬛⬛ ⬛⬛ ▦ ⬜
Prof   John Davies
Designer   J Braid
Facilities ⊗ �𝄃𝄃𝄃 ᴸᴬ ▆ ♀ ⛱ 🏠 🍴 ⛟ ♂
& Leisure snooker and billiards.
Location   0.5m W on A493

Hotel   ★★★ 71% Trefeddian Hotel, ABERDYFI
          ☎ 01654 767213 46 ⇄ ↑

ABERGELE   Map 06 SH97

Abergele Tan-y-Gopa Rd LL22 8DS
☎ 01745 824034 Fax 01745 824034
A beautiful parkland course with views of the Irish Sea and Gwyrch Castle. There are splendid finishing holes, a testing par 5, 16th; a 185 yd, 17th to an elevated green, and a superb par 5 18th with out of bounds just behind the green.
18 holes, 6520yds, Par 72, SSS 71, Course record 66.
Club membership 1250.
Visitors   must contact in advance. Limited play weekends.
Societies   must contact in advance.
Green Fees £23 per day (£29 weekends).
Prof   Iain R Runcie
Designer   Hawtree
Facilities ⊗ �𝄃𝄃𝄃 ᴸᴬ ▆ ♀ ⛱ 🏠 ♂
Location   0.5m W off A547/A55

Hotel   ★★★ 66% Kinmel Manor Hotel, St Georges
          Rd, ABERGELE ☎ 01745 832014 51 ⇄ ↑

ABERSOCH   Map 06 SH32

Abersoch LL53 7EY ☎ 01758 712622
Seaside links, with five parkland holes.
18 holes, 5819yds, Par 69, SSS 68, Course record 66.
Club membership 650.
Visitors   must contact in advance. Competition days Sun & Thu.
Societies   must apply in advance.
Green Fees not confirmed.
Prof   A D Jones
Designer   Harry Vardon
Facilities ⊗ ⑈ ᴸᴬ ▆ ♀ ⛱ 🏠 ⛏ ♘ 🛒 ♂ ♬
Location   S side of village

Hotel   ★★ 66% Deucoch Hotel, ABERSOCH
          ☎ 01758 712680 10 ⇄ ↑

ANGLESEY, ISLE OF   Map 06

Golf Courses on the island of Anglesey are listed below.

AMLWCH   Map 06 SH49

Bull Bay LL68 9RY ☎ 01407 830960 Fax 01407 832612
Wales's northernmost course, Bull Bay is a pleasant coastal, heathland course with natural rock, gorse and wind hazards. Views from several tees across Irish Sea to Isle of Man, and across Anglesey to Snowdonia.
18 holes, 6217yds, Par 70, SSS 70, Course record 60.
Club membership 825.

AA   71%
★★★
TREFEDDIAN HOTEL

Family owned/managed 3-star country hotel.
Close to sea in Snowdonia National Park.
Views of sand dunes, beaches, Cardigan Bay and
Aberdovey Championship Golf Links.
Bedrooms en-suite, some balcony.
Lift, indoor swimming pool, tennis, snooker.
Children's playroom. A Family Hotel. Ideal
base for touring North/Mid Wales. ½ mile
north of Aberdyfi village.
Telephone for full colour brochure.

ABERDYFI LL35 0SB WALES
Telephone: (01654) 767213
Fax: (01654) 767777

Visitors advisable to contact in advance.
Societies advance booking essential.
Green Fees £20 per day; £17.50 per round (£25/£22.50 weekends & bank holidays).
Prof John Burns
Designer W H Fowler
Facilities ⊗ ⑄ ⓑ ♥ ⓨ ⚐ ⛿ ⚐
Location 1m W of Amlwch on A5025

Hotel ★★ 63% Trecastell Hotel, Bull Bay, AMLWCH ☎ 01407 830651 13rm(11 ⇆ ↑)

BEAUMARIS   Map 06 SH67

Baron Hill LL58 8YW ☎ 01248 810231
Undulating course with natural hazards of rock and gorse. Testing 3rd and 4th holes (par 4's). Hole 5/14 plays into the prevailing wind with an elevated tee across two streams. The hole is between two gorse covered mounds.
9 holes, 5062mtrs, Par 68, SSS 69, Course record 62.
Club membership 400.
Visitors ladies have priority on Tue am & club competitions Sun.
Societies apply in writing to secretary.
Green Fees not confirmed.
Facilities ⊗ ⓑ ♥ ⓨ ⚐ ⚐
Location Take A545 from Menai Bridge to Beaumaris, course signed on approach to town

Hotel ★★ 67% Bulkeley Hotel, Castle St, BEAUMARIS ☎ 01248 810415 41rm(40 ⇆ ↑)

HOLYHEAD   Map 06 SH28

Holyhead Lon Garreg Fawr, Trearddur Bay LL65 2YL ☎ 01407 763279 Fax 01407 763279
Treeless, undulating seaside course which provides a varied and testing game, particularly in a south wind. The fairways are bordered by gorse, heather and rugged outcrops of rock. Accuracy from most tees is paramount as there are 43 fairway and greenside bunkers and lakes. Designed by James Braid. Indoor driving range.
18 holes, 6058yds, Par 70, SSS 70, Course record 64.
Club membership 1120.
Visitors must contact in advance.
Societies must contact in advance.
Green Fees £25 per day; £19 per round (£29/£25 weekends & bank holidays).
Prof Stephen Elliot
Designer James Braid
Facilities ⊗ ⑄ ⓑ ♥ ⓨ ⚐ ⛿ ⚐ ⇄ ⚐ ↑
Location 1.25m S on B4545

Hotel ★★★ 71% Trearddur Bay Hotel, TREARDDUR BAY ☎ 01407 860301 37 ⇆ ↑

LLANGEFNI   Map 06 SH47

Llangefni (Public) LL77 7LJ
☎ 01248 722193 Fax 01248 750156
Picturesque parkland course designed by Hawtree & Son.
9 holes, 1342yds, Par 28, SSS 28.
Visitors no restrictions.
Societies

Green Fees not confirmed.
Prof Paul Lovell
Designer Hawtree & Sons
Facilities ⊗ ♥ ⚐ ⛿ ⓨ ⚐
Location 1.5m off A5

Hotel ★★ 64% Anglesey Arms, MENAI BRIDGE ☎ 01248 712305 16 ⇆ ↑

RHOSNEIGR   Map 06 SH37

Anglesey Station Rd LL64 5QX
☎ 01407 811202 Fax 01407 811202
Links course, low and fairly level with sand dunes and tidal river.
18 holes, 6300yds, Par 68, SSS 68.
Club membership 500.
Visitors phone in advance, some times are reserved for members. Dress restrictions.
Societies telephone & confirm in writing.
Green Fees Summer:£15 per day (£20 weekends & bank holidays). Winter £10 per day (£15 weekends & bank holidays).
Prof Paul Lovell
Designer H Hilton
Facilities ⊗ ⑄ ⓑ ♥ ⓨ ⚐ ⛿ ⚐
Location NE side of village on A4080

Hotel ★★★ 71% Trearddur Bay Hotel, TREARDDUR BAY ☎ 01407 860301 37 ⇆ ↑

BALA   Map 06 SH93

Bala Penlan LL23 7YD
☎ 01678 520359 & 521361 Fax 01678 521361
Upland course with natural hazards. All holes except first and last affected by wind. First hole is a most challenging par3. Irrigated greens and good views of surrounding countryside.
10 holes, 4962yds, Par 66, SSS 64, Course record 64.
Club membership 229.
Visitors book in advance at weekends
Societies must contact in advance.
Green Fees £12 per day (£15 weekends & bank holidays).
Prof A R Davies
Facilities ⊗ by prior arrangement ⓑ by prior arrangement ♥ ⓨ ⚐ ⛿ ⚐
Location 0.5m SW off A494

Hotel ★★ 65% Plas Coch Hotel, High St, BALA ☎ 01678 520309 10 ⇆ ↑

BANGOR   Map 06 SH57

St Deiniol Penybryn LL57 1PX ☎ 01248 353098
Elevated parkland course with panoramic views of Snowdonia, Menai Straits, and Anglesey.
18 holes, 5068mtrs, Par 68, SSS 67, Course record 61.
Club membership 300.
Visitors must contact in advance.
Societies must contact in advance.
Green Fees £12 per day (£16 weekends).
Cards
Designer James Braid
Facilities ⊗ ⑄ ⓑ ♥ ⓨ ⚐ ⛿ ⚐
Location E side of town centre off A5122   ▶

Hotel   ★★ 64% Anglesey Arms, MENAI BRIDGE
☎ 01248 712305 16 ⇔ ॓

BETWS-Y-COED   Map 06 SH75

Betws-y-Coed LL24 0AL ☎ 01690 710556
Attractive flat meadowland course set between two rivers in
Snowdonia National Park.
9 holes, 4996yds, Par 64, SSS 63, Course record 63.
Club membership 350.
Visitors   must contact in advance.
Societies   must telephone in advance.
Green Fees   not confirmed.
Facilities   ⊗ ⅏ ⅃ ▆ ♀ ♨
Location   NE side of village off A5

Hotel   ★★★ 70% The Royal Oak Hotel,
Holyhead Rd, BETWS-Y-COED
☎ 01690 710219 26 ⇔ ॓

BODELWYDDAN   Map 06 SJ07

Kimnel Park LL18 5SR
☎ 01745 833548 Fax 01745 833544
Flat parkland pay and play course that is suitable for
beginners.
9 holes, 3100, Par 58, SSS 58.
Visitors   no restrictions.
Societies   telephone for details.
Green Fees   not confirmed.
Prof   Peter Stebbings
Designer   Peter Stebbings
Facilities   ⊗ ⅏ ⅃ ▆ ♀ ♨ ☂ ♒ ⎀
Location   y

Hotel   ★★★ 64% Oriel House Hotel, Upper Denbigh
Rd, ST ASAPH ☎ 01745 582716 19 ⇔ ॓

BRYNFORD   Map 07 SJ17

Holywell Brynford CH8 8LQ
☎ 01352 713937 & 710040 Fax 0707 660453
Exposed moorland course, with bracken and gorse flanking
undulating fairways. 720 ft above sea level.
18 holes, 6100yds, Par 70, SSS 70, Course record 68.
Club membership 505.
Visitors   advisable to book in advance particularly for
weekends.
Societies   by prior arrangement with the secretary.
Green Fees   £15 per day (£20 weekends & bank holidays).
Prof   Sean O'Conner
Facilities   ⊗ ⅏ ⅃ ▆ ♀ ♨ ⎙ ♒
Location   1.25m SW off B5121

Hotel   ★★★ 67% Holiday Inn Garden Court,
Gateway Services, Westbound A55,
NORTHOP HALL ☎ 01244 550011 55 ⇔ ॓

CAERNARFON   Map 06 SH46

Caernarfon Llanfaglan LL54 5RP
☎ 01286 673783 & 678359 Fax 01286 672535
Parkland course with gentle gradients.
18 holes, 5891yds, Par 69, SSS 68, Course record 64.
Club membership 730.

Visitors   must contact in advance.
Societies   must apply in advance, in writing or by
telephone.
Green Fees   £22 per day; £18 per round (£28/£24 weekends
& bank holidays).
Prof   Aled Owen
Facilities   ⊗ ⅏ ⅃ ▆ ♀ ♨ ⎙ ♒ ♒ ♨
Location   1.75m SW

Hotel   ★★★ 65% Celtic Royal Hotel, Bangor St,
CAERNARFON ☎ 01286 674477 110 ⇔ ॓

CAERWYS   Map 06 SJ17

Caerwys Nine Of Clubs CH7 5AQ ☎ 01352 720692
Following the natural contours of the land and with a south-
west aspect, this course could be considered a litle gem. Each
approach to every green is different and there are many
interesting and challenging holes.
9 holes, 3080yds, Par 60, Course record 61.
Club membership 150.
Visitors   no restrictions.
Societies   telephone then confirm in writing.
Green Fees   not confirmed.
Designer   Eleanor Barlow
Facilities   ⊗ ⅃ ▆ ⎙ ♒ ♨
Location   1.5m SW of A55, midway between St Asaph
and Holywell

Hotel   ★★ 64% Bryn Awel Hotel, Denbigh Rd,
MOLD ☎ 01352 758622
8rm(4 ⇔3 ॓) Annexe10 ⇔ ॓

CHIRK   Map 07 SJ23

Chirk Golf Club LL14 5AD
☎ 01691 774407 Fax 01691 773878
Overlooked by the National Trust's Chirk Castle, is a
championship-standard 18-hole course with a 664 yard, par 5
at the 9th - one of the longest in Europe. Also a 9-hole
course, driving range and golf academy.
*Manor Course: 18 holes, 7045yds, Par 72, SSS 73, Course
record 72.*
Club membership 750.
Visitors   advisable to contact in advance. May not play in
members preferred tee times 7-11 daily.
Societies   must telephone for provisonal booking.
Green Fees   £18 per round (£25 weekends).
Cards   ▆▆ ▆ ◹
Prof   Mrk Maddison
Facilities   ⊗ ⅏ ⅃ ▆ ♀ ♨ ⎙ ♒ ♒ ♨ ⎀
& Leisure   squash, fishing.
Location   5m N of Oswestry

Hotel   ★★★ 65% Hand Hotel, Church St, CHIRK
☎ 01691 772479 16 ⇔ ॓

COLWYN BAY   Map 06 SH87

Old Colwyn Woodland Av, Old Colwyn LL29 9NL
☎ 01492 515581
Hilly, meadowland course with sheep and cattle grazing on it
in parts.
9 holes, 5243yds, Par 68, SSS 66, Course record 63.
Club membership 267.
Visitors   welcome ex Sat. Contact in advance.
Societies   must contact in advance.

Green Fees £10 per day (£15 weekends & bank holidays).
Designer James Braid
Facilities ⛳
Location E side of town centre on B5383

Hotel ★★★ 66% Hopeside Hotel, Princes Dr, West End, COLWYN BAY ☎ 01492 533244 19 ⇨ ⌒

CONWY   Map 06 SH77

Conwy (Caernarvonshire) Beacons Way, Morfa LL32 8ER ☎ 01492 592423 Fax 01492 593363
Founded in 1890, Conwy has hosted national and international championships since 1898. Set among sandhills, possessing true links greens and a profusion of gorse on the latter holes, especially the 16th, 17th and 18th. This course provides the visitor with real golfing enjoyment against a background of stunning beauty.
18 holes, 6647yds, Par 72, SSS 72, Course record 69.
Club membership 1050.
Visitors advisable to contact secretary in advance. Limited play weekends.
Societies must contact in advance.
Green Fees £25 per day (£30 weekends & bank holidays).
Prof Peter Lees
Facilities ⊗ ⤢ ⛳ ♥ ♀ ⛳ ⌒ ⚑ ❦ ⚒ ✐
Location 1m W of town centre on A55

Hotel ★★★ 71% The Groes Inn, Tyn-y-Groes, CONWY ☎ 01492 650545 14 ⇨ ⌒

CRICCIETH   Map 06 SH43

Criccieth Ednyfed Hill LL52 0PH
☎ 01766 522154
Hilly course on Lleyn Peninsula. Good views.
18 holes, 5787yds, Par 69, SSS 68.
Club membership 350.
Visitors must contact in advance.
Societies telephone in advance.
Green Fees not confirmed.
Facilities ⊗ ⤢ ⛳ ♥ ♀ ⛳ ⌒ ✐
Location 1m NE

Hotel ★★★⚘ 68% Bron Eifion Country House Hotel, CRICCIETH ☎ 01766 522385 19 ⇨ ⌒

DENBIGH   Map 06 SJ06

Bryn Morfydd Hotel Llanrhaedr LL16 4NP
☎ 01745 890280 Fax 01745 890488
In a beautiful setting in the Vale of Clwyd, the original 9-hole Duchess course was designed by Peter Alliss in 1982. In 1992, the 18-hole Dukes course was completed: a parkland course designed to encourage use of finesse in play.
Dukes Course: 18 holes, 5650yds, Par 70, SSS 67, Course record 74.
Duchess Course: 9 holes, 2098yds, Par 27.
Club membership 450.
Visitors must book in advance, good standards of dress apply.
Societies apply in writing.
Green Fees not confirmed.

Cards ⬛ ⬛ ⬛ ⬛ ⬛
Prof Ivor Jones
Designer Peter Allis/Duncan Muirhead
Facilities ⊗ ⤢ ⛳ ♥ ♀ ⛳ ⌒ ⚑ ❦ ⚒ ✐
& Leisure heated outdoor swimming pool.
Location On A525 between Denbigh and Ruthin

Denbigh Henllan Rd LL16 5AA
☎ 01745 814159 Fax 814888
Parkland course, giving a testing and varied game. Good views.
18 holes, 5712yds, Par 69, SSS 68, Course record 64.
Club membership 725.
Visitors must contact in advance.
Societies apply in writing.
Green Fees not confirmed.
Prof Mike Jones
Designer John Stockton
Facilities ⛳ ⌒ ⚒ ✐
Location 1.5m NW on B5382

Hotel ★★★ 64% Oriel House Hotel, Upper Denbigh Rd, ST ASAPH ☎ 01745 582716 19 ⇨ ⌒

DOLGELLAU   Map 06 SH71

Dolgellau Pencefn Rd LL40 2ES
☎ 01341 422603
Undulating parkland course. Good views of mountains and Mawddach estuary.
9 holes, 4671yds, Par 66, SSS 63, Course record 62.
Club membership 280.
Visitors no restrictions
Societies must contact in advance.
Green Fees £15 per round.
Cards ⬛ ⬛ ⬛ ⬛ ⬛
Facilities ⊗ ⛳ ♥ ⛳ ⌒ ⚒ ✐
Location 0.5m N

Hotel ★★ 64% Royal Ship Hotel, Queens Square, DOLGELLAU ☎ 01341 422209 24rm(18 ⇨ ⌒)

EYTON   Map 07 SJ34

Plassey LL13 0SP ☎ 01978 780028
Pleasant 9-hole course set in naturally contoured parkland with water hazards. It is within Plassey Leisure Park and Craft Centre and all park facilities are available to golfers.
9 holes, 2300yds, Par 32, SSS 32.
Club membership 200.
Visitors must contact in advance,
Societies telephone then confirm in writing.
Green Fees not confirmed.
Designer Welsh Golf Union
Facilities ⊗ ⤢ ⛳ ♥ ♀ ⛳ ⌒ ⚒ ✐
& Leisure heated indoor swimming pool, fishing, sauna, solarium.
Location 2.5m off A483 Chester/Oswestry

Hotel ★★★ 67% Cross Lanes Hotel & Restaurant, Cross Lanes, Bangor Rd, Marchwiel, WREXHAM ☎ 01978 780555 16 ⇨ ⌒

FLINT
Map 07 SJ27

Flint Cornist Park CH6 5HJ
☎ 01244 812974 Fax 01244 811885
Parkland course incorporating woods and streams. Excellent views of Dee estuary and the Welsh hills.
9 holes, 6984yds, Par 69, SSS 69, Course record 65.
Club membership 260.
Visitors   must contact in advance, not Sun.
Societies   not weekends.
Green Fees £10 per day.
Designer   H G Griffith
Facilities   ⊗ ⅏ ⅊ ♥ ☕ △ ↩
& Leisure   hard tennis courts.
Location   1m W

HARLECH
Map 06 SH53

Royal St Davids LL46 2UB
☎ 01766 780361 Fax 01766 781110
Championship links, with easy walking and natural hazards.
18 holes, 6552yds, Par 69, SSS 73, Course record 64.
Club membership 800.
Visitors   pre booking essential, must hold current handicap certificate.
Societies   telephone secretary in advance. Handicap certificates required.
Green Fees £25-£33 (£30-£38 weekends & bank holidays).
Cards   💳 VISA
Prof   John Barnett
Facilities   ⊗ ⅏ ⅊ ♥ ♀ △ ☕ ♥ ⚒ ✓
Location   W side of town on A496

Hotel   ★★ 64% Ty Mawr Hotel, LLANBEDR
☎ 01341 241440   10 ⇆ ♪

HAWARDEN
Map 07 SJ36

Hawarden Groomsdale Ln CH5 3EH
☎ 01244 531447 & 520809
Parkland course with comfortable walking and good views.
18 holes, 5842yds, Par 69, SSS 69.
Club membership 550.
Visitors   arrange visit with the professional.
Societies   by prior arrangement.
Green Fees not confirmed.
Prof   Chris Hope
Facilities   ⊗ ⅏ ⅊ ♥ ♀ △ ☕
Location   W side of town off B5125

Hotel   ★★★ 72% The Gateway To Wales Hotel, Welsh Rd, Sealand, Deeside, CHESTER
☎ 01244 830332   39 ⇆ ♪

LLANDUDNO
Map 06 SH78

Llandudno (Maesdu) Hospital Rd LL30 1HU
☎ 01492 876450 Fax 01492 871570
Part links, part parkland, this championship course starts and finishes on one side of the main road, the remaining holes, more seaside in nature, being played on the other side. The holes are pleasantly undulating and present a pretty picture when the gorse is in bloom. Often windy, this varied and testing course is not for beginners.

18 holes, 6545yds, Par 72, SSS 72, Course record 66.
Club membership 1045.
Visitors   must book in advance.
Societies   must apply in advance to secretary.
Green Fees £25 per day, £18 per round after 1pm (£30/£22 weekends & bank holidays).
Prof   Simon Boulden
Facilities   ⊗ ⅏ ⅊ ♥ ♀ △ ☕ ♥ ⚒ ✓
Location   S side of town centre on A546

Hotel   ★★★ 67% Imperial Hotel, The Promenade, LLANDUDNO
☎ 01492 877466 100 ⇆ ♪

North Wales 72 Bryniau Rd, West Shore LL30 2DZ
☎ 01492 875325 Fax 01492 875325
Challenging seaside links with superb views of Anglesey and Snowdonia.
18 holes, 6247yds, Par 71, SSS 71, Course record 65.
Club membership 525.
Visitors   must contact in advance.
Societies   must contact in advance.
Green Fees £23 per day, £16 per round (£30/£20 weekends and bank holidays).
Prof   Richard Bradbury
Designer   Tancred Cummins
Facilities   ⊗ ⅏ ⅊ ♥ ♀ △ ☕ ♥ ⚒ ✓
Location   W side of town on A546

Hotel   ★★ St Tudno Hotel, Promenade, LLANDUDNO
☎ 01492 874411   20 ⇆ ♪

Rhos-on-Sea Penrhyn Bay LL30 3PU
☎ 01492 548115 (Prof) & 549100 (clubhouse)
Seaside course, with easy walking and panoramic views.
18 holes, 6064yds, Par 69, SSS 69, Course record 68.
Club membership 400.
Visitors   advised to telephone beforehand to guarantee tee times.
Societies   booking essential, telephone in advance.
Green Fees £10 per day (£20 weekends).
Prof   Mike Macara
Designer   J J Simpson
Facilities   ⊗ ⅏ ⅊ ♥ ♀ △ ☕ ♥ ✓
Location   0.5m W of LLandudno, off the A55

Hotel   ★★★ 66% Hopeside Hotel, Princes Dr, West End, COLWYN BAY
☎ 01492 533244   19 ⇆ ♪

LLANFAIRFECHAN
Map 06 SH67

Llanfairfechan Llannerch Rd LL33 0ES
☎ 01248 680144
Hillside course with panoramic views of coast.
9 holes, 3119yds, Par 54, SSS 57, Course record 53.
Club membership 197.
Visitors   contact in advance, booking necessary at weekends.
Societies   apply in writing.
Green Fees £5 per day (£10 Sun & bank holidays).
Facilities   ♀ △
Location   W side of town on A55

Hotel ★★68% Castle Bank Hotel,
Mount Pleasant, CONWY
☎ 01492 593888 9rm(8 🐾)

LLANGOLLEN Map 07 SJ24

Vale of Llangollen Holyhead Rd LL20 7PR
☎ 01978 860906 Fax 01978 860906
Parkland course, set in superb scenery by the River Dee.
18 holes, 6656yds, Par 72, SSS 73, Course record 67.
Club membership 760.
Visitors must contact in advance. Restricted club
competition days. Handicap certificate required.
Societies apply in writing to the secretary.
Green Fees £30 per day; £20 per round (£35/£25 weekends
& bank holidays).
Cards 🖮 💳 🔗 🔗
Prof David Vaughan
Facilities ⊗ 🍴 🛒 💄 ♀ 🏌 🛍 ⚷
Location 1.5m E on A5

Hotel ★★★♣♣69% Bryn Howel Hotel & Restaurant,
LLANGOLLEN
☎ 01978 860331 36 ⇆ 🐾

MOLD Map 07 SJ26

Old Padeswood Station Rd, Padeswood CH7 4JL
☎ 01244 547401 & 550414 Fax 01244 545082
Situated in the beautiful Alyn Valley, half on flat parkland
and half undulating. Striking mountain views.
18 holes, 6685yds, Par 72, SSS 72, Course record 66.
Club membership 600.
Visitors welcome, subject to tee availability.
Societies telephone in advance.
Green Fees £18 per round (£20 weekends & bank holidays).
Prof Tony Davies
Designer Jeffries
Facilities ⊗ 🍴 🛒 💄 ♀ 🏌 🛍 🕺 🛍 ⚷
Location 3m SE off A5118

Hotel ★★64% Bryn Awel Hotel, Denbigh Rd,
MOLD ☎ 01352 758622
8rm(4 ⇆3 🐾) Annexe10 ⇆ 🐾

Padeswood & Buckley The Caia, Station Ln, Padeswood
CH7 4JD ☎ 01244 550537 Fax 01244 541600
Gently undulating parkland course, with natural hazards and
good views of the Welsh Hills.
18 holes, 5982yds, Par 70, SSS 69, Course record 66.
Club membership 700.
Visitors weekdays only, contact secretary in advance
Societies apply in writing.
Green Fees £20 per round.
Prof David Ashton
Designer Williams Partnership
Facilities ⊗ 🍴 🛒 💄 ♀ 🏌 🛍 🕺 🛍 ⚷ ⚷
Location 3m SE off A5118

Hotel ★★64% Bryn Awel Hotel, Denbigh Rd,
MOLD ☎ 01352 758622
8rm(4 ⇆3 🐾) Annexe10 ⇆ 🐾

MORFA NEFYN Map 06 SH24

Nefyn & District LL53 6DA
☎ 01758 720966 Fax 01758 720476
A 27-hole course played as two separate 18's, Nefyn is a
cliff top links where you never lose sight of the sea. A
well-maintained course which will be a very tough test
for the serious golfer, is still user friendly for the casual
visitor. Every hole has a different challenge and the old
13th fairway is approximately 30 yards arcross from sea-
to-sea. The course has an added bonus of a pub on the
beach roughly halfway round for those whose golf may
need some bolstering!
Old Course: 18 holes, 6201yds, Par 71, SSS 71, Course
record 67.
New Course: 18 holes, 6548yds, Par 71, SSS 71, Course
record 67.
Club membership 800.
Visitors advisable to contact in advance.
Societies apply by telephone.
Green Fees £30 per day, £25 per round (£35/£30
weekends & bank holiday).
Prof John Froom
Designer James Braid
Facilities ⊗ 🍴 🛒 💄 ♀ 🏌 🛍 🕺 🛍 🛒 ⚷
Location 0.75m NW

Hotel ★★★78% Plas Bodegroes,
Nefyn Rd, PWLLHELI
☎ 01758 612363 9 ⇆ 🐾 Annexe2 ⇆ 🐾

NORTHOP Map 07 SJ26

Northop Country Park CH7 6WA
☎ 01352 840440 Fax 01352 840445
Designed by former British Ryder Cup captain, John Jacobs,
the parkland course gives the impression of having been
established for many years. No two holes are the same and
designed to allow all year play.
18 holes, 6750yds, Par 72, SSS 73, Course record 64.
Club membership 500.
Visitors must contact in advance.
Societies apply in writing or by telephone in advance.
Green Fees £30 per round (£35 weekends & bank holidays).
Cards 🖮 💳 🔗
Prof Matthew Pritchard
Designer John Jacobs
Facilities ⊗ 🍴 🛒 💄 ♀ 🏌 🛍 🕺 🛍 ⚷ ⚷ ⚷
& Leisure hard tennis courts, sauna, gymnasium.
Location 150 yds from Connahs Quay turnoff on A55

Hotel ★★★★70% St Davids Park Hotel, St Davids
Park, EWLOE ☎ 01244 520800 145 ⇆ 🐾

PANTYMWYN Map 07 SJ16

Mold Cilcain Rd CH7 5EH
☎ 01352 740318 & 741513 Fax 01352 741517
Meadowland course with some hard walking and natural
hazards. Fine views.
18 holes, 5528yds, Par 67, SSS 67, Course record 64.
Club membership 600.
Visitors contact in advance. Restricted play at weekends
Societies provisional booking by telephone.
Green Fees £18 per round (£25 per day, £20 per round
weekends & bank holidays).
Prof Richard Hughes ▶

Designer	Hawtree
Facilities	⊗ ⅷ ㊖ 🖳 ♀ ⟁ 🖴 📷 ⛴ ⛙ ⚷
Location	E side of village

Hotel	★★ 64% Bryn Awel Hotel, Denbigh Rd, MOLD ☎ 01352 758622 8rm(4 ⇌3 🌑) Annexe10 ⇌ 🌑

PENMAENMAWR   Map 06 SH77

Penmaenmawr Conway Old Rd LL34 6RD
☎ 01492 623330 Fax 01492 622105
Hilly course with magnificent views across the bay to
Llandudno and Anglesey. Dry-stone wall natural hazards.
9 holes, 5350yds, Par 67, SSS 66, Course record 64.
Club membership 600.

Visitors	advisable to contact in advance. May not play Sat.
Societies	must contact in advance.
Green Fees	£12 weekdays (£18 Sun and BH).
Facilities	⊗ ⅷ 🖳 ♀ ⟁ 🖴
Location	1.5m NE off A55

Hotel	★★★ 64% The Castle, High St, CONWY ☎ 01492 592324 29 ⇌ 🌑

PORTHMADOG   Map 06 SH53

Porthmadog Morfa Bychan LL49 9UU
☎ 01766 514124 Fax 01766 514638
Seaside links,very interesting but with easy walking and
good views.
18 holes, 6363yds, Par 71, SSS 71.
Club membership 900.

Visitors	must contact in advance. Handicap certificate required.
Societies	apply by telephone initially.
Green Fees	£20 per day (£26 weekends & bank holidays).
Prof	Peter L Bright
Designer	James Braid
Facilities	⊗ ⅷ 🖳 ♀ ⟁ 🖴 ⛙ ⚷
& Leisure	snooker.
Location	1.5m SW

Hotel	★★★♨♨ 68% Bron Eifion Country House Hotel, CRICCIETH ☎ 01766 522385 19 ⇌ 🌑

PRESTATYN   Map 06 SJ08

Prestatyn Marine Rd East LL19 7HS
☎ 01745 854320 Fax 01745 888353
Very flat seaside links exposed to stiff breeze. Testing holes:
9th, par 4, bounded on 3 sides by water; 10th,
par 4; 16th, par 4.
18 holes, 6564yds, Par 72, SSS 72, Course record 66.
Club membership 660.

Visitors	welcome except Sat & Tue mornings. Must contact in advance.
Societies	prior booking required.
Green Fees	£20 per day (£25 Sun & bank holidays).
Prof	Malcolm Staton
Designer	S Collins
Facilities	⊗ ⅷ 🖳 ♀ ⟁ 🖴 ⛴ ⚷
Location	0.5m N off A548

Hotel	★★ 61% Hotel Marina, Marine Dr, RHYL ☎ 01745 342371 29 ⇌ 🌑

St Melyd The Paddock, Meliden Rd LL19 8NB
☎ 01745 854405
Parkland course with good views of mountains and Irish Sea.
Testing 1st hole (423 yds) par 4. 18 tees.
9 holes, 5829yds, Par 68, SSS 68, Course record 65.
Club membership 400.

Visitors	must contact in advance.
Societies	must telephone in advance.
Green Fees	not confirmed.
Prof	Andrew Carr
Facilities	⊗ ⅷ 🖳 ♀ ⟁ 🖴
Location	0.5m S on A547

Hotel	★★ 61% Hotel Marina, Marine Dr, RHYL ☎ 01745 342371 29 ⇌ 🌑

PWLLHELI   Map 06 SH33

Pwllheli Golf Rd LL53 5PS ☎ 01758 701644
Easy walking on flat seaside course with outstanding views
of Snowdon, Cader Idris and Cardigan Bay.
18 holes, 6091yds, Par 69, SSS 69, Course record 66.
Club membership 880.

Visitors	restricted Tue,Thu & weekends.
Societies	must telephone in advance.
Green Fees	not confirmed.
Cards	🔲 🔲 🔲 🔲 🔲
Prof	G D Verity
Designer	Tom Morris
Facilities	⊗ ⅷ 🖳 ♀ ⟁ 🖴 ⚷
Location	0.5m SW off A497

Hotel	★★★ 78% Plas Bodegroes, Nefyn Rd, PWLLHELI ☎ 01758 612363 9 ⇌ 🌑 Annexe2 ⇌ 🌑

RHUDDLAN   Map 06 SJ07

Rhuddlan Meliden Rd LL18 6LB
☎ 01745 590217 Fax 01745 590472
Attractive, gently undulating parkland course with good
views. Well bunkered with trees and water hazards. The 476
yard 8th and 431 yard 11th require both length and accuracy.
The clubhouse has been refurbished.
18 holes, 6482yds, Par 71, SSS 71, Course record 66.
Club membership 1060.

Visitors	must contact in advance. Sun with member only.
Societies	telephone to book reservation.
Green Fees	£24 per day; £18 per round (£30 per round Sat).
Cards	🔲 🔲 🔲 🔲
Prof	Andrew Carr
Designer	Hawtree & Son
Facilities	⊗ ⅷ 🖳 ♀ ⟁ 🖴 ⛴ ⛙ ⚷
& Leisure	snooker.
Location	E side of town on A547

Hotel	★★★ 66% Kinmel Manor Hotel, St Georges Rd, ABERGELE ☎ 01745 832014 51 ⇌ 🌑

RHYL   Map 06 SJ08

Rhyl Coast Rd LL18 3RE ☎ 01745 353171
Seaside course.
9 holes, 6220yds, Par 70, SSS 70, Course record 65.
Club membership 500.
Visitors   must contact in advance. Limited availability at
weekends due to club competitions.
Societies   must contact in advance.
Green Fees   £12-£15 per 18 holes (£15-£20 weekends &
bank holidays).
Prof   Tim Leah
Designer   James Braid
Facilities   ⊗ ⑂ ⓑ ⚑ ♀ ♨ 🏠 ⛳ ⚷
Location   1m E on A548

Hotel   ★★ 61% Hotel Marina, Marine Dr, RHYL
☎ 01745 342371   29 ⇄ ⌂

RUABON   Map 07 SJ34

Penycae Ruabon Rd, Penycae LL14 1TP ☎ 01978 810108
An architecturally designed and built 9-hole parkland course
offering a challenge for players of all standards. After a lazy
Par 4 start the second Par 3 is wooded to one side and
guarded by water on the other. The 6th, a 317yds Par 4
makes a very difficult approach to the green. The 7th is
another Par 3, elevated and wooded to one side. The 8th
crosses water twice as the river meanders down the fairway.
9 holes, 2140yds, Par 64, SSS 62, Course record 62.
Club membership 200.
Visitors   advisable to book in advance.
Societies   telephone or write in advance.
Green Fees   not confirmed.
Designer   John Day
Facilities   ⊗ ⑂ by prior arrangement ⓑ ⚑ ♀ ♨ 🏠 ⛳ ⚷
Location   1m off A5

Hotel   ★★★ 65% Hand Hotel, Church St, CHIRK
☎ 01691 772479   16 ⇄ ⌂

RUTHIN   Map 06 SJ15

Ruthin-Pwllglas Pwllglas LL15 2PE
☎ 01978 790692 Fax 01978 790692
Hilly parkland course in elevated position with panoramic
views. Stiff climb to 3rd and 9th holes.
10 holes, 5362yds, Par 66, SSS 66.
Club membership 380.
Visitors   welcome except for competition days.
Societies   apply in writing.
Green Fees   £12.50 per round (£18 weekends).
Facilities   ♨
Location   2.5m S off A494

Hotel   ★★★ 64% Ruthin Castle, RUTHIN
☎ 01824 702664   58 ⇄ ⌂

ST ASAPH   Map 06 SJ07

Llannerch Park North Wales Golf Range, Llannerch Park
LL17 0BD ☎ 01745 730805
9 holes, 1587yds, Par 30.
Visitors   pay & play.
Societies   telephone in advance.
Green Fees   £2.50 per 9 holes.

Designer   B Williams
Facilities   ⚑ 🏠 ⛳ ⚷
Location   200yds S off A525

WREXHAM   Map 07 SJ35

Clays Farm Golf Centre Bryn Estyn Rd, Llan-y-Pwll
LL13 9UB ☎ 01978 661406 Fax 01978 661417
Gently undulating parkland course in a rural setting with
views of the Welsh mountains and noted for the difficulty of
its par 3s.
18 holes, 5908yds, Par 69, SSS 69, Course record 64.
Club membership 420.
Visitors   must contact in advance.
Societies   prior arrangement in writing.
Green Fees   £13 per round (£17.50 weekends).
Cards   ▨ ▨ ▨ ▨ ▨ ▨
Prof   David Larvin
Designer   R D Jones
Facilities   ⊗ ⑂ ⓑ ⚑ ♀ ♨ 🏠 ⛳ ♋ ⚷
Location   Off A534

Hotel   ★★★★ 66% Llwyn Onn Hall Hotel, Cefn Rd,
WREXHAM ☎ 01978 261225   13 ⇄ ⌂

Wrexham Holt Rd LL13 9SB
☎ 01978 351476 Fax 01978 364268
Inland, sandy course with easy walking. Testing dog-legged
7th hole (par 4), and short 14th hole (par 3) with full carry to
green.
18 holes, 6233yds, Par 70, SSS 70, Course record 64.
Club membership 600.
Visitors   may not play competition days, and are advised
to contact in advance. A handicap certificate is
required.
Societies   welcome Mon & Wed-Fri. Apply in writing.
Green Fees   not confirmed.
Prof   Roy Young
Designer   James Braid
Facilities   ⊗ ⑂ ⓑ ⚑ ♀ ♨ 🏠 ⚷
Location   2m NE on A534

Hotel   ★★★★ 66% Llwyn Onn Hall Hotel, Cefn Rd,
WREXHAM ☎ 01978 261225   13 ⇄ ⌂

MID WALES

This region includes the counties of Ceredigion,
Carmarthenshire, Pembrokeshire and Powys which reflect
the recent national changes.

ABERYSTWYTH   Map 06 SN58

Aberystwyth Brynymor Rd SY23 2HY
☎ 01970 615104 Fax 01970 615104
Undulating meadowland course. Testing holes: 16th (The
Loop) par 3; 17th, par 4; 18th, par 3. Good views over
Cardigan Bay.
18 holes, 6109yds, Par 71, SSS 71, Course record 67.
Club membership 450.
Visitors   must contact in advance.
Societies   write or telephone in advance.
Green Fees   not confirmed.
Prof   Mark Newson
Designer   Harry Vardon   ▶

Facilities ⊗ ⅢⅢ 🏃 ♉ ♈ ⚕ 🏠 ⚘ ⚔

Location N side of town

Hotel ★★★ 68% Belle Vue Royal Hotel, Marine Ter, ABERYSTWYTH ☎ 01970 617558 34 ⇆ ☔

AMMANFORD   Map 03 SN61

Glynhir Glynhir Rd, Llandybie SA18 2TF
☎ 01269 850472 & 851365 Fax 01269 851365
Parkland course with good views, latter holes close to Upper Loughor River. The 14th is a 394-yd dog leg.
18 holes, 6000yds, Par 69, SSS 70, Course record 66.
Club membership 700.

Visitors no visitors Sun. Contact professional in advance (01269 851010).

Societies welcome weekdays only. Contact in advance.

Green Fees £17 per day (£22 Sat & bank holidays).

Prof Duncan Prior

Designer F Hawtree

Facilities ⊗ Ⅲ by prior arrangement 🏃 ♉ ♈ ⚕ 🏠 ⚘ ⊟ ⚔

Location 2m N of Ammanford

Hotel ★★ 68% Mill at Glynhir, Glyn-Hir, Llandybie, AMMANFORD ☎ 01269 850672 11 ⇆ ☔

BORTH   Map 06 SN69

Borth & Ynyslas SY24 5JS
☎ 01970 871202 Fax 01970 871202
Seaside links, over 100 years old, with strong winds at times although part of the course is sheltered amongst the dunes. Some narrow fairways and plenty of natural hazards.
18 holes, 6116yds, Par 70, SSS 70, Course record 65.
Club membership 550.

Visitors must contact in advance, may play weekends ring to check no competitions in progress.

Societies telephone in advance.

Green Fees £25 per day; £20 per round (£32/£25 weekends & bank holidays).

Prof J G Lewis

Facilities ⊗ Ⅲ 🏃 ♉ ♈ ⚕ 🏠 ⚘ ⚔

Location 0.5m N on B4353

Hotel ★★★★♨ Ynyshir Hall, EGLWYSFACH ☎ 01654 781209 8 ⇆ ☔

BRECON   Map 03 SO02

Brecon Newton Park LD3 8PA ☎ 01874 622004
Parkland course, with easy walking. Natural hazards include two rivers on its boundary. Good river and mountain scenery.
9 holes, 5256yds, Par 66, SSS 66, Course record 61.
Club membership 360.

Visitors advisable to contact in advance, limited availability at weekends.

Societies apply in writing.

Green Fees £10 per day.

Designer James Braid

Facilities ⊗ Ⅲ 🏃 ♉ ♈ ⚕

Location 0.75m W of town centre on A40

Hotel ★★ 70% Castle of Brecon Hotel, Castle Square, BRECON ☎ 01874 624611 30 ⇆ ☔ Annexe12 ☔

Cradoc Penoyre Park, Cradoc LD3 9LP
☎ 01874 623658 Fax 01874 611711
Parkland with wooded areas, lakes and spectacular views over the Brecon Beacons. Challenging golf.
18 holes, 6331yds, Par 72, SSS 72, Course record 65.
Club membership 700.

Visitors must contact secretary in advance. Limited availability on Sundays

Societies apply in writing or telephone in advance to secretary.

Green Fees £20 per day (£25 weekends & bank holidays).

Prof Richard Davies

Designer C K Cotton

Facilities ⊗ Ⅲ 🏃 ♉ ♈ ⚕ 🏠 ⚘ ⚔

Location 2m N on B4520

Hotel ★★ 70% Castle of Brecon Hotel, Castle Square, BRECON
☎ 01874 624611 30 ⇆ ☔ Annexe12 ☔

BUILTH WELLS   Map 03 SO05

Builth Wells Golf Links Rd LD2 3NF
☎ 01982 553296 Fax 01982 551064
Well guarded greens and a stream running thorough the centre of the course add interest to this 18-hole undulating parkland course. The clubhouse is a converted 16th-century Welsh long house.
18 holes, 5386yds, Par 66, SSS 67, Course record 63.
Club membership 380.

Visitors contact secretary.

Societies by prior arrangement.

Green Fees £20 per day; £15 per round (£25/£20 weekends & bank holidays).

Prof Roy Truman

Facilities ⊗ Ⅲ 🏃 ♉ ♈ ⚕ 🏠 ⚘ ⚔

Location N of A483

Hotel ★★ 66% Pencerrig Country House Hotel, Llandrindod Rd, BUILTH WELLS
☎ 01982 553226 20 ⇆ ☔

BURRY PORT   Map 02 SN40

Ashburnham Cliffe Ter SA16 0HN
☎ 01554 832269 & 833846
This course has a lot of variety. In the main it is of the seaside type although the holes in front of the clubhouse are of an inland character. They are, however, good holes which make a very interesting finish. Course record holder, Sam Torrance.
18 holes, 6916yds, Par 72, SSS 74, Course record 70.
Club membership 730.

Visitors must be bona fide member of affiliated golf club and produce handicap certificate, very limited weekend times.

Societies telephone for initial enquiry.

Green Fees not confirmed.

Prof Robert Ryder

Designer J H Taylor

Facilities ⊗ Ⅲ 🏃 ♉ ♈ ⚕ 🏠 ⚘ ⚔

Location 5m W of Llanelli, A484 road

Hotel ★★ 66% Ashburnham Hotel, Ashburnham Rd, Pembrey, LLANELLI
☎ 01554 834343 & 834455
Fax 01554 834483 12 ⇆ ☔

CAERSWS   Map 06 SO09

Mid-Wales Golf Centre SY17 5SB
☎ 01686 688303 Fax 01686 688303
A 9-hole, Par 3 course with sand bunkers and three ponds.
9 holes, 2554yds, Par 54, SSS 54.
Club membership 95.
Visitors   welcome, restricted during competitions on Sun am.
Societies   telephone in advance.
Green Fees £6 per 18 holes; £4 per 9 holes (£8/£5 weekends & bank holidays).
Designer   Jim Walters
Facilities   🖥 ♥ ♀ 🛆 🖼 ↑↑ 🚃 ⌀ ⟨
Location   0.75m off A470 out of Caersws

Hotel   ★★ 64% Elephant & Castle, Broad St,
NEWTOWN ☎ 01686 626271
23 ⇄ ⋔ Annexe11 ⇄ ⋔

CARDIGAN   Map 02 SN14

Cardigan Gwbert-on-Sea SA43 1PR
☎ 01239 621775 & 612035 Fax 01239 621775
A links course, very dry in winter, with wide fairways, light rough and gorse. Every hole overlooks the sea.
18 holes, 6687yds, Par 72, SSS 73.
Club membership 600.
Visitors   may not play between 1-2pm. Handicap certificate preferred. Contact in advance
Societies   must telephone in advance.
Green Fees £20 per day (£25 weekends & bank holidays).
Cards   〰 ▭▭ 🜨 ⬛ ⌀
Prof   Colin Parsons
Designer   Hawtree
Facilities   ⊗ ⫙ 🖥 ♥ ♀ 🛆 🖼 ↑↑ 🍴 🚃 ⌀
& Leisure   squash.
Location   3m N off A487

Hotel   ★★★ 66% Cliff Hotel, GWBERT-ON-SEA
☎ 01239 613241   70 ⇄ ⋔

CARMARTHEN   Map 02 SN42

Carmarthen Blaenycoed Rd SA33 6EH ☎ 01267 281588
Hilltop course with good views.
18 holes, 6245yds, Par 71, SSS 71, Course record 67.
Club membership 700.
Visitors   must have a handicap certificate, telephone for times at weekends.
Societies   apply in writing minimum of ten days in advance.
Green Fees £18 (£25 weekends & bank holidays).
Prof   Pat Gillis
Designer   J H Taylor
Facilities   ⊗ ⫙ 🖥 ♥ ♀ 🛆 🖼 ↑↑ ⌀
Location   4m N of town

Hotel   ★★ 65% Falcon Hotel, Lammas St,
CARMARTHEN ☎ 01267 234959 & 237152
Fax 01267 221277   14 ⇄ ⋔

Derllys Court Llysonnen Rd SA33 5DT
☎ 01267 211575 Fax 01267 211575
Gently undulating parkland course with challenging par 3s (5th and 8th) and a testing par 5 involving a shot across a lake.

9 holes, 2859yds, Par 35, SSS 66, Course record 33.
Club membership 60.
Visitors   welcome at all times.
Societies   telephone in advance.
Green Fees £9 per 18 holes; £5 per 9 holes (£10/£6 weekends & bank holidays).
Cards   ▭▭ 🜨 VISA ▭ 🔌 ⌀
Designer   Peter Johnson
Facilities   ⊗ ⫙ 🖥 ♥ ♀ 🛆 🖼 ↑↑ 🚃 ⌀
Location   Just off A40 between Carmarthen/St Clears

Hotel   ★★ 65% Falcon Hotel, Lammas St,
CARMARTHEN ☎ 01267 234959 & 237152
Fax 01267 221277   14 ⇄ ⋔

GWBERT-ON-SEA   Map 02 SN15

Cliff Hotel SA43 1PP
☎ 01239 613241 Fax 01239 615391
This is a short course with 2 Par 4's and the remainder are challenging Par 3's. Particularly interesting holes are played across the sea on to a small island.
9 holes, 1545yds, Par 29.
Visitors   telephone to book in advance.
Societies   telephone in advance.
Green Fees from £6.50 per round.
Cards   ▭▭ VISA ⌀
Facilities   🛆 🖼 ↑↑ 🚃 ⌀
& Leisure   heated outdoor swimming pool, squash, fishing, sauna, solarium, gymnasium.

Hotel   ★★★ 66% Cliff Hotel, GWBERT-ON-SEA
☎ 01239 613241   70 ⇄ ⋔

HAVERFORDWEST · Map 02 SM91

Haverfordwest Arnolds Down SA61 2XQ
☎ 01437 764523 Fax 01437 764143
Fairly flat parkland course, a good challenge for golfers of all handicaps. Set in attractive surroundings with fine views over the Preseli Hills.
18 holes, 6005yds, Par 70, SSS 69, Course record 58.
Club membership 770.
Visitors restricted at weekends.
Societies apply in writing or telephone for booking form.
Green Fees £18 per round (£22 weekends).
Cards ⬤ ▥
Prof Alex Pile
Facilities ⊗ ⅢⅢ ▙ ⬤ ♀ ⌂ 🏌 🛒 ♨
Location 1m E on A40

Hotel ★★ 66% Hotel Mariners,
Mariners Square, HAVERFORDWEST
☎ 01437 763353 29 ⇔ 🐾

HAY-ON-WYE · Map 03 SO24

Summerhill Hereford Rd, Clifford HR3 5EW
☎ 01497 820451
Undulating parkland course set deep in the Wye Valley on the Welsh Border overlooking the Black Mountains.
9 holes, 2929yds, Par 70, SSS 67.
Visitors welcome anytime.
Societies contact for information.
Green Fees not confirmed.
Prof Graham Priday
Facilities ⌂ 🏌 ♨
Location B4350 Whitney toll bridge road

Hotel ★★★ 66% The Swan-at-Hay Hotel,
Church St, HAY-ON-WYE
☎ 01497 821188 15 ⇔ 🐾 Annexe3 ⇔ 🐾

KIDWELLY · Map 02 SN40

Glyn Abbey Trimsaran SA17 4LB
☎ 01269 861825 Fax 01269 861825
In the Gwendraeth valley, a 18-hole parkland course with greens well protected by the planting of 35,000 trees.
18 holes, 6173yds, Par 70, SSS 69, Course record 68.
Visitors advisable to book for weekends.
Societies must contact in advance.
Green Fees £15 per day, £10 per round (£20/£12 weekends).
Designer Hawtrees
Facilities 🏌 🛒 ♨
Location 4.5m E, off B4317

Hotel ★★ 66% Ashburnham Hotel,
Ashburnham Rd, Pembrey, LLANELLI
☎ 01554 834343 & 834455
Fax 01554 834483 12 ⇔ 🐾

KNIGHTON · Map 07 SO27

Knighton Frydd Wood LD7 1DB ☎ 01547 528646
Upland course with some hard walking. Fine views over the Welsh/English border.
9 holes, 5362yds, Par 68, SSS 66, Course record 66.
Club membership 150.

Visitors may not play on Sun until after 4.30pm.
Societies must contact in advance.
Green Fees £10 per day (£12 weekends & bank holidays).
Designer Harry Vardon
Facilities ⊗ by prior arrangement ⅢⅢ by prior arrangement ▙ ⬤ by prior arrangement ♀ ⌂
Location 0.5m S off B4355

Hotel ★★★ 62% The Knighton Hotel, Broad St,
KNIGHTON ☎ 01547 520530 15 ⇔ 🐾

LETTERSTON · Map 02 SM92

Priskilly Forest Castlemorris SA62 5EH
☎ 01348 840276 Fax 01348 840276
Testing parkland course surrounded by rhododendrons. Beautiful panoramic views. Challenging dog-leg 4th with hazards both sides.
9 holes, 5874yds, Par 70, SSS 68, Course record 76.
Club membership 70.
Visitors advance booking advisable at weekends during summer.
Societies telephone in advance.
Green Fees not confirmed.
Designer J Walters
Facilities ▙ ⬤ ♀ ⌂ 🏌 🛒 🐾 🛒 ♨
& Leisure fishing.
Location Off B4331 between Letterston and Mathry

Hotel ★★ 63% Abergwaun Hotel,
The Market Square, FISHGUARD
☎ 01348 872077 11rm(7 ⇔ 🐾)

LLANDRINDOD WELLS · Map 03 SO06

Llandrindod Wells The Clubhouse LD1 5NY
☎ 01597 823873 (sec) & 822247 (shop) Fax 01597 823873
An upland links course, designed by Harry Vardon, with easy walking and panoramic views. One of the highest courses in Wales. (1,100 ft above sea level).
18 holes, 5759yds, Par 69, SSS 69, Course record 65.
Club membership 450.
Visitors no restrictions.
Societies must telephone in advance.
Green Fees £15 per day, £12 per round (£22/£18 weekends).
Designer H Vardon
Facilities ⊗ ⅢⅢ ▙ ⬤ ♀ ⌂ 🏌 🐾 🛒 ♨
& Leisure Driving tees.
Location 1m SE off A483

Hotel ★★★ 67% Hotel Metropole,
Temple St, LLANDRINDOD WELLS
☎ 01597 823700 121 ⇔ 🐾

LLANDYSSUL · Map 02 SN44

Saron Saron SA44 5EL ☎ 01559 370705
Set in 50 acres of mature parkland with large trees and magnificent Teifi Valley views. Numerous water hazards and bunkers.
9 holes, 2400yds, Par 32, Course record 34.
Visitors may play at all times no arrangements required.
Societies telephone for details.
Green Fees £7 per 18 holes, £5 per 9 holes.
Designer Adas
Facilities 🏌 ♨
Location Off A484 at Saron

Hotel   ★★ 72% Ty Mawr Country Hotel & Restaurant, BRECHFA
☎ 01267 202332 5rm(4 ⇆ ♠)

LLANGATTOCK   Map 03 SO21

Old Rectory NP8 1PH
☎ 01873 810373 Fax 018373 810373
Sheltered course with easy walking.
9 holes, 2200yds, Par 54, SSS 59, Course record 53.
Club membership 80.
Visitors   telephone for information.
Societies   telephone for booking.
Green Fees not confirmed.
Facilities ⊗ ⅲ ⤶ ♥ ♀ ⚲ ⌖ ⊨
& Leisure outdoor swimming pool.
Location   SW of village

Hotel   ★★ 72% Gliffaes Country House Hotel, CRICKHOWELL
☎ 01874 730371 & 0800 146719 (Freephone)
Fax 01874 730463   19 ⇆ ♠ Annexe3 ⇆ ♠

LLANGYBI   Map 02 SN65

Cilgwyn SA48 8NN ☎ 01570 493286
Picturesque parkland course in secluded valley, with natural hazards of ponds, stream and woodland.
9 holes, 5309yds, Par 68, SSS 66, Course record 66.
Club membership 300.
Visitors   no restrictions, apart from Sun when advisable to telephone.
Societies   apply in advance by letter or telephone.
Green Fees not confirmed.
Facilities ⤶ ♥ ♀ ⚲ ⊨ ⌀
Location   5m N of Lampeter on A485

Hotel   ★★★★ 70% Falcondale Mansion, LAMPETER ☎ 01570 422910   19 ⇆ ♠

LLANIDLOES   Map 06 SN98

St Idloes Penrallt SY18 6LG ☎ 01686 412559
Hill-course, slightly undulating but walking is easy. Good views, partly lined with trees. Sand and grass bunkers.
9 holes, 5540yds, Par 66, SSS 66, Course record 61.
Club membership 339.
Visitors   may not play on Sun mornings.
Societies   apply in writing to the secretary at least one month in advance.
Green Fees not confirmed.
Facilities ⊗ by prior arrangement ⅲ by prior arrangement ⤶ ♥ ♀ ⚲ ⊨ ⌖ ⌀
Location   1m N off B4569

LLANRHYSTUD   Map 06 SN56

Penrhos Golf & Country Club SY23 5AY
☎ 01974 202999 Fax 01974 202100
Beautifully scenic course incorporating lakes and spectacular coastal and inland views. Many leisure facilities.
Penrhos: 18 holes, 6641yds, Par 72, SSS 73, Course record 71.
Academy: 9 holes, 1827yds, Par 31.
Club membership 300.

Visitors   must telephone, no jeans allowed on main course.
Societies   must telephone in advance.
Green Fees £25 per day; £18 per round (£30/£22 weekends).
Cards ▬ ▬ ▬ ⚙
Prof   Paul Diamond
Designer   Jim Walters
Facilities ⊗ ⅲ ⤶ ♥ ♀ ⚲ ⊨ ⌖ ⊨ ⬧ ⤙ ⌀ ⎰
& Leisure hard tennis courts, heated indoor swimming pool, sauna, solarium, gymnasium, bowling green.
Location   Turn off A487 onto B4337 in Llanrhystud. Course 0.25m on left

Hotel   ★★★★ 73% Conrah Hotel, Ffosrhydygaled, Chancery, ABERYSTWYTH
☎ 01970 617941   11 ⇆ ♠ Annexe9 ⇆ ♠

MACHYNLLETH   Map 06 SH70

Machynlleth Ffordd Drenewydd SY20 8UH
☎ 01654 702000
Lowland course with mostly natural hazards.
9 holes, 5726yds, Par 68, SSS 68, Course record 65.
Club membership 250.
Visitors   Thur ladies day, Sun morning mens competition.
Societies   telephone in advance.
Green Fees not confirmed.
Designer   James Braid
Facilities ⤶ ♥ ♀ ⚲ ⌀
Location   0.5m E off A489

Hotel   ★★ 66% Wynnstay Arms Hotel, Maengwyn St, MACHYNLLETH ☎ 01654 702941   23 ⇆ ♠

MILFORD HAVEN   Map 02 SM90

Milford Haven Woodbine House, Hubberston SA73 3RX
☎ 01646 692368 Fax 01646 697762
Parkland course with excellent greens and views of the Milford Haven waterway.
18 holes, 6030yds, Par 71, SSS 70.
Club membership 520.
Visitors   no restrictions, advisable to contact in advance.
Societies   telephone to book.
Green Fees £15 per round (£20 weekends & bank holidays).
Cards ▬ ▬ ▬ ⚙
Prof   J Lynch
Facilities ⊗ ⅲ ⤶ ♥ ♀ ⚲ ⊨ ⌖ ⬧ ⤙ ⌀
Location   1.5m W

Hotel   ★★ 61% Lord Nelson Hotel, Hamilton Ter, MILFORD HAVEN
☎ 01646 695341   32 ⇆ ♠

NEWPORT   Map 02 SN03

Newport (Pemb) The Golf Club SA42 0NR
☎ 01239 820244 Fax 01239 820244
Seaside links course, with easy walking and good view of the Preseli Hills and Newport Bay.
9 holes, 5815yds, Par 70, SSS 68, Course record 64.
Club membership 350.
Visitors   telephone in advance.
Societies   must telephone in advance.
Green Fees £15 per 18 holes, £10 per 9 holes.
Prof   Colin Parsons   ▶

403

Designer James Baird
Facilities ⊗ ⅧⅢ ┗ 💺 ♀ 🛆 🏠 🍴 🚩 🏡 🥄 🏌 ✐
Location 1.25m N

Hotel ★★64% Trewern Arms, NEVERN
☎ 01239 820395 10 ➪ ⏵

NEWTOWN Map 06 SO19

St Giles Pool Rd SY16 3AJ ☎ 01686 625844
Inland country course with easy walking. Testing 2nd hole, par 3, and 4th hole, par 4. River Severn skirts four holes.
9 holes, 6012yds, Par 70, SSS 70, Course record 67.
Club membership 350.
Visitors advisable to contact in advance.
Societies must contact in advance.
Green Fees £12.50 per day (£15 weekends & bank holidays).
Prof D P Owen
Facilities ⊗ ⅧⅢ ┗ 💺 ♀ 🛆 🏠 🍴 ✐
& Leisure fishing.
Location 0.5m NE on A483

Hotel ★★64% Elephant & Castle, Broad St, NEWTOWN
☎ 01686 626271 23 ➪ ⏵ Annexe11 ➪ ⏵

PEMBROKE DOCK Map 02 SM90

South Pembrokeshire Military Rd SA72 6SE
☎ 01646 621453
Parkland course overlooking the Cleddau River.
18 holes, 6100yds, Par 71, SSS 70, Course record 65.
Club membership 350.
Visitors must contact in advance, especially during season.
Societies apply in advance.
Green Fees £12 per day (£15 weekends).
Designer Committee
Facilities ⊗ ⅧⅢ by prior arrangement ┗ 💺 ♀ 🛆 🍴
Location SW side of town centre off B4322

Hotel ★★61% Old Kings Arms, Main St, PEMBROKE ☎ 01646 683611 21 ➪ ⏵

ST DAVID'S Map 02 SM72

St David's City Whitesands Bay SA62 6PT
☎ 01437 720312 & 721751
Links course with alternative tees for 18 holes. Panoramic views of St David's Head and Ramsey Island.
9 holes, 6117yds, Par 70, SSS 70, Course record 67.
Club membership 200.
Visitors prior booking with secretary is encouraged but no always necessary, please check for weekends, Ladies Day Fri pm.
Societies book with the secretary in advance.
Green Fees not confirmed.
Facilities 💺 🛆 ✐
Location 2m W overlooking Whitesands Bay

Hotel ★★★75% Warpool Court Hotel, ST DAVID'S ☎ 01437 720300 25 ➪ ⏵

TENBY Map 02 SN10

Tenby The Burrows SA70 7NP
☎ 01834 844447 Fax 01834 844447
The oldest club in Wales, this fine old seaside links, with sea views and natural hazards provides good golf all the year round. Hosts for the Welsh Amateur Championship in 1999.
18 holes, 6224yds, Par 69, SSS 71.
Club membership 800.
Visitors subject to competition & tee reservation. Must produce handicap certificate.
Societies must apply in advance.
Green Fees £26 per day (£30 weekends & bank holidays).
Prof Mark Hawkey
Designer James Braid
Facilities ⊗ ⅧⅢ ┗ 💺 ♀ 🛆 🏠 🍴 ✐
Location Close to railway station in the town

Hotel ★★★74% Atlantic Hotel, The Esplanade, TENBY
☎ 01834 842881 & 844176
Fax 01834 842881 ex 256 42 ➪ ⏵

Trefloyne Trefloyne Park, Penally SA70 7RG
☎ 01834 842165
Idyllic parkland course with backdrop of mature mixed woodlands and distant views of Tenby, Carmarthen bay and Caldey Island. Opened in 1996, natural features and hazards such as the Old Quarry make for exciting and challenging golf.
18 holes, 6635yds, Par 71, SSS 73.
Club membership 263.
Visitors must contact in advance, must play a reasonable standard of golf and adhere to golf etiquette and dress code of club. Must contact in advance.
Societies must book in advance by telephone or in writing.
Green Fees £17.50 per day (£21.50 weekends and bank holidays).
Cards 💳 💳 💳 💳 💳
Prof Steven Laidler
Designer F H Gillman
Facilities 💺 ♀ 🛆 🏠 🍴 🥄 🏌 ✐
& Leisure lessons by PGA Professional.
Location Within Trefloyne Park, just west of Tenby

Hotel ★★★66% Fourcroft Hotel, North Beach, TENBY ☎ 01834 842886 46 ➪ ⏵

WELSHPOOL Map 07 SJ20

Welshpool Golfa Hill SY21 9AQ ☎ 01938 850249
Undulating, hilly, heathland course with bracing air. Testing holes are 2nd (par 5), 14th (par 3), 17th (par 3) and a memorable 18th.
18 holes, 5708yds, Par 70, SSS 68, Course record 68.
Club membership 400.
Visitors must book in advance, restricted at weekends.
Societies must book in advance.
Green Fees £12.50 per day (£20.50 weekend & bank holiday in summer, £15.50 weekend & bank holiday in winter).
Designer James Braid
Facilities ⊗ ⅧⅢ ┗ 💺 ♀ 🛆 🏠 ✐

Location 3m W off A458

Hotel ★★★ 68% Royal Oak Hotel, WELSHPOOL
☎ 01938 552217 24 ⇄ ↟

SOUTH WALES

Cardiff Area Telephone Number Changes

From the 22 April 2000, all dialling codes listed as
(01222) will change to (029),
followed by an eight-digit local number, starting with 20.
For example, (01222) 123456 will
become (029) 2012 3456.

This region includes the counties of Blaenau Gwent,
Bridgend, Caerphilly, Cardiff, Merthyr Tydfil,
Monmouthshire, Neath Port Talbot, Newport, Rhondda
Cynon Taff, Swansea, Torfaen and Vale of Glamorgan which
reflect the recent national changes.

ABERDARE   Map 03 SO00

Aberdare Abernant CF44 0RY
☎ 01685 872797 Fax 01685 872797
Mountain course with parkland features overlooking Cynon
Valley.
18 holes, 5875yds, Par 69, SSS 69, Course record 64.
Club membership 550.
Visitors no restrictions
Societies apply in writing in advance to the secretary.
Green Fees £14 per day summer, £12 per day winter
(£18/£16 weekends & bank holidays).
Prof A Palmer
Facilities ⊗ ╟ ┗ ▆ ♀ ⚐ 🏠 ✔
Location 0.75m E

Hotel ★★★ 68% Tregenna Hotel, Park Ter,
MERTHYR TYDFIL
☎ 01685 723627 & 382055
Fax 01685 721951 24 ⇄ ↟

ABERGAVENNY   Map 03 SO21

Monmouthshire Gypsy Ln, Llanfoist NP7 9HE
☎ 01873 852606 Fax 01873 852606
This parkland course is very picturesque, with the
beautifully wooded River Usk running alongside. There
are a number of par 3 holes and a testing par 4 at the
15th.
18 holes, 5978yds, Par 70, SSS 69, Course record 65.
Club membership 700.
Visitors must play with member at weekends. Must
contact in advance & have handicap
certificate.
Societies must contact in writing.
Green Fees £25 per day (£30 weekends & bank
holidays).
Prof B Edwards
Designer James Braid
Facilities ⊗ ╟ ┗ ▆ ♀ ⚐ 🏠 ▜ ✔
Location 2m S off B4269

Hotel ★★ 71% Llanwenarth Arms Hotel,
Brecon Rd, ABERGAVENNY
☎ 01873 810550 18 ⇄ ↟

Wernddu Golf Centre Old Ross Rd NP7 8NG
☎ 01873 856223 Fax 01873 852177
A parkland course with magnificent views, wind hazards on
several holes in certain conditions and water hazards on four
holes. There is a 26 bay floodlit driving range.
18 holes, 5403yds, Par 68, SSS 67, Course record 64.
Club membership 550.
Visitors advisable to book in advance.
Societies telephone in advance.
Green Fees not confirmed.
Cards ▬ ▬▬ ▩ 🗲
Prof Alan Ashmead
Designer G Watkins
Facilities ⊗ ╟ ┗ ▆ ♀ ⚐ 🏠 ▜ ✔ ⟨
& Leisure 9 hole pitch & putt.
Location 1.5m NE on B4521

Hotel ★★★ 55% Angel Hotel,
15 Cross St, ABERGAVENNY
☎ 01873 857121 29 ⇄ ↟

BARGOED   Map 03 ST19

Bargoed Heolddu CF81 9GF
☎ 01443 830143 & 836411 (Prof)
Mountain parkland course, challenging par 70 course with
pamoramic views.
18 holes, 6049yds, Par 70, SSS 70, Course record 65.
Club membership 600.
Visitors must contact professional in advance, must play
with member at weekends.
Societies must contact in advance.
Green Fees £20 per day/round.
Prof C Coombs
Facilities ⊗ ╟ ┗ ▆ ♀ ⚐ 🏠 ⚒ ✔
Location NW side of town

Hotel ★★★ 68% Maes Manor Hotel,
BLACKWOOD ☎ 01495 224551 & 220011
Fax 01495 228217 8 ⇄ Annexe14 ⇄

BARRY   Map 03 ST16

Brynhill Port Rd CF62 8PN
☎ 01446 720277 Fax 01446 720277
Meadowland course with some hard walking. Prevailing
west wind.
18 holes, 6336yds, Par 72, SSS 71.
Club membership 750.
Visitors must contact in advance. May not play on Sun.
Societies phone secretary for details.
Green Fees £20 per day.
Prof Peter Fountain
Facilities ⊗ ╟ ┗ ▆ ♀ ⚐ 🏠 ✔
Location 1.25m N on B4050

Hotel ★★★ 65% Mount Sorrel Hotel, Porthkerry Rd,
BARRY ☎ 01446 740069 43 ⇄ ↟

RAF St Athan St Athan CF62 4WA
☎ 01446 797186 Fax 01446 751043
This is a very windy course with wind straight off the sea to
make all holes interesting. Further interest is added by this
being a very tight course with lots of trees.
9 holes, 6480yds, Par 72, SSS 72.
Club membership 450. ▶

Visitors   contact in advance, Sun mornings club competitions only.
Societies   apply in advance.
Green Fees   £12 per day (£17 weekends).
Facilities   ⊗ ⫴ ⪢ ▆ ♀ ⚲ 🏠
Location   Between Barry & Llantwit Major

Hotel   ★★ 68% West House Country Hotel & Restaurant, West St, LLANTWIT MAJOR
☎ 01446 792406 & 793726
Fax 01446 796147   21 ⇄ ❀

St Andrews Major Argae Ln, Coldbrook Rd East, Cadoxton CF63 1BL ☎ 01446 722227
A new 9-hole, Pay and Play course with 6 Par 4s, 1 par5 and 2 par3s.
9 holes, 3000yds, Par 70, SSS 68.
Club membership 520.
Visitors   must contact in advance.
Societies   telephone in advance.
Green Fees   £8 per 9 holes; £13 per 18 holes.
Designer   Richard Hurd
Facilities   ⊗ ⪢ ▆ ♀ ⚲ 🏠 🛈 ♂ ⚘
Location   Off Barry new link road

Hotel   ★★★♨ 77% Egerton Grey Country House Hotel, Porthkerry, BARRY
☎ 01446 711666   10 ⇄ ❀

BETTWS NEWYDD   Map 03 SO30

Alice Springs NP5 1JY
☎ 01873 880244 & 880914 Fax 01873 880838
Two 18-hole undulating parkland courses set back to back with magnificent views of the Usk Valley. The Queen's course has testing 7th and 15th holes.

Queens Course: 18 holes, 5517yds, Par 67, SSS 67, Course record 65.
Kings Course: 18 holes, 5596yds, Par 70, SSS 67, Course record 65.
Club membership 550.
Visitors   should contact the club in advance for weekend play.
Societies   must telephone in advance.
Green Fees   £22 per day, £16 per round (£25/£20 weekends).
Cards   ▬ ▬ ▬ ▬ ▬ ▬
Prof   Paul Williams
Designer   Keith R Morgan
Facilities   ⊗ ⫴ ⪢ ▆ ♀ ⚲ 🏠 🛈 ♂ ⚘ ⚘ ♂ ⚘
Location   N of Usk on B4598 towards Abergavenny

Hotel   ★★★ 74% Three Salmons Hotel, Bridge St, USK ☎ 01291 672133
10 ⇄ ❀ Annexe14 ⇄ ❀

BLACKWOOD   Map 03 ST19

Blackwood Cwmgelli NP2 1EL
☎ 01495 222121 (Office) & 223152 (Club)
Heathland course with sand bunkers. Undulating, with hard walking. Testing 2nd hole par 4. Good views.
9 holes, 5332yds, Par 67.
Club membership 310.
Visitors   contact club or turn up and pay greens staff, may not play at weekends & bank holidays unless with member.
Societies   by prior arrangement for members of a recognised golf club.
Green Fees   £13 per round.
Facilities   ⚲
Location   0.25m N of Blackwood, off A4048

| Hotel | ★★★ 68% Maes Manor Hotel, BLACKWOOD ☎ 01495 224551 & 220011 Fax 01495 228217 8 ⇌ Annexe14 ⇌ |

BRIDGEND   Map 03 SS97

Coed-Y-Mwstwr The Clubhouse, Coychurch CF35 6AF
☎ 01656 862121 & 864 934
Challenging holes on this 9-hole course include the par 3 3rd (170yds) involving a drive across a lake and the par 4 5th (448yds) which is subject to strong prevailing winds.
9 holes, 5834yds, Par 69, SSS 68, Course record 71.
Club membership 260.

Visitors	must have handicap certificate, advisable to contact in advance.
Societies	by prior application.
Green Fees	not confirmed.
Designer	Chapman/Warren
Facilities	⊗ 🏌 ☕ ♀ 🛎 🍴 ⚷
& Leisure	Indoor driving net.
Location	1m out of Coychurch, turn at village garage. 2m W of junct 35 on M4

| Hotel | ★★★ 74% Coed-Y-Mwstwr Hotel, Coychurch, BRIDGEND ☎ 01656 860621   23 ⇌ 🐾 |

Southerndown Ewenny CF32 0QP
☎ 01656 880476 Fax 01656 880317
Downland championship course with rolling fairways and fast greens. The par-3 5th is played across a valley and the 18th, with its split level fairway, is a demanding finishing hole. Superb views.
18 holes, 6417yds, Par 70, SSS 72, Course record 64.
Club membership 710.

Visitors	must contact in advance & have handicap certificate.
Societies	by arrangement with secretary.
Green Fees	£25 per day (£35 weekends).
Prof	D G McMonagle
Designer	W Fernie
Facilities	⊗ 🏌 🏌 ☕ ♀ 🛎 🍴 🏌 🛏 ⚷ ⚐
Location	3m SW on B4524

| Hotel | ★★★ 67% Heronston Hotel, Ewenny Rd, BRIDGEND ☎ 01656 668811   67 ⇌ 🐾 Annexe8rm(7 ⇌ 🐾) |

CAERLEON   Map 03 ST39

Caerleon NP6 1AY ☎ 01633 420342
Parkland course.
9 holes, 2900yds, Par 34, SSS 34, Course record 29.
Club membership 120.

Visitors	contact for details.
Societies	telephone.
Green Fees	not confirmed.
Prof	Alex Campbell
Designer	Steel
Facilities	🏌 ☕ ♀ 🛎 🍴 ⚷ ⚐
Location	3m from M4 turn off for Caerleon

| Hotel | ★★★★ 71% Celtic Manor Hotel, Golf & Country Club, Coldra Woods, NEWPORT ☎ 01633 413000   73 ⇌ 🐾 |

CAERPHILLY   Map 03 ST18

Caerphilly Penchapel, Mountain Rd CF83 1HJ
☎ 01222 883481 & 863441 Fax 01222 863441
Undulating mountain course with woodland affording good views especially from 10th hole, 700 ft above sea level.
13 holes, 6032yds, Par 73, SSS 71.
Club membership 700.

Visitors	telephone in advance, must produce a current handicap certificate or letter from club secretary, may not play at weekends except with member, no visitors bank holidays.
Societies	apply in writing in advance to the secretary.
Green Fees	£20 per day.
Prof	Richard Barter
Facilities	⊗ 🏌 by prior arrangement 🏌 ☕ ♀ 🛎 🍴 ⚷
Location	0.5m S on A469

| Hotel | ★★★ 73% Manor Parc Country Hotel & Restaurant, Thornhill Rd, Thornhill, CARDIFF ☎ 01222 693723   12 ⇌ 🐾 |

Mountain Lakes & Castell Heights Blaengwynlais
CF83 1NG ☎ 01222 861128 & 886666 Fax 01222 863243
The 9-hole Castell Heights course within the Mountain Lakes complex was established in 1982 on a 45-acre site. In 1988 a further 18-hole course, Mountain Lakes was designed by Bob Sandow to take advantage of 160-acres of mountain heathland, combining both mountain top golf and parkland. Most holes are tree lined and there are 20 'lakes' as hazards. Host of major PGA tournaments.
Mountain Lakes Course: 18 holes, 6046mtrs, Par 74, SSS 73, Course record 69.
Castell Heights Course: 9 holes, 2751mtrs, Par 35, SSS 32, Course record 32.
Club membership 500.

Societies	written or telephone notice in advance.
Green Fees	not confirmed.
Prof	Sion Bebb
Designer	Bob Sandown
Facilities	⊗ 🏌 by prior arrangement 🏌 ☕ ♀ 🛎 🍴 🏌 🛏 🍴 ⚷ ⚐
Location	Near Black Cock Inn, Caerphilly Mountain

| Hotel | ★★★ 73% Manor Parc Country Hotel & Restaurant, Thornhill Rd, Thornhill, CARDIFF ☎ 01222 693723   12 ⇌ 🐾 |

Virginia Park Golf Club Virginia Park CF83 3SW
☎ 01222 863919 & 585368
Beside Caerphilly leisure centre, the course is totally flat but with plenty of trees and bunkers and 2 lakes. It is a tight, challenging course with 6 par 4 and 3 par 3 holes. Also a 20-bay flodlit driving range.
9 holes, 2566yds, Par 33.
Club membership 250.

Visitors	telephone in advance.
Societies	telephone then write to confirm.
Green Fees	not confirmed.
Facilities	🏌 ☕ ♀ 🛎 🍴 🏌 ⚷ ⚐
Location	Off Pontyewindy Rd

| Hotel | ★★★ 73% Manor Parc Country Hotel & Restaurant, Thornhill Rd, Thornhill, CARDIFF ☎ 01222 693723   12 ⇌ 🐾 |

CAERWENT   Map 03 ST49

Dewstow NP6 4AH ☎ 01291 430444 Fax 01291 425816
Two picturesque parkland courses with easy walking and
spectacular views over the Severn estuary towards Bristol.
Testing holes include the Par three 7th, Valley Course, which
is approached over water, some 50 feet lower than the tee,
and the Par four 15th, Park Course, which has a 50ft totem
pole in the middle of the fairway, a unique feature. There is
also a 26-bay floodlit driving range.
*Valley Course: 18 holes, 6141yds, Par 72, SSS 70, Course
record 68.*
*Park Course: 18 holes, 6226yds, Par 69, SSS 69, Course
record 68.*
Club membership 850.
Visitors   may book two days in advance (six days in
              advance in winter).
Societies   apply in writing or telephone for details.
Green Fees   £22 per day; £13 per 18 holes; £8.50 per 9 holes
              (£16 per round; £10 per 9 holes weekends &
              bank holidays).
Cards   🖃 📇 🆚 ⚋ 📇 📇
Prof   Kim Dabson
Facilities   ⊗ �🝙 🝙 💺 ♀ ♨ 🝙 🍴 ❧ 🛒 ⟂ ℓ
Location   0.5m S of A48 at Caerwent

Hotel   ★★★★ 68% Marriott St Pierre Hotel &
              Country Club, St Pierre Park, CHEPSTOW
              ☎ 01291 625261 148 ⇆ ℝ

CARDIFF   Map 03 ST17

Cardiff Sherborne Av, Cyncoed CF2 6SJ
☎ 01222 753320 Fax 01222 680011
Parkland course, where trees form natural hazards.
Interesting variety of holes, mostly bunkered. A stream flows
through course and comes into play on 5 separate holes.
18 holes, 6016yds, Par 70, SSS 70, Course record 66.
Club membership 900.
Visitors   Must contact in advance.
Societies   Thu only, pre-booking essential.
Green Fees   £35 per day (£40 weekends).
Prof   Terry Hanson
Facilities   ⊗ �🝙 🝙 💺 ♀ ♨ 🝙 ℓ
& Leisure   snooker.
Location   3m N of city centre

Hotel   B Posthouse Cardiff, Pentwyn Rd, Pentwyn,
              CARDIFF ☎ 01222 731212 142 ⇆ ℝ

Cottrell Park Cottrell Park, St Nicholas CF5 6JY
☎ 01446 781781 Fax 01446 781707
Two well designed courses, opened in 1996, set in undulating
parkland with mature trees and spectacular views, especially
from the par 35 9-hole course. An enjoyable yet testing game
of golf for players of all abilities.
*Mackintosh: 18 holes, 6110yds, Par 72, SSS 71, Course
record 65.*
Button: 9 holes, 2660yds, Par 70, SSS 69.
Club membership 1050.
Visitors   must have a valid handicap certificate, advance
              bookings up to one week.
Societies   welcome on Mon & Tue, apply in writing,
              min 12.
Green Fees   Mackintosh: £37.50 per day, £22.50 per round
              (£50/£30 weekends) Button: £11.25 per round
              (£15 weekends).

Cards   🖃 📇 🆚 ⚋ 📇 Barclays CONNECT 📇 📇
Prof   Mike Pycroft
Designer   MRM Sandow
Facilities   ⊗ �🝙 🝙 💺 ♀ ♨ 🝙 🍴 ❧ 🛒 ℓ
Location   M4 junct 33 to Culverhouse Cross A48 to
              Cowbridge, through St Nicholas on right hand
              side

Hotel   ★★★★ 71% Copthorne Cardiff-Caerdydd,
              Copthorne Way, Culverhouse Cross, CARDIFF
              ☎ 01222 599100 135 ⇆ ℝ

Llanishen Cwm Lisvane CF4 5UD
☎ 01222 755078 Fax 01222 755078
Mountain course, with hard walking overlooking the Bristol
Channel.
18 holes, 5296yds, Par 68, SSS 66, Course record 63.
Club membership 600.
Visitors   must play with member at weekends & bank
              holidays. Must contact in advance.
Societies   contact in advance.
Green Fees   £24 per round.
Prof   Adrian Jones
Facilities   ⊗ �🝙 🝙 💺 ♀ ♨ 🝙 ℓ
Location   5m N of city centre off A469

Hotel   B Posthouse Cardiff, Pentwyn Rd, Pentwyn,
              CARDIFF ☎ 01222 731212 142 ⇆ ℝ

Peterstone Peterstone, Wentloog CF3 8TN
☎ 01633 680009 Fax 01633 680563
Parkland course with abundant water features and several
long drives (15th, 601yds).
18 holes, 6555yds, Par 72, SSS 71, Course record 67.
Club membership 714.
Visitors   contact in advance suggested.
Societies   telephone enquiries welcome.
Green Fees   not confirmed.
Cards   🖃 📇 🆚 📇
Prof   Richard Harries
Designer   Bob Sandow
Facilities   ⊗ �🝙 🝙 💺 ♀ ♨ 🝙 🛏 🛒 ℓ
Location   3m from Castleton off A48

Hotel   ★★★ 72% St Mellons Hotel & Country Club,
              Castleton, CARDIFF
              ☎ 01633 680355 21 ⇆ ℝ Annexe20 ⇆ ℝ

Radyr The Clubhouse, Drysgol Rd, Radyr CF4 8BS
☎ 01222 842408 Fax 01222 843914
Hillside, parkland course which can be windy. Good views.
Venue for many championships.
18 holes, 6031yds, Par 69, SSS 70, Course record 62.
Club membership 920.
Visitors   must play with member at weekends.
Societies   must contact in advance.
Green Fees   £36 per day.
Cards   🖃 📇 🆚 ⚋ 📇 📇 📇
Prof   Robert Butterworth
Facilities   ⊗ �🝙 🝙 💺 ♀ ♨ 🝙 🍴 ❧ 🛒 ℓ
& Leisure   Table tennis, snooker room.
Location   M4 junct32, 4.5m NW of city centre off A4119

Hotel   ★★★★ 68% Thistle Cardiff, Park Place,
              CARDIFF ☎ 01222 383471 136 ⇆ ℝ

St Mellons St Mellons CF3 8XS
☎ 01633 680408 Fax 01633 681219
This parkland course comprises quite a few par-3 holes
and provides some testing golf. It is indeed a challenge
to the single handicap golfer.
18 holes, 6275yds, Par 70, SSS 70, Course record 63.
Club membership 700.
Visitors   must contact in advance. With member only
              at weekends.
Societies   must contact in advance.
Green Fees £32 per round.
Prof   Barry Thomas
Facilities   ⊗ ⅷ 🖫 ⬛ ♀ Ꮬ ⮴ ꕥ ⛳ ⯑ ⛟ ⌀
Location   5m NE off A48

Hotel   ★★★ 72% St Mellons Hotel & Country
              Club, Castleton, CARDIFF
              ☎ 01633 680355
              21 ⇄ ⌀ Annexe20 ⇄ ⌀

Whitchurch Pantmawr Rd, Whitchurch CF4 6XD
☎ 01222 620985 (Sec) Fax 01222 529860
Well manicured parkland course, slightly undulating, with
fine views over the city centre and the Bristol Channel
beyond.
18 holes, 6321yds, Par 71, SSS 71, Course record 62.
Club membership 750.
Visitors   contact secretary/professional in advance.
Societies   Thu only. Must contact in advance.
Green Fees £35 per day (£40 weekends & bank holidays).
Cards   ⚊ ▣ ▣ ▨ ▨
Prof   Eddie Clark
Designer   F Johns
Facilities   Ꮬ ⮴ ⯑ ⌀
Location   4m N of city centre on A470, near junct 32 of
              M4

Hotel   ★★★★ 68% Thistle Cardiff,
              Park Place, CARDIFF
              ☎ 01222 383471 136 ⇄ ⌀

CHEPSTOW   Map 03 ST59

ST PIERRE See page 411

Shirenewton Shirenewton NP6 6RL
☎ 01291 641642 Fax 01291 641831
Parkland course with magnificent views over the Severn
estuary and extending to the Devon coastline.
18 holes, 6820yds, Par 72.
Club membership 300.
Visitors   welcome, advisable to reserve tee times, must
              book at weekends
Societies   contact K Evans for further information.
Green Fees not confirmed.
Cards   ⚊ ▣ ▣ ▨
Prof   Renton Doig
Facilities   ⊗ ⅷ 🖫 ⬛ ♀ Ꮬ ⮴ ꕥ ⛳ ⯑ ⛟ ⌀
Location   Junct 22 of M4 off A48

Hotel   ★★ 67% Beaufort Hotel,
              Beaufort Square, CHEPSTOW
              ☎ 01291 622497 18 ⇄ ⌀

CLYDACH   Map 03 SN60

Inco SA6 5PQ ☎ 01792 844216
Flat meadowland course to be extended to 18 holes.
15 holes, 5994yds, Par 70, SSS 69.
Club membership 300.
Visitors   no restrictions.
Societies   must contact in advance.
Green Fees not confirmed.
Facilities   🖫 ♀ Ꮬ
Location   0.75m SE on B4291

Hotel   ★★ 62% Oak Tree Parc Hotel, Birchgrove Rd,
              BIRCHGROVE ☎ 01792 817781 10 ⇄ ⌀

CREIGIAU (CREIYIAU)   Map 03 ST08

Creigiau Llantwit Rd CF4 8NN ☎ 01222 890263
Downland course, with small greens and many interesting
water hazards.
18 holes, 6015yds, Par 71, SSS 70, Course record 67.
Club membership 1020.
Visitors   must contact in advance. May only play at
              weekends with member.
Societies   Wed only, minimum number 20, must book in
              advance.
Green Fees not confirmed.
Prof   Iain Luntz
Facilities   ⊗ ⅷ 🖫 ⬛ ♀ Ꮬ ⮴ ⯑ ⌀
Location   6m NW of Cardiff on A4119

Hotel   ★★★★ 71% Miskin Manor Hotel,
              Groes Faen, Pontyclun, MISKIN
              ☎ 01443 224204 34 ⇄ ⌀ Annexe8 ⇄ ⌀

CWMBRAN   Map 03 ST29

Green Meadow Golf & Country Club Treherbert Rd,
Croesyceiliog NP44 2BZ ☎ 01633 869321 & 860655
Undulating parkland course with panoramic views. The 7th
hole is played partly down hill with the front half of the
green enclosed with water; the 13th is exposed to winds with
large mature trees along righthand side of green.
18 holes, 6029yds, Par 71, SSS 72.
Club membership 400.
Visitors   by prior arrangement advised especially at
              weekends, tel 01633 862626. Correct standard
              of dress compulsory.
Societies   telephone for brochure, Golf Shop 01633
              862626.
Green Fees not confirmed.
Prof   Dave Woodman
Designer   Peter Richardson
Facilities   ⊗ ⅷ 🖫 ⬛ ♀ Ꮬ ⮴ ꕥ ⛳ ⯑ ⛟ ⌀ ⎍
& Leisure   hard tennis courts.
Location   5m N of junct 26 M4, off A4042

Hotel   ★★★★ 64% Parkway Hotel, Cwmbran Dr,
              CWMBRAN ☎ 01633 871199 70 ⇄ ⌀

Pontnewydd Maesgwyn Farm, West Pontnewydd NP44 1AB
☎ 01633 482170
Mountainside course, with hard walking. Good views across
the Severn Estuary.
10 holes, 5353yds, Par 68, SSS 67, Course record 63.
Club membership 250.   ▶

Visitors must play with member weekends & bank holidays.
Green Fees not confirmed.
Facilities ⓑ ♀ ⚘
Location N side of town centre

Hotel ★★★★ 64% Parkway Hotel, Cwmbran Dr, CWMBRAN ☎ 01633 871199 70 ⇥ ♜

DINAS POWIS — Map 03 ST17

Dinas Powis Old High Walls CF64 4AJ
☎ 01222 512727 Fax 01222 512727
Parkland/downland course with views over the Bristol Channel and the seaside resort of Barry.
18 holes, 5486yds, Par 67, SSS 67, Course record 60.
Club membership 550.
Visitors must contact in advance (call G Bennett 01222 513682)
Societies telephone in advance.
Green Fees £25 (£30 weekends).
Prof Gareth Bennett
Facilities ⊗ ∭ ⓑ ☕ ♀ ⚘ 🏠 ⚷
Location NW side of village

Hotel ★★★ 65% Mount Sorrel Hotel, Porthkerry Rd, BARRY ☎ 01446 740069 43 ⇥ ♜

GLYNNEATH — Map 03 SN80

Glynneath Pen-y-graig, Pontneathvaughan SA11 5UH
☎ 01639 720452
Attractive hillside golf overlooking the Vale of Neath in the foothills of the Brecon Beacons National Park. Reasonably level farmland/wooded course.
18 holes, 5707yds, Par 69, SSS 68, Course record 64.
Club membership 650.
Visitors restricted starting times at weekend.
Societies must contact in advance.
Green Fees £15 per day (£20 weekends & bank holidays).
Prof Huw Thomas
Designer Cotton/Pennick/Lawri
Facilities ⊗ ⓑ ☕ ♀ ⚘ 🏠 ⚘ ⚷
Location 2m NE on B4242

Hotel ★★ 62% Oak Tree Parc Hotel, Birchgrove Rd, BIRCHGROVE ☎ 01792 817781 10 ⇥ ♜

HENSOL — Map 03 ST07

Vale of Glamorgan Golf & Country Club Hensol Park CF72 8JY ☎ 01443 222221 Fax 01443 222220
Two courses set in 200 acres of glorious countryside with views over Hensol Park lake and castle. The 18-hole par 72 Lake Course features towering trees, bunkers and water on ten holes. The signature hole, the 12th, has an island green reached via a stone bridge. The club is also home to the Welsh Golf Academy.
Lake: 18 holes, 6507yds, Par 72, SSS 71.
Hensol: 9 holes, 3115yds, Par 72, SSS 71.
Club membership 1100.
Visitors must have a handicap certificate and may only play with member at weekends.
Societies apply in writing.
Green Fees not confirmed.
Cards ▰ ▰ ▰ ▰ ▰ ▰
Prof Peter Johnson

Designer Peter Johnson
Facilities ⊗ ∭ ⓑ ☕ ♀ ⚘ 🏠 ⚘ ⚘ 🏌 ⚷ ♟
& Leisure hard tennis courts, heated indoor swimming pool, squash, fishing, sauna, solarium, gymnasium, many facilities in process of being built.
Location 2 mins from junct 34 of M4

Hotel ★★★★ 71% Miskin Manor Hotel, Groes Faen, Pontyclun, MISKIN ☎ 01443 224204 34 ⇥ ♜ Annexe8 ⇥ ♜

LLANWERN — Map 03 ST38

Llanwern Tennyson Av NP6 2DY
☎ 01633 412029 Fax 01633 412029
Parkland Course.
18 holes, 6115yds, Par 70, SSS 69, Course record 63.
Club membership 650.
Visitors welcome, but with member only at weekends.
Societies telephone and confirm in writing.
Green Fees £20 per day (£25 weekends with member).
Cards ▰ ▰ ▰
Prof Stephen Price
Facilities ⊗ ∭ ⓑ ☕ ♀ ⚘ 🏠
Location 0.5m S off A455

Hotel ★★★★ 71% Celtic Manor Hotel, Golf & Country Club, Coldra Woods, NEWPORT ☎ 01633 413000 73 ⇥ ♜

MAESTEG — Map 03 SS89

Maesteg Mount Pleasant, Neath Rd CF34 9PR
☎ 01656 734106 & 732037 Fax 01656 734106
Reasonably flat hill-top course with scenic views.
18 holes, 5929yds, Par 70, SSS 69, Course record 69.
Club membership 789.
Visitors must be a member of a recognised golf club & have a handicap certificate.
Societies apply in writing.
Green Fees £17 per day (£20 weekends & bank holidays).
Prof Chris Riley
Designer James Braid
Facilities ⓑ ☕ ♀ ⚘ 🏠 ⚘ ⚷
Location 0.5m W off B4282

Hotel ★★★ 68% Aberavon Beach Hotel, PORT TALBOT ☎ 01639 884949 52 ⇥

MAESYCWMMER — Map 03 ST19

Bryn Meadows Golf & Country Hotel The Bryn CF82 7FN
☎ 01495 225590 or 224103 Fax 01495 228272
A heavily wooded parkland course with panoramic views of the Brecon Beacons.
18 holes, 6132yds, Par 72, SSS 69, Course record 68.
Club membership 540.
Visitors may not play Sun mornings. Must contact in advance.
Societies Tue & Thu only.
Green Fees not confirmed.
Prof Bruce Hunter
Designer Mayo/Jeffries
Facilities ⚘ 🏠 ⚘ ⚘ 🏌 ⚘ ⚷ ♟
& Leisure heated indoor swimming pool, sauna, solarium, gymnasium.

▶

ST PIERRE

ST PIERRE PARK, CHEPSTOW *Monmouthshire*
☎ **01291 625261 Fax 01291 629975**   Map 03 ST59

*J*ohn Ingham writes: Just over the Severn Bridge, and a mile down the old Newport road, is St Pierre, the parkland course where huge trees stand in the way of any golf shot not hit on the perfect line!

Set in 400 yards of glorious deer park, with a lake preserved as a wild life sanctuary, a clubhouse which was once a great mansion and the 800-year-old church of St Pierre nearby, you cannot help but be impressed by the place, and the atmosphere.

There are two courses to sample. The Old was designed by C K Cotton in 1962 while the Mathern was created by Bill Graham, a Geordie businessman who snapped up the place after driving past in his car after World War II. He immediately saw the potential as the fast motorway link with London and the south was being created.

The courses have staged several successful tournaments including the old Dunlop Masters which I used to cover for a London newspaper. Competitors would get pretty cross when they found their towering drives achieved nothing because the ball, when they got up to it, was 'snookered' by huge trees, several hundred years old. Among other hazards there was none more fearsome than the lake that guards the short 18th hole - a 'mere' 245 yards across water. Television cameras here filmed Tony Jacklin and Peter Oosterhuis almost holing in one, But they missed Arwyn Griffiths who arrived on the last tee needing a par-3 for an amazing course record 63. Unhappily, Mr Griffiths found the ordeal too much and took a ghastly 11 shots, although he still won the amateur event and was thus able to celebrate at the very excellent 19th hole!

Accommodation is sumptuous within the historic buildings, making it a very special place for a few days away from it all.

While there are stories of spirits walking in the night I suspect they had something to do with the tough Old course which at 6700yards cannily sorts out even the best players while the shorter Mathern, at 5732 yards with a par 68 can also throw up a few nightmare situations if you become stymied behind a whopping oak tree!

Visitors	Must book 10 days in advance. Hotel residents only at weekends.
Societies	Must make an advance reservation.
Green fees	Prices on application.
Facilities	⊗ ⊪ ⅃ ☕ ♀ ⇔ ⚘ 🖥 ⚐ ⅃ ⚒ 🏌 ♂ ↺ ℓ Professional (Craig Dun).
Leisure	hard tennis courts, indoor swimming pool, sauna, solarium, gymnasium.
Location	Chepstow NP6 6YA (3m SW off A48).

36 holes. Old Course: 18 holes, 6700yds, Par71 SSS 73. Course record 64 Mathern Course: 18 holes, 5732yds, Par 68, SSS 67

WHERE TO STAY AND EAT NEARBY

HOTELS:
CHEPSTOW
★★★★⊛ 68% St Pierre Hotel & Country Club ☎ 01291 625261 148 ⇄ ↾

★★★62% The Old Course, Newport Rd. ☎ 01291 626261. 31 ⇄ ↾

★★68% Castle View, 16 Bridge St ☎ 01291 620349. 9 (8 ⇄ 1 ↾) Annexe 4 ⇄

★★ 67% The George Hotel, Moor St ☎ 01291 625363. 14 ⇄ ↾

TINTERN
★★★⊛ 72% Parva Farmhouse Hotel ☎ 01291 689411. 9 ⇄ ↾

★★⊛ 70% Royal George Hotel ☎ 01291 689205 5 (2 ⇄ ↾) Annexe 14 ⇄ ↾

WHITEBROOK
★★⊛ ⊛ ⊛ 73% The Crown at Whitebrook ☎ 01600 860254 10 ⇄ ↾

Location On the A4048 Blackwood to Ystrad Mynach rd

Hotel ★★★ 68% Maes Manor Hotel, BLACKWOOD ☎ 01495 224551 & 220011 Fax 01495 228217 8 ⇄ Annexe14 ⇄

MARGAM — Map 03 SS78

Lakeside Water St SA13 2PA ☎ 01639 899959
A parkland course with bunkers and natural hazards. Eight Par 4's and ten Par 3's.
18 holes, 4390yds, Par 62, SSS 63, Course record 65.
Club membership 250.
Visitors no restrictions.
Societies apply in advance by letter or telephone.
Green Fees £9.50 per round.
Cards ⊙ ▦ ▨
Prof Mathew Wootton
Designer Matthew Wootton
Facilities ⊗ ⊪ ⅃ ♥ ♀ ♨ ♞ ♟ ♥ ⌁
Location Off junct 38 of M4

Hotel ★★★ 68% Aberavon Beach Hotel, PORT TALBOT ☎ 01639 884949 52 ⇄

MERTHYR TYDFIL — Map 03 SO00

Merthyr Tydfil (Cilanws) Cilsanws, Cefn Coed CF48 2NU
☎ 01685 723308
Mountain-top course with good views. Requires accuracy off the tee.
18 holes, 5625yds, Par 69, SSS 68, Course record 65.
Club membership 210.
Visitors may not play on Sun.
Societies by prior arrangement.
Green Fees £10 per day (£15 weekends).
Facilities ⊗ ⊪ ⅃ ♥ ♀ ♨
Location Off A470 at Cefn Coed

Hotel ★★★ 74% Nant Ddu Lodge Hotel, Cwm Taf, Nant Ddu, MERTHYR TYDFIL ☎ 01685 379111 12 ⇄ ♞ Annexe10 ⇄ ♞

Morlais Castle Pant, Dowlais CF48 2UY
☎ 01685 722822 Fax 01685 722822
Beautiful moorland course overlooking National Park with excellent views of Brecon Beacons and surrounding countryside. The interesting layout of the course makes for a testing game.
18 holes, 6320yds, Par 71, SSS 71.
Club membership 500.
Visitors must contact in advance for weekends.
Societies apply in writing.
Green Fees not confirmed.

Prof H Jarrett
Facilities ⊗ ⊪ ⅃ ♥ ♀ ♨ ♨
Location 2.5m N off A465. Follow signs for Mountain Railway. Course entrance opposite railway car park

Hotel ★★★ 74% Nant Ddu Lodge Hotel, Cwm Taf, Nant Ddu, MERTHYR TYDFIL ☎ 01685 379111 12 ⇄ ♞ Annexe10 ⇄ ♞

MONMOUTH — Map 03 SO51

Monmouth Leasebrook Ln NP5 3SN
☎ 01600 712212 (clubhouse) & 772399 (sec) Fax 01600 77 2399
Parkland course in scenic setting. High, undulating land with good views.
18 holes, 5698yds, Par 69, SSS 69, Course record 68.
Club membership 600.
Visitors advisable to contact in advance, bank holidays only with member.
Societies advance notice advisable, write or telephone secretary.
Green Fees £20 per day; £15 per round (£20 per round only weekends).
Facilities ⊗ ⊪ ⅃ ♥ ♀ ♨ ♨ ♞ ♥ ♨ ⌁
Location 1.5m NE off A40

Hotel ★★ 68% Riverside Hotel, Cinderhill St, MONMOUTH ☎ 01600 715577 & 713236 Fax 01600 712668 17 ⇄ ♞

Rolls of Monmouth The Hendre NP5 4HG
☎ 01600 715353 Fax 01600 713115
A hilly and challenging parkland course encompassing several lakes and ponds and surrounded by woodland. Set within a beautiful private estate complete with listed mansion and panoramic views towards the Black Mountains. The short 4th has a lake beyond the green and both the 17th and 18th holes are magnificent holes with which to end your round.
18 holes, 6733yds, Par 72, SSS 73.
Club membership 131.
Visitors must telephone in advance.
Societies must contact in advance.
Green Fees not confirmed.
Facilities ♨ ♨ ♞ ⌁
Location 4m W on B4233

Hotel ★★ 68% Riverside Hotel, Cinderhill St, MONMOUTH ☎ 01600 715577 & 713236 Fax 01600 712668 17 ⇄ ♞

MOUNTAIN ASH   Map 03 ST09

Mountain Ash Cefnpennar CF45 4DT
☎ 01443 479459 Fax 01443 479459
Mountain course on heathland with panoramic views of the
Brecon Beacons.
18 holes, 5553yds, Par 69, SSS 67, Course record 63.
Club membership 600.
Visitors contact in advance for details.
Societies must contact in writing.
Green Fees £15 per day.
Prof Marcus Wills
Facilities ⊗ ⫼ ⓑ 🍽 ♀ 🛆 🏠 ⌁
Location 1m NW off A4059

Hotel ★★★ 68% Tregenna Hotel,
Park Ter, MERTHYR TYDFIL
☎ 01685 723627 & 382055
Fax 01685 721951   24 ⇔ 🐾

NANTYGLO   Map 03 SO11

West Monmouthshire Golf Rd, Winchestown NP3 4QT
☎ 01495 310233
Established in 1906, this mountain and heathland course was
officially designated in 1994 by the Guiness Book of Record
as being the highest above sea level, with the 14th tee at a
height of 1513ft. The course has plenty of picturesque views,
hard walking and natural hazards. Testing 3rd hole, par 5,
and 7th hole, par 4.
18 holes, 6013yds, Par 71, SSS 69, Course record 65.
Club membership 350.
Visitors welcome, must be guest of member for play on
Sun.
Societies apply in writing or contact golf shop 01495
313052.
Green Fees not confirmed.
Facilities ⊗ ⫼ ⓑ 🍽 ♀ 🛆 🏠 ⌁
Location 0.25m W off A467

Hotel ★★★ 55% Angel Hotel, 15 Cross St,
ABERGAVENNY ☎ 01873 857121   29 ⇔ 🐾

NEATH   Map 03 SS79

Earlswood Jersey Marine SA10 6JP ☎ 01792 812198
Earlswood is a hillside course offering spectacular scenic
views over Swansea Bay. The terrain is gently undulating
parkland with natural hazards and is designed to appeal to
both the new and the experienced golfer.
18 holes, 5084yds, Par 68, SSS 68.
Visitors no restrictions.
Societies advisable to contact in advance.
Green Fees £8 per round.
Prof Mike Day
Facilities 🍽 🛆 🏠 ⌁
Location Approx 4m E of Swansea, off A483

Hotel ★★ 65% Castle Hotel, The Parade,
NEATH ☎ 01639 641119 & 643581
Fax 01639 641624   28 ⇔ 🐾

Neath Cadoxton SA10 8AH ☎ 01639 643615 & 632759
Mountain course, with spectacular views. Testing holes: 10th
par 4; 12th par 5; 15th par 4.
18 holes, 6492yds, Par 72, SSS 72, Course record 66.
Club membership 700.

Visitors with member only at weekends & bank
holidays.
Societies should either telephone or write in advance.
Green Fees not confirmed.
Prof E M Bennett
Designer James Braid
Facilities ⊗ ⫼ ⓑ 🍽 ♀ 🛆 🏠 ⌁
& Leisure snooker.
Location 2m NE off A4230

Hotel ★★ 65% Castle Hotel, The Parade,
NEATH ☎ 01639 641119 & 643581
Fax 01639 641624   28 ⇔ 🐾

Swansea Bay Jersey Marine SA10 6JP
☎ 01792 812198 & 814153
Fairly level seaside links with part-sand dunes.
18 holes, 6605yds, Par 72, SSS 72.
Club membership 500.
Visitors welcome.
Societies telephone enquiry or letter stating requirements.
Green Fees £16 per round (£22 weekends & bank holidays).
Prof Mike Day
Facilities ⊗ ⫼ by prior arrangement ⓑ 🍽 ♀ 🛆 🏠 ⌁
Location 4m E of Swansea off A483

Hotel ★★ 65% Castle Hotel, The Parade,
NEATH ☎ 01639 641119 & 643581
Fax 01639 641624   28 ⇔ 🐾

NELSON   Map 03 ST19

Whitehall The Pavilion CF46 6ST ☎ 01443 740245
Windy hilltop course. Testing 4th hole (225 yds) par 3, and
6th hole (402 yds) par 4. Pleasant views.
9 holes, 5666yds, Par 69, SSS 68, Course record 63.
Club membership 300.
Visitors must be a member of a recognised golf club &
have a handicap certificate. Must contact in
advance to play at weekends.
Societies must contact in writing 4 weeks in advance.
Green Fees not confirmed.
Facilities ⊗ ⓑ 🍽 ♀ 🛆
Location Turn off A470 to Nelson and take A4054 S

Hotel ★★★ 68% Llechwen Hall Hotel, Llanfabon,
PONTYPRIDD ☎ 01443 742050 & 740305
Fax 01443 742189   12 ⇔ 🐾

NEWPORT   Map 03 ST38

Celtic Manor Hotel & Country Club Coldra Woods
NP6 2YA
☎ 01633 410294 & 410395 Fax 01633 412910 & 410272
*Roman Road: 18 holes, 6495yds, Par 69, SSS 72, Course
record 68.*
Coldra Woods: 18 holes, 3809yds, Par 59, SSS 61.
Wentwood Hills: 18 holes, 7000yds, Par 72.
Club membership 400.
Visitors may play subject to availability, must book in
advance
Societies telephone with details in advance.
Green Fees Coldra Woods: £15 per 18 holes, £10 per 9
holes. Roman Road: £35 per 18 holes, £20 per 9
holes. Wentwood Hills: £45 per 18 holes.
Cards 🔲🔲🔲🔲🔲🔲
Designer Robert Trent Jones   ▶

Facilities ⊗ 🍴 🏌 🍷 ♀ 👤 🏠 🍴 ⛳ 🛒 ⚷ ☖
& Leisure heated indoor swimming pool, sauna, solarium, gymnasium, golf tuition, health & fitness club.
Location Off junct 24 on M4

Hotel ★★★★ 71% Celtic Manor Hotel, Golf & Country Club, Coldra Woods, NEWPORT ☎ 01633 413000 73 ⇆ 🐾

Newport Great Oak, Rogerstone NP1 9FX
☎ 01633 892643 Fax 01633 896676
An undulating parkland course, in an ideal situation on an inland plateau 300ft above sea level with fine views over the surrounding wooded countryside. There are no blind holes, but plenty of natural hazards and bunkers.
18 holes, 6431yds, Par 72, SSS 71, Course record 64.
Club membership 800.
Visitors must contact in advance, handicap certificate required. Not on Sat, limited time Sun.
Societies must contact in writing or telephone
Green Fees £30 per day (£40 Sun).
Prof Paul Mayo
Facilities ⊗ 🍴 🏌 🍷 ♀ 👤 🏠 🛒 ⚷ ☖
Location 1m NW of junct 27 on M4 on B4591 just beyond 'Promotive' Garage

Hotel ★★★★ 71% Celtic Manor Hotel, Golf & Country Club, Coldra Woods, NEWPORT ☎ 01633 413000 73 ⇆ 🐾

Parc Church Ln, Coedkernew NP1 9TU
☎ 01633 680933 Fax 01633 681011
A challenging but enjoyable 18-hole course with water hazards and accompanying wildlife. The 38-bay driving range is floodlit until 10pm.
18 holes, 5619yds, Par 70, SSS 68, Course record 71.
Club membership 400.
Visitors must contact in advance 01633 680933.
Societies telephone in advance.
Green Fees £12 per 18 holes; £6 per 9 holes (£15/£7 weekends).
Prof B Thomas/J Skuse
Designer B Thomas/T F Hicks
Facilities ⊗ 🍴 🏌 🍷 ♀ 👤 🏠 🛒 ⚷ ☖
Location 3m SW of Newport, off A48

Hotel ★★★ 64% Kings Hotel, High St, NEWPORT ☎ 01633 842020 47 ⇆ 🐾

Tredegar Park Bassaleg Rd NP9 3PX
☎ 01633 894433 Fax 01633 897152
A parkland course with River Ebbw and streams as natural hazards. The ground is very flat with narrow fairways and small greens. The 17th hole (par 3) is played on to a plateau where many players spoil their medal round.
18 holes, 6095yds, Par 71, SSS 70.
Club membership 750.
Visitors must be a member of a golf club affiliated to a national golf union, please contact in advance.
Societies apply to secretary.
Green Fees £23 per day (£30 weekends & bank holidays).

Cards 💳 💳 💳
Prof M L Morgan
Facilities ⊗ 🍴 🏌 🍷 ♀ 👤 🏠 🛒 ⚷
Location 2m SW off A467 exit 27 of M4

Hotel ★★★ 64% Kings Hotel, High St, NEWPORT ☎ 01633 842020 47 ⇆ 🐾

OAKDALE   Map 03 ST19

Oakdale Llwynon Ln NP2 0NF ☎ 01495 220044
9 holes, 1344yds, Par 28, Course record 27.
Visitors no restrictions pay & play.
Societies telephone for further information and arrangements.
Green Fees not confirmed.
Prof Clive Coombs
Designer Ian Goodenough
Facilities 🍷 🏠 🛒 ⚷ ☖
Location B4251 E of Blackwood

PENARTH   Map 03 ST17

Glamorganshire Lavernock Rd CF64 5UP
☎ 01222 701185 Fax 01222 701185
Parkland course, overlooking the Bristol Channel.
18 holes, 6181yds, Par 70, SSS 70, Course record 64.
Club membership 1000.
Visitors contact professional in advance.
Societies must contact in advance.
Green Fees £30 (£35 weekends & bank holidays).
Cards 💳 💳
Prof Andrew Kerr-Smith
Facilities ⊗ 🍴 🏌 🍷 ♀ 👤 🏠 🛒 ⚷ ☖
& Leisure squash.
Location S side of town centre on B4267

Hotel ★ 67% Walton House Hotel, 37 Victoria Rd, PENARTH ☎ 01222 707782 13rm(11 ⇆ 🐾)

PENCOED   Map 03 SS98

St Mary's Hotel Golf & Country Club St Mary Hill CF35 5EA ☎ 01656 861100 Fax 01656 863400
A parkland course with many American style features. The Par 3 10th called 'Alcatraz' has a well deserved reputation.
St Mary's Course: 18 holes, 5291yds, Par 69, SSS 68, Course record 63.
Sevenoaks Course: 9 holes, 2426yds, Par 35, SSS 34.
Club membership 830.
Visitors St. Mary's Course: must contact in advance, handicap certificate not required between 9-4 Mon-Fri, after 1pm weekends. Seven Oaks: no restrictions
Societies telephone Kay Brazell.
Green Fees St Mary's: £14 per round (£16 weekends & bank holidays), Seven Oaks: £4 per round (£5 weekends & bank holidays).
Cards 💳 💳 💳 💳 💳 💳
Prof John Peters
Facilities ⊗ 🍴 🏌 🍷 ♀ 👤 🏠 🍴 🛒 ⚷ ☖
& Leisure hard tennis courts.

Hotel ★★★ 72% St Mary's Hotel & Country Club, St Marys Golf Club, PENCOED ☎ 01656 861100 24 ⇆ 🐾
See advertisement on page 406.

PENRHYS   Map 03 ST09

Rhondda Golf Club House CF43 3PW
☎ 01443 441384 Fax 01443 441384
Mountain course with good views.
18 holes, 6205yds, Par 70, SSS 71, Course record 67.
Club membership 600.
Visitors   contact secretary for weekend play.
Societies   contact for details.
Green Fees £20 per day (£25 weekends & bank holidays).
Prof   G A Bebb
Facilities   ⊗ ⑪ ♨ ☕ ♀ △ 🏠 ⬥ ⬱ ♂ ⚲
Location   0.5m W off B4512

Hotel   ★★★ 67% Heritage Park Hotel,
Coed Cae Rd, Trehafod, PONTYPRIDD
☎ 01443 687057   44 ⇨ ℱ

PONTARDAWE   Map 03 SN70

Pontardawe Cefn Llan SA8 4SH
☎ 01792 863118 Fax 01792 830041
Meadowland course situated on plateau 600 ft above sea-
level with good views over Bristol Channel and Brecon
Beacons.
18 holes, 6038yds, Par 70, SSS 70, Course record 64.
Club membership 500.
Visitors   must contact in advance, but may not play on
              weekends.
Societies   apply in writing.
Green Fees £20 per day.
Prof   Gary Hopkins
Facilities   ⊗ ⑪ ♨ ☕ ♀ △ 🏠 ⚲
Location   N side of town centre M4 junc 45 off A4067

Hotel   ★★ 62% Oak Tree Parc Hotel,
Birchgrove Rd, BIRCHGROVE
☎ 01792 817781   10 ⇨ ℱ

PONTLLIW   Map 02 SS69

Allt-y-Graban Allt-y-Grabam Rd SA4 1DT
☎ 01792 885757
A challenging parkland course with fine panoramic views,
opened in 1993.It is a 9-hole course but with plans for 12
holes. There are 6 par-4 holes and 3 par-3 holes. The 6th is a
challenging hole with a blind tee shot into the valley and a
dogleg to the left onto an elevated green.
9 holes, 2210yds, Par 66, SSS 66, Course record 63.
Club membership 158.
Visitors   no restrictions.
Societies   telephone in advance.
Green Fees £8 per round (£9 weekends).
Prof   Steven Rees
Designer   F G Thomas
Facilities   ♨ ☕ ♀ △ 🏠 ⬥ ⬱ ⚲
Location   From junct 47 on M4 take a A48 towards
              Pontardulais. Turn left after Glamorgan Arms

Hotel   ★★★ 63% The Lakeside, Phoenix Way,
Swansea Enterprise Park, SWANSEA
☎ 01792 310330 120 ⇨ ℱ

PONTYPOOL   Map 03 SO20

Pontypool Lasgarn Ln, Trevethin NP4 8TR
☎ 01495 763655
Undulating, mountain course with magnificent views.
18 holes, 6046yds, Par 69, SSS 69.
Club membership 638.
Visitors   must have a handicap certificate, restricted
              availability at weekends, advisable to call in
              advance.
Societies   apply in writing or by phone, deposit payable.
Green Fees £20 per day, £14 per round (£24/£18 weekends).
Prof   James Howard
Facilities   ⊗ ⑪ by prior arrangement ♨ ☕ ♀ △ 🏠 ⬱ ⚲ ⬥
Location   1.5m N off A4043

Hotel   ★★ 68% Mill at Glynhir, Glyn-Hir,
Llandybie, AMMANFORD
☎ 01269 850672   11 ⇨ ℱ

Woodlake Park Golf & Country Club Glascoed NP4 0TE
☎ 01291 673933 Fax 01291 673811
Undulating parkland course with magnificent views over
Llandegfedd Reservoir. Superb green constructed to USGA
specification. Holes 4, 7 & 16 are Par 3's which are
particularly challenging. Holes 6 & 17 are long Par 4's which
can be wind affected.
18 holes, 6278yds, Par 71, SSS 72, Course record 67.
Club membership 450.
Visitors   book in advance.
Societies   telephone or write for society package.
Green Fees £27.50 per day, £20 per round.
Cards   ▭▭▭ ▬▬
Prof   Adrian Pritchard
Facilities   ⊗ ⑪ ♨ ☕ ♀ △ 🏠 ⬱ ⬥ ⚲
& Leisure   fishing.
Location   Overlooking Llandegfedd Reservoir

Hotel   ★★ 68% Mill at Glynhir, Glyn-Hir,
Llandybie, AMMANFORD
☎ 01269 850672   11 ⇨ ℱ

PONTYPRIDD   Map 03 ST09

Pontypridd Ty Gwyn Rd CF37 4DJ
☎ 01443 409904 Fax 01443 491622
Well-wooded mountain course with springy turf. Good views
of the Rhondda Valleys and coast.
18 holes, 5721yds, Par 69, SSS 68.
Club membership 850.
Visitors   must play with member on weekends & bank
              holidays. Must have a handicap certificate.
Societies   weekdays only. Must contact in advance.
Green Fees not confirmed.
Cards   ▭▭ ▬▬ ▭▭ ▭ ▭
Prof   Wade Walters
Facilities   ⊗ ⑪ ♨ ☕ ♀ △ 🏠 ⬥ ⬱ ⚲
Location   E side of town centre off A470

Hotel   ★★★ 68% Llechwen Hall Hotel,
Llanfabon, PONTYPRIDD
☎ 01443 742050 & 740305
Fax 01443 742189   12 ⇨ ℱ

PORT TALBOT   Map 03 SS78

British Steel Port Talbot Sports & Social Club, Margam
SA13 2NF ☎ 01639 814182 & 871111
A 9 hole course with two lakes. All the holes are affected by
crosswinds and the 7th, Par 3, is alongside a deep stream, so
is very tight.
9 holes, 4726yds, Par 62, SSS 63, Course record 60.
Club membership 250.
Visitors   contact in advance, may not play at weekends.
Societies   by prior arrangement.
Green Fees not confirmed.
Facilities   ⊗ ⅃ 🛡 ♀ ⅄
& Leisure   hard tennis courts.

Hotel   ★★★ 68% Aberavon Beach Hotel,
                  PORT TALBOT ☎ 01639 884949 52 ⇆

PORTHCAWL   Map 03 SS87

Royal Porthcawl CF36 3UW
☎ 01656 782251 Fax 01656 771687
This championship-standard heathland/downland links
course is always in sight of the sea. With holes facing
every point of the compass, the golfer is always tested by
the wind and the course has hosted many major
tournaments.
18 holes, 6406yds, Par 72, SSS 74.
Club membership 800.
Visitors   must contact in advanced & produce
                  handicap certificate limit men 20, ladies 30.
                  Restricted at weekends & bank holidays.
Societies   apply in writing.
Green Fees not confirmed.
Cards   ▭ ▭ 🗐
Prof   Peter Evans
Designer   Charles Gibson
Facilities   ⅄ 🏠 ⽊ 🏳 ❧ ⚒ ⍾
Location   1.5m NW of town centre

Hotel   ★★★ 60% Seabank Hotel,
                  The Promenade, PORTHCAWL
                  ☎ 01656 782261 65 ⇆ 🐾

PYLE   Map 03 SS88

Pyle & Kenfig Waun-Y-Mer CF33 4PU
☎ 01656 783093 Fax 01656 772822
Links and downland course, with sand-dunes. Easy walking.
Often windy.
18 holes, 6688yds, Par 71, SSS 73, Course record 68.
Club membership 1080.
Visitors   by arrangement midweek, guests of members
                  only at weekends.
Societies   for large numbers apply in writing, small
                  numbers telephone booking accepted.
Green Fees £30 per day/round.
Cards   ▭ ▭ ▭ 🗐
Prof   Robert Evans
Designer   Colt
Facilities   ⊗ ⅃ ⅃ 🛡 ♀ ⅄ 🏠 ⽊ ❧ ⚒ ⍾ ⍾
Location   S side of Pyle off A4229. Access via
                  junct 37 on M4

Hotel   ★★★ 60% Seabank Hotel, The Promenade,
                  PORTHCAWL ☎ 01656 782261 65 ⇆ 🐾

RAGLAN   Map 03 SO40

Raglan Parc Parc Lodge, Station Rd NP5 2ER
☎ 01291 690077
New parkland course with well laid greens and a mature back
9 that are already the source of local praise. Several testing
holes where a combination of wind and water make golf
challenging. Easy walking.
18 holes, 6604yds, Par 72, SSS 73, Course record 67.
Club membership 350.
Visitors   advisable to contact in advance.
Societies   advance arrangement required.
Green Fees not confirmed.
Facilities   ⊗ ⅃ ⅃ 🛡 ♀ ⅄ 🏠 🚗
Location   Off junct of A449/A40

Hotel   ★★★ 66% Llansantffraed Court Hotel,
                  Llanvihangel Gobion, ABERGAVENNY
                  ☎ 01873 840678 21 ⇆ 🐾

SOUTHGATE   Map 02 SS58

Pennard 2 Southgate Rd SA3 2BT
☎ 01792 233131 & 233451 Fax 01792 234797
Undulating, cliff-top seaside links with good coastal views.
18 holes, 6265yds, Par 71, SSS 72, Course record 69.
Club membership 1020.
Visitors   advisable to contact Professional in advance.
Societies   by prior arrangement, telephone in advance.
Green Fees £24 (£30 weekends & bank holidays).
Cards   🗐
Prof   M V Bennett
Designer   James Braid
Facilities   ⊗ ⅃ ⅃ 🛡 ♀ ⅄ 🏠 ⽊ ⚒
& Leisure   squash, snooker.
Location   8m W of Swansea by A4067 and B4436

Hotel   ★★⚶ Fairyhill, REYNOLDSTON
                  ☎ 01792 390139 8 ⇆ 🐾

SWANSEA   Map 03 SS69

Clyne 120 Owls Lodge Ln, The Mayals, Blackpyl SA3 5DP
☎ 01792 401989 Fax 01792 401078
Challenging moorland course with scenic views of Swansea
Bay and The Gower.
18 holes, 6334yds, Par 70, SSS 71, Course record 64.
Club membership 800.
Visitors   must be member of a club with handicap
                  certificate. Groups over 8 advised to book in
                  advance
Societies   must contact in advance.
Green Fees £25 (£30 weekends & bank holidays).
Prof   Jonathan Clenett
Designer   H S Colt & Harries
Facilities   ⊗ ⅃ ⅃ 🛡 ♀ ⅄ 🏠 ⚒
Location   3.5m SW on B4436 off A4067

Hotel   ★★★ 69% Langland Court,
                  Langland Court Rd, LANGLAND
                  ☎ 01792 361545 14 ⇆ 🐾 Annexe5 ⇆ 🐾

Langland Bay Langland Bay SA3 4QR
☎ 01792 366023 Fax 01792 361082
Parkland course overlooking Gower coast. The par 4, 6th is
an uphill dog-leg open to the wind, and the par 3, 16th (151
yds) is aptly named 'Death or Glory'.

18 holes, 5857yds, Par 70, SSS 69.
Club membership 850.
Visitors no restrictions. Tue is Ladies Day. No societies at weekends
Societies must telephone in advance.
Green Fees £28 (£30 weekends).
Prof Mark Evans
Designer Henry Cotton
Facilities ⊗ �𝄞 ᴸ 🏌 ♥ 🍴 ☖ 🍴 ◊
Location 6m W on A4067

Hotel ★★★ 69% Langland Court,
Langland Court Rd, LANGLAND
☎ 01792 361545 14 ⇄ 🐾 Annexe5 ⇄ 🐾

Morriston 160 Clasemont Rd SA6 6AJ
☎ 01792 796528 Fax 01792 796528
Pleasant parkland course with a very difficult Par 3 15th hole.
18 holes, 5891yds, Par 68, SSS 68, Course record 64.
Club membership 700.

Visitors may not play Sat. Must contact in advance.
Societies apply in writing.
Green Fees £18 per day/round (£30 weekends).
Prof D A Rees
Facilities ⊗ �𝄞 ᴸ 🏌 ♥ 🍴 ☖ 🍴 ◊
Location 5m N on A48

Hotel ★★ 62% Oak Tree Parc Hotel, Birchgrove Rd,
BIRCHGROVE ☎ 01792 817781 10 ⇄ 🐾

TALBOT GREEN — Map 03 ST08

Llantrisant & Pontyclun Off Ely Valley Rd CF72 8HZ
☎ 01443 228169
Parkland course.
12 holes, 5712yds, Par 68, SSS 68, Course record 66.
Club membership 600.
Visitors must have handicap certificate, must contact in advance, not at weekends
Societies apply in writing.
Green Fees £15 per round.
Facilities ⊗ ⒨ ᴸ 🏌 ♥ 🍴 ☖ ◊
Location N side of village off A473

Hotel ★★★★ 71% Miskin Manor Hotel,
Groes Faen, Pontyclun, MISKIN
☎ 01443 224204 34 ⇄ 🐾 Annexe8 ⇄ 🐾

THREE CROSSES — Map 02 SS59

Gower Cefn Goleu SA4 3HS
☎ 01792 872480 (Off) 879905 (Pro) Fax 01792 872480
Set in attractive rolling countryside, this Donald Steel designed course provides good strategic hazards, including trees, water and bunkers, outstanding views and a challenging game of golf.
18 holes, 6441yds, Par 71, SSS 72.
Club membership 500.
Visitors tee booking upto 7 days in advance, reservations recommended, some weekend vacancies, dress code and course etiquette must be adhered to.
Societies by prior notice for established golfers.
Green Fees not confirmed.
Prof Mark Whittingham
Designer Donald Steel
Facilities ⊗ ⒨ ᴸ 🏌 ♥ 🍴 ☖ 🛒 ◊
Location Sign posted from the village of Three Crosses

Hotel ★★ 74% Beaumont Hotel, 72-73 Walter Rd,
SWANSEA ☎ 01792 643956 16 ⇄ 🐾

TREDEGAR — Map 03 SO10

Tredegar and Rhymney Cwmtysswg, Rhymney NP2 3BQ
☎ 01685 840743 (club) & 843400 (office)
Fax 01685 843440
Mountain course with lovely views. The course is being developed into an 18 hole course.
9 holes, 5504yds, Par 68, SSS 68, Course record 69.
Club membership 194.
Visitors cannot play Sun morning
Societies must contact in advance.
Green Fees not confirmed.
Facilities ☖
Location 1.75m SW on B4256

Hotel ★★★ 68% Tregenna Hotel, Park Ter,
MERTHYR TYDFIL ☎ 01685 723627 &
382055 Fax 01685 721951 24 ⇄ 🐾

UPPER KILLAY Map 02 SS59

Fairwood Park Blackhills Ln SA2 7JN
☎ 01792 203648 Fax 01792 297849
Parkland championship course on the beautiful Gower
Peninsula.
18 holes, 6741yds, Par 72, SSS 72, Course record 68.
Club membership 720.
Visitors	welcome except when championship or club matches are being held. Must contact in advance.
Societies	must contact in advance.
Green Fees	£25 per day (£30 weekends & bank holidays).
Prof	Gary Hughes
Designer	Hawtree
Facilities	⊗ ⵜ ⓛ 🍺 ♀ 👟 🏠 🍴 🚲 ⛳ ✎
Location	1.5m S off A4118

Hotel ★★ 73% Windsor Lodge Hotel,
Mount Pleasant, SWANSEA
☎ 01792 642158 & 652744
Fax 01792 648996   18 🛏 🐾

WENVOE Map 03 ST17

Wenvoe Castle CF5 6BE ☎ 01222 594371
Parkland course which is hilly for first 9 holes. Pond, situated
280 yds from tee at 10th hole, is a hazard.
18 holes, 6422yds, Par 72, SSS 71, Course record 64.
Club membership 600.
Visitors	must be a member of a recognised golf club & have a handicap certificate. Must play with member at weekends.
Societies	must contact in writing.
Green Fees	not confirmed.
Prof	Robin Day
Facilities	⊗ ⵜ ⓛ 🍺 ♀ 🏠 ✎
Location	1m S off A4050

Hotel ★★★♨ 77% Egerton Grey Country House
Hotel, Porthkerry, BARRY
☎ 01446 711666   10 🛏 🐾

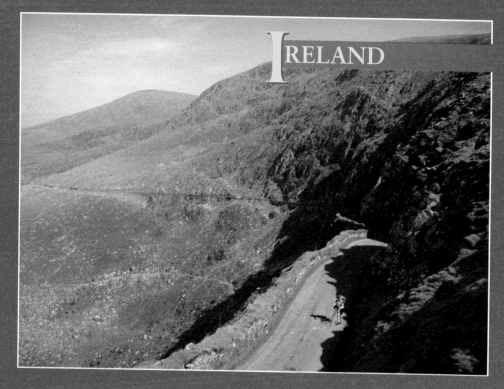

IRELAND

John Ingham writes: Anyone who doesn't love Ireland, doesn't love golf or the blarney that goes with it at the 19th hole. It's here, at the essential pit stop that rounds up the day, that I personally tell the most outrageous lies, exaggerating the utter brilliance of my play.

Frankly, I blame the refreshments provided in hospitable southern Ireland for the fact that not a single Eire golfer has ever won the Open championship. It wasn't the moist climate that prevented Christy O'Connor Snr from winning this major title, and it certainly wasn't the quality of the golf courses to be found, both north and south.

It was northern man, Fred Daly who won in 1947 but I'm not sure he was any better than O'Connor, or Harry Bradshaw (who once tied an Open) or indeed better than the modern set of Irish stars like Darren Clarke, or the fairly new men, Padraig Harrington and Paul McGinley.

The greatest Irish tests of golf are beside the sea. And many of their really great players, amateurs included like Joe Carr,

learned how to play the links in sweeping winds. And these are the conditions they usually face at Open championship time. So why don't the Irish win big? I think they may, with Clarke a good bet.

It would be disgraceful to suggest that the first teetotal Irish star <u>will</u> win, and if he does, I'll be the first to buy him a celebration drink. And maybe that says its all. The Irish play the game because they love it, are amused by it. Not for them the gim slog of Nick Faldo, the Englishman. And yet, Ben Hogan, the most frightening serious golfer I ever saw, had Irish blood in him!

So where to go in Ireland? Well, the lists I approve rate Royal Portrush, Newcastle Co Down, Ballybunion (Old), Portmarnock, Connemara, Dingle....but I have a chum who reckons Ballyliffin tops. It's 15 miles north of Derry and to play it costs about £11 in old money, if you arrive on the right day. No I'll tell you the best Irish course - it's Ballybunion, and Tom Watson says so, that's who!

419

NORTHERN IRELAND

Northern Ireland Telephone Number Changes

From the 22 April 2000, the dialling code for the whole of Northern Ireland will be **(028),** followed by an eight-digit local number. For example, **(01232)** 123456 will become **(028) 90**12 3456, **(012477)** 123456 will become **(028) 247** 12345.

CO ANTRIM

ANTRIM
Map 01 D5

Massereene 51 Lough Rd BT41 4DQ
☎ 01849 428096 Fax 01849 487661
The first nine holes are parkland, while the second, adjacent to the shore of Lough Neagh, have more of a links character with sandy ground.
18 holes, 6559yds, Par 72, SSS 71, Course record 66. Club membership 969.
Visitors must contact in advance.
Societies book in advance.
Green Fees not confirmed.
Prof Jim Smyth
Designer F Hawtree
Facilities ⊗ ⫟ ⯙ ⬝ ♥ ⚥ △ 🖻 ⋔ ⌀
Location 1m SW of town

Hotel ★★★★70% Galgorm Manor, BALLYMENA
☎ 01266 881001 23 ⇄ ⸙

BALLYCASTLE
Map 01 D6

Ballycastle Cushendall Rd BT54 6QP
☎ 01265 762536 Fax 01265 769909
An unusual mixture of terrain beside the sea, with magnificent views from all parts. The first five holes are inland type; the middle holes on the Warren are links type and the rest, on high ground, are heath type.
18 holes, 5406mtrs, Par 71, SSS 69, Course record 64. Club membership 950.
Visitors are welcome during the week.
Societies apply in writing.
Green Fees £20 per round (£28 weekends).
Prof Ian McLaughlin
Facilities ⊗ ⫟ ⯙ ⬝ ♥ ⚥ △ 🖻 ⌀
Location Between Portrush & Cushendall (A2)

BALLYCLARE
Map 01 D5

Ballyclare 23 Springdale Rd BT39 9JW
☎ 01960 322696 Fax 01960 322696
Parkland course with lots of trees and shrubs and water hazards provided by the river, streams and lakes.
18 holes, 5745mtrs, Par 71, SSS 71, Course record 66. Club membership 580.
Visitors must contact in advance.
Societies must contact in advance.
Green Fees £16 per round (£22 weekends & bank holidays).
Designer T McCauley

Facilities ⊗ ⫟ ⬝ ♥ ⚥ △ 🖻 ⌀
Location 1.5m N

Hotel ★★★★67% Stormont Hotel, 587 Upper Newtonards Rd, BELFAST
☎ 01232 658621 109 ⇄ ⸙

BALLYGALLY
Map 01 D5

Cairndhu 192 Coast Rd BT40 2QG
☎ 01574 583324 Fax 01574 583324
Built on a hilly headland, this course is both testing and scenic, with wonderful coastal views. The 3rd hole has a carry of 180 yds over a headland to the fairway.
18 holes, 5611mtrs, Par 70, SSS 69, Course record 64. Club membership 905.
Visitors may not play on Sat.
Societies must apply in writing.
Green Fees £15 Mon-Thu; £20 Fri (£24 Sat & Sun).
Cards ▭ ▪ ▬ ▫
Prof Robert Walker
Designer Mr Morrison
Facilities ⊗ ⫟ ⯙ ⬝ ♥ ⚥ △ 🖻 ⋔ ⌀
Location 4m N of Larne on coast road

Hotel ★★★65% Londonderry Arms Hotel, 20 Harbour Rd, CARNLOUGH
☎ 01574 885255 35 ⇄ ⸙

BALLYMENA
Map 01 D5

Ballymena 128 Raceview Rd BT42 4HY ☎ 01266 861487
Parkland course of level heathland with plenty of bunkers.
18 holes, 5299mtrs, Par 68, SSS 67, Course record 64. Club membership 895.
Visitors may not play on Tue or Sat.
Societies must contact in advance.
Green Fees not confirmed.
Prof Ken Revie
Facilities ⊗ ⫟ ⯙ ⬝ ♥ ⚥ △ 🖻 ⋔ ⛳ ⌀
Location 2m E on A42

Hotel ★★★★70% Galgorm Manor, BALLYMENA
☎ 01266 881001 23 ⇄ ⸙

Galgorm Castle Golf & Country Club Galgorm Rd BT42 1HL ☎ 01266 46161 Fax 01266 651151
18 hole championship course set in 220 acres of mature parkland in the grounds of a historic castle. The course is bordered by two rivers which come into play and includes five lakes. a course of outstanding beauty offering a challenge to both the novice and low handicapped golfer.
18 holes, 6736yds, Par 72, SSS 72, Course record 68. Club membership 400.
Visitors ring to book times.
Societies apply in writing or telephone in advance.
Green Fees £27 per day; £18 per round (£37.50/£24 weekends).
Cards ▭ ▪ ▬ ▫
Prof Lesley Callen
Designer Simon Gidman
Facilities ⊗ ⫟ ⯙ ⬝ ♥ ⚥ △ 🖻 ⋔ ⛳ ⬟ 🛥 ⌀ ⌁
& Leisure fishing.
Location 1m S of Ballymena on A42

Hotel ★★★★70% Galgorm Manor, BALLYMENA
☎ 01266 881001 23 ⇄ ⸙

CARRICKFERGUS   Map 01 D5

Carrickfergus 25 North Rd BT38 8LP
☎ 01960 363713 Fax 01960 363023
Parkland course, fairly level but nevertheless demanding, with
a notorious water hazard at the 1st. Well maintained and with
nice views.
18 holes, 5759yds, Par 68, SSS 68.
Club membership 850.
Visitors   restrictions at weekends.
Societies   must contact in advance.
Green Fees   not confirmed.
Prof   Raymond Stevenson
Facilities   🏌 🏠
Location   9m NE of Belfast on A2

Hotel   ★ 67% Dobbins Inn, 6-8 High St,
CARRICKFERGUS
☎ 01960 351905 15 ⊟ ♠

Greenisland 156 Upper Rd, Greenisland BT38 8RW
☎ 01232 862236
A parkland course estling at the foot of Knockagh Hill with
scenic views over Belfast Lough.
9 holes, 5536mtrs, Par 71, SSS 68.
Club membership 740.
Visitors   contact club in advance. Play restricted Sat and
Thu.
Societies   by prior arrangement.
Green Fees   £12 per day (£18 weekends & bank holidays).
Facilities   ⊗ ⅲ ㄴ ♥ ♀ 🏌

Hotel   ★ 67% Dobbins Inn,
6-8 High St, CARRICKFERGUS
☎ 01960 351905 15 ⊟ ♠

CUSHENDALL   Map 01 D6

Cushendall 21 Shore Rd ☎ 012667 71318
Scenic course with spectacular views over the Sea of Moyle
and Red Bay to the Mull of Kintyre. The River Dall winds
through the course, coming into play in seven of the nine
holes.
9 holes, 4386mtrs, Par 66, SSS 63.
Club membership 714.
Visitors   Ladies day Thursday, time sheet at weekends.
Societies   must contact in writing.
Green Fees   not confirmed.
Designer   D Delargy
Facilities   ⊗ ⅲ ㄴ ♥ ♀ 🏌
Hotel   ★★★ 65% Londonderry Arms Hotel,
20 Harbour Rd, CARNLOUGH
☎ 01574 885255 35 ⊟ ♠

LARNE   Map 01 D5

Larne 54 Ferris Bay Rd, Islandmagee BT40 3RT
☎ 01960 382228 Fax 01960 382088
An exposed part links, part heathland course offering a good
test, particularly on the last three holes along the sea shore.
9 holes, 6686yds, Par 70, SSS 69, Course record 64.
Club membership 430.
Visitors   may not play on Sat.
Societies   apply in writing or telephone in advance.
Green Fees   not confirmed.
Designer   G L Bailie
Facilities   🏌

Location 6m N of Whitehead on Browns Bay rd

Hotel   ★★★ 65% Londonderry Arms Hotel,
20 Harbour Rd, CARNLOUGH
☎ 01574 885255 35 ⊟ ♠

LISBURN   Map 01 D5

Aberdelghy Bell's Ln, Lambeg BT27 4QH
☎ 01846 662738 Fax 01846 603432
This parkland course, extended to 18 holes in 1997 has no
bunkers. The hardest hole on the course is the 340metre 3rd,
a dog leg through trees to a green guarded by water. The par-
3 12th high on the hill and the 14th hole over the dam
provide a challenge. The par-4 15th hole is a long dog leg.
18 holes, 4139mtrs, Par 66, SSS 62, Course record 64.
Club membership 150.
Visitors   restricted Sat 7.15am-1pm.
Societies   telephone in advance.
Green Fees   £7 per 18 holes (£9 weekends & bank holidays).
Prof   Ian Murdoch
Designer   Alec Blair
Facilities   ♥ 🏌 🏠 ↿ 🏌
Location   1.5m N of Lisburn off A1

Hotel   B Posthouse Belfast, Kingsway, Dunmurry,
BELFAST ☎ 01232 612101 82 ⊟ ♠

Lisburn Blaris Lodge, 68 Eglantine Rd BT27 5RQ
☎ 01846 677216
Meadowland course, fairly level, with plenty of trees and
shrubs. Challenging last three holes.
18 holes, 6647yds, Par 72, SSS 72, Course record 67.
Club membership 1421.
Visitors   must play with member at weekends. Must tee
off before 3pm weekdays.
Societies   must contact in writing.
Green Fees   not confirmed.
Prof   Blake Campbell
Designer   Hawtree
Facilities   ⊗ ⅲ ♀ 🏌 🏠 ↿ 🏌
Location   2m from town on A1

Hotel   ★★★★ 67% Stormont Hotel,
587 Upper Newtonards Rd, BELFAST
☎ 01232 658621 109 ⊟ ♠

MAZE   Map 01 D5

Down Royal Park Dunygarton Rd BT27 5RT
☎ 01846 621339 Fax 01846 621339
The 9-hole Valley course and the 18-hole Down Royal Park
are easy walking, undulating heathland courses. Down
Royal's 2nd hole is 628yards and thought to be among the
best par 5 holes in Ireland.
*Down Royal Park Course: 18 holes, 6824yds, Par 72,
Course record 73.*
Valley Course: 9 holes, 2500yds, Par 33.
Club membership 80.
Visitors   no restrictions, except dress code.
Societies   reservations in advance.
Green Fees   £15 per round (£17-£20 weekends & bank
holidays). 9 hole course: £4 (£4.50 weekends).
Cards   ⊟ ▦ 📷
Facilities   ⊗ ⅲ ㄴ ♥ ♀ 🏌 ↿ 🍴 🏌
& Leisure   Budget B & B accomodation.
Location   Inside Down Royal Race Course   ▶

421

Hotel ★★★ 68% White Gables Hotel,
14 Dromore Rd, HILLSBOROUGH
☎ 01846 682755 31 ⇔ ⋔

NEWTOWNABBEY   Map 01 D5

Ballyearl Golf & Leisure Centre 585 Doagh Rd, Mossley
BT36 8RZ ☎ 01232 848287
9 holes, 2520yds, Par 27.
Visitors no restrictions.
Societies telephone in advance.
Green Fees not confirmed.
Prof Jim Robinson
Designer V Lathery
Facilities ⋓ ⚲ 🏠 ⋔
& Leisure squash, gymnasium.

Mallusk Antrim Rd BT36 ☎ 01232 843799
Attractive 9-hole parkland course featuring 3 small par 4s
and several water hazards, notably on the tricky,
dog-leg 7th hole.
9 holes, 4444yds, Par 62, SSS 62, Course record 62.
Club membership 150.
Visitors no restrictions.
Societies contact for details.
Green Fees not confirmed.
Designer David Fitzgerald
Facilities ⋓ ⚲ 🏠 ⋈
& Leisure hard tennis courts, sauna.

PORTBALLINTRAE   Map 01 C6

Bushfoot 50 Bushfoot Rd, Portballintrae BT57 8RR
☎ 012657 31317 Fax 012657 31852
A seaside links course with superb views in an area of
outstanding beauty. A challenging par-3 7th is ringed by
bunkers with out-of-bounds beyond, while the 3rd has a blind
approach. Also a putting green and pitch & putt course.
9 holes, 5914yds, Par 70, SSS 67, Course record 68.
Club membership 850.
Visitors must contact in advance.
Societies must contact in advance.
Green Fees not confirmed.
Facilities ⊗ ⫯ ⅃ ⋓ ⚲ 🏠 ⋔ ♂
Location Off Ballaghmore rd

Hotel ★★ 69% Beach House Hotel,
The Sea Front, PORTBALLINTRAE
☎ 012657 31214 32 ⇔ ⋔

PORTRUSH   Map 01 C6

ROYAL PORTRUSH See page 423

WHITEHEAD   Map 01 D5

Bentra Municipal Slaughterford Rd BT38 9TG
☎ 01960 378996
A well matured course designed with the experienced golfer
and novice in mind with wide fairways and some particularly
long holes.
9 holes, 2885mtrs, Par 37, SSS 35.

Visitors no restrictions.
Societies contact in advance.
Green Fees £7.50 per 18 holes (£11 weekends).
Facilities ⊗ ⫯ ⅃ ⋓ ⚲ 🏠 ⋔ ♂ ⎰

Hotel ★ 67% Dobbins Inn,
6-8 High St, CARRICKFERGUS
☎ 01960 351905 15 ⇔ ⋔

Whitehead McCrae's Brae BT38 9NZ
☎ 01960 353631 & 353792 Fax 01960 353631
Undulating parkland course with magnificent sea views.
18 holes, 5946yds, Par 69, SSS 68, Course record 67.
Club membership 940.
Visitors may not play on Sat. Must play with member on
Sun.
Societies must contact in advance.
Green Fees £15 per round (£20 Sun & bank holidays).
Prof Colin Farr
Designer A B Armstrong
Facilities ⅃ ⋓ ⚲ 🏠 🏠
Location 1m from town

Hotel ★ 67% Dobbins Inn,
6-8 High St, CARRICKFERGUS
☎ 01960 351905 15 ⇔ ⋔

CO ARMAGH

ARMAGH   Map 01 C5

County Armagh The Demesne, Newry Rd BT60 1EN
☎ 01861 525861 Fax 01861 525861
Mature parkland course with excellent views of Armagh city
and its surroundings.
18 holes, 6212yds, Par 70, SSS 69, Course record 63.
Club membership 1000.
Visitors time sheet operates at weekends.
Societies must contact in advance.
Green Fees not confirmed.
Cards [cards]
Prof Alan Rankin
Facilities ⊗ ⫯ ⅃ ⋓ ⚲ 🏠 🏠 ♂ ⎰
Location On the Newry road

Hotel ★★★★ 67% Stormont Hotel,
587 Upper Newtonards Rd, BELFAST
☎ 01232 658621 109 ⇔ ⋔

LURGAN   Map 01 D5

Craigavon Golf & Ski Centre Turmoyra Ln, Silverwood
BT66 6NG ☎ 01762 326606 Fax 01762 347272
Parkland course with a lake and stream providing water
hazards.
18 holes, 6496yds, Par 72, SSS 72.
Club membership 400.
Visitors restricted Sat am.
Societies telephone in advance.
Green Fees not confirmed.
Facilities ⋓ ⚲ 🏠 ⋔ ♂ ⎰
& Leisure gymnasium, artificial ski slope.
Location 2m N at Silverwood off the M1   ▶

ROYAL PORTRUSH

PORTRUSH *Co Antrim* ☎ **01265 822311**
Fax 01265 823139   **Map 01 D4**

John Ingham writes: It was more than thirty years ago that I first saw Royal Portrush, but the memory lingers on. That week in 1960, the great Joe Carr won the British Amateur Championship for his third, and last, time. But everyone there was a winner; the sun shone, and the course glistened as the foaming ocean was almost blown inland on to the briar roses that dotted the rough.

What a splendid seaside paradise this is, I wrote in a London evening newspaper, whose readers were keen to follow players such as Joe Carr and Michael Bonallack. There among the gallery was the late Fred Daly, winner of the 1947 Open and the only Irishman ever to win.

The man who designed this course was Harry S Colt, a name that appears as a creator of many fine courses. This one is considered among the six best in the United Kingdom. It is spectacular, breathtaking, but one of the tightest driving tests known to man because, if you get in the long stuff, you may stay there. On a clear day, you have a fine view of Islay and the Paps of Jura - seen from the 3rd tee. Then there's the Giant's Causeway, from the 5th, as good a downhill dogleg hole as you'll find anywhere.

While the greens have to be 'read' from the start, there are fairways up and down valleys, and holes called Calamity Corner and Purgatory for good reason. The second hole, called Giant's Grave, is 509 yards but there's an even longer one waiting for you at the 17th, while the last hole, a 479-yarder, nearly cost Max Faulkner his 1951 Open title. He hit a crooked drive, and had to bend his second shot with a wooden club. Dressed in primrose-coloured slacks, his colourful plumage and out-going attitude attracted most of the small crowd.

The Open did not return to Portrush and championship golf is the loser because the place is a gem. Founded in 1888, it was also the venue of the first professional golf event held in Ireland, when in 1895, Sandy Herd beat Harry Vardon in the final.

You'll love it.

Visitors	must contact in advance, have a letter of introduction from their own club and a handicap certificate. Restricted Wed & Fri pm. Sat & Sun am
Societies	must apply in writing.
Green fees	Dunluce Links £60 (£70 weekends) Valley Links £24 per day (£32 weekends)
Facilities	⊗ ℳ ⓛ ⬛ ♀⚁ ⬛ ⚐ ⚑ Professional (Dai Stevenson)
Location	Bushmills Road Portrush BT56 8JQ (0.5m from Portrush on main road to Bushmills)

45 holes. **Dunluce Links: 18 holes, 6641 yds, Par 72, SSS 73, course record 66
Valley Links: 18 holes, 6054 yds, Par 70, SSS 70**

WHERE TO STAY AND EAT NEARBY

HOTELS:
PORTRUSH
★★★ 63% Causeway Coast, 36 Ballyreagh Rd.
☎ 01265 822435. 41 ⇌ ☞

RESTAURANT:
PORTRUSH
⚙ ⚙ Ramore, The Harbour.
☎ 01265 824313.

Hotel ★★★★ 67% Stormont Hotel,
587 Upper Newtonards Rd, BELFAST
☎ 01232 658621 109 ⇆ ♠

Lurgan The Demesne BT67 9BN
☎ 01762 322087 Fax 01762 325306
Testing parkland course bordering Lurgan Park Lake with a
need for accurate shots. Drains well in wet weather and suits
a long straight hitter.
18 holes, 6257yds, Par 70, SSS 70, Course record 66.
Club membership 856.
Visitors may not play Sat, contact in advance.
Societies must contact in advance, not Sat.
Green Fees £15 per round (£20 weekends & bank holidays).
Prof Des Paul
Designer A Pennink
Facilities ⊗ ⅏ ⅃ ♭ ☕ ♀ ⚘ 🏠 ⚐
Location 0.5m from town centre near Lurgan Park

Hotel ★★★★ 67% Stormont Hotel,
587 Upper Newtonards Rd, BELFAST
☎ 01232 658621 109 ⇆ ♠

PORTADOWN
Map 01 D5

Portadown 192 Gilford Rd BT63 5LF ☎ 01762 355356
Well wooded parkland course on the banks of the River
Bann, which features among the water hazards.
18 holes, 5649mtrs, Par 70, SSS 70, Course record 65.
Club membership 1004.
Visitors may not play on Tue & Sat.
Societies apply in writing.
Green Fees not confirmed.
Prof Paul Stevenson
Facilities ⊗ ⅏ ⅃ ♭ ☕ ♀ ⚘ 🏠 ⚐
& Leisure squash.
Location SE via A59

Hotel ★★★★ 67% Stormont Hotel,
587 Upper Newtonards Rd, BELFAST
☎ 01232 658621 109 ⇆ ♠

TANDRAGEE
Map 01 D5

Tandragee Markethill Rd BT62 2ER
☎ 01762 841272 Fax 01762 840664
Pleasant parkland course, the signature hole is the demanding
par 4 11th known as 'The Wall Hole', the real strength of
Tandragee is in the short holes.
18 holes, 5747mtrs, Par 71, SSS 70, Course record 65.
Club membership 1340.
Visitors contact in advance.
Societies must contact in advance.
Green Fees Men: £15 (£20 weekends & bank holidays);
Ladies: £11 (£18 weekends & bank holidays).
Prof Paul Stevenson
Designer John Stone
Facilities ⊗ ⅏ ⅃ ♭ ☕ ♀ ⚘ 🏠 ⚐ ⚐ ☇
& Leisure sauna, gymnasium.
Location On B3 out of Tandragee towards Markethill

Farm ▇▇▇ Brook Lodge Farmhouse,
house 79 Old Ballynahinch Rd, Cargacroy,
LISBURN
☎ 01846 638454 6rm(4 ♠)

CO BELFAST

BELFAST Map 01 D5

See also The Royal Belfast, Hollywood, Co Down.

Balmoral 518 Lisburn Rd BT9 6GX
☎ 01232 381514 Fax 01232 666759
Parkland course, mainly level, with tree-lined fairways and a
stream providing a water hazard.
18 holes, 6276yds, Par 69, SSS 70, Course record 64.
Club membership 912.
Visitors may not play Sat or Sun before 2.30pm.
Societies Mon & Thu. Must contact in advance.
Green Fees not confirmed.
Prof Geoff Bleakley
Facilities ⚘ 🏠 ⚐ ☇
Location 2m S next to Kings Hall

Hotel ★★★★ 67% Stormont Hotel,
587 Upper Newtonards Rd, BELFAST
☎ 01232 658621 109 ⇆ ♠

Cliftonville 44 Westland Rd BT14 6NH
☎ 01232 744158 & 746595
Parkland course with rivers bisecting two fairways.
9 holes, 6242yds, Par 70, SSS 70, Course record 66.
Club membership 430.
Visitors may not play: after 5pm unless with member, on
Sat or on Sun mornings.
Societies must contact in writing.
Green Fees not confirmed.
Prof Peter Hanna
Facilities ⊗ ⅏ by prior arrangement ♭ ☕ ♀ ⚘ 🏠 ⚐
Location Between Cavehill Rd & Cliftonville Circus

Hotel ★★★★ 67% Stormont Hotel,
587 Upper Newtonards Rd, BELFAST
☎ 01232 658621 109 ⇆ ♠

Dunmurry 91 Dunmurry Ln, Dunmurray BT17 9JS
☎ 01232 610834 Fax 01232 602540
Maturing very nicely, this tricky parkland course has several
memorable holes which call for skilful shots.
18 holes, 5832yds, Par 69, SSS 69, Course record 64.
Club membership 900.
Visitors telephone in advance. May only play Sat after
5pm, restricted Fri (Ladies Day).
Societies must contact in writing.
Green Fees not confirmed.
Prof John Dolan
Facilities ⊗ ⅏ ⅃ ♭ ☕ ♀ ⚘ 🏠 ⚐ ☇

Hotel ★★★★ 67% Stormont Hotel,
587 Upper Newtonards Rd, BELFAST
☎ 01232 658621 109 ⇆ ♠

Fortwilliam Downview Ave BT15 4EZ
☎ 01232 370770 (Office) & 770980 (Pro)
Fax 01232 781891
Parkland course in most attractive surroundings. The course
is bisected by a lane.
18 holes, 5789yds, Par 70, SSS 68, Course record 65.
Club membership 1000.
Visitors contact professional in advance.
Societies must contact in advance.

Green Fees £22 per round (£29 weekends & bank holidays).
Prof Peter Hanna
Facilities ⊗ ⫫ ᴸᴮ ♥ ♀ ⌂ ☎ ⌐ ⌀
Location Off Antrim road

Hotel ★★★ 66% Lansdowne Court Hotel,
657 Antrim Rd, BELFAST
☎ 01232 773317 25 ⇌ ⬧

Malone 240 Upper Malone Rd, Dunmurry BT17 9LB
☎ 01232 612758 (Office) & 614917 (Pro)
Fax 01232 431394
Two parkland courses, extremely attractive with a large lake, mature trees and flowering shrubs and bordered by the River Lagan. Very well maintained and offering a challenging round.
Main Course: 18 holes, 6599yds, Par 71, SSS 71.
Edenderry: 9 holes, 6320yds, Par 72, SSS 70.
Club membership 1300.
Visitors advisable to contact pro-shop in advance. Main Course: Unable to play Sat, Sun morning or Tues. Edenberry: no restrictions
Societies apply in writing or fax to club manager. Large group normally Mon & Thu only.
Green Fees Main Course: £33 per day (£38 weekends); Edenberry: £17 per day (£22 weekends).
Cards ▭ ▬▬ ▬▬ ▢
Prof Michael McGee
Designer C K Cotton
Facilities ⊗ ⫫ ᴸᴮ ♥ ♀ ⌂ ☎ ⌐ 🔨 ⌀
& Leisure squash, fishing, bowls green.
Location 4.5m S opposite Lady Dixon Park

Hotel ★★★★ 67% Stormont Hotel,
587 Upper Newtonards Rd, BELFAST
☎ 01232 658621 109 ⇌ ⬧

Mount Ober Golf & Country Club 24 Ballymaconaghy Rd BT8 4SB ☎ 01232 401811 & 795666 Fax 01232 705862
Inland parkland course which is a great test of golf for all handicaps.
18 holes, 5419yds, Par 67, SSS 66, Course record 67.
Club membership 400.
Visitors must contact in advance at weekends & bank holidays, may play Sat after 3.30pm and Sun after 10.30am.
Societies book by telephone or fax.
Green Fees £12 per round (£14 weekends & bank holidays).
Cards ▭ ▬▬
Prof Geoff Loughrey/Steve Rourke
Facilities ⊗ ⫫ ᴸᴮ ♥ ♀ ⌂ ☎ ⌐ ⌀ ⌀
& Leisure ski slopes, American billiards hall.
Location Off Saintfield Road

Hotel ★★★★ 67% Stormont Hotel,
587 Upper Newtonards Rd, BELFAST
☎ 01232 658621 109 ⇌ ⬧

Ormeau 50 Park Rd BT7 2FX
☎ 01232 641069 Fax 01232 646250
Parkland.
9 holes, 2653mtrs, Par 68, SSS 65.
Club membership 520.
Visitors welcome weekdays except Tue after 2pm. May play Sat after 5.30pm & Sun by arrangement.
Societies contact in advance.

Green Fees not confirmed.
Prof Bertie Wilson
Facilities ⊗ ⫫ ᴸᴮ ♥ ♀ ⌂ ☎ ⌐ ⌀
Location S of city centre

Shandon Park 73 Shandon Park BT5 6NY
☎ 01232 401856
Fairly level parkland offering a pleasant challenge.
18 holes, 6261yds, Par 70, SSS 70.
Club membership 1100. •
Visitors may not play on competition days. Must contact in advance and have a handicap certificate.
Societies may play Mon & Fri only, applications to club.
Green Fees not confirmed.
Prof Barry Wilson
Facilities ⊗ ⫫ ᴸᴮ ♥ ♀ ⌂ ☎ ⌐ ⌀
Location Off Knock road

Hotel ★★★★ 67% Stormont Hotel,
587 Upper Newtonards Rd, BELFAST
☎ 01232 658621 109 ⇌ ⬧

DUNDONALD   Map 01 D5

Knock Summerfield BT16 2QX
☎ 01232 483251 & 482249 Fax 01232 483251
Parkland course with huge trees, deep bunkers and a river cutting across several fairways. This is a hard but fair course and will test the best of golfers.
18 holes, 6435yds, Par 70, SSS 71, Course record 66.
Club membership 900.
Visitors with member only on Sat, Mon & Thu are Society Days, Tue is Ladies Day, advisable to contact in advance.
Societies must contact in advance.
Green Fees £20 per day (£25 weekends & bank holidays).
Prof Gordon Fairweather
Designer Colt, Allison & McKenzie
Facilities ⊗ ⫫ ᴸᴮ ♥ ♀ ⌂ ☎ ⌐ ⌀ 🔨 ⌀

Hotel ★★★★ 75% Culloden Hotel, Bangor Rd, HOLYWOOD ☎ 01232 425223 79 ⇌ ⬧

NEWTOWNBREDA   Map 01 D5

The Belvoir Park 73 Church Rd BT8 7AN
☎ 01232 491693 Fax 01232 646113
This undulating parkland course is not strenuous to walk, but is certainly a test of your golf, with tree-lined fairways and a particularly challenging finish at the final four holes.
18 holes, 6516yds, Par 71, SSS 71, Course record 65.
Club membership 1000.
Visitors must contact in advance, may not play Sat.
Societies must contact in writing.
Green Fees £33 per day, excluding Wed (£38 Sun & holidays).
Prof Maurice Kelly
Designer H Holt
Facilities ⊗ ⫫ ᴸᴮ ♥ ♀ ⌂ ☎ ⌐ ⌀ 🔨 ⌀
Location 3m from city centre off Saintfield/Newcastle rd

Hotel ★★★★ 67% Stormont Hotel,
587 Upper Newtonards Rd, BELFAST
☎ 01232 658621 109 ⇌ ⬧

CO DOWN

ARDGLASS
Map 01 D5

Ardglass Castle Pl BT30 7TP
☎ 01396 841219 Fax 01396 841841
A scenic cliff-top seaside course with spectacular views and some memorable holes.
18 holes, 5498mtrs, Par 70, SSS 69, Course record 65.
Club membership 800.
Visitors must contact in advance.
Societies must contact in advance, welcome weekdays & restricted times Sun.
Green Fees not confirmed.
Cards 💳 🖥
Prof Philip Farrell
Facilities ⊗ 🎿 🖫 💺 🍸 ⚖ 🏠 🕈 🏌 ♂
Location 7m from Downpatrick on the B1

Hotel ★★★★ 64% Slieve Donard Hotel, Downs Rd,
NEWCASTLE ☎ 013967 23681 130 ⇄ ⋔

ARDMILLAN
Map 01 D5

Mahee Island Mahee Island, Comber BT23 6EP
☎ 01238 541234
An undulating parkland course, almost surrounded by water, with magnificent views of Strangford Lough and its islands, with Scrabo Tower in the background. The first professional here was Fred Daly (1933-4) who became British Open Champion in 1947.
9 holes, 5590yds, Par 68, SSS 67, Course record 68.
Club membership 500.
Visitors may not play on Wed after 5pm or Sat before 5pm.
Societies contact in advance.
Green Fees £10 per 18 holes (£15 weekends).
Facilities ⚖ 🏠 🕈 ♂
& Leisure pool table.
Location Off Comber/Killyleagh road to the left 0.5m from Comber

Hotel ★★★★ 67% Stormont Hotel,
587 Upper Newtonards Rd, BELFAST
☎ 01232 658621 109 ⇄ ⋔

BALLYNAHINCH
Map 01 D5

Spa 20 Grove Rd BT24 8PN
☎ 01238 562365 Fax 01238 564158
Parkland course with tree-lined fairways and scenic views of the Mourne Mountains.

18 holes, 6003mtrs, Par 72, SSS 72, Course record 66.
Club membership 907.
Visitors must contact in advance. No play on Sat.
Societies must contact in advance.
Green Fees £15 per round (£20 weekends & bank holidays).
Designer F Ainsworth
Facilities ⊗ 🎿 🖫 💺 🍸 ⚖ 🏠 🕈 🏌 ♂
Location 1m S on the Grove Rd

Hotel ★★★★ 64% Slieve Donard Hotel, Downs Rd,
NEWCASTLE ☎ 013967 23681 130 ⇄ ⋔

BANBRIDGE
Map 01 D5

Banbridge 116 Huntly Rd BT32 3UR
☎ 01820 662211 Fax 01820 669400
A picturesque course with excellent views of the Mourne mountains. The holes are not long, but are tricky.
18 holes, 5003mtrs, Par 69, SSS 67, Course record 62.
Club membership 700.
Visitors may not play Sat or before 11am on Sun. Ladies Day Tue.
Societies must contact in writing.
Green Fees Male: £15 per day (£20 weekends & bank holidays), Female: £12 per day (£15 weekends & bank holidays).
Designer F Ainsworth
Facilities ⊗ 🎿 🖫 💺 🍸 ⚖ 🏠 ♂
Location 0.5m along Huntly road

Hotel ★★★★ 64% Slieve Donard Hotel, Downs Rd,
NEWCASTLE ☎ 013967 23681 130 ⇄ ⋔

BANGOR
Map 01 D5

Bangor Broadway BT20 4RH
☎ 01247 270922 Fax 01247 453394
Undulating parkland course in the town. It is well maintained and pleasant and offers a challenging round, particularly at the 5th.
18 holes, 6424yds, Par 71, SSS 71, Course record 62.
Club membership 1147.
Visitors may not play Sat & weekdays 1-2.
Societies must contact in advance, Mon/Wed by telephone, Fri by letter.
Green Fees £20 (£25 Sun & bank holidays).
Prof Michael Bannon
Designer James Braid
Facilities ⊗ 🎿 🖫 💺 🍸 ⚖ 🏠 🕈 🏌 ♂
Location 1m from town on Donaghadee Road

Hotel ★★★ 63% Royal Hotel, Seafront, BANGOR
☎ 01247 271866 50 ⇄ ⋔

Blackwood Golf Centre 150 Crawfordsburn Rd,
Clandeboye BT19 1GB
☎ 01247 852706 Fax 01247 853785
The golf centre is a pay and play development with a computerised booking system for the 18-hole championship-standard Hamilton course. The course is built on mature woodland with man-made lakes that come into play on 5 holes. The Temple course is an 18-hole Par 3 course with holes ranging from the 75yd 1st to the 185yd 10th, which has a lake on the right of the green. Banked by gorse with streams crossing throughout, this Par 3 course is no pushover.

Hamilton Course: 18 holes, 6304yds, Par 71, SSS 70.
Temple Course: 18 holes, 2450yds, Par 54.
Visitors pay as you play, computerised booking system for the Hamilton Course, bookable 7 days in advance.
Societies telephone in advance.
Green Fees £15 (£20 weekends).
Cards ▭ ▭ ▭ ▭ ▭
Prof Roy Skillen/Debbie Hannha
Designer Simon Gidman
Facilities ⊗ ∭ ⌶ ♙ ♀ ☂ ⚐ ♂ ℩
Location 2m from Bangor, off A2 to Belfast

Hotel ★★★ 70% Clandeboye Lodge Hotel, 10 Estate Rd, Clandeboye, BANGOR
☎ 01247 852500 43 ⇋ ໂ

Carnalea Station Rd BT19 1EZ
☎ 01247 270368 Fax 01247 273989
A scenic course on the shores of Belfast Lough.
18 holes, 5574yds, Par 68, SSS 67, Course record 63.
Club membership 1200.
Visitors restricted Sat.
Societies must contact in advance.
Green Fees £15 per round (£19 weekends & bank holidays).
Prof Tom Loughran
Facilities ⊗ ∭ ⌶ ♙ ♀ ☂ ⚑ ⚐ ♂
Location 2m W adjacent to railway station

Hotel ★★★ 69% Old Inn, 15 Main St, CRAWFORDSBURN
☎ 01247 853255 33 ⇋ ໂ

Clandeboye Tower Rd, Conlig, Newtownards BT23 3PN
☎ 01247 271767 Fax 01247 473711
Parkland/heathland courses. The Dufferin is the championship course and offers a tough challenge demanding extreme accuracy, with its mass of gorse, bracken and strategically placed trees that flank every hole.The slightest error will be punished. The Ava compliments the Dufferin perfectly. Accuracy is also the key with a notable 2nd hole.
Dufferin Course: 18 holes, 6469yds, Par 71, SSS 71.
Ava Course: 18 holes, 5755yds, Par 71, SSS 68.
Club membership 1300.
Visitors must contact in advance.
Societies Mon-Wed, Fri & after 3pm Sat & Sun. Must contact in advance.
Green Fees Dufferin: £25 per round (£30 weekend); Ava: £20 per round (£25 weekend).
Cards ▭
Prof Peter Gregory
Designer William Robinson
Facilities ⊗ ∭ ⌶ ♙ ♀ ☂ ⚑ ⚐ ♂
& Leisure grass tennis courts.
Location 2m S on A1

Hotel ★★★ 63% Royal Hotel, Seafront, BANGOR
☎ 01247 271866 50 ⇋ ໂ

Helen's Bay Golf Rd, Helen's Bay BT19 1TL
☎ 01247 852815 & 852601 Fax 01247 852815
A parkland course on the shores of Belfast Lough with panoramic views along the Antrim coast. The 4th hole Par 3 is particularly challenging as the green is screened by high trees.
9 holes, 5181mtrs, Par 68, SSS 67.
Club membership 820.

Visitors welcome Sun, Mon, Wed, Thu (before 1.30pm), Fri (after 11.30am during Jul & Aug) & Sat after 6pm. Book in advance with secretary.
Societies welcome Sun, Mon, Wed, Thu (before 1.30pm), Fri & Sat after 6pm. Telephone secretary in advance.
Green Fees not confirmed.
Facilities ⊗ ∭ ⌶ ♙ ♀ ☂ ♂
Location A2 from Belfast

Hotel ★★★ 69% Old Inn, 15 Main St, CRAWFORDSBURN
☎ 01247 853255 33 ⇋ ໂ

CARRYDUFF Map 01 D5

Rockmount 28 Drumalig Rd, Carryduff BT8 8EQ
☎ 01232 812279 Fax 01232 815851
A demanding 18-hole course set in open parkland with mature trees, several streams, and a tricky lake at the 11th hole. Panoramic views.
18 holes, 6373yds, Par 71, SSS 71, Course record 68.
Club membership 700.
Visitors welcome except for Sat or Wed afternoon.
Societies welcome except for Wed & Sat, book by telephone.
Green Fees £18 (£22 Sun).
Cards ▭ ▭
Designer Robert Patterson
Facilities ⊗ ∭ ⌶ ♙ ♀ ☂ ⚑ ▾ ⚒ ♂
Location 10m S of Belfast

Hotel ★★ 59% Balmoral Hotel, Blacks Rd, Dunmurry, BELFAST
☎ 01232 301234 44 ⇋ ໂ

CLOUGHEY Map 01 D5

Kirkistown Castle 142 Main Rd, Cloughey BT22 1JA
☎ 012477 71233 Fax 012477 71699
A seaside semi-links popular with visiting golfers because of its quiet location. The course is exceptionally dry and remains open when others in the area have to close. The Par 4 10th is particularly distinctive with a long drive and a slight dogleg to a raised green with a gorse covered motte waiting for the wayward approach shot.
18 holes, 6167yds, Par 69, SSS 70, Course record 65.
Club membership 931.
Visitors must contact in advance, restricted weekends.
Societies contact in writing or by phone.
Green Fees not confirmed.
Cards ▭ ▭ ▭ ▶

Prof	Jonathan Peden
Designer	James Braid
Facilities	⊗ ⅲ ㊇ 🍺 ♀ ♨ 🏠 ⛳ ✦ ⚕

Hotel ★★★ 69% Old Inn, 15 Main St, CRAWFORDSBURN ☎ 01247 853255 33 ⇥ 🐾

DONAGHADEE   Map 01 D5

Donaghadee Warren Rd BT21 0PQ ☎ 01247 883624
Undulating seaside course requiring a certain amount of concentration. Splendid views.
18 holes, 5570mtrs, Par 71, SSS 69, Course record 65.
Club membership 1190.

Visitors	contact in advance.
Societies	telephone in advance.
Green Fees	£14 per round (£20 Sunday & bank holidays).
Prof	Gordon Drew
Facilities	⊗ ⅲ ㊇ 🍺 ♀ ♨ 🏠 ⛳ ⚕

Hotel ★★★ 69% Old Inn, 15 Main St, CRAWFORDSBURN ☎ 01247 853255 33 ⇥ 🐾

DOWNPATRICK   Map 01 D5

Bright Castle 14 Coniamstown Rd, Bright BT30 8LU
☎ 01396 841319
Parkland course in elevated position with views of the Mountains of Mourne. A good challenge for the energetic golfer.
18 holes, 7300yds, Par 74, SSS 74, Course record 69.
Club membership 60.

Visitors	no restrictions.
Societies	must contact in advance.
Green Fees	not confirmed.
Designer	Mr Ennis
Facilities	⊗ ⅲ ㊇ 🍺 ♨ 🚜 ⚕
Location	5m S

Hotel ★★★★ 64% Slieve Donard Hotel, Downs Rd, NEWCASTLE ☎ 013967 23681 130 ⇥ 🐾

Downpatrick 43 Saul Rd BT30 6PA
☎ 01396 615947 Fax 01396 617502
This undulating parkland course provides a good challenge.
18 holes, 6100yds, Par 70, SSS 69, Course record 66.
Club membership 800.

Visitors	must contact in advance.
Societies	must telephone in advance.
Green Fees	not confirmed.
Designer	Hawtree & Son
Facilities	⊗ ⅲ ㊇ 🍺 ♀ ♨ 🏠 ⛳ 🦶 🚜 ⚕
Location	1.5m from town centre

Hotel ★★ 65% Enniskeen House Hotel, 98 Bryansford Rd, NEWCASTLE ☎ 013967 22392 12 ⇥ 🐾

HOLYWOOD   Map 01 D5

Holywood Nuns Walk, Demesne Rd BT18 9LE
☎ 01232 423135 Fax 01232 425040
Hilly parkland course with some fine views and providing an interesting game. Several feature holes, including the short 6th "Nuns Walk" and the treacherous 12th "White House".

18 holes, 5480mtrs, Par 69, SSS 68, Course record 64.
Club membership 1100.

Visitors	must contact in advance.
Societies	must contact in writing.
Green Fees	Men: £15 per round (£20 weekends); Women: £10 (£20 weekends).
Prof	Michael Bannon
Facilities	⊗ ⅲ ㊇ 🍺 ♀ ♨ 🏠 ⛳ 🚜 ⚕ ⚘
Location	Just outside Belfast, off the Bangor dual carriageway, behind the town of Holywood

Hotel ★★★ 69% Old Inn, 15 Main St, CRAWFORDSBURN ☎ 01247 853255 33 ⇥ 🐾

The Royal Belfast Station Rd, Craigavad BT18 0BP
☎ 01232 428165 Fax 01232 421404
On the shores of Belfast Lough, this attractive course consists of wooded parkland on undulating terrain which provides a pleasant, challenging game.
18 holes, 6185yds, Par 70, SSS 69.
Club membership 1200.

Visitors	may not play on Wed or Sat before 4.30pm; must be accompanied by a member or present a letter of introduction from their own golf club. Must contact in advance.
Societies	must contact in writing.
Green Fees	£30 per round (£40 weekends & bank holidays).
Prof	Chris Spence
Designer	H C Colt
Facilities & Leisure	⊗ ⅲ ㊇ 🍺 ♀ ♨ 🏠 ⛳ ⚕ hard tennis courts, squash.
Location	2m E on A2

Hotel ★★★★ 75% Culloden Hotel, Bangor Rd, HOLYWOOD ☎ 01232 425223 79 ⇥ 🐾

KILKEEL   Map 01 D5

Kilkeel Mourne Park BT34 4LB
☎ 016937 65095 Fax 016937 65095
Picturesquely situated at the foot of the Mourne Mountains. Eleven holes have tree-lined fairways with the remainder in open parkland. The 13th hole is testing and a well positioned tee shot is essential.
18 holes, 6615yds, Par 72, SSS 72, Course record 69.
Club membership 650.

Visitors	may not play Sat, possible to play Sun, must contact in advance.
Societies	must contact in advance.
Green Fees	£18 (£20 weekends).
Designer	Babington/Hackett
Facilities & Leisure	⊗ ⅲ ㊇ 🍺 ♀ ♨ ⚕ ⚘ fishing.
Location	3m from Kilkeel on Newry road

Hotel ★★★★ 64% Slieve Donard Hotel, Downs Rd, NEWCASTLE ☎ 013967 23681 130 ⇥ 🐾

Call the AA Hotel Booking Service on
0870 5050505 to book at AA recognised hotels and B & Bs
in the UK and Ireland, or through our Internet site:
http://www.theaa.co.uk/hotels

MAGHERALIN   Map 01 D5

Edenmore Edenmore House, 70 Drumnabreeze Rd
BT67 0RH ☎ 01846 611310 Fax 01846 613310
Set in mature parkland with gently rolling slopes. The front
nine holes provide an interesting contrast to the back nine
with more open play involved. Many new paths and features
have been recently added.
18 holes, 6244yds, Par 71, SSS 70, Course record 71.
Club membership 350.
Visitors   telephone in advance, may not play until after
               2pm Sat & with member only Sun.
Societies   telephone in advance.
Green Fees not confirmed.
Designer   F Ainsworth
Facilities   ⊗ 🍴 🏌 ⛳ 🏠 🛈 ✆

Hotel   B Posthouse Belfast, Kingsway, Dunmurry,
            BELFAST ☎ 01232 612101   82 ⇔ 🌾

NEWCASTLE   Map 01 D5

ROYAL COUNTY DOWN See page 431

NEWRY   Map 01 D5

Newry 11 Forkhill Rd BT35 8LZ
☎ 01693 63871 Fax 01693 63871
Short 18-hole course enjoying panoramic views of the
Mourne Mountains and across Newry.
18 holes, 3000mtrs, Par 53, SSS 52, Course record 51.
Club membership 150.
Visitors   welcome anytime.
Societies   apply in writing or telephone.
Green Fees not confirmed.
Cards   🔲 🔲 🔲 🔲 🔲
Prof   Larry Heaney
Designer   Michael Heaney
Facilities   ⊗ 🍴 🏌 🏠 ⛳ 🚶 🏌
& Leisure   hard and grass tennis courts, outdoor and indoor
            heated swimming pools, clay pigeon shooting.
Location   1m from Newry just off the main Dublin road

Hotel   ★★ 65% Enniskeen House Hotel,
            98 Bryansford Rd, NEWCASTLE
            ☎ 013967 22392 12 ⇔ 🌾

NEWTOWNARDS   Map 01 D5

Scrabo 233 Scrabo Rd BT23 4SL
☎ 01247 812355 Fax 01247 822919
Hilly and picturesque, this course offers a good test of golf
for golfers of all abilities. It benefits from good drainage and
remains dry and playable most of the year.
18 holes, 5722mtrs, Par 71, SSS 71, Course record 65.
Club membership 1002.
Visitors   may not play on Saturdays. Contact in advance.
Societies   must contact in advance.
Green Fees £15 per round (£20 Sun).
Prof   Paul McCrystal
Facilities   ⊗ 🍴 🏌 🏠 ⛳ 🏌 ✆
Location   Borders of Newtownards on the Ards Peninsula,
            follow signs for Scrabo Country Park

Hotel   ★★★★ 67% Stormont Hotel,
            587 Upper Newtonards Rd, BELFAST
            ☎ 01232 658621 109 ⇔ 🌾

WARRENPOINT   Map 01 D5

Warrenpoint Lower Dromore Rd BT34 3LN
☎ 016937 53695 Fax 016937 52918
Parkland course with marvellous views and a need for
accurate shots.
18 holes, 6108yds, Par 71, SSS 70, Course record 61.
Club membership 1285.
Visitors   must contact in advance.
Societies   must contact in advance.
Green Fees £20 per round (£27 weekends & bank holidays).
Cards   🔲 🔲 🔲
Prof   Nigel Shaw
Facilities   ⊗ 🍴 🏌 🏠 ⛳ 🏠 🛈 ✆
& Leisure   squash.
Location   1m W

Hotel   ★★★★ 64% Slieve Donard Hotel, Downs Rd,
            NEWCASTLE ☎ 013967 23681 130 ⇔ 🌾

CO FERMANAGH

ENNISKILLEN   Map 01 C5

Ashwoods Golf Centre Sligo Rd BT74 7JY
☎ 01365 325321 & 322908
Only 1 mile from Lough Erne, this course is open
meadowland. It has been well planted with many young
trees.
14 holes, 1930yds, Par 42.
Visitors   no restrictions.
Societies   must book in advance.
Green Fees £5 per 14 holes.
Cards   🔲 🔲 🔲
Prof   Pat Trainor
Designer   P Loughran
Facilities   ⊗ 🍴 🏌 🏠 🏠 🛈 🚶 ✆ 🏌
Location   1.5m W

Hotel   ★★★ 70% Killyhevlin Hotel, ENNISKILLEN
            ☎ 01365 323481   43 ⇔ 🌾

Castle Hume Castle Hume BT93 7ED
☎ 01365 327077 Fax 01365 327076
Castle Hulme is a particularly scenic and challenging course.
Set in undulating parkland with large rolling greens, rivers,
lakes and water hazards all in play on a championship
standard course.
18 holes, 6400yds, Par 72, SSS 70, Course record 69.
Club membership 225.
Visitors   may play any time subject to advance
            arrangement.
Societies   telephone in advance.
Green Fees not confirmed.
Cards   🔲 🔲
Designer   B Browne

▶

Facilities ⊗ by prior arrangement ⬛ 🍽 ♀ ♿ 🏧 ⛽ 🏌 🛒 ✏
& Leisure fishing.
Location 4m from Enniskillen on the Belleek Rd

Hotel ★★★ 70% Killyhevlin Hotel, ENNISKILLEN
☎ 01365 323481 43 ⇆ 🍴

Enniskillen Castlecoole BT74 6HZ ☎ 01365 325250
Meadowland course in Castle Coole estate.
18 holes, 5588mtrs, Par 71, SSS 69, Course record 67.
Club membership 600.
Visitors restricted Tue and weekends. Contact Hon
Secretaryor bar steward.
Societies must contact club steward in advance.
Green Fees £15 per day (£18 weekends & bank holidays).
Facilities ⊗ by prior arrangement 🍽 by prior arrangement
⬛ 🍽 ♀ ♿ ⛽ 🛒 ✏
Location 1m E

Hotel ★★★ 70% Killyhevlin Hotel, ENNISKILLEN
☎ 01365 323481 43 ⇆ 🍴

CO LONDONDERRY

AGHADOWEY Map 01 C6

Brown Trout Golf & Country Inn 209 Agivey Rd BT51
4AD ☎ 01265 868209 Fax 01265 868878
A challenging course with two par 5s. During the course of
the 9 holes, players have to negotiate water 7 times and all
the fairways are lined with densely packed fir trees.
9 holes, 5510yds, Par 70, SSS 68, Course record 66.
Club membership 250.
Visitors no restrictions.
Societies must contact by telephone, restricted tee-off
times Sun.
Green Fees £10 per day (£15 weekends & bank holidays).
Cards 💳 💳 💳 💳 💳
Prof Ken Revie
Designer Bill O'Hara Snr
Facilities ⊗ 🍽 🏧 ⬛ 🍽 ♀ ♿ 🛒 🏌 ✏
& Leisure fishing, gymnasium.
Location Junc of A54 & B66

Hotel ★★ 67% Brown Trout Golf & Country Inn,
209 Agivey Rd, AGHADOWEY
☎ 01265 868209 17 ⇆ 🍴

CASTLEDAWSON Map 01 C5

Moyola Park 15 Curran Rd BT45 8DG
☎ 01648 468468 & 468830 (Prof) Fax 01648 468468
Parkland course with some difficult shots, calling for length
and accuracy. The Moyola River provides a water hazard at
the 8th. Newly designed par 3, demands good shot placement
to a green on an island in the Moyola river, players
capabilities will be tested by the undulating green.
18 holes, 6522yds, Par 71, SSS 70, Course record 67.
Club membership 1000.

Visitors contact professional in advance, G.U.I. dress
code applies, Ladies day Wednesday, Sat & Sun
after 2pm, book in advance to avoid
dissappointment.
Societies must contact in advance, preferably in writing
Green Fees not confirmed.
Prof Vivian Teague
Designer Don Patterson
Facilities ⊗ 🍽 🏧 ⬛ 🍽 ♀ ♿ 🏧 ⛽ 🏌 ✏
Location 3m NE of Magherafelt

Hotel ★★★★ 70% Galgorm Manor, BALLYMENA
☎ 01266 881001 23 ⇆ 🍴

CASTLEROCK Map 01 C6

Castlerock 65 Circular Rd BT51 4TJ
☎ 01265 848314 Fax 01265 849440
A most exhilarating course with three superb par 4s, four
testing short holes and five par 5s. After an uphill start,
the hazards are many, including the river and a railway,
and both judgement and accuracy are called for. A
challenge in calm weather, any trouble from the elements
will test your golf to the limits.
Mussenden Course: 18 holes, 6499yds, Par 73, SSS 72,
Course record 67.
Bann Course: 9 holes, 2588mtrs, Par 34, SSS 33.
Club membership 1120.
Visitors contact in advance and must be members of
a recognised club.
Societies must contact in advance.
Green Fees Mussenden: £25 per round (£35 weekends
& bank holidays); Bann: £10 per round (£14
weekends & bank holidays).
Prof Robert Kelly
Designer Ben Sayers
Facilities ⊗ 🍽 🏧 ⬛ 🍽 ♀ ♿ 🏧 ⛽ ✏
Location 6m from Coleraine on A2

Hotel ★★★ 63% Causeway Coast Hotel,
36 Ballyreagh Rd, PORTRUSH
☎ 01265 822435 41 ⇆ 🍴

KILREA Map 01 C5

Kilrea Drumagarner Rd
A relatively short undulating inland course with tight
fairways and small greens. The opening hole is a long par 3,
particularly into the wind.
9 holes, 4514yds, Par 62, SSS 62, Course record 61.
Club membership 300.
Visitors welcome but restricted Tue pm, Wed pm during
summer and Sat all year.
Societies contact D P Clarke (Sec), 37 Townhill Rd,
Portglenone, Co Antrim BT44 8AD.
Green Fees not confirmed.
Facilities ♿

Hotel ★★ 67% Brown Trout Golf & Country Inn,
209 Agivey Rd, AGHADOWEY
☎ 01265 868209 17 ⇆ 🍴

Entries with a shaded background
identify courses that are
considered to be particularly interesting

ROYAL COUNTY DOWN

NEWCASTLE *Co Down* ☎ 013967 23314
Fax 013967 26281   **Map 01 D5**

Charlie Mulqueen writes: Where the mountains of Mourne sweep down to the sea – that's the location for one of the game's most beautiful and challenging golf courses, Royal Co Down alongside the lovely seaside town of Newcastle. There can be few grander places when the sun shines on the Mournes and on the Irish Sea and on the furze bushes that dot the sides of almost every fairway, turning the whole scene into one of riotous colour in early summer.

The most prestigious Championships, including the British Amateur, men's and ladies', and the Curtis Cup have come to Newcastle where the game began in 1889. Legend has it that Old Tom Morris was commissioned to lay out a course at a cost not exceeding £4. Another of golf's early greats, Harry Vardon, reconstructed the links in 1908, the same year it was made 'Royal' by Edward VII. Slight changes here and there over the decades have served only to make Newcastle a finer and fairer challenge.

Most people's favourite hole at Newcastle is the 9th, a none too difficult par five of less than 500 yards, but it has been suggested that the chief hazards of the hole are the distracting views of the sea and Slieve Donard, the highest of the Mourne Mountains – a breathtaking sight perhaps unrivalled in all of golf. .

However, nobody should run away with the idea that this is anything other than an outstanding test of golf where length, accuracy and a sure touch on the many fiercely undulating greens are all essential attributes. The 13th is such a beautiful hole that it was copied at a course in Cincinatti, Ohio…Newcastle is that kind of place, a jewel among golf courses.

Visitors	advisable to contact in advance. May not play Annesley course on Saturdays. May not play on Championship Course Sat, Sun am or Wed after 9am
Societies	telephone for availability and confirm in writing.
Green fees	Championship £65 (£95 weekends); Annesley £15 (£22 weekends) 〓 ▦ 〓 ▨
Facilities	⊗ ⓑ ♥ ♀ ⌂ 🛅 ⛏ ✓ Professional (Kevan Whitson)
Location	Newcastle BT33 0AN

36 holes. **Championship Course 18 holes, 7037yds, Par71 SSS 74. Course record 66 Annesley Links Course 18 holes, 4681yds, Par 66 SSS 63**

WHERE TO STAY AND EAT NEARBY

HOTELS:

NEWCASTLE
★★★★ 62% Slieve Donard Hotel, Downs Road ☎ 013967 23681 130 ⇌ ⋔

★★ 65% Enniskeen Hotel, 98 Bryansford Rd ☎ 013967 22392 12 (1 ⇌ ⋔ 3 ⋔ 8 ⇌)

LIMAVADY
Map 01 C6

Benone 53 Benone Ave BT49 0LQ
☎ 015047 50555 & 50919
9 holes, 1458yds, Par 27.
Visitors no reservations.
Societies telephone in advance.
Green Fees not confirmed.
Facilities 🍺 ♨ ⛳ ♪
& Leisure hard tennis courts, heated outdoor swimming
pool, bowling green.
Location Between Coleraine/Limavady on A2

Radisson Roe Park Hotel & Golf Resort Roe Park
BT49 9LB ☎ 015047 22222 Fax 015047 22313
A parkland course opened in 1992 on an historic Georgian
estate. The course surrounds the original buildings and a
driving range has been created in the old walled garden. Final
holes 15-18 are particularly memorable with water, trees,
out-of-bounds, etc to provide a testing finish.
18 holes, 6318yds, Par 70, SSS 35.
Club membership 500.

Visitors advance booking recommended. Handicap
certificate required.
Societies contact in advance.
Green Fees not confirmed.
Cards 💳 💳 💳 💳 💳 💳
Prof Seamus Duffy
Designer Frank Ainsworth
Facilities ⊗ ⟨ 🍴 🍺 ♀ ♨ 🏠 ♪ 🏌 🎯 ♪ ♪
& Leisure heated indoor swimming pool, fishing, sauna,
solarium, gymnasium.
Location Just outside Limavady on A2
Ballykelly/Londonderry road

Hotel ★★★★ 71% Radisson Roe Park Hotel &
Golf Resort, LIMAVADY
☎ 015047 22222 64 ⇆ 🏨

LONDONDERRY
Map 01 C5

City of Derry 49 Victoria Rd BT47 2PU
☎ 01504 346369 Fax 01504 310008
Two parkland courses on undulating parkland with good
views and lots of trees. The 9-hole course will particularly
suit novices.
*Prehen Course: 18 holes, 6406yds, Par 71, SSS 71, Course
record 68.*
Dunhugh Course: 9 holes, 4708yds, Par 63.
Club membership 823.
Visitors must make a booking to play on Prehen Course
at weekends or before 4.30pm on weekdays.

Societies must contact in advance.
Green Fees £20 per day (£25 weekends & bank holidays).
Cards 💳
Prof Michael Doherty
Facilities ⊗ ⟨ 🍺 🍴 ♀ ♨ 🏠 ♪
Location 2m S

Hotel ★★★★ 67% Everglades Hotel, Prehen Rd,
LONDONDERRY ☎ 01504 346722 64 ⇆ 🏨

Foyle International Golf Centre 12 Alder Rd BT48 8DB
☎ 01504 352222 Fax 01504 353967
Foyle International boasts a championship course, a 9 hole
par 3 course and a driving range. It is a fine test of golf with
water coming into play on the 3rd, 10th and 11th holes. The
6th green overlooks the Amelia Earhart centre.
18 holes, 6678yds, Par 72, SSS 71, Course record 70.
Club membership 250.
Visitors welcome any time, no retrictions.
Societies booking up to 12 months in advance with
deposit.
Green Fees £11 (£14 weekends & bank holidays). Par 3
£4/£4.50.
Cards 💳 💳 💳 💳
Prof Kieran McLaughlin
Designer Frank Ainsworth
Facilities ⊗ ⟨ 🍴 🍺 ♀ ♨ 🏠 ♪ 🏌 🎯 🚲 ♪ ♪
& Leisure 9 hole par3.
Location 1.5m from Foyce Bridge driving torwards
Moville

Hotel ★★★ 69% Trinity Hotel, 22-24 Strand Rd,
DERRY CITY ☎ 01504 271271 40 ⇆ 🏨

PORTSTEWART
Map 01 C6

Portstewart 117 Strand Rd BT55 7PG
☎ 01265 832015
Three links courses with spectacular views, offering a
testing round on the Strand course in particular.
Strand Course: 18 holes, 6784yds, Par 72, SSS 72.
Old Course: 18 holes, 4733yds, Par 64, SSS 62.
3: 9 holes, 2622yds, Par 32.
Club membership 1460.
Visitors preferred on weekdays.
Societies must contact in advance.
Green Fees not confirmed.
Prof Alan Hunter
Facilities ⊗ ⟨ 🍴 🍺 ♀ ♨ 🏠 ♪ ♪

Hotel ★★★ 63% Causeway Coast Hotel,
36 Ballyreagh Rd, PORTRUSH
☎ 01265 822435 41 ⇆ 🏨

CO TYRONE

COOKSTOWN
Map 01 C5

Killymoon 200 Killymoon Rd BT80 8TW
☎ 016487 63762 & 62254
Parkland course on elevated, well drained land.
18 holes, 5481mtrs, Par 70, SSS 69, Course record 64.
Club membership 950.

Visitors   booking essential through proshop on
016487 63460.
Societies   must contact in advance.
Green Fees not confirmed.
Prof   Gary Chambers
Facilities   ⊗ �em ⮂ 🏌 🛒 ♀ ⚑ 🏠 ♂

Hotel   ★★ 67% Royal Arms Hotel, 51 High St,
OMAGH ☎ 01662 243262   19 ⇄ ⬛

DUNGANNON   Map 01 C5

Dungannon 34 Springfield Ln BT70 1QX
☎ 01868 722098 or 727338 Fax 01868 727338
Parkland course with five par 3s and tree-lined fairways.
18 holes, 5950yds, Par 71, SSS 68, Course record 62.
Club membership 600.
Visitors   contact in advance, may not play before 4pm
Sat.
Societies   apply in writing to secretary.
Green Fees £15 per day (£18 weekends).
Prof   Alistair Fleming
Designer   Sam Bacon
Facilities   ♀ ⚑ 🏠 ♂
Location   0.5m outside town on Donaghmore road

Hotel   L The Cohannon Inn, 212 Ballynakilly Rd,
DUNGANNON ☎ 01868 724488   50 ⇄ ⬛

FINTONA   Map 01 C5

Fintona Ecclesville Demesne, 1 Kiln St BT78 2BJ
☎ 01662 841480 & 840777 (office) Fax 01662 841480
Attractive 9-hole parkland course with a notable water
hazard - a trout stream that meanders through the course
causing many problems for badly executed shots.
9 holes, 5765mtrs, Par 72, SSS 70.
Club membership 400.
Visitors   advised to contact in advance at weekends.
Societies   apply in writing well in advance, weekends not
advisable as competitions played.
Green Fees £15 per day.
Facilities   ⊗ by prior arrangement �em by prior arrangement
⮂ by prior arrangement 🛒 ♀ ⚑
Location   8m S of Omagh

Hotel   ★★ 67% Mahons Hotel, Mill St,
IRVINESTOWN ☎ 013656 21656 18 ⇄ ⬛

NEWTOWNSTEWART   Map 01 C5

Newtownstewart 38 Golf Course Rd BT78 4HU
☎ 016626 61466 & 62242 (pro shop) Fax 016626 62506
Parkland course bisected by a stream. Deer and pheasant are
present on the course.
18 holes, 5468mtrs, Par 70, SSS 69, Course record 66.
Club membership 700.
Visitors   contact in advance.
Societies   must contact secretary in advance.
Green Fees not confirmed.
Cards   ⊟ ▬▬
Facilities   ⊗ by prior arrangement �em by prior arrangement
⮂ by prior arrangement 🛒 ♀ ⚑ 🏠 ⛳ 🛺 ♂
♂
& Leisure tennis courts.
Location   2m SW on B84

Hotel   ★★ 67% Royal Arms Hotel, 51 High St,
OMAGH ☎ 01662 243262   19 ⇄ ⬛

OMAGH   Map 01 C5

Omagh 83a Dublin Rd BT78 1HQ
☎ 01662 243160 Fax 01662 241442
Undulating parkland course beside the River Drumnagh, with
the river coming into play on 4 of the holes.
18 holes, 5674mtrs, Par 71, SSS 70.
Club membership 850.
Visitors   play restricted Sat, no need to contact unless
large numbers.
Societies   must contact in advance.
Green Fees £10 per day (£15 weekends & bank holidays).
Facilities   ⮂ 🛒 ♀ ⚑
Location   On S outskirts of town

Hotel   ★★ 67% Royal Arms Hotel, 51 High St,
OMAGH ☎ 01662 243262   19 ⇄ ⬛

STRABANE   Map 01 C5

Strabane Ballycolman Rd ☎ 01504 382271 & 382007
Testing parkland course with the River Mourne running
alongside and creating a water hazard.
18 holes, 5537mtrs, Par 69, SSS 69, Course record 62.
Club membership 650.
Visitors   by arrangement.
Societies   must telephone in advance.
Green Fees not confirmed.
Designer   Eddie Hackett/P Jones
Facilities   ⊗ by prior arrangement �em by prior arrangement
⮂ 🛒 ♀ ⚑

Hotel   ★★ 67% Royal Arms Hotel, 51 High St,
OMAGH ☎ 01662 243262   19 ⇄ ⬛

REPUBLIC OF IRELAND

CO CARLOW

BORRIS   Map 01 C3

Borris Deerpark ☎ 0503 73310
Testing parkland course with tree-lined fairways situated
within the McMorrough Kavanagh Estate at the foot of
Mount Leinster.
9 holes, 6120mtrs, Par 70, SSS 69, Course record 66.
Club membership 400.
Visitors   advised to contact in advance, weekends very
restricted.
Societies   applications in writing.
Green Fees IR£12 per 18 holes.
Facilities   ⊗ �em ⮂ 🛒 ♀ ⚑ ♂

Hotel   ★★★★ 🍴 Mount Juliet Hotel,
THOMASTOWN
☎ 056 73000 32 ⇄ ⬛ Annexe24 ⇄ ⬛

CARLOW
Map 01 C3

Carlow Deerpark ☎ 0503 31695 Fax 0503 40065
Created in 1922 to a design by Tom Simpson, this testing
and enjoyable course is set in a wild deer park, with
beautiful dry terrain and a varied character. With sandy
sub-soil, the course is playable all year round. There are
water hazards at the 2nd, 10th and 11th and only two par
5s, both offering genuine birdie opportunities.
18 holes, 5974mtrs, Par 70, SSS 69, Course record 62.
Club membership 1200.

Visitors	are welcome, although play is limited on Tue and difficult on Sat & Sun. Must contact in advance.
Societies	must book in advance.
Green Fees	not confirmed.
Cards	▭▭ ▭▭
Prof	Andrew Gilbert
Designer	Tom Simpson
Facilities	⊗ 〴 ╚ ☕ ♀ ⏶ 🏠 ☂ ⋄
Location	2m N of Carlow on N9

Hotel	★★★ 72% Dolmen Hotel, Kilkenny Rd, CARLOW ☎ 0503 42002 40 ⇆ ♜

CO CAVAN

BALLYCONNELL
Map 01 C4

Slieve Russell Hotel Golf & Country Club
☎ 049 26444 & 26458 Fax 049 26474
An 18-hole course opened in 1992 and rapidly
establishing itself as one of the finest parkland courses in
the country. A 9-hole course was recently opened to
complement it. On the main course, the 2nd plays across
water while the 16th has water surrounding the green.
The course finishes with a 519 yard, Par 5 18th.
18 holes, 6650yds, Par 72, SSS 72, Course record 67.
Club membership 550.

STOP PRESS * STOP PRESS * STOP PRESS * STOP PRESS
Republic of Ireland - Telephone Number Changes

Some telephone codes have changed during the production of the guide. Only the new number can be dialled when contacting golf
courses located in the areas listed below.

National Dialling Code (NDC)	Numbering Area	Leading Digits of Current Numbers	New Prefix
41	Drogheda	2, 3, 4, 7, 8	98
41	Ardee	5, 6	68
42	Dundalk	2, 3, 5, 7, 8	93
42	Carrickmoss	6, 90, 91, 92, 94, 98	96
42	Castleblayney	4, 95	97
49	Cavan	3, 6, 7	43
49	Cootehill	5	55
49	Oldcastle	4	85
49	Belturbet	2	95
65	Ennis	2, 3, 4, 6	68
65	Ennistymon	7, 8	70
65	Kilrush	5	90
66	Tralee	2, 3, 4, 8	71
66	Dingle	5	91
66	Cahirciveen	7	94
66	Killorglin	6, 9	97

Number Changes in the Cork Area
In the Cork area there will be a two-phase process. Local numbers beginning with 40, 43 or 33 will be prefixed with a 2 or
a 7 (see Phase 1 below). In phase two, these new 2 or 7 numbers will be prefixed with a 4 (see Phase 2 below), as will the
other first digits.

National Dialling Code (NDC)	Numbering Area	Leading Digits of Current Numbers	New Prefix
PHASE 1			
21	Cork	40	2
21	Coachford	43, 33	7
PHASE 2			
21	Cork	2, 3, 5, 8, 9	4
21	Midleton		4
21	Kinsale	7	4

IN CASE OF DIFFICULTIES, PLEASE CONSULT DIRECTORY ENQUIRIES

Visitors	must book in advance for Saturdays.

Visitors must book in advance for Saturdays.
Societies write or telephone in advance, not allowed Sat.
Green Fees IR£30 per round (IR£38 Sat).
Cards 🔲🔳🔳
Prof Liam McCool
Designer Paddy Merrigan
Facilities ⊗ ⅢⅢ ℄ ⬛ ♀ ⚲ ⛳ ⛳ ⛳ ⚷ ℓ
& Leisure hard tennis courts, heated indoor swimming pool, squash, sauna, solarium, gymnasium, snooker and pool room.
Location 1.5m E of Ballyconnell

Hotel ★★★★ 67% Slieve Russell Hotel Golf and Country Club, BALLYCONNELL
☎ 049 26444 151 ⇆ ℟

BELTURBET   Map 01 C4

Belturbet Erne Hill ☎ 049 22287
Beautifully maintained parkland course with predominantly family membership and popular with summer visitors.
9 holes, 5480yds, Par 68, SSS 65, Course record 64.
Club membership 150.
Visitors must contact in advance.
Societies must contact secretary in advance.
Green Fees not confirmed.
Facilities ℄ ⬛ ♀ ⚲

Hotel ★★★★ 67% Slieve Russell Hotel Golf and Country Club, BALLYCONNELL
☎ 049 26444 151 ⇆ ℟

BLACKLION   Map 01 C5

Blacklion Toam ☎ 072 53024
Parkland course established in 1962, with coppices of woodland and mature trees. The lake comes into play on two holes and there are some magnificent views of the lake, islands and surrounding hills. It has been described as one of the best maintained and scenic inland course in Ireland.
9 holes, 5614mtrs, Par 72, SSS 69.
Club membership 250.
Visitors groups of 8 or more must contact in advance on Thursdays or Saturdays. No societies Sunday
Societies must contact in advance.
Green Fees IR£8 (IR£12 weekends & bank holidays).
Designer Eddie Hackett
Facilities ℄ ⬛ ♀ ⚲ ⚷
& Leisure fishing.

Hotel ★★★ 71% Sligo Park Hotel, Pearse Rd, SLIGO ☎ 071 60291 109 ⇆ ℟

CAVAN   Map 01 C4

County Cavan Drumelis ☎ 049 31541 Fax 049 31541
Parkland course.
18 holes, 5519mtrs, Par 70, SSS 69, Course record 66.
Club membership 830.
Visitors welcome but restricted at weekends.
Societies contact for details.
Green Fees not confirmed.
Prof Garan Carroll
Designer Eddie Hackett
Facilities ⊗ ⅢⅢ ℄ ⬛ ♀ ⚲ 🏠 ⚷
Location On Killeshandra rd

Hotel ★★★ 65% Kilmore Hotel, Dublin Rd, CAVAN ☎ 049 32288 39 ⇆ ℟

VIRGINIA   Map 01 C4

Virginia ☎ 049 47235 & 48066
9 holes, 4139mtrs, Par 64, SSS 62, Course record 57.
Club membership 500.
Visitors may not play Thu & Sun.
Societies must apply in writing to secretary.
Green Fees IR£8.
Facilities ⚲ ⛳ 🏠
& Leisure fishing.
Location By Lough Ramor

Hotel ★★ 67% Conyngham Arms Hotel, SLANE
☎ 041 24155 16rm(15 ⇆ ℟)

CO CLARE

CLONLARA   Map 01 B3

Clonlara Golf & Leisure ☎ 061 354141 Fax 061 354143
A 12-hole parkland course, Par 47, on the banks of the River Shannon with views of Clare Hills. Set in grounds of 63 acres surrounding the 17th century Landscape House, there is also a leisure complex for self-catering holidays.
12 holes, 5187mtrs, Par 71, SSS 69.
Club membership 100.
Visitors players only no accompanying persons.
Societies welcome subject to availability prior notice required.
Green Fees IR£5 per 12 holes Mon-Sat (IR£7 Sun & bank holidays).
Designer Noel Cassidy
Facilities ℄ ⬛ ♀ ⚲ ⛳ 🏠 ⚷
& Leisure hard tennis courts, fishing, sauna, games room, childrens play area.
Location 7m NE of Limerick

Hotel ★★★★ 71% Castletroy Park Hotel, Dublin Rd, LIMERICK ☎ 061 335566 107 ⇆ ℟

ENNIS   Map 01 B3

Ennis Drumbiggle ☎ 065 6824074 Fax 065 6841848
On rolling hills, this immaculately manicured course presents an excellent challenge to both casual visitors and aspiring scratch golfers, with tree-lined fairways and well protected greens.
18 holes, 5338mtrs, Par 70, SSS 69, Course record 65.
Club membership 1000.
Visitors advisable to contact in advance, course available Mon-Sat at most times.
Societies apply in writing.
Green Fees IR£18 per round.
Cards 🔲🔳
Prof Martin Ward
Facilities ⊗ ⅢⅢ ℄ ⬛ ♀ ⚲ 🏠 ⛳ ⚷
Location Close to town, well signposted

▶

Hotel ★★★65% Auburn Lodge Hotel, Galway Rd,
ENNIS ☎ 065 21247 100 ⇄ 🐾

KILKEE   Map 01 B3

Kilkee East End ☎ 065 56048
Well established course on the cliffs of Kilkee Bay, with
beautiful views.
18 holes, 6500yds, Par 72, SSS 71, Course record 68.
Club membership 390.
Visitors must book in advance.
Societies apply in writing.
Green Fees not confirmed.
Facilities ⓧ 🎋 🛗 ⬛ ♀ 🛆 📸 🍴 🖚 ♂
& Leisure squash, sauna.

Hotel ★★60% Halpin's Hotel, Erin St, KILKEE
☎ 065 56032 12 ⇄ 🐾

KILRUSH   Map 01 B3

Kilrush Parknamoney ☎ 065 51138 Fax 065 52633
Parkland course that was extended to 18 holes in the summer
of 1994.
18 holes, 5986yds, Par 70, SSS 70, Course record 68.
Club membership 425.
Visitors welcome, contact in advance.
Societies by prior arrangement.
Green Fees not confirmed.
Cards 💳
Facilities 🛆 📸 🍴 🖚 ♂

Hotel ★★60% Halpin's Hotel, Erin St, KILKEE
☎ 065 56032 12 ⇄ 🐾

LAHINCH   Map 01 B3

Lahinch ☎ 065 81003 Fax 065 81592
Originally designed by Tom Morris and later modified
by Dr Alister MacKenzie, Lahinch has hosted every
important Irish amateur fixture and the Home
Internationals. The par five 5th - The Klondike - is
played along a deep valley and over a huge dune; the par
three 6th may be short, but calls for a blind shot over the
ridge of a hill to a green hemmed in by hills on three
sides.
Old Course: 18 holes, 6696yds, Par 72, SSS 73.
Castle Course: 18 holes, 5594yds, Par 70, SSS 70.
Club membership 1840.
Visitors must contact in advance.
Societies apply in writing
Green Fees Old Course IR£50 per round ; Castle Course
IR£25 per round.
Cards 💳 💳
Prof R McCavery
Designer Alister MacKenzie
Facilities ⓧ 🎋 🛗 ⬛ ♀ 🛆 📸 🍴 ♂
Location 2m W of Ennisstymon on N67

Hotel ★★70% Sheedy's Restaurant & Hotel,
LISDOONVARNA ☎ 065 74026 11 ⇄ 🐾

Entries with a shaded background
identify courses that are
considered to be particularly interesting

MILLTOWN MALBAY   Map 01 B3

Spanish Point ☎ 065 84198 & 84219 Fax 065 84909
A 9-hole links course with 3 elevated greens and 4 elevated
tees. Overlooking Spanish Point beach.
9 holes, 4600mtrs, Par 64, SSS 63, Course record 59.
Club membership 250.
Visitors contact in advance. No green fees allowed
before 1pm Sun.
Societies apply in writing to the secretary 065 84219.
Green Fees IR£10 per day (IR£15 weekends Jun-Sep).
Prof Q
Facilities 🛗 ⬛ ♀ 🛆 🍴 ♂
Location 2m SW of Miltown Malbay, on N67

Hotel ★★★66% West County Conference & Leisure
Hotel, Clare Rd, ENNIS
☎ 065 23000 152 ⇄ 🐾

NEWMARKET-ON-FERGUS   Map 01 B3

Dromoland Castle Golf & Country Club
☎ 061 368444 & 368144 Fax 061 363355/368498
Set in 200 acres of parkland, the course is enhanced by
numerous trees and a lake. Three holes are played around the
lake which is in front of the castle.
18 holes, 6098yds, Par 71, SSS 72, Course record 67.
Club membership 500.
Visitors must contact in advance.
Societies contact in writing.
Green Fees IR£28 per day (IR£33 weekends and bank
holidays).
Cards 💳 💳 💳
Prof Philip Murphy
Designer Wigginton
Facilities ⓧ 🎋 🛗 ⬛ ♀ 🛆 📸 🍴 🐴 🖚 ♂
& Leisure hard tennis courts, fishing, sauna, solarium,
gymnasium.
Location 2m N, on main Limerick/Galway rd

Hotel ★★★61% Clare Inn Golf and Leisure Hotel,
NEWMARKET-ON-FERGUS
☎ 065 23000 161 ⇄ 🐾

SCARRIFF   Map 01 B3

East Clare Bodyke ☎ 061 921322
Beside Lough Derg, East Clare was opened in June 1992 as a
9-hole course in 148 acre site with natural trees and water on
well-drained land. An 18-hole championship course deigned
by Arthur Spring is in preparation.
9 holes, 52yds, Par 70, SSS 70 or 32 holes.
Club membership 130.
Visitors no restrictions unless there is a club competition
or a society playing.
Societies apply in writing, deposit required.
Green Fees not confirmed.
Facilities 🛆 🍴

Hotel ★★★66% West County Conference & Leisure
Hotel, Clare Rd, ENNIS
☎ 065 23000 152 ⇄ 🐾

Call the AA Hotel Booking Service on
0990 050505 to book at AA recognised hotels and B & Bs
in the UK and Ireland, or through our Internet site:
http://www.theaa.co.uk/hotels

SHANNON AIRPORT — Map 01 B3

Shannon ☎ 061 471849 Fax 061 471507
Superb parkland course with tree-lined fairways, strategically placed bunkers, water hazards and excellent greens, offering a challenge to all levels of players - including the many famous golfers who have played here.
18 holes, 6874yds, Par 72, SSS 74, Course record 65.
Club membership 1000.

Visitors	must contact in advance & have handicap certificate. Restricted play at certain times.
Societies	must contact in writing.
Green Fees	not confirmed.
Cards	⊟ 🖛
Prof	Artie Pyke
Designer	John Harris
Facilities	⊗ ⅋ ⅃ ⅃ ⅃ ♀ ♙ ⚑ 🏳 ⚓ ♣ ∫
Location	2m from Shannon Airport
Hotel	★★★ 61% Fitzpatrick Bunratty Hotel, BUNRATTY ☎ 061 361177 115 ⇔ 🐾

CO CORK

BANDON — Map 01 B2

Bandon Castlebernard ☎ 023 41111 Fax 023 44690
Lovely parkland course in pleasant rural surroundings.
18 holes, 5663mtrs, Par 70, SSS 69, Course record 66.
Club membership 900.

Visitors	welcome but may not play during club competitions. Must contact in advance.
Societies	must apply in writing or telephone well in advance.
Green Fees	IR£20 per day (IR£25 weekends & bank holidays).
Cards	🖛
Prof	Paddy O'Boyle
Facilities	⊗ ⅋ ⅃ ♀ ⅃ ⚑ 🏳 ♣
& Leisure	hard tennis courts.
Location	2.5km W
Hotel	★★★ 68% Innishannon House Hotel, INISHANNON ☎ 021 775121 12 ⇔ 🐾 Annexe1 ⇔ 🐾

BANTRY — Map 01 B2

Bantry Bay Bantry Bay
☎ 027 50579 & 50583 Fax 027 50579
Designed by Christy O'Connor Jnr and extended in 1997 to 18 holes, this challenging and rewarding course is idyllically set at the head of Bantry Bay. Testing holes include the par 5 of 487mtrs and the little par 3 of 127mtrs where accuracy is all-important.
18 holes, 5910mtrs, Par 71, SSS 72, Course record 71.
Club membership 550.

Visitors	advance booking recommended. At weekends and bank holidays visitors between 11.30-1.30pm and 3-4.30pm. Catering Mar-Oct only.
Societies	must apply in writing.
Green Fees	not confirmed.
Cards	⊟ 🖛
Prof	Finbar London
Designer	Christy O'Connor/Eddie Hackett
Facilities	⊗ ⅋ ⅃ ⅃ ♀ ⅃ ⚑ 🏳 ⚓ ♣
Location	3km N of Bantry town on the N71 Glengarrif road
Hotel	★★★ 58% Westlodge Hotel, BANTRY ☎ 027 50360 90 ⇔ 🐾

BLARNEY — Map 01 B2

Muskerry Carrigrohane
☎ 021 385297 Fax 021 385297
An adventurous game is guaranteed at this course, with its wooded hillsides and the meandering Shournagh River coming into play at a number of holes. The 15th is a notable hole - not long, but very deep - and after that all you need to do to get back to the clubhouse is stay out of the water.
18 holes, 6327yds, Par 71, SSS 71.
Club membership 712.

Visitors	may not play Wed afternoon & Thu morning. Some limited opportunities at weekends after 3.30pm. Must contact in advance.
Societies	must telephone in advance and then confirm in writing.
Green Fees	IR£23 per round, IR£12.50 before 10.30am (IR£25 per round weekends).
Cards	🖛
Prof	W M Lehane
Designer	Dr A McKenzie
Facilities	⊗ ⅋ ⅃ ⅃ ♀ ⅃ ⚑ 🏳 ♣
Location	2.5m W of Blarney
Hotel	★★★ 69% Blarney Park Hotel, BLARNEY ☎ 021 385281 91 ⇔ 🐾

CARRIGALINE — Map 01 B2

Fernhill Hotel & Golf Club
☎ 021 372226 Fax 021 371011
Parkland course.
18 holes, 5000mtrs, Par 69, SSS 68.
Club membership 150.

Visitors	available any time.
Societies	telephone in advance.
Green Fees	not confirmed.
Designer	M L Bowes
Facilities	⊗ ⅋ ⅃ ⅃ ♀ ⅃ ⚑ 🏳 ⚓ ♣ ∫
& Leisure	hard tennis courts, heated indoor swimming pool, fishing, sauna, 3 hole academy.
Location	2m from Ringaskiddy

CASTLETOWNBERE — Map 01 A2

Berehaven Millcove ☎ 027 70700
Seaside links founded in 1902.
9 holes, 2398mtrs, Par 68, SSS 66, Course record 63.

Visitors	welcome. Please check for major events.
Societies	telephone in advance.
Green Fees	IR£12 per day.
Cards	⊟ 🖛

▶

Facilities	⊗ by prior arrangement ﹰ by prior arrangement ﹰﹰﹰﹰﹰﹰﹰ
& Leisure	hard tennis courts, sauna.
Location	2m E on Glen Garriff Rd

Hotel	★★★▲▲ 74% Sea View Hotel, BALLYLICKEY ☎ 027 50073 50462 Fax 027 51555 17 ➡ ℝ

CHARLEVILLE   Map 01 B2

Charleville ☎ 063 81257 & 81515 Fax 063 81274
Wooded parkland course offering not too strenuous walking.
West Course: 18 holes, 6212yds, Par 71, SSS 69, Course record 65.
East Course: 9 holes, 6902yds, Par 72, SSS 72, Course record 72.
Club membership 1000.

Visitors	only prebooked at weekends.
Societies	contact in advance.
Green Fees	IR£15 per day (IR£20 weekends).
Cards	▭▭ ▭▭
Prof	David Keating
Designer	Eddie Connaughton
Facilities	⊗ ﹰﹰﹰ ﹰ ﹰ ♀ ♨ ⌂ ﹰ ﹰ ﹰ ﹰ
Location	2m W from town centre

Hotel	★★★▲▲ Longueville House Hotel, MALLOW ☎ 022 47156 & 47306 Fax 022 47459 20 ➡ ℝ

CLONAKILTY   Map 01 B2

Dunmore Dunmore, Muckross ☎ 023 33352
A hilly, rocky 9-hole course overlooking the Atlantic.
9 holes, 4464yds, Par 64, SSS 61, Course record 57.
Club membership 250.

Visitors	must contact in advance, may not play weekends.
Societies	apply in writing.
Green Fees	not confirmed.
Designer	E Hackett
Facilities	⊗ ﹰﹰﹰ ﹰ ﹰ ♀ ♨ ﹰ ﹰ ﹰ
Location	3.5m S of Clonakilty

Hotel	★★ 64% Courtmacsherry, COURTMACSHERRY ☎ 023 46198 13rm(9 ➡1 ℝ)

CORK   Map 01 B2

Cork Little Island ☎ 021 353451 Fax 021 353410
This championship-standard course is always kept in
superb condition and is playable all year round. It has
many memorable and distinctive features including holes
at the water's edge and holes in a disused quarry.
18 holes, 5910mtrs, Par 72, SSS 70, Course record 67.
Club membership 750.

Visitors	may not play 12.30-2pm or on Thu (Ladies Day), and only after 2pm Sat & Sun.
Societies	must contact in advance.
Green Fees	IR£40 per day (IR£45 weekends).
Cards	▭▭ ▭▭ ▭▭ ▭▭
Prof	Peter Hickey
Designer	Alister Mackenzie
Facilities	⊗ ﹰﹰﹰ ﹰﹰ ﹰ ♀ ♨ ⌂ ﹰ ﹰ
Location	5m E, on N25

Hotel	★★★★ 65% Jurys Hotel, Western Rd, CORK ☎ 021 276622 185 ➡ ℝ

Fitzpatrick Silver Springs Tivoli ☎ 021 507533
Five Par 4s and 4 Par3s make up this short 9-hole course.
The 4th has a 189 metre drive with out of bounds on the
righthand side.
9 holes, 1786mtrs, Par 32, Course record 26.
Club membership 70.

Visitors	no restrictions.
Societies	apply by telephone.
Green Fees	not confirmed.
Prof	Freddy Twomey
Designer	Eddie Hackett
Facilities	⊗ ﹰ ﹰ ♀ ♨ ﹰ ﹰﹰ ﹰ
& Leisure	hard tennis courts, heated indoor swimming pool, squash, sauna, solarium, gymnasium.
Location	1m E of city centre

Hotel	★★★★ 64% Fitzpatrick Silver Springs Hotel, Tivoli, CORK ☎ 021 507533 109 ➡ ℝ

Fota Island Carrigtwohill ☎ 021 883700 Fax 021 883713
Fota Island Golf Club is in the heart of the 780 acre island in
Cork Harbour which is recognised as one of Ireland's most
outstanding landscapes. The course is gently undulating
parkland routed among mature woodlands with occasional
views of the harbour. The overall design is very traditional,
featuring pot bunkers, a double green and undulating putting
surfaces. The 10th and 18th holes are narrow Par 5's that
require great accuracy and shotmaking skills. Fota has hosted
the Irish Club Professional Championship, the Irish PGA
Championship and the Irish Amateur Open.

18 holes, 6500yds, Par 72, SSS 72, Course record 67.
Club membership 400.

Visitors	advisable to contact in advance.
Societies	contact in advance.
Green Fees	not confirmed.
Cards	〰 💳 💳 💳
Prof	Kevin Morris
Designer	McEvoy/O'Connor
Facilities	⊗ 🍽 🏌 ♟ ♀ ⚐ ⛳ ☂ ♣ 🛒 ♂ ↾
Location	Off N25 E of Cork City. Take exit for Cobh, course 500m on right
Hotel	★★★ 66% Midleton Park, MIDLETON ☎ 021 631767 40 ⇆ 📻

The Ted McCarthy Municipal Golf Course Blackrock
☎ 021 294280
Municipal course which stretches alongside the river estuary, with some holes across water.
18 holes, 4818mtrs, Par 67, SSS 66.
Club membership 380.

Visitors	please contact in advance, may not play mornings at weekends.
Societies	please telephone in advance.
Green Fees	IR£11 (IR£12 weekends & bank holidays).
Designer	E Hackett
Facilities	⊗ 🍽 🏌 ♟ ♀ ⚐ ⛳ ☂ ♂
Location	2m from city centre
Hotel	★★★★ 64% Fitzpatrick Silver Springs Hotel, Tivoli, CORK ☎ 021 507533 109 ⇆ 📻

DONERAILE
Map 01 B2

Doneraile ☎ 022 24137 & 23427 (sec)
Parkland.
9 holes, 5528yds, SSS 66.
Club membership 500.

Visitors	no restrictions
Societies	welcome.
Green Fees	IR£10 per round.
Facilities	🏌 ♟ ♀ ⚐ ♂
Location	Off T11
Hotel	★★★ 63% Springfort Hall Hotel, MALLOW ☎ 022 21278 50 ⇆ 📻

DOUGLAS
Map 01 B2

Douglas ☎ 021 895297
Level inland course overlooking the city of Cork. Suitable for golfers of all ages and abilities. The course is under re-development for 1999 and therefore the measurements/details given below are due to change.
18 holes, 5383mtrs, Par 70, SSS 68.
Club membership 810.

Visitors	advisable to play Mon & Wed-Fri, contact in advance.
Societies	must contact in writing, dates allocated early Feb.
Green Fees	not confirmed.
Prof	Gary Nicholson
Designer	Harry Vardon
Facilities	♟ ⚐ ☂ ♂
Hotel	★★★★ 65% Jurys Hotel, Western Rd, CORK ☎ 021 276622 185 ⇆ 📻

FERMOY
Map 01 B2

Fermoy Corrin Cross
☎ 025 32694 (office) & 31472 (shop) Fax 025 33072
Rather exposed heathland course, bisected by a road.
18 holes, 5596mtrs, Par 70, SSS 69.
Club membership 950.

Visitors	contact in advance, must telephone in advance for weekends bookings
Societies	advisable to write or telephone in advance.
Green Fees	IR£13 (IR£16 weekends).
Prof	Brian Moriarty
Designer	John Harris
Facilities	⊗ 🍽 🏌 ♟ ♀ ⚐ ⛳ ☂ 🛒 ♂
Location	2m SW
Hotel	★★★🍴🍴 Longueville House Hotel, MALLOW ☎ 022 47156 & 47306 Fax 022 47459 20 ⇆ 📻

GLENGARRIFF
Map 01 B2

Glengarriff ☎ 027 63150 Fax 027 63575
Founded 1935.
9 holes, 2042mtrs, Par 66, SSS 62.
Club membership 300.

Visitors	welcome, details not supplied
Societies	apply to club.
Green Fees	not confirmed.
Facilities	🏌 ♟ ♀ ⚐ ☂ ♂
Location	On N71

►

Hotel   ★★★ 58% Westlodge Hotel, BANTRY
                ☎ 027 50360 90 ⇨ 🐾

KANTURK   Map 01 B2

Kanturk Fairyhill ☎ 029 50534
Scenic parkland course set in the heart of the Duhallow
region with superb mountain views. It provides a good test of
skill for golfers of all standards, with tight fairways requiring
accurate driving and precise approach shots to small and
tricky greens.
18 holes, 6262yds, Par 72, SSS 70, Course record 70.
Club membership 320.
Visitors   Ladies day Wed.
Societies   apply in writing or telephone the Secretary.
Green Fees not confirmed.
Designer   Richard Barry
Facilities 🏌 ♥ 🍴 🏖 ⚒
Location   1m from Kanturk on Fairyhill road, 2m off main
                Mallow/Killarney road from Ballymacquirke
                Cross

Guest   ▬▬▬▬ Assolas Country House, KANTURK
house   ☎ 029 50015 6 ⇨ 🐾 Annexe3 ⇨ 🐾

KINSALE   Map 01 B2

Kinsale Farrangalway ☎ 021 774722 Fax 021 773114
In addition to the existing 9-hole (Ringenane) course, a new
18-hole (Farrangalway) course was opened in 1994. Set in
unspoilt farmland and surrounded by peacefull rolling
countryside, it offers a stiff yet fair challenge to be enjoyed
by all standards of golfers. New putting green.
Farrangalway: 18 holes, 6440yds, Par 71, SSS 71, Course
record 70.
Ringenane: 9 holes, 5332yds, Par 70, SSS 68, Course record
67.
Club membership 740.
Visitors   welcome but may not be able to play at
                weekends. Contact in advance.
Societies   apply in writing.
Green Fees IR£22 (IR£27 weekends) IR£13 earlybird (until
                10am).
Prof   Ger Broderick
Designer   Jack Kenneally
Facilities ⊗ 🎿 🏌 ♥ 🍴 🏖 🏡 ⚒ ⚒
Location   On main Cork/Kinsale rd

Hotel   ★★★ 68% Trident Hotel, Worlds End,
                KINSALE ☎ 021 772301 58 ⇨ 🐾

Old Head ☎ 021 778444 Fax 021 778022
Opened for play in 1997 and designed by Ron Kirby and Joe
Carr, the Old Head course is spectacularly situated on a
promontory jutting out into the Atlantic. As well as bringing
the sea and cliffs into play, you have to contend with strong
prevailing winds - a fine test for all serious golfers.
18 holes, 6700yds, Par 72, SSS 73.
Club membership 150.
Visitors   tee time must be booked in advance.
Societies   pre booking necessary, rates for groups over 24.
Green Fees IR£150 per 36 holes; IR£90 per 18 holes.
Cards   ▬▬ 🔲 🔲
Designer   R Kirby/J Carr/P Merrigan/E Hackett
Facilities ⊗ 🎿 🏌 ♥ 🍴 🏖 🏡 ⚒ ⚒ ⚒

Location   From Cork city/airport, follow R600 to Kinsale,
                then signed to golf course

Hotel   ★★★ 73% Actons Hotel, Pier Rd, KINSALE
                ☎ 021 772135 76 ⇨ 🐾

LITTLE ISLAND   Map 01 B2

Harbour Point Clash Rd ☎ 021 353094 Fax 021 354408
A new championship-standard course in rolling countryside
on the banks of the River Lee at Cork's scenic harbour. A
distinctive and testing course for every standard of golfer.
18 holes, 5883metres, Par 72, SSS 71, Course record 71.
Visitors   must contact in advance.
Societies   telephone for bookings.
Green Fees IR£20 per round, IR5 for second round
                (IR£24/IR£10 weekends).
Cards   ▬▬ 🔲
Prof   Brendan McDaid
Designer   Patrick Merrigan
Facilities ⊗ 🎿 🏌 ♥ 🍴 🏖 🏡 ⚒ 🐾 🚜 ⚒ ⚒
& Leisure   practice area.
Location   5m E of Cork, take Rosslare road E from Cork
                city & exit at Little Island

Hotel   ★★★★ 64% Fitzpatrick Silver Springs Hotel,
                Tivoli, CORK ☎ 021 507533 109 ⇨ 🐾

MACROOM   Map 01 B2

Macroom Lackaduve ☎ 026 41072 Fax 026 41391
A particularly scenic parkland course located on undulating
ground along the banks of the River Sullane. Bunkers and
mature trees make a variable and testing course and the 12th
has a 50 yards carry over the river to the green.
18 holes, 5574mtrs, Par 72, SSS 70.
Club membership 600.
Visitors   restricted some weekends, contact in advance.
Societies   apply in writing.
Green Fees not confirmed.
Designer   Jack Kenneally
Facilities ⊗ 🎿 🏌 ♥ 🍴 🏖 ⚒ ⚒
Location   Through castle entrance in town square

Hotel   ★★ 72% Castle Hotel, Main St, MACROOM
                ☎ 026 41074 42 ⇨ 🐾

MALLOW   Map 01 B2

Mallow Ballyellis ☎ 022 21145 Fax 022 42501
Mallow Golf Club was first established in the late
1800's. A well wooded parkland course overlooking the

Blackwater Valley, Mallow is straightforward, but no less of a challenge for it. The front nine is by far the longer, but the back nine is demanding in its call for accuracy and the par 3 18th provides a tough finish.
18 holes, 5769metres, Par 72, SSS 71, Course record 67. Club membership 1400.

Visitors	must contact in advance.
Societies	apply in advance.
Green Fees	not confirmed.
Cards	▭ ▭
Prof	Sean Conway
Designer	D W Wishart
Facilities	⊗ 🍴 ⮿ ♥ ♀ ☂ 🏠 ❦ ✓
& Leisure	hard tennis courts, squash, sauna, snooker/billiards room, TV room.
Location	1m E of Mallow town
Hotel	★★★🎖 Longueville House Hotel, MALLOW ☎ 022 47156 & 47306 Fax 022 47459 20 ⇆ ♞

MIDLETON   Map 01 C2

East Cork Gortacrue ☎ 021 631687 Fax 021 613695
A well wooded course calling for accuracy of shots.
18 holes, 5491yds, Par 69, SSS 67, Course record 64. Club membership 530.

Visitors	may not play Sun mornings.
Societies	must telephone.
Green Fees	IR£15.
Prof	Don MacFarlane
Designer	E Hackett
Facilities	⊗ 🍴 ⮿ ♥ ♀ ☂ 🏠 ❦ ✓ ♝
& Leisure	squash.
Location	On the A626
Hotel	★★★ 66% Midleton Park, MIDLETON ☎ 021 631767 40 ⇆ ♞

MITCHELSTOWN   Map 01 B2

Mitchelstown Limerick Rd ☎ 025 27139
Attractive, gently undulating parkland course set in the Golden Vale, noted for the quality of the greens, the magnificent views of the Galtee Mountains and its friendly atmosphere. Ideal for golfers seeking tranquility and a golfing challenge.
18 holes, 5160mtrs, Par 67, SSS 68, Course record 65. Club membership 400.

Visitors	advisable to check in advance (information line 025 24231)

Societies	apply in writing or telephone.
Green Fees	IR£12 per day (IR£15 weekends) IR£40 per week.
Designer	David Jones
Facilities	⮿ ⮿ ♀ ☂ ✓
Location	0.75m on Limerick rd from Mitchelstown
Hotel	★★★🎖 Longueville House Hotel, MALLOW ☎ 022 47156 & 47306 Fax 022 47459 20 ⇆ ♞

MONKSTOWN   Map 01 B2

Monkstown Parkgariffe, Monkstown
☎ 021 841376 Fax 021 841376
Undulating parkland course with five tough finishing holes.
18 holes, 5441mtrs, Par 70, SSS 68, Course record 66. Club membership 960.

Visitors	restricted weekends, must contact in advance.
Societies	apply in writing or telephone. Large groups (24+) should book before Xmas.
Green Fees	not confirmed.
Prof	Batt Murphy
Facilities	⊗ 🍴 ⮿ ♥ ♀ ☂ 🏠 ❦ ✓ ♝
Location	0.5m SE of Monkstown village
Hotel	★★★★ 65% Jurys Hotel, Western Rd, CORK ☎ 021 276622 185 ⇆ ♞

OVENS   Map 01 B2

Lee Valley Golf & Country Club Clashanure
☎ 021 331721 Fax 021 331695
An undulating test of all golfing abilities designed by Ryder Cup star Christy O'Connor Junior. Seven of the 18 holes have water and the unusual feature of two fairy forts which are over 300 years old - can they be blamed for errors on the testing Par 5 8th and 12th holes?! The 508yard, Par 5 8th is already regarded as one of the best holes in Ireland with its spectacular feature from tee to green.
18 holes, 6434yds, Par 72, SSS 70, Course record 62. Club membership 400.

Visitors	telephone in advance. Avoid Sat/Sun before 11.15am.
Societies	telephone in advance.
Green Fees	Apr-Oct IR£27 per round (IR£29 weekends); Nov-Mar IR£18 per round (IR£23 weekends).
Cards	▭ ▭ ▭
Prof	John Savage
Designer	Christy O'Connor
Facilities	⊗ 🍴 ⮿ ♥ ♀ ☂ 🏠 ❦ ✓ ♝ 🛒 ✓ ♝
Location	8m from Cork on Cork/Killarney road N22
Hotel	★★ 64% Vienna Woods Hotel, Glanmire, CORK ☎ 021 821146 20 ⇆ ♞

SKIBBEREEN   Map 01 B2

Skibbereen & West Carbery Licknavar
☎ 028 21227 Fax 028 22994
Slightly hilly course in scenic location.
18 holes, 6004yds, Par 71, SSS 69, Course record 67. Club membership 640.

Visitors	advisable to contact in advance.
Societies	apply in writing or telephone.

▶

Green Fees May-Oct IR£25 per day, IR£18 per round; Nov-Apr IR£20 per day, IR£12 per round.
Cards
Designer Jack Kenneally
Facilities ⊗ 🏌 💺 ♀ ⚐ ⛳ 🛒 ✎
Location 1m W on Baltimore road

Hotel ★★★ 61% Baltimore Harbour Resort Hotel & Leisure Cntr, BALTIMORE ☎ 028 20361 64 ⇄ ☏

YOUGHAL   Map 01 C2

Youghal Knockaverry ☎ 024 92787 Fax 024 92641
For many years the host of various Golfing Union championships, Youghal offers a good test of golf and is well maintained for year-round play. There are panoramic views of Youghal Bay and the Blackwater estuary.
18 holes, 5646mtrs, Par 70, SSS 69, Course record 67.
Club membership 600.
Visitors may not play Wed (Ladies Day) and should contact in advance for weekends.
Societies must apply in writing a few months in advance.
Green Fees not confirmed.
Cards
Prof Liam Burns
Designer Cd. Harris
Facilities ⊗ ⊪ 🏌 💺 ♀ ⚐ 🏠 ⛳ ✎

Hotel ★★ 64% Devonshire Arms Hotel and Restaurant, Pearse Square, YOUGHAL ☎ 024 92827 & 92018 Fax 024 92900 10 ⇄ ☏

CO DONEGAL

BALLINTRA   Map 01 B5

Donegal Murvagh, Laghy
☎ 073 34054 Fax 073 34377
This massive links course was opened in 1973 and provides a world-class facility in peaceful surroundings. It is a very long course with some memorable holes, including five par 5s, calling for some big hitting. Donegal is the home club of former Curtis Cup captain, Maire O'Donnell.
18 holes, 6243mtrs, Par 73, SSS 73, Course record 68.
Club membership 750.
Visitors must contact in advance, limited availability at weekends.
Societies must contact in advance.
Green Fees IR£20 per day (IR£27 per round weekends & bank holidays).
Cards
Designer Eddie Hackett
Facilities ⊗ ⊪ 🏌 💺 ♀ ⚐ 🏠 ⛳ 🛒 ✎
Location 6m S of Donegal on Ballyshannon road

Hotel ★★★ 77% Sand House Hotel, ROSSNOWLAGH ☎ 072 51777 46 ⇄ ☏

BALLYBOFEY   Map 01 C5

Ballybofey & Stranorlar Stranorlar ☎ 074 31093
A most scenic course incorporating pleasant valleys backed by mountains with three of its holes bordered by a lake. There are three Par 3s on the first nine and two on the second. The most difficult hole is the long uphill Par 4 16th. The only Par 5 is the 7th.
18 holes, 5366mtrs, Par 68, SSS 68, Course record 64.
Club membership 450.
Visitors may play on weekdays. Advisable to book in advance
Green Fees not confirmed.
Facilities ♀ ⚐
& Leisure squash.
Location 0.25m from Stranorlar

Hotel ★★★ 70% Kee's Hotel, Stranorlar, BALLYBOFEY ☎ 074 31018 53 ⇄ ☏

BALLYLIFFEN   Map 01 C6

Ballyliffin Clonmany ☎ 077 76119 Fax 077 76672
The Old course is a links course with rolling fairways, surrounded by rolling hills and bounded on one side by the ocean. Nick Faldo said 'This is the most natural golf links I have ever played.' It has an old-fashioned charm with its uniquely contoured fairways. The new 18-hole course, the Glashedy (opened summer 1995), offers a modern (and arguably 'fairer') championship test.
Old Links: 18 holes, 6612yds, Par 71, SSS 72, Course record 66.
Glashedy Links: 18 holes, 6426yds, Par 72, SSS 71, Course record 68.
Club membership 1034.
Visitors telephone in advance.
Societies telephone in advance.
Green Fees Old Links: IR£19 (IR£22 weekends); Glashedy: IR£28 (IR£33 weekends).
Cards
Designer Tom Craddock/Pat Ruddy
Facilities ⊗ ⊪ 🏌 💺 ♀ ⚐ 🏠 ⛳ 🛒 ✎
Guest ◻◻◻◻ Mount Royd Country Home,
house CARRIGANS ☎ 074 40163 4 ☏

BUNCRANA   Map 01 C6

Buncrana Municipal Ballmacarry ☎ 077 62279
A 9-hole course with a very challenging Par-3 3rd with all carry out of bounds on either side.
9 holes, 2125yds, Par 62, SSS 60, Course record 59.
Club membership 100.
Visitors during open competitions only visitors with club handicaps.
Societies write in advance.
Green Fees not confirmed.
Facilities ♀ ⚐ 🏠
Guest ◻◻◻◻ Mount Royd Country Home,
house CARRIGANS ☎ 074 40163 4 ☏

North West Lisfannon, Fahan
☎ 077 61027 Fax 077 63284
A traditional-style links course on gently rolling sandy terrain with some long par 4s. Good judgement is required on the approaches and the course offers a satisfying test coupled with undemanding walking.

18 holes, 5968yds, Par 70, SSS 70, Course record 64.
Club membership 580.

Visitors	contact in advance for weekends. Wed - Ladies Day
Societies	telephone in advance.
Green Fees	IR£15 per day (IR£20 weekends).
Prof	Seamus McBriarty
Facilities	⊗ 〠 ⅃ ▆ ♀ ☖ ♪ ♨ ✎
Location	1m S of Buncanna
Guest house	[QQQQ] Mount Royd Country Home, CARRIGANS ☎ 074 40163 4 ☞

BUNDORAN   Map 01 B5

Bundoran ☎ 072 41302 Fax 072 42014
This popular course, acknowledged as one of the best in
the country, runs along the high cliffs above Bundoran
beach and has a difficult par of 69. Designed by Harry
Vardon, it offers a challenging game of golf in beautiful
surroundings and has been the venue for a number of
Irish golf championships.
18 holes, 5599mtrs, Par 69, SSS 70, Course record 66.
Club membership 560.

Visitors	must contact in advance.
Societies	must contact in advance.
Green Fees	IR£17 (IR£20 weekends & bank holidays).
Prof	David T Robinson
Designer	Harry Vardon
Facilities	▆ ▆ ♀ ☖ ☖ ♪ ♨ ✎
Location	Just off Main St, Bundoran on the Sligo/Derry road, 22m N of Sligo

Hotel	★★★ 77% Sand House Hotel, ROSSNOWLAGH ☎ 072 51777 46 ⇔ ☞

CRUIT ISLAND   Map 01 B5

Cruit Island Kincasslagh ☎ 075 43296
A links course on a small island. It is perched along the cliffs
overlooking the Atlantic. The course is short but always
challenging as the wind blows 90% of the time. It is
crowned by a magnificent 6th hole which is played across a
cove to an island green. With the prevailing wind in your
face and the Atlantic waves crashing in front, it is not for the
fainthearted.
9 holes, 4833mtrs, Par 68, SSS 66, Course record 62.
Club membership 350.

Visitors	restricted Sun & Thu mornings for Club competitions.
Societies	apply in writing to secretary.
Green Fees	IR£10-IR£12.
Designer	Michael Doherty
Facilities	▆ ▆ ♀ ☖
Location	8km N of Dungloe

Hotel	★★★ 65% Arnold's Hotel, DUNFANAGHY ☎ 074 36208 30 ⇔ ☞

DUNFANAGHY   Map 01 C6

Dunfanaghy Kill ☎ 074 36335 Fax 074 36335
Overlooking Sheephaven Bay, the course has a flat central
area with three difficult streams to negotiate. At the Port-na-
Blagh end there are five marvellous holes, including one

across the beach, while at the Horn Head end, the last five
holes are a test for any golfer.
18 holes, 5066mtrs, Par 68, SSS 66, Course record 63.
Club membership 335.

Visitors	must book in advance, time sheet in operation all year.
Societies	must telephone in advance.
Green Fees	IR£13 (IR£17 weekends).
Cards	▭ 〔VISA〕
Designer	Harry Vardon
Facilities	▆ ▆ ♀ ☖ ☖ ♪ ♨ ✎
Location	On N56

Hotel	★★★ 65% Arnold's Hotel, DUNFANAGHY ☎ 074 36208 30 ⇔ ☞

GREENCASTLE   Map 01 C6

Greencastle Moville ☎ 077 81013
A typical links course along the shores of Lough Foyle,
surrounded by rocky headlands and sandy beaches. In 1992
to celebrate its centenary, the club increased its size from 9 to
18 holes.
18 holes, 5118mtrs, Par 69, SSS 67.
Club membership 600.

Visitors	no restrictions.
Societies	telephone in advance.
Green Fees	not confirmed.
Facilities	♀ ☖

Hotel	★★★★ 67% Everglades Hotel, Prehen Rd, LONDONDERRY ☎ 01504 346722 64 ⇔ ☞

GWEEDORE   Map 01 B6

Gweedore Derrybeg ☎ 075 31140
This 9-hole links course provides plenty of challenge with
two subtle Par 3s and the Par 5 5th/14th at 556yards into the
prevailing west wind is a monster.
9 holes, 6201yds, Par 71, SSS 69.
Club membership 175.

Visitors	golf club must be notified if large numbers wish to play.
Societies	apply in writing.
Green Fees	IR£8 per day (IR£10 weekends & bank holidays).
Cards	〔VISA〕
Facilities	▆ ▆ ♀ ☖ ✎

LETTERKENNY   Map 01 C5

Letterkenny Barnhill ☎ 074 21150 Fax 074 21175
The fairways are wide and generous, but the rough, when
you find it, is short, tough and mean. The flat and untiring
terrain on the shores of Lough Swilly provides good holiday
golf. Many interesting holes include the intimidating 1st with
its high tee through trees and the tricky dog-leg of the 2nd
hole. The last 7 holes are on undulating ground, steep climb
from 11th green to 12th tee.
18 holes, 6239yds, Par 70, SSS 71, Course record 65.
Club membership 700.

Visitors	preferred Mon-Fri, except Wed evenings after 5pm. Advisable to contact in advance for weekends and bank holidays.
Societies	apply by writing or telephone.
Green Fees	IR£15 per day.
Prof	James Gallagher
Designer	Eddie Hacket

▶

Facilities ⊗ by prior arrangement ≡ by prior arrangement
🏌 ♣ ♀ ⚑ ⚐ ♂
Location 2m from town on Rathmelton road

Hotel ★★★ 70% Kee's Hotel, Stranorlar,
BALLYBOFEY ☎ 074 31018 53 ⇆ ☏

MOVILLE
Map 01 C6

Redcastle Redcastle ☎ 077 82073 Fax 077 82214
A testing course enjoying a picturesque setting on the shores
of Loch Foyle. The two challenging Par 3 holes should be
approached with the necessary respect.
9 holes, 3076yds, Par 36.
Club membership 200.
Visitors welcome except club times advisable to
telephone.
Societies enquiries welcome by telephone or in writing.
Green Fees not confirmed.
Facilities ⊗ ≡ 🏌 ♣ ♀ ⚑ ⚐ ♂ ♂
& Leisure hard tennis courts, heated indoor swimming
pool, fishing, sauna, gymnasium.
Location Main Londonderry/Moville road

NARIN
Map 01 B5

Narin & Portnoo ☎ 075 45107
Seaside links with every hole presenting its own special
feature. The Par 4 5th, for instance, demands a perfectly
placed drive to get a narrow sight of the narrow entrance to
the elevated green. Cross winds from the sea can make some
of the Par 4s difficult to reach with two woods.
18 holes, 5322mtrs, Par 69, SSS 68, Course record 63.
Club membership 510.
Visitors weekends by arrangement.
Societies telephone in advance.
Green Fees not confirmed.
Facilities 🏌 ♣ ♀ ♧ ♂ ♂
Location 6m from Ardara

Hotel ★★★ 63% Abbey Hotel, The Diamond,
DONEGAL ☎ 073 21014 49 ⇆ ☏

PORTSALON
Map 01 C6

Portsalon ☎ 074 59459 Fax 074 59459
Another course blessed by nature. The three golden beaches
of Ballymastocker Bay lie at one end, while the beauty of
Lough Swilly and the Inishowen Peninsula beyond is a
distracting but pleasant feature to the west. Situated on the
Fanad Peninsula, this lovely links course provides untiring
holiday golf at its best.
18 holes, 5880yds, Par 69, SSS 68.
Club membership 400.
Visitors telephone in advance.
Societies telephone in advance.
Green Fees IR£15 per round (IR£18 weekends & bank
holidays).
Facilities ⊗ 🏌 ♣ ♀ ♧ ♂
Location 20m N of Letterkenny

Hotel ★★★♨ 71% Fort Royal Hotel,
Fort Royal, RATHMULLAN
☎ 074 58100 11 ⇆ ☏ Annexe4 ⇆

RATHMULLAN
Map 01 C6

Otway Saltpans ☎ 074 58319
9 holes, 4234yds, Par 64, SSS 60, Course record 60.
Club membership 92.
Visitors welcome.
Societies contact for details.
Green Fees not confirmed.
Facilities ♀ ♧
Location W shore of Loch Swilly

Hotel ★ 59% Pier Hotel, RATHMULLAN
☎ 074 58178 & 58115 Fax 074 58115 10 ⇆ ☏

ROSAPENNA
Map 01 C6

Rosapenna Downings ☎ 074 55301 Fax 074 55128
Dramatic links course offering a challenging round.
Originally designed by Tom Morris and later modified by
James Braid and Harry Vardon, it includes such features as
bunkers in mid fairway. The best part of the links runs in the
low valley along the ocean.
18 holes, 6271yds, Par 70, SSS 71.
Club membership 200.
Visitors no restrictions.
Societies must contact in advance.
Green Fees not confirmed.
Prof Simon Byrne
Designer Old Tom Morris
Facilities ⊗ ≡ 🏌 ♣ ♀ ♧ ⚑ ⚐ ♂ ♂ ♂
& Leisure hard tennis courts.

Hotel ★★★ 65% Arnold's Hotel, DUNFANAGHY
☎ 074 36208 30 ⇆ ☏

CO DUBLIN

BALBRIGGAN
Map 01 D4

Balbriggan Blackhall ☎ 01 8412229 Fax 01 8413927
A parkland course with great variations and good views of
the Mourne and Cooley mountains.
18 holes, 5922mtrs, Par 71, SSS 71.
Club membership 650.
Visitors must contact in advance. With member only at
weekends.
Societies must apply in writing.
Green Fees IR£16 per round.
Designer Paramoir
Facilities ⊗ ≡ 🏌 ♣ ♀ ♧ ♂ ♂
Location 1km S off Balbriggan on N1

Hotel ★★★ 61% Boyne Valley Hotel & Country
Club, Stameen, Dublin Rd, DROGHEDA
☎ 041 37737 35 ⇆ ☏

BALLYBOUGHAL
Map 01 D4

Hollywood Lakes
☎ 01 8433406 & 8433407 Fax 01 8433002
A parkland course opened in 1992 with large USGA-type,
sand-based greens and tees. There are water features on
seven holes. The front nine requires accuracy while the
second nine includes a 636yard Par 5.

18 holes, 6246mtrs, Par 72, SSS 72, Course record 67.
Club membership 450.

Visitors	welcome Mon-Fri but may only play weekends from 12.30pm.
Societies	telephone then write in advance.
Green Fees	IR£18 per round (IR£23 weekends & public holidays).
Cards	▭▭▭
Designer	Mel Flanagan
Facilities	⊗ ⫴ ↳ 🍺 ♀ 🛆 🏠 🖐 ⚙ ⛳
Location	3m off main Dublin/Belfast road
Hotel	★★★ 69% Marine Hotel, Sutton Cross, DUBLIN 13 ☎ 01 8390000 28 ⇨ ℩

BRITTAS   Map 01 D4

Slade Valley Lynch Park
☎ 01 4582183 & 4582739 Fax 01 4582784
This is a course for a relaxing game, being fairly easy and in pleasant surroundings.
18 holes, 5388mtrs, Par 69, SSS 68, Course record 65.
Club membership 800.

Visitors	must contact in advance.
Societies	telephone in advance.
Green Fees	IR£15-IR£17 per round.
Prof	John Dignam
Designer	W Sullivan & D O Brien
Facilities	⊗ ⫴ ↳ 🍺 ♀ 🛆 🏠 ⛳
Location	9m SW of Dublin on N81
Hotel	★★★ 61% Downshire House Hotel, BLESSINGTON ☎ 045 865199 14 ⇨ ℩ Annexe11 ⇨ ℩

CASTLEKNOCK   Map 01 D4

Luttrellstown Castle Dublin15
☎ 01 8089988 Fax 01 8089989
Set in the grounds of the magnificent 560-acre Luttrellstown Castle estate, this championship course has retained the integrity of a mature and ancient parkland. It is renowned for the quality of its greens and the log-built Clubhouse which provides excellent facilities.
18 holes, 6032mtrs, Par 72, SSS 73, Course record 66.
Club membership 400.

Visitors	bookings made in advance only, no denims.
Societies	must phone in advance.
Green Fees	IR£42 per round (IR£50 weekends).
Cards	▭▭ ▭▭ ▭▭ 🅿
Prof	Graham Campbell
Designer	N Bielenberg
Facilities	⊗ ⫴ ↳ 🍺 ♀ 🛆 🏠 🖐 🚣 🐎 ⚙ ⛳ ℩
& Leisure	hard tennis courts, heated outdoor swimming pool, fishing, clay shooting.
Location	Porterstown rd
Hotel	★★★ 69% Finnstown Country House Hotel & Golf Course, Newcastle Rd, LUCAN ☎ 01 6280644 25 ⇨ ℩ Annexe26 ⇨ ℩

CLOGHRAN   Map 01 D4

Forrest Little ☎ 01 8401183
Testing parkland course.
18 holes, 5865mtrs, Par 70, SSS 70.

Visitors	preferred weekday mornings.
Green Fees	not confirmed.
Prof	Tony Judd

Facilities	♀ 🏠 ⛳
Location	6m N of Dublin on N1
Hotel	★★★ 69% Marine Hotel, Sutton Cross, DUBLIN 13 ☎ 01 8390000 28 ⇨ ℩

DONABATE   Map 01 D4

Balcarrick Corballis
☎ 01 8436228 & 8436957 Fax 01 8436957
Splendid 18-hole parkland course located close to the sea. A strong prevailing wind often plays a big part on every hole. Many challenging holes, notably the 7th - nicknamed 'Amen Corner'.
18 holes, 6273mtrs, Par 73, SSS 71.
Club membership 600.

Visitors	must contact in advance.
Societies	telephone in advance.
Green Fees	not confirmed.
Designer	Barry Langan
Facilities	⊗ ⫴ ↳ 🍺 ♀ 🛆
Hotel	B Posthouse Dublin, Cloghran, DUBLIN ☎ 01 8080500 249 ⇨ ℩

Corballis Public Corballis ☎ 01 8436583
Well maintained coastal course with excellent greens.
18 holes, 4971yds, Par 65, SSS 64.

Visitors	no restrictions.
Societies	apply in writing or telephone.
Green Fees	IR£9 per round (IR£12 weekends).
Facilities	↳ 🛆 🏠 ℩ 🐎 ⛳
Hotel	B Posthouse Dublin, Cloghran, DUBLIN

Donabate Balcarrick ☎ 01 8436346 & 8436001
Level parkland course.
18 holes, 5704yds, Par 70, SSS 69, Course record 67.
Club membership 900.

Visitors	welcome, weekdays & late Sunday afternoon.
Societies	must apply in writing.
Green Fees	not confirmed.
Prof	Hugh Jackson
Facilities	⊗ ⫴ ↳ 🍺 ♀ 🛆 🏠 ℩ 🐎 ⚙
Hotel	B Posthouse Dublin, Cloghran, DUBLIN ☎ 01 8080500 249 ⇨ ℩

The Island Corballis
☎ 01 8436104 & 8436205 Fax 01 8436860
Links course on a promontory, with sea inlets separating some of the fairways. Accuracy as well as length of shots are required on some holes and sand hills provide an additional challenge. ▶

18 holes, 6078mtrs, Par 71, SSS 72, Course record 67.
Club membership 800.

Visitors	preferred on Mon, Tue & Fri. Telephone for appointment.
Societies	must apply in advance.
Green Fees	IR£80 per day; IR£50 per round (IR£60 per round weekends).
Cards	🖃 VISA
Prof	Kevin Kelliher
Designer	Hackett/Hawtree
Facilities	⊗ 🎇 ⅊ ♿ 🍴 🛄 🛅 ⛳ 🧺 ✈
Location	Take main Dublin/Belfast road N1, pass airport, take turn for Donabate/Portrane, follow signs
Hotel	B Posthouse Dublin, Cloghran, DUBLIN ☎ 01 8080500 249 ⇄ ☂

DUBLIN   Map 01 D4

Carrickmines Carrickmines ☎ 01 2955972
Meadowland course.
9 holes, 6100yds, Par 71, SSS 69.
Club membership 500.

Visitors	with member only Sat, Sun & bank holidays.
Societies	contact for details.
Green Fees	not confirmed.
Facilities	⛳
Location	7m S of Dublin
Hotel	★★★ 65% Royal Marine Hotel, Marine Rd, DUN LAOGHAIRE ☎ 01 2801911 104 ⇄ ☂

Castle Woodside Dr, Rathfarnham
☎ 01 4904207 Fax 01 4920264
A tight, tree-lined parkland course which is very highly regarded by all who play there.
18 holes, 5732mtrs, Par 70, SSS 70, Course record 63.
Club membership 1200.

Visitors	welcome but may not play at weekends & bank holidays.
Societies	must apply in writing 6 months in advance.
Green Fees	IR£35 per round.
Prof	David Kinsella
Designer	Barcroft-Pickman & Hood
Facilities	⊗ 🎇 ⅊ ♿ 🍴 🛄 🛅 ⛳
Location	Off Dodder Park Road
Hotel	★★★★ 72% Jurys Hotel Dublin, Pembroke Rd, Ballsbridge, DUBLIN 4 ☎ 01 6605000 294 ⇄ ☂

Clontarf Donnycarney House, Malahide Rd
☎ 01 8331892 Fax 01 8331933
The nearest golf course to Dublin city, with a historic building as a clubhouse, Clontarf is a parkland type course bordered on one side by a railway line. There are several testing and challenging holes including the 12th, which involves playing over a pond and a quarry.
18 holes, 5459mtrs, Par 69, SSS 68, Course record 67.
Club membership 1100.

Visitors	welcome daily but must contact in advance.
Societies	Tue & Fri. Must contact in advance.
Green Fees	not confirmed.
Prof	Joe Craddock
Designer	Harry Colt
Facilities	⊗ 🎇 ⅊ ♿ 🍴 🛄 🛅 ⛳
Location	2.5m N via Fairview

Hotel	★★★ 67% Doyle Skylon Hotel, Drumcondra Rd, DUBLIN 9 ☎ 01 8379121 92 ⇄ ☂

Corrstown Corrstown, Kilsallaghan
☎ 01 8640533 & 8640534 Fax 01 8640537
The 18 hole course has a small river meandering through, coming into play at several holes culminating in a challenging Island green finish. Orchard course has mature trees and rolling pastureland offering golfers a relaxing enjoyable game.
River Course: 18 holes, 6077mtrs, Par 72, SSS 71.
Orchard Course: 9 holes, 2792mtre, Par 70, SSS 69.
Club membership 900.

Visitors	advisable to contact in advance. May play weekends after 2pm.
Societies	telephone or write in advance.
Green Fees	River: IR£17 per round (IR£20 weekends); Orchard: IR£15 per 18 holes, IR£8 per 9 holes.
Cards	🖃 VISA
Prof	Pat Gittens
Designer	Eddie Connaughton
Facilities	⊗ 🎇 ⅊ ♿ 🍴 🛄 🛅 ⛳ 🧺 ✈
Location	W of Dublin Airport via St Margarets
Hotel	★★★ 67% Doyle Skylon Hotel, Drumcondra Rd, DUBLIN 9 ☎ 01 8379121 92 ⇄ ☂

Deer Park Hotel & Golf Course Howth
☎ 01 8322624 Fax 01 8392405
Claiming to be Irelands largest golf/hotel complex, be warned that its popularity makes it quite busy at times and only hotel residents can book tee-off times.
St Fintans: 9 holes, 3373yds, Par 37.
Deer Park: 18 holes, 6830yds, Par 72.
Grace O'Malley: 9 holes, 3130yds, Par 35.
Short Course: 12 holes, 1810yds, Par 36.
Club membership 200.

Visitors	no restrictions. There may be delays especially Sun mornings.
Societies	must contact by telephone.
Green Fees	IR£10 per 18 holes (IR£12.25 weekends); IR£5 per 9 holes (IR£6.50 weekends).
Cards	🖃 AMERICAN EXPRESS VISA 💳
Designer	Fred Hawtree
Facilities	⊗ 🎇 ⅊ ♿ 🍴 🛄 🛅 ⛳
& Leisure	heated indoor swimming pool, sauna.
Location	On right 0.5m before Howth Harbour
Hotel	★★★ 69% Marine Hotel, Sutton Cross, DUBLIN 13 ☎ 01 8390000 28 ⇄ ☂

Edmonstown Edmondstown Rd, Edmondstown
☎ 01 4931082 Fax 01 4933152
A popular and testing parkland course situated at the foot of the Dublin Mountains in the suburbs of the city. An attractive

stream flows in front of the 4th and 6th greens calling for an accurate approach shot.
18 holes, 5393mtrs, Par 70, SSS 70.
Club membership 750.

Visitors	must contact in advance as there are daily times reserved for members. Limited times after 3.30pm weekends.
Societies	must contact in advance.
Green Fees	IR£25 per round (IR£30 weekends & bank holidays).
Cards	🖰 VISA
Prof	Andrew Crofton
Designer	McAllister
Facilities	⊗ ⅷ ⤶ ♥ ♀ ⚘ 🖰 ⛳ 🏍 ⚐

Hotel	★★★ 68% Doyle Montrose Hotel, Stillorgan Rd, DUBLIN ☎ 01 2693311 179 ⇆ ⋔

Elm Park Golf & Sports Club Nutley House, Nutley Ln, Dennybrook ☎ 01 2693438 Fax 01 2694505
Interesting parkland course requiring a degree of accuracy, particularly as half of the holes involve crossing the stream.
18 holes, 5355mtrs, Par 69, SSS 68, Course record 64.
Club membership 1750.

Visitors	must contact in advance.
Societies	apply in advance.
Green Fees	IR£35 (IR£45 weekends).
Prof	Seamus Green
Facilities	⊗ ⅷ ⤶ ♥ ♀ ⚘ 🖰 ⚐
& Leisure	hard and grass tennis courts.
Location	3m from city centre

Hotel	★★★★ 72% Jurys Hotel Dublin, Pembroke Rd, Ballsbridge, DUBLIN 4 ☎ 01 6605000 294 ⇆ ⋔

Foxrock Torquay Rd, Foxrock ☎ 01 2895668 & 2893992
A well-treed parkland course.
9 holes, 5667mtrs, Par 70, SSS 69.
Club membership 650.

Visitors	welcome but contact in advance, no green fees Tue & weekends.
Societies	apply in writing to William Daly.
Green Fees	not confirmed.
Prof	David Walker
Facilities	♀ ⚘ 🖰 ⚐

Hotel	★★★ 65% Royal Marine Hotel, Marine Rd, DUN LAOGHAIRE ☎ 01 2801911 104 ⇆ ⋔

Grange Rathfarnham ☎ 01 4932889
Wooded parkland course which provides both interest and challenge.
18 holes, 5517mtrs, Par 68, SSS 69.

Visitors	preferred on weekdays.
Green Fees	not confirmed.
Prof	W Sullivan
Facilities	♀ 🖰
Location	6m from city centre

Hotel	★★★ 68% Doyle Montrose Hotel, Stillorgan Rd, DUBLIN ☎ 01 2693311 179 ⇆ ⋔

Howth St Fintan's, Carrickbrack Rd, Sutton ☎ 01 8323055 Fax 01 8321793
A heathland course with scenic views of Dublin Bay. It is very hilly and presents a good challenge to the novice or expert golfer.

18 holes, 5618mtrs, Par 72, SSS 69.
Club membership 1200.

Visitors	contact in advance. May not play Wed and weekends.
Societies	must contact in advance.
Green Fees	IR£20 per round (IR£22 Fri).
Cards	🖰
Prof	John McGuirk
Designer	James Braid
Facilities	⤶ ♥ ♀ ⚘ 🖰 ⚐

Hotel	★★★ 69% Marine Hotel, Sutton Cross, DUBLIN 13 ☎ 01 8390000 28 ⇆ ⋔

Milltown Lower Churchtown Rd
☎ 01 4976090 Fax 01 4976008
Level parkland course on the outskirts of the city.
18 holes, 5638mtrs, Par 71, SSS 69, Course record 64.
Club membership 1400.

Visitors	must contact in advance but may not play weekends.
Societies	apply in writing.
Green Fees	not confirmed.
Cards	🖰
Prof	John Harnett
Designer	Freddie Davis
Facilities	⊗ ⅷ ⤶ ♥ ♀ ⚘ 🖰 ⚐

Hotel	★★★★ 72% Jurys Hotel Dublin, Pembroke Rd, Ballsbridge, DUBLIN 4 ☎ 01 6605000 294 ⇆ ⋔

Newlands Clondalkin 22
☎ 01 4593157 & 4593498 Fax 01 4593498
Mature parkland course offering a testing game.
18 holes, 5714mtrs, Par 71, SSS 70.
Club membership 1000.

Visitors	must contact in advance and may play Mon, Thu, Fri and Wed mornings only.
Societies	must contact in writing.
Green Fees	IR£32 per round.
Prof	Karl O'Donnell
Designer	James Braid
Facilities	⊗ ⅷ ⤶ ♥ ♀ ⚘ 🖰 ⚐

Hotel	★★★ 67% Doyle Green Isle Hotel, Naas Rd, DUBLIN 22 ☎ 01 4593406 90 ⇆ ⋔

The Open Golf Centre Newton House, St Margaret's
☎ 01 8640324 Fax 01 8341400
A 27-hole Pay and Play parkland course that is testing for the low handicap golfer but not too intimidating for high handicapper.
Yellow & Red Course: 18 holes, 5973yds, Par 71, SSS 69, Course record 66.
Blue Course: 9 holes, 2479yds, Par 31.

Visitors	no restrictions. Booking essential.
Societies	telephone for booking form.
Green Fees	IR£9.50 per 18 holes (IR£13.50 weekends & bank holidays).
Cards	🖰
Prof	Roger Yates
Designer	M Hawtree
Facilities	⚘ 🖰 ⚐ 🏍 ⚐ ⅃
Location	Adjacent to Dublin airport

Hotel	★★★ 69% Marine Hotel, Sutton Cross, DUBLIN 13 ☎ 01 8390000 28 ⇆ ⋔ ▶

Rathfarnham Newtown
☎ 01 4931201 & 4931561 Fax 01 4931561
Parkland course designed by John Jacobs in 1962.
9 holes, 5815mtrs, Par 71, SSS 70, Course record 69.
Club membership 680.
Visitors   must contact in advance, by arrangement only Sunday.
Societies   restricted to Mon, Wed & Fri.
Green Fees IR£22.50 per round (IR£28 Sun by arrangement).
Prof   Brian O'Hara
Designer   John Jacobs
Facilities   🛠 🍽 ♀ 👤 🏠 🚕 ✦

Hotel   ★★★★ 72% Jurys Hotel Dublin,
              Pembroke Rd, Ballsbridge, DUBLIN 4
              ☎ 01 6605000 294 ⇆ 📞

Royal Dublin North Bull Island, Dollymount
☎ 01 8336346 Fax 01 8336504
A popular course with visitors, for its design subtleties, for the condition of the links and the friendly atmosphere. Founded in 1885, the club moved to its present site in 1889 and received its Royal designation in 1891. A notable former club professional was Christie O'Connor, who was appointed in 1959 and immediately made his name. Along with its many notable holes, Royal Dublin has a fine and testing finish. The 18th is a sharply dog-legged par 4, with out of bounds along the right-hand side. The decision to try the long carry over the 'garden' is one many visitors have regretted.
18 holes, 6030mtrs, Par 72, SSS 71, Course record 63.
Club membership 800.

Visitors   must contact in advance & have handicap certificate. May not play Wed, Sat until 4pm summer.
Societies   must book one year in advance.
Green Fees IR£60 per round Mon, Tue, Thu (IR£70 Fri-Sun).
Cards   💳 💳 💳
Prof   Leonard Owens
Designer   H S Colt
Facilities   ⊗ 🍽 🛠 🍽 ♀ 👤 🏠 🚕 ✦
Location   3.5m NE of city centre

Hotel   ★★★ 69% Longfield's Hotel, Fitzwilliam St, DUBLIN 2 ☎ 01 6761367 24 ⇆ 📞

St Anne's North Bull Island, Dollymount ☎ 01 8336471
Links course, recently extended from 9 holes to 18.
18 holes, 5652mtrs, Par 70, SSS 69.
Club membership 500.

Visitors   telephone for restrictions.
Societies   must apply in writing.
Green Fees not confirmed.
Facilities   ♀ 👤 ✦

Hotel   ★★★ 69% Longfield's Hotel, Fitzwilliam St, DUBLIN 2 ☎ 01 6761367 24 ⇆ 📞

St Margaret's Golf & Country Club St Margaret's
☎ 01 8640400 Fax 01 8640289
A championship standard course which measures nearly 7,000 yards off the back tees, but flexible teeing offers a fairer challenge to the middle and high handicap golfer. The modern design makes wide use of water hazards and mounding. The Par 5 8th hole is set to become notorious - featuring lakes to the left and right of the tee and a third lake in front of the green. Ryder Cup player,Sam Torrance, has described the 18th as 'possibly the strongest and most exciting in the world'.
18 holes, 6917yds, Par 73, SSS 73, Course record 69.
Club membership 200.

Visitors   telephone in advance.
Societies   apply in writing or telephone
Green Fees not confirmed.
Cards   💳 💳 💳 💳
Designer   Craddock/Ruddy
Facilities   ⊗ 🍽 🛠 🍽 ♀ 👤 🏠 🚕 🏌 🛺 ✦ ♟
Location   9m NW of city centre

Hotel   ★★★ 69% Marine Hotel, Sutton Cross, DUBLIN 13 ☎ 01 8390000 28 ⇆ 📞

Stackstown Kellystown Rd, Rathfarnham
☎ 01 4942338 & 4941993
Pleasant course in scenic surroundings.
18 holes, 5925mtrs, Par 72, SSS 72, Course record 70.
Club membership 1042.
Visitors   preferred Mon-Fri.
Societies   telephone in advance and confirm in writing.
Green Fees not confirmed.
Prof   Michael Kavanach
Facilities   ♀ 👤 🏠
& Leisure sauna.
Location   9m S of city centre

Hotel   ★★★ 68% Doyle Montrose Hotel, Stillorgan Rd, DUBLIN ☎ 01 2693311 179 ⇆ 📞

Swords Open Golf Course Balheary Av, Swords
☎ 01 8409819 & 8901030 Fax 01 8409819
Parkland course situated beside the River Broadmeadow in unspoilt countryside, 10 miles from Dublin.
18 holes, 5677mtrs, Par 71, SSS 70.

Club membership 350.
Visitors timesheet bookings available all year, telephone to book, may play at any time
Societies telephone well in advance.
Green Fees IR£9 per round (IR£12 weekends & bank holidays).

Designer R Stillwell/T Halpin
Facilities 🏌 ⛳ ⛳ ⚐ 🚻

Hotel ★★★ 67% Doyle Skylon Hotel, Drumcondra Rd, DUBLIN 9 ☎ 01 8379121 92 ⇌ ↑

DUN LAOGHAIRE   Map 01 D4

Dun Laoghaire Eglinton Park, Tivoli Rd
☎ 01 2803916 Fax 01 2804868
This is a well wooded parkland course, not long, but requiring accurate club selection and placing of shots. The course was designed by Harry Colt in 1918.
18 holes, 5298mtrs, Par 69, SSS 68, Course record 63.
Club membership 1040.

Visitors may not play Sat until after 5pm. Must contact in advance.
Societies must apply in writing.
Green Fees IR£30 per day.
Prof Owen Mulhall
Designer Harry Colt
Facilities ⊗ 🏳 🏌 ⛳ ⛳ 🚻 ⚐ 🚻
Location 0.75m from town ventre and ferry port

Hotel ★★★ 65% Royal Marine Hotel, Marine Rd, DUN LAOGHAIRE ☎ 01 2801911 104 ⇌ ↑

KILLINEY   Map 01 D4

Killiney Ballinclea Rd ☎ 01 2852823 Fax 01 2852823
The course is on the side of Killiney Hill with picturesque views over south Dublin and the Wicklow Mountains.
9 holes, 5655mtrs, Par 70, SSS 70.

Club membership 450.
Visitors welcome Mon, Wed, Fri & Sun afternoons.
Green Fees not confirmed.
Prof P O'Boyle
Facilities 🏌 🏳 ⛳ ⛳ 🚻 ⚐ 🚻

Hotel ★★★ 68% Fitzpatrick Castle Hotel, KILLINEY ☎ 01 2840700 113 ⇌ ↑

KILTERNAN   Map 01 D4

Kilternan Golf & Country Club Hotel
☎ 01 2955559 Fax 01 2955670
Interesting and testing course overlooking Dublin Bay.
18 holes, 4952mtrs, Par 68, SSS 66, Course record 66.
Club membership 819.

Visitors may not play before 1.30pm at weekends. Contact in advance.
Societies apply in writing/telephone in advance.
Green Fees IR£16 per round (IR£20 weekends & bank holidays).
Cards 💳 💳 💳 💳
Prof Gary Hendley
Designer Eddie Hackett
Facilities ⊗ 🏳 🏌 🏳 ⛳ ⛳ 🚻 ⚐ 🚻
& Leisure hard tennis courts, heated indoor swimming pool, sauna, gymnasium, ski club, jacuzzi, creche & steam room.

Hotel ★★★ 68% Fitzpatrick Castle Hotel, KILLINEY ☎ 01 2840700 113 ⇌ ↑

LUCAN   Map 01 D4

Finnstown Fairways Finnstwon Country House Hotel, Newcastle Rd ☎ 01 6280644 Fax 01 6281088
A flat parkland 9-hole course based in grounds originally laid out in the 18th century. Very challenging 6th and 7th holes among many mature trees.
9 holes, 2695yds, Par 66, SSS 66.
Visitors now operates as a pay & play course, all visitors welcome, numeric ticket system.
Societies must reserve in advance.
Green Fees IR£10 (IR£15 weekends).
Cards 💳 💳 💳 💳
Prof Barry Power
Designer Robert Browne
Facilities ⊗ 🏳 🏌 🏳 ⛳ ⛳ 🚻 ⚐ 🚻
& Leisure hard and grass tennis courts, heated indoor swimming pool, solarium, gymnasium.
Location Off N4, 8 m W of Dublin

Hotel ★★★ 69% Finnstown Country House Hotel & Golf Course, Newcastle Rd, LUCAN ☎ 01 6280644 25 ⇌ ↑ Annexe26 ⇌ ↑

Hermitage Ballydowd ☎ 01 6265049 & 6268491
Part level, part undulating course bordered by the River
Liffey and offering some surprises.
18 holes, 6034mtrs, Par 71, SSS 70.
Club membership 1100.
Visitors contact for details.
Societies must telephone well in advance.
Green Fees IR£34 per round.
Cards ▬ ▭
Prof Simon Byrne
Designer Eddie Hackett
Facilities 🎡 ⬛ ⬛ ♀ ⬛ ⬛ ⬛ ♂

Hotel ★★★ 69% Finnstown Country House Hotel &
Golf Course, Newcastle Rd, LUCAN
☎ 01 6280644 25 ➪ ☏ Annexe26 ➪ ☏

Lucan Celbridge Rd ☎ 01 6282106 Fax 01 6282929
Founded in 1897 as a nine hole course and extended to 18
holes in 1988. Lucan involves playing over a lane which
bisects the 1st and 7th holes. The first nine is undulating
while the back nine is flatter and features water hazards and a
538mtr 5 par 18th hole.
18 holes, 5958mtrs, Par 71, SSS 71.
Club membership 780.
Visitors may play Mon, Tue & Fri.
Societies must apply in writing.
Green Fees IR£25 per round.
Designer Eddie Hackett
Facilities ⊗ 🎡 ⬛ ⬛ ♀ ⬛ ♂

Hotel ★★★ 64% Lucan Spa Hotel, LUCAN
☎ 01 6280495 6280497
Fax 01 6280841 65 ➪ ☏

MALAHIDE   Map 01 D4

Malahide Beechwood, The Grange
☎ 01 8461611 Fax 01 8461270
Splendid parkland course with raised greens and water
hazards affecting many of the holes, demanding
accuracy from tee to green.
Main Course: 18 holes, 5742mtrs, Par 69, SSS 68.
Club membership 1100.

Visitors must contact in advance.
Societies must contact in advance.
Green Fees IR£30 (IR£40 weekends & bank holidays).
Cards ▬ ▭
Prof David Barton
Designer E Hackett
Facilities ⊗ 🎡 ⬛ ⬛ ♀ ⬛ ⬛ ♂
Location 1m from coast road at Portmarnock

Hotel ★★★★ 76% Portmarnock Hotel & Golf
Links, Strand Rd, PORTMARNOCK
☎ 01 8460611 103 ➪ ☏

PORTMARNOCK   Map 01 D4

PORTMARNOCK See page 451

RATHCOOLE   Map 01 D4

Beech Park Johnstown ☎ 01 4580522 Fax 01 4588365
Relatively flat parkland with heavily wooded fairways.
18 holes, 5730mtrs, Par 72, SSS 70, Course record 67.
Club membership 750.
Visitors restricted on some days, telephone in advance.
Societies apply in writing.
Facilities ♀ ⬛

Hotel ★★★ 69% Finnstown Country House Hotel &
Golf Course, Newcastle Rd, LUCAN
☎ 01 6280644 25 ➪ ☏ Annexe26 ➪ ☏

RUSH   Map 01 D4

Rush ☎ 01 8438177 Fax 01 8438177
Seaside borders three fairways on this links course. There are
28 bunkers and undulating fairways to add to the challenge
of the variable and strong winds that blow at all times and
change with the tides. There are no easy holes!
9 holes, 5598mtrs, Par 70, SSS 69.
Club membership 350.
Visitors restricted Wed, Thu, weekends & bank holidays.
Societies apply in writing.
Green Fees IR£15.
Facilities ⊗ 🎡 ⬛ ⬛ ♀ ⬛ ♂

Hotel B Posthouse Dublin, Cloghran, DUBLIN
☎ 01 8080500 249 ➪ ☏

SAGGART   Map 01 D4

City West Hotel & Golf Resort
☎ 01 4588566 & 4010900 (shop) Fax 01 4588565
18 holes, 6314yds, Par 70, SSS 70, Course record 65.
Visitors time sheet in operation, telephone in advance.
Societies apply in writing/telephone in advance.
Green Fees IR£25 per 18 holes (IR£30 weekends).
Cards ▬ ▭ 🌑
Prof Mac Cregon
Designer Christy O'Connor Jnr
Facilities ⊗ 🎡 ⬛ ⬛ ♀ ⬛ ⬛ ⬛ 🚲 ♂
& Leisure fishing, sauna, solarium, gymnasium.
Location Naas road, southbound N7

Hotel ★★★ 63% Bewley's Hotel at Newlands Cross,
Newlands Cross, Naas Rd, DUBLIN 22
☎ 01 464 0140 200 ➪ ☏

SKERRIES   Map 01 D4

Skerries Hacketstown ☎ 01 8491567 Fax 01 8491591
Tree-lined parkland course on gently rolling countryside,
with sea views from some holes. The 1st and 18th are
particularly challenging. The club can be busy on some days,
but is always friendly. ▶

PORTMARNOCK

PORTMARNOCK *Co Dublin* ☎ 01 8462968
Fax 01 8462601   **Map 01 D4**

John Ingham writes: The night before our fourball tackled Portmarnock was spent, as I recall, in Dublin. Guinness in that city seems smoother, while the conversation with locals, ranged from why no southern Irish player ever won the Open to how such a small nation can boast so many great writers, wits and actors.

I can thoroughly recommend this preparation, prior to facing one of the world's great golfing challenges - providing you only intend playing eighteen holes in one day! Frankly, you will have to reach into the base of your golf bag to pull out every shot if you want to play to your handicap on this superb links.

An opening birdie, downwind, made me wonder what the fuss was about. Two hours later, with a backswing too fast and the breeze now something near a gale, I decided that a test of 7182 yards off the back tees was too man-size for me. Maybe it would be more enjoyable on a calm, summer evening!

I remember the course not for the way it humiliated me, but for the 1960 Canada Cup where I watched Sam Snead and Arnold Palmer winning with such skillful play. Even so, both took 75 in one round while scores by the mighty Gary Player ranged from 65 to 78.

There are no blind shots, unless you drive into sandhills. This is natural golf with no unfair carries off the tee and the only damage to your card is self-inflicted. True, there are a couple of holes of 560 yards and the 522-yard 16th is frightening as you tee up in a fierce wind.

It's incredible to think that Portmarnock was 'discovered' almost by accident in 1893 by a Mr Pickeman and the course architect, Ross. They had rowed a boat from Sutton to the peninsula where they came across a wilderness of bracken, duneland and natural-looking bunkers made by God. They were inspired to create the course, built a shack for a clubhouse and talked about the only real hazard left - a cow that devoured golf balls.

Today it's so very different - with a modern clubhouse filled with members delighted to belong to such an internationally well-known establishment.

Visitors	contact in advance and confirm in writing. Restricted Saturday, Sunday and public holidays. Handicap certificate required
Societies	must contact in advance in writing
Green fees	IR£70 per round (IR&90 weekends & BH). ▭ ▬ ▬ ▬ ▢
Facilities	⊗ ♨ ⛳ ♀ (all day) ⛴ 🏠 🏌 🐾 🛒 ♂ Professional (Joey Purcell)
Location	12m from Dublin. 1m from village down Golf Rd

27 holes Old Course: 18 holes, 7182 yds, Par 72, SSS 73, course record 64
New Course: 9 holes, 3370yds, Par 37

WHERE TO STAY AND EAT NEARBY

HOTELS:
PORTMARNOCK
★★★★🏵 🏵 76% Portmarnock Hotel & Golf Links. ☎ 01 8460611. 103 🛏 ๒

18 holes, 6081mtrs, Par 73, SSS 72.
Club membership 800.

Visitors	must contact in advance but may not play at weekends.
Societies	must contact well in advance in writing.
Green Fees	IR£25 per round (IR£30 weekends).
Cards	⬜ ⬛ ⬜
Prof	Jimmy Kinsella
Facilities	⊗ ⵊ 🝮 🍺 ♀ 🏔 🏠 ⛳ 🛒 ✐
Location	E of Dublin-Belfast road

Hotel	★★★ 61% Boyne Valley Hotel & Country Club, Stameen, Dublin Rd, DROGHEDA ☎ 041 37737 35 ⇆ ♟

TALLAGHT   Map 01 D4

Ballinascorney Ballinascorney
☎ 01 4516430 Fax 01 4598445
Set in the valley of Glenasmole, this very scenic course offers a variety of terrain, where every hole is different, many would be considered feature holes.
18 holes, 5466yds, Par 69, SSS 67, Course record 63.
Club membership 500.

Visitors	please contact in advance, welcome weekdays and weekends after 4pm.
Societies	contact for details.
Green Fees	IR£15 (IR£20 weekends & bank holidays).
Cards	⬛
Designer	Eddie Hackett
Facilities	🝮 🍺 ♀ 🏔 🏠 ⛳ 🛒 ✐
& Leisure	hill walking, fishing.
Location	8m SW of Dublin city centre

Hotel	★★★ 67% Doyle Green Isle Hotel, Naas Rd, DUBLIN 22 ☎ 01 4593406 90 ⇆ ♟

CO GALWAY

BALLINASLOE   Map 01 B4

Ballinasloe Rosglos ☎ 0905 42126 Fax 0905 42538
Well maintained parkland course, recently extended from a par 68 to a par 72.
18 holes, 5865metres, Par 72, SSS 70, Course record 69.
Club membership 884.

Visitors	preferably Mon-Sat, contact in advance.
Societies	contact in advance.
Green Fees	IR£12 per day.
Prof	Barry Flangan
Designer	E Hackett/E Connaughton
Facilities	⊗ 🝮 🍺 ♀ 🏔 🏠 🛒 ✐

Hotel	★★★ 72% Hayden's Hotel, BALLINASLOE ☎ 0905 42347 48 ⇆ ♟

BALLYCONNEELY   Map 01 A4

Connemara ☎ 095 23502 & 23602 Fax 095 23662
This championship links course is situated on the verge of the Atlantic Ocean in a most spectacular setting, with the Twelve Bens Mountains in the background. Established as recently as 1973, it is a tough challenge,

due in no small part to its exposed location, with the back 9 the equal of any in the world. The last six holes are exceptionally long and offer a great challenge to golfers of all abilities. A further championship 9 holes due to open summer 1999.
18 holes, 6611mtrs, Par 72, SSS 75, Course record 67.
Club membership 970.

Visitors	advisable to book in advance.
Societies	telephone in advance.
Green Fees	May-Sep: IR£30; Oct-Apr IR£25; Jan-Mar & Nov-Dec IR£20.
Cards	⬜ ⬜ ⬛
Prof	Hugh O'Neill
Designer	Eddie Hackett
Facilities	⊗ ⵊ 🝮 🍺 ♀ 🏔 🏠 ⛳ 🌴 🛒 ✐ 🎿
Location	9m SW of Clifden

Hotel	★★★ 76% Abbeyglen Castle Hotel, Sky Rd, CLIFDEN ☎ 095 21201 36 ⇆ ♟

GALWAY   Map 01 B4

Galway Blackrock, Salthill
☎ 091 522033 Fax 091 529783
Designed by Dr Alister MacKenzie, this course is inland by nature, although some of the fairways run close to the ocean. The terrain is of gently sloping hillocks with plenty of trees and furze bushes to catch out the unwary. Although not a long course, it provided a worthy challenge as the venue of the Celtic International Tournament in 1984 and continues to delight the visiting golfer.
18 holes, 6376yds, Par 70, SSS 71, Course record 67.
Club membership 1050.

Visitors	preferred on weekdays, except Tue.
Societies	must apply in writing.
Green Fees	IR£20 per round (IR£25 weekends).
Prof	Don Wallace
Facilities	⊗ ⵊ 🝮 🍺 ♀ 🏔 🏠 ⛳ 🌴 ✐
Location	2m W in Salthill

Hotel	★★★ 59% Lochlurgain Hotel, 22 Monksfield, Upper Salthill, GALWAY ☎ 091 529595 13 ⇆ ♟

Glenlo Abbey Bushypark ☎ 091 526666 Fax 091 527800
A parkland course overlooking the magnificent Lough Corrib but only 10 minutes from the centre of Galway city. 9 fairways but large double green with two flags and four tee postions allows 18 diffent holes. The Par 3, 4th hole is on an island-like green extending into the lough.
9 holes, 6009mtrs, Par 71, SSS 71.

Visitors	advisable to contact in advance at peak times.
Societies	telephone in advance.
Green Fees	not confirmed.
Cards	⬜ ⬜ ⬜
Prof	Gary Todd
Designer	Jeff Howes
Facilities	⊗ ⵊ 🝮 🍺 ♀ 🏔 🌴 🏠 ✐ 🎿
& Leisure	fishing, clay pigeon, shooting, lake boating.
Location	On N59 Galway/Clifden road 4km from Galway City Centre

Hotel	★★★★ 🏔 Glenlo Abbey Hotel, Bushypark, GALWAY ☎ 091 526666 45 ⇆ ♟

GORT
Map 01 B3

Gort Kilmacduagh Rd, Castlequarter ☎ 091 632244
Replacing the original 9-hole course, this new 18-hole course, opened in June 1996, offers golfers a real challenge. The 564yd 9th and the 516yd 17th are played into a prevailing wind and the par 4 dog-leg 7th will test the best.
18 holes, 6538yds, Par 71, SSS 69.
Club membership 450.

Visitors   advisable to telephone in advance.
Societies   must contact in advance.
Green Fees not confirmed.
Designer   Christy O'Connor Jnr
Facilities   ⊗ ⅃ 占 ☕ ♀ ♨ ⚒ ⚑

Hotel   ★★★ 67%   Galway Ryan Hotel, Dublin Rd, GALWAY ☎ 091 753181   96 ⇆ ☏

LOUGHREA
Map 01 B3

Loughrea Bullaun Rd, Graigue
☎ 091 841049 Fax 091 847472
An excellent parkland course with good greens and extended in 1992 to 18-holes. The course has an unusual feature in that it incorporates a historic souterrain (underground shelter/food store).
18 holes, 5261metres, Par 69, SSS 67, Course record 68.
Club membership 615.
Visitors   contact in advance, may not generally play Sun.
Societies   written application required. Anytime weekdays, 9-11.30 Sat, no play Sun.
Green Fees IR£12 per day.
Designer   Eddie Hackett
Facilities   ⊗ ⅃ 占 ☕ ♀ ♨ ⚑

Hotel   ★★★ 72%   Hayden's Hotel, BALLINASLOE ☎ 0905 42347 48 ⇆ ☏

MOUNTBELLEW
Map 01 B4

Mountbellew Ballinasloe ☎ 0905 79259
A 9-hole wooded parkland course with 2 quarries and penalty drains to provide hazards.
9 holes, 5143mtrs, Par 69, SSS 66.
Visitors   welcome.
Societies   by prior arrangement.
Green Fees not confirmed.
Location   Of N63 midway between Roscommon/Galway

Hotel   ★★★ 72%   Hayden's Hotel, BALLINASLOE ☎ 0905 42347 48 ⇆ ☏

ORANMORE
Map 01 B3

Athenry Palmerstown ☎ 091 794466 Fax 091 794971
Wooded parkland course, recently extended to 18 holes.
18 holes, 5552metres, Par 70, SSS 70, Course record 68.
Club membership 800.
Visitors   advisable to telephone in advance, may not play Sun.
Societies   must apply in writing for booking to the secretary.
Green Fees not confirmed.
Cards   ▭ VISA
Prof   Declan Cummingham
Designer   Eddie Hackett
Facilities   ⊗ ⅃ 占 ☕ ♀ ♨ 🏠 ⚑ ⚒ ⚑
Location   0.5m off Galway to Dublin road

Hotel   ★★★ 67%   Galway Ryan Hotel, Dublin Rd, GALWAY ☎ 091 753181   96 ⇆ ☏

Galway Bay Golf & Country Club Renville
☎ 091 790500 Fax 091 792510
A championship golf course surrounded on three sides by the Atlantic Ocean and featuring water hazards on a number of holes. Each hole has its own characteristics made more obvious by the everchanging seaside winds. The design of the course highlights and preserves the ancient historic features of the Renville Peninsula. A spectacular setting distractingly beautiful and cleverly designed mix of holes presents a real golfing challenge, demanding total concentration.
18 holes, 6091mtrs, Par 72, SSS 71.
Club membership 400.
Visitors   contact in advance.
Societies   contact in advance.
Green Fees not confirmed.
Cards   ▭ ▭ VISA ▭
Prof   Eugene O'Connor
Designer   Christy O'Connor Jnr
Facilities   ⊗ ⅃ 占 ☕ ♀ ♨ 🏠 ⚑ ⚒ ⚑ ☏
& Leisure   sauna.
Location   N18 S towards Limerick/Shannon, turn right for Oranmore at rdbt, through village, follow signs

Hotel   ★★★ 69%   Galway Bay Golf & Country Club Hotel, ORANMORE ☎ 091 790500   92 ⇆ ☏

OUGHTERARD
Map 01 B4

Oughterard ☎ 091 552131 Fax 091 552377
Well maintained parkland course with mature trees and shrubs. Some very challenging holes.
18 holes, 6660yds, Par 70, SSS 69, Course record 67.
Club membership 1000.
Visitors   contact secretary or professional in advance.
Societies   must apply in writing.
Green Fees IR£15 per day.
Cards   ▭ ▭ VISA ▭
Prof   Michael Ryan
Designer   P Merrigan
Facilities   ⊗ ⅃ 占 ☕ ♀ ♨ 🏠 ⚑ ⚒ ☏
Location   1m from town on Galway road

▶

Hotel ★★★ 63% Ross Lake House Hotel, Rosscahill,
OUGHTERARD ☎ 091 550109 & 550154
Fax 091 550184 13 ⇄ ☏

PORTUMNA   Map 01 B3

Portumna ☎ 0509 41059
Parkland course with mature trees.
18 holes, 5474mtrs, Par 68, SSS 67, Course record 67.
Club membership 650.
Visitors   restricted Sun & public holidays.
Societies   must contact in writing.
Green Fees IR£14 per day.
Designer   E Connaughton
Facilities ⊗ ⫵ ᴸ ♭ ♀ ♨ ⸱ ⧨ ♣ ♠ ✐
Location   2.5m from town on Woodford/Ennis road

Hotel ★★★ 60% County Arms Hotel, BIRR
☎ 0509 20791 24 ⇄ ☏

RENVYLE   Map 01 A4

Renvyle House Hotel ☎ 095 43511
Pebble Beach course at Renvyle House is an exceptionally
demanding 9 hole course. Exposed to Atlantic winds,
crosswinds are a regular feature. A lake comes into play on 3
holes on one of which is a drive over water. On 4 holes
pebble beach and the sea demand precision.
9 holes, 2000yds, Par 32.
Visitors   must contact in advance.
Societies   contact in advance.
Green Fees not confirmed.
Prof   Gus Murphy
Facilities ⊗ ⫵ ᴸ ♭ ♀ ♨ ⧨ ⇌ ✐
& Leisure   hard tennis courts, heated outdoor swimming
                pool, fishing.

TUAM   Map 01 B4

Tuam Barnacurragh ☎ 093 28993 Fax 093 26003
Parkland course with plenty of trees and bunkers.
18 holes, 5513mtrs, Par 72, SSS 70, Course record 72.
Club membership 800.
Visitors   preferred Mon-Fri, must contact in advance. No
                visitors Sat.
Societies   telephone/write in advance.
Green Fees IR£15 per round.
Prof   Larry Smyth
Designer   Eddie Hackett
Facilities ⊗ ⫵ ᴸ ♭ ♀ ♨ ⸱ ⧨ ♣ ♠ ✐
Location   0.5m from town on Athenry road

Hotel ★★★★ 65% Ardilaun House Hotel, Taylor's
Hill, GALWAY ☎ 091 521433 90 ⇄ ☏

CO KERRY

BALLYBUNION   Map 01 A3

BALLYBUNION See page 455

BALLYFERRITER   Map 01 A2

Ceann Sibeal ☎ 066 9156255 Fax 066 9156409
This most westerly golf course in Europe has a magnificent
scenic location. It is a traditional links course with beautiful
turf, many bunkers, a stream that comes into play on 14 holes
and, usually, a prevailing wind.
18 holes, 6700yds, Par 72, SSS 71, Course record 72.
Club membership 432.
Visitors   telephone in advance.
Societies   must contact in advance.
Green Fees not confirmed.
Cards   ▭ ▬
Prof   Dermot O'Connor
Designer   Hackett/O'Connor Jnr
Facilities ⊗ ⫵ ᴸ ♭ ♀ ♨ ⧨ ⸱ ⧨ ✐

Hotel ★★★ 72% Dingle Skellig Hotel, DINGLE
☎ 066 51144 115 ⇄ ☏

CASTLEGREGORY   Map 01 A2

Castlegregory Stradbally ☎ 066 39444
A links course sandwiched between the sea and a freshwater
lake and mountains on two sides. The 3rd hole is visually
superb with a 365yard drive into the wind.
9 holes, 2569mtrs, Par 68, SSS 68, Course record 67.
Club membership 200.
Visitors   advisable to contact in advance.
Societies   apply in advance.
Green Fees IR£15 per 18 holes, IR£10 per 9 holes.
Cards   ▬
Designer   Dr Arthur Spring
Facilities ♭ ♀ ♨ ⧨ ✐
& Leisure   fishing.
Hotel ★★★ 67% The Brandon Hotel, TRALEE
☎ 066 23333 160 ⇄ ☏

GLENBEIGH   Map 01 A2

Dooks ☎ 066 9768205 Fax 066 9768476
Old-established course on the sea shore between the
Kerry mountains and Dingle Bay. Sand dunes are a
feature (the name Dooks is a derivation of the Gaelic
word for sand bank) and the course offers a fine
challenge in a superb Ring of Kerry location.
18 holes, 6010yds, Par 70, SSS 68.
Club membership 750.
Visitors   must contact in advance.
Societies   contact in advance.
Green Fees IR£25 per round.
Cards   ▭ ▬
Facilities ⊗ ⫵ ᴸ ♭ ♀ ♨ ⧨ ✐
Location   On N70, between Killorglin and Glenbeigh

Hotel ★★★ 64% Gleneagle Hotel,
KILLARNEY ☎ 064 31870 200 ⇄ ☏

KENMARE   Map 01 B2

Kenmare Kilgarvan Rd ☎ 064 41291 Fax 064 42061
Extended to a championship 18-hole course in 1993 this
challenging parkland course enjoys a magnificent setting
where the cascading waters of the Sheen and Roughty rivers
join the Atlantic. Although it can be exacting on a good
golfer, it is never unfair to the weak or the novice golfer.

▶

BALLYBUNION

BALLYBUNION *Co Kerry*

☎ **068 27146 Fax 068 23787**   **Map 01 A3**

John Ingham writes: Since golf is a state of mind over muscle and a great day on the links is exhilarating, it is my view that memorable fairways tend not to be decorated with artificial lakes that are fun only for ducks and golf ball manufacturers.

Some of the best courses look natural, even though they may have been helped along by skilful architects such as Colt, Hawtree or Mackenzie. And in the Emerald Isle, it is entirely appropriate that, back in 1906, a Mr Murphy built Ballybunion on the West Coast of Ireland. Believe me, there are few greater adventures waiting to be tackled and not to play this old course is a crime.

In an American list of the world's top 100 courses, Ballybunion is in there at number eight and the reason is simple: it probably represents the ultimate links on as wild a stretch as you will find. The Atlantic waves crash into the shore and no golfer will ever feel closer to nature as he hunts his ball and flights it through crosswinds and breathtaking views. This course is a star even in a part of Ireland that is wall-to-wall golf courses of the highest calibre. The experience of taking on this classic will be remembered as long as you live.

There are now two courses at Ballybunion, separated only by a 19th hole that has heard all the wondrous stories before, as well as hosting such great names as Tom Watson, five times winner of the Open. Likeable Tom can't speak highly enough of the place and claims that before anyone builds a golf course, they should play Ballybunion.

Visitors	must contact in advance.
Societies	must book in advance
Green fees	Old Course: £IR60 per round; Cashen Course: £IR35 per round. Both courses IR£80. 🍽 🚃.
Facilities	⊗ 〽 ♨ ☕ ♀ ⚐ 🛎 ⛳ ⚙ Professional (Brian O'Callaghan).
Leisure	sauna
Location	Sandhill Rd

36 holes. Old Course: 18 holes, 6603 yds, Par 71, SSS 72. Course record 67
Cashen Course: 18 holes, 6216 yds, SSS 72 Par 72

WHERE TO STAY AND EAT NEARBY

HOTELS:

BALLYHEIGE

★ ★ ★ ❀ 64% The White Sands ☎ 066 33102 81 ⇌ ♟

TRALEE

★ ★ ★ 67% The Brandon ☎ 066 23333 160 ⇌ ♟

★ ★ ★ 64% Abbey Gate, Maine St. ☎ 066 29888 100 ⇌ ♟

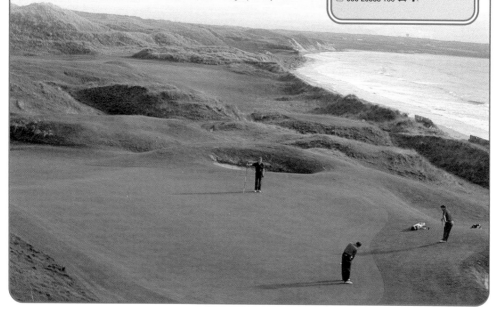

18 holes, 5615yds, Par 71.
Club membership 400.
Visitors enquire for weekends.
Societies contact in advance.
Green Fees not confirmed.
Designer Eddie Hackett
Facilities 🕃 ♥ ⚑ ♣ 🏠 ⛳ ⚐

Hotel ★★★★♨♨ Park Hotel Kenmare, KENMARE
☎ 064 41200 49 ⇆ ⛳

KILLARNEY Map 01 B2

Beaufort Churchtown, Beaufort ☎ 064 44440 Fax 064 44752
A championship standard Par 71 parkland course designed
by Dr Arthur Spring. This relatively new course is in the
centre of south-west Ireland's golfing mecca. Old ruins of an
11th century castle dominate the back nine and the whole
course is overlooked by the MacGillycuddy Reeks. The Par 3
8th and Par 4 11th are two of the most memorable holes.
18 holes, 6587yds, Par 71, SSS 72.
Club membership 200.

Visitors booking advisable for weekends.
Societies advance booking essential.
Green Fees IR£25 per round, IR£10 additional round
(IR£33/IR£13 weekends).
Cards 💳 🟦 VISA
Prof Hugh Duggan
Designer Arthur Spring
Facilities 🕃 ⚑ ♥ ⚑ ♣ 🏠 ⛳ 🏇 🏌 ⚐
Location 7m W of Killarney, off N72 w

Hotel ★★★ 67% Castlerosse Hotel, KILLARNEY
☎ 064 31144 110 ⇆ ⛳

Killarney Golf & Fishing Club Mahony's Point
☎ 064 31034 Fax 064 33065
Both of the courses are parkland with tree-lined
fairways, many bunkers and small lakes which provide
no mean challenge. Mahoney's Point Course has a
particularly testing par 5, 4, 3 finish and both courses
call for great skill from the tee. Killarney has been the
venue for many important events, including the 1996
Curtis Cup, and is a favourite of many famous golfers.
*Mahony's Point: 18 holes, 5826mtrs, Par 72, SSS 72,
Course record 68.*
*Killeen: 18 holes, 6006mtrs, Par 72, SSS 72, Course
record 65.*
Lackabane: 18 holes, 6381mtrs, Par 72, SSS 72.
Club membership 1300.
Visitors must contact in advance & have a handicap
certificate.

Societies must telephone in advance.
Green Fees available on request.
Cards 💳 🟦 AMEX VISA 🅿
Prof Tony Coveney
Designer H Longhurst/Sir Guy Campbell
Facilities 🕃 ⚑ ♥ ⚑ ♥ ⚑ ♣ 🏠 ⛳ ⚐ ⛳
& Leisure sauna, gymnasium.
Location On N 72, Ring of Kerry road

Hotel ★★★★ 78% Aghadoe Heights Hotel,
KILLARNEY ☎ 064 31766 60 ⇆ ⛳

KILLORGLIN Map 01 A2

Killorglin Stealroe ☎ 066 9761979 Fax 066 9761437
A parkland course designed by Eddie Hackett as a
challenging but fair test of golf, surrounded by magnificent
views.
18 holes, 6497yds, Par 72, SSS 71, Course record 68.
Club membership 280.
Visitors pre booking of tee time advisable, must be
confirmed in writing.
Societies book by telephone, confirm in writing.
Green Fees not confirmed.
Cards 💳 🟦 AMEX VISA 🅿
Designer Eddie Hackett
Facilities 🕃 ⚑ ♥ ⚑ ♥ ⚑ ♣ 🏠 ⛳ 🏇 🏌 ⚐
& Leisure fishing.
Location 3km from Killorglin, on N70 to Tralee

Hotel ★★★ 67% The Brandon Hotel, TRALEE
☎ 066 23333 160 ⇆ ⛳

PARKNASILLA Map 01 A2

Parknasilla ☎ 064 45122 Fax 064 45323
Recently re-designed course with new tees and greens on
every hole. The view from the eighth tee is breathtaking with
the green on the edge of the sea while the ninth tee is almost
surrounded by water.
9 holes, 5400mtrs, Par 70, SSS 69.
Club membership 150.

Visitors may not play on competition days. Must contact
in advance.
Societies must contact in advance.
Green Fees not confirmed.
Cards 💳
Designer Arthur Spring
Facilities ♣ 🏠 ⛳ 🏊 ⚐
& Leisure hard tennis courts, heated indoor swimming
pool, sauna.
Location 2m E of Sneem village on Ring of Kerry road

Hotel   ★★★★ 79%   Great Southern Hotel,
PARKNASILLA
☎ 064 45122 26 ⊯ ♞ Annexe59 ⊯ ♞

TRALEE   Map 01 A2

Tralee West Barrow ☎ 066 36379 Fax 066 36008
The first Arnold Palmer designed course in Europe, the
magnificent 18-hole links are set in spectacular scenery
on the Barrow peninsula. Perhaps the most memorable
hole is the par four 17th which plays from a high tee,
across a deep gorge to a green perched high against a
backdrop of mountains.
18 holes, 5939mtrs, Par 71, SSS 71, Course record 66.
Club membership 1098.
Visitors   may play before 4.20pm on weekdays but
only after 10.30am on Wed & 11am-1.30pm
on Sat & bank holidays. Must have a
handicap certificate and contact in advance.
Societies   weekdays only; must contact in writing.
Green Fees not confirmed.
Cards   ⬜ ⬜
Designer   Arnold Palmer
Facilities   ⊗ ⋔ ⓛ ⬛ ♀ ♨ ⌂ ♂
Location   8m NW of Tralee on Spa-Fenit road

Hotel   ★★★ 67%   The Brandon Hotel, TRALEE
☎ 066 23333 160 ⊯ ♞

WATERVILLE   Map 01 A2

Waterville House & Golf Links
☎ 066 74102 Fax 066 74482
On the western tip of the Ring of Kerry, this course is
highly regarded by many top golfers. The feature holes
are the par five 11th, which runs along a rugged valley
between towering dunes, and the par three 17th, which
features an exceptionally elevated tee. Needless to say,
the surroundings are beautiful.
18 holes, 6549yds, Par 72, SSS 72, Course record 71.
Visitors   must contact in advance.
Societies   must contact secretary/manager in advance.
Green Fees not confirmed.
Prof   Liam Higgins
Designer   Eddie Hackett
Facilities   ⊗ ⋔ ⓛ ⬛ ♀ ♨ ⌂ ⚐ ⚓ ♬ ♂ ⚐
& Leisure   heated outdoor swimming pool, fishing,
sauna.

Hotel   ★★★ 62%   Derrynane Hotel,
CAHERDANIEL ☎ 066 75136 74 ⊯

CO KILDARE

ATHY   Map 01 C3

Athy Geraldine ☎ 0507 31729
A meadowland course approaching its centenary year having
been founded in 1906.
18 holes, 6159yds, Par 71, SSS 69, Course record 69.
Club membership 475.

Visitors   time sheet in operation on Sundays
Societies   contact for infromation.
Green Fees IR£13 (IR£17 weekends).
Facilities   ⋔ by prior arrangement ⓛ ⬛ ♀ ♨ ♂
Location   2m N of Athy

Guest   ▬▬▬▬▬ Coursetown Country House,
house   Stradbally Rd, ATHY ☎ 0507 31101 5 ♞

CARBURY   Map 01 C4

Highfield Highfield House ☎ 0405 31021 Fax 0405 31021
A relatively flat parkland course but with interesting
undulations, especially by the fast flowing stream which runs
through many holes. The 7th doglegs over the lake, the 10th
is a great Par 5 with a challenging green, the 14th Par 3 is
over rushes onto a plateau green (out of bounds on left) and
the 18th Par 3 green is tucked between bunkers and a huge
chestnut tree.
18 holes, 5707mtrs, Par 72, SSS 69.
Club membership 400.
Visitors   welcome, must contact in advance for weekend
play.
Societies   telephone or apply in writing.
Green Fees IR£10 per day (IR£14 weekends & bank
holidays).
Cards   ⬜
Prof   Peter O'Hagan
Designer   Alan Duggan
Facilities   ⊗ ⓛ ⬛ ♀ ♨ ⌂ ♬ ⚓ ♂
Location   9m from Enfield

Hotel   ★★★ 71%   Keadeen Hotel, NEWBRIDGE
☎ 045 431666   55 ⊯ ♞

CASTLEDERMOT   Map 01 C3

Kilkea Castle ☎ 0503 45555 Fax 0503 45505
A beautiful course opened in the summer of 1994 in the
grounds of a 12th-century castle - visible from all over the
course. The River Griese and two lakes create numerous
water hazards.
18 holes, 6200mtrs, Par 71, SSS 71.

Visitors   must contact in advance for details.
Societies   welcome, contact for details.
Green Fees IR£25 per 18 holes; IR£15 per 9 holes.
Cards   ⬜
Designer   McDard/Cassidy
Facilities   ⊗ ⋔ ⓛ ⬛ ♀ ♨ ⌂ ♬ ♂
& Leisure   hard tennis courts, heated indoor swimming
pool, fishing, sauna, solarium, gymnasium.

▶

DONADEA   Map 01 C4

Knockanally Golf & Country Club ☎ 045 69322
Home of the Irish International Professional Matchplay
championship, this parkland course is set in a former estate,
with a Palladian-style clubhouse.
18 holes, 6485yds, Par 72, SSS 72.
Club membership 500.
Visitors   may not play on Sun 8.30am-noon.
Societies   must contact in writing or telephone.
Green Fees not confirmed.
Prof   Peter Hickey
Facilities   ♀ ⌂ ☎ ⛳ ♂
& Leisure   fishing.
Location   3m off main Dublin-Galway road

Hotel   ★★★ 64% Lucan Spa Hotel, LUCAN
                  ☎ 01 6280495 6280497
                  Fax 01 6280841   65 ⇄ ♠

KILDARE   Map 01 C3

Cill Dara Cill Dara, Little Curragh
☎ 045 521295 & 521433
Only 1 mile from the famous Curragh racecourse, this 9-hole
parkland course is unusual in having links type soil as well as
plenty of trees.
9 holes, 5738mtrs, Par 71, SSS 70, Course record 64.
Club membership 500.
Visitors   welcome, Wed is Ladies Day and may only play
                  after 1.30pm Sun (winter) and 4pm Sun
                  (Summer).
Societies   apply in writing to Mr M O'Boyle, Professional.
Green Fees not confirmed.
Prof   Mark O'Boyle
Facilities   ⊗ ⫟ ⓑ ☕ ♀ ⌂ ☎
Location   1m E of Kildare

Hotel   ★★★ 71% Keadeen Hotel, NEWBRIDGE
                  ☎ 045 431666   55 ⇄ ♠

The Curragh Curragh
☎ 045 441238 & 441714 Fax 045 441714
A particularly challenging course, well wooded and with
lovely scenery all around.
18 holes, 6035mtrs, Par 72, SSS 71, Course record 63.
Club membership 1040.
Visitors   must contact in advance, preferred on Mon,
                  Wed, Thu & Fri.
Societies   apply in writing.
Green Fees IR£18 per day (IR£22 weekends & bank
                  holidays).
Prof   Gerry Burke
Facilities   ⊗ ⫟ ⓑ ☕ ♀ ⌂ ☎ ⛳ ♂
Location   Off N7 between Newbridge & Kildare

Hotel   ★★★ 71% Keadeen Hotel, NEWBRIDGE
                  ☎ 045 431666   55 ⇄ ♠

KILL   Map 01 D4

Killeen ☎ 045 866003 Fax 045 875881
Set in pleasant countryside, the attractive course is
characterised by its many lakes. It provides a challenge to
test the skills of the moderate enthusiast and the more
experienced golfer.

18 holes, 5561mtrs, Par 71, SSS 71, Course record 70.
Club membership 170.
Visitors   please ring for tee-times
Societies   must contact in advance.
Green Fees IR£17 per round (IR£20 weekends & bank
                  holidays).
Cards   ▭ ▭
Designer   Pat Ruddy
Facilities   ⊗ ⫟ ⓑ ☕ ♀ ⌂ ☎ ⛳ ♂
Location   Off N7 at Kill signposted

Hotel   ★★★ 76% Barberstown Castle, STRAFFAN
                  ☎ 01 6288157   23 ⇄ ♠ Annexe4 ⇄ ♠

NAAS   Map 01 D4

Bodenstown Sallins ☎ 045 897096
The old course in Bodenstown has ample fairways and large
greens, some of which are raised, providing more than a fair
test of golf. The Ladyhill course is a little shorter and tighter,
but still affords a fair challenge.
Bodenstown: 18 holes, 6132mtrs, Par 71, SSS 71.
Ladyhill: 18 holes, 5428mtrs, Par 71, SSS 68.
Club membership 700.
Visitors   may not play on Bodenstown course at
                  weekends.
Societies   must contact by telephone.
Green Fees not confirmed.
Designer   Richard Mather
Facilities   ⊗ ⫟ ⓑ ☕ ♀ ⌂ ♂
Location   4m from town near Bodenstown graveyard

Hotel   ★★★ 61% Downshire House Hotel,
                  BLESSINGTON
                  ☎ 045 865199   14 ⇄ ♠ Annexe11 ⇄ ♠

Craddockstown Blessington Rd
☎ 045 897610 Fax 045 896968
A gradually maturing parkland course featuring four testing
par 3 holes, all over 140 metres in length, sand-based greens,
and many trees. Easy walking.
18 holes, 5645mtrs, Par 71, SSS 69, Course record 67.
Club membership 600.
Visitors   should ring in advance to verify tee times
                  available, limited at weekends.
Societies   apply in writing.
Green Fees IR£15 per round (IR£20 weekends).
Designer   A Spring
Facilities   ⊗ ⫟ ⓑ ☕ ♀ ⌂ ♂
Location   Off the main dual carriageway (N7/N97), head
                  towards Naas, turn left on to Blessington Road

Hotel   ★★★ 71% Keadeen Hotel, NEWBRIDGE
                  ☎ 045 431666   55 ⇄ ♠

Naas Kerdiffstown
☎ 045 897509 Fax 045 896109 & 874644
Scenic parkland course well bunkered, with a substantial
number of trees, greens are both sand based and natural.
18 holes, 5663mtrs, Par 71, SSS 69, Course record 65.
Club membership 1000.
Visitors   may not play on Sun, Tue or Thu.
Societies   must contact in advance.
Green Fees IR£18 per round (IR£24 weekends & bank
                  holidays).
Cards   ▭ ▭
Designer   E Hackett/A Spring

Facilities ⊗ ⛴ ♨ ♀ ⚲ ♂
Location 1m from town on Sallins-Johnstown road

Hotel ★★★ 61% Downshire House Hotel,
BLESSINGTON
☎ 045 865199 14 ⇄ ↑ Annexe11 ⇄ ↑

Woodlands Cooleragh, Coill Dubh
☎ 045 860777 Fax 045 860988
Reconstructed 9-hole course opened in March 1997 offering
an interesting challenge with completely new greens, tees
and an extra 1000 yards coming into play. Extended to 18
hole course opening July 1999.
9 holes, 6408yds, Par 72, SSS 71.
Club membership 454.
Visitors must contact in advance, unable to play most
weekends (member competitions).
Societies telephone in advance for details.
Green Fees IR£10 per day (IR£12 weekends & bank
holdiays).
Designer Tommy Halpin
Facilities ⊗ � ⛴ ♨ ♀ ⚲ ⌂ ♂
Location Off the Clane/Edenderry road

Hotel ★★★ 71% Keadeen Hotel, NEWBRIDGE
☎ 045 431666 55 ⇄ ↑

STRAFFAN Map 01 D4

Castlewarden ☎ 01 4589254 & 4589838 Fax 01 4588992
Founded in 1990, Castlewarden is maturing into a delightful
parkland course with water features and excellent greens.
18 holes, 6496yds, Par 72, SSS 70.
Club membership 765.
Visitors welcome contact for details. Tues Ladies Day.
Societies by prior application.
Green Fees Apr-Sep IR£17 am, IR£20 pm (IR£20
weekends); Oct-Mar IR£17 (IR£20 weekends).
Prof Gerry Egan
Designer Tommy Halpin
Facilities ⊗ ⛴ ♨ ♀ ⚲ ⌂ ↑ ♂
Location Between Naas/Rathcoole

Hotel ★★★ 62% Ambassador Hotel, KILL
☎ 045 877064 36 ⇄ ↑

The K Club ☎ 01 6017300 Fax 01 6017399
Known as The K-Club, this course is growing in
reputation. Designed by Arnold Palmer, its 6,456 metre
length is a challenge to even the best golfers. Covering
177 acres of prime Kildare woodland there are 14 man-
made lakes as well as the River Liffey to create water
hazards. There is the promise of a watery grave at the
monster 7th (Par 5, 520 metres) and at the 17th the tee
shot is to the green on the water's edge. There is also a
practise area and driving range.
18 holes, 6163mtrs, Par 72, SSS 72, Course record 64.
Club membership 520.
Visitors contact in advance to book prefered tee
times, restricted at members times.
Societies telephone & write in advance, societies not
allowed on weekends & Wed afternoon.
Green Fees IR£130.
Cards 💳
Prof Ernie Jones
Designer Arnold Palmer

Facilities ⊗ ⛴ ♨ ♀ ⚲ ⌂ ↑ ⌂ ♨ ♂
& Leisure hard tennis courts, heated indoor swimming
pool, squash, fishing, sauna, solarium,
gymnasium.
Location From Dublin take N4 and axit R406,
entrance to hotel on right in Straffan

Hotel ★★★★★♨ The Kildare Hotel & Country
Club, STRAFFAN
☎ 01 6017200 36 ⇄ ↑ Annexe9 ⇄ ↑

CO KILKENNY

CALLAN Map 01 C3

Callan Geraldine ☎ 056 25136 & 25949
Meadowland.
18 holes, 6377yds, Par 72, SSS 70, Course record 67.
Club membership 500.
Visitors welcome. Must contact in advance.
Societies must apply in writing.
Green Fees not confirmed.
Cards 💳
Prof John O'Dwyer
Facilities ⊗ ⛴ ♨ ♀ ⚲ ⌂ ↑ ♂
& Leisure fishing.

Hotel ★★★ 68% Hotel Kilkenny, College Rd,
KILKENNY ☎ 056 62000 80 ⇄ ↑

KILKENNY Map 01 C3

Kilkenny Glendine ☎ 056 65400 Fax 056 23593
One of Ireland's most pleasant inland courses, noted for
its tricky finishing holes and its par threes. Features of
the course are its long 11th and 13th holes and the
challenge increases year by year as thousands of trees
planted over the last 30 years or so are maturing. As host
of the Kilkenny Scratch Cup annually, the course is
permanently maintained in championship condition. The
Irish Dunlop Tournament and the Irish Professional
Matchplay Championship have also been held here.
18 holes, 5857mtrs, Par 71, SSS 70, Course record 64.
Club membership 1000.
Visitors must contact in advance.
Societies must contact in advance.
Green Fees IR£20 per round (IR£25 weekends & bank
holidays). ▶

Prof	Noel Leahy
Facilities	⊗⍟🖫💺♀♨🏠🏌🐾⚓✦⚘
Location	1m from centre on Castlecomer road
Hotel	★★★ 68% Hotel Kilkenny, College Rd, KILKENNY ☎ 056 62000 80 ⇥ 🐾

THOMASTOWN   Map 01 C3

MOUNT JULIET GOLF COURSE See page 461

CO LAOIS

ABBEYLEIX   Map 01 C3

Abbeyleix Rathmoyle ☎ 0502 31450 Fax 0502 30108
A pleasant, parkland 9 hole course.
9 holes, 5626mtrs, Par 70, SSS 69.
Club membership 300.
Visitors   welcome weekdays.
Societies   apply in writing.
Green Fees IR£8 per day (IR£10 weekends).
Facilities   🖫💺♀♨⚘

Hotel   ★★★ 67% Newpark Hotel, KILKENNY
               ☎ 056 22122 111 ⇥ 🐾

MOUNTRATH   Map 01 C3

Mountrath Knockanina
☎ 0502 32558 & 32643 (office) Fax 0502 32643
A picturesque course at the foot of the Slieve Bloom
Mountains in central Ireland. The 18 hole course has fine
fairways and well bunkered greens, the river Nore flows
through the course.
18 holes, 5493mtrs, Par 71, SSS 69, Course record 68.
Club membership 500.
Visitors   check for availability at weekends, other days no
               problem but safer to check.
Societies   must contact in advance.
Green Fees IR£10.
Facilities   ⊗ by prior arrangement 🖫💺♀♨⚘
Location   1.5m from town on Dublin-Limerick road

Hotel   ★★★ 71% Keadeen Hotel, NEWBRIDGE
               ☎ 045 431666 55 ⇥ 🐾

PORTARLINGTON   Map 01 C3

Portarlington Garryhinch ☎ 0502 23115 Fax 0502 23044
Lovely parkland course designed around a pine forest. It is
bounded on the 16th and 17th by the River Barrow which
makes the back 9 very challenging.
18 holes, 5673mtrs, Par 72, SSS 69, Course record 70.
Club membership 562.
Visitors   welcome but restricted Tue-Ladies Day, Sat &
               Sun societies and club competitions. Must
               contact in advance
Societies   must apply in writing.
Green Fees IR£14 per round (IR£17 weekends).

Designer	Eddie Hackett
Facilities	⊗⍟🖫💺♀♨⚘
Location	4m from town on Mountmellick road
Hotel	★★★ 71% Keadeen Hotel, NEWBRIDGE ☎ 045 431666 55 ⇥ 🐾

PORTLAOISE   Map 01 C3

The Heath
☎ 0502 46533 & 46622 (Pro shop) Fax 0502 46866
One of the oldest clubs in Ireland. The course is set in pretty
countryside and offers a good challenge.
18 holes, 5736mtrs, Par 71, SSS 69, Course record 69.
Club membership 800.
Visitors   contact in advance, preferred on weekdays.
Societies   apply in writing.
Green Fees IR£10 (IR£17 weekends and bank holidays).
Prof   Eddie Doyle
Facilities   ⊗⍟🖫💺♀♨🏠⚘✦
Location   3m N on N7

Hotel   ★★★ 71% Keadeen Hotel, NEWBRIDGE
               ☎ 045 431666 55 ⇥ 🐾

RATHDOWNEY   Map 01 C3

Rathdowney ☎ 0505 46170 Fax 0505 46170
A 18 hole course recently opened. Undulating terrain, 12th &
15th are particularly tough par 4 holes, 6th is a challenging
par 5 (550yds) into the prevailing wind. A good test for
golfers of all abilities.
18 holes, 5894mtrs, Par 71, SSS 70.
Club membership 320.
Visitors   welcome. Ladies have priority on Wed, Sat &
               Sun mornings are reserved for member &
               societies.
Societies   must apply in writing and pay deposit to confirm
               booking.
Green Fees not confirmed.
Designer   Eddie Hackett
Facilities   ♀♨⚘
Location   0.5m SE. Follow signs from town square

Hotel   ★★★ 68% Hotel Kilkenny, College Rd,
               KILKENNY ☎ 056 62000 80 ⇥ 🐾

CO LEITRIM

BALLINAMORE   Map 01 C4

Ballinamore ☎ 078 44346
A very dry and very testing 9-hole parkland course along the
Ballinamore/Ballyconnell Canal.
9 holes, 5680yds, Par 68, SSS 66, Course record 66.
Club membership 100.
Visitors   restricted occasionally.
Societies   must contact in writing.
Green Fees not confirmed.
Designer   A Spring
Facilities   🖫💺♀♨
& Leisure   fishing.

Hotel   ★★ 64% Royal Hotel, BOYLE
               ☎ 079 62016 16 ⇥ 🐾

MOUNT JULIET

THOMASTOWN *Co Kilkenny*
☎ 056 73000 Fax 056 73019   Map 01 C3

*C*harlie Mulqueen *writes:* Nick Faldo and David Leadbetter are just two of the game's luminaries to have fallen in love with Mount Juliet, the only Jack Nicklaus designed golf course in Ireland. Faldo, perhaps, is somewhat biased given that he completed a hat-trick of Irish Open successes there in 1993.

Mount Juliet stands as a monument to the architectural ability of Nicklaus. The estate was acquired in the late '80s by Tim Mahony, who gave the Golden Bear a free hand. In return, Nicklaus delivered a 6641 yards, par 72 course of great quality and considerable charm. The hundreds of mature trees help to give the impression that the course has been here for centuries rather than just since 1991 - an occasion marked by a memorable exhibition between Nicklaus and Ireland's own great Christy O'Connor Senior. Since 1993 it has hosted the Murphy's Irish Open.

Mount Juliet's 'signature hole' arrives as early as the third, played from an elevated tee across an awesome lake to an island green. The golfer confronts a lot more water as the round progresses, especially at the perilous 13th, which has certainly proved unlucky for many of the contestants in each of the last three Irish Opens. Nor can even the best relax until they have completed the 470 yards, par four 18th. Again a lake comes into play all the way down the left and very frequently it requires two full woods to reach the long, narrow green. South African David Frost took 10 here in the opening round of the 1993 Irish Open and still hit back to finish third!

When the golf is over, the 1500 acres of the Mount Juliet estate offers many more attractions; horse riding, clay pigeon shooting or archery, fishing in the delightful River Nore or dinner in the superb 18th-century mansion transformed into a luxury hotel. And if the golf hasn't been up to requirements, up you get bright and early the following morning for a lesson on the magnificent David Leadbetter academy. Mount Juliet has it all - it's a must!

Visitors	telephone in advance
Societies	book in advance by telephone or in writing.
Green fees	not confirmed.
Facilities	⊗ ⟫⛳ 🍴 ♥ ♀ 🍺 ⚓ ⛏ 🏠 ⛏ ♂ ♀ Professional (Mark Reid) golf academy
Leisure	tennis, indoor swimming pool, private fishing, sauna, solarium, gym, equestrian centre.
Location	Dublin/Waterford road (off the N9)

18 holes, 6641yds, Par72 SSS 72
Course record 65

WHERE TO STAY AND EAT NEARBY

HOTELS:

THOMASTOWN
★★★★ ❀❀ ♨♨ Mount Juliet Hotel,
☎ 056 73000. 32 ⇄ 🐾 Annexe 24 ⇄ 🐾

KILKENNY
★★★ 68% Hotel Kilkenny, College Rd
☎ 056 62000. 80 ⇄ 🐾
★★★ 67% Newpark Hotel
☎ 056 22122. 111 (86 ⇄ 🐾 25 🐾)

CO LIMERICK

ADARE

Map 01 B3

Adare Manor ☎ 061 396204 Fax 061 396800
An 18-hole parkland course, Par 69, in an unusual setting. The course surrounds the ruins of a castle, a friary and an abbey.
18 holes, 5800yds, Par 69, SSS 69.
Club membership 600.

Visitors	welcome weekdays, weekends only by arrangement and subject to availability.
Societies	by prior arrangement, preferably in writing.
Green Fees	not confirmed.
Cards	🔲
Designer	Ben Sayers/Eddie Hacket
Facilities	🅱 ☕ 🍴 🔥 ⛳ 🏌 ⚡
& Leisure	fishing.

LIMERICK

Map 01 B3

Castletroy Castletroy
☎ 061 335753 & 335261 Fax 061 335373
Parkland course with out of bounds on the left of the first two holes. The long par five 10th features a narrow entrance to a green guarded by a stream. The par three 13th has a panoramic view of the course and surrounding countryside from the tee and the 18th is a daunting finish, with the drive played towards a valley with the ground rising towards the green which is protected on both sides by bunkers. In recent years the club has hosted the finals of the Irish Mixed Foursomes and the Senior Championships.
18 holes, 5802mtrs, Par 71, SSS 71.
Club membership 1062.

Visitors	must contact in advance & have handicap certificate but may not play Sun or 1-2.30pm weekdays.
Societies	apply in writing.
Green Fees	IR£23 (IR£30 weekends).
Cards	🔲
Facilities	🅧 🍴 🅱 ☕ 🍴 🔥 ⛳ 🏌 ⚡
Location	3m from city on Dublin road

Hotel   ★★★★ 71% Castletroy Park Hotel, Dublin Rd, LIMERICK ☎ 061 335566 107 ⇥ 🏮

Limerick Ballyclough ☎ 061 415146 Fax 061 319219
Tree-lined parkland course which hosted the 1991 Ladies Senior Interprovincial matches. The club are the only Irish winners of the European Cup Winners Team Championship.
18 holes, 5938mtrs, Par 72, SSS 71, Course record 67.
Club membership 1300.

Visitors	may not play after 4pm or on Tue & weekends.
Societies	must contact in writing.
Green Fees	IR£22.50 per round.
Cards	🔲
Prof	John Cassidy
Designer	A McKenzie
Facilities	🅧 🍴 🅱 ☕ 🍴 🔥 ⛳ 🏌 ⚡
Location	3m S on Fedamore Road

Hotel   ★★★ 72% Jurys Hotel, Ennis Rd, LIMERICK ☎ 061 327777 95 ⇥ 🏮

Limerick County Golf & Country Club Ballyneety
☎ 61 351881 Fax 61 351384
Limerick County was designed by Des Smyth and presents beautifully because of the strategic locaton of the main features. It stretches over undulating terrain with one elevated section providing views of the surrounding countryside. It features over 70 bunkers with six lakes and several unique design features.
18 holes, 6712yds, Par 72, SSS 74, Course record 70.
Club membership 400.

Visitors	welcome but prebooking essential.
Societies	book by telephone or in writing.
Green Fees	not confirmed.
Prof	Philip Murphy
Designer	Des Smyth
Facilities	🅧 🍴 🅱 ☕ 🍴 🔥 ⛳ 🏌 ⚡
& Leisure	sauna.
Location	5m SE of Limerick on R512

Hotel   ★★★ 62% Greenhills Hotel, Caherdavin, LIMERICK ☎ 061 453033 59 ⇥ 🏮

NEWCASTLE WEST

Map 01 B3

Killeline Cork Rd ☎ 069 61600 Fax 069 77428
Set in 160 acres of gently contoured parkland in the heart of the Golden Vale with views to the Galtee Mountains. Because of its design and many mature trees, accuracy in playing is the key to good scoring.
18 holes, 6671yds, Par 72, SSS 68.
Club membership 400.

Visitors	welcome weekdays, by arrangement weekends, must contact in advance
Societies	telephone in advance.
Green Fees	not confirmed.
Cards	🔲
Prof	Kevin Dorrien
Facilities	🅧 🍴 🅱 ☕ 🍴 🔥 ⛳ 🏌 ⚡
& Leisure	heated indoor swimming pool, sauna, solarium, gymnasium.
Location	0.25m off main Limerick/Killarney route

Hotel   ★★★ 78% Dunraven Arms Hotel, ADARE ☎ 061 396633 75 ⇥ 🏮

Newcastle West Ardagh
☎ 069 76500 Fax 069 76511
A new course set in 150 acres of unspoilt countryside, built to the highest standards on sandy free draining soil. A practice ground and driving range are included. Hazards on the course include lakes, bunkers, streams and trees. A signature hole is likely to be the Par 3 6th playing 185 yards over a lake.

18 holes, 6317yds, Par 71, SSS 72, Course record 67.
Club membership 730.

Visitors   advisable to contact in advance, but available most days.
Societies   contact in advance.
Green Fees   IR£18 per day.
Cards   ⬜ ⬜
Designer   Dr Arthur Spring
Facilities   ⊗ ⬛ ⬛ ♉ ♈ 👜 ⛳ ♐
Location   2m off N21 between Limerick & Killarney

Hotel   ★★★ 78% Dunraven Arms Hotel, ADARE
☎ 061 396633 75 ⇆ ℟

CO LONGFORD

LONGFORD   Map 01 C4

County Longford Glack, Dublin Rd
☎ 043 46310 Fax 043 47082
A lovely 18-hole parkland course with lots of trees.
18 holes, 6044yds, Par 70, SSS 69, Course record 69.
Club membership 819.

Visitors   very welcome, but advisable to telephone in advance for Tue and Sun play.
Societies   by prior arrangement.
Green Fees   not confirmed.
Facilities   ⊗ ⬛ ⬛ ⬛ ♉ ♈ 👜 ⛳ 🛒 ♐ ♐
Location   E of town

Hotel   ★★★ 64% Abbey Hotel, Galway Rd,
ROSCOMMON ☎ 0903 26240 & 26505
Fax 0903 26021 25 ⇆ ℟

CO LOUTH

ARDEE   Map 01 D4

Ardee Townparks ☎ 041 53227
Pleasant parkland course with mature trees and a stream.
18 holes, 6100yds, Par 69, SSS 69.

Visitors   may normally play on weekdays (except Wed).
Green Fees   not confirmed.
Facilities   ♉

Hotel   ★★★ 69% Ballymascanlon House Hotel,
DUNDALK ☎ 042 71124 75 ⇆

BALTRAY   Map 01 D4

County Louth ☎ 041 9822329 Fax 041 9822969
Generally held to have the best greens in Ireland, this
links course was designed by Tom Simpson to have well
guarded and attractive greens without being overly
dependant on bunkers. It provides a good test for the
modern champion, notably as the annual venue for the
East of Ireland Amateur Open.
18 holes, 6613yds, Par 73, SSS 71.
Club membership 1100.

Visitors   must contact in advance.
Societies   by prior arrangement.
Green Fees   IR£45 per round (IR£55 weekends).
Cards   ⬜ ⬜ ⬜
Prof   Paddy McGuirk
Designer   Tom Simpson
Facilities   ⊗ ⬛ ⬛ ⬛ ♉ ♈ 👜 ⛳ 🏇 🐾 🛒 ♐
& Leisure   hard tennis courts.
Location   5m NE of Drogheda

Hotel   ★★ 67% Conyngham Arms Hotel,
SLANE ☎ 041 24155 16rm(15 ⇆ ℟)

DUNDALK   Map 01 D4

Ballymascanlon House Hotel
☎ 042 9371124 Fax 042 9371598
Now a testing 18-hole parkland course with numerous water
hazards and two difficult holes through woodland, this very
scenic course is set at the edge of the Cooley Mountains.
18 holes, 5548yds, Par 68, SSS 66.

Visitors   must telephone in advance to check availability.
Societies   booking by telephone or letter.
Green Fees   not confirmed.
Cards   ⬜ ⬜ ⬜ ⬜
Designer   Craddock/Ruddy
Facilities   ⊗ ⬛ ⬛ ⬛ ♉ ♈ 👜 🛒 ♐
& Leisure   grass tennis courts, heated indoor swimming pool, sauna, gymnasium.
Location   3m N of Dundalk on the Carlingford road

Hotel   ★★★ 69% Ballymascanlon House Hotel,
DUNDALK ☎ 042 71124 75 ⇆

Dundalk Blackrock ☎ 042 21731 Fax 042 22022
A tricky course with extensive views.
18 holes, 6115mtrs, Par 72, SSS 72.
Club membership 1000.

Visitors   must contact in advance and may not play Tue or Sun.
Societies   must apply in writing in advance.
Green Fees   not confirmed.
Prof   James Cassidy
Facilities   ♉ 👜 ⛳ ♈
& Leisure   sauna.
Location   2.5m S on coast road

Hotel   ★★★ 69% Ballymascanlon House Hotel,
DUNDALK ☎ 042 71124 75 ⇆

Killinbeg Killin Park ☎ 042 39303
Opened in 1991 and designed by Eddie Hackett, this
undulating 18-hole parkland course has mature woodland and
river features.
18 holes, 5293yds, Par 69, SSS 65.
Club membership 100.
Visitors no restrictions.
Societies apply by telephone or in writing in advance.
Green Fees not confirmed.
Designer Eddie Hackett
Facilities ⊗ by prior arrangement ⫚ by prior arrangement
🏌 🍺 ♀ ⌂ ⛳ ♂
Location Bridge-a-Crinn

Hotel ★★★ 69% Ballymascanlon House Hotel,
DUNDALK ☎ 042 71124 75 ⇆

GREENORE   Map 01 D4

Greenore ☎ 042 73212 & 73678 Fax 042 73678
Situated amidst beautiful scenery on the shores of
Carlingford Lough, the trees here are an unusual feature on a
links course. There are quite a number of water facilities,
tight fairways and very good greens.
18 holes, 6514mtrs, Par 71, SSS 71.
Club membership 500.
Visitors must contact in advance at weekends. A letter of
introduction is desirable, but not essential.
Societies must contact in advance.
Green Fees not confirmed.
Facilities ⊗ ⫚ 🏌 🍺 ♀ ⌂ ♂

Hotel ★★★ 69% Ballymascanlon House Hotel,
DUNDALK ☎ 042 71124 75 ⇆

TERMONFECKIN   Map 01 D4

Seapoint ☎ 041 9822333 Fax 041 9822331
A very long championship links course of 7,000 yards with a
particularly interesting 17th hole.
18 holes, 6339mtrs, Par 72, SSS 71.
Visitors phone in advance for restrictions.
Societies telephone in advance.
Green Fees Summer: IR£25 (IR£30 weekends & bank
holidays); Winter: IR£30 (IR£35 weekends &
bank holidays).
Cards 💳 💳
Prof David Carroll
Designer Des Smyth
Facilities ⊗ ⫚ 🏌 🍺 ♀ ⌂ 🏠 ⛳ 🏡 🛒 🚲 ♂
Location 4m NE of Drogheda

Hotel ★★ 67% Conyngham Arms Hotel, SLANE
☎ 041 24155 16rm(15 ⇆ 🐾)

CO MAYO

BALLINA   Map 01 B4

Ballina Mossgrove, Shanaghy
☎ 096 21050 Fax 096 21050
Undulating but mostly flat inland course.
18 holes, 6103yds, Par 71, SSS 69, Course record 69.
Club membership 478.

Visitors welcome but may not play Sun before 3.30pm.
Restrictions apply depending on
competitions/society visits.
Societies apply in writing or telephone in advance.
Green Fees not confirmed.
Cards 💳 💳
Designer E Hackett
Facilities 🏌 🍺 ♀ ⌂ ⛳ ♂
Location 1m outside town on Bonnocolon Rd

BALLINROBE   Map 01 B4

Ballinrobe Cloonagashel ☎ 092 41118 Fax 092 41889
A championship parkland 18 hole course, set in the mature
woodlands of a historic estate at Cloonacastle. The layout of
the course incorporates seven man made lakes with the river
Robe flowing at the back of the 3rd and 5th greens.
Ballinrobe is full of charm and character typified by the 19th
century period residence now used as the clubhouse.
18 holes, 6043mtrs, Par 73, SSS 72, Course record 69.
Club membership 570.
Visitors welcome daily, telephone to reserve Tee-time.
Societies must telephone or write to Secretary in advance.
Green Fees IR£15-IR£18 per day.
Cards 💳 💳
Prof David Kearney
Designer Eddie Hackett
Facilities ⊗ 🏌 🍺 ♀ ⌂ 🏠 ⛳ 🏡 🛒 🚲 ♂ ℓ
Location Off N84 onto R331 to Claremorris

Hotel ★★★ 65% Breaffy House Hotel,
CASTLEBAR ☎ 094 22033 62 ⇆ 🐾

BALLYHAUNIS   Map 01 B4

Ballyhaunis Coolnaha ☎ 0907 30014 Fax 094 81829
Undulating parkland course with 9 holes, 10 greens and 18
tees.
9 holes, 5413mtrs, Par 70, SSS 68, Course record 68.
Club membership 340.
Visitors welcome all times but must avoid members
competitions on Sun & Thu.
Societies must apply in writing or telephone.
Green Fees not confirmed.
Facilities 🍺 ♀ ⌂ ♂ ℓ
Location 3m N on N83

Hotel ★★★ 65% Breaffy House Hotel,
CASTLEBAR ☎ 094 22033 62 ⇆ 🐾

BELMULLET   Map 01 A5

Carne Carne ☎ 097 82292 Fax 097 81477
18 holes, 6119mtrs, Par 72, SSS 72, Course record 72.
Club membership 420.
Visitors welcome, booking essential to guarantee tee-
time.
Societies booking advisable.
Green Fees not confirmed.
Designer Eddie Hackett
Facilities ⊗ ⫚ 🏌 🍺 ♀ ⌂ ⛳ 🛒 🚲 ♂
Location 2m from Belmullet

> Entries with a shaded background
> identify courses that are
> considered to be particularly interesting

CASTLEBAR　　　　　　　　　　　Map 01 B4

Castlebar Hawthorn, Rocklands
☎ 094 21649 Fax 094 26088
Mature testing treelined parkland course.
18 holes, 5698mtrs, Par 71, SSS 70, Course record 67.
Club membership 800.
Visitors　very welcome weekdays, must contact in
　　　　　　　advance for weekend play.
Societies　must contact in advance.
Green Fees not confirmed.
Facilities　⊗ ᴸᴱ 🍺 ♀ 🛠 ⛳ 🕯 🎣 🏌
Location　　1m from town on Belcarra road

Hotel　　★★★ 65% Breaffy House Hotel,
　　　　　　CASTLEBAR ☎ 094 22033 62 ⇆ ⌨

CLAREMORRIS　　　　　　　　　　Map 01 B4

Claremorris Castlemagarrett ☎ 094 71527
A 9-hole parkland course on hilly terrain. A new 18-hole
course is due to open in 1998 and will feature plenty of
mature trees and numerous water hazards.
18 holes, 6600mtrs, Par 73, SSS 72.
Club membership 300.
Visitors　may play weekdays and weekends on request
　　　　　　　Contact Willie Feeley 094 71868
Societies　welcome weekdays, contact 094 62554 for
　　　　　　　details.
Green Fees not confirmed.
Cards　　 💳 💳 💳 💳 💳 💳
Designer　Tom Craddock
Facilities　⊗)Ⅲ ᴸᴱ 🍺 ♀ 🛠
Location　　1.5m from town, on N17 S of Claremorris

Hotel　　★★★ 57% Belmont Hotel, KNOCK
　　　　　　☎ 094 88122 49 ⇆ ⌨

KEEL　　　　　　　　　　　　　　Map 01 A4

Achill Achill Island, Westport ☎ 098 43456
Seaside links in a scenic location on the edge of the Atlantic
Ocean.
9 holes, 2723yds, Par 70, SSS 66, Course record 69.
Club membership 170.
Visitors　welcome but cannot play on some Sundays
Societies　must write or telephone in advance.
Green Fees not confirmed.
Facilities　🕯 🏌

Hotel　　★★★ 67% Hotel Westport,
　　　　　　The Demesne, Newport Rd, WESTPORT
　　　　　　☎ 098 25122 129 ⇆ ⌨

SWINFORD　　　　　　　　　　　Map 01 B4

Swinford Brabazon Park ☎ 094 51378
A pleasant parkland course with good views of the beautiful
surrounding countryside.
9 holes, 5542mtrs, Par 70, SSS 68.
Club membership 420.
Visitors　must contact in advance in peak season.
Societies　must apply in writing or telephone in advance.
Green Fees not confirmed.
Facilities　🛠 🏌

Hotel　　★★★ 65% Breaffy House Hotel,
　　　　　　CASTLEBAR ☎ 094 22033 62 ⇆ ⌨

WESTPORT　　　　　　　　　　　Map 01 B4

Westport Carrowholly
☎ 098 28262 & 27070 Fax 098 27217
This is a beautiful course with wonderful views of Clew
Bay, with its 365 islands, and the holy mountain called
Croagh Patrick, famous for the annual pilgrimage to its
summit. Golfers indulge in a different kind of penance
on this challenging course with many memorable holes.
Perhaps the most exciting is the par five 15th, 580 yards
long and featuring a long carry from the tee over an inlet
of Clew Bay.
18 holes, 6667yds, Par 73, SSS 71, Course record 65.
Club membership 750.
Visitors　　must contact in advance. No visitors during
　　　　　　　　members times.
Societies　　apply in writing or telephone well in
　　　　　　　　advance.
Green Fees IR£19 per round (IR£24 weekends).
Prof　　　　Alex Mealia
Designer　　Fred Hawtree
Facilities　　⊗)Ⅲ ᴸᴱ 🍺 ♀ 🛠 🏠 🕯 🎣 🏌
Location　　2.5m from town

Hotel　　★★★ 67% Hotel Westport,
　　　　　　The Demesne, Newport Rd, WESTPORT
　　　　　　☎ 098 25122 129 ⇆ ⌨

CO MEATH

BETTYSTOWN　　　　　　　　　　Map 01 D4

Laytown & Bettystown ☎ 041 27170 Fax 014 28506
A very competitive and trying links course, home of famous
golfer, Des Smyth.
18 holes, 5652mtrs, Par 71, SSS 70.
Club membership 950.
Visitors　　may not play 1-2pm. Must contact in advance.
Societies　　must contact in writing.
Green Fees IR£23 per round (IR£28 weekends).
Cards　　　💳
Prof　　　　Robert J Browne
Facilities　　⊗)Ⅲ ᴸᴱ 🍺 ♀ 🛠 🏠 🕯 🏌
& Leisure　hard tennis courts, badmington.

Hotel　　★★ 67% Conyngham Arms Hotel, SLANE
　　　　　　☎ 041 24155 16rm(15 ⇆ ⌨)

DUNSHAUGHLIN　　　　　　　　　Map 01 D4

Black Bush Thomastown ☎ 01 8250021 Fax 01 8250400
Three 9-hole courses, giving three possible 18-hole
combinations, set in lovely parkland, with a lake providing a
hazard at the 1st. Recently added creeks, trees and bunkers
make for challenging and accurate shot-making.
Course 1: 18 holes, 6930yds, Par 73, SSS 72.
Course 2: 9 holes, 3400yds, Par 35, SSS 34.
Club membership 950.
Visitors　　must contact in advance but cannot play 1-2pm
　　　　　　　　weekdays.
Societies　advance booking required.
Green Fees not confirmed.　　　　　　　　　　▶

Black Bush

Cards	
Prof	Shane O'Grady
Designer	Bobby Browne
Facilities	⊗ ⅷ ᴸ ♟ ♀ ♧ 🏠 ⚓ ⚲ ♂ ☟
Location	1.5m from village on Dunshaughlin-Ratoath raod

Hotel	★★★ 69% Finnstown Country House Hotel & Golf Course, Newcastle Rd, LUCAN ☎ 01 6280644 25 ⇄ ♙ Annexe26 ⇄ ♙

KELLS   Map 01 C4

Headfort ☎ 046 40857 40146 Fax 046 49282
A delightful parkland course which is regarded as one of
the best of its kind in Ireland. There are ample
opportunities for birdies, but even if these are not
achieved, Headfort provides for a most pleasant game.
Currently a further challenging 18 holes are being
developed.
18 holes, 6007mtrs, Par 72, SSS 71, Course record 67.
Club membership 1162.

Visitors	restricted Tues Ladies Day. Must contact in advance.
Societies	must apply in writing.
Green Fees	IR£20 (IR£25 weekends & bank holidays).
Cards	
Prof	Brendan McGovern
Facilities	⊗ ⅷ ᴸ ♟ ♀ ♧ 🏠 ⚓ ♂
Hotel	★★★ 62% Ardboyne Hotel, Dublin Rd, NAVAN ☎ 046 23119 27 ⇄ ♙

KILCOCK   Map 01 C4

Kilcock Gallow ☎ 01 6287283 Fax 01 6284294
A parkland course with wide, gently undulating fairways, flat
greens and light rough only.
18 holes, 5775mtrs, Par 71, SSS 70, Course record 69.
Club membership 600.

Visitors	must contact in advance for weekends, no problem weekdays.
Societies	telephone for dates available.
Green Fees	not confirmed.
Designer	Eddie Hackett
Facilities	⊗ ⅷ ᴸ ♟ ♀ ♧ ⚓ ♂
Location	2m from end of M4

Hotel	★★★ 64% Lucan Spa Hotel, LUCAN ☎ 01 6280495 6280497 Fax 01 6280841 65 ⇄ ♙

NAVAN   Map 01 C4

Royal Tara Bellinter
☎ 046 25508 & 25244 Fax 046 25508
Pleasant parkland course offering plenty of variety. Situated
close to the Hill of Tara, the ancient seat of the Kings of
Ireland.
New Course: 18 holes, 5757mtrs, Par 71, SSS 70.
Bellinter Nine: 9 holes, 3184yds, Par 35, SSS 35.
Club membership 1000.

Visitors	prior arrangement is advisable. Tue is ladies day.
Societies	apply in writing or telephone.
Green Fees	IR£18 per round (IR£22 weekends & bank holidays).
Prof	Adam Whiston
Facilities	⊗ ⅷ ᴸ ♟ ♀ ♧ 🏠 ⚓ ⚲ ♂ ☟
Location	6m from town on N3

Hotel	★★★ 62% Ardboyne Hotel, Dublin Rd, NAVAN ☎ 046 23119 27 ⇄ ♙

TRIM   Map 01 C4

County Meath Newtownmoynagh
☎ 046 31463 Fax 046 37554
Originally a 9-hole course opened in 1971, it was extended to
18-holes in 1990. It is maturing into a very challenging and
formidable course with four testing Par 5's. At present new
sand-based greens are under construction, 9 will be ready in
1999 and the other 9 and extra bunkers will be ready for the
year 2000. Luxurious clubhouse with panoramic views
across the course.
18 holes, 6720mtrs, Par 73, SSS 72, Course record 68.
Club membership 900.

Visitors	welcome; some restrictions telephone for details.
Societies	not Sun, enquiries welcome.
Green Fees	IR£15 (IR18 weekends & bank holidays).
Designer	Eddie Hackett/Tom Craddock
Facilities	⊗ ⅷ ᴸ ♟ ♀ ♧ ♂
Location	3m outside Trim on Trim/Longwood rd

Hotel	★★ 67% Conyngham Arms Hotel, SLANE ☎ 041 24155 16rm(15 ⇄ ♙)

CO MONAGHAN

CARRICKMACROSS   Map 01 C4

Mannan Castle Donaghmoyne
☎ 042 63308 Fax 042 63195
Parkland and picturesque, the course starts with a Par 3, then
a dogleg Par 4, next a Par 5 with majestic cypress trees as a
back drop to the green. The 4th needs a good tee shot to
make the approach shot to the green. The long Par 5 5th
requires a straight hitter; the 6th doglegs left and the 7th
overlook the whole course. Downhill to the 8th with trouble
on the right and straight and long into the 9th.
9 holes, 5900mtr, Par 72, SSS 70.
Club membership 477.

Visitors	may play anytime except competition times Sat, Sun & Wed from 2-2.30pm.
Societies	apply in writing to the secretary.
Green Fees	not confirmed.
Designer	F Ainsworth
Facilities	⌂
Location	4m N

Hotel   ★★★ 69% Ballymascanlon House Hotel, DUNDALK ☎ 042 71124 75 ⇋

Nuremore ☎ 042 61438 & 64016 Fax 042 61853
Picturesque parkland course of championship length incorporating the drumlins and lakes which are a natural feature of the Monaghan countryside. Precision is required on the 10th to drive over a large lake and between a narrow avenue of trees. Signature hole 18th.
18 holes, 6400yds, Par 71, SSS 69, Course record 67.
Club membership 200.

Visitors	welcome all times but must contact Maurice Cassidy in advance.
Societies	must contact in advance.
Green Fees	IR£20 per day (IR£25 weekends & bank holidays).
Cards	▬ ▨ ▨
Prof	Maurice Cassidy
Designer	Eddie Hackett
Facilities	⊗ ⫼ ⅃ ♥ ♀ ⌂ ⋔ ⌂ ↘ ♣ ♂
& Leisure	hard tennis courts, heated indoor swimming pool, squash, fishing, sauna, gymnasium.
Location	1m S of Carrickmacross, on main N2

Hotel   ★★★★ 75% Nuremore Hotel, CARRICKMACROSS ☎ 042 61438 72 ⇋ ℾ

CASTLEBLAYNEY   Map 01 C4

Castleblayney Onomy ☎ 042 40451 Fax 042 40451
Scenic course on Muckno Park estate, adjacent to Muckno Lake and Blayney Castle.
9 holes, 5378yds, Par 68, SSS 66, Course record 68.
Club membership 275.

Visitors	no visitors allowed during major weekend competitions.
Societies	must contact in advance.
Green Fees	IR£8 per day (IR£10 weekends & bank holidays).
Designer	Bobby Browne
Facilities	⅃ ♥ ♀ ⌂
& Leisure	fishing.

Hotel   ★★★ 69% Ballymascanlon House Hotel, DUNDALK ☎ 042 71124 75 ⇋

CLONES   Map 01 C5

Clones Hilton Park ☎ 047 56017 Fax 042 42333
Parkland course set in Drumlin country. Due to limestone belt, the course is very dry and playable all year round. There is a timesheet in operation on Saturday and Sunday.
9 holes, 5206mtrs, Par 68, SSS 67, Course record 62.
Club membership 330.

Visitors	must contact in advance.
Societies	apply in writing.
Green Fees	IR£10 per day (IR£12 weekends).
Facilities	⊗ ⫼ ⅃ ♥ ♀ ⌂
Location	3m from Clones on Scotshouse rd

Hotel   ★★★ 65% Four Seasons Hotel & Leisure Club, Coolshannagh, MONAGHAN ☎ 047 81888 44 ⇋ ℾ

MONAGHAN   Map 01 C5

Rossmore Rossmore Park, Cootehill Rd ☎ 047 81316
An undulating 18-hole parkland course amidst beautiful countryside.
18 holes, 5534mtrs, Par 70, SSS 68, Course record 62.
Club membership 800.

Visitors	must contact in advance, tel club house: 047 81316 if over 10 in a group
Societies	must apply in writing.
Green Fees	IR£15 per day.
Designer	Des Smyth
Facilities	⊗ ⅃ ♥ ♀ ⌂ ⌂ ♂ ♣
Location	2m S on Cootehill road

Hotel   ★★★ 65% Four Seasons Hotel & Leisure Club, Coolshannagh, MONAGHAN ☎ 047 81888 44 ⇋ ℾ

CO OFFALY

BIRR   Map 01 C3

Birr The Glenns ☎ 0509 20082 Fax 0509 22155
The course has been laid out over undulating parkland utilising the natural contours of the land, which were created during the ice age. The sandy subsoil means that the course is playable all year round.
18 holes, 5700mtrs, Par 70, SSS 70, Course record 62.
Club membership 750.

Visitors	contact in advance,
Societies	advance contact to secretary.
Green Fees	IR£12-IR£14 per day.
Cards	▬ ▬ ▨ ▨ ▨
Facilities	⊗ ⫼ ⅃ ♥ ♀ ⌂ ⌂ ⋔ ↘ ♣ ♂ ♣

Hotel   ★★★ 60% County Arms Hotel, BIRR ☎ 0509 20791 24 ⇋ ℾ

EDENDERRY   Map 01 C4

Edenderry ☎ 0405 31072
A most friendly club which offers a relaxing game in pleasant surroundings. In 1992 the course was extended to 18 holes. ▶

18 holes, 6029mtrs, Par 72, SSS 72, Course record 66.
Club membership 700.
Visitors   restricted Thu & weekends, ring for times.
Societies   may not play on Thu & Sun; must contact the secretary in writing.
Green Fees IR£15-IR£20 (IR£20-IR£22 weekends).
Designer   Havers/Hackett
Facilities   ⊗ ⁜ ⅏ 🍽 ♀ ♨ ♂

TULLAMORE   Map 01 C4

Tullamore Brookfield ☎ 0506 21439 Fax 0506 41806
Well wooded parkland course.
18 holes, 6500yds, Par 70, SSS 71, Course record 68.
Club membership 989.
Visitors   must contact in advance, restricted on Tue & at weekends.
Societies   must contact in writing.
Green Fees IR£18 (IR£22 weekends & bank holidays).
Prof   Donagh McArdle
Designer   James Braid/Paddy Merrigam
Facilities   ⊗ ⁜ ⅏ 🍽 ♀ ♨ 🏠 ⛳ ♞ ♂
Location   2.5m SW on Kinnity road

Hotel   ★★★64% Prince Of Wales Hotel, ATHLONE ☎ 0902 72626 73 ⇄ ☏

CO ROSCOMMON

ATHLONE   Map 01 C4

Athlone Hodson Bay ☎ 0902 92073
A picturesque course with a panoramic view of Lough Ree. Overall, it is a tight, difficult course with some outstanding holes and is noted for its magnificent greens. Many championships have taken plave here including the 1998 All Ireland Cups and Shields finals.
18 holes, 5854mtrs, Par 71, SSS 71.
Club membership 1000.
Visitors   must contact in advance.
Societies   apply in writing.
Green Fees IR£18 (IR£20 weekends)..
Cards   🖵 💳
Prof   Martin Quinn
Facilities   ⊗ ⁜ ⅏ 🍽 ♀ ♨ 🏠 ⛳ 🛒 ♞ 🛺 ♂
Location   4m from town beside Lough Ree

Hotel   ★★★69% Hodson Bay Hotel, Hodson Bay, ATHLONE ☎ 0902 92444 97 ⇄ ☏

BALLAGHADERREEN   Map 01 B4

Ballaghaderreen ☎ 0907 60295
Mature 9-hole course with an abundance of trees. Accuracy off the tee is vital for a good score. Small protected greens require a good short-iron plan. The Par 3, 2nd hole at 178 yards has ruined many a good score.
9 holes, 5727yds, Par 70, SSS 66.
Club membership 250.
Visitors   no restrictions.
Societies   apply in writing or telephone during office hours.

Green Fees not confirmed.
Designer   Paddy Skerritt
Facilities   🍽 ♀ ♨ ♂
Location   2m S of town

Hotel   ★★64% Royal Hotel, BOYLE ☎ 079 62016 16 ⇄ ☏

BOYLE   Map 01 B4

Boyle Roscommon Rd ☎ 079 62594
Situated on a low hill and surrounded by beautiful scenery, this is an undemanding course where, due to the generous fairways and semi-rough, the leisure golfer is likely to finish the round with the same golf ball.
9 holes, 5324yds, Par 67, SSS 66, Course record 65.
Club membership 280.
Visitors   no restrictions.
Societies   must contact in writing.
Green Fees IR£10 per day.
Designer   E Hackett
Facilities   ⅏ 🍽 ♀ ♨ ⛳
Location   2m from Boyle on the Roscommon road

Hotel   ★★64% Royal Hotel, BOYLE ☎ 079 62016 16 ⇄ ☏

CARRICK-ON-SHANNON   Map 01 C4

Carrick-on-Shannon Woodbrook ☎ 079 67015
A pleasant 9-hole course overlooking the River Shannon. A fine test of golf for both those with low and high handicaps.
9 holes, 5545mtrs, Par 70, SSS 68.
Club membership 400.
Visitors   welcome, contact in advance to avoid competitions.
Societies   must contact in advance.
Green Fees IR£10 per day.
Designer   Eddie Hackett
Facilities   ⅏ 🍽 ♀ ♨ ⛳ ♂ ♣
Location   4m W beside N4

Hotel   ★★64% Royal Hotel, BOYLE ☎ 079 62016 16 ⇄ ☏

CASTLEREA   Map 01 B4

Castlerea Clonalis ☎ 0907 20068 & 20705
The clubhouse is virtually at the centre of Castlerea course with 7 tees visible. A pleasant parkland course incorporating part of the River Francis very near the centre of town.
9 holes, 4974mtrs, Par 68, SSS 66, Course record 62.
Club membership 234.
Visitors   welcome, but Sunday by arrangement only.
Societies   contact for details.
Green Fees not confirmed.
Facilities   ⅏ 🍽 ♀ ♨ ♂
Location   On Dublin/Castlebar road

Hotel   ★★★64% Abbey Hotel, Galway Rd, ROSCOMMON ☎ 0903 26240 & 26505 Fax 0903 26021 25 ⇄ ☏

> Entries with a shaded background identify courses that are considered to be particularly interesting

ROSCOMMON — Map 01 B4

Roscommon Mote Park
☎ 0903 26382, 26931 & 25281 (catering) Fax 0903 26043
Located on the rolling pastures of the old Mote Park estate, this recently extended 18-hole course successfully blends the old established nine holes with an exciting and equally demanding new 9-hole lay-out. Numerous water hazards, notably on the tricky 13th, multi-tiered greens and an excellent irrigation to give an all-weather surface.
18 holes, 6290mtrs, Par 71, SSS 70, Course record 64.
Club membership 650.
Visitors contact in advance.
Societies apply in writing.
Green Fees IR£15 per day.
Facilities ⊗ 〜 ⅃ ⬤ ♀ △ ♦ ☄ ♂
Location 0.5m S of Roscommon town

Hotel ★★★ 64% Abbey Hotel, Galway Rd, ROSCOMMON ☎ 0903 26240 & 26505 Fax 0903 26021 25 ⇔ ʁ

STROKESTOWN — Map 01 C4

Strokestown Cloonfinlough ☎ 078 33323 & 33084
Picturesque 9-hole course set in parkland with fine views of Cloonfinlough Lake. The three Par 3's are long and quite testing.
9 holes, 2615mtrs, Par 68.
Club membership 250.
Visitors may play any times except during competitions.
Societies apply in writing or telephone at least 2 weeks in advance.
Green Fees not confirmed.
Facilities △
& Leisure fishing.
Location 1.5m from Strokestown

Hotel ★★★ 64% Abbey Hotel, Galway Rd, ROSCOMMON ☎ 0903 26240 & 26505 Fax 0903 26021 25 ⇔ ʁ

CO SLIGO

BALLYMOTE — Map 01 B4

Ballymote Ballinascarrow ☎ 071 83158 & 83089
Although Ballymote was founded in 1940, the course dates from 1993 and has matured well into a parkland course with ample fairways and large greens. Wonderful views of Ballinascarow Lake. Ideal for family groups.
9 holes, 5302mtrs, Par 68, SSS 67.
Club membership 250.
Visitors must contact in advance.
Societies telephone in advance.
Green Fees IR£10 per day.
Prof Leslie Robinson
Designer Eddie Hacket
Facilities ⬤ △ ☄ ♂
& Leisure fishing.
Location 1m N

Hotel ★★ 64% Royal Hotel, BOYLE ☎ 079 62016 16 ⇔ ʁ

ENNISCRONE — Map 01 B5

Enniscrone ☎ 096 36297 Fax 096 36657
In a magnificent situation with breathtaking views of mountain, sea and rolling countryside, this course offers some unforgettable golf.It was host to the West of Ireland championship and the Ladies Irish Close in 1997. It offers an exciting challenge among its splendid sandhills and a particularly favourite hole is the tenth, with a marvellous view from the elevated tee and the chance of a birdie with an accurate drive.
18 holes, 6620yds, Par 72, SSS 72, Course record 66.
Club membership 750.
Visitors must contact in advance, may not play before 11am or between 1.00 & 4pm on Sun.
Societies must telephone in advance.
Green Fees Mon-Thu IR£25 per day (per round Jun-Sep); Fri IR£25 per round (IR£34 per round weekend).
Cards ▬
Prof Charlie McGoldrick
Designer E Hackett
Facilities ⊗ 〜 ⅃ ⬤ ♀ △ ⊞ ☄ ♦ ☄ ♂ ↑
Location 0.5m S on Ballina road

SLIGO — Map 01 B5

County Sligo Rosses Point
☎ 071 77134 or 77186 Fax 071 77460
Now considered to be one of the top links courses in Ireland, County Sligo is host to a number of competitions, including the West of Ireland Championships and Internationals. Set in an elevated position on cliffs above three large beaches, the prevailing winds provide an additional challenge.Tom Watson described it " as a magnificent links, particularly the stretch of holes from the 14th to the 17th."
18 holes, 6037mtrs, Par 71, SSS 72, Course record 66.
Club membership 1069.
Visitors advisable to contact in advance, available most days except Captains or Presidents days.
Societies must contact in writing & pay a deposit.
Green Fees not confirmed.
Prof Leslie Robinson
Designer Harry Colt
Facilities ⊗ 〜 ⅃ ⬤ ♀ △ ⊞ ☄ ♦ ☄ ♂
Location Off N15 to Donegal

Hotel ★★★ 65% Tower Hotel, Quay St, SLIGO ☎ 071 44000 58 ⇔ ʁ

Strandhill Strandhill ☎ 071 68188 Fax 071 68811
This scenic course is situated between Knocknarea Mountain and the Atlantic, offering golf in its most natural form amid the sand dunes of the West of Ireland. The 1st, 16th and 18th are Par 4 holes over 364 metres in length; the 2nd and 17th are testing Par 3s which vary according to the prevailing wind; the Par 4 13th is a testing dogleg right. This is a course where accuracy will be rewarded.
18 holes, 5516mtrs, Par 69, SSS 68.
Club membership 450.

▶

Visitors must contact in advance.
Societies apply in advance.
Green Fees not confirmed.
Facilities ⊗ ⫶ ⬛ ⬛ ♀ ⬟ ⬜ ⛾ ⬟ ⚒ ✧
Location 5m from town

Hotel ★★★ 71% Sligo Park Hotel, Pearse Rd, SLIGO ☎ 071 60291 109 ⇔ ♞

TOBERCURRY   Map 01 B4

Tobercurry ☎ 071 85849
A 9-hole parkland course designed by Edward Hackett. The 8th hole, a Par 3, is regarded as being one of the most testing in the west of Ireland.
9 holes, 5490mtrs, Par 70, SSS 69.
Club membership 300.
Visitors restricted on Sun.
Societies telephone in advance on 071 85770.
Green Fees IR£10 per day.
Designer Eddie Hackett
Facilities ⊗ ⫶ ⬛ ⬛ ♀ ⬟ ✧
Location 0.25m from Tobercurry

CO TIPPERARY

CAHIR   Map 01 C3

Cahir Park Kilcommon ☎ 052 41474 Fax 052 42717
Parkland course dissected by the River Suir which adds a challenge to the par 4 8th and par 3 16th.
18 holes, 5740mtrs, Par 71, SSS 71.
Club membership 350.
Visitors may play any time except during competitions.
Societies by prior arrangement, apply in writing.
Green Fees not confirmed.
Prof Dominic Foran
Designer Eddie Hackett
Facilities ⊗ ⫶ by prior arrangement ⬛ ♀ ⬟ ✧
Location 1m from Cahir on the Clogheen road

Hotel ★★★ 70% Cahir House Hotel, The Square, CAHIR ☎ 52 42727 31 ⇔ ♞

CARRICK-ON-SUIR   Map 01 C2

Carrick-on-Suir Garvonne ☎ 051 640047 Fax 051 640558
18 hole parkland course with the backdrop of the Comeragh Mountains on one side and views of the Suir valley on the other.
18 holes, 6061mtrs, Par 73, SSS 71, Course record 69.
Club membership 600.
Visitors may not play on Sun morning
Societies contact for details.
Green Fees not confirmed.
Designer Eddie Hackett
Facilities ⊗ ⫶ ⬛ ⬛ ♀ ⬟ ⚒ ✧
Location 2m SW

Hotel ★★★ 73% Minella Hotel, CLONMEL ☎ 052 22388 70 ⇔ ♞

CLONMEL   Map 01 C2

Clonmel Lyreanearla, Mountain Rd
☎ 052 24050 & 21138 Fax 052 24050
Set in the scenic, wooded slopes of the Comeragh Mountains, this is a testing course with lots of open space and plenty of interesting features. It provides an enjoyable round in exceptionally tranquil surroundings.
18 holes, 5845mtrs, Par 72, SSS 71.
Club membership 850.
Visitors must contact in advance.
Societies must contact in advance.
Green Fees not confirmed.
Prof Robert Hayes
Designer Eddie Hackett
Facilities ⊗ ⫶ ⬛ ⬛ ♀ ⬟ ⛾ ⬟ ⚒ ✧
Location 3m form Clonmel off N24

Hotel ★★★ 73% Minella Hotel, CLONMEL ☎ 052 22388 70 ⇔ ♞

NENAGH   Map 01 B3

Nenagh Beechwood ☎ 067 31476 Fax 067 34808
Interesting gradients call for some careful approach shots. Some magnificent views.
18 holes, 5491mtrs, Par 69, SSS 68, Course record 64.
Club membership 820.
Visitors must contact in advance.
Societies must apply in writing.
Green Fees IR£15 per day.
Prof Gordon Morrison
Designer Eddie Hackett
Facilities ⊗ ⫶ ⬛ ⬛ ♀ ⬟ ⛾ ✧
Location 3m from town on old Birr rd

Hotel ★★★ 68% Nenagh Abbey Court Hotel, Dublin Rd, NENAGH ☎ 067 41111 46 ⇔ ♞

ROSCREA   Map 01 C3

Roscrea Golf Club Derryvale
☎ 0505 21130 Fax 0505 23410
An 18-hole parkland course.
18 holes, 5750mtrs, Par 71, SSS 70, Course record 69.
Club membership 420.
Visitors telephone in advance, on Sun by arrangement.
Societies apply in writing to Hon Secretary.
Green Fees IR£14 per day (IR£17 weekends).
Designer A Spring
Facilities ⊗ ⫶ ⬛ ⬛ ♀ ⬟ ⛾ ✧
Location N7, Dublin side of Roscrea

Hotel ★★★ 67% Grant's Hotel, Castle St, ROSCREA ☎ 0505 23300 25 ⇔ ♞

TEMPLEMORE   Map 01 C3

Templemore Manna South ☎ 0504 31400
Parkland course with newly planted trees which offers a pleasant test to visitors without being too difficult. Walking is level too.
9 holes, 5419mtrs, Par 70, SSS 69, Course record 68.
Club membership 220.

Visitors may not play during Special Events & Open weeks. Semi Open events available such as four ball
Societies must contact in advance.
Green Fees IR£8 per round (IR£12 weekends & bank holidays).
Facilities ⊗ ┗ ☕ ⛳ ♨
& Leisure hard tennis courts.
Location 0.5m S

Hotel ★★★ 60% County Arms Hotel, BIRR ☎ 0509 20791 24 ⇆ 🐾

THURLES   Map 01 C3

Thurles Turtulla ☎ 0504 21983 & 22466 Fax 0504 24647
Superb parkland course with a difficult finish at the 18th.
18 holes, 5904mtrs, Par 72, SSS 71, Course record 65.
Club membership 920.
Visitors welcome, limited availability at weekends, Tuesday is Ladies day.
Societies apply in writing to Hon Secretary.
Green Fees not confirmed.
Prof Sean Hunt
Facilities ⊗ ⽊ ┗ ☕ ♨ ⛳ 🏠 ⛺ ✀ ⟋
& Leisure squash, sauna, gymnasium.
Location 1m from town on Cork road

Hotel ★ 59% Royal Hotel, Bridge St, TIPPERARY TOWN ☎ 062 33244 16 ⇆ 🐾

TIPPERARY   Map 01 C3

County Tipperary Dundrum House Hotel, Dundrum ☎ 062 71116
The course had been built into a mature Georgian estate using the features of woodland and parkland adorned by the Multeen River. Designed by Philip Walton. The 4th hole is one of the most testing Par 5's in Ireland.
18 holes, 6709yds, Par 72, SSS 72, Course record 70.
Club membership 190.
Visitors booking is advisable especially at weekends.
Societies apply in writing.
Green Fees not confirmed.
Designer Philip Walton
Facilities ⊗ ⽊ ┗ ☕ ♨ ⛳ 🏠 ⛺ 🛒 ✀ ⟋
& Leisure hard tennis courts, fishing.
Location 7m W of Cashel off N8

Hotel ★ 59% Royal Hotel, Bridge St, TIPPERARY TOWN ☎ 062 33244 16 ⇆ 🐾

Tipperary Rathanny ☎ 062 51119
Recently extended to 18-holes, this parkland course has plenty of trees and bunkers and water at three holes to provide additional hazards.
18 holes, 5761mtrs, Par 71, SSS 71, Course record 66.
Club membership 700.
Visitors advisable to contact by phone, weekend play available but limited on Sun.
Societies apply in writing.
Green Fees IR£15 per round (£17 weekends).
Facilities ⊗ ⽊ by prior arrangement ┗ ☕ ♨ ⛳ 🏠 ⛺ 🛒 ⟋
Location 1m S

Hotel ★ 59% Royal Hotel, Bridge St, TIPPERARY TOWN ☎ 062 33244 16 ⇆ 🐾

DUNGARVAN   Map 01 C2

Dungarvan Knocknagranagh
☎ 058 41605 & 43310 Fax 058 44113
A championship-standard course beside Dungarvan Bay, with seven lakes and hazards placed to challenge all levels of golfer. The greens are considered to be among the best in Ireland.
18 holes, 6560yds, Par 72, SSS 71, Course record 66.
Club membership 625.
Visitors welcome weekdays, booking advisable weekends.
Societies telephone then write to confim booking.
Green Fees IR£17 per round (IR£22 weekends & bank holidays).
Cards ▭ ▦ ▭
Prof David Hayes
Designer Moss Fives
Facilities ⊗ ⽊ ┗ ☕ ♨ ⛳ 🏠 ⛺ 🛒 ⟋
Location Off N25 between Waterford & Youghal

Hotel ★★★ 56% Lawlors Hotel, DUNGARVAN ☎ 058 41122 & 41056 Fax 058 41000 89 ⇆ 🐾

Gold Coast Golf & Leisure Ballinacourty
☎ 058 42249 & 44055 Fax 058 43378
A parkland course bordered by the Atlantic Ocean with unrivalled panoramic views of Dungarvan Bay. The mature tree-lined fairways of the old course are tastefully integrated with the long and challenging newer holes to create a superb course.
18 holes, 6171mtrs, Par 72, SSS 72.
Club membership 450.
Visitors book in advance, times available throughout the week.
Societies apply by telephone in advance.
Green Fees IR£16 per round (IR£20 weekends).
Cards ▭ ▦ ▭ 🅿
Designer Maurice Fives
Facilities ⊗ ⽊ ┗ ☕ ♨ ⛳ 🏠 ⛺ 🐾 🛒 ✀ ⟋
& Leisure hard tennis courts, heated indoor swimming pool, sauna, gymnasium.
Location Left of N25, 2m bfore Dungarvan

Hotel ★★★ 56% Lawlors Hotel, DUNGARVAN ☎ 058 41122 & 41056 Fax 058 41000 89 ⇆ 🐾

West Waterford ☎ 058 43216 & 41475 Fax 058 44343
Designed by Eddie Hackett, the course is on 150 acres of rolling parkland by the Brickey River with a backdrop of the Comeragh Mountains, Knockmealdowns and Drum Hills. The first nine holes are laid out on a large plateau featuring a stream which comes into play at the 3rd and 4th holes. The river at the southern boundary affects several later holes.
18 holes, 6004mtrs, Par 72, SSS 74, Course record 70.
Club membership 185.

▶

Visitors pre book for tee times.
Societies telephone or write in advance.
Green Fees not confirmed.
Designer Eddie Hackett
Facilities ⌘⚒🏌️♨️🍴♀️⛱🏠⛳🚬🏌️‍♂️♨️
& Leisure hard tennis courts.
Location Approx 3m W of Dungarvan, off N25

Hotel ★★★ 56% Lawlors Hotel, DUNGARVAN
☎ 058 41122 & 41056 Fax 058 41000 89 ⇥ ♠

DUNMORE EAST   Map 01 C2

Dunmore East ☎ 051 383151 Fax 051 383151
Overlooking the village of Dunmore East, with panoramic views of the village, bay and Hook peninsula. This course promises to offer idyllic surroundings and challenging golf for the high or low handicap golfer.
18 holes, 6655yds, Par 72, SSS 70, Course record 69.
Club membership 300.
Visitors welcome, no restrictions.
Societies telephone in advance.
Green Fees IR£12 per day (IR£15 weekends & bank holidays).
Cards 💳
Prof Derry Kiely
Designer W H Jones
Facilities ⊗⚒🏌️♨️🍴♀️⛱🏠⛳🚬🏌️‍♂️♨️

Hotel ★★★ 66% Dooley's Hotel, 30 The Quay,
WATERFORD ☎ 051 873531 113 ⇥ ♠

LISMORE   Map 01 C2

Lismore Ballyin ☎ 058 54026 Fax 058 53338
Picturesque tree-dotted sloping course on the banks of the Blackwater River. Rothwell's is a diffiuclt hole with a sloping green and trees to either side.
9 holes, 5790yds, Par 69, SSS 67, Course record 67.
Club membership 350.
Visitors may not play Sun before noon. Restricted Wed, Thu & weekends.
Societies must apply in writing.
Green Fees not confirmed.
Facilities ⊗🏌️♨️🍴♀️⛱♨️

Hotel ★★★ 56% Lawlors Hotel, DUNGARVAN
☎ 058 41122 & 41056 Fax 058 41000 89 ⇥ ♠

TRAMORE   Map 01 C2

Tramore Newtown Hill ☎ 051 386170 Fax 051 390961
This course has matured nicely over the years to become a true championship test and has been chosen as the venue for the Irish Professional Matchplay Championship and the Irish Amateur Championship. Most of the fairways are lined by evergreen trees, calling for accurate placing of shots, and the course is continuing to develop.
18 holes, 5918mtrs, Par 72, SSS 72, Course record 65.
Club membership 1200.
Visitors pre-booking required.
Societies contact in advance.
Green Fees IR£25 per round (IR£30 weekends & bank holidays).
Cards 💳
Prof Derry Kiely
Designer Capt H C Tippet
Facilities ⊗⚒🏌️♨️🍴♀️⛱🏠⛳🚬🏌️‍♂️♨️

& Leisure squash.
Location 0.5m from Tramore on Dungaruan coast road

Hotel ★★★ 63% Majestic Hotel, TRAMORE
☎ 051 381761 57 ⇥ ♠

WATERFORD   Map 01 C2

Faithlegg House Dunmore East ☎ 051 382241
Some wicked slopes and borrows on the immaculate greens, a huge 432yard 17th what has a host of problems and a doglegged approach to the two-tier 18th green are just some of the novel features on this course. Set on the banks of the River Suir, the course has been integrated into a landscape textured with mature trees,flowing parkland and five lakes.
18 holes, 6057mtrs, Par 72, SSS 72, Course record 69.
Club membership 65.
Visitors no restrictions.
Societies apply in writing or telephone at least a month in advance.
Green Fees not confirmed.
Prof Ted Higgins
Facilities ♀️⛱🏠⛳

Hotel ★★★ 62% Jurys Hotel, Ferrybank,
WATERFORD ☎ 051 832111 98 ⇥ ♠

Waterford Newrath ☎ 051 876748 Fax 051 853405
Undulating parkland course in pleasant surroundings.
18 holes, 5722mtrs, Par 71, SSS 70, Course record 66.
Club membership 931.
Visitors must contact in advance.
Societies must apply in writing.
Green Fees not confirmed.
Prof Eamonn Condon
Designer W Park/J Braid
Facilities ⊗⚒🏌️♨️🍴♀️⛱🏠⛳🚬🏌️‍♂️♨️
Location 1m N

Hotel ★★★ 62% Jurys Hotel, Ferrybank,
WATERFORD ☎ 051 832111 98 ⇥ ♠

Waterford Castle The Island, Ballinakill
☎ 051 871633 Fax 051 871634
Parkland course with mature trees, 4 lakes, sandbased tees and greens and good bunkering.
18 holes, 5827mtrs, Par 72, SSS 71, Course record 70.
Club membership 500.
Visitors must contact in advance, pre booking required.
Societies apply in advance.
Green Fees not confirmed.
Designer Den Smyth
Facilities 🏌️♨️🍴♀️⛱🏠⛳🚬♨️♞
& Leisure hard tennis courts, heated indoor swimming pool.
Location 2m E of Waterford City, on Island approached by private ferry

Hotel ★★★ 62% Jurys Hotel, Ferrybank,
WATERFORD ☎ 051 832111 98 ⇥ ♠

CO WESTMEATH

ATHLONE
Map 01 C4

Glasson Golf & Country Club Glasson
☎ 0902 85120 Fax 0902 85444
Opened for play in 1993 the course has earned a reputation
for being one of the most challenging and scenic courses in
Ireland. Designed by Christy O'Connor Jnr it is reputedly his
best yet! Surrounded on three sides by Lough Ree the views
from everywhere on the course are breathtaking.
18 holes, 6664yds, Par 72, Course record 65.
Club membership 220.
Visitors   must book in advance.
Societies   book in advance.
Green Fees   IR£27 per round (IR£30-£IR32 Fri-Sun).
Cards
Designer   Christy O'Connor Jnr
Facilities
Location   6m N of Athlone on N55

Hotel   ★★★ 64% Prince Of Wales Hotel,
ATHLONE ☎ 0902 72626 73

DELVIN
Map 01 C4

Delvin Castle Clonyn
☎ 044 64315 & 64733 Fax 044 64733
Situated in the mature parkland of Clonyn Castle, the course
is well known for its unique historic setting with a 16th
century ruin in the back nine holes and an imposing
Victorian castle in the front nine.
18 holes, 5800mtrs, Par 70, SSS 68.
Club membership 400.
Visitors   no restrictions. Advance booking
recommemded.
Societies   apply in writing in advance.
Green Fees   not confirmed.
Prof   David Keenaghan
Designer   John Day
Facilities
Location   On N52, Dundalk to Mullingar road

Hotel   ★★★ 62% Ardboyne Hotel, Dublin Rd,
NAVAN ☎ 046 23119 27

MOATE
Map 01 C4

Moate ☎ 0902 81271
Extended in 1994 to 18 holes, the course is parkland with
trees. Although the original 9-holes did not have water
hazards the new section has a lake.

---

18 holes, 5642mtrs, Par 72, SSS 70, Course record 67.
Club membership 550.
Visitors   welcome, advisable to telephone in advance.
Societies   welcome, prior arrangement not needed.
Green Fees   not confirmed.
Designer   B Browne
Facilities
Location   1m N

Hotel   ★★★ 64% Prince Of Wales Hotel,
ATHLONE ☎ 0902 72626 73

Mount Temple Mount Temple Village
☎ 0902 81841 & 81545 Fax 0902 81957
A traditionally built, highly-rated, all year round course with
parkland and unique links-type greens and natural undulating
fairways. A challenge for all levels of golfers as the wind
plays a major part in the scoring on this course.
18 holes, 5950mtrs, Par 71, SSS 71, Course record 73.
Club membership 150.
Visitors   welcome but must book for weekends.
Societies   telephone in advance.
Green Fees   not confirmed.
Cards
Designer   Michael Dolan
Facilities   by prior arrangement
Location   4m off N6 to Mount Temple village, 5m from
Athlone

Hotel   ★★★ 64% Prince Of Wales Hotel,
ATHLONE ☎ 0902 72626 73

MULLINGAR
Map 01 C4

Mullingar ☎ 044 48366 Fax 044 41499
The wide rolling fairways between mature trees provide
parkland golf at its very best. The course, designed by
the great James Braid, offers a tough challenge and
annually hosts one of the most important amateur events
in the British Isles - the Mullingar Scratch Cup. It has
also been the venue of the Irish Professional
Championship. One advantage of the layout is that the
clubhouse is never far away.
18 holes, 6406yds, Par 72, SSS 71, Course record 63.
Club membership 1000.
Visitors   preferred if booked in advance, Sundays are
Medal days, Wednesday Ladies day.
Societies   apply in writing.
Green Fees   not confirmed.
Prof   John Burns
Designer   James Braid
Facilities
Location   3m S

Hotel   ★★★ 64% Prince Of Wales Hotel,
ATHLONE ☎ 0902 72626 73

Call the AA Hotel Booking Service on
0870 5050505 to book at AA recognised hotels and B & Bs
in the UK and Ireland, or through our Internet site:
http://www.theaa.co.uk/hotels

CO WEXFORD

ENNISCORTHY   Map 01 D3

Enniscorthy Knockmarshall ☎ 054 33191 Fax 054 37367
A pleasant course suitable for all levels of ability.
18 holes, 6115mtrs, Par 72, SSS 72.
Club membership 900.
Visitors   must telephone for booking.
Societies   must book in advance.
Green Fees Summer: IR£20 (IR£22 weekends); Winter:
            IR£15 (IR£15 weekends).
Prof   Martin Sludos
Designer   Eddie Hackett
Facilities   ⊗ ⫼ 🖫 🍷 ♨ 🏠 ⛳ ♂ ⛿
Location   1m from town on New Ross road

Hotel   ★ 60% Murphy-Flood's Hotel,
         Market Square, ENNISCORTHY
         ☎ 054 33413 21rm(5 ⇆13 🐾)

GOREY   Map 01 D3

Courtown Kiltennel ☎ 055 25166 Fax 055 25553
A pleasant parkland course which is well wooded and
enjoys views across the Irish Sea near Courtown
Harbour.
18 holes, 5898mtrs, Par 71, SSS 71, Course record 65.
Club membership 1200.

Visitors   must contact in advance.
Societies   advisable to contact in advance.
Green Fees May-Sep: IR£20 (IR£25 weekends); Oct-
            Apr: IR£15 (IR£20 weekends).
Prof   John Coone
Designer   Harris & Associates
Facilities   ⊗ ⫼ 🖫 🍷 ♨ 🏠 ⛳ ♀ 🏌 ⛿
Location   3m from town, off Courtown Road

Hotel   ★★★🏌 Marlfield House Hotel, GOREY
         ☎ 055 21124 19 ⇆ 🐾

NEW ROSS   Map 01 C3

New Ross Tinneranny ☎ 051 421433 Fax 051 420098
Recently extended to 18-holes, this well kept parkland course
has an attractive backdrop of hills and mountains. Straight
hitting and careful placing of shots is very important,
especially on the 2nd, 6th, 10th and 15th, all of which are
challenging holes.

18 holes, 5751yds, Par 71, SSS 70.
Club membership 700.
Visitors   welcome, booking required for weekend play.
Societies   apply to secretary/manager.
Green Fees not confirmed.
Designer   Des Smith
Facilities   🖫 🍷 ♀ ♨ ⛿
Location   3m from town centre

Hotel   ★★ 59% The Old Rectory Hotel, Rosbercon,
         NEW ROSS ☎ 051 421719   12 ⇆ 🐾

ROSSLARE   Map 01 D2

Rosslare Rosslare Strand ☎ 053 32203 & 32238
This traditional links course is within minutes of the
ferry terminal at Rosslare, but its popularity is not
confined to visitors from Fishguard or Le Havre. It is a
great favourite with the Irish too. Many of the greens are
sunken and are always in beautiful condition, but the
semi-blind approaches are among features of this course
which provide a healthy challenge.
Old Course: 18 holes, 6587yds, Par 72, SSS 72, Course
record 66.
New Course: 9 holes, 3153yds, Par 35, SSS 70.
Club membership 1000.
Visitors   book in advance.
Societies   apply in writing/telephone.
Green Fees Old: IR£22 (IR£30 weekends & bank
            holidays). New: IR£15 per 18 holes, IR£10
            per 9 holes.
Cards   🗠 VISA
Prof   Austin Skerritt
Designer   Hawtree/Taylor
Facilities   ⊗ ⫼ 🖫 🍷 ♀ ♨ 🏠 ⛳ 🐾 🏌 ⛿
& Leisure   sauna.
Location   6m N of Rosslare Ferry Terminal

Hotel   ★★★★ 78% Kelly's Resort Hotel,
         ROSSLARE
         ☎ 053 32114 Annexe99 ⇆ 🐾

St Helen's Bay Golf & Country Club St Helens, Kilrane
☎ 053 33234 & 33669 Fax 053 33803
A championship-standard golf course designed by Philip
Walton. Parkland with water hazards, bunkers and trees
incorporated generously.
18 holes, 5813mtrs, Par 72, SSS 72, Course record 69.
Club membership 300.
Visitors   contact in advance.
Societies   telephone/write in advance.
Green Fees not confirmed.
Designer   Philip Walton
Facilities   ⊗ ⫼ 🖫 🍷 ♀ ♨ 🏠 ⛳ 🚶 🐾 🏌 ⛿ ♂
& Leisure   hard tennis courts, sauna, gymnasium.
Location   5 minutes from the ferryport

Hotel   ★★★ 57% Hotel Rosslare, ROSSLARE
         HARBOUR ☎ 053 33110 25 ⇆ 🐾

WEXFORD   Map 01 D3

Wexford Mulgannon ☎ 053 42238
Parkland course with panoramic view of the Wexford
coastline and mountains.
18 holes, 6100yds, Par 71, SSS 69.
Club membership 800.

Visitors	must contact in advance but may not play Thu & weekends.
Societies	must contact in writing.
Green Fees	not confirmed.
Prof	G Ronayne
Facilities	♀ ♨ 🏠

Hotel	★★★ 72% Talbot Hotel, Trinity St, WEXFORD ☎ 053 22566 100 ⇄ 🐾

CO WICKLOW

ARKLOW   Map 01 D3

Arklow Abbeylands ☎ 0402 32492 Fax 0402 32492
Scenic links course.
18 holes, 5404mtrs, Par 68, SSS 67, Course record 66.
Club membership 450.

Visitors	may play Mon-Fri and 3hrs Sat 9am-12 noon, must book in advance.
Societies	must apply in writing or telephone in advance.
Green Fees	IR£20 per round.
Designer	Hawtree & Taylor
Facilities	⊗ ⫚ ⅃ 🐾 ♥ ♀ ♨ 🏠 ⁀ ♂ ↾
Location	0.5m from town centre

Hotel	★★★♨ Marlfield House Hotel, GOREY ☎ 055 21124 19 ⇄ 🐾

BALTINGLASS   Map 01 D3

Baltinglass Dublin Rd ☎ 0508 81350 Fax 0508 81350
On the banks of the River Slaney, the 9-hole course has 4
Par-4s over 400 yards which have to be played twice.
Reputed to be one of the hardest 9-hole courses in the
Republic.
9 holes, 5554mtrs, Par 68, SSS 69, Course record 68.
Club membership 400.

Visitors	advisable to check availability for weekends.
Societies	apply in writing.
Green Fees	IR£10 per 18 holes (IR£12 weekends & bank holidays).
Facilities	⊗ ⫚ ⅃ 🐾 ♥ ♀ ♨ ♂
Location	500 metres N of Baltinglass

Rathsallagh ☎ 045 403316 Fax 045 403295
Designed by Peter McEvoy and Christy O'Connor Jnr, this is
a spectacular course which will test the pro's without
intimidating the club golfer. Set in 252 acres of lush parkland
with thousands of mature treesn naturalwater hazards and
gently rolling landscape.
18 holes, 6916yds, Par 72, SSS 74.
Club membership 220.

Visitors	must have appropriate attire & book in advance. Restricted weekends.
Societies	telephone in advance.
Green Fees	not confirmed.
Designer	McEvoy/O'Connor
Facilities	⊗ ⫚ ⅃ 🐾 ♀ ♨ 🏠 ⁀ ♥ ↾ ♂ ↾
& Leisure	hard tennis courts, heated indoor swimming pool, sauna.
Location	15m SE of Naas

Hotel	★★★ 61% Downshire House Hotel, BLESSINGTON ☎ 045 865199 14 ⇄ 🐾 Annexe11 ⇄ 🐾

BLAINROE   Map 01 D3

Blainroe ☎ 0404 68168 Fax 0404 69369
Parkland course overlooking the sea on the east coast,
offering a challenging round to golfers of all abilities.
18 holes, 6070mtrs, Par 72, SSS 72, Course record 71.
Club membership 868.

Visitors	must contact in advance.
Societies	must telephone in advance.
Green Fees	IR£28 (IR£38 weekends).
Cards	🔲
Prof	John McDonald
Designer	C Hawtree
Facilities	⊗ ⫚ ⅃ 🐾 ♥ ♀ ♨ 🏠 ⁀ ♂ ♂
Location	S of Wicklow, on coast road

Hotel	★★★♨ Tinakilly Country House & Restaurant, RATHNEW ☎ 0404 69274 40 ⇄ 🐾

BLESSINGTON   Map 01 D3

Tulfarris House Hotel & Country Club
☎ 045 867555 Fax 045 867561
Designed by Paddy Merrigan, this course is on the
Blessington lakeshore with the Wicklow Mountains as a
backdrop.
18 holes, 7116mtrs, Par 72, SSS 74.
Club membership 150.

Visitors	tee booking advisable; may not play Sun 8-11.30pm.
Societies	must contact in writing or telephone in advance.
Green Fees	IR£30 per round (IR£40 weekends & bank holidays).
Cards	🔲 🔲 🔲 🔲 🔲 🔲
Prof	A Williams
Designer	Patrick Merrigan
Facilities	⊗ ⫚ ⅃ 🐾 ♥ ♀ ♨ 🏠 ⁀ ♥ ♥ ♂ ♂ ↾
& Leisure	hard tennis courts, heated indoor swimming pool, fishing, sauna, gymnasium, Holiday homes.
Location	Via N81, 2m from Blessington village

Hotel	★★★ 61% Downshire House Hotel, BLESSINGTON ☎ 045 865199 14 ⇄ 🐾 Annexe11 ⇄ 🐾

BRAY   Map 01 D4

Bray Ravenswell Rd ☎ 01 2862484 Fax 01 2862484
A 9-hole parkland course with plenty of trees and bunkers.
9 holes, 5761mtrs, Par 70, SSS 70, Course record 65.
Club membership 500.

Visitors	restricted Mon, Sat & Sun.
Societies	contact in advance.
Green Fees	not confirmed.
Prof	Michael Walby
Facilities	⅃ 🐾 ♥ ♀ ♨ 🏠 ⁀ ♂

Hotel	★★★ 68% Fitzpatrick Castle Hotel, KILLINEY ☎ 01 2840700 113 ⇄ 🐾

Old Conna Ferndale Rd
☎ 01 2826055 & 2826766 Fax 01 2825611
Parkland course set in wooded terrain with panoramic views
of Irish Sea and Wicklow mountains.
18 holes, 6550yds, Par 72, SSS 72, Course record 70.
Club membership 900.

Visitors	advisable to contact in advance but may not play weekends. Smart dress essential on course & in clubhouse.
Societies	must telephone well in advance.
Green Fees	IR£27.50 per round (IR£40 weekends).
Cards	
Prof	Paul McDaid
Designer	Eddie Hackett
Facilities	
Location	2m from Bray
Hotel	★★★ 60% Royal Hotel & Leisure Centre, Main St, BRAY ☎ 01 2862935 91

Woodbrook Dublin Rd ☎ 01 2824799 Fax 01 2821950
Pleasant parkland with magnificent views and bracing sea
breezes which has hosted a number of events, including the
Irish Close and the Irish Open Championships. A testing
finish is provided by an 18th hole with out of bounds on both
sides.
18 holes, 6017mtrs, Par 72, SSS 71, Course record 65.
Club membership 1100.

Visitors	must contact in advance and have a handicap certificate.
Societies	must contact in advance.
Green Fees	not confirmed.
Cards	
Prof	Billy Kinsella
Designer	Peter McEvoy
Facilities	
Location	11m S of Dublin on N11
Hotel	★★★ 60% Royal Hotel & Leisure Centre, Main St, BRAY ☎ 01 2862935 91

BRITTAS BAY   Map 01 D3

The European Club ☎ 0404 47415 Fax 0404 47449
A links course that runs through a large dunes system.
Since it was opened in 1992 it is rapidly gaining
recognition as one of Irelands Best Courses.
18 holes, 7105yds, Par 71, SSS 71, Course record 69.
Club membership 100.

Visitors	pre-booking advised especially for weekends, no denim.
Societies	must book in advance.
Green Fees	IR£45 per round.
Cards	
Designer	Pat Ruddy
Facilities	
Location	1.5m from Brittas Bay Beach
Hotel	★★★★♨ Tinakilly Country House & Restaurant, RATHNEW ☎ 0404 69274 40

DELGANY   Map 01 D3

Delgany ☎ 01 2874536 Fax 01 2873977
An undulating parkland course amidst beautiful scenery.
18 holes, 5474mtrs, Par 69, SSS 68, Course record 61.

Club membership 890.

Visitors	may play Mon, Wed (until 10am), Thu & Fri. Contact in advance.
Societies	contact in advance.
Green Fees	IR£23 per round (IR£27 weekends).
Cards	
Prof	Gavin Kavanagh
Designer	H Vardon
Facilities & Leisure	snooker, practice nets.
Location	0.75m from village
Hotel	★★★ 60% Royal Hotel & Leisure Centre, Main St, BRAY ☎ 01 2862935 91

GREYSTONES   Map 01 D3

Charlesland Golf & Country Club Hotel ☎ 01 2876764
Championship length, Par 72 course with a double dog-leg at
the 9th and 18th. Water hazards at the 3rd and 11th.
18 holes, 5907mtrs, Par 72, SSS 72.
Club membership 744.

Visitors	must contact in advance.
Societies	must apply in advance.
Green Fees	not confirmed.
Prof	Paul Heeney
Designer	Eddie Hackett
Facilities & Leisure	sauna.
Hotel	★★★★♨ Tinakilly Country House & Restaurant, RATHNEW ☎ 0404 69274 40

Greystones ☎ 01 2874136 Fax 01 2873749
A part level and part hilly parkland course.
18 holes, 5322mtrs, Par 69, SSS 68.
Club membership 995.

Visitors	may only play Mon, Tue & Fri morning. Must contact in advance.
Societies	must contact in writing.
Green Fees	IR£25 per round (IR£30 Friday).
Cards	
Designer	P Merrigan
Facilities	
Hotel	★★★★♨ Tinakilly Country House & Restaurant, RATHNEW ☎ 0404 69274 40

KILCOOLE   Map 01 D3

DRUIDS GLEN See page 477

Kilcoole ☎ 01 2872066 2872070 Fax 01 2871803
9 holes, 5506mtrs, Par 70, SSS 69.
Club membership 250.

Visitors	restricted Sat & Sun 8-10am.
Societies	apply in writing or telephone.
Green Fees	IR£15 per 18 holes (IR£18 weekends).
Facilities	
Location	N11 Kilcoole/Newcastle
Hotel	★★★ 63% Hunter's Hotel, RATHNEW ☎ 0404 40106 16

DRUIDS GLEN

KILCOOLE Co Wicklow

☎ 01 2873600 Fax 01 2873699   Map 01 D3

Visitors	advance booking essential
Societies	advance booking essential
Green fees	IR£80 per round — 🍽 🚾
Facilities	⊗ 〉Ⅲ 🝙 💺 ♀ ⚑ ⌇
Designer	Tom Cradduck/Pat Ruddy
Location	20m S of Dublin, 3m off the N11 motorway, immediately S of Glen of Downs

18 holes, 6547yds, Par71 SSS 72

WHERE TO STAY AND EAT NEARBY

HOTELS:

ENNISKERRY

★★🌐 67% Enniscree Lodge Hotel. ☎ 01 2863542. 10 ⇆ ↟

RATHNEW

★★★🌐🌐 ♨♨ Tinakilly Country House & Restaurant ☎ 0404 69274 40 ⇆ ↟

★★★ 🌐 63% Hunters Hotel ☎ 0404 40106 13 ⇆ 3 ↟

John Ingham writes: Those who never came face-to-face with Druids, ancient pagan high priests who practised, in full regalia, in dense forests in the fifth century BC, probably missed something. There was evidence of these people in Wales where the good folk talked of them - in hushed tones. Years later, other fanatics came along. They were called golfers and across the water, in Ireland, these two groups have become twinned, like modern cities.

You ask why? Well, a short drive (four wheel type) from Dublin takes you to Druids Glen Golf Club. Built around an old estate inhabited back in the mists of time by Sir Thomas Wentworth, the good chap didn't confuse us by naming it after himself, and the location is a delight.

How does a club come to be named after pagans? It seems the dreaded Druids sailed in and once even tried to repel St Patrick. Today, not in hushed tones, they say a Druids altar remains as proof of their infiltration to the nearby Glen. So, with a wonderful-looking clubhouse and grounds transformed into a scenic delight of fairways and greens, it's there, twenty miles from Dublin, between the Wicklow Hills and the sea.

So the provenance of the place is beyond dispute and now the 18 holes are highlighted by streams, lakes and all manicured into an idyllic setting made available to the professional tour which play the Irish Open there. The experts heaped praise, with Colin Montgomerie, a severe critic of anything less than 5-star, particularly fulsome - after winning the 1997 title!

Off the back tees, the course is more than 7000yards with three holes of more than 500 yards. So a par round of 71 is to talk about and anything less to die for. Water is a hazard, and you are not allowed to recover drowning balls, or to stand on cliff edges.

No expense has been spared to restore the big house and the dining room has an extra touch. It offers views of the sea, and on a clear day, of the Welsh mountains beyond. So those long gone Welsh Druids are not forgotten!

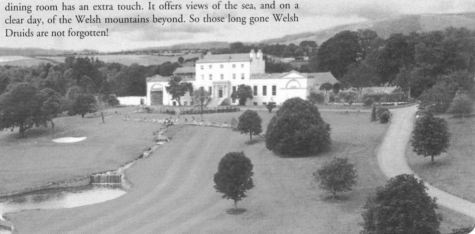

RATHDRUM Map 01 D3

Glenmalure Greenane ☎ 0404 46679 Fax 0404 46783
A moorland course with elevated tees and greens where
accuracy is required. The 3rd, known as the Helicopter Pad,
is difficult. GUI affiliated.
18 holes, 5300yds, Par 71, SSS 67, Course record 71.
Club membership 250.
Visitors unable to play Sunday 8-11am
Societies telephone at least 3 days in advance.
Green Fees IR£18 per day (IR£22 weekends & bank
holidays).
Designer P Suttle
Facilities ⊗ ⅷ 🄻 🍺 💼 🍸 🛆 ⚐ 🛒 🐾 🛺 ♂
Location 2m W

Hotel ★★★ 64% Woodenbridge Hotel, WOODEN
BRIDGE ☎ 0402 35146 23 ⇆ ♜

ROUNDWOOD

Roundwood Newtown, Mountkennedy
☎ 01 2818488 & 2802555 Fax 01 2843642
Heathland and parkland course with forest and lakes set in
beautiful countryside with views of the coast and the
Wicklow Mountains.
18 holes, 6685yds, Par 72, SSS 72.
Club membership 120.
Visitors no restrictions
Societies pre booking necessary.
Green Fees IR£25 per day; IR£20 per round (IR£30/IR£25
weekends & holidays).
Facilities ⊗ 🄻 💼 🛆 ⚐ 🐾 🛺 ♂
Location 2.5m off N11 at Newtown Mountkennedy on
N765

Hotel ★★★ 64% The Glendalough Hotel,
GLENDALOUGH ☎ 0404 45135 44 ⇆ ♜

SHILLELAGH Map 01 D3

Coollattin Coollattin ☎ 055 29125
Plenty of trees provide features on this 18-hole parkland
course.
18 holes, 6148yds, Par 70, SSS 68.
Club membership 760.
Visitors may not play weekends. Must contact in
advance.
Societies contact for details.
Green Fees IR£20 per round (IR£25 weekends).
Designer Peter McEvoy
Facilities ⊗ ⅷ 🄻 💼 🍸 🛆 ♂

Hotel ★★★♨ Marlfield House Hotel, GOREY
☎ 055 21124 19 ⇆ ♜

WICKLOW Map 01 D3

Wicklow Dunbur Rd ☎ 0404 67379
Situated on the cliffs overlooking Wicklow Bay this parkland
course does not have many trees. It was extended to 18 holes
in 1994, it provides a challenging test of golf with each hole
having its own individual features.
18 holes, 5556mtrs, Par 71, SSS 70.
Club membership 500.
Visitors welcome, restrictions on Wed/Thu evening and
Sun. Recommended to call in advance for times
Societies contact for details.
Green Fees IR£20 per round.
Prof David Daly
Designer Craddock & Ruddy
Facilities ⊗ ⅷ 🄻 💼 🛆 🏠 ♂

Hotel ★★★♨ Tinakilly Country House &
Restaurant, RATHNEW
☎ 0404 69274 40 ⇆ ♜

WOODENBRIDGE Map 01 D3

Woodenbridge Woodenbridge, Arklow
☎ 0402 35202 Fax 0402 35202
A level parkland course with undulating fairways and greens,
traversed by two lovely meandering rivers.
18 holes, 6344yds, Par 71, SSS 71, Course record 71.
Club membership 550.
Visitors may not play Thu and Sat, prior booking
strongly recommended.
Societies Mon, Tue & Fri only, book well in advance.
Green Fees not confirmed.
Cards ▭ 🟦
Designer Paddy Merrigan
Facilities ⊗ ⅷ 🄻 💼 🍸 🛆 🛺 ♂
Location 4m NW of Arklow

Hotel ★★★ 64% Woodenbridge Hotel, WOODEN
BRIDGE ☎ 0402 35146 23 ⇆ ♜

GOLF DRIVING RANGES

BEDFORDSHIRE
Bedford, Bedford Golf Club (01234 320022)
Bedford, Mowsbury Driving Range
(01234 771041)
Chalgrave, Chalgrave Manor Golf Club
(01525 876556)
Ivinghoe, John Lambel Driving Range
(01296 662720)
Leighton Buzzard, Aylesbury Vale
(01525 240196)
Luton, Stockwood Park Golf Centre
(01582 413704)
Tilsworth, Tilsworth Golf Centre
(01525 210721/2)
Wyboston, Wyboston Lakes Range
(01480 223004)

BERKSHIRE
Ascot, Lavender Park Golf Centre
(01344 884074/886096)
Binfield, Blue Mountain Golf Centre
(01344 300200)
Chaddleworth, West Berkshire Golf Club
(01488 638574)
Maidenhead, Bird Hills Golf Range
(01628 771030/75588)
Newbury, Donnington Valley Hotel & Golf
Course (01635 32488)
Reading, Reading Golf Club (0118 947 2909)
Sindlesham, Bearwood Golf Club
(0118 976 0060)
Wokingham, Downshire Golf Range
(01344 422708)

BUCKINGHAMSHIRE
Aylesbury, Aylesbury Park Golf Club
(01296 399196)
Beaconsfield, Beaconsfield Golf Club
(01494 676545)
Bletchley, Windmill Hill Golf Complex
(01908 378623)
Colnbrook, Colnbrook Driving Range
(01753 682670/685127)
Denham, Buckinghamshire Golf Club
(01895 835777)
Loudwater, Wycombe Heights Golf Range
(01494 812862)
Milton Keynes, Abbey Hill Golf Club
(01908 562408)
Wavendon, Wavendon Golf Centre
(01908 281811)

CAMBRIDGESHIRE
Cambridge, Gog Magog Golf Club
(01223 247626)

Hemingford Abbots, Hemingford Golf Centre
(01480 492939)
Peterborough, Elton Furze Golf Club
(01832 280189)
Pidley, Lakeside Lodge (01487 740540)
Ramsey, Edrich Golf Driving Range
(01487 813519)
St Neots, Abbotsley Golf & Squash Club
(01480 215153)
Thorney, Thorney Golf Centre
(01733 270570)

CHESHIRE
Chester, Carden Park Hotel Golf Resort
(01829 731000)
Hartford, Hartford Golf Range (01606 871162)
Heaton Mersey, Cranford Golf Driving Range
(0161 432 8242)
Knutsford, Mere Golf & Country Club
(01565 830219)
Prestbury, Prestbury Golf Club
(01625 434562)
Warrington, Drive Time Golf Range
(01925 234800)

CORNWALL
Falmouth, Falmouth Golf Club
(01326 311262)
Launceston, Trethorne Golf Club
(01566 86324)
Lostwithiel, Lostwithiel Golf & Country Club
(01208 873822/873550)
St. Austell, Porthpean (01726 64613)
Redruth, Treleigh, Radnor Golf Centre
(01209 211059)
Rock, St Enodoc Golf Club (01208 863216)
Truro, Killiow Park (01872 270246)

CUMBRIA
Crosby-on-Eden, Eden (01228 573003)
Penrith, Penrith Golf Club (01768 891919)

DERBYSHIRE
Buxton, Buxton & High Peak Golf Club
(01298 23453)
Chesterfield, Grassmoor Golf Centre
(01246 856044)
Horsley, Horsley Lodge Golf Range
(01332 780838)
Long Eaton, Trent Lock
(0115 9464398/9461184)

DEVON
Exeter, Woodbury Park Golf Club
(01395 233382)
High Bickington, Libbaton (01769 560269)

Ilfracombe, Ilfracombe & Woolacombe Golf
Range (01271 866222)
Ivybridge, Dinnaton (01752 892512/892452)
Tedburn St. Mary, Fingle Glen Golf Range
(01647 61817)

DORSET
Bere Regis, East Dorset Golf Club
(01929 472244)
Christchurch, Iford Bridge Golf Range
(01202 473817)
Wareham, Hyde, East Dorset Golf Centre
(01929 472244)
Verwood, Crane Valley Golf Range
(01202 814088)
Weymouth, Wessex Golf Centre
(01305 784737)

CO. DURHAM
Chester-le-Street, Roseberry Grange
(0191 370 0660)
Durham, Ramside Hall (0191 386 9514)
Newton Aycliffe, Aycliffe Driving Range
(01325 310820)
Stockton-on-Tees, Knotty Hill Golf Centre
(01740 620320)

ESSEX
Bulphan, Langdon Hills Driving Range
(01268 548444)
Canvey Island, Castle Point (01268 510830)
Colchester, Colchester Golf Range
(01206 230974)
Earls Colne, Essex Golf & Country Club
(01787 224466)
Epping, Nazeing Golf Club (01992 893798)
Leigh-on-Sea, Leigh Driving Range
(01702 710586)
Toot Hill, Toot Hill Golf Club (01277 365523)
Witham, Benton Hall Golf Course
(01376 502454)

GLOUCESTERSHIRE
Cirencester, Cirencester (01285 653939)
Gloucester, Brickhampton Court
(01452 859444)
Minchinhampton, Minchinhampton
(01453 833866)
Thornbury, Thornbury Golf Centre
(01454 281144)

GREATER LONDON
Addiscombe, Croydon Golf Centre
(0181 656 1690)
Arkley, A1 Golf Range (0181 447 1411)
Bushey, Bushey Golf Range (0181 950 2215)

Carshalton, Oaks Sports Centre
(0181 643 8363)
Chadwell Heath, Warren Park
(0181 597 1120)
Chessington, Chessington Golf Centre
(0181 391 0948)
Elstree, Elstree Golf Range (0181 953 6115)
Greenford, Lime Trees Park (0181 842 0442)
Hounslow, Airlinks (0181 561 1418)
Ilford, Barkingside, Fairlop Waters
(0181 500 9911)
Kingston, Jack Nicklaus Golf Centre
(0181 949 9200)
Northolt, Ealing Golf Range (0181 845 4967)
Northolt, London Golf Centre
(0181 845 3180)
Orpington, Lullingstone Park (01959 533793)
Orpington, Ruxley Park Golf Centre
(01689 871490)
Richmond, Richmond Driving Range
(0181 332 9200)
Ruislip, Ruislip Driving Range (01895 638081)
Twickenham, Twickenham (0181 783 1748)

GREATER MANCHESTER
Altrincham, Altrincham (0161 928 0761)
Bardsley, Bardsley Park Golf Centre
(0161 627 2463)
Castleton, Castle Hawk Golf Range
(01706 659995)
Middleton, Manchester (0161 643 3202)
Standish, Standish Court (01257 425777)
Wigan, Up Holland, Beacon Park Driving
Range (01695 622700)

HAMPSHIRE
Alton, Worldham Park (01420 543151)
Basingstoke, Basingstoke Golf Centre
(01256 350054)
Botley, Botley Park Hotel & Country Club
(01489 796000)
Crondall, Oak Park (01252 850880)
Dibden, Dibden Golf Centre (01703 207508)
Liphook, Old Thorns (01428 724555)
Ower, Paulton's Golf Centre (01703 813992)
Portsmouth, Portsmouth Golf Centre
(01705 664549)
Southampton, Chilworth, Southampton Golf
Range (01703 740544)
Tadley, Tadley Driving Range (0118 9815213)
Winchester, South Winchester
(01962 877800)

HEREFORDSHIRE
Kington, Kington ((01544 230340)
Ross-on-Wye, Ross-on-Wye (01989 720267)

HERTFORDSHIRE
Berkhamsted, Shooters Golf Centre
(01442 872048)
Bishop's Stortford, Great Hadham
(01279 843558)

Bushey, Hartsbourne (0181 950 1133)
Graveley, Chesfield Downs (01462 482929)
Hemel Hempstead, Little Hay Golf Range
(01442 833798)
Royston, Kingsway (01763 262727/262943)
Royston, Whaddon Golf Centre
(01223 207325)
Stevenage, Stevenage Golf Range
(01438 880424)
Ware, Whitehill Golf Centre (01920 438495)
Welwyn Garden City, Gosling Sports Park
(01707 331056)

KENT
Ashford, Homelands Bettergolf Centre
(01233 661620)
Biddenden, Chart Hills (01580 292222)
Chatham, Chatham Golf Centre
(01634 848925)
Chelmsfield, Chelmsfield Lakes Golf Centre
(01689 896266)
Dartford, Birchwood Park (01322 662038)
Dartford, Swanley, Olympic Golf Centre
(01322 669201)
Edenbridge, Edenbridge Golf Range
(01732 865097)
Folkestone, Etchinghill Golf Course
(01303 863863)
Hever, Hever (01732 700771)
Maidstone, Langley Park Driving Range
(01622 863163)
Orpington, St. Paul's Cray, Ruxley Park Golf
Centre (see under Greater London)
Sittingbourne, The Oast Golf Centre
(01795 473527)
Sittingbourne, Upchurch, River Valley Golf
Range (01634 379592)
Westerham, Westerham (01959 563700)

LANCASHIRE
Blackburn, Blackburn Driving Range
(01254 581996)
Blackpool, Heron's Reach, De Vere Hotel
(01253 766156)
Blackpool, Phoenix Driving Range
(01253 854846)
Bolton, Kearsley Golf Range (01204 575726)
Chorley, Euxton Park Golf Centre
(01257 261601)
Preston, Preston Driving Range
(01772 861827)
Tarleton, Leisure Lakes Golf Range
(01772 815842)
Upholland, Beacon Park (01695 622700)

LEICESTERSHIRE
Botcheston, Forest Hill (01455 824800)
Greetham, Greetham Valley (01780 460666)
Leicester, Humberstone Heights
(0116 2763680)
Leicester, Whetstone Golf Range
(0116 2861424)

Loughborough, Charnwood Golf Centre
(01509 610022)
Lutterworth, Kilworth Springs (01858 575082)

LINCOLNSHIRE
Belton, DeVere Belton Woods
(01476 593200)
Gainsborough, Gainsborough (01427 613088)
Holbeach, Gedney Hill (01406 330922)
Horncastle, Horncastle (01507 526800)
Lincoln, Lincoln Bowls (01522 522059)
Scunthorpe, Messingham, Grange Park
(01724 764478)
Skegness, The Elms Golf Centre
(01754 881230)

LONDON SEE ALSO GREATER LONDON
N9 Edmonton, Lea Valley Leisure Centre
(0181 803 3611)
N14 Southgate, Trent Park (0181 366 7432)
E4 Chingford, Chingford Golf Range
(0181 529 2409)

MERSEYSIDE
Formby, Formby Golf Centre (01704 875952)
Hoylake, Royal Liverpool (0151 632 3101
Moreton, Wirral Golf & Drive Centre
(0151 677 6606)
Southport, Hillside (01704 567169)

NORFOLK
Norwich, Bawburgh, Norwich Golf Centre
(01603 740404)
King's Lynn, Eagles Golf Centre
(01553 827147)
King's Lynn, Middleton Hall (01553 841800)
Norwich, Sprowston Park (01603 410657)
Norwich, Wensum Valley (01603 261012)

NORTHAMPTONSHIRE
Chacombe, Cherwell Edge (01295 711591)
Daventry, Staverton Park (01327 302000)
Northampton, Collingtree Park
(01604 700000)
Northampton, Delapre Golf Complex
(01604 764036)

NOTTINGHAMSHIRE
Newark, John Lee Golf Centre
(01636 702161)
Nottingham, Richard Harrod Leisure Centre
(0115 961 2949)
Nottingham, Cotgrave Place Golf Range
(0115 933 3344)
Nottingham, Ramsdale Park Golf Centre
(0115 965 5600)
Nottingham, Riverside Golf Centre
(0115 986 2179)
Oxton, Oakmere Park (0115 965 3545)

OXFORDSHIRE
Abingdon, Drayton Park (01235 550607)
Chipping Norton, Lyneham ((01993 831841)

Frilford, Frilford Heath (01865 390864)
Horton-cum-Studley, Studley Wood
 (01865 351122)
Oxford, Oxford Golf Centre (01865 721592)
Witney, Witney Lakes (01993 779000)

SHROPSHIRE
Oswestry, Mile End (01691 671246)
Telford, Telford Hotel Golf & Country Club
 (01952 429977)
Whitchurch, Hill Valley Golf & Country Club
 (01948 663584)

SOMERSET
Congresbury, Mendip Spring (01934 852322)
Farrington Gurney, Farrington Golf Range
 (01761 241274)
Langport, Long Sutton Golf Range
 (01458 241017)
Monkton Combe, Combe Grove Manor Golf
 Range (01225 835533)
Taunton, Swingrite Golf Range, Holway
 (01823 442600)
Taunton, Oake Manor (O1823 461993)
Taunton, Taunton Vale, West Monkton
 (01823 412220)
Wells, Wells (Somerset) (01749 675005)
Yeovil, Halstock Driving Range
 (01935 891689)

STAFFORDSHIRE
Burton-upon-Trent, Craythorne
 (01283 564329)
Cannock, Beau Desert (01543 422626)
Litchfield, Seedy Mill Golf Range
 (01543 417333)
Newcastle-under-Lyme, Keele Golf Centre
 (01782 717417)
Stoke-on-Trent, Trentham (01782 658109)

SUFFOLK
Halesworth, Halesworth (01986 875567)
Ipswich, Fynn Valley (01473 785267)
Stowmarket, Stowmarket (01449 736473)
Woodbridge, Ufford Park Hotel Golf & Leisure
 (01394 383555)

SURREY
Camberley, Pine Ridge (01276 675444)
Cobham, Silvermere Driving Range
 (01932 866007)
Esher, Sandown Golf Centre (01372 461234)
Farnham, Blacknest Golf Club (01420 22888)
Godalming, Broadwater Park (01483 429955)
Old Woking, Hoebridge Golf Centre
 (01483 722611)
Woking, Windlemere Golf Range
 (01276 858727)

SUSSEX (EAST)
Ditchling, Mid Sussex Golf Course
 (01273 846567)

Eastbourne, Eastbourne Golfing Park
 (01323 520400)
Hastings, Hastings (01424 852981)
Hellingly, Wellshurst Golf Range
 (01435 813456)
Horam, Horam Park (01435 813477)
Hove, West Hove (01273 419738)
Ticehurst, Dale Hill (01580 200112)

SUSSEX (WEST)
Chichester, Chichester Golf Range
 (01243 533833)
Crawley, Pease Pottage Driving Range
 (01293 521706)
Crawley, Tilgate Forest Driving Centre
 (01293 530103)
Haywards Heath, Haywards Heath
 (01444 414457)
Horsham, Horsham Golf Park (01403 271525)
Pulborough,West Chiltington Driving Range
 (01798 813574)
Rustington, Rustington Golf Centre
 (01903 850790)
Slinfold, Slinfold Park (01403 791555)

TYNE & WEAR
Newcastle-upon-Tyne, Parklands
 (0191 236 4867)
Washington, Washington Moat House
 (0191 402 9988)

WARWICKSHIRE
Coventry, Brandon Wood (01203 543141)
Lea Marston, Lea Marston Driving Range
 (01675 470468)
Nuneaton, Purley Chase (01203 393118)
Stratford-upon-Avon, Stratford Oaks Golf
 Range (01789 731980)
Warwick, Warwick Golf Centre
 (01926 494316)

WEST MIDLANDS
Bromsgrove, Bromsgrove Golf Centre
 (01527 575886)
Coventry, John Reay Golf Centre
 (01 203 333920/333405)
Dudley, Sedgley Driving Range
 (01902 880503)
Dudley, Swindon (01902 897031)
Halesowen, Halesowen Golf Range
 (0121 550 2920)
Meridian, Marriott Forest of Arden Golf &
 Country Club (01676 522335)
Solihull, Four Ashes Golf Centre
 (01564 779055)
Wishaw, The Belfry (01675 470301)
Wolverhampton, Three Hammers
 (01902 790940)
Wolverhampton, Perton Park Golf Range
 (01902 380103)

WILTSHIRE
Calne, Bowood (01249 822228)
Westbury, Thoulstone Park (01373 832825)
Swindon, Broome Manor Golf Complex
 (01793 532403)
Swindon, Wrag Barn Golf Range
 (01793 861327)
Tollard Royal, Rushmore Park (01725 516326)
Trowbridge, Wingfield Golf Range
 (01225 776365)

WORCESTERSHIRE
Bishampton, The Vale Driving Range
 (01386 462781)
Ombersley, Ombersley Golf Range
 (01905 620747)
Redditch, Abbey Park Hotel (01527 68006)
Worcester, Worcester Golf Range
 (01905 421213)

YORKSHIRE EAST RIDING
Bridlington, Bridlington Links (01262 401584)
Hull, Hull Golf Centre (01482 492720)

YORKSHIRE (NORTH)
Harrogate, Rudding Park (01423 872100)
Middlesbrough, Middlesbrough Driving Range
 (01642 315533)
York, York Driving Range (01904 690421)

YORKSHIRE (SOUTH)
Bawtry, Austerfield Park (01302 710841)
Barnsley, Sandhill Golf Range (01226 753444)
Sheffield, Rother Valley Golf Centre
 (0114 247 3000)
Sheffield, Concord Park (0114 234 9802)

YORKSHIRE (WEST)
Huddersfield, Bradley Park (01484 223772)
Knaresborough, Scotton Golf Range
 (01423 868943)
Leeds, Leeds Golf Centre (0113 288 6000)
Leeds, Oulton Park (0113 282 3152)
Pontefract, Mid Yorkshire (01977 704522)
Wetherby, Wetherby (01937 580089)

CHANNEL ISLANDS

GUERNSEY
L'Ancresse Vale, Royal Guernsey
 (01481 46523)
St Peter Port, St Pierre Park (01481 728282)

JERSEY
La Moye, La Moye (01534 743401)
St. Ouens Bays, Les Mielles Golf & Country
 Club (01534 482787)

ISLE OF MAN
Douglas, Mount Murray (01624 661111)

SCOTLAND

HIGHLANDS & ISLANDS
Cruden Bay, Cruden Bay (01779 812285)
Inverness, Loch Ness (01463 713335)
Spey Bay, Spey Bay (01343 820424)

CENTRAL
Arbroath, Arbroath (01291 872069)
Bathgate, Whitburn, Polkemmet Country Park
  (01501 743905)
Edinburgh, Bruntsfield Links Golfing Society
  (0131 336 1479)
Edinburgh, Port Royal (0131 333 4377)
Edinburgh, Lasswade, Melville Golf Centre
  (0131 663 8038)
Errol, Middlebank Golf Range (01821 670320)
Glenrothes, Glenrothes Golf Range
  (01592 775374)
Gullane, Gullane ((01620 842255)
Perth, Murrayshall Country House Hotel
  (01738 552784)
Stirling, Stirling (01786 464098)

SOUTHERN LOWLANDS & BORDERS
Cumbernauld, Cumbernauld Golf Range
  (01236 737000)
Cumbernauld, Westerwood (01236 457171)
Glasgow, Bishopbriggs Golf Range
  (0141 762 4883)
Glasgow, Renfrew, Normandy Golf Range
  (0141 886 7477)
Glasgow, Uddingston, Nevada-Bobs
  (0141 641 8899)
Stevenston, Auchenharvie Driving Range
  (01294 603103)

WALES

NORTH
Abersoch, Abersoch (01758 712622)
Bodelwyddan, Kinmel Park Golf Complex
  (01745 833548)
Holyhead, Holyhead (01407 763279)
Penymynydd, Bannel Golf Range
  (01244 544639)
St. Asaph, North Wales Golf Range
  (01745 730805)
Wrexham, Clays Farm Golf Centre
  (01978 661406/661416)

CENTRAL
Caersws, Mid-Wales (01686 688303)
Haverfordwest, Mayfield Golf Range
  (01437 890308)
Llanrhystud, Penrhos Golf & Country Club
  (01974 202999)
Middletown, Welsh Border Golf Range
  (01743 884247)
Newport, Parc (01633 680933)

SOUTH
Abergavenny, Wernddu Golf Centre
  (01873 856223)
Barry, South Wales Golf Range
  (01446 742434)
Bridgend, Pencoed, St. Mary's Driving Range
  (01656 861100)
Caerleon, Caerleon Driving Range
  (01633 420342)
Caerphilly, Mountain Lakes (01222 861128)
Caerwent, Dewstow (01291 430444)
Cwmbran, Green Meadow (01633 869321)

NORTHERN IRELAND

CO ANTRIM
Ballymena, Galgorm Castle Golf & Country Club
  (01266 46161)
Whitehead, Whitehead Driving Range
  (01960 353631)

CO ARMAGH
Armagh, County Armagh (01861 525861)
Lurgan, Craigavon Golf Centre
  (01762 326606)
Tandragee, Tandragee (01762 841272)

CO BELFAST
Belfast, Knockbracken Golf Centre
  (01232 792108)
Belfast, Mount Ober, Golf, Ski & Leisure
  (01232 401811)
Belfast, Newtonabbey, Ballyearl Golf Centre
  (01232 848287)

CO DOWN
Bangor, Blackwood (01247 852706)
Holywood, Holywood (01232 423135)
Kilkeel, Kilkeel (016937 65095)
Warrenpoint, Newry & Mourne Golf Centre
  (016937 73247)

CO FERMANAGH
Enniskillen, Ashwoods Golf Centre
  (01365 325321)

CO LONDONDERRY
Limavady, Radisson Roe Park Hotel & Golf
  Resort (015047 22222)
Londonderry, Foyle International Golf Centre
  (01504 352222)

CO TYRONE
Omagh, Clanabogan Driving Range
  (01662 245409)

REPUBLIC OF IRELAND

(From UK dial 00353 and ignore first digit of
numbers below)

CO CORK
Cork, Fota Island (021 883700)
Kinsale, Old Head (021 778444)
Little Island, Harbour Point (021 353094)

CO DONEGAL
Rosapenna, Rosapenna (074 55301)

CO DUBLIN
Castleknock, Luttrellstown Castle
  (01 8089988)
Dublin, Leopardstown Golf Centre
  (01 289 5341/895671)
Dublin, St Margaret's Golf & Country Club
  (01 8640400)
Dublin, Ward Golf Centre (01 8348711)

CO GALWAY
Galway, Galway Range (091 526737/26753)
Galway, Glenlo Abbey (091 526666)
Oranmore, Galway Bay Golf & Country Club
  (091 790500)

CO KILDARE
Celbridge, Celbridge Golf Centre
  (01 628 8833)
Straffan, The K Club (01 6017300)

CO KILKENNY
Kilkenny, Kilkenny (056 65400)

CO LAIOS
Portlaiose, The Heath (0502 46622)

1

A	B	C	D

6

Rathlin Island

Ballyliffen
Greencastle Portrush Portballintrae
Tory Island Rosapenna Morville Portstewart Ballycastle Cushendall
Dunfanaghy Portsalon Castlerock Aghadowey
Gweedore Buncrana Limavady Kilrea **M2** Ballygally
Cruit Island Rathmullan LONDONDERRY Ballymena **M1** A36 Larne Carrickfergus
Aran Island Letterkenny Newtownabbey Whitehead Holywood
Nairn Ballybofey Strabane Castledawson Ballyclare Bangor
Newtonstewart Antrim Dundonald Donaghadee
Cookstown BELFAST Newtownards
Omagh Lisburn Newton-breda Ardmillan
Ballintra Dungannon Maze Carryduff Cloughey
Bundoran Fintona Portadown Lurgan Ballynahinch
Enniskillen Armagh Tandragee Magheralin Downpatrick
Banbridge Newcastle Ardglass
5 SLIGO Blacklion Clones Monaghan Newry Kilkeel
Castleblayney Warrenpoint Greenore
Belmullet Enniscrone Ballyconnell Belturbet Carrickmacross DUNDALK
Ballina Ballymote Ballinamore Cavan Ardee **M1** Termonfeckin
Achill Toberdurry Boyle Carrick- Virginia Baltray Bettystown
Keel Castlebar Swinford Ballaghaderreen on-Shannon Kells Balbriggan
Clare Westport Ballyhaunis Castlerea Strokestown Navan Skerries
Inishturk Claremorris Longford Delvin Dunshaughlin Rush Lambay
Inishbofin Renvyle Ballinrobe Roscommon Mullingar Trim Cloghran Malahide
4 Ballyconneely Tuam Mountbellew **1** Portmarnock
Oughterard Athlone N6 Moate **2** DUBLIN
GALWAY Oranmore Ballinasloe Carbury Donadea **3** **M** DUN LAOGHAIRE
Loughrea Tullamore Edenderry Clane **6** Killiney
Gorumna Gort Portuna Portarlington Kildare Naas **8** **12** BRAY
Island Birr PORT LAOISE Blessington **10** Greystones
Inishmore Scarriff Mountrath Roundwood Delgany
Lahinch Roscrea Abbeyleix Castledermot Rathdrum Kilcoole
Milltown Malbay Newmarket- Ennis Nenagh Rathdowney CARLOW Athy Baltinglass Wicklow
on-Fergus Clonlara Templemore Woodenbridge Blainroe
3 Kilkee Shannon Thurles KILKENNY Shillelagh Brittas Bay
Airport LIMERICK Borris Arklow
Kilrush Adare Callan Gorey
Ballybunion Newcastle Tipperary Carrick- Thomastown Enniscorthy Courtown Harbour
West Cahir on-Suir
Charleville New WEXFORD
Castlegregory TRALEE Mitchelstown CLONMEL Ross Rosslare
Great Blasket Ballyferriter Killorglin Doneraile Lismore WATERFORD N25
Island Glenbeigh Kanturk Tramore Dunmore East
2 Parknasilla Killarney Mallow Fermoy Dungarven
Waterville Kenmare Blarney Midleton Youghal
Castletown Macroom CORK Little Island
Bearhaven Glengarriff Ovens Douglas Monkstown
Dursey Bantry Bandon Carrigaline
Clonakilty Kinsale
Skibbereen

Clear

○ Town Names
● Golf Course

0   20   40 miles
0   20   40   60 kilometres

1	Ballyboughal
2	Donabate
3	Clonsilla
4	Castlerock
5	Lucan
6	Straffan
7	Rathcoole
8	Kill
9	Tallaght
10	Brittas
11	Kilternan
12	Saggart

2

○	Town Names
●	Golf Course
BLAE G	Blaenau Gwent
BRDGND	Bridgend
MYR TD	Merthyr Tydfil
NEWPT	Newport
RHONDD	Rhondda Cynon Taff
TORFN	Torfaen
V GLAM	Vale of Glamorgan

CERED

Llangybi

Gwbert on Sea
Cardigan
SN
Newport
Llandyssul

Strumble Head
Letterston
St David's   PEMBROKESHIRE
Ramsey
Island
St Brides Bay
Carmarthen   CARMARTHEN
A40
A48

Skomer Island
Haverfordwest
Milford
Haven
Skokholm
Island
Pembroke
Dock   Tenby
A477   Kidwelly
Burry Port   A484
Pontlliw
Three Crosses   SWA
Upper Killay   A4
Southga

Caldey
Island

Carmarthen
Bay

SM

SW
Perranporth
ST AUSTELL
Truro
A30
St Ives
Lelant   Camborne
St Just   Penzance
Budock Vean
Falmouth
Mawnan Smith
Land's End   A30
Praa
Sands
Mount's
Bay   Mullion
Lizard
Point

SS
Ilfracombe
Mortehoe
Saunton
Westward Ho!
Lundy
Hartland Point
High
Bickington
Woolfardisworthy   A39   Great
Torrington
Bude
Holsworthy
Okehampton

SW
Land's End
Isles of Scilly
St Mary's

Camelford   Launceston
A30

Trevose Head   Rock   St Minver   CORNWALL   Da
Constantine Bay   Padstow   Wadebridge   Bodmin
Moor   Tavistock
Mawgan Porth   Bodmin   A38
Newquay   A392   A30   St Mellion   Yelverto
Holywell Bay   Lostwithiel   Saltash
A3075   ST AUSTELL   Looe   PLYMOUTH   Sparkwell
Carlyon   Torpoint   Ivybrid
Bay
SEE INSET   SX
Dodman Point

For continuation pages refer to numbered arrows

For continuation pages refer to numbered arrows

5

1 – Aldenham
2 – Watford
3 – Rickmansworth
4 – Chalfont St Giles
5 – Chorleywood
6 – Bushey
7 – Elstree
8 – Hadley Wood
9 – Enfield
10 – Gerrards Cross
11 – Stoke Poges
12 – Wrexham Street
13 – Uxbridge
14 – Hillingdon
15 – West Drayton
16 – Hounslow
17 – Isleworth
18 – Hampton Wick
19 – Kingston upon Thames
20 – New Malden
21 – Surbiton
22 – Carshalton
23 – Croydon
24 – Coulsdon
25 – Chipstead
26 – Kingswood
27 – Walton-on-the-Hill
28 – Banstead
29 – Chessington
30 – Weybridge
31 – Addlestone
32 – Walton-on-Thames
33 – Hampton
34 – Chertsey
35 – West Byfleet
36 – East Horsley
37 – Shepperton
38 – Chobham
39 – Caterham
40 – Downe
41 – Halstead
42 – Addington
43 – Farleigh
44 – Westerham

○ Town Names
● Golf Course

5   6   7   8   9   0   1   2   3   4   5   6   7   8   **11** 9   0   A595   1

A17   Point of Ayre   Seascale

Isle of Man   A3   ● Ramsey
Maughold Head

Peel ●   A4   ISLE
OF
MAN   A2

A1   ● Onchan
Port St Mary   A3   A5   DOUGLAS

Port Erin ●   ● Castletown
Dreswick Point

*I r i s h
S e a*

Silecrof

SC

MEI

Carmel Head   Amlwch ●   *Great
Ormes
Head*
Llandudno ●   COLWYN   Rhyl   Prestatyn
BAY
Holyhead ●   Anglesey   Conwy ●   A5

Holy Island   Llangefni ●   Beaumaris ●   Abergele ●   Rhuddlan
Penmaenmawr ●   A55   St Asaph
Rhosneiger ●   A5   Llanfairfechan ●   Bodelwyddan   Caerw
Bangor ●
ISLE OF   Denbigh ●
ANGLESEY   Caernarfon ●   A4086   A5   CONWY   Ruthin
A543   A525
*Caernarfon
Bay*   SH   A498   A470   Betws-y-coed ●   ENBIGHS

Morfa   A499   A470
Nefyn ●   A487   A4212   Bala ●
Lleyn Peninsula   A497   Porthmadog ●   A494
Criccieth ●
Pwllheli ●   Harlech ●   GWYNEDD
Abersoch ●   A470

Bardsey   A496
Island   Dolgellau ●   A470   A458

A487   POWYS

○ Town Names   A493   Machynlleth ●   A470   Caersws ●
● Golf Course   Aberdyfi ●   Newtov
Cardigan Bay   Borth ●   A44   A483
0   10   20 miles
SN   Llanidloes ●   A470
0   10   20   30 kilometres   Aberystwyth ●   A487

CEREDIGION

2   Llanrhystud ●   A485

5   6   7   8   9   0   1   2   3   4   5   6   7   8   9   0   1

For continuation pages refer to numbered arrows

9

5 6 7 8 9 0 1 2 3 4 5 6 7 8 9 0

TA

Spurn Head

A1031

Sutton-on-Sea
Woodthorpe
A52

A158

A52

Skegness

TF

The
Hunstanton
Wash

Sutton
Bridge

King's
Lynn
Middleton

A10

5

Brancaster

A149

A148

A148

Fakenham

A1065

Dereham
A47

A47

Mattishall

N O R F O L K

A140

A1067

Weston
Longville

A47

Sheringham

Cromer
West
Runton

Mundesley

TG

A149

A1151

The
Broads

A47

0 10 20 miles
0 10 20 30 kilometres

○ Town Names
● Golf Course

5 6 7 8 9 0 1 2 3 4 5 6 7 8 9 0

Tiree
Ulva
Isle of Mull
Iona
A849
NM
Craignure
Lismore
Eriska
A828
Oban
Firth of Lorne
A816
Luing
Scarba
Dalmally
A85
A819
ARGYLL
AND BUTE
Inveraray
A83

Colonsay
Scalasaig
Oronsay
Lochgilphead
A886
A815
A814
A82
Luss
Helensburgh
Cardross
Bor
Dunoon
Gourock
DUMBAR
Greenock
Langt
Innellan
Port Glasgow
M8
Port
Bannatyne
Skelmorlie
Kilmacolm
Bishop
Bridge of Weir
Johnston
Rothesay
Largs
Lochwinnoch
Kingarth
A760
Uplawmo
Sound
of Bute
Millport
Kilbirnie
Beith
Lochranza
West
Kilbride
A737
NORTH
AYRSHIRE
Corrie
Stevenston
Irvine
A71
Brodick
KILMARNOC
Arran
Firth of
Baras
Machrie
Clyde
Troon
Lamlash
Holy I
Prestwick
Whiting
Bay
Ayr
A77

Jura
Sound of Jura
A846
Coul Point
Islay
A847
Port Ellen
Gigha
Gigha
Island
NR
A83
Kintyre
Kilbrannan Sound
A841
Carradale
Blackwaterfoot
Machrihanish
Southend
Mull of
Kintyre
Ailsa Craig
Patna
Maybole
Turnberry
Girvan
SOUTH
AYRSHIRE
A77

Tighnabruaich
Tarbert

North Channel
NW
Loch Ryan
Newton Stewart
Stranraer
A77
A75
Glenluce
Wigtow
Portpatrick
A176
A747
Luce Bay
Monre
Mull of
Galloway

○	Town Names
●	Golf Course
C EDIN	City of Edinburgh
C GLAS	City of Glasgow
CLACKS	Clackmannanshire
W DUNS	West Dunbartonshire
E DUNS	East Dunbartonshire
E RENS	East Renfrewshire
INVER	Inverclyde
N LANS	North Lanarkshire
RENS	Renfrewshire

0   10   20 miles
0   10   20   30 kilometres

NORTH SEA

Arbroath
Carnoustie
Monifieth
Barry
Tayport
NO
DUNDEE CITY
DUNDEE
A92
A90
PERTH
Firth of Tay
Leuchars
St Andrews Bay
St Andrews
FIFE
A914
(A921)
M90
A91
A915
A917
Crail
Fife Ness
Lundin
Links
Anstruther
Elie
GLENROTHES
Isle of May
M90
A92
SN

Dunfermline
Firth of Forth
North Berwick
A198
Gullane
Aberlady
Longniddry
EDINBURGH
WEST
EDIN
EAST
LOTHIAN
Haddington
Gifford
A1
Dunbar
St Abb's Head
A1107
Eyemouth
MIDLOTHIAN
A68
LAMMERMUIR
Hills
Duns
A6105
Berwick-upon-Tweed
NU

Peebles
A72
11
BORDERS (SCOTTISH)
NT
Lauder
A697
A6112
A698
Coldstream
Holy Island
Galashiels
Melrose
A8089
Kelso
A1
Bamburgh
Belford
Seahouses
St Boswells
Wooler
Selkirk
Minto
Jedburgh
The Cheviot Hills
Embleton
Hawick
A68
A6088
Alnwick
A697
Alnmouth
A1
A1068
Warkworth
Rothbury
Swarland
A697

Moffat
A74
Longhorsley
A1

DUMFRIES
AND
GALLOWAY
Newcastleton
NORTHUMBERLAND
Morpeth
Newbiggin-
by-the-Sea
A74(M)
A75
Bellingham
A696
Bedlington
Blyth
Cramlington
Ponteland
Whitley Bay
Tynemouth
Matfen
Backworth
South Shields
Greenhead
A69
Gosforth
Wallsend
Brampton
Hexham
Prudhoe
Ryton
NEWCASTLE UPON TYNE
CARLISLE
A689
Crosby-
on-Eden
A689
Stocksfield
Chopwell
Whickham
Felling
Gateshead
Boldon
SUNDERLAND
NY
Allendale
Burnopfield
Birtley
Washington
Seaham
Beamish
Alston
Consett
Stanley
Houghton-
le-Spring
NZ
Chester-le-
Street
CUMBRIA
M6
A686
A689
DURHAM
Crook
A167
A1(M)
8
Penrith
A66
DURHAM
A68
A689
HARTLEPOOL
A19
A689
Appleby-in-
Westmorland
A66
Barnard
Castle
A688
MIDDLESBROUGH
Lake District
A591
A66
A66
DARLINGTON
A172
7

For continuation pages refer to numbered arrows

0   10   20 miles
0   10   20   30 kilometres

○ Town Names
● Golf Course
C EDIN City of Edinburgh

15

Dunnet Head
Island of Stroma
Duncansby Head
A836
Thurso
A9
Noss Head
A89 (A9)
Wick
A9
(A895)
ND
Lybster

Firth

Lossiemouth
Hopeman
Spey Bay
Cullen
Banff
Macduff
Fraserburgh
Inverallochy
Garmouth
Buckie
A98
A92
A90
Elgin
A95
A941
Keith
NJ
Turriff
A950
Peterhead
Rothes
A97
A947
A952
A90
(A952)
NK
MORAY
Dufftown
Huntly
A920
Cruden Bay
A95
A941
A96
A920
Ellon
Insch
Oldmeldrum
A90
(A92)
Newburgh on Ythan
ABERDEENSHIRE
Inverurie
Newmachar
A97
Alford
Kemnay
Kintore
A939
A944
A944
ABERDEEN CITY
ABERDEEN
A938
A97
Tarland
A980
Torphins
Peterculter
A93
Portlethen
A93
Ballater
Aboyne
Banchory
A90
Braemar
A957
Stonehaven
ains

Auchenblae
A92
Glenshee
(Spittal of)
NO
Edzell
A90
A93
ANGUS
Brechin
Montrose
A924
Kirriemuir
A935
A926
A932
Lunan Bay
Blairgowrie
Alyth
Forfar
A90
A933
12

○ Town Names
● Golf Course

0   10   20 miles
0   10   20   30 kilometres

16

2 3 4 5 6 7 8

9
8
7
6 HY
5
Westray ●
4
3
Mainland
2
1 KIRKWALL ●
Stromness ●
0
Hoy
9
8 ND

Orkney
Islands

2 3 4 5 6 7 8

0 10 20 miles
0 10 20 30 kilometres

2 3 4 5 6 7

2
1 HP
0
9
Yell
8
7
Island of
Whalsay ●
6
5
Mainland
4 LERWICK ●
3 HU
2
1

Shetland
Islands

2 3 4 5

0 10 20 miles
0 10 20 30 kilometres

Jersey

0 1 2 3 miles
0 1 2 3 4 kilometres

St Ouen ●

La Moye ●

ST HELIER ○

St Clement ●
Grouville ●

L'Ancresse
Vale ●

St Peter Port ●

Alderney ●
St Anne

Herm
Sark ○
Guernsey

Jersey

Guernsey

0 1 2 3 miles
0 1 2 3 4 kilometres

INDEX

H

S

T

Y